# Storm on the Horizon

# Storm on the Horizon

*The Challenge to American Intervention,*

*1939–1941*

Justus D. Doenecke

ROWMAN & LITTLEFIELD PUBLISHERS, INC.
*Lanham · Boulder · New York · Oxford*

ROWMAN & LITTLEFIELD PUBLISHERS, INC.

Published in the United States of America
by Rowman & Littlefield Publishers, Inc.
4720 Boston Way, Lanham, Maryland 20706
http://www.rowmanlittlefield.com

12 Hid's Copse Road
Cumnor Hill, Oxford OX2 9JJ, England

British Library Cataloguing in Publication Information Available

**Library of Congress Cataloging-in-Publication Data**

Doenecke, Justus D.
    Storm on the horizon : the challenge to American intervention, 1939–1941 / Justus D. Doenecke.
        p.    cm.
    Includes bibliographical references and index.
    ISBN 0-7425-0784-X (alk. paper)
        1. United States—Foreign relations—1933–1945.   2. Intervention (International
law)—History—20th century.   3. World War, 1939–1945—United States.   4. World War,
1939–1945—Diplomatic history.   I. Title.

    E806 .D628   2000
    327.73'09'044—dc21                                                                00-038738

Printed in the United States of America

⊗™ The paper used in this publication meets the minimum requirements of American National
Standard for Information Sciences—Permanence of Paper for Printed Library Materials, ANSI/NISO
Z39.48–1992.

*To Carol*

# Contents

# Preface

"We are passing," said Herbert Hoover, "through the most serious moment in the history of the world since the year 410 A.D.—the year of the fall of the Roman Empire and the capture of Rome by the barbarian king, Alaric." The former president was addressing the bar association of Nassau County, New York, on 25 May 1940, just as German troops had reached the English Channel.[1]

By December 1941, when the United States entered World War II as a full-scale belligerent, most Americans found the world situation even more perilous. Adolf Hitler totally dominated the European continent. Though major German air losses and the intense Russian campaign had caused the Führer to abandon immediate plans for invading Britain, England's fate was precarious. In Asia, the situation appeared equally threatening. By the end of 1941, Imperial Japan not only controlled eastern China. It extended its rule to Indochina and was ready to strike at the Philippines, Singapore, and the Netherlands East Indies.

Hence, during the years 1939–41, the fate of the world lay "in the balance," and it is little wonder that historian Gerhard L. Weinberg has used that very phrase to introduce one of his studies.[2] To Americans, any wrong move might bring imminent peril. Late in 1939, the *Saturday Evening Post* editorialized, "The decision we make may alter the history of the world for a thousand years."[3] The issue was a crucial one: how best to survive as the Eurasian land mass came under the increasing domination of a predatory Axis.

In one of the most impassioned debates in the nation's entire history, many citizens, including Hoover himself, opposed the ever-increasing efforts of Franklin Delano Roosevelt to intervene on the side of the Allies. Any move of the president was fought resolutely by people who found such policies literally endangering the United States. Such people feared that the administration's agenda, even be it piecemeal, would inevitably lead to full-scale participation, which in turn would destroy the nation itself.

On one side stood a group often called "isolationist," although it is far more accurate to call it "anti-interventionist" or "noninterventionist," or—for heuristic purposes—to use such terms as "Roosevelt critics," "FDR foes," or "administration adversaries." The nation's leading scholar of isolationism defines the stance as involving opposition to "American intervention in European wars," with "noninterventionist views generally extended to Asia and Latin America." Its proponents were also unilateralists, opposing American involvement in such "entangling alliances" as collective security agreements or such international organizations as the League of Nations.[4] Only a few wore the label *isolationist* with pride, one being the *New York Daily News*, which felt no compunction about describing its position as such.[5] Most FDR critics, however, claimed that the term had misrepresented their position, for they never sought "isolation" from the rest of the world. "I am an isolationist from war," said Congressman Hamilton Fish (Rep.-N.Y.), "but not an isolationist from arbitration, mediation, and peaceful methods of settling international disputes."[6]

Certainly the term *isolationist* does little justice to either the complexity of the anti-interventionist stance or the reasoning behind it, particularly if one adds pacifists, people who in principle opposed participation in any given conflict.[7] Said the prominent New York minister John Haynes Holmes, in deeming war itself a crime, "There are no circumstances or causes that can justify murder."[8] In the period 1939–41, isolationists and pacifists cooperated to a surprising degree, often advancing similar arguments in their opposition to Roosevelt's foreign policies. If a marriage of convenience was at work, sufficient overlap existed to call the common position "anti-interventionist."

Since the 1960s, undoubtedly partly because of the Vietnam War, scholarship on anti-interventionism has blossomed, and an annotated bibliography completed in 1987 listed close to sixteen hundred entries.[9] Interspersed in such accounts are various explanations for this phenomenon, though all have their limitations. Some find the stance rooted in such ethnic groups as German and Irish Americans; however, the great majority of anti-interventionists came from Anglo-Saxon backgrounds. Others see anti-interventionism grounded in the Great Plains and upper Mississippi Valley. Certainly an explanation based on midwestern and agrarian roots holds true for such leading anti-interventionists as Senator Gerald P. Nye (Rep.-N.Dak.). Within the "interventionist" Northeast, however, many people, including city dwellers, opposed the president's diplomacy, and this stance transcended such predictable ethnic groups as German and Irish Americans. At times, party affiliation played a crucial role, with Democrats leaning far more to intervention than Republicans. All the same, by 1940 it was a Senate Democrat, Burton K.

Wheeler of Montana, who led the attack in his chamber against FDR; on the other side, Wendell Willkie, presidential standard-bearer for the Grand Old Party that year, soon showed himself to be a strong interventionist. Several social scientists have portrayed anti-interventionism as a form of psychological marginality, in which a xenophobic "in-group" struck blindly at a world it never made.[10] Still in all, this explanation is greatly oversimplified, neglecting the many anti-interventionists who were clearly tied by family, education, and occupation to the nation's most elite political and economic institutions.

In the long run, to best understand anti-interventionism during the 1939–41 period, one should focus on far more than geographic regions, socioeconomic factors, ethnic groups, or even party politics. Rather, one must examine an ideology possessing roots deep in the American past. From the time of the nation's founding, and for many years thereafter, its leaders believed that continental and commercial expansion could go hand in hand—in fact, be protected—by totally avoiding international power politics. Moreover, since at least 1776, Americans as a people had felt both separate from—indeed, superior to—a Europe perceived as corrupt, effete, maybe downright degenerate. If, in reality, they found themselves slaughtering Indians and enslaving blacks, they saw themselves launching a community of pristine republicanism, one that by the early nineteenth century remained untainted by the twin evils of the Old World: anarchistic revolution and predatory imperialism. By the 1920s, a hundred years later, it was the dreams of British imperialist Cecil Rhodes and the visions of the Russian Bolshevik V. I. Lenin that could embody such perils.[11]

During the years 1939–41, this entire posture was put to the test. Most historians have stressed prominent personalities, leading action groups, and major debates that often centered on such matters as neutrality legislation and conscription.[12] This book skirts none of these matters but rather puts them in a wider framework, one focusing on underlying military, economic, and geopolitical assumptions.[13] How did anti-interventionists perceive the ideology, armed potential, and territorial aspirations of Germany, the British Empire, Japan, and the Soviet Union? To what degree did they envision Nazi Germany as a bulwark against the Soviets? What role would the United States play in a world increasingly composed of competing economic blocs and military alliances? What weapons and strategies could best defend their nation's sphere of influence, and how far should this sphere extend? What was the optimum military readiness? What would be the likely scenarios if the United States fought a full-scale war against Germany or Japan or both? Were noninterventionists "doves" in Europe, "hawks" in Asia? What prospects did they see for a negotiated peace, particularly in Europe, and what would be the context of such a peace? Why did they fear that a defense boom would injure the American economy, not aid it? These are just a few of the questions addressed in a study that examines the mental universe of President Roosevelt's strongest critics.

# Acknowledgments

Few books involving major research are written without assistance. This has been especially true in my case, particularly as I have researched this project for well over a quarter of a century.

My greatest debt is to my wife Carol, for whom no dedication is sufficient. My obligation to her is inestimable, as her contribution has ranged over the years from reading innumerable drafts to copying countless items in untold collections.

Several scholars have read the manuscript intensely and critically, spending countless hours to aid a colleague in diplomatic history. Irwin F. Gellman, despite unusual burdens, has scrutinized the entire manuscript at least once and some chapters a second time. The same holds true for George H. Nash, who, like Irwin, offered detailed commentary that extended to the most minute material. J. Garry Clifford examined the bulk of these chapters, sent me pages of detailed analysis, and continually probed framework and focus. He also lent me his notes of the William R. Castle papers that were later supplemented by my personal examination. Wayne S. Cole, the dean of scholars of World War II anti-interventionism, aided greatly in framing the project, both in analyzing the preface and conclusion and engaging in many encouraging conversations over the years. I've also benefited from Raymond A. Esthus's critique of my chapters on East Asia and Raymond G. O'Connor on naval incidents. I could not have been blessed with more perceptive and conscientious readers. It is such generosity that makes the enterprise of scholarship so rewarding.

Equally indispensable is my indebtedness to the various foundations that helped finance this research. Foremost is the Institute for Humane Studies of Menlo Park, California, where I was senior research fellow in the academic year

1977–78 and resident summer fellow in 1975, 1976, 1978, and 1981. The names of Leonard P. Liggio, former IHS president, and Kenneth S. Templeton Jr., former IHS vice president, stand out in this regard. Again, I owe both an obligation that can never be repaid. To work in such gracious and supportive surroundings was indeed a privilege. I am also grateful to the John Anson Kittredge Educational Fund of Cambridge, Massachusetts, and in particular to Walter Muir Whitehill and Ernest R. May, for aid in 1973 and 1980. In 1981, the Herbert Hoover Library Association of West Branch, Iowa, supported research in the Herbert Hoover papers. The Earhart Foundation of Ann Arbor, Michigan, awarded me a travel grant in 1995, and I must single out Anthony Sullivan, its secretary and program director. For these, too, I am most thankful.

The staff of any library can either aid or hinder a project, and in this regard I have been singularly blessed. Personnel of the Jane Bancroft Cook Library of the University of South Florida (USF) at Sarasota have offered superb service. Special mention must be given to Holly Barone, Kim Grohs, and Gail Novak, all of whom assisted in countless ways, extending themselves far beyond the call of duty. The staffs of USF libraries at Tampa and St. Petersburg have also been most cooperative.

Certain other librarians and administrators, along with their institutional coworkers, deserve to be singled out. These include Rosemary Allen Little, librarian of public administration, politics, and law at Princeton University's Firestone Library; Robert S. Wood of the Herbert Hoover Presidential Library at West Branch, Iowa; Milorad M. Drachkovitch, Robert Hessen, Charles Palm, Adorjan I. de Galffy, and Elena Danielson, all of the Hoover Institution on War, Revolution and Peace, Stanford University; Judith Schiff of Sterling Library, Yale University; Gene M. Gressley of the University of Wyoming; Martin Schmitt of the University of Oregon; Gladys MacKenzie, entrusted with the papers of the National Council for the Prevention of War at the Swarthmore College Peace Collection; and Archie Motley of the Chicago Historical Society. In addition, I am most appreciative of the efforts of the staffs of the Houghton Library, Harvard University; Providence College; the Bancroft Library of the University of California at Berkeley; Cornell University; the archives division of the New York Public Library; the manuscript division of the Library of Congress; the State Historical Society of Wisconsin, Madison; and the Franklin D. Roosevelt Presidential Library at Hyde Park, New York. Certain library staffs were extremely kind in allowing me to examine firsthand the campus newspapers of their institutions during my research trips: Amherst College, Brown University, Bryn Mawr College, City University of New York, Dartmouth College, Fordham University, George Washington University, Georgetown University, Haverford College, Johns Hopkins University, Mount Holyoke College, New York University, Smith College, Union Theological Seminary of New York, and Vassar College.

Certain individuals, on campus and off, have been more than encouraging. They include Arthur M. Schlesinger Jr., Leo P. Ribuffo, James T. Patterson, Forrest and Ellen McDonald, Betty Miller Unterberger, William Hamilton, and Stephen Fischer-Galati. Over the years I was also able to interview such prominent anti-interventionists as Frank Cullen Brophy, R. Douglas Stuart Jr., Abraham Kaufman, Henry Regnery, Eugene Davidson, Page Hufty, Felix Morley, Frank Waldrop, Bonner Fellers, and Lawrence and Dora Dennis. Adria Holmes Katz has given me permission to cite papers from the collection of John Haynes Holmes. At New College of the University of South Florida, I have benefited from superb academic leadership; again, certain names of administration and staff should be singled out: Laszlo Deme, Eugene Lewis, Robert Benedetti, Anthony P. Andrews, Gordon Michalson, Gordon Bauer, James Feeney, and Susan Janney. For permission to reproduce, with modifications, the contents of one article, I am indebted to Arthur J. Vidich, editor of the *International Journal of Politics, Culture, and Society*.

Finally, I wish to express my deep appreciation to Stephen M. Wrinn, acquisitions editor of Rowman & Littlefield; to Mary Carpenter, assistant editor; and to Mary C. Hack and Renee Jardine, production editors. I have never experienced such enthusiastic support for a project of this magnitude. I am truly grateful.

# Acronyms

| | |
|---|---|
| AFC | America First Committee |
| CDAAA | Committee to Defend America by Aiding the Allies |
| CR | *Congressional Record* |
| CT | *Chicago Tribune* |
| FOR | Fellowship of Reconciliation |
| HFAC | House Foreign Affairs Committee |
| HHPL | Herbert Hoover Presidential Library |
| IDU | *In Danger Undaunted* |
| KAOWC | Keep America Out of War Congress |
| MEPWDC | Make Europe Pay War Debts Committee |
| NCFSD | National Committee on Food for the Small Democracies |
| NCPW | National Council for the Prevention of War |
| NYDN | *New York Daily News* |
| NYT | *New York Times* |
| NYWT | *New York World-Telegram* |
| SCPC | Swarthmore College Peace Collection |
| SFE | *San Francisco Examiner* |
| SFN | *San Francisco News* |
| SFRC | Senate Foreign Relations Committee |
| WFL | *Weekly Foreign Letter* |
| WIL | Women's International League for Peace and Freedom, U.S. Section |
| WTH | *Washington Times-Herald* |

# A Note to the Reader

Due to constraints of space, the material in the index is often constricted to the data presented in the text itself. Additional data, however, often appears in the endnotes. For example, in chapter one, endnote eight, Hamilton Fish and Edwin M. Borchard are cited in the index but references to Hugh Johnson, William R. Castle, and John Bassett Moore are not. For a full investigation of any given topic or theme, the reader should examine the particular endnote.

At times, certain members of Congress are only cited in the endnotes. When first mentioned, the individual is identified by first and last name, state, and party affiliation. After that first citation, there is no further endnote reference. For example, for full data on "Keefe" as cited in chapter 10, endnote 90, see the initial reference to "Frank B. Keefe (Rep.-Wis.)" as given in chapter 3, endnote 67. The same situation holds true for other historical figures. For instance, for the occupation and full name of "Neilson," chapter 15, endnote 4, see the initial reference to "revisionist writer Francis Neilson," chapter 1, endnote 129.

# Introduction:
# The Many Mansions
# of Anti-interventionism

The anti-interventionists of World War II have seldom done well before the bar of history. To most professional historians, and to much of the general public ever since, it was criminal folly to have opposed major American efforts to check Hitler's Reich and Imperial Japan. In the heat of World War II, such people were often accused of being naive, obstructionist, or even downright lunatic. At best, according to such establishment weeklies as *Time* and *Life* and such left-leaning dailies as New York's *PM*, they were unwitting handmaidens of the Axis. Interior Secretary Harold Ickes referred to aviator Charles A. Lindbergh, the nation's best-known anti-interventionist, as "No. 1 Nazi fellow traveler."[1] The Friends of Democracy, Inc., a pro-administration action committee, attacked the leading anti-interventionist group by issuing a pamphlet titled "The America First Committee—Nazi Transmission Belt."

In reality, such attacks were most unwarranted, though even today negative stereotypes remain in the popular imagination. During the 1930s, however, the United States ardently opposed intervention. Public opinion polls indicated that at least until September 1938, when the Munich conference took place, the American people as a whole favored a strong neutrality policy, supporting above all an embargo on war supplies to any belligerent.[2] As late as the summer of 1939, anti-interventionists controlled Congress. Federal legislation prohibited the extension of credits and sale of arms to any belligerent, even if a general consensus existed that said nation had experienced outright aggression.

In the Senate, anti-interventionists ran the gamut from arch-conservatives to disillusioned progressives and individuals often to the left of Franklin D. Roosevelt.[3] Certainly, Robert A. Taft ranked as one of the more conservative critics of FDR's foreign policy. A strong critic of the New Deal, the Ohio Re-

1

publican said in 1933, "There is very little the Government can do to really modify the tremendous economic forces involved in a world-wide business depression."[4] Hiram Johnson of California stood far more squarely in the progressive fold, being the running mate of Theodore Roosevelt in 1912 and remaining particularly outspoken in promoting the public ownership of utilities. In 1932, though a Republican, he endorsed FDR and backed much of his earlier legislation, though by 1937 he broke with the New Deal over such matters as Supreme Court "packing," sit-down strikes, and above all foreign policy.[5] Gerald P. Nye took a somewhat similar route. A foe of big business and of Wall Street in particular, the maverick Republican from North Dakota fought continually with President Herbert Hoover. Originally friendly to FDR's domestic agenda, by 1939 he was blasting government spending and "tinkering."[6] Another liberal, Robert Marion La Follette Jr. (Prog.-Wis.), remained firmly in the Roosevelt camp, endorsing three out of four of his election bids while being more radical on such matters as labor.[7]

In the House, similar diversity existed. Admittedly it was the conservative Republicans who predominated, people strongly anti–New Deal and often hailing from west of the Alleghenies. Almost anomalous among this group was their leader, Hamilton Fish. A Harvard-educated blueblood from FDR's own congressional district, Fish supported social security and minimum wage laws while opposing court "packing," government reorganization, and massive relief programs.[8] Yet some in their midst were quite radical. Vito Marcantonio (Am. Lab.–N.Y.), far to the left of the New Deal, first called World War II an "imperialist" struggle, although he sought a declaration of war soon after the Soviet Union entered the conflict.[9] Usher Burdick (Rep.-N.Dak.) had been state president of the Farm Holiday Association, a group radical enough in the early thirties to run sheriffs off foreclosed land.[10]

Certain Republican leaders possessed strong noninterventionist sentiments, among them former president Hoover, retired diplomat William R. Castle, and Alfred Landon, governor of Kansas from 1933 to 1937 and presidential candidate in 1936.[11] The most prominent labor leader in the nation, John L. Lewis, found Roosevelt's foreign policy repellent, as did many business and labor journals.[12] University students often opposed involvement, being far more adamant on the issue than their professors.[13] There were, however, some prominent scholars resisting involvement, including—in the field of international law alone—Edwin M. Borchard of Yale, Philip Jessup of Columbia, and John Bassett Moore, former justice on the World Court.[14] Within the Roosevelt administration itself, some figures could be most cautious in public but somewhat adamant in private, the most pronounced being Joseph P. Kennedy, ambassador to Britain until December 1940.[15] Others include John Cudahy, ambassador to Belgium from January to November 1940; military advisers Stanley Embick and Truman Smith; and anglophobe assistant secretary of state Adolf A. Berle.[16]

Aviator Charles Augustus Lindbergh, one of the most famous people in the world, was so outspoken on the matter that he served as the leading drawing card of the president's opponents. Beginning in 1935, eight years after his famous flight to Paris, Colonel Lindbergh lived four years in Europe, reporting on German air power for American military intelligence. In the late 1930s, he maintained that war between Germany and the Western powers would be suicidal, for a predatory Soviet Union lurked on the sidelines. His wife, Anne Morrow Lindbergh, articulately supported her husband's position, though her arguments took on a more humanitarian thrust.[17]

Powerful elements of the American press bitterly fought FDR. The arch-conservative William Randolph Hearst remained in control of the nation's leading newspaper chain. In 1940, Hearst owned seventeen dailies, including such highly influential papers as the *San Francisco Examiner* and the *Chicago Herald-American*. At least two Hearst papers, the *New York Journal-American* and the *New York Mirror*, possessed circulations well above half a million. Beginning in late February 1940, Hearst wrote his own front-page column, "In the News," commenting on matters ranging from Cleopatra's role in history to contemporary military tactics. His views were strongly reinforced by Hearst columnist Boake Carter, a radio commentator who wrote two anti-interventionist primers: *Why Meddle in the Orient?* (1938) and *Why Meddle in Europe?* (1939).[18]

Roy W. Howard directed another anti-interventionist chain, Scripps-Howard, that possessed nineteen dailies in 1940. Howard personally edited the chain's flagship, the *New York World-Telegram*, with a circulation of over four hundred thousand in 1940. Though his chain had backed Roosevelt enthusiastically in the 1932 and 1936 elections, it broke with him in 1940, in part because of the president's foreign policy. In March 1941 *Time* claimed that the publisher had converted to interventionism, yet the chain remained sharply critical of the president.[19]

Though the Scripps-Howard chain featured certain pro-FDR writers, including Raymond Clapper and Eleanor Roosevelt, it gave his foes a major forum. One such critic was General Hugh Johnson, who in 1933 had headed the National Recovery Administration (NRA), the linchpin of the early New Deal. Eight years later, Johnson was totally estranged from the president. His *Hell-Bent for War* (1941) assailed Roosevelt's foreign policy: it claimed that Germany was overextended, found little danger in Hitler's economic penetration of the Western hemisphere, and accused the British of fighting in part to preserve their empire.[20] Beginning in December 1939, Scripps-Howard carried John T. Flynn, a financial writer best known among intellectuals for his attacks on Wall Street speculation, who made no secret of finding FDR attempting to lift the United States out of the depression by seeking martial adventures.[21]

The firm's management found one columnist, the polemical scholar Harry Elmer Barnes, so provocative that he contributed exclusively to the *New York*

*World-Telegram.* A prolific historian and sociologist, Barnes wrote thirty books and over a hundred essays in a lifetime spanning seventy-nine years. He began a career of controversy by writing pro-Allied propaganda in World War I and ended it by denying Hitler's Final Solution. When World War II broke out, Barnes claimed that the British and French "deserved" Hitler, called the conflict a "back room brawl," and hoped that neither side would be victorious. In May 1940, the *World-Telegram* dismissed Barnes, declaring that the editorial page needed lighter material.[22]

Anti-interventionism also found a champion in the *New York Daily News.* In 1941, with two million readers daily and three and a half million on Sunday, this tabloid led the entire nation in circulation. Staunchly pro–New Deal through the 1940 election, it was published by Captain Joseph Medill Patterson. The *News's* editorial writer, Reuben Maury, who won a Pulitzer Prize in 1940, opposed Roosevelt's foreign policy in the *News* while supporting it in *Collier's* magazine.[23]

Patterson's first cousin, Colonel Robert R. McCormick, published the *Chicago Tribune.* He veered sharply from Patterson's militant support of the New Deal but shared his opposition to the president's overseas policies. Possessing a daily circulation in 1940 of close to a million, the *Tribune* was the most widely distributed full-sized paper in the nation, second overall only to that of Patterson's *News.*[24] Patterson's sister, Eleanor Medill ("Cissy") Patterson, published the *Washington Times-Herald,* which had a circulation of two hundred thousand in 1941. Not only did she share her brother's views to such a degree that she usually ran *News* editorials verbatim, but her foreign editor, Frank Waldrop, also frequently contributed an anti-interventionist column of his own.[25]

These newspaper magnates found additional support: H. L. Mencken, the caustic cofounder of the *American Mercury* and columnist for the *Baltimore Sun;* Felix Morley, chief editorial writer of the *Washington Post* until March 1940; Raymond Moley, former FDR brain truster and contributing editor of *Newsweek;* George Sokolsky, columnist for the *New York Sun;* William Henry Chamberlin, foreign correspondent for the *Christian Science Monitor* until 1940; freelance journalist Freda Utley; Burton Rascoe, critic for the *American Mercury;* and Porter Sargent, publisher of an anti-interventionist bulletin.[26]

Several conservative journals opposed involvement. The *Saturday Evening Post,* which drew well over three million readers in 1941, published weekly editorials opposing Roosevelt's policies. Chief editorial writer Garet Garrett (originally Edward Peter), who joined the weekly in the middle of 1940, and foreign correspondent Demaree Bess were particularly vocal on foreign policy. In May 1941, the *Post* claimed that the passage of lend-lease had closed the debate, implying that the public should rally around the administration. Yet until the Japanese attacked Pearl Harbor, it still maintained its attack.[27]

*Scribner's Commentator,* a monthly digest, was even more anti-interventionist. Published by Charles S. Payson, husband of millionaire Joan Whitney, and edited by George T. Eggleston, it fired its volleys in many different directions, all arch-rightist in tone. It carried industrialist Henry Ford's attack on "international bankers," articles blasting the French Republic and praising the Portugal of António de Oliveira Salazar, book reviews by philosophical anarchist Albert Jay Nock, and warnings against "fifth columns" of refugees, some essays mentioning Jews as a distinct category.[28]

Some journals far more friendly to Roosevelt's domestic policies suspected his pro-Allied sentiments, at least when World War II first began. Of these, the *New Republic*, edited by Bruce Bliven and possessing a circulation of a little over thirty thousand in 1940, undoubtedly claimed the most influence. In late April 1940, as Norway came under siege, the liberal weekly started to shift, a circumstance aided by pressure from its owner and founder, Dorothy Whitney Elmhirst, who had long lived in Britain. Within months John T. Flynn, whose financial column increasingly warned of the perils of militarization, was fired.[29]

The monthly *Common Sense*, edited by Alfred M. Bingham and Selden Rodman, possessed a moderate noninterventionism, combining its endorsement of aid to Britain with calls for a negotiated peace. Frank Hanighen, its Washington correspondent, had gained prominence as coauthor of *Merchants of Death* (1934), a muckraking account of the global munitions industry.[30]

In June 1940, the *Progressive*, an eight-page tabloid published in Madison, Wisconsin, came under the direct control of Senator Robert M. La Follette Jr. and his brother, former Wisconsin governor Philip La Follette.[31] It served as a refuge for such exiles from interventionist journals as publisher Oswald Garrison Villard, who had just resigned from the *Nation*, and pacifist Ernest L. Meyer, who had left the *New York Post*. Also contributing were air power advocate Major Al Williams, who also wrote for Scripps-Howard, and liberal economist Stuart Chase, author of the anti-interventionist *The New Western Front* (1939).[32]

*Uncensored* could well have been the most imaginative liberal journal. A mimeographed weekly sponsored by the Writers Anti-War Bureau, it offered news not usually found in the daily press. In 1940, it was edited by Sidney Hertzberg, a prominent socialist journalist who had served on the staff of the *New York Times*, *Time*, and *Current History*. Although the journal operated, in Hertzberg's words, on "a frayed shoestring" and reached only a thousand subscribers, it found its articles attacking Roosevelt foreign policy reproduced by the *Progressive* and the Socialist Party's *Call*.[33]

By the fall of 1939, all political parties on the left strongly opposed "entanglement." Among them were the socialists, whose presidential candidate since 1928 had been Norman Thomas, formerly a Presbyterian minister.[34] In his book *Keep America Out of War: A Program* (1939), written with fellow radical Bertram D. Wolfe and published just after hostilities commenced, Thomas made his position clear. "We set it down as our opinion that this Second World War is the continuation of the First," he stated, going on to describe "age-old power politics" and "modern imperialist conflicts."[35] The *Call*, an eight-page weekly tabloid, served as the party's major vehicle. Thomas's weekly column, "Your World and Mine," attacked the "delusions" of fellow liberals, while Lillian Symes's "Hold That Line" assailed the interventionist press. The weekly *American Guardian* acted as the *Call*'s Great Plains version. Published in Oklahoma City and having a circulation of close to fifty thousand in 1940, it was edited by Oscar Ameringer, a veteran Oklahoma socialist, who once titled a self-descriptive column "Isolationist: Hard-Boiled and Unashamed."[36]

For a belated, intermittent, and thoroughly expediential recruit to anti-interventionist ranks, one could find no better example than the Communist Party of the United States of America. When, in late summer 1939, the Soviet Union and Germany signed a nonaggression pact, the party abruptly ceased its long-standing cries for collective security and, following the dictates of Moscow, called for strict isolation.[37] At the beginning of the conflict, the *Daily Worker*, a tabloid published in New York, acted as the official Communist Party organ, but several other journals echoed the Stalinist position as well.[38] Especially close to the party was the weekly *New Masses*, which usually remained silent concerning Germany while saving its most frequent and bitter abuse for Britain.[39] In June 1940, a four-page weekly bulletin, *In Fact*, was launched. Claiming to expose "the war-mongering press," it was edited by George Seldes, former foreign correspondent and author of *Iron, Blood, and Profits* (1934), an indictment of the munitions trade.[40] That August, the new weekly *Friday*, a picture magazine patterned on *Life* and *Look*, promoted the communist position.[41] March 1941 saw the birth of the Milwaukee-based *US Week*, a twenty-four-page communist rival to *Time* and *Newsweek*.[42] Once the Soviet Union entered the war, all these vehicles turned vehemently interventionist overnight. Henceforth, it would be hard to find a prominent critic of FDR whom they did not thereafter portray as pro-Axis.

Various Trotskyist journals offered another left perspective. Products of a most arcane political world, they possessed a richly diverse group of writers, who were prone to excommunicate alleged deviators.[43] Within Trotskyism's ranks were the *Partisan Review*, in whose pages editor Dwight Macdonald, en route to philosophical anarchism, predicated his anti-interventionism on the premise that revolutionary socialism was the only way to destroy fascism; the *Socialist Appeal*, organ of the Socialist Workers Party, in which columnist James Burnham, soon to be author of *The Managerial Revolution* (1941), denounced "isolationists" for tacitly endorsing the defense of Canada; and the *New International*, in which Hal Draper went so far as to warn that even the war referendum movement masked aggressive imperialism.[44]

In a class by itself lay the mimeographed four-page *Weekly Foreign Letter*, written by Lawrence Dennis, former infantry officer, lower-level diplomat, and financial expert. By 1934, Dennis saw salvation from the Great Depression lying in the corporate state. He was not afraid to use the term *fascism* in espousing a one-party government, strident nationalism, continental autarchy, and centralized economic controls. In February 1939, Dennis joined the *Weekly Foreign Letter*, which had just been founded eight months previously. He shared editorial responsibilities with V. D. Gravenhoff, a White Russian, until mid-March 1940, whereupon he became sole author. The bulletin, which received $1,200 from the German embassy, was far more extreme than most other noninterventionist journals. It attacked the "isolationists" from within, claiming they were foolish to endorse limited aid to Britain and to hold Roosevelt accountable to his antiwar pledges. Only by combining a program of absolute nonparticipation with promises of a welfare state or the annexation of the entire continent could the president's adversaries, he argued, secure a mass base. Though his circulation remained a few hundred, it reached certain leading anti-interventionists, many of whom were far more in the political mainstream than Dennis himself.[45]

Anti-interventionism found a strong voice in certain religious journals. The *Christian Century* was certainly one of the important Protestant periodicals in the world, though its circulation in 1940 was only twenty-nine thousand. Editor Charles Clayton Morrison, a Disciples of Christ minister, vigorously supported social reform (including the New Deal), liberal theology, and pan-Protestant church union. He felt impassioned enough about the outlawry of war to write a book by that title. Although, in 1941, he denied that either he or his journal was pacifist, his editorials opposed all of FDR's moves overseas. Even the most militant of pacifists were far more welcome as contributors than were interventionists.[46] If the absolutist pacifists had a leader with national visibility, it was John Haynes Holmes, Unitarian minister of the Community Church of New York, who edited the Chicago-based bimonthly *Unity.*[47]

Much of the Roman Catholic press felt similarly.[48] The Jesuit weekly *America*, edited by Francis X. Talbot, often backed New Deal measures; yet it was so opposed to U.S. involvement in World War II that it carried an article attacking Britain by the anti-Semitic and pro-Mussolini poet Ezra Pound.[49] James M. Gillis edited the Paulist monthly *Catholic World*, whose opposition to Italy's Benito Mussolini and Spain's Francisco Franco did not hinder it from being acerbic concerning both Roosevelt's foreign policy and the New Deal.[50] The lay weekly *Commonweal*, far more liberal domestically, expressed similar criticism of FDR's diplomacy, though at times its entire staff was so divided that certain editorials had to be signed.[51]

*Social Justice*, a weekly tabloid launched in 1936, reflected the views of Father Charles E. Coughlin, whose broadcasts from Royal Oak, Michigan, had once reached forty million people, giving him the largest radio audience in the world. By 1938, Coughlin's early calls for inflation and a currency based solely on silver gave way to vehement anti-Semitism (he reprinted *The Protocols of the Learned Elders of Zion* in his journal) and praise for fascist regimes. In August 1941, his journal even charged that "because Jewish International bankers own or control the gold of the world, *it is their war.*"[52] In 1939, *Social Justice* was first edited by E. Perrin Schwartz, former city editor of the *Milwaukee Journal,* and then by Louis B. Ward, a business consultant personally closer to Coughlin. At all times, however, the radio priest (who contributed the column "From the Tower") was firmly in control. Its foreign editor was Major James Strachey Barnes, an Englishman who had joined the Italian fascist party and been decorated by Mussolini.[53]

Obviously, peace organizations opposed Roosevelt's policies.[54] On the surface, the Women's International League for Peace and Freedom, U.S. Section (WIL), was more moderate, as it was open to both pacifists and nonpacifists and thereby encompassed those who believed in strict neutrality and those who would favor some forms of collective security. Indeed, its honorary international president, educator Emily Greene Balch, favored such nonmilitary forms of international coercion as moral, diplomatic, and economic pressure. Its national secretary, Dorothy Detzer, however, spoke out continually against all interventionist measures, even when she could not rally her own organization behind her. In 1938, the WIL had reached a membership peak of just over fourteen thousand. By April 1940, its enrollment had dropped to slightly under thirteen thousand.[55]

Other peace groups produced their own journals. The National Council for the Prevention of War (NCPW), an umbrella organization of pacifist and nonpacifist groups, sponsored *Peace Action,* an eight-page monthly bulletin edited by executive secretary Frederick J. Libby. A Quaker pacifist, Libby said in 1940 that he would not participate in any war in which the United States might engage. His newsletter combined pragmatic argument with scriptural injunction, thereby reasoning on the basis of global power relationships as well as on abstract ethical imperatives.[56]

The Fellowship of Reconciliation (FOR) sponsored its own monthly organ, *Fellowship,* which expressed a far more overt pacifism. By the end of 1940, the FOR, which was the nation's major pacifist body, listed eight thousand active members and two thousand inactive ones. In 1941, *Fellowship*'s editor was John Nevin Sayre, an Anglican clergyman who chaired the international FOR. A. J. Muste, a former Dutch Reformed minister and Marxist who became FOR secretary in April 1940, contributed often to the journal.[57]

Obviously the house of anti-interventionism contained many mansions, and the bitterest of enemies might agree on only one premise: the necessity of avoiding full-scale American involvement in World War II. Reasons could be contradictory: opposition to fundamental social reform or fear of radical social change; lack of the needed armament or Jesus's injunctions against "the sword"; a global analysis that predicted eventual victory of the world's totalitarian powers or one that predicted their defeat. All these factors, and many others besides, came into play once Germany invaded Poland, an event that took place on 1 September 1939.

# 1

# War, Phony and Real

The attack began before dawn. At 0445 hours German tanks crossed the Polish frontier. The Luftwaffe immediately crushed the Polish air force. That evening Prime Minister Neville Chamberlain told the House of Commons that Britain had sent an ultimatum to Reichchancellor Hitler demanding an immediate troop withdrawal. When two days later, 3 September 1939, Germany rejected Britain's withdrawal deadline of 11 A.M., Chamberlain broadcast that "all my long struggle to win peace has failed." By the end of the day, Britain and France had declared war on Germany, thus turning the Poland invasion into World War II. Hitler justified his attack on the grounds that the Poles would not cede the German-speaking areas of Danzig and the Polish Corridor.[1]

Once war broke out, blame for the conflict varied.[2] Certain nonintervention-ists accused Hitler of triggering the conflict as did over 80 percent of Gallup poll respondents.[3] Wrote Oswald Garrison Villard of the Allies, "Theirs is the righteous cause; they were willing to negotiate; the records show that Hitler went around lying and in haste." Using data just released in Britain's *White Book*, the *Chicago Tribune* argued that Hitler had sought war, whereas Britain desired only peace and the integrity of Poland.[4] The socialist *Call* conceded the legitimacy of Germany's claim to Danzig and the Corridor but found Hitler's attack putting Poland's sheer existence at stake. Charles A. Lindbergh saw "the fault of the war about evenly divided in Europe." The liberal monthly

*Common Sense* thought it irrelevant to assess guilt, asserting no one in Europe really wanted a clash.[5]

A surprising number of anti-interventionists had little sympathy for the Allies. To understand their position, one must examine their views on Danzig and the Corridor, Hitler's earlier diplomatic overtures to Poland, the Anglo-French guarantee to the Poles of March 1939, the Munich pact of September 1938, and the German-Soviet accord of August 1939. To begin with, several figures accepted a major German claim—namely, that the Polish crisis was rooted in the status of Danzig and the Polish Corridor. The Versailles treaty of 1919 had designated Danzig, whose population was overwhelmingly German, as a free city, self-governing under the general supervision of a high commissioner responsible to the League of Nations. At the same time, Danzig was incorporated into the Polish customs system, and Poland represented the city in foreign affairs. To assure Poland "free and secure access" to the Baltic Sea, the language of Woodrow Wilson's Fourteen Points, Poland obtained a "corridor" lying along the Vistula River. Although the Corridor contained more Poles than Germans, it severed the relatively small territory of East Prussia from Germany proper. No German leader ever supported Polish domination of either Danzig or its surroundings.[6]

Even after the German attack, noninterventionists often maintained that the German position on the Corridor was just. In 1919, they recalled, President Wilson had warned that depriving Germany of such areas would lead to another war. Prime Minister Lloyd George's famous Fontainebleu memorandum to Clemenceau, dated 25 March 1919, prophesied that putting German nationals under foreign rule would create conflict.[7]

Still more important to such anti-interventionists, Danzig and the Corridor remained unquestionably German. Danzig, said Congressman Hamilton Fish (Rep.-N.Y.), was "97 percent German, 97 percent Prussian, and 97 percent Nazi." To Yale law professor Edwin M. Borchard, "Morally Hitler has a good case."[8]

Of course, attacks on Poland's domination of the Corridor were far from limited to the anti-interventionists. In 1933, for example, FDR himself told the British that the Corridor should be returned to Germany.[9] Yet all polls taken in August and September 1939 indicated that Americans, by a large margin, found Hitler's claims to Danzig and the Corridor unjustified.[10]

Even when the fighting started, several anti-interventionists maintained that Hitler had sought peace with Poland. Such a view was based on the German-Polish negotiations launched in late October 1938. German foreign secretary Joachim von Ribbentrop offered Josef Lipski, Polish ambassador to Berlin, a series of terms, including Danzig's incorporation into Germany, a German-controlled road and rail link with East Prussia, German guarantee of the Polish frontier, a twenty-five-year extension of the 1934 nonaggression pact between the two countries, and Polish membership in the Anti-Comintern Pact that included Germany, Japan, and Italy. Realizing that such terms would result in

Poland's subordination to the Reich, Polish foreign minister Josef Beck refused.[11] The entire spring and summer of 1939 were consumed by relentless
German pressure, both propagandistic and military, against the Poles.

Hitler's formal terms—as filtered through the popular press—appealed to
some anti-interventionists, including more than the obvious profascist elements.[12] Harry Elmer Barnes found Germany's formal demands "very reasonable." Frank C. Waldrop of the *Washington Times-Herald* suggested that
Poland should have linked itself with either Russia or Germany and have declared Warsaw an open city.[13]

Several anti-interventionists bestowed major responsibility for the conflict
on Britain and France, accusing them of foolishly encouraging Polish resistance. Such critics pointed to one Allied assurance to Poland after another, each
increasing the degree of commitment. Although France had entered into a
formal alliance with Poland in 1925, only on 31 March 1939 did the British
government promise Anglo-French aid in case independence was threatened.
On 25 August, the British intensified their commitment, entering into a mutual assistance pact with Poland and, in a secret protocol, specified Germany
as the potential aggressor.[14]

Less than a month before war began, Congressman Fish sought negotiation
of the Danzig crisis. President of the American delegation to the Interparliamentary Union Conference, which met in mid-August 1939, Fish first spoke
with European leaders, including the foreign ministers of Britain, France, and
Germany. On the 17th, he introduced a resolution at the Oslo meeting calling
for arbitration, mediation, and a cooling-off period of thirty days.[15] Because
of the opposition from British and Norwegian representatives, he withdrew
his proposal. In September, Fish blamed the British for rejecting a proposal
that might have "saved Poland from being crucified by invasion and war."[16]

During the last week of peace, some noninterventionists were particularly
blunt. Borchard claimed that Britain's "churlish refusal" to accept Hitler's demands created another case in which "Hitler will again appear to be right and
the Allies wrong." Felix Morley, chief editorial writer for the *Washington Post*,
found the British fighting to save "face," not Poland. Writing of British intransigence, poet Anne Morrow Lindbergh wrote, "Is this courage or is it stupidity?" To her husband Charles, "Poland is beyond help under any circumstances."[17] Once the British and French entered the conflict, attacks on their
Polish guarantee became even more strident. General Hugh Johnson called
Britain's declaration of war "one of the greatest and most stupid blunders in
history—if not the greatest."[18]

To many, the fundamental error went far beyond the Anglo-French guarantee to Poland. Rather it lay in failing to follow through on the genuine détente
established by the Munich conference of late September 1938. At that time
Britain and France acceded in the transfer of the Sudetenland to Germany, an
event that within six months led to the dismemberment of Czechoslovakia.

True, some anti-interventionists attacked Munich bitterly, including Senator William E. Borah (Rep.-Idaho), who referred to "the dismembered body of Czechoslovakia, the only real republic in that portion of the world."[19] Others defended the pact.[20] By signing the agreement, they said, the Western powers had bought time to defend themselves.[21] Furthermore, Munich might turn German expansion in an easterly direction, thereby creating conflict with the Soviet Union. "Having given Hitler at Munich the keys to Eastern Europe," wrote Lawrence Dennis, "the British decided six months later to forbid him to use the keys."[22] According to journalist William Henry Chamberlin, France had missed its opportunity to crush Germany single-handedly during the Rhineland crisis of 1936. Hence, it had only one reasonable policy left: to acquiesce in German expansion eastward.[23]

The German-Soviet accord of 23 August 1939 created even more diverse reaction. Earlier that month, an Anglo-French military mission had traveled to Moscow, seeking to explore the possibilities of containing an obviously expanding Germany. When the Russians insisted on the right to transport troops across Poland as part of any agreement, the head of the British mission balked. In the 23 August agreement, Germany and the Soviet Union, hitherto the bitterest of enemies, signed a nonaggression pact. Both parties pledged to refrain from attacking the other and promised neutrality if either party were attacked by a third. A secret codicil was attached that divided Eastern Europe into spheres of influence.[24]

Not surprisingly, American communists endorsed the agreement. The pact, predicted party head Earl Browder, would break the Axis, while commentator Theodore Draper alleged that the pact had temporarily shattered "the appeasement front."[25] Conversely, Father Charles E. Coughlin found the pact embarrassing. When news of the agreement was released, he told a radio audience that Americans must henceforth treat communism and Nazism alike. Sooner or later, he went on, Stalin's and Hitler's star would set.[26]

A few opponents of intervention saw the agreement as reducing the chances for conflict, the *New York Daily News* maintaining it showed Stalin's unwillingness to enter a general war.[27] And even if the pact did not advance the cause of peace, it could still be defended. Senator Borah, former chairman of the Senate Foreign Relations Committee, thought the British deserved such treatment, for they had excluded the Soviets from the Munich conference, while seeking their aid in protecting Poland. Historian Harry Elmer Barnes went further. He conceded the Soviet Union was guilty of aggression but asserted that it was the Soviets' desire for peace and security that induced them to sign the 23 August agreement.[28]

The agreement, some anti-interventionists correctly suspected, involved secret understandings. The *New York Daily News* suggested that the pact might involve the partition of Poland.[29] To Hugh Johnson, the agreement included the return of the Baltic states to Russia and the partition of Rumania.[30] Within ten years, *Social Justice* predicted, Hitler would control the Balkans, dividing its rich markets with Stalin, while the USSR would command Turkey, Iraq, and Persia.[31]

On 27 September, Soviet troops advanced from the east, meeting the Germans at Brest-Litovsk two days later. Again, the communists strongly defended the move, quoting British politician David Lloyd George and playwright George Bernard Shaw on the matter.[32] Several noninterventionists expressed outrage.[33] To jurist John Bassett Moore, Russia had become "the chief exponent of the spirit of aggression." The *New York Daily News* stressed such Soviet perfidies as the shooting of priests. At the same time, it argued, Britain had gone to war fully aware that the Soviets would not come to Poland's aid.[34]

Why, some anti-interventionists asked, had not the Allies declared war on Russia as they had on Germany?[35] In noting the observation made by British Foreign Secretary Lord Halifax—namely, that the Soviet-Polish border simply followed the ethnic Curzon line drafted at the 1919 Paris conference—the *Christian Century* accused Britain of acquiescing in the Soviet annexation of more than a third of Poland."[36] Socialist leader Norman Thomas requested Roosevelt to extend his neutrality proclamation banning arms and munitions to the USSR, though he maintained that Poland's Jews and White Russians would be better satisfied under Stalin than they had been under either Hitler or the old Polish autocracy.[37]

Among the anti-interventionists, Poland had its share of sympathizers.[38] "My heart bleeds," said Congressman Lewis D. Thill (Rep.-Wis.), for a people who "so valiantly defended their homeland against German and Russian attacks." Senator James J. Davis (Rep.-Pa.) warned, "Nazi ruthlessness is eradicating a people from the face of the earth." To Hamilton Fish, Poland had been "crucified." In February 1941, the usually reticent Charles A. Lindbergh told the Senate Foreign Relations Committee that he was "very much opposed to what happened in the German invasion of Poland." Before the Soviets invaded Poland, the communist *Daily Worker* urged "maximum aid."[39]

Roman Catholic journals voiced particular concern, no doubt partly because of Poland's historic prominence as a Catholic nation.[40] Even *Social Justice* saw Warsaw displaying "a heroism unsurpassed in the annals of militant patriotism," whereas Hitler embodied "the pagan plottings of anti-Christ."[41] The fact that Coughlin's journal was published in a suburb of Detroit, a heavily Polish area, was undoubtedly a factor in its position.

As news spread of German atrocities against Poland's Jews, anti-interventionists vehemently denounced Hitler's anti-Semitic policies.[42] Hitler's new "Jewish State" there, predicted Villard, would become "nothing more than a huge concentration camp and charnel house." Calling for mass protest meetings, he continued, "The Jews are treated literally as no German would be allowed under the law to treat a dumb animal."[43] Not since Genghis Khan and Attila, suspected Hugh Johnson in January 1940, had there been such barbarism.[44] In February 1941, Herbert Hoover, speaking to the Jewish Welfare Fund of Chicago, called for the creation of a new refugee state in Central Africa.[45]

A few noninterventionists were more reserved. Pacifist leader Dorothy Detzer conceded that atrocity stories concerning Poland might well be true, but she accused the British of deliberately timing news releases so as to influence neutrality debates in Congress.[46] *Catholic World* even saw the Germans as possible victims. In reviewing *Polish Acts of Atrocity Against the German Minority in Poland*, published by the German Library of Information, the Paulist monthly judged that Berlin's claims were as credible as those who stressed Nazi atrocities.[47]

Many anti-interventionists were unsympathetic to Poland, and several focused on Poland's long history of anti-Semitism.[48] More Jews had been persecuted in Poland, said Senator Burton K. Wheeler (Dem.-Mont.), than in any other country in the world.[49]

Furthermore, such noninterventionists depicted the Polish government as oppressive, its ruling class exploitative.[50] Harry Elmer Barnes cited socialist writer Max Nomad in claiming that Poland's regime was "hated by the majority of its own people."[51] According to the *Christian Century*, civil liberties had ceased to exist when General Joseph Pilsudski had launched his coup in 1926.[52] *Call* columnist Lillian Symes contended that the Allies were fighting for the restoration of "a semi-fascist government of less military significance than Czechoslovakia."[53]

Poland's recent conduct in Europe was severely questioned. The *Christian Century* recalled that even before the Paris Peace Conference of 1919 had even adjourned, Poland had attacked Galicia and within a year had invaded Soviet Russia.[54] After Munich, Congressman John Marshall Robsion (Rep.-Ky.) noted, Poland had seized seven thousand square miles of Czech territory.[55] Barnes accused the nation's leaders of envisioning a "Great Poland" stretching from the Baltic to the Black Sea.[56] Anti-interventionists occasionally pilloried Poland's war leaders for fleeing to Rumania. Pundit H. L. Mencken, for example, accused them of looting the gold resources of their own nation.[57]

To several figures, Poland's fall did not simply result from its leadership. Publisher Robert R. McCormick indicted Britain and France for remaining totally inert during the German invasion.[58] Joseph P. Kennedy asserted England would rather "sell 100 Polands down the river than risk the life of a British soldier or the loss of a British pound." Even if Poland was restored, declared Mencken, Britain would make it a "puppet state" similar to Egypt and India.[59] Congressman Bruce Barton (Rep.-N.Y.) found Western aid infeasible. A look at the atlas, he said, showed that there was no way France and England could come to Poland's aid.[60]

Once Poland's fate was decided, certain anti-interventionists sought to alleviate its disasters. Herbert Hoover launched a full-scale campaign to feed starving Poles, establishing the Commission for Polish Relief and raising some $6 million.[61] In February 1940, Senator Alexander Wiley (Rep.-Wis.), pointing to Polish forces fighting in France, urged $15 million in congressional aid. Fish found surplus American wheat and cotton able to clothe and feed the Poles.[62] Indeed, some anti-interventionists remained optimistic concerning Poland's ultimate survival.[63] Congressman Thill predicted that the division of Poland would not last forever: "The world is too small for both Hitler and Stalin."[64]

Yet, irrespective of their analysis, all such commentators concurred with one claim of the *Chicago Tribune*: the United States had not created the Danzig situation; it therefore had no stake in it. Even if the U.S. so desired, it could not eject Hitler from the old free city of Danzig, much less force Stalin to return his portion of Poland.[65] Senator Robert A. Taft sympathized with the invaded Poles but saw "no reason why we should run on the field and play quarterback."[66]

Despite the loss of Poland, many anti-interventionists did not think the Allies would be defeated. The American public itself was equally optimistic; a *Fortune* poll taken in October predicted an Allied victory 64 percent to 7 percent, with 29 percent uncertain.[67] At best Hitler's foes would emerge victorious, at worst experience stalemate.[68] Said General Hugh Johnson in November, "An ignorant and brutal upstart has shot craps with destiny once too often."[69]

Several reasons were given. First, Allied ground forces appeared invincible. Not only did the French possess the largest effective army in the world; it was the best. The Allies, wrote columnist Boake Carter, could put three soldiers in the field for every one the Germans could muster.[70] Second, so both Herbert Hoover and Charles A. Lindbergh noted, the Maginot line served to deter the Germans.[71] Third, as Hoover stressed, Allied naval strength appeared far superior. The French and British would continue to control the seas.[72]

Only one factor was debated: air power. Boake Carter foresaw German factories demolished by British and French bombs; ten million Germans, he predicted, would die.[73] Arguing to the contrary, Colonel Lindbergh envisioned Germany as soon possessing complete air supremacy.[74] The discussion was often taken to another level, for several anti-interventionists denied that air power alone could ever conquer a nation. Hugh Johnson, writing in October, called German raids on British naval forces "flops"; new defenses made mass raids on large cities too dangerous even to attempt.[75] The *Chicago Tribune*, which acknowledged German air superiority, found that pursuit planes and antiaircraft weapons could defend cities against air attack.[76] Dennis and Gravenhoff were particularly skeptical of bombing, for even if Germany should capture the Netherlands and use it as an air base, the Luftwaffe could not inflict much damage on Britain. Ninety percent of London itself consisted of open spaces; therefore, over three-fourths of any bombs dropped there would be wasted.[77]

To the noninterventionists, the Allies held advantages in resources. Britain and France, maintained Boake Carter, dominated the world's entire financial resources and 70 percent of its material ones.[78] As Hoover noted, the Allied nations possessed 115 million people, Germany only 80 million. In regard to foodstuffs, he found France practically self-supporting, Britain well supplied from its dominions. Germany, in contrast, was starting the war "on bread cards."[79] In fact, *Commonweal* believed conditions in Germany so bad that it suggested a relief organization. The strategic situation itself, wrote *Newsweek* editor Raymond Moley, worked to Allied advantage. Germany, he said, feared the enormous sacrifice that an attack on the western front would entail, for "if she weakens herself Russia will move westward."[80] Conversely, several anti-interventionists saw Germany internally weak, lacking essential foodstuffs and such raw materials as iron ore and oil. Besides, it risked rampant inflation.[81]

Even if Germany won the war, according to such reasoning, it could not dominate Europe for long.[82] Senator Taft envisioned any dictator facing countless occupation difficulties.[83] Senator Robert Rice Reynolds (Dem.-N.C.) concurred, stressing the colossal task Germany would face in holding down the French and British empires.[84] Moreover, there were the punative lessons of history, as shown by ill-fated would-be conquerors ranging from Julius Caesar to Napoleon.[85]

Several saw a possibility of Hitler's Reich dissolving internally.[86] John T. Flynn spoke of economic collapse or a leftist revolt.[87] In due time, predicted Senator William J. Bulow (Dem.-S.Dak.), the German people would overthrow their Nazi rulers. Drawing on José Ortega y Gasset's *Revolt of the Masses* (1930), Congressman Barton claimed that a long war would trigger popular revolts in both Germany and the Soviet Union. Already, wrote Boake Carter in September, some eight million Czechs were prepared to revolt.[88]

To Oswald Garrison Villard, a close observer of German affairs, Germany lacked the strength for a long-term struggle. Arriving there just before the outbreak of war, he remained three and a half weeks and then reported on his trip to both the public and Roosevelt himself.[89] From what he observed, Germany was a most unhappy land, the bulk of its people worn, tired, depressed, and in some cases hopeless. While denying the possibility of an early collapse, he said that internal differences within the Reich, centering on opposition to Nazi policy, would eventually result in Hitler's defeat. At one point, he noted that 75 percent of the people he met in Germany opposed Hitler's regime and that as many as 90 percent were against the war.[90] His firsthand account, *Within Germany* (1940), received favorable reviews.[91]

A few went further in emphasizing Germany's internal problems.[92] Early in December 1939, Norman Thomas found discontent reaching the high command. In January 1940, the *New York Daily News* discovered Germany rationing hot water.[93]

Amid such optimism, there was one warning: the Allies must not go on the offensive.[94] Any such blunder, Hoover warned, would exhaust British and French manpower. At the very outset of the conflict, Colonel Lindbergh feared that the British and French would attempt to bomb German cities, a move that could only draw terrible retaliation. Only one prominent anti-interventionist urged an Allied offensive: William Randolph Hearst. Britain and France, suggested the publisher in March 1940, should place themselves under such capable "war dictators" as French foreign minister Edouard Daladier, then secure Turkish support and attack through Italy, thereby assuring control of the Mediterranean.[95]

Throughout the winter of 1939–40, anti-interventionists saw only deadlock ahead.[96] They frequently pointed to lack of combat in Western Europe, a circumstance that changed only in April 1940. Congressman John Rankin (Dem.-Miss.) quipped that the troops "are merely playing pinochle."[97] If, said Senator Edwin Johnson (Dem.-Colo.), the Allies could neither crack the Siegfried line nor starve the Germans, who were supplied with unlimited Soviet assistance, victory would be extremely difficult. German submarines, lacking bases on the Atlantic, would soon be neutralized.[98] The *New York Daily News* kept stressing that any fight to the finish would result in unspeakable ills—starvation, communism—and that both sides realized it.[99] "England and France are in no position," wrote Hugh Johnson, "to fight any kind of war except an interminable affair of siege, blockade and starvation. Do you want to encourage that?" Lawrence Dennis and V. D. Gravenhoff denied that any German leader advocated "lightning war" against the Allies. Rather, Germany's "extremely logical" plan was based on submarine and air offensives against Allied shipping and naval bases.[100]

Several foes of intervention found the whole situation on the Western front absurd. Hearst's *San Francisco Examiner* called the conflict "about as senseless as two men quarreling in a boat which is about to carry them over Niagara Falls." The Allies, it was argued, lacked a fighting spirit. "There is something phony about this war," said Senator Borah, coining a famous phrase, for he was accusing the Allies of pulling their punches against Germany. Why, asked Hugh Johnson, had the Allies not bombed the Krupp works at Essen? Socialist editor Oscar Ameringer answered such queries by claiming, "The plutocrats are not going to bomb their own."[101]

Other noninterventionists, however, rejoiced in the static situation.[102] At the present pace, remarked Senator Lynn Frazier (Rep.-N.Dak.), Hitler could never smash the Allies. To *New Republic* editor Bruce Bliven, "The mass slaughter of human beings is about the most dreadful thing I know," and he deemed it best for the Allies to "sit still and starve Germany out." The title of his article: "I Like a Phony War."[103]

Certain figures in the Roosevelt administration were less optimistic.[104] Admiral Harold Stark, chief of naval operations, was in a decided minority in seeing stalemate ahead.[105] Secretary of State Cordell Hull envisioned the defeat of Britain and France, the partition of Eastern Europe between Germany and the Soviet Union, and the severing of all trade between the United States and Europe.[106] Assistant Secretary Adolf Berle and Interior Secretary Harold Ickes saw little reason for the Allies to count on a victory.[107] In November, both the state department and military experts, noted Ickes, predicted a German drive to the Channel through the Netherlands.[108]

Roosevelt's own attitude fluctuated. He told Ickes in October that German morale would crack; at other times he gave the Allies only a fifty-fifty chance of victory.[109] Within higher British circles only Colonel Hastings Ismay, military secretary to the war cabinet, predicted that France would collapse in the face of a German onslaught.[110]

Almost as soon as the war started, some noninterventionists saw peace in the offing. Early in September, Norman Thomas declared that the war might stop with the conquest of Poland. On 9 October, John Rankin predicted peace within a few days.[111] Others were a bit more vague but still hopeful.[112] "Some sort of peace," commented Hearst's *San Francisco Examiner* in mid-October, might come by Christmas, after which a world conference would undo the "obvious and almost universally hated injustices of the Versailles Treaty."[113] Signs included a warm German reception for a false armistice report, the return home of a hundred thousand French troops, German seizing of two supposed British peace agents on the Dutch border, and the scuttling of the German battleship *Graf Spee* off the Argentine coast, which showed Hitler could not endure the heavy casualties involved in a battleship fight.[114] Just before he died on 19 January 1940, Borah told a reporter he expected peace that spring, followed by a general revision of the Versailles treaty.[115]

Some were wary. As early as October, Herbert Hoover predicted that the impasse would only last until the spring.[116] Anne Morrow Lindbergh foresaw the conquest of Poland and merciless bombing of London and Paris. She thought in terms of "a new Spain," referring to the civil war that had just ended. To her husband Charles, it was again "The Charge of the Light Brigade." In March 1940, Villard feared that Hitler would soon attack Britain by both air and sea.[117]

A few anti-interventionists divined an Allied initiative, though not necessarily in Western Europe. In mid-February, the *New York Daily News* anticipated an Allied move in the Middle East. Noting the sudden appearance of thirty thousand Anzac troops at Suez, it contemplated a drive to sever the Soviet Union's Baku oil fields from Hitler. To block the move, Germany and Russia might push into Rumania, attacking the strategically vital Constantinople.[118]

For many, if not most, anti-interventionists, the greatest danger to the world came not from Germany but from the Soviet Union.[119] Who, queried Anne Morrow Lindbergh, was "the potential invader of Europe, the real threat of European civilization?" "Ask the Balkans and the Baltic states. Ask Finland; ask Rumania; ask Turkey." With Europe "bled white by wars and prostrated by devastation, her [Russia's] advance will be slow, inevitable, and deadly—like a flow of lava."[120]

So far, some argued, Hitler was already a loser, not a winner. On the political right, such opinions were expected.[121] Read one editorial headline in the *Chicago Tribune*: "The Winner, Red Josef."[122] But liberal noninterventionists too saw Stalin as the victor.[123] Norman Thomas found the German dictator doing "the fighting," the Soviet dictator "the annexing."[124]

Even Germany was not excluded from going Red.[125] Villard envisioned a communist takeover within five years.[126] Hearst correspondent H. R. Knickerbocker gave Hitler's Reich six years.[127] Dire consequences, several warned, would not be limited to Germany alone. Once the belligerents had been "bled white," predicted Representative Fish, "the Communist vulture will sweep down on the bloody remains of Europe."[128]

Stalin's aims appeared insatiable.[129] Reynolds spoke of Russia "creeping down" on Persia and India.[130] Congressman George A. Dondero (Rep.-Mich.) suspected Soviet designs on China and the Philippines. Norman Thomas warned of "a kind of world hegemony." By the war's end, the *New York Daily News* predicted, the United States "may be the only non-Communist nation left in the world."[131] To *Social Justice*, the West faced a series of revolutions, led in France by such "Communists" as Leon Blum, in Britain by such "rocking chair Communists" as Anthony Eden and Winston Churchill, and in the United States by such figures as financier Bernard Baruch and labor leaders Harry Bridges and Walter Reuther.[132]

Within interventionist circles, such apprehension was occasionally shared.[133] To Ickes, Hitler had "a big and unmanageable bear by the tail that will destroy him in his turn even if he succeeds in destroying France and England."[134] Assistant Secretary of State Berle found Stalin and Hitler ruling "from Manchuria to the Rhine, much as Genghis Khan once ruled."[135] Walter Lippmann, undoubtedly the most respected columnist among the interventionists, defined what he saw as the real issue of the war: "What shall be the boundary of Europe against the expanding invasion of Russian imperial Bolshevism?"

Only Roosevelt dissented slightly, denying that Germany could ever go "Communist in the Russian manner," for it had always honored the values of private property and family independence.[136]

Fortunately, so many hoped, a negotiated peace might be in the offing, one that could end the bloodshed and deflect the wide-sweeping ambitions of the Soviets.

# 2

# Early Hopes for Peace

On 6 October 1939, in the wake of his conquest of Poland, Hitler addressed the Reichstag. The German dictator called for an end to hostilities in the West, followed by a general peace conference to discuss such matters as disarmament, colonies, international economic reorganization, "the Jewish problem," the redivision of Eastern Europe "according to the various nationalities," and the formation of a Polish state friendly to Germany.[1]

Several anti-interventionists gave credence to Hitler's bid, among them Norman Thomas, John Haynes Holmes, and Harold E. Fey, field editor of the *Christian Century* and former FOR field secretary.[2] Commented the Protestant weekly itself, "Hitler wants peace. He wants it badly; he wants it now."[3]

Such pacifists were not alone.[4] Hearst's *San Francisco Examiner* suspected that Hitler might negotiate peace and then turn supreme command over to Reichsmarschall Hermann Goering.[5] Professor Borchard remarked that the Führer realized how seriously war would affect Germany's internal life.[6]

Not all anti-interventionists were so optimistic. When, in mid-September, Hitler first made peace overtures, retired diplomat William R. Castle called him a liar and his address "piffle."[7] In January, Villard wrote, "I do not suppose that in all history there has ever been a worse man or a less trustworthy one with whom to make solemn agreements." The liberal editor placed his hopes on elements of the German army and foreign office.[8] To the *New Republic*, Hitler simply wanted to celebrate his victories, not to negotiate with his enemies.[9] Several anti-interventionists, including the *New York Daily News*, put little credence in the Goering option.[10]

Some noninterventionists saw the Allies primarily at fault, finding them both obstinate and unrealistic. Once war commenced, Britain asserted it would never negotiate with Hitler. On 12 October, Chamberlain rejected the

Führer's peace bid of six days earlier: "After our past experience it is no longer possible to rely on the unsupported word of the present German Government." His nation, he said, would continue fighting until Hitler's regime was removed and independence restored to the European countries he had conquered. Furthermore, any peace must so restrict Germany as to prevent further efforts to conquer Europe and seek world domination.[11]

Anti-interventionists quickly responded to the prime minister.[12] Insistence on the destruction of the Nazi regime and the restoration of Czechoslovakia and Poland, warned the *San Francisco Examiner*, would cancel Hitler's peace offer.[13] Villard deplored a speech of First Lord of the Admiralty Winston Churchill that, so he alleged, prevented "a friendly attitude on the part of Hitler" toward Dutch and Belgian proposals.[14] If England and France persisted in restoring the Polish government, warned Wheeler, democracy would be "driven from the face of the earth." To Borah, Allied intransigence proved that France and Britain sought territory and power, not the elimination of Nazism. Only a few anti-interventionists thought that Britain genuinely desired peace, among them the journal *Uncensored*, journalist C. Hartley Grattan, and even Villard.[15]

Unknown to the general public, both in the United States and overseas, Chamberlain did keep open contacts with Germans whom he saw as "moderate," including conservative generals and Reichsmarschall Goering. The British blockade, he hoped, could ultimately destroy the German economy, thereby prompting the overthrow of Hitler. Unlike Roosevelt, the prime minister saw time on the side of the Allies. Rejecting the aim of total victory, he stressed the need to eliminate Nazism and maintain Britain as a world power. Responding to any "specious appeal" from Hitler could only divide the Allies while leading to strong pressure from the neutrals. Historian David Reynolds writes, "Historically British leaders had conceived of a strong but peaceful Germany as a potential source of stability in central Europe. Eliminating the Nazi menace at the cost of exposing the Continent to the Soviet threat was hardly a desirable prospect."[16]

Chamberlain was far from alone. Foreign Secretary Halifax privately hoped a peace might be made on the basis of partial German retirement from Poland, restoration of an independent Czech state, the surrender of half Germany's air force, and—in his words—"a lot more."[17] Even Churchill, who found the prime minister's military strategy too passive, said in October 1939 that he did not oppose a "genuine" German offer. Indeed, the first lord of the admiralty thought that Goering might be glad to play the role of George Monk, the general who fostered the transition from Cromwell's Commonwealth rule to the later Stuarts.[18]

Those who publicly endorsed negotiation were much applauded. There was, maintained John Haynes Holmes, more peace sentiment in both Britain and France than the American press acknowledged.[19] Anti-interventionists gave much attention to Lloyd George's peace approaches.[20] On 3 October, in addressing the House of Commons, the former prime minister claimed that a tolerable settlement could be imposed by the major neutral powers, who could enforce disarmament, the redistribution of colonies, and the restoration of Czechoslovakia and Poland.[21]

The "Welsh wizard" found endorsements in a wide span of anti-interventionist journals, ranging from the Hearst press to *New Masses*.[22] In November, Congressman Rankin praised the truce bid of the man he called "the Baptist lay leader of the British Empire." Until the United States entered the war, some noninterventionists speculated hopefully on Lloyd George's return to power and a possible peace bid, although others—such as Oswald Garrison Villard and William Henry Chamberlin—were dubious.[23]

When playwright George Bernard Shaw urged Britain give up the "pretense" of war, leaving the Russians and Germans to come to terms, he, too, found anti-interventionist support, particularly among American communists.[24] Those of pacifist leanings pointed to other Britons as well. The *Christian Century* noted the twenty thousand–member Scottish miners union, two Scottish railwaymen's organizations, and various clergy.[25] In its December 1939 issue, *Fellowship* magazine led with a parliamentary speech by prominent Laborite George Lansbury. In January 1940, *Peace Action* covered comments by Eamon De Valera, prime minister of Ireland.[26] These voices had all called for immediate peace. So, too, had various Englishmen featured by the American left, such as various trade unions, writer H. G. Wells, and James Maxton and his Independent Labor Party. In November 1939, *New Masses* cited a Gallup poll reporting that 25 percent of the British people opposed the war.[27]

Certain noninterventionists discussed concrete terms. If, said Castle, the Germans and Russians reconstituted an ethnic Poland, Britain would have to accede to their moves. Villard thought that Hitler would probably consent to a small Poland and Czechoslovakia, not "the Humpty Dumpty of the old Poland or the old Czechoslovakia." Borchard envisioned Poland as a "rump state" and the possible cession of British colonies in return for German acquiescence in strong British aviation and submarine forces. "Something," he continued vaguely, "may be done for Czechoslovakia."[28] Germany, said the socialist *American Guardian*, would demand a $5 billion bribe plus access to raw materials and world markets.[29]

Pacifists spoke in more Wilsonian concepts. Direct negotiation between the belligerents, averred Frederick J. Libby, could likely reach agreement on such matters as arms reduction, economic and financial cooperation, political independence for small nations, and "a sort of association of nations." To the

Fellowship of Reconciliation, the forthcoming peace conference could focus on such matters as tariffs, currency, equal access to raw materials, international control of colonies, and ultimately world government. Ernest Fremont Tittle, a leading Methodist clergyman from Evanston, Illinois, offered an entire agenda ranging from peaceful revision of the Versailles treaty to a general agreement to outlaw economic warfare. The Reverend Harold E. Fey elaborated on a similar program, one that included a Polish state, possible federalism for the Balkans, and the liberation of some colonies, such as India, and international control of others. John Haynes Holmes urged the plan outlined in Sir Arthur Salter's *Security: Can We Retrieve It?* (1939), which endorsed abrogation of the Versailles treaty, establishment of free trade between Britain and Germany, and common access to colonial resources.[30]

Not only pacifists talked of turning swords into plowshares or flirted with Wilsonianism. The *New York Daily News* suggested some terms, vague to be sure, but including a United States of Europe, incorporation of unnamed small nations into larger ones, and a return of some of Germany's former colonies.[31] According to Harry Elmer Barnes, no "reasonable man" could object to colonial restitution or an economic conference. In endorsing "a peace without victory," Barnes called for a world organization potent enough to deal with the "tough realities" of the day. John Cudahy, American ambassador to Belgium, thought Britain and France must permit German penetration of their world markets, even though the move would reduce their living standards.[32] The *Chicago Tribune* sought independent states for the Poles, Czechs, and other nationalities; similarly the British must acquiesce in a general disarmament and the abolition of Versailles boundaries.[33] Any negotiated peace, said *Commonweal*, must provide greater access to the raw materials of all empires, tariff reduction, and credits for financial rehabilitation and commercial development.[34]

At this stage only a small minority of anti-interventionists opposed American participation in the possible peacemaking. In February 1940, Herbert Hoover admonished, "Intervention of any kind is more likely to aggravate the situation than to improve it." A month later Norman Thomas, while continuing to call for neutral mediation, warned against the American underwriting of any peace terms or the use of the U.S. military to enforce any settlement.[35]

Needless to say, all during the fall and winter of 1939–40, anti-interventionists suspected pending negotiations. By late September, various rumors concerning papal intervention had emerged.[36] Such noninterventionists as Norman Thomas and the *New York Daily News* backed the initiative.[37] Similarly, they relied on the collective action of Western Europe's neutral powers.[38] On the day that the German-Soviet pact was announced, King Leopold of Belgium invited the foreign ministers of seven small states, the so-called Oslo powers, to meet in Brussels within forty-eight hours, there to present a peace plan to Europe's major powers.[39] On 6 November, Leopold paid a hurried visit to the Hague, where he met with Queen Wilhelmina of the Netherlands. Fearing imminent German invasion, the two monarchs issued a public appeal, offering mediation to the belligerents. At the very least, they might delay the Germans until winter, when invasion would become too difficult.[40]

Anti-interventionists were encouraged by the Dutch-Belgian initiative.[41] Not surprisingly, those closest to pacifism welcomed the bid.[42] So too did some senators.[43] To D. Worth Clark (Dem.-Idaho), the mediation offer seemed the last chance to save Europe. In responding, the Allies asserted that they would be glad to entertain proposals that promised a genuinely just peace. FDR was characteristically vague, pledging American friendship but avoiding even the suggestion of commitment. Pope Pius XII supported the proposal.[44]

Roosevelt, more than any other figure, was mentioned as potential mediator. Early in October, diplomatic legations in Berlin representing varied neutral powers hinted that Hitler would accept unconditionally an FDR mediation proposal.[45] Ambassador Kennedy cabled the president, saying that "some of my English friends" believed that only Roosevelt, whom he called a combination of the Holy Ghost and prizefighter Jack Dempsey, could save the world.[46] In November, British ambassador Lothian saw an early peace depending on FDR. The moderate interventionist William Allen White, nationally respected editor of the *Emporia* (Kans.) *Gazette*, endorsed the president though he also wanted Herbert Hoover part of any negotiations.[47]

Those of pacifist leanings lobbied FDR.[48] In January 1940, Villard lunched with the president, urging him to join with various neutrals in requesting the war aims of all belligerents, then to convene "a meeting of plenipotentiaries with or without an armistice."[49] In early December, the decidely nonpacifist *New York Daily News* headlined an editorial "We Think the Time Has Come for Roosevelt to Mediate." In fact, it said, the president should threaten economic reprisals if he were snubbed.[50]

Although surprising in retrospect, other pronounced Roosevelt critics called for presidential intercession, among them Senators Edwin Johnson and Burton K. Wheeler and Congressman Fish.[51] Hugh Johnson said, "There is nobody more competent to deal with this kind of deadly poker player than Mr. Roosevelt."[52] Senator Nye also backed the president's mediation, though he warned that any change in the United States's neutrality status would lead the Germans to consider FDR "one of the gang of defenders of the older imperial systems of the world."[53] A few anti-interventionists expressed mistrust of the president, among them law professor Edwin M. Borchard and pacifist leader Frederick J. Libby, both of whom found the president far too biased.[54]

The president's responses, though cautious, could appear encouraging.[55] In October, when Norman Thomas approached Roosevelt directly on the matter, the president's reply was guarded, saying he must act "with the greatest circumspection."[56] In mid-November, a delegation of the National Peace Conference (NPC), a coalition of pacifist and internationalist organizations, impressed on Roosevelt the need for a continuous mediation conference. In responding to their appeal, FDR implied that more was being done than he could mention.[57] Two days before Christmas, in a message to Pius XII, Roosevelt denied that any world leader could move forward on a specific peace plan but that the "time for that would surely come."[58] When Villard had called on the neutral powers to ask the belligerents to state their war aims, a move he hoped would be followed by negotiation, the president replied that he was thinking "along similar though not identical lines."[59]

At times anti-interventionists spoke of U.S. mediation without mentioning the president.[60] One idea centered on establishing machinery whereby such neutral powers as the United States would engage in continuous mediation. During World War I, the International Congress of Women, headed by reformer Jane Addams, had offered such a proposal.[61] When, on 6 September, the NPC unanimously called on the U.S. to initiate a conference of neutral nations toward that end, individual pacifist groups and leaders gave their endorsement.[62] A variety of people endorsed the bid of publisher David Lawrence, soon a strong interventionist, who frequently wrote that the United States should request a nine-power peace conference.[63]

All such efforts failed. In mid-October, Hull announced that the U.S. did not contemplate any peace efforts. With Hitler currently occupying Czechoslovakia, Austria, and much of Poland, not to mention imposing a Nazi regime on his own people, the secretary found chances for a real peace dubious. Later in the month, FDR said he would only act when all belligerents officially requested.[64]

Despite his public posture, however, the president was already involved in surreptitious peace feelers. In early fall 1939, with Roosevelt's tacit approval, independent oil operator William Rhodes Davis met with Reichsmarschall Goering in Berlin. Goering proposed that FDR mediate the conflict and retain the existing neutrality act (which contained an arms embargo) in return for a free hand in the Far East. Although FDR remained suspicious, Davis feared that continued war would only exhaust Europe, leaving communism in its wake.[65]

During the first week of December, FDR told Assistant Secretary of State Berle that he, in Berle's words, "proposed to make peace next Spring on the basis of having everybody produce everything they need; take what they need; and let the countries which needed the balance draw it as needed, through the cartels."[66] The president also told British ambassador Lothian that, before his term ended, he wanted to intervene as "a kind of umpire [and] . . . lay down the conditions for an armistice." To overcome German fears of a new Versailles, he would stress four basic freedoms: freedoms of speech and religion, freedom from fear, and freedom of trade and access to raw materials.[67]

Early in 1940, Roosevelt initiated more peace moves. First, he asked General Motors executive James D. Mooney to travel to Germany and approach certain high-level officials whom he had long known. Mooney was to indicate that, both sides being willing, Roosevelt would be glad to mediate.[68] Second, the president asked forty-six neutral nations to present their views on arms control and economic stability; his ultimate object involved the proposing of joint mediation, peace terms, and a place at the conference table.[69] Third, the president announced the appointment of Myron Taylor, board chairman of United States Steel, as special representative with ambassadorial rank to the Vatican, a move that obviously concerned possible coordination of peace efforts. When, on 9 February, various neutral powers called a meeting to preserve their rights, state department officials saw in its formation a chance for mediation.[70]

Most important of all, on 9 February 1940, Roosevelt announced that Undersecretary of State Sumner Welles would visit Europe. As Hull was often ill and Welles was personally closer to the president, the undersecretary was often singled out for special assignments. The ostensible assignment: to report on conditions there.[71] Undoubtedly FDR's focus extended far beyond the gathering of information. Such a mission, if successful, could possibly end the European conflict before it escalated beyond repair. Furthermore, it could strengthen his political hand if he decided to seek reelection in 1940 as a peace candidate.[72] At the very least, it might wean Mussolini, a man Welles much admired, away from Hitler.[73] In forty-one days, the dapper urbane Welles covered fourteen thousand miles, meeting the leaders of Italy, France, Britain, and Germany, though not Hitler himself.[74]

Several anti-interventionists suspected interventionist motives behind the president's move, and U.S. entry into war was not ruled out.[75] Certainly Welles's mission appeared all too similar to an earlier venture by Woodrow Wilson's confidant and troubleshooter Colonel E. M. House.[76] On 22 February 1916, House had signed an agreement with British foreign secretary Sir Edward Grey. He indicated that if Germany turned down an American invitation to a peace conference, the United States would probably enter the war on the Allied side. Moreover, if the conference was held and the Germans rejected "terms not unfavorable to the Allies," the U.S. would join the Allies as a belligerent.[77]

The *Daily Worker* accused the undersecretary of seeking to convert the existing conflict into war against the Soviet Union.[78] According to the *Chicago Tribune*'s Washington correspondent, Arthur Sears Henning, the mission signified a Roosevelt ploy to mold the structure of the world as effectively as Metternich did at Vienna in 1815. If an international federation resulted from the proceedings, FDR would consider himself the logical choice for its first president.[79]

Welles himself was personally attacked.[80] Hiram Johnson approvingly cited a friend who called Welles "a rat, with all a rat's cunning."[81] Recalled were his controversial activities in Cuba, where, as U.S. ambassador in 1933, he helped topple a regime. To Norman Thomas, Welles was "the man whose maneuvers in Cuba prepared the way for Battista [*sic*] and fascism."[82]

A few found the Welles mission a self-aggrandizing sham. It was "fantastic," said columnist Boake Carter, "to imagine he can get one umpteenth of what Joe Kennedy can get from Chamberlain in one-half hour of conversation." Herbert Hoover suspected that once Welles returned, Roosevelt would suggest a six-week truce, during which time peace terms would be discussed. Even if they were refused, the president would have gained votes in the forthcoming election.[83]

Anti-interventionists were, however, by no means all of one mind, some being more hopeful concerning Welles's mission and denying any parallel with Colonel House.[84] Those of pacifist leanings expressed particular support.[85] Frederick J. Libby claimed that Roosevelt's long-awaited peace offensive had now been launched: "There is no halting place on this road short of ultimate success."[86] The *Christian Century* saw "some sort of free Poland and Czechoslovakia" in the works.[87]

Even several centrist and rightist opinion-makers expressed hopes in the mission. The *New York Daily News* hoped that America's "peace effort" had begun.[88] William Randolph Hearst gave Roosevelt "the greatest credit." Father Coughlin surmised that the trip might restore full diplomatic relations between the United States and Germany.[89]

In a private report to the president, Welles asserted that the Allies should not bargain with a dictator they could not trust but that the United States and other neutral nations must take the lead in any movement toward peace. Roosevelt thanked the undersecretary for his pains but minimized any peace prospect. The mission remained as stillborn as a negotiated peace itself. The British and French strongly opposed the visit, with Chamberlain warning FDR that it would simply fuel German peace propaganda, arouse false hopes within the democracies, and encourage the neutral Scandinavian nations to obstruct a proposed Allied expeditionary force to help the Finns.[90] Certainly Welles's varied conversations convinced FDR that Hitler would never endorse the type of settlement he sought.[91]

Had the president desired to take a further initiative, he could have had a majority of the public behind him. A Gallup poll released early in March found a 58:42 ratio in favor of negotiations between the belligerents and a 55:45 ratio for American participation in a peace conference. As far as terms were concerned, 62 percent opposed German retention of Czechoslovakia, and 70 percent were against its keeping Poland.[92] Given German strength and intention, the possibility of realizing such terms was most unlikely. Despite the frequency and intensity of their call for mediation, anti-interventionist efforts were singularly ineffective. Furthermore, by launching the Welles mission in February 1940, Roosevelt had outmaneuvered them. Even more troublesome was the matter of Allied war aims, often seen as more imperialistic than those of the Germans.

# 3

# A Matter of War Aims

It was crucial, felt many noninterventionists, to debunk the Allied cause, so as to reveal any lofty war aims as a mask for aggrandizement and imperialism. To be countered were such figures as Kansas editor William Allen White, who called the conflict "a clash of ideologies," in which "these European democracies were carrying our banner, fighting the American battle."[1]

Foes of intervention argued just the opposite. World politics remained dominated by the law of the jungle. Burton B. Kendrick, a historian at the University of North Carolina, denied that such ideals as justice and democracy existed in the political world. "Birth, growth, conflict, defeat, decay, death—these are the facts of life. They exist and their existence calls neither for tears nor laughter."[2]

Europe, such people maintained, had never stopped fighting.[3] In the words of Charles A. Lindbergh, "The history of Europe has always been interwoven with conflict. Experience would warn us to be surprised if much more time had passed without a war." Occasionally an anti-interventionist offered an entire list of Europe's wars. That of Congresswoman Frances Bolton (Rep.-Ohio), for example, began in 1801.[4]

Reasons for Europe's supposed proclivity for conflict ranged from unsatisfied minorities to demands for land, food, and raw materials.[5] Hence, it was not surprising to portray the current conflict as just another traditional European clash. Pacifist minister John Haynes Holmes found the fighting a continuation of World War I, "the old war of Lloyd George against the Kaiser, just as Richelieu's struggle against Maximilian in 1637 was the same old war that Emperor Ferdinand began against Frederick of Bohemia in 1618."[6]

A surprising number perceived World War II as an outright imperialistic struggle, differing little, if at all, from many conflicts of the past.[7] A Gallup poll revealed the nation itself split evenly on the topic, half finding the struggle one for power and wealth, half seeing the cause of democracy at stake.[8] Within the past quarter century, V. I. Lenin had outlined the nature of such a crisis in his tract *Imperialism: The Highest Stage of Capitalism* (1917), an indictment of the powers participating in World War I.[9] Both the communists and the extreme right stressed the theme of imperialist war, albeit in vastly different ways. Radical Congressman Vito Marcantonio (Am. Lab.–N.Y.) saw a deeply rooted conflict between "the Rome-Tokyo-Berlin Axis" and "the Wall Street–Downing Street Axis."[10] Congressman Martin L. Sweeney (Dem.-Ohio), a pugnacious follower of Father Coughlin, found control of the world's gold at issue. At issue, claimed Father Coughlin, was whether the Bank of England would remain supreme.[11]

Scholars, too, were vocal.[12] Harry Elmer Barnes found the war centering on "the old thieves" versus "the new thieves," the former possessing "the manners," the latter "the best case."[13] Students concurred. Marguerite Higgins, Berkeley, class of 1941, and soon a prominent war correspondent, remarked that American students should stay out of war "run by Chamberlain-Daladier-Hitler inc. in the interest of their empires." Another University of California student, future film critic Pauline Kael, called the conflict "a war of rival imperialisms for the economic and political domination of the world."[14]

To some noninterventionists, control of the world itself was at issue.[15] Senator Nye compared the conflict to "the long imperial war by which England ousted France from world empire, and, before that, France ousted Spain." To James Gillis of the *Catholic World*, the war was being waged for nothing less than "the redistribution of the surface of the earth." *Uncensored* mentioned "the control of native populations in Africa, Asia and Europe."[16]

Others cited more narrow economic factors.[17] Educational consultant Porter Sargent said, "Capitalist imperialism is now face to face with socialist imperialism." James D. Mooney, vice president of General Motors, asserted that Germany and Italy were fighting "to keep from being starved to death." Senator La Follette queried whether Britain sought to destroy Germany's form of government, doing so to replace it with one that would leave its trade and interests in southeastern Europe untroubled.[18]

In Charles Lindbergh's eyes, the Germans sought "territory and power," the British and French preservation of their "influence and empire." If the French and English vowed they were "fighting to maintain their possessions and their ethics, and to keep the status quo of their last victory," the Germans could equally "claim the right of an able and virile nation to expand—to conquer territory and influence by force of arms as other nations have done at one time or another." Unlike so many other anti-interventionists, the colonel did not criticize imperialism per se; rather, he sought to see this "influence and empire" shared. Once the necessary redistribution took place, the Western nations, acting together, would be strong enough to serve as a world police force. "Germany," Lindbergh continued, was "as essential to this group as England or France, for she alone can either dam the Asiatic hordes or form the spearhead of their penetration into Europe."[19]

If there was a traditional aggressor, it was Britain.[20] "I see no reason why England should dominate the world," said John Haynes Holmes. During the past 150 years, said Senator Ernest Lundeen (Farmer-Lab.–Minn.) in 1939, the British had engaged in fifty-four wars, the French in fifty-three.[21] Senator Sheridan Downey (Dem.-Calif.) began with a reference to the year 1066: "Do not underrate the English people; they have been engaged in these conquests for a thousand years." James Gillis concurred with Hitler's claim that the German people "have not conquered by war forty million square miles on this earth as England has."[22]

According to some foes of intervention, Germany was simply aping Britain's longtime behavior.[23] To Idaho novelist Vardis Fisher, Germany was repeating British aggression in India and South Africa. Pacifist leader A. J. Muste cited British jurist Sir Arthur Salter, who saw the "so-called" democracies controlling thirty million square miles and 80 percent of the earth's resources, the Axis and its allies only one million square miles and 15 percent of the world's wealth. Congressman James F. O'Connor (Dem.-Mont.) found contemporary relevance in President Wilson's comment, made in September 1919:

> The seed of war in the modern world is industrial and commercial rivalry. The real reason that the war that we have just finished took place was that Germany was afraid her commercial rivals were going to get the better of her, and the reason why some nations went into the war against Germany was that they thought Germany would get the commercial advantage of them.[24]

Obviously, such noninterventionists asserted, the British were fighting to preserve their supremacy over the "upstart" German nation.[25] Ambassador Kennedy cabled Roosevelt that Britain was fighting "for her possessions and a place in the sun just as she has in the past."[26] William A. Orton, an economist at Smith College, labeled the conflict Britain's Second Punic War against a new power attempting to "muscle in." To columnist Raymond Moley, Germany, Italy, and Japan were joining together "to crack the British Empire, which, for 150 years has been a worldwide imperial, capitalistic trading organization." The pro-Soviet sociologist Edward A. Ross put the matter quite succinctly: "Germany got tired of this hogging of world space by Britain."[27]

Some indictments of Britain were more specific. Robert La Follette Jr. suspected that London sought to replace Germany's regime with one that would leave British trade and interests in southeastern Europe untouched. *New Masses* editor Joseph Starobin found the war motivated by Britain's desire to

maintain control of German capitalism and redirect the Reich against the Soviet Union. The war, argued the *New York Daily News*, was rooted in the fact
that "Germany was gradually recovering the 1914 boundaries of the Central
Powers, and England told her to stop." By November 1941, it went decidedly
further, finding the underlying reason for the war lying in Britain's need for
food and oil.[28]

To such people, the course of the war itself manifested evidence of British
imperialism. As early as October 1939, Senator Reynolds blamed the British
for sending "a million sons of French mothers to death" to provide the continued superiority of its empire. In March 1941, Nye noted that British troops
were currently occupying Iceland, Crete, and Libya and were pressing into Eritrea, Italian Somaliland, and Ethiopia. Yet only with respect to the "desolate
stretches" of Iceland had England promised to return territory.[29] That month,
*Uncensored* noted items in the *Times* of London showing that recent British financial arrangements with the Dutch East Indies, the French Cameroons, and
the Belgian Congo tied those nations to a currency system based on the sterling bloc. Such agreements implied that a victorious Britain might end up
with the French, Belgian, and Dutch empires in tow. In September, Frank Waldrop observed that the British empire had gained nearly eight hundred thousand more square miles of territory than had Germany. Britain controlled the
exile governments of Western Europe, which took in diamonds (from
Antwerp), securities (from Paris), and peoples of "the docile races, listless in
the custody of a few strong-minded and well-armed white men." New tracts
of empire included Libya and Italian Somaliland (strategic locale), Iran and
Iraq (oil), the Dutch East Indies (rubber, tin, spices), and the Congo ("Africa's
richest prize").[30]

Most noninterventionists frequently expressed abhorrence of Hitler's regime.
Pacifist leader A. J. Muste was far from alone in saying, "I do not want to minimize the evil of a German victory. I recoil from every prospect of it."[31]

Some reaction was more qualified. When French scientist Alexis Carrel
warned that a German victory meant the fall of Western civilization, his friend
Colonel Lindbergh demurred. "Germany," the aviator replied, "is as much a
part of Western civilization as France or England."[32] According to one observer, the Harvard biblical scholar Henry J. Cadbury, who was a staunch
Quaker pacifist, told audiences a German victory was inconsequential.[33]

Accounts of Nazi brutalities, both in the waging of war and the subsequent
occupation, soon reached American shores. In particular, the persecution of
Jews, both within Germany and its occupied lands, was becoming increasingly
severe, culminating in January 1942, just a month and a half after the United

States entered the war, at the Wannsee conference held outside Berlin, where plans for what is now called the Holocaust were solidified.[34]

At the beginning of the conflict, however, a few anti-interventionists scoffed at reports of German atrocities. Congressman Jesse P. Wolcott (Rep.-Mich.) doubted whether German troops either shot hostages indiscriminately or cut the tongues of Roman Catholic priests. When, in a broadcast delivered on 26 May 1940, Roosevelt mentioned German strafing of civilians from the air, William R. Castle was skeptical.[35]

Others attempted to relativize such German activity. Wheeler did express horror at Germany's persecution of its Jews. At the same time, he noted that few Americans were calling for war with Mexico, although he found its oppression of Roman Catholics unmatched. In warning against atrocity propaganda, Hugh Johnson wrote, "War itself is an atrocity." Ralph Townsend, a minor state department official from 1930 to 1933, compared American silence concerning British imprisonment of Mahatma Gandhi with its outrage over German internment of Protestant pastor Martin Niemoeller, American acquiescence concerning British bombing of French civilians with indignation when the Germans engaged in such activity. Harry Elmer Barnes was particularly acid: "Had Hitler tortured and then killed every one of the half million Jews living in Germany in 1933 such a foul and detestable act would still have left him a piker compared to Britain's blockade of 1918–19." The historian called the blockade "far and away the greatest atrocity in all human history."[36]

The alleged inequities of the Versailles treaty were often stressed.[37] "Not since Rome punished Carthage," said Senator Rush Dew Holt (Dem.-W.Va.), "was there such a treaty placed on any people." According to the *New York Daily News*, the treaty made "geographical hash of Europe." The Allies, recalled Herbert Hoover, "secured a total area larger than the United States east of the Mississippi."[38] *Social Justice* serialized Edwin D. Schoonmaker's *Democracy and World Dominion* (1938), a work that combined attacks on "Jewish" Bolshevism with the claim that the war guilt clause was "unheard of in all the annals of war."[39]

Many anti-interventionists linked the settlement directly to the rise of Nazism.[40] As pacifist leader Kirby Page put the issue, "If you sow a Versailles Treaty, you reap a Hitler."[41] To Senator Henrik Shipstead (Rep.-Minn.), Britain and France were as responsible for the German leader as "the royal, corrupt monarchy of France [was] responsible for Marat and for Robespierre."[42]

Such attitudes did not lack articulation within the Roosevelt administration. Despite their strong sympathy for the Allies, both FDR and Hull blamed the rise of Hitler and Mussolini on those European powers who betrayed Wilsonian principles. William E. Bullitt, U.S. ambassador to France, and Undersecretary Berle both opposed any war waged to create another Versailles and feared that a decisive Allied victory could lead to just that result. A year before World War II started, Welles—backed by Berle and J. Pierrepont Moffat, chief of the state department's Division of European Affairs—had sought a general settlement on the grounds that the 1919 settlement was both unjust and untenable.[43]

The Versailles peace, certain anti-interventionists argued, embodied the worst of both worlds: it was neither too severe nor too lenient to preserve peace. To author Albert Jay Nock, the victors had only one choice: "to exterminate the Germans or to understand them." Yet they picked a third option, to "reduce them to servitude and use them as labor-motors." The treaty needed revision as time passed, said Charles A. Lindbergh, or Britain and France would be forced to keep Germany weak.[44]

Others, while not attacking Versailles directly, blamed Allied policies for German behavior.[45] D. Worth Clark criticized "European capitalism" for strangling the Weimar Republic, France and England for forming "a ring of steel" around Germany.[46] Given such a perspective, Hitler was simply trying to rectify Versailles.[47] As the *New York Daily News* saw the issue, the conflict embodied "a war to undo the effects of the 1919–20 treaty makers' passion for punishing conquered nations by cutting them off from the sea."[48]

Germany, not the Allies, it was argued, was the power with the more limited ambitions, these being restricted to the European continent.[49] Even here, however, German war aims were not perceived as modest. In the fall of 1939, the *New Republic* pointed to designs on French Alsace-Lorraine, Belgian Eupen-Malmedy, Danish Schleswig, Austrian Tyrol, and the whole of Hungary. To the *Chicago Tribune*, Germany sought recognition of its conquest of Poland and economic leadership in southeastern Europe, perhaps in Scandinavia as well. The German people, said Villard, would accept reduced sovereign entity for both Poland and Czechoslovakia. The *New York Daily News* thought Hitler might well improve the lot of occupied Poles, Bohemians, Moravians, and Slovaks, though certainly not restore their independence. Both Lawrence Dennis and Boake Carter praised German rule in the new collaborationist state of Slovakia for granting national autonomy and fostering high living standards.[50]

Some saw more sweeping goals. Barnes found Germany wanting "more Munichs." To pacifist leader John Swomley, a German victory would simply lead to Versailles in reverse. John T. Flynn posited that Germany sought to recover its old empire, as well as that of Austria, and to strip Britain of its important colonies.[51] By August 1941, the financial columnist conceded that Germany would incorporate into the Reich such conquests as France, oil-rich Rumania, and the fertile Ukraine.[52]

In commenting on Rumania and the Ukraine, Flynn was not alone. Several anti-interventionists stressed Hitler's drive for Eastern Europe.[53] To radio commentator Boake Carter, German hegemony in central Europe was as inevitable as U.S. mastery of the Western Hemisphere. Castle emphasized Hitler's desire for the Ukraine, adding that the Russian peasant could not be worse off under Hitler's domination than under Stalin's.[54] The *New York Daily News* saw Germany still focused on the Kaiser's dream of a German-dominated Mitteleuropa, with the Nazis ruling everything from the Baltic to the Black Sea. As Germany's population, sixty-five million in 1933, lacked sufficient space, the *News* found "some justice" in Hitler's desire to expand east.[55]

Others envisioned Germany driving even farther. Senator Nye noted the oil of Iran and Iraq and the "unexploited wealth of Africa." *Call* writer Lillian Symes added the "treasures of India," the cotton of Egypt, and such African resources as manganese, timber, rubber, and tin.[56]

Noninterventionists differed over Hitler's intentions concerning Britain itself. In May 1940, Hearst denied that the German leader wanted to conquer Britain; his only true objective lay in the east. "Hitler has no heart in this war," he remarked. Flynn, claiming that Germany would find a conquered England a liability, said the Reich merely sought to reign over the old German and Austrian empires and to strip Britain of its important colonies. Economist Stuart Chase invoked the teachings of German geographer Karl Haushofer, pioneer in the new field of geopolitics, to assert that Germany did not seek to bring the British to their knees but rather to hold the "Heartland" against all attack.[57]

Arguing contrariwise, Dennis found the defeat of Britain, while not proposed by Hitler, the most popular aim of the war. The goal had long been favored by Germany's Kaiser, aristocracy, masses, and army. In April 1940, the *New York Daily News* went further, declaring that Hitler would have originally settled for Danzig and a passage to East Prussia through the Corridor; now he might well demand dissolution of the British Empire.[58] In April 1941, Father Coughlin's *Social Justice* saw, as did Congressman Usher Burdick and William Randolph Hearst, Hitler seeking a United States of Europe patterned on the United States. A common federal authority would control the army and navy, the banking system, and postage and communications.[59]

Occasionally administration opponents described how Europe might be parceled. *Uncensored* envisioned France rewarded for its collaboration, losing Alsace-Lorraine, but ruling the channel ports and Belgium's Walloon section. A puppet Netherlands would absorb Flanders. Italy would exercise political control over the newly created state of Croatia. Spain and Portugal might be organized into a united monarchy, with General Franco as military leader and Salazar as premier. "Keeping it running will be quite a job even for Adolf Hitler," it said.[60] Father Coughlin spoke of a Europe divided into three sections: a Germanic bloc that would include Austria, Hungary, the Scandinavian nations, the Netherlands, northern Belgium, and a small section of France; a Slavic bloc, composed of Russia, the Balkans, and Turkey; and a Latin bloc consisting of France, Italy, southern Belgium, Spain, Portugal, and part of North Africa.[61]

Anti-interventionists differed over the possible severity of Germany's rule over Europe. If Germany won the war, commented correspondent William

Henry Chamberlin, its form of military state socialism would be extended over the entire continent. A central authority in Berlin would order each nation to concentrate on specific priorities: France, agriculture; Norway, fisheries; Rumania, oil and wheat; Czechoslovakia, textiles and glass. "A right objective, the economic unification of Europe, would be achieved by terribly wrong means," he judged. Early in 1941, Lawrence Dennis stressed Hitler's desire to revive Napoleon's continental system. An organized Mitteleuropa, Dennis continued, would be able to bargain as a unit with overseas countries, thus securing better trading terms. In fact, a German-engineered social revolution would give masses everywhere secure employment, high wages, medical care, recreation, and good housing.[62]

Several noninterventionists, however, denied that Germany sought political domination of all Europe. Diplomat John Cudahy said Hitler did not seek to incorporate Holland and Belgium into the Reich.[63] *Peace Action* took at face value Hitler's 1941 interview with Cudahy, published in *Life*, in which the Führer spoke of reorganizing Europe along economic lines. *Social Justice* correspondent J. S. Barnes claimed Germany would retain economic and political supremacy over conquered areas while permitting cultural and administrative autonomy of the smaller ethnic groups.[64]

Anti-interventionists disagreed on one major claim made by many of their foes—namely, that Hitler sought world domination.[65] To some, such as Hearst, Dennis, and Henry Elmer Barnes, Hitler had no such goal.[66] Charles A. Lindbergh specifically denied that Germany had military aspirations in the Western Hemisphere.[67] Others did believe, as did Roosevelt, that Hitler wanted world conquest.[68] *New York Times* military correspondent Hanson Baldwin, for example, asserted that the Third Reich harbored "well-defined views of world empire."[69] Such commentators, however, found such a goal impossible to achieve. Hitler's bravado, said Wheeler, no more impressed him than earlier boasts of Lenin and Trotsky that they were going to make a world revolution.[70]

When advocates of collective security pointed with alarm to Hitler's *Mein Kampf* (1925), they found the work derided. Congresswoman Jessie Sumner (Rep.-Ill.) called it Hitler's "campaign literature," a garbled version of Oswald Spengler. Senator Holt asked whether the Führer's memoir differed from those Soviet writers "who proclaimed their desire for a world revolution, the day of control of communism."[71]

Similar treatment was met out to Hermann Rauschning, a former Nazi politician who had broken with the regime in 1935. In his *Revolution of Nihilism* (1939) and *The Voice of Destruction* (1940), Rauschning stressed the anarchistic and expansionist aspects of the regime, which could "no more dispense with its pursuit of hegemony than with its government by violence at home."[72]

Few anti-interventionists believed Rauschning.[73] Only William R. Castle gave *The Voice* credence, saying it showed Hitler was "determined to have Germany dominate the world."[74] Lundeen called *The Voice* "curdling bedtime stories."[75] Harry Elmer Barnes equated it with Lord Bryce's spurious report on World War I atrocities and André Cheradame's *The Pan German Plot*.[76] Senator Nye accused Rauschning of falsifying conversations with Hitler made years before: "We all know with what skepticism all such alleged evidence must be regarded."[77]

Then there was the speech supposedly made by Walther Darré, sometime late in 1939, in which Hitler's minister of agriculture said, "We will introduce . . . a new aristocracy of German masters. . . . We have actually in mind a modern form of medieval slavery which we must and will introduce because we urgently need it to fulfill our great tasks." Darré spoke of Germany's desire to control American industry and trade. The *New York Times* printed excerpts, believing it authentic. *Life* magazine reproduced the text with the caveat that it might not have been delivered exactly as recorded. Secretary Ickes pointed to passages threatening the economic ruin of the United States.[78] Darré subsequently denied making the address. Of the populace polled by Gallup, 80 percent found the speech credible.[79]

Noninterventionists rebutted immediately. University of Chicago physiologist Anton J. Carlson classified it with such bogus documents as the *Protocols of Zion*. Senator D. Worth Clark compared it to World War I atrocity reports, those "faked and forged pictures of Belgian children with their hands cut off, of mutilated women, and of crucified men."[80]

Even if Germany did win the European war, so such commentators maintained, its hegemony would remain precarious. According to Flynn, Hitler's Reich, divided by hatreds and drained by war, would be unable to dominate a continent. Even should Germany be foolish enough to incorporate Britain, France, Spain, and Italy, it would find them liabilities, unable to support their own populations. In due time, said John Haynes Holmes, "the national frontiers shall be eliminated, the separate nationalistic prides and prejudices purged away through the sheer experience of suffering, and out of the fire of disaster and death a united Europe emerge."[81]

The *New York Daily News* predicted, "Europe can be expected to begin coming unglued as soon as Hitler's Nazism shows itself unable to make life comfortably livable for most people under its hooked-cross banner." Soon after a German victory, one might reasonably expect the death of an exhausted Hitler, followed by such dissension among his successors that the newly created empire would fall apart.[82]

In offering such analyses, the anti-interventionists failed to convince much of the American public, which, as soon as war had broken out, was revealed by a Gallup poll to be far more negative about German aims. In late September 1939, 63 percent of the public predicted that a victorious Germany would eventually start a war against the United States; in early June 1940, 65 percent took that position. In April 1941, a *Fortune* poll found over 69 percent convinced that Hitler sought to dominate the U.S.[83]

If many noninterventionists could remain tacitly sanguine about Germany's supposed war aims, finding them either reasonable or impossible to achieve, they were seldom satisfied with Britain's official statements of policy.[84] The British, they believed, were at best stonewalling, at worst envisioning a Carthaginian peace. "The holy war boys and girls," mused historian Barnes, "almost imply that Harold Laski is Prime Minister and Bernard Shaw Foreign Minister."[85]

On 3 September 1939, when Britain declared war on Germany, Neville Chamberlain addressed the House of Commons: "I trust I may live to see the day when Hitlerism has been destroyed and a liberated Europe has been re-established." Anti-interventionists responded quickly. The prime minister, commented the *Chicago Tribune*, should not have issued "an ultimatum" at the outset but rather have stressed treaty obligations and pledges of good faith. Father Gillis, editor of the *Catholic World,* conceded that Hitler was a murderer but insisted that the Germans had to find out this fact for themselves. The *New York Daily News* remonstrated with Chamberlain's reference to the destruction of Hitlerism, saying such language invariably led to "the extermination of the German people." Oswald Garrison Villard was in a decided minority in welcoming Chamberlain's commitment to a stable international system.[86]

Lord Lothian, Britain's ambassador to the United States when war commenced, offered a quasi-official statement of war aims. Speaking late in October 1939 to the annual dinner of the American section of the Pilgrims, an Anglo-American society, he endorsed "autonomous freedom" for all nations of Europe, including the elimination of the Gestapo within their borders. The *New York Daily News* accused Lothian of harboring utopian goals: fighting until Austria, Czechoslovakia, the Baltic states, and Albania were restored and secret police eliminated everywhere in Europe.[87]

In a radio speech on 7 November 1939, Lord Halifax, Britain's foreign minister, gave his rendition of British war aims, claiming that his nation was fighting against "brute force, bad faith, injustice, oppression and persecution." The *New York Daily News* responded, "If you can make anything out of that, you're a better maker-outer than we are." Gillis called Halifax "a good honest man, and religious" but wondered why he never espoused these values when Mussolini annexed Ethiopia and Albania.[88]

Few British advocates aroused such hostility as did Alfred Duff Cooper, former first lord of the admiralty, appointed minister of information in May 1940.[89] Early that year, while visiting the United States on a speaking tour, Duff Cooper announced, "We are not fighting for the Czechs, the Poles or the Abyssinians, or anybody, but for ourselves." At first only the communists responded, the *Daily Worker* accusing him of seeking world domination.[90]

Further remarks met with wider opposition. The entire German people, said Duff Cooper in April, bore heavy responsibility for its nation's crimes; hence, "it would be a good thing to break Germany up into small states." In attacking Germany's political heritage, he called Frederick the Great "perverted," branded Bismarck a "mountebank," and found William II "the vain cripple . . . the slave of the half crazy Ludendorff."[91]

This time noninterventionists responded rapidly. *Commonweal*, noting that Duff Cooper had charged the "whole German people" with responsibility for Nazi crimes, denied that people of one nation essentially differed from those of another. *Uncensored* recalled one Duff Cooper remark made in April 1939: "Hatred of any race was a sign of mental deficiency."[92]

Despite the statements of various British leaders, anti-interventionist pressure for more concrete British aims grew louder, reaching a crescendo early in 1941 during the debate over lend-lease.[93] Anti-interventionists cited peace queries from the British themselves, including the *Times* [London], military writer B. A. Liddell Hart, an archbishop, and such prestigious publications as the *New Statesman and Nation, Time and Tide,* and the *Manchester Guardian.*[94]

Such pressure for war aims stemmed from motives that were obviously mixed, with genuine concern intermingled with a deliberate effort to embarrass Britain at a time when direct assistance was most fervently debated. On 27 January 1941, Senators Nye and Wheeler submitted a resolution calling on all belligerents to publicize their war aims, peace conditions, and any secret treaties involving territorial spoils. In World War I, so the resolution noted, the secret treaties of Britain and France clearly revealed that "their purpose was to conquer people and not to preserve democracy or to end all war."[95] The WIL National Board asked Roosevelt to press both Britain and the Axis to state peace terms; the peace organization was acting in the hope of bringing the war to a close on the basis of mutual disarmament.[96]

By March 1941, Lothian had died and Lord Halifax had become his successor. When the new emissary spoke to the Pilgrims that March, he stressed that Britain sought liberation of occupied countries and global economic cooperation. Anti-interventionists disapproved. To *Uncensored,* Halifax had implied that Britain and the dominions would not give up their preferential tariffs, much less even consider redistributing raw materials. According to the *Christian Century,* Halifax admitted that "Britain is fighting to retain the status quo within Britain and within the empire." The *New York Daily News* found the ambassador demanding the policing of Germany "until the Germans see the light as we see it," an effort bound to fail.[97]

When, in May, Foreign Secretary Anthony Eden offered his assessment, he fared no better. On 29 May 1941, while speaking at the Mansion House on British war aims, he said, "Our political and military terms for peace will be designed to prevent repetition of Germany's misdeeds." Although the *Christian Century* welcomed his stress on worldwide social security and economic health and on Europe's own economic reorganization, several anti-interventionists still found a new Versailles in the works.[98]

Amid the concrete responses to the various British spokesmen, anti-interventionists stressed one major theme: the war did not involve ideology. Certainly Britain was not fighting fascism per se. Destroying Hitler the man was by no means the same as crushing Nazism the system. Commented the *New Republic* in September 1939, "Obviously terms might be set with Hitler out of the way that would be nearly as bad as those set with Hitler in power." That November, Raymond Moley maintained that Britain simply sought a ministerial crisis in Germany.[99] A month later, *Uncensored* alleged that the British stood ready to conclude a peace with a Nazi regime headed by the "moderate" Hermann Goering.[100] "Such a peace," it continued, "would leave fascism entrenched in Germany, buttressed by economic aid from the Allies as a defense against expansionist Russia."[101] On the eve of Germany's attack on Norway, the Socialist Party saw only one way that any Allied victory could lead to a genuine defeat of Hitler: French and German workers must keep Allied troops from overthrowing the type of German revolution that took place in 1918, when Germany's last despotism was overthrown.[102] As late as March 1941, Lawrence Dennis claimed that "the more enlightened British," as well as FDR and his chief troubleshooter Harry Hopkins, merely sought a Europe led by a Germany denuded of Hitler and operating under Anglo-American tutelage.[103]

The Allies, some noninterventionists believed, sought to restore the Hapsburg monarchy, or even that of the Hohenzollerns.[104] In October 1939, *Uncensored* noted Duff Cooper's prediction of a possible merger of Catholic Austria and Bavaria under Otto von Hapsburg, grandson of Emperor Franz Joseph and pretender to the Austro-Hungarian crown.[105] Such a restoration, it soon said, would be packaged as a Danubian Federation that would include Austria, Hungary, Czechoslovakia, parts of Poland, and adjoining fragments of Central and Eastern Europe.[106] Indeed, Otto himself had recently called for such an arrangement, and in December 1940, Churchill privately endorsed the idea.[107]

Among administration critics, such schemes drew little enthusiasm.[108] The *Christian Century* asked, "Having fought one war to get rid of a Kaiser, are the Allies now fighting another to bring a Kaiser back?"[109] The *New Republic* reported that Otto represented the very government, led by Chancellor Engelbert Dollfuss, that in 1934 had bombarded the municipal workers' houses of Vienna.[110]

Besides, mere elimination of Hitler and Nazism in themselves could not bring peace.[111] Bullets could not kill ideologies.[112] "Kaiserism" and "Prussian militarism," argued pacifist minister Kirby Page, did not end in World War I. To *Commonweal*, "Hitlerism," however one defined it, could not be eliminated from the world by "paragraphs in a peace treaty." Villard asserted that real cleaning of Germany must come from within: "Only the Germans can do away with the Nazis and their totalitarian state." Furthermore, he continued, to eradicate Nazism by force was useless unless one eliminated Russian communism as well, for both were "sisters under the skin."[113] "Behind Hitler are substitute quarterbacks six deep," wrote Hugh Johnson. As to whether the Germans sought democracy: "The Heinies never had done much of that kind of yearning. They seem always to have liked to be goosestepped and verboten. And the only difference in this regard between Hitler and the Kaiser is the cut of his moustache and the droop of the drawers."[114]

To many anti-interventionists, the issue transcended the installation of a Hapsburg ruler and the elimination of Nazism. Any repetition of 1919 was especially to be abominated.[115] Nye approvingly quoted George Bernard Shaw's claim, "If we won, it would be Versailles all over again, only worse—with another war less than twenty years off." Conversely, several anti-interventionists, including Frederick J. Libby, doubted whether Britain would ever have the power to restore the Paris settlement.[116]

Certainly much anxiety existed over possible dismemberment of Germany.[117] The French were perceived as particularly villainous.[118] Both Villard and the *New York Daily News* accused them of seeking to seize the left bank of the Rhine and split Germany into Catholic and Protestant states.[119] In March 1940, Libby pointed to a map published in *Newsweek* as evidence that they sought detachment of the Rhineland and the subdivision of Prussia.[120]

For some anti-interventionists, the alleged Allied strategy of massive destruction was even more fatal. Villard quoted British author H. G. Wells as saying that Berlin must be destroyed, something that only encouraged Germany to fight. Harold E. Fey, executive secretary of the FOR, feared bloody reprisals on German leaders. A few anti-interventionists spoke in terms of forced population control, perhaps genocide. One anti-interventionist cited a demand to sterilize all men of German blood. *Uncensored* quoted a young French soldier on the Maginot line, who supposedly said, "On this continent there exists a *breed* which must be exterminated." When the lend-lease bill was passed, Wheeler asked whether Churchill sought "the annihilation of 80,000,000 German people."[121]

To some anti-interventionists, Britain was not the only culprit. Some leaders of their own nation, the United States, possessed the most sweeping of imperial designs, in the process betraying their nation's birthright.

# 4

# American Goals:
# An Object of Suspicion

By late 1940, the label "imperialism" was applied to the United States. "Many interventionists," claimed historian Howard K. Beale, "want to intervene because they wish to establish an Anglo-American domination of the world."[1]

Here the left grew particularly vocal. A. J. Muste wrote, "We shall be the next nation to seek world-domination—in other words, to do what we condemn Hitler for trying to do." If the United States went to war, said Norman Thomas, within ten years it would fulfill Leon Trotsky's prophecy of becoming the most ruthless power in the world. *Uncensored* accused the country of seeking a huge customs union, one that would include all of Latin America and the British Dominions.[2]

The left, however, was not alone in making such accusations. Queried advertising executive Chester Bowles, "Are we to dominate the world by force and establish our ideas of justice in Africa, India and the Far East?" Senator George Aiken (Rep.-Vt.) referred to American interventionists who "envision their flag waving in glory over the oil fields of Asia Minor and the plantations of the East Indies." Dennis predicted that prolonged war would weaken both Germany and Britain, thereby permitting the United States to fall heir to British possessions in the Western Hemisphere and become the world's leading sea power.[3]

Noninterventionists singled out certain figures as promoting either an autonomous American empire or one in league with Britain. Among these were interventionist columnists Dorothy Thompson and Walter Lippmann, publisher Henry R. Luce, Secretary of War Henry L. Stimson, and Harvard political scientist William Yandell Elliott.[4] An often-quoted *Life* editorial of February 1941, proclaiming the "American Century," so terrified Villard that he foresaw the United States as another seeker after "world domination," "just as great a menace to mankind as Germany, or Russia, or Japan."[5] When Secretary of the Navy Frank Knox, speaking to the American Bar Association on 1 October 1941, asserted that the world's sea power must remain with the United States and Britain for the next hundred years, administration critics were again outraged. Libby accused FDR's secretary of the navy of making the U.S. "the senior partner dominating the world."[6]

The left paid particular attention to a speech that Virgil Jordan, president of the National Industrial Conference Board, gave on 10 December 1940 to the Investment Bankers Association, meeting in Hollywood, Florida. The United States, he said, was committed—if necessary—to replacing the British Empire. "Whatever the outcome of the war, America has embarked upon a career of imperialism, both in world affairs and in every other aspect of her life," with particular areas of expansion lying in the Southern Hemisphere and the Pacific. *New Masses* called the address "the most cynical revelation of American war aims we have yet seen, a real insight into the minds of the men who rule and have ruled this country."[7]

Even the idealistic language of Franklin D. Roosevelt was suspect. In his annual message to Congress on 6 January 1941, the chief executive endorsed the Four Freedoms as America's postwar aims. Included were "freedom of speech and expression"; "freedom of every person to worship God in his own way"; "freedom from want—which, translated into world terms means economic understandings which will secure to every nation a healthy peacetime life for its inhabitants"; and "freedom from fear—which, translated into world terms, means a world-wide reduction of armaments to such a point and in such a thorough fashion that no nation will be in a position to commit an act of physical aggression against any neighbor." After each freedom, the president added the phrase "everywhere in the world," then stressed that his "is no vision of a distant millennium. It is a definite basis for a kind of world attainable in our own time and generation."[8]

Surely, to the president's opponents, the scope of such aims was most awesome, particularly as it implied the guaranteeing freedom of religion and expression to the entire world.[9] Professor Borchard commented, "At least crusades of a thousand years ago had a more limited objective."[10] For Robert Maynard Hutchins, president of the University of Chicago, the Four Freedoms meant "a program of perpetual war in Latin America, war in the Far East, war in the South Seas, and even war with Britain."[11] Certainly any effort at enforcement would be highly irresponsible.[12]

Besides, it was argued, the Four Freedoms did not even exist at home. Senator Robert La Follette Jr. recalled his recent role as chairman of a Senate subcommittee investigating violent intimidation of trade unions: "I urge," he said, "that we make the 'four freedoms' prevail in America before we try to ram them down the throats of people everywhere in the world." Furthermore, entering the war conflict would betray the four freedoms, not promote them. Congressman George Holden Tinkham (Rep.-Mass.) denied that "freedom from want" could be obtained by the "waging of war and the subsidizing of world wars," or "freedom from fear" by suspending the Bill of Rights.[13]

Even setting the Four Freedoms aside, noninterventionists found the price of sweeping victory far too high.[14] To journalist Upton Close (writing under the pseudonym Josef Washington Hall), Britain would be too tired and bankrupt to impose any new order upon Europe; therefore, the United States would have to assume the task. Merely to reestablish the balance of power would fail, for it had been this very balance that had "kept Europe divided for a hundred years." Flynn feared that the United States would be policing Europe for a century. What, Taft wondered, would the U.S. do with eighty million Germans?[15] Historian Charles A. Beard asked,

> Does Congress intend to supply money, ships, and commodities of war until the French Republic is restored, until the integrity of its empire is assured, until all the lands run over by Hitler are once more vested with full sovereignty, until Russia has returned to Finland and Poland the territories wrested from them, until democracy is reestablished in Greece, until the King of Albania has recovered his throne? Is Congress prepared to pour our American wealth until the Chungking Government in China has conquered the Nanking Government, until Japan is expelled from the continent, until Chinese Communists are finally suppressed, and until Soviet Russia is pushed back within the old Russian borders?[16]

To administration critics, the most Wilsonian of peace aims could be the most dangerous of all. On 22 July 1941, Undersecretary Welles spoke at the Norwegian legation, describing an ideal postwar order in terms of international arms control, an end to aggressive armament, and equal access to the world's raw materials. The *Chicago Tribune* responded that the Germans, too, had endorsed equal access to the world's markets and that therefore a war over the matter seemed unnecessary. The Versailles treaty, it continued, already had made provision for international control of arms.[17] When Welles called for a new international organization that November, the *Tribune* argued that such a goal could only be obtained at the price of reducing Germany, the Soviet Union, Italy, and Japan to impotence.[18]

Among the concerns over American aims, international organization loomed as a major one. Only a minute number of prominent anti-interventionists had favored U.S. membership in the League of Nations.[19] Nye sought some new "more international organization" that would see to it that "no men go mad." This body, he stressed, must not be "under control by some lone empire," an obvious allusion to Britain. Veteran League foe Hearst suggested an arbitration tribunal, to which all nations would refer disputes, though in 1935 he had staunchly opposed U.S. membership in the World Court.[20]

Most anti-interventionists held the League of Nations in strong contempt.[21] Critics accused it of serving as a major instrument of the Versailles conquerors.[22] According to journalist Carleton Beals, the international body, acting as the tool of Britain and France, "crucified small nation after nation, abetting injustice, while hypocritically and piously denouncing them." Besides, it was argued, the organization could only embroil the United States in continual conflict. The very concept of collective security, said writer John Chamberlain, was "a pernicious, war-breeding" one. By refusing even to consider two legitimate sides to any conflict, the system, said Borchard, "constitutes a charter for perpetual war." The legal scholar was particularly distressed with Article 16 of the League Covenant, which authorized economic and military action against an offending state.[23]

To such people, Clarence K. Streit's Union Now movement appeared particularly ominous. Formerly the *New York Times* correspondent in Geneva, Streit in 1939 established the Inter-democracy Federal Unionists, which in 1940 was took on the name Federal Union. By March 1941, the organization had 60 chapters in the United States plus 250 in Britain. Moreover, a Gallup poll estimated that eight million U.S. citizens believed in an international organization along his lines.[24]

His first book, *Union Now* (1939), became a veritable manifesto for his cause. In it Streit proposed a federal union of democracies, among them the United States, six units of the British Empire, the Low Countries, four Scandinavian countries, and Switzerland. In January 1941, Streit updated his work, giving it the title *Union Now with Britain*. An immediate union with the Commonwealth nations would serve as an eventual nucleus for a Federal Union of the World. Certain nations not originally slated for membership, including such "outside peoples" as the Germans and Italians, could join later. Streit asserted his new union would offer both countries relief from armaments as well as admission to the greatest market in the world. Federation citizens would enjoy the benefits of a common currency, defense force, customs union, and postal and communications system. In local matters, member nations would retain complete authority. The union's structure would replicate the American federal system, complete with a lower house, based on population, and a senate, in which each nation would be represented. The executive might consist of a five-person board or a single chairman. Streit preferred two concurrent executives serving like Roman consuls, and he envisioned FDR and Churchill filling these slots. Although a member state might be socialist or capitalist, a republic or monarchy, each would have to conform to a Bill of Rights that guaranteed freedom of speech, worship, and the press and the right to peaceful assembly. Streit called on the president of the United States to issue a Declaration of the Dependence of Free Men, invite other democracies to sign it, and then call a constitutional convention.[25]

Pending the convention, an intercontinental congress would be convened. There would be one representative for each member democracy and an additional representative for every five million inhabitants. The United States would hold twenty-seven seats, other nations a total of twenty-two. Until direct election of the U.S. legislators could be arranged, the president could either appoint them or suggest a slate to the American Congress. Among Streit's own candidates were Herbert Hoover, Republican leader Wendell Willkie, and James Cox, former governor of Ohio and Democratic presidential candidate in 1920.[26]

Such a scheme, asserted Streit, would not precipitate a full-scale American military intervention; rather, it would preclude it. While maintaining that U.S. entry into the war was otherwise inevitable, he boasted that his plan "offers the only reasonable promise of overthrowing dictatorship without need of any great American expeditionary force whether in Europe, Africa, Asia or Latin America." With the Union established, Hitler could be blockaded in Europe and the conquered nations would gain incentive to throw off his yoke. Thus, his plan could tempt Axis powers to negotiate individually with the Union.[27]

At any rate, Streit argued, "isolation" was infeasible, for once Hitler possessed the British fleet, he warned, he would gain "world control." To protect "our vital North Atlantic seaboard," the United States would have to move its own fleet from the Pacific, in the process abandoning Australia, New Zealand, and perhaps even Alaska to Japan. Such loss of the sea would cost the U.S. most of its trade, with ensuing "chaos in factory and farm" and "panicky demands for dictatorship from within."[28]

To administration antagonists, Federal Union seemed the logical outcome of FDR's foreign policy, the ultimate goal to which it was leading. The America First Committee (AFC), by 1941 the leading anti-interventionist body, even promoted the slogan "British Union Now? Soviet Union Next?" A congressional investigation into the whole matter, it suggested, was much needed. *Social Justice* carried a story "Fifth Column Discovered!" Representative Tinkham called the group "disloyal and traitorous." In October 1940, Senator Holt listed various prominent supporters, indicated their previous ties to Britain, and cited a *Newsweek* article stating that Franklin and Eleanor Roosevelt were holding private discussions with Streit.[29]

By October 1941, the *Saturday Evening Post* depicted American and British leaders mounting a concentrated effort to advance Streit's scheme. Included were the president's wife; John Winant, U.S. ambassador to Britain; Leslie Hore-Belisha, former British war secretary, who suggested a common American-British citizenship; and Colonel Josiah Wedgwood, a prominent Labor Party leader.[30] That March the weekly had quoted an English journalist who predicted that in 1944, after the defeat of Germany, FDR would take up temporary residence in Britain while the king and queen moved to Mount Vernon.[31]

Certainly, Union Now became another stick with which to beat the British.[32] According to several anti-interventionists, Streit's plan was steeped in conspiracy. Boake Carter, Rush Holt, and publisher Porter Sargent imagined the plan fulfilling the Anglo-Saxon unity schemes of Cecil Rhodes.[33] John B. Trevor, president of the American Coalition of Patriotic Societies, included the supposed designs of Scottish-born steel magnate Andrew Carnegie. Erstwhile reformer Amos Pinchot saw the hand of the British Labor Party at work. Even the more urbane *Uncensored* understood Union Now not as a vast experiment in democratic federalism but as a sinister plot, advanced by "the Men of Munich" and designed to enable the United States to underwrite the British Empire. If proponents of union were really serious, said the *Chicago Tribune*, nothing prevented Britain from applying for American statehood. Economically, the U.S. would profit, gaining forty million more customers for its manufactures and agricultural products.[34]

To the organization's critics, national sovereignty was a crucial matter.[35] Challenging Streit's claims, Sargent maintained that the United States would inevitably be outvoted; India alone would ensure Britain a substantial margin.[36] Moreover, some foes argued, the scheme was downright reactionary. In July 1939, even before the European conflict broke out, liberal broadcaster Quincy Howe warned that it would lead to "a grand crusade against social changes that are overdue in both Europe and Asia."[37] Others expressed a different fear, that of Great Power imperialism. Streit, said journalist Freda Utley, ignored the colonial question, taking an entirely legalistic approach. Columnist George Sokolsky asked, "Are we to control the Malay States and is Hong Kong to become an American colony and is the Union of South Africa to throw the Boer nationalist movement into our laps?"[38]

At best, the proposal appeared overly ambitious. Were it to go into effect, remarked the *New York Daily News*, "Justly and magnanimously, we'd tell Japan not to expand anywhere; we'd give Germany the same orders; we'd treat the colored folks in Africa as kindly as Augustine St. Clare in 'Uncle Tom's Cabin' treated the slaves in contrast to the wicked Simon Legree." Norman Thomas found Streit's plan, or any other proposal for world government, totally impractical, because any such system could not be achieved without dictatorship. Instead, he stressed, world reconstruction must center on economic cooperation, involving equal access of all nations to raw materials, fiscal systems, and commerce and providing for the rights of colonial peoples.[39] Most important, anti-interventionists of many political persuasions feared that Union Now would accelerate U.S. participation in the war. Trevor warned that Union Now would lead to American troops defending British possessions in Asia and Africa, the policing of the seven seas by the U.S. fleet, and the exploitation of American economic resources so as to pay all wartime bills of the British Empire.[40]

A few anti-interventionists refused to condemn Streit out of hand. Chester Bowles, for example, called Union Now at least "an honest effort" to discuss the postwar order.[41] Some anti-interventionist clergy appeared mildly in-trigued.[42] The more Americans Streit "can prepare for a surrender, even a diminution, of jealously held sovereign rights," said the *Christian Century* in December 1939, "the more quickly will we reach a time when it will be prac-ticable to work for a rational world order." In March 1941, the Protestant jour-nal hoped that Streit's plan might enable the United States to obtain a consid-erable measure of control over British policy, though it feared that the U.S. would assume responsibility for maintaining an imperialist system that was historically doomed.[43]

Occasionally noninterventionists went further.[44] When the European war first began, the *Washington Post's* Felix Morley recommended that France and Britain acquiesce in Hitler's domination of Poland and then work on building a practical Anglo-French-American union along Streit's lines.[45] Harry Elmer Barnes found strength in Streit's original proposal. His plan encompassed a population of about 350 million, which would control about half the world's surface, govern nearly half the human race, carry on two-thirds of the world's trade, and possess at least 50 percent of the world's raw materials, including over 60 percent of basic war materials.[46]

Streit was not alone in advancing federalist views. A few anti-intervention-ists toyed with similar notions. Whoever won the conflict, wrote economist Stuart Chase in the *Progressive*, Europe was bound to become more central-ized, federated, and socialized. As far as the behavior of the victors went, "The gentlemen in London will be kinder, the gentlemen in Berlin will be more ef-ficient." Germany, in fact, possessed an appeal to workers, peasants, and mem-bers of the lower middle class "sick and tired of plutocrats, landlords, and ex-ploiters." Extending his analysis beyond Europe, Chase envisioned the postwar world comprised of four power blocs: the United States, Japan, Germany, and Russia. Smaller nations would either have to "snuggle under the aluminum wings of one of the four" or surrender their own sovereignty. Even the British Empire could no longer qualify as a compact fighting unit.[47]

Harry Elmer Barnes saw a somewhat similar revolution currently at work, one comparable to such events as the decline of the Roman Empire and the downfall of the medieval world. The trend toward state control of a nation's economy seemed inevitable. So did a greater proportion of production for use, not profit. Nations faced a stark choice: they must either adopt the Mid-dle Way of a democratic planned economy, exemplified by Sweden and Fin-land, or find themselves subject to totalitarian revolution. As part of the new revolution, individual states would inevitably be supplanted by large-scale po-litical units that would embrace entire continents.[48]

Among the more liberal anti-interventionists, especially those with pacifist instincts, some sentiment for world government existed. Few went as far as Dorothy Detzer, who told the WIL, "The thing we must eventually stand for is a world state."[49] In October 1941, the WIL itself endorsed a resolution introduced by Congressman Rudolph G. Tenerowitz (Rep.-Mich.), which supported world federation.[50] The *Christian Century*, while pushing regionalism, promoted a world league, but one limited to control of armament plants, codification of international law, and the sponsoring of various studies.[51]

For the problems of the European continent, federated blocs appeared to offer some solution.[52] After the war, suggested international law professor Philip Jessup, a Western European federation should be formed, consisting of England, France, Belgium, Luxembourg, and possibly the Scandinavian countries.[53] Norman Thomas saw such a European union as a model for the regional unification of all powers.[54] Congressman John M. Vorys (Rep.-Ohio) hinted at a European cooperative commonwealth.[55] Senator Burton Wheeler and the *New York Daily News* found a United States of Europe the only solution to the continent's recurring wars.[56]

Alfred M. Bingham, coeditor of the liberal weekly *Common Sense*, offered the most extensive scheme presented by an anti-interventionist. In his book *The United States of Europe* (1940), published just before Hitler's blitzkrieg, Bingham favored organizing the continent along federal lines. Government would reside in a Council of States, which would contain representatives of various countries according to their "relative weight," and a European Assembly, based on population. The executive would emerge from the Council of States.

Such a Europe would possess a common army and navy, establish forts throughout the continent, and control such strategic seas as Gibraltar and Suez. Various administrative agencies would supervise disarmament, mandates, nationalities, citizenship, raw materials, a monetary system, and a postwar reconstruction agency. The new entity would possess visible symbols of sovereignty—including a flag, coinage, and postage—as well as a capital city. Bingham even suggested a site: just north of Basel at the juncture of France, Germany, and Switzerland.

This new system, Bingham claimed, met principal grievances of the Nazi regime, as it advanced the internationalization of colonies and assured access to raw materials. "A German government still ostensibly Nazi," he surmised, "could accept the guarantees of autonomy for minority groups and emigration for individuals." Were Hitler to be overthrown, he continued, two German federations—northern and southern—might enter a United States of Europe as separate entities; conversely, for the Allies to divide Germany into many states would "perpetuate the dangerous neurotic features of German nationalism, and make trouble for the future." The best hope, he said, "may be a chastened Nazi regime, with a sufficient change in the top leadership to make rational negotiation possible."[57]

Bingham explained how such a peace could be obtained. A peace conference would be called, first consisting of the neutral powers and backed by the pope; it would establish permanent machinery, both to mediate and to design various aspects of a permanent settlement. Although "some token restoration of independence to Poles, Czechs and Slovaks" was needed, it was, he said, absurd to restore the old boundaries, even if the Russians withdrew from newly conquered territories.[58]

Opponents of interventionism differed over Bingham's proposals. Freda Utley called it "realistic, comprehensive, and profound." Unlike Streit, she said, Bingham realized that federation could not wait for the establishment of democracy within each constituent state.[59] In critiquing Bingham's book, journalist John Chamberlain accused him of imposing FDR's National Recovery Administration on the entire European continent. Although democracy would still exist in Bingham's Europe, it would be "a sterile sort of democracy—an eternal round of plebiscites on the proposals put forward by experts. The race would breed two predominant types: samurai and yes-men, each a little less than human." Economist Peter F. Drucker, not a party to the debate over intervention, went even further, writing in Bingham's own journal that the plan would make Germany master of Europe. Social revolution and civil war would break out in every nontotalitarian country there, for such nations would be deprived of their internal and external defenses.[60]

After Hitler's blitzkrieg against Western Europe, Bingham's *Common Sense* opposed immediate entrance into the war and endorsed a negotiated peace. Even if total victory became feasible, he wrote, it was not worth the human cost. Though Bingham personally grew fatalistic concerning American claims of remaining aloof, he remained convinced that military stalemate would foster negotiations that would center on fairer distribution of the world's resources.[61]

Of all the belligerents, only the British leaders stressed European federation as a positive war aim. On 26 November 1939, Prime Minister Chamberlain spoke of establishing such a unit. It would ensure a constant flow of trade, general though gradual disarmament, and the right of each nation to choose its own form of government. The *Christian Century* first welcomed Chamberlain's proposal but soon expressed the fear that such a body would simply become a victor's alliance, designed to dominate Europe permanently. Any genuine system, it continued, must include all of Europe, particularly those states whose disabilities produced the present catastrophe.[62]

Ambassador Lothian too asserted that at least part of Europe needed "some form of economic federation, perhaps of political federation."[63] How, asked journalist C. Hartley Grattan in response, could countries with long-established traditions of independence surrender authority over armies and tariffs? Moreover, he added, Spain, Italy, and the Soviet Union were unlikely to cooperate with any central authority.[64] On the one hand, according to the *New York Daily News*, the Allies sought "a glorified League of Nations," possessing a central governing or supervisory body. On the other hand, they endorsed the restoration of Poland, Czechoslovakia, and Austria and sought to guarantee the independence of all other small nations.[65] In the long run, the first aim would probably dominate, as economic pressures were invariably pushing all Europe into "bigger states and fewer states."[66]

Even if intervention's foes could accept some concept of European federation, however, and even if a small minority within their ranks refused to condemn Streit as an arch-traitor, they greatly feared any suggestion of collective security, and beginning in September 1939 some wrote entire books attacking this concept.

Foremost was historian Charles A. Beard, long one of its most articulate opponents. Beard, who always thrived on controversy, had strongly supported the Roosevelt administration in its early years, for he believed firmly in centralized planning and economic self-sufficiency.[67] By 1935, however, he saw the administration avoiding radical and necessary measures, such as nationalizing the nation's banks, to pursue mere piecemeal reform. Beard feared that the United States might well find a convenient remedy for continued depression in foreign conflict, particularly one fought in the Pacific.[68]

The title of his article for *Harper's Magazine* of September 1939, also published as a small book that year, encapsulated Beard's thesis. *Giddy Minds and Foreign Quarrels* is taken from the famous advice given by Shakespeare's Henry IV as his son was about to ascend the English throne: "busy giddy minds with foreign quarrels; that action, hence borne out, may waste the memory of the former days." No blanket critic of FDR's leadership, Beard praised such Roosevelt polices as abrogating the Platt amendment, which had turned Cuba into a quasi-protectorate of the United States; withdrawing marines from the Caribbean; granting conditional independence to the Philippines; abandoning the chimera of the China market; and recognizing the Soviet Union. At the same time, he was sharply critical of the munitions embargo to Spain's Loyalist government; Roosevelt's speech of 5 October 1937, which called for "quarantining" aggressor nations; the naval appropriation bill of 1938; backstage involvement in the Munich conference; and the current effort to repeal the arms embargo. All such activity, said Beard, proved that the president sought to collaborate with Britain and France in "their everlasting wrangle" with Germany, Italy, and Japan.[69]

Not surprisingly, FDR's critics praised the essay, which reached the public just as war began again in Europe.[70] Similarly, interventionists were quick to offer objections, defending collective security and affirming the need for foreign trade.[71] Communist writer A. B. Magil took a unique tack. Such "liberal isolationism," said the *New Masses* editor, was essentially utopian, based on a return to the era of premonopoly capitalism.[72]

Just as Western Europe was overrun, Beard offered a more comprehensive prescription for what he called Continental Americanism. He began *A Foreign Policy for America* (1940) by praising the nation's founders for promoting simple commerce while avoiding destructive military and political entanglements. After the American Civil War, however, he claimed the United States lost its bearings, becoming ensnared in navalism, colonialism, and the quixotic quest for massive foreign markets. By the time of the First Hague Conference of 1899, another destructive tendency had emerged: "internationalism," a policy that promised nothing less than the peace of the entire world, to be pursued by permanent links with the European state system. To the negative examples offered in *Giddy Minds*, Beard added the Welles mission and demands for aiding Finland. He also attacked "imperialists" who sought war against Japan and retention of the Philippines as a base for commercial expansion.[73]

Anti-interventionists immediately endorsed the work.[74] NCPW staffer Ruth Sarles, for example, found Beard's definition of Continental Americanism simply "common sense."[75] Yet criticism was strong. Columbia University historian Allan Nevins, for example, accused Beard of outright distortion of certain historical facts (e.g., his claim that in 1898 Spain had promised to free Cuba) and betraying a "frigid indifference" to Hitler's invasion of Western Europe.[76]

Readers often compared the book to *Isolated America* (1940), an interventionist volume written by Raymond Leslie Buell, staff member of the interventionist magazine *Fortune* and former president of the Foreign Policy Association.[77] Challenging Beard's claim that the United States could prosper by remaining totally self-sufficient, Buell stressed political vulnerability amid an Axis-dominated world and U.S. economic dependence on foreign goods. Theologian Reinhold Niebuhr accused Beard of "moral indifferentism," while finding Buell affirming the ethical basis of American democracy. In addition, said Niebuhr, Buell showed how major fascist gains would seriously damage its American economy. Radio commentator Elmer Davis also favored the *Fortune* editor, maintaining that Beard offered no foolproof formula for survival, in either politics or economics. Communist Bruce Minton saw both Beard and Buell neglecting the underlying class basis behind the current "imperialist war."[78]

Even those who preferred Buell did not always find him without flaw. Political scientist Max Lerner agreed with his claim that 150 years of technological change had forced the United States to rethink its entire relationship to Europe. Lerner, however, feared that Buell's alternative—massive aid to the Allies—could lead to major economic dislocation and a garrison state. Norman Cousins, literary editor of *Current History*, challenged Beard's assumption that a victorious Germany would "have no part of us," but he found Buell's internationalism possibly leading to war. Walter Millis, an editor of the *New York Herald Tribune*, had written a popular account of U.S. entry into World War I so revisionist that in October and November 1939 the *Chicago Tribune* offered excerpts in its Sunday supplements. A convert to intervention, Millis came down squarely on Buell's side though he regarded his vision of a more just world order as a bit naive.[79]

At the same time Beard's *Foreign Policy* was being debated, Anne Morrow Lindbergh's *The Wave of the Future: A Confession of Faith* (1940) was published. Poet, aviator, heiress, and wife of Charles A. Lindbergh, she had been greatly shaken by the events of the spring.[80] In *The Wave's* forty-one pages, she deeply opposed the current "aggression, terror, class or race persecution" but found the "Democracies"—a term she put in quotation marks—by no means innocent. Their moral case, she argued, resembled that of the rich young man in Jesus's famous parable. If the "Have Nations" had shared more of the world's possessions with the "Have-nots," or if the democracies had given "reasonable economic and territorial concessions" to Germany's budding republic, neither Nazism nor the ongoing war would have taken place. The evils currently existing in Germany could occur in any nation experiencing war, revolution, defeat, frustration, and suffering. The complacent status quo of the 1930s could not last: "A world in which young people, willing to work, could not afford a home or family, in which one found on every side dissatisfaction, maladjustment and moral decay—that world was ripe for change." To resist inevitable change was "to sin against life itself." Inadvertently coining a phrase that would haunt her the rest of her life, she wrote, "There is no fighting the wave of the future any more than as a child you could fight against a gigantic roller that loomed ahead of you someday."[81]

Certainly, wrote Anne Lindbergh, the current struggle did not pit good versus evil; rather, the "Forces of the Past" were fighting the "Forces of the Future." She went so far as to see "some new, and perhaps ultimately good, conception of humanity trying to come to birth, often through evil and horrible forms and abortive attempts." This new conception was "in its essence, good; but because we are blind we cannot see it, and because it was slow to change, it must force its way through the heavy crust violently—in eruptions. Some of these eruptions take terrible forms, unrecognizable and evil forms."[82]

Anne Lindbergh specifically denied that the evils of Nazism embodied these "Forces of the Future." Noting that the dictators were using these "new social and economic forces," she wrote, "They have felt the wave of the future and they have leapt upon it. The evils we deplore in these systems are not in themselves the future; they are scum on the wave of the future." Comparing current totalitarian behavior to the French Revolution, she recalled Edmund Burke's famous denunciation of its atrocities but added, "Few seriously question the fundamental necessity or 'rightness' of the movement."[83]

Given such premises, Mrs. Lindbergh found only one policy acceptable: isolation. Civilization, she maintained, could not be saved simply by entering the war, nor could democracy, liberty, or "our way of life." If Americans did not promote these values at home, fighting to preserve them overseas was useless: "They will crumble away under the very feet of our armies." Conversely, if Americans sacrificed their selfish interests, "giving up part of the ease of living and the high material standards we have been noted for," there might

ensue "a gain in spirit, in vigor, and in self-reliance, for which no price could
be too high." Let Americans foster a peaceful democratic revolution, not engage in crusading abroad.[84]

The book immediately became a best-seller. Fifty thousand copies were
purchased in the first two months alone. Several noninterventionists, particularly within the religious and pacifist ranks, warmly endorsed the work.[85]
The more moderate Wall Street lawyer John Foster Dulles wrote her, "In a
prose which I cannot equal and to an audience which I cannot reach, you have
expressed some of the fundamental problems which have been troubling me
for a good many years past. It is never easy or popular to tell people to pause
and think at a time when emotion is dominant." Poet W. H. Auden simply
called it "a beautiful book."[86]

Other anti-interventionists, however, were more reserved. *Common Sense*
regarded *Wave* as "one of the most successful efforts to put the present act of
the human drama into words" but was troubled by her imprecise prose. Norman Thomas called the book a good one, though he hoped the author overrated "the hopeful element" in the both European revolution and the totalitarian state. Socialist Lillian Symes thought Anne Lindbergh a liberal reformer
who lacked an understanding of basic economic forces. The *Christian Century*
praised her for placing the war in the context of a vast and inevitable revolution. It did, however, take issue with any "wave" analogy that depicted humanity only as helpless victim or fortunate beneficiary.[87]

Some reviewers shared the Protestant journal's concern over a certain determinism. The bimonthly journal of the Institute for Propaganda Analysis,
edited by Columbia Teachers College professor Clyde Miller, found her views
similar to those of the collectivist elitist Lawrence Dennis: "The very title of
her book suggests her belief that the revolution will win inevitably." Even the
noninterventionist *Commonweal* stressed that "man" was "free," possessing the
potential to "put the moral mark on any environment, to moderate it and organize for truly human purposes."[88]

Not surprisingly, interventionists harped on what they saw as a fatuous fa-
talism. Playwright Clare Boothe, wife of Henry Luce, insisted that "the world
has progressed only because it has not allowed the waves to sweep over it."
Said E. B. White, monthly columnist for *Harper's Magazine*, "I think I shall go
on resisting any change I disapprove of, for I do not think change *per se* is anything much, nor that change is necessarily good." Herbert Agar, editor of the
*Louisville Courier-Journal*, saw her mind "painfully divided against itself"; it
had produced "some ugly examples of confused thought."[89]

More significantly, one interventionist after another accused Anne Lindbergh of softness toward fascism:[90] a Hitlerian view of "the Wagnerian saga,"
according to the *New Republic*, "appeasement" and "demagoguery," commented Margaret Marshall, book columnist for the *Nation*. Foreign correspondent Reuben Markham called the wave of the future sheer totalitarian-

ism. Harvard political scientist William Yandell Elliott spoke of "anthropolog-ical primitivism." One commentator attacked Lindbergh's explanation for to-talitarianism, asserting the phenomenon was rooted in greed and revenge, not frustration and privation.[91]

In June 1941, using the pages of the *Atlantic Monthly*, Mrs. Lindbergh re-sponded to her critics. She reiterated acute revulsion to the horrors of Europe, which she described in more concrete terms: "the suppression of free speech, of free action, the relinquishing of individual rights to the control of one man, the end of democratic government, the wielding of hate as a weapon, the unrestricted use of force and terror, mob riots, class warfare, racial and re-ligious persecution."

Furthermore, she became more concrete in describing the "wave." It marked no inevitable wave of communism, fascism, and Nazism "to which we must bow down in abject submission." Far from accepting a fascist-dominated Europe, she denied that such an order was all-powerful, inevitable, or perma-nent. An occupied Europe could never function successfully, for prosperity is "not a flower that grows from oppression."

Rather, she stressed, the wave involved "a movement and adjustment to a highly scientific, mechanized, and material era of civilization, with all its at-tendant implications, and as such it seems to me inevitable." To say that the revolution was in its essence good simply meant that "the effort to adjust to the mechanized world is a necessary one." In discussing her claim that the evils in fascism were "the scum" on the wave's surface, she remarked, "Certainly it is necessary to deal with the scum; but I feel that if we do not deal with the wave first we shall have no power to deal with the scum." She wanted Britain— "with its justice, tolerance and compassion"—to survive but wondered whether continued war would contribute to that end.[92]

If some found Anne Lindbergh's *Wave* far too vague, the same could not be said of Lawrence Dennis's treatise on world politics, *The Dynamics of War and Revolution* (1940), a work far less comforting to defenders of competitive cap-italism and parliamentary democracy.[93] Dennis began his career on the lower rungs of the American establishment. Receiving his formal education at Phillips Exeter and Harvard and serving overseas as an infantry officer in World War I, Dennis worked several years in the foreign service, followed by employment abroad with J. & W. Seligman and the National City Bank of New York. In 1930, he began to attack the overseas activities of American invest-ment banking, publishing his broadsides in such liberal journals as the *Nation* and the *New Republic*. By the middle of the decade, he started to advocate a "desirable fascism" and, in Hitler's early years of power, expressed admiration for him. According to Dennis's schema, a new American ruling elite would as-sume power legally, call private enterprise to "the colors as conscripts in war," reorganize the Congress on vocational lines, and replace the two-party system with a single party "holding a mandate from the people." Specific economic measures included nationalization of banks and major monopolies, redistribution of wealth and income through progressive taxation, and subsidization of small enterprises and farming. In the new society, all institutions—press, radio, cinema, schools, and churches—must foster a "national plan" designed to coordinate the entire economy.[94]

Dennis's self-defined version of "fascism" made him somewhat of a "loner," even among administration critics. By late 1939, his only consistent outlet lay in his weekly mimeographed bulletin, the *Weekly Foreign Letter*. Occasionally anti-interventionists spoke of him highly or recommended his work.[95] He was also involved in some ghostwriting for more prominent and centrist anti-interventionists.[96] He was acquainted with the Lindberghs, but it remains unclear how much they were influenced by him.[97]

In *Dynamics*, Dennis again stressed that world capitalism had played itself out. To alleviate poverty and stagnation, "capitalist imperialism" must be replaced by "socialist revolution," a concept that—to Dennis—included Russian-style communism, fascism, Nazism, and even the New Deal. Several major "socialist imperialist" blocs would emerge: "The United States over the Western Hemisphere, Germany over a considerable part of Europe, Italy over a considerable part of the Mediterranean and North Africa, France over its self-sufficient territory in Europe and some of North Africa, Russia over eastern Europe and central Asia and Japan with/or China over the Far East."[98]

Even such a new order would not bring stability, for international politics was invariably Darwinistic. Society, so he stated, always needed war to keep it from stagnating. Just as capitalistic and democratic countries had fought each other in the past, so, too, would socialist countries battle against each other in the future. The harshness of the new rule "may be, usually is, mitigated with time."[99]

To Dennis, World War II was simply "another British bid to Americans to come over to Europe to help the British and the French to put and keep the Germans in their place, which is the doghouse." While approvingly citing Marx to the effect that anti-Semitism was "the socialism of fools" and criticizing the United States in his bulletin for not admitting "a few hundred thousand refugees," he found efforts to hinder Germany's natural expansion both futile and dangerous.[100]

Were America truly humanitarian, Dennis argued, it would persuade the Allies to "stop the war," promising in return full responsibility for rehabilitating Britain itself as well as "the defense of such parts of the empire, under our flag, as we might decide, on strategic grounds, we could reasonably carry out." The U.S. would "have to take over" Canada and Australia and revamp its own economy to absorb twenty million British immigrants. Britain in turn must abandon its possessions in Africa, Asia, and the Mediterranean "to those best able to grab and hold them." The United Kingdom would become "another Sweden," with the royal family possibly retained "like the quintuplets in Canada." In return, a new Anglo-Saxon world would be created, one "not only invincible in a military way but workable in an economic way."[101]

Even if American intervention was temporarily successful in defeating immediate enemies, wrote Dennis, in the long run it could not preserve its capitalist system. "The quickest and surest route to an American Fascism or Nazism," he wrote, "is a war to end Nazism in Europe." As the conflict continued, taxes would bilk owners of wealth while business would be continually weakened by increasing regimentation; the bureaucratic elite and organized labor would expand. In time the inevitable "bereavement and sacrifices" and the ensuing disillusionment would create "a drastic phase of revolutionary change" based on "hate for the persons, ideas and institutions responsible for our entry into war." At the same time, "such hate may give birth to a new American folk unity and dynamism."[102]

A few anti-interventionists offered qualified approval.[103] So, too, did Supreme Court chief justice Harlan Fiske Stone, who called it "the most thought-provoking book I've read in many a day." Harry Elmer Barnes found Dennis's ideology contrary to his own "prejudices" but recognized an unrivaled critique of "the terminal stage" of capitalism and liberalism.[104]

Yet practically no reviewers treated the book uncritically. Karl Korsch, a German-born revisionist Marxist, concurred with Dennis's claim that democracy in the concrete was synonymous to capitalism. However, as Korsch went on, the leaders of Dennis's contemporary "revolution"—Hitler, Mussolini, and Stalin—were in reality "reactionaries," seeking the destruction of genuine revolutionary forces. To William Henry Chamberlin, the book was well written, provocative, and somewhat on target concerning capitalism's failures. Problems lay in Dennis's willingness to "accept fascism at the valuation of its professed upholders," a tendency that blinded him to the terror systems adopted by both the Nazi and Communist Parties. Freda Utley endorsed his picture of the declining capitalist order, but she held other presumptions more suspect, including Dennis's belief in ethical relativism and rule by elites and his assertion that the Soviet Union was a genuinely socialist power. Alfred M. Bingham, while praising Dennis's mastery of social forces, criticized sloppy definitions and an "obvious yearning for a superman."[105] William Z. Foster, chairman of the American Communist Party, saw no merit in the work, although he still devoted some thirty-four columns of the *Communist* to its contents. Foster attacked Dennis for denying that the USSR was a democracy; linking the USSR with Germany, Italy, and Japan as "socialist" states; portraying Germany as a "revolutionary" power; and predicting that genuinely "socialist" nations would fight each other. At least one reviewer, former *Commonweal* editor Michael Williams, called Dennis "a poisonous propagandist for the diabolically evil forces of the atheistic world revolution"; he concretely faulted Dennis for denying the reality, much less the validity, of moral and ethical principles in statecraft.[106]

Several reviewers who were by no means anti-interventionist, however, bestowed some value to the work. Editor Charles R. Walker praised Dennis's analysis of democratic capitalism. Dennis fell short, said Walker, when it came to asserting that genuine fascism could solve unemployment without the dynamics of war. Harvard political scientist Pendleton Herring found Dennis often penetrating but claimed that his amoral realpolitik ignored the fact that the "dynamo of democracy" generated "the highest human voltage mankind has ever seen."[107] Frederick L. Schuman, government professor at Williams College, engaged him in debate. In an open letter to the *Nation,* Schuman endorsed several Dennis tenets, including the death of competitive capitalism and traditional power politics, the West's lack of will, and the inevitability of what German philosopher Oswald Spengler called "Caesarism." Schuman's remedy called for just the opposite: a "dynamic and revolutionary America," linked to a "dynamic and revolutionary Britain." By immediately declaring war on Germany, both nations could "remake the world in a fashion which might be preferable (to you and me as Americans) to the fashion in which the Nazis will remake it."[108] In his rejoinder, Dennis found much in common with Schuman's "method, attitude, and conclusions," but he fully expected Hitler to conquer Britain and continue "cooperative relationships with the other dynamic totalitarians." Asserting that Schuman sought alliance with Britain so as to check the foes of capitalism, Dennis saw it futile to fight for such a goal. A people as favored as Americans possessed the natural resources, geographic isolation, and sheer size to become again "dynamic"—that is, if they adopted "some variant of an expansive totalitarian collectivism directed by a non-hereditary functional elite." Political scientist Max Lerner, in commenting on both writers, attacked Dennis for scorning democracy, Schuman for advancing "Caesarism." Democracy, said Lerner, "is substance as well as dream," "something to die for, to live for, to give our talent and energy to extending."[109]

Amid all such speculation, however, a more immediate task lay at hand: to combat the initial policies of President Roosevelt that risked leading the nation into the conflict.

# 5

# Initial Engagements

On 21 September 1939, in addressing a special session of Congress, Roosevelt urged repeal of the existing arms embargo. At the same time, he wanted the United States to maintain its ban on war credits and require all items to be transported in foreign vessels. Buyers of American goods must take title before leaving the U.S. "Cash-and-carry," as the policy was immediately called, should avert the torpedoing of American vessels and the destruction of American property in combat zones. "By repeal of the embargo," said the president, "the United States will more probably remain at peace than if the law remains as it is today." Furthermore, Roosevelt called on Congress to give him authority to establish war zones from which American vessels, planes, and citizens would be banned.

Though FDR was far from explicit, his bill obviously had one aim: to aid the Allies. Roosevelt did remind Congress that the current embargo deprived sea powers (i.e., Britain and France) of a natural advantage over land powers (i.e., Germany), but he would go no further. Instead, he stressed gains to American industry, asking why the United States should send "all manner of articles across the ocean for final processing there, when we could give employment to thousands by doing it here."[1] *Time* magazine was far more blunt about FDR's real motive, noting that the current American arms embargo had given Hitler "almost the equivalent of an Atlantic fleet, because Great Britain and France can get no arms from the U.S."[2]

At the beginning of the debate over the president's bill, *Newsweek* foresaw a battle as intense as that over the League of Nations in 1919. After Key Pittman (Dem.-Nev.) and William E. Borah led off the debate before a packed Senate gallery, however, arguments soon became repetitive, and much public interest quickly waned.[3] Speeches in both houses did continue almost a month, during which seventy senators contributed more than a million words.[4]

The president's adversaries were not as strong as many thought. Until the fall of 1940, when the America First Committee (AFC) was founded, the Keep America Out of War Congress (KAOWC) was the only national organization specifically created to retain strict neutrality and hence to oppose Roosevelt's foreign policy. It had been founded in March 1938 when the NCPW, FOR, WIL, and Socialist Party all had joined forces with several other peace groups. From September 1939 until late 1941, John T. Flynn served as national chairman. Concentrating on trade unions, pacifists, and socialists, it possessed its own youth affiliate.[5]

The KAOWC adamantly opposed cash-and-carry, but it lacked the membership and the mass backing to be effective. Philip La Follette, former governor of Wisconsin, proposed a nationwide organization supposedly to be financed by meat packer Jay Hormel. His plans, however, aroused opposition by such Republican isolationists as Senator Arthur H. Vandenberg (Rep.-Mich.), who feared the rise of a La Follette–dominated third party.[6]

Roosevelt's political skill neutralized much potential opposition. The American Legion contented itself with a general "stay out of war" resolution. The American Federation of Labor favored cash-and-carry, provided that "it can be shown that such a step will not lead us into war." An influential ad hoc body was soon organized to back the president: the Non-partisan Committee for Peace through the Revision of the Neutrality Law. It was led by the prominent journalist, William Allen White, a Republican long active in the Progressive movement and a man who wielded considerable influence. According to a Gallup poll, 62 percent believed that the United States should do everything possible to aid the Allies "short of war."[7]

Several figures later prominent in anti-interventionist ranks backed Roosevelt's proposal, though occasionally with reservations.[8] They raised a bevy of arguments. It was "Pharisaical," said Robert A. Taft, for the United States to supply steel, machinery, cotton, alcohol, and nitrate while "our hands are too clean to complete the process of manufacture." The Ohio senator saw such shipments quite permissible under international law, invoking the names of Daniel Webster and John Hay in the process.[9]

The *New York Daily News* noted the potential employment for ten million Americans still lacking jobs and contributed as well a defense argument, declaring that the United States needed factories geared to war production and workers who knew how to operate such machinery. Moreover, retention of the arms embargo would inevitably lead to smuggling, which in turn would cause Germany and Britain to sink American vessels.[10]

Lying in back of all arguments was one underlying fact: retention of the arms embargo aided Germany; its elimination helped the Allies.[11] "Our 'Neutrality' Act—A Help to Hitler," read the headline of one *Daily News* editorial. If Hitler could not crack the Maginot line or the British blockade, it warned, he might well cut loose his air force against London or Paris. The German dictator would be far less likely to commit such "civilian murder and city devastation" if he knew that the Allies had access to American aircraft factories, giving them that "much more chance to retaliate by raining bombs on Berlin, Munich, Hamburg, or some other beautiful and valuable German city."[12]

Most figures later prominent in the anti-interventionist movement were far less supportive. Borah's initial speech expounded several major arguments used by the bill's foes. The proposal would endanger the United States: "The spy, the dynamite, and the air bomb will have standing invitations to visit the munitions plants." The U.S. would be acting immorally, entering "that dirty trade" of arms commerce. War-stricken European nations could never supply the funds to repay the United States. Most of all, the bill took the first step on the road to war. Said the Idaho senator, "Hearing and heeding the Macedonian cry for arms, will we, if a more critical hour should occur, turn a deaf ear to the Macedonian cry for armies?"[13]

Other arguments were raised. Sinking even foreign ships might endanger American neutrality. American vessels themselves might be sunk by mistake. Suppose belligerent nations violated an inter-American declaration, proclaimed at Panama in October 1939, by arming their own merchant ships in pursuit of American trade. They could be "subject to extermination" by the U.S. Navy. Britain and France possessed huge factories where cannon and shells were made far more cheaply than in the United States. In fact, it was the U.S. that lacked crucial munitions, not the Allies. The proposal might even endanger the Allies, not Germany. If Hitler saw the United States coming to their aid, he would immediately launch air attacks on France and England.[14]

Much attention centered on the bill's economic consequences. Cited frequently was the president's famous Chautauqua address, delivered on 14 August 1936, which referred to wartime trade as "fool's gold."[15] Boom would inevitably be followed by bust.[16] Massive war trade would cause the United States to accumulate the world's gold supply, a circumstance that—contrary to appearance—really crippled the nation's prosperity by tying up a crucial medium of exchange.[17] The American merchant marine would be endangered, as many vessels would be taken off the seas.[18]

The lack of neutrality, the president's critics claimed, was absolutely blatant.[19] Fish compared the matter to "changing the rules after the kick-off in a football game." Borah quoted Bernard Baruch, the original author of cash-and-carry, who denied that the scheme was genuine neutrality. "Not by 20 sea miles," said the financier. "It amounts to giving active assistance to whatever nation has command of the seas."[20] Congressman George A. Dondero asked, "If two men are fighting in the street and you are standing nearby and give one of them a knife, are you neutral?"[21] Candid pro-Allied comments by such administration defenders as Senator Frederick Van Nuys (Dem.-Ind.) were quoted as evidence as to Roosevelt's real intentions.[22]

Above all, feared administration foes, the bill seemed to be the first step toward American entry into the conflict.[23] Bennett Clark commented that "cash and carry" had already degenerated into "credit and carry" and would soon be followed by "crash and carry," and ultimately "clash and carry." Recent activities of Allied purchasers were seen as destructive precedents.[24]

The remembrance of World War I was not reassuring. Once the Allies ran out of cash, so the bill's opponents maintained, they would seek loans. In 1915 and 1916, the Wilson administration first permitted short-term banking credits, then major loans.[25] Soon the entire American economy was dependent on a war boom, and Senator Nye was quick to recall the frankness of leading Wilson officials on the matter.[26] Congressman Bruce Barton went even further. Recalling the sinkings of American ships early in 1917, he said, "The German people had been made insane with anger because it was our guns, our shells, our gas, and our airplanes that were murdering their sons."[27] Journalist C. Hartley Grattan quickly rushed to press with a book bearing the ominous title *The Deadly Parallel* (1939). Repeal of the arms embargo, he warned, "*will mark the beginning of the collapse of American neutrality.*"[28]

In making such claims, anti-interventionists relied heavily on what Roosevelt himself called "the age-old and time-honored doctrine of international law." Such law, the president said, permitted neutrals to trade with belligerents in "goods and products of all kinds." Recalling the 1807 embargo of Thomas Jefferson, FDR asserted that the action of the third president had precipitated a ruinous economy and a destructive war.[29]

Certain scholars responded quickly. Edwin M. Borchard, professor at Yale Law School, was particularly disturbed by the president's proposal. A prolific author on various aspects of international law and a leading consultant on matters of international arbitration, Borchard possessed a singular attachment to traditional legal principles, while at the same time stressing underlying economic issues. Many of the conflicts of the interwar period, he believed, could be eliminated by the cancellation of war debts, tariff reduction, arms limitation, and redistribution of foreign markets and raw materials. Before World War I, he argued, carefully defined international law protected nations from purposeless involvement, permitted commercial prosperity, limited the scope of fighting, and allowed for neutral mediation. President Woodrow Wilson and Secretary of State Robert Lansing, however, defied all precedents, refusing to press for genuine neutral rights and in the process making U.S. entry into World War I inevitable. Postwar efforts to freeze the status quo and check "aggressors" simply ensured that all nations would be embroiled in endless conflict. If understood correctly, Borchard maintained, the League of Nations was an armed alliance, the Kellogg–Briand pact a foolproof device to involve the United States in continual conflict. To oppose the expansion of Germany, Italy, and Japan could be compared to sitting on a safety valve. During the debate over neutrality revision and the others to follow, Borchard continually offered advice to a host of congressional figures, including Senators Borah, La Follette, Hiram Johnson, and John A. Danaher (Rep.-Conn.) and Congressman James A. Shanley (Dem.-Conn.).[30]

In many battles against intervention, Borchard was supported by two academic colleagues. First was a scholar many years his senior, John Bassett Moore, who from 1921 to 1928 had been the first American judge on the World Court and had long served on the faculty of Columbia University. Although he certainly did not consider himself an "isolationist," Moore was critical of what he saw as international moralism and, like Borchard, could be quite biting. Such traditional devices as international arbitration and conciliation, he thought, were always the best means of preserving peace and limiting conflict.[31] Second, there was Philip C. Jessup, also a Columbia professor, who had written major works on neutrality. Jessup sharply differed with Moore and Borchard, who had been his teachers, over such matters as sanctions against aggressors (which Jessup favored) and presidential discretion in penalizing an aggressor (which he also supported). Yet he followed his mentors in opposing Roosevelt's policies once war broke out.[32]

If Borchard advocated one policy, it was legal neutrality, which, he conceded, was not the same as practical even-handedness. Several months before the European war began, he said, "Neutrality is not expected to place equal handicaps on both belligerents. It is an institution designed to protect your people from involvement in foreign quarrels by enabling you to justify your conduct and thus avoid the charge that you are consciously discriminating between the belligerents, thus exposing yourself to a charge of participating in the war." As far as morality went, the neutral power was neither "a sort of referee having the privilege of pronouncing moral judgments" nor a judge "between good and evil"; rather, it was "obliged to disregard moral considerations which that state is not in a position to examine."[33]

In regard to cash-and-carry, Borchard maintained that the relaxing of a nation's neutral obligations, if done with the motive or even the effect of aiding one belligerent at the expense of another, involved a marked violation of international law and—more important—was itself "an act of war and intervention." Germany, he feared, might in desperation justly take reprisals. Borchard had opposed the original passage of the neutrality acts on the grounds that they surrendered time-honored international rights.[34] He now stressed that the only changes a neutral power could make while a war was in progress were those in the direction of tightening that nation's neutrality.[35]

Others echoed Borchard's fears. Law professors Jessup and Charles Cheney Hyde, also of Columbia University, found the United States not only acting hypocritically but possibly exposing itself to brutal retaliation by a victorious

Germany. Roscoe Pound, former dean of Harvard Law School, warned that any change in the neutrality act would put the United States into the war. Danaher accused the president of seeking to engage the nation in a conflict that "might involve our very livelihood and our very continued existence."[36]

Several FDR opponents offered related arguments. They found little precedent for making radical changes in neutral practice once a major war had broken out, and they offered a host of citations from President Wilson to Sir Edward Grey, British foreign minister at the beginning of World War I.[37] Neutral nations, they said, had no obligation to trade with belligerents and, furthermore, had often refused to do so from the time of the American Revolution.[38] Roosevelt's discussion of Jefferson's embargo was seen as flawed, some saying that the move did not really damage the American economy.[39] Congressman Albert J. Engel (Rep.-Mich.) went so far as to say that since Hitler had been in power, "Germany has apparently scrupulously obeyed the rules of international law." Conversely, Professor Jessup accused the United States of emulating Germany's chancellor in diluting the rules of international law by discriminating between belligerents.[40]

Several administration foes expressed skepticism at the entire concept of an international law, but they leveled their criticisms only at FDR's use of the concept, not Borchard's. Publisher Porter Sargent called international law, as Roosevelt invoked it, "largely the creation of the British with the acquiescence of their satellites to foster British ends and embarrass rebel peoples." Charles A. Beard found the matter so tangled that it was hard to discern what Roosevelt meant. The *Christian Century* denied that there was any definite body of accepted rules for the protection of neutral rights, known to all nations and obeyed by all belligerents.[41]

Where, it was asked, was the mechanism needed to enforce international law? Finding no refuge in what he saw as a chimera, C. Hartley Grattan personally wrote Borchard, "The belligerents are committed to anarchy, will act as anarchists, will twist the law, cite the precedents which suit them, and otherwise make the law a mare's nest of the first order. . . . [U]nlike violators of national law, violators of international law cannot be either convicted or jailed by the good law of the prosecuting attorney."[42]

Several anti-interventionists wanted to reverse the president's request, seeking even tighter legislation. True neutrality, insisted the Jesuit *America*, must include a ban on foodstuffs as well as munitions, and it quoted Napoleon to the effect that "an army crawls on its belly."[43] Pacifist leader Dorothy Detzer sought the embargoing of "basic war materials," a category that included oil, cotton, and steel. The Reverend John Haynes Holmes opposed a single "pound of goods" shipped anywhere in the service of this war."[44] Senator Nye wanted a total embargo; any lost trade with European belligerents could be compensated by commerce with Latin America.[45]

Others suggested a stronger arms embargo. The embargo, said Norman Thomas, should not only be applied to belligerents but to Japan, Italy, and the Soviet Union as well. Senator Henry Cabot Lodge (Rep.-Mass.) endorsed its extension to all neutral powers.[46]

Herbert Hoover wanted to distinguish between offensive and defensive weapons. Such "offensive" weapons as bombers, poison gas, and submarines should not be sent overseas, and he pointed to the "barbarism" created by such munitions in China, Spain, Ethiopia, and Poland.[47] Charles A. Lindbergh, who had been in touch with Hoover on the matter, concurred (as confidentially did the more interventionist Kansas editor William Allen White). The aviator conceded that certain weapons were "borderline cases" but found the bomber an unequivocally offensive weapon.[48]

Interventionists responded immediately, denying that that one could distinguish between the offensive and defensive nature of planes and tanks.[49] Several of their political opponents agreed with them. If Germany were about to invade France or vice versa, said Senator Bennett Clark, antiaircraft guns could serve as an offensive weapon to shoot down the enemy's defensive planes.[50] William P. Lage, New York attorney and Borchard's coauthor for *Neutrality for the United States* (1937), accused Hoover and Lindbergh of "attempting to mollify their consciences while at the same time giving expression to the American desire for the defeat of Hitler." Hoover privately admitted that his proposal was unlikely to "develop into anything very practical" but hoped that "some day something may come of it." He also believed that "defensive" arms sales would "give an emotional outlet to the American people," thereby reducing the pressures for intervention.[51]

Many FDR foes supported an amendment introduced on 4 October by Senator Charles W. Tobey. The New Hampshire Republican wanted to retain the arms embargo while restoring cash-and-carry for all other items. If the United States sent arms to belligerents, he said, "We may find ourselves on the brink of entrance into a war which will cost us billions of dollars, many thousands of men, economic instability, and greatly increase the depth and length of the post-war depression." His proposal drew much support.[52]

Other amendments were offered. Taft, who had spoken in favor of cash-and-carry, suggested several. One obligated Congress to declare a war zone that covered all waters within three hundred miles of Europe; it was safer, he said, to send U.S. ships to belligerent Bermuda than to neutral Belgium.[53] Others specified that a foreign government provide cash before the American-made goods left port, that credits be prohibited to individuals and corporations of belligerent nations, and that no U.S. government agency finance exports to belligerents.[54] Fearing an artificial war boom, Senator La Follette introduced an amendment to limit U.S. foreign trade to the average of peacetime years.[55] Senator Edwin Johnson wanted the president, whenever he found a state of war existing between foreign states, to issue a proclamation naming the nations involved.[56]

All such amendments were defeated. Roosevelt's proposal passed the Senate on 27 October 63 to 20, the House on 2 November by 243 to 181. A Gallup poll showed a 58:42 ratio in favor of lifting the arms embargo.[57]

Some noninterventionists took the defeat hard. Hiram Johnson felt "run over by a truck." To pacifist leader Dorothy Detzer, it was "as though my baby had died." Wrote Professor Borchard to Borah, "The campaign to get us into the war is now on."[58]

Others remained optimistic. John T. Flynn credited the KAOWC and the "Neutrality Bloc" with saving "cash-and-carry" by defeating an administration offer of a ninety-day credit period. The nation, he said, had been aroused and public opinion changed. Vandenberg claimed a "great moral victory," asserting that the Senate forced FDR and his supporters "to become vehement in their peace devotions." *Uncensored* maintained that neutrality forces "came out far ahead." It found the cash-and-carry provisions were, contrary to Roosevelt's wishes, fairly stringent; Americans showed themselves determined to keep out of war; and most antiembargo senators and representatives were on record against intervention.[59]

Once the 1939 neutrality bill was signed, the American merchant marine experienced a severe blow. With American shipping barred from all combat areas, some ninety-two vessels remained in harbor, and six thousand seamen suffered unemployment. Moreover, bankruptcy faced every steamship line in the U.S., with annual revenue losses estimated at $52.5 million. When the chief victim, the United States Lines, asked the U.S. Maritime Commission for permission to allow nine of its ships to enter combat zones flying the Panamanian flag, it ruled that such transfer of registry was wholly within the law. It had already permitted the sale of 106 vessels to Brazilian, Honduran, Panamanian, and other interests. The commission pointed out that the vessels involved were nearly twenty years old and were currently being replaced by new craft. As the United States Lines had promised not to carry U.S. crews or passengers, American lives would not be lost if the "reflagged" vessels were ever sunk.

At first FDR and Hull approved the deal, but once barraged with protests, they rescinded the decision pending "full investigation." "It would have been a mistake," said Roosevelt, "to furnish the means to a sister Republic to adopt a different form of neutrality from our own. Panama ought not to send Panama flag ships into the war zones any more than we do." Meanwhile, American ships could be transferred to foreign registry only in cases of a bona fide sale.[60]

Only one anti-interventionist defended Panamanian registration. According to Hugh Johnson, the move did not violate the spirit of the new law, which did not seek to surrender U.S. commerce on any part of the high seas.[61] Most noninterventionists, however, saw evidence of the administration's bad faith. On 8 November, the *Daily Worker* carried the headline "Trying to Get around

It Already." To the *New Republic*, the ploy embodied "a dangerous attempt to circumvent cash-and-carry. "There is plenty of work for them," it said in referring to U.S. ships, "in other parts of the world, with 100 merchant vessels already sent to the boom of the ocean since the war began." The scheme, mused the *New York Daily News*, involved an effort to "make a profit out of a war from which our lawmakers do not want Americans to make open and aboveboard profits." The United States, it suggested, should return to the old neutrality principle by which American sailors and shippers could trade anywhere at their own risk. Panamanian registry, warned Norman Thomas, would invite German submarines into the Panama Canal region.[62]

Several FDR critics were downright acid. Hiram Johnson called the move a "contemptible expediency." *Commonweal* thought the Maritime Commission ruling "a case of duplicity rarely paralleled in this country in recent years." The Panama caper, commented the communist *New Masses*, proved that "embargo repeal was obtained by cynical subterfuge and calculated trickery," the product of "the newly organized firm of Wall Street & Roosevelt." Said John Bassett Moore, "the transfer of our ships to Panama renders it unnecessary for a person like myself to go to a playhouse to see a burlesque." In turn, Moore received the following sarcastic message from Borchard: "We might tell the Administration that the thousands of American seamen who are thus threatened with unemployment might also become naturalized as Panamanians. A little cocoanut oil would make their skins darker, and two or three words of Spanish could easily be taught to them. They would then sail as Panamanian citizens, and thus our trade would go on."[63]

Despite the anxieties of the anti-interventionists that the new commerce would soon lead to American belligerency, at first only the French placed substantial orders. Britain lacked the foreign exchange and could produce planes more quickly than the Americans. For Neville Chamberlain, the repeal of the arms embargo lay more in its negative effect on German morale than on any actual armaments Britain found itself needing. Roosevelt and his treasury secretary, Henry Morgenthau Jr., privately expressed disappointment over the lack of major Allied orders. Both men saw such purchases essential in resisting a major German offensive the president found inevitable that spring, not to mention playing a vital role in encouraging American manufacturers to convert plants to military use. Only in March 1940, with its productive capacity strained to the full and acting under strong French pressure, did the British place a major order for American aircraft. The limited nature of Anglo-American cooperation was not solely due to American isolationism. Neither country saw a full-scale commitment as desirable, much less necessary.[64]

In part, Chamberlain's own apparent indifference lay in his belief that by spring Hitler would resign. Goering would then lead a transitional government that would make peace. Once the German Führer departed, Germany would be accommodating on a host of issues, including Poland, Czechoslova-

kia, Jews, and disarmament. The only "real trouble" would come from the recalcitrant French. The United States might not be needed at all, something the
egotistical prime minister found just as well, for American "meddling" was the
last thing he wanted.[65]

Chamberlain's optimism was rooted in assumptions long held by British intelligence—namely, that the German economy was working at such a high
pace that it would inevitably face exhaustion. Because it lacked essential raw
materials and foodstuffs, it would crack under British blockade within eighteen months. One simply had to wait for a German collapse.[66]

All during the debates over cash-and-carry, some anti-interventionists remained strongly suspicious of Britain. Response to the *Athenia* sinking
showed how deep such attitudes were. On 3 September, the very day the
British declared war, Cunard passenger ship *Athenia*, bound for Canada from
Liverpool, was reportedly torpedoed off the Hebrides Islands. Of the thousand passengers, some three hundred were American citizens. One hundred
eighty-three people drowned; the rest were rescued. The British said the ship
was sunk by a German torpedo, but the Germans insisted that the British had
sunk it themselves, doing so for propaganda purposes. Sixty percent of
Gallup poll respondents accused the Germans; only 9 percent denied their
culpability.[67]

Certain anti-interventionists combined calls for restraint with expressions
of absolute horror, accusing the Germans of wantonly sinking the craft. Boake
Carter, implying that Germany had attacked the ship, called the sinking a
criminal act.[68]

Others were less sure. Herbert Hoover doubted whether a sub had sunk the
boat, saying, "It is such poor tactics that I cannot believe even the clumsy
Germans would do such a thing." Robert Rice Reynolds denied Germany had
any motive for sinking the boat; at best, such an act "could only further in-
flame the world, and particularly America, against Germany, with no appre-
ciable profits from the sinking." Conversely, said the North Carolina senator,
Britain could well have a secret motive: "to infuriate the American people."[69]
*Social Justice* declared outright that British guns sank the ship.[70] Only during
the Nuremberg trials of 1946 did Admiral Erich Raeder, commander-in-chief
of the German navy, testify that one of his inexperienced commanders had
sunk the vessel by accident.[71]

For international law experts among the anti-interventionists, further evidence of British cupidity was found in the *Altmark* incident. On 16 February
1940, the British destroyer *Cossack* entered Norwegian territorial waters and
removed 326 British sailors from the German prison ship *Altmark*. John Bas-

sett Moore accused Britain of violating Norway's neutrality, for no belligerent ship, be it man-of-war or merchantman, was subject to capture in neutral waters, even if it entered those waters for purposes of safety.[72] Philip C. Jessup concurred: "Our sympathies for the Allied cause against the Nazis should not blind us to the just rights of a small neutral." Such views were picked up by anti-interventionists at large, the *Chicago Tribune* accusing the British of endangering Norwegian peace and security.[73]

From the outset of the conflict, the president's critics found the Roosevelt administration unneutral in matters pertaining to the high seas. Within weeks after war was declared, Borchard learned that the United States had decided to admit "defensively armed" British vessels to its ports. As German submarines could easily confuse American ships with British ones, the "overt" warlike act sought by the interventionists would follow. Furthermore, by supplying these armed ships with the means to operate, he continued, the U.S. itself had become a de facto naval supply base. To John Bassett Moore, not only was the U.S. position unsupported by legal authority; it was directly contrary to what its own Supreme Court had decided.[74]

Others similarly found the United States acting in a most one-sided fashion. Hugh Johnson accused Britain of flouting the Declaration of Panama, which had forbidden belligerent ships to enter waters within three hundred miles of neutral hemispheric powers. The *Altmark* and *Graf Spee* incidents revealed that Britain never intended to respect neutral waters within the specified three hundred–mile limit. Boake Carter charged the United States with partiality. When a British cruiser captured the German freighter *Düsseldorf* off the Chilean coast, the United States did not protest, although the move constituted a legal act of war. On many such matters, the state department did lodge official protests, although certainly the Roosevelt administration was leaning over backward to accommodate the Allies.[75]

If such concerns hitherto were sporadic, Allied seizure of American ships triggered absolute outrage. During the first two months of war, said *Newsweek,* the Allies had detained forty-eight American ships. At times other numbers were offered. On 1 November, the *Chicago Tribune* denounced the Maritime Commission, claiming it had suppressed evidence that the British had searched 580 non-British ships since the war began. According to Congressman Engel, Britain and France had seized twenty-two U.S. vessels by early November.[76]

On 25 November 1939, British ambassador Lothian announced that British officials would inspect neutral ships at the port of loading. If the origin, destination, and nature of the cargo were approved, the vessel would receive a naval certificate, or "navicerts," that supposedly would minimize chances of its seizure on the high seas. At first the state department stressed that the arrangement was strictly a private one between the American exporter and the British government.[77]

Exactly one week later, the British put into effect a blockade of German exports. Britain planned to strangle Germany economically, thereby gaining sufficient time to build up a huge bomber force that would administer the coup de grâce. Under its terms, any neutral ship sailing from an enemy or enemy-occupied port might be forced to discharge its goods in an Allied port. The same held true for goods shipped from one neutral country to another if these goods had originally been bought in Germany or had drawn on German goods in the manufacturing process.[78]

Anti-interventionists found the British blockade outrageous.[79] Hugh Johnson compared it to the extortion of Al Capone.[80] Over a month before Britain made its announcement, Borchard called all such actions illegal.[81]

On 8 and 14 December, Hull said that the United States could not view such measures with equanimity but lodged no formal protest.[82] In early January, after the British had taken U.S. vessels to Kirkwall, Scotland, for examination, Hull protested, saying Britain would be held for loss or damage suffered during detention.[83]

Some noninterventionists saw the complicated odyssey of an American freighter, *The City of Flint*, as exemplifying the administration's double-standard, although this time Britain was not involved. On 3 October 1939, the ship left New York, bound for Liverpool and Glasgow, its hold loaded with foodstuffs, tractors, lumber, and oil. Some cargo was deemed contraband. Six days later, a boarding party from the pocket battleship *Deutschland* assumed control of the vessel and detained forty-one Americans, as it had the British crew of the *Stonehenge*, a ship that it had sunk earlier. The Germans took the ship, on which it put the Danish flag, as a prize vessel into the Norwegian port of Tromsö. In the port the Germans raised their own flag, but the Norwegian authorities, on establishing its true identity, refused to permit sailing until American flags had been repainted on its sides. The British seamen were taken off, but before the *Flint* could be turned over to its original crew, the Germans managed to escape with the ship, including the forty-one Americans, and sailed to Murmansk, where in turn the Russians interred the Germans and held the ship. Stalin ordered the Russians to release the *Flint* and expedite its immediate departure. On 28 October, with the Americans still in tow, the freighter left Murmansk, finally being forced by the Norwegians into the port of Haugesund, where the Germans were imprisoned for violating Norway's neutral waters. The ship was returned to the American crew.[84]

The Roosevelt administration protested. It realized full well, however, that the ship's plight offered a telling argument for a major provision of the pending neutrality act, one that would have prohibited the American vessels from sailing into belligerent waters. Moreover, administration anger was directed far more at the Russians, who appeared obstinate and circuitous, than to the Germans, who were quick to grant Secretary Hull every assurance he requested.[85]

The United States, administration critics claimed, had overreacted. Quite predictably the communist *New Masses* defended Soviet behavior. As early as 1915, recalled Senator Bennett Champ Clark (Dem.-Mo.), the British and French had repeatedly acted as did the Germans. The *New Republic* found the *City of Flint* was "apparently loaded with contraband consigned to Britain"; therefore, under international law, it could be seized or destroyed by its enemies. Philip Jessup, who had written books on prize court procedures, said that legally the Soviets could hold the *Flint* until a German prize court had decided on the fate of vessel and cargo.[86]

Overall, alleged several anti-interventionists, the British had been by far the greater offenders. The United States, therefore, was applying a double standard in not protesting sufficiently.[87] Hugh Johnson accused the British of "hijacking" thirty U.S. ships to Germany's one, claiming the state department began to issue press releases only in the case of the *Flint*. Is it pro-Nazi, he asked, to call attention to British conduct, particularly as previous state department silence about past British seizures was one reason the United States had entered World War I? "A plague on both your houses," invoked Hearst's *San Francisco Examiner*, bringing up for good measure British atrocities in India as well as German ones in Czechoslovakia.[88]

Controversy with Britain was just beginning. By early January 1940, the British had confiscated American mail at Bermuda en route to neutral ports. Interventionist Senator Harry S. Truman (Dem.-Mo.) said the British had struck "one hell of a note," and such leading administration backers as Key Pittman concurred.[89] Of course, administration critics were particularly outspoken. The Hague Convention, attested Borchard, had ruled such mails immune from seizure. Referring to Bermuda as the site of many of the mail seizures, the *Chicago Tribune* ominously warned that "only by a serious fault of diplomacy does that island remain in its present jurisdiction." When, in mid-February, the Associated Press reported that an American clipper had been boarded by a boatload of British marines, Bennett Clark accused the British of "using high-handed procedure in taking American mails at the point of a bayonet and rifling them."[90]

Noninterventionists offered varied solutions for British offenses. Lundeen called for seizing Bermuda, Nye for barring the island to American traffic. Representative Melvin Maas (Rep.-Minn.) proposed that American warships carry the mail, doing so, he said, to prevent the British from filching valuable business information. According to Congressman Jacob Thorkelson (Rep.-Mont.), a demagogue best known for anti-British and anti-Jewish ranting, the United States should ship no goods to England until it allowed free delivery of American cargoes to neutral nations. The *New Republic*, predictably expressing itself in milder terms, called for prompt adjudication by the Hague court of arbitration.[91]

In an unexpectedly vigorous protest to London delivered on 2 January, Hull accused the British of violating the 1907 Hague Convention that forbade such activity. Britain rejected this protest, asking why no similar note was sent to Germany. Hull in turn warned that American air service to Bermuda might be suspended if British authorities continued to open U.S. mail aboard its own planes. Pan American Airways helped resolve the matter by announcing that after 25 March, its clippers would not stop at Bermuda on eastbound trips but rather fly to the Portuguese-owned Azores in one hop.[92]

In January 1940, *Uncensored* raised another issue: a blacklisting of those American firms trading with Germany. Since the outbreak of the war, it noted, Britain's Ministry of Economic Warfare had drafted four such listings; the French, two. Between them, the two Allied powers cited Latin American firms, many of them engaged in doing business with the United States for years. Canadian firms, however, remained free to trade with anyone. As with the blockade, Borchard found the blacklist illegal.[93]

Britain's decision, made in January 1940, to curtail imports of American tobacco also drew scorn. In making this move, the British had two motives: first, the desire to conserve dollars by purchasing within the sterling areas; second, to assure a British market to two strategically vulnerable nations, Turkey and Greece. Because the overwhelming majority of congressional delegations from Virginia, Kentucky, and North Carolina had voted for repealing the arms embargo, the *Chicago Tribune* noted, "If the farmers of the tobacco growing states don't like what happened they know where to ask questions."[94]

Neville Chamberlain had little sympathy with American complaints. He wrote privately:

> Then the U.S. goes right back on us because while we spend all our dollars on buying war stores from them we have none left to buy tobacco. And they declare they are insulted when we examine their mails which are the vehicle of a carefully organised system of aid & relief to our enemies. Heaven knows I don't want the Americans to fight for us—we should have to pay too dearly for that if they had a right to be in on the peace terms—but if they are so sympathetic they might at least refrain from hampering our efforts and comforting our foes.

The British Foreign Office felt similarly. The United States, it maintained, had passed a neutrality law that forced Britain to restrict its purchasing or sell its securities. Roosevelt's proclamation of a combat zone strained British shipping resources, thereby operating to Germany's advantage. The Declaration of Panama kept the war away from the Western Hemisphere while extending U.S. economic and political penetration in Latin America.[95]

On all these matters, so administration critics believed, Hull's protests were far too weak.[96] "Our protests are now made for home consumption," said Porter Sargent. The *Chicago Tribune* questioned how far the secretary was willing to back up his words. Had the Germans been the offenders, said *Social Justice*, headlines would ring with government protests. Far more cautious, the

*New York Daily News* did not think the United States should "get tough" but added that Britain should realize that the U.S. was no minor European power.[97]

Despite anti-interventionist suspicions, leading administration officials were genuinely concerned over such measures, opposing in particular the navicert system and finding economic intelligence gleaned by Britain's censor used to its advantage. Cordell Hull and Special Assistant Secretary Breckinridge Long accused Britain of sheer stupidity; it was creating hostility among the American public by giving the impression of not playing fair. To Adolf Berle, Britain was "treating us as though we were a small nation—say, Czechoslovakia." Undersecretary of State Sumner Welles replied that his nation reserved all rights under international law. Roosevelt himself cabled Winston Churchill, first lord of the admiralty, warning that the British policies were being severely criticized by the American public: "The general feeling is that the net benefit to your people and to France is hardly worth the definite annoyance caused by you."[98]

A few administration officials even suspected sinister designs. J. Pierrepont Moffat and Adolf Berle saw the British establishing a closed Anglo-French trading bloc. Such distrust was misplaced; Neville Chamberlain never sought to take advantage of the war to create a trading orbit, always believing the Empire needed both European and American commerce.[99]

The British did modify their ways, at least to Hull's satisfaction. Mail censorship in the British West Indies was suspended. Examination of American ships at Gibraltar was speeded up. U.S. ships were no longer hauled into British ports. The blockade was loosened for certain American manufacturers. The navicert system no longer discriminated commercially against American craft. Once Germany seized Denmark, Norway, and the Low Countries, it closed their ports to American ships. Britain, therefore, had no further need to inspect U.S. cargoes in the north Atlantic.[100]

By March 1940, the president's adversaries were pointing to other matters that, in their eyes, proved that his administration was acting in a highly unneutral manner. On 19 March 1940, James H. R. Cromwell, newly appointed minister to Canada, addressed a luncheon in Toronto. In remarks that were broadcast throughout the dominion, he accused Germany of enslaving the Poles, whereas the British Empire was advancing a democratic economic and social order. He further castigated those Americans who failed to distinguish between the belligerents as being "shortsighted and cynically minded."[101]

Hull immediately wired Cromwell that such comments were "likely to disturb relations between this and other governments," warning him not repeat the offense. The speech, said the secretary, "contravened standing instructions to American diplomatic officers" to refrain from "public discussion of controversial policies of other governments, particularly with governments engaged in war, without the prior knowledge and permission of this government." *Newsweek* noted that few diplomats had been so publicly chastised.[102]

Nevertheless, anti-interventionists fumed.[103] Calls for Cromwell's resignation were frequent.[104] To *Uncensored*, Cromwell was a "diplomatic dope." "Never before," said Hamilton Fish, "has an American Minister in a foreign land attempted to destroy American neutrality by making a speech in a warring nation denouncing another belligerent nation." The vehemently anti-British Congressman George Holden Tinkham (Rep.-Mass.) wrote Hull a scathing epistle: "Disloyalty and sedition should no longer be tolerated by the American people."[105]

Cromwell's wealthy background and large contributions to the Democratic Party were noted. "Let's have no more playboy diplomats," warned the *New Republic*. As the husband of the heiress Doris Duke, Cromwell was accused by the *Chicago Tribune* of seeking "to use graves of American soldiers for a dizzier social climb." According to Congressman John Jennings Jr. (Rep.-Tenn.), "Our playboy Minister to Canada, Mr. Duke Cromwell, after wending his way through the highballs, was caught among the sheep with wool in his teeth." As Nye, Borchard, and *New Masses* all saw it, Roosevelt himself was behind the Toronto address.[106]

A few administration foes reacted more moderately. Cromwell, commented the *Christian Century*, undoubtedly spoke for most Americans in expressing sympathy for the Allies. He erred, however, it went on, when he embraced Allied war aims and identified their cause with that of liberty and democracy. Senator Alexander Wiley discovered some good coming from Cromwell's statement: it would make all U.S. diplomats "better Americans," he remarked. Even Father Coughlin said attacks on the emissary should be limited to "just criticism," for Cromwell's writings on capitalism revealed him discharging the obligations of his fortune more creditably than many others.[107]

No sooner was the Cromwell matter resolved when a book by columnists Joseph Alsop and Robert Kintner appeared that April. Titled *American White Paper*, it covered the past eighteen months of U.S. diplomacy. In this work, the authors found Roosevelt and the Congress of necessity being forced "to do good by stealth." If necessary, they hinted, the president would send naval and air assistance to the Allies although not an American expeditionary force.[108]

The president's critics stressed those portions that implied that Roosevelt sought to lead the nation into the conflict. Senator Lundeen remarked, "Every act of Mr. Roosevelt confirms the view of the authors that the President is determined to drag our country into Europe's war." To *Uncensored*, American troops would definitely be sent overseas if other forms of military assistance were inadequate. "For practical purposes, then, it may be assumed that there are no limits to Roosevelt's determination to seek an Allied victory." Norman Thomas urged FDR to clarify himself on the matter. The book, noted Senator Nye, revealed that the United States had never made a peace move.[109]

In June 1940, the New York firm of Howell, Soskin published *The German White Paper*. Originally the work was called "Polish Documents Bearing on Events That Led Up to the War." The book contained memoranda, recently captured by the Germans, written by Polish diplomats stationed such in places as the United States, Britain, and France. Journalist C. Hartley Grattan, noted for his World War I revisionism, wrote the foreword. The Germans, Grattan stressed, had deliberately chosen documents that they hoped would help clear their nation of war guilt and conversely prove that American diplomats had encouraged the Allies to precipitate the conflict. Moreover, he claimed, the documents "fit neatly into the Roosevelt line of 'action short of war' in support of Britain and France."[110]

The Polish ambassadors to Washington and London reported that the United States had promised to support Britain and France if they took up arms against Hitler. True, American promises varied: shipping a thousand planes within ten days; placing the entire financial and material resources of the U.S. at Allied disposal; eventually entering the war as a full-scale belligerent. Washington allegedly warned the Allies against discussing territorial changes with the totalitarian powers. The Poles in particular had been reassured by the fact that in January 1939, the United States was already spending $1.25 billion on military preparations. William C. Bullitt, American ambassador to France, was frequently cited as being particularly partisan, although Joseph P. Kennedy, U.S. ambassador to Britain, received similar billing.[111]

The Roosevelt administration was quick to deny the authenticity of the documents, even though diplomat Breckinridge Long suspected "more truth than fiction" in them. Two interventionist columnists, Drew Pearson and Robert S. Allen, thought they were genuine, as did *New York Times* Washington correspondent Arthur Krock. The president described the work as sheer propaganda, to be taken with "three grains of salt." Bullitt added, "With even more salt." Hull and the state department gave the material no credence. Count Jersy Potocki, Poland's ambassador to the United States, denied ever having conversed with Bullitt on American participation in the war. Kennedy refused to comment publicly, though he told Charles A. Lindbergh that the white paper had described his own role accurately and implied its account of Bullitt was correct.[112]

Not surprisingly, anti-interventionists pounced on the materials as authentic.[113] Rush Holt accused Bullitt of speaking under the influence of "foreign liquor." To Senator Lundeen, such American assurances "surely helped bring on the second world war." Were the documents to prove valid, said the *Christian Century*, they imposed a "moral responsibility on Mr. Roosevelt of terrific proportions." Hinting at impeaching the president, Hamilton Fish said, "If these charges are true, they would constitute virtually a treasonable act."[114]

Some found the documents be credible. The *Washington Post*, whose chief editorial writer was still the increasingly anti-interventionist Felix Morley, said that "the excerpts so far published sound plausible." The *Chicago Tribune* saw the material deserving serious study.[115] Even if forgeries, Senator Reynolds stated, they "sound very much like many things we have heard over the radio from any people in high office from time to time."[116] He and Fish introduced resolutions calling for a full investigation.[117] At first the *New York Daily News* downplayed their importance, declaring, "What really matters is what the President says and does while the war goes on." In January 1941, it wanted Bullitt to testify on the matter.[118]

Others seemed more certain. The socialist *Call* approvingly quoted Sir Wilmott Lewis, London *Times* correspondent in Washington, who stated that the papers were authentic.[119] Harry Elmer Barnes, who reportedly had chosen Grattan to edit the documents, said the published edition "should be read by every American interested in his country's destiny."[120]

Why, anti-interventionists asked, had Germany released the documents? Villard and Hearst writer Paul Mallon tied the action to the Welles mission, which they found the Germans hoping to sabotage.[121] The extreme left put its own spin on the materials. According to George Seldes's weekly newsletter *In Fact*, the white paper linked Bullitt and Kennedy to a shady anti-Soviet plot; it accused the British of betraying Poland. To communist *New Masses*, the materials revealed that FDR sought U.S. entry in the European war early enough to preserve the British Empire and to prevent the advance of socialism throughout Europe.[122]

To some journals leaning toward the interventionist camp, the documents' significance was highly exaggerated. The materials, said *Time*, only proved that "U.S. diplomats sometimes talk with an unprofessional lack of reticence"; it was nonsense to claim that American officials had conspired to foment war. Bullitt's views, commented *Newsweek*, had never been secret and hence were discounted in every capital in the world.[123]

Several administration critics concurred. Former diplomat Castle found the representations of both Bullitt and Kennedy accurate. He continued, however, "What has been published does not show, as the Germans pretend, that we instigated the war or anything like it."[124] Similarly, to *Commonweal*, the documents revealed nothing not already known, particularly in regard to Bullitt's sympathy for the Allied cause. The Jesuit weekly *America* went further, asserting that any German-sponsored material was highly suspect.[125]

The names of Bullitt and Kennedy led to a wider issue, the supposed interventionism of both ambassadors. Anti-interventionists of the right denied that Bullitt had ever abandoned his earlier sympathies with communism.[126] Conversely, those on the left believed him too anti-Russian.[127] Even the more moderate Castle wrote in his diary, "I wish there was some way to eliminate that fellow from public life as he will always be a danger."[128] Not content with material in the *German White Paper*, Fish indirectly cited *Gringoire*, a pro-Nazi and anti-Semitic French weekly, to the effect that Bullitt pressured Daladier and Juliesz Lukasiewicz, Polish ambassador to France, to fight Germany.[129] Bullitt fought back, rhetorically asking in a speech delivered August 1940 on the steps of Philadelphia's Independence Hall, "How many Americans today are playing the dictators' game without knowing it?"[130]

Although surprising in retrospect, Ambassador Kennedy was first portrayed as a militant interventionist. Hugh Johnson, recalling the partisanship of Wilson's ambassador to Britain, asked whether the United States had "a new Walter Hines Page at the Court of St. James."[131] The *Chicago Tribune* commented, "The American ambassador is frequently one of the most serviceable members of the British diplomatic service."[132] Unlike Bullitt, Kennedy did receive praise from several Roosevelt opponents. In December 1939, the *Christian Century* eulogized the ambassador for urging the U.S. to stay out of war.[133] William Randolph Hearst personally endorsed him for the presidency.[134]

All during this time, a crisis was emerging in the Baltic. In October 1939, the Soviet Union demanded that Finland cede territory on the Karelian Isthmus and in the Arctic region. It also sought to lease Hangö harbor and certain islands in the Gulf of Finland. In return, it offered Finland territory along the central portion of the Russian-Finnish frontier. When the Finns refused on 30 November, the Soviets launched a full-scale attack. Russian warships shelled Finland's coast, its bombers raiding Helsingfors.

Yet, for three months, it appeared as if the Finns might be able to repel the invasion, at least if they received material and volunteers from outside. Even within the administration, only an occasional voice, such as Breckinridge Long, expressed skepticism concerning Finland's ability to hold out. Roosevelt strongly condemned the Soviets, released forty-four pursuit planes, and granted $10 million nonmilitary credits. He permitted some private loans on his own authority, then asked Congress for more funds. Under his aegis, the Senate Banking Committee proposed a token loan of $20 million, out of which Finland could purchase trucks, raw materials, and agricultural goods. The Finns could not, however, buy what they really needed, which were American arms.[135]

The general population, anti-interventionists included, exhibited far more sympathy for the Finns than for the Poles.[136] Adolf Berle was no doubt accurate in noting in his diary on 5 December, "The neutrality of this country is not as solid as it was a week ago." Publisher Roy Howard found the spontaneous indignation greater than that created by the "rape" of Belgium in 1914 or the sinking of the *Lusitania* a year later. To Norman Thomas, the invasion was "a piece of stupid and outrageous brutality which matches or exceeds any performance of Hitler."[137] John Haynes Holmes placed the Finnish flag in his Manhattan pulpit and included their national anthem as part of his worship service.[138]

Not surprisingly, the communist press staunchly backed the Soviets.[139] Moreover, a few noncommunist foes of interventionists either found the Soviet demands just or warned the Finns against resistance. Borchard did not see Russian demands as excessive, finding it quite natural for it to seek protection against the looming German danger. Publisher Porter Sargent, while claiming to admire Finland's "valiant and vigorous defense of freedom," maintained that the Soviet Union could not afford to tolerate neighboring territory in hostile hands. At the beginning of the crisis, the *New York Daily News*, fearing the total liquidation of Finland, called on it to surrender some port rights or naval sites.[140]

Once the attack took place, the *New York Daily News* and the *Chicago Tribune* hoped that the Allies might rescue Finland. In mid-December, they suggested that British warships in the North Sea block Russian sea communications between Murmansk and Petsamo, the only place where Russia had gained ground. If Hitler truly feared the Bolshevik threat, he would encourage Norway and Sweden to aid Finland.[141]

Soon both papers expressed far more caution. Early in January, the *Chicago Tribune* thought that Allied military involvement might backfire, putting all of Scandinavia in great peril. Moreover, if such aid were forthcoming, the Russians might invite their German allies into the conflict, thereby imperiling Finland even more.[142] The *New York Daily News* noted that Churchill was planning to ship British troops to Finland via Norway or Sweden. The move, it said, could only result in "terrific" carnage. Early in March, the *News* suggested Swedish mediation. Rather than experience certain defeat, the Finns could enter in league with Norway and Sweden, thereby making the Scandinavian area "that much more of a north-Europe battlement against Red and Brown Bolshevism."[143]

As in the matter of cash-and-carry, the Finland issue caused some fissures among many who usually stood united. Most of the debate took place over the bill introduced by Senator Prentiss M. Brown (Dem.-Mich.), who proposed the $20 million credit from the Export–Import Bank.

Several anti-interventionists favored a modest loan, among them Hearst's *San Francisco Examiner*.[144] Hamilton Fish sought $20 million, to be spent under Roosevelt's personal direction.[145] Since neither side had officially declared war, it was argued, anti-interventionists denied that the restrictions of the November 1939 neutrality act applied to the conflict.[146] In defending financial aid, certain legislators posited an early version of the domino theory. If Finland fell, Sweden, Norway, and Denmark all lay in peril of Moscow, with northern Europe and the Balkans threatened as well and the possibility existing of a Soviet ships on the Atlantic.[147] Certainly, said Representative Richard T. Buckler (Farmer-Lab.-Ill.), the defeat of Finland would put Stalin "on the way to ruling all of Europe."[148]

Other noninterventionists stood strongly opposed such loans.[149] The U.S. Constitution lacked any provision that permitted foreign loans for war purposes.[150] The proposal left too much discretion to the Export–Import Bank.[151] Although Finland had admittedly paid interest on its war debt, it had not repaid the $8.2 million principal of the debt itself.[152]

Some arguments were more diffuse. Let the British and French supply the loans.[153] Domestic poverty remained America's priority. Norman Thomas remarked, "We have more refugees from our own dust bowl than there are refugees from Finland; our unemployed far outnumber all the Finns there are in the world!"[154] The allocation was too small to aid any nation fighting the Soviets.[155] If the United States so opposed communism, said Reynolds, "we should begin cleaning house here at home." Slaps at Mexico were not excluded.[156]

Certain claims appeared more telling. In stating that the a loan was illegal, Borchard found such action "exposing the United States to legitimate reprisals now or hereafter, on the part of the Soviet Union."[157] The precedent was ominous, said others, foreshadowing similar loans throughout the world.[158] Most important of all, many anti-interventionists argued, the move simply meant one more step forward.[159] Had there not been such loans in World War I, said Senator Pat McCarran (Dem.-Nev.), "We should not have row on row of white crosses in Flanders fields." Pacifists became particularly alarmed, one calling the measure "the Trojan horse of intervention."[160]

Socialists lacked one mind on the issue, the *Call* stressing Finland's need for arms, the party's executive committee speaking in terms of sending money and supplies directly to Finnish labor organizations. Yet, Norman Thomas, in calling for Finnish nonviolent resistance to the Soviet Union, found even an unrestricted U.S. loan dangerous.[161]

At times, alternatives were offered. One option centered on total cancellation of Finland's war debt.[162] Another focused on severing various forms of trade with the Soviet Union.[163] An embargo, it was argued, should be levied on American copper, tools, dies, and machinery, all used in Red Army operations.[164] A similar solution involved severing American gold purchases and wheat exports.[165]

Much attention riveted on still another option: voluntary contributions to Finland.[166] At the behest of the Finns, the ubiquitous Herbert Hoover established the Finnish Relief Fund, which enlisted the support of over twelve thousand newspapers. By early March, it had amassed some $3.5 million.[167]

Even here, several anti-interventionists demurred. The private charitable drive, said the *New Republic*, was backed by individuals who were seeking to enlist the United States in an anti-Soviet crusade. Norman Thomas called Hoover antilabor and pro-British. From the opposite end of the political spectrum, the *Chicago Tribune* remembered that Hoover had risen to prominence through aid to Belgium: "We cannot forget that Belgian relief was the first step on the march that ended in the Argonne forest."[168]

A proposal to sever diplomatic relations with the Soviet Union drew intense controversy.[169] In December, Senator Vandenberg submitted a resolution asking the president to report to the Senate on whether Russia had flagrantly broken the Roosevelt–Litvinov agreements of 1933, by which the Soviets promised to abandon subversive activities and committed themselves to settling major debts. If the Russians had indeed violated the accord, Roosevelt should recall the entire American delegation from Moscow.[170] In February, 105 members of the House voted to amend an appropriations bill so that the salary of an American ambassador in Moscow would be eliminated.[171] Within the administration, as high an official as Undersecretary of State Welles favored the notion.[172]

This proposal secured no consensus. Several anti-interventionists opposed a diplomatic rupture. Wheeler feared the loss of a potentially strong trading partner. Retaining an embassy in Moscow, asserted Hugh Johnson, might expedite a peace. Norman Thomas feared that the United States would be deprived of any effective vehicle to make protests. Breaking diplomatic relations, said Senator Clyde Reed, could not "stay the wings of a single Red plane." Castle warned his friend Hoover, who favored the move, that the measure might even lead to war.[173] The *New York Daily News* conceded that the Soviets had murdered five million of its own citizens and was maintaining an agency in the United States that "unabashedly works to undermine our Government." It continued to say, however, that recognition did not necessarily imply approval of a government's philosophy or methods. Moreover, "Hadn't we better stay in position to act as mediator in this European war—and hope that the chance so to act may come soon?" Expressing a view prevalent in the administration, Ambassador Lawrence Steinhardt wrote from Moscow that any such gesture compared to striking "an elephant with a feather."[174]

The Brown bill passed the Senate on 13 February by forty-nine to twenty-seven, the House on 28 February by voice vote. On 12 March, the Finns were forced to sign a peace agreement, in which they ceded strategic parts of their territory as well as rich forest resources, 10 percent of the arable land, their fourth largest industrial center, and 625 miles of railroad.

Certain noninterventionists reacted to the surrender by attacking the Allies.[175] Even before the capitulation, some were heaping scorn. The *Christian Century*, referring to the "effective aid" promised by Britain and France, asked, "Where is it?"[176] Once the conflict had ended, aviation writer Al Williams blamed the British leaders for not letting "their war lose itself in a great religious and moral world campaign against Red Russia." To *Uncensored*, the Finnish struggle deflected Soviet supplies from Germany and kept the Soviets occupied while the Allies contemplated an attack in the Near East. "Realists will decide that it was a case of Britain expecting every Finn to do his duty," it remarked.[177] Lawrence Dennis concurred, though he conceded that any British invasion of Finland was suicidal: "Setting a game little terrier on a big bear is not our idea of good clean sport."[178]

Others suggested Finland never had a chance. Even had it sufficient time to use the American loan, claimed John T. Flynn, its defeat would have merely been postponed a month. The *New York Daily News* found the Finns acting wisely. An Allied Expeditionary Force of necessity would have overextended itself as German troops poured into Sweden. "In the end, Scandinavia would have become a bloody shambles, while the Allied fighting would have become greatly extended." Only a federation of all Scandinavian countries, said William Randolph Hearst, could have prevented the recent invasion. The Finnish fiasco provided another example of the Versailles folly, which had left too many insignificant states too weak to defend themselves.[179]

Occasionally a note of optimism resounded. People of such spirit, said the *Christian Century*, could not be permanently defeated. The *New Republic* saw Finland giving the Allies a temporary respite; by occupying the energies of the Soviet Union, the conflict delayed any aid the Soviets might be giving the German Reich. The Finns, remarked Herbert Hoover, had pricked the bubble of the mighty Russian army and thereby relieved the small nations of Europe of their fears. The *New York Daily News* hoped that the peace in Finland might signify that the general conflict had begun to ebb. John Bassett Moore even asserted that Stalin's terms revealed his actions "better than some other countries . . . that professed to regard him with abhorrence."[180]

Overall, a more assertive policy could have done little for the Finns. The United States was not producing enough arms for its own defense, much less for that of the Allies and Finland. Furthermore, transportation logistics and the time factor worked strongly against the Finns.[181] If anti-interventionists were divided, so was FDR's administration. Roosevelt, who at first considered a stronger aid message, was unwilling to buck Hull, who exaggerated anti-interventionist strength.[182] Pressure for an arms loan, the president believed, would revive charges that he sought to enter the war, undermine his guarded aid to Britain and France, and weaken reelection chances.[183] The military too opposed the sale of any surplus arms.[184] According to Gallup polls, a slight majority of Americans favored U.S. government loans for nonmilitary supplies but balked when it came to weapons.[185]

Throughout the debates, Borchard had been disturbed by the sudden interventionism of Hoover and Hamilton Fish, who had offered a bill to launch a Finnish loan.[186] "It seems extraordinary how fragile is a matter of principle and how few people seem to realize how their sympathies may run away with their principles." Still, when the crisis ended, he said, "I think a door to our intervention has been closed. They [the administration] will have to find other doors."[187]

All such debates were suddenly called short in the spring of 1940, for Adolf Hitler launched his long-awaited blitzkrieg. By the end of June 1940, the bulk of Western Europe lay in his hands.

# 6

# The Fall of Western Europe

In the early dawn of 9 April 1940, German columns moved across the Danish border, and warships appeared in Copenhagen harbor. There was little resistance, and within a day the Danes surrendered. More significantly, on that same day, the Germans made six landings in Norway: Oslo, Kristiansand, Bergen, Trondheim, Stavanger, and Narvik. As the first week of combat ended, Hitler's forces occupied all major ports, securing possession of every important airfield.

On 8 April, just a day earlier, the British had begun mining Norway's coast, trying to force German ore transports from Narvik to the open seas. A week later, to counter the German invasion, the British started landing troops along Norway's Atlantic shore, although these forces did not arrive until the Germans had established strongholds. Furthermore, the British forces numbered only one-tenth of the Germans they sought to evict. Though Hitler's command structure was confused, the grossly incompetent British generals had to evacuate by early May. Late that month, the Western powers temporarily seized Narvik, but the German offensive in Belgium soon forced them to withdraw. The Germans did take heavy losses at sea, losing several of their larger surface ships.[1]

The fiasco resulted in a major shakeup in British leadership. On 10 May, Chamberlain resigned as Britain's prime minister. King George VI appointed Winston Churchill, a far more aggressive personality, to succeed him.

Several noninterventionists expressed absolute shock over Germany's attack on Norway. Anne Morrow Lindbergh wrote in her diary, "I felt that familiar sick-at-the-pit-of-the-stomach shock that all moves of Germany give instinctively to you."[2] Herbert Hoover was discouraged, both over the extent of Nazi penetration and British tardiness. Oswald Garrison Villard went further, even praising Roosevelt "for his admirable characterization of this latest German crime."[3]

Yet, for many, it was the British who were ultimately at fault. Pacifist John Swomley, FOR youth secretary for New England, denounced Britain and France for continuing the "butchery" in the face of German and neutral peace offers.[4] The British were frequently accused of prompting the German attack by mining Norwegian waters.[5] Lawrence Dennis not only stressed British mines; he also denied Hitler had any desire to fight in Scandinavia. *Uncensored* printed a chronology showing British aspirations in Scandinavia and its violations of the area's neutrality.[6] Several within the Roosevelt administration concurred in such indictments: Sumner Welles and Breckinridge Long held the British responsible for the German strike.[7]

Occasionally anti-interventionists blamed both sides.[8] *America*, for example, pointed out that neither Germany nor the Allies had respected neutral powers. To the *New York Daily News*, the fight resembled "the proverbial struggle between the shark and the elephant." In such a conflict, it commented, "small nations have no rights."[9]

A few speculated on the motives behind Britain's Norwegian campaign. The *Christian Century* thought the British sought to distract Germany from its Western front. *New Masses* accused them of planning to extend the war to Sweden, "perhaps very soon." Although, said *Uncensored*, the British mining aimed at blocking German access to the rich iron ore deposits of Sweden, Germany could still obtain this ore from the Swedish port of Luleä. Furthermore, it was becoming steadily less dependent on outside sources. To Dennis, spreading the war to the Scandinavian peninsula simply gave the British navy and air force "a theater in which to do stunts"; the action lacked decisive military value. By forcing the issue, he continued, Britain would simply compel Germany and the Soviet Union into a "business alliance" that would ultimately lead to the Bolshevization of Germany itself. Editor and critic Burton Rascoe presented a particularly bizarre analysis, suspecting that the British secretly approved of Germany's entrance into Norway and its domination of Denmark, Norway, and possibly Sweden.[10]

The British even received strategic advice, although belatedly. A pessimistic Hoover thought the British should mine the Kattegat and Skagerrak, doing so as to isolate the Scandinavian peninsula. Hearst went further, claiming that Britain should have been active on other fronts, taking aggressive measures in the Mediterranean, lining up Turkey and the Balkans, and compelling Italy to abandon the Axis.[11]

On 10 May 1940, the same day Churchill took office, Hitler commenced his main attack through Belgium and the Netherlands. Although both sides were roughly equal in manpower, the Germans totally dominated in aircraft. The

Dutch capitulated in five days, the Belgians in eighteen. By 20 May, Hitler's forces had reached the English Channel.

Ever since the war began, anti-interventionists had strongly praised the neutrality of the Low Countries and the Scandinavian nations, some finding them as a model for American policy.[12] When Churchill sought to enlist the neutral powers in Allied ranks, the *Chicago Tribune* backed a Dutch reply that asserted their moral right to remain aloof.[13] Indeed, several anti-interventionists blamed the Allies for infringing on their sovereignty. One writer in *America* accused the Western powers of deliberately throttling Belgian and Dutch commerce, doing so by holding merchant vessels for weeks in British harbors. Hearst found British raids on the Low Countries to be merely creating hostility. Borchard spoke of "the Allied illegality of cutting off trade between Germany and neutrals."[14]

When the Low Countries were invaded, several anti-interventionists expressed both shock and outrage, as in the case of Norway.[15] To *America*, the move was "dastardly."[16] Commented Anne Morrow Lindbergh of the Germans, "They *must* be stopped."[17] On 24 May, her husband Charles said to her, "I can't keep those troops out of my mind. I know what hell is going on there, what hell."[18]

Only evacuation by sea remained. Between 27 May and 4 June, almost 340,000 British and French troops were evacuated by boat from the channel port of Dunkirk, an enterprise carried out under intensive German air bombardment and brilliant rearguard actions.

On 28 May, King Leopold of Belgium surrendered his army, in part because of a calamitous French defeat farther south. If his motives were debatable, the consequences were clear. The engagement for the channel ports was lost by the Allies that very morning, for until then the Belgian army had been holding the northern arm of a rough crescent centering on Dunkirk. Even before these events took place, a clear majority of Americans found the Allies to be losing the war.[19]

By surrendering, the Belgian monarch created the bitterest of controversies. French prime minister Paul Reynaud called Leopold's decision "without precedent in history." The premier of Belgium demanded that the king be deposed. On the day he stepped down, Leopold wrote Roosevelt a letter that would be made public months later. Stressing that the Belgian army was exhausted and surrounded, he argued that continued fighting "would have today led to our extermination without a profit for the allies."[20]

Some foes of intervention justified Leopold's action, maintaining he had no choice.[21] When Leopold surrendered, said the *New York Daily News*, nine-tenths of Belgium already lay in German hands, a half-million civilians had been made homeless by the Battle of Flanders, and the capture of Ypres seemed imminent. John Cudahy, U.S. ambassador to Belgium and later an outspoken anti-interventionist, commented, "When the truth is known about King Leopold his decision to surrender will be applauded."[22] One writer in *Scribner's Commentator* called Leopold "the real martyr" of Dunkirk. Wrote J. Perry Carmer, "His was the army that held the line while the British took to the boats." Only William Randolph Hearst struck a dissenting note. He accused Leopold of surrendering several thousand men fighting in Flanders, together with important strongholds, while the British were risking their own homeland to protect Belgium and Holland.[23]

If many anti-interventionists praised the Belgians, a few attacked Allied leadership. Socialist journalist Devere Allen blamed Britain for triggering the German invasion by landing expeditionary forces and then by making the Low Countries fight its battles. Concerning Britain's hasty departure from France, Dennis wrote scathingly, "It was so noble of the British to run out with 330,000 soldiers while the French covered their retreat."[24]

In late May, when the fate of Britain's continental army remained in doubt, its cabinet considered peace terms. Foreign Secretary Halifax was open to any conditions that would preserve British integrity and independence, that is, no cession of either the fleet or the Royal Air Force. Prime Minister Churchill did not rule out negotiation, but only "provided we retained the essentials and the elements of our vital strength." On 26 and 27 May, he voiced willingness to recognize German "overlordship of central Europe" and cession of Malta, Gibraltar, and some African colonies to the Reich. Yet if the new prime minister might eventually trade British territory to Germany and Italy, such bargaining held little promise while France was falling.[25]

On 5 June, the Germans resumed their offensive against French armies in the south, within a day breaking through the lower Somme and reaching the River Aisne. The French government fled to Tours, then Bordeaux. On 22 June, Germany and France signed an armistice in the Compiègne forest, by which France agreed to surrender all its naval forces and demobilize land and air forces. Terms also provided for Nazi occupation of approximately two-thirds of France, including Paris, the entire the Atlantic coast, most industrial and mining areas, and nearly all grain-producing regions.

Marshal Philippe Pétain assumed full legislative and executive powers on 12 July, combining in himself the offices of president and premier under a unique title: chief of state. Abjuring the "false idea of the natural equality of men," he proposed to substitute "a society based on a hierarchy of ability and service to the state." Rather than "*liberté, fraternité, égalité,*" the watchwords became "*travail, famille, patrie.*" The new regime, sovereign in unoccupied France, was formally renamed État Français, informally called the Vichy government. It soon became clear that former premier Pierre Laval was the most powerful figure in the new government, assuming the titles, respectively, of minister of state (23 June), deputy prime minister (27 June), designated successor of Pétain (12 July), and foreign minister (24 October 1941). Until the Allied invasion of North Africa, the United States maintained full diplomatic relations with Vichy.

Most Americans were shocked by the French defeat, the anti-interventionists no exception. Hiram Johnson called the fall of France "a horrible thing to contemplate." Journalist William Henry Chamberlin, who had covered the defeat for the *Christian Science Monitor*, was reminded of the fall of Constantinople in the fifteenth century.[26]

In retrospect, the defeat was far from inevitable. Germany had entered the war short of essential raw materials and was economically unable to sustain a long conflict. By May 1940, it possessed a third less fuel than in September 1939. Contrary to myth, France had prepared for mobile warfare and defense in depth. Though the Germans had more planes, the French possessed more tanks and motorized units. It was the French strategy of advancing into Belgium plus the German blitzkrieg tactic that assured Hitler's victory.[27]

A few FDR critics blamed their own president for France's demise. According to the *Chicago Tribune*, he had promised that all U.S. material resources would be at the disposal of the Allies; hence, the French naturally took American support for granted. Hiram Johnson accused Roosevelt of having "gone far beyond what the responsible head of a government should, and repeatedly indulged in demonstrations that he might better have left unsaid."[28]

Of course, anti-interventionists—like the rest of the population—engaged in military analysis of France's defeat, though their comments were usually quite conventional.[29] Colonel Robert R. McCormick pointed to a two-to-one disadvantage in manpower, four-to-one in tanks (here he was incorrect), six-to-one in airplanes. William Henry Chamberlin added more statistics: a four- or five-to-one German superiority in industrial power, a preeminence in divisions of 160 to 60, and an added bonus of eleven armored divisions. Lawrence Dennis cited British military writer and fascist supporter J. F. C. Fuller, who in *Towards Armageddon* (1937) opposed constructing the Maginot line while recommending the formation of highly mobile army groups. Rather than remain on the defensive, said the *New York Daily News*, France had foolishly responded to "screams" about German outrages by ordering its best troops into Belgium.[30]

Such military analyses did not conceal one overarching fact: anti-interventionists of all persuasions had serious misgivings about modern France. One indictment centered on its entire twentieth-century record of behavior. To Harry Elmer Barnes, France bore the major responsibility for creating Hitler, doing so by its "vindictive diplomacy" of 1919–33.[31] Hugh Johnson accused France of tossing "both Prague and Warsaw to the wolves," violating its own treaty obligations in the process.[32] *Uncensored* noted French seizure of mail from an American ship, though the occurrence was denied by Secretary Hull. Back in World War I, Boake Carter could not help recalling, the French had even charged the United States for cemeteries used to bury its war dead.[33]

Certain Roman Catholic anti-interventionists pointed to France's long record of anticlericism. Father James Gillis, for example, could not forget the "persecution" of his church under René Waldeck-Rousseau, prime minister from 1899 to 1902. In fact, so Gillis wrote, Freemasonry still kept Catholics from enjoying their rightful place in government.[34]

Its empire tainted France's reputation even further.[35] The swords of its imperialists, said Senator Lundeen, were "dripping with blood." To Norman Thomas, forced labor and disease conveyed by white settlers had reduced the population of French Equatorial Africa from twenty million to three million. Furthermore, he remarked, the French had conducted ruthless warfare against the Riffs of Morocco. Rush Holt, noting the two thousand casualties from the French bombing of Syria's capital in 1925, quoted a journalist who wrote, "The screaming and bursting shells that spattered the streets of Damascus with the blood of innocent men, women, and children sent a thrill of horror throughout the civilized world."[36]

To conservatives, the fall of France showed the folly of the Popular Front, a French "New Deal" launched in the summer of 1936. Lasting just over a year, it was led by a leftist coalition headed by socialist premier Léon Blum. Its agenda included a forty-hour work week, paid vacations lasting two weeks, compulsory arbitration, nationalization of armament factories, and a public works programs. While visiting France, actress Lillian Gish witnessed "that great country grow soft, demanding more and more, while working less and less."[37] French politicians, commented prominent Iowa Republican Hanford MacNider, espoused "the doctrines of Moscow." To the more subtle Lawrence Dennis, the changes initiated by the "partially Communist" Blum government were long overdue, but they produced destructive social cleavages.[38] Congressman John C. Schafer (Rep.-Wis.) added foreign policy to the indictment, accusing the Blum government of making "an offensive and defensive alliance with the ungodly, un-Christian Communist butchers in Moscow," even though the agreement had been signed by Premier Pierre Laval a year before Blum took control. The extreme rightist journal *Scribner's Commentator* was particularly militant on this issue, denouncing Blum for blocking completion of the Maginot line, authorizing the fatal nationalization of the aircraft industry, and alienating Italy, Spain, and Belgium.[39]

A host of anti-interventionists found an accurate indictment in Count René de Chambrun's *I Saw France Fall: Will She Rise Again?* (1940), an account by a prominent French officer who was also Laval's son-in-law. If his firsthand narration focused primarily on secret dispatches and harrowing escapes, it blamed the Blum regime for wrecking France's moral fiber and serving as an unwitting instrument of Stalin's foreign policy.[40] Stanton B. Leeds's book, *These Rule France: The Story of Edouard Daladier and the Men Around Daladier* (1940), possessed a somewhat similar focus. Leeds, an American who had lived in France for sixteen years, offered a personal attack on Blum while lauding Pétain.[41]

Some administration foes, however, defended the Popular Front. *Uncensored* specifically denied that France's dire plight was caused by "communized war industries" or the "sabotage of Popular Front Government." Rather, nationalization of defense industries did not in itself limit production, nor did the forty-hour week slow down aircraft manufacture.[42] Frank Hanighen, who had made a special survey of the French economy, saw nationalization taking place too late, not too early. The so-called "French New Deal," he said, suffered because Blum did not institute currency reform and supervise the private banks.[43] The *Progressive* blamed rightist regimes of the early thirties for the lag in French production. Quoting Air Minister Pierre Cot, it claimed that during the Popular Front, production in the basic war industries was overtaking the Nazis.[44]

Even before France entered the war, several anti-interventionists denied its status as a democracy. The French Republic, said Senator Wheeler, had really died in March 1939, when the Chamber of Deputies gave the government permission to rule through November by decree. Bennett Clark called Daladier as much a dictator "as any of the rest of them." To Norman Thomas, writing in December 1939, "France today is virtually fascist." Control of all workers from age eighteen to forty, observed John T. Flynn, was in the hands of the minister of labor; the state determined wages and place of work.[45]

Particularly galling was France's treatment of refugees and pacifists.[46] In November 1939, the *New Republic* reproached the French government for interning thousands of German antifascist refugees in concentration camps, where they lived in an inhumane situation. Barnes found their conditions worse than those in German concentration camps, for prisoners had to sleep on hard stadium seats and barely possessed enough food to keep them alive. That October *Uncensored* reported the arrest of some thirty intellectuals who had demanded an immediate peace, including the philosopher Émile-Auguste Chartier Alain. Dorothy Detzer, on learning that the French WIL had been practically dissolved, called France a "complete dictatorship."[47]

According to certain noninterventionists, France had abolished civil liberties. Wrote publisher Porter Sargent in February 1940, "In France, the penalty for free speech is the guillotine." Pointing to French suppression of its own Communist Party, which numbered over three hundred thousand members and had seventy-two seats in the Chamber of Deputies, the *New Republic* asked, "When the French get through fighting for democracy, under leaders whose allegiance to it is dubious, how much democracy are they going to have left?" The *New York Daily News* not only cited the communist prohibition but accused France of arresting people for saying kind words about Hitler.[48]

Edouard Daladier, prime minister when the war began, was strongly attacked.[49] Barnes referred to "the weak and double-crossing Daladier and the cynical stooge [Foreign Minister Georges] Bonnet." Finding him far less sinister, William Henry Chamberlin nonetheless labeled Daladier—along with Maurice Gamelin, French commander at the time Germany invaded the Low Countries—"unimaginative mediocrities," unable to grasp the nature of modern war.[50] To Frank Hanighen, the prime minister served as the political tool of the generals. Hearst, more friendly, called Daladier a "fine man," who, if unhampered by party opposition, would make a powerful dictator in war or peace.[51]

When, on 21 March 1940, Paul Reynaud succeeded Daladier as premier, *Uncensored* presented the difference in ministries as simply "between a tisket and a tasket." Moreover, it thought that Reynaud, a man closely tied to heavy industry, sought economic rapprochement with Hitler. Hanighen saw the new prime minister as the instrument of Winston Churchill, who had convinced him to send French troops into Belgium and oppose Daladier's desire for a separate peace.[52]

On 29 July 1940, the Vichy regime convened a court of seven judges to try those responsible for the defeat. In less than two weeks, it began sessions at Riom, a town in central France. Among the accused were Daladier, Reynaud, and Gamelin.

American extremists of all shades supported the Riom trials. *New Masses* had no sympathy for the defendants. "The thieves have fallen out," it said, predicting that even Pétain and General Maxime Weygand would soon face the docket. Writing from the opposite side of the political spectrum, journalist Stanton B. Leeds referred to "those Blum-sponsored incompetents who wrecked France, who let her be drawn into a fight before she was ready." Even the relatively moderate *Chicago Tribune* maintained that such trials might "tell us a great deal about European politics in the recent past that otherwise would have remained forever in the realm of conjecture."[53] John Haynes Holmes, who considered the Vichy government fascist, called the trials shameless. "Nevertheless," he rationalized, "we cannot help feeling that, apart from the persons and circumstances involved, this is a good thing—*to put on trial the makers of war!*"[54]

Anti-interventionists levied one accusation that was particularly severe: trading with the enemy. While the French and German armies were at war, they charged, industrialists of both nations exchanged the materials out of which shells and cannons were made. "Within the sound of artillery duels," wrote Hanighen, "trainloads of these materials have met and passed each other, each bound for enemy territory." Coke came from Germany and iron ore from France, with the meeting point at Athus, a railroad junction in Belgium. Devere Allen, returning to the United States after a year in Europe, reported that French barges traversed down the Rhine around Strasbourg without German interference, carrying apples from Normandy and dates from southern France to export markets.[55]

Once France was conquered, however, a few anti-interventionists expressed great confidence in Marshal Pétain. On first hearing that the French leader would seek peace terms, Anne Morrow Lindbergh wrote in her diary, "They can trust him; he is devoted to France, has known victory and defeat. I feel relieved that they have such a man at such a terrible time." The Jesuit *America* praised France's new ruler. "Great in war and great in peace, he is first in the hearts of his people."[56]

When the new government began, the marshal's role became disputed.[57] The *New York Daily News* referred to "the senile Marshal Pétain, . . . probably nothing but a Hitler puppet nowadays, with all the strings jerked from Berlin: a sad spectacle." John Haynes Holmes accused Pétain of playing "the tragic role of traitor." Dennis predicted that Pétain would eventually be replaced by a new elite, one that could provide "bread and circuses" for the masses, honor and power for the new rulers, and administrative efficiency for the economy.[58]

Similar disagreement concerned the nature of the Vichy regime. In July 1940, *Social Justice* lauded the new France as genuinely fascist, a regime dedicated to bringing "mental, spiritual, and social development" to a country that had been ruled in the spirit of the "atheist Voltaire." Hoover thought the French were "well on the way to totalitarian government." The *Christian Century* doubted whether, in the long run, France would remain fascist, for it found "the average Frenchman probably the world's most inveterate individualist."[59] By September, the Protestant journal suspected that loss of empire and "capitalistic domination in industry" could eventually lead to greater prosperity as well as the recovery of cultural and spiritual leadership. (The *Century* foresaw the creation of a joint French-Italian-Spanish "Latin bloc" that might check German power.)[60] In January 1941, William Henry Chamberlin simply found Vichy a mixture of anti-Semitism, old-fashioned conservatism, and diluted fascism.[61]

Throughout 1941, some anti-interventionists, without totally embracing Vichy or its formal leader, gave it the benefit of the doubt. In January, Porter Sargent combined his pro-Vichy posture with a touch of veiled anti-Semitism by writing, "The much abused Pétain Government, not popular in lower New York, has been trying to remedy abuses." A month later, *America* saw Pétain as "a most important factor in the obstruction of Hitler." France's leader, it claimed, had refused power to the "universally detested" Laval, placed General Maxime Weygand in the most strategic spot in Africa, and encouraged General Francisco Franco to seek self-determination for Spain. In April, Hearst called Pétain a loyal Frenchman, doing his best to protect French independence and territorial integrity. Not surprisingly, *Social Justice* became one of Vichy's leading defenders. The regime, it said, had replaced universal manhood suffrage with a corporate state, moved against the "God-haters" who gave allegiance to "the bloodstained rag" of Moscow, and sought to curtail the activities of "foreign" Jews (in contrast to French Jews). Only Norman Thomas appeared to be a marked critic, accusing Vichy of complicity with Hitler and noting that the new French government had turned two prominent social democrats, Rudolf Hilferding and Rudolf Breitscheid, over to Germany.[62]

Roosevelt himself was less than enamored with the new France. Disillusioned by most French leadership in the interwar period, he was bitterly disappointed when the nation fell so swiftly.[63] During 1941, the United States maintained diplomatic relations with the Vichy regime. Furthermore, it continued to supply wheat to unoccupied France and provisions to Vichy-controlled North Africa. By midyear, however, Roosevelt had grown increasingly alarmed over France's collaboration with Germany, symbolized by the meeting that May between Hitler and Admiral Jean Darlan, Pétain's powerful naval minister. On 15 May, the president publicly warned against collaboration, much less entering into any kind of alliance "which would deliver up France and its colonial empire" to German control. Early in June, Hull cautioned the Vichy government to avoid cooperating with Germany beyond the specified terms of capitulation; he hinted at breaking diplomatic relations.[64]

Even as the Vichy regime was drawing ever closer to Hitler, certain non-interventionists tacitly defended its increasingly pro-German stance. France, commented Hearst, had to look out for itself. While England could offer nothing, the Reich could grant participation in a United States of Europe, in which France would remain a world power possessing an extensive empire. In the eyes of the *Chicago Tribune*, France had received only verbal promises from the United States; therefore, it was forced to make the best terms possible with Germany. Frederick J. Libby found the French government pursuing the only policy by which it could survive.[65]

Only the *New York Daily News* offered a slight note of optimism. "France," it said, "is tied to Hitler's chariot wheels" because of its inability to buy more food from the United States and ship it through the British blockade. It predicted, however, that Germany would become "fat and drowsy from too much milking of France and other countries," at which time "the lean and hungry Frenchmen will move in and slash the Germans down."[66]

In a radio speech delivered on 12 August 1941, Pétain pledged his regime to collaboration with Hitler's "new order." *America*, heretofore pro-Vichy, noted that "the high-minded Marshal is by no means surrounded by men as high-minded and idealistic as himself." As to a U.S. diplomatic break with Vichy, William R. Castle asked, "Why break relations with Vichy if we have not done so with Germany?"[67]

If some anti-interventionists empathized with the Vichy government, most held no sympathy for the Italy of Benito Mussolini. On 10 June 1940, Italy entered the war as Germany's ally and attacked southern France. That same day, speaking at Charlottesville, Roosevelt said, "On this tenth day of June, 1940, the hand that held the dagger has stuck it into the back of its neighbor."[68]

Until that point, anti-interventionists lacked any consensus concerning the Italian nation or its dictator. Some views were quite predictable. *Social Justice*, for example, often praised the regime. Its foreign correspondent, J. S. Barnes, wrote in December 1939 that Il Duce had yet to be proven wrong.[69] Also unsurprisingly, Norman Thomas remarked that Mussolini only remained neutral because he was holding out for the greatest reward. If and when he ever intervened on the Allied side, the socialist leader continued, the *New York Times* and other groups would undoubtedly find something noble to say about him! Three months before Italy entered the conflict, the *New York Daily News* envisioned Mussolini as organizing central Europe into a large customs union. A month later it called Mussolini "the smartest of the European power politicians"; his nation was simply "sitting back and making what money it can out of the war."[70]

When Italy attacked France, reaction varied. "What business is it whether Italy goes Nazi or Ally?" asked Senator Lundeen. "How does this feeble international meddling square with the sturdy Farewell Address of the Father of our Country?"[71]

Far more noninterventionists were critical. To Congressman Harold Knutson (Rep.-Minn.), Italy was a "buzzard." Anne Morrow Lindbergh thought Mussolini was playing "a lying and deceitful game." *America* remarked that Mussolini had "struck a dagger into the back of his own people," hurling forty-five million unwilling people into war on the side of a man whose views they detested.[72]

A few reacted negatively to both Mussolini's move and Roosevelt's response. Charles A. Lindbergh compared the crowds gathering to hear the Italian dictator to "a pack of animals ready for the kill," though he also called Roosevelt's Charlottesville speech "demagogic." Similarly, Castle wrote of Italy's strike, "It makes one despise Mussolini," but he, too, blamed FDR for preventing "decent relations" with Italy. Within the administration, several policymakers found the Charlottesville speech insulting, Long and Welles among them.[73]

Some saw the United States partly responsible for Italy's growing strength. *Uncensored* attacked the administration for sending scrap iron to Italy—in fact, over the previous four months twice as much as shipped to Japan: "The steel dagger with which Mussolini executed his 'stab in the back' might well have been marked 'Made in U.S.A.'" The *New Republic* noted that American capitalists had befriended Mussolini, making reckless investments under his regime. Even Lundeen said, "We helped to set Mussolini up in business," doing so first by making substantial loans to Italy, then by canceling $12 billion of them in 1926.[74]

Occasionally anti-interventionists castigated Western diplomats for having been far too severe on Italy. The Ethiopian crisis, claimed Charles Lindbergh, had unnecessarily thrown Italy into German arms. Had the British and French foreign secretaries, Sir Samuel Hoare and Pierre Laval, been permitted to compromise with Mussolini, said the *Chicago Tribune*, Europe might have remained at peace. Writing before the attack, Hearst conceded Italy's ambition for an empire that included the better part of North Africa, Albania, Yugoslavia, Piedmont, Corsica, Nice, and perhaps all of Provence. Yet he found such aims quite understandable, for after World War I, Italy had been "thrown out of the international gambling joint, not only without due division of the swag but with her pockets rifled and her distinguished service in the stacked card game of strip poker unrecognized."[75]

In May and June 1940, as Hitler's blitzkrieg swept through Western Europe, former president Herbert Hoover launched a major relief effort. Hoover had always been more moderate than many anti-interventionists, supporting U.S. membership in the World Court and the League of Nations and finding that the neutrality acts of the 1930s could "place us in practical economic alliance with the aggressor." In the fall of 1939, as noted, Hoover favored defensive arms sales to the Allies. In May 1940, as the Low Countries were being conquered, he reversed his criticism of military appropriations, going so far as to back FDR's call for $1.8 billion on national defense. Six months later he advocated "all the support for England that we can."[76]

When war broke out, Hoover focused increasingly on projects to feed nations occupied or under siege, as shown by efforts on behalf of Poland and Finland. In late September 1939, at the request of the Polish government, he organized the Commission for Polish Relief. Though Roosevelt was always wary of his predecessor, Hoover's renewed political influence forced FDR and the American Red Cross to supply far more aid to both nations than they had ever intended.[77]

In addition to humanitarian motives on Hoover's part, he obviously had political ones as well. By directing relief efforts the year before the Republican convention, he could show himself as "above politics" while still keeping his name before the public. The bread lines of the recent depression and the memories of "Hoovervilles" might fade whereas his massive relief efforts in Belgium during World War I would be recalled. In the words of historian Hal Elliott Wert, "Hoover's World War II relief activities served to resurrect a tarnished reputation. For Hoover, these projects represented a second chance, an opportunity for personal justification and political renewal."[78] If Hoover had any luck, he could again be a major player on the diplomatic scene, laboring with both the British and the Germans to mitigate, perhaps end, the conflict.

With the German spring offensive under way, Hoover worked behind the scenes with representatives of Poland, Belgium, the Netherlands, Luxembourg, and Norway. His aim: to send American food through the British blockade and in the process persuade the governments in exile to request his help openly. Such activity met with British resistance. As in the Napoleonic wars and World War I, continental blockade became a linchpin of British strategy—along with mass bombing, subversion, and psychological warfare. Only by such means, Britain believed, could the trench warfare that had proven so deadly in World War I be avoided. When Churchill assumed the reins of power, Britain became—if anything—even more adamant concerning the blockade. Because Washington cooperated with British policy, if at times half-heartedly, it was Hoover who gave the occupied countries their hope for direct relief. In May 1940, a Hoover-sponsored Commission for the Relief of Belgium was reconstituted.[79]

Hoover soon found support for feeding Belgium from Ambassador Cudahy. In an interview given in London early in August, the diplomat warned that starvation awaited Belgium that coming winter. "No words in English will be able to describe it," he said. Hence, the British should allow food through their blockade. Cudahy continued to voice his views, including them in his book *The Armies March: A Personal Report* (1941).[80] Anti-interventionists were quick to express sympathy to Cudahy's pleas.[81]

On 11 August 1940, at Yellowstone, Montana, Hoover launched a far more ambitious effort: to feed some twenty-seven million Europeans, mostly women and children. Unless food was immediately made available, he warned, Norway, Holland, Belgium, Finland, and Poland faced "wholesale starvation, disease and death." Possibly France, too, would be "in difficulties." The Germans, he continued, must agree to safeguards concerning transportation and distribution while Britain had to guarantee passage through the blockade. Soon his preliminary body, the European Food Distribution Committee, was predicting that eight million (Cudahy's estimate) were approaching starvation in Belgium, eighteen million (Hoover's own figure) elsewhere in Europe. It was, however, unable to provide indisputable data.[82]

In a most revealing letter to interventionist radio commentator Raymond Gram Swing, Hoover outlined his early strategy. Feeding occupied Europe, he wrote on 19 August 1940, could make no difference in the war's outcome. Had the British adopted Hoover's proposal, the Germans "in their present arrogant mood would have unquestionably refused the whole thing." The moral responsibility quite correctly would have fallen on the Reich, "where of course it belongs." At that point, public pressure would eventually force the Germans to accept Hoover's plans or provide relief themselves.[83]

At first, Hoover was optimistic, thinking that Britain would permit food to pass through its blockade once it had won the still-contested air war.[84] He soon found the British adamant in opposition. In this war, stressed Winston Churchill on 20 August, "the front lines run through the factories." Feeding a factory worker in Belgium was in reality feeding the enemy war machine. Mentioning the Hoover food plan by name, the prime minister said, "The

Nazis are boasting that they have created a new unified economy in Europe. They have repeatedly stated that they possess ample resources of food and that they can feed their captive peoples."[85]

Early in October, Hoover responded. The European peoples, he stressed, were not asking the American government for appropriations, charity, ships, or even the right to purchase food in the United States. Rather, they sought permission to import food from other parts of Europe, if there was any food there, or from elsewhere overseas. A neutral international organization could supervise the operation, protecting all supplies from the occupying armies. On 15 November 1940, in a nationwide broadcast, he denied that his scheme involved feeding the Germans, for at any point only three days' supply would be on hand. The British themselves, he noted, were permitting food ships to pass through their blockade of Spain. In an article for *Collier's*, Hoover warned that if the occupied peoples were not fed, their skilled workers would be forced to take jobs in German munitions factories.[86]

On 18 November, the ex-president's National Committee on Food for the Small Democracies (NCFSD) was formally constituted. Within the United States, the organization gained real support. Even the interventionist *Time* magazine called Hoover "an eloquent keeper of the U.S. public conscience," and such notables as General John J. Pershing and Admiral William V. Pratt, not particularly stalwart in opposing Roosevelt's measures, endorsed his efforts.[87] Soon Hoover could list among his supporters 504 college presidents and educators; 60 publishers, editors, and columnists; and innumerable clergy of all faiths. Some 2,500 local committees sprang into operation.[88] Within the administration, Berle privately supported the feeding, writing in his diary, "I would supply food to anybody who is really hungry—including Germans."[89]

On 11 December, Hull challenged Hoover, denying that any starvation would occur in Europe for five or six months. The United States, he maintained, "would not attempt to formulate a policy on the subject until half that period had passed." Hoover was far less certain, telling journalist William Henry Chamberlin early in January 1941 that he anticipated famine in Belgium and that Norway was in serious condition.[90] In a public speech given in February, Hoover predicted the "extinction of millions."[91] By then the Belgian government in exile had approved his test plan, which involved operating soup kitchens for one million adults and two million children. In February, Hoover spoke to the secretary of state concerning the role food could play in Spain, North Africa, and unoccupied France. "We must use food," he said, "amongst neutrals and semi-neutrals both for purposes of confidence and affection and also as a Sword of Damocles."[92]

Late in February 1941, Hoover thought he had won a major victory, for the German government consented to the establishment a Food Commission supervised by Americans and headquartered in Brussels. Furthermore, it agreed to refrain from confiscating imported supplies, cease removing food from

Belgium, and import potatoes and grain. American supervisors could oversee the distribution. Germany's concurrence failed to benefit Hoover, as most Americans—horrified by atrocity and deportation accounts—mistrusted the Germans intensely.[93]

On 10 March, the British gave their formal refusal. It was, they claimed, the responsibility of the German government to assure the material welfare of the countries it had overrun; any form of outside relief would simply strengthen the enemy's war effort. Let the Germans use the roads of Western Europe to carry food, rather than troops, fuel, and bombs for the campaign against Britain. If they so acted, the needed surplus nutriment could be transported, particularly to Norway, Denmark, and the Netherlands. Even if food shortages were likely, the British would regard it as "false humanitarianism" to admit foodstuffs, knowing that the action would prolong the war and in the long run add to "the sum of human misery." While no one could impugn Hoover's efforts, such action was incompatible with "a speedy British victory and the release of Europe from enemy domination."[94] On the same day, Hoover issued a reply, pointing to the plan's safeguards.[95]

Among anti-interventionists, feeding occupied Europe became a favorite cause, and one would be hard put to find any who disapproved. The nation's leading pacifist organizations backed the effort, as did many Roman Catholic journals and clergy.[96] The *Christian Century* spoke for much of the Protestant clergy promoting Hoover's cause at every opportunity, at one point calling the starvation of eighteen million noncombatants "the incomparable atrocity."[97] Also in support were retired diplomats, major newspaper publishers and journalists, members of Congress, many members of the America First National Committee, and the AFC itself.[98]

In addition, some Hoover backers favored the feeding of unoccupied France, a nation not covered by the ex-president's committee.[99] In November 1940, Dennis accused "all true lovers of world liberty" of deliberately starving the French so as "to hasten the downfall of Hitler." In January 1941, the *Chicago Tribune* reported forty million Frenchmen cold and hungry. Senator Edwin Johnson quoted approvingly the comment of Admiral Jean Darlan, Vichy's vice premier, who said in March that Germany was more humanitarian toward France than was Britain. He also cited Ambassador Bullitt's claim that Britain's blockade simply involved "playing the German game."[100] In June 1941, Borchard remarked, "This policy of starving France has helped to throw her people into the arms of Germany, the only reed on which France can lean."[101] In June 1941, under American pressure, Churchill did agree to permit some medical goods and foodstuffs to enter Pétain's France.[102]

All during 1940 and 1941, noninterventionists continually found European conditions deplorable. Publisher Frank Gannett saw Europe threatened with the worst famine in all history. Representative Louis Ludlow (Dem.-Ind.) said that the Belgians were forced to eat cats and dogs. Fear of disease was particularly strong. When interventionists maintained that the blockade might spawn massive plagues that could reach Germany, the *Christian Century* asked, "Who can steer an epidemic?" Besides, the Protestant weekly continued, "Looked at from any angle, the inhumanity of starving your friends to hurt your enemies reaches depths of moral degradation which cannot possibly serve any worthy end." Such a scourge, warned the *New York Daily News*, was "apt to jump the Atlantic Ocean, just as the Spanish influenza did in the last war." Pointing to Madison Grant's *The Passing of the Great Race* (1916), it asserted that a Europe enfeebled by famine might well be "easy pickings" for "the yellow hordes of Asia."[103]

Some comments concerning British opposition were particularly biting.[104] To Hugh Johnson, British behavior was "positively obscene."[105] The *Chicago Tribune* accused FDR and Churchill of sanctioning "the slaughter of babies." To Father James Gillis, Britain's rationale bespoke "the kind of logic that was used to justify the sinking of the *Lusitania*." "Must we become the most hated nation on earth?" queried Senator George Aiken. Representative Usher Burdick wanted Congress to withhold further assistance unless it lifted the blockade.[106]

At best, the food blockade was counterproductive. Remarked Senator Henrik Shipstead of the starving Europeans, "It will not do very much good to save them for democracy after they are dead." If, commented the *New York Daily News*, Britain ever launched its much-prophesied European offensive, it would badly need the goodwill of the continent's population. When opponents of the plan alleged that starvation would cause the occupied peoples to revolt, the *Christian Century* caustically referred to "unarmed, ravenous people . . . attempting with their bare hands to wrest machine guns and planes" from their conqueror. As for the claim that the Germans, moved by self-pity or self-interest, would feed the occupied people out of their own supplies, the *Century* denied that Hitler's Reich would risk its own starvation. To Lawrence Dennis, decimation of occupied populations by famine and malnutrition would only enhance the relative strength of the occupiers. Moreover, he continued, the more Europe was devastated by American bombs and starved by the British blockade, the closer the entire world moved toward Bolshevism.[107]

Certainly, said the plan's supporters, Britain was acting in a most hypocritical fashion. Why, asked Senator Reynolds, should the British object to feeding the starving children of Belgium when the United States was attempting to save British children by evacuating them at that very time? "We cannot permit Mr. Hoover to send food to aid starving peoples in occupied Europe," remarked Harry Elmer Barnes, "but we let down the bars to shipments to Russia, which can send even war materials to Germany." Both *Uncensored* and *Friday*, a weekly totally supporting the communist line, accused Britain of opposing the Hoover plan but winking at wheat shipments to Franco's Spain.[108] The U.S., too, was portrayed as lacking in candor, mocking its own rhetoric concerning freedom of the seas.[109]

By autumn 1941, Hoover realized that his effort had failed. The governments in exile, including the Belgians, were publicly repudiating his committee; only the Poles stood up to Britain. Summer harvests, claims historian James H. George Jr., relieved the immediate need for cross-blockade relief. At no point did the polls ever indicate majority support for Hoover's program.[110]

During the balance of the year, George continues, the NCFSD was relatively inactive. Senator Vandenberg consistently tried to have the Senate Foreign Relations Committee hold hearings on the proposal, but he was unsuccessful. On 19 October, in a speech at Chicago, Hoover attempted to revive interest but offered no new initiatives.[111] When Japan attacked Pearl Harbor, his proposal remained buried in committee, with no chance of being released.

Although Hoover had drawn much support, his plan remained tangential to the fundamental debates over intervention. The fall of Western Europe led the Roosevelt administration to embark on a series of measures that had not been remotely envisioned earlier that year. Although FDR's proposal met with occasional anti-interventionist endorsement, most foes of involvement remained more suspicious of the president than ever. Even his proposals for military defense were scrutinized most carefully.

# 7

# Protecting the Republic

Just as war was breaking out in Europe, Oswald Garrison Villard offered an entire defense policy based on a strict continentalism. In *Our Military Chaos* (1939), he wrote that even if Germany won a European conflict, it would be as unable to send an army to the planet Mars as to the United States. Similarly, a Japan victorious in Asia would be too exhausted to undertake further military ventures overseas. The real problem with the U.S. military, he maintained, lay not in too little effort but rather in too much. He found the problem rooted in the lack of any comprehensive policy, for the budget-breaking expenditures had no relation to any established military program. A popular war referendum was needed. So, too, was a blue-ribbon commission, composed of both civilians and military officers, that would define what was to be defended, how and where it would be protected, and just what sums were needed. To Villard himself, the ultimate choice lay in "whether we are only to defend our shores, or to prepare again to fight abroad."[1]

Anti-interventionists of pacifist leanings strongly endorsed the book, FOR executive Harold E. Fey calling Villard "a pacifist who can meet military authorities on their own ground."[2] Hugh Johnson, more cautious concerning the work, praised Villard's call for an impartial, nonpartisan, and extra-governmental commission to examine defense policy.[3]

Other commentators were more critical. To Lindsey Rogers, political scientist at Columbia, Villard was too simplistic in offering such suggestions as a cabinet secretary for national defense: "What is needed first is not unified administration, but more thought." George Fielding Eliot, a military writer soon active in interventionist ranks, concurred with Villard's attack on waste but argued that defense of U.S. shores was best assured by a navy "prepared to act offensively against enemy forces." Livingston Hartley, former state department official and outspoken interventionist, endorsed the call for a defense secretary, but he asserted that the United States should incorporate Latin America, particularly Brazil, into its plans. Military writer R. Ernest Dupey found little merit in the entire work, saying of Villard's chapter "The Huge Growth of Our Military Forces," "Would it were true!"[4]

Villard continued his attack in the *American Mercury*. The army, he maintained in April 1940, was wasteful, antiquated, poorly administered, and possessed too many officers. Not only was it caste-ridden, having one officer to fourteen soldiers, but its defense lacked even 25 percent efficiency. For example, scores of army posts were outmoded though Congress retained them for political reasons.[5]

Even presidential promises met with Villard's scorn. In attacking FDR's fireside chat of 26 May 1940, in which Roosevelt took credit for existing preparations, Villard accused him of ignoring the lack of planes, antiaircraft guns, mortars, and armored and scout vehicles. In May, Villard did endorse Roosevelt's appointment of a civilian armament board.[6]

In the spring of 1940, as Western Europe fell to the Nazi onslaught, noninterventionists bemoaned the nation's lack of preparedness. Obviously some partisanship contributed to the criticism. Senator Wiley, for example, remarked, "The President and Hitler came into power at the same time. Hitler prepared, the President slept."[7]

The critique, however, still remained.[8] Amos Pinchot mourned, "We have no Army to speak of, a very small air force, inadequate coast defenses, practically no antiaircraft guns, and a paralyzing public debt which will make adequate military preparations possible only at the cost of a serious sacrifice in the standard of living."[9] Besides, anti-interventionists argued, the United States lacked such crucial resources as chromite, bauxite, and quicksilver. There was not a single heavy tank and only thirty-eight light and medium ones. There were fewer than forty million modern rifles and only a few dozen modern cannon. The army needed shoes, blankets, and canteens.[10] According to Congressman Robsion, the U.S. had only one mechanized division, composed of about fifteen thousand men, and pitifully little antiaircraft equipment.[11] As Senator Danaher saw it, the nation had not even retrained its labor force: "A man who makes pins does not know how to bore a gun barrel." *Chicago Tribune* publisher Robert R. McCormick was most succinct: "We have practically no army."[12]

Comparisons were made to European powers. Even recently defeated Belgium, it was maintained, had been better prepared. In May 1940, William Randolph Hearst contrasted the U.S. regular army of 227,000, ill armed and insufficiently equipped, to "little Switzerland," which had 480,000 men fully prepared. As late as March 1941, Charles A. Lindbergh found the United States as unready as France and England had been in 1939.[13]

Such comments were not off the mark. If the U.S. led the world in production, it ranked twentieth in military power, even behind the Netherlands. Noninterventionists often quoted top administration officials themselves: General George C. Marshall, army chief of staff, on the lack of antitank guns; Assistant Secretary of War Louis Johnson on the shortage of new Garland rifles; General Hugh Drum, former deputy chief of staff, on the need for the type of equipment used currently in France.[14]

By the spring of 1940, Roosevelt was already responding to such criticism. On 16 May, as German armies poured into northern France, he asked Congress to authorize the production of at least fifty thousand military planes a year, a sum that dwarfed recommendations of his own service officers. Although he had requested twenty thousand planes in 1938, his pleas now suddenly intensified.[15] He also sought $1.18 billion in defense appropriations; over half was slated for a "larger and more thoroughly rounded Army."[16]

In his attempt to gain support, the president presented some frightening scenarios. A European air squadron could depart from the Cape Verde Islands off the African coast, refuel in Latin America, then strike such American cities as St. Louis, Kansas City, and Omaha—all within just over eighteen hours. Similar attacks could be made via Alaska, Greenland, or the Azores. Ten days later, in his "fireside chat," FDR used a metaphor from the recent Spanish Civil War, warning against "the fifth column that betrays a nation unprepared for treachery." He also assailed those who had "closed their eyes to events abroad."[17] Within two weeks, Congress exceeded FDR's request by $320 million, and when on 31 May Roosevelt called for more massive funds, Congress appropriated an additional $1.7 billion.[18]

Still in all, for anti-interventionists, lack of planning remained a sore point. What areas did the United States intend to defend? In opposing Roosevelt's request of May 1940, *Uncensored* asked, "If we do not know where our vital interests begin, how can we decide intelligently what our defense needs are?"[19] Certainly Roosevelt's massive buildup involved risks of their own. Columnist Frank Waldrop went so far as to accuse the war department of planning for a new American Expeditionary Force, a "pay-roll army" involving "masses of men, underarmed, undertrained, and oversized." Only by planning offensive war, wrote Lawrence Dennis, could one spend in one year the $9 or $10 billion currently projected for defense.[20]

Moreover, it was sheer folly to take on powerful enemies.[21] "Go to war?" asked Taft. "With what?" Noting that from 1925 to 1940 the United States had spent only $21 million a year on the army, Dennis commented: "A nation that has been spending this little on its army has no business indulging in righteous indignation over what happens in Europe or in impulses to do something military about it."[22]

Such people countered with their own military proposals. Waldrop spoke in general terms of "a really mechanized, mobile, fast-moving, professional defense striking force of the sort to repel boarders in this hemisphere." The *New York Daily News*, suspecting Hitler of world conquest, envisioned a ground force of at least a million highly trained men. The army, it said, could become "a West Point for the masses."[23] In June 1940 McCormick sought eighteen national guard divisions, eight regular army divisions of 15,000 men each, and an army totaling 280,000 men ready to go anywhere on the North American continent.[24]

Anti-interventionists became particularly uneasy when, on 20 June, just two days before France sued for an "honorable peace," Roosevelt announced two appointments to his cabinet. The first was Henry L. Stimson, age seventy-two, slated to head the war department. A staunch Republican, Stimson had been secretary of war once before, from 1911 to 1913 under President William Howard Taft, and had more recently served as Herbert Hoover's secretary of state. He was an ardent interventionist who publicly endorsed compulsory military training, the immediate repeal of the 1939 neutrality act, and the opening of all U.S. ports to British and French ships needing repairs. In seeking a marked acceleration of aircraft shipments to the Allies, he mentioned the possibility of American ships convoying such armaments.[25]

The departing secretary of war, Harry Woodring, had long been in the anti-interventionist camp.[26] For example, in January 1940, his praise of the 1939 "cash-and-carry" act centered on its role in lessening American involvement in the war. Supposedly, three months before he was removed, Woodring told friends in Topeka that "a comparatively small clique of international financiers" sought full-scale American entry into the European conflict. In stepping down, Woodring publicly claimed that increased aid to Europe's democracies endangered national defense; in fact, he denied that the United States had any quarrels overseas.[27] He claimed to have been fired because he opposed Roosevelt's efforts to supply the Allies, particularly the transfer of such weapons as B-17s, called Flying Fortresses, to Britain. Five days after the secretary's departure, however, Roosevelt wrote him to the effect that the bombers should stay in the U.S.[28]

Roosevelt's second appointment was Frank Knox, publisher of the *Chicago Daily News*, whom he chose to head the navy department. Republican vice-presidential candidate just four years previously, Knox had recently called for an army of a million men and the largest air force in the world. Moreover, he would put "at the disposal of the British all the munitions and supplies needed to keep the battle going."[29]

Anti-interventionists harped on the advanced years of both nominees, noting the irony of Roosevelt's well-known attack in 1937 on "over-aged" Supreme Court justices.[30] More significant, their entire past record was strongly assailed. Knox and Stimson, Wheeler said, embodied the "heart of Wall Street."[31] Anti-Roosevelt statements by candidate Knox were dug up with relish, including the publisher's claim that FDR was "overconfident, incautious, self-willed, uncertain, and unreliable," a man whose leadership in time of war "would be disastrous."[32] Nye condemned Knox for having "denounced every single social reform which has been made." Holt recalled that Stimson had favored conscription in 1916, opposed President Wilson's peace efforts of that year, and—as President Coolidge's mediator in Nicaragua—favored the sending of marines to protect $15 million of American investments.[33]

Most important of all was the current interventionist views of both nominees.[34] The Japanese were right, wrote William R. Castle, in considering Stimson "their greatest enemy," continuing that "we need the friendship of Japan." But Knox, too, appeared threatening. Wheeler accused him, by promoting aid to Britain, of encouraging "Hitler, Mussolini, and Churchill to keep on bombing cities, killing innocent women and children, filling the hospitals with men made insane by war."[35]

Occasionally an anti-interventionist endorsed one or both appointments. The *New York Daily News* called Knox "an able and energetic man, with an excellent record of service in both the Spanish-American and World Wars." To the *News*, Stimson, though "a bit on the elderly side for what may be a mankilling job," was—like Knox—a man of "courage and honesty." Vandenberg favored Knox's confirmation, though not Stimson's, noting that the Chicago publisher had spoken against U.S. convoys. On 9 July, Stimson was confirmed by a vote of fifty-eight to twenty-eight; on the next day, Knox was approved sixty-six to sixteen.[36] Within the administration, the balance was now decisively tipped in favor of the more militant interventionists.[37]

The firing of Woodring raised a related issue: interventionist efforts to supply the Allies with vital weapons that, so anti-interventionists argued, the United States itself needed. In March 1940, Congressman John C. Schafer proposed an amendment to a military appropriations bill: no foreign power should be allowed to purchase any type of aircraft or related equipment. On hearing that the army might sell the Allies planes capable of flying four hundred miles per hour, including the Curtiss P-40 fighter, he warned, "A friendly country today may be an enemy tomorrow, or be under the control of an unfriendly country."[38]

On 6 June, the navy department, with the president's approval, announced that some fifty Curtiss-Wright scout bombers were being sold to the besieged French. "If we give unlimited arms and war supplies to the Allies," asked Lundeen, "how are we going to train our own Army? With cornstalks and broomsticks?" Even if just limited to training pilots, such aircraft, argued columnist Al Williams, was crucial.[39]

Within two weeks, the administration had released twenty of the navy's fastest torpedo boats and submarine chasers to the British. Also scheduled were military aircraft and huge stocks of the army's World War I rifles, seventy-five-millimeter guns, mortars, machine guns, and ammunition.[40]

Anti-interventionists offered many objections: France had already fallen. Article VIII of the Hague Convention of 1907 forbade such acts. The United

States could face legal action from Germany. The move violated U.S. criminal codes. American naval crews and fliers would be shipped next. Indeed, the nation was committing an act of war.[41] Representative Schafer called for the resignation of Henry Morgenthau because—as acting secretary of the navy—the treasury secretary had approved the sale.[42]

The controversy soon blew over, for Roosevelt canceled the release on 24 June, doing so on the grounds that his attorney general had found that the transfer violated a law enacted in 1917.[43] On 28 June, the Senate passed an amendment to the Naval Expansion Bill, introduced by Senator David I. Walsh (Dem.-Mass.) and subsequently signed by FDR, forbidding the disposal of any army or navy matériel unless either the chief of staff or the chief of naval operations certified the weapons involved as unessential to American defense.[44]

All during this time, Britain's chances of survival appeared poor. In the 24 June issue of *Life* magazine, which reported on the Germans entering Paris, the interventionist weekly found it "almost beyond hope that England can stand off Germany very long." In July, it described Britain as facing a "life-and-death" fight on its own shores.[45] On 11 June, Captain Alan G. Kirk, U.S. naval attaché in London, predicted invasion by 1 August. Britain, he said, was no more prepared to defend itself than Long Island, New York. In mid-June, Breckinridge Long did not rule out a British collapse within a month.[46] Key Pittman wrote off Europe altogether, saying Britain must "fight from the New World with our Navy."[47]

Hence, within the Roosevelt administration itself, strong reluctance to aiding Britain existed. Even the shipment of a thousand planes, argued Long, could only last the Allies a week. The United States, advised war department planners on 22 May, should confine its defense to the American continent and possessions east of Midway. Chief of Staff George C. Marshall in particular objected to expending American matériel in what appeared a hopeless cause. He vetoed the sale of any fighter plane requested by Churchill, disapproved of any ship transfer, and agreed only to send rifles, machine guns, and field pieces left over from World War I.[48] The loss of even a hundred American planes, cautioned army air force chief General Henry ("Hap") Arnold, would set pilot training back six months, cut the U.S. supply by one-fourth, and expose Hawaii, the Canal Zone, and the Caribbean to attack. Even shipping seventy-five-millimeter guns would put the nation behind by two years.[49] Major Walter Bedell Smith, a member of the General Staff Corps, warned that if the U.S. eventually needed such weapons, "everyone who was a party to the deal might hope to be found hanging from a lamp post." Treasury Secretary Henry Morgenthau Jr., who favored aiding the Allies, mourned, "We haven't got one airplane today that has got the things they [the Allies] needed if they went up against a German plane. Not one. Guns are of such small caliber that they can't pierce the armor of the Germans. We have not got one bomber flying that has a gun on its tail to defend itself."[50]

At this stage, in fact, historians J. Garry Clifford and Samuel R. Spencer Jr. find Marshall's views compatible with the "Gibraltar America" ideas soon espoused by the America First Committee. "It seems plain," said Assistant Secretary Berle, "that our job is to collect the strongest and solidest defense force we can, and not to fritter away small detachments to the other side of the Atlantic."[51]

The Gallup poll of late May 1940 revealed caution, 64 percent opposing aid to Britain and France if such assistance risked U.S. entry into the war.[52] In regard to the five thousand planes retained by the American armed forces, less than 50 percent polled by Gallup wanted any sale at all.[53] By mid-June, Gallup indicated 35 percent predicting a German-Italian victory; 32 percent, an Allied one; and 33 percent, undecided.[54]

Quite possibly only in mid-July did Roosevelt himself really believe that the British might survive and thereby meet administration criteria for massive aid.[55] Early in July, Roosevelt had seen Britain's chances as one in three; by late July, fifty-fifty.[56] Here a mission to Britain of a close friend, Colonel William J. Donovan, played a crucial role, for Donovan submitted an optimistic report.[57]

Debate over torpedo craft and submarine chasers soon took on much wider ramifications, and to understand anti-interventionist sentiment, one must examine various appraisals of sea power.[58] As part of its general rearmament program, the Roosevelt administration requested a vastly strengthened navy. In January 1940, for example, the administration sought to increase naval strength some 25 percent, to be gained by a congressional allocation of $1.3 billion. All during the spring of 1940, it kept up the pressure.

Until the fall of France and often thereafter, many noninterventionists resisted. To the *New Republic*, such efforts reflected a "militarism gone mad." The *Christian Century* concurred, accusing Roosevelt of shifting away from needed electrification, highway construction, and farm relief. Hamilton Fish attacked the naval lobby. Just before naval appropriations were due, said the New York congressman in April 1940, Americans would be told that Japan was building sixty-five-thousand-ton battleships, that its navy was larger than that of the United States, and that "we are almost in the same category as China or Abyssinia or Poland." Besides, Fish argued, a prospective enemy was bound to see massive naval increases as provocative. The U.S. should not "extend the Monroe Doctrine 10,000 miles to the Far East."[59]

Then there was the factor of military effectiveness. All during the debates over intervention, certain anti-interventionists deemed battleships, in particular, obsolete.[60] They never appeared in any engagements, said the Hearst press; they could not be tended at most dry docks and were incapable of passing through the Panama Canal.[61] In particular, such critics remarked, air power had made the battleship antiquated.[62] Warships, commented Charles A. Lindbergh, invariably suffered heavy losses when coming within striking distances of enemy aviation. It took a battleship ten days, remarked Senator Reynolds, to travel from San Francisco to New York; a fleet of bombers, transporting tons of high explosives, could make the same trip in eleven hours.[63] Such criticism was often prompted by a comment of Secretary of the Navy Charles Edison, who, early in May 1940, asserted that U.S. naval vessels needed revamping because their topsides were vulnerable to air attack.[64] Harry Elmer Barnes had his own authority, Admiral Yates Stirling, former chief of staff of the U.S. Fleet, who maintained that the navy was building unseaworthy ships at exorbitant cost.[65] Recent incidents were cited as evidence of the battleship's impotence, including the sinking of the British *Royal Oak* in Scapa Flow and the German *Bismarck* in the north Atlantic and the British pulverization of the Italian fleet at Taranto.[66]

Cost, too, was a factor in the air–sea comparison.[67] An entire air fleet, said Senator Reynolds, could be purchased for about $80 million, something that certainly could not be said of a major naval force. Danaher asserted that the $120 million spent on two battleships could be far better spent on twelve hundred planes ready for delivery within a few months.[68]

To such people, talk of a two-ocean navy appeared particularly irresponsible.[69] According to Colonel McCormick, a "one-ocean navy," using the Panama Canal, could be just as effective. If navies on both major oceans simultaneously attacked the United States, he continued, American ships could defend on one side while attacking on the other. In a broadcast in September 1940, the Chicago publisher went further, saying, "Surface sea power is dying, and it is a very good thing for us that it is." The Americans, he said, had not been a seafaring people since the days of the clippers. The United States lacked the needed reserve forces; it had contributed little to naval design; its shipbuilders were "the worst in the world"; and its merchant seamen were organized "in a communist union ready to sabotage our nation on orders from Moscow." In the future, predicted McCormick in June 1941, the navy's role would be limited to providing floating landing fields, from which dive bombers and torpedo planes could destroy any surface craft.[70]

Yet among anti-interventionists, consensus remained elusive. Certainly, there was no massive bloc of congressional anti-interventionists opposing the major appropriations. Even Fish, a strong critic of a large navy, ended up voting for them.[71] In the House, only left-wing Congressman Vito Marcantonio dissented from the Ship Construction Bill and Aviation Expansion Bill of May 1940.[72]

Certainly administration critics stressed the potential of the existing American navy, implying that massive increases were not needed.[73] In March 1940, Fish found the United States already possessing the greatest navy in its history, one already equal to that of the British, three and a half times as large as Germany's, twice as large as Italy's, and 50 percent larger than Japan's.[74] In August

1941, Wheeler said that he had not found an American naval officer who believed that the U.S. fleet was outnumbered by Germany's. Furthermore, German craft was not built for long-range service but simply for action on the Baltic Sea or along Europe's coast.[75]

Such confidence in the U.S. Navy had more erudite proponents. Two major contributors to *Common Sense*, Fleming MacLiesh and Cushman Reynolds, called the fleet the most powerful in existence; its gunnery was probably the best, its ships able to venture further than those of any other nation. To Hanson Baldwin, the combined sea power of all four of the United States's potential enemies—Germany, Japan, Russia, and Italy—was somewhat superior, but it was not sufficient to endanger American security.[76] Certainly the U.S. Navy could not be outbuilt, even if Hitler engaged all Europe, including a conquered England, to the task.[77]

Some noninterventionists wanted the fleet, or at least certain aspects of it, expanded.[78] In the Senate, David Walsh was particularly outspoken. Chairman of its Senate Naval Committee, the Massachusetts Democrat specifically denied that air power had made the battleship obsolete. Heavily gunned and armored battleships, he maintained, could withstand any armor-piercing projectiles.[79] In May 1940, Taft pointed to the slowness of U.S. naval construction as compared to that of the Japanese.[80] Hearst stressed the building of naval cruisers, emphasizing the factor of speed.[81]

Certain administration critics, such as Charles A. Lindbergh and William Castle, specifically called for a two-ocean navy.[82] The *New York Daily News* engaged in a veritable crusade on its behalf.[83] Using the motto "two ships for one," meaning that the United States should have a two-to-one superiority over any potential rival, the *News* saw such a navy insuring continued access to a host of goods: coffee, rubber, rare metals needed for steel alloys, and drugs produced in the tropics.[84] In July 1940, it endorsed FDR's signing of "a two-ocean Navy bill," providing for a navy of three million tons.[85] Even after calling for accommodation with Japan, the *News* sought naval dominance in the Pacific.[86]

If anti-interventionists had a favorite weapon, it lay in aviation.[87] As Al Williams wrote, "The nation that rules by air will rule the world." Architect Frank Lloyd Wright found a "super-air force" as essential to the nation's welfare as "a true non-war-breeding organic internal economy."[88] To such people, the controversial aviation pioneer General Billy Mitchell was a prophetic figure and he was often so treated.[89]

The airplane appeared to offer the ideal defense, dovetailing nicely with the anti-interventionist stress on hemispheric protection. Furthermore, air power promised victory independent of other military branches, made minimal demands on the American populace, and supposedly acted as an instrument of surgical precision, thereby incapacitating an enemy without slaughter.[90]

Al Williams was particularly vocal in this regard, and various anti-interventionists cited him with approval. Williams wrote a daily aviation column for the Scripps-Howard press and a weekly one for the *Progressive*. A flight trainer for the navy during World War I, he designed a combat plane and flew in air races when the conflict ended. By 1929, he was the most famous naval aviator in the nation. In 1932, he entered the Marine Corps Aviation Reserve, receiving the rank of major within three years. Yet his outspoken persistence on behalf of an independent air force and, above all, a unified defense plan for all services drew official reprimands. In July 1940, Williams was forced to resign from the corps, to which he replied, "Free speech, hell! That freedom is only for those in power."[91]

Williams's book *Airpower* (1940) was a veritable manifesto on the topic. The bulk of the text focused on appraisals of specific aircraft. His firsthand observations of European politics, however, based on trips made in 1936 and 1938, made it a most controversial work. An arch-conservative, Williams considered France's Popular Front communist, opposed British pressure on Mussolini during the Ethiopian crisis, and strongly defended the new Spanish government of General Francisco Franco. He went so far as to blame the destruction of Guernica on "the dynamite and incendiarism of the Reds and anarchists."[92]

Similarly, the New Deal met with Williams's scorn. He saw contemporary American interventionism rooted in the effort to alleviate the nation's economic disasters. Not only was Roosevelt's domestic policy a failure but the president had also acted irresponsibly in placing a moral embargo on Italy during the Ethiopian war, "tolerating" the Sino-Japanese conflict for years, and failing "to enforce the law against recruiting American manpower for the Spanish Loyalist Army." The aviator opposed U.S. gold purchases from England and Russia, the latter power being "the bloodiest sponsor of mass murder in the pages of history." Now, he said, the administration was seeking to enter the conflict directly. Once the public realized that "America's political and financial clothing was becoming shabby and worn," "our international politicians began weaving a dread war cloak of ominous hue for America's unwilling shoulders, designed to hide the threadbare and shiny spots of our nation's economic garb."[93]

More particularly, said Williams, the entire U.S. defense system remained in deplorable shape, "about one-quarter built and more than twice paid for."[94] He called the United States a seventh-rate army power, a seventh-rate sea power, and a fifth- or sixth-rate air power. American leaders had not even sketched a coordinated national defense plan. Particularly opposed to sending "our first-line warplanes" overseas, Williams blamed the Roosevelt administration, "British and French money," and "the interventionist financiers of

Wall Street" for betraying the nation to such a degree that Benedict Arnold would "look like a sportsman and the exposures of 1914–1918 look like nursery rhymes."[95]

Not unexpectedly, several anti-interventionists strongly endorsed his work.[96] Hanson Baldwin found the book to contain much valuable information, though he accused Williams of overstating his case, acting as "a partisan with a grievance."[97] Other reviewers were less certain. *Newsweek* praised his description of various aircraft in recent military campaigns, while finding him a man of "vituperative rhetoric," "shrill to the point of fanaticism." George Fielding Eliot challenged Williams's assertion that the day of sea power was over, for—Eliot claimed—"the seas remain the great commercial highway of the world." While conceding air power as an essential element of warfare, Eliot pointed to Germany's recent campaign in Western Europe as evidence that it was most effectively used in coordination with ground forces. Writing in the *New Republic*, Max Gissen saw Williams as "clear and forthright" on such matters as "fixed-pitch versus controllable-pitch propellers" but said his politics were uncomfortably close to Father Coughlin's *Social Justice*.[98]

In his crusade for air power, Williams had many allies. Hearst's press was particularly adamant on the issue. For example, an editorial in his *San Francisco Examiner*, published in November 1939, was titled "The Best Defense for U.S."[99] Like several other anti-interventionists, Hearst cited Lieutenant Colonel Thomas R. Phillips, a general staff officer who boasted that the bomber repelled all threat of invasion.[100]

The *New York Daily News* was equally enthusiastic. In December 1939, it stated that U.S. defense depended on the purchase of fast pursuit planes, which cost one-fifth as much as the overrated bomber. If placed in major strategic points—for example, Cuba, New York, Jacksonville, Cold Harbor, Hawaii, the Aleutians, and possibly Samoa—enemy bombers might be "cut down" before they reached American coasts.[101]

Recent military events were frequently cited to prove air power's superiority. Aviation, said Senator Reynolds, played the primary role in subjugating Poland, Finland, and Norway.[102] On 10 May, some seventy-two German paratroopers had captured the fort of Eben Emael, the key to Belgium's entire defense system. Temporary air supremacy made the miraculous evacuation at Dunkirk possible. Both the Battle of Britain and the strikes on German cities revealed air power's invincibility.[103] In the German capture of Crete for the first time in history, a major military victory had been gained entirely by an air force.[104]

By the middle of 1940, therefore, FDR critics were among the most vocal in deploring the paucity of American planes.[105] In May, Colonel McCormick wanted five thousand new aircraft. The United States, Al Williams warned, lacked a single squadron capable of matching the performance of German Spitfighters, Messerschmitts, and Heinkels. "We are defenseless in the air," he wrote two months later.[106]

As in the case of evaluating air strength, anti-interventionists quoted American military leaders themselves. Among them was Navy Secretary Edison, who in May 1940 reported that the U.S. had been provided with only eighty-seven new planes since war began; Army Air Corps General Hap Arnold, who noted that only fifty-two U.S. planes were equipped for modern warfare; and an army colonel who found the United States needing 50,000 pilots, 750,000 ground personnel, and 9,000 antiaircraft guns.[107]

Particular attention was given to the views of Captain Eddie Rickenbacker, World War I ace and general manager of Eastern Air Lines. In August 1940, Rickenbacker called for a quarter-million planes and half a million pilots to protect the nation from air invasion.[108] A particular hero to anti-interventionists, Rickenbacker was nominated by the *Chicago Tribune* to direct aviation procurement.[109] When the America First Committee was first organized, Rickenbacker served on the national committee but withdrew almost immediately, giving no reason.[110]

As part of his address given to a joint session of Congress on 16 May 1940, Roosevelt, as noted, called for building fifty thousand military planes.[111] Some anti-interventionists, including the *New York Daily News*, strongly supported the move.[112] An army of a million, it stressed, should be supplemented by technical training of about a hundred thousand pilots and fifty thousand fighter planes.[113] The *Chicago Tribune* welcomed the president's air program and endorsed the president's call for training a large number of flyers, although it found him evasive on such crucial matters as artillery, ammunition, and antiaircraft weapons.[114]

More noninterventionists demurred. To Colonel Lindbergh, it was childish to speak in terms of fifty thousand planes when the cost was so prohibitive. Arguing that the aircraft would cost at least $7 billion, John T. Flynn asked, "Who is to pay for it? How? And when?" The sum, Al Williams feared, could go even higher, reaching $10 billion. Lindbergh also raised another matter, that of trained personnel. To implement the president's request, he said, at least a quarter of a million men were needed, not simply the twelve thousand FDR mentioned.[115]

As often concerning Roosevelt, his adversaries suspected ulterior motives. Dennis denied the United States could use even ten thousand planes; fifty thousand planes, he argued, could only be used effectively by an army of three million mobile troops. Flynn called the president's proposal a "gigantic war-scare hoax." Such requests, Lindbergh believed, were predicated on the U.S. fighting in the European war.[116] The more moderate Hanson Baldwin saw no threat warranting Roosevelt's request. The United States, he maintained, had nothing to fear from Japan, a weak air power. Germany possessed eight thousand planes at most, with only a handful being able to cross the southern Atlantic. At any rate, argued Williams, the new aircraft were earmarked for Europe, where they could do little to defend the U.S.[117]

Yet in 1941, demands for increased air power remained. Most planes on hand, Lindbergh asserted in January, were obsolete. In an article published in *Collier's* late in March, the aviator claimed that the weekly warplane production of Germany surpassed the total inventory of American fighting planes.[118] In June 1941, the America First Committee considered plane production distressingly small, particularly that of long-range bombers. It also noted Boake Carter's claim that the United States was sending overseas up to 70 percent of the weapons needed to meet any invasion. By September 1941, Al Williams was finding American bombers first-rate but maintained that the fliers still needed a year's training.[119]

A good many noninterventionists—Lundeen, Williams, and Representative James Van Zandt (Rep.-Pa.) among them—called for a separate department of the air, citing Billy Mitchell as authority.[120] The proposal had no more militant and persistent advocate than the *New York Daily News*.[121] The British and Germans served as the *News*'s models, both nations possessing the most powerful air forces in the world.[122] Of all the first-class military powers of the world, only caste-bound Japan, stated the *News*, did not have an independent air force.[123]

Some anti-interventionists, however, found air power's potential exaggerated, and at times even outspoken air proponents tempered their enthusiasm. Aviation was insufficient, it was often argued; it must be used in conjunction with other forces. In the words of Colonel McCormick, "It is only a part—tho a vital part—of the army." Another time the Chicago publisher said, "If the ground forces are equal, superiority in the air will be decisive; if air forces are equal, superiority on the ground will decide." The *New York Daily News* concurred, saying, "The air plane cannot besiege a city as effectively as an army can." Furthermore, the infantry must hold territory "after the planes and tanks have blasted their way."[124]

Any belief in the sufficiency of air power, wrote Lawrence Dennis, resembled faith in the prowess of such comic strip figures as Superman or Popeye. Not a single military leader, he continued, believed that planes alone could defeat Germany. "Wars are not won with or by machines but by men—good fighting men," he wrote. Hugh Johnson went so far as to take on the ghost of Billy Mitchell. Calling the aviation prophet "an air enthusiast with the showmanship of P. T. Barnum," Johnson maintained that Mitchell had been unable to sink a battleship in tests that replicated combat conditions and that his bombing raids on naval bases had flopped.[125]

Moreover, to air power critics, not all recent events showed its efficacy. The Spanish Civil War proved that the bombing of cities alone could not win a war. In Finland, the Russians dropped 6,667 bombs but killed only eighteen civilians.[126] In referring to Germany's recent conquest of Western Europe, the *New York Daily News* commented, "Bombing did not topple these countries; the infantry did." To Lawrence Dennis, the fall of France offered sufficient evidence: "What the Germans have done to the French in 1940 with planes they did in 1870 without planes or tanks. And Caesar did it a couple of thousand years ago without fire arms. The Germans have had in 1940 superiority in the air, but it would have been useless without superiority on the land in quality and quantity of fighting men."[127]

Continued evidence appeared daily. The Japanese controlled the air over China but still could not defeat the government of Chiang Kai-shek. Although Malta and Gibraltar had been bombed innumerable times, they remained invulnerable bases for the British Empire. The survival of the British Isles themselves, commented Hearst, showed that "we have overestimated the importance of air power as an aggressive force operating at a distance from its base."[128] All these observations led to one conclusion. While air power might be the one essential weapon in American defense, it could not in itself cause Germany's defeat.[129]

Ironically, such anti-interventionist air advocates as Lindbergh and Williams helped prepare the way for Roosevelt's own deepening emphasis on air power. The president might be calling for fifty thousand planes while Lindbergh found ten thousand sufficient, but both presented aircraft as the linchpin of hemispheric defense.[130]

A year before war broke out, in the midst of the Munich crisis, FDR had found that any German defeat lay in a simultaneous air pounding by Britain, France, and the Soviet Union. In the president's opinion, recorded Ickes, "This kind of war would cost less money, would mean few casualties, and would be more likely to succeed than a traditional war by land and sea." Certainly a "huge air force" would preclude the need for a "huge army," something that—according to Treasury Secretary Morgenthau—FDR saw as both "undesirable and politically out of the question."[131]

Though FDR always remained a strong navalist, he—like Lindbergh—exaggerated the scope and strength of German aircraft, whose number of front-line planes hid weaknesses in training, reserve, and industrial capacity. German field marshal Erhard Milch, the dominant figure in German aircraft production, claimed that had France attacked just after his nation invaded Poland, the Luftwaffe would have been relegated to the sidelines. In February 1940, the U.S. naval attaché to Germany estimated German air production at eighteen hundred to two thousand planes per month; in reality the average for all 1940 was under nine hundred a month.[132] In fact, though Germany possessed the largest fleet of bombers in Europe, it did not attempt to develop long-range heavy bombers until 1942, and even then its effort was half-hearted.[133]

The Roosevelt administration never placed total faith in air power. On 20–21 June 1940, as France was signing surrender terms in the Compiègne forest,

Senator Edward R. Burke (Dem.-Nebr.) and Representative James S. Wadsworth (Rep.-N.Y.) sponsored the first peacetime conscription bills in American history. Both proposals called for registering some forty million men between ages twenty-one and forty-five for possible military training. At the time the Burke–Wadsworth bill was introduced, the regular army consisted of 255,000 men, the national guard of 230,000. The bill would increase the regular army to 500,000, the National Guard to 400,000.[134]

Roosevelt at first appeared hesitant about supporting the proposal, which was the brainstorm of the prominent lawyer Grenville Clark and the Military Training Camps Association. In accepting his party's nomination on 19 July, the president asserted that "some form of selection by draft is as fair and necessary today as it was in 1917 and 1918." Two weeks later, at a press conference, he forthrightly endorsed "a selective training bill." The United States, said FDR, did not just require weapons; it needed the trained men to use them. He went on: "You cannot get a sufficiently trained force of all kinds at the front, in the Navy yards and the arsenals, transportation, supply system, and munitions output, you cannot get it just by passing an Act of Congress when war breaks out, and you cannot get it by the mere volunteer system." Hence, immediate conscription was crucial. General George C. Marshall, army chief of staff, backed the president fully.[135]

Several prominent anti-interventionists also favored conscription. On 15 June, Charles A. Lindbergh told a radio audience, "The men of this country must be willing to give a year of their lives to military training—more if necessary." Columnist Frank Waldrop found conscription needed as the United States itself embarked on a new wave of imperialism. Robert Rice Reynolds, chairman of the Senate Armed Services Committee, went so far as to promise that the bill would improve the nation's health, for the conscripts would receive medical and dental care plus "three good wholesome meals every day."[136]

The *New York Daily News*, in backing conscription, argued that only the draft could "round up the cream of our strong, smart, young and brutal male population, and put it as fast as we can through a course of training in the methods of total war."[137] It called for the universal military training of every American male, beginning at age nineteen.[138]

Hugh Johnson voiced particular enthusiasm. In 1917, serving under Judge Advocate General Enoch Crowder, Johnson had directed the entire selective service effort. Now he found volunteer recruitment lagging dangerously. Moreover, in conscription lay the most efficient way to raise an army, as draftees cost only a fraction of the sum needed to maintain volunteers. Johnson's main defense of conscription was, however, staunchly anti-interventionist: "With our strength of men and resources we can take a defensive position which nobody will ever dare threaten." He hoped that he would again be called to direct the draft, but, having tangled with the president continually in his newspaper column, he remained persona non grata at the White House.[139]

Among the anti-interventionists, the proconscription view attracted only a decided minority. Far more opposed Burke–Wadsworth. To such people, the bill often smacked of totalitarianism.[140] William Henry Chamberlin saw the move a greater danger to the United States than Hitler. Harry Elmer Barnes called the draft "the first step to American fascism," saying that it would "give us millions of half-trained and half-baked little militarists, more cocky and conceited than one of Hitler's storm troopers. They would think themselves perfect Napoleons."[141] Wheeler even doubted the bill's constitutionality.[142]

Loss of liberty became a major argument. Not only would the nation's young men be deprived of elementary civil liberties; Americans as a whole would lose fundamental rights.[143] To Taft, the logical conclusion of peacetime conscription was "the conscription of everything—property, men, industries, and all labor."[144]

Besides, the mechanics of the bill appeared most unfair. The selection process was arbitrary, salaries low. Urban munitions workers could be deferred while rural youth were mustered.[145] Not only did the procedure unnecessarily disrupt many lives; employment after service would invariably be difficult.[146] Administrative problems were heavy, cost and provisioning steep, and the nation's economy weakened in the process.[147] Training was skimpy, facilities miserable.[148] The needed equipment might be lacking for two years.[149]

More important from a strategic point of view, mass armies appeared outmoded. To Wheeler, sheer numbers of troops did not compensate for lack of effectiveness; they actually increased the danger. "Millions of men," said Wiley, if lacking the means of stopping "these superdreadnoughts and the air armada," were "sheep before the wolf."[150]

Anti-interventionists could not help noting that neither Canada nor Australia had resorted to this device.[151] Furthermore, as Hitler's spring blitzkrieg had shown, conscription in Belgium, Holland, and France had done those nations little good. In fact, fifty thousand trained and well-equipped Germans had defeated two million French conscripts.[152]

Certainly, as will later be shown, FDR's foes always maintained that danger of invasion was not compelling.[153] Any potential enemy, maintained Fish, faced a superior American navy and air force. According to Senator Downey, military experts argued that when soldiers and matériel were transported five thousand miles, their potential was reduced five to ten times.[154]

How, it was asked more pointedly, could Hitler threaten the United States when he could not conquer Britain?[155] A few anti-interventionists suspected that a new American Expeditionary Force lay in the wings. Asked Vandenberg, "Why this positively frenzied speed to upset the volunteer system? What is in the wind?"[156]

Perhaps, asked the socialists, hemispheric imperialism lay behind it all. The *Call* offered a unique analysis, claiming that the new conscripts would be sent to Latin America. The greatest war danger, wrote Norman Thomas, resided in

U.S. action against Mexico or an even more distant South American land.[157]

The anti-interventionist alternative? Again the stress lay on a small highly trained mobile force designed to protect the United States from attack. The nation's first line of defense, maintained Taft, lay with the navy, followed by innumerable bombers, antiaircraft guns, and a mechanized professional army.[158] Numbers of troops varied, ranging from 150,000 to 750,000.[159] The Hearst press took a slightly different tack, endorsing the Swiss system of universal military training.[160]

As far as an immediate alternative to Burke–Wadsworth was concerned, the anti-interventionists focused on one option: continuation of the voluntary system. Fish introduced a cleverly worded amendment authorizing the president to make two calls for volunteers, the first two months after the bill's enactment, the second on 1 January 1941. Only if four hundred thousand volunteers were not forthcoming could the president begin drafting. He said that his amendment would actually speed up induction, whereas under the House's Wadsworth bill, the army could not induct any draftees until 15 November or after sixty days, and then it would take only seventy-five thousand men.[161]

The volunteer system had several supporters.[162] Some with pacifist leanings were particularly enthusiastic.[163] *Uncensored* noted Senate testimony, given by the nation's military leaders on 12 July, to the effect that every previous quota had been filled by volunteers.[164] Former American conflicts—including, surprisingly, the Civil War—were used as evidence that the old system had worked well.[165]

Those anti-interventionists favoring conscription found little good in Fish's approach. Hugh Johnson called the Fish amendment "cheap political monkey-business." When "traditional volunteering" was tried in the War of 1812, Washington was burned and Detroit surrendered.[166]

On 5 September, the House approved the Fish amendment but soon gave it up in conference committee. On the 16th, conscription legislation, having passed both houses, was signed by the president. Only those between the ages of twenty-one and thirty-five were required to register. In mid-August, the Gallup poll had indicated 66 percent in favor of the draft.[167]

Even after Congress adopted Burke–Wadsworth, some noninterventionists voiced concern over the nation's defenses. To Senator Lodge, it would take from six to seven years to build a two-ocean navy, six years alone to finish the double set of locks needed to protect the Panama Canal. Dennis pointed to the absence of any concerted defense scheme. To defend America, one needed a highly specialized professional army, based on the ideas of German general Hans von Seeckt and French general Charles de Gaulle.[168]

Little wonder anti-interventionists kept proposing their own solutions. The *Chicago Tribune* called for promoting the submachine gun, abolishing the army's present division of services (e.g., infantry, cavalry, engineers), and downplaying the role of the tank—which, it claimed, could not protect the infantryman in close combat. The *Saturday Evening Post* pushed a two-ocean navy and an "impervious antiaircraft wall." Rather than rush into conscription, said Senator Wiley, the United States should make its ships immune from torpedoes and bombs, develop an adequate naval air fleet, train ground forces in blitzkrieg techniques, and acquire tanks and antiaircraft guns.[169]

Even in the spring of 1941, Hanson Baldwin found the U.S. attempting to expand the army too rapidly. Not only were powder and ammunition dangerously low but the needed tanks and field artillery could not be delivered for months. In the past, he asserted, throwing masses of semi- or untrained men into combat had simply resulted in casualties. Now the situation risked repeating itself, for all army units drew most heavily on raw recruits.[170]

All this time, interventionists—finding Britain in dire peril—demanded the shipment of major American weapons to the besieged isles. On 12 September, the Committee to Defend America by Aiding the Allies (CDAAA) said Britain needed twenty-five Flying Fortresses, twenty torpedo (mosquito) boats, and "as many pursuit planes as possible." Tanks, Lee-Enfield rifles, and the new Norden bombsight were added. So were loans to enable payment of all such items. The CDAAA had avoided any position on the draft, for it feared that the ensuing controversy would simply delay aid to Britain, its first priority.[171]

Such proposals greatly alarmed its political foes.[172] Above all, the United States's own military needs were stressed. The *Saturday Evening Post* mourned, "We have not a rifle, a gun, an airplane, or a rowboat to spare, nor any industrial capacity." National guardsmen were training with imaginary machine guns devised by plumbers out of gas pipe. Both Senator Edwin Johnson and pacifist Frederick J. Libby warned that such weapons might well be needed in any conflict with Japan. Bennett Clark accused the administration of risking enemy capture of the Norden bombsight, "the most vital military secret that the United States has ever had."[173]

On 5 September 1940, General Hugh Johnson officially launched the America First Committee with a nationwide radio broadcast. He noted that the existing U.S. Army possessed fewer than three hundred first-line combat planes and only fifty-nine heavy bombers; it lacked enough modern equipment to outfit a hundred thousand men. When, on 3 October, the AFC started placing advertisements in the press, it stressed the danger of sending weapons overseas: "We need guns. We need men. We need ships enough for a two-ocean navy independent of any other power. Let nobody take them away from us. Let nobody give them away."[174]

Other arguments were raised as well: Such sales violated the Hague convention of 1907 as well as American legislation of 1917 and 1940. The transfer involved an act of war against Germany, thereby inviting counter-measures that could rapidly draw the United States into full-scale embroilment.[175]

To both the anti-interventionists and their critics, the issue of rearmament led logically to a much greater question, this one dealing not so much with *how* to defend the nation but with the geographical *scope* of any such defense. How much of the Western Hemisphere belonged in the defense orbit of the United States? What was the optimum sphere of influence by which the nation could best assure its own safety?

# 8

# Military Defense
# of the Hemisphere

On 3 October 1939, exactly a month after Britain and France had declared war on Germany, an inter-American conference, designated the Consultation of Ministers for Foreign Affairs of the American Republics, issued the Declaration of Panama. Drafted under U.S. prompting, the declaration proclaimed a "security belt" reaching several hundred miles from the shores of the neutral American republics. Within this zone, any hostile action by any non-American belligerent was strictly forbidden. In case of violation, mutual consultation would lead to enforcement.[1]

Critics opposed the Panama declaration on several grounds.[2] First, they found the declaration warlike. Because such British possessions as Canada, Newfoundland, and the Bahamas were within the new zone, Congressman Paul Shafer (Rep.-Mich.) warned, "If we attempt to enforce this guardianship, it will mean war for the United States." Similarly, the *Chicago Tribune*, envisaging U.S. naval vessels patrolling several hundred miles off the Atlantic, accused the administration of "provocative steps," likely at any time to produce the torpedoing of a U.S. destroyer. Furthermore, it argued, nations did hold an unquestioned right to send their own warships to their own possessions; in fact, interference was an act of war.[3]

Certainly, it was argued, enforcement was difficult.[4] Policing an area three to six hundred miles off the American coast, said Senator Wallace White (Rep.-Maine), meant taking on "the most gigantic task ever assumed by any nation in history."[5] In addition, FDR opponents found the declaration blatantly illegal. The manifesto, posited John Bassett Moore, had "no foundation in law or in common sense" and furthermore violated the very principle of freedom of the seas. Moore raised an additional factor—namely, that the dec-

laration was hypocritical. On 21 December, after the administration announced that it would ask Germany to heed the new zone, Moore mused that
the United States had never protested the activities of British cruisers already
carrying on "hostile operations to the very verge of the three-mile limit, if not
within it." In reality, the jurist contended, the declaration could serve as a device to protect Allied possessions in the Western Hemisphere. Noting that several British bases lay within the neutrality zone, Borchard remarked, "These
are presumably to be kept immune from attack by England's enemies."[6]

Of the critics of the Panama declaration, only the chauvinistic *Chicago Tribune* suggested an alternative policy. The Gulf of Mexico, it said, should be
proclaimed a Pan-American lake, and all warships of any nonhemispheric belligerent should be permanently banned. Such acts would only require agreement of the United States, Mexico, and Cuba, although other American republics might also desire to endorse it. It also called for extending the
neutrality cordon to the Caribbean, which the U.S. Navy was able to guard.
While doing so, the administration should demand the cession of the British
and French islands.[7]

Within the Roosevelt camp itself, there were major misgivings. Hull objected
to the declaration on grounds similar to those of the anti-interventionists: the
neutrality zone was unenforceable, had no legal standing, and could well involve the U.S. in war through an incident on the high seas. The fact that his state
department rival, Sumner Welles, had designed the plan only increased his
misgivings.[8] The navy, too, protested, finding the patrolling task impossible.[9]

By December 1939, the declaration had already proven ineffective, for the
British sank a major German battleship, the *Graf Spee*, in Montevideo harbor.
On U.S. prompting, the American republics issued a joint note of protest although it was obvious they lacked the means to take further action. Roosevelt
himself showed little anxiety, undoubtedly in part because there was relative
calm on the Atlantic afterward. Toward the end of 1940, the president accepted Hull's proposal for a more flexible zone whose range would be determined by current circumstance. Although Germany publicly rejected the neutrality belt, both Hitler's Reich and the Allies ended up privately honoring it.
Hence, as one historian notes, the announcement proved an "extremely potent
weapon in Roosevelt's diplomatic arsenal."[10]

In the wake of Germany's conquest of Western Europe, apprehension quickly
developed concerning the fate of French and Dutch possessions in the Western Hemisphere. Such Caribbean islands as French Martinique and Dutch
Curaçao, it was feared, might well come under German domination. A Gallup
poll showed 87 percent in favor, if necessary, of taking immediate posses-

sion.[11] As Britain was fighting for its survival, anxieties centered as well on its many islands in the West Indies.

On 17 June 1940, the Senate unanimously passed a resolution introduced by Key Pittman. Reaffirming the Monroe Doctrine, the resolution specified that the United States would not recognize the transfer of any geographic region in the Western Hemisphere from one "non-American power" to another "non-American power." Further, in the event that such transfer should appear likely, the U.S. would consult immediately with other American republics. A day later the House adopted the identical resolution, introduced by Congressman Sol Bloom (Dem.-N.Y.), chairman of its Foreign Affairs Committee, by a vote of 381 to 8.[12] The pronouncement determined little, however; it was Hitler's desire to avoid challenging Washington, not any joint resolution of Congress, that decided matters.[13]

Several administration critics supported the Pittman–Bloom resolution. Congressman John Vorys, for example, said, "We are simply repainting our 'no trespassing' sign so that would-be trespassers will be sure to see it."[14]

The Germans were quick to reply. On 1 July, Foreign Secretary Joachim von Ribbentrop denied any German aspirations and then stated that the Monroe Doctrine could in principle be valid legally only under one condition: if the American nations did not "interfere" in European affairs. Four days later, Hull in turn replied that the United States pursued no involvement in the "purely political affairs of Europe," while cooperating with all nations to advance "the cause of international law and order."[15]

Several anti-interventionists adopted Ribbentrop's logic of two separate spheres. Fish commented, "We want America for Americans and Europe for Europeans, and that is a good American doctrine."[16] Other arguments were used as well: Efforts to legislate on the Monroe Doctrine were unnecessary. The consultation provisions of the resolution unduly restrained the United States. The resolution was far too encompassing. The *Washington Daily News*, a Scripps-Howard paper, described the bill as involving "a responsibility that stretches from pole to pole, from ocean to ocean, and from Hell to breakfast." Congressman Andrew Schiffler (Rep.-W.Va.), who had endorsed the Senate resolution, feared that Iceland and parts of the USSR could be included. Congressman Robert Chiperfield (Rep.-Ill.) cited a state department geographer whose findings implied that Greenland, the Antarctic, New Zealand, and the Samoan and Solomon islands were part of the hemisphere.[17]

Besides, it appeared that the United States had invoked the Monroe Doctrine in a most hypocritical manner. To political writer Katherine Rodell, the United States had first been the offender when it entered World War I, more recently when it permitted the French and English to land troops in Aruba and Curaçao. Furthermore, the Monroe Doctrine appeared to have been more honored in the breach than in the observance. It had not, Porter Sargent argued, prevented Britain's seizure of the Falkland Islands or Guatemalan territory, France from taking St. Barthélemy island, or the Dutch from ruling Aruba and Curaçao.[18]

More important, the resolution appeared warlike. The *Christian Century* feared that the Monroe Doctrine might be interpreted as bestowing "a duty to help police every American government all the way south to the Straits of Magellan." Asked Congressman Charles L. Gifford (Rep.-Mass.), "Does this mean that we will fight with a foreign nation if it attempts to take possession of that which it may have a legal right to possess?"[19]

Anti-interventionists soon confronted another matter, the Havana Conference of July 1940. Here, at a meeting of Pan-American foreign ministers, the delegates—led by Secretary Hull—unanimously declared an attack on one to be an attack on all. In case of a threatened strike, any American republic could move unilaterally in seizing any colony under threat. The assemblage signed a declaration, the Act of Havana, that provided for an Inter-American Commission for Territorial Concessions in the New World. The new body would assume temporary control of any European possessions facing transfer to another sovereignty.[20]

Reactions to Havana varied. Only the United States possessed a navy and air force powerful enough, said the *Chicago Tribune*, to prevent the transmittal of holdings from one European state to another. To imply that any hemispheric alliance could control such territories jointly could only breed confusion and feebleness. John T. Flynn offered a more radical critique. If a European power should lose such a possession, the American republics should promote its permanent independence. A writer in the socialist *Call* saw the Havana meeting bestowing on a market-hungry U.S. hegemony over all lands south of the Rio Grande. Conversely, the *Christian Century* praised Hull's skillful and successful diplomacy, arguing, "This defense measure is good in itself and may turn out to be very useful."[21]

Though the Pittman–Bloom resolution had overwhelming congressional support, the questions raised by a minority of dissenters were disturbing indeed. The administration might offer most sweeping definitions of the areas to be covered by the Monroe Doctrine, something that could create endless anxiety. Even the Havana declaration had its pitfalls.

Such reactions could not mask one thing: certain anti-interventionists themselves sought domination of European possessions in the hemisphere.

When, on 9 April 1940, Germany conquered Denmark, several anti-interventionists sought U.S. purchase of its largest colony, Greenland. Both Lundeen and Fish filed bills to that effect.[22]

A certain geographic determinism was manifested. Lundeen cited claims of Arctic explorers Vilhjalmur Stefansson and Admiral Robert E. Peary to the effect that Greenland belonged to the United States. To Fish, "progress" could not be halted. For over a hundred years, he said, Denmark had failed to develop its vast colony, which still possessed a population of less than twenty thousand.[23] Other factors also made Greenland attractive, including a trade potential; considerable fish, fur, and graphite; and the world's largest deposits of cryolite.[24]

To such advocates of American ownership, however, defense was the crucial factor.[25] In enemy hands, Lundeen claimed, Greenland would threaten the populous Eastern Seaboard. A flight from Greenland to New York, noted Fish, took only six hours. A *Chicago Tribune* writer stressed the importance of establishing an American naval base near Cape Farewell, lying at Greenland's lower tip.[26] The *New York Daily News* noted that its fjords could be used for submarine bases, some of its flat areas turned into air outposts. "We should neither delay nor mumble our words," it proclaimed, but declare a protectorate until Denmark again became free.[27]

Other anti-interventionists downplayed Greenland's role, finding little danger if it was in hostile hands. Suppose, wrote Frank Waldrop, Hitler was "just nutty enough to claim Greenland and declare the Eskimos a suppressed German minority"; the German dictator still had no friendly ocean between him and his objective. Besides, said Waldrop, the British would prevent any such move. Senator Reynolds stressed that the distance between Greenland and New York equaled that between New York and London. Colonel Lindbergh thought that secondary bases might be placed in Greenland but found any invasion of the United States from that locale hazardous. In the summer of 1933, while surveying its coast for several weeks, the aviator had found its climate severe, summer season short, and seas and terrain icy.[28]

The Make Europe Pay War Debts Committee, later called the Islands for War Debts Defense Committee (IFWDDC), articulated a more general demand for European possessions.[29] Founded on 3 December 1939, the organization was secretly fostered by German American propagandist George Sylvester Viereck and financed, at least in part, with German funds.[30] Arguing that the European powers owed the United States $14 billion, the committee demanded cession of their island possessions in the Western Hemisphere. Some Allied leaders, including French premier Edouard Daladier, had themselves made overtures in that direction, but the diplomats lacked followthrough.[31] The militant anti-interventionist Lundeen was national chairman, and anti-interventionists dominated the group.[32] Encouragement came from Frank Knox, publisher of the *Chicago Daily News* and soon to be secretary of the navy, though he did not join, and former treasury secretary and senator William G. McAdoo, who had long backed the proposal.[33]

In mid-October 1939, Lundeen called on his nation to use force in the matter. Unless England and France paid their war debts, he threatened, "we will send the armed forces" in accordance with "the Jacksonian theory." Not a retaliatory shot would be fired, for the Allies "are pretty busy on the western front, at the west wall, the Siegfried line, and the Maginot line."[34]

Senator Robert Rice Reynolds was also adamant on the issue. The only Southern Democrat who was consistently anti-interventionist, in May 1941 Reynolds became chairman of the Senate Military Affairs Committee, although he lacked the political clout usually wielded by one holding such office.[35] Reynolds presented a veritable shopping list of possessions, including Bermuda, Newfoundland, the Mexican territory of Lower California, and the disputed island of Wrangel in the Arctic, although he did not call for taking them by force.[36]

Other anti-interventionists also sought Caribbean islands.[37] In defending Reynolds's position, the *Chicago Tribune* found any asking price inconsiderable in relation to the debt owed the United States. The *Tribune* envisioned an American military presence stretching from Greenland to the coast of Brazil.[38] Fish would even pay France "a part of the utterly useless gold buried out in the State of Kentucky."[39] Those of more liberal politics suggested plebiscites by local inhabitants, joint administration by the Latin American nations, and chances for repurchase after the war.[40]

Defenders of such schemes pointed to a survey by the American Institute of Public Opinion. Taken in November 1939, it revealed that 66 percent favored exchanging cancellation of war debts for major Caribbean islands, with 34 percent opposed.[41] The Senate Naval Affairs Committee endorsed the plan, combining its endorsement with calls for air bases in the southeast corner of the Caribbean, fortification of the Panama Canal, and the possible building of a canal across Nicaragua.[42]

Strategic arguments were foremost: The islands would protect the Panama Canal. Germany might attempt military domination. Even British fortification of its own Caribbean possessions, warned the *Chicago Tribune*, could put the Unites States in danger.[43]

Given such dangers, U.S. military action was essential.[44] The *New York Daily News* called on the American fleet to seize the French and Dutch possessions. If the two European nations were eventually restored to full sovereignty, the United States should present them with a bill for expenses incurred while in protective custody.[45]

Certain islands in particular were stressed. The *Chicago Tribune* called Bermuda "a dagger" pointed at the U.S., for it could house bomber bases within easy flying range of New York City.[46] It also found the Galapagos Islands of no value to Ecuador but possible protection for the Panama Canal.[47] Reynolds focused on St. Pierre and Miquelon, two French islands off the coast of Newfoundland; their acquisition, he said, would enable the United States to meet any attack from Iceland, Greenland, or the northeast in general.[48]

A few noninterventionists opposed any such action.[49] Borchard feared that the U.S. might experience legal difficulties over the matter. Venezuela, he noted, had already protested against any transfer of Trinidad on the basis of history and contiguity. To Hugh Johnson, the transfer of "a few islands" and "banana belt" countries would not "scratch the surface" of the World War I debts. More important, obtaining them without the consent of their own people would put the United States "in the class of pickle-puss Adolf and walrus mug Joe Stalin."[50]

On 2 September 1940, much of this debate became a bit moot. The White House announced that the United States was sending fifty overage destroyers to Britain. Beginning on 15 May, in his first letter to FDR as prime minister, Churchill had asked for "the loan of the forty to fifty of your older destroyers."[51] Such craft were vital, he said, for patrol against invasion and facilitating antisubmarine escorts on the Atlantic.[52] In this and subsequent messages, he also requested such weapons as aircraft, rifles, and torpedo boats.

In return for the destroyers, the U.S. would receive ninety-nine-year leases for the immediate construction of military bases in Newfoundland, Bermuda, the Bahamas, Jamaica, St. Lucia, Trinidad, Antigua, and British Guiana. When Roosevelt met with George VI of England in June 1939, he had raised the matter, acting in the belief that no European empire had any business being there anyway.[53] Now Roosevelt was maintaining that the bargain "was probably the most important thing that has come for American defense that has been taken since the Louisiana Purchase."[54]

The destroyer issue had been debated in the United States since the beginning of August. During the negotiations the previous month, four prominent lawyers—including Dean Acheson—wrote to the *New York Times*, claiming that American statutes permitted the sale on the ground that the ships had not been specifically built for Great Britain. Attorney General Robert H. Jackson, in a much-publicized opinion, offered similar reasoning.[55]

The leading interventionist organization, the Committee to Defend America by Aiding the Allies, endorsed the move. Of the 176 destroyers with which Britain had begun the war, only seventy were left.[56] Yet, the CDAAA went on, the British were facing a huge task: deterring invasion of their own isles, providing for the defense of Gibraltar, preventing Axis shipping from leaving continental Europe and the Mediterranean, and protecting convoys on which its imports and exports depended. In early August, a Gallup poll showed 60 percent favoring the destroyer sale. By late October, Gallup indicated a fifty-fifty split over the general matter of helping Britain at the risk of war, but within a month the ratio was sixty-forty in favor of such aid.[57]

As with many administration actions, not all of FDR's usual critics were hostile to the arrangement or his supporters friendly.[58] Once the bargain was solidified—in fact, even during the negotiations—some applauded the arrangement.[59] The *New York Daily News* called the move "the greatest single achievement—or at any rate the most important—of Franklin D. Roosevelt's administration to date."[60] The *Chicago Tribune*, boasting that the bargain had fulfilled a policy it had advocated since 1922, praised the acquisition as "the greatest contribution of this newspaper to the country's history since the nomination of Lincoln."[61] "Thank God," said Colonel McCormick, the Caribbean was now "an American lake."[62] By mid-October, the *Tribune* publisher cited the new leases in boasting that the United States had become "the most powerful nation in the world."[63]

Again, however, far more anti-interventionists voiced alarm.[64] John T. Flynn called for Roosevelt's impeachment. Both Senator Lodge and his fellow Bay State Republican, Congresswoman Edith Nourse Rogers, sought an investigation.[65]

Any agreement involving the transfer of destroyers, such critics argued, was bound to embroil the United States in conflict.[66] The next steps, predicted Senator La Follette, involved "middle-aged" battleships, then "youngish" cruisers, and finally "right aged" sons.[67] Furthermore, claimed the president's opponents, the accord usurped congressional power. The *St. Louis Post-Dispatch* began its editorial with the words, "Mr. Roosevelt today committed an act of war. He also became America's first dictator."[68]

As in the case of cash-and-carry, legal issues were raised.[69] Among the statutes supposedly violated were the Hague Convention of 1907, ratified by the Senate in 1908, which forbade a neutral from supplying a belligerent with "warships";[70] the Treaty of Washington of 1871, which prohibited the departure of any vessel intended to conduct war;[71] and the Walsh Amendment of 28 June 1940, which required the chief of naval operations to issue a certificate denying that such material was essential to U.S. defense.[72] Moreover, it was claimed, Attorney General Jackson misconstrued an act of 15 June 1917 that made it unlawful to send any American vessel to a belligerent.[73]

Criticism of Jackson grew particularly strong.[74] Edward S. Corwin, Princeton scholar and author of major works on the presidency, asserted that according to Jackson's reasoning, the president as commander in chief would have the power to transfer the entire navy to a foreign government. "No such dangerous opinion," he continued, "was ever before penned by an Attorney General of the United States." Charles Francis Adams, formerly Hoover's secretary of the navy, found the decision so dishonest that he privately called for Jackson's impeachment.[75]

Some anti-interventionists found the bargain itself a bad one. First, the bases arrangement was not lasting; eventually all the islands would revert back to Great Britain. Besides, Boake Carter remarked, Britain received the ships within sixty days, whereas it would take three to ten years to equip the hemispheric bases properly.[76]

There was also the matter of cost. In February 1941, Bennett Clark quoted columnists Drew Pearson and Robert S. Allen to the effect that some 125 acres slated in Bermuda would really cost $1.5 million, or $12,000 an acre.[77] Senator Reynolds cited the same two journalists in maintaining that the United States gained thousands of acres of mere swamp in Trinidad, for which the owners demanded an exorbitant price.[78]

Some FDR adversaries believed that the United States still needed the destroyers.[79] Why, asked Hugh Johnson, if the destroyers were so obsolete, was it argued that the life of the British navy depended on them?[80] It was claimed that the destroyers had recently been put into first-class condition; that the craft were valuable for training in seamanship, navigation, gunnery, and engineering; and that it would take two years to construct replacements for the fifty ships.[81] If, said Senator Nye, the Panama Canal blew up while the U.S. fleet was stationed in the Pacific, the fifty destroyers could be put to good use in the Atlantic.[82]

Some alternatives were offered. Borchard sought the direct transfer of either Newfoundland and the West Indies, or, less preferably, Britain's retention of the bases. To Professor Corwin, it seemed the president should ask Congress to ratify the agreement.[83] Hugh Johnson and Hamilton Fish raised the old islands-for-war-debts issue.[84] Lundeen similarly renewed his demand for cession of the British and French West Indies; he sought a time limit and urged that the United States engage in actual threats. The *New York Daily News* kept pushing the seizure of Martinique, adding for good measure Devil's Island, Dutch and French Guiana, St. Pierre and Miquelon, and the French Leeward and Windward Islands.[85] Hanson Baldwin suggested U.S. ownership of British Honduras and possibly Trinidad, Jamaica, Bermuda, and certain unnamed islands in the Pacific. Dorothy Detzer favored a scheme advanced by the Scripps-Howard papers by which the U.S. should purchase the islands, place them under the Pan-American flag, and in time conduct a plebiscite.[86]

Several anti-interventionists opposed any additional U.S. presence in the Caribbean. *New Masses* accused the United States of having "actually taken the first measure of aggression in South America," for Brazil, Venezuela, and Columbia were now placed within the range of American guns.[87] To Oswald Garrison Villard, even such a provisional change in status quo necessitated consulting a local population bitterly hostile to the U.S. color line, particularly because blacks in some British islands enjoyed a considerable measure of social equality.[88] Noting the 50 percent unemployment in a similar area, Puerto Rico, Frederick J. Libby remarked, "Empire is not our forte." Roosevelt himself opposed direct U.S. sovereignty over the islands, calling their population "two million headaches, . . . who would be a definite economic drag on this country, and who would stir up question[s] of racial stocks by virtue of their new status as American citizens."[89]

Had Roosevelt's adversaries known of the hesitant, even suspicious manner in which he conducted the negotiations, they might have seen a president more protective of their interests. All during June, Roosevelt feared above all that the British and French would surrender their fleets to Germany. Hence, he turned away Churchill's plea just when the destroyers were most needed. On 5 June, Churchill cabled Mackenzie King, prime minister of Canada, with one eye to the United States in the process, "If . . . America continued neutral, and we were overpowered I cannot tell what policy might be adopted by a pro-German administration such as would undoubtedly be set up."

Not only did the debacle in France strengthen Roosevelt's worst fears; Churchill's warnings about defeat only strengthened the president's reluctance to provide the destroyers. Little wonder that when the transaction was announced, the British government issued a statement that if the nation fell, the Royal Navy would be neither sunk nor surrendered. Furthermore, Roosevelt himself initially doubted the constitutionality of such a move, particularly in light of the Walsh amendment. Despite the arguments of American anti-interventionists, the British cabinet correctly thought the exchange was far from equal.[90]

As far as the actual deal was concerned, its impact on the war was slight. As the British lacked experienced crews and the ships needed much refitting, only thirty destroyers were in use by the following May. The precise sites and terms for the bases were not settled until March, and the rifles, B-17 aircraft, and torpedo boats did not arrive immediately.[91]

The anti-interventionists mourned that the destroyer–bases deal brought the United States closer to war. The president, however, was "hedging his bets" (to use the words of historian David Reynolds), though the Axis powers read the agreement as an American commitment. The arrangement certainly contributed to the formation of the tripartite pact, the alliance among Germany, Italy, and Japan signed in September 1940.[92]

During all such debates, interventionists continually stressed dangers to Latin America. After the Munich pact, one historian argues, FDR's main anxieties centered far more on the hemisphere than on Britain or France. Early in 1939, the Army War College called for the creation of a Hemisphere Defense Force composed of over a hundred thousand men, special equipment for projected Latin American operations, and the acquisition of necessary shipping. That May, FDR foresaw a possible war in which Germany would neutralize the British fleet, secure domination of Latin America, and—in coordination with Japan—wage open warfare against the United States.[93] Historian David Haglund writes, "In those dark days of late May and early June 1940, the consensus of the administration was that England—brave as it might be—*might* be finished and that the United States might shortly be fighting the battle of its life in Latin America. This was not a prospect that pleased him, yet Roosevelt accepted it as a probable, if gloomy, scenario."[94]

Others among the president's backers felt similarly.[95] In June 1940, Drew Pearson and Robert S. Allen asked, "Can We Keep Hitler Out of the Americas?" The two columnists warned of Axis influence in Bolivia, Peru, Argentina, and Brazil. A month later, *Time* feared that Germany might launch an invasion of the United States from South America via the Caribbean, doing so by initiating a flanking drive to close the Panama Canal. In August, William Bullitt predicted that Hitler would reach South America before Christmas.[96]

According to the CDAAA, the eastern shoulder of Brazil was particularly vulnerable. Enemy parachutists could seize the airports of Natal (not to be confused with the African province of the same name) and Pernambuco, then invade the nation itself. Brazil possessed only six million people (most of whom, said the CDAAA, were "negroes and mulattos") and lacked a decent communications system.[97]

Some noninterventionists stressed U.S. defense of Latin America, in toto or in part. In mid-June 1940, Charles A. Lindbergh endorsed the building of military bases "wherever they are needed for our safety, regardless of who owns the territory involved."[98] Within a year, the aviator recommended war if any foreign power attempted to establish a base in either North or South America. He called for U.S. air bases as far south as the Amazon valley, specifically in such locales as Colombia, Venezuela, the Galapagos Islands, and the Guianas.[99] Ten thousand U.S. planes, he maintained, could raid enemy communications lines to South America.[100]

Others, too, spoke in terms of massive hemispheric involvement.[101] Congressman James E. Van Zandt, former national commander of the Veterans of Foreign Wars, called on the nation to "militarize South America before turning our attention to the plight of European nations."[102] The United States, said Philip La Follette, should "draw a line from the Arctic Circle to the tip of Cape Horn and within the area it bounds enforce the Monroe Doctrine."[103] Wiley advocated agreements that would permit the use of air bases in Venezuela and harbors in Brazil. William E. Castle sought a defense treaty with such nations as Brazil, Chile, Uruguay, and Argentina; the U.S. would gain access to their airports and receive permission to land troops on their territory. At the same time, he declared that complete protection of the hemisphere was beyond U.S. capacity, especially if a foreign presence came in the wake of an internal revolution.[104] The *Chicago Tribune* made detailed recommendations, which included U.S. possession of all the bases near its own shores and the Panama Canal; Cuban control of Jamaica; the transfer of the Falklands to Argentina; and permission to develop such bases as Pernambuco.[105]

A few endorsed stark imperialism. Louis B. Ward, editorial director of *Social Justice*, sought a military protectorate over both continents. Boake Carter spoke of "military control" of Mexico, the West Indies, and Central America down to the Canal Zone. "Partial military control" of Canada and South American nations would be assumed as well. In late July 1941, D. Worth Clark told reporters that the United States should take full possession of the Western Hemisphere, including Canada. The Idaho senator mused, "We could make some kind of arrangement to set up puppet governments which we could trust to put American interests ahead of those of Germany or any other nation in the world."[106]

Other anti-interventionists emphasized U.S. circumscription. The nation, claimed Fish, should draw the line at Argentina, Uruguay, Paraguay, and possibly Brazil. Business leader Graeme Howard recommended the creation of a North American Federation, to be composed of the United States, Canada, the Central American and Caribbean nations, Venezuela, and Colombia. Chicago investor Sterling Morton spoke of guarantees to Peru and lands north of the Amazon. In October 1940, AFC head General Robert E. Wood, board chairman of Sears, Roebuck, said the U.S. must insist that "no government in Mexico, Central America and the Caribbean South American countries will be tolerated unless it is friendly to the United States and that, if necessary, we are prepared to use force to attain that object." Seven months later, Wood asserted he would defend Latin America to the bulge of Brazil.[107]

Some military experts concurred. To best defend the United States, wrote Hanson Baldwin, one must establish bases on Bermuda, the Azores, and the Panama Canal and create a string of outposts that would reach to such locales in Brazil as Behia, Belém, or Sao Luiz de Maranhao.[108] To Fleming MacLiesh and Cushman Reynolds, an air and naval base at Pernambuco, linked with other bases running through Trinidad and the West Indies, could hamstring any expeditionary force striking at the southern part of South America.[109]

Still other noninterventionists thought in far more limited terms. In August 1940, Taft favored sending troops to some Caribbean islands so as to protect the Panama Canal, but only if Congress had previously been consulted. That October, Norman Thomas endorsed U.S. bases in the Caribbean and around the Panama Canal. Several months later, the socialist leader said he would protect Cape Verde or the Canary Islands.[110]

Threats coming from South America, some argued, might be greatly exaggerated. According to retired general William C. Rivers, even a Germany victorious in Europe lacked the battle fleet needed to reach Latin America. If, commented Senator Sheridan Downey, the Germans landed a hundred thousand troops there, these forces would lack guns and supplies and find their transportation lines cut by U.S. "airplane fleets." Moreover, said the California Democrat, South American countries were proud, independent, and defiant, unlikely to "submit their heads to the noose of any European dictatorship."

Senator Nye developed a worst-case scenario, hypothesizing a U.S. Navy defeated in the Caribbean and Hitler's capture of the Panama Canal. Even then, maintained the North Dakota senator, the surrounding jungle was impassable; hence, it would be impossible for a German army to march north. The U.S. Navy alone, said Taft, could prevent a German army from coming to South America. Hearst went so far as to find the South American republics a military liability, as they lacked a trained navy or an adequate army.[111]

Hugh Johnson warned against policing a continent of nations that at best were suspicious and hostile. Besides, the United States could not afford to police every nation from the North Pole to Cape Horn. Going much further, Senator Dennis Chavez (Dem.-N. Mex.) recalled that the U.S. had often acted aggressively in Latin America, citing as evidence such events as the war with Spain and the landing of Marines in Haiti, Nicaragua, and Santo Domingo.[112] Journalist Carleton Beals was emphatic on this point, writing in *Pan America* (1940) that Latin American nations could no longer serve as "our oyster to be devoured, or as shock troops for our safety, or as pawns in the game of world politics." There should, he continued, be no change without joint Pan-American agreement. Concrete recommendations included inter-American control of the Panama Canal, eventual political independence or statehood for Puerto Rico, a plebiscite for the Virgin Islands, and cancellation of British or French debts whenever the European powers set free their New World population.[113]

Had the more strict anti-interventionists been privy to administration thinking, they scarcely would have been reassured. Chief of naval operations Admiral Harold Stark, General Marshall, Undersecretary Welles, and FDR desired nothing less than "preventive occupation" of any strategic areas menacing either the United States itself or the Panama Canal. Otherwise, they feared, a network of Nazi satellite regimes would emerge throughout Latin America. Referring in May 1940 to possibilities of "Nazi-inspired revolution" in Brazil and "widespread disorders" in Mexico, Marshall considered preventive occupation of European possessions in the Western Hemisphere, "offensive-defensive operations in South America," and "limited offensive operations" south of the Rio Grande.[114] That July, the war department drew up contingency plans to take both Martinique and Guadeloupe; 9,600 ground troops and fifteen fighting ships would be involved.[115]

When, in June 1940, Marshall called for federalizing the national guard, he referred to the "indirect, subversive methods" that could emerge in Latin America; in particular, he said, the Panama Canal could be threatened. Norman Thomas responded that such a move was bound to appear imperialistic to the indigenous population.[116] Villard warned against suppressing a revolutionary movement thought friendly to dictatorships overseas. Would the United States, for example, hold Rio de Janeiro unless a republican government were established in Brazil?[117]

To such liberal anti-interventionists, the situation in Uruguay appeared particularly alarming. When, in mid-June 1940, U.S. minister Edwin C. Wilson feared a Nazi coup, Roosevelt sent the heavy cruiser *Quincy*, stationed at Guantanamo, and the *Wichita*, part of the Atlantic fleet, to Uruguay's capital, Montevideo.[118]

A variety of anti-interventionists were quick to voice alarm. Roosevelt, feared Libby, might make war on Uruguay. Dorothy Detzer wrote, "A couple of years ago Norman Thomas was jokingly speaking of 'dear American boys dying for Patagonia'—well, that's just what may happen." *New Masses* cited Scripps-Howard columnist Raymond Clapper, who feared that the United States might be engaged in "protective occupation."[119] If the U.S., Taft warned, sent an army to that country while the Germans had control of the South Atlantic, that force would be expendable.[120]

Apprehensions also centered on Brazil. During a fifth-column panic in the spring of 1940, the country's president, Getulio Vargas, announced that his nation would remain strictly neutral in the current European conflict. On receiving a British warning that six thousand Nazi forces could be headed there with the possible intent of seizing the government, Roosevelt directed Admiral Stark to devise plans for moving at least ten thousand U.S. troops to Brazil by air, followed by a hundred thousand by sea. Operation Pot of Gold would involve four battleships, two carriers, nine cruisers, and three squadrons of destroyers. Brazil immediately sought cooperation with the United States on defense matters, and the plan was never executed.[121]

Because of rumors concerning this U.S. action, some anti-interventionists thought the worst.[122] Libby offered a scenario whereby Brazil's Germans might start a revolution in the southern part of that nation, the Brazilian government would recognize the rebels, and the U.S. National Guard would attempt intervention.[123] The procommunist weekly *In Fact* cited journalist Clapper, who spoke of a possible U.S. military occupation to keep Brazil's iron ore out of German hands.[124]

If some anti-interventionists worried that the United States might intervene militarily any time it perceived a fascist coup in the offing, others warned against aligning the nation with a fascism they already saw prevalent there. As early as December 1939, Dorothy Detzer accused the U.S. of defending police states so reactionary that they even failed to offer their people the advantages of fascism. In January 1941, Wheeler indicted his country for "trying to appease all the dictators in South America."[125]

The entire region, it was argued, was the antithesis of representative government. The *Christian Century* questioned whether the southern half of the hemisphere was truly democratic. Congressman Fred Bradley (Rep.-Mich.) made a pointed comparison to corrupt Democratic Party machines: "There's about as much democracy in most of those countries as there is in Chicago or Jersey City." Pacifist Nicholas Broughton recalled that even the continent's greatest heroes, Simon Bolívar and José de San Martín, had been dictators. Authoritarian or not, warned Chicago financier Sterling Morton, Latin American nations would confiscate the property of others, assured that if retribution should draw near, "the strong arm of Uncle Sam will ward it off." If the "stream of milk" from the U.S. "milk cow" dried up, the Good Neighbor would again become the hated Colossus of the North.[126]

Certain nations were singled out. Santo Domingo, asserted Hugh Johnson, was as bloody and ruthless as anything Hitler ever dreamed. *New Masses* accused Brazil's ruler Getúlio Vargas of eulogizing Hitler and Mussolini.[127]

Mexico was subject to particular debate. Journalist Paul Arden contended that at least 80 percent of Mexico's population opposed U.S. foreign policy, sought to trade with any European victor, and found their nation's German settlers among the most adaptable and law-abiding foreign elements in their land. Lawrence Dennis remarked that ideologically and institutionally "Mexico is closer to Moscow or Berlin than to Washington and Wall Street." In May 1940, the *New York Daily News* maintained that Germany had two hundred agents in Mexico and that the Soviet Union was also active there. "Mexico is already on the ragged edge of complete Communism," it said. Besides, it was just conceivable that Mexico might serve "as the jumping-off point for an invasion of the United States—or at least for some kind of violation of the Monroe Doctrine." Arguing to the contrary, Hearst, who in 1916 had called for war with Mexico, called on the United States to be as friendly toward Mexico as it was toward Canada. Mexico, he went on, had been "close friends now for nearly a hundred years."[128]

Anti-interventionists focused on Alaska as well. In 1940, the U.S. military was building installations at Fairbanks, Anchorage, Sitka, Kodiak, Dutch Harbor, Annette Island, and Yakutat. Such construction greatly increased in 1941, with work continuing on navy posts at Sitka, Kodiak, and Dutch Harbor; airfields at Annette Island, Juneau, and Nome; and army posts named Fort Ray, Fort Greeley, Fort Mears, and Fort Raymond.

No real consensus existed on the matter. Some Roosevelt critics continually called for more Alaskan bases, particularly airfields.[129] Finding threats in both Japan and the Soviet Union, in April 1940, Senator Reynolds sought an air station at either Anchorage or Dutch Harbor.[130] That same month Hugh Johnson pointed with alarm to five Russian military stations at Kamchatka and German technical missions at Vladivostok and Komandorski.[131] Fleming MacLiesh and Cushman Reynolds stressed that the Aleutian Islands lay almost on the Great Circle Route between Yokohama and San Francisco.[132] To Colonel Lindbergh, it was essential that the United States maintain defense bases there, though he found little likelihood that "the wilds of Canada" could be crossed and the U.S. itself invaded. Hanson Baldwin suggested various bases in Alaska but denied the U.S. could possibly—or needed to—protect its entire coastline. "If an enemy," he continued, "ever attempted an overland campaign strike for Seattle he would leave behind him a trail bleached in bones, and in the words of one officer, the soldiers who started would not reach Seattle."[133]

Some anti-interventionists were less concerned. Fish noted that the closest distance from Soviet Russia to the Bering Strait was some twenty-five hundred miles, making it impossible for an enemy army ever to reach Alaska. If enemy troops crossed the Bering Strait, said Senator Alva Adams (Dem.-Colo.), they would be in barren country, without means of transportation.[134]

In late June 1941, the administration implied that Alaska was threatened. Hence, so it argued, U.S. fighter planes should be granted use of Soviet bases in Siberia and the Bering Sea.[135] The CDAAA soon warned that if Japan occupied eastern Siberia, Alaska would become the most vulnerable spot in the Western Hemisphere.[136]

The AFC strongly opposed such moves. Noting the U.S. military bases being built in Alaska's panhandle, on the Aleutian Islands, and on the mainland, it said that American submarines, surface raiders, and bombers could immediately smash any invasion attempt and bomb any bridgehead an enemy might establish. Furthermore, bases in Siberia would be difficult to construct, as they could not be reached by railroad, only by ships and planes. The new U.S. superbomber, the B-19, could reach the industrial cities of a hostile Japan directly, making Alaska superfluous in the process. At one point, the America First Committee claimed that occupation of the Siberian bases could only be justified if the United States were taking offensive action in the Far East.[137]

Alaska and Mexico were not the only debated invasion routes. Alarm also centered on Africa and the Western Mediterranean islands. In May 1941, Roosevelt warned that Germany threatened the city of Dakar in French Senegal and "the island outposts of the New World," the Portuguese-owned Azores and Cape Verde Islands. The Cape Verdes, FDR warned, lay "only seven hours' distance from Brazil by bomber or planes carrying troops."[138]

Such interventionists as the CDAAA developed the president's argument. In enemy hands, said the interventionist action group, the whole string of Atlantic islands—Cape Verde, Madeira, and the Canaries—would permit German U-boats and bombers to assault Britain's major Atlantic and African sea lanes and threaten U.S. commerce with Brazil, Uruguay, and Argentina as well. Furthermore, noted CDAAA staffer Livingstone Hartley, British shipping to the Red Sea, India, Singapore, and Australia would all be menaced. The CDAAA coyly stated that if Germany crossed the Pyrenees, "many experts" had suggested that the United States should seize the islands. Such a move, it maintained, would undermine the confidence of France, Spain, Portugal, and Japan in a German victory and would help restrain Japan from striking at the Dutch East Indies and Singapore.[139] On this issue, the public leaned toward intervention. According to one poll, over half the population said the U.S. should keep Germany out of such African islands.[140]

Throughout the conflict, particularly in 1941, Roosevelt's adversaries found U.S. moves on any such sites warlike.[141] His administration was particularly suspected of making plans for nothing less than seizing Dakar and the Atlantic islands.[142] Were the United States to occupy such areas, warned *Uncensored*, it would only be exposing itself to "defeat in detail," for its forces could be bombed from Spanish Rio de Oro.[143] The Portuguese had stationed some sixteen thousand troops on the island, equipped with batteries and motorized vehicles. Furthermore, German planes stood only a few hours away.[144]

Conversely, anti-interventionists portrayed any German threat via West Africa and Brazil as absurd.[145] To attack the United States from Dakar, troops would need a supply line from Europe via the African base, extending over practically two thousand miles of ocean, as sea transportation was the only possible route.[146] Transport was no small undertaking, argued Philip La Follette, for German troops in Africa would require forty thousand field guns, a hundred thousand vehicles, nine million pounds of food per day, ten thousand airplanes, and nine million tons of shipping. If such forces did attempt to cross from Africa to South America, they would—so Boake Carter said—be sunk by the U.S. Navy.[147]

Invading Brazil presented its own problems. Charles A. Lindbergh claimed that one required dozens of previously prepared airfields, equipped with tanks and fuel, and crews of skilled mechanics, all of which had to be transported by sea. One must further presuppose that Germany had already won the war in Europe; that its conquered countries remained so docile that it could devote attention to an interhemispheric struggle; that it could ignore Asia, "always at her back door"; and that it had Africa "well in hand."[148]

Suppose Germany did take the eastern bulge of Brazil, critics argued. Its problems would just begin. Were Hitler to station a million troops there, these forces would lie just as far from the United States as when they began operations. Furthermore, "There is no link by rail with the rest of South America," said Hanson Baldwin. "There are no roads, no facilities."[149] How, asked Fish, could panzer divisions survive in the Amazon swamp in a territory as vast as Germany, France, and England combined? Then the Germans would still have to trek north. "Practically all of this 5,530-mile hike," said the *New York Daily News*, "would be through mountains, jungles or deserts, not to mention hostile populations, heat, snakes, tropical disease germs, tarantulas and gila monsters." Were Germany to attack across the Caribbean, warned Taft, U.S. naval domination would make the effort ten times as difficult as crossing the English channel.[150]

Conversely, asserted the AFC research bureau, any U.S. seizure of Dakar would be far from easy. In the words of Colonel Frederick Palmer, a noted military expert, the effort embodied "an invitation to massacre in detail." Landing on a defended shore involved the most difficult of all military operations. At least a hundred thousand men, four hundred thousand tons of shipping, a hundred ships, and a powerful naval escort were required, all serving as a perfect target for dive-bombers and submarines. Even to land in Freetown, Sierra Leone—five hundred miles south of Dakar—could, remarked *Uncensored*, cost the attacker many troops.[151]

If the United States did take Dakar, the African city would be difficult to hold. "How can we protect Dakar from recapture," asked Vincent Gilroy, former editor of *The Democrat*, "unless we advance, step by step, North, South, East and West . . . until the entire continent of Africa is the field of our operations?" Similarly, John T. Flynn noted the difficulty of supplying U.S. troops and ships and holding the population under American control. War and merchant ships would be diverted from aiding Britain.[152]

Dakar itself was deemed a worthless area, a useless bridgehead, being sixteen hundred miles from North Africa and twenty-five hundred miles from Axis bases in Libya. It lacked road and railroad access; 98 percent of its materials needed to come by ship. Furthermore, the British could destroy the port by a blockade and bombardment from nearby Bathurst.[153] The AFC research bureau called Dakar "a steaming, squalid, hurricane-swept tropical port in French Senegal which is loyal to Vichy," sorely needing a major air base and lacking a single dry dock. Hanson Baldwin found it lacking storage facilities for coal, oil, or gasoline, much less an ammunition dump of any size.[154]

General Marshall himself found any such move "strategically unsound." Writing Admiral Stark, he said, "We are not prepared to undertake any large scale defensive operations on land for some time to come." A *Fortune* poll of October 1941 found fewer than half the population supporting its defense.[155]

It would also be difficult, so administration critics argued, to defend the islands on the western Atlantic. Such outposts, admitted *Uncensored*, could be used by hostile submarines and bombers, but the liberal newsletter denied that their occupation was vital to hemispheric defense; it preferred bases in Brazil. The exposed Azores would be as difficult for the United States to hold as would be Bermuda for an enemy.[156]

The AFC research bureau also feared a domino effect. "If we occupy the Azores, must we not then occupy Portugal to protect the Azores? If we occupy the Cape Verde Islands and Dakar, must we then not occupy portions of the African coast to protect those outposts?"[157]

Only one anti-interventionist, Colonel McCormick, favored a base at the Azores, arguing that such a post was necessary to prevent any move from Dakar. Were Hitler to conquer Portugal and establish a puppet government on those islands, he said, the U.S. Navy should occupy them. The Azores, commented the *Chicago Tribune* itself, flanked any European approach to Africa, could easily be defended against air attack from continental Europe, and lay within easy steaming distance of a fleet based at Bermuda.[158]

On 22 May 1941, in response to Pétain's collaborationist speech of the previous week, Roosevelt secretly prepared expeditionary forces for possible preemptive strikes. Within a month, the Azores and other Atlantic islands might be seized.[159] The war department opposed the proposal, focusing instead on the importance of Brazil. For over a month, a task force was prepared, troops even being issued tropical clothing. Yet, probably acting on rumors concerning a massive German onslaught on Russia, FDR suspended the Azores project, pushing instead the Iceland incursion.[160]

When he met with Churchill that August, Roosevelt promised to occupy the Azores as soon as Britain had made arrangements with Portuguese president António de Oliveira Salazar, though continued Russian resistance and a paucity of forces persuaded both men to postpone such plans.[161] General Marshall, finding his forces unprepared, always argued against such use of American forces outside their hemisphere. In part because of such warnings, Roosevelt dropped plans for invading either the Azores or Dakar.[162] Even in October, noted a *Fortune* poll, less than 50 percent of the public favored American defense of the two areas.[163]

Americans as a whole were far more willing to fight Germany over Latin America than over the domination of Europe. As early as September 1939, Gallup polls indicated that 72 percent of the public backed the use of American force against any German incursion within fifteen hundred miles of the Panama Canal. Furthermore, some 53 percent would fight to repel an invasion of Brazil, Chile, or any other major South American nation.[164]

Anxieties concerning political and military threats to Latin America were greatly exaggerated.[165] Beginning in 1938, British intelligence planted fabricated stories of Nazi plots there. In May 1940, General Marshall, stressing the limited range of all existing bombers, claimed that American cities might face sporadic air strikes, but only enemy air bases in close proximity could expose them to continuous attack. In January 1941, Colonel Joseph T. McNarney, a member of the General Staff, and Captain Richmond Kelly Turner, director of the Navy's War Plans Division, drew up a memorandum for the Joint Army and Navy Board that included the statement "The United States can safeguard the North American continent and probably the western hemisphere, whether allied with Britain or not."[166]

Within the American military, however, strong anxieties concerning Brazil remained. Rear Admiral Ernest J. King, appointed commander of the Atlantic Patrol Force, continually worried about an invasion of Brazil via Senegal. Marshall, learning in May 1941 from the Army Intelligence Division that Germany would probably invade West Africa, wanted to send nine thousand U.S. troops to Natal. To counter the German move, he and Stimson sought to station U.S. troops there; only Hitler's attack on the Soviet Union reduced anxieties over any such strike. In addition, in March 1941, the military drew up contingency plans to occupy all Central American countries south of Mexico as well as Ecuador, Colombia, and Venezuela—said action taking place within forty-eight hours.[167]

According to the administration, the German threat was not only military—it was economic as well. Here, too, debate remained impassioned.

# 9

# Economic Survival
# in the Americas

The Roosevelt administration often pointed with alarm to the German economic penetration of Latin America.[1] As early as January 1939, the president himself saw Germany as being able to isolate the United States by means of economic control. Increasingly he feared that Germany might form a continental trading union to negotiate with Latin America and thereby threaten U.S. security.[2]

Not only did as much as half of South America's total exports depend on a European market, noted Undersecretary Welles in January 1941, but Germany's barter system, with its attendant political manipulation, could impose a commercial and financial stranglehold on these nations. Large-scale subversive movements could soon follow, then actual physical invasion.[3]

In his book *You Can't Do Business with Hitler* (1941), Douglas Miller elaborated on Welles's warning. According to Miller, recently U.S. economic attaché to Berlin, German economic strangulation of the United States would begin slowly. Latin America had long sold twice as much to Europe as to the U.S., already was home to numerous German and Italian nationals, and derived its culture from such German-controlled nations as Spain, Portugal, France, and Italy. Fearful of "revolution from within and aggression from without," South America would eagerly buy German arms, especially as many of its inhabitants still cherished suspicions against the Colossus of the North. Soon one would see a series of Nazi-inspired revolutions "exploding like a pack of firecrackers."[4]

In an attempt to combat possible German barter agreements, on 21 June 1940 Roosevelt endorsed the establishment of an Inter-American Trading Corporation. This body would engage in joint marketing of the important staples throughout the Americas. Under such aegis, the United States could conduct the trade relations of the twenty Latin American republics in a manner similar to the way Washington regulated the commerce of the forty-eight states.[5]

Noninterventionists were negative, maintaining that creation of such a cartel was highly impractical. To make the system work, said *Uncensored,* strict control of all agricultural produce was needed, a complex matter when the wheat and cotton of Argentina, Canada, and Brazil was added to that of the United States Cost was also a factor. To John T. Flynn, purchasing the coffee of Brazil, the copper of Chile, and the nitrates of Peru would cost at least a billion dollars a year. In enforcement, too, lay a huge problem. Would the United States, asked free market economist Frank Chodorov, send its fleet to chase German merchantmen from South American waters when Germany undersold it? "Are we ready to back up our economic war measures with force?"[6]

Other objections to the cartels appeared. It was futile, wrote Hugh Johnson, to become business agent for some twenty-odd Latin American republics that lacked the naval and air bases needed for their own protection. These nations, argued the *Christian Century,* had no more desire to enter into such a scheme than did North American capital.[7]

Roosevelt soon abandoned the project. In August 1940, the president told a press conference that his nation sought no inclusive arrangement with all of Latin America. In continuing efforts to protect American markets against totalitarian dumping, he said, the administration would consider each problem individually. Hull feared for the fate of his reciprocity program, which faced congressional renewal later in the year, and did not seek further controversy. The treasury department, although committed to currency stabilization, found the cartel scheme too grandiose. As Great Britain appeared increasingly capable of survival, such efforts at hemispheric cartelization became increasingly irrelevant.[8]

Still and all, the administration found increased trade between the United States and Latin America eminently desirable. Hence, on 22 July 1940, Roosevelt asked Congress for half a billion dollars, lent through the Export-Import Bank, to relieve Latin America's economic difficulties. The war, noted Hull, had made it difficult for Latin American countries to pay for necessary imports; therefore, immense stores of export commodities were piling up.[9]

A few anti-interventionists favored such loans, but endorsements were half-hearted.[10] To the *Christian Century,* the loans indicated a recognition that a problem existed, but they were not in themselves a solution.[11] Journalist Frank Hanighen found the sums far too modest, the Roosevelt administration far too fixated on "the vested interests and the upper classes."[12]

More administration critics, however, opposed the proposal.[13] As with the cartel scheme, cost was a factor. Flynn wrote, "We can do a nice job in the direction of ruining ourselves if we undertake to pay the bills involved in the ruin of South America."[14] Furthermore, such loans might subsidize economic rivals. When, for example, the United States announced a $20 million loan that would enable Brazil to erect a steel mill, the *Chicago Tribune* claimed that the move would simply create competition for domestic steel producers.[15] On 26 September, Congress approved the measure, though it forbade loans for war materials to countries still owing money to the U.S. government. In 1941, the U.S. made an accord with Brazil and Mexico, offering stable export prices at relatively high levels.[16]

To many of the administration's adversaries, the United States certainly could compete with Germany in Latin America.[17] Agricultural expert George Peek wrote, "Quality is remembered long after price is forgotten." Hugh Johnson saw no threat in Germany's much-touted barter policies, for those Latin American nations that traded with the Reich would soon possess an overabundance of aspirins, bicycles, and cameras. "Ignorant nations," he predicted, "will no longer trade tusks of ivory and wedges of gold for calico, squarefaced gin and strings of beads." According to the research bureau of the America First Committee, the U.S. already possessed 50 percent of the Caribbean's trade; nearly 30 percent of Brazil's; nearly 25 percent of such Pacific Coast countries as Bolivia, Ecuador, Chile, and Peru; and over 10 percent of such Atlantic-oriented nations as Argentina, Paraguay, and Uruguay.[18]

From the outset of the war, several anti-interventionists called for closer economic ties with Latin America.[19] If the two continents, said the *New York Daily News*, could pool resources and develop adequate distribution, "every man, woman and child in the Western Hemisphere could be well fed, well clothed, well housed." Noting in October 1940 that Britain's South American trade had been heavily reduced, it remarked, "We ought to go after that trade, and aim to keep the bulk of it after the war."[20]

Various techniques were proposed. Robert La Follette Jr. spoke in general terms of U.S. financial assistance, economist Stuart Chase of linking the entire hemisphere into one self-sufficient economic unit. If the Axis dominated Eurasia, the *Chicago Tribune* suggested that the United States must organize its hemisphere's commerce along monopolistic lines. *Social Justice* editor Louis B. Ward favored the broadening of the development of the Pan American Union and the creation of an Inter-American Bank. Historian J. Martin Klotsche advocated spending the sums currently slated for the Allies on Latin American trade. If necessary, said General Robert E. Wood and Norman Thomas, the U.S. could establish export cartels and mass purchasing organizations against the Germans. Educator Robert M. Hutchins saw the nation adopting Secretary Knox's proposal of an immediate customs union with the Latin American nations.[21]

Particular attention was given to the rubber of Brazil and the tin of Bolivia.[22] The United States was currently deriving 90 percent of its crude rubber and 75 percent of its tin from Malaya and the Netherlands East Indies.[23] If the U.S. purchased both resources within the hemisphere, it could bolster

Latin American economies while avoiding dependence on areas threatened by Japan. Said the AFC research bureau, "We need not go to war for rubber or tin; American boys need not fight and die in Dong Dang or Bangkok," as it pointed to tin smelters currently being built in Texas. Hugh Johnson stressed that Durango, Mexico, produced tin. Congress, said Hamilton Fish in May 1940, should appropriate $2 million to erect a tin smelter in Bolivia and survey Latin America's potential for rubber production.[24] Taft favored development loans from the Export-Import Bank.[25]

Other Latin American products received attention. *Uncensored* suggested buying manganese in Cuba and Brazil and chromium, platinum, and tungsten throughout the entire continent. Senator Robert La Follette recommended shifting U.S. cocoa purchases from Africa, where the product was "cheaper but distinctly inferior," to such nations as Venezuela and Ecuador. Fleming MacLiesh and Cushman Reynolds endorsed purchases of cocoa beans, tapioca, long-staple cotton, cashew nuts, and such vegetable fibers as sisal and henequen.[26]

Some proposals were more comprehensive. New Mexico senator Dennis Chavez offered an entire list of proposals, including the subsidizing of U.S. shipping; constructing a canal through Nicaragua and possibly Tehuantepec, Mexico; building additional transcontinental highways; making long-term investments in transportation, communication, and water power; and enlarging the Panama Canal's facilities. Taft suggested insuring short-term credits, reducing steamship rates, increasing coffee purchases from Brazil, and possibly lowering taxes on profits from the export trade.[27]

Anti-interventionists found comfort in Carleton Beals, whom the interventionist *Time* magazine had called the best informed writer on Latin America. Educated at the University of California and Columbia University, Beals had written books on everything from Porfirio Díaz to Huey Long. In 1940, he called the present war a fight over raw materials, "a struggle bound to grow bitter, whoever wins."[28]

In *Pan America*, Beals stressed hemispheric integration, with Latin America focusing on production of the raw materials needed for common defense. To Beals, the admittedly needed U.S. investment must have expiration deadlines. More important, the producing country must always control and eventually own all such stocks. He suggested a variety of trading methods, including preferential tariffs, markets, and contracts, and guaranteed quotas and prices. Some anti-interventionists, such as the AFC research bureau, strongly touted his work.[29]

Other anti-interventionists, however, were far less sanguine.[30] *Uncensored* offered a barrage of figures. Europe, it noted, normally received 93 percent of Argentina's beef, 80 percent of its corn, 40 percent of its hides, and most of its wheat; from Brazil alone, Europe bought 40 percent of its coffee and most of its cotton. At its height, remarked broadcaster Fulton Lewis Jr., the trade of Central and South America only consumed 6.7 percent of U.S. business.[31]

America First leader Wood put the point simply. The products of Latin America's tropical belt, he noted, complemented U.S. manufactured goods. Hence, Mexican metals, Venezuelan oil, Brazilian coffee, and Central American bananas were sure to find many buyers to the north. It was in confronting the products of the temperate zone—Brazil's cotton, Argentina's meat, cotton and wool, and Chile's copper and nitrates—that the United States would find trouble. "We cannot sell unless we buy," the general declared, "and that is a far greater obstacle than all nazidom." Furthermore, argued the *New York Daily News*, any markets gained during the war would be transitory, for "most of the world will be broke after this orgy of shoveling tangible wealth into the fire." For the U.S. to compete with Europe, it must either subsidize its exports or cut the wages of its own workers "to the bone."[32]

Some anti-interventionists went further. A German victory, said Hanson Baldwin, could lead to a reduction in the American standard of living as well as "a fierce economic war for our markets in South America" and possibly a military conflict. Irrespective of who won the current global struggle, warned both Joseph P. Kennedy and the *New York Daily News*, the United States faced a bitter trade rivalry there.[33]

The conclusion became obvious: whatever power alignments existed in Europe, Latin America depended on its business. Should the Germans end up in control of Europe, Latin Americans would still have to deal with them and possibly with Japan, too.[34]

To Lawrence Dennis, the entire debate over the Latin American market was irrelevant. The region, he said, "is economically very small peanuts for Hitler and for us"; for Europe it was a matter of "life and death." If Hitler knocked out Britain, he would speedily incorporate Eurasia and Africa into his totalitarian system, giving him—on the basis of 1937 figures—56.3 percent control of total world exports and imports. His Latin American trade, only 5.9 percent of the total, would be the least of his concerns. If the Germans really sought to conquer the world, Dennis continued, they would not waste economic resources in trying to undersell the United States in Latin America or establishing useless military bases five hundred miles south of the Panama Canal. Rather, they would concentrate on building a navy or air force strong enough to defeat the U.S. The entire Axis would be wiser to engage an American Expeditionary Force in scattered points in Europe, Africa, and Asia, where U.S. forces would be overwhelmed.[35]

Admittedly, by 1938, Germany's bilateral trade policies in Latin America had led to significant economic gains. Hitler's Reich had become the market for 10.5 percent of all the area's exports and supplied 17.5 percent of all imports. Yet despite the United States's relative decline in its own exports to other hemispheric republics, it was never in real danger in being replaced as the region's leading supplier. In general, U.S. exports were not of major magnitude, in the late 1930s averaging between $500 and $600 million. Besides, British sea power was increasingly terminating whatever market potential Germany hoped to possess.³⁶

The administration's efforts at rechanneling hemispheric trade patterns might have been relatively half-hearted, but its concern over a wider German economic threat was palpable indeed. In December 1939, Roosevelt warned William Allen White that a combined German-Russian victory would so jeopardize U.S. trade as to imperil "your civilization and mine." When, on 27 May 1941, Roosevelt declared a national emergency, he stressed that a German victory would force the American worker to compete with "slave labor" throughout the world. With Hitler "fixing" wages and hours, "the dignity and power and standard of living of the American worker and farmer would be gone." Similarly, the American farmer, no longer able to sell in a competitive market, "would face obvious disaster and complete regimentation." The president went on: "Freedom to trade is essential to our economic life. We do not eat all the food we can produce; we do not burn all the oil we can pump; we do not use all the goods we can manufacture. It would not be an American wall to keep Nazi goods out; it would be a Nazi wall to keep us in." Roosevelt ended the address on a most somber note. "Our Bunker Hill of tomorrow," he said, "may be several thousand miles from Boston."³⁷

The president's sentiments were echoed by other prominent interventionists, among them Cordell Hull, William C. Bullitt, and columnists Walter Lippmann and Dorothy Thompson.³⁸ According to a *Fortune* poll taken that month, much of the business community shared similar anxieties.³⁹

In his *You Can't Do Business with Hitler*, state department attaché Douglas Miller offered the most frightening account of all. Hitler's Reich, he warned, would force subject nations to supply it with food and raw materials while imposing German manufactured goods on them at will. All commercial transactions ranging from "the North Cape in the Land of the Midnight Sun to the tip of South Africa" would be coordinated by a central bureaucracy in Berlin. Obviously such massive power would ruin the U.S. economy. Once Germany had integrated Latin American into its economic empire, it would cut the United States off from vital raw materials, dangerously curtailing any defense program. In addition, the nation would suddenly experience tremendous overproduction in such crucial items as cotton, grain, and tobacco, thereby facing the dilemma of trading on Hitler's terms or curtailing production. With U.S. political and social institutions shattered and all hopes for "a fuller and freer existence" lost, only "State Socialism" lay ahead. "America," Miller mourned, "would pass from a civilized era into a long night of siege."⁴⁰

Though Miller received his share of laudatory reviews, anti-interventionists struck back. Financial writer Samuel Crowther found the argument flawed. If

Germany's Führer wanted economic self-sufficiency for his nation, Crowther observed, he would have to limit imports. If, on the other hand, he really sought control of the markets of the world, he would be forced—merely in order to trade—to maximize them. In any case, autarchy and commercial expansion were incompatible: to put the issue simply, the Germans could not have it both ways.[41]

The administration also cast one eye on Asia, where—so it feared—another entire section of the world might be subject to an autarchic economic system. Suppose, FDR asked the American Society of Newspaper Editors in April 1940, "the Yangzi remains permanently closed to American products," not to mention the China treaty ports, Cochin China [southern Indochina], Xianggang [Hsiang River], Siam, the Straits Settlements, and the Dutch Indies? As historian Jonathan G. Utley paraphrased the administration's view, "This was a question not of a few supplies, but of the preservation of a world order that had brought unparalleled prosperity for the industrial nations in general and the United States in particular."[42]

The administration, so anti-interventionists feared, might be leading Americans to believe economic survival depended on outright war. Such rhetoric, wrote Raymond Moley, would intensify criticism of the United States "from Tokyo to Lisbon," for Americans would aptly be charged with focusing on "the world situation" only because of their own pocketbooks.[43] Certainly, to FDR's critics, the commercial price of intervention was far too high. Asked Merle Thorpe, editor of *Nation's Business*, "When has war helped a nation's trade in the long run?" "The tremendous destruction of war is greater in 1 year," said Senator Taft, "than the benefits derived by us in 20 years of foreign trade."[44]

Whatever took place, several anti-interventionists argued, the future was bleak. Even if Britain won, remarked pacifist leader Florence Brewer Boeckel, the United States would invariably face an economically united Europe. Sheer continuation of the conflict, warned Joseph P. Kennedy, meant the loss of all foreign markets.[45]

One possible solution to Axis victory lay in autarchy.[46] Anti-interventionists differed on the percentage of American income dependent on trade, their estimates ranging from 3 to 7 percent.[47] "If worse came to worse," said Kennedy, "we could gear ourselves to an intelligent self-contained national economy and still enjoy a fair amount of prosperity." "We have the best home market in the world," remarked General Wood. To political scientist Brooks Emeny, the nation already possessed half the world's industrial capacity. If the war continued much longer, it would own 75 percent.[48] As far as imports went, Peek only found a few items taken in bulk. Though they did include tin and rubber, the United States could produce substitutes.[49] Offering a mild dissent, John T. Flynn maintained that U.S. trade, though seldom rising above $5 billion, was important for both the nation and the world. Yet, if Hitler ended up dominating Europe, the United States would not have to lose its trade with Canada or Latin America, areas that in 1938 comprised almost half of U.S. commerce.[50]

Economist Stuart Chase's entire book, *The New Western Front*, had been written to stress U.S. self-sufficiency. Chase denied that Italy, France, Russia, and Japan "rolled into one" could approach the nation's industrial potential. Except for the Soviet Union, Chase observed, the United States was the most integrated continental empire in the world, possessing easy access to all the raw materials it needed. Americans, he asserted at one point, can "feed and clothe ourselves without any imports whatever."[51]

Herbert Hoover found autarchy quite feasible. Reasoning that Axis victories invariably diminished U.S. exports, the former president called for more home industries. New American factories, producing for domestic consumption, would hire the newly displaced workers and, at the same time, free the nation from foreign dependence. While he did "not relish it," he saw the United States as 97 percent self-sufficient, if necessary. "And the cost of it would be less over twenty years than one year of war."[52]

In addition to economic self-sufficiency, there was some flirtation with barter. Senator Lodge saw both bartering and dumping as effective retaliation against German penetration. "This is a game at which two can play," said Peek. To Lawrence Dennis, the United States could adjust itself better to the Axis "New Economics" than any other nation—could, in fact, be dominant commercially. If the Germans sought to manipulate the price of cotton, wheat, and tobacco, the United States "can destroy them, as Brazil has done with millions of bags of coffee, give them away to our own people or eliminate them altogether by better agricultural management."[53]

Among the anti-interventionists, Flynn again voiced dissent. Germany's own barter practices in South America served as a negative example as they turned out to be unprofitable.[54] Besides, the system put traders at a fatal disadvantage in dealing with an unfettered foreign competitor, particularly one with gold in its pockets.[55]

One anti-interventionist offered a related strategy: that of dividing the world into spheres of influence. In 1940, Graeme Howard, vice president in charge of overseas operations for General Motors, offered a commercial manifesto, *America and a New World Order*.[56] Several noninterventionists endorsed the book.[57] The auto executive proposed dividing the world into recognizable economic blocs, suggesting as entities continental Europe, the British Empire, the USSR, Latin America, North America, and Japan's "New Order" in Asia. Cooperative regionalism, said Howard, could substitute mutual interdependence for "international economic chaos, revolution and conflict." True, the United States faced keen postwar competition from England, Germany, Italy, and Japan, all nations whose survival depended on exports. It could, however, still sell its cotton, lard, tobacco, and wheat surpluses overseas as well as supply loans for productive projects. In addition, it could mediate the world's conflicts and thereby keep such nations as Germany, Japan, Italy, Russia, and Spain out of the "international doghouse." All such nations,

Howard insisted, had no quarrel "other than the quarrels we ourselves wish to initiate," and the U.S. would be wise to avoid further "bellicose criticism" of their regimes.[58]

Many of the administration critics stressed neither autarchy, barter, nor regionalism. Rather, they simply asserted that the United States could not only survive in an Axis-dominated world but could meet any new economic rival.[59] As Hugh Johnson remarked, "There is only one rule for success. It is goods of better quality, at lower prices than competitors can offer."[60]

Agricultural leader George Peek raised a related factor—namely, that the U.S. possessed the greatest international purchasing power in the world. Proclaiming with pride, "This is our high card," he noted that the United States bought massive amounts of coffee, sugar, and wool within the hemisphere, not to mention 40 percent of the world's tin, 50 percent of Southeast Asia's rubber, and 90 percent of Japan's entire exports. Germany, he continued, would find it difficult to disrupt this market.[61]

Furthermore, John T. Flynn argued, Germany possessed within itself the seeds of its own economic destruction. Citing interventionist columnist Walter Lippmann as an authority, Flynn denied that Hitler could ever manage a peacetime empire. Debts would be unmanageable, industrial structure dislocated, the entire German nation on the verge of starvation. Excessive regulation would first make private profit impossible and then destroy capitalism itself. Once the government was forced directly to appropriate businesses, collapse would become inevitable. After a disorderly struggle for power, the Reich was likely to go communist.[62]

Some anti-interventionists went so far as to claim that it was Germany—not the United States—that would end up the dependent country.[63] In contending that the nation always held the natural advantage, the AFC research bureau cited a study sponsored by the Brookings Institution, Cleona Lewis's *Nazi Germany and World Trade*.[64] According to Lewis's findings, the ravaged European continent would be on such short rations that Germany simply would be unable to exclude U.S. imports. Similarly, without American raw materials, European industries would be crippled. Conversely, as Europe's exports were not indispensable to the U.S. economy, the bargaining power would naturally lie with the Western Hemisphere. The United States could even force the Germans to pay in dollars.

Even before World War II, said the AFC, Germany depended on imports of certain food and raw materials. The war merely accentuated the Reich's dilemma, making it even more economically dependent. Of all twenty nations under Nazi sway, only three—Bulgaria, Rumania, and Yugoslavia—complemented the Nazi economy by supplying these two elements. Some nations—Denmark, Hungary, the Netherlands, and Sweden, for example—needed food themselves. Still others required both food and raw materials, among them such significantly industrialized states as Belgium, France, Italy, Switzerland,

and Czechoslovakia. If the Nazis controlled every nation bordering the Mediterranean, they still would possess few raw materials.[65]

The AFC research bureau soon dealt with the economic implications of Hitler's possible conquest of the Soviet Union. Quoting again from Lewis's study, it asserted that domination of undeveloped Soviet plains would hardly improve Germany's position. The USSR had not exported much food since World War I; its own deficiencies had been considerable, and it could supply Germany with just 14 percent of the food it needed. Only by deliberately starving the Soviets could Hitler receive much food from the USSR, but starvation would only lower Russia's productivity. As far petroleum went, despite its huge oil output, the Soviet Union was actually short of regular and aviation gasoline. Moreover, the Soviets possessed little surplus coal and iron and could not make up Germany's deficiencies in such major raw materials as tin and tungsten.[66]

A few anti-interventionists were even more explicit in claiming that a German-dominated postwar order could operate to U.S. advantage. To pacifist Nicholas Broughton, the breakup of the British Empire could lead to greater U.S. trade with an independent Canada and other self-governing dominions. The United States, he argued, would no longer be hampered by Britain's imperial preference system, by which the empire was exclusively open to British manufactured goods.[67]

Such critics found little merit in Roosevelt's own argument concerning "slave labor"—namely, that the low wages within Axis-dominated countries created a real threat.[68] After all, a host of administration foes argued, the U.S. had long traded with a number of totalitarian and low-wage countries, including China, Japan, India, and the Soviet Union.[69] The United States, maintained Frank Chodorov, would counter the bargains made by German slave labor with the products of its own free laborers, who in turn had far more wages to spend. True, Germany controlled twice as many buyers as the United States, but these buyers were paupers.[70]

Even access to raw materials presented little problem. In January 1941, *Uncensored* strongly challenged FDR's claim, made in his recent message to Congress, that the populations and resources of Europe, Asia, Africa, and Australia—in the president's words—"exceeds the sum total of the population and the resources of the whole of the Western Hemisphere—yes, many times over." While conceding that the United States only had 6 percent of the world's population and the entire Western Hemisphere just double that, it stressed that the nation retained vast shares of the world's resources. "Judged by their potential capacity to produce," it said, "Americans should never be faced with the grim choice of guns or butter."[71] Certainly, several anti-interventionists argued, the U.S. either possessed what it needed or could easily stockpile scarce goods.[72]

In some ways, the president's adversaries had the better of the immediate argument over trade. During the 1930s, only 3 percent of the U.S. gross national product had gone to nations outside North America. American businesses invested slightly under 6 percent of their wealth abroad. As far as the balance of trade with Germany was concerned, it lay substantially in Washington's favor.[73]

In regard to resources, the United States was already involved in major stockpiling. In June 1940, the Metals Reserve Company, a subsidiary of the Reconstruction Finance Corporation (RFC), began engaging in massive purchases of foreign tin, copper, and tungsten. Another RFC firm, the Rubber Reserve Company, undertook the same activity. In May 1941, the Office of Production Management altered stockpiling priorities to assure a three year's supply of such materials as chromite, manganese, and graphite.[74] Both Roosevelt and Welles conceded the U.S. was not dependent on Southeast Asian tin and rubber, for sources were available elsewhere.[75] Moreover, if the administration saw markets as a linchpin of its policy, it would have remained reluctant to embargo Japan, for its exports to that land were several times larger than its sales to beleaguered China.

Hopefully, for both interventionists and their foes, economic survival amid a hostile world would remain moot. Much depended on Britain's chances for survival after the fall of France, the possibilities of a negotiated peace, and the individual who assumed the presidency in January 1941.

# 10

# War, Peace, and Elections

Debates over military and economic survival took place amid a background that was certainly grim. Once France fell, British leaders had every reason to fear an imminent German strike. On 15 May, in his very first message to Roosevelt as prime minister, Churchill said, "We expect to be attacked here, both from the air and by parachute in the near future." Twelve days later, the British military warned Churchill that if Germany obtained air supremacy, the Royal Navy could not fend off invasion. Even worse, land defenses were insufficient to repel enemy forces. Within a month, the belief in inevitable invasion was widespread.[1] Churchill biographer Martin Gilbert entitles his chapter covering July 1940 "The Great Invasion Scare." On 4 September, the prime minister gave the British three-to-one odds of staving off the assault. Less than three weeks later, Churchill received an intelligence summary: "The threat of invasion to this country cannot be said to have lessened."[2]

By mid-August, the famous air war known as the Battle of Britain had begun in earnest. On 15 September, aerial combat reached its climax, with thirteen hundred German sorties against London. The Germans found costs so high that two days later Hitler postponed invasion indefinitely. Britain was by no means secure, however, and until May 1942 it experienced sustained bombing in what was called the blitz.

American officials kept a wary eye on developments. In mid-July, General Raymond E. Lee, American military attaché and head of intelligence in London, believed invasion was in the offing, though he predicted the British would repel it.[3] Within six months, according to the U.S. Joint Planning Committee, Britain would not be an active combatant.[4] To Adolf Berle, there was "a long bitter stalemate" ahead, with each side "pounding the other to a bloody pulp." Only occasionally was there slight optimism. Early in September, the American military was noting the growing strength of the Royal Air Force and the development of an army sufficient to fight in Africa and the Near East.[5] In the same month, Bullitt would not rule out a British invasion of the European continent within a year.[6]

To Americans in general, Britain's fate remained black. A *Fortune* poll conducted in July found slightly over 40 percent predicting a German victory.[7] That August, the same poll indicated 39.8 percent denying that Germany would conquer Britain but 37.5 percent thinking it would.[8]

Even some most sympathetic to Britain were discouraged. Early in June, for example, *Life* magazine forecast several hundred thousand German troops landing "in fast motorboats at night." A month later it offered an article that described a hypothetical invasion.[9]

Anti-interventionists were divided over the matter of Britain's fate. Some comments were bleak. In mid-May, Chicago business leader Sterling Morton expected the invasion of England, if only by paratroopers, within the next few weeks. On the day King Leopold surrendered, Joseph P. Kennedy saw negotiation on Germany's terms as the only hope for both France and Britain. On 25 July, the ambassador gave three weeks for Hitler to arrive in London.[10] Al Williams repeatedly warned of a German invasion, stressing in particular the role bombing would play.[11] "The invasion of England is poised," the aviation columnist wrote early in August.[12] On 1 August, Lawrence Dennis predicted invasion within the month.[13]

Even in May and June of 1940, other FDR critics envisioned Britain's successful resistance. To William Randolph Hearst, the English Channel could successfully "engulf" armies as the Red Sea had "engulfed the hosts of Pharaoh."[14] The *Chicago Tribune* claimed Britain could prevent a major landing by blowing up its docks.[15] If, said publisher McCormick, the Germans disembarked near Hastings, the well-trained regular English army, "reinforced by the splendid Australians and the indomitable Canadians," could hold a narrow front.[16] By 24 July, the *New York Daily News* could predict that British ships, planes, and minefields might "pile up so many German dead in the water that the attack will crumble." If the Germans did get ashore, the British possessed over a million trained soldiers waiting to meet them, plus "an unknown number of home guards, 'parashoots,' bloodthirsty school kids with .22's, and old gentlemen who used to do some hunting or some World War soldiering."[17]

Even in Britain's blackest moments, a few anti-interventionists denied that Germany could ever really succeed. Senator Taft continued his prediction that Europe could never succumb to one-man rule.[18] Hugh Johnson quoted Napoleon's maxim: "Empires always die of indigestion." John T. Flynn found Germany's heavy war expenditures inadvertently revealing the desperate condition of its economy; the entire German system was headed for a crack-up.[19] Even if Germany won its immediate campaigns, commented Hanson Bald-

win, it would still confront the mistrust of Russia and Italy, find the domination of conquered peoples difficult, and experience the exhaustion resulting
from any war. "Wolves for long do not lie down with lions."[20]

Even before the arrival of autumn, such anti-interventionists expressed
confidence that Britain would hold out.[21] A combination of the Royal Air
Force and pestilence on the continent, maintained Hearst in September,
would give Hitler no stomach for further aggression. The publisher found
German aircraft incapable of transporting sufficient invasion troops.[22] In the
same month, the *Chicago Tribune* pointed to approaching stormy weather and
to the supremacy of British fighters over German bombers.[23]

In October, some continued to deny the possibility, much less the success,
of an invasion. The *New York Daily News*, noting the increasing fogs and
storms in the Channel, guessed that Britain could at least hold off Germany
for the winter.[24] Radio broadcaster Quincy Howe denied that Hitler ever considered an invasion of Britain, and was certainly unable to win the war.[25]

Others spoke in more general terms. In December, Sterling Morton questioned whether Britain could ever be conquered. Even if it was, Germany faced
an unparalleled policing job. "The more Hitler conquers," asserted Republican
leader Alf Landon, "the weaker he becomes." The task of permanently governing "a free, courageous, and patriotic people like the French, Dutch, and Norwegians" was "insurmountable."[26] Hitler, said the *Chicago Tribune*, had gone
farther and faster than Napoleon but still faced three things that had stymied
Bonaparte: British sea power, a Russian alliance that was unreliable, and the
"volcanic powers latent in people who had lost their liberty."[27] As early as October, Villard expected the German people to suffer a terrible winter, experiencing inadequate food supplies, exposed cities, and incessant air raids.[28] In
fact, he argued, the majority of the Führer's own people were sullen, under-
nourished, and "sick and tired of the whole business."[29]

Certainly, Britain's fate remained unclear. Italy's entrance into the war
caused Britain severe problems in Africa and the Mediterranean. In June,
Italian aircraft raided Malta and bombed Aden and Port Said. A month later
Italians stationed in Ethiopia overran British Somaliland. That September
Italy's forces in Libya began the long-awaited invasion of Egypt, followed in
late October by an invasion of Greece via Albania. American naval experts offered a most pessimistic analysis, predicting Axis domination of the Mediterranean, to be followed by the failure of British blockading efforts and then
military disaster.[30] Only in December did the British begin their counterat-
tack in North Africa, reaching Tobruk on 22 January 1941 and Beda Fomm
on 6 February.

Little wonder some administration foes forecast defeat or at least an impasse. Frederick J. Libby, estimating that German air superiority remained at
least four-to-one, predicted that Germany would win the Battle of Britain. If
it just maintained its bombing, William R. Castle feared, it could "bring the

British people to their knees through sheer hunger." Senator Taft saw the destruction of the British fleet and the breakup of its empire as a distinct possibility. To Hugh Johnson, Britain's only hope lay in revolution within the conquered nations. Even without invasion, argued Lawrence Dennis, Britain faced starvation. He saw Britain losing North Africa, Ethiopia, and the Mediterranean and then, after defeat, experiencing proletarian revolution.[31] The *New York Daily News* forecast Germany closing Britain's Mediterranean lifeline at both sides, thereby boxing in the British fleet, blockading the southern end of the Suez Canal, and cutting off the British-dominated Near East from the home country. If such tactics succeeded, the war might continue for years, resulting in mutual starvation and "Stalin picking up the pieces." C. Hartley Grattan drew up a whole scenario for British dissolution, including massive unemployment, chaos for the pound sterling, drastic curtailment in agriculture and mining, and loss of major colonies.[32]

At times, noninterventionists found Britain already defeated. "The totalitarian domination of Germany and Italy," predicted Herbert Hoover in September, "will cover most of the Continent from Russia to the Atlantic." In addition, Germany would control many Allied dependencies in Africa and the East Indies.[33]

The Dakar fiasco simply added to the pessimism. On 23 September 1940, British naval forces and Free French officers landed at the Vichy-held port of Dakar, but after two days of desultory fighting, they were forced to abandon operations. The British repulse, commented the *New York Daily News*, was "the most ominous setback Great Britain has yet suffered," a move that might persuade Spain to join the Axis and obviously encourage the Japanese.[34]

A month later Britain's fate appeared little better.[35] In October, Anne Morrow Lindbergh wrote that eventually Britain would have to meet Hitler's terms. With Gibraltar and Suez still threatened, the *New York Daily News* stated, "The British Empire's near future looks dark—darker at the moment than that of Great Britain proper." The *Chicago Tribune* expected the Germans to strike at such areas as Gibraltar, Egypt, the Balkans, Russia, or Greece.[36]

November and December brought more discouragement. Charles A. Lindbergh remarked privately that England could not win the war unless Germany collapsed internally.[37] Though the British were showing courageous resistance, the Germans were by far inflicting the most damage.[38] Libby commented, "We are too late. Britain can not win, even with our help," though he argued a peacetime Germany could not remain totalitarian. According to Ambassador Kennedy, almost every British port was seriously damaged; therefore, its food supply would last only two months. Furthermore, the ambassador continued, the loss of North Africa was inevitable if the Germans wanted to pursue it. The *Chicago Tribune* did not rule out the actual invasion of the British Isles.[39]

Given such prognoses—a high chance of British survival, a low chance of British victory—anti-interventionist talk increasingly centered on stalemate.[40]

Both sides, maintained the *New York Daily News*, could withstand any pressure the other could exert. As Villard remarked, "Hitler is not winning this war and isn't going to win it—nobody is except famine, disease, utter misery and probably Communism."[41]

All during Hitler's blitzkrieg of Western Europe, anti-interventionists talked continually of mediation. Neville Chamberlain, his dream of an imminent peace suddenly shattered, concurred with Joseph Kennedy in believing that Britain's sheer survival depended on Roosevelt's appeal for an armistice. The Duke of Windsor secretly added his support to such an enterprise.[42]

Within the United States, two pacifist groups—the Fellowship of Reconciliation and the Women's International League—called for negotiation by the president himself. In April 1940, the Federal Council of Churches, the leading Protestant organization, requested the neutral nations to create a permanent coordinating body dedicated to consultation; both Frederick L. Libby and the *Christian Century* concurred.[43] In May, the *New York Daily News* endorsed Pius XII's recent call for peace, calling him "the wisest statesman in Europe today."[44] As U.S. participation in the war would make no difference, "Why not patch up some kind of peace with Hitler, then put the Allies' best diplomats, go-betweens, agents provocateurs, stool pigeons, finks and finooglers on the job of busting up the Hitler-Stalin friendship?"[45]

Even as Norway, the Low Countries, and France were being overrun, hopes remained high.[46] Senator Wheeler hinted at a British peace with Hermann Goering. Lawrence Dennis saw peace sentiment existing among both right-wing "appeasers" and the British Labor Party. Auto executive James D. Mooney, whom FDR had sent to Europe on a scouting mission several months earlier, cautiously reported that negotiation was not impossible. Needed was "a formula providing security for the English and French and removing the threat of starvation for the Germans." Frank Waldrop foresaw Hitler ruling Europe from the Arctic Circle to the Pyrenees but believed that all this conquest was "impoverished, sullen, fractured and useless in its present state to anybody." Britain, he suggested, should offer the Führer the Belgian Congo, France's African colonies, and a free hand in the East "before he integrates all that vast power into a machine to use on England."[47]

Some peace terms appeared a bit cosmic. The plan of Albert W. Palmer, president of Chicago Theological School, included immediate disarmament, a world court, equal access of all nations to markets and raw materials, and an American rehabilitation fund of $4 billion for both Europe and China.[48] *Common Sense* looked toward a European federation and the beginning of world government.[49] Frederick J. Libby sought general disarmament, independence restored to occupied countries, a German sphere of influence in southeastern Europe, and the perpetuation of such powerful blocs as the British and French empires, Russia, Germany, Italy, the United States, and "an oriental federation."[50]

On 19 July 1940, Hitler addressed the Reichstag. As at the end of the Polish campaign, he called on Britain to end the struggle. "I can see no reason why this war must go on," he said, though he mentioned no concrete peace terms.[51]

Churchill adamantly refused to negotiate.[52] By now the British had rescued the bulk of their continental army, German attention was still focused on France, and American aid appeared possible. If the prime minister privately might have feared that victory was unattainable, he still thought Britain could hold out for more acceptable terms.[53] Furthermore, Churchill mistakenly believed that the German war machine was approaching maximum efficiency, that the British blockade would begin taking a heavy toll, and that an American declaration of war was imminent.[54] A Gallup poll within Britain revealed strong support for continuing the war.[55]

Some anti-interventionists sought a positive response to Hitler's bid. Britain, suggested Villard, should call Hitler's bluff; hopefully, threatened famine in Europe, war weariness among the German people, and a Soviet threat in the Balkans would create an honorable peace. Just before the Führer's speech, the *New York Daily News* called on Britain to treat any proposal seriously. Five to ten years of armed truce would give the British time to prepare for a final showdown; the alternative simply meant famine throughout all Europe.[56]

Others were more tentative. Anne Morrow Lindbergh noted that the speech containing no real terms, though she dreaded "the suffering and the terror and horror" continued fighting would involve.[57] The *Chicago Tribune* endorsed the British rejection; Hitler's "collected works" revealed "a unique disdain for good faith."[58]

For the rest of the year, calls for negotiation continued from voices as disparate as Norman Thomas and Charles A. Lindbergh, *Social Justice,* and the WIL.[59] The *New York Daily News* and the Hearst press suggested papal intervention; General Wood and Frederick Libby would include Roosevelt as well.[60]

Britain could make a settlement by which it could keep its fleet and colonies, said Wood in October, though admittedly Germany would be left possessing economic control of Western Europe.[61] If the United States affirmed that it would not enter the war, remarked the general two months later, peace could be made by the spring of 1941.[62] He proposed peace terms involving the liberation of Norway, Denmark, Holland, and Belgium and the continuation of the British Empire, with perhaps the ownership of two former German colonies submitted to neutral mediation.[63]

In December, William Henry Chamberlin endorsed a compromise peace made at the expense of the Soviet Union. The *Chicago Tribune* warned Britain that chances of sustaining a long war were less than equal. *Fortune* staffer John Chamberlain, a bit more cautious, sought "a real negotiated peace, not a fake one that would leave her government and armament in hands sympathetic to Hitler."[64]

The alternative appeared to be Red revolution. Writing in his diary that October, Felix Morley confided that from the beginning of the conflict he had felt that Germany would win. Labor Party obstinacy, so he feared, could create a "communist England" though he blamed the United States as well.[65] William R. Castle, John Bassett Moore, John Cudahy, and Charles A. Lindbergh shared the anxiety.[66]

Rumors appeared everywhere. In October, Devere Allen's Nofrontier News Service reported that secret peace negotiations via Spain had recently been "in full tide" but that the destroyer bases deal and possible access for the American fleet in Singapore terminated the negotiations.[67] A month later, Amos Pinchot heard "on good authority" that Britain could keep its empire and control of the Mediterranean, admittedly a "gamble" but one preferable to mutual annihilation. Joseph P. Kennedy forecast that British defeats would lead to negotiation under a Lloyd George premiership.[68] In December, Borchard supposedly had learned from sources in Germany and Switzerland that the Nazis sought to end the war. *Uncensored* noted that "responsible Washington sources" were seriously entertaining the idea of a negotiated peace.[69]

In early October, a resolution of Congressman John G. Alexander (Rep.-Minn.) received mild anti-interventionist support. His proposal included the cessation of hostilities under joint neutral supervision and the advancement of a world federation—all under the aegis of the American president and other leaders of neutral nations. Territorial questions, he later added, would be referred to a convention that would draw up a constitution for a United States of the World along the lines of the U.S. Constitution.[70]

At the end of 1940, Burton Wheeler made a major proposal. Its terms included restoration of Germany's 1914 boundaries; the return of former German colonies; an autonomous Poland and Czechoslovakia; the restoration of an independent France, Holland, Norway, Belgium, and Denmark; the return of Alsace-Lorraine to France; protection of religious and racial minorities in all countries; internationalization of the Suez Canal; no indemnities or reparations; and arms limitation. "The President," he maintained, "should make a determined effort to bring the warring nations of Europe together" by insisting that "a just peace be worked out."[71] According to a hostile journalist, Wheeler conceded that a negotiated peace might simply serve as an armed truce but asserted that the United States had "gotten along" with tyrants in the past and would be forced to do so in the future.[72]

Several anti-interventionists were always pessimistic about such proposals. As early as April, William R. Castle, after hearing Norman Thomas speak, claimed he could not "follow him so earnestly in wishing for a negotiated peace rather than continuance of the war." William Henry Chamberlin judged war passions to be so intense that a compromise peace remained "perhaps the least probable outcome of the war."[73]

Roosevelt soon voiced his opposition to any such overtures. In a nationwide address given on 28 December 1940, the president attacked the entire notion:

> Is it a negotiated peace if a gang of outlaws surrounds your community and on threat of extermination makes you pay tribute to save your skins? Such a dictated peace would be no peace at all. It would only be another armistice, leading to the most gigantic armament race and the most devastating trade wars in history. And in these contests the Americas would offer the only real resistance to the Axis Powers.[74]

Anti-interventionists quickly responded. Libby deplored the president's opposition, citing columnist Ernest K. Lindley to the effect that peace sentiment was growing in Britain. Norman Thomas challenged Roosevelt's claim that any negotiation meant total victory for Hitler. The Führer, said the socialist leader, had no occupation troops in Britain, did not seek its navy, and was forced to divert his own strength to bolster his weak ally Mussolini. One anti-interventionist journal, *America*, did back the president, concurring in FDR's claim that Germany sought only to "dominate and enslave the human race."[75]

All the time anti-interventionists discussed the fate of the war and promoted a negotiated peace, a presidential campaign was under way, one in which such matters played an increasingly crucial role. Amid widespread dissatisfaction over a stagnant economy, not to mention bottlenecks in defense, the Republicans hoped to capture the White House and Congress. Within the ranks of the Grand Old Party, almost every would-be standard-bearer voiced anti-interventionist sentiments.

Senator Robert A. Taft of Ohio was particularly vocal on this issue. Though he had just entered Congress a year earlier, in January 1940 *Time* found "the wisemen" deeming him "today the No. 1 Republican Presidential possibility." In some ways, Taft had been a relative moderate concerning intervention, having supported repeal of the arms embargo and a government loan to Finland. In May 1940, he publicly preferred the defeat of Britain to American participation in the European war, even adding, "I don't understand why, if peace is once restored, we could not trade as well with Germany as with England." Taft biographer James T. Patterson has called this address, made at St. Louis on 20 May, the most damaging speech of his campaign, as it dismissed any notion that the Nazis posed a threat to the United States.[76] It was, however, this very staunchness that brought support from many anti-interventionists, including the *Christian Century*, liberal advertising executive Chester Bowles, and the usually cynical Lawrence Dennis.[77]

More popular among the voters, at least those who voted in primaries, was Thomas E. Dewey, Manhattan's district attorney who had gained a national reputation as a racket buster.[78] In April 1940, *United States News* predicted Dewey as the probable nominee.[79] Dewey condemned Roosevelt for "misery, lack of jobs, heavier taxes, and the eventual undermining of the nation itself," although the New York crime buster wavered on foreign policy.[80] That January, he had looked forward to "the moment when we might, without entanglement, use our good offices to effect a genuine peace." Yet in late March, he warned the United States to "reject every entanglement in the affairs of Europe," and he called on his nation to "remain genuinely neutral." In fact, he urged the U.S. to "keep its hands wholly out of the European war and out of any negotiations that may take place between the warring nations, now or at any other time." Early in May, Dewey again backtracked, declaring that the United States could not so isolate itself as to be unaffected by events in other nations. On 21 June, the eve of the Republican convention, he endorsed the "extension to the victims of aggression of all proper aid," but abhorred "foreign entanglements." On arrival at the convention, Dewey told reporters he opposed selling U.S. warships and revealed he was thinking primarily in terms of surplus World War I ammunition.[81]

Though the New Yorker showed more vacillation than Taft, some FDR opponents saw him as the decidedly superior vote getter. Moreover, he was deemed sufficiently militant to receive strong noninterventionist support.[82] In endorsing him for the GOP nomination, the *New York Daily News* approvingly labeled Dewey "an isolationist, meaning that if elected he will be 100% for arming to the teeth for defense of this country, but against buying any further into Europe's war."[83] Similarly, in an editorial entitled "The Voters Want Dewey," the *Chicago Tribune* found him the clearest of the candidates in opposing what it saw as FDR's attempt to involve the United States in war.[84] Others thought Dewey far too superficial.[85] For example, the outspoken daughter of Theodore Roosevelt, Alice Roosevelt Longworth, deemed his speeches and foreign policy to be lacking intelligence.[86]

Of the contenders most often mentioned for the Republican nomination, Senator Arthur H. Vandenberg of Michigan had shown himself to be the most consistently anti-interventionist, even opposing cash-and-carry. His biographer C. David Tompkins went so far as to write, "After Senator Borah's death in early 1940, Vandenberg became the Republican isolationist leader."[87]

As editor of the *Grand Rapids Herald*, Vandenberg had endorsed American possession of the Philippines, the Open Door policy, and entry into the League of Nations. His service on the Nye Committee had caused him to regret U.S. participation in World War I and warn that additional involvement would lead to dictatorship at home. Borah had promised to deliver the principal nominating speech at the party convention. When Vandenberg entered the Wisconsin primary, Nye toured the state for him. John T. Flynn also gave a reluctant endorsement. Milton Mayer was less enamored, finding him more of a political opportunist than a genuine anti-interventionist. The liberal journalist found danger in such Vandenberg positions as the abrogation of the 1911 trade treaty with Japan and severance of U.S. diplomatic relations with the Soviets when Finland was invaded.[88]

In late November 1939, the *New York Daily News* predicted Vandenberg's nomination. So, too, did over 60 percent of some fifty Washington correspondents polled early in December by *Look* magazine.[89] In August 1939, FDR had thought he would be a hard candidate to beat.[90] Yet once he lost the Wisconsin and Nebraska primaries, he no longer seemed a major contender.

Almost all the GOP dark horses were anti-interventionist. Labor leader John L. Lewis, whose relations with FDR had become extremely embittered, sought to launch a boom for Herbert Hoover.[91] Amos Pinchot came out strongly for New York State publisher Frank Gannett, who, like Vandenberg, claimed Borah's endorsement.[92] Editor Verne Marshall of Cedar Rapids, Iowa, placed the name of a prominent Iowa businessman, Colonel Hanford Mac-Nider, in nomination at the party convention. Hugh Johnson considered Congressman Bruce Barton of New York most able. Hamilton Fish, increasingly the leader of the House anti-interventionists, briefly entered the race himself. *Social Justice* found Senator Arthur Capper (Rep.-Kans.) acceptable and suggested Charles Lindbergh's candidacy.[93]

The party nomination went to Wendell Willkie, a utilities lawyer and Wall Street magnate who had been a Democrat all but four years of his life and who came into the convention with only a handful of pledged delegates.[94] Almost until the moment of his nomination, which took place on 28 June on the sixth ballot, Willkie was known primarily as a liberal business leader who opposed specific New Deal programs while endorsing some government intervention in the economy. Although urging American membership in the League of Nations in the 1920s, he only spoke out directly on foreign policy in April 1940, after Hitler attacked Denmark and Norway. Willkie accused FDR of tardiness in aiding the Allies, criticized other Republicans for their "isolationism," and asked Cordell Hull "what help—short of troops—the American people can give." In recognition that many Americans still harbored deep-lying anti-interventionist sentiments, he did announce in his last preconvention speech in Brooklyn, "It is the duty of the President of the United States to recognize the determination of the people to stay out of war and to do nothing by word or deed to undermine that determination."[95] The more anti-interventionist Charles L. McNary, senator from Oregon, was chosen as running mate.[96]

Had the foes of intervention coordinated their efforts, they might have stopped the Willkie boom. Before the balloting began, Dewey offered Vandenberg the vice-presidential nomination. Vandenberg simply reciprocated the invitation, even offering to "flip a coin to see which end of the ticket we each take." No future communication occurred between the two men, though historian Donald Bruce Johnson claims that they "probably could have won the nomination as a joint slate." Similarly, Taft's chances plummeted when such anti-interventionists as Vandenberg, Dewey, Hoover, and MacNider stayed in the race. Had Dewey accepted the vice-presidential bid on a Taft ticket, speculates historian Patterson, the Ohio Republican might have won the nomination. In the hopes of promoting his own fortunes, Hoover encouraged Dewey to remain a contender.[97]

Even before Willkie's nomination, some administration opponents voiced suspicion of the party's new standard-bearer.[98] Late in June, five Republican senators and about forty House members, primarily from the Midwest and West, attended a meeting to oppose Willkie's nomination. Eight signed an appeal requesting the delegates to nominate a candidate whose views, both foreign and domestic, were far more in line with the party's congressional record.[99]

The debate over intervention carried over into a struggle over the platform. In the final draft, the party found itself "firmly opposed to involving this nation in foreign war." At the same time, it favored "the extension to all peoples fighting for liberty, or whose liberty is threatened, of such aid as shall not be in violation of international law or inconsistent with the requirements of our own national defense." According to Alf Landon, who headed the platform subcommittee on national defense and foreign policy, the document was flexible enough to "allow our candidate to campaign effectively, in view of the changing world conditions." Indeed, it embodied the position of the moderate anti-interventionist Herbert Hoover.[100] Most administration critics were far less sanguine. H. L. Mencken acidly remarked, "It is so written that it will fit both the triumph of democracy and the collapse of democracy, and approve both sending of arms to England or sending only flowers."[101]

As nominee, Willkie kept straddling the foreign policy issue. On the one hand, he endorsed economic aid to China and the development of air bases in the Pacific. In his acceptance speech of mid-August, he found some form of selective service absolutely necessary. "If Britain falls," he continued, "we are utterly and savagely alone." On the other hand, while endorsing the results of the destroyer bases deal, he attacked the way it had been negotiated as "the most arbitrary and dictatorial action ever taken by any President." When FDR said he would do all he could to keep war away from American shores, Willkie often retorted that Roosevelt's reelection meant that American troops would soon be on the transports.[102]

Anti-interventionists were torn over the Republican nominee. Some backed the candidate wholeheartedly.[103] The *Chicago Tribune* titled an editorial "Willkie and Peace, or Roosevelt and War." Even though the candidate had forthrightly repudiated Father Coughlin, the 4 November issue of *Social Justice* ran the headline "VOTE FOR WILLKIE TO AVERT WAR AND DICTATORSHIP."[104]

Others, while endorsing the Hoosier businessman, wanted him to be far more strident.[105] Hiram Johnson, who endorsed Willkie as the lesser of two evils, said that by backing conscription, "He slapped every one of us in the face, who were thinking American, and acting American."[106] Still others remained critical of Willkie all during the campaign.[107] Wheeler called him "an acknowledged Wall Street lawyer and one who openly espoused the policy of American intervention in Europe's blood baths until a few weeks—if not days—ago."[108]

A broad spectrum of FDR's critics hoped that the Democrats, too, would choose a less interventionist nominee. In 1939, Sterling Morton had supported the anti–New Deal senator Edward Burke of Nebraska, later coauthor of the conscription law. Novelist Sinclair Lewis endorsed Robert Maynard Hutchins, president of the University of Chicago, whose domestic liberalism won him mild support from presidential aide Harry Hopkins. At one point during the Democratic convention, Hopkins told the educator that FDR wanted him as a running mate.[109] Joseph P. Kennedy briefly tested the waters. In January, *Social Justice* praised Vice President John Nance Garner, who had announced his candidacy, calling him the type of "old line American" who carved out the frontier. When the convention met, Coughlin's weekly praised Senator Carter Glass of Virginia for nominating Postmaster General James A. Farley.[110] Villard felt content with a host of candidates, some of whom had become strongly interventionist. In mentioning the names of Wheeler and Bennett Clark, he found the latter absolutely trustworthy on the "all-important question of war and peace."[111]

The greatest speculation centered on Senator Wheeler, until recently an arch-liberal who had first achieved fame by leading a Senate inquiry into the "Teapot Dome" scandal.[112] Throughout FDR's first term, Wheeler had backed most of the New Deal. By leading the opposition to the president's court-packing proposal in 1937, however, he gave Roosevelt his first major setback. In the process he created a rift that was never closed. Though he opposed American entry into the World Court and cash-and-carry, he first took on Senate leadership among the anti-interventionists by opposing the sending of U.S. Army and Navy matériel to belligerents.[113]

At the outbreak of war, a modest Wheeler-for-president organization had been established, operating in relatively few states and possessing few funds.[114] Always a political realist, Wheeler realized that he could only be nominated if

Roosevelt refused to run.[115] It is still debated whether FDR offered him the vice-presidential slot to secure his allegiance.[116]

In his bid, Wheeler sought to trade on his anti-interventionism. Defining his position in April 1940, he sought a negotiated peace while accepting an Allied victory moderate enough to preserve Germany itself intact.[117] On 12 June, Wheeler threatened to form a third party, promising he would oppose interventionist standard-bearers on either major ticket.[118]

To some degree, Wheeler's bid for anti-interventionist support was successful. Anti-interventionists of all political persuasions supported his candidacy.[119] John L. Lewis toyed with promoting a Wheeler boom. In January 1940, the labor leader invited him to address the United Mine Workers in Columbus, Ohio, and early that July endorsed him directly.[120]

The ultimate issue was never in doubt. Roosevelt, acting with characteristic coyness, arranged to be "drafted" for another term, accepting the party's nomination on 18 July. As with the Republicans, the platform involved a compromise. The United States, it said, would aid the Allies with "all the material at our command, consistent with the law and not inconsistent with the interests of our own national self-defense." At the same time, it would "not participate in foreign wars, and we will not send our Army, naval or air forces to fight in foreign lands outside the Americas, except in case of attack."[121]

Not surprisingly, many anti-interventionists opposed Roosevelt's renomination, sharing Charles A. Lindbergh's opinion that those "who have failed to solve even our peacetime problems" were currently leading the nation steadily toward "that climax of all political failure—war."[122] Even some who had not been ardent Republicans felt similarly.[123] To the *Christian Century*, Roosevelt's acceptance speech undercut his own party's platform by proposing "the English channel as the front line of our defense," while his claims of indispensability made him "the Führer" of an "inchoate fascism." Socialist writer Richard Rovere thought it disingenuous for Roosevelt to attack "appeaser fifth-columnists" in his acceptance speech. After all, wrote the radical journalist, the president had approved the Munich conference, offered irresponsible overtures to Mussolini, and acquiesced in Japanese expansion.[124]

To John T. Flynn, FDR not only sought to "cook up a war scare" and "militarize the country" but was also engaged in nothing less than attempting to create a totalitarian regime. Flynn contributed a major campaign broadside, *Country Squire in the White House* (1940). Although much of his book involved an attack on the New Deal, the chapter "The President Goes to War" accused FDR of being "one of those lovers of peace who is too ready to choose war." Current defense plans, Flynn argued, merely "take the minds of our people off the failure to solve our own problems and will furnish a new excuse to spend another ten or fifteen billion dollars to return his party to power."[125]

Anti-interventionists were quick to endorse Flynn's work.[126] Porter Sargent devoted an entire bulletin to its contents.[127] The *Chicago Tribune* not only embraced the book but commenced serializing it.[128] Other reviewers found Flynn too one-sided.[129] John Chamberlain, by no means a strong interventionist, differed with Flynn's whole thrust toward disarmament. "Dependence on the Panama Canal," he said, "inevitably implies enough armament to win a prospective battle of Peru or the Guineas."[130]

Conversely, some anti-interventionists were so enthusiastic about the New Deal they were willing to risk Roosevelt's foreign policy.[131] While the *New York Daily News* considered both candidates interventionists, it saw FDR the better informed and more experienced, particularly in naval matters.[132]

Others found little difference between the candidates.[133] To *Uncensored*, "The great body of noninterventionist Americans who depend on the two-party system have been hoaxed."[134] In contrasting Roosevelt and Willkie, Lawrence Dennis found the choice lying "between a knave and a fool." Mencken wrote of Willkie, "When he swallowed the Roosevelt foreign policy all the rest of the New Deal rumble-bumble went down with it, and he has since presented the spectacle of a man choking on his own false teeth."[135] Some of pacifist leanings were particularly unenthusiastic. The FOR's A. J. Muste feared Willkie would "play a role similar to Woodrow Wilson after the election of 1916."[136]

Predictably, many anti-interventionists on the Democratic left supported Norman Thomas.[137] To journalist Richard Rovere, the Socialist leader was the only candidate who opposed conscription, rearmament, and intervention, all milestones on the road to fascism. Wheeler later hinted to Thomas of his support.[138]

In the election of 5 November, Roosevelt polled 27.3 million votes, almost 5 million more than Willkie. His electoral vote was even more impressive, 449 to Willkie's 82. Though the Hoosier drew more votes than any previous GOP candidate, he captured only ten states. Roosevelt had successfully neutralized Willkie's attacks on his interventionism by continually stressing his peace goals. On 30 October, for example, the president had told a Boston rally, "I have said this before, but I shall say it again and again and again: Your boys are not going to be sent into any foreign wars."[139]

Even now, historians differ on the role foreign policy played in the election.[140] Certainly many anti-interventionists believed Willkie lost the election by failing to fight the president more vigorously in this regard.[141] Had Willkie taken the stand of the America First Committee, wrote Lawrence Dennis, he might have secured a majority in such close states as New York, Illinois, Ohio, and Missouri. In Hearst's opinion, Dewey could have done better.[142] Within weeks Willkie's subsequent embrace of Roosevelt's plan to aid Britain would add to the bitterness.

There was only one result in which anti-interventionists could take heart: the return to the Senate of every outspoken opponent of the president's foreign policy and of many House members as well.[143] To Frederick J. Libby, in the senatorial races lay "proof that the election was a clear mandate to keep the country out of war." Conversely, the Socialist Party expressed relief that certain staunch interventionists were defeated.[144]

Overall, Roosevelt's adversaries found the consequences of the 1940 race most awesome. Hiram Johnson remarked to his son, "It is going to be hell here the next six months or a year. If we can escape the concentration camps we'll be lucky."[145] Had he learned that he would soon have to vote on a bill with the innocent title of "lend-lease," he would not have been reassured.

# 11

# Lend-Lease
# and the "Futile War"

During the election of 1940, the America First Committee established itself as the primary anti-interventionist organization in the United States, ready to do battle with the Committee to Defend America by Aiding the Allies. The ubiquitous John T. Flynn headed the semiautonomous New York chapter. The organization remained in existence until Germany declared war on the United States, battling all of Roosevelt's interventionist moves except term extension for draftees. Only on 11 December 1941 did it formally disband. By then it had 450 units and at least a quarter of a million members. Such legislators as Nye, Holt, Fish, Wheeler, and Bennett Clark spoke at their rallies, as did Charles Lindbergh and Norman Thomas.[1]

The AFC's financial base lay in the Chicago business community. General Robert E. Wood, board chairman of Sears, Roebuck, served as acting chairman. Widely respected as one of the nation's most progressive business leaders, Wood had backed much of the New Deal, balking only on such issues as spending and labor policy. Foreign intervention, the general believed, would ruin American capitalism.[2] R. Douglas Stuart Jr., a Yale law student, was first national director, then executive secretary. Publishers Colonel McCormick and Captain Patterson helped finance the committee.

The more vocal members of the AFC national committee were staunch conservatives, including Charles A. Lindbergh (who joined in April 1941), William R. Castle, Major Al Williams, General Hugh Johnson, and George Peek. Nonetheless, pacifists and liberals assumed crucial positions in drafting position papers. Ruth Sarles, director of the research bureau, had edited the NCPW's *Peace Action.* Socialist lawyer James Lipsig bore sole responsibility for the bureau's *Did You Know?* bulletins, a series of position papers.[3]

For an extremely brief period, the AFC had a rival. In mid-December 1940, Verne Marshall, editor of the *Cedar Rapids* (Iowa) *Gazette*, established a similar organization, the No Foreign War Committee. The leader's mercurial personality, however, soon led to its demise, particularly when Marshall—an extreme rightist—tacitly accused the Roosevelt administration of ignoring a secret German peace plan.[4] Anti-interventionists needed the resources of mass organization, for the United States was about to launch the most extensive assistance program a nation at peace ever extended to a country at war.

By the beginning of winter 1940–41, Germany had grown ever stronger. Its allies now included Hungary and a truncated Rumania, the latter occupied by Wehrmacht troops. Britain was experiencing heavy shipping losses—over four hundred thousand tons that October. In December, Secretary of War Stimson told government officials that British sea power might be swept from the Atlantic within ninety days.[5] Moreover, Britain's dollar reserves were running low, threatening its capacity to purchase American supplies. As early as August 1940, the British government foresaw imminent financial collapse ahead. Privately, Ambassador Lothian alerted Churchill on 12 November, "It is obvious that our capacity to carry on the war on the current basis must abruptly come to an end."[6]

On 8 December 1940, Churchill cabled Roosevelt, warning that Britain would soon lack the cash needed to buy American arms. He pointed to heavy losses at sea, the danger of the Vichy government (which controlled West Africa) joining the Axis, and the possibility of a Japanese thrust in the direction of Singapore and the Dutch East Indies.[7] At a press conference held on the 17th, Roosevelt spoke of a plan whereby the United States itself would "lease or sell" what it thought the British needed.[8]

Nine days later, in one of his fireside chats, the president offered his full rationale. The British Empire, Roosevelt asserted, spearheaded "resistance to world conquest." If England fell, "the Axis powers will control the continents of Europe, Asia, Africa, Australasia, and the high seas—and they will be in a position to bring enormous military and naval resources against this hemisphere." Rather than exposing the United States to "the point of a gun," he sought all possible aid to Britain. Warning against those "American citizens, many of them in high places," who were often unwittingly "aiding and abetting" the work of destructive foreign agents, he branded any negotiated accord "a dictated peace," in reality "another armistice, leading to the most gigantic armament race and the most devastating trade wars in all history." More than Britain's dollar crisis was at issue; Roosevelt could use the Allied orders as the means of galvanizing a sluggish defense industry into greater output.[9]

Within another four days, Roosevelt's bill reached Congress. Though the concept was phrased in innocent terms ("lend-lease") and colored in patriotic pleas (the House bill was deliberately labeled HR 1776), its scope was sweeping. The president could provide military articles and information to any country "whose defense the President deems vital to the defense of the United States." If he so desired, the terms *defense article* and *defense information* could cover virtually everything, military secrets included. No limits were set on the quantity of weapons loaned or the sums to be allocated. Friendly belligerents could use American ports. *Newsweek* inadvertently concurred with the America First Committee in finding that FDR wanted authority to lend "anything from a trench shovel to a battleship." No American, said *Time*, had ever asked for the powers Roosevelt requested.[10]

To some of the president's foes, the end of the world could hardly be less foreboding.[11] Historian Howard K. Beale saw "the very fate of our democratic government at stake." The *Christian Century* called it "the most un-American proposal which the American people have ever had seriously to consider."[12]

The bill, it was argued, made the United States an appendage of Great Britain. If Britain was fighting America's battles, remarked Congressman Paul Shafer, "we had best accept a dominion status and be done with it." Representative William P. Lambertson (Rep.-Kans.) quipped about the Duchess of Windsor, "Since England is broke, we should pay for the lifting of Wally's face." Congressman Robert R. Rich (Rep.-Pa.) suggested that Britain might someday use lend-lease planes against the U.S., while Vito Marcantonio envisaged U.S. bombers used "in massacring the Indian tribes who are seeking independence and freedom from British exploitation." On a more serious note, the research bureau of the America First Committee argued that lend-lease dollars were designed to maintain the British pound in the world market.[13]

Many critics stressed the massive extension of presidential powers as well as the bill's all-encompassing language.[14] To John Bassett Moore, "The question is whether we shall have a government of law or a government of men." Hamilton Fish quoted A. Lawrence Lowell—former president of Harvard, political scientist, and usually a strong interventionist—who maintained that the bill could practically give away the entire American navy and air force as well as the nation's entire military manufacturing power.[15]

With certain scholars so apprehensive, it was hardly surprising for others to voice alarm.[16] "I would not give such powers to the Archangel Gabriel," Villard wrote. Both the *New York Daily News* and John Haynes Holmes saw the bill as making FDR dictator of the United States. The Reverend Norman Vincent Peale, secretary of the National Committee to Uphold Constitutional Government, asserted that HR 1776 gave the president "the power to commit the American people to any war anywhere, and without action by Congress."[17]

Anti-interventionists continually stressed that lend-lease aid to Britain would certainly weaken the United States. Hanford MacNider called it "the triple-threat bill—lease, lend, and lose America's defenses." Joseph P. Kennedy, who formally endorsed the bill, stated that American production was by no means adequate for the U.S., let alone aiding Britain. The AFC found any attempt to expand beyond current defense plans too taxing, and it pointed especially to bottlenecks existing in various types of skilled labor.[18] In particular, the U.S. would be giving away planes essential to an effective air force, though antiaircraft guns and naval craft were mentioned as well.[19] Senator Walsh introduced an amendment opposing transfer of any American naval craft.[20] At times even the comments of leading administration experts—such as George Marshall and Henry L. Stimson—were used to stress the nation's shortages.[21]

Domestic consequences were also noted.[22] Lend-lease could cause the real income of American consumers, according to the AFC, to plummet for a host of reasons, including increased taxes on consumption, forced saving, rising prices, and curtailment of many government services. By specifying repayment of arms in kind after the war, the British, reported Frank Hanighen, could maintain their production while American arms plants, which would include practically all American industry, would have to shut down. *Uncensored* predicted another postwar depression. Civil liberties would also suffer, with the possibility existing that all criticism of the administration could be labeled rebellion or treason.[23] Senator Danaher sought an amendment forbidding any law interfering with freedom of speech.[24]

As with cash-and-carry, several anti-interventionists saw lend-lease as violating international law and agreements.[25] To William C. Dennis, president of Earlham College and former state department official, lend-lease epitomized "the law of the jungle, the Vigilantes, and the Indiana White Caps." International law, he maintained, specified that private sales to belligerents were permitted but public transactions were not.[26] The Washington Treaty of 8 May 1871, which settled the *Alabama* claims; the 1907 Hague Convention; the Kellogg–Briand Pact renouncing war as "an instrument of national policy"; the Panama Declaration of 1939—lend-lease breached all such agreements.[27]

Above all, to its opponents, the bill was tantamount to war.[28] Norman Thomas found it so belligerent that even a German who hated Hitler could not support the legislation.[29] To a group of Harvard scholars, the bill involved irrecoverable military collaboration with other nations, but evaded the means of collaboration, the human and material cost, and the ends involved.[30] Congresswoman Jeanette Rankin (Rep.-Mont.) introduced an amendment calling for further authorization before the president could order troops outside the hemisphere.[31] Several critics stressed that Germany had not acted belligerently toward the United States.[32]

Not only was a new American Expeditionary Force feared.[33] The sheer mechanics of the bill could ensnare the United States. The legislation, said Vandenberg, would permit a British battleship, the *Renown*, to be repaired in the Brooklyn Navy Yard, which in turn would "invite Axis submarines into the Hudson River, and Axis mines off Sandy Hook, and Axis wings over New York City."[34] AFC national director R. Douglas Stuart Jr. expected German sabotage of U.S. industrial production, with the consequent inflammation of national feeling.[35]

Robert A. Taft was particularly vocal. He warned that the president, "sitting beneath the scenes," could "pull the strings which fire the guns and drop the bombs on armed forces and helpless civilians alike." Once lend-lease passed, Roosevelt could land a regiment of American soldiers at Gibraltar, claiming that its defense involved the defense of the United States.[36] Recalling the famous *Alabama* claims issue, he introduced an amendment to prevent American ports from being used by the British fleet; otherwise, the Germans could mine these ports and pursue British vessels into U.S. harbors.[37]

Anti-interventionists stressed one matter above all: convoys—that is, in technical naval language, those warships "escorting" a "convoy" of merchant ships. If the United States leased strategic war goods to the British, such escorting appeared the next step—and a fatal one. To many the bill itself implied American convoying of British ships and the sending of American craft into war zones.[38] Senator Guy M. Gillette (Dem.-Iowa) favored an amendment prohibiting American merchant vessels from carrying materials to belligerents in those combat zones specified in the 1939 neutrality act.[39]

Although Roosevelt had secretly been considering convoying and a diplomatic break with the Axis, he told a press conference in mid-January that convoys were about the "last thing we have in our minds." At the same time, the administration never retreated from the position that the president had the constitutional power to order such escorting without congressional approval.[40] On 6 February, the House, by a vote of 111 to 74, defeated an anti-convoy amendment introduced by Representative Karl Mundt (Rep.-S.Dak.). Ultimately the administration accepted an amendment to HR 1776 specifying that the act itself did not authorize such convoys.[41]

Some anti-interventionist concerns, however, were more subtle. The Roosevelt administration had been quick to emphasize Britain's desperate financial condition, which in reality was most dire. Roosevelt himself, tempted by a vision of British imperial opulence, first suggested the British sell their assets in the Western Hemisphere, though he was soon disabused of the notion. As Secretary of the Treasury Henry Morgenthau Jr. put the issue, "When it comes to finding the dollars to pay for anything like what they need, they just haven't got it."[42]

Many of the president's adversaries, however, felt the British were far from broke. Charles A. Beard suggested that Britain pledge its vast assets in the United States, which others valued at sums of $2 to $10 billion.[43] General Wood cited specific British-owned firms operating in the United States, among them Lever Brothers, the American Viscose Corporation, and Dunlop Tire. By selling such assets, said Wood, Britain could survive another year. (Under Morgenthau's pressure, the British did dispose of American Viscose, doing so at a price well below market value.)[44]

Only if Britain were to market its entire holdings in the Western Hemisphere, including extensive railroad interests in Argentina, anti-interventionists argued, should credit be extended.[45] Some told Britain to draw on its resources throughout the entire globe.[46] Taft estimated the British held $14 billion worth of assets, which was "a very large proportion of the property of the world."[47] Even before FDR's formal lend-lease proposal, *Uncensored* had proposed mortgaging the British Empire's gold production.[48] The immense wealth held by prominent British citizens, such as the Astors and the Duke and Duchess of Windsor, was noted.[49] Retired advertising executive William Benton proposed using the entire British Museum as collateral.[50]

Several anti-interventionists pointed to Britain's supposed prosperity in time of war. A number of claims were made: During the war, Britain had managed to increase imports 33 percent while losing only 2 percent of its export trade.[51] The British Empire was producing 60 percent of the world's gold, which the United States was buying "at very fancy prices."[52] Despite the conflict, Britain had added to its commercial shipping to retain its monopoly the U.S.–South America route.[53] British cargo facilities totaled over twenty-six million tons, ten million more than at the beginning of the year.[54] If the shipping shortage was so marked, asked the *Chicago Tribune*, why not use the 150 vessels of the St. Lawrence fleet? Even resentment over Britain's continued trade with the dominions was sharp, as Wheeler noted that India, one of the richest nations of the world, "had not yet passed any lend-lease bill."[55]

Each lend-lease opponent, it seemed, had a different alternative to FDR's comprehensive legislation. Merwin K. Hart, president of the New York State Economic Council and an arch-rightist, merely called for the continuation of cash-and-carry.[56] Others spoke in terms of a straight loan, with sums ranging from $2 to $10 billion.[57] Taft, for example, suggested offering $2 billion in loans to Britain, Canada, and Greece.[58]

Others considered outright gifts.[59] Edwin Johnson would authorize the president to turn over $2 billion worth of munitions to Britain for "testing." Herbert Hoover would give Britain all the defense material the United States could spare and some $2 to $3 billion to make other purchases. The U.S., said Senator George Aiken, should donate outright the larger part of a $2 billion lend-lease appropriation in the form of materials to Canada.[60] General Wood suggested that Britain exhaust its U.S. resources, after which it would receive gifts or loans of planes, artillery, and tanks, all carried in Britain's own vessels. More moderate than some anti-interventionists, Wood did favor selling American merchant ships to Britain, provided the U.S. merchant marine would not be crippled in the process.[61]

Several anti-interventionists proposed bargaining over certain British colonies within the Western Hemisphere.[62] The British, said the *New York Daily News*, should simply give the United States its pick of sites as well as other "conveniently located pieces of the empire." Wood spoke of the transfer of Newfoundland or British Honduras.[63] Fish's eye was on the West Indies.[64] Representative Melvin J. Maas proposed an amendment enabling the U.S. to purchase all British possessions in the Western Hemisphere, with the obvious exceptions of Canada and Nova Scotia.[65]

Other goods and concessions were sought. Congressman William J. Barry (Dem.-N.Y.) noted such British raw materials as manganese, chromium, tin, and nickel. Nye wanted Britain's commercial shipping. Wiley desired revision of the Hay-Pauncefote treaty (1901) with Britain, which provided free access to the Panama Canal for ships of all nations on equal terms.[66]

A few anti-interventionists used the debate over lend-lease to suggest total impartiality in the conflict. Journalist and maritime historian Lincoln Colcord argued, "We should not have taken sides." In fact, he accused the America First Committee of "trying to carry water on both shoulders," for it was endorsing aid to Britain in principle when strict neutrality was called for.[67] Similarly Lawrence Dennis, in an obvious reference to the sentiment embodied in the AFC, said that the noninterventionists should never have abandoned absolute neutrality. By endorsing "all-aid-short-of-war," they could only fight rearguard actions and postpone the inevitable.[68]

Other anti-interventionists supported the continued flow of war goods to Britain. General Wood sought to rush steel and remove bottlenecks on planes.[69] Colonel McCormick wanted Britain to have whatever it required, though he did not think it needed anything.[70] Charles A. Lindbergh, far more cautious, favored continuing current aid to Britain but stressed the need for negotiated peace; hence, such assistance should neither be increased nor continued indefinitely.[71]

Time and spending limits were often raised, however, as were limits on what the president could send.[72] Vandenberg and Vorys, for example, proposed that the service chiefs certify the transfer of any military goods.[73] Much support was given to the varied forms of an amendment introduced by Senator Allen Ellender (Dem.-La.), which, in its original form, stated that nothing in the act authorized the use of American armed forces outside the United States or its territories.[74]

On 8 March 1941, the Senate passed the lend-lease bill 60 to 31 (with two paired for and against), and three days later the House approved the bill as amended 317 to 71. That same day, Roosevelt signed the legislation.[75] On 7 March the Gallup poll had reported 61 percent of the American public favoring the bill.[76] Vandenberg correctly saw the implications of what had taken place. "We have said to Britain: '*We will see you through to victory*'—and it would be unbelievably dishonest for us to stop short of full participation in the war if that would be necessary to a British victory."[77]

Within the administration itself, there was at least one dissenter. Admiral Emory Land, chairman of the U.S. Maritime Commission, warned an unappreciative FDR, "If we don't watch our step, we shall find the White House en route to England with the Washington Monument as a steering oar."[78]

Ironically, given the extensive debate, for the rest of 1941 lend-lease was neither outstandingly novel nor notably altruistic. If, for two years, Roosevelt had envisaged the European democracies as America's front line, the supplies were no gift, as repayment was postponed, not waived. Later administration discussions revealed that "consideration" would not necessarily be in money or even in kind; instead, it involved a commitment to the U.S. conception of the postwar world economy. The United States would press Britain into abolishing its commercial system of imperial preference, thereby eliminating discriminatory tariffs against American goods.[79]

In 1941, Britain received no immediate benefit. Only later was the British Commonwealth given some $31 billion in supplies and the Soviet Union some $11 billion. Throughout 1941 lend-lease provided only 1 percent of Britain's munitions total. (Another 7 percent came from the United States under older contracts, which the British paid for in cash.)[80]

The bill did mark a significant turning point. Presidential speech writer Robert E. Sherwood was later reminded of the *Webster's Dictionary* definition of *common-law marriage:* "An agreement between a man and a woman to enter into the marriage relation without ecclesiastical or civil ceremony, such agreement being provable by the writings, declarations, or conduct of the parties."[81] By assuming responsibility for Britain's long-term purchases, Roosevelt relieved the British government of a costly and cumbersome burden and demonstrated his faith in Britain's survival. With that irrevocable commitment, a genuine Anglo-American alliance was forged. The later extension of lend-lease to the Soviet Union was equally significant. Without lend-lease, claim historians Thomas A. Bailey and Paul B. Ryan, "The Russians probably could not have beaten Hitler on their front, at least not as soon as they did."[82]

One need not accept any notion of conspiracy to acknowledge that lend-lease took the country to the edge of the European conflict. Having gambled its wealth on Britain's survival, the United States was not apt to stand by and watch its investment go down if an Axis victory appeared imminent. Historian Warren F. Kimball notes that today few can quarrel with the stated purpose of the bill, though he finds legitimate an objection raised by the anti-interventionists. Because of its long-term implications, "one is still disturbed and even shocked by the lack of candor displayed by the Roosevelt administration during the evolution of its legislation."[83]

While the United States debated lend-lease—indeed, all during the winter of 1941—the British were experiencing major setbacks. Early in the year, such British ports as Plymouth, Southampton, and Clydeside continued to be hit hard. The British suffered in ship tonnage as well, losing 517,000 tons in March. When, early in February, General Erwin Rommel assumed command of the Afrika Korps, the numerically inferior Germans won one engagement after another, leaving the British about as vulnerable as they were when the desert war had started. In Greece, the British were increasingly committing troops to a most risky venture, while at the same time exposing their North African units to Rommel's units. For example, on 6 January 1941, Churchill ordered reinforcements to Greece and, on 4 March, a four-division contingent commanded by General Maitland Wilson left from Egypt. Only one unequivocally bright spot appeared: East Africa, where the British were taking Italian Somaliland, Ethiopia, and Eritrea.

Throughout the winter, many anti-interventionists judged Britain to be in no danger of conquest. Germany supposedly lacked the needed bases from which to launch an assault, much less sufficient gasoline for an all-out air blitz.[84] Furthermore, said Colonel McCormick, Germany possessed a limited amount of ammunition, was unable to transport heavy guns and tanks by air, and would find its paratroopers repulsed by British motorized units.[85] His *Chicago Tribune* was so optimistic that it endorsed Churchill's diversion of General Archibald Wavell's forces to Salonika, claiming that Libya was of scant military importance.[86] In January, the *New York Daily News* had imagined Britain in such dire peril that its government faced transfer to Canada. By mid-March, it found an invasion of England increasingly unlikely, for Britain still controlled the air and had a strong navy.[87] Lincoln Colcord did not rule out a German invasion but had little expectation of its success. Even if Hitler were successful, the resulting occupation would be difficult. "To hold forty million Britishers in subjection," wrote Frederick J. Libby, "is a task too formidable for any British tyrant to attempt, much less a foreigner."[88]

By early 1941, some anti-interventionists were predicting that ultimately Germany could not win the war, thereby concurring with close to a third of the American public.[89] From the Athenians at Syracuse to the Russians in Manchuria, Colonel McCormick noted, "the greatest catastrophes" faced nations embarking on distant military adventures."[90] Besides, Hitler was already overextended. To Senator Wheeler, the great mass of Russian peasants could be kept in subjection, but not such "intelligent people" as the Dutch, Belgians, or French.[91] Norman Thomas thought that the Nazis might not even rule Germany for more than a generation, adding, "Even the terrible Tartar Empires were civilized by China in the end."[92] Even if Hitler did conquer Europe, said the *Christian Century*, he needed raw materials and foodstuffs, which would force him continually to seek new and destructive military ventures. He faced "the eternal Russian threat" on his flank and would find the patrolling of subject populations exhausting.[93]

Suppose, speculated journalist William Henry Chamberlin, Germany continued to dominate Europe. Its rule would remain uneasy. Admittedly, he wrote, a Europe organized under German economic leadership has the potential of being a more productive unit, but so far Hitler's empire had been hopelessly lopsided, oversupplied in men and machines while lacking sufficient foodstuffs and raw materials.[94]

A few analyses were even more upbeat. Senator Bulow saw the end of Hitler in sight. If England could only hold out until July, speculated Castle, Germany might break down. In Hearst's opinion, Britain would actually add to its empire, ending up controlling Iceland, Greenland, a few Pacific islands, the Dutch East Indies, and most of Africa.[95]

To many foes of intervention, Britain was still far from victory. The island nation, argued the *New York Daily News,* could fight Hitler only to a draw. Villard found Britain's Mediterranean and African successes invaluable in bolstering morale, but he saw no possibility of either a continental invasion or an internal collapse within Germany. Neither British victories in Africa nor Greek victories in Albania, said *Uncensored,* could decide the outcome, which could only be resolved in the current air battle over Britain itself. Highly relevant in this regard, however, was an apparent decline in British production, particularly in planes.[96] Colonel Truman Smith, an anti-interventionist who was a member of the military intelligence division of the General Staff, predicted that by early summer, the Reich would launch "a new air-and-land onslaught."[97]

Lawrence Dennis ascribed Britain's early victories in North Africa to inherent weaknesses in Mussolini's regime, not to British prowess. Italy suffered from the same weakness as the U.S. Republican Party: "too many 'nice' but technically useless people in positions of command."[98] Issue after issue of the *Weekly Foreign Letter* centered on the coming British defeat.[99]

Some anti-interventionists found Germany impregnable.[100] Ambassador John Cudahy saw Britain's chances for surviving the spring as "almost nil." "It is a desperate fight," remarked the *New York Daily News,* "and the odds against the British and their friends are heavier than they were in 1914–18." Joseph P. Kennedy estimated that Britain had mobilized one and a half million men under arms, Germany six million. In January 1941, Charles A. Lindbergh had publicly denied that Germany could invade Britain without a previous internal collapse of the Reich. Privately he estimated that the British had only five thousand fighter planes to Germany's twenty-five thousand.[101]

America First continually stressed Britain's precarious position. Late in January, it cited unnamed "high circles" in the U.S. Army who forecast a German air offensive in April involving three to four thousand planes daily. After such "softening," invasion was possible. Britain, it said, had only a 50 percent chance of surviving the summer. By mid-February, the AFC was anticipating a successful joint German-Bulgarian attack on Greece and the subsequent neutralization of Yugoslavia.[102]

A few noninterventionists predicted radical upheaval within Britain itself. Even if it won the war, said John T. Flynn, the ensuing poverty and class struggle would be so great that its ruling aristocracy could well opt for fascism. America would be facing another fascist power, this one owning more land in the Western Hemisphere than did the United States itself.[103] *Social Justice* foresaw "Socialism in its various manifestations—Communism, National Socialism and Fascism," all serving as "a people's defense mechanism against bankruptcy and insolvency in human efforts." Soon Churchill would yield to labor minister Ernest Bevin, who was already Britain's "virtual boss."[104] Lawrence Dennis, more cautious, just predicted increased strikes as class cleavages increased.[105]

Such pessimism was not limited to anti-interventionists alone. In late December 1940, *Life* noted German preparations to invade Britain, quoting Lord Beaverbrook, minister of aircraft production, on the likelihood of it happening before spring. Roosevelt warned Churchill in mid-January 1941 that Britain might be invaded within the month; Germany might seize the Balkans, Ukraine, and Portuguese islands as well.[106] When, in late January, Harry Hopkins went to London as the president's personal representative, he reported that most of the British cabinet, as well as high military figures, believed a German invasion of Britain imminent, though he personally denied it would succeed.[107] Early in February, Hull feared Germany might invade within ninety days.[108] At one point that same month, attaché Raymond Lee did not think invasion could be long delayed.[109]

During this time, anti-interventionist enthusiasm for a negotiated peace remained strong.[110] Vandenberg told *Foreign Correspondent*, a British propaganda weekly, that the United States should guarantee such a settlement provided it met with the approval of the American people. If Hitler refused to negotiate, the U.S. should enter the war.[111] Lindbergh, in testimony before the House Foreign Affairs Committee, said, "I prefer to see neither side win."[112] Any British victory, he maintained, would involve years of war and an invasion of Europe, which in turn would create prostration, famine, and disease throughout the entire continent.[113]

Other reasons were given as well, including anxieties over the Bolshevization of Europe and commercial isolation of Britain.[114] In his plea for negotiation, Castle found England's chances of survival "almost nil." Former diplomat William C. Dennis asserted that peace would free England to do what Lord Lothian had advised long before: desist from further attempts to control the European continent. Libby denied that such a settlement would depend on Hitler's word; rather it rested "on the consent and cooperation of the peoples concerned."[115]

As in the past, several anti-interventionists sought American mediation.[116] The *New York Daily News* and Norman Thomas both mentioned Roosevelt by name.[117] Charles A. Lindbergh would have had the president initiate a move but opposed any subsequent U.S. participation in the proceedings.[118] As in the past, Pope Pius XII was deemed an intermediary.[119]

Certain peace terms were suggested, some modest, some elaborate. If, said Senator Bulow, Britain would announce that it would only destroy Hitlerism—not Germany itself—the Führer's subjects would soon revolt. Methodist missionary E. Stanley Jones spoke of a worldwide cooperative commonwealth, equal access to the world's raw materials, and the redistribution of the world's "land opportunities."[120] The *Christian Century* offered a plethora of items, basically Wilsonian in nature, including the liberation of occupied nations, the outlawry of war, regional federations of nations, and a world league.[121]

Some real optimism existed over the matter.[122] Despite FDR's denunciation of "appeasement," *Uncensored* found Washington grasping the desperateness of Britain's situation; therefore, it claimed, the Roosevelt administration was secretly considering peace negotiations. It quoted Churchill himself as possibly threatening an "uneasy truce" should American aid fail. The *Christian Century* pointed to a variety of peace feelers: an early statement of Lord Tavistock, disclosure of attempted Spanish mediation, and the uproar over oil magnate William Rhodes Davis, who in 1939 had carried a supposed peace proposal from Hermann Goering to FDR. In Churchill's appeal to the Italian people, the Protestant weekly said, he virtually offered a negotiated peace on the single requirement that they get rid of "one man." In fact, Hitler himself had assured the German people that peace would be followed by general disarmament.[123]

Several anti-interventionists held little hope for negotiation.[124] In a radio speech delivered in January, Kennedy accused Germany of rejecting peace.[125] Even Amos Pinchot, who favored the initiative, referred to "Hitler's complete unreliability."[126] In late January 1941, a Gallup poll indicated that 79 percent of the American public wanted Britain to keep on fighting; only 15 percent said it should desist. Moreover, 74 percent predicted any German invasion would fail.[127]

Advice and projections were always easy to come by. It would not be an easy spring.

# 12

# A Troubled Spring

The passage of the lend-lease bill far from alleviated Britain's predicament. Britain remained threatened, particularly on the high seas. Shipping losses amounted to 381,000 tons in April, 436,500 in May, and 415,000 in June. On a single night early in April, Germany sank ten of twenty-two ships in a British convoy. Admiral Harold R. Stark, Roosevelt's chief of naval operations, believed Britain could not last out the year without the United States convoying lend-lease goods at least partly across the Atlantic.[1]

The Committee to Defend America by Aiding the Allies was quick to voice alarm. At the current rate of sinkings, the CDAAA noted in mid-March, one-third of the tonnage currently engaged in supplying the British Isles would be lost. Either more ships should be provided to Britain, or U.S. craft must guard the lifeline.[2] In the latter case, it argued, Germany would not declare war, for such action would only increase American aid to its enemies and permit the United States to strike at Hitler's Reich directly.[3]

By mid-May, the CDAAA was stressing that such setbacks not only weakened the British Isles but also affected its offensive capacity on other battle-fronts.[4] If June and July brought a slight reduction in the sinkings, the CDAAA noted quite accurately that the Battle of the Atlantic was far from won. The urgency of the convoy issue was real.[5]

Given the increasing demand for convoys, the president's critics became understandably uneasy.[6] Much of the daily press, including some major interventionist newspapers, pointed to rumors concerning the matter.[7] A number of anticonvoy resolutions were proposed in Congress, the most publicized effort being led by Senator Charles W. Tobey.[8] The New Hampshire Republican received letters from American naval personnel who said they had already been assigned to convoy duty.[9] After much discussion, on 30 April, the Senate Foreign Relations Committee tabled Tobey's bill committee thirteen to nine.[10]

Yet, for Roosevelt's adversaries, such anxieties were only compounded when, on 10 April, the president announced an agreement with the Danish government permitting the United States to occupy Greenland for defensive purposes. In his press conference, FDR invoked the Monroe Doctrine.[11] The Danish minister in Washington, Henrik de Kauffmann, lacked the authority to make such an agreement, which was disavowed by the Nazi-dominated government at home.

For the U.S., the action was unprecedented and ran counter to conventional international procedure. But no matter. Assistant Secretary Adolf A. Berle articulated administration views when he warned that hostile planes from Greenland could strike at New York. Conversely, in friendly hands, Berle found the island invaluable; it expedited the delivery of short-range aircraft to Britain and its weather stations were essential to later bombing raids on Germany.[12] By August, close to 80 percent of *Fortune* poll respondents favored its defense by U.S. armed forces.[13]

Certain anti-interventionists criticized the Greenland arrangement, arguing that the move inevitably brought the war closer to the United States. *Uncensored* endorsed the agreement while fearing the measure would expedite American convoys. Such naval operations, the newsletter continued, were an open invitation for armed clash, particularly as Hitler had declared the waters between Greenland and Iceland to be in the zone of his own blockade.[14]

Others expressed little anxiety.[15] Hearst's *San Francisco Examiner* adjudged Greenland an area of little military value but denied that occupation would bring the U.S. closer to war. The *New York Daily News* backed FDR's move, finding it preferable for the United States, not Germany, to have its "hooks" there. Greenland, it continued, stood only about a thousand miles from Maine and was within easy bombing distances of new American bases in Newfoundland. Conversely, military writers Fleming MacLiesh and Cushman Reynolds saw little at stake: Greenland's anchorage would be untenable for any power not already controlling the seas; Cape Farewell lay within the radius of an American fleet operating from Boston; U.S. Coast Guard cutters, patrol planes, and submarines could offer ample protection.[16]

On 11 April, Roosevelt infuriated his opponents when he issued a proclamation removing the Red Sea from combat zone status, thereby permitting American shipping there. By mid-May, twenty-seven American merchant ships were en route to the area, laden with supplies for British troops in Africa and the Middle East. Senator Wheeler found the policy "asinine," as it might force the United States to fight single-handedly in all parts of the world.[17]

Then, scarcely over a week later, Roosevelt established a "neutrality patrol" in the western Atlantic, though he lacked the ships to make it effective. By flashing locations of German U-boats, the patrol would alert British merchantmen to veer away while inviting British cruisers and destroyers to attack. The U.S. neutrality or security zone reached as far as twenty-six degrees west longitude; it included all of Greenland plus the Azores, what historian Waldo Heinrichs calls "the great basin of the North Atlantic."[18] Since this vast expanse overlapped a German combat zone proclaimed on 25 March, an eventual clash appeared inevitable.[19]

In a press conference held on 25 April, FDR tried to minimize the move by distinguishing between a "patrol," which was limited to scouting, and an "escort," which offered the possibility of actual combat. U.S. patrols, he continued, would be sent "as far on the waters of the seven seas as may be necessary for the defense of the American Hemisphere."[20] Four days later, at another press conference, FDR claimed to possess the legal authority to send American warships into combat zones, although, he continued, he might not take such action. By early June, *Newsweek* reported that 52 percent of those polled favored convoys; only 41 percent opposed them.[21]

At best, so administration foes found, the president had acted provocatively.[22] To Herbert Hoover, either convoys or patrols would mean "joining in this war, once and for all," with the consequence of less—not more—aid for the British.[23]

Some critics raised logistical factors. Villard noted that in convoy travel, the faster ships were held down to the speed of the slower, which was usually about ten or eleven knots, and therefore stood prey to German submarines and Stuka dive-bombers. Unless convoys were protected by interceptor planes, argued the AFC, long-range bombers and submarines would continue to sink them. Those interventionists requesting convoys should ask for planes instead. To guarantee the safety of all trans-Atlantic cargoes, said *Uncensored*, a large part of the American fleet would have to move from the Pacific, which meant scrapping existing Far Eastern policy.[24]

Unloading too was deemed a critical factor.[25] A considerable percentage of U.S. munitions, Taft noted, was destroyed after it had arrived in Britain, for docks and warehouses experienced continual bombardment.[26]

All this time, anti-interventionists denied that American convoys were needed. If, advised the *Chicago Tribune*, Britain moved naval units from the Mediterranean—where it had just won some victories—to the Atlantic, it could protect those ships carrying American munitions. On 7 May, Vandenberg cited a letter from Admiral Emory S. Land, chairman of the United States Maritime Commission. According to Land, of the 158 British vessels sunk in all parts of the world between 1 January and 30 April 1941, only twelve were cleared from U.S. ports, and eight were bound for Britain.[27] Headlined a *Christian Century* editorial, "Admiral Land Lets the Cat Out of the Bag."[28]

Land, obviously embarrassed by the use of his material by the anti-interventionists, soon retorted, "There is reason to believe that actual losses run substantially greater than reported losses."[29] The British themselves stated they had suffered major losses in April, that Vandenberg's figures were incorrect, and that even if convoys protected munitions, ships carrying steel and food remained exposed to U-boats.[30]

The matter of economic competition was also raised.[31] Why, it was asked, did Britain need American convoys when its ships remained engaged in profitable—and competitive—trade? Congressman Philip A. Bennett (Rep.-Mo.) pointed to the sale of Scottish, English, and Irish liquors.[32] Shafer noted British soaps, china, earthenware, clothing materials, and tobacco. Britain, he warned, was "embarking on a trade-war program that may eventually crush the United States economically."[33]

In April, Roosevelt also sought congressional authority to purchase or lease some eighty-three European ships lying idle in New York harbors. Involved were one Belgian ship, thirty-six Danish, fourteen French, two Estonian, one Lithuanian, one Rumanian—and two German and twenty-six Italian—some half a million tons in all. Congressman Schuyler O. Bland (Dem.-Va.), who introduced the bill in the House, asserted that almost every nation was willing to turn the ships over to the United States. Furthermore, the German and Italian ships, the only craft creating controversy, belonged to the U.S. by reason of forfeiture.[34]

Anti-interventionists raised various arguments against the bill, many centering on the status of the German and Italian craft.[35] Fish called the move "the grossest breach of international law in history."[36] According to Vorys, the United States had violated "the ancient law and right of sanctuary."[37] Borchard denied any right to seizure unless sabotage was an issue. Ironically, he went on, sabotage only became relevant when it was possible that the U.S. would illegally seize the ships.[38] Congressman Leo Allen (Rep.-Ill.) warned of retaliation: Germany or Italy might seize the property of American citizens, even perhaps the U.S. embassy in Greece.[39] Opponents feared, above all, that the United States would turn the confiscated ships over to the British, a matter on which Congressman Bland hedged.[40]

Vandenberg was particularly outspoken, labeling the move a "provocative step toward war." The British themselves, he argued, had refused to recognize the right of temporary seizure when the government of Chile seized three interned Danish vessels. In fact, they threatened to capture the craft at sea.[41]

Such aid to Britain, FDR critics further maintained, was not needed. In light of the many ships the United States was providing to the British, the twenty-six Italian and two German ships represented "only a drop in the bucket." The U.S. itself had the greater need.[42] On 7 May, however, the bill passed the House and on the 15th the Senate.[43]

On 27 May 1941, FDR gave a major address in which he asserted that the European war centered on nothing less than Hitler's drive for world domination. He warned against German control of certain areas, among them Iceland, Greenland, Labrador, Dakar, the Cape Verdes, and the Azores. Reasserting "the ancient American doctrine of freedom of the seas" and noting that American patrols were helping ensure the delivery of war goods to the British, he proclaimed an "unlimited national emergency."[44]

As yet, FDR was most vague. In a subsequent press conference, he specifically denied he sought amendment, much less repeal, of the 1939 neutrality act. He denied contemplating any immediate executive orders that would use any of the broad powers conferred on him by the proclamation.[45] "He was trusting to luck," scholar James MacGregor Burns writes, "to his long-tested flair for timing, and to the fortunes of war. He had no plans."[46] Comments Roosevelt scholar Frank Freidel, "Just what the proclamation might mean no one knew."[47]

Some anti-interventionists were optimistic concerning the president's address. The AFC, for example, expressed relief that FDR had "resisted the war-makers" and later took credit for his relative mildness.[48] Still, some apprehension remained.[49] Congressman Roy O. Woodruff (Rep.-Mich.) labeled the speech "a declaration of undeclared war."[50]

No administration opponent was pleased with FDR's invocation of freedom of the seas. To the AFC research bureau, the president was seeking to aid one belligerent without danger of interference by the other. If American ships transported contraband, obviously German ships would attempt to stop them, as accepted rules of international law so provided. U.S. craft could not even claim exemption from visit and search, much less capture.[51] *Uncensored* called the whole concept of freedom of the seas a chimera, for it existed on the sufferance of whatever power controlled the particular seas in question. Congressman Bennett compared the United States policy to "the position of a citizen who insists upon exercising his right of freedom of streets regardless of how many bullets are flying across them." Britain itself, maintained Senator Nye, had never sought freedom of the seas; it wanted "dominance and sovereignty over them."[52]

The anti-interventionists had reason to be suspicious of Roosevelt's moves. From late March through May, the president told such intimates as Harold Ickes and Henry Morgenthau that he hoped an incident on the high seas might result in providing convoys or possibly even a state of war with Germany.[53]

The Atlantic was not the only focus of anti-interventionist attention, nor was Roosevelt the only American leader under scrutiny. Events in the Balkans aroused anxiety as did the activities there of Colonel William J. ("Wild Bill") Donovan. Donovan was a flamboyant figure, having been a hero in World War I, federal prosecutor in the 1920s, and prominent New York State Republican leader. In late 1940 and early 1941, Donovan undertook a secret mission to southeastern Europe and the eastern Mediterranean. His assignment: to report on the strategic situation to both Roosevelt and Churchill. From 23 to 25 January 1941, he met in Belgrade with leading Yugoslav officials. At a luncheon with Prince Regent Paul, Donovan hinted that Yugoslavia would receive American aid if the neutral ruler chose to fight the Germans. The prince, influenced by his pro-German wife, ignored the hint. After lunch, Donovan visited General Dušan Simović, commander of the Yugoslav air force and a strong foe of Germany, showing Simović a telegram signed by Roosevelt also hinting at U.S. support.[54]

On 25 March, Prince Paul joined the Axis by signing the tripartite pact. Four days later, as four British divisions established a beachhead in Greece, Simović overthrew Prince Paul and his government, renounced the treaty with Germany, and placed the young king, Peter II, on the throne. On 6 April, Germany attacked both Yugoslavia and Greece. By mid-month, the greater part of Yugoslavia had been conquered; both the king and Simović had fled. On 27 April, the Germans entered Athens, and within a day the British had evacuated Greece itself. The German attack on Crete began on 20 May, ending in conquest on 1 June. Roosevelt himself thought that Britain might lose the Mediterranean.[55]

Demaree Bess, foreign correspondent for the *Saturday Evening Post* and an anti-interventionist, soon blamed the 29 March coup and Yugoslavia's subsequent fate on direct U.S. involvement. "Our representatives," he said, "made commitments for us which virtually established a new American frontier on the Danube." Donovan had assured the Yugoslavs that the United States would guarantee that they came out on the winning side, a pledge—wrote Bess—that could only be fulfilled by all-out war against Germany. American ambassador Arthur Bliss Lane also met with Bess's scorn, for he supposedly had worked tirelessly to undermine Paul's pro-German diplomacy.[56]

Some FDR foes quickly turned Bess's article into another indictment against the president.[57] Others were slightly cautious about his account.[58] If the *Post* was reliable, claimed *Uncensored*, the United States had engaged in "a quixotic but dangerous attempt to play a hand in a deadly serious game without any particular cards to turn over in the showdown."[59] Certainly anti-interventionists shared a unanimous sentiment that the U.S. bore heavy responsibility for Yugoslavia's fall. In Fish's words, the United States had encouraged it "to fight the mighty Nazi armies without our raising a finger to help them."[60]

To a lesser extent, Donovan was also attacked for giving similar assurances to Bulgaria, which joined the tripartite pact on 1 March 1941 and opened its borders to German troops the same day.[61] Frank Hanighen accused Roosevelt's troubleshooter of attempting an abortive countercoup in Iraq, designed to overthrow the pro-Nazi regime there.[62] Even the colonel's past record met with strong attack. He was accused of hindering the Teapot Dome investigation of 1923–24 and the work of Nye's probing of the munitions industry during the mid-1930s.[63]

In reality, Donovan's critics had misperceived the issue. It was the British, not "Wild Bill" and the United States, who had taken the initiative in encouraging Balkan resistance to Hitler. They assumed that their own forces in the Middle East could operate successfully in that region and perhaps encourage a resistance that might make Turkey an active ally. The U.S. played only a limited role.[64]

The Balkans imbroglio led anti-interventionists to a wider point, the fact that none of the nations there were democracies. *Social Justice*, itself a defender of fascist regimes, was outspoken. Attacking the Orthodox Serbs' treatment of the Roman Catholic Croatians, it called Yugoslavia "a totalitarian gangster in the worst sense of the term," which—in proportion to population—could well have been "the scene of more racial persecution, more mass murder and arrests and more mass terrorism" than any other country in Europe. Turning to Greece, Father Coughlin's weekly spoke in terms of a one-party system, muzzled press, and concentration camps.[65]

More moderate anti-interventionists, too, stressed the lack of Greek democracy. "The Greeks don't even want self-government," flippantly remarked Samuel B. Pettengill, columnist and former Democratic congressman from Indiana. "They crave a domestic yoke." The *Christian Century* indicted Rumania on similar grounds, finding it a land riddled with anti-Semitism, "reeking" of political corruption, and possessing a "heartless landlord system" that "exploited a helpless peasantry."[66]

Several noninterventionists found German conquest of the Balkans inevitable. Even before the German successes, Hoover had predicted that the Nazis would overrun Yugoslavia and Greece. To Lawrence Dennis, such small nations faced the dilemma of becoming either "economic provinces of a Greater Germany or else satellites of Russia."[67]

At the same time, some asserted, the Balkans might well be strategically irrelevant. The *Chicago Tribune* called Greece a sideshow, of little value to either belligerent. Even the Dardanelles, argued the *New York Daily News*, was overrated, its possession bestowing neither oil nor food. Similarly, if Hitler seized Suez and Gibraltar, he would experience stalemate unless he could either starve or invade Britain itself.[68]

Not all reactions were so sanguine.[69] Castle thought that the expulsion of British forces from Greece might force it to seek a peace.[70] Commenting on the fall of Crete, the *Chicago Tribune* asked, "Is Egypt Next?"[71]

All during this time, the gaze of the anti-interventionists went beyond the Atlantic and the Balkan mainland. During the spring of 1941, several continued to stress German weakness. Hitler's Reich, said Congressman Mundt, could not win so long as the British Isles and its navy withstood attack. The *New York Daily News* called one British naval victory off Cape Matapan, Greece, late in March the blackest day the Axis had yet experienced; the engagement promised to rank with Aboukir, Trafalgar, and possibly Jutland.[72]

At times a longer view was taken. Anne Morrow Lindbergh wrote, "Prosperity is not a flower which grows from oppression." Wheeler predicted that Nazi rule was bound to fail, for Europe's diverse nationalities and religious groups would prove too troublesome.[73] If Germany did win, forecast the *New York Daily News*, Hitler would soon die, as "he will have run his race and spent all his creative force." At that point, the Nazi leaders would fight among themselves, destroying their new United States of Europe in the process.[74]

Far more noninterventionists saw Britain itself as being in serious trouble. On 8 April, a raid on Coventry marked the end of a temporary bombing lull. From 16 to 19 April, London was hit, creating over two thousand fatalities and striking 148,000 homes. The night of 10–11 May, the last night of the blitz, saw the heaviest attack of all: 1,436 were killed, 1,792 seriously injured, and one-third of the streets rendered impassable.

One gloomy comment followed another. Late in April, *Uncensored* noted British plane production falling far behind Germany's; it cited a report that the Germans were fitting out heavily armored four-motor planes so as to bomb Britain from nearby French bases. Britain, the *Chicago Tribune* said in mid-May, was suffering twenty-five times as much as the Germans. AFC staffer Ruth Sarles asserted that "official quarters" in Washington, including the visiting air force chief General Hap Arnold, found Britain in "a very bad way." Liverpool remained the only effective port, pilots in training lacked air space, and shaken morale had weakened production.[75]

To many such people, it appeared Britain could well go under.[76] In April, Senator Nye judged victory odds to favor the Axis. Continued ship sinkings, feared Hanson Baldwin, would cause Britain to fall. Certainly, he maintained, the British could not defeat the Nazis without full participation of the American army and air force.[77] A month later, General Wood predicted German domination of the Mediterranean areas, including Gibraltar, Malta, and Egypt. Hitler would probably get "what he wants" in Europe but would not be able to destroy the British Empire.[78] Libby thought the war was in its last stages, for in every category—manpower, air strength, food, equipment—Britain was hopelessly outclassed.[79] Not surprisingly, Lawrence Dennis's *Weekly Foreign Letter* and Father Coughlin's *Social Justice* kept stressing British defeat.[80]

Early in April, Herbert Hoover appeared the most pessimistic of all. Though forecasting that the British would drive the Italians out of all Africa, thereby securing naval control of the Mediterranean, he thought the Germans might try to invade Britain within six months. Conversely, the British lacked sufficient planes to crack German morale. By mid-May, the former president did express some hope, enough to keep endorsing American military aid. While opposing convoys, he called for continuing the sending of tanks, munitions, food, merchant ships, and bombers.[81]

Such anxieties were echoed within the Roosevelt administration itself. Until early June, American leaders thought German activity in the Atlantic presaged either an invasion of the British Isles or moves against such an Atlantic outpost as Gibraltar.[82] Furthermore, an official report from American military intelligence greatly exaggerated Luftwaffe strength, finding it to possess eleven thousand front-line combat planes when in reality Germany had just over three thousand bombers and fighters.[83] According to Harold Ickes, "the best military opinion" saw the British as having difficulty remaining in North Africa. By the end of May, not only did the interior secretary share this fear himself but he also spoke of German domination of Gibraltar, Portugal, and Spain. The interventionist *Life* showed pictures of a possible German invasion of Britain. In April, however, a Gallup poll found 50 percent predicting a British victory; in May, 55 percent.[84]

Until early summer, FDR took few initiatives. The president felt constrained by public opinion, lacked the warships needed to intervene decisively on the Atlantic, and feared a Japanese advance in Southeast Asia. In addition, he was unclear as to where Hitler would move next: the Near East, Morocco, Dakar, or the Soviet Union. He had still to be assured that the United States and Britain shared common peace aims.[85]

During the spring of 1941, anti-interventionists continued to back a negotiated peace.[86] In so doing, a few refused outright to endorse a British victory, thereby taking the position always maintained by Charles Lindbergh. Nye hoped both sides would become economically and physically exhausted, for only then could one secure a lasting settlement. If Hitler lost, commented Philip La Follette, the Germans would have to overturn him. "In fifteen years," he continued in referring to the war, "it will not matter who won this struggle."[87]

In any such negotiation, it was argued, Britain would not fare that badly. "England has been offered a peace which would respect and insure the integrity of the British Empire," Hearst wrote; Churchill should realize that never, in its entire history, had his nation ever conquered Europe. If, remarked General Wood, Britain could secure terms by which it kept its navy, its independence, and most of its colonies, it should seek terms at once.[88]

Somewhat less upbeat, the *New York Daily News* conceded that such a settlement would invariably result in an armed truce, with Hitler initially dominant in Europe, the Soviet Union and Japan sharing most of Asia, the United

States remaining supreme in the Western Hemisphere, and Britain possibly keeping all of its present empire. But, the *News* continued, except for the four hundred years of Pax Romana, most of recorded history showed peace to be a mere interval between wars. If the current conflict persisted long enough, "we shall all sink together into communism or a new dark age."[89]

The spring of 1941 marked their height of optimism concerning such negotiation.[90] Some signs appeared particularly auspicious. In late May, Wheeler and the *New York Daily News* reported on the Paris press communicating Hitler's desire that FDR mediate the conflict.[91] Early in June, Senator Tom Connally said that peace talks were in progress. "As far as we are concerned," said the Texas Democrat, "if England keeps her independence and her navy, that is all we can ask. It is their war, after all."[92] When John Winant, who had replaced Kennedy as U.S. ambassador to Britain that February, returned to Washington for consultations, a few anti-interventionists incorrectly suspected that he brought German peace terms with him.[93]

Heightening all such speculation was the flight, made on 10 May 1941, of Rudolph Hess to Britain.[94] The deputy Führer, acting without Hitler's backing, was involved in an effort to initiate peace talks just a little over a month prior to Germany's attack on the Soviet Union.[95]

Some anti-interventionists saw the flight marking an official German bid. *Uncensored* thought Hess had brought peace terms to Churchill. Herbert Hoover thought the flier had offered Britain an alliance against Russia. Supposedly, said Hoover, Churchill had been greatly impressed, but FDR denied that any Hitler terms could be trusted. To the communist *Daily Worker*, the flight showed both Britain and Germany fearing that the war was terminating the entire capitalist order.[96] Historian Will Durant suggested Hess had proposed German withdrawal from the Scandinavian countries and occupied countries of Western Europe in return for domination of the Ukraine.[97]

Others were more cynical concerning any peace prospects. The *Christian Century* believed that the deputy Führer was so outraged over the prospect of German-Soviet partnership that he had broken with Hitler.[98] Soon the Protestant journal said, "Hess was in an abnormal mental condition. Who among the German leaders is not?"[99] *America* suspected that he was the victim of a Nazi purge. Similarly, Dennis wrote, "Hess's case is simply that of a bewildered and naive idealist in revolt against the new Nazi Russo-German policy which ran counter to all he held dear in the Nazi program."[100] The *New York Daily News* did not rule out the possibility that he might be a decoy, giving the British phony secrets.[101] *New Masses* featured an article asserting that the flight might have been made with Hitler's knowledge. As Nazi rule was shaky, with extreme dissatisfaction existing among the German masses, it said, Hess fled like "a rat leaving a sinking ship."[102]

All this time, pacifists were extremely busy. In May, Charles Boss, executive secretary of the Methodist Commission for World Peace, organized the Ministers' No War Committee, with himself as executive secretary and Albert W. Palmer, president of Chicago Theological Seminary, as chairman. Boasting a membership of twelve hundred, it announced a nationwide series of programs, featuring such prominent clergy as E. Stanley Jones, Harry Emerson Fosdick, and George Buttrick. On 9–10 May, the group launched the Churchman's Campaign for Peace Through Mediation. Jones, a prominent missionary, served as a major organizer. Five-sixths of the FOR attended the organizing session, and the *Christian Century*'s Charles Clayton Morrison gave it full backing. In June, the American Friends Service Committee called for a general peace based on universal disarmament and international organization.[103]

In Congress several anti-interventionists made concrete proposals. In May, Congressman Jerry Voorhis (Dem.-Calif.) introduced a resolution requesting that a conference of parliamentary bodies draw up a basis for a lasting settlement.[104] Congressman Rudolph G. Terenowitz called for immediate action by the Congress, acting with the legislatures of other nations, to bring about the cessation of hostilities and the organization of peace.[105]

One of the more publicized efforts came from Congressman John M. Vorys, who late in April advocated "an American peace offensive."[106] The United States, he said, should state its postwar peace aims, call for an immediate armistice, and offer to mediate. The ensuing negotiations would not be dictated by a single power but would lead to a free European commonwealth. If Hitler refused equitable terms, Vorys continued, he would lose his following among his own people, whose wartime losses had made them genuine peace partisans. True, the German leader might not be trustworthy, but terms could be enforced by economic retaliation, impounding arms on both sides, and joint or international control of strategic positions. In addition, the promise of food, money, and matériel could be used to keep the peace.[107]

Others, too, sought American initiative, with some mentioning Roosevelt or Pius XII by name.[108] For example, on 20 May, Mundt suggested that FDR call a mediation conference of neutral powers.[109] Even the communists promoted a negotiated peace. Late in May, Mike Gold, novelist and *Daily Worker* columnist, endorsed the terms outlined by Sidney Bradshaw Fay. The Harvard historian opposed large reparations and the division of Germany into small units while calling for a federation of European states and the restoration of all nations conquered by Hitler.[110]

Several noninterventionists supported semiofficial peace agendas. Among the more popular were the five points of Secretary of State Cordell Hull, outlined in a broadcast delivered on 18 May. The secretary proposed his favorite panacea: a postwar reconstruction program that included (1) an end to excessive trade restrictions; and (2) nondiscrimination in commercial relations; (3) equal availability of raw materials to all nations; (4) protection of consuming countries and their people; and (5) loans conducive to trade. Congressman Louis Ludlow introduced a House resolution in which the president, backed by the twenty-one American republics, would offer Hull's five points as the tentative basis for stopping the war. A mediation movement, he maintained, might gain tremendous momentum. Congressman Mundt endorsed Hull's five peace proposals but added a few more of his own: a clearinghouse to settle controversies, revitalization of the League of Nations, and expansion of Clarence Streit's Union Now to include all nations. If preliminary discussion so warranted, direct invitations could be sent to Germany and Britain.[111]

Occasionally personal agendas were offered. Sterling Morton's included the restoration of Norway; a buffer state in the Low Countries; a "semi-independent" France that would accept the loss of Alsace-Lorraine; German domination of the Balkans, either by straight annexation or the creation of buffer states; a German interest in the Suez Canal; German hegemony over Italy and its colonies; and British retention of territorial gains made in Abyssinia. Within two years, Britain could increase the strength of its island fortress, making it practically impregnable, while the United States could complete its two-ocean navy, develop a massive merchant marine, and train several million more men. The socialist *Call* spoke in terms of British independence, retention of much of the British Empire, loss of former German colonies and the Mediterranean, and joint German-British control over the Suez Canal.[112]

In his "national emergency" speech of 27 May 1941, Roosevelt again stressed his opposition to negotiated peace. In such bargaining, he said, "Germany would literally parcel out the world—hoisting the swastika itself over vast territories and populations and setting up puppet governments of its own choosing, wholly subject to the will and the policy of a conqueror."[113] Gallup polls, moreover, usually showed strong public disapproval, revealing a faith that the British would pull through. In early May, a Gallup poll found 62 percent preferring U.S. entry into the war to Britain's surrender.[114]

Even when the fate of Britain appeared most precarious, however, a good many of the more vocal anti-interventionists sought to discredit its cause. Here the rhetoric was at its most impassioned.

# 13

# Great Britain: An Unfit Ally

While Britain's fate remained in doubt, many noninterventionists expressed strong sympathy for the beleaguered nation.[1] The *Chicago Tribune*, undoubtedly aware of its reputation as an Anglophobe journal, specifically denied any hostility. England, it said, had followed the United States far on the road to self-government and freedom. In August 1940, Norman Thomas expressed hope that the British would stave off the Nazi invasion. The U.S., he continued, should not reimpose an embargo on Britain or cease purchasing its gold. In the same month, the *New York Daily News* supported Churchill when he spoke in Commons of the intertwining of American-British interests.[2] That April Charles A. Lindbergh had told an America First rally, "It will be a tragedy for the entire world if the British Empire collapses." In May 1940, William Randolph Hearst ordered E. D. Coblentz, supervisor of his chain's editorial division, to kill any editorials unfriendly to England. Just less than a year later, Hearst reprinted an address he had given in 1927 in which he advocated a guarantee of mutual support with Britain to maintain the peace of the world.[3]

Administration critics, however, fully realized that popular sympathy for Britain could result in the consequence they most feared: full-scale entry into the war.[4] Hence, it was to their interest, and they fully realized it, to "balance" positive accounts of Britain's leadership, diplomacy, and heritage with negative ones, doing so in the hopes that such "modification" would create a more cautious foreign policy. The great outburst of philanthropic and media support, manifested in such varied ways as the Bundles for Britain relief program and such films as *A Yank in the R.A.F.* (1941), irritated some anti-interventionists. Even Anne Morrow Lindbergh, far from unsympathetic to the British war effort, reacted negatively to "the smart women wearing British lions conspicuously on their bosoms."[5] Furthermore, within the opposition camp, there existed bitterly anti-British individuals who became almost livid on the subject of "perfidious Albion."

At all times, concern over British manipulation existed.[6] To Harry Elmer Barnes, speaking in May 1940, "Great Britain is our most dangerous enemy today, because we are 'suckers' for her propaganda."[7] Often cited was a 1938 exposé by former British intelligence officer Sidney Rogerson, *Propaganda and the Next War.*[8]

The more-strident Anglophobes found the British peril to be extremely serious. Two authors held such pronounced views that the bulk of their comments involved a veritable indictment of that nation. First was novelist Theodore Dreiser, who had become increasingly procommunist, although not yet a party member. In his book *America Is Worth Saving* (1941), he offered a leftist interpretation, denouncing an "International of Privilege," interpreting the war as a frenzied struggle for world markets, stressing America's domestic poverty, and praising Soviet society. He continually returned to the crimes of Britain and its empire, which he presented as the greatest evil facing the world. Indeed, the United States had long been "England's first enemy."[9]

Equally anti-British was Porter Sargent's *Getting US into War* (1941), a compilation of weekly bulletins "exposing" British propaganda that circulated primarily to private school and university leaders. Publisher of the annual *Handbook of Private Schools,* a standard reference work, Sargent was a Harvard-educated Bostonian who, without sharing Dreiser's domestic politics, saw the world's ills rooted in British perfidy.[10] A host of noninterventionists endorsed the bulletins.[11] The book received similar praise.[12]

The United States itself, so some pugnacious critics maintained, was actually subservient to Britain.[13] To H. L. Mencken, the U.S. was serving as "the client and goon" of its traditional enemy, "acting precisely like a English colony."[14] The *Chicago Tribune* accused American "colonials" of believing, even more than the Canadians, that it was their duty to assist Britain.[15] If, said John Bassett Moore, the United States sought to participate in all wars waged by Britain, it would be more sensible to "add ourselves to the number of self-governing dominions under the British crown."[16] In November 1940 Senator Homer Bone (Dem.-Wash.) observed that relations with Britain were becoming so tight that he snidely endorsed a Society for the Promotion of Dominion Status for the United States. The *New York Daily News* assailed the Roosevelt administration for seeking to preserve the British Empire, just as Wilson had supposedly done earlier. By September 1941, it proclaimed the United States "unofficially a part of the British Empire," a situation that, it said, had existed since the Spanish-American War. That November, John Haynes Holmes asserted: "This is evidently a war to make the world safe for the British Empire, and U.S.A. is evidently expected to do the job!"[17]

To such extremists, Britain remained fundamentally hostile to the United States, said enmity being long-standing.[18] To Senator Sheridan Downey, for example, Britain had threatened the safety of the United States more than any other country; by contrast, Germany had never sought to interfere with American rights. Not only, said journalist Carleton Beals, had Britain's monopolistic system held most of the world in bondage but thanks to it, the U.S. "has long seen its own economy warped, distorted, depressed, its property endangered, the national defense weakened."[19]

Asked Porter Sargent, "Has any other country ever landed one uniformed soldier in North America?" Senator Holt also listed Britain as the only nation that ever sought to invade the United States. Going further back, *Social Justice* added that during the War of 1812, Britain had committed atrocities on the women and children of Hampton, Virginia.[20] Other British misdeeds included attempted suppression of the American Revolution, opposition to the Monroe Doctrine, and support of the Confederacy.[21]

World War I provided a prime example of British deception.[22] Said Congressman Sweeney, Britain "took our blood and our money in the last war and left us holding the bag."[23] Wheeler quoted from Churchill's *The Aftermath* (1929) to show Lloyd George's resistance to Wilson's peace effort.[24]

After the war, according to the more Anglophobic among the anti-interventionists, Britain still treated the United States poorly. Dreiser wrote of efforts to exclude the U.S. from newly opened oil fields in the Middle East. During the Washington Naval Conference of 1921–22, argued Senator Dennis Chavez, "we scrapped battleships while Britain threw away a few blue prints." In discussing the Manchurian crisis of 1931–33, Barnes accused British foreign minister Sir John Simon of leaving Secretary of State Henry L. Stimson "out on a limb." Similarly, Senator La Follette blamed Britain for not cooperating with American efforts to restrain Italian aggression in Ethiopia. It was British pressure during the Spanish Civil War, commented Barnes, that, more than anything else, kept the United States from sending supplies to Loyalist Spain.[25]

Britain supposedly presented a trade threat as well. Even when war began, Britain's foes continued indictments of commercial hostility that had been made since the twenties, if not before.[26] In March 1939, several anti-interventionists argued, Britain had sought again to edge the United States out of world commerce.[27] At that time an agreement was made at Düsseldorf in which the Federation of British Industries and the Reichgruppe Industries concurred in sharing certain overseas markets. Furthermore, the two powers would, in the words of the text, be "eliminating undesirable competition" and "taking concrete steps to increase world consumption of the products in which German and British industries are interested."[28] Norman Thomas saw the arrangement as an effort to use state-subsidized trade to capture U.S. customers in South America. Senator Charles Tobey called it "a British-Nazi conspiracy to enter into a trade-pooling agreement for the purpose of fleecing us of our South American trade." Philip La Follette even cited *The Economist* [London], which stated that the Federation of British Industries "contemplates seeking British Government subsidies to help German trade against America."[29]

Düsseldorf was just one example. In December 1939, *Uncensored* faulted the administration for maintaining a price of $35 for an ounce of gold, thereby giving British importers competitive advantage in the world market. In March 1940, William Philip Simms, Scripps-Howard foreign editor, noted that the British had ordered all their exporters—when selling such items as rubber, tin, jute, and whiskey—to demand payment in dollars. Such a practice, alleged Senator Reynolds, had made "England the master of international commerce, and at the expense of the United States"; he called for immediate retaliation.[30]

Indeed, said some antagonists, the British were stealing from the United States at the very time that America was sacrificing to aid their war effort. In March 1940, Fish accused them of "monopolizing the markets of the world," in particular by destroying the cotton markets of the American South and replacing them with Egyptian cotton.[31] Latin America was a particular sore point.[32] Congressman Frances Case (Rep.-S.Dak.), speaking in November 1941, remarked that every dock in Central and South America was piled high with boxes labeled "Britain delivers the goods."[33]

Lend-lease simply made the situation worse.[34] Noting British sales of such items as bicycles and shoes, in September 1941 the *Chicago Tribune* challenged Roosevelt's claim that materials supplied to the British did not compete with U.S. exports.[35] Senator Nye claimed that British manufacturers were molding American lend-lease steel into machines that they would sell back to the United States and to South American republics. Congressman Robert F. Jones (Rep.-Ohio) warned against industrial espionage. The British, he said, "are in every airplane factory, in every tank factory, in every ordinance plant, in every engine plant."[36]

Neither the state department nor the staff of lend-lease administrator Harry Hopkins could find much to substantiate these allegations. To meet such charges, however, they forced the British in mid-September to promise that American lend-lease goods would not be reexported. Even goods similar to those provided in the lend-lease program would not be permitted to enter new markets at the expense of U.S. merchants. By such means, American manufacturers supplanted Britain in many markets, particularly in Latin America.[37]

British control of major natural resources remained another sore point. In February 1941, Wheeler found the empire to possess a virtual monopoly of many such items. A month later, the *Chicago Tribune* protested against what it saw as artificially high prices for rubber, diamonds, and cocoa. The *Tribune* singled out tin for special attention, in the process blaming the state department for being overly solicitous in failing to challenge British control.[38]

Besides, so such anti-interventionists reasoned, the British were not simply stealing American trade and monopolizing resources—they were making inroads on American shipping, doing so just as the American merchant marine was declining.[39] In February 1941, *Uncensored* noted that Britain had requisitioned ships of occupied countries, thereby assuming control of 45 percent of the world's ocean tonnage. Moreover, it had sent increasing numbers of ships to trade routes far removed from belligerent waters, in the process threatening U.S. commercial prospects.[40]

The end of the war implied even greater commercial conflict.[41] The United States, warned pacifist leader A. J. Muste, was already saving its newest ships for this rivalry. Sometimes a noninterventionist acknowledged that postwar Britain needed to remain economically aggressive. If it defeated Germany, Senator La Follette predicted, it would be forced to exercise its control of world trade to preserve its nation and empire. Charles A. Lindbergh, hearing that the British feared the competition of Pan American Airlines in Africa, wrote in his diary, "After all, they have got to live *after* the war as well as *through* it; and that is not as simple a problem for them as it is for us (not that it looks so very simple for us at the time)."[42]

Yet even before the war, the Roosevelt administration itself was far from benign concerning at least some aspects of a British commercial threat. Since summer 1937, Washington had been suspicious of an Anglo-German arrangement by which Britain would have access to Mitteleuropa while the Reich's goods could penetrate the empire. Sumner Welles, for example, protested against the Düsseldorf agreement.[43] Hull and his staff, never believing that Britain could be short of dollars while operating a vast empire, continually sought to use lend-lease as a lever with which to crack Britain's imperial preference system, whose potency they much exaggerated.[44] He and Welles both were most disappointed, for example, when Article 4 of the Atlantic Charter, which seemed at first glance to look toward a general lowering of tariffs, contained the language "due respect" for "existing obligations." In August, Churchill stated that "a vast breaking down of tariffs and other barriers" was essential to any "great future of the world." Yet only in 1942, in the forging of a major lend-lease accord, did the British agree to a clause calling for "the elimination of all forms of discriminatory treatment in international commerce."[45]

To some anti-interventionists, the British were not only working at cross-purposes to the United States—they were plotting to reincorporate the U.S. into their own massive empire. Crucial in this regard was the entire network of Rhodes scholarships. The first will of Britain's most successful imperialist had called for the establishment of a secret society that would promote British settlement over the entire continents of Africa and South America, the Middle East, Canada, the Pacific Islands, the Malay archipelago, and the seaboard of China and Japan. Ultimately it envisioned the recovery of the United States. The document had been drafted while Cecil Rhodes was still an Oxford student and before he had made his fortune. To the end of his life, Rhodes dreamed of a federal union of the U.S. and Britain under British aegis.[46]

To John T. Flynn, the Rhodes organization was "the greatest fifth column in the world." The *Christian Century* saw the scholarships "as effective a method of propaganda as was ever devised." Porter Sargent quoted from the book *Last Will and Testament of Cecil J. Rhodes* (1902) to compare Rhodes's schemes to that of the Jesuits.[47]

At least two anti-interventionists deemed Britain a possible military threat to the United States. When asked by interventionist Claude Pepper (Dem.-Fla.) if he ever feared Britain and France attacking the U.S., former diplomatic consul Ralph Townsend replied, "You never know. The sentiment in Great Britain was very much against us in the 1920s." In August 1941, Lindbergh suggested that "before this war is over, England herself may turn against us, as she has turned against France and Finland."[48]

Anti-interventionists not only emphasized Britain's predatory nature toward the United States but also attacked the entire British record in the world at large. Albert Jay Nock quoted Thomas Jefferson, who had called the British government "the most flagitious which has existed since the days of Philip of Macedon."[49] Senator Chavez cited legal philosopher Jerome Frank's *Save America First* (1938) to the effect that the British balance-of-power doctrine had produced more wars than it had prevented.[50]

Britain's entire twentieth-century diplomatic record was denounced. "Without an exception," said Townsend, "the British betrayed every ally in the World War, and did so by plan rather than by accident." According to such critics, the British allowed the Turks to destroy Armenia and drive the Greeks into the sea at Salonika. They undercut the Weimar Republic and, in a sense, created Hitler, for they surrounded Germany with military alliances, doing so at the instigation of France.[51] There was hardly a reactionary ruler in Europe, wrote Theodore Dreiser, whom the British had not backed. "England's aim was to keep down the masses of all the new states of Europe and make them accept kings and dictators subservient to her."[52]

Through the thirties, anti-interventionists argued, Britain had kept acting in a highly irresponsible fashion. In the Rhineland crisis of 1936, it prevented French general Maurice Gamelin from confronting the Germans. During the Ethiopian crisis, it sold huge quantities of gasoline and oil to the invading Italians. When the Spanish Civil War broke out, Britain and France both withheld supplies from the besieged Spanish republic.[53] As Senator Borah saw the issue, Britain had connived at the Führer's repudiation of the military provisions of the Versailles treaty, agreed to the creation of the new German navy, urged France to disregard its treaty for the protection of Czechoslovakia, and schemed at Hitler's seizure of Austria.[54]

Moreover, it was argued, Britain had helped to bankroll Germany's entire rearmament. Wheeler accused British industrialists and financiers of lending Hitler $2 billion on short-term credits and $1 billion in long-term loans.[55] Others maintained that Britain helped supply the Reich's entire war machine.[56] Rush Holt, for example, cited *Merchants of Death*, the muckraking indictment of the international munitions trade by H. C. Englebrecht and Frank Hanighen, to allege that the British and French both aided in arming Hitler.[57]

Indeed, several argued, Britain had deliberately fostered Nazi Germany to contain communism. Once the Soviet five-year plans "gave the Tories the jitters," wrote Sargent, the British welcomed Mussolini and Hitler. Even after World War II broke out, Borah said, "Britain wants Hitler to become supreme in all Central Europe. Britain regards Hitler as a stabilizing influence and a barrier against communism."[58]

Even after war began, economic dealings between Britain and Germany appeared to be continuing. The Bank of England, noted *Uncensored* in November 1939, still accepted German paper as collateral for loans to British banks. Because Britain regarded German credits as sound, it could quite possibly sell them to neutrals, thus helping promote a lively trade with its official enemy.[59] Furthermore, Britain was as yet trading with the USSR, an ally of Germany.[60] In October 1939, Nye, noting an exchange of Russian timber for British rubber and tin, asked whether "British rubber going to Russia will turn up as rubber tires on German airplanes or German armored cars."[61] *Uncensored* found the entire arrangement "reminiscent of the World War days when contraband nickel (essential alloy for armaments) was shipped into Bremen with the permission of the French government, when a constant supply of German magnetos sparked French airplane engines, and when German soldiers were impaled on German-made barbed wire bought by the British."[62]

A few anti-interventionists labeled the United States as Britain's collaborator in this endeavor. In his 1941 book, Dreiser titled a chapter "Have English and American Finance Co-operated with Hitler to Destroy Democracy?" Nye accused American industrialists of helping Germany rearm in "utter violation" of Versailles. *Labor* magazine, the journal of the Railroad Brotherhoods, maintained that American bankers, too, furnished Hitler with hundreds of millions of dollars. Bennett Clark saw the U.S. sales as aiding in the creation of Germany's formidable air force, while Harry Elmer Barnes focused on patent agreements.[63]

If opponents held the British diplomatic record in such contempt, one could hardly expect that they would treat British leaders warmly. Anti-interventionists, however, were of two minds concerning Neville Chamberlain. For allowing German expansion in Eastern Europe, the prime minister, said the *Chicago Tribune*, was "the world's champion boob."[64] Moreover, it continued, he was foolish to fight Germany without a strong French air force, Belgium and the Netherlands as allies, and recourse to Czech fortifications.[65] Liberal and leftist anti-interventionists concurred, seeing the prime minister as sacrificing Spanish freedom to British investment efforts and making only halfhearted efforts to create an alliance with the Soviets.[66]

At times, some anti-interventionists, including again the *Chicago Tribune* and the *New York Daily News,* praised the prime minister.[67] After Chamberlain's death in November 1940, Hearst saw the former prime minister as right even when his public wanted him to be wrong. Even *Social Justice* praised him for attempting to arbitrate such "tension spots" as Danzig, the Saar, "the stolen colonies," and "the mad rearmament race."[68]

Greater anti-interventionist consensus centered on Lord Halifax, whose policies were opposed by all sides of the anti-interventionist spectrum.[69] Halifax headed the foreign ministry from February 1938 until December 1940, when he was appointed British ambassador to the United States. His ardent pleas for American lend-lease, including direct approaches to the American public and the Congress, resulted in strong criticism.[70]

In fact Halifax's entire record was portrayed as cloudy at best. As governor-general of India from 1925 to 1931, Halifax, according to *Uncensored*, had violently suppressed every manifestation of political activity there, jailing forty-seven thousand Indians, including Mahatma Gandhi.[71] Even more controversial was his diplomatic record, for he was presented as an arch-appeaser.[72] Wheeler remarked, "It should be remembered that Lord Halifax was shooting wild boar with Goering at a time when in the United States some of us, including myself, were denouncing Hitler from one end of the country to the other."[73] Several anti-interventionists stressed Halifax's ties to Sir George Ambrose Lloyd, whose book *The British Case* (1940) found no quarrel with fascism per se; Halifax had written the preface.[74]

Even his personality and mien were against him. As Halifax was known for his piety, Sargent called him "a high churchman, medieval in mind and outlook, Jesuitical in his methods, autocratic, aristocratic." He was "in close touch with God with whom he is said to communicate several times a day." Marcantonio referred to "his cadaverous appearance of an unwrapped Egyptian mummy."[75] As with Neville Chamberlain, Halifax did receive an occasional compliment, however. To John Haynes Holmes, for example, he was "a man of exalted idealism," "one of the noblest men now in public life."[76]

In retrospect, Halifax might have been a somewhat inept envoy, ignorant of the American political system and at best lukewarm toward FDR. The "holy fox" only became popular after the United States entered the war, at which point he turned into a skilled negotiator.[77] Roosevelt initially feared that the foreign secretary had been too much of an appeaser to serve as British ambassador. Harold Ickes found Halifax's record of "appeasement" sticking in his "craw," though in hindsight he called the policy "the most reasonable and logical." Harry Hopkins, who liked Halifax as a man, labeled him "a hopeless Tory," who should have as little to do with any forthcoming peace as possible.[78] During the time the Anglo-American alliance was being formed, Halifax played a minor role.[79]

Similar ambiguity existed concerning Lord Lothian, ambassador to the United States before Halifax. As with Chamberlain and Halifax, Lothian's friendly attitude toward Germany aroused hostility.[80] Even after war broke out again in 1939, asserted Wheeler, Lothian had expressed confidence in Hermann Goering.[81] Senator Lundeen inserted into the *Congressional Record* an anti-Lothian pamphlet written by German-American propagandist George Sylvester Viereck, who used the pseudonym James Burr Hamilton. The tract compared the diplomat's more recent interventionist statements with earlier ones far more favorable to Nazi Germany.[82]

When Lothian called for U.S. support in the new conflict, noninterventionists again attacked him.[83] In January 1940, in a speech before the Chicago Council of Foreign Relations, Lothian hinted at mutual American-British dependence, at which point the vehemently anti-British George Holden Tinkham demanded his recall.[84] In November 1940, the ambassador drew more criticism. He broadcast from London thanking the United States for its aid but supposedly declaring, "we also need planes, men, and ships if we are to be sure of defeating the Nazi threat to liberty."[85]

Again as with Chamberlain and Halifax, some anti-interventionists, including Hearst and Lindbergh, sincerely admired Lothian.[86] To this day, the role of Lothian remains debated; he is portrayed as either a skilled ambassador or an envoy hopelessly out of touch with American life.[87]

Anti-interventionists were also of two minds concerning Lord Beaverbrook, the prominent Canadian-born publisher who was minister of aircraft production in 1940 and of supply in 1941.[88] In prewar days, claimed *Uncensored*, Beaverbrook had been an "empire isolationist"; he still might deal with Hitler. When, in March 1940, Beaverbrook suggested that the United States and Britain might be "joined together again" when the conflict was over, the *New York Daily News* accused him of seeking to reunite "this onetime colony . . . to the mother country." Occasionally Beaverbrook garnered praise, both Hearst and the *Chicago Tribune* welcoming his defense appointments.[89]

Winston Churchill, who became prime minister in May 1940, attracted by far the greatest attention—and not surprisingly—the greatest hostility. Commented Norman Thomas, "Churchill is a great man in many ways, but Churchill is an imperialist to the core."[90]

Some militant Anglophobes judged Churchill to have been a negative force almost from birth. As a young officer, he had supposedly helped suppress nationalist risings in India and the Sudan.[91] Similarly, while a reporter during the Spanish-American War, he had participated in atrocities against Cubans struggling for independence in which capacity he expressed, in Rush Holt's words, a "delicious yet tremulous sensation" in killing American boys.[92] While first lord of the admiralty during World War I, he backed the costly Gallipoli campaign while denouncing the United States for apparent tardiness in entering the war.[93] Then, in 1936, Churchill supposedly told a minor American publisher that U.S. participation in the conflict had prevented a needed truce with Germany.[94] He also sought to stifle the Bolshevik Revolution, attacked Gandhi, and embraced Mussolini's rule over Italy and invasion of Ethiopia.[95] In 1937, he said of Germany's Führer, "One may dislike Hitler's system and yet admire his patriotic achievement. If our country were defeated I hope we should find a champion as indomitable to restore our courage and lead us to our place among the nations."[96]

Once World War II began, Churchill became first lord of the admiralty and then on 10 May 1940, prime minister. Criticism soon accelerated.[97] In both these offices, his military strategy was deemed foolhardy. Anti-interventionists accused him of botching the Norwegian campaign, pushing a dangerous offensive in Belgium and France, and being responsible for the loss of Yugoslavia and Greece.[98]

His desire for total victory and supposed intrigue appeared particularly dangerous.[99] "I just don't trust him," Joseph Kennedy confided to his diary. "He always impressed me that he was willing to blow up the American Embassy and say it was the Germans if it would get the United States in." To the *New York Daily News*, his ascendancy indicated that "hopes of a peace before a vast explosion and a colossal war are about gone."[100]

Occasionally anti-interventionists did praise aspects of Churchill's rule.[101] The *Chicago Tribune* found Churchill to be the best possible replacement for Chamberlain.[102] Noting his speech of 4 June 1940 ("We shall fight on the beaches"), it said that the new prime minister had already demonstrated he was worth "a quarter of a million or more soldiers."[103] In February 1941, while conceding such military blunders as Norway and Gallipoli, Castle saw it fatal to remove him from office: "Changing horses in the middle of a war is pretty poor business." *Uncensored* criticized him for losing Crete and neglecting war production but maintained, "Winston Churchill has given Englishmen leadership of a calibre they have lacked since the heyday of David Lloyd George."[104]

Churchill's critics did not always speak in a vacuum. When he first assumed office, some leading officials within the Roosevelt administration were less than enthusiastic. Not only did Welles and Berle find the new prime minister far too heavy a drinker but FDR himself apparently told Ickes that Churchill was "drunk half the time." Only in midsummer 1940 did such opinions change. Even then, diplomat Averell Harriman recalled, Roosevelt always saw Churchill as a nineteenth-century imperialist. Hopkins noted that the president loved Winston as "a man for the war" but was horrified at his "reactionary attitude" concerning the subsequent peace.[105]

Noninterventionists also attacked other British leaders. Anthony Eden, Churchill's foreign minister, was cast as at best a lightweight, at worst the architect of British defeat.[106] Several were accused of being profascist: Neville Henderson, prewar ambassador to Germany; Oliver Stanley, who became secretary of state for war in 1940; and Sir Samuel Hoare, lord privy seal in 1939 and 1940.[107]

At times a British leader received praise. Hearst said that Leslie Hore-Belisha, who resigned as secretary for war in January 1940, should be considered for prime minister.[108] The *New York Daily News* pushed Lloyd George for the cabinet.[109] Lawrence Dennis found Laborites, particularly Hugh Dalton and Ernest Bevin ("the British John L. Lewis"), to be the ablest figures in the war cabinet. In fact, Dennis felt Bevin should be groomed for the prime ministership.[110]

*Social Justice* lauded the Duke of Windsor, who had bucked the owners of the Welsh mines by protesting against the squalid conditions. So, too, did Hearst, who in December 1940 wanted the duke to replace the late Lothian as ambassador to the United States. The duke, Hearst continued, was "a progressive," "a brain for the problems of his time."[111]

Extremists within anti-interventionist ranks were not content with attacking Britain's leaders; the entire people were vilified. Hollywood actor Francis X. Bushman wrote of the British: "To me they STINK. They are so contemptuous of us, that even the so called cultured cannot hide it UNTIL they need to come to SHYLOCK as to a pawn shop for cash." Anyone who trusted them, said author Albert Jay Nock, would be "sold down the river at a moment's notice"; victims included the Jews, Arabs, Poles, and French. "A Britisher is not a national," remarked *Social Justice*. "He is an internationalist dwelling in the capitals of the world and worshiping the god of gold in the temple of the Bank of England." While Americans sacrificed for the British cause, their new wards were accused of still living most frivolously, indulging themselves with golf, racing, and joy rides. The AFC, while hoping the British would not lose, was unsparing in spreading anti-British stories, including them in one bulletin after another, each tale stressing their singular ungratefulness.[112]

Certainly, such critics asserted, Britain was no democracy.[113] "In spite of all the hullabaloo of centuries," wrote Al Williams, "the English commoner has never been a free man in fact. . . . In England, liberty is regarded as an alienable gift by the government, not an unalienable gift of God." Because of an archaic and unfair electoral system, commented Harry Elmer Barnes, the House of Commons did not represent the British people. Furthermore, the cabinet did not itself speak for the Commons. The columnist found an even greater obstacle to democracy lying in the all-powerful bureaucracy or civil service, never touched by elections or changes in the ruling party.[114]

As evidence, anti-interventionists drew on comments made by prominent Britons, including novelists J. B. Priestley and H. G. Wells and diplomat Anthony Eden, all of whom denied Britain was a genuine democracy.[115] Even had it been so before it had entered the war, emergency regulations now made it a regimented state. In an interview with the *Boston Globe* held in November 1940, Joseph P. Kennedy curtly commented, "Democracy is finished in England. It may be here. Because it comes to a question of feeding people. It's all an economic question." The ambassador continued that England faced "national socialism." Writing in November 1941, Barnes saw Britain as being more thoroughly regimented than Germany or Italy was in 1939. He cited Mencken's portrayal of Britain as "a sort of Asiatic despotism, with every citizen completely at the mercy of the politician."[116]

For several, the word *dictatorship* was not too strong.[117] The *Chicago Tribune* continually stressed this theme. In "the British war dictatorship," it noted as the conflict broke out, all by-elections for Parliament had been terminated; in addition, Britain planned to cancel the major election scheduled for November 1940.[118] By October 1940, the *Tribune* reported British life as so tightly controlled that the state determined where one lived and worked as well as what one purchased, heard on the radio, and read in the press.[119]

The *Tribune* was far from alone. Because manufacturing and selling were licensed and taxes "automatically zooming," said Hugh Johnson, liberty of contract had disappeared: "The appalling total of all this seems to make Hitler a piker and Mussolini a maundering monk." In February 1940, the *New York Daily News* alleged that the war pushed Britain "a long way toward totalitarianism": "When the government begins to tell people to douse their lights, send their children to the country, and how much meat they can eat, that is state control of the individual where he lives."[120]

One measure was continually cited. On 22 May 1940, after three hours of debate, Parliament passed a new Emergency Powers Defense Bill that, in the words of historian A. J. P. Taylor, "gave the government practically unlimited authority over all British citizens and their property." Certainly its sweeping provisions guaranteed control over major facets of British life, including industry and banking. *Newsweek* warned of "temporary state socialism as far reaching as Soviet Russia's or Nazi Germany's."[121]

Anti-interventionists of all persuasions were quick to comment.[122] The *Christian Century* editorialized, "Britain Establishes a War Dictatorship."[123] To the *Chicago Tribune*, Britain had become "a Hitler government to fight Hitler," abandoning the famous charter of 1215 to avoid the defeat of 1066.[124] Such legislation, it was said, was irrevocable, even when Britain reverted back to peacetime conditions.[125]

The extreme right and extreme left saw the implications differently. To Dennis, powerful Laborites had launched the overthrow of British capitalism and were establishing a socialist dictatorship.[126] Conversely, *New Masses* concluded that the 22 May legislation marked the "British M-Day" or Mobilization Day. Under the new "gleischaltung rules," workers might be commandeered for anything that suits His Majesty.[127]

For most critics, it was British socialism—not monopoly capital—that would emerge from the war. Britain, stated Norman Thomas, would of necessity emerge from the conflict highly collectivized. Wheeler, undoubtedly less sanguine about the matter, saw the British Labor Party as seeking to impose "International Socialism" on the postwar world, in the process abolishing all "national sovereignties" and treating the world as a "single economic unit."[128] Several rightists underscored the supposedly prominent role of Harold J. Laski, a Marxist political theorist who, they claimed, would be the eminence gris in the new international socialist order.[129]

Not all anti-interventionists foresaw a socialist order ahead. Ambassador Kennedy, for example, denied that the profit system was in danger.[130] The *Progressive*, much to its regret, could not envision a Labor government assuming power after the war.[131]

Britain was often indicted for terminating traditional civil liberties.[132] In August 1939, Parliament passed a most severe law; it involved detention without trial, outlawing the possession of certain books and articles, and strict control of public meetings.[133] Senator James J. Davis accused the nation of blacking out freedom of speech and the press—indeed, freedom itself.[134] In August 1940, the *San Francisco Examiner* quoted Lloyd George's protest against "the Nazification of Britain," in which the former prime minister called threats of punishment and persecution "principles of the Gestapo."[135] In January 1941, the *Chicago Tribune* alleged of both Britain and Canada, "It is possible now for their people to be in concentration camps without trial, merely by the word of authority."[136]

When anti-interventionists wanted to attack administration policy toward dissent, however, they would often hold up Britain as a positive model. At this point Britain ceased to be an oppressive nation; it manifested extreme tolerance.[137] In October 1939, *Uncensored* discovered a tolerance for conscientious objectors unknown in World War I.[138] Over a year later, William Henry Chamberlin compared Britain favorably to France; Britain had systematically published German communiqués in its press, permitted listening to German radio, and had "maintained a civil liberties record in the midst of a grim life-and-death struggle."[139] In November 1940, Joseph Kennedy reported to Herbert Hoover that Britain manifested more free speech and less vituperation than the United States.[140]

Again the anti-interventionists were far from alone. Among themselves, interventionists were often highly critical of the British. Roosevelt did share a sense of community with the British, referring to them as his "cousins" and believing strongly in Anglo-American naval cooperation to confront German power. At the same time, he held the characteristic American suspicion of Britain's upper class. In January 1939, he told Lothian that the "wealthy class" in Britain so feared communism that it threw itself in "the arms of Nazism."[141]

To FDR, Britain was both indispensable partner and malign force. In an off-the-record session with the American Society of Newspaper Editors, held in mid-April 1940, Roosevelt combined his affirmation of mutual interest with the qualification that he could not be fooled by "all their tricks." He alerted Wendell Willkie, "It is always the same with the British. They are always foxy and you have to be the same with them."[142]

Several others within the administration felt much stronger. Berle could hardly write a memo without showing anxiety. "While we want to give every help to the British," he commented in October 1940, "we must not make the mistake we made in 1917 and become virtually their adjuncts."[143] The American services were ever suspicious of British machinations. Not only was Major General Stanley D. Embick, army representative on the Joint Defensive Board, continually warning against a British alliance but his boss General Marshall could never shake his own wariness in dealing with them.[144]

In their effort to discredit Britain, the more strident anti-interventionists experienced an uphill battle. Even had British propaganda not been effective, as it certainly was, much of the public would still see the defeat of Germany, and with it the accompanying British victory, as being more important than keeping out of war. A Gallup poll taken in April 1941 revealed that some 68 percent would enter the war if Germany and Italy could be defeated in no other way. In May, 54 percent of those polled favored immediate entry if Roosevelt said that otherwise the British would be defeated.[145]

The ideological debate was still not finished. If one could brand Britain with a crude and unrepentant imperialism and, in fact, successfully portray its empire as the world's most despotic power, American opinion might still be won over.

# 14

# The British Empire:
# A Dubious Cause

If the more militant noninterventionists stressed one point concerning Britain, it was that the island nation ruled over a massive and exploitative empire. Father James Gillis, while endorsing aid to Britain itself, called its empire "an impossible organization, created and sustained by monstrous injustice." Literary critic Burton Rascoe found himself "deeply" supportive of the British war effort but took slaps at the empire's "profiteer rulers."[1]

Such people made little apology for continually using the word *empire* in describing Britain's realm. In the language of the *Chicago Tribune*, which included the French empire in its description, "that is exactly what they are, that is what they are proudly admitted to be, and that is what they will remain if the people of Britain and France, or at least the governments of Britain and France, can successfully defend them." To these critics, the word *commonwealth* embodied a deceptive euphemism, the word *dominion* being similarly suspect.[2]

Often attacks were made in most sweeping terms. Wheeler called Britain "the greatest aggressor in the pages of history."[3] To Nye it was "the ace aggressor of all time."[4] Lundeen referred to "the bleeding British Empire, this empire with nearly 600,000,000 people, this empire whose sword has been dripping with the blood of enslaved and oppressed peoples for a thousand years."[5] To D. Worth Clark, British imperialism was not essentially different from German Nazism, Italian fascism, and Russian communism.[6]

The sheer scope of the British Empire was stressed. Anglophobic congressman Martin Sweeney spoke in terms of Britain dominating three-fourths of the world's land area and half the world's population. House colleague John Marshall Robsion saw three hundred million British subjects as little more than slaves.[7] H. L. Mencken asserted that the British Empire "owned and operated the sea," was dominant at both ends of the Americas, and "ran" Europe, Africa, and more than half of Asia. All over the globe, maintained the *Chicago Tribune*, Britain ruled by military occupation and military courts, bombing open towns to sustain its rule.[8] Even a far more moderate figure could express concern. Chester Bowles said of the British, "Like every other nation, they have been ruthless and hard and cruel."[9]

British treatment of subject peoples, it was stated, remained poor. Norman Thomas described the British as establishing a "slum empire" in Africa and the West Indies, where the indigenous population and resources had been totally and stupidly exploited.[10] A writer for the *Call* argued that subjects in Africa were practically treated as slaves, needing passes to change jobs, no matter how badly they were treated.[11] Official reports were cited, including the government's Committee on Colonial Nutrition and the Royal Commission Investigating Conditions in the British West Indies.[12]

A few went so far as to compare the British record unfavorably to that of the Germans. True, commented the *New York Daily News*, Germany had disturbed the peace of the world five times in the past century, but the British Empire had "hung up a higher per-century record of peace disturbance than that." To Ralph Townsend, British methods did not seem to differ significantly from those Hitler used in Czechoslovakia and Poland. Bennett Clark made his comparison to the Japanese, who were allegedly imitating in Asia precisely the methods the British used there. Norman Thomas differed, though he maintained it was quite ridiculous to be sentimental over British virtues. Congressman Marcantonio felt similarly, saying the difference was too small to warrant positing any juxtaposition between democratic and Nazi forces.[13]

Certainly, these anti-interventionists argued, subject populations possessed such little loyalty to their British rulers that they would never rally to the Allied cause. If, in fact, they were truly content, they would have enlisted voluntarily in British ranks. Novelist Vardis Fisher said that Ireland and India were not assisting Britain, the Union of South Africa had almost rebelled, and at first Canada was "very lukewarm." Of five hundred million living under the British flag, remarked Congressman Robsion, only seventy million would fight on its behalf.[14]

Event after event, region after region was brought up. Nye offered a whole litany of British offenses, ranging from the corruption of Warren Hastings, governor-general of India, in the 1770s to the violation of Lord Passfield's 1930 pledges that the tribal lands of Kenya would be reserved to the "natives" forever. Senator Wallace White accused the British of smashing the ports of China "to force opium down the throats of the Chinese."[15] Nye found Britain guilty of violating the neutrality of the Suez Canal, imposing the autocratic rule of Lord Cromer on Egypt, and making false promises to the Egyptian people.[16] Bowles, reflecting on the Boer War, asserted that the only crime of the Dutch settlers "lay in the fact that they wanted to farm the land where British financiers knew there was gold."[17]

The British were accused of playing a double game in the Palestine mandate, making mutually exclusive promises to the Jewish and Arab populations.[18] Several saw the British as persecuting the Jews there, Holt arguing that British "terrorism" against the Jews of Palestine was "just as bad as the terrorism against the Jews and Czechs in Czechoslovakia."[19] One of the most bizarre condemnations came from Father Coughlin, whose *Social Justice* was notoriously anti-Semitic. In the aftermath of the British white paper of 1939, which limited further Jewish immigration to Palestine, the radio priest claimed to sympathize with "the poor Jews" of Palestine who, after investing their "hard-earned money," found the British government turning against them.[20]

Two examples of supposed British tyranny were continually cited: India and Ireland. From the outset, it was maintained, British rule had been oppressive in both lands.[21] "The British conception of ruling India," wrote Albert Jay Nock, "has never for one moment risen above the conception of a *Polizeistatt.*" Senator Tobey spoke of "the black hole of Calcutta." Citing Indian claims, Ralph Townsend in 1941 said that a quarter of a million people had been jailed during the past two decades. Two out of every ten Britons, Wheeler estimated, were involved in the exploitation of some 350 million Indian subjects. Drawing in part from firsthand observation, the Montana Democrat commented, "There is greater poverty in India than can be found in any other place in the world."[22] Contemporary incidents of repression were given full play, including RAF bombings of villages on the northwest frontier.[23]

Similarly, Indian nationalism received much encouragement. Bowles, later American ambassador to India, asserted that 350 million people had "clamored" for freedom for several generations. If the United States became a belligerent, said Sterling Morton, it should prepare to fight a Britain that would not free India.[24]

Among all wings of anti-interventionism, tremendous sympathy existed for Jawaharlal Nehru's Indian National Congress movement.[25] Certainly anti-interventionists did all they could to give visiting Indians a forum.[26] The left-wing American Youth Congress featured Rajni Patel, a political scientist with a degree from Cambridge and president of the All-Indian Student Congress, who denounced the conflict as an imperialist war.[27] Also on the college circuit was Reginald Babu Lal Singh, Oxford graduate, member of the foreign department of the Indian National Congress, and adherent of Gandhi's pacifism. "Non-violence will triumph over violence," Singh said, "because human beings are not by nature sadistic."[28]

To some anti-interventionists, major resistance appeared imminent.[29] In November 1939, for example, Congressman John G. Alexander thought India was on the point of insurrection.[30] On 13 October 1940, such predictions were in part realized, for Mahatma Gandhi announced renewed *satyagrata*, or civil disobedience—a campaign for full independence.[31] For his own part in the campaign, Nehru was imprisoned, resulting in widespread anti-interventionist protest.[32] As long as Nehru stayed in jail, remarked Norman Thomas, it was quite impossible to believe that the triumph of British imperialism would solve the world's problems.[33]

Certain British promises were most suspect. When, in October 1939, British viceroy Lord Linlithgow pledged Britain to discuss dominion status after the war, the *Christian Century* recalled similar false assurances after World War I.[34] Nor, according to the Protestant weekly, did the appointment of Lord Lloyd as secretary of state for the colonies appear a good sign, for Lloyd was "the most diehard Tory imperialist in India." In October 1940, Britain reiterated its support for postwar dominion status, but the Protestant journal condemned it for not endorsing full independence.[35]

Yet, surprisingly enough, at times several anti-interventionists complimented the British on their rule. If Britain left India, warned Hearst's *San Francisco Examiner,* riots could well break out between Hindus and Moslems, making it easy for a predatory Russia to impose an even greater tyranny. The *New York Daily News* offered downright praise. The British kept peace among over forty-five races speaking two hundred languages and divided into twenty-four hundred castes and tribes. Besides, they did "an excellent job of cleaning up and disinfecting the Indian population." If India suddenly received the self-determination Gandhi demanded, "it would more than likely turn into self-extermination." Frank Waldrop concurred, attacking the naive Gandhi for seeking "a peaceful, goat's milk–drinking civilization in which people weave their own breechclouts, speak kindly to one another, avoid birth control, think beautiful thoughts, and live happily."[36]

In their hostility to British rule in India, the anti-interventionists were not alone. Within the state department, some already advocated full dominion status. India in particular was a sore point with the president.[37] Several months before the United States became a full-scale belligerent, Roosevelt himself pushed for Indian self-government, and Article 2 of the Atlantic Charter was framed in part with India in mind. During the war, the president continually raised the issue in correspondence or through emissaries.[38]

Prime case number two was Ireland, and here the rhetoric was equally extreme. Commented D. Worth Clark in October 1939: "Paint me a picture of 6

years of persecution of the Jews, the Catholics, and the Protestants in Germany, paint it as gory and as bloody as you please, and I will paint you one 10 times as brutal, 10 times as savage, 10 times as bloody in the 500 years of British destruction, pillage, rape, and bloodshed in Ireland." The *Chicago Tribune* accused England of suppressing Ireland for centuries, only desisting when the Irish made good their revolution.[39]

The British repression just after World War I, implemented through the Black and Tans, was noted by people as diverse as liberal advertising executive Bowles and Coughlinite congressman Sweeney.[40] Several anti-interventionists cited the findings of the American Commission on Conditions in Ireland, a group of prominent reformers who in 1921 attacked British policy.[41]

Even after World War II began, Britain was accused of persecution. Discussing Ulster in September 1939, journalist Frank Hanighen noted a report of the British Council for Civil Liberties, which asserted that the Bill of Rights had been permanently abolished in Northern Ireland, that the Roman Catholic minority had been oppressed, and that in general an intolerable state of affairs persisted in the region. Hanighen, who had personally investigated conditions, said he could confirm the council's report.[42]

When war came, anti-interventionists often endorsed Ireland's neutrality, though they did not speak for the broader American public.[43] By the end of 1940, Britain was seeking access to Irish ports. The Irish Free State refused.[44] Critics of Britain remained vocal on the matter.[45] If four million Irishmen had no rights that forty million Englishmen were bound to respect, commented the *Saturday Evening Post*, what rights had forty million Englishmen that eighty million Germans must honor? In June 1941, *Scribner's Commentator* accused Roosevelt of refusing to supply food to Ireland, whose situation was "painful." It acidly suggested that "a few ships" could miraculously be found if the Irish permitted British naval bases in its ports.[46]

Even if the Irish granted permission, some anti-interventionists saw logistical problems. Bases in southern Eire, *Uncensored* remarked in December 1940, would be of comparatively little use to Britain, as shipping did not pass that way. Moreover, it would take six months to fit any such ports. The real reasons behind Britain's pressure, it continued, were quite different: a rationalization for its navy's failure to break up the German submarine attacks and a ploy to bring Eire into the war, thereby transforming Irish Americans into interventionists.[47] If the British truly sought bases there, stated Hanighen, the port of Lough Folye, just across the border in Northern Ireland, would serve just as well as Lough Swilly in the south.[48]

Some voices were more moderate. Britain, asserted the *Chicago Tribune*, could not allow Ireland to serve as a German base. Noting in January 1941 that bombs had recently been dropped on Dublin, the *New York Daily News* said Ireland must choose between Britain and Germany, continuing, "Britain nowadays, for all its bloody record in Ireland in other times, is very gentle with all its possessions except India when India gets too fresh." If the Germans attempted to invade Ireland, the *News* remarked, the Irish could only throw them back with the aid of the British navy and the quarter million British ground troops stationed in Northern Ireland.[49]

Always there were rumors of direct U.S. involvement in Ireland. In July 1941, Taft and Wheeler pointed to reports that the United States was constructing a naval base in northern Ireland for British use.[50] Senator Danaher suspected an American occupation of northern Ireland in the works. The AFC research committee cited the construction of U.S. bases there, noting that one construction contract had gone to a subsidiary of J. P. Morgan.[51]

Even Canada, long the friendliest of American neighbors, did not escape anti-interventionist attack. On 14 April 1939, Roosevelt had pledged defense of all the Americas, singling out Canada by name. That September, a Gallup poll showed a majority favoring war if a European power invaded that nation.[52]

On 3 September 1939, Canada entered the war alongside Britain, a move that many administration critics viewed with suspicion.[53] As it was Canada, not Germany, that first declared war, several noninterventionists—including *America* magazine, Hugh Johnson, Gerald Nye, and Edwin M. Borchard—labeled it the aggressor.[54] "The Canadians jumped into the war like a bunch of sheep without any provocation," wrote Harry Elmer Barnes. "If this is independence, then Germany is democratic."[55] When, on 12 September, Roosevelt warned that the United States could not "stand idly by" if Canada was threatened "by another empire," Hugh Johnson denied any commitment to defend that land.[56]

Charles A. Lindbergh expressed the greatest concern of all. In a radio speech in October 1939, he conceded that "we must protect our sister American nations from foreign invasion, both for their welfare and our own." Nonetheless, he questioned the right of any people "to draw this hemisphere into a European war simply because they prefer the Crown of England to American independence." Mentioning Canada by name, he asked, "Can we rightfully permit any country in America to give bases to foreign warships, or to send its army abroad while it remains secure in our protection at home?" "Sooner or later," he noted, "we must demand the freedom of this continent and its surrounding islands from the dictates of European power."[57] Several anti-interventionists gave Lindbergh strong support, including Boake Carter and Hugh Johnson.[58] Some advocates of collective security found the colonel to be behaving in an outrageous fashion, calling for nothing less than American domination of its northern neighbor.[59]

Even without Lindbergh, the issue of annexing Canada drew some attention. The socialist *American Guardian* had already stated that only by such a union could the United States protect itself. The *New York Daily News* denied the U.S. should make the attempt, though individual Canadian provinces were welcome to apply for statehood. Historian Charles Callan Tansill suggested that the Canadians themselves hold a plebiscite on joining the United States.[60]

More debate was provoked when, on 4 June 1940, Churchill told Parliament that defeat in the British Isles would be followed by a retreat to Canada. The *Christian Century* queried, "This country has already given a pledge of protection to Canada; would it be expected to protect the transplanted British throne as well? Would this nation welcome the idea of using the American continent as a base for another world war to reestablish the British empire?"[61]

Nevertheless, several FDR critics sought closer ties with Canada.[62] The *Chicago Tribune* endorsed a defensive alliance, declaring that Canada was the only nation (besides the United States) possessing a demonstrated capacity for waging modern warfare.[63] Moving the seat of the British Empire, Hearst stated, in reality testified to its expansion and regeneration, for it would be separated from Europe's "constantly recurring tribal wars."[64]

On 18 August 1940, after meeting in Ogdensburg, New York, Roosevelt and Canadian prime minister Mackenzie King announced a permanent joint board of defense. The agreement, at least in part, served as a device to acquire control over any remnants of the British fleet seeking refuge in the New World.[65] Several anti-interventionists endorsed the move.[66] Hearst, in calling for Senate ratification, referred to the agreement as "a beneficial thing," though it meant that "the United States will defend Canada more than Canada will defend the United States." The *Chicago Tribune* wanted additional joint action, including the building of a four-lane highway across western Canada to Alaska; a common pool of such resources as nickel, aluminum, zinc, and copper; and combining of their massive wheat surpluses, a move that would give both nations the "whip hand" with the coming of peace. By October, it was calling the agreement the most important event since the Revolutionary War.[67]

To the *New York Daily News*, the arrangement provided "insurance against invasion." Otherwise a frightening scenario might take place: if Hitler conquered Europe that winter, he would immediately grab Newfoundland, continue to Montreal, cross the St. Lawrence plains to Lake Champlain, and go down "excellent roads" to Albany and New York City, thereby isolating the industrial East from the rest of the nation. Surplus divisions could fan out from Albany up the strategic Mohawk Valley and across to Boston.[68]

Colonel McCormick, too, initially feared an attack through Canada via the Champlain–Hudson Valley. A strike on New England "could be reinforced by more troops than we *now* have available to eject them." Parachute troops, aided by "the communist fifth column of New York," could capture the forts of the city, and its harbor could be lost before American troops could be brought up. Hence, the Chicago publisher called for forming a defensive alliance with Canada, raising nine divisions of regulars and eighteen of the national guard, conducting military training in the schools, and keeping the U.S. fleet intact and close to shore. Soon, however, McCormick was maintaining that Newfoundland and Nova Scotia could be easily protected. Were a hostile army somehow able to advance further, it could still be blocked by the St. Lawrence River and the mountains of Maine.[69]

Not all noninterventionists cheered the Ogdensburg agreement.[70] Villard found the agreement "one of the most unprecedented events" in all American history"; it was "the first time that we have sought to make an effective defense union with a country actively engaged in a war in which we are supposed to be neutral." To Congressman Roy O. Woodruff, the arrangement "smacks too much of dictatorship to suit a good many people." *New Masses* expressed the greatest outrage, practically accusing FDR of declaring war.[71] "A virtual military alliance," said the *Christian Century*, "has been concluded with a nation that is already at war and that may, in a future already previsioned by Mr. Churchill, become the seat and military center of a warring empire."[72] Ironically, once FDR was assured that the British fleet was safe, he lost interest in the entire matter.[73]

During the following year, the matter of Canada still incurred debate. Some Roosevelt adversaries stressed closer ties.[74] A German victory in Europe, stated Lawrence Dennis, would force the full integration of both Canada and Britain's hemispheric possessions into the American "system."[75] In late May 1941, Arthur Vandenberg avowed, "Certainly Detroit, Mich., cannot wait until an invasion reaches Windsor, Ont., before it starts to shoot." Sociologist Edward A. Ross hoped to see the nine provinces of Canada seek American statehood so that all North America, from the Rio Grande to the North Pole, could constitute a single defense unit.[76] Senator D. Worth Clark created some embarrassment when, in late July 1941, he included Canada in his call for U.S. control of the hemisphere.[77]

Others sought restraint. In late May, Burton Wheeler and Felix Morley stressed that the defense of Canada should involve no aggressive action against powers in Europe, Africa, or Asia. Libby warned against being dragged into war if Canada became the seat of the British Empire: "We have not been consulted regarding that war and must not be responsible for its outcome."[78]

As far as civil liberties were concerned, Canada—like Britain—could be considered a negative object lesson as to what war could do to a nation. Hugh Johnson, writing just as the conflict began, judged that in Canada the Magna Carta was "already in the ash can," the Bill of Rights "out the window." He continued, "You have to do that in war today. We did some of it in 1918." By January 1940, Sargent was noting that the Mounties were raiding residences for subversive books. Furthermore, newspapers had been banned and radio broadcasts censored. According to an AFC bulletin issued a year later, any person who predicted a German victory stood guilty of violating Defense of Canada Regulations, regardless of the spirit in which the remark was made. In

May 1941, the *Call* quoted a Canadian labor leader who asserted that war had brought fascism to Canada.[79]

Again, the Roosevelt administration itself possessed many antiempire sentiments. Historian Warren Kimball accurately paraphrases the president's own attitude: "The monster of colonialism threatened to bite if not devour the world by plunging it into another huge war." During World War I, Roosevelt believed, colonialism had worked against reasonable settlement, and the 1919 negotiations in Paris had revealed a squalid scramble for territory. In December 1939, he told Lothian that Britain should state publicly that it had abandoned empire building and was firmly committed to self-government. In 1941, in addressing correspondents, he said, "We believe that any nationality, no matter how small, has the inherent right to its own nationhood." When the United States became a full-time belligerent, FDR continually challenged the entire imperialist system.[80]

Indeed, his feelings were so strong on the matter that British historian D. Cameron Watt can write of the president's conviction "that all arguments in favour of colonial rule were initiated by the self-interest of those who advanced them." If nothing else, the president's very fear of an isolationist resurgence made him determined not to fight for British aims. The state department harbored similar sentiments: if the British Empire brought progress to indigenous peoples, it still was an *empire* and as such needed to be gradually dissolved.[81]

Neither the anti-interventionists nor their foes realized how much the empire drained Britain itself. The white dominions had long been moving toward self-government. On the eve of the war, only 1 percent of Britain's income came from this source. At the same time, Britain had the task of defending vulnerable territory in every part of the globe, certainly a major strategic liability. India alone absorbed a third of the British army while contributing little in return. According to the map, the empire was the largest the world had yet seen, holding a quarter of the world's population. In reality, as historian Clive Ponting notes, it resembled a Potemkin village.[82]

Ultimately, the fact that Britain was an imperialist power did little to modify the strongly pro-British sympathies of the American people. Hopefully, in anti-interventionist eyes, the threat of any alliance with the Soviet Union might cause the nation to rethink its current course.

# 15

# The Soviets: A Greater Enemy

Ever since the Bolshevik Revolution of November 1917, relations between the United States and the newly founded Union of Soviet Socialist Republics, commonly called the Soviet Union or Russia, had usually been strained. The Soviets recalled the stationing of American troops at Vladivostok and Archangel in 1918 and the U.S. refusal to recognize their government until 1933. To more conservative Americans, the Soviet Union stood for the persecution of religion, failure to pay the debts incurred by the czarist regime, and the liquidation of the entire Kulak class. For many liberals, Russia only became "the God that failed" in the middle 1930s. Reformers, however, were deeply disillusioned by the famines in the Ukraine, the liquidation of the top army command, the obviously trumped-up accusations of Stalin's purge trials, and the establishment of labor camps in what was later known as the Gulag.[1] President Roosevelt himself told delegates of the left-wing American Youth Congress, gathering on the White House lawn in February 1940, that the Soviet Union manifested "a dictatorship as absolute as any in the world."[2] Unquestionably, hostility to the Soviet Union was a deeply rooted phenomenon, by no means simply prompted by the Molotov–Ribbentrop pact of 23 August 1939 and the Soviet attack on Finland of 30 November.[3]

Many anti-interventionists saved their strongest invective for the Soviet Union, not for Nazi Germany. Al Williams called the Soviet Union "the bloodiest sponsor of mass murder in the pages of history." The *New York Daily News* asserted, "The Soviets' Christian victims have far outnumbered the Nazis' Jewish victims."[4]

Journalist Freda Utley, a British subject who would soon become an American citizen, was particularly adamant: "The Russian brand of national socialism is even more oppressive, and far more destructive of life and material prosperity, than the German. So that absorption by the U.S.S.R. is even more feared than Nazi domination by the little states close to Russia." A former communist who had worked for the Comintern for six years, Utley had bitterly repudiated Stalinism after her husband had disappeared in the Gulag in 1936.[5]

In late summer 1940, Utley's book *The Dream We Lost: Soviet Russia Then and Now* was published. After detailing the appalling conditions of workers and peasants, she predicted that Stalin would be utterly unable to oppose Hitler, for his regime was too weak, his unpopularity with his people too great, and his army of dubious strength. She nonetheless warned that continued war between Britain and Germany could ultimately make the Russian dictator victorious. Hence, in her last chapter, she called for a negotiated peace. Otherwise, she asserted, Europe would come "to resemble those ancient lands along the Tigris and Euphrates where a Mongol conquest put an end to the oldest of civilizations."[6]

Utley even found German hegemony over the continent preferable to continuing the war. In comparing Stalinism and Hitlerism, she judged the Reich "a little more likely to bear the seed of a better ordered world than Stalin's bastard socialism." Admittedly, she said, Hitler had imprisoned and expelled tens of thousands, but Stalin had consigned hundreds of thousands to concentration camps. "The very fact that so many Germans and German Jews have been allowed to leave the country and tell the world about it, instead of being shot or interred for life in concentration camps, proves the *comparative* mildness of the Nazi regime." Give the Nazis economic opportunity and peace, she wrote, and Germany could well turn toward democracy. Utley did admit her wish might end up being "a vain delusion" but thought it "the only hope for Europe."[7]

Several anti-interventionists approved of her account.[8] Norman Thomas endorsed Utley's claim that Stalin's rule was even more cruel than Hitler's but found one contradiction: If Stalin's regime operated as incompetently as she maintained, how could he ever dominate Western Europe?[9] Even those who were not pronouncedly anti-interventionist found some merit in the book, though certain endorsements were qualified.[10] Russian expert Michael T. Florinsky of Columbia University found her treading "on dangerous ground" in her vision of a National Socialist Germany giving up its racial theories, militant spirit of conquest, and persecution of the Jews. China scholar Nathaniel Peffer accused her of seeking either a German victory or "a drawn peace that leaves the Nazis masters of the whole European continent." Socialist commentator Richard Rovere questioned her claim that Nazism worked more effectively than Russian communism. Her call for a negotiated peace, Rovere remarked, was "a counsel of despair, for she feels that England is altogether incapable of achieving her war aims."[11]

Others too highlighted the record of Josef Stalin. To the *New York Daily News*, he was "even more of a beast" than Hitler, and the *News* was not alone in this regard. The *Chicago Tribune* found him possessing an "unparalleled record of brutality and treachery"; he was "the man responsible for more human misery than any since the Mongolian invasions." In the 1920s, Senator Hiram Johnson had ardently sought U.S. recognition of the Soviets. By 1941, he was saying of the Russian dictator, "The greatest blood-letting that was ever committed on this earth occurred through him." Congressman John Robsion called Stalin "the bloodiest, most cruel and ruthless despot that the world has ever known." Moreover, remarked the Kentucky Republican, the Soviet dictator had worked harder at destroying the United States than any other person in the world.[12]

Throughout 1940 and much of 1941, noninterventionists continued to warn of Soviet expansion.[13] By remaining on the sidelines, asserted William Henry Chamberlin, Stalin would be the ultimate victor.[14] Frank Waldrop noted such concrete Soviet aims as conquest of Persia and the Dardanelles.[15] Others talked in terms of all Europe.[16] Harry Elmer Barnes included Britain and the U.S. as well. General Robert E. Wood warned of "the end of capitalism all over the world." The *Christian Century* feared the entire world would become "Stalinist."[17]

Hence, for some administration critics, Germany had to remain strong.[18] It alone, maintained Charles A. Lindbergh, "can either dam the Asiatic hordes or form the spearhead of their penetration into Europe."[19] The time might come, warned the *New York Daily News*, when the Allies would want Hitler's Reich to "side with them against Russia, in a concerted attempt to throw the Russian hordes and the murder and robbery that go with them back into Asia." The newspaper called the Führer "the bulwark against Bolshevism." The British, it speculated, might with American help win the current struggle, but Europe would be rendered so prostrate as to become "easy prey for the Russian Reds." Would the United States then be called on to supply the manpower for a new war?[20]

A few anti-interventionists denied any Soviet threat. Felix Morley, in calling for a Western European league to contain the Soviets, posited that the Russians needed tranquillity to govern their sprawling empire. Republican leader Hanford MacNider believed the Soviets would always be too weak to dominate the world. According to Oswald Garrison Villard, Stalin could not even run an efficient government at home.[21]

Particularly irritating, however, was continued American trade with the USSR.[22] John Haynes Holmes accused the American petroleum industry of supplying gasoline for planes used in bombing the Finns.[23] Americans, claimed Senator Danaher in May 1940, were paying $35 for gold that "some Communist Russian" produced for $8. Hoover opposed U.S. shipment of gasoline, cooper, and alloys. "We swat Hitler and the Japs and cuddle up to Big Joe," asserted columnist Samuel Pettengill. "Figure it out for yourself."[24]

On 6 August 1940, after negotiations between Undersecretary of State Sumner Welles and Soviet ambassador Constantine Oumansky, the United States renewed its annual trade agreement with the Soviets. Since 1937, the USSR had been bound to make at least $40 million worth of U.S. purchases each year. By this new accord, some $7 million worth of embargoed American machine tools were released, and within two days American tankers loaded with gasoline were on their way.[25]

Anti-interventionists quickly expressed anger. Bennett Clark saw the "Russian bear—with its claws still dripping from patriotic Finnish blood"—receiving $5 million worth of machine tools "now imperatively needed for the defense of the United States."[26]

On 21 January 1941, the United States lifted the moral embargo of December 1939, which had forbidden Soviet purchases of planes, aviation parts, and patent processes for producing high-quality aviation gasoline.[27] Anti-interventionists again voiced outrage.[28] Russia, protested Congressman Shanley, had become the United States's leading customer in certain major strategic materials: tin, rubber, copper tubing, molybdenum, gasoline, and machine tools.[29] In light of a new German-Soviet trade agreement, the *Chicago Tribune* warned that American-made planes, originally shipped to Russia, might soon be among the German bombers flying over Britain.[30]

Throughout the debate, the *New York Daily News* took a minority position among the anti-interventionists, as it continually favored American overtures to the Soviets.[31] In April 1941, for example, the *News* suggested that the United States "promise Stalin as much of Germany as he can get, just as in return for going to war England promised Poland as much of Poland as it could keep."[32]

From the time that the German-Russian alliance was formed, many anti-interventionists denied it would last. A German attack on the Soviets was often predicted or at least seen as possible.[33] In December 1939, *Uncensored* envisaged a huge coalition—Germany, Britain, France, and Italy—all lined up against the Soviet Union.[34] Germany would attack the Soviets, said John T. Flynn in January 1941, to secure the grain it needed.[35]

Already, anti-interventionists kept saying, tension existed. In December 1939, Flynn anticipated the USSR sealing Germany off from the Ukraine, not to mention the oil of Rumania and the iron ore of Scandinavia. That January *Call* writer Henry Haskell divined an imminent Soviet attack on Rumania. Noting the Soviet occupation of the Rumanian province of Bessarabia in June 1940, the *Chicago Tribune* foresaw that within months, Hitler might attack the Soviet Union with the greatest military force the world had yet known. Citing the imminent abdication of Rumanian King Carol, the *New York Daily News* referred to Napoleon's major victory over Austria and Russia: "Is it possible Hitler is thinking of another Austerlitz, with Soviet Russia as the patsy this time?" At one point, the *News* headlined an editorial, "They Spell It 'Romania,' But It Looks as If They Won't Be Spelling It at All Pretty Soon."[36]

In any such confrontation, the odds—as several anti-interventionists speculated—lay overwhelmingly with Germany. Freda Utley found the Soviets so

weak that Stalin might prefer to serve as Hitler's Russian gauleiter rather than
risk a war that would topple him.[37] If Hitler would just promise land to the
Soviet peasants, asserted the *New York Daily News*, they would probably welcome him as a deliverer.[38]

Speaking in the minority, Lawrence Dennis repeatedly saw no conflict
ahead. The visit of Soviet foreign minister Vyacheslav Molotov to Berlin in
November 1940 proved that Hitler and Stalin were in "permanent business
partnership . . . to remake the western world." The Soviets possessed a vested
interest in a German victory, Dennis wrote, for its defeat would destroy
Stalin's regime as well, and they had secretly given approval to Hitler's domination of Hungary, Yugoslavia, Rumania, and Bulgaria.[39]

Several administration critics concurred. As late as mid-June 1941, *Uncensored*, which had anticipated friction, suspected such talk hid a week of bargaining, with Stalin holding out for a high price. Besides, it said, Hitler might
well be hiding plans for a move elsewhere, perhaps a new bombing assault on
the British Isles. Norman Thomas thought the Führer wanted unrestricted use
of the Dnieper–Dunia Canal, which ran from Odessa to Riga, but maintained
that he would not fight over the matter.[40]

Such anti-interventionists were not alone. When the USSR attacked Finland, Roosevelt himself suspected "a fairly definite arrangement" to partition
Europe, Africa, and the Near East.[41] The president and his closest advisers
thought that Germany would first invade Britain, and only then assault the
Soviet Union.[42] By March 1941, there was some minor dissent within the administration, with Adolf Berle predicting, "The Germans will tackle Russia,
and probably will smash her."[43]

On 22 June 1941, Hitler's legions launched the greatest onslaught in the history of warfare. They attacked the Soviet Union with 3.2 million men, organized into 148 divisions that ranged a thousand miles from the Arctic Circle to
the Black Sea. "This is the real war," wrote Flynn. It made the British struggle
"a mere flea bite."[44]

Anti-interventionists saw various motives at work. The New York AFC
stressed the dictator's desire for the Ukraine, with its huge amounts of grain,
coal, manganese, and iron, and for Baku, which produced close to 20 percent
of the world's petroleum. The *New York Daily News* suggested that Hitler invaded to keep his massive army occupied. "He didn't know what else to do to
keep his men in fighting trim." It later asserted that Hitler planned to chase
Stalin a thousand miles into the Urals, develop a large Ukrainian grain supply,
and reorganize Russian industries, thereby protecting himself from any attack
from the West.[45] Norman Thomas emphasized raw materials, fear of a Russian

double cross, and a desire to win over anticommunist sentiment in the West, including that of the Roman Catholic Church.[46]

In late June, Dennis cheerfully admitted surprise, finding the attack rooted in a variety of factors: Germany's latest peace offensive, Britain's indifference to the Hess mission, Roosevelt's determination to prevent peace, Stalin's growing demands as the price of more supplies, and indications from Vichy, Madrid, Rome, and the Balkans that an economic United States of Europe could be secured by war against the Soviets.[47]

Publisher William Randolph Hearst blamed the Russians themselves. The USSR, wrote Hearst, had double-crossed Germany by seizing a variety of territories—the Baltic states, parts of Finland, half of Poland. Furthermore, it had defaulted on promised oil and grain shipments to Germany, while demanding even more land and concessions. The socialist *Call*'s Henry Haskell found the Nazi strike due in large part to the U.S. policy. Seeing a powerful Anglo-American alliance in the making, Germany did not want the Russian army at its rear.[48]

Some FDR foes hoped for a war of mutual exhaustion. In retrospect, much attention has been given to Senator Harry Truman's famous statement: "If we see that Germany is winning we ought to help Russia, and if Russia is winning we ought to help Germany, and that way let them kill as many as possible, although I don't want to see Hitler victorious under any circumstances."[49]

It was the anti-interventionists in particular who voiced such sentiments.[50] The more damage the German and Russian armies did to each other, according to Congressman Roy Woodruff, "the safer the world of free and honest men and women and children will be." Hiram Johnson remarked, "I would take both Hitler and Stalin, confine them securely in an elevated cage, and let them fight it out."[51]

When the invasion first took place, Roosevelt acted cautiously, dodging questions about extending lend-lease to the Soviets. By mid-July, he had unfrozen some $39 million of Russian funds and directed the release of machine tools. He also refrained from invoking the 1939 neutrality pact, thus enabling American ships to carry munitions to Russian ports.[52]

At the end of July 1941, the president authorized his leading adviser, Harry Hopkins, to visit Moscow, there to see whether the Soviets were strong enough to hold out against the German onslaught and to appraise whether the United States should risk sending military aid. Before Hopkins commenced his mission, he was skeptical of Russian strength. Once he arrived, he estimated that prompt American aid could enable the Soviets to stop the German advance. Even if the Germans captured Moscow, he continued, the defenders were determined to continue fighting.[53]

On 18 September, Roosevelt sent to Congress a supplementary lend-lease bill that included aid to the Soviets. On 10 October, Congressman Robert F. Rich's amendment, banning aid to the Soviets, was defeated 21 to 162. The legislation was passed in the House 323 to 67, in the Senate, 59 to 13.[54]

Despite the belief of most military analysts that the Soviets faced imminent defeat, many interventionists strongly supported such assistance.[55] Should Hitler dominate Russia, warned the CDAAA, the danger to both Britain and the United States would be far greater. As far as the immediate danger went, Germany could strike from the Caucasus or through Iraq, flank the British position in Iraq and the Persian Gulf, and move on India through Afghanistan. Should Siberia fall under Axis control, Singapore would be vulnerable. Conversely, an undefeated Russia would be able to fight until military and economic attrition, combined with "blows in the West," caused Germany's collapse.[56]

While conceding American abhorrence of communism, the CDAAA denied that the Soviet Union endangered the security of the Western Hemisphere. When the Soviets obtained victory, the interventionist group maintained, they would be so weakened that they might not even be communist any longer. Furthermore, they possessed no bases on the North Atlantic, lacked the sea power to threaten Alaska, and could not reach the South Atlantic. A loosely knit and backward nation, the USSR had shown it could not expand effectively, as seen by failures to install communist regimes in Hungary and Spain. Germany, in contrast, was so tightly centralized and industrially efficient that within two years it had brought most of Europe under the Nazi flag.[57]

A minority of the president's critics favored such aid.[58] In addition to the communists, whose sudden conversion to interventionism was the least of surprises, the *Militant* called for defense of the Soviet Union. The USSR itself, said the Trotskyist weekly, must be distinguished from "the bureaucrats" who "had usurped the seats of power."[59] *Commonweal* found the case for aiding the Soviet Union "unassailable," fearing that "the Nazi régime will directly, or indirectly, control and determine the political and social order of the world." Villard, in calling the attack "indescribably base," deemed Roosevelt and Welles courageous to announce that the United States would provide all possible help.[60]

Several anti-interventionists wanted to limit any such relief. Wheeler found no objection to giving money or matériel to Russia but sought assurance that American ships would not be sunk on their way to Vladivostok.[61] The *Christian Century* wanted the U.S. to give the Soviet Union enough aid to hold off Hitler, not enough to create a "Russian avalanche." Taft was inclined to favor assistance provided it was not used against Finland, though he did muse, "Apparently we are to follow Bundles for Britain with Packages for Petrograd." Mundt suggested that the British administer all such assistance, with the United States reimbursing their supplies. He warned, "Let us not have Uncle Sam become the generalissimo of the war nor the bedmate of communism."[62]

Yet most noninterventionists strongly opposed American aid to the Soviets. One of the most extreme comments came from Charles Lindbergh, who said in San Francisco on 2 July, "I would a hundred times rather see my country ally herself with England, or even with Germany with all her faults, than the cruelty, the Godlessness, and the barbarism that exists in Soviet Russia."[63] At a New York City rally in October, the aviator recalled that in 1938 he had hoped Britain and France would "permit Germany to expand eastward without declaring war."[64]

On moral grounds alone, it was argued, the Soviets did not deserve aid.[65] Bestowing military assistance simply made a travesty of any war against totalitarian dictatorship. Representative Fish accused "fire-eaters" of proposing to turn the "lend-lease" bill into a "Lenin-lease" bill. Sterling Morton confessed his disdain of "Mufflers for Moscow." To the *New York Daily News*, the German-Russian struggle was simply the latest event in a conflict stemming back to the Teutonic knights of the thirteenth century—no "more of our business than any of the previous wars were." Boake Carter called for a joint American-British-Japanese alliance to check both Germany and the Soviets. Commented Chester Bowles, "The Administration and the interventionists will, however, soon begin to attempt to build up Russia as a fine, God-fearing benefactor of the downtrodden. Or at worst a rather nice amiable benefactor with which we happen to have a slight disagreement on various details of economic and social organization."[66]

In attempting to secure backing for Russian aid, the president, in a press conference of 30 September, asserted that Article 124 of the 1936 Soviet constitution protected the free exercise of religion, a claim his critics challenged immediately.[67] Noninterventionists were quick to respond.[68] Roman Catholics were vocal, one poll showing 90 percent of the clergy opposed to aiding the Soviets.[69] Less than two years previously, the *Christian Century* recalled, Roosevelt had told the American Youth Congress how much he detested Russia's "banishment of religion." Stalin, mused socialist writer Lillian Symes, might order compulsory attendance at mass on penalty of liquidation or twenty years' hard labor. *Uncensored* accused Roosevelt of showing "symptoms of juridical cretinism."[70]

In Congress, too, the response was quick. Fish suggested that Roosevelt baptize Stalin in the White House swimming pool. Congresswoman Edith Nourse Rogers sought to amend the aid bill: no assistance would be implemented until the Soviet Union guaranteed freedom of religion and ended communist propaganda within the United States.[71]

Germany, some argued, was more tolerant of Christianity than were the Soviets. For every specimen of blasphemy spoken or written in Hitler's Reich, said *Catholic World*, a thousand had been officially approved in the land of Lenin and Stalin. In challenging Roosevelt's implicit comparison, *Commonweal* stressed that the German people could go to church, that its army had chaplains, and that the sacraments were administered. It did concede, however, that in neither country was it safe for a party member publicly to profess

Christianity or participate in community worship and charity.[72] On 25 October, *Uncensored* noted that Hitler might establish a Christian state in occupied Russia, with possible options including toleration for all Christian groups; acceptance of Lutheranism, Roman Catholicism, and "the Greek Orthodox religion of old Russia"; and encouragement for the Uniate Church, a move likely to be supported by the Vatican.[73]

In opposing American aid, the *Chicago Tribune* questioned the logistics of supply: It was physically impossible for the United States to deliver munitions. Germany occupied Greece and held the keys to the Dardanelles. Archangel was icebound, Murmansk cut off by the Finnish advance. The railroad from Iran to the Soviet Union ran through steep mountain grades and had a 250-mile gap. Loading facilities at Vladivostok were meager, and the Trans-Siberian Railroad operated a poorly equipped single-track line.[74]

Given such anxieties, even continued aid to Britain was suspect. In noting a pending lend-lease appropriation bill, the AFC warned that Britain might still turn its own supplies over to Russia while receiving American lend-lease. Similarly, General Wood asked, "Are we to continue our aid to Britain without some assurance that everything we send will not be relayed to Stalin?"[75]

At the outset of the Russian attack, several anti-interventionists stressed that the Soviets had no chance. The Germans were advancing too fast, were too well equipped, and possessed too much strategic genius for the USSR to survive. In late June, just after the Army Group South of General Gerd von Rundstedt captured Dubno, Herbert Hoover claimed, "These Russians will be promptly mopped up."[76]

Early in July, as the Germans broke through Soviet lines on the Latvian border, Hiram Johnson wrote to his son, "I never did believe the Russians were good fighters or good soldiers."[77] Hanson Baldwin, referring to the famous Russian defeat in World War I, saw in the offing "a Tannenburg far more decisive and disastrous than the first." Certainly a German victory was "well on the way to accomplishment." Late that month, columnist George Sokolsky forecast that Russian troops would revolt against their Stalinist leaders, establishing a pro-German government similar to France's Vichy regime.[78]

Such analysis persisted all through August. On the 9th, just after Russian pockets at Smolensk and Uman surrendered and over four hundred thousand Soviet prisoners were taken, *Uncensored* quoted unnamed "Washington observers" who deemed the Red Army doomed. By the end of the month, as the Soviets were evacuating the industrial center of Dnepropetrovsk and blowing the great dam on the Dnieper at Zaporozhe, Flynn wrote in his diary, "Russia in bad way. Looks as if that war in its last stages." When Hitler reached the Caspian Sea and the Ural Mountains, Hoover predicted, he might initiate peace moves with Stalin, both of them henceforth fighting Churchill.[79]

Early in September, when the siege of Leningrad began, many FDR adversaries stressed the reverses suffered by the Soviets.[80] The New York Chapter of

America First could not find a single military expert who believed that they could hold out, much less win the war. Before winter set in, noted its weekly bulletin, German armies would conquer Moscow and Baku; Stalin might then retire beyond the Urals. In mid-month, just after the Germans took Kiev, Colonel McCormick announced to a radio audience, "It looks as if the communist menace to the world has been destroyed." With the collapse of the Soviet Union expected by British and American experts alike, Libby thought Hitler would be able to consolidate all Europe, including Turkey, into a single economic bloc. Though Britain would encourage acts of sabotage through "Fifth Column activities," it could not trigger an effective revolt against him.[81] To Hanson Baldwin, Germany had lost the battle of time, but the columnist still put odds on its victory.[82]

Freda Utley appeared most vocal of all. In a memo drafted in the initial weeks of fighting, she predicted a rapid German victory. The Reich, she wrote, need not conquer the entire nation; the Ukraine, rich in grain and oil, and the Caucasus, also abundant in petroleum, were sufficient. In fact, Germany probably would not require large-scale occupation garrisons, for it could rely on Ukrainians embittered by the mass starvations. Writing in the September issue of the *American Mercury*, she speculated that a rump Soviet state might relocate to Asia, Stalin flee to Mexico, and Russia face a new threat from Japan.[83]

During October, certain noninterventionists envisaged Germany successful everywhere.[84] The Soviets, asserted Frank Waldrop, had already lost the war; the Russian people were about to "deliver a bloody bill to Stalin." R. Douglas Stuart Jr. of America First was so confident of German victory that he feared a desperate Roosevelt move to prevent a peace. *Uncensored* forecast a German "knockout" within two months. John Cudahy found the USSR "just about gasping." Again more cautious, Baldwin saw Germany ultimately advancing to the Volga, though the move might take a year.[85]

In mid-November, on the day before Rostov-on-Don was taken, the *Chicago Tribune* predicted that winter would not hamper German operations in the Crimea and the oil-rich Caucasus. Furthermore, because the communists had treated the Ukrainians so miserably, they were passively casting their lot with the invader. *Uncensored* expected a Nazi occupation of the Donets Basin and further advance on the Black Sea.[86]

To some Roosevelt foes, massive German conquests of the Soviet heartland really aided the United States and Britain, not threatened them. Late in June, Taft found the invasion postponing for many months any attack Hitler could possibly make on the U.S. The *New York Daily News* called the attack Britain's "biggest break in the war." Even if Germany captured Moscow, maintained the *Chicago Tribune*, the most favorable season for invading Britain would have passed.[87]

By 1 August 1941, the AFC's research bureau reported that Hitler's conquest of the USSR would contribute little to German wealth. Once Germany deprived the Soviet Union of most of its oil, Russia's "economic life would be reduced to a hopeless state of non-productivity, which would be small help to the Nazis in war or peace." Moreover, the USSR was short on food, not having been a major food exporter since World War I. "To get much food out of Russia," remarked the AFC, Hitler "must keep the tractors running full blast and starve the Russians, thus lowering their productivity." And unless Soviet industry disappeared, the nation had little coal and iron to export.[88]

Even a victorious Hitler, such anti-interventionists kept saying, would not have it easy. Representative Chiperfield stressed that the German leader needed to rest his troops, replace lost planes, and police a vast area before turning his attention again to England and Western Europe. According to Hoover, Hitler would need one million men "to garrison the place against the conspiracies of the OGPU."[89] *Uncensored* anticipated social disruption at home.[90]

Occasionally voices of apprehension were heard. Several anti-interventionists warned that any truce between Germany and the USSR would seriously harm the West. In early October, for example, Congressman James O'Connor feared that the Soviet leader "might double-cross us overnight" by making peace with Hitler: "Remember, human monsters are all yellow."[91]

At times certain noninterventionists were not so quick to see a German victory, much less a "quisling" peace, in the offing. Germany's Führer, they predicted, would lose the Russian campaign, for a combination of huge distances and the Soviets' scorched-earth policy were bound to defeat him. In June, the *Chicago Tribune* stressed the massive distances, poor communications, and the USSR's vast army.[92] The *New York Daily News* remarked, "Hitler won't find Russia full of filling stations for his panzers, any more than Napoleon found it full of feed for his horses."[93] The Reich, noted Senator Alexander Wiley early in August, had been greatly weakened in planes, ships, and morale and had already lost a million men in the invasion. "If Hitler keeps on pursuing his course in Russia," remarked the Wisconsin Republican, "the Russian bear may do so much damage there will not be any Hitler." The more Hitler spread himself, Wheeler asserted, the weaker he became. "Leningrad may fall," commented *Christian Century* in September, just as the German siege of that city began. "Moscow may fall; Odessa may fall—but Russia will not fall."[94] On 8 November, five days after the Germans had captured Kursk, Hiram Johnson believed that although Germany had "whipped" the USSR, it was hard to see how the Reich could withstand the losses in men and material. Less than three weeks later, Baldwin found the struggle still undecided; even the German capture of Moscow might not be fatal to the Soviet cause. Four days before the Pearl Harbor attack, the *New York Daily News*, noting Hitler's recent reverse at Rostov, found him facing a severe winter ahead.[95]

To several administration critics, a Soviet victory would not necessarily constitute good news.[96] If Stalin won, warned Norman Thomas, he would dictate the peace.[97] Helicopter manufacturer Igor Sikorsky, a native Russian, feared that a victorious USSR could reach the Balkans and Scandinavia. Robsion mentioned the Baltic states.[98] John Haynes Holmes predicted the USSR would occupy East Prussia and the Dardanelles and would probably take over Manchukuo and Mongolia. In December 1941, the *Christian Century* gave ten-to-one odds that Germany would be in Soviet hands. Senator William Bulow saw the Soviets' eye on Britain. George Sokolsky worried that U.S. arms shipped to the Soviets might eventually "find their way into the making of a social revolution in this country."[99]

Conflict between the Soviets and the West was bound to follow. "Where would Stalin stop?" asked the *Chicago Tribune*. "Would another war begin with British and American troops trying to stem forces they had supported?" Queried the *Saturday Evening Post*, "Having saved the world from Nazism, should we not be morally obligated to go on and save it from Bolshevism?"[100]

At least one anti-interventionist faced a genuine dilemma. This was William Henry Chamberlin, who had served as *Christian Science Monitor* correspondent in Moscow from 1922 to 1936, before being transferred to Tokyo and Paris. Like his personal friend and fellow journalist Freda Utley, he had begun his career as a radical, welcoming the Soviet experiment and marrying a native Russian. Disillusioned by Stalinism, however, he later became one of the Soviets' most bitter foes.[101]

In 1940, Chamberlin published *Confessions of an Individualist*. In this work he staunchly opposed collective security. If, he warned, it would take the Allies three years to crush Germany (which was the British estimate), millions would have been killed or wounded, thousands of ships sunk, and scores of beautiful cities devastated—a price he found too high. The Red Army would be in a position to seize all of Poland and much of the Balkans. To avoid another and sterner Versailles, Germany might well go communist. "Great Britain and France, already strained to the uttermost, would find themselves confronted by a hostile land mass stretching from the Rhine to the Pacific." Far better to "keep clear of adventurous crusades" than to risk such an outcome.[102]

As expected, Roosevelt's adversaries praised Chamberlin's work.[103] Vera Micheles Dean, research director and editor of the Foreign Policy Association, was more ambivalent. While lauding Chamberlin's "faith in the intrinsic worth of human personality," she asserted that he had underestimated Soviet weakness and naively assumed Hitler's ambitions were limited to Central Europe. She rejected his belief that, in her words, the United States could view Europe with "unconcern and detachment."[104]

Between Hitler's invasion of Russia and U.S. entry into war, Chamberlin wavered on the matter of Soviet victory. In July 1941, he wrote that the Red Army could retreat a thousand miles, exploiting its vast hinterland and industrial centers to its east.[105] Two months later, he estimated that Hitler's defeat would be "little short of a miracle." Nevertheless, in late October, Chamberlin hailed Russia's "amazing resistance," something that he credited to an indoctrinated youth, a modernized army, a seasoned munitions industry, and the sheer vastness of the nation. Speculating about a free Russia participating in a free Europe, he called for American aid to the USSR as a matter of "hard-boiled, calculating American self-interest." In November, speaking at Stanford University, he saw risks in U.S. assistance, among them a victorious Stalin overrunning Europe.[106]

From the time of Hitler's invasion, certain noninterventionists used the Soviet theater of war as a means of attacking the British, whom—so they asserted—were singularly inactive while the USSR was experiencing a major onslaught.[107] In mid-October, Pettengill accused Britain of throwing Russia "to the dogs" to save its empire and quite possibly to make peace with Germany.[108] The *Chicago Tribune* was vehement on the matter, blaming Churchill for sitting behind a twenty-mile dike of water, waiting for Hitler to defeat the Russians and absorb their resources before attacking Britain. Regarding the British forces, it declared, "The armies of an empire of 500 million people are wearing out nothing but their pants seats."[109] Hearst demurred, maintaining that any effort to invade Europe meant the sacrifice of a large part of Britain's defense forces.[110]

Even British aid to the Soviets was viewed with a jaundiced eye. Congressman Robert F. Jones indicted the British for making all deliveries to Russia at world prices with contracts in sterling. In claiming that Britain was not sending planes to the Soviets, Representative Robsion said, "She never fights except to save her own skin."[111]

At no time after Hitler's invasion of Russia did the anti-interventionist posture dominate general public sentiment. On 30 June, R. Douglas Stuart Jr., the AFC's executive secretary, wrote Herbert Hoover, "The outbreak of war between Russia and Germany has had a notable influence on public opinion. People realize there is no choice for us. If Germany wins, Russia will go Fascist. If Russia wins, Germany will go Communist. The American people are not anxious to fight to make the world safe for communism."[112]

In a Gallup poll taken in July 1941, however, 72 percent of the respondents endorsed a Russian victory, only 4 percent a German one. In fact, administration critics could take heart in just one statistic: the percentage favoring immediate U.S. entry into the war dropped from 24 percent to 21 percent. On 5 August a Gallup poll found only 35 percent supporting the inclusion of Russia in the lend-lease program. Yet, when asked whether the United States should *sell* war supplies to the Soviets, 70 percent endorsed the move. In late September, Gallup noted a 49:44 ratio in favor of credits if the Soviets could not pay cash.[113] *Fortune* magazine, canvassing the public in October, found 51.4 percent of the respondents saying the U.S. should work alongside the Russians. An additional 21.9 percent believed that the Soviets should be treated as full partners. Only 13.5 percent took the position held by most anti-interventionists: the United States should cut off all aid to the Russians.[114] Gallup polls in both June and September also showed a majority predicting Soviet victory.[115]

Within the administration, prognosis concerning Soviet success varied. Stimson, Knox, Stark, and Bullitt all anticipated Soviet defeat by the year's end.[116] In June, Laurence A. Steinhardt, U.S. ambassador to Moscow, gave the Russians only two months to hold out.[117] On the other hand, Joseph C. Grew, American ambassador to Japan, thought the Russians would fight harder than many believed.[118] Berle and Hull supported lend-lease, undoubtedly believing that the USSR would survive.[119] By mid-August, a reluctant Sumner Welles had been won over.[120]

At first the Allied military was usually pessimistic. The British War Office and chiefs of staff believed that once Germany had reached the Urals, Soviet resistance would cease.[121] Of the top American military, only George Marshall saw the possibility of Soviet survival, and even he opposed any shipment of scarce American aircraft. To the chief of staff, greater priorities included the Philippines and Brazil.[122] At times Marshall envisioned Soviet defeat ahead, writing Sumner Welles in mid-July, "The German Army is on the verge of disrupting the Russian forces."[123] Stimson concurred with Marshall's opposition, privately protesting against depleting American forces.[124] Colonel Truman Smith of G-2 predicted a quick German victory over the Soviets, after which the Reich would attempt to negotiate a peace with Britain. If Britain refused, Hitler would either invade the British Isles or seek to eliminate British influence in the entire Mediterranean region.[125] Only early in August did more optimistic reports reach the president; these centered more on German setbacks, not actual defeats.[126]

Despite the intensity of the debate over Russia, American lend-lease had little initial impact. Only in late September did Lord Beaverbrook, representing Britain, and W. Averill Harriman, representing the United States, make an agreement in Moscow by which the U.S. pledged a billion dollars of aid.[127] Delivery was always difficult. Roosevelt and Hopkins themselves saw such aid as more a pledge of American "good faith" than of immediate value to the Soviet war effort. As for the winter of 1941–42, they realized that U.S. supplies would play a negligible part in the battle for Moscow. Little could arrive until after the military outcome had already been decided. Of course, by 1944, lend-lease would play a major role in the Soviet victory, as the $10 billion worth of U.S. equipment and supplies filled critical gaps in the Russian output. The tide of battle, however, had swung in the Soviets' favor long before American aid had arrived in quantity.[128]

During the entire debate over aiding the Soviets, anti-interventionists supported one of the USSR's most embittered and understandable enemies, Finland. On 26 June, in the wake of the German onslaught, the Finns attacked the

USSR. "For the liberty of the Fatherland," President Risto Ryti announced, Finland was going to war alongside Germany and "her leader of genius, Reichchancellor Hitler." On 30 August, it reclaimed Vyborg. Soon it was making long thrusts into Soviet territory all along the frontier. Its leading general, Field Marshal Carl Gustav Emil von Mannerheim, proclaimed publicly that Finland could no longer be satisfied with old, inadequate frontiers: "New days are dawning ever brighter before our eyes."[129]

The British told the Finns on 22 September not to advance into "purely Russian territory."[130] Within a month and a half, Hull announced that the administration had recently called on the Finns to withdraw their troops from the USSR. The United States, he claimed, had notified Finland on 18 August that the Soviet Union wanted to discuss peace on the basis of territorial compensation. Finland did not reply, and its troops continued to advance. On 25 November, the Finns signed the anti-Comintern pact with the Axis countries. On 6 December, Britain declared war on Finland, and the U.S. took six Finnish ships into custody.[131]

Finland still had much anti-interventionist support. The country, said the *Chicago Tribune*, was fighting for its freedom. The *Christian Century* noted that "nine out of ten Americans would rejoice to see the Finns march triumphantly into Leningrad." Hearst's *San Francisco Examiner* reprinted major portions of Finland's white book, justifying its reentry into war. Opposing American aid to the Soviet Union, the newspaper's editorial headline read, "Our Honor Periled by Aid to Finland's Foe." Congressman Fred Bradley queried, "Shall we now furnish Russia with planes to bomb Finland?"[132]

Many anti-interventionists severely criticized Hull's November warning. Finland, they stated, was acting in self-defense. According to Representative Clare Hoffman (Rep.-Mich.), the Finns had refused to "submit themselves to the tender mercy of the man who has starved and murdered his own subjects by the thousands." For Finland to make a separate peace with Russia, commented the *Call*, would expose itself to massacre by its erstwhile Nazi allies.[133]

Furthermore, FDR critics found the American warning hypocritical. How, asked Wheeler, could the United States demand that Finland not protect its own soil while the U.S. extended the war to Greenland, Iceland, and Asia and Britain invaded Libya, Ethiopia, Iraq, and Iran? Hoover wondered whether his nation had "lost all sense of human and moral proportions." Taft remarked, "We will be deeply ashamed in all time to come." Said Senator Shipstead, "We are being placed in the position of Uncle Sam being the errand boy for Joe Dlugashvili [*sic*], alias Joe Stalin, otherwise Joe the Steel Man, and Winston Churchill."[134]

The British in particular were strongly assailed. Stated Hiram Johnson, "I could not find it in my heart to blame this little nation, but I saw, with indignation, Britain bombing her ports." Waldrop asserted that Britain's blocking of Red Cross supplies made Finland dependent on the Nazis. "The British," he continued, "learned a long time ago to stand aloof of other nations except to the extent they could be used for Britain's interest."[135]

In retrospect, as historian George C. Herring Jr. notes, American neutrality in the Russo-German war involved risks that at the time appeared too great to shoulder. True, the burdens of governing a large, alien, and hostile territory might weaken, not strengthen, Hitler's Reich. In the short term, however, the consequences could have been catastrophic for the Allies. The Germans would have obtained vast quantities of food and raw materials, the Near East would be exposed to Nazi penetration, and Japan would have been given a free hand in the Far East. The balance of power would have shifted from the United States and Britain to the Axis powers. One could also argue that Roosevelt's personal rationale in aiding the Soviets was quite self-serving: the exhaustion of German forces on the Russian front would decrease the need for any American troops on the European continent.[136]

To the anti-interventionists, even a German conquest of the USSR placed the U.S. in less danger, not more. Therefore, the occupation of Iceland and the lengthening of selective service terms were most unnecessary.

# 16

# A Pivotal Summer

By the summer of 1941, the administration focus had centered increasingly on Iceland, where Roosevelt feared a German takeover. A sovereign state in personal union with Denmark, Iceland had been scheduled for full independence in 1944. The island instead became totally orphaned in April 1940, when Germany occupied its mother country. First, Britain and Canada stationed troops there. Then, in summer 1941, encouraged by the British, Iceland accepted American "protection," and on 7 July a brigade of nearly four thousand American marines arrived.

Historian Waldo Heinrichs aptly calls Iceland "the turntable of the Atlantic."[1] Were the Germans to occupy that strategic island, said Roosevelt as he announced the move, they would pose an intolerable threat to all "the independent nations of the New World." Hostile naval and air bases there would menace Greenland, threaten shipping in the North Atlantic, and interrupt the steady flow of munitions, the last item "a broad policy clearly approved by Congress." In friendly hands, Iceland possessed two critical advantages: it provided indispensable refueling bases for convoys, and it controlled the Denmark Strait, a passage between Greenland and Iceland where German ships had been active.[2]

The CDAAA backed Roosevelt strongly. If the United States had not sent troops, it argued, the Battle of the Atlantic would be lost, and Britain itself would face defeat. The American position in Greenland would be untenable, as German bases would be lodged within six hundred miles of Canada.[3] A Gallup poll estimated 75 percent favoring U.S. convoys to that area.[4]

In 1940, some anti-interventionists had called for U.S. occupation of Iceland. In April, Hearst noted that its excellent harbors made for a valuable base.

Two months later, Lundeen—ever the imperialist—said Iceland was "an American island belonging to the Western Hemisphere, and it ought to be under our flag."[5] That August, the *Chicago Tribune*, while denying Iceland lay in the Western Hemisphere, expressed hope that the United States could obtain it after the war. At the very least, the U.S. should insist that no other power be permitted to use it for military purposes.[6]

Columnist Frank Waldrop dissented, claiming that four-fifths of Iceland was uninhabitable. It lacked any harbor, was too remote to serve as an air base, and produced "nothing but hay, geysers, and herring." Moreover, its 108,000 citizens were "highly literate, quarrelsome, individualistic Aryans," who "would be mighty mean to an invader."[7]

Once Roosevelt made his announcement, the *New York Daily News* stood alone among the anti-interventionists in partially endorsing the move. The U.S. Navy, it said, had testified to Iceland's strategic value. Moreover, the occupation would relieve an estimated sixty to eighty thousand troops for service elsewhere and, when fogs were not too thick, facilitate the provisioning of American ships. Opposing the president's promise to return the island to Denmark after the conflict, it called for a permanent U.S. protectorate. The *News* did object to the fact that FDR did not consult Congress, and, more important, it found the move "a long step toward war."[8]

Many of the president's critics, far less ambivalent than the *News*, strongly opposed his action. To Charles A. Lindbergh, the decision was "the most serious step we have yet taken." Norman Thomas sought a congressional investigation of the matter. The *Christian Century* headlined its editorial: "The President Enters the War." American troops sent to Iceland, commented the AFC's R. Douglas Stuart Jr., would have been considerably safer had Germany been informed beforehand of the occupation; otherwise, the Reich might have attacked U.S. vessels accidentally discovered in its declared war zone.[9]

Castle denied that Hitler had threatened Iceland. Furthermore, to Robert A. Taft, an American occupation was a liability. Were Germany to conquer the British Isles, the entire U.S. force in Iceland might easily be defeated, as it would be in easy reach of a German-dominated Ireland and Scotland but too far to be defended by the American fleet.[10] Even if Iceland were lost, said Colonel McCormick, the rough terrain of Greenland and Labrador would hold off any invader. *Uncensored* raised a different point. Unless the British were going to abandon the island, a Nazi attack would be fantastic. Had there been danger, the already seasoned British troops obviously would have remained.[11]

Roosevelt's use of presidential power was also questioned. Taft found no legal or constitutional right to send American troops; the president's legal power was limited to U.S. citizens and property. "The mere fact that power may be usurped is no evidence of legal right," he continued. "If the occupation of Iceland is defense, then any act the President cares to order is defense."[12]

The agreement made with Iceland, several administration foes argued, was illegal. Borchard doubted whether Iceland had officially seceded from Denmark or whether Denmark had recognized this secession. Unless either fact was verified, Iceland was not an independent country, and Roosevelt had committed an international offense. Civil liberties lawyer John Finerty, Flynn's replacement as national chairman of the Keep America Out of War Congress, denied that Iceland had ever invited the United States; certainly Denmark had not given its approval. Villard challenged Roosevelt's claim that defense exigencies gave the U.S. the right to declare special jurisdiction in the waters around Iceland. As the high seas were the common property of all nations, Roosevelt's assertion was "nothing less than bizarre."[13]

By October, Boake Carter was writing that American troops were ruining Iceland's decent and orderly life. The "lure of gold" and fantastic wages had driven farmers to town, causing fields to be abandoned. Hence, there could only be dislocation and ruin when the conflict ended. Pacifist leader Dorothy Detzer sought an investigation into the number and task of U.S. troops in Iceland, noting that its president had pointed to "serious difficulties between natives and our soldiers."[14]

If the Iceland move met with anti-interventionist attack, lengthening the term served by conscripts drew far greater hostility. The Burke–Wadsworth Act of 1940 had limited the time of service for draftees to twelve months. Furthermore, it prohibited draftees from being stationed outside the Western Hemisphere.

By 1941, however, General Marshall was expressing alarm. Testifying before the Senate Military Affairs Committee on 9 July, he urged Congress to extend indefinitely the terms of draftees, National Guardsmen, and reserve officers. Otherwise, he continued, "our present trained forces will largely melt away." More specifically, the chief of staff opposed efforts to restrict the term of service to six months—or any other precise limit, for that matter. A few days after Marshall made his report, the war department requested that the hemispheric restrictions be lifted. On 23 July, in testimony before the House Military Affairs Committee, Marshall stressed certain potential dangers: war clouds gathering in the Far East, the Axis threat to Alaska, and Nazi uprisings in Bolivia, Brazil, and Colombia.[15]

In a special message sent to Congress on 21 July, Roosevelt backed Marshall. The peril, he warned, was "infinitely greater" than it had been a year before. Each German conquest brought Nazi domination that much closer. "Within two months, disintegration, which would follow failure to take Congressional action, will commence in the armies of the United States." Rather than take the time to amend the 1940 act, Congress should parallel his own declaration of 27 May by "acknowledging" a national emergency. The move would give the president authority to hold soldiers "for the duration."[16]

The public was far from receptive: a Gallup poll of 29 July indicated that only 51 percent favored eliminating the one-year limit.[17] In bargaining with congressional leaders, Roosevelt was forced to retain the ban on serving outside the hemisphere, though he did manage to secure endorsement for lifting the one-year restriction.

A few noninterventionists saw logic in the administration's claims. More than a year's training, Boake Carter stated, was needed for such groups as engineers and antiaircraft gunners. However, the Hearst columnist did oppose permission to send forces overseas.[18] The *New York Daily News* backed Marshall's assertion that the loss of three-fourths of the officers, due for release when the year's term was up, would damage the budding army. Taking issue with Marshall's similar concerns about the loss of two-thirds of the draftees, it argued for rotation.[19]

Usually anti-interventionists balked. Some found the existing army sufficiently strong; Congressman Dewey Short (Rep.-Mo.) pointed to a force of close to four and a half million men. The Missouri Republican suggested that just as enlistments were staggered over all twelve months, so too could be the demobilizations.[20] Vorys challenged the claim that two-thirds of the army would vanish. By March 1942, he asserted, only one-tenth would be lost, and this number could be replaced by draftees who had seven months' training.[21] The *Chicago Tribune* claimed that a volunteer force of less than half a million, if properly armed and trained, would be able to defend the nation. Al Williams was satisfied with a hundred thousand.[22]

The administration, said its critics, had reversed its position. Bennett Clark noted that Marshall had originally found eighteen months of training sufficient. Wheeler claimed not to have much faith in a chief of staff who, on one day, said the United States needed 375,000, a few days later called for 450,000, and the next time spoke in terms of 1.7 million. If an expert testified this way on the witness stand, Wheeler asserted, a judge would tell the jury to disregard his comments.[23]

The administration, said its critics, was acting under Allied pressure. Danaher pointed to Marshall's interview in the 24 June issue of the *Washington Post*, in which the chief of staff had promised that the bulk of trainees could return home once they spent twelve months in uniform. Only after Churchill, General Sir Archibald Wavell, and General Sir Claude J. E. Auchinleck had spoken, noted the Connecticut senator, did Marshall change his position.[24] Wavell, in relinquishing his post as commander in chief of British forces in the Middle East, and his replacement Auchinleck had stated early in July that a second American Expeditionary Force would be needed.[25] Early in August, Churchill created a mild flurry by arguing that the United States was "advancing with rising wrath and conviction to the very verge of war."[26] The *Call* observed that Charles de Gaulle, leader of the Free French, endorsed the Wavell–Auchinleck view.[27]

Furthermore, FDR's foes accused the administration of breaking faith with the draftees.[28] They frequently cited the claim of the staunch interventionist Senator Claude Pepper, who noted that men might be kept in the army for ten years.[29] To the *New York Daily News*, "a dirty trick" was being played.[30]

Miserable training conditions only compounded the breach of promise. Congressman William Blackney (Rep.-Mich.) found frequent instances whereby draftees were required to walk long distances, perhaps as much as a mile, for meals and toilets.[31] The *Chicago Tribune* endorsed exposés on camp morale published in *Life* and the *Nation*, both interventionist journals.[32] Marked salary inequities, it was noted, existed between soldiers and civilian factory workers, not to mention Canadian troops. Moreover, soldiers could be used as strike breakers.[33] Lawrence Dennis observed draftees, mustered out after a year's training, "who are not fit to take part in anything more military than a Boy Scout's jamboree."[34] Administration critics asserted that other countries, ranging from Canada to Germany, trained their recruits in far less time.[35] An internal army report conceded that the service was experiencing a major morale problem.[36]

The whole matter of equipment was stressed. Pointing to the lack of proper matériel, Bennett Clark cited maneuvers in which an ordinary truck bore the sign: "This is a tank."[37] The United States, said the *Chicago Tribune*, lacked a single dive-bomber, possessed only a few attack planes and light bombers, and had no medium-sized tanks or self-propelling gun mounts. Not a single division in the U.S. Army equaled a Nazi contingent.[38]

Anti-interventionists challenged Roosevelt's claim that the United States was in greater danger in 1941 than it had been in 1940. In late July, the *Christian Century* asked rhetorically, "Is the Nation in Peril?" and answered with a resounding no. Senator Alva Adams queried, "Can we imagine Germany, surrounded by hostile peoples whom she has overrun, with her hands more than filled in meeting Russia, and with the British fleet on the other side, undertaking to invade the United States?"[39]

Allied successes on the battlefield were presented as evidence that further American preparations were not needed. Within a year, Senator Wiley stressed, Britain had conquered Italian East Africa, Ethiopia, and French Syria. It was "out-Coventrying, on Germany's soil, the German Luftwaffe's bombardment of Coventry."[40] Moreover, England did not appear that alarmed.[41] The AFC pointed to a number of factors: Hitler's indefinite postponement of invading Britain, Germany engaged in fighting its strongest opponent on the European continent, a fall in British sea losses during the summer, and a much stronger British air defense.[42]

Nor was the Far East neglected. George Bender (Rep.-Ohio) stressed that China was holding out. Singapore and the Netherlands East Indies, said

Wiley, were equipped and garrisoned. Moreover, despite Japan's recent move into Indochina, it had been weakened in both finances and manpower. Conversely, the United States had strengthened its navy, fortified its island possessions, and severed fuel oil to Japan.[43]

In addition, the U.S.'s own defenses appeared much improved. To Wiley, the new American bases had turned the Caribbean into "an American lake." In the final analysis, said Senator Walsh, the nation's protection depended on sea and air power, not just ground forces. Congressman Bartel J. Jonkman (Rep.-Mich.) pointed to the example of Frederick the Great, who—when limited by treaty to a hundred thousand—created a magnificent army by providing intensive training.[44]

Marshall's desire to lift the ban on service overseas met with particular anxiety. A new American Expeditionary Force, it was feared, might well be in the making. "If this is an army for an expedition abroad," commented Congressman Daniel A. Reed (Rep.-N.Y.), "then we should be beginning now to lay out our hospital program." General Wood used the term "fraud."[45]

The AFC research bureau denied that Iceland, Siberia, Dakar, the Azores, or the Cape Verde Islands were endangered. After examining all the supposed routes by which the United States could be invaded, it found the nation well protected. Nor could any mythical danger of invasion from Europe be used to justify American entry into combat zones along the coasts of Northern Ireland, Scotland, or Norway. It cited Hanson Baldwin, who wrote, "The argument that we have to establish bases in another hemisphere to protect our own land quickly reaches a strategic absurdity."[46]

As frequently in the past, noninterventionists stressed the possible abuses of presidential power. In particular, Roosevelt's request that Congress declare a national emergency caused much concern. Such a proclamation, said the AFC research bureau, "would create an amorphous situation in which drastic powers without definite limits would become available for exercise by the Administration." Some 223 supplementary laws might be tapped, including those that could control labor, industry, agriculture, transportation, communication, and the merchant marine.[47]

The AFC national committee took no official stand on term extension, largely because its chairman, General Wood, did not want to be put in the position of challenging the army chief of staff. Many local chapters, however, strongly resisted the proposals. The AFC did promote the slogan "National Defense at Any Expense, but Keep Our Boys at Home." Its research bureau conceded that it was impossible to train a mass army within a year but presented its own option to Marshall's plan: retain all existing army divisions and national guard units, bringing them up to full strength by enlistments, if necessary, and giving them extensive training. At the same time, all draftees and new officers should be placed in entirely new units. By this device, regular army and national guard units would be instructed quickly. The United States could have nine fully prepared army divisions, ready for any contingency, plus many partially trained units. Under present policy, existing units were spread so thin that the U.S. only possessed two well-prepared and -equipped divisions.[48]

As in the original debate over the draft in the summer of 1940, administration adversaries offered a major alternative: a return to the volunteer system. General Wood called for a special reenlistment bounty, suggesting $150 per man. If a sufficient number could not be induced to reenlist, special provision could be made to keep those draftees stationed in such places as Hawaii, Panama, and Trinidad from three to six more months.[49]

Others offered suggestions as well. Villard simply called for putting all 472,000 three-year regulars into equipped divisions. If they were provided with the best officers, the United States would have an army ready for service. General Thomas S. Hammond, president of the Whiting Corporation and chairman of the Chicago AFC chapter, outlined a scheme by which selectees would enlist for three years in the army, then spend three years in the national guard, followed by three more years in the reserve. Hearst repeated his pleas for the Swiss system of a citizen army.[50]

The *Christian Century* considered calling for the demobilization of the draft army. Citing recent columns of Walter Lippmann, it noted the impossibility of arming Britain, the Soviet Union, and China while building a domestic mass force in the United States at the same time. The interventionist columnist also argued that expansion of the American army could not be rushed through effectively and that the army lacked the competent officers, much less the equipment, needed to train soldiers effectively.[51]

As in the case of previous legislation, congressional anti-interventionists offered many amendments. Taft sought to limit national guard term extension to two years, draftee extension to six months.[52] Edwin Johnson called for a raise of $7.50 per month ("so modest that I am almost ashamed to offer it").[53] Fish proposed a measure that would permit the release of all married soldiers, national guardsmen, and selectees; set a maximum of two million men for the army; and retain the one-year limit on service provided that no more than forty-five thousand be discharged in any one month.[54]

The bill's sponsors encountered some difficulties. On 7 August, by the comfortable margin of forty-five to thirty, the Senate offered only an eighteen-month extension, provided for a pay raise after one year's service, and sought to expedite the release of men over age twenty-eight. On 12 August, the House narrowly passed the same bill, 203 to 202. The news that the Vichy government was on the verge of capitulating to Germany, analyzed AFC staffer Ruth Sarles, served at the last moment to swing sufficient votes to pass the bill.

Two historians, J. Garry Clifford and Samuel R. Spencer Jr., have seen Roosevelt's leadership as erratic. He failed to explain the need for longer service and had left Washington during the final voting to meeting with Churchill in

Newfoundland. A Gallup poll indicated that 71 percent favored a one-year draft for men between the ages of eighteen and thirty-two.[55]

The vote has often been misunderstood. Even if the eighteen-month extension had been turned down, undoubtedly a compromise would have been reached, and draftees would still have had to serve from six to twelve more months.[56] AFC leaders were far from despondent. The CDAAA, on the other hand, found little comfort in the closeness of the tally, claiming it would encourage the Axis in further aggression.[57]

During the debate over lengthening the terms of conscription, one event appeared to mark the most dangerous step thus far: a summit meeting between the president and Winston Churchill. From 9 to 12 August, the two men, together with civilian and military advisers, rendezvoused off the coast of Newfoundland near Argentia, a base recently transferred to the United States as part of the destroyer bases deal. Useful if inconclusive discussion focused on production priorities as well as the wider matter of beating Germany and heading off Japan. The informal meeting of British and American leaders, however, far transcended any concrete agreements made, which were of limited importance and soon modified by the demands of war. It was the face-to-face encounters that expedited common planning once the U.S. entered the war.[58]

For years, attention has focused more on the eight-point declaration of Anglo-American war aims, which has gone down in history as the Atlantic Charter, than on the informal conversations.[59] For Churchill, the Eight Points aligned the United States and Britain more closely while bringing the Americans a step closer to war. Contrariwise, Roosevelt, who did not fully trust the British, saw the joint declaration as a device to head off the kind of secret and concrete agreements that had been so troublesome after World War I. Moreover, it might rally people in occupied countries to defy the Nazis, and, by pledging an equitable peace, even move the German people to resist Hitler. Then, too, a peace statement ringing with exalted phrases could distract attention from the weighty discussions of military assistance and spike anti-interventionist criticism of the meeting.

Anti-interventionists dissected the Eight Points most carefully, often stressing the danger or naiveté involved. Concerning point 1, in which the United States and Britain denied seeking any "aggrandizement, territorial or other," the AFC research bureau responded that the document was not signed by such Allied governments in exile as the Netherlands. Therefore, nothing could prevent territorial acquisition on their part. Nor did it deter any of the British dominions or the Soviet Union from seizing territory held by other nations.[60]

In point 2, the two countries expressed their "desire to see no territorial changes that do not accord with the freely expressed wishes of the peoples concerned." *Uncensored* found the whole issue moot, for nations fighting for the status quo ante bellum obviously had no interest in territorial changes.[61] To John T. Flynn, the words remained meaningless unless applied to such nations as "India, Indo-China, the Dutch Indies, British Malaya, Lithuania, Latvia, Estonia, and Finland."[62]

According to point 3, the United States and Britain agreed to "respect the rights of all peoples to choose the form of government under which they will live; and they wish to see sovereign rights and self government restored to those who have been forcibly deprived of them." Hearst listed an entire group of nations for whom the Eight Points would not apply, among them India, Persia, Egypt, Arabia, Syria, Tunis, Algeria, Morocco, Madagascar, and Tripoli. Moreover, would democracy be advanced, asked the AFC research bureau, by the restoration of such monarchs as Zog of Albania, Haakon VII of Norway, Peter of Yugoslavia, and George of Greece?[63]

Point 4 involved an effort, with "due respect" for "existing obligations, to further the enjoyment by all states, great and small, victor or vanquished, of access, on equal terms, to the trade and to the raw materials of the world which are needed for their economic prosperity." The *New York Daily News* saw an American commitment to distribute its vast natural wealth overseas, something only done by removing all immigration restrictions and tariff barriers. "The rest of the world," it said, "will flood in gladly and start sharing our wealth with loud cheers."[64]

The "due respect" phrase was particularly disconcerting. To *Uncensored*, it entailed the preservation of the British Empire, the Ottawa commercial agreement, American tariff and gold policies, and international British cartels over rubber and tin. To Henry Noble McCracken, president of Vassar College, the power to guarantee equal access to the earth's raw materials necessarily implied imperialistic control of the countries in which these materials were located.[65]

In responding to point 5, which spoke of "improved labor standards, economic advancement and social security," the AFC warned that the provision necessitated a functioning economic league or possibly even agreements to divide world markets.[66]

Far more controversy was created by the next point, which stated, "Sixth, after the final destruction of the Nazi tyranny, they hope to see established a peace which will afford to all nations the means of dwelling in safety within their own boundaries, and which will afford assurance that all the men in all the lands may live out their lives in freedom from fear and want." Point 6, said the AFC research bureau, was conspicuously silent concerning the destruction of fascism as "a way of life," much less the breakup of Italian fascism, Soviet totalitarianism, the Spanish dictatorship, or Japanese tyranny. Even more disturbing was the phrase "final destruction of Nazi tyranny," as it implied the complete destruction of Germany, an effort that would require full-scale belligerency.[67] By point 6, feared the AFC, the president had "committed us to active participation in the present war."[68]

A few peace leaders found slight hope in the language. Ruth Sarles interpreted the statement as neither requiring the "destruction of Nazism in Germany" nor "the break-up of the German state." Similarly, Libby expressed gratitude that point 6 aimed at the "destruction of the Nazi tyranny," not the "overthrow of Hitler and the Nazi regime." The effort to overthrow the German government and to force democracy on the German people, he continued, had always been unreal, for democracy—properly understood—could not be imposed on a people from without.[69]

Point 7 referred to the right of "all men to traverse the high seas and oceans without hindrance."[70] In war, said *Uncensored*, freedom of the seas always becomes a "hoary hoax," for the British and U.S. fleets inevitably dominated access. Furthermore, reported the AFC research bureau, both the 1939 neutrality act and U.S. acquiescence in British restrictions involved self-limitations of this right.[71] The *New York Daily News* went further, noting that the United States even backed the British in preventing American food shipments to France "until old Marshal Pétain has finally leaped into the arms of Hitler."[72]

Point 8 might have been the most controversial of all, as it implied international peacekeeping:

Eighth, they believe that all of the nations of the world, for realistic as well as spiritual reasons, must come to the abandonment of the use of force. Since no further peace can be maintained if land, sea or air armaments continue to be employed by nations which threaten, or may threaten, aggression outside of their frontiers, they believe, pending the establishment of a wider and permanent system of general security, that the disarmament of such nations is essential. They will likewise aid and encourage all other practicable measures which will lighten for peace-loving peoples the crushing burden of armaments.

Such a schema, some anti-interventionists argued, was inherently unworkable. "Would," *America* asked, "the nations of the world rise to the high idealism of the American and British democracies?" Lawrence Dennis, pointing to the phrase "abandonment of the use of force," wrote, "The pursuit of this absurd chimera by war will be the screwiest and bloodiest and costliest futility yet committed by democracy. Alongside it, prohibition was sane and successful."[73]

The one-sided nature of the proposed disarmament was found especially offensive. According to the AFC research bureau, the two leaders visualized an international police force, probably Anglo-American, with just potential aggressors demilitarized.[74] Norman Thomas spoke in terms of an armed imperialism. Hearst correspondent Karl von Wiegand, writing from Germany, reported that famine alone could follow any plan to disarm the Nazis. *Uncensored* noted that the German press did not even bother to comment on the points; it merely printed them in full, with the eighth point in boldface.[75] Among the anti-interventionists, only pacifist Libby, a member of the Society of Friends, concretely endorsed point 8, saying that the sentence involving abandonment of force "might well have been borrowed from the Quaker book of Discipline, because it is the ultimate in disarmament."[76]

Certainly, for many anti-interventionists, the Eight Points were most alarming. They might possibly hold the character and force of executive agreements such as the Taft–Katsura note of 1905, the House–Grey memorandum of 1916, and the Lansing–Ishii agreement of 1917. Drawing on such constitutional scholars as Edward S. Corwin, the AFC research bureau did note that the president possessed the legal power to "undertake many dangerous actions on his own initiative. All the Senate or the House could do would be to voice approval or disapproval of any or all of them, or appoint a committee to inquire into their formulation or adoption."[77] The precedent of Woodrow Wilson's diplomacy appeared haunting.[78] The research bureau made a detailed comparison between Roosevelt and Churchill's eight-point manifesto and Wilson's Fourteen Points, though AFC vice chairman Janet Ayer Fairbank noted, "The American people are more cynical and a lot more realistic than they were in 1918."[79]

Conversely, some anti-interventionists found the Eight Points meaningless. "A lot of words," said Nye. "Eight platitudes," remarked Dennis. "A rehash of old ideas," commented Castle.[80] To others they were too weak. Anne Morrow Lindbergh wrote in her diary, "As usual, beautiful words, ideals—*how* is it to be done?" "Alien nations," said Hearst, would endorse the Eight Points so long as the belligerents needed American aid but would disregard them once the war ended. The *Christian Century* noted the verbs used (*desire, wish, will endeavor, hope, will aid, encourage*) and those omitted (*pledge, promise*). Furthermore, the *Century* saw the agreement as silent on many crucial matters, including colonial issues, reparations, European unification, general disarmament, and a new association of nations.[81]

At times a few anti-interventionists expressed support of the charter.[82] General Wood thought the peace plan might even find a receptive hearing in Germany.[83] Some liberals and pacifists were particularly pleased.[84] The WIL officially expressed "very deep gratitude" for the Eight Points, particularly for those providing for a permanent system of general security and raising the living standard for all nations.[85] Libby called the statement "a step toward peace," saying it struck a conciliatory note absent in official British utterances. Indeed, he continued, "We can look forward hopefully to peace negotiations on the basis of the Eight Points."[86] He was particularly pleased that all peoples would be given the right to self-government and access to the markets and raw materials of the world. Fellow pacifist A. J. Muste dissented from Libby's view: the Eight Points contained some fundamental principles of a lasting peace, but the statement was too vague, in reality serving as an instrument of intervention.[87]

Regardless of how anti-interventionists reacted to the Eight Points, suspicions remained concerning the real reason for the summit meeting: secret agreements that might well be committing the United States to full-fledged belligerency.[88] To Boake Carter, the conference "smacks of the sort of secret Hitler–Mussolini meetings at the Brenner Pass, where the two dictators blandly decided how many lives should be carved up to accomplish their aggressive purposes."[89] Chesly Manly of the *Chicago Tribune* saw a joint military invasion of Europe as being in the works.[90] Norman Thomas thought the U.S. had agreed to fight for Singapore and the Dutch East Indies.[91] The *Christian Century* speculated on an entire agenda: aid to Russia; intervention against Japan, given an attack on Singapore, the Dutch East Indies, Siberia, and Thailand; unspecified "action" concerning France; and an eventual American Expeditionary Force.[92]

Some in Congress were equally apprehensive.[93] AFC staffer Fred Burdick reported that the president's critics shared a consensus that Roosevelt had committed the nation to another AEF.[94] Congressman George Holden Tinkham considered charging the chief executive with treason, for FDR had made "a declaration of war, without Congress, on a British battleship." Several members suspected that the meeting would lead to a U.S.-British military mission to Russia.[95]

The America First Committee was particularly distressed. It was, said its research bureau, no coincidence that the Newfoundland meeting was followed by a joint note to Stalin concerning future allocation of resources and by the announcement that American planes were being ferried to Africa via Brazil. Ruth Sarles saw a number of warlike options lying ahead: the breaking off of U.S. relations with Vichy, the sending of U.S. troops to Liberia and Sierra Leone, and outright belligerency if Japan moved toward the Netherlands East Indies or Singapore. The New York chapter suspected the aerial ferrying of supplies into the nonwar zones of Africa or actual entry into the shooting war.[96]

In the opinion of other FDR critics, no secret agreement was involved.[97] Congressman Harold Knutson found the United States to be farther from war than ever. The joint statement, said General Wood, was utterly devoid of commitments on Roosevelt's part—no promise of convoys, troops, or further occupation of distant points.[98] R. Douglas Stuart Jr. was slightly more cautious, saying, "We all knew that Churchill went fishing, but from what they tell us the big one got away." Chicago lawyer Clay Judson noted that the U.S. had not yet declared that its navy was joining the British or convoying vessels. Nor was it occupying Dakar or sending troops to Europe.[99]

Anti-interventionists would not have been reassured had they sat in on a British cabinet meeting held 19 August. Here Churchill maintained that at the Argentia conference "the President said he would wage war, but not declare it, and that he would become more and more provocative. If the Germans did not like it, they could attack American forces." Roosevelt also promised that the United States would assume responsibility for escorting North Atlantic convoys within the defensive zone west of twenty-six degrees west. Churchill reported, "The President's orders to these escorts were to attack any U-boat which showed itself, even if it were 200 or 300 miles away from the convoys. . . . Everything was to be done to force an 'incident.'"

For the British, the conference proved a bitter anticlimax. When Roosevelt returned to Washington, he did nothing to implement any such policy. On 28 August, Churchill cabled Hopkins that the president's continued statements that the United States was no nearer war had caused "a wave of depression" in the cabinet. The Newfoundland conference had only decided on detailed contingency plans in case FDR did order convoys. As historian David Reynolds writes, "Churchill and his colleagues did not travel 3,000 miles across the U-boat infested Atlantic in the hope of a press release."[100]

The main value of the meeting lay in the personal relationships established by the two national leaders and by their military staffs as well. As far as editorial opinion was concerned, a government survey found strongly favorable reaction both to the meeting and to the Atlantic Charter. A *Fortune* poll that October revealed just over half the respondents voicing unequivocal approval.[101] To most anti-interventionists, any informal alliance was bound to be dangerous, particularly since, as anti-interventionists never ceased arguing, any war with Germany could entail tragic consequences.

# 17

# Projections of Conflict

All during the debates over conscription and war aims, anti-interventionists continually returned to one theme above all: it was the height of folly ever to think of invading Europe. Under no circumstances should an American Expeditionary Force be attempted.

Some anti-interventionists offered gruesome descriptions of the horrors produced by World War I.[1] Borah referred to "chunks of human flesh . . . quivering on the branches of trees." Hugh Johnson spoke of "glistening white human bones sticking through the quivering shreds of bloody flesh." Congressman Louis Thill quoted Alan Seeger's poem "I Have a Rendezvous with Death." Representative John Main Coffee (Dem.-Wash.) cited Stephen Vincent Benét's pacifist work "1936."[2] Several anti-interventionists, including Stuart Chase and the *New York Daily News*, approvingly noted *Johnny Got His Gun* (1939), a bitter antiwar novel written by procommunist Dalton Trumbo.[3]

If grim descriptions of past butchery were not enough, the sheer logistical problems of invading Europe seemed overwhelming.[4] Charles A. Lindbergh predicted the United States would face a "superhuman task of crossing an ocean and forcing a landing on a fortified continent against armies stronger than our own and hardened by years of war."[5] With Britain being pounded by Nazi bombers, Al Williams noted, the U.S. could not deliver the needed fighters, much less operate from Britain.[6] Using the term "ghastly gamble," Frank Waldrop noted exposure to air attack, lack of landing harbors, and beachheads defended by artillery, planes, and machine guns.[7]

Any assault, estimated the *New York Daily News*, required 420 American divisions. Even then victory was uncertain: "It is possible that our boys may suffer one or more super-Dunkirks, rather than enjoy a victory march to Berlin.

And the Atlantic Ocean is a trifle wider and harder to evacuate large forces across than is the English Channel."[8]

Comparisons were continually made to World War I. To Iowa editor Verne Marshall, it would now take twice the manpower; to *Social Justice*, two to three times; to Lawrence Dennis, four to five.[9] The factor of transportation was also raised. In World War I, recalled Villard, the United States had used the vessels of fourteen different countries; in 1941 the ships of Japan, Italy, and France were unavailable. Furthermore, he continued, it then required twelve tons of shipping to supply a single soldier. Currently four to five times that much was needed. The world itself, said Senator Wheeler, did not contain enough ships to move a million men, plus their equipment, across the Atlantic.[10]

There was also the matter of allies. In the last conflict, the U.S. had twenty allies; this time it had only the British Empire by its side. Even in World War I, Germany was able to stave off an army of two to three million Frenchmen, a million Englishmen, the armed forces of Italy, and a vast army on the eastern flank of Russia. At the beginning of 1941, however, Germany already dominated the continent.[11]

Even if an AEF turned out to be successful, noninterventionists found the price too high. Projections varied from two to twenty million men[12] and from 150 to 280 divisions.[13] One out of every three men between the ages of eighteen and forty-five, predicted Villard, would participate in the onslaught.[14] Similarly the number of fatalities was expected to be extremely steep, this time the range lying between one to ten million.[15] "We cannot," wrote Hanson Baldwin, "re-conquer a continent without wholesale death."[16]

The financial cost was equally formidable. Edwin Johnson spoke in 1939 of $40 billion, Hamilton Fish in 1940 of $100 billion, and Hanson Baldwin in 1941 of $300 billion.[17] Furthermore, the time needed to secure Europe would be long indeed.[18] No such effort, wrote Stuart Chase in December 1940, could begin before 1944; the war itself would last twenty years.[19] "American children yet unborn," commented Fish, "may be serving in that war in China, Africa, and Europe. And the end means bankruptcy and ruin, and probably after that communism."[20] It would take ten years just to build the needed forty tons of shipping, said Hoover.[21]

Colonel McCormick outlined an entire invasion scenario. The United States, he asserted in October 1940, could ultimately beat the German army, but the toll could be prohibitive. Noting that the northern European coastline stretched from Kiel to Brest, he maintained that any invasion at a single point could not easily be reinforced, especially in the face of enemy air superiority. Therefore, a series of feints, attacks, and counterattacks was required until a front had been established at least a hundred miles long, possibly from Calais to Denmark. By this time, all docks from the Zuider Zee to Bordeaux would be destroyed, all harbors obstructed. The cost: a conflict lasting four hundred days, a price of $400 billion, a million deaths, and several million ruined lives. In total, the United States would have to mobilize twenty million men as well as creating separate armies to "watch" Japan and, oddly enough, Mexico. Certainly, the "liberated" people would be "ungrateful" to "an army which would have to destroy their every town, every city, every structure in order to deliver them."[22]

McCormick raised a crucial factor: the long-term consequences of victory. Enforcing a postwar division of Germany, speculated Sterling Morton, might take five hundred years while creating a spirit of revenge in the process.[23] Would the United States be required to use its military might, the *New York Daily News* asked, to restore such monarchs as George II of Greece, Peter of Yugoslavia, Wilhelmina of Holland, and Leopold of Belgium to full power?[24] H. L. Mencken wrote, "If Hitler is put down by force we'll get no more thanks than we got then, and a bill two or three times as large. And if Hitler is not put down we'll face the just and bitter enmity of the strongest military power on earth, and the disdain and derision of all the rest of the human race."[25]

Only one anti-interventionist remained mildly optimistic at any such an endeavor. Were the United States to become a full-scale belligerent, asserted Hanson Baldwin, it would begin action by convoy operations in the Atlantic, using naval forces augmented by patrol planes and long-range bombers. At the same time, the U.S. would supply ships and planes to Britain and the Mediterranean and seize the Azores, Canaries, Cape Verdes, and points in Africa. Once a combined Anglo-American-Greek force of four million men was assembled, it could begin landings in the southern Mediterranean, possibly at Sardinia, Sicily, or southern France. After the war, the United States would have to accept some sort of international body, "a union with Britain," and a jointly administered police force to keep world peace.[26]

Even without invasion, Baldwin saw Germany as vulnerable. Hitler's new empire lacked essential war materials, and ersatz substitutes could not indefinitely replace such resources as nickel and copper. Furthermore, dissidence existed within Germany, bitterness aroused by Nazi methods and "the slavery of souls."[27]

Interventionists themselves minimized any need for an AEF, accusing their opponents of raising a spurious issue. In April 1941, the CDAAA specifically denied that the war could be won by "masses of men." Rather, "mechanized striking power," particularly in the air, remained crucial. Even if an AEF of two million were added to British forces, the new contingent would be inferior to the German army. If, however, Britain received sufficient weapons, its forces would surpass German striking power.[28]

As early as November 1940, Admiral Stark took issue with such views. Britain, he thought, might conceivably defeat Germany by means of bombing and blockade. But only by the sending of large American naval, air, and land forces to Europe did Britain really stand a chance. Final victory still would not be certain.[29]

By September 1941, the war department had drafted a contingency plan that involved successful invasion, preponderantly American, of the European continent. Even if Germany dominated Moscow, the Volga, and Russian territory west of the White Sea, the department found an AEF technically feasible.[30] A so-called Victory Program, drafted by Major Albert C. Wedemeyer of the War Plans Division, would entail five field armies, 215 divisions, seven million tons of shipping, and six million men, all to engage in "offensive task forces" organized for European combat. At one point, the report concurred with the anti-interventionists—namely, in the assumption that Germany could not be defeated without direct American intervention. Ironically, Wedemeyer himself was an anti-interventionist, sympathetic to the America First Committee.[31] No formal authorization for the program was ever given, and all during the fall, the army feared manpower cutbacks. One official military history called the plan "a hypothesis without real influence."[32] Four days before the Pearl Harbor attack, a person still unknown leaked the projection to the *Chicago Tribune*, which created a sensation by incorrectly claiming that the scheme proved that the administration had already committed the nation to full-scale belligerency.[33]

It remains highly questionable whether Roosevelt himself sought an AEF until the Japanese attacked Pearl Harbor. Privately, he had always maintained that an expeditionary force was politically impossible. More important, he genuinely believed that strategic bombing, with the deliberate aim of hitting German towns as well as industrial centers, would make a large-scale army superfluous.[34] Furthermore, he realized full well that the United States still lacked the matériel to be a major participant. Moreover, a land invasion of Germany would simply strengthen loyalties to the Nazi regime.[35] As Roosevelt wrote Stimson late in August 1941, his primary concern centered on "the reservoir of mutual munitions power available to the United States and her friends" being sufficient to defeat the Axis.[36] Quite possibly Roosevelt did not abandon his belief in a "low casualty–high tech war" until the Casablanca Conference of January 1943.[37]

While Churchill and the British chiefs hoped for an American declaration of war, they saw its value centering on aircraft, tanks, ships, and supplies, not on another AEF. General Marshall was not so sanguine, finding a massive ground assault on Festung Europa absolutely necessary; millions of casualties might be needed, for strategic bombing and blockade alone could never defeat Germany.[38]

Roosevelt's critics kept stressing a converse point as well—namely, that Germany could never invade the United States. Certain interventionists had voiced just such fears. In September 1939, Harold Ickes privately expressed belief that the U.S. was on Hitler's timetable.[39] Early that October, Assistant Secretary of War Louis Johnson publicly pronounced the U.S. as threatened as Poland, a comment attacked by foes of intervention.[40] In March 1940, William Bullitt quietly agreed that the United States was in danger.[41] That same month, Roosevelt wanted to make sure the Virginia–Washington, D.C., railroad bridge was secure in case of sudden attack "by a foreign enemy or by a sudden domestic uprising."[42]

Even the Atlantic appeared perilous. On 22 September 1939, the president had confirmed rumors of submarines off Key West and Boston, to which Senator Holt replied that the supposed menace was merely "snapping turtles striking their heads out of the water looking for air."[43] Rumors of the supposed sinking of two British ships, the *Southgate* and *Coulmore,* off the American coast were later proven to be unfounded.[44]

Particularly after the fall of France, many scare stories arose concerning such a threat. Even one as sophisticated as A. A. Berle could momentarily accept their credibility.[45] In the spring of 1940, when the fate of the French and British fleets were still in doubt, army planners feared that a vastly increased German navy could transport a considerable number of troops across the Atlantic.[46] *Life* magazine showed Germans bombing the Panama Canal, landing in Brazil, defeating the American fleet, and invading New Jersey to overrun the industrial Northeast.[47] In the second half of 1940, *Liberty* magazine presented a fictionalized series that dealt with such an assault, as did a novel written by popular historian Hendrik Willem Van Loon.[48]

All the time Hitler was conquering Western Europe, noninterventionists mocked such anxieties. Advertising executive Chester Bowles facetiously referred to "the possibility of German parachutists capturing New York's City Hall and blowing up Boulder Dam." "Every time an automobile backfires," scoffed Hamilton Fish, Washingtonians "envision the panzer divisions marching up Pennsylvania Avenue." "People are seeing airplanes flying over the Rocky Mountains," stated Wheeler, "seeing submarines on their coasts, and are thinking they are about to be bombed." The *Christian Century* described American mothers "armed with rifles, ready to shoot down parachutists."[49] In the words of John Haynes Holmes, "The country is going mad." Even the prudent Berle spoke of "a steady wave of hysteria" within the nation.[50]

Noninterventionists argued that Hitler would always be preoccupied with the European continent. Before he could begin an American invasion, remarked *Uncensored* in June 1940, he must overcome a host of problems: conquering England and France; keeping in subjugation some 142 million occupied Europeans; working out "his self-proclaimed destiny in the East," where he confronted Russia, Italy, and Turkey; and whipping up "his war-weary people into a frenzy of hatred against the United States." To attack the United States, commented Philip La Follette in February 1941, eighty million exhausted Germans needed sufficient reserve strength to risk leaving twice as many embittered subject peoples in their rear; furthermore, "a vast and unpredictable Russian military machine" was on their flank.[51] Retired marine general Smedley Butler had joked in October 1939, "Nobody in Europe can afford to leave home. Why, if Hitler leaves Germany with a million soldiers to come over here, if he ever got back he'd find everyone speaking either French or Russian. Those babies would move in on him while he was gone."[52]

Again, in February 1941, Herbert Hoover, meeting with Cordell Hull, challenged the secretary's claim that Germany intended to attack North and South America, much less conquer the world. The USSR and the Balkans together, he noted, possessed far more undeveloped resources than did the entire Western Hemisphere. While the Soviet Union could be conquered with two army corps, an attack on the hemisphere would require tremendous amounts of equipment.[53]

More than Hitler's continental concerns, however, entered into play. To administration critics, the United States seemed to possess an airtight defense: three thousand miles of ocean between itself and Europe. Said Taft in May 1941, "An ocean is the most effective barrier of defense that the world provides."[54] Anti-interventionists often cited a report dated 15 May 1940, issued by the Senate Committee on Naval Affairs.[55] Denying that the U.S. was menaced by foreign armies, it countered, "The United States at the present time is not vulnerable to direct attack by any means whatsoever save those with which a thoroughly modern Navy and air force can deal adequately."[56]

Several anti-interventionists wrote entire books on how the United States could best defend itself. Undoubtedly, Hanson W. Baldwin, military correspondent for the interventionist *New York Times*, received the most general respect. An Annapolis graduate who spent three years on active duty, Baldwin had worked for the *Baltimore Sun*, of which his father was managing editor, before joining the *New York Times* in 1929.[57] His writings received many endorsements from the president's adversaries.[58] Privately, Baldwin told anti-interventionists that he opposed American entry into the war.[59]

Baldwin's systematic treatment of U.S. defense, *United We Stand!*, was published in the spring of 1941. In it he firmly denied that the nation could be invaded. No potential hostile power possessed territory or bases in the Western Hemisphere; the Atlantic stretched three thousand miles, the Pacific from four to seven thousand. "Invaders can reach this country only by ship or plane; armies cannot swim to victory."[60]

Suppose, he speculated, that the USSR, Germany, Japan, and Italy all planned a joint attack on the United States. Eleven million troops, or between six and seven hundred divisions, would be needed. Also required would be from thirty to sixty thousand planes, although the flying range of most of these would be limited. Only a handful of the world's bombing planes, said

Baldwin, possessed an operating radius of more than two thousand miles, and most of these were American. The great majority, probably 90 percent, had operating radii of from three to nine hundred miles. For a mass bombardment, five hundred miles out and five hundred back was about the limit, as German operations had recently shown. A few points on the Atlantic coast could be bombed by one-way raiders, but these ranges meant little militarily.[61]

Any united fleet would scarcely outmatch the United States's own. Even if it possessed twenty-five battleships to the U.S.'s fifteen, this sum included two German pocket battleships plus only three Russian battleships—all unable to cross the seas. The disembarkation "might well result in a far worse shambles than Gallipoli."[62]

Genuine defense, Baldwin argued, required neither the emplacement of heavy guns nor profuse construction of airfields nor naval patrols covering every square mile of coast. Essential, rather, was sufficient control of certain strategic points, those crucial to guarding vital areas and preventing the construction of enemy bases. Northern approaches to the hemisphere would be guarded by bases in the Labrador–Newfoundland–Nova Scotia area; southern approaches would be protected by bases in Brazil. Turning to the Pacific coast, Baldwin sought use of Ecuador's Galapagos Islands and Costa Rica's Cocos Islands as well as the U.S. islands of Oahu, Midway, Wake, and Guam. Add bases in the Alaskan-Aleutian-Hawaiian area, and the Pacific sector would be practically impregnable.[63] In August 1941, he suggested bases in Northern Ireland, Scotland, Freetown, and possibly the Azores and Cape Verde.[64]

FDR foes praised his volume, as did such interventionists as historian Walter Millis and *Time* magazine.[65] *New Republic* editor Malcolm Cowley lauded Baldwin's detailed comments on the armed forces but saw the defense of Britain as far more vital to American safety than Baldwin was willing to admit.[66]

At the same time Baldwin's book appeared, Fleming MacLiesh and Cushman Reynolds's *Strategy of the Americas* was published. MacLiesh was a licensed air pilot and poet. Reynolds edited *Uncensored* after Sidney Hertzberg stepped down to prepare bulletins for the America First Committee.

Claiming that defense of the entire hemispheric land mass was neither practicable nor necessary, MacLiesh and Reynolds quoted the adage of Frederick the Great: "If you defend everything, you defend nothing." All that was required was effective control of strategic points, so as to prevent any enemy from establishing a bridgehead. Much of their vision resembled Baldwin's, as it involved U.S. bases in Alaska, Newfoundland, Nova Scotia, Prince Edward Island, Cape Verde, and the bulge of Brazil and such Pacific islands as Hawaii, Midway, and Wake.[67]

As Baldwin had done, MacLiesh and Reynolds also drew up a worst-case scenario. Seizure of Pernambuco, Brazil, would just begin Germany's problems. Long- and medium-range American bombers, convoyed by pursuit planes from nearby bases, could blast the isolated beachhead continually.

Even an invasion force of ten thousand soldiers would be dependent on highly vulnerable supply lines and subject to American fire. If Hitler attempted a more northern route, he would face an even greater concentration of American power. The Caribbean, with its three narrow water passages and U.S. bases, presented superb strategic advantages. Any strike along the Atlantic seaboard or in eastern Canada would bring him up against American coastal artillery and a first-class mechanized army. Suppose, they wrote, Hitler's aircraft carriers launched nighttime raids against Washington, Philadelphia, New York, and Boston. Carriers could transport at most seventy small planes, which would be required to run a gauntlet of antiaircraft guns and powerful concentrations of interceptor, fighter, and attack planes. Such raids would lack any military value, as the ensuing damage could not compensate for the enormous losses. Even if every American battleship was sent to the bottom, U.S. bomber squadrons could still cripple gun turrets, blast supply lines, put carriers out of action, wipe out any bridgeheads, and sink transports, destroyers, and flotilla craft.[68] Anti-interventionists praised the work, which received other favorable reviews as well.[69]

In his own version of a prospective invasion, John T. Flynn stressed problems of matériel. An attacking force of even a hundred thousand troops, he said, required 750,000 tons of shipping. With each ship averaging five thousand tons, this force would need 150 vessels, convoyed by a flotilla of seven battleships, seven light cruisers, several mine layers, and at least seventy destroyers. Such an immense armada, moving slowly over three thousand miles of seas, would stand at the mercy of the American navy and air force. Were Hitler to invade with a million men, Flynn continued, his problems would simply increase. He would need forty-four thousand guns; over a hundred thousand vehicles, including forty-five hundred tanks; and nearly ten thousand planes. Each day his army would use up nine thousand tons of rations and supplies, 1.5 million gallons of gasoline, and 150,000 gallons of oil. After the army arrived on shore, it would have to keep open a continuous flow of provisions, fuel, and arms. Transportation alone lay "beyond the power of any country."[70]

Administration adversaries stressed one theme continually: shipping needs alone, they said, would prevent the Germans from invading.[71] Wheeler, finding an invasion force to need two million troops for success, denied that all the ships of the world could carry a force half that size.[72] Even moving two hundred thousand troops, Hugh Johnson agreed, would take 2.4 million tons of shipping, a "mathematical impossibility."[73] "Could the U.S. Be Invaded? Yes, but What a Job!" was the headline of a *Chicago Tribune* article.[74]

Air attack was deemed no threat. No bomber in existence or under construction, said *Uncensored* in May 1940, could fly a bomb load two thousand miles, drop it, and return to its base.[75] Over a year later, the AFC cited General Johnson Hagood, executive officer of supply in World War I, who had recently written, "The best known authorities have agreed that the average American is in much more danger of an automobile or a gangster than he is of a German bomb even if we should be drafted into the war."[76]

Of all the anti-interventionists, no one was more frequently quoted on air defense than Charles Lindbergh.[77] In May 1940, the aviator conceded that bombing planes could be built with sufficient range to cross the Atlantic and return, but "the cost is high, the target large and the military effectiveness small." Furthermore, he continued, few such bombers would exist; they would have to be accompanied by thousands of smaller ones and pursuit planes; and planes could only transport relatively small forces of men over thousands of miles.[78]

None of the four major air routes, Lindbergh maintained, threatened the United States. The northern route, via Greenland and Iceland, was too mountainous, the seas too filled with ice, the Arctic climate too severe. The Great Circle route over Newfoundland and Iceland spanned nearly nineteen hundred miles; an enemy still would have to refuel in either Newfoundland or Canada. The southern route, over Bermuda and the Azores, involved an even longer nonstop flight over water. The South Atlantic route, between Africa and Brazil, extended only sixteen hundred miles (he once personally measured the route from Cape Verde) and possessed relatively good weather conditions, but an invader could be repulsed by a U.S. air base in South America.[79]

Moreover, so FDR critics claimed, bombers needed fighters accompanying them. "Bringing down such a bomber unprotected by escort fighters," Nye said, "would be as easy for our pursuit ships and interceptors as it would be for an expert rifle shot to fell a sitting target." Some bombers, he conceded, might reach the United States, but they presented no serious danger to its productive capacity.[80] Boake Carter noted that German air raids on Britain had been ineffective, for the Reich lacked the fighters required to defend German bombers. As the range of most fighters was nine hundred miles, they certainly would be unable to make the four thousand–mile route from the Azores to the Americas and back.[81]

What if the Germans used aircraft carriers? Without the protection of a fleet, said Nye, a carrier was the most vulnerable type of warship afloat. Even under such escort, carriers were none too secure. According to Taft, the Germans did not possess a sufficient number anyhow.[82] Similarly, major airstrips were required. Villard conceded Roosevelt's claim that fliers could reach the United States from Greenland and South America within a few hours; he stressed, though, that both areas were deficient in the huge support bases that must supply the thirty mechanics needed to tend each plane.[83]

Besides, it was argued, effective coastal defense could repel any initial landing.[84] American bombers, commented Colonel McCormick, could prevent any invasion of the eastern seaboard. (The Chicago publisher had been a line officer in World War I and saw himself as a military strategist.)[85] To Hiram

Johnson, striking a "slow, lumbering and defenseless armada" would be "like shooting fish in a barrel." For any invasion to succeed, Smedley Butler argued, harbors were essential: "You can't stop 25 miles out at sea, drop a 5-ton armored tank overboard, and tell it to swim ashore and meet you on Broadway." To clog up New York Harbor, which was the only large harbor on the Atlantic coast, all one had to do was to dump two days' garbage in the channel! Villard cited General Hagood to the effect that an invading army could disembark at one of only five ports—New York, Boston, Norfolk, San Francisco, and Seattle—for an army required docks and powerful cranes.[86] Moreover, suggested D. Worth Clark, such havens could be so mined so that battleships and planes would not be needed to deter a foreign fleet.[87]

Suppose enemy troops were able initially to land on U.S. shores. They would be repulsed quickly.[88] Sterling Morton envisioned Germans being bayoneted as they disembarked.[89] The state of Florida alone, asserted Senator Downey, could decimate over ten thousand soldiers as they landed on its beaches.[90] Congresswoman Jeanette Rankin quoted an American Legionnaire who said that if the Germans invaded fifty thousand at a time, "the police could take care of them, but if they came over in 6,000 loads, the Boy Scouts could handle them."[91] Different estimates were given as to the defensive manpower involved, with Villard offering the highest number, six hundred thousand.[92]

The sheer expanse of the United States, maintained the *New York Daily News*, would stifle any expeditionary force that might get a foothold on its shores. "Look what the Chinese are doing to the Japanese." Moreover, superior U.S. transportation facilities could shuttle defense force armies from coast to coast, welcoming the aggressors "with bloody hands to hospitable graves."[93] Even in World War I, wrote Frank Waldrop, a two million–strong AEF needed the support of three navies, the merchant marine of five nations, and domination of friendly shores. "Can they really gang up on us?" he asked.[94]

Similarly, certain campaigns of World War II were presented to show invasion difficulties. Senator Chavez pointed to problems Germany encountered in transporting troops a few hundred miles to Norway.[95] *Uncensored* warned against "unscrupulous interventionists who imply that a murderous marauder baffled by the English Channel would find the Atlantic Ocean a duck pond."[96] Wheeler, noting the example of British resistance, asked in August 1941, "If it is as easy as all that for the Germans to come over and land men and have them blow up everything in the city of New York and in Buffalo, why in the name of God do not the British send men over to Germany and blow up Berlin and then pick them up again and bring them back?"[97]

Hitler, it was further argued, would need much more time to prepare.[98] In September 1940, Congressman John Jennings estimated it taking five years to organize an expeditionary force, by which time the United States would possess a two-ocean navy. No attack, said *Uncensored* in January 1941, could come before 1943, at which time the U.S. would have twenty-three battleships.[99]

A related concern centered on the British fleet, a major issue with the interventionists. Stimson warned, "We are in very great danger of invasion by air in the event the British Navy should be destroyed or surrendered." If Britain fell, so the CDAAA argued, the Axis powers would (without having any British craft) possess a battleship superiority of three to four over the United States and more than eight times the nation's shipbuilding capacity. Having the British navy would make the danger that much more ominous, for possible invasion of the U.S. itself could be in the offing. From 30 July to 1 August 1940, the CDAAA ran advertisements declaring "Between Us and Hitler Stands the British Fleet," an argument used particularly frequently during the destroyer bases deal.[100]

Noninterventionist opposition responded quickly, using the fleet matter as another opportunity to indict England.[101] Britain, Nye recalled, was "the only power that has ever brought aggression to the Americas."[102] Even more moderate voices, including Norman Thomas, pointed to Britain's supposed record of aggression. In reality, remarked Hanson Baldwin, American security never lay with the British fleet but was embodied in such factors as geographic isolation, the United States's own inherent strength, the balance of power in Europe, and the preoccupation of the Orient with its own development.[103]

Even if, however, Albion was as perfidious as the more extreme anti-interventionists believed, it would never surrender its flotilla.[104] Nye cited Churchill's own pledge to that effect. *Uncensored* noted unnamed "military experts" who predicted that in any major battle in the English Channel, one-third of Britain's ships would be sunk; the rest might make a run to empire or American ports. If necessary, the entire fleet might be scuttled. In the process, Hitler, too, would experience severe losses.[105]

Were Germany to possess the British fleet, crossing the Atlantic would still be by no means easy.[106] According to MacLiesh and Reynolds, Hitler would still face incredible preparation: training crews, plotting strategy, coordinating use of guns and shells, conducting the maneuvers of a combined British-German-French-Italian fleet. Even if a massive air armada lay at his disposal, only part of it could fly across the Atlantic and return to home base without refueling. Preparation alone would take two years, during which time the United States's own naval schedule would be completed.[107]

In the worst of circumstances, a few anti-interventionists argued, the U.S. could still maintain its defenses.[108] Were the Germans to seize the British navy, said Colonel McCormick, "We could stop the fleet anyway." Taft cited Roosevelt himself to the effect that no enemy, even one that possessed the British navy, would be stupid enough to invade without the needed strategic bases.[109] Pacifist Nicholas Broughton envisioned "an understanding between ourselves and Germany similar to the one we had with Great Britain." If the Reich was recalcitrant, Germany might be confronting an American-Japanese détente wherein Japan "would guard the Pacific while we patrolled the Atlantic."[110]

Within the administration, powerful voices stressed that the nation was fully capable of self-defense. In January 1941, the military Joint Planning Committee reported, "The United States can safeguard the North American continent and probably the western hemisphere, whether allied to Britain or not." Pleading for caution in regard to military commitments, it warned against sacrificing American interests.[111]

That same month, Roosevelt accused the anti-interventionists of misstating the issue. In his State of the Union address to Congress, FDR denied that any enemy "would be stupid enough to attack us by landing troops in the United States across thousands of miles of ocean." The real issue centered on domination of strategic bases that could serve as launching pads and that would be occupied "by secret agents and their dupes."[112]

From the beginning of the European conflict, polls indicated fears that a victorious Germany would attack the Western Hemisphere. Yet, in April 1941, a *Fortune* poll found well over half the recipients denying that Hitler was able to invade the United States.[113] To much of the American public, U.S. security was dependent on other factors, among them the survival of Great Britain in the summer and fall of 1941.

# 18

# Waging Undeclared War

During the second half of 1941, the British wound up their campaign in East Africa, seizing Gondar in Ethiopia late in September. They were less successful in North Africa, where the troops of General Alan Cunningham were fighting indecisively against Rommel's Afrika Korps, which recovered almost the entire coast east of Tunisia. In August, British civilian losses totaled 169, the equivalent of a low toll for a single night when the blitz was at its most intensive.[1] Fortunes also improved on the Atlantic, with shipping losses rising above two hundred thousand tons only in September.

As Britain, however, depended on its convoys escaping an ever-increasing number of German U-boats, such losses were crucial. On 25 June, Churchill warned that invasion of the British Isles could take place any time from 1 September on. In October, General Marshall, still not sanguine, ordered a survey of British land defenses.[2]

Several anti-interventionists stressed German weakness. In July, Norman Thomas saw the British Empire surviving as long as the war lasted. In September, Herbert Hoover found Britain growing daily more impregnable to attack; conversely, Hitler's Europe lacked needed food and material. To the *Chicago Tribune*, Britain was simply "sitting pretty" as Germany and the USSR wore themselves out.[3]

During the rest of the fall, such optimism continued, reflected in public opinion polls showing up to 85 percent of the respondents predicting a German defeat.[4] Anti-interventionists noted accounts of sabotage and uprisings within the occupied countries and widespread depression within Germany itself. One *Christian Century* editorial headline ran, "Nazi-Occupied Lands Seethe with Revolt."[5] In early November, Senator Shipstead said, "Germany may have within her borders more seeds of destruction than we have any idea of." Drawing on firsthand observations, Cudahy pointed to inadequate food and clothing, a depleted transportation system, and "a crying shortage of labor." The former ambassador, who had interviewed Hitler that June, observed, "I never saw a man who looked so ill as he did when I saw him." In fact, he called the German Führer "only a passing fad." Speaking somewhat vaguely, Fish predicted that the German leader would eventually die and his empire collapse.[6]

All this time, predictions of stalemate remained. "To defeat Germany," asserted Congressman Shanley, "would be difficult, with industrial areas in Russia now in her hands. But Hitler will fall down when it comes to achieving peace." Citing Demaree Bess's article in the *Saturday Evening Post*, "Put Up or Shut Up," Villard denied that the world contained enough Englishmen to defeat Germany.[7]

Britain, several FDR foes stated, was too weak to fight alone.[8] In July, Hoover predicted that once the Germans had defeated Russia, they would propose a peace that Britain would invariably turn down, at which point the United States would enter the war as a full-scale belligerent. Britain, suspected the *New York Daily News* in mid-November, planned to fight a defensive war through 1942, hoping that the Soviets would keep Germany occupied until a joint American-British invasion was launched in 1943. Early in December, Alf Landon suspected that Britain might intentionally be seeking others to do its fighting, permitting the Soviet Union and the United States to engage in major hostilities: "If Russia and America do fight it out with Germany, is there any possibility that we may wind up bankrupt, both as a people and as a government, with England sitting in the best financial position of any country in the world?"[9]

Even full-scale American participation, some argued, could not defeat the Germans.[10] Britain and the Soviet Union together, claimed Freda Utley, had not made a dent on the German war machine; how could it be assumed that England and the United States, the latter some three thousand miles away from the fighting, possessed the potential to defeat Hitler? Germany, she continued, had actually secured about twice as many war materials from occupied France than Britain had from the U.S. Because of Germany's long head start, the thousands of American planes scheduled for delivery in 1942 and 1943 still could not give England the needed air superiority. Bombing was ineffective to achieve victory, for as George Bernard Shaw had noted, it did not destroy morale; rather, it made people "fighting mad." To Felix Morley, U.S. involvement—beyond what was necessary to let Britain negotiate a peace on equal terms—was "utter madness. Of such madness, however, the administration is fully capable."[11]

Several administration critics on the extreme right frequently changed their analyses. In July, Lawrence Dennis predicted the launching of a British Expeditionary Force, but by September he denied that either Hitler or Roosevelt would soon precipitate full-scale war. "FDR will have most of the naval honors along with the British. The Germans will have the military or land honors." If the United States really wanted to make trouble for Hitler, it stood a better chance by continuing its present policy of supplying arms, tanks, and planes to the Reich's enemies.[12] In July, *Social Justice* spoke in terms of a joint British-American attack on the European continent. As the Nazis were fighting on two fronts, the invaders might be able to secure a solid foothold either in a German-occupied nation or in northern Germany itself. Early in September, Coughlin's journal denied that the United States would enter the war; it foresaw Britain itself joining the Axis. Yet within two weeks, it again shifted its position, asserting that to save an international banking system based on "gold" and "debt," Roosevelt would plunge his nation into a losing war.[13]

Little wonder that during the summer and fall of 1941, anti-interventionists kept calling for a negotiated peace.[14] Those of pacifist leanings were particularly vocal. In October, Charles Clayton Morrison demanded explicit peace aims, saying no Eight or Fourteen Points would suffice. If the German people were offered "a decent peace," said A. J. Muste, much bloodshed would be avoided.[15] The prominent Methodist leader Ernest Fremont Tittle called for an international conference.[16]

Despite the obvious animosity against him, Roosevelt was still mentioned as a facilitator.[17] John Haynes Holmes, in his capacity as chairman of the Citizens Peace Petition Committee, requested the president "to use the influence which he possesses as the elected representative of the American people for the cessation of hostilities and the achievement of a just peace."[18]

AFC executive R. Douglas Stuart asked educator Robert M. Hutchins to lead a mediation drive. Hutchins consented to lend his name to a mediation movement but refused to assume leadership.[19] In mid-November, John T. Flynn sought a peace offensive, led by such prominent clergy as Protestant minister Harry Emerson Fosdick and Roman Catholic archbishop Francis Beckman of Dubuque.[20]

As always, rationale varied. "A Europe at peace," said Wheeler, "means that the Hitler empire will crack and crumble." The German leader, Castle speculated, could not survive in peacetime: As the Führer's government was based on war and conquest, the starvation accompanying any peace would lead to his overthrow. The Reverend Holmes predicted that Hitler would abandon his conquests if Britain would abandon its own, including its rule of India. If he himself did not respond, Holmes continued, the German people would accept the terms on their own.[21]

Some anti-interventionists were less sanguine but found no alternative. A continent dominated by Hitler, said Alfred M. Bingham, was not "a pleasant prospect to look forward to, but it is at least possible that we shall have to make the best of it as the most we can hope for." Suppose the peace were one of armed watchfulness, commented the *Chicago Tribune*; the burdens would still be far less than those of "an interminable war with no foreseeable results." The *New York Daily News* agreed with presidential adviser Joseph Davies, recent American ambassador to Russia, who found Hitler's word not "worth a tinker's damn," but it spoke of a peace that Germany itself would find in its interest to keep. Even if such a settlement just served as an armed truce, it could last ten years, long enough for at least some world leaders to lose power. Freda Utley agreed, conceding that one could never trust Hitler. A fully armed United States and a rejuvenated Britain, however, would be strong enough to maintain the integrity of their territories and spheres of influence—indeed, probably to force Germany into a peace of equals.[22]

From July through September, some optimism prevailed. In July, Taft thought that Hitler might make a reasonable peace proposal by the fall. Just over a month later, Libby suspected that Germany and Britain were already involved in secret peace negotiations. Late in September, Charles A. Lindbergh saw at least an even chance of a negotiated peace by the following spring.[23]

If anything, October bought even more such predictions.[24] Cudahy found the Germans so eager for settlement that the general staff would force Hitler ("only a passing phase") to negotiate.[25] To Borchard, Russia's defeat would likely lead to the overthrow of Churchill's government, at which point Britain would make a "reasonable peace."[26] Ruth Sarles noted Washington rumors, the activity of Lloyd George, and Hitler's own desire, which, she remarked, was opposed by the German military. A victorious Führer might propose a peace while resigning as chancellor.[27] Even in October, Dennis also believed Hitler ready to make a peace; Lloyd George was already making himself available for negotiation. *Social Justice* predicted peace by the end of the year, citing as evidence Germany's domination of Europe and imminent victory over the Soviets. It was no mere coincidence, Father Coughlin's weekly continued, that neither London nor the major German cities had been bombed efficiently in many months.[28] If Hitler, said Chester Bowles, restored the democratic powers of Western Europe, Britain might jump at negotiation, particularly if the Soviets were defeated.[29]

Each anti-interventionist had his own idea of what the peace terms could be. Libby found a basis for negotiation in a supposed German proposal, published on 7 August in the *New York Times* and supposedly communicated via Ankara, whose terms included complete German withdrawal from Norway, Denmark, the Netherlands, Belgium, and France.[30] According to the *Chicago Tribune*, Germany sought retention of Alsace-Lorraine and a joint crusade with Britain against Bolshevism. In October, *Uncensored* speculated that the German people would accept a peace that allowed the Reich to retain only Austria and the Polish Corridor, both areas where the majority had favored Anschluss. Its source was *Inside Germany Reports*, the journal of the American Friends of German

Freedom. Cudahy saw Hitler as offering "the restoration of the Western European democracies" while insisting on "control of the continent."[31]

Certain individual peace agendas were prepared. Libby envisioned a settlement based on the Eight Points that "would have the support of all peoples, including Germany." To enforce such a peace, various international committees would have to focus on such matters as economic grievances, tariffs, disarmament, and currency.[32] Edwin Borchard spoke of tariff adjustment, customs unions, and the allocation of economic spheres of influence so as to make every industrial nation self-sufficient. All distinction between victor and vanquished would be dropped; so would "all ideas of coercion, which were fundamental to the peace enforcers of 1919."[33]

Late in November, Chester Bowles outlined an entire peace agenda, one that included the removal of Hitler, Mussolini, and Churchill from any peace negotiations; German withdrawal behind former western frontiers, which might include Alsace-Lorraine; the restoration of the British and Italian empires; fixing the political and economic future of Central and Eastern Europe by a conference of the powers involved; American sharing of resources; and a disarmament program in which the former belligerent nations and the United States would participate. Although such a peace, said Bowles in a memo to Herbert Hoover, would leave the Nazis in possession of much of the European continent, the German people should be preoccupied for many years. Bowles reluctantly conceded to U.S. guarantees of Europe's boundary lines and an alliance with Britain. Yet, he maintained, such a combination might readily involve other nations, thereby winning over the British and "middle-of-the-road" interventionists to acquiesce in his proposal. The military provisions, he hoped, would gradually drop into the background.[34] Hoover saw no immediate possibility of its implementation, but he thought that the schema might be made effective before the winter was over.[35]

Not all administration critics favored negotiations, much less were optimistic about them. Several strongly opposed such agitation. Negotiation, for example, never became part of the AFC official program. To America First vice chairman Hanford MacNider, the recommendation of a negotiated peace involved just as much "misguided meddling" as Roosevelt's activity.[36] Americans, said Charles A. Lindbergh, were not sufficiently acquainted with European conditions to accept any practical plan. "We would find ourselves in the position of guaranteeing a peace that could not possibly last."[37]

Interventionists continually stressed their opposition. Even a short truce, the CDAAA argued in July, would permit Hitler to make up his shortages of raw materials and consolidate his striking force. Conversely, the British, their will for victory gone, would be unable to continue their unprecedented national effort.[38] Sharing such fears, Harold Ickes found the British susceptive to a Lloyd George government that would bargain with the Germans. In his Labor Day speech, Roosevelt attacked the "appeasers and Nazi sympathizers"

who "even ask me to negotiate with Hitler—to pray for crumbs from his victorious table. They do, in fact, ask me to become the modern Benedict
Arnold and betray all I hold dear." Again the polls supported the president on
the matter.[39]

All the time that campaigns were analyzed and negotiation debated, American
conflict with Germany was steadily intensifying on the high seas. On 21 May,
the Germans sank their first U.S. ship. The *Robin Moor*, a merchant vessel flying the American flag, was headed for British South Africa carrying steel rails
and trucks. Such craft had been spared torpedoing outside the belligerent
danger zones recognized under the neutrality act of 1939; hence, the ship's
owners had reason to expect immunity. No lives were lost. Only in early June
did Americans receive the news.[40]

The CDAAA used the incident to call for immediate American "policing" of
the entire Atlantic. Germany, it conceded, had been entitled to stop and search
the vessel but had no right to sink it without providing for the safety of passengers and crew.[41]

Anti-interventionists held no brief for the sinking, the AFC calling the Ger-
man behavior "unjustified and ruthless" and former senator David A. Reed
(Rep.-Pa.) finding it "pure piracy."[42] Still and all, the fear continually arose that
Roosevelt would use the incident to intensify American involvement. The *New
York Daily News* suspected a new *Lusitania* incident, recalling that the Cunard
liner's manifest, which revealed that the ship had been carrying munitions,
was not published until years later.[43] The *Daily Worker* headlined an editorial,
"The People Want No 'Incidents.'"[44] Though America First expressed relief
that Congress showed little anxiety, its research bureau stressed that, contrary
to the claims of interventionists, the *Robin Moor* was carrying contraband and
thereby ran the risks that such cargoes involved.[45]

On 17 June 1941, Roosevelt announced that the United States had not put
into operation plans for arming merchant vessels, although such designs had
existed since 1918. The AFC replied that any arming of merchant vessels
turned them into auxiliary warships and therefore would lead to conflict.[46]
Three days later, in a message to Congress, Roosevelt called the *Robin Moor* incident "a first step in assertion of the supreme purpose of the German Reich
to seize control of the high seas." Invoking the doctrine of freedom of the seas,
he maintained that the U.S. would not yield to "piracy."[47] Unlike Woodrow
Wilson in the case of the *Sussex*, he did not do what the AFC most feared: use
the *Robin Moor* incident to take more radical measures. In the words of historian James MacGregor Burns, "The President still had no strategy except a
strategy of no strategy."[48]

Columnist George Sokolsky replied that Britain itself had never agreed to freedom of the seas, quoting Churchill's *The Aftermath* (1929) on the matter. The AFC research bureau accused the president of violating international law by attempting to help one belligerent defeat another.[49]

On 25 July 1941, in a conference with the top German naval commander, Admiral Erich Raeder, Hitler denied seeking a warlike incident while the Russian campaign was still in progress; he would, however, never call a submarine commander to account if he accidentally torpedoed an American ship.[50]

Such torpedoing soon became a reality. On 17 August, the *Sessa*, an American freighter sailing under Panamanian registry, was shelled near Greenland while transporting foodstuffs and lumber to Iceland. On 6 September, some survivors were rescued, though twenty-four members of its crew were lost, including one American. Word reached the United States on 9 September when a U.S. Navy patrol picked up three survivors. On 5 September, the U.S. freighter *Steel Seafarer*, flying the American flag, was bombed in the Red Sea. There were no fatalities. Americans learned about the incident three days later.[51]

Anti-interventionists addressed themselves to both incidents. Finerty of the KAOWC claimed that the *Sessa* was carrying contraband. Villard argued that the *Sessa* had been warned. In the case of the *Steel Seafarer*, General Wood noted that it, too, was supplying contraband and that the ship had entered the Red Sea, obviously belligerent waters and some twelve thousand miles from American shores.[52]

The practice of Panamanian registry was strongly attacked. Between the outbreak of war and 1 July 1941, according to the AFC, sixty-three ships had been transferred to the Panamanian flag. "Little Panama," whose land area was less than that of Indiana, had suddenly become one of the leading shipping nations of the world. Finding an obvious contradiction in U.S. policy, the AFC recorded, "On the one hand, the Administration seeks to place American ships in the war trade forbidden by our laws, placing them under *foreign* flags, and, on the other hand, claims that *American* ships are being attacked when those foreign-flag ships run the risks to which that policy necessarily subjects them." Besides, said the AFC, such practice harmed U.S. defense, for in February 1941 the Maritime Commission indicated an acute shortage of ships needed to carry vital defense materials. Finerty soon alleged that Panamanian registry violated the law, even if the Maritime Commission had claimed sanction from "some Attorney General." Furthermore, he charged, because President Arnulfo Francisco Arias of Panama had opposed arming these ships, the United States had helped manipulate the overthrow of his government that very October. General Wood was more direct: "American ship owners hid behind a foreign flag to make some money. Are American men to die for their 'dividends'"?[53]

Early in September, Americans learned that the U.S. destroyer *Greer* had been attacked by an unidentified submarine en route to Iceland. The immediate response of FDR's critics was predictable. "We have," said Senator McCarran, "been sticking our nose out so far that we can expect anything." The further American ships entered into war zones, added Danaher, "the more likely we are to be embroiled in war."[54]

Roosevelt bided his time on such matters until 11 September, when he told a nationwide radio audience that, exactly one week earlier, a German submarine had fired on the *Greer*. Also mentioning the attacks on the *Robin Moor*, *Sessa*, and *Steel Seafarer*, FDR found "a Nazi design to abolish freedom of the seas, and to acquire absolute control and domination of these seas for themselves." The next German steps would include "domination of the United States" and "domination of the Western Hemisphere by force of arms," to be followed by their ultimate goal: "world conquest and permanent world domination by sword."

The president issued a warning. To ward off "the rattlesnakes of the Atlantic," American ships and planes would henceforth "strike their deadly blow—first"; that is, they would shoot on sight and ask questions later. Furthermore, U.S. patrolling vessels and planes would "protect all merchant ships—not only American ships but ships of any flag—engaged in commerce in our defensive waters," an area (though he did not say so) that currently extended to some four hundred miles off the Scottish coast. For roughly three-quarters of the Atlantic, therefore, American naval and air vessels would escort friendly convoys, in the process eliminating any Axis forces encountered on the way. Historical precedents, Roosevelt said, included actions against piracy by John Adams and Thomas Jefferson. An undeclared war in the Atlantic had officially begun.[55]

On the following day, the CDAAA supported the president's speech, asserting that American ships must not be "sitting targets" for Hitler's raiders. Once the U.S. Navy took the offensive, it predicted, German submarines would hesitate to court destruction. Besides, it continued, the U.S. was defending its rights on the high seas.[56]

Following FDR's speech, a Gallup poll indicated 62 percent in support of the president's position.[57] Two prominent anti-interventionists backed the president. Roosevelt, maintained Hamilton Fish, was right in defending American vessels going to Iceland, though he deplored the fact that they were there.[58] Herbert Hoover found FDR justified in protesting the sinking of merchant ships without adequate protection for crew. He did warn against sending American warships into danger zones, however.[59]

Most noninterventionists opposed Roosevelt on this matter. Certainly, they argued, the president was guilty of hypocrisy. "An amazing speech," wrote Anne Morrow Lindbergh in her diary. "A wizard he is to make so plausible the thesis that we will continue to give all possible aid to the enemies of Hitler while being affronted if Hitler does not respect our rights as a 'neutral'!" To Castle, it was the U.S. that was breaking international law: "Even the President of the United States cannot make law to suit himself from day to day." Professor Philip Jessup found no relationship between FDR's new policy and the activities of Adams and Jefferson. The AFC, he suggested, should indirectly broach the matter of impeachment. Nye, Bennett Clark, and America First all wanted the *Greer* incident investigated.[60] Norman Thomas sought the total withdrawal of American forces from Iceland.[61] The *Christian Century* recalled that a much more serious incident, Japan's attack on the *Panay* in December 1937, had been peacefully resolved.[62]

On 14 October, the chief of naval operations, Admiral Harold Stark, released an official report noting that the *Greer* had sought out the German sub, trailed it doggedly for hours, and given British planes information to facilitate their attack.[63] The CDAAA still justified the *Greer*'s action: "The fact that a British plane dropped bombs near the submarine earlier in no way gave the submarine any right to fire on an American warship."[64]

To many of the president's critics, the Stark report again revealed Roosevelt's duplicity.[65] The *Chicago Tribune* carried the editorial headline "The Truth Comes Out."[66] Amos Pinchot compared the *Greer* incident to Bismarck's famous Ems telegram, which triggered the Franco-Prussian war.[67]

Some anti-interventionists suddenly saw the German action as quite rational.[68] To Senator Danaher, it was the Americans who were committing "flagrant acts of war." Nye said, "What the German submarine did was probably less than we would have done under like circumstances." Hoover now called the *Greer* "the aggressor." Wheeler cited a sailor on the *Greer* who had written him to the effect that his ship, under orders, had fired first.[69]

As far as FDR's shoot-on-sight orders were concerned, administration foes were even more furious.[70] Fifty-eight prominent Americans signed a petition calling Roosevelt's speech a "grave threat to the democratic principle of majority rule."[71] General Wood accused the president of initiating "an undeclared war, in plain violation of the Constitution."[72] A detailed AFC position paper charged FDR with violating the 1939 neutrality act and misrepresenting the concept of "freedom of the seas." The AFC accused the president not of eliminating submarines but of eliminating Congress. The New York chapter found FDR to be "annexing" the waters of the Atlantic, a part of the Pacific, and portions of the Red Sea—indeed, almost everything but the Mediterranean: "Never in the history of the country has there been so gross usurpation of power by any executive save Huey Long."[73]

Roosevelt's term *piracy* was disputed. To Lincoln Colcord, the Americans were the real pirates for committing "repeated acts of war without declaring war." To Chicago attorney Clay Judson, *piracy* could easily apply to Britain, for it was the power preventing the United States from sending food to the babies of occupied Europe. Similarly, the *Chicago Tribune* compared Germany, which seldom interfered with peaceful American commerce, to Britain, which was interfering "every moment of every day in every port and every ocean," in the process keeping American farmers and manufacturers from exporting their products to occupied Europe.[74]

Noninterventionists challenged other Roosevelt claims as well. Axis domination of Eurasia, said both the AFC and the socialist *Call*, would not lead to a shipbuilding gap. In fact, one American steel company in 1941 could produce more steel than all of Germany. Similarly, freedom of the seas was again found to be a misnomer, being neither traditional American doctrine nor recognized in international law. In the words of the AFC, the president really sought "freedom to aid at will one belligerent nation without danger of interference by the other belligerent."[75]

On 11 September, the day FDR gave his shoot-on-sight speech, the freighter *Montana*, heading toward Iceland, was torpedoed 260 miles southwest of its destination. Its entire crew was saved. Chartered to a private American firm, it flew the Panamanian flag. The event was reported a day later. Few anti-interventionists commented. Finerty asserted that the ship was probably traveling in convoy, which would give the Germans legal rights to sink it.[76]

On 17 September 1941, the U.S. Navy began escorting its first British convoy. On the same day, Hitler gave instructions to avoid any incident before the middle of October. Just a week later, the Royal Navy withdrew completely from the western Atlantic, leaving escorting there to the Americans and the Canadians.[77]

On 19 September, the merchant ship *Pink Star*, also under Panamanian registry, was sunk between Greenland and Iceland under circumstances almost identical to the *Montana*. Of the twelve men lost, not one was an American. Within ten days, the public learned of the incident. To Roosevelt the United States had an obligation to protect ships flying the Panamanian flag, for "today freedom of the seas includes very definitely the protection of this Western Hemisphere and all of the twenty-one Republics therein."[78]

Anti-interventionists responded quickly. As in previous cases, they emphasized that the *Pink Star* carried contraband and was armed.[79] Fish, noting the Panamanian registry, held the U.S. no more responsible for such ships than for those "flying the Swedish flag" or representing "the Swiss Navy."[80] Congressman Bradley stressed that the *Pink Star* was sailing in a Canadian convoy into an area that the German government had declared a blockade zone. Germany, said Amos Pinchot, had a right, possibly a duty, to sink such vessels.[81]

While the president was implementing his convoy orders, on 27 September still another sinking took place. A German U-boat struck the *I. C. White*, a tanker that belonged to the Standard Oil Company of New York but that flew the Panamanian flag. Sailing alone from Curaçao to Cape Town carrying a cargo of fuel oil, it was hit some six hundred miles east of Pernambuco, Brazil. Three of its crew were lost, all Americans. The public learned of the event within the week. Roosevelt's adversaries again stressed the matter of contraband and the fact the ship was armed.[82]

Aid to Britain was still limited by the 1939 neutrality act, which forbade American vessels from entering combat zones previously designated by the president. Could such ships sail directly to England, without having to transfer cargoes at Iceland, the embattled isle would receive substantially more lend-lease matériel. Moreover, interventionists argued, these freighters could assist in their own defense if they could mount one or two guns.[83]

Fully aware of the narrowness of the House vote on extending draft terms, the president did not to seek immediate repeal of the entire 1939 act. Rather, he would simply alter section 2, which banned American vessels from belligerent zones; section 3, which authorized the president to proclaim combat zones around belligerent countries; and section 6, which prohibited the arming of U.S. merchant vessels. The administration decided to test opinion in the House, where opposition seemed stronger, by asking it to approve the arming of merchant ships. If the House did so, the Senate would then be requested to repeal all three sections, at which time the House would again vote, this time on the comprehensive Senate bill.[84] A few anti-interventionists thought that the president had the authority to act on his own, though of course they hoped he would not do so.[85]

On 9 October, Roosevelt proposed the arming of American merchant ships—an old practice, he said, never prohibited by international law or, until 1937, by any federal statute. By such means, aid could be delivered with far greater effectiveness against the "tremendous forces now marching toward conquest of the world." The president did concede that "the arming of merchant vessels does not guarantee their safety," but "it most certainly" added to it. Most of the vital goods authorized by Congress were being delivered, he noted; nevertheless, too many craft were still being sunk. He added a general wish that Congress would give its "earnest and early attention" to eliminating the ban on entering combat zones, thereby permitting American merchant ships to reach belligerent ports. FDR denied that he was calling for a declaration of war; he was simply concerned with the "essential defense of American rights" and "the freedom of the seas."[86]

The CDAAA, in defending the arming of merchant ships, maintained that such vessels could keep a submarine submerged, thereby limiting their speed to eight knots and giving American craft a good prospect of escaping. If U.S. ships encountered a bomber, their guns would keep the plane so high that attack was less likely. Recalling that Woodrow Wilson had armed such ships on his own authority in 1917, CDAAA spokesman Livingstone Hartley praised the president for submitting the issue to Congress, something that gave lie to any claims that FDR was dictatorial.[87]

A few noninterventionists supported the move. To Fish, the measure would probably be ineffective, but, he continued, "our ships have the right to defend themselves on the seven seas, outside the war zones.[88] General Wood did not feel he could conscientiously testify against the arming of merchant ships, as long as administration leaders were advancing the proposal as a defense measure.[89]

Most critics, however, saw such arming not as protecting American seamen but as endangering them. Representative Shafer made the analogy of sending "a 10-year-old boy out into the jungles to hunt ferocious tigers with a sling-shot." Congressman Short compared the proposal to a boxing match between comedian Eddie Cantor and heavyweight champion Joe Louis. By eliminating all warning, said Charles A. Beard, a sea war would be far more merciless.[90]

Objections were detailed: There was difficulty in firing guns from the deck of a moving ship, particularly with aircraft or U-boats in the vicinity. Armed merchantmen were easy targets, for in convoys the fastest ship was forced to travel at the speed of the slowest. Mines presented a danger, as did as such raiders as the *Graf Spee* or the *Scharnhorst*.[91] The United States only possessed four hundred four- and five-inch guns, most nearly forty years old and often ineffective in World War I.[92] Prevailing shortages made it impossible to arm two hundred ships in a merchant marine of some twelve hundred vessels.[93]

The technology of the submarine was stressed. Modern subs possessed directional sound devices that enabled them to strike before their presence became known.[94] There had never been a case in which a lone merchantman had successfully defended itself against such craft.[95]

Then there was the matter of professional testimony. Some British officers denied the efficacy of such protection, claiming that it was too difficult to coordinate the entire crew of a ship.[96] American experts, too, were quoted, as was Navy Secretary Knox, who said that the guns slated for arming merchant ships were needed for naval vessels.[97] Admiral Stark himself asserted that armed ships were more likely to escape but conceded, "Occasionally you might lose a lot of lives where you would not otherwise."[98] The experience of World War I was recalled: Armed ships then could not defend themselves, even though the U-boats and aircraft were far less efficient.[99]

If all these factors were not enough, a battery of international law experts—including Charles Cheney Hyde, Philip Jessup, John Bassett Moore, and Edwin M. Borchard—found that such arming violated international law. Once a merchant ship was armed, it lost all immunity as a neutral vessel.[100] Furthermore, argued Borchard, "There is no *right* to send United States munitions to Great Britain."[101]

Most anti-interventionists also opposed Roosevelt's effort to eliminate war zones. The president, warned General Robert E. Wood, was "asking Congress to issue an engraved drowning license to American seamen." In a private letter, the general portrayed Hitler as "trying hard" not to sink U.S. ships bound for Iceland, though the Führer would certainly attack if they ventured all the way to the British Isles.[102]

Critics continued to harp on Roosevelt's assertion concerning freedom of the seas. As Lincoln Colcord saw it, such freedom did not exist in wartime. When the United States spoke in such terms, it only meant that it supported Britain's control of the seas. "It would be more honest and useful for us to say so," he said. Finerty added that Roosevelt's request violated existing treaties with Italy and Germany; the AFC reprinted an entire treaty of 1928 with Germany.[103]

As the Senate began debate, the Germans sank two more merchant ships. On 16 October, the *W. C. Teagle*, a large Standard Oil tanker, and the *Bold Venture* went down. Both vessels were en route to Britain, carried Panamanian registry, and were hit some five hundred miles south of Iceland. No American lives were lost on either ship. The public learned of the incidents within the week.[104]

Few anti-interventionists commented on the matter. Both ships, noted Finerty, were loaded with contraband; furthermore, the *Bold Venture* was part of a British convoy. Danaher stated that the *Bold Venture* was armed.[105]

On the next day, 17 October, the navy department announced that the *USS Kearny*, a crack destroyer scarcely a year in service, had been torpedoed. Coming to the aid of some fifty merchant ships that had left a Canadian port in convoy early that month, it was struck by German subs about four hundred miles from Iceland. The ship was damaged, not sunk, but eleven lives were lost, the first American fatalities on a U.S. ship since the war began. The news was reported immediately.[106]

Administration adversaries proposed various alternatives to the administration bill. Villard sought to keep each American ship unarmed and then hold Germany to strict accountability.[107] Finerty would have preferred to donate several ships rather than "donate the lives of our seamen." "Give them the guns to man them if they want," he said at another point, "and if necessary give them the crew to man them."[108] In its own report, the minority bloc of the House Foreign Affairs Committee suggested placing such American merchant ships under British registry. The move, it maintained, would save American lives; eliminate the subterfuge of Panamanian registry; enable the United States to provide Britain with merchant ships, armed or unarmed as it chose; provide Britain with shipping space equal to any other program; conform to existing legislation; and serve as a genuine "lend-lease," with provisions for permitting American ownership and return to the U.S. on demand.[109]

The naval incidents, particularly the attack on the *Kearny*, all had their effect. On the same day the *Kearny* was hit, 17 October, the House, voting 259 to 138, allowed the arming of American merchant ships. Two days later, a Gallup poll showed 72 percent favoring such arming, and 46 percent supporting the entering of combat zones.[110]

Responding to the House action, Hitler publicly confirmed secret orders on 18 October: "If . . . an American ship shoots . . . it will do so at its own peril. The German ship will defend itself, and our torpedoes will find their mark."[111]

Now the matter lay before the Senate. The bill, which added the abolition of war zones to the arming of merchant ships, was seen as particularly crucial.[112] Ex-senator Reed commented, "I regard it as the most critical decision that had to be made since 1861." The *Christian Century* entitled its editorial on neutrality repeal "The Last Stand." Said an AFC pamphlet, "The war party is demanding a one way passage to Davy Jones' Locker for American seamen—a one way passage to the battlefield of Europe for a huge new AEF."[113]

In the meantime, the sinking of merchant ships continued. On 19 October, the freighter *Lehigh*, bound from Bilbao, Spain, to the African Gold Coast, was sunk without warning some seventy-five miles off Freetown, an area not staked out as a combat zone by any belligerent. A British destroyer rescued all thirty-nine crew members. The ship belonged to the United States Lines, flew the American flag, and was carrying only ballast. Within three days, Americans knew of the sinking.[114]

This time even Roosevelt foes found Germany to be totally in the wrong. Villard called the sinking the "one absolutely indefensible case." To Vandenberg it was "the act of a wanton pirate," for which Germany must be held strictly accountable. If the practice continued, warned Taft, "we shall have a cause for war."[115]

On 27 October, in a Navy Day address, Roosevelt stated that with the strike against the *Kearny*, an American war vessel, the nation itself had been attacked. Furthermore, the president claimed to possess a secret map that revealed Hitler's plans to weld South and Central America into five vassal nations. Moreover, he had covert evidence that Hitler planned to abolish all existing religions and establish an international Nazi church.[116]

Before and after the president's speech, anti-interventionists were quick to comment on the *Kearny* sinking. "So we are in the war," said the *New York Daily News*. Hoover noted the destroyer was "convoying British ships—not even American-flag vessels." Senator Wheeler remarked, "The *Kearny* gave chase; she tossed off depth charges; she was out for the kill."[117]

The *Chicago Tribune* had one solution to such incidents: Roosevelt should demand that British armed forces withdraw from Iceland, thereby giving complete control to the United States and depriving Hitler of any excuse for interfering with American communications. Addressing a different point, Vorys mused that if a submarine could sink such a well-armed destroyer, what chance had "tramp steamers armed with old World War guns"?[118]

FDR's opponents questioned his claims concerning Nazi designs.[119] The president, noted General Wood, had refused to permit public inspection of the presumed Nazi documents. The *Chicago Tribune* asserted that sweeping contingency plans, such as those FDR said the Germans possessed, had been drafted by every general staff in the world against every conceivable enemy. Were the chief executive to examine the files of his own war and navy departments, he could find plans for attacking Britain and seizing Canada.[120] The map is now suspected of being a doctored British plant.[121]

Anti-interventionists also criticized Roosevelt's comments on religion. Five days before the president's speech, remarked D. Worth Clark, the *Christian Science Monitor* had printed a story stating, "The Bible would be superseded by *Mein Kampf* and other symbols of the church by a sword." Obviously, deduced the Idaho senator, someone had woven the *Monitor* article into the president's speech. Socialist writer Devere Allen accused the president of stealing his material from Nazi theorist Alfred Rosenberg's *The Myth of the Twentieth Century* (1930), a work that he claimed the Nazis themselves had long ignored.[122]

Again the issue of presidential war-making power remained crucial. Wheeler found no peacetime legal sanction giving the president authority to send an American warship to assist a belligerent convoy. To Philip La Follette, FDR was treating American ships as his personal property, not those of the American people. John Cudahy compared Roosevelt to Hitler, who plunged his country into war and told the Reichstag about it afterward. America First cited Supreme Court decisions ruling that war making remained with Congress, including even the provocative Curtiss–Wright (1936) judgment that stressed the broad inherent powers the president possessed in the realm of foreign affairs.[123]

Lawrence Dennis attributed Machiavellian designs to the president. Denying that Roosevelt sought a full-scale war, Dennis found FDR to be hoping to see Britain and Germany so weaken each other that the United States would "fall heir to British possessions in this hemisphere" and "hold sway as the indisputably first sea power in the world." Hence, the debate over neutrality revision, he said, was "largely an unreal farce."[124]

Some administration critics not only argued that Britain was doing relatively well on the battlefront but also found British shipping to be in good shape.[125] Taft saw the British commanding many more ships than the U.S., the tonnage ratio being twenty-five million tons to four or five million, in Britain's favor.[126] According to the AFC, the British possessed more shipping than when the war began. It quoted Churchill, who told the House of Commons on 1 October that sinkings of British, Allied, and neutral ships during the past four months had only been one-third those of April, May, and June. England's privations in the Atlantic, the AFC continued, had become almost negligible. Moreover, American and British shipyards were turning out new ships at an unprecedented rate, exceeding by many times the combined rate of losses.[127]

In general, so it was argued, the British were doing quite well. German reservists, not regular troops, were stationed across the Channel; the Luftwaffe was not over London but over Moscow; German panzer divisions were fighting on a two thousand–mile battlefront, in the process experiencing casualties numbering in the millions.[128] After two years of war, the British forces, including Australians and New Zealanders, had tallied only 142,000 casualties in all, some 3 percent of its total armed strength.[129]

As the Senate was debating its own version of Roosevelt's proposals, more sinkings took place. On the night of 29–30 October, the armed U.S. Navy tanker *Salinas* was torpedoed southwest of Iceland while traveling in convoy.

No serious injury, much less loss of life, was involved, and the *Salinas* reached port safely. The event was reported several days later.[130]

On 31 October, a far more pivotal incident took place. A German U-boat torpedoed the U.S. destroyer *Reuben James*, part of a five-destroyer escort, six hundred miles west of Ireland. The attack took place at daybreak, so the U-boat commander probably knew he was firing on an American ship. Of the 160 men on board, only 45 were rescued. The news was released immediately. The president condemned the sinking but took no further action.[131]

Anti-interventionists made familiar responses.[132] Senator Aiken held FDR personally responsible for every life lost. Wheeler cited Arthur Krock, *New York Times* Washington correspondent, to the effect that the *Reuben James*, acting as part of a convoy, was aiding another ship when attacked. Congressman Robert Rich accused the administration of "committing murder on the men in our own Navy." "We can't expect the Germans," said Amos Pinchot, "to refrain from doing what we would do in their place." Nye remarked, "The sinking had about as much to do with the defense of our shores as the sinking of a freighter by an iceberg." Norman Thomas found Hitler "extraordinarily patient" in the face of repeated acts of war.[133]

On 7 November, after eleven days of bitter debate, the Senate voted fifty to thirty-seven to arm American merchantmen and permit the entry of U.S. ships into war zones. Bennett Clark sought to separate the question of opening belligerent ports and combat zones from that of arming merchant ships, but he was voted down.[134] The legislation then went back to the House, which now had to consider the war zone issue.

The second House vote produced, if anything, even stronger anti-interventionist anxieties than had the previous House and Senate bills. Knute Hill (Dem.-Wash.) called the tally "a declaration of war by Congress."[135] William Pfeiffer (Rep.-N.Y.) envisioned U.S. ships entering such far-flung areas as Murmansk, the Black Sea, and the Suez Canal.[136]

On 13 November, just eleven minutes before the time limit on debate was reached, House Majority Leader John W. McCormack (Dem.-Mass.) produced a letter from the president. Arming American merchant ships was necessary, Roosevelt declared, because of "the continued sinking of American flag ships in many parts of the ocean." By convoying in the combat zones, time and money could be saved, thereby increasing the quantity of supplies being sent to "those nations fighting Hitlerism." As Clark had done in the Senate, Congressman Everett McKinley Dirksen (Rep.-Ill.) sought to divide the bill, which—he hoped—could result in securing the arming of ships and retaining the existing war zones. This move, too, was unsuccessful.[137]

The House voted 212 to 194 to eliminate the war zones.[138] Four days later Roosevelt signed the bill. For practical purposes, the neutrality act of 1939 was dead.

A shift of ten votes would have defeated the measure. Those members of Congress opposing revision, said General Wood, represented about half of the

American voters. Moreover, the margin was far too narrow to encourage any declaration of war, something that the public, according to the polls, continued to oppose.[139] The polls did show approval of American convoys to Britain, with 59 percent of the respondents in agreement. Furthermore, the Gallup poll indicated 47 percent favored the sending of an AEF if such a move was needed to defeat Germany; 46 percent were opposed.[140]

On the day of the House action, Hitler held a naval conference at which he approved a new set of orders for German "surface forces." Once American naval vessels began action, including "shadowing," the German commander must not be "too late in using his weapons."[141]

Some anti-interventionists still hoped that the United States could avoid full-scale war.[142] The *Christian Century* hoped that the sheer closeness of the vote might slow Roosevelt down. Flynn thought the president would wait at least a month before using any new powers.[143] FDR, commented Pinchot, would be held responsible if more lives and ships were lost.[144] Other anti-interventionists were less optimistic, the *Chicago Tribune* entitling its editorial on the tally "The Vote for War."[145]

Nonetheless, even in late November and early December, Roosevelt remained cautious. On 22 November, with characteristic ambivalence, he spoke of creating routes to Britain and the USSR: "The use of American flag ships must come very soon but should be worked into gradually." Three days later, the administration decided that American vessels traveling to Lisbon should not be armed but that U.S. merchant ships bound for Archangel needed such protection. In giving his orders, Roosevelt cryptically asserted, "Ships under the American flag go to Great Britain as soon as they become available but that this procedure progress gradually with only a small number of ships being so routed in the beginning. This number may be increased at a later date if in accordance with Administration policies and instructions." Presumably, these vessels would have been included in British convoys, thereby postponing a decision about whether to send a convoy of American ships under its own escorts. The orders were not publicized—hardly the all-out effort to provoke war that Churchill believed FDR had promised him in August. If the president was trying to protect the Atlantic supply line, he was doing so in the least provocative way.[146]

Of course, in the end, it was Hitler who would decide what constituted provocation. But the German dictator was never in any hurry to start a war with the United States while his European problems remained unsettled. In September 1941, military intelligence in Washington predicted that Germany would not use its large submarine force in the North Atlantic "until she is ready to provoke the United States or until hostilities with America begin."[147]

While all such debates were being conducted—in fact, from the time that Hitler invaded Poland—anti-interventionist attention was not solely focused overseas. FDR critics saw the domestic consequences of full-scale involvement as possibly the most fatal of all.

# 19

# The Domestic Front

All during the debate over American policy, critics of intervention expressed long-range concerns over the nation's domestic life. Some were so anxious about developments on the home front that they genuinely saw tyranny in the offing. In November 1940, for example, John T. Flynn referred to "a condition of terror, growing alarm that it is only a question of a little time when we shall have to meet the Nazi terror in our own streets and our own homes."[1]

Admittedly, Hitler's blitzkrieg in Western Europe had produced some genuine panic. Particularly alarming was an incipient spy scare.[2] *New Masses* told of German Americans in St. Louis finding swastikas painted on their homes and religious proselytizers being driven from a Texas border town as suspected Nazi sympathizers. Even the *New Republic*, by now increasingly interventionist, told of a tribe of Miami Indians who felt compelled to write the secretary of Indian affairs, informing him that they were not fifth columnists.[3]

To administration opponents, Roosevelt was exploiting war scares so as to use military spending as a means of recovery.[4] Journalist C. Hartley Grattan went further, writing, "Mr. Big is doing his damndest to get us in [the war]."[5]

Concern increased as the debate over lend-lease heated up.[6] In January 1941, Idaho novelist Vardis Fisher was reminded of the recent radio broadcast of producer Orson Welles, a sensationalist dramatization of H. G. Wells's *War of the Worlds* (1898), which portrayed the United States being invaded by Martians.[7] To Congressman Woodruff, the administration "would have us believe that Mr. Hitler is practically ready to sail into New York harbor within a few days after England submits to his bombs." The more sober Alan Valentine, president of the University of Rochester, deplored "prophecies of mass air attacks at 45,000 feet, of gas bombing, of planes bombing Detroit from bases in Newfoundland, of economic collapse in this hemisphere if England is defeated."[8]

Even after lend-lease was enacted, administration critics saw their opponents as continually attempting to create panic. Noting that FDR had recently asserted that Denver and Omaha could lie within striking distance of German air power, Fish said in April 1941, "The people near the Mississippi Valley are now demanding battleships for the Mississippi River for protection, and soon they will be asking for submarines in the Dust Bowls."[9]

The many violations of civil liberties committed during World War I, non-interventionists feared, might well be repeated. Borchard, writing in February 1941, remarked, "We have about the same attitude that prevailed here between January and April 1917, when any sane man was looked on askance." Wheeler hauntingly remembered, "Men were hanged for their opinions. Others were taken into cellars and beaten."[10]

Already the signs appeared ominous. When, in April 1941, Harold Ickes called Oswald Garrison Villard and Norman Thomas allies of Germany's Führer, Villard in turn accused the interior secretary of attempting to choke off opposition: "The Ickes tactics are exactly those of Adolf Hitler." Castle indicted Secretary Stimson for stating that criticism of the war effort should be suppressed. The United States, commented the retired diplomat, was not far from being a dictatorship.[11]

At times Roosevelt himself was seen as leading the witch hunt. When the president called for unspecified government action against "a few slackers or troublemakers in our midst," Villard wrote, "Such words are unprecedented in our history. It was the first time that a President of the United States has threatened to use the power of government in peacetime to suppress criticism and dissent—this in a democracy!" Robert Maynard Hutchins saw Roosevelt as "conducting a war of nerves . . . against his own people."[12]

Given such an environment, so anti-interventionists claimed, little room for dissent existed.[13] Several quoted Mark Twain's *Mysterious Stranger* (1916), in which the prominent novelist warned against wartime panic.[14] After the 1940 election, Norman Thomas predicted, the government would crack down on antidraft agitation "and all other opposition or criticism." Harry Elmer Barnes predicted "a scapegoat period after the war which will make Hitler seem a Judophile by comparison."[15] "As this psychosis rises," feared Herbert Hoover in April 1941, "every word of caution uttered by honest Americans will be denounced as being 'a call from Hitler.'"[16]

Even domestic fascism was not unthinkable. Porter Sargent warned, "We may become fascist by fighting fascism, as Huey Long prophesied." While the Old World faced "the prospect of a Communist totalitarianism," remarked Harry Elmer Barnes, the resulting fascism in the United States might "last longer than our Federal Constitution has lasted." "More terrible than Hitler," wrote pacifist Milton Mayer, "is the Hitler, the Fascist, the animal, in all of us."[17]

Analogies were made to both Germany and the Soviet Union. In June 1941, Representative Vito Marcantonio recalled news flashes emerging from Nazi Germany in 1936: "Four million so-called aliens fingerprinted and registered; 500 noncitizens rounded up and imprisoned without bail; strike broken by troops using bayonets against workers; concentration camps being prepared; work-or-fight order given to workers, minister of justice urges concentration camps and wholesale deportations." By November, socialist leader Maynard Krueger found the nation already in its "Brüning" stage.[18]

Lawrence Dennis, who had written *The Coming American Fascism* (1936), nonetheless could not see FDR as an incipient totalitarian despot. FDR "may be a Kerensky," Dennis wrote in July 1940, "but he won't be a Lenin for he lacks the personality, ideology, system and lieutenants for a dictator." Close to a year later, however, Dennis accused the president of using the war emergency to establish an American dictatorship. Signs included army intervention in a California strike, the Russell–Overton "seize-property" proposal, and a barrage of alarmist statements about subversive activities.[19]

Evidence of oppression came from many quarters. In September 1939, *Uncensored* noted that the National Protective League, organized recently by Toledo industrialists, was offering a $25 bounty for information leading to the arrest of "foreign agents." Modeled after the vigilante American Protective Association of World War I, the group was endorsed by no less than the director of the Federal Bureau of Investigation (FBI), J. Edgar Hoover. A month later, *Commonweal* observed the American Legion's call for registration and fingerprinting of all aliens and the outlawing of the German American Bund and the Communist Party. It also noted the American Labor Party's purge of communists and John L. Lewis's call for similar cleaning of his Congress of Industrial Organizations. In February 1940, Porter Sargent offered his own list: the conviction of communist leader Earl Browder on spurious charges; the roundup of eighteen followers of Father Coughlin's paramilitary group, the Christian Front; the closing of a Russian bookshop; the disbanding of the Friends of the Soviet; and the cutting off of foreign scientific periodicals. He claimed that nothing less than a new Red scare was in the offing. That July, *Commonweal*'s coeditor Philip Burnham expressed concern over House passage of a bill to deport Harry Bridges, the longshoremen's union leader and militant leftist, and an appropriations bill denying relief aid to communists and German American Bundists; membership in both groups, he noted, was quite legal. In August 1940, Nye condemned the arrest without charges of Gerald Harris, vice president of the Farmers' Union of Alabama in Birmingham, for intending to speak against conscription at a county Farmers' Union convention. That same month, William Henry Chamberlin observed that Fulton Oursler, editor of *Liberty*, told an audience that he endorsed suspension of all civil liberties and suppression of the foreign-language press.[20]

In 1941, both *Uncensored* and a writer in *New Masses* gave credence to a column by Arthur Krock, Washington correspondent for the *New York Times*, that maintained that "members of the inner White House circle" sought national censorship, including the banning of anti-interventionist speeches given by members of Congress.[21] Krock was also cited concerning suspension of congressional elections in 1942. In November, Norman Thomas pointed to the Supreme Court decision written by Justice Felix Frankfurter, who ruled that the Jehovah's Witnesses could be compelled to salute the flag.[22]

One practice was most disturbing: the turning over of anti-interventionist letters, written to government leaders in protest against interventionist policies, to federal enforcement agencies. In October 1940, constitutional scholar Edwin S. Corwin referred to the possibility of an American Gestapo, noting that O. John Rogge, assistant attorney general, delivered antiadministration correspondence to the criminal division of the department of justice, including a letter by noted music scholar Daniel Gregory Mason.[23]

The American Civil Liberties Union (ACLU) was presented as an expert witness. Sargent cited an ACLU statement: "The guns of reaction are booming." In June 1940, Dorothy Detzer quoted Roger Baldwin, its director, to the effect that within the past month more violations of civil liberties had been reported than during the entire war period of 1917–18.[24]

Certain legislation, though never enacted, appeared downright dangerous. In 1939, the House passed a bill introduced by Congressman Sam Hobbs (Dem.-Ala.) that included provisions for imprisoning aliens without trial.[25] In June 1940, the Senate added crippling amendments to the La Follette civil liberties bill. In November 1941, the House judiciary committee reported out an amendment to the antisabotage law: a mandatory death penalty would be required if an "offense resulted in death or serious injury to any other person or placed any other person in grave danger of death or serious injury." In the same month, the House voted for a measure enabling the Federal Communications Agency to revoke a radio license if there was a "reasonable probability" the operator was subversive. Representative Hatton W. Sumners (Dem.-Tex.) sought a law that would make illegal even the voicing of opinions that would please a foreign principal.[26]

If such proposals were never enacted, others were, and much alarm was created in the process. Liberal anti-interventionists were particularly frightened by the Alien Registration Act, a bill passed by Congress in June 1940. It outlawed membership in any group teaching the violent overthrow of the U.S. government. Known as the Smith Act after its House sponsor, Congressman Howard W. Smith (Dem.-Va.), it also strengthened existing laws governing the admission and deportation of aliens as well as requiring their fingerprinting.[27] Sargent warned that such legislation would make illegal his keep-out-of-war bulletins. Norman Thomas called the bill "the most vicious, fascistic measure yet enacted by our war-hysterical Congress." It permits, he said, "in time of excitement a more drastic control of public discussion than the Espionage Act of the first World War."[28] Thomas also opposed congressional passage of a bill, introduced by Congressman Jerry Voorhis, an erstwhile anti-interventionist, that required the registration of organizations that were subject to foreign control, engaged in civilian military operations, or advocated the overthrow of the United States by force. The socialist leader feared that the bill was so sweeping that his own party, as well as trade unions, international veterans societies, and even the English-Speaking Union, might fall under its jurisdiction.[29]

Some noninterventionists offered their own solutions. The real remedy to such spies, traitors, and saboteurs, observed *Commonweal's* Philip Burnham, lay in "normal precautions and a mild registration system." "If foreign agents are violating the law," wrote Dennis, "they could be promptly apprehended, tried, convicted and punished" without the use of unverifiable innuendoes.[30]

Even the direction of American culture appeared to be a matter of grave concern. In the spring of 1940, Archibald MacLeish, poet and librarian of Congress, castigated his fellow artists for apathy toward the fascist menace. In particular, he attacked novelists John Dos Passos and Ernest Hemingway for implying that not only "the war issues but *all* issues, all moral issues, were false—were fraudulent—were intended to deceive."[31]

The response was vehement.[32] *Uncensored* called MacLeish "the literary department of the Washington war party." A contributor to *Partisan Review* recalled that MacLeish had been strongly isolationist through 1935. The real "irresponsibles," according to socialist writer Lillian Symes, were "those naive enough to believe that we can fight this war without any essential damage to, or alterations in, the prevailing democratic structure."[33]

Even greater alarm was voiced over the comment of Nicholas Murray Butler, seventy-five-year-old president of Columbia University, who in October 1940 defined the current war as one "between beasts and human beings." His institution, he continued, would cooperate fully with the government in its "attempt to strengthen the defenses of our American system of economic, social and political liberty." Any faculty whose personal convictions would "hamper and embarrass the ideals of the University" in this regard, Butler said, should resign.[34]

Critics found the speech a prime example of war-engendered hysteria. Bennett Champ Clark called Butler "a senile reactionary." To the *Chicago Tribune*, Butler was "Columbia's Fuehrer." John Haynes Holmes accused the educator of trying to do for Columbia "what Hitler had done completely to German universities."[35] After the immediate ruckus, Butler appeared to backtrack, as he declared that his students and faculty possessed full freedom of expression.[36]

Anti-interventionists could point to one instance after another where— they maintained—censorship, either formal or informal, was becoming a reality. Early in 1941, Porter Sargent observed, the following anti-intervention-ist columnists had been dropped from their journals: Dorothy Dunbar Brom-ley and Ernest L. Meyer from the *New York Post,* Harry Elmer Barnes from the *New York World-Telegram,* Oswald Garrison Villard from the *Nation,* John T. Flynn from the *New Republic,* and H. L. Mencken from the *Baltimore Sun.*³⁷ The *Christian Century* noted efforts to suppress the radio broadcasts of Hugh Johnson as well as short-wave programs from foreign capitals.³⁸

In late February 1941, the administration established an Office of Govern-ment Reports. Lowell Mellett, a strong New Dealer who had managed the Scripps–Howard News Alliance, was chosen director. Its aim: to keep local communities informed of defense preparedness.³⁹ *Uncensored* found Mellett "an honest, liberal minded, capable journalist," but it warned that censorship could be imposed by a quiet appeal to publishers' patriotism, friendly hints to reporters that sources might be closed, and the Espionage Act of 1917, which was still on the books.⁴⁰

By the middle of 1941, even liberal administration critics found their speak-ing engagements terminated, their meetings banned. When the Youth Com-mittee Against War sought to hold its convention in Madison, Wisconsin, in December 1940, the University of Wisconsin and the First Congregationalist Church both refused to lend their facilities. Similarly in 1941, Ohio University and the University of California at Los Angeles would not permit Norman Thomas to speak on their campuses. That November, Wheeler found during a tour of California that the Fraternal Order of Eagles had denied him a hall.⁴¹ The America First Committee often experienced trouble finding locales for its rallies, as seen by objections made by the county commissioners of Miami and the city council of Oklahoma City.⁴²

For some of the more outspoken noninterventionists, the FBI was a target for criticism.⁴³ In January 1940, *Uncensored* spoofed the arrest of seventeen members of Father Coughlin's paramilitary Christian Front, marking in par-ticular FBI director Hoover's rejoinder to criticism: "It took only 23 men to overthrow Russia."⁴⁴ A month later, Nye opposed adding "G-men" to an "al-ready overloaded government payroll."⁴⁵ The FBI, noninterventionists charged, reciprocated by investigating the North Dakota senator though he had been supposedly cleared by Hoover.⁴⁶

John T. Flynn was especially outspoken, writing, "Communism is subversive, let us say. But what is communism? What is a Communist? Who is to define a man's political views and activities and determine whether they are subversive or not?" To such critics, the FBI's own director was far from sacrosanct. "J. Edgar Hoover runs a Gestapo in the United States," wrote Flynn, a circumstance he laid directly at Roosevelt's door.⁴⁷ In a special supplement on the FBI, *Uncen-sored* accused Hoover of spying on senators, cabinet members, and diplomats.⁴⁸

Of equal concern was the House Committee on Un-American Activities (HUAC), established in 1938 and chaired by the flamboyant Martin Dies

(Dem.-Tex.). Even before war broke out, many liberals had fought the committee bitterly. The coming of the conflict did little to assuage their anxieties.[49] In October 1939, *Commonweal* criticized Dies's effort to purge nearly three thousand known communists from key positions in the government. Several months later, Barnes called the Dies committee "part and parcel of the same un-American drive that has been more dramatically focused by the Christian Front." When Congressman Dies remarked that "a triple gangup of Nazi, Fascist and Communist agents" was "trying to disrupt national defense and prevent the United States from giving aid to Great Britain," *America* countered quickly: "An American who is opposed to a declaration of war, immediately, against Germany, does not draw his conviction from Nazi propaganda."[50]

In an effort to clear itself of any profascist tint, the America First Committee asked for an FBI probe of its Chicago membership lists. After initial reluctance, the bureau investigated.[51] When the New York City AFC made a similar request, director Hoover turned it down, declaring that such investigation was outside the scope of its activities.[52] In a letter to General Wood, Hoover stated, "At no time has the FBI directly or indirectly at any place in the United States tapped the wires, interfered with the mail, or checked the membership lists of the America First Committee." When Charles A. Lindbergh was told the FBI was tapping his phone, he wrote in his diary that he would gladly clarify any conversations for the bureau. "It really makes very little difference as far as I am concerned," he said. "My main interest lies in knowing whether or not these tactics are being used by the Administration."[53] All this time, however, the FBI was supplying the administration with reports on the AFC.[54]

Similarly, the AFC welcomed a HUAC probe.[55] In the fall of 1941, the committee started to investigate the AFC but dropped its investigation when Japan attacked Pearl Harbor and the organization immediately disbanded.[56]

Anti-interventionist anxieties concerning civil liberties were well founded. Far too often Roosevelt's response to critics involved use of the FBI, the department of justice, and his own personal investigator, John Franklin Carter. The president did not always meet the arguments of his critics directly; at times he used the loyalty issue to intimidate opponents.[57] Even Harold Ickes mourned, "Some of our superpatriots are simply going crazy."[58] One historian, Leo P. Ribuffo, sees the administration fostering a Brown Scare, in which it deliberately and falsely linked reputable anti-interventionists to fascist sympathizers.[59]

Throughout the thirties, many and loud were the accusations that Roosevelt sought to regiment the nation's economy, and rightist and business circles used the words *fascist* and *communist* with abandon.[60] Such attacks took on a special intensity during the years 1939–41, and this time more than anti–New Deal Liberty Leaguers were involved.[61]

War, it was said, inevitably meant regimentation, and even a president of the most democratic leanings could not escape that fact. The first act of any nation at war, wrote John T. Flynn, was to turn its premier or president into a dictator. In fact, America was moving toward the same totalitarian model Germany embodied. Drawing on material in Gustav Stolper's highly respected *German Economy, 1870–1940* (1940), Flynn saw the United States, like Hitler's Reich, combining "rationalization of industry under government supervision" with "social welfare measures to ease over the jolts of capitalism in trouble."[62]

Some FDR critics were even more apprehensive than Flynn. Predicting the destruction of "all our liberties," John Haynes Holmes wrote, "I fear war more than I fear Hitler." To Frederick J. Libby, Roosevelt himself was "more dangerous to the people of the United States" than the German leader. War, stated Trotskyist James Burnham, marked the end of "bourgeois democracy." Senator Tobey quoted Charles Evans Hughes, chief justice of the Supreme Court, who maintained that the United States could not survive as a democracy if it entered the war. Joseph P. Kennedy concurred.[63]

In describing the American experience of World War I, Herbert Hoover was not afraid to use the term "clamps of fascism" to describe wartime controls. The ex-president recalled, "We became an effective dictatorship." Not only did the government partially suppress much freedom of speech and the press, "it told the people what to eat and what to wear."[64]

To liberals, some predictions were particularly frightening, for—they feared—the social gains made by the New Deal would be canceled. Senator La Follette saw workers as being confronted "with a choice of starving or working where, when, and under what conditions they ought to work." Citing congressional testimony of financier Bernard Baruch, who had directed the mobilization effort of World War I, La Follette continued, "Farmers would have their prices fixed. Business would be put in a strait jacket." Libby saw an atmosphere "in which both employers and workers can be held in line, double taxes will be accepted, non-defense expenditures eliminated, a comprehensive price ceiling will be agreed to and a spirit of self-sacrifice will prevail generally." If necessary, "national unity" would be imposed by coercion.[65]

Some comments were even more sweeping. "We have the economic power," commented Harry Elmer Barnes, "to build a Utopia in this country in four or five years, or we may have ten or fifteen years of war that will completely wipe out civilization." If it didn't dissipate its energies in war, the United States possessed the potential to develop a cooperative society that would solve the problems of distribution. Borchard feared for private property itself. Because of administration needs to assume dictatorial powers over prices, wages, and production, American capitalism, asserted Dennis, would be eliminated. "Education will cease," warned Robert M. Hutchins, to be replaced by vocational and military training. Stuart Chase offered an entire catalog of evils: "M-Day, the liquidation of political democracy, of Congress, the Supreme Court, private enterprise, the banks, free press and free speech; the persecution of German Americans and Italian Americans, witch hunts, forced labor, fixed prices, rationing, astronomical debts and the rest."[66] Feared Freda Utley, "If the war goes on to the point of one side trying to win absolute victory over the other, I think we shall have a form of authoritarian state more closely approximating the Soviet tyranny than anything else that has yet developed."[67]

Certain noninterventionists blamed business itself for manipulating the defense effort on its own behalf. Citing conservative editor David Lawrence, who claimed that defense mobilization threatened the wages and hours law, the *Christian Century* found "a big business fifth column" seeking to use military preparation "as cover for an attack to overthrow recent democratic advances in the economic and social sphere." To Trotskyist Dwight Macdonald, reaction reigned triumphant, for both major parties were using the cause of national defense to foster a series of destructive measures: "anti-alien laws, 'coordination' of North and South America under the State Department, 'fifth column' attacks on Reds and unions, relaxing of war profits curbs and sabotaging of the Wagner Act and wages and hours law, universal conscription in peacetime, etc., etc."[68]

More conservative leaders expressed still greater alarm. Hugh Johnson spoke in terms of increased debt, taxes, and confiscation of property, with American democracy probably being destroyed in the process. "Under the smokescreen of national defense," stated Alf Landon, "a little group of new dealers" sought to establish a "collective state," one that involved state-managed cartels and elimination of "the 80-acre farmer and the small business man." Congressman Karl Mundt offered still another gloomy scenario, one that involved conscription of all manpower, full nationalization of the banking system, repeated reevaluation of gold reserves, confiscation of liquid private property by capital levies, the fixing of prices and wages, and government operation of all basic industries as well as of transportation, communication, and hydroelectric power.[69]

Were Congress to declare a national emergency, warned the AFC research bureau, labor conditions would be determined by fiat and the eight-hour day jeopardized. The president would assume direct control of the merchant marine, industry, radio broadcasting, banking, railroads, agriculture, and property rights. If Congress decided that a power shortage existed, it could prohibit the use of washing machines, refrigerators, milking machines, and other electrical appliances.[70]

Given such anxieties, a variety of anti-interventionists were particularly concerned about the various war mobilization plans espoused in Washington. Much anxiety centered on "M-Day," or Mobilization Day, when the United States would go on a complete wartime footing and all American life would be regimented.[71] The purpose of such thinking was obvious: to avoid the mistakes of World War I by having a full-scale blueprint at hand if the United States ever entered a conflict.

Such plans had been drafted by Washington officials in 1931, 1933, 1936, and 1939, though none had the sanction of law. Assistant Secretary of War Louis Johnson, who by 1939 was entrusted with directing this program, had repeatedly suggested an advisory board of industrial leaders to check the blueprints as they were periodically revised. Only on 4 August 1939, however, did FDR establish a War Resources Board (WRB), whose chief assignment was to review the war department's existing Industrial Mobilization Plan, hence perfecting plans already made to put the nation on a war footing. Chaired by Edward Stettinius Jr., board chairman of United States Steel, its members included Dr. Karl Compton, president of the Massachusetts Institute of Technology; Walter S. Gifford, president of the American Telephone and Telegraph Company; John Lee Pratt, a director of General Motors; and Harold G. Moulton, president of the Brookings Institution. General Robert E. Wood, board chairman of Sears, Roebuck and later the AFC's acting chairman, was also a member.[72]

Anti-interventionists balked almost instantaneously. To Hugh Johnson, the WRB represented "the highest type" of businessman; at the same time, he found the appointment an "incredible political blunder," as the members were closely tied to the financial interests of the du Ponts and J. P. Morgan.[73] Similarly, although the *New Republic* called the members "singularly patriotic," it asserted, "They are hardly the men whom one would elect to govern the economic life of the country."[74]

Other objections were more pronounced, for to some Roosevelt critics the WRB embodied regimentation on a grand scale.[75] Both *Social Justice* and the *Saturday Evening Post* saw complete dictatorship ahead. Senator Vandenberg quoted an unidentified newspaper account as evidence that labor and business would be regimented; strikes outlawed; prices, wages, and hours set by the government; and light, heat, and food rationed. He continued, "The Bill of Rights would need a gas mask, and individual liberty of action would swiftly become a modern memory." Bennett Clark, the most prominent congressional critic, saw implicit threats to ruin businesses that ignored government-set priorities. Such activity, he argued, would be "blushed at in Germany or Italy." Senator Downey estimated that one-third of the nation's wealth would be "blown away," prices raised up to 150 percent, and a new dictatorship created that "would virtually make us all serfs." Villard, citing the *Saturday Evening Post*'s Garet Garrett, spoke of using up two-thirds of the nation's wealth. *Uncensored* hearkened to rumors that wages would be lowered and political meetings banned. The *Washington Times-Herald* attacked the secrecy surrounding the committee; in wartime "some second lieutenant of ordnance" might close down most of the city's newspapers.[76]

All this time, administration opponents pointed with alarm to books and articles friendly or neutral to such planning, including political scientist Harold J. Tobin's "Preparing Civilian America for War" and radio newscaster Larry Nixon's edited volume *What Will Happen and What to Do When War Comes.*[77] The last chapter in Nixon's work, written by journalist Malcolm Logan, predicted a coming dictatorship. *Look* magazine presented a frightening pictorial essay, "War Comes to America," based on Nixon's work.[78]

Economist Leo Cherne's *Adjusting Your Business to War* (1939), containing a foreword by Assistant Secretary Louis Johnson, drew particular alarm.[79] The book was candid in declaring that the war and navy departments expected Congress to give the president legal authority on such matters as the fixing of prices and the commandeering of materials and plants.[80] Were Cherne's scheme to be implemented, warned Porter Sargent, the president "would end up more powerful than Hitler."[81]

Because of Johnson's preface, the Cherne study embarrassed the Roosevelt administration. During a cabinet meeting held on 26 September 1939, Secretary of War Woodring, a bitter rival of Johnson, called the president's attention to the work, expressing considerable dissatisfaction over Johnson's introduction. FDR said little at the meeting but told the subsequent press conference no such book had his administration's imprimatur.[82]

The WRB report, completed on 12 October 1939, remained secret though it was relatively innocuous. Totally rejecting the idea of any "superagency" to control a war economy, it called for a number of temporary agencies that could be disbanded promptly at the end of an emergency.[83] By 1941, the entire scheme was a dead letter.[84]

Despite the dissolution of the WRB and the tentative nature of all mobilization proposals, anti-interventionists still kept up their fire.[85] In January 1940, pacifist editor Harold E. Fey warned, "Dictatorship is being definitely planned for the United States in the event of war or of some as yet undefined national emergency short of war."[86] A month later, Villard accused Roosevelt of having already approved legislation that would destroy liberty "the day war is declared." Dennis, writing in May 1940, saw the industrial mobilization plan as a conspiracy "to replace the American system with a totalitarian dictatorship." By April 1941, the *Call* found existing wartime controls so strong as to offer a front-page headline: "M-DAY PLAN COMES TO U.S.; SNEAKED OVER ON WORKERS."[87]

Any Mobilization Day edict, several critics feared, would remain long after a conflict ended. Not only were such codes inevitable in wartime, commented Flynn, but once the fighting stopped, the United States would face the same kind of disorder that characterized Italy in 1922 and Germany in 1933, thereby making continued controls irresistible. Pacifist Kirby Page referred to a war department pamphlet that, so he maintained, proposed a wartime dictatorship that could last indefinitely.[88]

Even without any M-Day in the works, certain administration proposals caused much alarm.[89] On 3 January 1940, Charles Edison, acting secretary of the navy, wrote to House speaker John Bankhead (Dem.-Ala.) to the effect that the president needed the authority to commandeer ships, factories, and war materials. If Edison's proposal were implemented in peacetime, feared Borah, "you could also provide suspension of the Bill of Rights; you could prohibit free press and the right to trial by jury." The *Christian Century* offered an editorial, "The Navy Wants a Dictator."[90]

Noninterventionists expressed apprehension over the abortive Russell–Overton amendment, introduced late in August 1940, just after the Burke–Wadsworth bill had passed the Senate. Cosponsored by Senators Richard Russell (Dem.-Ga.) and John H. Overton (Dem.-La.), the bill would have given the president authority to seize uncooperative industrial plants, thereby showing that the president was not afraid to draft wealth as well as men. When the proposal passed the Senate, Flynn commented, "The notion that our terrified businessmen can enjoy the luxury of being frightened out of their wits by Mr. Roosevelt's propaganda department and not pay for it is as naïve as anything business men have done for years."[91]

During the Senate debate, the firmly interventionist Josh Lee (Dem.-Okla.), a strong Roosevelt backer, supported the amendment as a means of allowing the government to take over "a man, a factory, or even a radio station or newspaper for propaganda purposes if the nation is in danger." Senator Claude Pepper, if anything even more interventionist than Lee, favored an additional grant of power whereby the president might, at his discretion, suspend the operation of any statutes that, in his opinion, interfered with his defense measures. "If this be dictatorship," he said, "make the most of it." The *Christian Century*, in citing his remarks, entitled its editorial simply "Candor on the Prospects for Dictatorship." *America*'s editorial on the Lee–Pepper proposals saw the nation being "Nazified."[92]

The wartime debt alone, so FDR adversaries asserted, would create a revolutionary situation.[93] Eventually the sum would be so high, Borchard warned, that it would be repudiated, causing "a social upheaval the consequences of which no man can foresee." To Senator Lundeen, it seemed the inevitable convulsion would create a dictatorship. Dennis predicted that rising taxes, together with sharp cuts in living standards, would lead to the overthrow of incompetent "rascals" by competent ones.[94]

Even without massive debts, revolution might result. Herbert Hoover predicted an outraged public reacting violently. Veterans returning from the conflict, said Senator La Follette, would be so radicalized that the Russian troops of World War I would appear conservative by comparison. Bennett Clark referred to veterans "not only wracked with wounds but shocked and poisoned by the revolutionary excesses which every expert and student expects to signal the end of this war." By 1945, speculated the pacifist columnist Ernest L. Meyer in a harrowing scenario, twenty thousand unemployed veterans of a victorious AEF would launch a bonus march to Washington, where they would be fired on by state troopers while the president laid a wreath at the tomb of the unknown soldier.[95]

All this time, anti-interventionists argued, poverty still permeated the nation.[96] It was claimed that 40 percent of all Americans lacked a decent living standard, that sixty-two million Americans were impoverished, and that ten million remained unemployed.[97] According to the National Resources Board, 55 percent of Americans lived on an income of less than $1,500 a year, not enough—estimated *Fortune* magazine—to support a family of four.[98] Wheeler quoted Roosevelt's famous phrase of 1937: "one-third of a nation ill-fed, ill-housed, and ill-clad." Not a single internal problem, said Chester Bowles when the European war first broke out, could be solved by again embarking on an expeditionary force to Europe, be the matter medical care and security for the aged, abolition of child labor, shorter hours, increased wages, or education for all who desired to learn. Hamilton Fish, in opposing a $650 million naval bill in March 1940, noted that the United States was trimming all forms of relief. That December, Lawrence Dennis wrote interventionist correspondent Dorothy Thompson, "Your passion for an unhappy minority is proportionate to their distance from you. It is great enough to condemn millions of our youth to die for Jews in Poland and Chinese in Asia but not great enough to insure adequate nourishment to American babies within a block of where you live."[99]

To Roosevelt's foes, a war boom was no solution. The resulting prosperity, they believed, would be temporary and ultimately fatal.[100] After World War I, the nation had experienced postwar inflation, strikes, and unemployment; it would certainly do so again. The *Christian Century* summarized the entire saga:

> First, a tremendous factory expansion to produce for a foreign war. Second, a rush of workers for the high pay which such emergency work will offer. Third, big profits for the shareholders in the "lucky" corporations. Fourth, the necessity to keep the expanded plant going if there is not to be an industrial crash. Fifth, peace—and no more use for the expanded plant. Sixth, the crash.

Conceding in April 1941 that the sudden prosperity had already brought "joy" to many communities, Nye warned that the return of peace would produce "ghostlike, idle new industrial plants with thousands of unemployed." Robert M. Hutchins foresaw a postwar United States with at least ten million unemployed. Although subsequent repudiation and inflation might rid the nation of an enormous debt, it would wipe out its entire middle class as well.[101]

When the European war first broke out, the economy responded sluggishly, causing some anti-interventionists to find the new wealth a chimera.[102] As far as any Wall Street boom was concerned, said the still anti-interventionist *New Republic*, "All the lambs who were sheared in 1929 and in 1937 have rushed into the market to be shorn again." It predicted another recession within four months, one "likely to be ever sharper than the tumble we took after our spree in the summer of 1917."[103] John T. Flynn thought such industries as steel, copper, and even grains would benefit moderately from a year of war; others, such as cotton and cotton textiles, faced severe damage. On balance, he concluded, the conflict would bring the nation's economy no immediate benefits.[104] *Uncensored* predicted, "The metal industries and industries dependent on metal production will grab the empty profits of war by dragging the farm boys into the factories, only to turn them loose again after the boom is over."[105]

Even in 1940, some doubts remained as to any new prosperity.[106] The expected British and French war orders had not been submitted. The *Call* titled an article "War Business Flops."[107] Certainly any new prosperity appeared most uneven.[108] Whereas the aviation industry had a backlog of unfulfilled orders, thousands of tobacco workers—so *Uncensored* noted in February 1940—risked starvation. And though the steel industry had already experienced one boom, migratory farm workers on the Pacific coast faced new hardships for lack of an export fruit market.[109] In April 1941, Nye said that American farmers continued to face decreasing markets abroad and depressed farm prices at home. In comparing long-range winners and losers, Dennis found corporate bureaucracies, together with skilled labor, to be growing more powerful; however, small businessmen, "coupon clipping rentiers," inefficient small storekeepers, and farmers were sinking into "poverty, powerlessness, despair and dependence on a government dole."[110]

Certainly, FDR critics argued, unemployment would still remain.[111] Expert witnesses were cited. In the spring of 1940, Colonel F. C. Harrington, chief administrator for the Works Progress Administration, feared that unemployment in the fiscal year 1941 could reach nine million, a forecast that caused Frank Hanighen to assert, "I believe that this country is facing the same sort of depression which I witnessed in Britain and France in the year preceding the outbreak of war." In August 1941, Leon Henderson, administrator of the Office of Price Administration and Civilian Supply, estimated that during the next few months, unemployment would increase by two million, a 25 percent increase in the total number of unemployed. Peter Nehemkis Jr., special assistant to the chief of the defense contract service, had noted ten entire industries forced to close down or enter a new line of production. "As the tempo of the war economy gains increased momentum," Nehemkis stated, "you may expect to find, for a time, not less but more unemployment; not less but more idle machines." Officials of the Office of Production Management remarked that diverting strategic materials away from civilian industries would cause at least five thousand factories to shut down.[112]

Converting plants from peacetime to wartime production was far from easy. Factories producing radios, radiators, or inexpensive automobiles, argued Lawrence Dennis, could not easily be transformed into those making munitions, tanks, or warplanes. Transformation might literally take years, in the meantime producing terrible unemployment and trade dislocation.[113]

Moreover, the economic consequences of such conversion were highly destructive. Even in 1941, *Uncensored* found American industrial potential decidedly limited, so much so that only "a tremendous domestic setback" could enable the U.S. economy to add British war orders to its own domestic needs. Once factories were producing armaments instead of consumer goods, prices for even secondhand automobiles, refrigerators, radios, and washing machines would skyrocket. The nation's living standards were bound to be reduced.[114]

At the same time, massive defense orders could be highly destructive. To superimpose a huge arms program for Britain on the United States's own defense program, said the AFC research bureau as late as October 1941, would bring the nation to the verge of another depression. Such firms as Bethlehem Steel, General Motors, and Curtiss-Wright already had massive backlogs of orders, resulting in bottlenecked production and a defense jam.[115]

Even if the economy experienced a genuine war boom, some anti-interventionists found the new prosperity most immoral.[116] As the war was ending its very first week, the *New York Daily News* noted impressive gains in the commodity and stock markets. Then it added that if the conflict continued, "our unemployment problem will be pretty largely solved. Millions of us will be making munitions and war gear for the Europeans to kill one another with, or growing food for their soldiers to eat." In January 1940, *Uncensored* noted the irony of an advertising caption: "Transports for TRADE and bombers for DEMOCRACY/Look to Lockheed for leadership in both." "The distinction between bombers for democracy and bombers for, say, fascism," it maintained, "is a new departure for dealers in death," particularly as Lockheed in 1935 had sought to sell bomber designs that could have easily ended up in Hitler's hands.[117]

At times, anti-interventionists saw the war boom as all too real—indeed, dangerously so.[118] As early as September 1939, a *Christian Century* editorial began, "Wall Street and the wheat pit are off on a joy-ride." Just over a year later, noting the marked increase in profits for Du Pont, Douglas Aircraft, and Bethlehem Steel, it commented, "Bethlehem's star is rising as the Star of Bethlehem goes into eclipse." In January 1941, Norman Thomas admitted that prosperity existed but found it lopsided: Even those workers who received large wages would find their gains partly nullified by price increases. That May, Thomas made another prediction: the boom would leave at least four million unemployed. In November, Dennis acknowledged a rise in real wages, employment, and farm prices but predicted "growing class warfare over who gets what." As labor increased its demands, he wrote, collective bargaining would become impossible, a fascist regime inevitable.[119]

Given such awesome consequences, anti-interventionists felt all efforts must be made to avoid full-scale participation in a major conflict. Such a threat might come, some feared, over a relatively neglected area: East Asia.

# 20

# The Asian Cauldron

In July 1937, just outside Peking, an accidental skirmish between Chinese and Japanese forces triggered a full-scale if undeclared war on the Chinese mainland. The Japanese soon captured such coastal cities as Shanghai as well as territory several hundred miles inland. They conducted war in such a manner that Americans would refer for years to the conquest of China's capital as the "rape of Nanking." By 1940, public outrage was frequently expressed.[1]

Some noninterventionists strongly condemned the Japanese activity.[2] As early as November 1938, Herbert Hoover called Japan's war on China "as horrible as that of Genghis Khan." In February 1940, the *Chicago Tribune* saw Japan's methods in China as the equal of Hitler's persecutions and Stalin's murder of millions.[3] By November, even the strongly pro-Japanese Ralph Townsend, former U.S. consular official in China, conceded that the Japanese were "not angels" in China.[4] In August 1941, the New York AFC chapter agreed that the Japanese were "behaving badly" there.[5] Just before the Pearl Harbor attack, William Randolph Hearst referred to Japan as an aggressor.[6]

Of all the president's critics, few had been as empathetic to Japan as William R. Castle Jr. Formerly chief of the state department's division of Western European affairs and undersecretary of state, Castle developed his sympathy toward Japan while American ambassador there in 1930. An ardent Republican and a man particularly close to Herbert Hoover, Castle left the state department in 1933. He retained his contacts with Japanese diplomats and prominent civilians, however, and remained something of a Washington "insider."[7] "Many of the condemned are great people," he said of the Japanese in September 1939. Yet he strongly opposed the Japanese invasion of China, confiding to his diary in June 1940, "Why did those damn Japanese bomb Chungking again yesterday?"[8]

To some anti-interventionists, even a less "barbarous" Japan would still have presented a clear danger to U.S. interests. In 1939, publisher Roy Howard warned against Japan's "tieup" with the anti-Comintern powers, while accusing it of violating American rights in China.[9] To the *New York Daily News*, it appeared that Japan sought to monopolize the China market, rule all Asia, turn the Pacific into "a Japanese lake," and eventually conquer the United States.[10] In January 1940, while endorsing a British and French victory in Europe, it warned, "Our big, decisive war is most likely coming on the Pacific, anyway."[11] "Europe's political business is none of our business," it continued in February; "Japan is the real danger to the United States."[12] Conversely, like certain other anti-interventionists, the *News* endorsed aid to China. The Chinese, it said, were "a quiet, peaceable people," who sought "to be left alone so that they can work their farms" and "dream about what remarkable people their ancestors were."[13]

Certain other anti-interventionist critics denied that China needed American aid. That country, asserted the *Chicago Tribune*, was "an old hand at fending for itself against invaders." Lawrence Dennis predicted that the Chinese would eventually force Japan out of their land, whereas sudden Japanese withdrawal would throw some two million demobilized soldiers back into an impoverished homeland.[14]

Several Roosevelt foes called for the withdrawal of the small contingents of American marines in China, stationed there to protect U.S. lives and property.[15] American troops in China, asserted the *Chicago Tribune* in September 1939, were too few to defend themselves but too many to be needlessly sacrificed. "We have no China front," it maintained.[16] When, in November 1939, the British war office started pulling its own troops out of northern China, the *New York Daily News* warned against replacing them with U.S. forces.[17]

Furthermore, some anti-interventionists were quite negative about besieged China. Raymond Moley thought the Chinese would betray the United States if they had the chance. Burton Wheeler stressed the continuation of slavery there.[18] One derogatory article, published in *Scribner's Commentator*, accused the Chinese of selling their own infants in time of distress. In fact, the author found nothing of merit in the entire nation.[19]

In time, the *New York Daily News* joined the attack. By June 1940, it had changed its entire posture toward the Pacific, now fearing that continued confrontation with Japan could serve as a dangerous back door to war. Suddenly the Chinese were accused of stripping "the good earth," practicing ancestor worship, and possessing the potential for becoming "a much more perilous Yellow Peril than the Japanese ever were." It called on the West to end its self-destruction; otherwise, the "yellow race" might be the next rulers of the entire world, "not a bad thing" except that the Chinese and Japanese had created similar shambles in Asia. In referring to the current war between the British and the Germans (the "two most vital and vigorous peoples in Europe") and the "starvation" of the European continent, it warned, "European racial suicide today may be paving the road for another Mongol invasion a few years hence."[20]

Even those of more moderate persuasion harbored suspicions concerning China.[21] In February 1940, for example, Hugh Johnson denied that China would ever repay a $20 million loan.[22] Certainly, it was argued, China was no democracy. According to Ralph Townsend, who had served in the American consular service there, all of its recent rulers had gained power through repression and assassination. The *New York Daily News* found political parties in China mere "cliques, lodges, more or less secret societies, as we see them—faintly comparable to our big city machines, but not to our national political organizations."[23]

China's ruler, Chiang Kai-shek, was denounced. Author Burton Rascoe called him "a cheap gangster who would sell out, as he has sold out, time and time again, for the perpetuations *[sic]* of the fortunes of his wife's family." Hugh Johnson called the generalissimo China's "present absolute dictator," a man by turns "democratic, dictatorial and Communist—whatever it takes to get the persimmon."[24]

Any effort to aid the Chinese, argued a few anti-interventionists, simply expedited the spread of communism in Asia.[25] Rival communist groups, Hearst wrote, had been murdering each other there for twenty years; he saw no more reason why the United States should "sympathize with Communist China than with Fascist Japan."[26] Dennis referred to China's rulers as "military gangsters, many of whom are communists and most of whom are rascals" and who would "enjoy nothing better than giving their erstwhile allies the bum's rush out of Asia." Should China emerge victorious from the conflict with Japan, predicted Townsend, it would succumb to Russian control, and millions of men would be required for garrison duty. Far better to let Japan and the USSR cancel out each other's influence.[27]

Others found China ungovernable, more of a geographic entity than a nation.[28] Driving Japan out of China, said Raymond Moley, was one thing; putting "Humpty-Dumpty together" was another. If the Sino-Japanese War should cease, observed Castle, "China would again become the sport of the war lords and despair of the rest of the world." Why, asked Congressman George Bender, could not China's four hundred million people form a mighty nation?[29] Jurist John Bassett Moore, claiming forty years of diplomatic experience in Far Eastern relations, saw China as merely "a geographic name, with somewhat uncertain application, rather than a coherent rational and political entity." "Why," he mused, "if we love the Chinese so much, [do] we exclude them from the United States?"[30]

Several noninterventionists stressed that the much-touted economic open door policy had vanished, never to return.[31] Speaking of earlier American arrangements with the other industrial powers, Hugh Johnson remarked, "We tried to share the loot, but we were new and inexperienced in this international chiseling." Harry Elmer Barnes called the open door "a British subterfuge to insure open season for all on robbing China." No matter what happened in China, wrote Lawrence Dennis, British and American capitalists were "on the way out."[32] Queried historian Charles Callan Tansill, "Is the American public ready to go to war to compel these stubborn children of Nippon to accept a political pabulum that they despise?"[33]

To such people, the Nine Power Pact was equal folly. Signed in 1922 by major powers as part of the Washington agreements, it committed signatories to commercial equality and administrative integrity in China; "frank and full communication" would take place in the event of possible violation. To Judge Moore, the agreement was "one of the greatest impostures ever committed to writing"—an agreement that no signatory had ever attempted to carry out nor would any ever do so. Not only did it not in reality guarantee the territorial integrity of China, wrote Hugh Johnson, but it had become as "dead as a dodo" as early as 1932, when Britain refused to cooperate with Secretary Stimson over Manchuria.[34]

If Japan had few outright supporters among anti-interventionists, several among them empathized with its economic predicament. Senator Wiley stressed the need for raw materials and markets. Senator Danaher questioned whether the United States could continually keep eight hundred Japanese limited to a single square mile, particularly as nations possessing a large land mass barred Japanese immigrants. Pacifist Kirby Page found its truculence psychologically understandable: "In Japan's shoes would American patriots be less aggressive and belligerent than the Japanese are now?"[35]

To certain noninterventionists, Japan was simply seeking a legitimate sphere of influence. Just as the United States, said Hearst, had sought to extend its influence over the Western Hemisphere, so it was only natural for Japan as well to seek expansion: "Are we not denying to other nations the rights which we claim in exaggerated form for ourselves?"[36] America, asserted Amos Pinchot, had no more right to demand that Japan relinquish its China conquest than Japan had to ask the U.S. to give up the Philippines and Puerto Rico. Porter Sargent went even further: "Japan's present purpose is to take up what China failed to do and drive the Western exploiter and usurper out of the East where he doesn't belong."[37]

Castle cogently articulated what he called "a Monroe Doctrine for Japan." "A highly industrialized territory," he wrote, "always dominates economically neighboring territories which are technically less advanced." Besides, greater continental coordination would result in general prosperity and therefore an increased demand for foreign goods.[38] (Another time, though, Castle characterized the Japanese as essentially a "home people." Indeed, whenever they violated their heritage by attempting to colonize China, they had found themselves stymied. Eventually China's four hundred million would defeat Japan's eighty million.[39])

Several anti-interventionists went still further. General Motors executive Graeme Howard stated that Japan needed a preferred position among the non-Occidental powers of the Orient.[40] "The American people should thank their lucky stars," wrote Lawrence Dennis, "that there is so much conquerable territory for the Japanese in the Far East, rather than seek to frustrate Japanese southward expansion."[41]

In 1941, the *New York Daily News* noted that the Japanese, as "the most occidental race in the Far East," had a "vital urge" to grow and expand, to dominate its seas and control its neighbors. No harm would come, it said, "if we were to mind our own business, stay in this hemisphere, and organize it with Canada's cooperation, and let the Japs organize Asia and the South Seas if they can. These two economic and political units could then trade with each other and the rest of the world, to their mutual profit, we think."[42]

Occasionally, it was alleged that Japan was bringing progress to a benighted China. Sterling Morton, for example, thought the island kingdom had restored peace and order to large sections of the former Chinese empire. The Chicago investor saw the Japanese puppet state of Manchukuo in particular as a positive model, a magnet pulling millions of Chinese who had emigrated there to escape warlords, excessive taxation, and bandits.[43]

Even some anti-interventionists who saw Japan as harboring extensive territorial ambitions felt no alarm. According to William Randolph Hearst, writing in June 1940, not only did Japan seek the Netherlands East Indies and the Philippines but its aspirations also extended to Alaska and the Pacific Coast. Yet he feared that the United States might provide Japan with an opportunity for war, just as France had recently supplied Italy with an excuse to gain Savoy, Nice, Corsica, and Tunisia.[44]

The nature of Japanese government and society fostered disagreement. Ralph Townsend found Japan more of a democracy than China. Until 1937, when the China war began, the Japanese Diet's authority matched that of the British government. Furthermore, he asserted, no one in Japan ever exercised the sweeping personal authority of President Roosevelt. The *New York Daily News* stressed Japan's kinship with the United States, noting its penchant for technology and commerce, not to mention love of baseball. "They are physically clean," it added. (The *News* still found certain aspects of Japan's war "barbarous," but it continued: "We cannot undertake to protect every aggressors' victim from the aggressors. In plainer English, we'll be behind the 8 ball if we get into a two-ocean war.") Though not going so far, NCPW staffer Mark Shaw pointed to positive features in Japan's recent heritage, including general compulsory education, recognition of property rights, and "a responsible constitutional government." Castle called Prince Konoye Fumimaro, Japan's erstwhile prime minister, "one of the most honorable men in public life," a man who would be the first to turn his nation back to a parliamentary system. Writing in October 1940, however, the retired diplomat saw Japan rapidly becoming a totalitarian state.[45] That May, Dennis had found Japan's civilian leadership to be more traditionalist than totalitarian. Even a year later, he was claiming that the Japanese military possessed neither an "up-to-the-minute, wave-of-the-future ideology nor a corresponding blitz, military technique."[46]

Within the Roosevelt administration itself, some voices occasionally sounded sympathetic to Japan. Early in 1940, Ambassador Joseph Grew believed that Japan was a "have-not" nation, lacking essential raw materials, dependent on overseas markets, and plagued by excess population. "Japan in China has a good case and a strong case if she knew how to present it," he commented privately, "but her stupidity in publicity and propaganda is only exceeded by her stupidity in methods."[47] Even Admiral Stark, in designing War Plan Dog, warned against reducing Japan to inferior military and economic status. Writing Secretary Knox that November, he remarked, "A balance of power in the Far East is to our interest as much as is a balance of power in Europe." Criticizing Dutch rule in the East Indies, the chief of naval operations questioned whether Japan really sought to invade that area.[48]

All during the debates over intervention, critics warned against defending Western imperialist holdings.[49] If, said Sterling Morton, the United States was going to guarantee Western empires in Asia, "perhaps the Javanese and the Annamites might first be consulted."[50] William Henry Chamberlin asked, "How many Americans, on a referendum vote, would wish to die for the Dutch East Indies, for Singapore, for Thailand or Senegal?" He continued, "I am anticipating the day when the possession of Tibet and Afghanistan will be represented as vitally necessary to the security of Kansas and Nebraska."[51] The Japanese might well think, commented *America*, that the U.S. held to a double standard. Foreign Minister Matsuoka Yosuke, the Jesuit weekly noted, found the United States protesting strongly over Manchuria in 1932 while being relatively silent over the German naval base erected in Shantung in 1898.[52]

Above all, administration critics argued, Americans must avoid—in the words of Harry Elmer Barnes—any effort "to make the Pacific safe for the British Empire." After all, they asserted, the British had many stakes in East Asia, the Americans few. As Hugh Johnson presented the issue, "Our stake in the Far East which might be menaced by Japan is to that of Great Britain as a molehill to a mountain."[53]

The entire British presence in Asia met with strong attack.[54] The New York AFC chapter claimed that Britain was "parked" in the Pacific simply for gold, oil, rubber, silver, diamonds—that is, those rich supplies that its capitalists had "stolen" from the Asian people.[55] Similarly, the *New York Daily News*, in referring to British interests in Hong Kong, Malaya, and India, said, "The British have no more historic or racial right to be in any of these places than the Germans have to be in France." Even recent history was brought into the anti-interventionist indictment. The *Chicago Tribune*, for example, accused the British of "deserting" Secretary of State Stimson in the Manchurian crisis of 1931–33.[56]

Certain administration critics suspected secret accords already existed between Britain and the United States.[57] In March 1940, Congressman Tinkham maintained, quite incorrectly, that two years earlier Britain and the United States had entered into a binding military alliance, with Britain to defend Canton and Enderbury islands.[58] That May, Al Williams warned that the British foreign office had assigned the United States the task of attacking Japan under the guise of maintaining the status quo in the Far East. A month later, Rush Holt proclaimed that the American fleet was serving in the Pacific to protect British interests.[59] In March 1941, Congressman Robsion pointed with alarm to press reports that American cruisers and destroyers lay off the coast of Australia and American bombers had been shipped to Singapore.[60]

Some anti-interventionists even cautioned against possible U.S. designs.[61] Roosevelt, feared Norman Thomas, was "policing the Far East for the benefit of American imperialism over Japanese imperialism." Warning that the United States could soon be in Singapore, Raymond Moley queried, "Are we going to be a nation or an empire?"[62]

Amid such suspicions, anti-interventionists might well have minimized American economic interests in much of Asia, particularly the lower region. By 1941, U.S. trade there exceeded Japan's. Even in the thirties, the United States was the best customer of Malaya, the third leading customer of Indochina, and the third major importer to the Dutch East Indies.[63]

From 1939 until the actual attack on Pearl Harbor, some anti-interventionists supported various forms of economic pressure. Here they were in accord with widespread public sentiment, for as early as August 1939 a Gallup poll showed 82 percent of its respondents opposing the sale of any war materials to Japan.[64]

In particular, the trade in war materials made people furious. In April 1940, the Socialist Party called the United States "a virtual partner of Japan in the assault on China."[65] According to Barnes, the nation was supplying over 50 percent of Japanese war materials; according to Villard and Senator Capper, 70 percent.[66] In the words of Congressman Robert T. Secrest (Dem.-Ohio), "We have been a party to this grinding of a nation of 400,000,000 humans to dust and abject slavery."[67]

A few anti-interventionists accused the U.S. of playing a double game, furnishing both sides with implements of destruction.[68] Danaher remarked in October 1939, "We have assisted Japan in making a war and China in continuing it." One Baptist clergyman wrote in the FOR's *Fellowship* three months later, "We have shipped munitions to Japan and prayers to China." In February 1941, Vito Marcantonio noted that China had been unable to buy a single significant American weapon while American exports to Japan had increased markedly over the past six months: "We give China just a bit to keep Japan busy, but never will we give China sufficient to make China win."[69]

Certain anti-interventionists accused the Roosevelt administration of hypocrisy while denying any inconsistency themselves. "Many a lover of democracy," remarked the AFC, had long wondered why the United States would "froth at the mouth against the Axis, and at the same time continue to appease Japan, a member of the Axis, by shipping it war material." Capper found little conflict between his opposition to lend-lease and his demands for an arms embargo on Japan; both positions were essentially peace measures, preventing arms from going to warring nations.[70]

All during 1940, a variety of embargoes were proposed.[71] Freda Utley sought to prohibit trade in "the sinews of war." Reynolds stressed "implements of death."[72] The *New York Daily News* used the term "war materials."[73] An American ban on military supplies, maintained Congressman August H. Andresen (Rep.-Minn.), would end the China campaign within sixty days.[74]

By 1941, some no longer wanted to limit embargoes to arms. Each anti-interventionist appeared to have a different preference for additional bans. William Henry Chamberlin spoke generally in terms of resources essential to American security. Congresswoman Jessie Sumner referred to "manufactured goods." In the late spring, Senators Nye and Wheeler listed oil.[75]

Scrap iron was particularly noted.[76] For the past two years, Fish said in April 1940, he had sponsored a bill prohibiting its shipment to Japan, but the proposal had been bottled in committee.[77] A month later, *Common Sense* asserted that such shipments might eventually put American troops in danger, saying that an epitaph might eventually read, "They died for the sake of the American junk business."[78]

While in its initial hawkish phase, the *New York Daily News* suggested the most radical pressure of all. "We think," it said in late August 1939, "there should be a long-distance naval blockade of Japan, based on Singapore, Hawaii and the Aleutian Islands." Because of the danger from the USSR, Japan would be so preoccupied that "an American embargo alone will be iron-clad enough to squeeze the military caste off the necks of the peaceable Japanese people."[79] By September, it was proposing a joint effort whereby Britain would string commerce raiders south from Singapore, and the U.S. Navy, basing its operations in Hawaii, would keep Japanese commerce out of the Western Hemisphere.[80]

Though many anti-interventionists supported pressure on Japan, others expressed the concern that such efforts not go too far. For example, in December 1939, a coalition of pacifist organizations urged the maintenance of normal trade relations with Japan.[81]

Various reasons were given for such a position. Japan, it was argued, could respond by blockading Chinese ports, shutting out all imports, applying martial law wherever its armies were located, and excluding all foreigners from China.[82] It could also retort by venturing southward, conquering such areas as

Borneo, the Dutch East Indies, the Philippines, and Singapore.[83] It might be pushed into the arms of such totalitarian states as Germany and Italy, even the Soviet Union, thereby upsetting the world balance of power, besides leading to an increased arms race.[84] In speaking of an oil embargo, former congressman Samuel B. Pettengill, speaking in August 1940, noted Tokyo's own warning that its reaction would be "very great," which in turn would cause the United States to build more battleships.[85]

A few maintained that Japan could certainly survive economic pressure. Historian Arthur J. May estimated that Japan possessed sufficient resources at home and alternate sources of supply. Though the severing of U.S. supply lines, said Hanson Baldwin, might eventually be effective, Japan probably had stored a year's reserve of fuel oil; it also had access to oil shale in Manchukuo and could receive small quantities of iron ore and other metals across the Strait of Tsushima.[86] Above all, it was argued, the United States conducted a rich trade with Japan, particularly in comparison with the minuscule amount of its trade with China.[87] In June 1941, the *New York Daily News* noted that Japan normally bought $200 million worth of American goods each year, China about $80 million. "It seems grotesque to fight the good customer on behalf of the not so good customer."[88]

The China trade and investment were continually denigrated.[89] In recent years, wrote Porter Sargent, less than 3 percent of U.S. commerce had been with China, including Hong Kong. Moreover, asserted lumber merchant George H. Cless, Americans had put less than $200 million into China, "slightly more than we paid for chewing gum last year." In fact, in all the Far East, American investments did not exceed $750 million, "materially less than our total cigarette bill last year." The sum, said Hugh Johnson, involved fewer dollars than "Harry Hopkins used to toss away in a single merry month of raking leaves" or, as Boake Carter remarked, than Americans spent annually to watch athletic events. Certainly, claimed the Hearst columnist, the cost to American taxpayers for one year's military and trade services in the Orient exceeded the nation's permanent investment there.[90]

By contrast, trade with Japan was often touted. For decades, said the *New York Daily News* in July 1941, Japan had been "far and away our best customer in the Far East." In January 1940, Hearst's *San Francisco Examiner* had found Japan to be the third largest purchaser of American goods.[91] According to Townsend, Japan normally bought about as much as all the rest of Asia combined, in some years more than all South American countries, and usually four to five times as much annually as China. Furthermore, of all the major powers, only the Tokyo government had never defaulted on a single dollar or debt.[92]

William J. Baxter, a Wall Street investment consultant active in America First, offered an elaborate rationale in his book *Japan and America Must Work Together* (1941). With its plethora of virtues—large population, stable family life, habits of thrift, long hours of work, and absence of trade unions—Japan was ideally suited for U.S. investment and exports. Like the Germans and Americans, the Japanese were part of "Nature's chosen people." Not only could Japan contain the spread of "Russian Communism" but it alone, he implied, was able to bring recovery to the depression-ridden United States, a nation that must either help the Japanese "Americanize" Asia or go to war over the matter.[93]

Such anti-interventionists denied that Japan had really closed the open door.[94] U.S. trade in Manchukuo alone, commented Hearst, was three times that with China. The *Chicago Tribune* foresaw a Japanese-dominated Asia creating a far greater need for American products, particularly cotton and foodstuffs. Though the United States would probably have to extend credits, it would end up in a favorable trading position.[95]

Moreover, in February 1941, the *New York Daily News* asserted that Japan had not stifled American trade elsewhere. Citing the U.S. Department of Commerce's figures, it noted that exports to such places as China, Japan, Thailand, and the Netherlands East Indies had increased from 1939 to 1940. Were Japan to dominate other nations, the *News* surmised, it probably would not shut the United States off from trading with the others.[96] Even the lower wages of Asian nations involved no threat. After all, said John T. Flynn, the United States had long competed with such "slave labor" countries as Japan, China, and "Britain's India."[97]

It was in Japan's own financial interest, anti-interventionists maintained, to maintain good commercial relations. Ralph Townsend thought the Japanese normally drew between one-fourth and one-third of their national income from foreign trade. Moreover, he continued, the U.S. offered the best values in many commodities and was the world's best market for others.[98]

Were the United States to sever trade with Japan, some anti-interventionists argued, certain sections of the nation would suffer inordinately. So, too, would certain industries. The *Chicago Tribune* predicted that the West Coast, particularly its shipping industry, would suffer from an embargo. Japan, stressed Hugh Johnson, was one of the nation's principal outlets for cotton, on which the entire economy of "our threatened and impoverished South" depended.[99] Townsend found cotton to be the nation's most overproduced commodity, with a surplus of twenty-five million bales, equaling roughly two years of American production. As business recovery in the cotton states depended on disposing of this surplus and as many normal European outlets were closed, he stated, Japan loomed more important than ever. The *Chicago Tribune* made a similar point concerning silk-related industries.[100]

Until the Japanese attacked Pearl Harbor, many anti-interventionists stressed that Japan could never threaten the continental United States.[101] They scoffed at rumors, prevalent in the spring of 1940, that the Japanese stood poised to capture San Francisco, Los Angeles, Seattle, and Portland, Oregon.[102] *Call* writer Henry Haskell found the possibility equal to that of an invasion of Germany by Luxembourg. "I suppose," mused Rush Holt, "she is going to fly her big tanks over the Canadian Rockies." Any invasion of the U.S. via Alaska, Fleming MacLiesh and Cushman Reynolds wrote, would be repulsed by "a good-sized army." The worst Japan could do, said Castle, was to strike at the Philippines.[103] Several anti-interventionists quoted what might be taken as an unimpeachable authority, Franklin D. Roosevelt himself. In an article written in 1923 in *Asia* magazine, the future president found invasion of the western shores on the Pacific probably impossible, certainly impractical.[104]

Sheer logistics, it was argued, worked against any strike on the American mainland. Japan, asserted the *Chicago Tribune*, was fully three hundred times as far from the United States as Hitler was from the still-unoccupied Britain. In fact, predicted Taft, the stationing of two hundred thousand U.S. troops on the Pacific Coast would make a Japanese landing impossible. According to Villard, Japan lacked the bases needed to launch an air strike across the Pacific.[105] MacLiesh and Reynolds envisioned an American fleet, operating out of Hawaii with "air wings," harrying any advancing Japanese force. Were a Japanese fleet to engage in a frontal attack on Pearl Harbor, the land-based guns there would outshoot Japan's sea-based ones. Anyone who had seen Japanese poverty firsthand, maintained Senator Wheeler, would realize that Japan could not attack the United States.[106]

Even the much-touted Japanese navy, some argued, embodied no threat. Certain noninterventionists, for example, strongly challenged a claim by Rear Admiral Joseph K. Taussig, commandant of the Fifth Naval District at Norfolk and former chief of staff of the U.S. Fleet. On 22 April 1940, in testifying before the Senate Naval Affairs Committee, the admiral had called for larger battleships, impregnable bases in Guam and the Philippines, and an agreement with Britain, France, and the Netherlands for joint action. The reason? The Japanese military sought world domination. Hull and Stark immediately disavowed his remarks, but the damage was done.[107]

Administration critics were incensed. Bennett Clark demanded Taussig's court-martial. Fish called Taussig's remarks "perhaps the most provocative, inflammatory, and dangerous remarks that have been made by any Navy officer in our time and generation."[108]

Certainly, a naval race in the Pacific appeared the height of folly. Flynn found the costs prohibitive. So long as the United States had the world's largest and strongest navy, said Hanford MacNider, Japan could not be a menace.[109] General Johnson Hagood predicted that the American fleet would be able to keep Japanese expeditionary forces from U.S. home waters while land fortifications—defended by mines, subs, and aircraft—would prevent the entry of stray ships. Militia would stop even small Japanese detachments from attacking mainland forts from behind.[110]

Not all anti-interventionists spoke so confidently. Hearst wanted at least a 5:3 naval ratio over Japan. Even the Spanish-American War, he recalled, was not concluded for a year though the American navy was twice the size of Japan's. In fact, the publisher became downright alarmist, finding even the cities of the American West Coast in jeopardy. If Japan invaded, he wrote in June 1940, it would be best to declare Los Angeles an open city, for the American army, lacking transportation facilities, would have to withdraw. "One can imagine the highways obstructed by long lines of refugees, composed mainly of real estate operators and motion picture stars, fleeing before an advancing army of Japanese vegetable gardeners."[111]

Although by spring 1940 the *New York Daily News* had opposed any naval confrontation in the western Pacific, it still pushed for a strong navy. Even then, it noted a year later, the United States might easily become overextended. If it took on Germany, Italy, Japan, and perhaps the Soviet Union all at once, "the Japs" could make a "shambles" out of Manila, San Francisco, and Los Angeles.[112]

Several noninterventionists used a possible Japanese menace to warn against commitments in Europe.[113] If, warned Wheeler in June 1940, the U.S. fought a naval war with Germany, it would be open to attack by Japan, "an axis power who hates us."[114] The *Chicago Tribune* called for a political settlement in the Pacific, so the United States could then use its fleet in the Atlantic, where it was most needed.[115] In 1940, Dennis declared that American involvement in Europe was exposing the Philippines to attack. The *New York Daily News* made the same claim concerning Hawaii.[116]

Conversely, military defeat of Japan itself was deemed extremely difficult. Libby saw such a war lasting five years, with victory still not assured. Even if U.S. troops embarked from Hawaii, predicted Senator Downey, it would take three to four "bloody years" to occupy islands some eight hundred miles away from Japan.[117] Barnes forecast that "somewhere between 100,000 and 1,000,000 American boys would be fed to the Pacific sharks or rot under the glare of the Oriental sun." The estimated financial cost: $100 billion.[118]

Most important of all, it was asserted, victory in any naval conflict was at best uncertain.[119] Factors of distance and time remained paramount.[120] To Senator David Walsh, chairman of the Senate Naval Affairs Committee, a battle on the other side of the Pacific might prove "naval suicide": the greater the distance from Hawaii, the more hazardous the engagement.[121] To fight Japan, said Senator Lundeen, the United States would have to extend its naval lines six or seven thousand miles and possess a navy three or four times its present size.[122] Villard quoted military writer George Fielding Eliot, who had himself become an interventionist, as saying that it would take the U.S. Navy two years to reach Guam with a hundred thousand men, and only then could a real war really be fought.[123]

Naval combat would be no easy matter. Even if, said *Uncensored*, American battleships blasted the entire Japanese line from Pearl Harbor to Singapore, the enemy still would not be defeated. Japan could unleash an air attack from bases in Indochina, draw the American fleet into battle around the Philippines, and even refuse to fight a major engagement, thereby leading the United States to levy a costly long-distance blockade that could go on for years.[124] Aviation expert Al Williams predicted that Japan would not engage the American fleet "in Nelson style" until its air and submarine forces had trimmed down American sea power.[125] Japan, warned the *New York Daily News*, might fight a major engagement in the Pacific, chase the remnants of the American fleet east of Hawaii, which would certainly fall after a siege, and institute naval bombardments against the U.S. Pacific Coast.[126]

Certainly, invasion of Japan itself would be most difficult.[127] The United States would undoubtedly win such a war, predicted Hanson Baldwin, if it was only fighting on one front. Yet the conflict would probably be "a long, hard, grueling war of attrition," leaving "a trail of blood" across the Pacific.[128] The effort would require a million troops, thereby probably making it "the most costly expedition in history."[129]

Senator Downey claimed Japan could not be invaded. Operating out of its own bases, and possessing submarines, airplanes, and armies, the island empire could easily destroy any army within a distance of four or five thousand miles.[130] The U.S. Pacific Fleet, Johnson Hagood argued, would be unable to operate at full strength, for it would face such diverse tasks as protecting Alaska and the American Pacific Coast, convoying across the ocean, and securing trade routes to British Malaya, a major source of rubber. If the U.S. landed two million men and penetrated a hundred square miles, problems would have just begun. The Japanese fleet, lying quietly among numerous shelters, would prevent reinforcements and supplies. "The American boys on shore," Hagood continued, would "begin to feel the pangs of hunger, and after holding out for sixty days, or perhaps a hundred, the whole thing would end up pleasantly, the umpires deciding that the little fellows had won."[131]

William Randolph Hearst believed Japan would choose to defend its excellently fortified shores with its planes, ships, and land batteries. Though the United States could destroy its paper houses, they were hardly worth bombing. It would still have to conquer Japan with ground troops, in the process facing superbly trained armies. Meanwhile, Japan's cruisers and carriers could bomb Seattle, Portland, San Francisco, and Los Angeles. Any conquest would take years. One should realize, the publisher stressed, that Japan had never been conquered, even by the apparently overwhelming forces of Kublai Khan.[132]

Even victory would present problems. The *Chicago Tribune* forecast that American bombers would destroy the populous Japanese cities, whose flimsy construction invited disaster, but questioned any "nobility" in such action.[133] Historian Arthur J. May denied that the United States would accept immense responsibilities in the Far East; hence, only the Soviet Union stood to benefit. Libby felt similarly: Even if the U.S. turned all Japan into a desert, it still could not triumph in the long run, for communism would sweep over both Japan and China. "Stalin would win our war." The *New York Daily News* commented on the defeated Japanese people: "Unless we sterilize them, they will proceed to breed, half-starve, hate, and build new armaments, and in due time the 'yellow peril' will bounce up again, more perilous than ever before."[134]

Rather than fight Japan, several Roosevelt adversaries proposed the U.S. instigate various defense strategies. Hugh Johnson sought a ring of outposts from the Aleutians through Hawaii to the Galapagos. Hearst called for fortification of the West Coast, retention of the navy in Pacific waters, and the establishment of new military and naval academies on the Pacific. Retired major general William C. Rivers wanted a defense line that included the Aleutians, and Johnson, Palmyra, and Midway islands, all in the eastern Pacific and part of a defense line proposed by Admiral William Leahy, chief of naval operations. Downey saw the United States's defenses extended as far as Pago Pago.[135]

Not only did anti-interventionists often call for caution in dealing with Japan itself but many also sought U.S. withdrawal from the Philippines, an American possession slated for independence in 1946. Until then, however, it held the status of "commonwealth" and lay under U.S. sovereignty. In 1934, Congress had passed the Tydings–McDuffie Act, which targeted Philippine independence in twelve years, provided for the removal of American military posts, and envisioned negotiation with the Filipinos over naval bases.

Not surprisingly, those of pacifist leanings favored American disengagement. A group of neutrality organizations meeting in December 1939, for example, called for the islands' earliest possible liberation as well as neutralization by international treaty.[136] The pacifists were far from alone. The *Chicago Tribune* found the Philippines to hold no vital U.S. interest. The *New York Daily News* suggested dividing the Pacific along the international dateline, thereby allotting them to the Japanese.[137]

The entire nature of the Philippines, wrote Frank Waldrop, made them a dubious ally. Composed of 7,091 individual islands and populated by forty-three ethnographic groups, they were not—said the columnist—a national unit in the same sense as either Japan or Britain. Moreover, they had long served as "a way station for all kinds of breeds and conquerors," including the Spaniards, Dutch, British, and Americans.[138] Besides, said the *New York Daily News*, the Filipinos were ungrateful, having "constantly hated what we've tried to do for them."[139] Certainly, so such anti-interventionists as Hugh Johnson and the *Chicago Tribune* stressed, they themselves wanted the Americans out.[140]

To Harry Elmer Barnes, it was apparent that Japan had long controlled the Philippines anyhow. Politically they dominated the National Assembly. Economically they were influential in fishing, hemp, mining, lumber, and the re-tail trade. Even Manuel Quezon, elected president of the Philippine commonwealth in 1935, courted their support.[141]

Conversely, FDR critics maintained, the United States held little economic stake there. They deemed the cost of maintaining the islands prohibitive. Neither the nation's best customer nor its most important source of raw materials, the Philippines—in the words of *Uncensored*—were a long-term drain on American finances, "the biggest headache in U.S. defense plans." The American taxpayer, remarked Hugh Johnson, spent $3 there for every $1 received in benefits. To Barnes, the Philippines were not worth a slight fraction of the cost involved in defeating Japan. Any conflict waged over their future, commented Flynn, would only serve the interests of a few dozen corporations. Boake Carter feared the influence of "the sugar barons of Manila," who—supported by the U.S. Navy—would demand that a new Singapore be built in the Philippines, then keep half the American fleet around Manila.[142]

At any rate, several anti-interventionists found the islands indefensible, the *Chicago Tribune* calling them a "military liability of the gravest sort to the United States."[143] Most naval experts, said the *New York Daily News*, denied that the islands could survive an attack by a destroyer flotilla.[144] Were the American navy to operate some six thousand miles from home base, warned Hugh Johnson, its striking power would be trimmed two-thirds, a discrepancy that could be offset only by a vast preponderance of tonnage. Even then, chances of victory were uncertain, for the Philippines were literally surrounded by Japanese-mandated islands, many of which were reportedly fortified.[145] During the debate over Burke–Wadsworth, Congressman Bruce Barton offered an amendment to exclude the Philippines from the definition of the United States and its possessions, declaring that military authorities had claimed the islands could not be defended.[146] Certainly, argued several anti-interventionists, the continual replenishment of U.S. military aid simply created more anxiety.[147]

Hanson Baldwin challenged such analysis, denying that Japan could conquer the islands easily. Such a campaign would require at least ten thousand men, three hundred planes, and a hundred transport ships. He did concede that the Philippines were short in aircraft and possessed inadequate docking and repair facilities, an ill-equipped and undermanned garrison, and a woefully inadequate army. When world conditions permitted, he continued, the U.S. should withdraw, substituting its unilateral guarantee with an international neutralization. If such were not possible, it should build a huge naval base and large land garrison and station at least thirty thousand troops and at least three hundred planes there.[148]

Of all the noninterventionists, probably no one was more cited than retired general William C. Rivers, former chief of the Philippine constabulary, who offered an entire battery of arguments supporting U.S. withdrawal. In fact, Rivers was so adamant on this subject that he joined semipacifist groups.

American trade with the Philippines, he said, was always disappointing. The islands lacked the rubber, oil, coal, and hardwood needed for lucrative commerce; in fact, they failed to raise sufficient rice for their own population. The United States itself had subsidized the Philippine sugar industry, even though it could purchase sugar cheaper in Cuba or Hawaii. Were the Japanese to conquer the islands, Rivers argued, Japan itself would be more vulnerable, not less, for its empire would be split into two parts, each separated by a stretch of almost two thousand miles and leaving a threatening China lying in between. At any rate, the Philippines' new rulers were hardly democratic. Rivers cited the Filipino Civil Liberties Union, which accused Quezon of seeking to create a totalitarian regime. The president had supposedly called for the abolition of political parties. As far as defending the Philippines was concerned, Rivers quoted Admiral Harry E. Yarnell, former commander in chief of the Asiatic fleet, on the need for dry docks, a naval base, and a fleet possessing a 2:1 ratio over Japan.[149]

A few noninterventionists sought to retain the islands or to fight if they were attacked.[150] Wheeler and Fish spoke of war if Japan attempted to conquer them.[151] Hearst's *San Francisco Examiner* called the Philippines the first U.S. line of defense, as nowhere was America's peace and security so seriously threatened. Moreover, it asserted, the Filipinos probably desired and certainly needed American protection.[152] Withdrawal, wrote Hearst himself, would only result in Japanese occupation. Deeming the Philippines ten times as important as Hawaii, he said they should be twice as well fortified. Once the United States constructed major bases there, it could threaten any naval expedition bound for its own west coast. Furthermore, if the islands remained an American possession, its population could contribute an army of one million.[153]

The U.S. military had been at best ambivalent about defending this vast archipelago. Joint army–navy plans devised in 1936 envisioned a Philippine garrison holding the entrances to Manila Bay until superior sea power came to the rescue. Any further commitment, commented General Stanley D. Embick, was "an act of madness"; Embick, who had commanded the Corregidor garrison three years earlier, had called then for neutralization of the islands. As late as May 1941, Stimson—who had been appointed governor general of the Philippines in 1928—found the islands indefensible.[154]

Only on 31 July 1941 did Marshall define their defense as official U.S. policy. The islands would play host to some 165 Flying Fortresses, B-17 bombers that would serve as a deterrent and if necessary an attack force. Suddenly the war department was tacitly affirming that the Philippines were defensible if sufficient time existed to complete a reinforcement program and train the Philippine army. By mid-September, the first contingent of nine bombers had arrived; in mid-November, twenty-six more had come.[155]

Exorbitant claims were made concerning the deterrent potential of the new aircraft. To Stimson and Marshall, they could break up the Axis alliance. In Hull's eyes, the B-17s gave "punch" to the American diplomatic effort. The war plans division saw them as "a powerful threat to Japan proper."[156] Douglas MacArthur, recently recalled to active service as commanding general of "U.S. Army Forces, Far East," had long been giving assurances that the islands were defensible.[157]

Among anti-interventionists, Guam, too, served as a matter of debate. An American possession, it was the largest island in the Marianas chain (the remaining ones belonging to Japan) and was administered by the navy department. In February 1939, Congress had voted down a $5 million appropriation to construct harbor works there. Both the state and war departments disparaged the harbor proposal, fearing that the move would antagonize Japan.[158]

A few anti-interventionists, including the Hearst press, endorsed Guam's fortification. Late in 1940, the *New York Daily News* maintained that the island should be made into an effective naval station: "It would at least give us an outpost to make some trouble in case of a fight." Hanson Baldwin sought a small submarine and patrol base.[159]

Most Roosevelt critics, however, strongly opposed Guam's fortification.[160] First, they claimed, there could be no salient more exposed.[161] It lay 3,000 miles west of Pearl Harbor, the westernmost U.S. naval base, but was only 1,350 miles from Tokyo. As the effective operating radius of the U.S. fleet from a major base was about 2,500 miles, Guam would be difficult to hold. In addition, many of the surrounding Japanese islands possessed good submarine and airplane harbors.[162]

Second, fortification was costly and possibly futile. Boake Carter, noting Admiral Stark's assertion that an expenditure of $250 million would secure Guam, found the sum more than the total of U.S. investment in the Philippines, Japan, and China combined. According to *Uncensored*, the proposed construction of Guam's Apra harbor, which would consist of improvements and a few bomb shelters, was far too weak to be effective.[163]

Besides, it was argued, the move was provocative, as much so—said Libby—as would be reciprocal action by Japan in the Galapagos Islands or by Germany in Bermuda.[164] To the *Chicago Tribune*, Guam appeared to be the linchpin in a major anti-Japanese alliance consisting of the United States, Britain, Australia, and New Zealand.[165]

In contrast to such suspicions concerning the Philippines and Guam, many anti-interventionists believed Hawaii to be impregnable.[166] "The greatest military outpost and maritime fortress in the whole world," Senator Downey called it. In October 1941, the *Chicago Tribune* specifically denied that the American base at Hawaii lay within striking power of the Japanese fleet.[167]

Even if the Japanese attempted an attack, it was argued, the effort would be futile. Troops at Schofield Barracks, declared Fleming MacLiesh and Cushman Reynolds, manned a greater concentration of antiaircraft guns than anywhere on the mainland. All of Oahu was protected by mountain ranges. The *New York Daily News* was equally optimistic. Heavily fortified and stocked with munitions and food supplies, Pearl Harbor alone, it said, could hold out until an American rescue fleet arrived.[168] Were the Japanese able to occupy Hawaii, *Uncensored* predicted they could not hold it easily. Only General Rivers offered a slight dissent, saying that the American fleet should leave Hawaii for territory east of the Panama Canal, probably the Caribbean.[169]

The impending crisis, certain anti-interventionists maintained, could be avoided if their own suggestions for peace were followed. In the two years before the war, they offered various proposals, in some cases full-scale plans, on how to alleviate the tension. In September 1939, Norman Thomas favored mediation between China and Japan, with the United States taking "an intelligent lead."[170] Four months later, Senator Wiley referred to a "round-table method" used successfully by Methodist missionary E. Stanley Jones in India.[171] Publisher Roy Howard called for a commission, composed of Americans possessing some respect for "oriental psychology," that would report to Congress and the president on the "fundamentals" of the entire Asian situation.[172] In February 1941, the *Christian Century* suggested a world parley.[173] That May, the Women's International League spoke of an "economic conference" between the U.S. and Japan centering on access to the resources of the Pacific.[174]

Several proposals centered on China. Before it joined the ranks of the interventionists, the *New Republic* suggested relinquishment of all foreign garrisons and extraterritorial privileges. By this arrangement, Japan would still be able to develop much of China's economy.[175] Pacifists concurred in such a Western withdrawal.[176] In January 1940, the *New York Daily News* suggested an agreement among the United States, Japan, Britain, the Soviet Union, and China that would keep the Chinese market open to all.[177] In September, claiming that the Japanese people were "seriously fed up with the war in China," the *News* called for American mediation between Chiang Kai-shek, the Japanese puppet ruler Wang Ching-wei, and Japan's leaders. The United States could be rewarded for its efforts by obtaining "a fair show for United States businessmen in China, Manchukuo and Japan."[178] Even in August 1941, it suggested a face-saving settlement by which the Japanese would abandon most of China while being permitted "a reasonable degree of expansion from their cramped, over-populated islands."[179]

One ad hoc task force was established. Early in the fall of 1941, at the invitation of publicist O. K. Armstrong, a small group of church leaders, writers, and scholars met in New York to discuss strengthening U.S. relations with Japan. It issued a public statement calling for reconciliation and formed a Committee on Pacific Relations, but the group lacked the strength or the time to be effective.[180]

In any discussion concerning terms, pacifists and liberals stressed the need to repeal the Japanese Exclusion Act of 1924. American recognition of racial equality was deemed crucial.[181] Norman Thomas endorsed a program of limited immigration, controlled by treaties and quotas, saying the United States could not receive great numbers. Dorothy Detzer saw lifting the 1924 act as part of a bargain concerning Japan's withdrawal from China. The FOR spoke in terms of establishing a customs union of "all Pacific and American peoples" and assisting general economic development.[182]

To best understand the context of all such general attitudes, a detailed knowledge of the varied events leading up to the Pearl Harbor attack is crucial.

# 21

# Toward the Pacific War

From the fall of 1939 through the spring of 1940, anti-interventionists lacked a common perspective on events in East Asia. Many saw Japan, not China, as the nation experiencing the most trouble.[1] In September 1939, Oswald Garrison Villard thought that Japan felt so betrayed by Germany that it was less inclined than ever to begin hostilities against the United States.[2] Four months later, the *Chicago Tribune* alleged that the recently installed Japanese government, headed by Admiral Yonai Mitsumasa and Foreign Minister Arita Hachiro, sought accommodation.[3] In March 1940, the *New York Daily News* found Japan to be "on the ragged edge of national bankruptcy."[4]

Tensions between the two nations, however, steadily increased. Concrete anxiety first centered on the 1911 U.S. commercial treaty with Japan, which included a most-favored-nation provision. In June 1939, in the Craigie–Arita agreement, the Chamberlain government surrendered to Japanese demands that its conquests in China be recognized. Opposing the move, Roosevelt and Hull believed that Japan must be shown that it could no longer conquer with impunity.[5] Hence, on 26 July, Hull sent out the necessary six-month notice of possible abrogation of the 1911 agreement.[6] After 26 January 1940, the secretary warned, the United States might sever the iron, steel, and oil needed for the Japanese war machine, thereby crippling its military effort. Moreover, the U.S. treasury would be free to curtail purchases of Japanese gold and silver, Japan's chief source of foreign exchange and essential to its commercial life.[7] Trade would thenceforth be conducted on a twenty-four-hour basis, not automatically severing valuable war supplies but keeping Japan in a high state of uncertainty. According to a Gallup poll, the American public approved cancellation of the treaty by over a four-to-one margin.[8]

Several noninterventionists supported abrogation, including Roy Howard and the *New York Daily News*.[9] To Dorothy Detzer, abrogation would express strong American disapproval of Japanese action without exerting further coercion.[10] One anti-interventionist, Senator Arthur Vandenberg, had long sought such a measure. Six days before Roosevelt's initial announcement, the Michigan Republican had introduced a resolution calling for rescinding the 1911 treaty and the reassembling of the Brussels conference of November 1937, an effort by the signers of the Nine Power Pact of 1922 to curb Japanese expansion. When columnist Walter Lippmann accused the Michigan senator of taking a major step on "the road to war," Vandenberg replied that his resolution would create just the opposite effect: a bellicose embargo would have been avoided. At the same time, conditions for a new Japanese-American treaty, one providing for American rights in Japan and China, would be fostered.[11] Indeed, he was discouraged when he saw the state department using his resolution to threaten the Japanese rather than as an opportunity to seek accommodation.[12]

Other anti-interventionists were apprehensive.[13] Borah thought abrogation would be insulting, and found the possibility of a discriminatory embargo disastrous.[14] Asked the *Chicago Tribune*, "Is there at Washington any desire to promote the nation's foreign trade?"[15] Even if the United States did not radically raise its duties, feared William Castle, contracts would be uncertain, and therefore trade would languish.[16] To Borchard, it seemed the U.S. had already broken the 1911 treaty by levying moral embargoes on Japan.[17] Hearst's *San Francisco Examiner* asserted that the indignities suffered by the U.S. in the Sino-Japanese war had not been great; in fact, they could easily be alleviated with the restoration of good relations. On the other hand, American hostility might force Japan into an alliance with the USSR.[18]

At times war was mentioned. Charles Callan Tansill accused Hull of seeking to reduce Japan to a second-class power. "Is the American public ready to go to war," questioned the Fordham historian, "to compel these stubborn children of Nippon to accept a political pabulum that they despise?" Lawrence Dennis and V. D. Gravenhoff predicted that Japan would not succumb to American demands concerning China, although it would avoid open clash.[19]

During the winter and spring of 1939–40, rumors floated concerning accommodation between Japan and Great Britain, causing a quite different set of anxieties among noninterventionists. The United States, feared the *Chicago Tribune* in January 1940, might end up fronting for "occidental imperialism" in China. That April, writer Burton Rascoe accused England of dividing the opium monopoly with Japan while establishing a common bulwark against the Soviet Union. *New Masses* noted that the British-dominated Anglo-Iranian Oil Company had just sold a million barrels of crude oil to Japan and that the British ambassador to Japan had given a conciliatory speech. "The British," said the communist weekly, "are once more engaged in sideswiping their most formidable American rival, American imperialism." Furthermore, both China and the Soviet Union were intended to be the victims.[20]

On 30 March 1940, the "All China government" of Wang Ching-wei, a pro-Japanese rival of Chiang Kai-shek, was inaugurated at Peking, though sovereignty was confined to the Japanese-occupied areas of Kiangsu, Chekiang, and Anhwei. Hull immediately announced that the United States would not recognize the new regime.[21] Before the signing of a formal peace treaty on 30 November 1940, Japan itself offered only de facto recognition although it was already treating it as a puppet.

Borchard opposed Hull's statement, fearing that imminent British recognition of the de facto protectorate might leave the United States "out on a limb."[22] In an editorial entitled "Victorious China," the *Chicago Tribune* immediately claimed that Wang had made the Japanese recognize a "free and independent China," something that Chiang, for all his hard fighting, had been unable to do. While acknowledging Japanese control of the new government's financial, industrial, and educational structures, the newspaper found Wang the possible "savior of his country."[23]

On 15 April 1940, Foreign Minister Arita, anticipating a request from the Netherlands for U.S. occupation of its East Indies, publicly warned against any change in the status quo there. Hull dreaded any Japanese move into this territory. He responded two days later by stressing American dependence on their rubber and tin. Any forceful alteration of the existing situation, he continued, would be prejudicial to the security of the entire Pacific region. On the following day, a spokesman for Japan asserted that his country fully concurred with Hull's statement.[24]

Anti-interventionists opposed raising the issue.[25] "Apparently," said Borchard, "we are getting to the point where no change can be made in the world's political control without offense to the United States."[26] Fish warned against extending the Monroe Doctrine some ten thousand miles from American shores. He continued that Hull's doctrine logically applied to the Netherlands itself.[27] The *Christian Century* feared that the U.S. would assume responsibilities for the Dutch islands. The state department, argued Castle, should have communicated the message privately, a move that would have served Hull's purpose equally while not irritating the Japanese.[28] The *New York Daily News* found Hull's statement to contain the seeds of possible war. If the U.S. Navy should try to stop a Japanese naval strike on the Indies, it might experience defeat in a salient even weaker than that of the Philippines.[29]

Certainly, argued certain administration critics, the Netherlands had not treated the indigenous population well. The *Daily News* accused the Dutch of exploiting the Indies "as systematically and as coolly as the Japanese could."[30] Upton Close concurred. "Even the nymphs of Bali shun a Hollander," he remarked. John T. Flynn pointed out that the fifty-three million inhabitants were ruled by a governor general and council named by "the democratic process" of appointment by Queen Wilhelmina.[31]

Until the United States entered the war, such interventionists as the CDAAA focused on the Dutch East Indies, warning that Japanese domination would sever America's tin supply. Administration critics strongly debated among themselves claims that Southeast Asia supplied essential resources. Because the U.S. needed this resource, *Social Justice* thought the country could well go to war over the matter. As, in the words of Upton Close, "we live, move and have our being" on rubber, the United States needed to protect its supply routes by aiding China, "gathering in" all Japanese merchant ships, and upsetting the booming Japanese trade in South America. Further, he proposed that the U.S. build "a naval base in the Aleutians from which we could fire every paper-and-matchwood city in Japan."[32]

Other FDR foes saw no threat in any Japanese designs. The Japanese, they asserted, depended on U.S. imports of both rubber and tin. Hugh Johnson denied that Japan would toss away half the world's market. John Chamberlain asserted that any nation owning the East Indian mines "must sell in Akron or Pittsburgh or also face prolonged depression."[33]

The *New York Daily News* was particularly adamant on the subject: "If we play ball with Japan, Japan will play ball with us, commercially at least. Japan always has." As late as June 1940, the *News* called for renewing the 1911 treaty and "soft-pedaling" moral indignation over "her aggression in China." Otherwise, particularly if Britain was in jeopardy, the United States might be facing "a possible German-Russian-Italian-Japanese gang-up against us."[34]

Besides, certain noninterventionists asserted, rubber could be obtained elsewhere. In October 1940, General Wood noted that the Germans were filling 90 percent of their rubber requirements with substitutes. A year earlier, Downey had stressed that Du Pont was producing synthetic rubber in the U.S. Fleming MacLiesh and Cushman Reynolds pointed to such production by Firestone, Du Pont, B. F. Goodrich, and Standard Oil of New Jersey. Firestone and Ford, the *Christian Century* noted in September 1941, were currently cultivating rubber in Africa and South America. Hugh Johnson observed that the United States could draw on six substitutes within the Western Hemisphere, all of which were far superior to rubber. "I have heard Texans claim," wrote editor John Chamberlain, "that rubber trees can thrive in the lower Rio Grande Valley."[35] Only *Social Justice* dissented, declaring that synthetic production was in the "dark ages" and that developing useful substitutes would take years.[36]

Some anti-interventionists thought tin too could be made artificially.[37] In October 1940, Hugh Johnson alleged that processes existed for making a product far superior, not to mention cheaper, than East Indian tin.[38] "About the worst that should happen," wrote MacLiesh and Reynolds, "would be that baked beans, condensed milk, tomato soup might be sold in cans coated with lacquer, aluminum or silver." Again *Social Justice* balked, saying that not one electric bulb could function without tin, that it was primarily imported from Malaya, and that the United States was endangering this supply by antagonizing Japan.[39]

In June 1940, France fell to Hitler's armies and Indochina became subject to Vichy administration. In part acting out of anxieties concerning the general fate of Southeast Asia, Roosevelt signed a treasury department proclamation on 25 July limiting the export of aviation gasoline and scrap metal.[40] In late December 1939, the United States had started to exert economic pressure by placing a moral embargo on the export of planes, plants, manufacturing rights, and technical information required to produce high-quality aviation gasoline.[41] The December move had met with fragmentary support among administration critics and no opposition.[42] The 25 July order was a somewhat different matter, for this time the president's opponents were most hostile.[43]

Morally, asserted the *Chicago Tribune*, the United States was justified in stopping supplies; politically, however, taking on another enemy was unwise.[44] Borchard warned, "While threatening Japan with dire consequences if she touches the Netherlands East Indies, our embargoes force her to look in that direction." To the *New York Daily News*, such actions would not prevent Japan from seizing either Indochina or the Dutch East Indies, moves that could be prevented only by concentrating a two-ocean navy in the Pacific. Castle regretted that Grew had not privately approached the Japanese.[45] Taking a more acquiescent tone, the *Christian Century* found the impact of the move slight, for Japan had received virtually no American gasoline since the moral embargo was imposed the previous year. Nevertheless, the measure would lend support to the hard-pressed British, whose nationals living in Tokyo had been imprisoned. *New Masses* denied that the move was prompted by the desire to halt Japanese aggression; rather, it involved haggling over exploitation rights.[46]

To ease Japan's need for oil, and thereby to control any impulse to seize the Dutch East Indies, the state department interpreted Roosevelt's ban as including only high-octane fuels, a move that permitted Japan to purchase the middle-octane gasolines that satisfied its needs. The navy department shared state's anxiety.[47] Roosevelt had rebuffed such militants as Henry Morgenthau Jr. to side with Sumner Welles, who feared that more overt action could push Japan into the Dutch East Indies.[48] The British, too, dreaded any move that might provoke the Japanese into attacking the islands, for they were the recipient of half their oil exports. At the same time, the move strengthened those middle-level officers in Japan who sought to accelerate their nation's southward advance.[49]

The closing of the Burma Road created additional debate. On 12 July, ten days after the Japanese leadership committed itself to moving into Indochina and Thailand, the British government announced its decision to cut off the Burma Road for three months, beginning on 18 July. Thanks to the road, Chiang's government had been receiving eighteen million tons of supplies per month. Militarily its closing bore little significance, for during the rainy season it would have been impassable anyway.[50]

Anti-interventionists reacted differently. Assuming incorrectly that the British took measures without consulting the United States, Dorothy Detzer accused the United States of acting "like small puppy dogs, determined to do everything that England wants, and quite uncritically."[51] In noting American opposition, Borchard mused, "They talk about the freedom of roads 8,000 miles away, while abandoning freedom of the seas." Castle found the state department protest unjustified, by either law or common sense. The *Chicago Tribune* went so far as to praise the British for closing the road to reduce conflict.[52]

On 8 October, the British reopened the route. The *Chicago Tribune* suspected collusion, linking the Burma Road matter to Hull's warnings, cooperative efforts of naval and army officers concerning the Netherlands East Indies, and a naval agreement by which the United States secured access to the base at Singapore.[53] Journalist Lincoln Colcord stated the U.S. had shown itself ready to fight if the Japanese invaded Singapore or the Dutch Indies.[54] In late February 1941, Wheeler interpreted the reopening, together with the possible sending of American troops to Singapore, as an effort to enter the war through the back door.[55]

The Roosevelt administration itself was by no means ready for any Singapore commitment.[56] When Churchill had proposed that the United States order a naval squadron to Singapore, Marshall, Welles, and Stark all opposed it, stressing the importance of the Atlantic theater over the Pacific one.[57] "Sending the fleet to Singapore," said Hull several months earlier, "would leave our entire Atlantic seaboard, north and south, exposed to possible European threats."[58]

Indochina remained a source of administration anxiety. On 22 September, its governor general permitted the Japanese to establish three air bases in the Tonkin area and maintain a small force at Haiphong. On the 23rd, the Japanese crossed the Indochina frontier at Lang Son. The French resisted, halting the Japanese invasion on the 25th. On the following day, Roosevelt limited steel and scrap iron shipments, effective 16 October, to the Western Hemisphere; only Britain was made an exception. Stimson confided to his diary, "This is a direct hit on Japan, a point which I had hoped we would hit for a long time."[59]

Anti-interventionists strongly opposed the president's move.[60] The *Chicago Tribune* saw no real difference between France's original "grabbing" of the territory and Japan's trying to wrest it. It suspected Roosevelt of seeking a war, as it found his prospects in the 1940 election dim.[61] Warning against possible American ambitions in the region, the *Tribune* said, "A democracy cannot rule subject peoples and remain a democracy." Commented the *New York Daily News*, "The Japanese would be pretty dumb if they didn't have designs on any French property lying near them." Given Japan's population problems, the *News* concluded, the United States was "badgering" the nation.[62] Castle asserted that Indochina's millions were being exploited by a few hundred Frenchmen who supported the German-controlled Vichy government.[63]

FDR antagonists shared Castle's antipathy toward French colonialism.[64] Porter Sargent pointed to decades of repression, stating that bombs, firing squads, and the guillotine had been used. Boake Carter soon went even further, citing an Associated Press dispatch from Manila that reported that the French had shot two thousand "natives" at the Saigon airport.[65]

Roosevelt himself was far from enamored with the French presence in Indochina, his only concern being strategic. He told reporters in 1945, "They have been there over a hundred years and have done nothing about educating [the people]. For every dollar they have put in, they have taken out ten." His own solution for the area lay in the form of a trusteeship, albeit with France as the trustee.[66]

Although such matters as the Burma Road and northern Indochina obviously produced tension in Japanese-American relations, it was the formation of the tripartite pact that marked a crucial turning point. By the terms of the agreement, signed on 27 September 1940, Japan recognized German and Italian leadership of a "new order in Europe" in return for their acquiescence of Japan's own sphere in "Greater East Asia." Signers pledged mutual armed support if any were attacked by "a Power at present not involved in the European war or in the Chinese-Japanese conflict." Obviously the three powers had the United States foremost in mind, though the Soviet Union was not overlooked.[67]

In administration eyes, the pact made one thing clear. As Roosevelt wrote Grew in January 1941, "I believe that the fundamental proposition is that we must recognize that the hostilities in Europe, in Africa, and in Asia are all parts of a single world conflict."[68] To Raymond Moley, the tripartite pact signified "the most frightening news since the war began."[69]

Most anti-interventionists believed the U.S. was finally reaping the folly of its own policies.[70] According to the *Christian Century*, the newly formed Axis suspected the United States of taking over the dying British Empire, doing so by occupying naval bases in Singapore, the Netherlands East Indies, South Africa, and Sierra Leone. Villard pointed to the increase in U.S. Pacific strength, including a possible base on Guam, appropriations for a two-ocean navy, negotiations for a share of the British base at Singapore, and protests concerning the status quo in Indochina and the Netherlands East Indies. The more the United States frustrated the Japanese, argued Lawrence Dennis, the more it drove them into the hands of their own "soldier socialists" as well as Germany and the USSR.[71]

A few administration critics deplored Japan's action. Calling the new alliance "a perfectly natural response" to U.S. pressure, Borchard found the pact to be encouraging American intervention.[72] Wesley Winans Stout, editor of the *Saturday Evening Post*, concurred: "To back down to Japan now would be to back down to Hitler, and that is not possible even were Burt Wheeler to be elected President in November." Hanson Baldwin saw Japan's membership in the Axis as menacing vital American interests but warned the U.S. against driving Japan to desperation or engaging in a two-ocean conflict. He suggested such steps as evacuation of remaining Americans from Japan and China, withdrawal of American gunboats from the Yangtze, retention of the

Asiatic fleet along the China coast, and transfer of U.S. marines from Shanghai, Tientsin, and Peking to the Philippines. The United States, he continued, might recall its ambassador to Tokyo while keeping minor diplomatic representation there.[73]

All during the fall of 1940, several noninterventionists suspected a Pacific war was imminent.[74] In October, Dennis thought that Japan might experience a palace revolution: Emperor Hirohito would be replaced by his seven-year-old son, and the current prime minister, Prince Konoye Fumimaro, would dominate a new regency. Colonel Hashimoto Kingoro, who would be the nation's actual ruler, might then fight the U.S.[75] The *Christian Century* alluded to a number of ominous signs, including the state department's advising all Americans to leave Japan and the Asian mainland, the recall of Pacific Fleet commander James O. Richardson for secret consultations, and the rushing of fifty-three merchant vessels for use as fleet auxiliaries.[76]

The United States, said Herbert Hoover, was behaving far too aggressively.[77] American provocation, Castle feared, only fell short of actual actions of war.[78] The U.S. could do nothing about Japan's ultimate aim to create a new order in Asia, he felt, although it could have helped steer that policy "in sane lines." The retired diplomat even doubted whether Japan sought to annex the Philippines, the Dutch East Indies, or Malaya; rather, it merely wanted to dominate them economically, so as to assure itself of raw materials. Furthermore, any Far Eastern crisis would so distract the administration that it would terminate needed war supplies to Britain. Stationing the American navy permanently in the Pacific simply assisted Hitler.[79]

Roosevelt's foes saw the United States as too weak to engage any Far Eastern conflict.[80] "We must be careful," said Wheeler, "not to get into a two-ocean war with our one-ocean navy." If the U.S. attempted to save Indochina or the Dutch East Indies, warned General William Rivers, it might be tempting the Germans or Italians to attack South or Central America.[81] To the dovish *New York Daily News*, a number of measures had now become essential, including the expansion of facilities in Hawaii, securing the right to use the Galapagos Islands, and developing air bases in the Aleutians.[82]

A few anti-interventionists denied that any major war lay in the offing. As Japan was becoming bogged down in China, noted Hearst, it had its "hands full" and had, therefore, decided not to make war on the United States.[83] Protestant editor Harold E. Fey, who just returned from a trip to the Far East, found Japan in such bad economic straits that American fears of war were ridiculous. The dire economic situation, he continued, was causing its army to evacuate much of China, leaving the pathetic Wang Ching-wei to fend as best he could. Dennis too predicted that a depression-stricken Japan would come to terms with China, though he saw the situation more dangerous as a result. Once Japan and China in turn reached an understanding with the Soviets, Japan would start seizing British and Dutch possessions. The USSR would levy its own price for its neutrality in the matter: a Japanese attack on the capitalist powers and respect for its own interests in northern China.[84]

In light of such reactions, possibly both the anti-interventionists and the administration overreacted to the tripartite pact. Historian Akira Iriye finds that the agreement never succeeded in committing Japan irrevocably to southern expansion or an anti-American stand. Even early in 1941, the Japanese army sought a compromise with the United States.[85]

Be that as it may, 60 percent of the American public, according to a Gallup poll, perceived Japan as a serious threat that September.[86] A *Fortune* poll for November 1940 showed close to half the respondents endorsing "strong measures against Japan" and less than a quarter opposed.[87] By then close to 60 percent of those polled favored sending massive military supplies to China.[88]

All during the winter of 1940–41, some anti-interventionists continued to foresee a war with Japan ahead.[89] Such predictions came from many quarters. The Axis pact and Japanese advances, asserted Castle in January, were making peace difficult.[90] *Social Justice* anticipated a Japanese attack on Singapore, possibly timed simultaneously with German attacks on Suez and Gibraltar, that would prompt American entrance into war. A month later, Boake Carter called the Far East the most dangerous spot in our world. His evidence included the American "scramble" to build bases in Guam and Samoa, major Japanese naval units appearing off French Indochina, and the announcement by the Netherlands East Indies that if invaded it would fight. In March, Dennis anticipated a naval war with Japan, for that nation could not afford to back down over Singapore and the Dutch Indies.[91]

Other noninterventionists were more hopeful, thereby being somewhat in accord with a Gallup poll taken in February 1941, in which only 14 percent would have supported war with Japan. The newly organized America First Committee denied that armed conflict was imminent. The United States, said the AFC, realized that Asian involvement would weaken its aid to Britain. Japan did not want to fight the U.S. or start hostile action against Britain or the Netherlands East Indies, particularly before Hitler began his spring campaign.[92] Even to seize the Dutch Indies, said FOR cosecretary John Nevin Sayre, would require three hundred thousand troops, which Japan could not spare from China.[93]

During the spring and early summer of 1941, such administration critics still remained optimistic.[94] Japan, said Boake Carter in April, sought to end the China war, for its strength was drained and its people weary.[95] Carter's boss, William Randolph Hearst, claimed that the Soviet-Japanese nonaggression pact, signed on 13 April, could make for peace.[96] The communist press, which in February had found war imminent throughout Southeast Asia, now feared American "appeasement" in the Far East.[97] "A group in the State Department," said *US Week* in June, sought to recognize Japan's claims in China in exchange for a Japanese promise not to fight in a Germany-U.S. conflict. *New Masses* noted the rumor that the American fleet was moving into the Atlantic, signifying that Japan had "promised to be good."[98]

By summer, however, other anti-interventionists saw crisis ahead. In late June, *Social Justice* noted American ships exploring the magnitude of Singapore, U.S. fighting men receiving commissions at Honolulu and Manila, and American "volunteers" assisting the air force in what it caustically called "the great democracy" of China. As the Japanese were shut out of the Anglo-American world by tariff and immigration barriers, said Dennis in July, they would eventually be forced to conquer such areas as French Indochina, Siam, Vladivostok, and the Philippines.[99]

In *United We Stand!*, the more sober Hanson Baldwin spoke of deterrence. Calling for "embargoes" on Japan by using the pretext of defense "priorities," he also endorsed additional long-range submarines and patrol planes and perhaps an additional heavy cruiser for the U.S. Asiatic fleet. This fleet, he went on, should pay friendly visits to Singapore, Australia, New Zealand, and possibly a port in East India. The United States should also make secret agreements with the Allies for its use of Singapore and the Netherlands East Indies. In a *Life* article published in August, Baldwin added other steps: gradually limiting the strategic commodities sent to Japan, helping maintain Soviet Far Eastern armies, and sending the maximum number of bombers to "our Anglo-Netherlands-American outposts."[100]

Tensions accelerated on 23 July when the Vichy government yielded to Tokyo's demands for military bases in Indochina. In return, Japan agreed to "protect" that colony from British and Free French "domination." Speaking for the United States, Sumner Welles accused Japan of pursuing "an objective of expansion by force or threat of force." Predicting Japanese seizure of additional territories, he expressed American concern over tin, rubber, and oil. On 26 July, acting together, the U.S. and Britain froze all Japanese assets; Roosevelt placed the armed forces of the Philippines under direct American command. Although the president's ultimate intent remained uncertain, historians William E. Langer and S. Everett Gleason are undoubtedly correct in calling the freezing order "probably the crucial step in the entire course of Japanese-American relations before Pearl Harbor."[101] Without so declaring, the United States had embargoed Japan's most crucial resource: oil.

Interventionists had long been concerned over Japanese control of Indochina. Once Japan possessed bases at Cam Ranh Bay and Saigon, they stressed, it stood within six hundred miles of Singapore and Manila. Furthermore, it would possess land access to Thailand and Rangoon, Burma, the city where American materials bound for China were being stored.[102] American leaders saw the Japanese step as part of a broader Axis threat, Hull and Roosevelt both believing that the move seriously hampered Britain's chances for victory in Europe. That month, a Gallup poll revealed more than half the respondents favoring war to keep Japan from seizing either the Dutch East Indies or Singapore. Similarly, a government survey of editorial opinion found strong support for the administration action.[103]

Certain FDR foes found his move belligerent. Japan, said *Commonweal*, might see no alternative but to call America's bluff, thereby creating the very war that Roosevelt's "appeasement" had tried to prevent. If the United States entered the war over Indochina and the Dutch East Indies, maintained Norman Thomas, an unforgivable crime would have been committed against the American people.[104]

Now that the Soviets were in the war, the Stalinist press no longer objected to Roosevelt's moves. To others of the left, the freezing order proved that the entire Asian struggle centered on resources. The administration, said the socialist *Call*, had shown it was acting on behalf of "dear old Standard Oil, U.S. Rubber and Electric Bond and Share." Both the freezing order and the appointment of General Douglas MacArthur as American military chief in the Far East, commented a writer in the Trotskyist *Militant*, signaled a war for "imperialist plunder" ahead.[105]

The United States apparently was not protecting any material interests of its own; rather, it was greatly overreaching itself on behalf of a foreign colony.[106] If it intervened in Indochina, cautioned the executive committee of the New York AFC, Japan could claim the right of preventing the construction of American bases in Brazil.[107] "We may deplore these moves," it continued concerning the latest Japanese actions, "but they are none of our vital business."[108] Borchard felt similarly, saying, "I wonder what difference it will make to an Indo-Chinese whether a French General or a Japanese General occupies the thatched hut in Cambodia."[109] Castle denied that the U.S. could prevent the establishment of Japanese bases in Indochina, for the move was made with Vichy's concurrence. Had the administration allowed Japan access to food and raw materials, the American press would not have to be disturbed about the sudden availability of Indochinese rice to Japan. "If the United States is going to object every time some hungry nation sets forth to grab itself some food," warned the *New York Daily News*, "it will precipitate endless wars."[110]

Indochina was not the only colony under anti-interventionist scrutiny. On 26 July, the day that the United States and Britain announced their freezing orders, the *Chicago Tribune* asked pointedly, "Are we to fight Japan for good old Singapore and queen Wilhelmina?" Both the British and the Dutch, it said, sought to put the Indies under the protection of the American flag; furthermore, the British desired to make Singapore "an outpost of the American republic."[111]

The *Tribune* struck a major anti-interventionist theme—namely, that American Far Eastern policy was increasingly centering on defense of Britain's

East Asian empire, whose focal point was Singapore.[112] Some interventionists themselves conceded as much. In Japanese hands, commented CDAAA spokesman Livingstone Hartley, Singapore could be the keystone of its new order in Eastern Asia, enabling it to force Britain and the United States out of the region. In addition, Britain's lifeline to Africa and the Near East would be severed, an action that in turn could lead to a sudden Axis attack through Spain. The long-range result: the Axis would possess all the petroleum, wheat, and cotton it needed. The British outpost was crucial in another way as well: Were Japan to control both Singapore and the Dutch East Indies, it would encircle the Philippines.[113]

More than ever, anti-interventionists maintained, peace was now crucial. Hearst denied that Japan sought war with the United States, predicting instead that the U.S. might well have its next "squabble" with Britain. Noting state department language concerning "flexibility" of enforcement, the *Call* downplayed any change in commercial patterns. Lawrence Dennis denied that either Tokyo or Washington wanted to fight, though both were playing "a dangerous game with loaded pistols." Maintaining that Japan could not easily be defeated, he mused, "We don't see how America can profit from the destruction of the only conservative regime in the Far East and the enhancement of the radical regimes of Moscow and Chungking."[114]

According to the *New York Daily News*, Japan was "sick" of the war in China and sought to settle its differences with the United States. As noted, the *News* made a sweeping proposal based on its own brand of realpolitik: "Japan and the United States ought to divide Pacific hegemony between them, the dividing line corresponding roughly with the International Dateline. The Philippines under such an agreement would fall in the Japanese sphere, true; but we think that would be fine and that we ought to seize with glad cries this chance to cut them adrift before 1946."[115]

On 6 August, public attention was centered on a different area: Thailand. When Hull stated publicly that Japanese activity would endanger American security in the Pacific, anti-interventionists again became apprehensive. The New York AFC chapter, warning against any effort to stop the Japanese in Siam, noted that Japan possessed a large army just across the Thai border and a greater fleet at hand than any the United States could mobilize. Chester Bowles found "whooping up this Siam problem" to be evidence that the administration was involved in guaranteeing the future safety of the British Empire and the downfall of Hitler.[116]

When Roosevelt and Churchill met off the Newfoundland coast on 9–12 August, noninterventionists became even more frightened. In a front-page story, the *Call* maintained that the two had agreed on the precise moment when they would go into action in the Far East. Wheeler suspected that Roosevelt would take the lead in combating Japanese threats to Malaya, thereby involving the United States in a Pacific war. Noting that some U.S. trade with Japan was continuing, he commented, "There is no reason why we should not live in peace with her."[117] AFC staffer Ruth Sarles believed Roosevelt and Churchill had made a mutual pledge to defend Singapore or the Dutch East Indies. Hearst thought the commitment also covered Outer Mongolia and eastern Siberia, in particular the protection of Vladivostok. In mid-August, the AFC executive committee unanimously endorsed a resolution that opposed war with Japan: "In the absence of attack on this country we should maintain peace."[118]

In reality, Roosevelt had promised Churchill little. During the meeting, the president and the prime minister had agreed to submit parallel American and British notes to Japan warning that further encroachment in the southwest Pacific might lead to conflict. Once FDR returned to Washington, however, he disappointed Churchill by omitting any reference to possible war. A Gallup poll released 5 August revealed only 24 percent supporting immediate war with Japan.[119]

In September, the interventionist CDAAA found time to be working on the U.S. side. Ahead lay an impending rainy season in Malaya and the Netherlands East Indies, the approach of winter in Siberia, the progressive effect of sanctions on Japan, and an increase in Allied military strength in the Far East—all representing an advantageous position that could only be seriously compromised by "any retreat from our present firm attitude towards Japan."[120]

All during the summer—in fact, until the first part of October—administration adversaries continued to express guarded optimism.[121] Frederick J. Libby claimed that Japan had proposed a Far Eastern settlement that marked genuine collaboration among the East Asian nations. *Uncensored* even specified the coming peace terms, which included U.S. recognition of Manchukuo and of Japanese domination of French Indochina, American loans and trade concessions to Japan, Japanese renunciation of the Axis, and Japanese, American, and British withdrawal from China. It found Roosevelt reluctant but believed Japan anxiously sought a settlement. In mid-September, suspected the *Chicago Tribune*, the United States had bought off Japan with a promise to recognize its conquest of Manchuria and "sundry other items of Chinese real estate." The *Christian Century* simply hoped that the negotiations would be conducted "in a spirit of generosity," so that Japan might be wooed away from Germany.[122]

A few anti-interventionists supported the continued pressure on Japan. Fish favored the administration embargo program, the freezing of Japanese assets, and restrictions on war goods with Japan, though he warned that further steps risked war. Congressman John M. Vorys went so far as to call for a whole series of measures: an American embargo, termination of the silk trade, the defense of the Philippines, and the withholding of oil, metal, and machinery.

"We can bring Japan to her knees without firing a shot," he said, "simply by re-fusing to buy from her certain things."[123]

Herbert Hoover maintained that Roosevelt's action was necessary while concurrently blaming administration leaders for "doing everything they can to get us into war through the Japanese back door." He was even willing to give the Japanese advice: take eastern Siberia, thereby relieving itself of the "terri-ble menace" of Vladivostok's air bases as well as giving them "a vast unpopu-lated area into which to expand." He even thought Japan would willingly give up everything south of the Great Wall for eastern Siberia and peace with the West, an arrangement surely in the American interest. At one point, he sug-gested a six-month freeze on military action, the relaxation of American sanc-tions, and a summit meeting in Honolulu. Using attorney Raoul Desverine as his intermediary, the ex-president unsuccessfully sought to promote his plan with diplomats on both sides.[124]

By mid-October, several anti-interventionists felt that U.S.-Japan negotia-tions were in trouble. The *Christian Century* accused Washington of engaging in stalemate, "keeping the Japanese on the anxious seat and daily advancing our own preparations for a two-ocean war." In mid-September, Lawrence Dennis had expressed doubt about whether Washington could offer Japan enough to call off its army. Japan, he continued, could not solve its unem-ployment problem without continuous expansion and conquest.[125]

Such anxieties were compounded when, on 16 October, the Konoye regime resigned after its ministers failed to agree on national policy. Two days later, Lieutenant General Tojo Hideki, long known as a pronounced militarist, formed a new Japanese cabinet, assuming the portfolios of prime minister, war, and home ministries. The American public remained ambivalent, a *For-tune* poll of that month indicating a nation split on defending the Dutch East Indies, Singapore, the Burma Road, and Thailand.[126]

By now more noninterventionists were seeing war in the offing.[127] To Flynn, the fall of the more moderate Konoye showed the situation "deteriorating swiftly." Lincoln Colcord predicted that the United States would fight in de-fense of Singapore or Vladivostok. The *Chicago Tribune* reported that the Japanese were offering considerable concessions to FDR, but that negotiations had stalled on the matter of two Japanese bases remaining in China.[128]

Others were more hopeful.[129] Late in October, Dennis saw Roosevelt as hes-itating on war with Japan, doing so on the advice of older navy men and ca-reer diplomats. Hoover, predicting the Japanese seizure of Vladivostok, denied that the Roosevelt administration would take any action, for neither the U.S. nor Britain sought war. Indeed, if the U.S. acquiesced in the Vladivostok move, Japan might secure "the face" needed to withdraw from China.[130]

Several FDR critics of pacifist leanings suggested terms. The WIL and NCPW proposed a quid pro quo: cessation of hostilities on the Asian main-land in exchange for such concessions as a fresh trade agreement with Japan.

Harold E. Fey wrote of demilitarization of the Pacific and opening equal access to oil and other materials.[131]

During November, intensive negotiations took place in Washington. On the 10th, Ambassador Nomura Kichisaburo submitted "Plan A," a proposal calling on the United States to restore normal trade with Japan and persuade Chiang to meet Japan's terms. If the generalissimo refused, the United States would agree to terminate all aid to China. In return, the Japanese would not automatically honor the tripartite pact but would rather decide any obligation "independently." Provisions concerning evacuation from China and Indochina and guaranteeing the open door within the Japanese empire were most vague.[132] Within five days, the American government rejected Plan A.

On 17 November, veteran Japanese diplomat Kurusu Saburo arrived in Washington to assist Nomura. Kurusu spoke in terms of a return to the status quo ante of July 1941, whereby the United States would lift its trade restrictions and Japan would withdraw from southern Indochina. By a decoding process known as "Magic," America soon learned that Kurusu had exceeded his instructions. Within three days, Nomura proposed "Plan B": Japan to advance no further in Southeast Asia and the western Pacific, remove all troops from southern to northern Indochina, and withdraw from Indochina after a general settlement or restoration of peace with China; the U.S. to discontinue support for Chiang, unfreeze Japanese assets, supply Japan with "a required quantity of oil," and press the Dutch to reopen the East Indies to Japanese trade. The United States found the terms unacceptable.[133] In the meantime, on 14 November, Roosevelt had ordered U.S. marines to leave garrisons in Shanghai, Peking, and Tientsin.

A few administration adversaries remained optimistic.[134] The *New York Daily News*, for example, speculated that Japan's sending of a special envoy indicated it did not wish to fight.[135] Yet as negotiations resumed, many anti-interventionists grew pessimistic, placing the onus strictly on Roosevelt.[136] Senator Nye maintained that relatively minor concessions in China, for example, permitting Japan air bases in such areas as Shanghai, could end the crisis. "The trouble is," he continued, "the Administration doesn't want to settle this thing." Taft wrote, "I know that Hull and Stimson are so very anti-Japanese that they may precipitate a war when it is wholly unnecessary."[137] Japan, said Dennis, had spoken in terms of abandoning the Axis alliance and withdrawing its army from China, but it insisted that the United States must abandon its economic boycott and recognize the Japanese occupation of French Indochina. FDR, however, he found to be intransigent.[138]

On 25 November, the Roosevelt administration abandoned thoughts of one ad hoc proposal it had briefly considered, a three-month modus vivendi. By such a temporary accord, both powers would have pledged to avoid military action in the South Pacific, Japan to evacuate southern Indochina "forthwith," and the United States to resume normal trade with Japan, and direct negotiations would have commenced between Japan and the Chiang government.[139]

Two things prevented the United States from making the proposal: first, the news that Japanese troops were sighted off Taiwan; second, the strong opposition of Britain and China.

A day later, Hull submitted proposals to the Japanese diplomats that were strictly "for the record." They included withdrawal of Japanese armed forces from China and Indochina, mutual lifting of trade restrictions, the unfreezing of assets, and the conclusion of a nonaggression pact among the United States, Japan, China, the Netherlands, the British Empire, the Soviet Union, and Thailand. The public simply learned that Hull had again submitted traditional principles centering on peaceful restraint and that talks were stalled but not broken.[140]

On 27 November, the administration received word that Japan was massing troops in Indochina. A day later, dispatches from Shanghai reported that seventy transports were moving some thirty thousand Japanese troops southward. Rumors abounded that Japanese troops were headed to the Isthmus of Kra in Thailand. Such measures were hardly reassuring to Western leaders quite aware that Singapore lay at the tip of this isthmus.

A few noninterventionists still did not think war inevitable.[141] The FOR proposed a release of Japanese assets and renewed Japanese access to nonmilitary supplies, thereby resuming much trade immediately. Dennis saw Roosevelt as being under British pressure to compromise with Japan, though he said that Australia and China were balking. AFC congressional representative Fred Burdick thought that the alarm generated by the *Chicago Tribune*'s exposé of a major war mobilization plan would make it more difficult to thrust the United States into a Pacific war.[142]

Fear was still more prevalent than hope, particularly as eyes were cast on Thailand. According to Hearst columnist Paul Mallon, such a move would bring British troops stationed in Malaya into conflict, then eventually involve the American fleet. Congressman Ross Rizley (Rep.-Okla.) remarked, "I don't know anybody in the country who wants to go to war over aggression in the Far East. As for fighting over Thailand, most people don't even know where it is."[143]

Even without the Thai crisis, most anti-interventionists reflected general public opinion in believing that war was simply a matter of time.[144] On 29 November, for example, Hoover envisioned the United States heading for a Pacific war (while planning an expeditionary force to Egypt as well). Several in Congress, to use the words of Fred Burdick, desired an "avalanche" of mail to the White House asking that the negotiations with Japan be publicized, doing so in the hopes of curbing the president and avoiding war.[145] Congressmen Mundt and Ludlow suggested a congressional inquiry into U.S. Far Eastern policy.[146]

The administration's diplomacy was accused of being both secret and irresponsible. Senator Danaher attacked the administration for supposedly having committed the United States to war over China or Thailand. On 1 December, Castle feared that negotiations had broken down. If war came, he asserted, Washington "will be at least equally guilty with Tokyo." Congressman William P. Lambertson accused the administration of presenting "an ultimatum" to Japan, though he confessed ignorance of the American proposals.[147] The *Christian Century* presented a more complicated picture, criticizing the U.S. for submitting a list of "unacceptable" though unidentified demands.[148] On 6 December, the day before the Pearl Harbor attack, the New York AFC chapter charged the administration with imposing irresponsible conditions, such as removal of Japanese troops from Thailand's borders and ending the China war.[149]

Such anxieties had some grounding in reality. On 3 December, Roosevelt gave a private verbal assurance to Britain. He would offer "armed support" if Japan invaded British or Dutch possessions, even though in reality he could not guarantee congressional support.[150] Through the Pacific crisis, the U.S. had seldom coordinated action with England. The United States would not concentrate its naval strength in East Asia, much less at Singapore. It excluded the British from its negotiation with Japan, not consulting them over such vital matters as the oil embargo.

During the entire fall, the president's foes warned that a Pacific war would endanger the Allied effort against Germany.[151] A Pacific conflict, noted Hoover, would be "God's gift to Hitler," for the U.S. Navy would be preoccupied in convoying across the Pacific and Indian oceans. Once the United States was committed in Asia, Senator Wiley feared, Germany would force it into a European conflict as well.[152] Journalist Lincoln Colcord anticipated the reverse—namely, that the moment the U.S. entered a war in the Atlantic, Japan would advance in Asia. The result would be the same: America would experience a conflict on two fronts.[153]

Within the Roosevelt administration itself, anxiety existed over a two-front war. Such cabinet members as Morgenthau, Stimson, and Knox consistently took a strident position, as did such lower-ranking but influential figures as Stanley K. Hornbeck, chief of the state department's division of Far Eastern affairs. As far back as September 1940, however, both Adolf Berle and Breckinridge Long noted that confrontation in the Pacific could tie American hands in Europe.[154] Though the U.S. Navy had always seen Japan as its natural enemy, the army always opposed fighting in Asia.[155] In those last few days before the Japanese attack, both Marshall and Stark admonished that challenging Japan could endanger the more crucial struggle against Germany.[156]

On 7 December 1941, the Japanese attacked Pearl Harbor, a strike that cost the United States the lives of 2,323 men and practically every airplane on Oahu. All eight battleships were disabled, two permanently destroyed.

Anti-interventionists immediately endorsed a war against Japan.[157] The only thing to do now, said Senator Wheeler, was "to lick hell out of them," though he privately felt he had no apologies for his anti-interventionism.[158] "We stand with our country," cried the *Christian Century*. Senator Danaher spoke of "war to the hilt." "When you are attacked, there is nothing to do but fight," asserted the *New York Daily News*.[159]

The Japanese received the bulk of the blame.[160] Sterling Morton, General Wood, and Norman Thomas referred to Japan's "treachery."[161] The *Chicago Tribune* used the term "perfidy." To Castle, Japan had simply gone "mad." Hearst remarked that Japan had long sought war; it was "swaggering around Asia" and "murdering a lot of unarmed Chinese men."[162]

Even those of pacifist leanings spoke out. Libby called Japan a "ruthless aggressor." "Criminality" and "wickedness" were Villard's words. John Haynes Holmes found the attack "outrageous," though he added it did not "change the history of what went on before."[163] Similarly, the Socialist Party condemned the "wanton attack," while claiming that underlying the event were long-standing imperialist rivalries.[164]

Usually anti-interventionists refused to renounce their prewar position.[165] Said the AFC national committee, "Our principles were right. Had they been followed, war could have been avoided."[166] The KAOWC expressed itself in similar terms. "We will be proven right historically," wrote Chester Bowles.[167] "The powers that be," regretted Amos Pinchot, "did not take our advice about war." *Scribner's Commentator* possibly hinted at a postwar revisionism when it said, "It is ours to do or die. It is for the historians of the dim future to reason why."[168]

Certainly, many anti-interventionists were most critical of American diplomacy toward Japan. Only Raymond Moley, George Sokolsky, and Dorothy Detzer went so far as to praise the way Roosevelt had conducted negotiations. Senator Vandenberg thought the United States could have conceded Japanese control of Manchukuo and permitted Japan more commercial and territorial concessions in China. General Wood privately suspected that Japan "was practically forced into action at the time by the notes from our own Executive and State Departments."[169]

Some anti-interventionists criticized the U.S.'s entire Asian policy.[170] According to Danaher, as the United States had levied economic sanctions and had supplied aviators to bomb the Japanese, Japan took steps that it "in national honor was bound to take in face of our conduct." Charles A. Lindbergh entered in his diary, "We have been prodding them into war for weeks. They have simply beaten us to the gun." "This continuous putting pins in rattlesnakes," remarked Hoover, had "finally got this country bitten." The former president was particularly concerned about Hull's "ultimatum" of 26 November, which "sooner or later" meant war.[171]

Those of pacifist leanings were particularly vocal. Citing the Japanese exclusion act of 1924, the American naval rivalry with Japan, and the fortification of Guam, Libby maintained that the United States drove Japan into a position where the only alternatives were "to back down or fight." The *Christian Century* accused America of failing to apply neutrality legislation in 1937, a move—it argued—that would have stalled Japan's war machine quickly. Furthermore, the United States was unresponsive to Japan's "terrible problem of providing a decent livelihood for her teeming population." Similarly, the FOR offered a whole catalog of offenses, ranging from initial Western incursions into Asia to selling war materials to Japan while making loans to China.[172]

To several anti-interventionists, the outlook was gloomy. Hoover feared the loss of Singapore and the Philippines, estimating that recapture might take ten years. With the loss of Japan's "stabilizing influence," feared Castle, Asia would revert to "the old type of special privilege in the Far East," in particular the influence of Britain and the Soviets. More optimistic, Hearst said that once the United States "washed up" Japan, it could "straighten things out" in Europe.[173]

Others stressed more long-range goals. The AFC warned against "secret treaties committing America to imperialistic aims or vast burden in other parts of the world." Frederick J. Libby and Dorothy Detzer hoped for an early peace, adding the wish that the U.S. would not "stoop to the bombing of helpless civilians in Japan." Calling for restraint in waging the conflict, *Commonweal* cautioned, "We cannot fight until wrong has left the world."[174]

Several FDR critics wondered why the base at Hawaii had been so unprepared. General Wood called the attack "a disgrace to both the Army and Navy." Colonel McCormick had not imagined "the shocking state of lack of discipline in the navy and army that led to the catastrophe." The *New York Daily News* sought a congressional investigation, asking whether "some dead wood in high U.S. Navy circles" needed to be retired.[175] Why, queried Lawrence Dennis, were not American destroyers patrolling several hundred miles around Hawaii?[176]

Some hints of conspiracy existed. "The administration," noted Borchard, "must have known that a quick attack would be the indicated Japanese war policy." Fearing that military commanders might be made scapegoats, Hoover had a series of questions for General Frank R. McCoy, a member of the investigating commission chaired by Associate Supreme Court Owen J. Roberts:

> Did the State Department appraise the Army and Navy of the ultimatum [of 26 November] and its serious import? If so, did the Washington heads of these departments transmit it to the forces in the field? Now the only reason why I write this is the feeling that perhaps some Admiral or some General in the Pacific may be a goat for action or lack of action higher up, and thus a great injustice done.[177]

The seeds of Pearl Harbor revisionism had already been planted.

# Conclusion

History has not been kind to the anti-interventionists of 1939–41. For years, except in occasional scholarly studies, they have been perceived in the most negative of terms.

In the retrospect of more than a half-century, however, it is far less easy to be supercilious or patronizing. Their heritage, like that of the interventionists they so bitterly fought, contains prophetic elements as well as foolish ones. They possessed a healthy suspicion of executive power, as manifested in such matters as the destroyer bases deal and the American occupation of Iceland. They were alert to presidential duplicity, as exhibited in the case of the *Greer*. They correctly saw an American Expeditionary Force as a most risky military venture, for one must ask what would have been its likely fate if the brunt of Hitler's Wehrmacht had not been blunted on the Russian steppes.[1] Though their anticommunism could border on the hysterical, noninterventionists correctly challenged pro-administration claims that Germany's defeat would have little bearing on Soviet expansion. They felt unjustly maligned, and deservedly so, when administration officials not only branded them en masse as potential traitors or Nazi dupes but used the FBI as an instrument of intimidation. Such practices, they correctly surmised, were creating a climate of opinion in which dissent was confused with disloyalty, a circumstance that bade ill for American democracy.

Despite stereotypes of apathy and ignorance, certain major vehicles of anti-interventionism were highly informed concerning the events of the day. The editorials of the *Chicago Tribune*, *New York Daily News*, and Hearst press reveal a detailed knowledge of the military campaigns and battlefront shifts.

Such journalists as Frank Hanighen, William Henry Chamberlin, and Hanson Baldwin offered sober commentary.

At the same time, many anti-interventionists could be quite off the mark. They harped on the proclivity of Europe for continual conflict, interpreted the current struggle as simply another imperialist war, and found Britain—not Germany—bearing the greater guilt in both immediate and long-range history. Journalist Elmer Davis made a telling point when, in conceding the checkered record of the British in such areas as Ireland and India, he wrote, "There is hope—some hope—of a decent peace if the Allies win; if the Germans win there is no evidence on which to base any hope at all."[2] Similarly, few noninterventionists realized the precariousness of all such overseas holdings, which had long made them a continual drain on the European powers. Many colonies could not be retained once the war ended.

Anti-interventionists often found Germany's war aims quite limited, perceiving them strictly in terms of traditional continental balance-of-power politics. At most, it was thought, Germany sought to dominate Central Europe. If it ventured further east, in the direction of the Soviet Union, either the two dictatorships would slaughter each other into bloody exhaustion or Hitler would rid the world of the communist scourge. Certainly such FDR critics woefully misunderstood the dynamism of the German regime or its potential threat to a wider world balance.

Anti-interventionists pointed to prospects for a negotiated peace at every opportunity and irrespective of changing battlefronts. Hitler's initial peace bids of October 1939 found much hearing. Curiously, though often suspicious of the president, some of his bitterest foes suggested him as mediator. At times, such people advanced peace aims as utopian as those posited in the Atlantic Charter and just as unlikely to see fulfillment. One might naturally expect pacifists and clergy to advance the most cosmic of schemes. More sober-minded figures, however—such as Sterling Morton, Chester Bowles, Robert E. Wood, and Burton Wheeler—also offered relatively far-reaching proposals.

To the anti-interventionists, overseas involvement invariably led to domestic ruin. An America at war was an America bereft of civil and economic liberties. While conceding—in fact at times emphasizing—the degree of poverty in the nation, they remained highly skeptical concerning any war boom: Dictatorship, not prosperity, may well be in store.

Anti-interventionists could be irresponsibly demagogic, attacking the British and their empire to such a degree that an untutored listener might place their behavior on a moral equivalency with that of the Axis. Though one might expect such comments from Porter Sargent and Rush Holt, Theodore Dreiser and Father Coughlin, more mainstream figures also shared deep suspicion. Journalist Carleton Beals, for instance, said that in any forthcoming peace, the United States "may as little likely expect generosity from England as from Germany."[3] At a time when the British Isles were under siege, certain anti-interventionists deliberately stressed historic tensions between the two countries. When, asked Congressman Dewey Short, "did Britain ever fight our battle? Was it in 1775 when some of our flesh and blood were spilled with Washington at Valley Forge to throw off the yoke of British oppression and to escape the hell of British tyranny?"[4]

The president's critics similarly indicted Allied leadership, with Winston Churchill held up to particular opprobrium. Dwight Macdonald found the prime minister only differing from one of the "Munichmen" in being "more energetic, able, and more realistically aware of the threat offered by Hitler to British imperialism."[5] Britain, several argued, was never a democracy, and emergency wartime legislation made it even less of a one. Early in October 1939, Arthur Vandenberg brandished an unidentified headline of the previous week: "British Find Liberties Vanish with War: Traditional Freedom Is Blackened Out."[6] A few administration critics found the British people themselves highly suspect.

Furthermore, the Roosevelt administration was perceived as mere dupes of British power, the object of sinister manipulation by Downing Street. Jurist John Bassett Moore found the United States so tied to the British it would have more freedom as a self-governing dominion.[7] Washington editor Frank Waldrop wrote in September 1941, "Those of us who are isolationists believe Churchill is bossing Roosevelt and leading us down the road to a profitless war as a mere British Empire goonsquad."[8] The Rhodes scholar program and Clarence Streit's Union Now plan were presented as centers of a British plot.

The worldview of FDR critics could border on the conspiratorial in other matters as well. In particular, some harped on Polish documents allegedly captured by the Germans, claiming they proved that the Roosevelt administration had plotted a general military conflagration by promising military and financial aid to the Allies if war erupted. In so doing, they inadvertently helped bolster one claim of World War II revisionism—namely, that FDR pressed Chamberlain to give irresponsible commitments to the Poles.[9]

Yet one should be careful in speaking of *the* anti-interventionist position. True, there occasionally existed an incredible marriage of convenience, as when the *Chicago Tribune* serialized an antiwar novella by fellow traveler Dalton Trumbo and the *Daily Worker* praised Charles Lindbergh's defense strategy. It is hard to realize in retrospect that every single American political party of the left opposed intervention from September 1939 until at least June 1941. At the same time, the Communist Party continually attacked such mainstream groups as America First, maintaining that its own American Peace Mobilization was the only truly authentic antiwar group.[10] Obviously the noninterventionists were a highly diverse coalition, one that ranged from communists and profascists to Christian pacifists, though the great bulk professed a brand of politics far more in the American mainstream.

In resisting Roosevelt's major proposals—lend-lease, the extension of the term of draftees, convoys to Britain—much agreement existed among administration foes. There was similar accord on certain relatively minor matters—islands-for-war-debts, for example, or the Ogdensburg agreement with Canada. Similarly, in dealing with the origins of the European war, anti-interventionists concurred as to the evils of the Versailles treaty, the legitimacy of German claims to Danzig and the Corridor, and the folly of any British-French guarantee to Poland. Chances for Allied victory usually appeared negligible, even were the United States to intervene as a full-scale belligerent. And suppose the U.S. and Britain did triumph—the costs to civilization would still be ruinous.

Anti-interventionists concurred in maintaining that the Axis posed neither a military nor economic threat to the United States. Often they defined military safety in terms of a "Fortress America," economic survival dependent on either national self-sufficiency or hemispheric integration. As Germany's expansion would simply make Hitler's Reich weaker, not stronger, they maintained, the winning hand always lay with the U.S. Conversely, so they believed, war mobilization would ruin the American economy, while an AEF would decimate the nation's armed forces.

If the anti-interventionists had one predominating fear, it was that the Soviet Union would emerge as the conflict's only victor. Its accompanying social system of communism, with its possible ecumenical appeal, made the peril appear far more threatening than that of the Axis nations, which could be presented as a bulwark against a Red onslaught. When, in June 1941, Hitler invaded the USSR, the president's critics often predicted its imminent demise while stressing the immorality of coming to its aid. It would hardly be exaggerating to find in the anti-interventionist posture a kind of rehearsal for the Cold War, although certain "old isolationists" retained their hostility to global commitments through at least 1949.[11]

The picture concerning Asia is more complicated. Certainly, the great majority of FDR's foes opposed the Japanese conquest of China, but they were equally hostile to European imperialism in the Far East. They debated economic pressure on Japan, some opposing continued shipment of war goods to that nation. Conversely, others found embargoes both self-destructive and dangerous, and a few acquiesced in a "Japanese Monroe Doctrine" for Asia. Some of the most articulate anti-interventionists opposed a continued American military presence in the Philippines and the fortification of Guam, arguing that both areas were militarily indefensible. As in the case of Europe, many found the continental United States secure from any Japanese attack, while seeing any American invasion of Japan as most costly. It was, they believed, far better for the U.S. and Japan to negotiate, particularly over the contentious issue of China.

Such disagreement over Asia leads one to a wider point: the degree to which administration critics differed among themselves on some quite significant issues. Even if one eliminates the more extreme in their ranks (e.g., Father

Coughlin, Lawrence Dennis, Ralph Townsend, the *Daily Worker*, hard-core pacifists), incredible diversity remained. Roosevelt's foes were divided on the wisdom of the Munich agreement, the justice of Poland's cause, and the desirability of aiding Finland, a matter that revealed the greatest fissure of all. As far as military defense went, they differed on defending Alaska, occupying Greenland, and integrating South America into a U.S.-dominated system. Some spoke in terms of controlling Greenland and the Caribbean, several seeking the outright seizure of such islands as Martinique. Others saw all South America as needing protection. Still others desired U.S. bases as far south as Brazil.

They could not concur on the effectiveness of air and sea power, particularly on the use of bomber and battleship, though many supported a large air force and expanding the American fleet. Powerful voices within their ranks, albeit a minority, were not averse to a large conscript army. They also disagreed as how best to meet Axis economic competition, some pushing barter, others autarchy. Certain Roosevelt initiatives could create dissidence within anti-interventionist ranks, among them the Welles mission of February 1940 and the Eight Points of the Atlantic Charter.

Administration critics lacked a common analysis regarding the prognosis of the war—indeed, concerning chances for British and Soviet survival. At the same time, most never changed their fundamental position as a result of shifting events. Irrespective of all Allied prospects, they maintained that the United States could only weaken itself fatally by massive overseas commitments, in the process moving toward the very totalitarianism it was fighting abroad.

Particularly in the early phases of the war, noninterventionists agreed at times with the Roosevelt administration, which itself could be divided. The president himself extended peace feelers in the winter of 1939–40 and recognized the Vichy regime. Far from being a tool of the British Empire, Roosevelt was profoundly wary, espousing opposition toward French domination of Indochina as well. The rise of Hitler and Mussolini, he maintained, lay in the West's betrayal of its own Wilsonian principles. Strong voices within the American military always remained suspicious of massive arms shipments overseas. Similarly, certain administration figures initially expressed pessimism concerning Britain's and later the Soviet Union's survival. Others recommended accommodation with Japan.

In the end, the anti-interventionists were defeated at every point. Of course, seldom—if ever—in American history have political "outsiders" determined major foreign policy. The years 1939–41 marked no exception. With consummate skill, Franklin Roosevelt set the agenda, defined the issues, and chose his timing. His critics were forced to respond to the president's initiatives. Besides, noninterventionists were far too diverse to offer any unified alternatives of their own, even too divided to offer any alternative vision of a positive international order. The America First Committee might take credit for a number of minor victories (e.g., an amendment to the original lend-lease bill prohibiting actual delivery of supplies), but such triumphs were trivial at best.[12]

To the degree that opinion polls reflected popular sentiment, administration critics found little comfort in their findings. Once issues shifted from the general question of directly entering the war to such more concrete proposals as cash-and-carry and convoys, the president's opponents drew only minority support. The polls might show consensus on such matters as the desirability of islands-for-war-debts in November 1939 or a negotiated peace in March 1940, but certainly not on such major legislation as lend-lease.[13]

When the United States entered the war without reservation, anti-interventionists felt a profound sense of personal tragedy. Their anxiety was compounded by the fact that on 11 December 1941, Germany and Italy had declared war on the United States. "I feel as if my world has pretty well come to an end," wrote Norman Thomas, "that what I have stood for has been defeated, and my own usefulness made small." John Haynes Holmes recalled a passage in Augustine's *City of God*, describing a conqueror who looked ever more like the conquered; the New York minister feared "nothing but disaster all around." Two days after the attack, Anne Morrow Lindbergh wrote in her diary, "I feel as if all I believed *was* America, all memories of it, all history, all dreams of the future were marching gaily toward a precipice—and unaware, unaware."[14]

# Notes

## PREFACE

1. Hoover, bar association of Nassau County, New York, *New York Times* (hereafter cited as *NYT*), 26 May 1940, 15.

2. Gerhard L. Weinberg, *World in the Balance: Behind the Scenes of World War II* (Hanover, N.H.: Brandeis University Press of New England, 1981).

3. "America," *Saturday Evening Post* 212 (7 October 1939): 22.

4. Wayne S. Cole, *Roosevelt and the Isolationists, 1932–1945* (Lincoln: University of Nebraska, 1983), 7.

5. See, for example, "An Isolationist," *New York Daily News* (hereafter cited as *NYDN*), 22 June 1940, 13. For similar use, see Representative George Holden Tinkham (Rep.-Mass.), House Foreign Affairs Committee (hereafter cited as HFAC), 21 January 1941, 246; Senator Hiram Johnson (Rep.-Calif.), speech, "Peace or War," NBC, 6 November 1941, in *Congressional Record* (hereafter cited as *CR*), A5042; Hiram Johnson to John Bassett Moore, 26 July 1940, the Papers of John Bassett Moore (hereafter cited as Moore Papers); "Isolation," *America* 61 (30 September 1939): 589.

6. Fish, speech, NBC, 23 September 1939, in *CR*, A20. For similar attitudes, see diplomat John Cudahy, testimony, Senate Foreign Relations Committee (hereafter cited as SFRC), 23 October 1941, 160, 161, 176; Lawrence Dennis, *Weekly Foreign Letter* (hereafter cited as *WFL*) 117 (24 October 1940): 4.

7. For a distinction between *isolationist* and *pacifist*, see Howard Brinton, "Pacifist Not Isolationist," *Fellowship* 6 (June 1940): 91.

8. Holmes, *Unity* 124 (15 January 1940): 154.

9. Justus D. Doenecke, *Anti-Intervention: A Bibliographical Introduction to Isolationism and Pacifism from World War I to the Early Cold War* (New York: Garland, 1987).

10. For the ethnic interpretation, see Samuel Lubell, *The Future of American Politics,* 3d ed., rev. (New York: Harper, 1965), 131-55. For the debate over Populism, see Ray Allen Billington, "The Origins of Middle Western Isolationism," *Political Science Quarterly* 60 (March 1945): 44-64; William G. Carleton, "Isolationism and the Middle West," *Mississippi Valley Historical Review* 33 (December 1946): 377-90; Warren F. Kuehl, "Midwestern Newspapers and the Isolationist Sentiment," *Diplomatic History* 3 (Summer 1979): 283-306. For case studies of agrarian figures, see Wayne S. Cole, *Senator Gerald P. Nye and American Foreign Relations* (Minneapolis: University of Minnesota Press, 1962);

Peter Baldwin Bulkley, "Daniel A. Reed: A Study in Conservatism," Ph.D. diss., Clark University, 1972. For the South, see Wayne S. Cole, "America First and the South, 1940–1941," *Journal of Southern History* 22 (February 1956): 36-47. For party patterns, see David L. Porter, *The Seventy-sixth Congress and World War II, 1939–1940* (Columbia: University of Missouri Press, 1979), 180-82. For xenophobia, see Bernard Fensterwald Jr., "The Anatomy of American 'Isolationism' and Expansion," *Journal of Conflict Resolution* 2 (June 1958): 111-39; (December 1958): 280-307; Daniel Bell, ed., *The Radical Right* (Garden City, N.Y.: Doubleday, 1963); Edward A. Shils, *The Torment of Secrecy* (Glencoe, Ill.: Free Press, 1956).

11. For more extensive discussion, see Michael H. Hunt, *Ideology and U.S. Foreign Policy* (New Haven, Conn.: Yale University Press, 1987), especially chap. 2; Justus D. Doenecke, *Not to the Swift: The Old Isolationists in the Cold War Era* (Lewisburg, Pa..: Bucknell University Press, 1979), 22-31.

12. See, for example, Wayne C. Cole, *America First: The Battle Against Intervention, 1940–1941* (Madison: University of Wisconsin Press, 1953); Cole, *Charles A. Lindbergh and the Battle Against Intervention in World War II* (New York: Harcourt Brace Jovanovich, 1974); Cole, *Roosevelt and the Isolationists*; Manfred Jonas, *Isolationism in America, 1939–1941* (Ithaca, N.Y.: Cornell University Press, 1986); J. Garry Clifford and Samuel R. Spencer Jr., *The First Peacetime Draft* (Lawrence: University Press of Kansas, 1986); Justus D. Doenecke, ed., *In Danger Undaunted: The Anti-Interventionist Movement of 1940–1941 as Revealed in the Papers of the America First Committee* (Stanford, Calif.: Hoover Institution Press, 1990) (hereafter cited as *IDU*).

13. For some preliminary findings, see Justus D. Doenecke, *The Battle Against Intervention, 1939–1941* (Malabar, Fla.: Krieger, 1997).

## INTRODUCTION

1. Harold Ickes, *New York Times*, 14 April 1941, 19.

2. Philip E. Jacob, "Influences of World Events on U.S. 'Neutrality' Opinion," *Public Opinion Quarterly* 4 (March 1940): 48–65.

3. Major studies of Congress include Cole, *Roosevelt and the Isolationists*; Porter, *Seventy-sixth Congress*. For overviews of the Senate, see Thomas N. Guinsburg, *The Pursuit of Isolationism in the United States from Versailles to Pearl Harbor* (New York: Garland, 1982); Ronald L. Feinman, *Twilight of Progressivism: The Western Republican Senators and the New Deal* (Baltimore: Johns Hopkins University Press, 1981).

4. James T. Patterson, *Mr. Republican: A Biography of Robert A. Taft* (New York: Knopf, 1972), 151.

5. Richard Coke Lower, *A Bloc of One: The Politics and Career of Hiram W. Johnson* (Stanford, Calif.; Stanford University Press, 1993); Peter Gerald Boyle, "The Study of an Isolationist: Hiram Johnson," Ph.D. diss., University of California, Los Angeles, 1970; Howard Arthur DeWitt, "Hiram W. Johnson and American Foreign Policy, 1917–1941," Ph.D. diss., University of Arizona, 1972.

6. Cole, *Nye*; John E. Wiltz, *In Search of Peace: The Senate Munitions Inquiry, 1934–1936* (Baton Rouge: Louisiana State University Press, 1963).

7. Patrick J. Maney, *"Young Bob" La Follette: A Biography of Robert M. La Follette, Jr., 1895–1953* (Columbia: University of Missouri Press, 1978); Alan Edmond Kent Jr., "Portrait in Isolationism: The La Follettes and Foreign Policy," Ph.D. diss., University of Wisconsin, 1956.

8. Richard Kay Hanks, "Hamilton Fish and American Isolationism, 1920–1944," Ph.D. diss., University of California, Riverside, 1971; Anthony C. Troncone, "Hamilton Fish, Sr., and the Politics of American Nationalism" Ph.D. diss., Rutgers University, 1993; Hamilton Fish, *Memoir of an American Patriot* (Washington, D.C.: Regnery Gateway, 1991).

9. Norman Jay Kaner, "Vito Marcantonio and American Foreign Policy," Ph.D. diss., Rutgers University, 1968; Louis Schaffer, *Vito Marcantonio: Radical in Congress* (Syracuse, N.Y.: Syracuse University Press, 1966).

10. Edward C. Blackorby, "Usher Lloyd Burdick," in *Dictionary of American Biography: Supplement Six, 1956–1960*, ed. John A. Garraty (New York: Scribner's, 1980), 85–87.

11. See, for example, Gary Dean Best, *Herbert Hoover: The Postpresidential Years, 1933–1964,* 2 vols. (Stanford, Calif.: Hoover Institution Press, 1983); Justus D. Doenecke, "The Anti-Interventionism of Herbert Hoover," *Journal of Libertarian Studies* 8 (Summer 1987): 311–40; Alfred L. Castle, "William R. Castle and Opposition to United States Involvement in an Asian War, 1939–1941," *Pacific Historical Review* 54 (August 1985): 337–51; Alfred L. Castle, *Diplomatic Realism: William R. Castle, Jr., and American Foreign Policy, 1919–1953* (Honolulu: Samuel N. and Mary Castle Foundation, 1998); Donald McCoy, *Landon of Kansas* (Lincoln: University of Kansas, 1966).

12. For Lewis, see Melvyn Dubofsky, "John L. Lewis and American Isolationism," in *Three Faces of Midwestern Isolationism,* ed. John H. Schacht (Iowa City, Iowa: Center for the Study of the Recent History of the United States, 1981), 23–33. For business and labor opinion, see William Arthur Weinrich, "Business and Foreign Affairs: The Roosevelt Defense Program, 1937–1941," Ph.D. diss., University of Oklahoma, 1971; John W. Roberts, *Putting Foreign Policy to Work: The Role of Organized Labor in American Foreign Relations, 1932–1941* (New York: Garland, 1995).

13. There is no general study of student opinion. For studies of left-wing activity, see Robert Cohen, *When the Old Left Was Young: Student Radicals and the First Mass Student Movement, 1929–1941* (New York: Oxford University Press, 1994); Eileen M. Egan, *Class, Culture, and the Classroom: The Student Peace Movement of the 1930s* (Philadelphia: Temple University Press, 1980); Dennis N. Mihelich, "Student Antiwar Activism during the Nineteen Thirties," *Peace and Change* 2 (Fall 1974): 29–40.

14. Richard H. Kendall, "Edwin M. Borchard and the Defense of Traditional American Policy," Ph.D. diss., Yale University, 1964; Justus D. Doenecke, "Edwin M. Borchard, John Bassett Moore, and Opposition to American Entry in World War II," *Journal of Libertarian Studies* 6 (Winter 1982): 1–34; Marshall R. Kuehl, "Philip C. Jessup: From America First to Cold War Interventionist," Ph.D. diss., Kent State University, 1985; Richard Megaree, "Realism in American Foreign Policy: The Diplomacy of John Bassett Moore," Ph.D. diss., Northwestern University, 1963.

15. Studies of Kennedy include Michael J. Beschloss, *Kennedy and Roosevelt: The Uneasy Alliance* (New York: Norton, 1980); David E. Koskoff, *Joseph P. Kennedy: A Life and Times* (Englewood Cliffs, N.J.: Prentice Hall, 1974); Richard J. Whalen, *The Founding Father: The Story of Joseph P. Kennedy* (New York: New American Library, 1964).

16. Patrick J. Hearden, "John Cudahy and the Pursuit of Peace," *Mid-America* 68 (April–June 1986): 99–114; Mark A. Stoler, "From Continentalism to Globalism: General Stanley Embick, the Joint Strategic Survey Committee, and the Military View of American National Policy during the Second World War," *Diplomatic History* 6 (Summer 1982): 303–21; Ronald Schaffer, "General Stanley D. Embick: Military Dissenter," *Military Affairs* 37 (October 1973): 89–95; Robert Hessen, ed., *Berlin Alert: The Memoirs and Reports of Truman Smith* (Stanford, Calif.: Hoover Institution Press, 1984); Jordan A. Schwarz, *Liberal: Adolf A. Berle and the Vision of an American Era* (New York: Free Press, 1987); Beatrice Bishop Berle and Travis Jacobs, eds., *Navigating the Rapids, 1918–1971: From the Papers of Adolf A. Berle* (New York: Harcourt Brace Jovanovich, 1973).

17. For Lindbergh's findings in Germany, see Hessen, *Berlin Alert.* Truman Smith was then U.S. military attaché to Germany. For superior material on the Lindberghs, see Cole, *Lindbergh; The Wartime Journals of Charles A. Lindbergh* (New York: Harcourt Brace Jovanovich, 1970); A. Scott Berg, *Lindbergh* (New York: Putnam's, 1998); Anne Morrow Lindbergh, *The Flower and the Nettle: Dairies and Letters, 1936–1939* (New York: Harcourt Brace Jovanovich, 1976); Anne Morrow Lindbergh, *War Within and Without: Diaries and Letters, 1939–1944* (New York: Harcourt Brace Jovanovich, 1980); Dorothy Herrmann, *A Gift for Life: Anne Morrow Lindbergh* (New York: Ticknor & Fields, 1993).

18. For Hearst circulation, see J. Percy Johnson, ed., *Directory of Newspapers and Publications* (Philadelphia: Ayer, 1940), 640, 645 (hereafter cited as *Ayer's,* followed by date of publication). By far the best work on Hearst's foreign policy is Rodney P. Carlisle, *Hearst and the New Deal: The Progressive as Reactionary* (New York: Garland, 1979). See also W. A. Swanberg, *Citizen Hearst* (New York: Scribner's, 1961). For Carter, see Boake Carter and Thomas H. Healy, *Why Meddle in the Orient? Facts, Figures, Fictions and Follies* (New York: Dodge, 1938); Boake Carter, *Why Meddle in Europe? Facts, Figures, Fictions and Follies* (New York: McBride, 1939). For the only scholarly work on Carter, see David H. Culbert, *News for Everyone: Radio and Foreign Affairs in Thirties America* (Westport, Conn.: Greenwood, 1976).

19. For Scripps-Howard circulation, see *Ayer's, 1941,* 676. There is no full-scale biography of Roy W. Howard. For superior sketches, see Alfred Lawrence Lorenz, "Roy W. Howard," in *Dictionary of Literary Biography,* vol. 29: *American Newspaper Journalists, 1926–1950,* ed. Perry G. Ashley (Detroit: Gale, 1984), 123–31; Irving Dilliard, "Roy Wilson Howard," in *Dictionary of American Biography: Supplement Seven, 1961–1965,* ed. John A. Garraty (New York: Scribner's, 1981), 369–70. For Howard and Roosevelt, see Graham J. White, *FDR and the Press* (Chicago: University of Chicago, 1979), 55–59. For the issue of a policy shift, see "Howard's Heart Change," *Time,* 10 March 1941, 59; "Neutrality Repeal," *San Francisco News* (hereafter cited as *SFN*), 25 September 1941, 14; "Undeclared War," *SFN,* 1 November 1941, 6.

20. For Johnson's book, see *Hell-Bent for War* (Indianapolis: Bobbs-Merrill, 1941). For his career, see John Kennedy Ohl, *Hugh S. Johnson and the New Deal* (DeKalb: Northern Illinois University Press, 1985). For endorsements from anti-interventionists, see business leader Robert E. Wood to Hugh Johnson, 30 April 1941, Box 56, the Papers of the America First Committee, Hoover Institution, Stanford, California (hereafter cited as AFC Papers); Nick Broughton, "Books in a World at War," *Peace Action* 7 (April 1941): 7.

21. Richard C. Frey Jr., "John T. Flynn and the United States in Crisis, 1928–1950," Ph.D. diss., University of Oregon, 1969; Michele Flynn Stenejem, *An American First: John T. Flynn and the America First Committee* (New Rochelle, N.Y.: Arlington House, 1976).

22. For Barnes on the New Deal, see Roy Carroll Turnbaugh Jr., "Harry Elmer Barnes: The Quest for Truth and Justice," Ph.D. diss., University of Illinois, 1977, 219–22, 234–35; for foreign policy, see 251. For Barnes on the war, see "Russian Tie-up with Nazis," *New York World-Telegram* (hereafter cited as *NYWT*), 3 October 1939, 18; "War Held No Armageddon," *NYWT,* 27 October 1939, 26; "Course of U.S. in the War," *NYWT,* 15 January 1939, 14. For correspondence concerning Barnes's firing, see Lee B. Wood to Harry Elmer Barnes, 1 and 11 May 1940, both in the Papers of Harry Elmer Barnes, University of Wyoming, Laramie (hereafter cited as Barnes Papers); Harry Elmer Barnes to Roy W. Howard, 7 May 1940 (hereafter cited as Howard Papers); Roy W. Howard to Harry Elmer Barnes, 11 May 1940 and 13 June 1940, the Papers of Roy W. Howard, Library of Congress, Washington, D.C.

23. For the *News's* circulation, see *Ayer's, 1942,* 669. There is no scholarly biography of Joseph Patterson. For brief sketches, see William V. Shannon, "Joseph Medill Patterson," in *Dictionary of American Biography: Supplement Three, 1941–1945,* ed. Edward T. James (New York: Scribner's, 1974), 645–46; "Joseph Medill Patterson," in *Current Biography, 1942,* ed. Maxine Block (New York: Wilson, 1943), 648–51; Ronald S. Marmarelli, "Joseph Medill Patterson," in *Dictionary of Literary Biography,* vol. 29, 269–84. For the debate over Maury, see George Britt, "Ethics for Editors," *New Republic* 105 (25 August 1941): 248–49; "Reuben Maury Replies," *New Republic* 105 (8 September 1941): 312.

24. For work on McCormick and his *Tribune,* see Frank J. Waldrop, *McCormick of Chicago: An Unconventional Portrait of a Controversial Figure* (Englewood Cliffs, N.J.: Prentice Hall, 1966); Jerome E. Edwards, *The Foreign Policy of Col. McCormick's Tribune, 1929–1941* (Reno: University of Nevada Press, 1971); Lloyd Wendt, *Chicago Tribune: The Rise of a Great American Newspaper* (Chicago: Rand McNally, 1979); Joseph Gies, *The Colonel of Chicago* (New York: Dutton, 1979); Richard Norton Smith, *The Colonel: The Life and Legend of Robert R. McCormick, 1880–1955* (Boston: Houghton Mifflin, 1997). For *Tribune* circulation, see *Ayer's, 1940,* 220.

25. Paul F. Healy, *Cissy: The Biography of Eleanor M. "Cissy" Patterson* (Garden City, N.Y.: Doubleday, 1966); Ralph G. Martin, *Cissy* (New York: Simon & Schuster, 1979). For *Times-Herald* circulation, see *Ayer's, 1941,* 155.

26. For biographies and autobiographies, see Felix Morley, *For the Record* (South Bend, Ind.: Regnery Gateway, 1979); Warren I. Cohen, *The Chinese Connection: Roger S. Greene, Thomas W. Lamont, George E. Sokolsky, and American–East Asian Relations* (New York: Columbia University Press, 1978); William Henry Chamberlin, *The Confessions of an Individualist* (New York: Macmillan, 1940); Robert Hobbs Myers, "William Henry Chamberlin: His Views of the Soviet Union," Ph.D. diss., Indiana University, 1973; Freda Utley, *Odyssey of a Liberal: Memoirs* (Washington, D.C.: Washington National Press, 1970). Comprehensive works are needed on Moley and Rascoe. Mencken has many biographies, including Charles A. Fecher, *Mencken: A Study of His Thought* (New York: Knopf, 1978). Sargent will be discussed in detail in chap. 14.

27. For *Post* circulation, see *Ayer's, 1942*, 842. For Garrett, see Carl Ryant, *Profit's Prophet: Garet Garrett* (Selinsgrove, Pa.: Susquehanna University Press, 1989). For Bess, see Demaree Bess, "Put Up or Shut Up," *Saturday Evening Post* 214 (22 November 1941): 14–15, 84–86; "Demaree (Caughey) Bess," in *Current Biography, 1943*, ed. Maxine Block (New York: Wilson, 1944), 40–41. For an interventionist attack on Bess's reporting, see "'Uncensored': Mr. Bess Visits German Europe," *Nation* 152 (18 January 1941): 62. On the *Post*'s supposed shift, see "The Peril," *Saturday Evening Post* 213 (24 May 1941): 28, 80. See also *NYT*, 17 May 1941, 1; 18 May 1941, 38; 21 May 1941, 12; "Satevepost Turns a Page," *Time*, 26 May 1941, 67; *Newsweek*, 2 June 1941, 17; Lillian Symes, "Hold That Line: *Satevepost* Capitulates," *Call*, 7 June 1941, 5. For claims that the *Post* was holding firm, see Robert L. Bliss, "The Saturday Evening Post," AFC Bulletin #283, 27 May 1941, Box 279, AFC Papers; Hanford MacNider to K. A. Greene, 31 October 1941, the Papers of Hanford MacNider, Herbert Hoover Presidential Library, West Branch, Iowa (hereafter cited as HHPL; MacNider Papers).

28. For its history, see Justus D. Doenecke, "*Scribner's Commentator*, 1939–1942," in *The Conservative Press in Twentieth-Century America*, ed. Ronald Lora and William Henry Longton (Westport, Conn.: Greenwood, 1999), 273–82. For its birth, see "Isolationist Organ," *Time*, 30 December 1940, 34. For Eggleston's own account, see *Roosevelt, Churchill, and the World War II Opposition: A Revisionist Autobiography* (Old Greenwich, Conn.: Devin-Adair, 1979). On bankers, see Henry Ford, "An American Foreign Policy," *Scribner's Commentator* 9 (December 1940): 30–36. On France, see "These Rule France" [picture essay], *Scribner's Commentator* 9 (January 1941): 13–20; Lois and Donaldson Thorburn, "Dear Elmer," *Scribner's Commentator* 8 (August 1940): 30–32, 41–42. On Portugal, see Paul R. Sanders, "Europe's Mildest Dictator," *Scribner's Commentator* 11 (November 1941): 31–36; On refugees, see Albert Hall, "Reviewing the Refugee Problem," *Scribner's Commentator* 10 (September 1941): 45–51; Howard M. Yates, *Scribner's Commentator* 10 (October 1941): 47–50. For work on Nock, see Robert M. Crunden, *The Mind and Art of Albert Jay Nock* (Chicago: Regnery, 1964); Michael Wreszin, *The Superfluous Anarchist: Albert Jay Nock* (Providence, R.I.: Brown University Press, 1972).

29. For a brief account, see John M. Muresianu, *War of Ideas: American Intellectuals and the World Crisis, 1938–1945* (New York: Garland, 1988), 127–30. For *New Republic* circulation, see *Ayer's, 1941*, 661. For contemporary suspicions concerning Mrs. Elmhirst's role, see Lillian Symes, "Hold That Line," *Call*, 15 February 1941, 5; Lawrence Dennis, *WFL* 131, (31 January 1941): 2; Sidney Hertzberg to Edmund Wilson, 29 August 1941, the Papers of Sidney Hertzberg, New York Public Library (hereafter cited as Hertzberg Papers); Norman Thomas to William Attwood, 1 February 1941, Norman Thomas to Bruce Bliven, 16 February 1941, both in the Papers of Norman Thomas, New York Public Library (hereafter cited as Thomas Papers); Fred Rodell, Yale law professor, to "Barbara," 1 February 1941, AFC Papers. For denial of Elmhirst intervention, see Bruce Bliven, *Five Million Words Later: An Autobiography* (New York: Day, 1970), 196–97. For a claim of Elmhirst intervention, see Michael Straight, *After Long Silence* (New York: Norton, 1983), 158–59. For the Flynn controversy, see Bruce Bliven to John T. Flynn, 4 November 1940, John T. Flynn to Bruce Bliven, 8 January 1941, the Papers of John T. Flynn, University of Oregon Library (hereafter cited as Flynn Papers); "A Communication: Mr. Flynn Speaks for Himself," *New Republic* 104 (3 February 1941): 148–50.

30. Donald L. Miller, *The New American Radicalism: Alfred M. Bingham and Non-Marxian Insurgency in the New Deal Era* (Port Washington, N.Y.: Kennikat, 1979); Alfred M. Bingham, *Insurgent America: Revolt of the Middle-Classes* (New York: Harper, 1935); Muresianu, *War of Ideas*, 130–33. For a summary of its foreign policy, see "Why Short of War?" *Common Sense* 10 (May 1941): 144–45. For Hanighen, see H. C. Engelbrecht and Frank Hanighen, *Merchants of Death: A Study of the International Armament Industry* (New York: Dodd, Mead, 1934).

31. For La Follette control, see Maney, *La Follette*, 234–35; Kent, "Portrait," 306–8. For a history of the journal, see John Alan Ziegler, "*The Progressive*'s Views on Foreign Affairs, 1909–1941: A Case Study of Liberal Economic Isolationism," Ph.D. diss., Syracuse University, 1970.

32. For Villard, see Stephen A. Thernstrom, "Oswald Garrison Villard and the Politics of Pacifism," *Harvard Library Bulletin* 14 (Winter 1960): 126–52; Michael Wreszin, *Oswald Garrison Villard: Pacifist at War* (Bloomington: Indiana University Press, 1965); Anthony Gronowicz, ed., *Oswald Garrison Villard: The Dilemma of the Absolute Pacifist in Two World Wars* (New York: Garland, 1983). For Williams,

see Maxine Block, ed., "Alford Joseph Williams, Jr., "*Current Biography, 1940* (New York: Wilson, 1941), 870–72. For Chase, see "Stuart Chase," in *Current Biography, 1940,* 162–64; James Carpenter Lanier, "Stuart Chase: An Intellectual Biography (1888–1940)," Ph.D. diss., Emory University, 1972; Stuart Chase with Marian Tyler, *The New Western Front* (New York: Harcourt Brace, 1939). There is no work on Ernest L. Meyer.

33. In January 1941, Cushman Reynolds became editor, and that July both Reynolds and Hertzberg shared the responsibility. By the summer of 1941, Hanighen became its Washington correspondent. Editorial sponsors included Barnes, Chase, Flynn, Meyer, Rascoe, Rodman, and Villard as well as columnist Dorothy Dumbar Bromley, *Fortune* editor John Chamberlain, and military writer Fleming MacLiesh. Among those intermittently with *Uncensored* were radio broadcaster Quincy Howe, editor George Leighton, Latin American expert Hubert Herring, author Ferdinand Lundberg, and journalists Marquis Childs, C. Hartley Grattan, and Richard Neuberger. For "shoestring," see Sidney Hertzberg to Morris L. Ernest, 30 January 1940. For circulation, see Hertzberg to Edmund Wilson, 29 August 1941. For examples of endorsements, see Boake Carter to Hertzberg, 30 November 1939; Abraham Kaufman, War Resisters League, to Hertzberg, 15 October 1940; advertising executive William Benton to Hertzberg, 3 October 1940, Hertzberg Papers.

34. Major work on Thomas and the Socialist Party includes W. A. Swanberg, *Norman Thomas: The Last Idealist* (New York: Scribner's, 1976); Bernard K. Johnpoll, *Pacifist's Progress: Norman Thomas and the Decline of American Socialism* (Chicago: Quadrangle, 1970); Stephen Mark Gens, "Paranoia Bordering on Resignation: Norman Thomas and the American Socialist Party," Ph.D. diss., University of Oklahoma, 1982; John Dennis McGreen, "Norman Thomas and the Search for an All-Inclusive Socialist Party," Ph.D. diss., Rutgers University, 1976.

35. Norman Thomas and Bertram D. Wolfe, *Keep America Out of War: A Program* (New York: Stokes, 1939), 145. Endorsements by anti-interventionists include Bruce Bliven, "KAOW," *New Republic* 102 (18 March 1940): 385; "Books in a World at War," *Peace Action* 6 (November 1939): 7. A second book, *We Have a Future* (Princeton, N.J.: Princeton University Press, 1941), stressed how socialism could stop the nation's drift toward the conflict.

36. For the story of Ameringer and the *Guardian*, see James R. Green, *Grass-Roots Socialism: Radical Movements in the Southwest, 1845–1943* (Baton Rouge: Louisiana State University Press, 1978); *If You Don't Weaken: The Autobiography of Oscar Ameringer* (New York: Holt, 1940). For circulation, see *Ayer's, 1941,* 780. For isolationism, see *American Guardian,* 19 January 1940, 4.

37. "Revised Reds," *Time,* 4 September 1939, 11. For descriptions of the party's condition, see Harvey Klehr, *The Heyday of American Communism: The Depression Decade* (New York: Basic Books, 1984); Maurice Isserman, *Which Side Were You On? The American Communist Party during the Second World War* (Middletown, Conn.: Wesleyan University Press, 1982); Samuel Walker, "Communists and Isolationism: The American Peace Mobilization, 1940–1941," *Maryland Historian* 4 (Spring 1973): 1–12.

38. Clarence Hathaway, former semiprofessional baseball player and tool and die maker, served as editor. In mid-1940, in an effort to avoid possible suppression, it formally cut party ties and became published by the nominally independent "Freedom of the Press, Inc." Louis F. Budenz, a labor journalist who joined the party in 1935, replaced Hathaway. At the time it had a daily circulation of close to fifty thousand and seventy-two thousand on Sundays. Isserman, *Which Side,* 72; *Ayer's, 1941,* 676. Benjamin J. Davis Jr. and Harold G. Bolt were also listed as editors though Budenz ran day-to-day operations. Hathaway was eventually expelled from the party. *NYT,* 13 January 1941, 1.

39. In November 1939, there were five editors: Crockett Johnson, A. B. Magil, Ruth McKenney, Joseph North, and Samuel Sillen. In 1940, it boasted a subscription of thirty-two thousand, placing it slightly ahead of the *New Republic.* See *Ayer's, 1941,* 661.

40. George Seldes, *Iron, Blood, and Profits: An Exposure of the World-Wide Munitions Racket* (New York: Harper, 1934). For Seldes's own account of *In Fact,* see his *Never Tired of Protesting* (New York: Stuart, 1968).

41. Editor Dan Gillmore, son of a retired admiral, denied he was a communist. Dan Gillmore, "A Reply to a Letter," *Friday,* 4 April 1941, 2. In 1940, circulation was 164,000. *Ayer's, 1941,* 650.

42. It was staffed by former employees of the interventionist New York daily *PM;* edited by Doris

Berger, daughter of a former socialist congressman from Milwaukee; and bankrolled by the William E. Dodd Foundation, a fund administered by two children of the former U.S. ambassador to Germany. See "Dodd's Memorial," *Time*, 31 March 1941, 42–43.

43. For an able description of American Trotskyism, see Constance Ashton Myers, *The Prophet's Army: Trotskyists in America, 1928–1941* (Westport, Conn.: Greenwood, 1977).

44. For *Partisan Review*, see James Burkhart Gilbert, *Writers and Partisans: A History of Literary Radicalism in America* (New York: Wiley, 1968); Michael Wreszin, *A Rebel in Defense of Tradition: The Life and Politics of Dwight Macdonald* (New York: Basic Books, 1994), chap. 5; Muresianu, *War of Ideas*, 133–35. For Burnham, see *The Managerial Revolution* (New York: Day, 1941); James Burnham, "Their Government," *Socialist Appeal*, 20 October 1939, 4. In February 1941, *Socialist Appeal*, which had been edited by Max Shachtman and Felix Morrow, became the *Militant*. For Draper, see "The Friends of the War Referendum," *New International* 5 (October 1939): 302–5.

45. For an extensive treatment of Dennis, see chap. 4 of this book. For the history of the bulletin, see Justus D. Doenecke, "*Weekly Foreign Letter*, 1938–1942," in Lora and Longton, *Conservative Press*, 283–94. For German financial support, see Klaus Kipphan, *Deutsche Propaganda in den Vereinigten Statten* (Heidelberg: Winter 1971), 174–75. For Dennis on mass base, see *WFL* 127, (2 January 1941): 1–3; 232 (6 February 1941): 1–2. Among the newsletter's subscribers were Oscar Ameringer, Harry Elmer Barnes, George T. Eggleston, H. L. Mencken, Gerald P. Nye, Albert Jay Nock, advertising executive Chester Bowles, international lawyer John Foster Dulles, pacifist leader Frederick J. Libby, publisher Porter Sargent, journalist Freda Utley, and German American propagandist George Sylvester Viereck. Subscription list, no date, Box 19, the Papers of Lawrence Dennis, Hoover Institution (hereafter cited as Dennis Papers).

46. There is no biography of Morrison. For brief portraits, see Justus D. Doenecke, "Charles Clayton Morrison," in *Biographical Dictionary of Modern Peace Leaders*, ed. Harold Josephson (Westport, Conn.: Greenwood, 1985), 664–66; "Apostle in Print," *Christian Century* 86 (16 March 1966), 323–25; "Voice of the Century," *Newsweek*, 23 June 1947, 72; Muresianu, *War of Ideas*, 54–59. For the *Christian Century* and foreign policy, see Donald B. Meyer, *The Protestant Search for Political Realism* (Berkeley: University of California Press, 1960), chap. 18. For peace views, see Morrison, *The Outlawry of War* (Chicago: Willett, Clark & Colby, 1927). On pacifism, see Morrison, testimony, SFRC, 6 February 1941, 630; "Light amid Chaos," *Christian Century* 57 (9 October 1940): 1241. For circulation, see *Ayer's, 1941*, 212.

47. The best source on Holmes is his own autobiography, *I Speak for Myself* (New York: Harper, 1959). For brief scholarly accounts, see Charles D. Benedetti, "John Haynes Holmes," in *Biographical Dictionary of Modern Peace Leaders*, 422–44; Ralph E. Luker, "John Haynes Holmes," in *Dictionary of American Biography: Supplement Seven*, 355–57. *Unity's* circulation in 1940 was six hundred. *Ayer's, 1941*, 226. In April 1941, it became a monthly. At that time, interventionist managing editor Curtis W. Reece and the journal's directors took *Unity* out of Holmes's hands, though Holmes continued to write anti-interventionist material under his own name. For Holmes's troubles with *Unity*, see John Haynes Holmes to Mrs. Helen B. Anthony, 24 April 1941; to editor, *Christian Leader*, 6 June 1941; to Llewellyn Jones, 14 April 1941, the Papers of John Haynes Holmes, Library of Congress (hereafter cited as Holmes Papers).

48. George Q. Flynn, *Roosevelt and Romanism: Catholics and American Diplomacy, 1937–1945* (Westport, Conn.: Greenwood, 1976), chap. 3.

49. Pound, "The Inedible: Russia Has It," *America* 62 (9 March 1940): 593–94. For a brief treatment, see Muresianu, *War of Ideas*, 73–78, 151–55. *America's* circulation was twenty-six thousand in 1941. *Ayer's, 1942*, 643.

50. There is no biography of Gillis. For brief sketches, see John Cogley, "James Martin Gillis," in *Dictionary of American Biography, Supplement Six*, ed. John A. Garraty (New York: Scribner's, 1980), 237–38; "Rev. James M(artin) Gillis," in *Current Biography, 1956*, ed. Marjorie Dent Candee (New York: Wilson, 1957), 214–16; Muresianu, *War of Ideas*, 78–82, 155–58.

51. Beginning in 1938, *Commonweal* was edited by Philip Burnham and Edward Skillin Jr., who had taken over an ailing journal and raised its circulation to a modest fourteen thousand by 1941.

*Ayer's, 1942,* 651. For divisions among the staff, see Edward R. Skillin Jr. to Justus D. Doenecke, 20 February 1970, in the author's possession. For a history, see Rodger Van Allen, *The* Commonweal *and American Catholicism: The Magazine, the Movement, the Meaning* (Philadelphia: Fortress, 1974). See also Muresianu, *War of Ideas,* 68–73, 149–51. On the editors, the only sketch existing is "Edward S. Skillin," in *Current Biography, 1949,* ed. Anne Rothe (New York: Wilson, 1950), 572–74.

52. Standard works on Coughlin include Sheldon Marcus, *Father Coughlin: The Tumultuous Life of the Priest of the Little Flower* (Boston: Little, Brown, 1973); Charles J. Tull, *Father Coughlin and the New Deal* (Syracuse, N.Y.: Syracuse University Press, 1965); Donald Warren, *Radio Priest: Charles Coughlin, the Father of Hate Radio* (New York: Free Press, 1996). Circulation of *Social Justice* was steadily declining, from 228,000 in 1939 to less than 185,000 by 1940. *Ayer's, 1940,* 441; *Ayer's, 1942,* 451. On Jewish bankers, see *Social Justice,* 8 August 1941, 3; emphasis the journal's. For wider matters of anti-Semitism and anti-interventionism, see Cole, *America First,* chap. 8; Cole, *Lindbergh,* chap. 21; Doenecke, *IDU,* 37–40, 390–401; Jonas, *Isolationism in America,* 253–56; and Edward S. Shapiro, "The Approach of War: Congressional Isolationism and Anti-Semitism, 1939–1941," *American Jewish History* 74 (September 1984): 45–65.

53. For Barnes, see Marcus, *Father Coughlin,* 290; Richard Griffiths, *Fellow Travellers of the Right: British Enthusiasts for Nazi Germany* (London: Constable, 1980), 16–17. Barnes gives his own views in *Fascism* (New York: Holt, 1931).

54. The best history of interwar pacifism remains Charles Chatfield, *For Peace and Justice: Pacifism in America, 1914–1941* (Knoxville: University of Tennessee Press, 1971).

55. Histories of the WIL include Carrie A. Foster, *The Women and the Warriors: The U.S. Section of the Women's International League for Peace and Freedom, 1915–1946* (Syracuse: Syracuse University Press, 1995); Anne Marie Pois, "The Politics and Process of Organizing for Peace: The United States Section of the Women's International League for Peace and Freedom, 1919–1939," Ph.D. diss., University of Colorado, 1988; Linda K. Schott, *Reconstructing Women's Thoughts: The Women's International League for Peace and Freedom* (Stanford, Calif.: Stanford University Press, 1997). For Balch, see Mercedes M. Randall, *Improper Bostonian: Emily Greene Balch* (New York: Twayne, 1964). Detzer sorely needs a biographer. For preliminary work, see Rosemary Rainbolt, "Women and War in the United States: The Case of Dorothy Detzer, National Secretary W.I.L.P.F.," *Peace and Change* 4 (Fall 1977): 18–22; Rainbolt, "Dorothy Detzer," in *Biographical Dictionary of Modern Peace Leaders,* 210–12. For Detzer's autobiography, see *Appointment on the Hill* (New York: Holt, 1948). For membership, see "Report of the National Organization Secretary to the Annual Meeting," Pittsburgh, 27–30 April 1940, the Papers of the Women's International League for Peace and Freedom, American Section, Swarthmore College Peace Collection (hereafter cited as WIL Papers; SCPC).

56. For scholarly work on Libby and the NCPW, see George Peter Marabell, "Frederick J. Libby and the American Peace Movement, 1921–1941," Ph.D. diss., Michigan State University, 1975; Justus D. Doenecke, "Frederick Joseph Libby," in *Biographical Dictionary of Modern Peace Leaders,* 562–64. Libby tells his own story in *To End War: The Story of the National Council for the Prevention of War* (New York: Fellowship Publications, 1969). For Libby's pacifism, see *NYT,* 6 February 1940, 6.

57. For Sayre, see Charles F. Howlett, "John Nevin Sayre and the International Fellowship of Reconciliation," *Peace and Change* 15 (April 1990): 123–49. The best study of Muste is Joann Ooiman Robinson, *Abraham Went Out: A Biography of A. J. Muste* (Philadelphia: Temple University Press, 1981), but for his views, see also A. J. Muste, *Nonviolence in an Aggressive World* (New York: Harper, 1940). Other contributors to *Fellowship* included Harold E. Fey, former educator in the Philippines and Sayre's predecessor as *Fellowship* editor, and Kirby Page, a prolific author who published a ninety-three-page manual, *How to Keep America Out of War* (pamphlet; Philadelphia: American Friends Service Committee et al., 1939). For Page's life, see Charles Chatfield and Charles DeBenedetti, eds., *Kirby Page and the Social Gospel: An Anthology* (New York: Garland, 1976); Harold E. Fey, ed., *Kirby Page, Social Evangelist: The Autobiography of a Twentieth Century Prophet for Peace* (Nyack, N.Y.: Fellowship, 1975). For membership, see minutes, executive committee, Fellowship of Reconciliation, 14 January 1941, 1, in the Papers of the Fellowship of Reconciliation, SCPC (hereafter cited as FOR Papers).

## CHAPTER 1: WAR, PHONY AND REAL

1. Chamberlain speech summary, *NYT*, 1 September 1939, 1, 3; German response, 2. For Chamberlain's text, see "Chamberlain Talk Announcing War," *NYT*, 4 September 1939, 8.

2. Former state department consul Ralph Townsend was almost alone in saying directly that Hitler might have had some justification for his invasion of Poland. Testimony, SFRC, 8 February 1941, 810.

3. Gallup poll, 30 August 1939, in Hadley Cantril with Mildred Strunk, *Public Opinion, 1935–1946* (Princeton, N.J.: Princeton University Press, 1951), 1075.

4. Oswald Garrison Villard, "Men and Events: London Blackout," *Nation* 149 (16 September 1939): 293; "The War Guilt," *Chicago Tribune* (hereafter cited as *CT*), 4 September 1939, 18. For a more modified opinion, see "The War the World Feared," *CT*, 2 September 1939, 10.

5. "Polish Corridor an Imperialist Jungle," *Call*, 16 September 1939, 2; Lindbergh, testimony, House Foreign Affairs Committee (hereafter cited as HFAC), 23 January 1941, 378; "Peace Terms Now," *Common Sense* 8 (October 1939): 16.

6. C. E. Black and E. C. Helmreich, *Twentieth Century Europe*, 3d ed. (New York: Knopf, 1966), 95.

7. For Wilson, see Congressman John M. Robsion (Rep.-Ky.), *CR*, 2 November 1939, 1925. For Lloyd George, see "The Fate of Poland," *Christian Century* 56 (20 September 1939): 1128; A. J. Muste, "At Versailles," *Christian Century* 58 (28 May 1941): 727; Hearst, "In the News," *San Francisco Examiner* (hereafter cited as *SFE*), 20 September 1940, 1; Nye, *CR*, 4 August 1941, 6672; Wheeler, *Williams* [College] *Record*, 15 April 1941, 1. *Social Justice*'s foreign correspondent J. S. Barnes noted that most of the British delegation at the Paris peace conference—including Lloyd George, Lord Curzon, Sir Eyre Crow, and General Jan Christian Smuts—opposed the Danzig/Corridor settlement. "The Real Issues of War," *Social Justice*, 9 October 1940, 7.

8. Fish, *CR*, 9 October 1939, 222; Edwin M. Borchard to James A. Shanley, 30 August 1939, the Papers of Edwin M. Borchard, Yale University Library (hereafter cited as Borchard Papers). See also Hugh Johnson, *SFN*, 5 July 1940, 17; William R. Castle to Edwin M. Borchard, 13 December 1940; John Bassett Moore to Edwin M. Borchard, 31 August 1939, Borchard Papers. Several months before war broke out, Borchard said that "Hitler has again been given a nearly perfect case to appear to the patriotism of the German people to break the barriers that England seeks to build around Germany." See Edwin M. Borchard to William P. Lage, 7 April 1939, Borchard Papers. For similar views of those more sympathetic to fascism, see poet Ezra Pound, "The Inedible: Russia Has It," *America* 62 (9 March 1940): 593–94; *Social Justice*, 4 September 1939, 7; Philip Johnson, "Poland's Choice Between War and Bolshevism Is a 'Deal' with Germany," *Social Justice*, 11 September 1939, 4.

9. Arnold A. Offner, "The United States and National Socialist Germany," in *The Fascist Challenge and the Policy of Appeasement*, ed. Wolfgang L. Mommsen and Lothar Kettenacker (London: Allen & Unwin, 1983), 415.

10. Cantril, *Public Opinion*, 1165.

11. P. M. H. Bell, *The Origins of the Second World War in Europe* (London: Longman, 1986), 250–51. For Hitler's terms to Foreign Minister Beck as conveyed on 5 January 1939, see "The German Demands on Poland," in *Documents on Nazism, 1919–1945*, ed. Jeremy Noakes and Geoffrey Pridham (New York: Viking, 1974), 55–58. For Hitler's first public divulgence of his terms, see text of Reichstag address, *NYT*, 29 April 1939, 10.

12. For outright profascist views, see "After Peace, What?" *Social Justice*, 30 October 1939, 9; George Sylvester Viereck, letter to editor, *New York Herald Tribune*, 27 September 1939, sect. 2, 11.

13. Harry Elmer Barnes to "Mr. Elliott," 14 February 1940, Barnes Papers; Waldrop, "The Voice of the Victim," *Washington Times-Herald* (hereafter cited as *WTH*), 8 July 1940, 6. See also Frederick J. Libby to Mrs. S. Foster Hunt, 1 June 1940, the Papers of the National Council for the Prevention of War, SCPC (hereafter cited as NCPW Papers); pacifist journalist Devere Allen, "Who Is Responsible for the War?" *Call*, 14 October 1939, 1; Senator D. Worth Clark (Dem.-Idaho), *CR*, 16 October 1939, 447.

14. "Chamberlain's Statement," *NYT*, 1 April 1939, 3; "The Text of the British-Polish Treaty," *NYT*, 26 August 1939, 4; Black and Helmreich, *Twentieth Century Europe*, 534.

15. The most thorough accounts of Fish's efforts are found in Hanks, "Hamilton Fish," 163–95, and Troncone, "Fish," chap. 18. For Fish and French officials, see *NYT*, 13 August 1939, 5. For his speech before Interparliamentary Union Conference, Oslo, 17 August 1939, see *CR*, A8–9. Fish was quoted as saying that "the great danger is that the Communists will provoke an incident in connection with Danzig to unleash war's furies." *Nation* 149 (19 August 1939): 183. See also *NYT*, 13 August 1939, 5; *NYT*, 18 August 1939, 4.

16. Fish, radio speech, NBC, 23 September 1939, in *CR*, A19–20. See also radio address, 18 April 1940, A2302. For Fish's later blame on Roosevelt for pressuring Britain and France into war, see Hamilton Fish, *FDR: The Other Side of the Coin* (New York: Vantage, 1976), 105–6.

17. Edwin M. Borchard to William Orton, 28 August 1939, Borchard Papers; the diary of Felix Morley, 2 September 1939, HHPL (hereafter cited as Morley Diary); Anne Morrow Lindbergh, entry of 18 August 1939, *War Within and Without*, 3; Charles A. Lindbergh, entry of 24 August 1939, *Wartime Journals*, 245.

18. Hugh Johnson, "One Man's Opinion," *SFN*, 5 July 1940, 17. See also "Neville Chamberlain Dead," *NYDN*, 12 November 1940, 25; William R. Castle to Edwin M. Borchard, 13 December 1940, Borchard Papers; the diary of William R. Castle, 1 September 1939, in Houghton Library, Harvard University, 28 February 1941 (hereafter cited as Castle Diary); Lawrence Dennis, *WFL* 93 (9 May 1940): 3; "The War Nobody Knows," *Christian Century* 56 (1 November 1939): 326; Congressman Harold Knutson (Rep.-Minn.), *CR*, 6 October 1941, 7682; Frank C. Waldrop, "Something in Common," *WTH*, 2 November 1939, 13; Waldrop, "Who Are We to Condemn?" 3 July 1940, 13; Waldrop, "The Voice of the Victim," 8 July 1940, 6; William Henry Chamberlin, "France in June: The Collapse," *Atlantic Monthly* 166 (September 1940): 302; Charles A. Lindbergh, testimony, SFRC, 6 February 1941, 559; Morley Diary, 2 September 1939; Gillis, "The War: What Else but the War?" *Catholic World* 150 (October 1939): 6.

19. Borah, *CR*, 2 October 1939, 73. See also Hugh Johnson, "Deadly Blundering," *NYWT*, 19 September 1939, 17; Hugh Johnson, "Join or Die," 23 January 1940, 17; Harry Elmer Barnes to "Mr. Elliott," 14 February 1940, Barnes Papers; Barnes, "Poland Victim of Exploiters," *NYWT*, 22 December 1939, 12; D. Worth Clark, *CR*, 14 October 1939, 447; John P. Delaney, "Stay Out of It!" *America* 61 (16 September 1939): 532–33; A. J. Muste to H. W. Foote, 28 October 1941, FOR Papers; Rep. Daniel Reed (Rep.-N.Y.), *CR*, 19 March 1941, 2372; Senator Rush Holt (Dem.-W.Va.), *CR*, 18 October 1940, 551; Nye, radio address, 30 September 1939, in *CR*, A83.

20. See, for example, attorney Amos Pinchot to Roy Howard, 1 February 1939; publisher Frank E. Gannett to Amos Pinchot, 11 February 1939, the Papers of Amos Pinchot, Library of Congress (hereafter cited as Pinchot Papers); "Chamberlain Resigns," *NYDN*, 4 October 1940, 37.

21. See, for example, Joseph P. Kennedy, radio speech, 29 October 1940, in *CR*, A6539; Chicago attorney Clay Judson, "Is This Our War?" n.d., Box 56, AFC Papers; General Robert E. Wood to P. I. B. Lavan, 20 December 1940, AFC Papers; "Munich and After," *CT*, 22 November 1940, 12; "But Boake Carter Says," *SFE*, 4 October 1940, 17. At one point, Hugh Johnson, who had attacked the agreement, claimed that the Western powers were too weak to do anything else. "One Man's Opinion," *SFN*, 13 December 1940, 25; Joseph P. Kennedy in entry of 11 June 1940, George Bilainkin, *Diary of a Diplomatic Correspondent* (London: Allen & Unwin, 1942), 105.

22. Dennis, *WFL* 117 (24 October 1940): 2. See also Dennis, *WFL* 85 (14 March 1940): 1, 3; Dennis, *The Dynamics of War and Revolution* (New York: Weekly Foreign Letter, 1940), 201–2.

23. Chamberlin, "France in June: The Collapse," 298. See also Chamberlin, *Confessions*, 264; Hearst, "In the News," *SFE*, 26 March 1940, 1; "Political Consequences of the Nazi-Soviet Pact," *Social Justice*, 18 September 1939, 7; memorandum of conversation, Herbert Hoover and Cordell Hull, 28 February 1941, the Papers of Herbert Hoover, HHPL (hereafter cited as Hoover Papers); Stanton B. Leeds, "The Lesson of France," *Scribner's Commentator* 8 (April 1941): 64.

24. For those parts of the treaty made public, see "Text of the Berlin-Moscow Treaty," *NYT*, 24 August 1939, 1. For the nonpublished terms, see "Secret Additional Protocol," in *World War II Policy and Strategy: Selected Documents with Commentary*, ed. Hans-Adolf Jacobsen and Arthur L. Smith Jr. (Santa Barbara, Calif.: ABC-Clio, 1979), 25–26.

25. Browder quoted in "Children of Moscow," *Time*, 18 September 1939, 12; Draper, "The Case of the Stupid Statesmen," *New Masses* 32 (5 September 1939): 3. In contrast, James Burnham, Trotskyist professor of philosophy at New York University, called the pact a definite capitulation to Hitler, who

received more advantages than the Soviet Union. It resulted from the determination of the Russian bureaucracy to destroy minority opposition and seize land. Burnham, *Washington Square College* [New York University] *Bulletin*, 23 October 1939, 4.

26. Coughlin, "What of the Future?" broadcast dated 27 August 1939, in *Social Justice*, 4 September 1939, 15. See also Father Edward Lodge Curran, address at Cincinnati, *Social Justice*, 25 August 1939, 3; Curran, "Here and There," *Social Justice*, 4 September 1939, 4. For earlier anxiety, see "What Is the Cost?" *Social Justice*, 12 June 1939, 6.

27. "How's the Nerves, Buddy?" *NYDN*, 31 August 1939, 25. See also "Surprise from Stalin," *NYDN*, 23 August 1939, 31; Dennis and Gravenhoff, *WFL* 56 (25 August 1939): 2. Dennis and Gravenhoff also predicted that the alliance would lead to "a let-up" on Germany's Jews. Jews were no longer needed as scapegoats once the British and capitalists were playing its role. *WFL* 64 (19 October 1939): 5.

28. Borah, *CR*, 2 October 1939, 73; Barnes, "Russian Tie-up with Nazis," *NYWT*, 3 October 1939, 18; Barnes, "Russian Pact with Nazis," *NYWT*, 20 October 1939, 26. Barnes cited with approval foreign correspondent John Gunther, "Behind the Pact," *Living Age* 357 (October 1939): 122–25.

29. "Surprise from Stalin," *NYDN*, 23 August 1939, 31. See also "Status Quo Ante 1914," *NYDN*, 25 August 1939, 25.

30. Johnson, "Deadly Blundering," *NYWT*, 19 September 1939, 17. See also Villard, "Issues and Men," *Nation* 149 (19 September 1939): 499.

31. "What the Hitler Stalin Pact Means for the World," *Social Justice*, 4 September 1939, 7. See also Coughlin, "A Statement to the Press," 4 September 1939, 1; "Political Consequences of the Nazi–Soviet Pact," 18 September 1939, 7.

32. Lloyd George, *Daily Worker*, 29 September 1939, 2; Shaw, 21 September 1939, 1. On Lloyd George, see also draft memo, 29 September 1939, Box 276, the Papers of Ernest Lundeen, Hoover Institution (hereafter cited as Lundeen Papers). For Lloyd George's statement, see *NYT*, 28 September 1939, 5. For Shaw, see *NYT*, 20 September 1939, 8.

33. For samples of outrage, see Waldrop, "No Surprise in Red Attack on Poland," *WTH*, 28 September 1939, 7; "Behind the Bombers' Curtain," *WTH*, 20 August 1940, 10; "What Stalin Has Lost" *New Republic* 101 (27 September 1939): 197; "Russia Shakes the World," *New Republic* 101 (27 September 1939), 200–201.

34. John Bassett Moore to Edwin M. Borchard, 11 October 1939, Borchard Papers; "British Diplomacy and the War," *NYDN*, 24 September 1939, 15; "The Social Revolution," 29 September 1939, 35; "Stalin Cuts Himself Another Piece of Cake," 4 October 1939, 39; "Red 'Missionaries' in Poland," 19 October 1939, 35; "Tragic Poland," 25 January 1940, 27. For an attack on a recent trade treaty with the Soviets, see "What about Russia?" *CT*, 25 October 1939, 14.

35. "What about Russia?" *CT*, 25 October 1939, 14; James Gillis, "What Are They Fighting For?" *Catholic World* 150 (December 1939): 259; Chester Bowles to Philip La Follette, 28 September 1939, the Papers of Philip La Follette, State Historical Society of Wisconsin, Madison, Wisconsin (hereafter cited as Philip La Follette Papers); Ben Marcin [pseud.], "Fight Bolshevism at Home Before Fighting It Abroad," *Social Justice*, 16 October 1939, 3; D. Worth Clark, *CR*, 24 February 1941, 1296; John P. Delaney, "Why Fight in Their War? Why?" *America* 62 (14 October 1939): 6. Of the more mainline anti-interventionists, retired diplomat William R. Castle took a different position, claiming that such a declaration of war would get England and France "nowhere" and might do much damage. Castle Diary, 18 September 1939. See also C. Hartley Grattan, "The Struggle for Peace," *Harper's Magazine* 180 (February 1940): 300–301. According to Ezra Pound, no force could get Russia out of eastern Poland in a hundred years. "The Inedible: Russia Has It," *America* 62 (9 March 1940): 594.

36. "Britain Approves Russia's Polish Grab," *Christian Century* 56 (8 November 1939): 1363. See also "The War Nobody Knows," *Christian Century* 56 (1 November 1939): 1327; Congressman John Rankin (Dem.-Miss.), *CR*, 1 November 1939, 1172. For an attack on Halifax, see Frank Waldrop, "Something in Common," *WTH*, 2 November 1939, 13. For Halifax's own statement, see *NYT*, 27 October 1939, 2.

37. Norman Thomas to Franklin D. Roosevelt, 23 September 1939, Thomas Papers; Norman Thomas, "Your World and Mine," *Call*, 11 November 1939, 2. For a similar comment about better conditions under Soviet rule, see "Russia Shakes the World," *New Republic* 101 (27 September 1939): 200–201.

38. See, for example, John Bassett Moore to George H. Ryden, 19 September 1939, Moore Papers.

39. Congressman Lewis D. Thill (Rep.-Wis.), *CR*, 30 October 1939, 595. Davis, *CR*, 4 March 1940, 2290; Fish, *CR*, 9 October 1939, 222; Lindbergh, testimony, SFRC, 6 February 1941, 511; *Daily Worker*, 5 September 1939, 6.

40. See, for example, "Remember Poland," *America* 62 (10 February 1940): 491; "Atrocities: 1940" *Catholic World* 150 (March 1940): 641; James McCawley, "Atrocities—Fact and Fiction," *Catholic World*, 152 (September 1940): 724–28.

41. On Warsaw, see "Causes, Effects and Potentialities of Christian Poland's Assassination," *Social Justice*, 2 October 1939, 15. On Hitler, see 6. For acknowledgment of German atrocities, see 25 November 1940, 12. For other manifestations of sympathy with Poland, see 16 October 1939, 20; 23 October 1939, 17; 4 March 1940, 16; "Poland—A 'Lost' People," 31 March 1941, 9.

42. See, for example, Holmes, "The Plight of the Jews," *Unity* 124 (1 January 1940): 137; Devere Allen, "Chaos in Conquered Poland," *Unity* 125 (18 March 1940): 26; Frank C. Waldrop, "This Winter in Poland," *WTH*, 4 December 1939, 7; writer Milton Mayer, "I Think I'll Sit This One Out," *Saturday Evening Post* 212 (7 October 1939): 97.

43. Villard, "Issues and Men: The Latest Anti-Jewish Horror," *Nation* 149 (December 1939): 735. Moreover, he said, every Jew in Germany or Czechoslovakia "sits in his home expecting with every ring of the doorbell that his death sentence has arrived." Villard, *NYT*, 6 January 1940, 12.

44. Johnson, "Polish Jews," *NYWT*, 11 January 1940, 13. See also Johnson, "One Man's Opinion," *SFN*, 1 February 1940, 13.

45. Hoover, *CT*, 12 February 1941, 5.

46. Dorothy Detzer to Emily Greene Balch, 4 November 1939, WIL Papers. Borchard accused William C. Bullitt, American ambassador to France, of telling Anthony J. Drexel Biddle Jr., U.S. ambassador to Poland, to exaggerate atrocity stories so as to influence the congressional debates on neutrality legislation. Edwin M. Borchard to William E. Borah, 29 September 1939, Borchard Papers. For another suspicion of atrocity accounts in Poland, see Fish, radio address, 18 April 1940, in *CR*, A2302.

47. "New Books," *Catholic World* 152 (November 1940): 253.

48. See, for example, John Haynes Holmes to Harry Ward, 31 October 1939, Holmes Papers; "Polish Persecution," *Uncensored* 19 (10 February 1940): 2.

49. Wheeler, *CR*, 11 October 1939, 287. See also John Haynes Holmes, "A Holy War!" *Unity* 124 (6 November 1939): 67; "Europe's Fateful Hour," *Christian Century* 56 (6 September 1939): 1063; Harry Elmer Barnes, "War Held No Armageddon," *NYWT*, 27 October 1939, 26.

50. See, for example, Upton Close [Josef Washington Hall], "Common Sense for Americans," *Living Age* 358 (August 1940): 511; "But Boake Carter Says," *SFE*, 16 September 1939, 13; "To the Brink," *St. Louis Post-Dispatch*, 11 June 1940.

51. Harry Elmer Barnes, "Poland Victim of Exploiters," *NYWT*, 22 December 1939, 12, citing Max Nomad [Max Podolsky], "Poland Without a Halo," *American Mercury* 48 (December 1939): 442–48. Barnes's column was endorsed by the dissident Trotskyite Max Schactman. See "In This Corner," *Socialist Appeal* 4 (6 January 1940): 3. See also Barnes, "World's Fate in Balance," *NYWT*, 13 October 1939, 2.

52. "The Fate of Poland," *Christian Century* 56 (20 September 1939): 1128. See also Flynn, "Other People's Money: First-Person Singular," *New Republic* 101 (6 September 1939): 131.

53. Lillian Symes to Oscar Lange, 7 November 1939, Thomas Papers.

54. "The Fate of Poland," *Christian Century* 56 (20 September 1939): 1128. See also Dorothy Detzer to Mrs. Robert E. Park, 1 November 1939, WIL Papers.

55. Robsion, *CR*, 2 November 1939, 1296.

56. Barnes, "Poland Victim of Exploiters," *NYWT*, 22 December 1939, 12. See also Harry Elmer Barnes to "Mr. Elliott," 14 February 1940, Barnes Papers; "Realism and the Coming Peace Treaty," *Christian Century* 58 (9 April 1941): 485.

57. H. L. Mencken, "Notes on a Moral War," *Baltimore Sun*, 8 October 1939. See also "Dying for Danzig," *CT*, 22 September 1939, 14; "What Hinders Peace?" *Christian Century* 56 (18 October 1939): 1264.

58. McCormick, address to American Legion banquet, *CT*, 26 September 1939, 4. For additional attacks on Britain, see *Social Justice*, 2 October 1939, 4; Coughlin, "From the Tower," *Social Justice*, 25 September 1939, 5; Theodore Draper, "Hanging the Kaiser in 1940," *New Masses* 34 (20 February 1940): 7.

59. Kennedy in William C. Rock, *Chamberlain and Roosevelt: British Foreign Policy and the United States, 1937–1940* (Columbus: Ohio State University Press), 236; H. L. Mencken, "Notes on a Moral War," *Baltimore Sun*, 8 October 1939.

60. Barton, *CR*, 18 June 1940, 8545. For similar views, see Senator Bennett Champ Clark (Dem.-Mo.), 14 October 1939, 402; Waldrop, "The Help That Never Came," *WTH*, 8 October 1939, C13; Dennis and Gravenhoff, *WFL* 60 (21 September 1939): 2–3; Senator Lynn D. Frazier (Rep.-N.Dak.), *CR*, 14 October 1939, 402. In March 1940, the *Chicago Tribune* conceded that it might have been impossible for Poland's allies to come to its aid, though the Poles should not have been led to believe such aid was possible. See "Reproaches from Mr. Stanley," 24 March 1940, 14.

61. For Hoover's activities, see George J. Lerski, comp., *Herbert Hoover and Poland: A Documentary History of a Friendship* (Stanford, Calif.: Hoover Institution Press, 1977), 43–45, 101–12; Hal Elliott Wert, "The Specter of Starvation: Hoover, Roosevelt, and American Aid to Europe, 1939–1941," Ph.D. diss., University of Kansas, 1991, chap. 1. See also Wert, "U.S. Aid to Poles Under Nazi Domination, 1939–1940," *Historian* 57 (Spring 1995): 511–24; Castle Diary, 29 February 1940, 27 March 1940, 16 April 1940.

62. Wiley, *CR*, 9 February 1940, 1288; Fish, *CR*, 24 January 1940, 643.

63. See, for example, Senator Arthur H. Vandenberg (Rep.-Mich.), *CR*, 4 October 1939, 104; William J. Bulow (Dem.-S.Dak.), *CR*, 12 October 1939, 313; "The Defense of Warsaw," *CT*, 24 September 1939, 1; "Lessons from Poland," *CT*, 17 September 1939, 16; "Poland Will Rise Again," *New Republic* 101 (4 October 1939): 227. For less optimistic views, see "What About Russia?" *CT*, 15 October 1939, 14; Delaney, "Why Fight in Their War? Why?" *America* 62 (14 October 1939): 6; "To the Editor and the Readers," *America* 62 (6 January 1940): 343.

64. Thill, *CR*, 30 October 1939, 595.

65. "Not Our War," *CT*, 2 September 1939, 10. The independent socialist weekly *American Guardian* considered the editorial important enough to put some of it on page 1 with approval. Issue of 8 September 1939.

66. Taft, "Nonpartisanship in Domestic and Foreign Policy, " speech at Milwaukee, 19 January 1940, in *CR*, A364. For a similar view, see John P. Delaney, "Stay Out of It!" *America* 61 (16 September 1939): 532–33.

67. *Fortune* poll of October 1939, Cantril, *Public Opinion*, 1185. For related polls, see 1185.

68. See, for example, Senator Henry Cabot Lodge (Rep.-Mass.), *CR*, 10 October 1939, 39; Lodge, speech to New York Herald Tribune Forum, 16 October 1939, in *CR*, A553; "Who Will Win?" *New Republic* 101 (13 September 1939): 145, quoting military writer George Fielding Eliot; Amos Pinchot to "Ranny" [Randolph Walker], 29 September 1939, Pinchot Papers.

69. Johnson, "One Man's Opinion," *SFN*, 8 November 1939, 17.

70. "But Boake Carter Says," *SFE*, 9 September 1939, sect. SF, 3. See also Senator Sheridan Downey (Dem.-Calif.), *CR*, 6 October 1939, 171; Hoover, interview with Roy Howard dated 3 October 1939, in *CR*, 13 October 1939, 366 (hereafter cited as Hoover, Roy Howard interview).

71. Hoover and Lindbergh in Lindbergh entry of 2 October 1939, *Wartime Journals*, 269; Lindbergh in Castle Diary, 2 September 1939. See also Senator Edwin C. Johnson (Dem.-Colo.), speech delivered Mutual, Minneapolis, entered *CR*, 28 September 1939, A62; Dennis and Gravenhoff, *WFL* 65 (26 October 1939): 1.

72. Hoover, Roy Howard interview. For a similar view, see Congressman Robsion, *CR*, 2 November 1939, 1296.

73. "But Boake Carter Says," *SFE*, 9 October 1939, 13. For further confidence in Allied air power, see Downey, *CR*, 6 October 1939, 171.

74. Lindbergh, entry of 22 October 1939, *Wartime Journals*, 280. Lindbergh added that he had long been convinced that the Germans would have soon complete supremacy of the air and "hold about the

same place in European air that England held on European seas." Indeed, he felt it desirable that Germany regain strength, for he found a strong Germany was essential to the welfare of Europe. He did not like to see England fall so far behind in air strength, because he regarded "a strong British Empire essential to world stability."

75. Hugh Johnson, "War Stalemate," *NYWT*, 13 October 1939, 25.

76. "Guide to the War," *CT*, 3 September 1939, 6. The *Tribune* did concede that though air power might not be decisive within the first thirty days, it might prove so in the final outcome, for the nation that controlled the air would know of enemy movements. For similar stress on ground protection, see Hoover, Roy Howard interview.

77. Dennis and Gravenhoff, *WFL* 73 (21 December 1939): 2–3; *WFL* 68 (16 November 1939): 2; *WFL* 79 (1 February 1940): 2.

78. "But Boake Carter Says," *SFE*, 20 September 1939, sect. SF, 3. For similar views, see historian Eric F. Goldman, *Johns Hopkins Newsletter*, 10 November 1939, 1; John T. Flynn, "Economic Odds on the Allies," *NYWT*, 12 December 1939, 22.

79. Hoover, Roy Howard interview. See also Thill, *CR*, 3 November 1939, 815.

80. "The Unlimited Claim to Relief," *Commonweal* 30 (13 October 1939): 545; Raymond Moley to H. C. Chatfield-Taylor, 16 December 1939, the Papers of Raymond Moley, Hoover Institution (hereafter cited as Moley Papers).

81. See, for example, "Inside Germany," *Uncensored* 2 (14 October 1939); "Who Will Win?" *New Republic* 101 (13 September 1939): 146; Edwin M. Borchard to Leslie H. Thompson, 12 October 1939, Borchard Papers. For a dissenting picture stressing German prosperity, see Porter, Bulletin #22, 15 December 1939; Sargent, *Getting US into War* (Boston: Porter Sargent, 1941), 198, 208 n. 4.

82. See, for example, Hugh Johnson, speech to Veterans of Foreign Wars, *SFE*, 9 October 1939, 11; Hiram Johnson, *CR*, 20 October 1939, 631; sermon of Harry Emerson Fosdick, Riverside Church, New York, 1 October 1939, *CR*, A339.

83. Taft, *CR*, 13 October 1939, 356. See also Taft speech, Vienna, Illinois, 20 September 1939, A76; "Nonpartisanship in Foreign and Domestic Policy," speech at Milwaukee, 19 January 1940, A364.

84. Reynolds, *CR*, 21 October 1939, 698.

85. For Caesar, see Congresswoman Jessie Sumner (Rep.-Ill.), *CR*, 1 November 1939, 1258; Congressman Knute Hill (Dem.-Wash.), *CR*, 13 November 1941, 8857. For Napoleon, see Hiram Johnson in *CR*, 20 October 1939, 631; B. C. Clark, *CR*, 17 February 1941, 1044; Hill, *CR*, 13 November 1941, 8857; Taft, "Shall the United States Enter the European War?" radio address, 17 May 1941, in *CR*, A2344; A. J. Muste, "A Plea to Enlist," *Fellowship* 6 (September 1940): 103.

86. For skepticism concerning any German revolution, see "The Indian Summer of This War," *CT*, 19 November 1939, 12.

87. Flynn, "War Economy Vital Factor," *NYWT*, 20 September 1939, 22. See also Flynn, "Other People's Money: War on the Home Front," *New Republic* 101 (30 September 1939): 188.

88. Bulow, *CR*, 12 October 1939, 312; Barton, *CR*, 26 October 1939, 1163; "But Boake Carter Says," *SFE*, 20 September 1939, Sect. SF, 3. Anne Morrow Lindbergh was one anti-interventionist who challenged any idea of internal collapse. See entry of 9 September 1939, *War Within*, 51. See also "How Long Will the War Last?" *NYDN*, 7 September 1939, 33, which pointed to a strong German general staff and the Soviet alliance.

89. See, for example, "Oswald Garrison Villard on the Present European Situation," attached to NCPW minutes, 20 December 1939, NCPW Papers; "Issues and Men: Germany Has Power," *Nation* 149 (25 November 1939): 582; "Issues and Men: Communism from Above," *Nation* 149 (16 December 1939): 681; "My Four Weeks in Nazi Germany," *Look*, 12 March 1940, 14–19; *Daily Northwestern*, 14 February 1940, 1–2. For reference to his meeting with Roosevelt, see Oswald Garrison Villard to Franklin D. Roosevelt, 7 January 1940, the Papers of Franklin D. Roosevelt, Roosevelt Presidential Library, Hyde Park, New York (hereafter cited as Roosevelt Papers).

90. Villard, *Yale Daily News*, 31 January 1940, 1, 3.

91. Oswald Garrison Villard, *Within Germany* (New York: Appleton-Century-Crofts, 1940). For praise, see Margaret Marshall, "Faith, Hope, and Clarity," *Nation* 150 (2 March 1940): 312; unsigned,

*NYT Book Review*, 18 February 1940, 6; John C. DeWilde, "Behind the Westwall," *Saturday Review of Literature*, 17 February 1940, 15; Bruce Bliven, "Behind the Westwall," *New Republic* 102 (25 March 1940): 416; Joseph Barnes, *New York Herald Tribune Book Review*, 11 February 1940, 6; Porter Sargent to Oswald Garrison Villard, 3 August 1940, the Papers of Oswald Garrison Villard, Harvard University (hereafter cited as Villard). *Time* printed a summary of the book with no editorial comment. See "Liberal Among Nazis," 29 January 1940, 28.

92. See, for example, "Our Army," *Call*, 11 November 1939, 4; Lillian Symes to Oscar Lange, 7 November 1939, Thomas Papers. For the claim that Germany could only be changed by revolution, see Paul Porter, "The Struggle of the Empires," *Call*, 23 September 1939, 2.

93. Thomas, "Your World and Mine," *Call*, 2 December 1939, 2; "Tragic Poland," *NYDN*, 25 January 1940, 27.

94. See, for example, "Can England Lick Germany in an Offensive War?" *NYDN*, 21 September 1939, 37.

95. Hoover, Roy Howard interview; Hoover and Lindbergh in Lindbergh, entries of 2 October 1939, *Wartime Journals*, 269; Lindbergh in Castle Diary, 2 September 1939; Hearst, "In the News," *SFE*, 26 March 1940, 1.

96. See, for example, Nye, *CR*, 13 October 1939, 365; Congressman Roy O. Woodruff (Rep.-Mich.), 13 October 1939, 387; Congressman James A. Shanley (Dem.-Conn.), *CR*, 31 October 1939, 1116; Norman Thomas to George V. Denny, 30 March 1940, Thomas Papers; Libby, "Shall We Try to Stop the War in Europe?" *Peace Action* 6 (March 1940): 1, based on "The Periscope," *Newsweek*, 18 March 1940, 11; "Invincible Uncle Sam," *NYDN*, 7 April 1940, 43; "The First World War," *St. Louis Post-Dispatch*, 31 March 1940; "Nazi Aims," *Uncensored* 21 (24 February 1940): 4.

97. Rankin, *CR*, 23 October 1939, 762. See also Frazier, *CR*, 13 October 1939, 401; B. C. Clark, *CR*, 14 October 1939, 402; Reynolds, *CR*, 21 October 1939, 692.

98. Johnson, speech delivered Mutual, Minneapolis, in *CR*, 28 September 1939, A62.

99. "Allies Can Win," *NYDN*, 22 December 1939, 23. See also "A War to Finality," 4 September 1939, 21; "The Third Quarter Is the Hardest," 9 September 1939, 15; "A Christmas Truce—Why Not?" 22 November 1939, 37. In March, it claimed the Allies had an even chance of winning a long conflict. "Will the Allies Win?" 11 March 1940, 21.

100. Hugh Johnson, "Where Are We?" *NYWT*, 20 September 1939, 25; Dennis and Gravenhoft, *WFL* 65 (26 October 1939): 1; *WFL* 68 (16 November 1939): 2.

101. "Finland Falls: But War Is Not Yet Over," *SFE*, 16 May 1940, 8; Borah, *NYT*, 19 September 1939, 13; Johnson, "One Man's Opinion," *SFN*, 28 February 1940, 13; Ameringer, "What Price Plutocracy?" *American Guardian*, 22 September 1939, 4. See also "But Boake Carter Says," *SFE*, 16 March 1940, 9.

102. One anti-interventionist, however, did not believe the phony war could last. Charles A. Lindbergh feared heavy losses. Anne Morrow Lindbergh, entry of 20 September 1939, *War Within*, 60.

103. Frazier, *CR*, 13 October 1939, 401; Bruce Bliven, "I Like a Phony War," *New Republic* 150 (18 October 1939): 291–92. See also Lillian Symes to Oscar Lange, 11 November 1939, Thomas Papers.

104. See, for example, Fred L. Israel, ed., *The War Diary of Breckinridge Long: Selection from the Years 1939–1944* (Lincoln: University of Nebraska Press, 1966), 10, 13; Long in Rock, *Churchill and Roosevelt*, 236; Joseph P. Kennedy to Roosevelt, 30 September 1939, in William L. Langer and S. Everett Gleason, *The Challenge to Isolation: The World Crisis of 1937–1940 and American Foreign Policy* (New York: Harper & Brothers, 1952), 252; Kennedy to Hull, 12 September 1939, in *Foreign Relations of the United States, 1939*, vol. 1: *General* (Washington, D.C.: U.S. Government Printing Office, 1956), 551–52. For an exception, see William C. Bullitt, entry of 11 February 1940, in *The Secret Diary of Harold L. Ickes*, vol. 3: *The Lowering Clouds, 1939–1941* (New York: Simon & Schuster, 1954), 133.

105. Stark in Joseph P. Lash, *Roosevelt and Churchill, 1939–1941: The Partnership That Saved the West* (New York: Norton, 1976), 87.

106. Hull in Breckinridge Long, entry of 2 September 1939, *War Diary*, 1.

107. Berle, entry of 23 March 1940, *Navigating*, 299; Long, entry of 23 March 1940, *War Diary*, 71; Ickes, entry of 26 August 1939, in *The Secret Diary of Harold L. Ickes*, vol. 2: *The Inside Struggle, 1936–1939* (New York: Simon & Schuster, 1954), 704.

108. Ickes, entry of 11 November 1939, *Secret Diary*, 3:60.

109. Roosevelt in Ickes, entry of 14 October 1939, *Secret Diary*, 3:37; David Reynolds, *The Creation of the Anglo-American Alliance, 1937–1941: A Study in Competitive Co-operation* (Chapel Hill: University of North Carolina Press, 1982), 67.

110. David Reynolds, "1940: Fulcrum of the Twentieth Century," *International Affairs* 66 (April 1990): 329.

111. Norman Thomas to John Newton Thurber, 8 September 1939, Thomas Papers; Rankin, *CR*, 9 October 1939, 210. See also Reynolds, *CR*, 21 October 1939, 692; "Peace Terms Now," *Common Sense* 8 (October 1939): 16–17.

112. See for example, Barnes, "U.S. Held Key to War Course," *NYWT*, 11 October 1939, 32; Hugh Johnson, "One Man's Opinion," *SFN*, 10 October 1939, 13.

113. *SFE*, 14 October 1939, 15. It continued that offsetting this possibility were White House assurances to the Allies pledging full American support.

114. For armistice report and French troops, see Barton, *CR*, 1 November 1939, 1163. For British agents, see *Christian Century* 56 (6 December 1939): 1491. For *Graf Spee*, see *SFE*, 25 December 1939, 15. The two British agents hoped to make contact with dissident figures in the German military. John Costello, *Ten Days to Destiny: The Secret Story of the Hess Peace Initiative and British Efforts to Strike a Deal with Hitler* (New York: Morrow, 1991), 64, 533 n. 38.

115. Borah, *WTH*, 3 February 1940, 2. See also Castle Diary, 26 September 1939.

116. Hoover in Lindbergh, 2 October 1939, *Wartime Journals*, 269. See also James Burnham, "Their Government," *Socialist Appeal*, 10 November 1939, 4; Roy W. Howard to Nelson T. Johnson, 19 January 1940, Howard Papers; Libby, "Immediate Mediation the Hope of the World," *Peace Action* 6 (January 1940): 1, drawing on British ambassador Lothian's speech to Chicago Council of Foreign Relations, *NYT*, 5 January 1940, 4; military writer Hanson Baldwin, "Factors Are Forming to Prevent War Deadlock," *NYT*, 7 January 1940, 4E; Porter Sargent, Bulletin #22, 15 December 1939, *Getting US into War*, 205–6.

117. Anne Morrow Lindbergh, entry of 3 September 1939, *War Within*, 47–48, quotation on page 48; Charles A. Lindbergh, entry of 1 September 1939, *Wartime Journals*, 249; Villard, "Issues and Men: Will Hitler Strike at England?" *Nation* 150 (16 March 1940): 366. See also Villard, "Issues and Men: Germany Has Power," *Nation* 149 (25 November 1939): 581; Villard, *Yale Daily News*, 31 January 1940, 1; "Villard Says Germans Are Confident," *Progressive*, 4 May 1940, 3.

118. "War on Two Fronts," *NYDN*, 14 February 1940, 29. See also "Now for the Real War—Maybe," *NYDN*, 5 April 1940, 31; Dennis and Gravenhoff, *WFL* 85 (14 March 1940): 5.

119. See, for example, Joseph P. Kennedy to Roosevelt, 30 September 1939, in Langer and Gleason, *Challenge to Isolation*, 252; report of Kennedy to army and navy officers, 15 December 1939, in Langer and Gleason, *Challenge to Isolation*, 345; Patrick J. Hearden, "Cudahy," 108. Such anxieties were not limited to anti-interventionists. See diary entry, 3 September 1939, in Claude Denson Pepper with Hays Gorey, *Eyewitness to a Century* (New York: Harcourt Brace Jovanovich, 1987), 92.

120. Anne Morrow Lindbergh, "A Prayer for Peace," *Reader's Digest* 36 (January 1940): 5.

121. See, for example, Reynolds, *CR*, 21 October 1939, 691; *SFE*, 10 October 1939, 1, 6, quoting George Bernard Shaw; Waldrop, "Who Is Now Boss in the Balkans?" *WTH*, 18 March 1940, 7; Dennis and Gravenhoff, *WFL* 60 (21 September 1939): 6. By late October, Dennis and Gravenhoff were suspecting that Germany and Russia might well have decided on an eventual partition of the Balkans. Involved might be a swift Russian war against Turkey. *WFL* 65 (26 October 1939): 6. Once the Finnish crisis took place, Dennis and Gravenhoff found Stalin in Hitler's power. *WFL* 75 (4 January 1940): 2.

122. "The Winner, Red Josef," *CT*, 10 March 1940, 12. On 17 November 1939, the *Tribune* also printed a Shaw article saying that the two neutrals, the United States and Russia, were the war's real winners. *CT*, 1, 9. For other claims that Russia had won or would win the war, see also Delaney, "Why Fight in Their War? Why?" *America* 62 (14 October 1939): 6; Chicago investor Sterling Morton, address to Illinois Manufacturers Association, 13 October 1939, the Papers of Sterling Morton, Chicago Historical Society (hereafter cited as Morton Papers); Barton, *CR*, 1 November 1939, 1163.

123. See, for example, "The Partition of Poland," *New Republic* 101 (4 October 1939): 230; Bliven, "I Like a Phony War," 291; Ameringer, *American Guardian*, 13 October 1939, 1.

124. Thomas, *Wesleyan* [University] *Argus*, 12 October 1939, 4.

125. See, for example, "Peace Talk," *NYDN*, 30 September 1939, 17; Senator Dennis Chavez (Dem.-N.Mex.), *CR*, 25 October 1939, 826; Hugh Johnson, "One Man's Opinion," *SFN*, 8 November 1939, 17; Hugh Johnson, "If Hitler Wins, America Will Be Next—'Bunk'," *Look*, 21 November 1939, 13–15. When a United Press report from London noted that Britain and the exiled Polish government would not ask Russia to restore the Polish territory it grabbed, the *New York Daily News* asked if the Allies intended to destroy Hitlerism and bolster Stalinism. "What Are the Allies' War Aims?" 21 October 1939, 15.

126. "Oswald Garrison Villard on the Present European Situation," attached to NCPW minutes, 20 December 1939, NCPW Papers; Ickes, entry of 4 February 1940, *Secret Diary*, 3:123.

127. Knickerbocker lecture quoted in *American Guardian*, 15 December 1939, 2. See also *SFE*, 11 October 1939, sect. SF, 5.

128. Hamilton Fish, radio speech of 27 November 1939, as reprinted in Fish, *The Red Plotters* (New York: Domestic and Foreign Affairs Publishers, 1947), 37. See also Robert A. Taft, *Congressional Digest* 18 (October 1939): 245; D. W. Clark, *CR*, 16 October 1939, 448.

129. See, for example, "Retrospect," *Christian Century* 56 (27 December 1939): 1598; Fish, *CR*, 1 November 1939, 1170; Fish, speech, NBC, 28 October 1939, in *CT*, 701; entry of 28 September 1939, revisionist writer Francis Neilson, *The Tragedy of Europe: A Day-to-Day Commentary of the Second World War*, 5 vols. (Appleton, Wis.: C. C. Nelson, 1940–46), 1:79; Dorothy Dunbar Bromley, [City College of New York] *Campus*, 10 November 1939, 1.

130. Reynolds, *CR*, 21 October 1939, 691. For other predictions of designs on India, see J. S. Barnes, "Big Drive to India Soviet Aim in 1940," *Social Justice*, 8 January 1940, 3, 18. See also J. S. Barnes, "Possible Developments of the War in Europe," *Social Justice*, 26 February 1940, 9; J. S. Barnes, "The Situation in India," *Social Justice*, 13; Dennis and Gravenhoff, *WFL* 70 (30 November 1939): 4.

131. Dondero, *CR*, 31 October 1939, 1133; Norman Thomas to Franklin D. Roosevelt, 8 October 1939, Thomas papers; "Stalin Is 59," *NYDN*, 14 October 1939, 15. For other *News* comments concerning the Soviet Union, see "Stalin Cuts Himself Another Piece of Cake," 4 October 1939, 39; "The Dry Peter the Great," 10 October 1939, 29; "The War on the Neutral Fronts," 24 November 1939, 49; "As We've Said Before—," 2 December 1939, 15; "Stalin is 60, Hitler Is 50," 22 December 1939, 33.

132. Ben Marcin [pseud. for *Social Justice* staff], "Fight Bolshevism at Home Before Fighting It Abroad," *Social Justice*, 16 October 1939, 3; *Social Justice*, 20 November 1939, 3. See also J. S. Barnes, *Social Justice*, 9 October 1939, 7. For the fictitious use of name "Ben Marcin," see Marcus, *Father Coughlin*, 254.

133. See, for example, Breckinridge Long, entries of 26 September 1939, *War Diary*, 20; 5 October 1939, 24–25; 11 October 1939, 26–27. See also entry of 1 September 1939 in Nancy Harvison Hooker, ed., *The Moffat Papers: Selections from the Diplomatic Journals of Jay Pierrepont Moffat, 1919–1943* (Cambridge, Mass.: Harvard University Press, 1956), 261.

134. Ickes, entry of 14 October 1939, *Secret Diary*, 3:37.

135. Ickes, entry of 13 September 1939, *Navigating*, 254. See also 3 March 1940, 292; 21 March 1940, 297.

136. Lippmann quoted in Thomas R. Maddux, *Years of Estrangement: American Relations with the Soviet Union, 1933–1941* (Tallahassee: University Presses of Florida, 1980), 107; Roosevelt to Joseph P. Kennedy, 30 October 1939, in *F.D.R.: His Personal Letters, 1928–1945*, ed. Elliott Roosevelt (New York: Duell, Sloan & Pearce), 949.

## CHAPTER 2: EARLY HOPES FOR PEACE

1. "Text of Chancellor Adolf Hitler's Address on His War Aims Before the German Reichstag," *NYT*, 7 October 1939, 8. See also "Text of Hitler's War Relief Speech," Berlin, *NYT*, 11 October 1939, 4.

2. Norman Thomas to Franklin D. Roosevelt, 8 October 1939, Thomas Papers; Holmes, "Anti-war Sentiment," *Unity* 124 (20 November 1939): 88; Holmes, "How Long Will This War Go On?" *Unity* 124 (4 December 1939): 103; Fey, "America's Greatest Opportunity," *Fellowship* 5 (November 1939): 3. For a more cautious statement of Thomas, see *Wesleyan* [University] *Argus*, 12 October 1939, 1.

3. "What Hinders Peace?" *Christian Century* 56 (18 October 1939): 1264–65. See also "The War Nobody Wants" (4 October 1939): 1191; "Neutral Monarchs Make New Peace Appeal" (22 November 1939): 1427–28.

4. See, for example, David Lawrence, "Peace Bids by Neutrals Traditional," *Washington Evening Star*, 9 October 1939; *Daily Worker*, 14 October 1939, 1; "The Asiatic Barbarism in Europe," *CT*, 4 December 1939, 14; "Peace Now or After Exhaustion?" *CT*, 5 December 1939, 14; Edwin Johnson, *SFE*, 8 October 1939, Sect. 1, 17; Edwin Johnson, *CR*, 9 October 1939, 174; Frazier, *CR*, 14 October 1939, 402.

5. *SFE*, 11 October 1939, sect. SF, 5. The Hearst press kept up its optimism into the following year. See *SFE*, 13 February 1940, 1. For an administration focus on Goering, see Breckinridge Long, entry of 11 October 1939, *War Diary*, 27–28.

6. Edwin M. Borchard to Leslie H. Thompson, 10 October 1939, Borchard Papers.

7. Castle Diary, 19 September 1939. Hitler denied that he coveted territory of Britain or France and claimed that Germany desired lasting peace. "Text of Chancellor Hitler's Speech at Danzig Professing His Desire for Peace," *NYT*, 20 September 1939, 18.

8. Villard, "Europe Longs for Peace: An Analysis of Europe Today," *Peace Action* 6 (January 1940): 4, 8; "Issues and Men," *Nation* 150 (27 January 1940): 101. Villard had said earlier that the vast majority of Britons were determined to eliminate the German menace by force of arms. "Issues and Men," *Nation* 150 (28 October 1939): 469.

9. "Hitler Proposes," *New Republic* 101 (18 October 1939): 283–84.

10. "Chamberlain's 89% No," *NYDN*, 4 October 1939, 39; Dennis and Gravenhoff, *WFL* 68 (16 November 1939): 3–4; *WFL* 75 (4 January 1940): 3; "What Price Plutocracy?" *American Guardian*, 22 September 1939, 4; "Peace at Hitler's Price," *New Republic* 101 (4 October 1939): 225. Gerhard L. Weinberg sees Goering as wanting more time for economic preparations and thereby genuinely interested in a respite in hostilities. *A World at Arms: A Global History of World War II* (New York: Cambridge University Press, 1994), 89.

11. Chamberlain, address to Commons, *NYT*, 13 October 1939, 4.

12. See, for example, "Hitler Is 50, Chamberlain Is 70," *NYDN*, 14 October 1939, 15; Paul Mallon, "The News Behind the News," *SFE*, 10 November 1939, 15; Frazier, *CR*, 14 October 1939, 402; D. Worth Clark, *CR*, 16 October 1939, 446.

13. *SFE*, 11 October 1939, sect. SF, 5.

14. "Oswald Garrison Villard on the Present European Situation," attached to NCPW minutes, 20 December 1939, NCPW Papers. Villard might well have been referring to a speech Churchill made on 12 November in which the admiralty chief said that "either all that Britain and France stand for in the modern world will go down, or that Hitler, the Nazi regime and the recurring German or Prussian menace will be broken and destroyed." See "Text of Churchill's War Broadcast," *NYT*, 13 November 1939, 4. The *New Masses* blamed Churchill for declining a Soviet-backed peace offer, hence "revealing thereby how sinister and thoroughgoing the war against Germany will become should Churchill come to the helm in England." See "The Peace Offer," 33 (10 October 1939): 23.

15. Wheeler, *SFE*, 8 October 1939, sect. 1, 17; Borah, *NYT*, 23 October 1939, 8; "Unity in Washington," *Uncensored* 6 (4 November 1939): 3; "Of Things to Come," *Uncensored* 9 (2 December 1939): 3; C. Hartley Grattan, "The Struggle for Peace," *Harper's Magazine* 180 (January 1940): 304; "Oswald Garrison Villard on the Present European Situation."

16. David Reynolds, "Churchill and the British 'Decision' to Fight On in 1940," in *Diplomacy and Intelligence During the Second World War*, ed. Richard Langhorne (New York: Cambridge University Press, 1985), 151–52. See also C. A. MacDonald, *The United States, Britain, and Appeasement, 1936–1939* (New York: St. Martin's, 1981), 177. On 10 September, Chamberlain had thought that Mussolini had viable peace proposals. See Rock, *Chamberlain and Roosevelt*, 215.

17. Andrew Roberts, *"The Holy Fox": A Life of Lord Halifax* (London: Macmillan, 1991), 177.

18. For Churchill on genuine offer, see Reynolds, *Creation*, 9, 84; Clive Ponting, *1940: Myth and Reality* (Chicago: Dee, 1990), 97; Martin Gilbert, *Winston S. Churchill*, vol. 6: *Finest Hour, 1939–1941* (Boston: Houghton Mifflin, 1983), 57.

19. John Haynes Holmes to Robert Whitaker, 16 October 1939, Holmes Papers.

20. For the role of Lloyd George, see Paul Addison, "Lloyd George and the Compromise Peace in the Second World War," in *Lloyd George: Twelve Essays*, ed. A. J. P. Taylor (London: Hamilton, 1971), 368. For interventionist attention, see "Life on the Newsfronts of the World: Ancients for Peace," *Life*, 16 October 1939, 22.

21. "Text of the Chamberlain and Lloyd George Statements in the House of Commons," *NYT*, 4 October 1939, 4. See also *NYT*, 10 October 1939, 5; 22 October 1939, 35. For a later reiteration of Lloyd George's call for negotiations, see Bilainkin, entry of 28 July 1940, *Diary*, 169.

22. Lloyd George, *SFE*, 15 October 1939, Sect. 1, 16; news stories in *SFE*, 14 October 1939, 15; 22 October 1939, 16; "The Role of the Neutrals," *New Masses* 33 (17 October 1939): 21. See also "What Hinders Peace?" *Christian Century* 56 (18 October 1939): 1264; *Daily Worker*, 13 October 1939, 1.

23. Rankin, *CR*, 1 November 1939, 1171. For optimism, see Hearst–Lloyd George correspondence, "In the News," *SFE*, 25 May 1941, A; memo, conversation of Herbert Hoover and Joseph P. Kennedy, 22 November 1940, Hoover Papers; Dennis, *WFL* 150 (12 June 1941): 3; *WFL* 168 (16 October 1941): 5; "Aid to Churchill," *Uncensored* 107 (18 October 1941): 2–3. For pessimism, see Villard, "Men and Events," *Nation* 150 (11 May 1940): 599; diary of William Henry Chamberlin, 19–26 April 1941, Providence College (hereafter cited as Chamberlin Diary).

24. For Shaw, see *NYT*, 10 October 1939, 4; 28 August 1939, 4. For communist backing, see *Daily Worker*, 25 September 1939, 1; *New Masses* 33 (7 November 1939): 21; Joseph Starobin, "God Better Save the King," *New Masses* 33 (14 November 1939): 16; J. B. S. Haldane, "Britain's Writers Under the Bombs," *Daily Worker*, 3 September 1940, 13. For other endorsements, see *American Guardian*, 29 September 1939, 1; Downey, *CR*, 9 October 1939, 190; Frazier, *CR*, 14 October 1939, 399; Holt, *CR*, 18 October 1939, 547.

25. "Let Mr. Chamberlain Be Specific!" *Christian Century* 56 (27 October 1939): 1295; "Neutral Monarchs Make New Peace Appeal," *Christian Century* 56 (22 November 1939): 1428. Those listed by the *Century* as asking FDR to mediate included Bishop of Chichester G. K. A. Bell, Methodist leader Leslie Weatherhead, Labor party members George Lansbury and Richard R. Stokes, classical scholar Cyril Bailey, and philosopher C. E. M. Joad.

26. Lansbury, "No New World by War," *Fellowship* 5 (December 1939): 2–3; "'Peace Now' Drive Gets New Support," *Peace Action* 6 (January 1940): 6.

27. For forty Labor candidates, Lanarkshire miners, the fifty thousand members of the Ayrshire Federation of the Labor Party, and the Scottish cooperative movement, see Joseph Starobin, "God Better Save the King," *New Masses* 33 (14 November 1939): 16. For Wells, see *Daily Worker*, 29 March 1940, 1. For Maxton and the ILP, see the *Call*, 30 September 1939, 2. For other accounts of various trade unions, see Allen Hunt, "Cannon, Not Butter, Says Chamberlain," *New Masses* 35 (9 April 1940): 13; "British Labor Calls for Peace," *New Masses* 35 (9 April 1940): 14.

28. Castle Diary, 26 September 1939; "Oswald Garrison Villard on the Present European Situation"; Edwin M. Borchard to Leslie H. Thompson, 12 October 1939, Borchard Papers. In January, Borchard thought that the British might be satisfied with "some kind" of Czechoslovakia or Poland but that FDR wanted a "knockout" on Germany. See Edwin M. Borchard to Oswald Garrison Villard, 31 January 1940, Borchard Papers.

29. "What Price Plutocracy?" *American Guardian*, 22 September 1939, 4.

30. Libby, "Truce, with Neutral Mediation, Only Solution," *Peace Action* 6 (October 1939): 2; "War in Europe: A Statement by the 1939 National Conference of the Fellowship of Reconciliation," *Fellowship* 5 (October 1939): 4; Harold E. Fey, "America's Greatest Opportunity," *Fellowship* 5 (October 1939): 3; Ernest Fremont Tittle, "How Can Hitler Be Stopped?" *Fellowship* 5 (October 1939): 6–7; Holmes, "How Can Hitler Be Stopped?" *Fellowship* 5 (September 1939): 4, citing Sir Arthur Salter, *Security: Can We Retrieve It?* (London: Macmillan, 1939).

31. "After This War, What?" *NYDN*, 15 October 1939, 47. The *News* continually maintained that economic pressures were pushing Europe in the direction of larger and fewer states. See "Status Quo Ante 1914," *NYDN*, 25 August 1939, 25.

32. Barnes, "World's Fate in Balance," *NYWT*, 13 October 1939, 26; Barnes, "Course of U.S. in the War," 16 January 1940, 14; Hearden, "Cudahy," 108.

33. The Czechs and Poles would been given commercial, but not political, rights to a Baltic port. In addition, "the Mongols" with "their Red banner" would be ejected from the lands they had seized. It said the economic claims of smaller nations could be satisfied without disturbing anyone's rights. See "Hope of Peace Persists," *CT*, 2 January 1940, 12. See also "Europe's Hope for Peace," 11 February 1940, graphic section, 1. In February, it called for peace pleas by the neutral peoples. See "Peace Now or After the Final Battle," 26 February 1941, 10.

34. "The Belgium-Holland Mediation Offer," *Commonweal* 30 (17 November 1939): 85.

35. Herbert Hoover to John Callan O'Laughlin, 18 February 1940, O'Laughlin–Hoover correspondence filed separately in Hoover Institution Archives (hereafter cited as Stanford Files). Norman Thomas to George Denny Jr., 30 March 1940, Thomas Papers. At the same time, the *Call* endorsed mediation. "Mediation Now," *Call*, 2 March 1940, 4.

36. For rumors of a "behind-the-scenes" effort by Pius to sponsor a peace conference, out of which would result a Polish buffer state designed according to ethnic lines, see *NYT*, 28 September 1939, 1, 5.

37. For endorsements of papal efforts, see Norman Thomas, "Your World and Mine," *Call*, 6 January 1940, 2; "What Are the Allies' War Aims?" *NYDN*, 17 September 1939, 33; "Peace Talk," *NYDN*, 30 September 1939, 17; "The Pope Calls for Peace," *NYDN*, 26 March 1940, 21; entry of 29 September 1939, Francis Neilson, *Tragedy*, 1:81. At one point, the *NYDN* even mentioned Mussolini, who was not yet a belligerent. "Peace Talk," 30 September 1939, 17. Weinberg notes that Mussolini wanted additional time to prepare for war with Britain and France. See *World at Arms*, 90.

38. See, for example, "Mediation Now," *Call*, 2 March 1940, 4.

39. "Text of King Leopold's Appeal for Peace Negotiations," and statement of Hubert Pierlot, Belgian foreign minister, *NYT*, 24 August 1939, 5. The seven nations included Belgium, the Netherlands, Luxembourg, Denmark, Sweden, Finland, and Norway. See, for example, "King Leopold of Belgium Makes Move for Peace," *Christian Century* 56 (8 August 1939): 1036; "Can the United States Stay Out of the War?" *Commonweal* 30 (15 September 1939): 465.

40. "Visit," *NYT*, 7 November 1939, 1, 21; "Text of Two Rulers' Offer," *NYT*, 8 November 1939, 4. For a previous secret bid to Roosevelt, see Ickes, entry of 17 October 1939, *Secret Diary*, 3:39; Roosevelt to Joseph E. Davies [October 1939], *F.D.R.: His Personal Letters*, 938–39. For the monarchs' fears, see *The Memoirs of Cordell Hull*, 2 vols. (New York: Macmillan, 1948), 1:712.

41. See, for example, *SFE*, 9 November 1939, 12; "The Appeal for Peace," *CT*, 9 November 1939, 14; "European Devil Dance," *NYDN*, 9 November 1939, 33; "Royal Gestures for Peace," *Daily Worker*, 9 November 1939, 6.

42. Frederick J. Libby, "Belgium and Holland Have Right to Protest," *Peace Action* 6 (November 1939): 2; John Nevin Sayre, [New York University] *Heights Daily News*, 10 November 1939, 1; "Neutral Monarchs Make New Peace Appeal," *Christian Century* 56 (22 November 1939): 1427–28; "Oswald Garrison Villard on the Present European Situation"; Villard, "Europe Longs for Peace: An Analysis of Europe Today," *Peace Action* 6 (January 1940): 1, 8; Villard, "Issues and Men," *Nation* 150 (27 January 1940): 101.

43. Senators Richard Russell (Dem.-Ga.), Alva Adams (Dem.-Colo.), James E. Murray (Dem.-Mont.), Ernest W. Gibson (Rep.-Vt.), and Clyde L. Herring (Dem.-Iowa) all endorsed the bid. *SFE*, 10 November 1939, 1, 9; 11 November 1939, 2.

44. Clark, *SFE*, 11 November 1939, 2. Roosevelt in Langer and Gleason, *Challenge to Isolation*, 265–66; Pius, *SFE*, 11 November 1939, 2.

45. *NYT*, 7 October 1939, 1, 3; Hearst correspondent Karl H. Von Wiegand, *SFE*, 3 October 1939, 1. The Germans officially denied such an appeal. *NYT*, 14 October 1939, 3.

46. Kennedy to Roosevelt, 3 November 1939, in Beschloss, *Kennedy and Roosevelt*, 194. See also Kennedy to Cordell Hull, 13 September 1939, in *Foreign Relations, 1939*, 1:423–24.

47. Lothian in Rock, *Chamberlain and Roosevelt*, 234. William Allen White to Bruce Bliven, 23 September 1939, in *Selected Letters of William Allen White*, ed. Walter Johnson (New York: Holt, 1947), 398.

48. See, for example, John Nevin Sayre, *United States News*, 30 October 1939, 4; report, national secretary to national board, WIL, 21–22 October 1939, 5; Dorothy Detzer to Greta Engkvist, 23 January 1940, WIL Papers; minutes, governing committee, Keep America Out of War Congress, 29 September 1939, the Papers of the Keep America Out of War Congress, SCPC (hereafter cited as KAOWC Papers); "Europe's Fateful Hour," *Christian Century* 56 (6 September 1939): 1063. For peace leaders encouraged by resolutions introduced by Senator Edwin C. Johnson calling for presidential initiative, see "To Stop War and Build Peace," *Peace Action* 6 (October 1939): 3; Dorothy Detzer to Emily Greene Balch, 9 October 1939, WIL Papers; minutes, annual meeting, WIL, 29 April 1940, Pittsburgh, 1, WIL Papers.

49. Conversation summarized in Oswald Garrison Villard to Franklin D. Roosevelt, 17 January 1940, Roosevelt Papers. For an earlier bid for presidential mediation, see Villard to Roosevelt, 20 October 1939, Roosevelt Papers. See also "Oswald Garrison Villard on the Present European Situation"; Ickes, entry of 4 February 1940, *Secret Diary*, 3:123. For another statement that both the German people and foreign office sought peace, see Villard, "Issues and Men: Germany Has Power," *Nation* 149 (25 November 1939): 581. For other references to Villard's call for a negotiated peace, see Villard comments, General Staff, Neutrality Bloc, 8 January 1940, KAOWC Papers; Villard to Cordell Hull, undated, Villard Papers; [University of Rochester] *Tower Times*, 23 February 1940, 1.

50. *NYDN*, 8 December 1939, 39. The newspaper said FDR's hand would be strengthened if he invited the pope and Mussolini to join his bid. See also "Why Not Make the Armistice Official?" 9 January 1940, 31; "Big Shots and Little Shots," 12 March 1940, 25. *News* columnist Doris Fleeson claimed that FDR was "bitterly angry" at Hitler for suggesting to certain correspondents that FDR mediate, but at the same time, "the President would like nothing better than a bona fide offer to assume the role of mediator of the Second World War." "Capitol Stuff," 16 October 1939, 4.

51. Johnson, *CR*, 9 October 1939, 174; Wheeler, *SFE*, 8 October 1939, sect. 1, 17; Fish, radio speech, NBC, 28 October 1939, in *CR*, A701. Wheeler's views were supported by senators Arthur Capper (Rep.-Kans.), Holt, and Reynolds, and Congressman Rankin. *CR*. See also Senator Ernest Lundeen (Farmer-Lab.–Minn.) in *Newsweek*, 23 October 1939, 28. See also Senators Pat McCarran (Dem.-Nev.) and Elbert D. Thomas (Dem.-Utah) and Congressman Rankin in *NYT*, 8 October 1939, 3. For Frazier, see *CR*, 14 October 1939, 402. At the convention of the American Federation of Labor in Cincinnati, the delegates endorsed their council's recommendation that FDR offer his services as mediator. *NYT*, 2 October 1939, 1, 8; *Time*, 16 October 1939, 28.

52. Hugh Johnson, *SFN*, 10 October 1939, 13. For a general call for U.S. mediation, see Johnson, *SFN*, 20 September 1939, 13.

53. Nye, *CR*, 13 October 1939, 363. For other linkages of negotiations to retention of the neutrality legislation, see Congressman James A. Shanley, *CR*, 31 October 1939, 1116; Harold E. Fey, "Save Neutrality! Save Peace!" *Christian Century* 56 (11 October 1939): 1236. Senator John A. Danaher (Rep.-Conn.) claimed in June 1940 that repeal of the arms embargo ruined an impending negotiated peace. *CR*, 3 June 1940, 7375.

54. Edwin M. Borchard to John Bassett Moore, 3 January 1940, Borchard Papers; Libby, "Truce, with Neutral Mediation, Only Solution," *Peace Action* 6 (October 1939): 2. Libby also blamed Roosevelt for not backing the mediation efforts of the Dutch and Belgian monarchs. See "Immediate Negotiation the Hope of the World," *Peace Action* 6 (January 1940): 1. Roosevelt, Libby said, would take no steps without Allied approval. Minutes, General Staff, Neutrality Bloc, 8 January 1940, KAOWC Papers. Libby always maintained this position. See also Libby, testimony, HFAC, 14 October 1941, 71. See also Hugh Johnson, "U.S. Peace Role," *NYWT*, 25 January 1940, 15.

55. See, for example, "The Role of the Neutrals," *New Masses* 32 (17 October 1939): 21; "But Boake Carter Says," *SFE*, 22 December 1939, 9; "F.D.R.'s Four F's," *Uncensored* 8 (25 November 1939): 1. The newsletter predicted that the British Foreign Office would tell Roosevelt when it sought peace. "In Washington," *Uncensored* 15 (13 January 1940): 1.

56. Norman Thomas to Franklin D. Roosevelt, 8 October 1939, Thomas Papers; Franklin D. Roosevelt to Norman Thomas, 17 October 1939, Roosevelt Papers. The previous day Secretary of State

Cordell Hull had written a draft reply. Memo, Hull to Roosevelt, 16 October 1939, Roosevelt Papers. For Thomas's continued optimism, see "Your World and Mine," *Call*, 2 December 1939, 2; 6 January 1940, 2; 13 January 1940, 2.

57. Walter Van Kirk to Dorothy Detzer, 16 November 1939, WIL Papers. Among the delegation were Walter Van Kirk, NPC director; Henrietta Roelofs, NPC president; John H. Lathrop, NPC vice president; and Mrs. Norman Thomas.

58. "President's Letter to Pope Pius," *NYT*, 24 December 1939, 6. For optimistic responses to Roosevelt's message, see John Haynes Holmes, "President, Pope, and Peace," *Unity* 124 (15 January 1940): 151; "Roosevelt Peace Stand Commendable," *SFE*, 26 December 1939, 1. See also Hearst correspondent H. R. Knickerbocker on FDR's role, [University of] *Michigan Daily*, 13 December 1939, 1.

59. Franklin D. Roosevelt to Oswald Garrison Villard, 17 January 1940; Roosevelt to Villard, 18 January 1940, Roosevelt Papers. Yet Villard may well have mistrusted the president. According to Borchard, Villard believed that FDR sought to take the United States into the war but did not yet dare. Edwin M. Borchard to John Bassett Moore, 31 January 1940, Borchard Papers.

60. In November, Senator Capper called on the United States to offer negotiations. *SFE*, 10 November 1939, 1, 9. See also Harry Elmer Barnes, "U.S. Influence for Peace," *NYWT*, 1 November 1939, 26; Dorothy Dunbar Bromley, [City College of New York] *Campus*, 10 November 1939, 1; Lundeen, *United States News*, 30 October 1939, 4.

61. For extensive discussion, see Randall, *Improper Bostonian*, chaps. 6–9.

62. Text, "Peace Forces Unite on Six-Point Program," *Peace Action* 6 (September 1939): 3. The NPC was founded in 1935 as a coalition encompassing some thirty pacifist and internationalist organizations. The WIL was particularly active in this body. At an emergency meeting of the WIL executive committee, held on 13 September 1939, with about sixty present, Dorothy Detzer called for WIL cooperation with the NPC. Minutes, WIL Papers. On 28 September 1939, the WIL executive committee met again. Detzer noted that at her request, Senator Capper and Representative Robert Allen (Dem.-Pa.) agreed to introduce a resolution in Congress asking for a conference of neutrals. Minutes, WIL Papers. On 22 October, the WIL national board called on all neutral nations to establish a conference that would sit continually offering mediation. Resolutions, WIL Papers. See also Libby, "President Should Initiate Neutral Mediation Commission," *Peace Action* 6 (September 1939): 2; "War in Europe: A Statement by the 1939 National Conference of the Fellowship of Reconciliation," *Fellowship* 5 (October 1939): 4; Harold E. Fey, "Save Neutrality! Save Peace!" *Christian Century* 56 (6 October 1939): 1234; annual session, Methodist General Commission on World Peace, 19–20 September 1939, in *Peace Action* 6 (October 1939): 3. Even early in 1940, peace groups and leaders sought U.S. involvement. See, for example, Libby, "Immediate Mediation the Hope of the World," *Peace Action* 6 (January 1940): 1–2; minutes, National Board, WIL, Washington, D.C., 20–21 January 1940, 1, WIL Papers; John Nevin Sayre, "Mediate Now," *Fellowship* 6 (February 1940): 26; Ernest Fremont Tittle, *Smith College Weekly*, 14 February 1940, 1. See also Alfred Bingham to Sidney Hertzberg, 6 December 1939, Hertzberg Papers.

63. "Peace Bids by Neutrals Traditional," *Washington Evening Star*, 9 October 1939. The nine powers would include Germany, Britain, France, Italy, Japan, the Soviet Union, and three neutral nations. "Peace Now!" *United States News*, 23 October 1939, 14. For the backing of Libby, see governing committee, KAOWC, 30 October 1939, KAOWC Papers; Libby, "Enlist for 'Peace Now' Until We Get It," *Peace Action* 6 (November 1939): 1. Libby reproduced David Lawrence's editorial of *United States News* of 23 October 1939. See "Let's Skip the War and Work for Peace Now!" *Peace Action* 6 (November 1939): 4–5. The *Daily Worker* featured calls for mediation by Lawrence and Heywood Broun. See "The People Can Halt the War Now!" 10 October 1939, 1. Columnist Broun, a recent convert to Roman Catholicism, endorsed the peace proposed by Pius XII and a conference sponsored by the neutral nations. Unlike many anti-interventionists, however, he favored repeal of the arms embargo. Broun, "It Seems to Me," *SFN*, 27 October 1939, 21.

64. For Hull, see *Newsweek*, 16 October 1939, 29; Hull, *Memoirs*, 1:711; Breckinridge Long, entry of 11 October 1939, *War Diary*, 27–28. For FDR, see *NYT*, 8 October 1939, 1, 39; 11 October 1939, 5; 14 October 1939, 1, 3. For doubts within the administration concerning any peace, see Long, entry of 13 September 1939, *War Diary*, 13.

65. Cole, *Roosevelt*, 335–37; Berle diary entry, 19 September 1939, *Navigating*, 256–57; 13 October 1939, 265; 16 October 1939, 266; entry of 12 October 1939, *Moffat Papers*, 273–76.

66. Berle, entry of 5 December 1939, *Navigating*, 275. Berle suspected that Roosevelt would call a general peace conference in early spring. Entry of 29 December 1939, 281.

67. MacDonald, *United States, Britain*, 177.

68. Franklin D. Roosevelt to James G. Mooney, 24 January 1940, Roosevelt Papers. For material on Mooney's entire activities, see Costello, *Ten Days*, 60–61, 64, 67–68, 134–35, 142, 144, 399–403; Ickes, entry of 13 December 1940, *Secret Diary*, 3:395.

69. Robert Dallek, *Franklin D. Roosevelt and American Foreign Policy, 1932–1945* (New York: Oxford University Press, 1979), 216.

70. "President's Letter to Pope Pius," *NYT*, 24 December 1939, 6; Berle, entry of 11 January 1940, *Navigating*, 283–84; 15 January 1940, 284–85; 27 January 1940, 288. For earlier state department plans, see Berle, entry of 29 December 1939, *Navigating*, 280–81; Frank Warren Graff, *Strategy of Involvement: A Diplomatic Biography of Sumner Welles* (New York: Garland, 1988) 382–84.

71. *NYT*, 10 February 1940, 1.

72. Warren F. Kimball, *Forged in War: Roosevelt, Churchill, and the Second World War* (New York: Morrow, 1997), 44–45; Dallek, *Roosevelt*, 216–18; Irwin F. Gellman, *Secret Affairs: Franklin Roosevelt, Cordell Hull, and Sumner Welles* (Baltimore: Johns Hopkins University Press, 1994), 171; Mark M. Lowenthal, "Roosevelt and the Coming of the War: The Search for United States Policy, 1937–1942," *Journal of Contemporary History* 16 (July 1981): 419–20; Langer and Gleason, *Challenge to Isolation*, 375; Arnold A. Offner, *The Origins of the Second World War* (New York: Praeger, 1975), 169–73; Reynolds, *Creation*, 71.

73. For focus on Mussolini, see Stanley E. Hilton, "The Welles Mission to Europe, February–March 1940: Illusion or Realism?" *Journal of American History* 58 (June 1971): 93–120; Gellman, *Secret Affairs*, 198; Welles, "Italy and Peace in Europe," *Foreign Relations, 1940*, vol. 1 (Washington, D.C.: U.S. Government Printing Office, 1959), 113–16. For praise by both Welles and Breckinridge Long, see Long, entry of 2 September 1939, *War Dairy*, 2, 4. Long had been Roosevelt's ambassador to Italy. For FDR's perception of Italy as a key to peace, see David F. Schmitz, *The United States and Fascist Italy, 1922–1940* (Chapel Hill: University of North Carolina Press, 1988), 205.

74. For accounts, see "Report by the Under Secretary of State (Welles) on His Special Mission to Europe," *Foreign Relations, 1940*, vol. 1 (Washington, D.C.: U.S. Government Printing Office, 1959), 21–117; Sumner Welles, *The Time for Decision* (New York: Harper, 1944), chap. 3; Graff, *Strategy of Involvement*, chap. 6; *Moffat Papers*, 291–304.

75. See, for example, Edwin M. Borchard to John A. Danaher, 12 and 17 February 1940, Borchard Papers; Hiram W. Johnson to Hiram W. Johnson Jr., 10 February 1940, the Papers of Hiram Johnson, University of California, Berkeley (hereafter cited as Johnson Papers); Dennis and Gravenhoff, *WFL* 81 (15 February 1940): 1–2; *WFL* 83 (29 February 1940): 1–2; Senator Robert R. Reynolds, *NYT*, 2 April 1940, 12.

76. See, for example, Norman Thomas to Wendell Willkie, 12 February 1940, Thomas Papers; "But Boake Carter Says," *SFE*, 16 February 1940, 8; Gerald P. Nye, "We're Already in the War," *Look*, 23 April 1940, 8; Morris Kamman, "Britain Expects FDR to Do His Duty," *New Masses* 34 (19 March 1940): 3–6; "Mr. Roosevelt Sends Mr. Welles to Europe," *CT*, 11 February 1940, 16; "Sending Mr. Welles to Europe," *CT*, 13 February 1940, 12; "As Mr. Welles Follows Col. House," *CT*, 19 February 1940, 12; "Mr. Welles in Europe," *CT*, 28 February 1940, 10; C. Hartley Grattan to Sidney Hertzberg, n.d., Hertzberg Papers; B. C. Clark in Sargent, Bulletin #37, 16 February 1940, *Getting US into War*, 287.

77. For the text of the House–Grey memorandum, see Arthur S. Link, *Wilson*, vol. 4: *Confusion and Crises, 1915–1916* (Princeton, N.J.: Princeton University Press, 1964), 134–35.

78. "Mr. Welles Completes His Trip," *Daily Worker*, 21 March 1940, 1. See also "The Specter of Peace," *New Masses* 35 (2 April 1940): 19; "Why Is Sumner Welles Going to Europe? Envoy to Probe for Anti-Soviet Front," *Socialist Appeal* (a Trotskyist paper), 17 February 1940, 1. The pro-Soviet interpretation also received surprising confirmation from Demaree Bess, European staff correspondent for the *Saturday Evening Post*. See "Our Election and Hitler's War," *Saturday Evening Post* 212 (11 May 1940): 9.

79. Henning cited in *CR*, 27 February 1940, 2073. For further attack, see "Mr. Welles Hits the Trail Back," *CT*, 16 March 1940, 14.

80. See, for example, Congressman John C. Schafer (Rep.-Wis.), *CR*, 12 March 1940, 2748; "How America Is Entrapped in Maze of Secret Diplomacy," *Social Justice*, 18 March 1940, 9.

81. Hiram W. Johnson to Hiram W. Johnson Jr., 10 February 1940, Johnson Papers. See also Dennis and Gravenhoff, *WFL* 81 (15 February 1940): 1–2; *WFL* 83 (29 February 1940): 1–2.

82. Norman Thomas, "Your World and Mine," 9 March 1940, *Call*, 3. See also Dorothy Detzer to Gertrude Baer, 21 March 1940, WIL papers; J. S. Barnes, "The Prospects of a Good Peace," *Social Justice*, 18 March 1940, 9; "Minister Non-Potentiary," *Uncensored* 21 (24 February 1940): 2.

83. "But Boake Carter Says," *SFE*, 16 February 1940, 8. Hoover in Castle Diary, 18 February 1940. See also  Castle Diary, 13 February 1940; "From Washington," *Uncensored* 22 (2 March 1940): 2; Sargent, Bulletin #37, 16 February 1940, *Getting US into War*, 287.

84. See, for example, Hugh Johnson, *SFN*, 13 February 1940, 13. See also Reynolds, *CR*, 2 April 1940, 3821; "Mr. Roosevelt Sends an Envoy to Europe," *Christian Century* 57 (21 January 1940): 236; Dorothy Detzer to Emily Greene Balch, 26 February 1940, WIL papers.

85. See, for example, John Haynes Holmes, "The President and Peace," *Unity* 125 (4 March 1940): 4; Norman Thomas to Franklin D. Roosevelt, 12 February 1940, Thomas Papers; Thomas, "Your World and Mine," *Call*, 9 March 1940, 3.

86. "Cautious Exploratory Peace Moves Begin," *Peace Action* 6 (February 1940): 1. See also Libby, *United States News*, 23 February 1940, 22.

87. "Mr. Roosevelt Sends an Envoy to Europe," *Christian Century* 57 (21 February 1940): 235.

88. "Roosevelt Moves for Peace," *NYDN*, 10 February 1940, 13. The *News* soon expressed concern over the derisive comments on the mission made by the British, French, and Italian press, which treated Welles as "a babe in the woods." The masses in all the belligerent nations, it noted, were still apathetic and morose about the conflict. See "The Hecatombs of Spring," 23 February 1940, 29. See also "Why Not 'Implement' Welles?" 5 March 1940, 23. By late 28 February, it found Welles's mission based on "a slender hope," for the Allies appeared determined to apply the "recipe" of General John J. Pershing who had said just two days previously that the Allies should have marched to Berlin in 1918. See "'On to Berlin,'" 28 February 1940, 29.

89. Hearst, "In the News," *SFE*, 5 March 1940, 2; Coughlin, "From the Tower," *Social Justice*, 25 March 1940, 3.

90. For Roosevelt, see Gellman, *Secret Affairs*, 192–93. For Britain, see Reynolds, *Creation*, 81; Rock, *Chamberlain and Roosevelt*, 267. For France, see Henry Blumenthal, *Illusion and Reality in Franco-American Diplomacy, 1914–1945* (Baton Rouge: Louisiana State University Press, 1986), 255–57.

91. Kimball, *Forged in War*, 45.

92. Gallup polls, *NYT*, 10 March 1940, 27. See also *NYT*, 29 October 1939, 29. For related polls, see Cantril, *Public Opinion*, 1136.

## CHAPTER 3: A MATTER OF WAR AIMS

1. Walter Johnson, *The Battle Against Isolation* (Chicago: University of Chicago Press, 1944), 47–48.

2. Kendrick, letter to *Common Sense* 10 (August 1941): 225.

3. See, for example, Downey, *CR*, 9 October 1939, 186; Robsion, *CR*, 5 February 1941, 642; Hugh Johnson, "International Sucker," *NYWT*, 30 September 1939, 19; "'Roll Up That Map,'" *NYDN*, 1 June 1940, 13; Barton, broadcast, NBC, 29 October 1939, in *CR*, A593; Hoover, "We Must Keep Out," *Saturday Evening Post* 212 (28 October 1939): 9; Chavez, *CR*, 12 October 1939, 316; "Required Reading for Europeans," *Saturday Evening Post* 212 (28 October 1939): 22; Colonel Robert R. McCormick, speech, Pottawatomic Park, St. Charles, Illinois, in *CT*, 4 September 1939, 5; Borchard, address to Yale Alumni, South Orange, New Jersey, 27 January 1940, in *CR*, A602; Nye, "Shall the United States Make Available to Eng-

land Some of Its World War Destroyers?" American Forum of the Air, 25 August 1940, in *CR*, A5661; Republican leader Hanford MacNider to Milo J. Warner, 20 December 1940, MacNider Papers.

4. Lindbergh, "What Substitute for War?" *Atlantic Monthly* 165 (March 1940): 304; Bolton, *CR*, 19 February 1941, A761–62. For the exact same list, see Waldrop, *WTH*, 12 November 1941. Historian Charles A. Beard made a list of two hundred years of Europe's wars that was published in the *Chicago Tribune*. See issue of 27 July 1941, 10.

5. For minorities, see Taft, *CR*, 13 October 1939, 355. For resources, see Senator Henrik Shipstead (Rep.-Minn.), address, Northfield, Minnesota, 4 July 1940, in *CR*, A4384.

6. Holmes, "If America Enters the War," *Christian Century* 57 (11 December 1940): 154. See also Holmes to Barnett R. Brickner, 24 October 1939, Holmes Papers. For other examples, see Sterling Morton to Ralph E. Church, 16 May 1940, Morton Papers; historian Eric F. Goldman, *Johns Hopkins University Newsletter*, 10 November 1939, 1; Borah, *CR*, 2 October 1939, 73; Capper, broadcast, CBS, 29 September 1939, in *CR*, A88; Vandenberg, *CR*, 4 October 1939, 99; Senator Guy Gillette (Dem.-Iowa), *CR*, 16 October 1939, 462; Bulow, *CR*, 21 February 1941, 1258; Chester Bowles to Philip La Follette, 28 September 1939, La Follette Papers.

7. See, for example, "America," *Saturday Evening Post* 212 (3 October 1939): 22. Only rarely did an anti-interventionist directly argue against such accusations. The Jesuit weekly *America* denied that neutrality was aided, or peace furthered, by thundering that the conflict was a mere scramble between capitalists for imperialist power or a hopeless mess in which no principles of right and justice were involved. To use such language, it said, was merely to play into communist hands. "Comment," *America* 63 (15 June 1940): 254.

8. For Gallup poll of 22 September 1939 and related polls, see Cantril, *Public Opinion*, 1076.

9. V. I. Lenin, *Imperialism: The Highest Stage of Capitalism*, new rev. trans. (New York: International, 1939).

10. Marcantonio, *CR*, 5 February 1941, 657. See also activist Helen Keller, *Call*, 21 October 1939, 2.

11. Sweeney, speech over NBC red network, 6 May 1941, in *CR*, A2154; Coughlin, "From the Tower," *Social Justice*, 25 September 1939, 5. See also "In the News," *Social Justice*, 25 March 1940, 3.

12. See, for example, philosopher E. L. Burtt, *Cornell [University] Daily Sun*, 20 April 1940, 1.

13. Barnes, [University of] *Michigan Daily*, 17 May 1940, 1. See also "Real Americanism: Neutrality Held Mark," *NYWT*, 5 April 1940, 26; "Europe's War and America's Democracy," *Virginia Quarterly Review* 16 (October 1940): 553.

14. Higgins, [University of California, Berkeley] *Daily Californian*, 19 September 1939, 4; Kael, *American Guardian*, 15 December 1939, 2.

15. For stress on empire, see Congressman Jerry Voorhis (Dem.-Calif.), *CR*, 2 October 1939, A124; Robsion, *CR*, 1 November 1939, 1295; Congressman John G. Alexander (Rep.-Minn.), *CR*, 9 December 1940, A6809; Reynolds, *CR*, 20 February 1941, 1212; diplomat J. Reuben Clark, quoted in "But Boake Carter Says," *SFE*, 4 April 1941, 9; Hearden, "Cudahy," *Mid-America* 68 (April–June 1986), 107–8.

16. Nye, *CR*, 13 October 1939, 383; Gillis, "The War: What Else but the War?" *Catholic World* 150 (October 1939): 6; "Economics of Empire," *Uncensored* 76 (25 March 1941): 4. For further stress on colonies, see sociologist Edward A. Ross, [University of Wisconsin] *Summer Cardinal*, 4 July 1940, 10.

17. See, for example, Robsion, *CR*, 1 November 1939, 1295; Congressman Clare Hoffman (Rep.-Mich.), *CR*, 18 March 1941, 2341; Congressman Philip A. Bennett (Rep.-Mo.), radio address over KMOX, St. Louis, 10 May 1941, in *CR*, A2360; Congressman Dewey Congressman Dewey Short (Rep.-Mo.), *CR*, 29 May 1941, 4566; historian Franklin C. Palm, [University of California, Berkeley] *Daily Californian*, 11 October 1939, 1; Herbert Zam, "A War for Profits," *Call*, 23 September 1939, 2; farm leader George N. Peek to R. Douglas Stuart Jr., 1 January 1941, AFC Papers; McCarran, *CR*, 22 February 1941, 1271.

18. Sargent, Bulletin #22, 15 December 1939, 266; James D. Mooney, speech to University Club, Cleveland, 1 June 1940, in *CR*, 7822; La Follette, *CR*, 12 October 1939, 321.

19. Lindbergh, "What Substitute for War?" *Atlantic Monthly* 165 (March 1940): 306–7. At another point, Lindbergh said that the war centered on "the division of territory and wealth among nations," which "has caused conflict in Europe since European history began." Speech, Soldier's Field, Chicago, 4 August 1940, in *CR*, 4794.

20. See, for example, B. C. Clark, *CR*, 1 November 1941, 8410. John Haynes Holmes to Barnett R. Brickner, 24 October 1939, Holmes Papers; Holmes to General John F. O'Ryan, 21 May 1940, Holmes Papers; Norman Thomas, "Your World and Mine: War Aims and Peace Terms," *Call*, 5 April 1941, 5; Sweeney, *CR*, 14 August 1940, 10359.

21. John Haynes Holmes to Sherwood Eddy, 17 October 1940, Holmes Papers; Lundeen, *CR*, 9 October 1939, 189. For the exact same figures, see McCarran, Armistice Day address, Las Vegas, 11 November 1939, in *CR*, 4 April 1940, 4009. According to Barbara McDonald, chairman of the AFC speakers bureau, over the past five hundred years Spain had been at war 67 percent of the time; England, 50 percent; Russia, 46 percent; Austria, 40 percent; Italy, 35 percent; and Prussia and Germany, 28 percent. Memorandum to all speakers, 11 March 1941, Barnes Papers.

22. Downey, *CR*, 9 October 1939, 186, 187, 191; Gillis, "The War: What Else but the War?" *Catholic World* 150 (October 1939): 6.

23. See, for example, Lundeen, *CR*, 27 August 1940, 10994; socialist economist Maynard Krueger, [University of Chicago] *Daily Maroon*, 24 May 1940, 1.

24. Fisher, [Boise] *Idaho Daily Statesman*, 17 January 1941; A. J. Muste to Mrs. H. W. Foote, 28 October 1941, FOR Papers; O'Connor, *CR*, 21 January 1941, 212.

25. See, for example, John T. Flynn diary notes, 27 June 1941, Box 32, Flynn Papers; Reynolds, *CR*, 21 October 1939, 692; H. L. Mencken, "Notes on a Moral War," *Baltimore Sun*, 8 October 1939; Mencken, [Georgetown University] *Hoya*, 25 October 1939, 2; Albert Jay Nock, "You Can't Do Business with Hitler," *Scribner's Commentator* 11 (November 1941): 84; Hearst, "In the News," *SFE*, 29 May 1941, 1; Neilson, entry of 6 June 1941, *Tragedy*, 2:364; Libby, "We Try to Stop the War in Europe?" *Peace Action* 6 (March 1940): 3.

26. Joseph P. Kennedy to Roosevelt, 30 September 1939, in Beschloss, *Kennedy and Roosevelt*, 193. At one point, he told a British correspondent Britain was fighting for "self-preservation." Bilainkin, entry of 8 April 1940, *Diary*, 59.

27. Orton, *Mt. Holyoke* [College] *News*, 14 February 1941, 1. Raymond Moley to Alf Landon, 20 March 1941, Moley Papers; Ross in [University of] *Wisconsin Summer Cardinal*, 4 July 1940, 10.

28. La Follette, *CR*, 12 October 1939, 321; Starobin, *Brooklyn College Vanguard*, 8 March 1940, 4; "A Long War Means a Spreading War," *NYDN*, 17 January 1940, 29; "Food—Oil—Jealousy," *NYDN*, 9 November 1941, 61.

29. Reynolds, *CR*, 21 October 1939, 692; Nye, *CR*, 4 March 1941, 1730. See also Thomas, "Your World and Mine," 5.

30. "Economics of Empire," *Uncensored* 76 (15 March 1941): 4; Waldrop, "Who's Getting What?" *WTH*, 20 September 1941, 18. Though, Waldrop continued, Germany had picked up nearly 150 million more people than Britain, this factor simply gave Hitler "the bad bargain of more mouths to feed and more industrial machinery of which he already had plenty before he began." The German dictator also had "under his uncertain thumb the most contrary, perverse, plot-minded, and revolutionary segment of the human race."

31. Muste, [University of] *Wisconsin Daily Cardinal*, 6 May 1941, 4.

32. Lindbergh, entry of 28 May 1940, *Wartime Journals*, 351. In 1941, under congressional questioning, Lindbergh did claim that privately he had been critical of Germany. Testimony, HFAC, 23 January 1941, 435.

33. Cadbury in Chamberlin Diary, 19–26 April 1941.

34. For the significance of the Wannsee Conference of January 1942, see Michael R. Marrus, *The Holocaust in History* (Hanover, N.H.: University Press of New England, 1987), 32–33.

35. Wolcott, *CR*, 9 October 1939, 215; Castle Diary, 27 May 1940.

36. Wheeler, *CR*, 11 October 1939, 288; Johnson, "Regarding Atrocities," *NYWT*, 16 September 1939, 15; Townsend, "Mercy—Strictly Political," *Scribner's Commentator* 9 (March 1941): 83–84; Barnes, "This Unholy War: Crimes of the British," *NYWT*, 29 March 1940, 22.

37. See, for example, Barnes, "New Peril Seen to Neutrality," *NYWT*, 1 December 1939, 32; Congressman Charles Hawks Jr. (Rep.-Wis.), *CR*, 14 October 1939, 401; Wheeler, *CR*, 6 August 1940, 9930; "No Hostility to England," *CT*, 1 November 1939, 14; Lindbergh, speech, 13 October 1939, in *CR*,

A302; Gillis, "The War: What Else but the War?" 8; Edwin M. Borchard to John Bassett Moore, 8 July 1940, Moore Papers. John T. Flynn expressed a minority view in claiming even "a much better peace" still could not have prevented Germany's collapse, for "her economic system was in distress and the war had crippled it beyond repair." In fact, Italy, a victor nation, "cracked up" before Germany did. Testimony, SFRC, 23 October 1941, 208.

38. Holt, *CR*, 18 October 1939, 548; "Shall We Fight for the Versailles Treaty?" *NYDN*, 1 December 1939, 31; Hoover, "We Must Keep Out," *Saturday Evening Post* 212 (28 October 1939): 76. See also Hoover, "The First American Crusade," *Saturday Evening Post* 214 (1 November 1941): 9–11, 35–39; "'You May Be Sure That I Shall Fight Shy': The First American Crusade," 214 (8 November 1941): 14–15, 41–50; "The Only Nation Since the Crusades That Has Fought the Battles of Other Peoples at Her Own Gigantic Loss," 214 (15 November 1941): 31, 128–31.

39. "Versailles Treaty Impossible Peace," *Social Justice*, 23 October 1939, 8; Schoonmaker, *Democracy and World Dominion* (New York: Smith, 1939). For further serialization of Schoonmaker, see *Social Justice*, 2 October 1939, 10; 30 October 1939, 18.

40. See, for example, William Henry Chamberlin, *Christian Science Monitor*, 7 August 1939; Bennett Clark, *CR*, 11 October 1939, 280; Senator Clyde Reed (Rep.-Kans.), *CR*, 11 October 1939, 280; Nye, 13 October 1939, 365; Daniel M. O'Connell, S.J., "War Objective," *Catholic World* 151 (April 1940): 72; Methodist missionary E. Stanley Jones, "What Is America's Role in This Crisis?" *Christian Century* 58 (9 March 1941): 388; "War in Europe," statement of 1939 National Conference of FOR, *Fellowship* 5 (October 1939): 3; Rankin, *CR*, 24 April 1941, 3282; Colonel Robert R. McCormick, letter to Lord Kemsley, entered *CR*, 28 November 1941, A5330; Socialist writer Bertram D. Wolfe, *Washington Square College* [New York University] *Bulletin*, 11 November 1939, 1; Dorothy Detzer to Frederick Brown Harris, 14 October 1939, WIL Papers; Holt, *CR*, 18 October 1939, 548.

41. Page, *Amherst* [College] *Student*, 27 November 1939, 1. See also Page, *Brown* [University] *Daily Herald*, 21 November 1939, 1.

42. Shipstead, *CR*, 25 February 1941, 1350.

43. Kimball, *The Juggler: Franklin Roosevelt as Wartime Statesman* (Princeton, N.J.: Princeton University Press, 1991), 68; John Lamberton Harper, *American Visions of Europe: Franklin D. Roosevelt, George F. Kennan, and Dean G. Acheson* (New York: Cambridge University Press, 1994), 54, 57–60.

44. Nock, review of Arthur Bryant, *Unfinished Victory* (London: Macmillan, 1940), in *Scribner's Commentator* 9 (April 1941): 17; Lindbergh, text of address, *NYT*, 16 September 1939, 9. See also Dennis, *WFL* 100 (27 June 1940): 2.

45. See, for example, free market economist Frank Chodorov, "Hitler—Economic Threat?" *Scribner's Commentator* 9 (March 1941): 33.

46. Clark, *CR*, 24 February 1941, 1295.

47. See, for example, Edwin M. Borchard to William E. Borah, 18 April 1939; Borchard to George Norris, 27 February 1941; Borchard to Hiram W. Johnson, 19 February 1941, Borchard Papers; Senator David I. Walsh (Dem.-Mass.), *CR*, 21 June 1940, 8784; Hearst, "In the News," *SFE*, 12 April 1940, 1; "Not America's War," *Christian Century* 56 (22 November 1939): 1433.

48. "Bloody Merry-Go-Round," *NYDN*, 29 November 1940, 35. The *News* accused the peacemakers of lopping off Bulgaria's Mediterranean outlet, excluding Russia from the Baltic, and erasing Austria-Hungary's long Adriatic coastline.

49. See, for example, Hoffman, *CR*, 6 February 1941, 722; "What Price Plutocracy?" *American Guardian*, 22 September 1939, 4.

50. "The Peace Offensive," *New Republic* 101 (11 October 1939): 256, which also mentioned Germany's former colonies; "Hitler's Terms," *CT*, 7 October 1939, 10; Villard, *Within Germany*, 54–55; "The Damned and Dangerous Fascination of War," *NYDN*, 29 December 1939, 19; Dennis, *WFL* 99 (20 June 1940): 3; "But Boake Carter Says," *SFE*, 16 March 1940, 9.

51. Barnes, "Course of U.S. in the War," *NYWT*, 15 January 1940, 14; FOR staffer John Swomley, *Wesleyan* [University] *Argus*, 22 April 1940, 3; Flynn, *Harvard* [University] *Crimson*, 8 May 1941, 1. The *New York Daily News* had called for Britain to voluntarily give Germany some African colonies, but it did not say which ones. See "Treaty of Versailles Torn Up," *NYDN*, 15 October 1939, 47.

52. Flynn, "Nazi Economy—A Threat?" *Scribner's Commentator* 10 (August 1941): 24. See also Flynn, "Stalin Moves in Europe," *NYWT*, 13 December 1939, 30.

53. See, for example, Amos Pinchot to W. Earl Hall, 1 December 1941, Pinchot Papers; Lindbergh, entry of 21 September 1939, *Wartime Journals*, 260; entry of 3 October 1939, 269; Cudahy, testimony, SFRC, 23 October 1941, 169, 177.

54. "But Boake Carter Says," *SFE*, 16 September 1939, 13; William R. Castle to R. D. Stuart Jr., 11 March 1941, Box 63, AFC Papers. See also Castle Diary, 28 February 1941.

55. "A Long War Means a Spreading War," *NYDN*, 17 January 1940, 29; "Stumblebum Diplomacy Here," 24 June 1940, 21.

56. Nye, *CR*, 26 February 1941, 1435; Symes, "Hold That Line: Whither Hitler?" *Call*, 29 June 1940, 4. See also Symes, "Hold That Line: American 'Opportunity'?" *Call*, 12 July 1941, 5.

57. Hearst, "In the News," *SFE*, 6 May 1940, 1; Flynn, *Harvard* [University] *Crimson*, 8 May 1941, 1; Chase, "What Are the Germans After?" *Progressive*, 29 November 1941, 1.

58. Dennis, *WFL* 68 (16 November 1939): 2; "The Germans Will Starve Last," *NYDN*, 6 May 1940, 21.

59. "A Prediction: Hitler's Peace Plan," *Social Justice*, 7 April 1941, 15; Burdick, *CR*, 12 August 1941, 7002; Hearst, see "In the News," *SFE*, 29 May 1941, 1.

60. "Washington Picture," *Uncensored* 89 (14 June 1941): 4. The projection came from Frank Hanighen's memo to the journal, 15 May 1941, Hertzberg Papers.

61. Charles E. Coughlin, "A Page of Comment," *Social Justice*, 20 May 1940, 20. For further projections in *Social Justice*, see J. S. Barnes, "The Real Issues of War," 9 October 1939, 7; J. S. Barnes, "After Peace, What?" 30 October 1939, 9; "Forecast of Peace Terms," 14 October 1940, 8; "Outlining the New Europe," 21 October 1940, 8; "A New Deal for the Old World," 28 October 1940, 13; "A Prediction: Hitler's Peace Plan," 7 April 1941, 15.

62. Chamberlin, "The Coming Peace," *American Mercury* 51 (November 1940): 264–65; Dennis, *WFL* 136 (6 March 1941): 5; *WFL* 99 (20 June 1940): 3. For further Dennis projections, see *WFL* 85 (14 March 1940): 4; 124 (12 December 1940): 3.

63. Cudahy, testimony, SFRC, 23 October 1941, 148. See also Lundeen, *CR*, 11 July 1940, 9512.

64. Cudahy, "Hitler or Americas," *Life*, 9 June 1941, 34–37; "Britain's War Aims; Germany's Peace Feelers," *Peace Action* 7 (May 1941): 5; J. S. Barnes, "The Real Issues of War," *Social Justice*, 9 October 1939, 7.

65. For the scholarly literature on Hitler's war aims, see Ian Kershaw, *The Nazi Dictatorship: Problems and Perspectives of Interpretation*, 2d ed. (London: Arnold, 1989), chap. 6; Meir Michaelis, "World Power Status or World Dominion? A Survey of the Literature on Hitler's 'Plan of World Dominion,'" *Historical Journal* 15 (1972): 331–60; John Lukacs, *The Hitler of History* (New York: Knopf, 1997), chap. 5. For stress on continental goals, see, for example, Eberhard Jäckel, *Hitler's Weltanschauung: A Blueprint for Power* (Middletown, Conn.: Wesleyan University Press, 1972), chap. 2; Geoffrey Stoakes, *Hitler and the Quest for World Domination: Nazi Ideology and Foreign Policy in the 1920s* (New York: Berg, 1986). For stress on world mastery, see, for example, Gerhard L. Weinberg, *Germany, Hitler, and World War II* (New York: Cambridge University Press, 1995); Milan Hauner, "Did Hitler Want World Domination?" *Journal of Contemporary History* 13 (January 1978): 15–32.

66. Hearst, "In the News," *SFE*, 29 May 1941, 1; Henry Elmer Barnes, "Keep Out of War and Investigate the War-Mongers" [draft], 47–48, Box 252, Lundeen Papers; Dennis, *WFL* 126 (26 December 1940): 4. See also General Robert E. Wood, "Our Foreign Policy," address to Chicago Council of International Relations, 4 October 1940, in *CR*, A6302.

67. Lindbergh, testimony, SFRC, 6 February 1941, 538.

68. Among those who believed that Hitler sought world conquest were Congressman Frank B. Keefe (Rep.-Wis.), *CR*, 3 September 1940, 11,373; Vandenberg, *CR*, 18 February 1941, 1102; attorney John Finerty, testimony, HFAC, 14 October 1941, 44. For Roosevelt, see "President's Call for Full Response on Defense," *NYT*, 30 December 1940, 6.

69. Baldwin, *United We Stand! Defense of the Western Hemisphere* (New York: McGraw-Hill, 1941), 41.

70. Wheeler cited in I. F. Stone, "Munichman from Montana," *Nation* 152 (11 January 1941): 36. See also Princeton America First Committee chapter, [Princeton University] *Daily Princetonian*, 28 October 1941, 4; Congressman Robert Rich (Rep.-Pa.), *CR*, 4 October 1940, 13225.

71. Sumner, *CR*, 1 November 1939, 1259; Holt, *CR*, 2 January 1941, 14,013.

72. Rauschning, *The Revolution of Nihilism* (Garden City, N.Y.: Garden City, 1939), 285. See also Rauschning, *The Voice of Destruction* (New York: Putnam, 1940). For historians' debate over Rauschning's evidence, see Thedor Schieder, *Hermann Rauschnings "Gesprache mit Hitler" als Geschichtsquelle* (Opladen: Westdeutscher, 1972); Wolfgang Hänel, *Hermann Rauschnings "Gesprache mit Hitler"—Eine Geschichtsfälschung* (Ingolstadt: Zeitgeschichte Forschungstelle, 1984).

73. See, for example, General Robert E. Wood, speech to National Association of Manufacturers, 13 December 1940, Box 286, AFC Papers.

74. Castle Diary, 17 April 1940. For similar respect for Rauschning, see Gillis, "Scandinavian Invasion: Crime or Blunder?" *Catholic World* 151 (May 1940): 129.

75. Lundeen, *CR*, 11 July 1940, 9512.

76. Barnes, "New Peril Seen to Neutrality," *NYWT*, 1 October 1939, 22. Barnes did find Hitler unreasonable in occupying non-German regions in Czechoslovakia and in conquering areas in Poland beyond the Corridor.

77. Nye, *CR*, 26 February 1941, 1435.

78. Darré, "Nazis Envision Chattel Slavery for People of Conquered Nations," *NYT*, 6 December 1940, 1, 10; "Secret Nazi Speech," *Life*, 9 December 1940, 43–44; Ickes, speech to Jewish National Workers' Alliance of America, 13 April 1941, in *CR*, A1770. See also *NYT*, 6 December 1940, 1; "Nazis Object," *Time*, 19 May 1941, 63.

79. Darré denial, *NYT*, 8 December 1940, 55; Gallup, *NYT*, 27 December 1940, 5.

80. A. J. Carlson, unpublished letter to *Life* [copy], 9 December 1940, Box 289, AFC Papers; Clark, *CR*, 24 February 1941, 1297. For other doubts of its authenticity, see Nye, *CR*, 25 February 1941, 1364; Norman Thomas, "Your World and Mine: Some Pro-War Propaganda," *Call*, 21 December 1940, 5; Cudahy, testimony, SFRC, 23 October 1941, 179.

81. Flynn, "Nazi Economy—A Threat?" *Scribner's Commentator* 10 (August 1941): 22–23; John Haynes Holmes to William Roger Greeley, 28 May 1940, Holmes Papers. At one point, Holmes claimed that he could not look upon a German victory with equanimity. Letter to John Middleton, 30 April 1940, Holmes Papers.

82. "After the Ball," *NYDN*, 9 June 1941, 19.

83. For general public opinion, including *Fortune* of April 1941, see Cantril, *Public Opinion*, 774–76. For Gallup polls, *NYT*, 29 September 1939, 13; 2 June 1940, 24.

84. *Commonweal*, for example, blamed the British and French for stating their war aims in the most hazy and negative terms. See "The Belgium-Holland Mediation Offer," 31 (17 November 1939): 85.

85. Barnes, "This Unholy War! Crimes of the British," *NYWT*, 29 March 1940, 22. Laski was a prominent socialist political scientist.

86. Chamberlain, text, *NYT*, 4 September 1939, 8; "The Spreading War," *CT*, 19 September 1939, 12; Gillis, "Crazy Leader of a Sane People," *Catholic World* 150 (October 1939): 4; "Peace Talk," *NYDN*, 30 September 1939, 17; Villard, "Men and Events," *Nation* 149 (14 October 1939): 12.

87. Lothian, text, *NYT*, 26 October 1939, 4; "The 'Phony War,'" *NYDN*, 27 October 1939, 37.

88. Halifax, text, *NYT*, 8 November 1939, 2; "European Devil Dance," *NYDN*, 9 November 1939, 9; Gillis, "What Are They Fighting For?" *Catholic World* 150 (December 1939): 259–60.

89. For attacks on Cooper as propagandist, see "Family Album," *Uncensored* 9 (2 December 1939): 1; Thomas, "Your World And Mine," *Call*, 4 November 1939, 3; "British Propaganda," *Call*, 18 May 1940, 3; Burton Rascoe to George Britt [copy], 5 September 1940, Hertzberg Papers.

90. Duff Cooper quoted in *Daily Worker*, 8 January 1940, 6. For similar Communist attacks, "Two Fronts," *New Masses* 35 (7 May 1940): 21; "Duff Cooper Gives the Game Away," *Daily Worker*, 24 April 1940, 6.

91. Duff Cooper, speech to London's Royal Society of St. George, *NYT*, 24 April 1940, 3; speech to constituency meeting, *NYT*, 26 April 1940, 11; *Time*, 6 May 1940, 29.

92. "Should the German People Be Punished?" *Commonweal* 32 (3 May 1940): 29; "British Propaganda," *Uncensored* 33 (18 May 1940): 3. See also Dennis, *WFL* 91 (25 April 1940): 5; Theodore Dreiser, *America Is Worth Saving* (New York: Modern Age Books, 1941), 220.

93. See, for example, Hoffman, *CR*, 13 January 1941, 129; Congressman George Bender (Rep.-Ohio), *CR*, 16 January 1941, 162; Bender, *CR*, 19 January 1941, 384; Keefe, *CR*, 30 January 1941, 421; Rich, *CR*, 4 February 1941, 560; O'Connor, *CR*, 21 February 1941, 212; "The Bitter Question," *Saturday Evening Post* 213 (8 March 1941): 24; "What Are British War Aims?" *St. Louis Post-Dispatch*, 2 March 1941; Charles A. Lindbergh, "Letter to Americans," *Collier's* 107 (29 March 1941): 75; "War Aims," *America* 64 (1 March 1941): 575; "Should America Formulate Peace Aims Now?" *Commonweal* 33 (28 March 1941): 555; "War Aims?—Churchill Still Keeps Them a Secret," *Daily Worker*, 15 February 1941, 6; Vandenberg, *NYT*, 2 January 1941, 1; "Q & A," *Uncensored* 66 (4 January 1941): 4; "What Are Our War Aims?" *NYDN*, January 29, 1941, 27.

94. For *Times*, see Herbert O'Brien, chairman, New York Committee to Keep America Out of War, testimony, SFRC, 7 February 1941, citing *Times* of that day. See 637. For Liddell Hart, see "A War for Sea Power," *Christian Century* 58 (16 April 1941): 521. For archbishop, see Wheeler, *CR*, 27 February 1941, 1472. For varied journals and for such leaders as Lord Ponsonby; Richard Stokes, Labor M.P. from Ipswich; editor Wickham Steed; and Eleanor Rathbone, Independent M.P. for the Combined English Universities, see "Statement of War Aims Urged by British Parliament and Press," *Peace Action* 7 (January 1941): 6–7.

95. Nye and Wheeler, *CR*, 27 January 1941, 311. For endorsement of the Nye-Wheeler resolution, see "What Are Our War Aims?" *NYDN*, 29 January 1941, 27.

96. Resolutions, WIL National Board, Baltimore, 18–19 January 1941, 2, in WIL Papers.

97. Halifax, text, *NYT*, 26 March 1941, 10; "Halifax and War Aims," *Uncensored* 78 (29 March 1941): 4; "Lord Halifax Reveals British War Aims," *Christian Century* 58 (9 April 1941): 485; "Our War Aims," *NYDN*, 27 March 1941, 29. See also "What Are Our War Aims?" *NYDN*, 29 December 1940, 35; "What Revolution?" *NYDN*, 13 January 1941, 19; "Halifax's Speech," *Militant*, 29 March 1941, 6.

98. Eden, excerpts, *NYT*, 30 May 1941, 4; "Eden Gives First Outline of British War Aims," *Christian Century* 58 (11 June 1941): 772–73.

99. "Are the Allies Shadow-Boxing?" *New Republic* 101 (27 September 1939): 197; Moley, speech to Harvard Club, Boston, 8 November 1939, in Hoover Papers.

100. For other accusations that the Allies would deal with Goering, see "America and a Federal Europe," *Christian Century* 57 (24 January 1940): 104; A. B. Magil, "Who's Afraid of Peace?" *New Masses* 35 (9 April 1940): 3, citing Duff Cooper, "Does England Expect Us to Fight?" *Current History* 51 (December 1939): 18–20, 63; G. S. Johnson, "Is Britain's Government Democratic?" *New Masses* 39 (8 April 1941): 10.

101. "Of Things to Come," *Uncensored* 9 (2 December 1939): 3–4. Evidence of such negotiations included the kidnapping of two British secret agents at Venloo, Holland, who supposedly were carried across the border by Goering's rivals, and the flight of German industrialist Fritz Thyssen, who realized that continued war meant his liquidation at the hands of Russian imperialists or German revolutionaries. See also "Of Things to Come," *Uncensored* 10 (9 December 1939): 3, where *Uncensored* found that the *British Blue Book* showed former ambassador to Berlin Sir Neville Henderson and former ambassador to Warsaw Sir Howard W. Kennard both whitewashing Goering.

102. Socialist Party, resolutions of 6–8 April 1940, in *CR*, A2293.

103. Dennis, *WFL* 136 (6 March 1941): 3.

104. For references to the Hohenzollerns, see Philip La Follette, testimony, SFRC, 4 February 1941, 286; Dwight Macdonald, "Sparks in the News," *Socialist Appeal*, 16 December 1939, 4. The *Christian Century* denied the possibility. "What Hinders Peace?" *Christian Century* 56 (4 October 1939): 1265. See also Berle, entry of 15 November 1939, *Navigating*, 270.

105. "War Aims," *Uncensored* 4 (28 October 1939): 1–2. In the same issue, it also noted the strong belief in France that only the restoration of monarchies in Central and Eastern Europe could check the absolutism of Hitler and Stalin. For further mention of the Hapsburgs or of a Bavarian-Austrian union, see "War Aims" [special supplement], *Uncensored* 60 (25 November 1939): 1; Frank Hanighen, "How France Is Taking the War," *New Republic* 101 (30 December 1939): 256; Sargent, Bulletin #22, 15

December 1939, *Getting US into* War, 211; "British Propaganda," *Uncensored* 33 (18 May 1940): 3; Libby, "Behind This War a Problem of Populations," *Peace Action* 6 (January 1940): 2; "What's Behind This Hapsburg Visit?" *Christian Century* 57 (27 March 1940): 403; Czech theologian Matthew Spinka, "A Hapsburg Trojan Horse," *Christian Century* 57 (20 March 1940): 379–81.

106. "Restoration Drama," *Uncensored* 23 (9 March 1940): 2.

107. *NYT*, 7 March 1940, 3; Gilbert, *Churchill*, 6:943–44.

108. See, for example, newsletter editor Franklin Roudybush to Sidney Hertzberg, ca. spring 1940, Hertzberg Papers; Henry Haskell, "A Socialist Peace for Europe," *Call*, 25 November 1939, 1.

109. "If Repeal Wins," *Christian Century* 56 (8 November 1939): 1369. In April 1940, the Protestant weekly considered the restored Hapsburg kingdom as "that 'Catholic buffer state' which the Vatican, only a little while ago, was hoping might be erected on the ruins of Poland." "Roman Catholic Interests in the German Reich," 57 (24 April 1940): 532.

110. "One for Goebbels," *New Republic* 102 (18 March 1940): 359.

111. Some interventionists, too, distinguished between Nazism and German militarism but saw their own policies as the only means of eliminating the latter, more fundamental enemy. Livingstone Hartley and Frank S. Goodwin, "Behind the Nazis," *Washington Office Information Letter* 44 (14 November 1941): 3–4, Box 35, the Papers of the Committee to Defend America by Aiding the Allies, Princeton University (hereafter cited as CDAAA Papers).

112. See, for example, Norman Thomas, *Vassar Miscellany News*, 21 May 1941, 4; C. Hartley Grattan, "The Struggle for Peace," *Harper's Magazine* 180 (February 1940): 300; "The President's Message," *Progressive*, 4 January 1941, 8; theologian Albert Palmer, testimony, SFRC, 22 October 1941, 96; Vassar president Henry Noble MacCracken, testimony, SFRC, 22 October 1941, 101; Holt, *CR*, 21 June 1940, 8815; *American Guardian*, 22 September 1939, 4; "What Hinders Peace?" *Christian Century* 56 (4 October 1939): 1265; AFC Speakers Bureau, "Questions Posed to Speakers of the William Allen White Committee," [1941], in Doenecke, *IDU*, 116.

113. Kirby Page, *How to Keep America Out of War*, 3; "The War Aims of the Nations," *Commonweal* 30 (13 October 1939): 54; Villard, "Issues and Men—If This Be Treason—," *Nation* 150 (3 February 1940): 130; Villard, "The President's Address," *Progressive*, 7 June 1941, 5. See also Villard, "Adolf Hitler Is Not the Sole Enemy," *Progressive*, 29 November 1941, 8.

114. Johnson, "None of Our Gravy," *NYWT*, 4 October 1939, 25; Johnson, *SFN*, 28 September 1940, 13.

115. For references to another Versailles, see Bruce Barton, broadcast, NBC, 29 October 1939, in *CR*, A593; John La Farge, "The Peace Aims of Europe Should Unify the States," *America* 63 (10 February 1940): 480; "The Allies' War Aims," *New Republic* 101 (4 October 1939): 226; Harry Elmer Barnes, "Course of U.S. in the War," *NYWT*, 15 January 1940, 14; Harry Elmer Barnes, "Peace at Once! Keeping Hitler Appeased," *NYWT*, 27 March 1940, 28; "The Voice of Versailles Again," *CT*, 3 June 1941, 12; "Treaty of Versailles Torn Up," *NYDN*, 15 October 1939, 47; "The Pendulum Swings Back," *NYDN*, 12 April 1941, 15; "How Will They Cut Up the Bearskin?" *NYDN*, 31 May 1941, 13; "Double Talk," *NYDN*, 1 June 1941, 41; Robert R. McCormick to Congressman Charles S. Dewey (Rep.-Ill.), 25 November 1941, in *CR*, A5330; John Swomley, *Wesleyan* [University] *Argus*, 22 April 1940, 3; John Haynes Holmes to Henry Smith Leiper, 20 November 1939, Holmes Papers.

116. Nye, *CR*, 12 October 1939, 382; Frederick J. Libby, "Our People Want Neither War nor Empire," *Peace Action* 7 (February 1941): 2. See also "The Search for a Lasting Peace II: Germany and Europe's Chaos," *Christian Century* 58 (19 February 1941): 249.

117. See, for example, Reynolds, *CR*, 21 October 1939, 693; Chavez, *CR*, 25 October 1939, 826; Henry Haskell, "A Socialist Peace for Europe," *Call*, 25 November 1939, 4; "What Hinders Peace?" *Christian Century* 56 (4 October 1939): 1265; Dennis, *WFL* 131 (30 January 1941): 4; *WFL* 68 (16 November 1941): 2. William Henry Chamberlin thought France might gain the Rhineland but would have to follow British lead in all such matters. "The Coming Peace," *American Mercury* 51 (November 1940): 268–69.

118. In January 1940, the *Christian Century* noted that *Le Temps*, frequently a voice of the French Foreign Office, had recently suggested that Russia too be partitioned. "America and a Federal Europe," *Christian Century* 57 (24 January 1940): 104.

119. "Oswald Garrison Villard on the Present European Situation," 20 December 1939, NCPW minutes; Villard, "Issues and Men: Collective Security Must Come," *Nation* 149 (23 December 1939): 711; "De Valera Also Raises His Voice for Peace," *NYDN*, 27 December 1939, 27; "A Long War Means a Spreading War," *NYDN*, 17 January 1940, 29.

120. Libby, "Shall We Try to Stop the War in Europe?" *Peace Action* 6 (March 1940): 3. See also Libby, "Behind This War a Problem of Populations," *Peace Action* 6 (January 1940): 2; Sargent, Bulletin #37, 16 February 1940, *Getting US into War*, 287.

121. Villard, "How Long Can Europe Endure?" *Christian Century* 57 (2 October 1940): 1207; Fey, "Save Neutrality! Save Peace!" *Christian Century* 56 (11 October 1939): 1234; sterilization, Christopher Hollis, "The Situation in Europe," *Catholic Digest* 4 (December 1939): 79; "From the Maginot Line," *Uncensored* 33 (18 May 1940): 4 (emphasis in original); Wheeler, *NYT*, 21 March 1941, 8. See also La Follette Jr., *CR*, 12 October 1939, 331; John A. Danaher to Philip C. Jessup, 18 June 1940, the Papers of Philip C. Jessup, Library of Congress (hereafter cited as Jessup Papers).

## CHAPTER 4: AMERICAN GOALS

1. Howard K. Beale, "Some Fallacies of the Interventionist View" (pamphlet; Washington, D.C.: author, 1941), 7.

2. Muste, "This Senseless War," *Fellowship* 7 (August 1941): 140; Thomas, *Cornell* [University] *Daily Sun*, 23 May 1941, 1; "Halifax and War Aims," *Uncensored* 78 (29 March 1941): 4. See also Norman Thomas to Ralph Harlow, 4 October 1940, Thomas Papers.

3. Chester Bowles to R. Douglas Stuart Jr., 30 July 1941, AFC Papers; Aiken, *CR*, 25 February 1941, 136; Dennis, *WFL* 170 (30 October 1941): 3.

4. For Lippmann and Luce, see Frederick J. Libby to Mrs. William F. Comfort, 7 April 1941, NCPW Papers. Similarly, the *Christian Century* pointed disapprovingly to columnist Walter Lippmann, who called the struggle a war for sea power, with the control of the Atlantic at stake. See "A War for Sea Power," *Christian Century* 58 (16 April 1941): 521. Under attack was Lippmann's article "The Atlantic and America," *Life*, 7 April 1941, 84–92. For the including of Stimson and Thompson, see Taft, radio address, "Shall the United States Enter the European War?" 17 May 1941, in *CR*, A2344. For Elliott, see "God, Inc.," *Uncensored* 110 (1 November 1941): 2; *Social Justice*, 8 December 1941, 20.

5. Villard, "America Is Not God," *Progressive*, 21 June 1941, 5. See also Norman Thomas, "Your World and Mine: Which 'American Century'?" *Call*, 22 March 1941, 5. For Luce's editorial, see "American Century," *Life*, 17 February 1941, 61–65. For its origin, see Robert E. Herzstein, *Henry R. Luce: A Political Portrait of the Man Who Created the American Century* (New York: Scribner's, 1994), chap. 16; Robert T. Elson, *Time Inc.: The Intimate History of a Publishing Enterprise, 1923–1941*, vol. 1 (New York: Atheneum, 1968), 460–64.

6. For Knox's speech, see "Secretary Knox's Address Before the Bar Association," *NYT*, 2 October 1941, 4. For Libby, see testimony, HFAC, 14 October 1941, 64. For protests, see, for example, attorney John Finerty, testimony, SFRC, 23 October 1941, 199; "The Knox War Theses," *Commonweal* 34 (17 October 1941): 605; "But Boake Carter Says," *SFE*, 8 October 1941, 11; Detzer, report of national secretary, WIL, 18 October 1941, WIL Papers; Vandenberg, *CR*, 27 October 1941, 8258; Capper, *CR*, 31 October 1941, 8386; B. C. Clark, *CR*, 1 November 1941, 8407; Edwin M. Borchard to John A. Danaher, 13 October 1941, Borchard Papers; "Eight Points vs. One Hundred Years," *Uncensored* 110 (8 November 1941): 1; "The Road to War," *NYDN*, 3 October 1941, 37; "A War on Two Fronts?" *NYDN*, 6 October 1941, 6; Mrs. Orris Gravener [Dorothy Meeders Robinson] and Dorothy Detzer to Franklin D. Roosevelt, 11 October 1941, WIL Papers; Amos Pinchot to K. C. Warder, 10 October 1941, and Philip C. Jessup to Amos Pinchot, 10 October 1941, both in Pinchot Papers.

7. Jordan in "Out of Their Mouths," *New Masses* 38 (13 December 1940): 4; "Question," *New Masses* 38 (28 January 1941): 20. See also "Design for Empire," *New Masses* 38 (31 December 1940): 3–5; Marcantonio, *CR*, 5 February 1941, 659; "A Frank Admission of FDR's War Aims," *Daily Worker*, 27 December 1940, 1, 4.

8. Roosevelt, annual message, *CR*, 6 January 1941, 46. In March 1941, Roosevelt conceded he might have gone too far by saying that "they may not be immediately attainable throughout the world." See "President's Address to the Democracies," *NYT*, 16 March 1941, 42.

9. See, for example, Alf Landon and B. C. Clark, testimony, SFRC, 8 February 1941, 689–90; "A Lot of Loose Talk," *CT*, 8 January 1941, 10; "The President's Message," *NYDN*, 7 January 1941, 19; Capper, radio broadcast, "Shall the United States Police the World?" in *CR*, 21 January 1941, A169; Marcantonio, *CR*, 4 February 1941, 539; Vandenberg, *CR*, 18 February 1941, 1101; Capper, *CR*, 22 February 1941, 1273; Shipstead, *CR*, 25 February 1941, 1349; Wheeler, *CR*, 9 June 1941, 4864; John Haynes Holmes to Franklin D. Roosevelt, 16 April 1941, Holmes Papers; ed. Paul Palmer, "New Deal World Tour," *Scribner's Commentator* 10 (May 1941): 8.

10. Edwin M. Borchard to John Bassett Moore, 13 January 1941, Borchard Papers. For a comparison to the original crusades, see "After the Crusade, What?" *NYDN*, 27 July 1941, 37.

11. Hutchins, sermon, Rockefeller Memorial Chapel, University of Chicago, 30 March 1941, in *CR*, A1581.

12. For similar attacks, see Congressman Noah Mason (Rep.-Ill.), *CR*, 24 January 1941, A235; Woodruff, *CR*, 29 May 1941, 4574; "The New Apocalypse," *Saturday Evening Post* 213 (22 March 1941): 26; Hiram Johnson, radio speech, NBC, 31 May 1941, in *CR*, A2596; Burdick, *CR*, 4 February 1941, 539; Archbishop Francis Joseph Beckman of Dubuque, "Brother Against Brother," *Time*, 4 August 1941, 46; Castle Diary, 24 July 1941; Robert La Follette Jr., *CR*, 24 February 1941, 1302; Amos Pinchot, "To the Editor," 3 March 1941, Pinchot Papers.

13. La Follette, *CR*, 24 February 1941, 1308; Tinkham, *CR*, 5 February 1941, 626. See also resolutions, National Board, WIL, Baltimore, 18–19 January 1941, 2, WIL Papers; Harry Elmer Barnes cited by Nye, 26 February 1941, 1431; Senator Charles Tobey (Rep.-N.H.), *CR*, 5 March 1941, 1791; Robsion, *CR*, 7 November 1941, 8689.

14. See, for example, Voorhis, *CR*, 21 March 1941, 2483; Keefe, *CR*, 30 January 1941, 421.

15. Upton Close [Josef Washington Hall], "Common Sense for Americans," *Living Age* 358 (August 1940): 511; Flynn, testimony, SFRC, 23 October 1941, 21; Taft, "Shall the United States Enter the European War?" radio address, 17 May 1941, in *CR*, A2344. See also historian Fred Harvey Harrington, [University of] *Wisconsin Daily Cardinal*, 12 April 1940, 1.

16. Beard, testimony, SFRC, 13 February 1941, A627. See also Senator Danaher, *Yale Daily News*, 7 January 1941, 5.

17. Welles, *NYT*, 23 July 1941, 1; "The Gentleman from Oxon Hill Road," *CT*, 24 July 1941, 8.

18. "Alternative Paths of Foreign Policy," *CT*, 23 November 1941, 12. For Welles's remarks, see *NYT*, 12 November 1941, 3.

19. See, for example, Cudahy, testimony, SFRC, 23 October 1941, 160; publisher Frank Gannett to Justin Wroe Nixon, 14 October 1941, the Papers of Frank Gannett, Cornell University, Ithaca, New York (hereafter cited as Gannett Papers); Felix Morley to R. E. Wood, 4 January 1941, the Papers of Felix Morley, Herbert Hoover Presidential Library, West Branch, Iowa (hereafter cited as Morley Papers); John Haynes Holmes to Rabbi S. E. Starrels, 20 November 1939, Holmes Papers.

20. Nye, [University of North Carolina] *Daily Tar Heel*, 19 November 1941, 1; Hearst, "In the News," *SFE*, 5 February 1941, 2.

21. For representative anti-League comments, see Charles A. Lindbergh, testimony, SFRC, 6 February 1941, 523; Charles Clayton Morrison, testimony, SFRC, 24 October 1941, 247; Raymond Moley to Alf Landon, 1 August 1941, Moley Papers; Norman Thomas to Margaret Snyder, 22 August 1941, Thomas Papers; Anne Morrow Lindbergh to Robert E. Wood, 11 October 1940, the Papers of Robert E. Wood, HHPL (hereafter cited as Wood Papers); Quincy Howe, "Is War Inevitable If Britain Falls?" *American Forum of the Air* 3 (9 February 1941): 5; Barnes, "Keep Out of War and Investigate the War-Mongers" [draft], 41, Box 252, Lundeen Papers. For milder comments, see publicist O. K. Armstrong, testimony, SFRC, 6 February 1941, 569; Albert W. Palmer, testimony, SFRC, 22 October 1941, 94; Maynard Krueger, testimony, SFRC, 24 October 1941, 230; Shipstead, *CR*, 16 October 1939, 451, 455.

22. See, for example, "Watch Out for Propaganda," *Social Justice*, 18 September 1939, 6; Barnes, "Armistice Day Reminders," *NYWT*, 11 November 1939, 16.

23. Beals, *Pan America: A Program for the Western Hemisphere* (Boston: Houghton Mifflin, 1940), 115; Chamberlain, "Beware the Wilsonian Ghost," *Progressive*, 22 November 1941, 5; Edwin M. Borchard to Dr. Alberto Ulloa, 17 November 1941, Borchard Papers; Edwin M. Borchard, letter to SFRC, 25 January 1941, committee hearings, 653. See also Congressman Melvin J. Mass (Rep.-Minn.), "Further Aid to Britain," *American Forum of the Air* 2 (23 November 1940): 12.

24. "The Case for Union," *Time*, 17 March 1941, 15–16.

25. *Time*, 17 March 1941, 16; Robert A. Divine, *Second Chance: The Triumph of Internationalism During World War II* (New York: Atheneum, 1967), 38–39. He did not think China, Japan, and India were yet ready for membership and saw no likelihood of the Soviet Union applying. See Clarence K. Streit, *Union Now with Britain* (New York: Harper, 1941), 188–93.

26. *Time*, 17 March 1941, 16.

27. Streit, *Union Now*, 46; *Time*, 17 March 1941, 16.

28. Streit, *Union Now with Britain*, 17.

29. Richard A. Moore, Bulletin #388, 3 July 1941, Box 279, AFC Papers; AFC Research Bureau, "Union Now?" *Did You Know* 16 (6 August 1941), in Doenecke, *IDU*, 248; *Social Justice*, 29 July 1940, 14; George Holden Tinkham to Secretary of the Navy, in *CR*, 17 June 1941, 5266; Holt, *CR*, 3 October 1940, 13,085–86. See also Nye, *CR*, 7 November 1941, 8627.

30. "Whose America?" *Saturday Evening Post* 214 (25 October 1941): 24. Hore-Belisha, in calling for union of the United States and Britain, said the Declaration of Independence must be replaced with a "declaration of interdependence." *NYT*, 18 September 1941, 8. Wedgwood endorsed a federal union that included the United States, Britain, the Low Countries, Norway, China, and even a Germany purged of Nazism. *NYT*, 10 October 1941, 4. In attacking Hore-Belisha, the *NYDN* claimed that not only would such a union lead to marrying the United States to Britain's eternal quarrels in Europe but it would also permit British goods to undersell the United States at home. "I'm Gonna Get My Big Brother to Lick You," *NYDN*, 15 June 1941, 41.

31. "A Vision of Unity," *Saturday Evening Post* 213 (22 March 1941): 26.

32. See, for example, Sargent, *Time*, 25 December 1939, 34; Nye, *CR*, 4 March 1941, 1725; "Cabbages and Kings," *Scribner's Commentator* 10 (July 1941): 3; "Postwar Union with Britain?" *NYDN*, 13 February 1941, 29; Eleanor Hart, "Times Have Changed," *Scribner's Commentator* 10 (July 1941): 51–53; Congressman Stephen Day (Rep.-Ill.), radio address, 15 June 1941, in *CR*, A2878. Day's book *We Must Save the Republic: A Brief for the Declaration of Independence and the Constitution of the United States* (Washington, D.C.: Shaw, 1941) was an all-out assault on Union Now.

33. "But Boake Carter Says," *SFE*, 24 November 1939, 9; 15 November 1939, 15; 12 January 1940, 9; Holt, *CR*, 3 October 1940, 13,086; Sargent, "The Dream of Cecil Rhodes," Bulletin #11, 16 October 1939, *Getting US into War*, 143–46. Journalist Edward Price Bell denied that Cecil Rhodes ever foresaw a conflict involving Germany; rather, he wanted joint British-German-American leadership. The noted journalist saw Union Now an offshoot of "New Dealism." Letter, *CT*, 29 April 1941, 10.

34. Trevor, "Union Now?" in *CR*, 5 June 1941, A2698; Amos Pinchot, open letter to President Roosevelt, 20 June 1941, Pinchot Papers; "Inside England," *Uncensored* 90 (21 June 1941): 1–2; "Britain as a State in Our Union," *CT*, 21 September 1940, 10. For an additional attack, see "Britain and Federalism," *CT*, 23 March 1941, 16. For explicit endorsements of *Uncensored*'s position, see Frank C. Waldrop, "Union How?" *WTH*, 25 July 1941, 13.

35. See, for example, Bennett Champ Clark, "Union Now?" *Rotarian* 57 (October 1940): 57; "Comment," *America* 64 (15 March 1941): 619; Waldrop, "Whose Union?" *WTH*, 13 August 1941, 8; "The Fetish of Independence," *Saturday Evening Post* 213 (19 April 1941): 28.

36. Sargent, "The Dream of Cecil Rhodes," Bulletin #11, 16 October 1939, *Getting US into War*, 143–46, 148.

37. Howe, "Union Now Means War Tomorrow," *Forum* 102 (July 1939): 31–32. See also John Haynes Holmes to Trufant Foster, 27 April 1940, Holmes Papers; Lundeen, *CR*, 11 July 1940, 9512; Dennis, "The Party-State and the Elite," *Nation* 152 (11 January 1941): 39; Congressman Paul Shafer (Rep.-Mich.), *CR*, 19 May 1941, A2380.

38. Utley, "What Kind of Peace for Europe?" *Saturday Review of Literature* 22 (25 May 1940): 7; Sokolsky, "These Days: Anglo-American Union," *New York Sun*, 25 January 1941, 16. See also Albert Jay Nock, "'Union Now': A Review," *Scribner's Commentator* 9 (May 1941): 21.

39. "Postwar Union with Britain?" *NYDN*, 13 February 1941, 29; Norman Thomas to Mercedes Randall, 2 March 1940, Thomas Papers. See also Norman Thomas to Dr. Minnee Maffett, National Federation of Business and Professional Women's Clubs, 26 August 1941, Thomas Papers.

40. Trevor, "Union Now?" in *CR*, 5 June 1941, A2698. See also Norman Thomas, testimony, HFAC, 22 January 1941, 347; Sidney Hertzberg, "Admission of Britain a Reactionary Move," *Living Age* 360 (June 1941): 319; Burton Roscoe to Admiral W. H. Standley [copy], 25 November 1940, Hertzberg Papers; Libby, "Discussions of Post-War World Begin," *Peace Action* 7 (September 1941): 4.

41. Chester Bowles to Roy Larsen, 30 April 1941, in Doenecke, *IDU*, 286. See also Stuart Chase to Sidney Hertzberg, 18 January 1940, and Sidney Hertzberg to Stuart Chase, 25 January 1940, both in Hertzberg Papers.

42. See, for example, Harold E. Fey, "Save Neutrality! Save Peace!" *Christian Century* 56 (11 October 1939): 1235. For a debate among FOR leaders, see Vernon Nash, "Federal Union and Mediation," *Fellowship* 6 (May 1940): 76–77; A. J. Muste, "What 'Federal Union' Lacks," 78.

43. "A Federated Europe?" *Christian Century* 56 (6 December 1939): 1496; "The Search for a Lasting Peace, IV: America's Stake," 58 (5 March 1941): 312.

44. For stronger endorsements, see Quaker leader Richard R. Wood, "Fresh Hope in Union Now," *Fellowship* 5 (October 1939): 23; Villard, "Issues and Men," *Nation* 149 (14 October 1939): 414; Villard, "Issues and Men: Collective Security Must Come," *Nation* 149 (23 December 1939): 711.

45. Morley Diary, 2 September 1939. In November 1940, he was listed as an endorser of Interdemocracy Federal Unionists. *Smith College Associated News*, 26 November 1940, 1. In June 1940, Morley voiced some skepticism, claiming Union Now would focus the United States away from the hemisphere and into a European grouping toward which the mass of American opinion was, to say the least, apathetic. "The Formula of Federation," *Asia* 40 (June 1940): 294.

46. Barnes, "Hope for Peace Seen in Union," *NYWT*, 29 December 1939, 12.

47. Chase, "The War as a Revolution," *Progressive*, 5 April 1941, 5; "Ideologies for Export," 31 May 1941, 5; "Why Germany Keeps On Winning," 6 September 1941, 1; "Balancing the Risks," 17 May 1941, 5.

48. Barnes, "The War and World Revolution," *Progressive*, 15 November 1941, 9.

49. Dorothy Detzer to Mrs. Louis N. Robinson, 21 August 1940, WIL Papers. See also John Haynes Holmes, "Is There Any Feasible Plan for Banning War from the World?" *Unity* 124 (19 February 1940): 186; Holmes to Shlomo Katz, 26 October 1939, Holmes Papers.

50. WIL National Board meeting, resolutions, 18–19 October 1940, Swarthmore, Pennsylvania, 2, WIL Papers. In April 1941, Norman Thomas offered a qualified endorsement of the Tenerowitz resolution, expressing the hope that it might start people thinking all "the right lines," but denying that world conditions permitted much action and fearing that Roosevelt might use the initiative to bring the nation into war. Norman Thomas to Edith Wynner, Campaign for World Government, 10 April 1941, Thomas Papers. In October 1939, Thomas had denied that conditions were ready for a federation of the world. *Smith College Weekly*, 25 October 1939, 2. For endorsement of the proposal, see John Haynes Holmes to Tracy Mygatt, 1 October 1941, Holmes Papers.

51. "A Sketch for a Possible Peace Treaty," *Christian Century* 58 (12 March 1941): 353.

52. See, for example, Stuart Chase quoted in Isabel Bacon La Follette, "A Room of Our Own: Stuart Chase a Visitor," *Progressive*, 17 February 1940, 7; Paul Porter, "The Struggle of the Empires," *Call*, 23 September 1939, 2; Cudahy, testimony, SFRC, 23 October 1941, 160; William A. Orton, *Williams* [College] *Record*, 27 April 1940, 5; Representative Anton Johnson (Rep.-Ill.), *CR*, 24 April 1941, A3007; Bender, *CR*, 24 April 1941, 3282; "Toward European Federation," *New Republic* 102 (8 January 1940): 38–40.

53. Jessup, *Bryn Mawr College News*, 24 April 1940, 2. He recommended similar federations for the Danubian, Balkan, and Baltic areas.

54. Norman Thomas to Ernest Minor Patterson, 27 February 1940, Thomas Papers; Thomas, *Brown* [University] *Daily Herald*, 26 April 1940, 1; Norman Thomas, "Your World and Mine: War Aims and Peace Terms," *Call*, 5 April 1941, 8. For more socialist endorsement, see Thomas, "Your World and

Mine: A Foreign Policy for America," *Call*, 24 May 1941, 5; Henry Haskell, "For a United Socialist Europe," *Call*, 21 October 1939, 4; *American Guardian*, 13 October 1939, 1. Communist Joseph Starobin commented that a United States of Europe would involve the military domination of capitalism and "a united front against the USSR." "The United States of Europe," *New Masses* 34 (13 February 1940): 5–7; quotation, 7.

55. Vorys, *CR*, 5 May 1941, 3592.

56. Wheeler, *CT*, 22 June 1941, 3; "The Case for Isolation," *NYDN*, 5 November 1939, 49. See also "Satellite Nations," *NYDN*, 17 March 1940, 47. In "A United States of Europe," 10 December 1939, 63, the *News* noted that Lothian and Chamberlain had recently endorsed the idea although the scheme could only work if England "stays on the sidelines."

57. Alfred M. Bingham, *The United States of Europe* (New York: Duell, Sloan & Pearce, 1940), 296, 299, 302.

58. Bingham, *United States,* 311.

59. Utley, "What Kind of Peace for Europe?" *Saturday Review of Literature* 22 (25 May 1940): 7, 20–21. For another favorable comparison of Bingham to Streit, see Harry Elmer Barnes, "Keep Out of War and Investigate the War-Mongers" [draft], n.d., 40, Box 252, Lundeen Papers.

60. Chamberlain, "Europe, Incorporated," *New Republic* 103 (1 July 1940): 32–33; Drucker, "Federation," *Common Sense* 9 (May 1940): 27.

61. "Why Short of War?" *Common Sense* 9 (May 1941): 144–45; Miller, *New American Radicalism*, 196.

62. Chamberlain broadcast, text, *NYT*, 27 November 1939, 2; "A Federated Europe?" *Christian Century* 56 (6 December 1939): 1495–96; "America and a Federal Europe," 57 (24 January 1940): 104. See also the *Century*'s response to the pledge of the inter-Allied council, meeting in London on 28 March 1940, to make peace on the basis of "an effective and lasting guarantee" of mutual security. "Post-War Security for France," 57 (10 April 1940): 468. For another endorsement of Chamberlain, see John La Farge, "The Peace Aims of Europe Should Unify the States," *America* 62 (10 February 1940): 480.

63. Lothian, address to the Pilgrim Society, *NYT*, 26 October 1939, 4. See also address, Council of Foreign Relations, *NYT*, 5 January 1940, 4.

64. Grattan, "The Struggle for Peace," *Harper's Magazine* 180 (February 1940): 301, 303. See also "Propaganda," *Saturday Evening Post* 212 (10 February 1940): 26.

65. "A Long War Means a Spreading War," *NYDN*, 17 January 1940, 29. Amos Pinchot feared that United States would be fighting to drive Germany out of Poland, France, Czechoslovakia, and other conquered nations. Letter to E. F. Hutton, 5 September 1940; to Hiram Johnson, 2 October 1940, Pinchot Papers.

66. "Status Quo Ante Bellum," *NYDN*, 25 August 1939, 25. See also "The Case for Isolation," *NYDN*, 5 November 1939, 49; "Satellite Nations," *NYDN*, 17 March 1940, 47; Bruce Barton to Harry Elmer Barnes, 21 November 1939, Barnes Papers.

67. For Beard's belief in a planned economy, see Richard Hofstadter, *The Progressive Historians: Turner, Beard, Parrington* (New York: Knopf, 1968), 322–34. For an unusually able exposition of Beard's whole career, including his foreign policy, see Ellen Nore, *Charles A. Beard: An Intellectual Biography* (Carbondale: Southern Illinois University Press, 1983).

68. Beard, "National Politics and War," *Scribner's Magazine* 97 (February 1935): 65–70.

69. Charles A. Beard, *Giddy Minds and Foreign Quarrels: An Estimate of American Foreign Policy* (New York: Macmillan, 1939), 57. For the magazine version, see "Giddy Minds and Foreign Quarrels," *Harper's Magazine* 179 (September 1939): 337–51.

70. See, for example, John Haynes Holmes to Harry L. Kadet, 11 October 1939, Holmes Papers; Norman Thomas, "Your World and Mine," *Call*, 4 November 1939, 3; Lillian Symes, "Hold That Line," *Call*, 28 September 1939, 4; Barnes, "Keep Out of War and Investigate the War-Mongers" [draft], 54, Box 252, Lundeen Papers; C. Hartley Grattan, *NYT Book Review*, 15 October 1939, 3; NCPW official Florence Brewer Boeckel, "Books in a World at War," *Peace Action* 6 (September 1939): 7; Edwin M. Borchard to Charles A. Beard, 1 September 1939, Borchard Papers; Congressman Francis H. Case (Rep.-S.Dak.), radio broadcast, 19 September 1939, in *CR*, A29; Page Hufty, "America First Book List," Bulletin #476, 7 August 1941, in Doenecke, *IDU*, 121. For excerpts, see Charles A. Beard, "What Should

Our Foreign Policy Be?" *Peace Action* 6 (September 1939): 5. For entire text, see entry of D. Worth Clark, *CR*, 10 July 1941, A3351–56.

71. Clarence A. Berdahl, Kenneth Colegrove, William Rice Sharp, and Quincy Wright, "Cooperation of States Held Necessary to World Peace," *NYT*, 12 November 1939, sect. 4, 8–9.

72. "The Beards Lose the Thread of History," *New Masses* 33 (12 December 1939): 25.

73. Beard, *A Foreign Policy for America* (New York: Knopf, 1940).

74. See, for example, Nye, *CR*, 21 June 1940, 8792; Hugh Johnson, "One Man's Opinion," *San Francisco News*, 7 May 1940, 13; Hufty, "America First Book List"; Holmes, "American Foreign Policy," *Unity* 124 (20 November 1939): 98.

75. Sarles, "Books in a World at War," *Peace Action* 6 (May 1940): 7.

76. Nevins, *NYT Book Review*, 26 May 1940, 1. See also Ralph Thompson, "Books of the Times," *NYT*, 15 May 1940, 23. For a specific attack on Nevins's review, see Edwin M. Borchard to Spencer Brodney, 28 June 1940, Borchard Papers.

77. See, for example, Quincy Wright, "America's Foreign Relations," *Survey Graphic* 29 (August 1940): 443–44; "Fundamentalist v. Modernist," *Time*, 10 May 1940, 90–93.

78. Buell on vulnerability, *Isolated America* (New York: Knopf, 1940), 229–45; Niebuhr, "American Foreign Policy," *Nation* 150 (25 May 1940): 656–58; Davis, "America and the War," *Saturday Review of Literature* 22 (10 May 1940): 5, 11–12; Bruce Minton, "Spokesmen of the Past," *New Masses* 36 (9 July 1940): 26–29.

79. Lerner, "In the Hour of Decision," *New Republic* 102 (3 June 1940): 765–67; Cousins, "The World Today in Books," *Current History* 51 (June 1940): 1–5; Millis, "Is It Internationalism or 'Continentalism'?" *New York Herald Tribune Book Review*, 19 May 1940, sect. 9, 3. For excerpts of Walter Millis's, *Road to War: America, 1914–1917* (Boston: Houghton Mifflin, 1935), see *CT*, Sunday issues of 8 October–12 November 1939.

80. Anne Morrow Lindbergh, letter to Mrs. Dwight [Elizabeth] Morrow begun 5 June 1940, *War Within*, 100; entry of 4 September 1940, 142.

81. Anne Morrow Lindbergh, *The Wave of the Future: A Confession of Faith* (New York: Harcourt Brace, 1940); quotations, respectively, 24, 22, 12, and 34.

82. Lindbergh, *Wave*, 16–18. See also entries of, 29 April 1940, and 27 May 1940, *War Within*, 80, 93.

83. Lindbergh, *Wave*, 18–19. See also entry of 29 April 1940, *War Within*, 81.

84. Lindbergh, *Wave*, 25, 40.

85. For best-seller status, see Berg, *Lindbergh*, 406. For favorable reviews, see, for example, Mary L. Dunn, *America* 64 (30 November 1940): 221; *Catholic World* 152 (January 1941): 510; Nicholas Broughton, "Books in a World at War," *Peace Action* 7 (October 1940): 7; Mario Collaci, "Books in Review," *Fellowship* 6 (December 1940): 161; Robert E. Wood to Anne Morrow Lindbergh, 11 October 1940, Wood Papers; "Anne Lindbergh Urges U.S. Pay Price of Peace," *Progressive*, 12 October 1940, 7; John Haynes Holmes to Ruth Benedict, 17 April 1941, Holmes Papers; Holmes to Mrs. George [Margot] Picksen, 16 February 1941, Holmes Papers; Frederick J. Libby to Anne Morrow Lindbergh, 27 September 1940, NCPW Papers; Philip C. Jessup to Anne Morrow Lindbergh, 24 October 1940, Jessup Papers. The *Reader's Digest* reproduced it in condensed form. See 37 (November 1940): 1–12.

86. John Foster Dulles to Anne Morrow Lindbergh, 8 October 1940, Box 19, the Papers of John Foster Dulles, Princeton University (hereafter cited as Dulles Papers); Auden in Berg, *Lindbergh*, 406.

87. "The Wave of the Future," *Common Sense* 10 (March 1941): 80; Norman Thomas to Comrade Waldron, 29 November 1940, Thomas Papers; Symes, "Hold That Line: Who's a Fascist?" *Call*, 1 February 1941, 5; "Wave of the Future," *Christian Century* 57 (30 October 1940): 1335. Dorothy Dunbar Bromley called the wave "pure socialism." Entry of July 1941, *War Within*, 209.

88. Miller, "War Aims in War Propaganda," *Propaganda Analysis* 4 (27 May 1941): 8; "On Using Freedom to Lose Freedom," *Commonweal* 33 (17 January 1941): 316.

89. Clare Boothe, "Half a Worm," *Current History and Forum* 52 (7 November 1940): 4; E. B. White, "One Man's Meat," *Harper's Magazine* 181 (November 1940): 330; Agar in *Time*, 6 January 1941, 11.

90. See, for example, Leon Bryce Bloch, *Living Age* 359 (December 1940): 384; philosopher Irwin Edman, "The Poetry of Appeasement," *New York Herald Tribune Book Review*, sect. 9, 20 October 1940,

2; Max Lerner, speech, Hampshire County Progressive Club, *Smith College Weekly*, 5 November 1940, 1; Dorothy Thompson, "An Open Letter to Anne Lindbergh," *Look*, 25 March 1941, 11. For a direct attack on Thompson's interpretation, see "Cabbages and Kings: Explain This," *Scribner's Commentator* 10 (May 1941): 4–5.

91. "Nazi Innocents," *New Republic* 103 (30 December 1940): 887; Marshall, "Books and the Arts," *Nation* 150 (12 October 1940): 336; Reuben H. Markham, *The Wave of the Past* (Chapel Hill: University of North Carolina Press, 1941), 15; Elliott, *Harvard* [University] *Crimson*, 7 January 1941, 3; Jean Rushmore Patterson, *Letter to Anne Lindbergh* (pamphlet; New York: Lenox Hill, 1940), 7.

92. Lindbergh, "Reaffirmation," *Atlantic Monthly* 167 (June 1941): 681–86. Quotations from 683–84.

93. Until the spring of 1940, Dennis's publishing house, Harper and Brothers, had planned to publish the volume but after the fall of France found it inexpedient; hence, Dennis had to publish it himself. See supplement to Dennis, *WFL* 97 (6 June 1940); Dennis to Ordway Tead, Harper and Bros., 30 April 1940, Dennis Papers.

94. For a brief biography, see "Lawrence Dennis," in *Current Biography, 1941*, ed. Maxine Block (New York: Wilson, 1942), 218–20. For his admiration of Hitler, see O. John Rogge, *The Official German Report: Nazi Penetration, 1924–1942; Pan-Arabism, 1939–Today* (New York: Yoseloff, 1961), 174–79. For his social vision, see Dennis, "Portrait of American Fascism," *American Mercury* 36 (December 1935): 407–8; *The Coming American Fascism* (New York: Harper, 1936), especially viii, 137, 198–99, 211–12. For the question of Dennis's fascism, see Justus D. Doenecke, "The Isolationist as Collectivist: Lawrence Dennis and the Coming of World War II," *Journal of Libertarian Studies* 3 (Summer 1979): 193.

95. See, for example, Robert E. Wood to Robert E. Wood Jr., 5 May 1941, Wood Papers; Lawrence Dennis to Robert E. Wood, 10 October 1941, copy in Barnes Papers; Lawrence Dennis to Harry Elmer Barnes, 29 September 1941, Barnes Papers; Edwin M. Borchard to John Bassett Moore, 22 November 1940, and John Bassett Moore to Edwin M. Borchard, 25 November 1940, both in Borchard Papers; Ruth Sarles to Sidney Hertzberg, 20 March 1940, Box 67, AFC Papers; Burton K. Wheeler to Robert E. Wood, 10 July 1941, Box 67, AFC Papers; Alfred M. Bingham to Lawrence Dennis, 31 March 1942, Dennis Papers; Harry Elmer Barnes, "Keep Out of War and Investigate the War-Mongers" [draft], 7, Box 252, Lundeen Papers. For appreciative words by one interventionist, see A. A. Berle to Lawrence Dennis, 8 May 1940, Dennis Papers.

96. Concerning ghostwriting for *Scribner's Commentator*, see Rogge, *Official German Report*, 282, 347–48; for Freda Utley, see Lawrence Dennis to John W. Blodgett Jr., 10 October 1941, Dennis Papers. Concerning a Dennis manuscript for General Wood and the America First Committee, see Doenecke, *IDU*, 21–22, 62 n. 78, 200–205.

97. For Dennis's meetings with the Lindberghs and for their views toward each other, see Lawrence Dennis to Harry Elmer Barnes, 29 September 1941, Barnes Papers; Charles A. Lindbergh, entry of 17 September 1941, *Wartime Journals*, 391; Dennis, *WFL* 131 (30 January 1941): 1; Anne Morrow Lindbergh, entry of 12 November 1941, *War Within*, 152. For stress on similarities between Dennis's thought and that of the Lindberghs, see Dorothy Thompson, quoted in *Life* 10 (20 January 1941): 27; Rogge, *Official German Report*, 282–83; Kenneth S. Davis, *The Hero: Charles A. Lindbergh and the American Dream* (Garden City, N.Y.: Doubleday, 1959), 401–2, 409, 509–11. Lindbergh later claimed that Dennis's influence was "negligible." See Cole, *Lindbergh*, 255. Dennis, on the other hand, claimed that Lindbergh undoubtedly learned much from him. Interview with Lawrence Dennis, 1967, Columbia Oral History Project, Columbia University, 14.

98. Lawrence Dennis, *The Dynamics of War and Revolution* (New York: Weekly Foreign Letter, 1940), xxvi–xxvii, 149. Included in his definition of socialist revolution was "more public ownership in displacement of private ownership" and "in general more collectivism and less individualism." See xxiv.

99. Dennis, *Dynamics*, xxvii, 7, 102–13, 214–16.

100. On the war, Dennis, *Dynamics*, 213; on anti-Semitism, *Dynamics*, xxxi; on refugees, *WFL* (30 January 1941): 5.

101. Dennis, *Dynamics*, 158–59.

102. Dennis, *Dynamics*, xv, 139, 188–89.

103. For reserved approval, see Robert E. Wood to Sterling Morton, 7 May 1941, and Sterling Morton to Robert E. Wood, 12 May 1941, both in Morton Papers.

104. Harlan F. Stone to Mr. Palmer, 1 September 1940, Dennis Papers; Harry Elmer Barnes, *Southern Economic Journal* 7 (April 1941): 559.

105. Korsch, "Lawrence Dennis's 'Revolution,'" *Partisan Review* 8 (May–June 1941): 244–47; Chamberlin, "Advocate of a Fascist America," *Christian Science Monitor*, 19 October 1940, 11; Utley, "Mr. Dennis's Dangerous Thoughts," *Common Sense* 9 (September 1940): 23–24; Bingham, *Modern Quarterly* 15 (Summer 1940): 83–87. In a private letter, Bingham found that certain events tended to confirm Dennis's thesis, while others "tend to confirm the view that the liberal humanistic ideals are more vital than ever." Alfred M. Bingham to Lawrence Dennis, 18 January 1941, Dennis Papers.

106. Foster, "American Fascism Speaks Out," *Communist* 20 (April 1941): 333–40; Williams, "Views and Reviews," *Commonweal* 33 (8 November 1940): 78–79. Williams's original review was far less critical. *Commonweal* 32 (13 September 1940): 428–29.

107. Walker, "Lowdown on the Democracies," *New Republic* 103 (25 November 1940): 728–29; Pendleton Herring, *Annals of the American Academy of Political and Social Science* 213 (January 1941): 197. See also Leon Whipple, "Dynamisms," *Survey Graphic* 29 (October 1940): 517.

108. Schuman, "Who Owns the Future? The Will to Survive," *Nation* 152 (11 January 1941): 36–39, quotation on 38. See also Frederick L. Schuman to Lawrence Dennis, 3 September 1940, Dennis Papers.

109. Dennis, "Who Owns the Future? The Party-State and the Elite," *Nation* 152 (11 January 1941): 39–41; Lerner, "The Dynamics of Democracy," 41–44, quotation on 42.

## CHAPTER 5: INITIAL ENGAGEMENTS

1. Roosevelt, address to Congress, 21 September 1939, *CR*, 11–12.

2. *Time*, 25 September 1939, 12.

3. *Newsweek*, 9 October 1939, 27. For major accounts of the bill, see Divine, *The Illusion of Neutrality* (Chicago: University of Chicago Press, 1962), chap. 9; Guinsburg, *Pursuit of Isolationism*, chap. 9; Porter, *Seventy-sixth Congress*, chap. 4; Cole, *Roosevelt and the Isolationists*, 320–30. Dallek claims Borah privately favored the bill but feared further warlike steps. See *Roosevelt*, 203.

4. *Newsweek*, 6 November 1939, 24.

5. The other peace groups included the Peace Section of the American Friends Service Committee, the World Peace Commission of the Methodist Church, and the War Resisters League. For a brief history of the KAOWC, see Justus D. Doenecke, "Non-interventionism of the Left: The Keep America Out of the War Congress, 1938–1941," *Journal of Contemporary History* 12 (April 1977): 221–36. For the background and history of left-wing youth activity, including the KAOWC-affiliated Youth Committee Against War, see Cohen, *Old Left*; Eagan, *Class, Culture*; and Mihelich, "Student Antiwar Activism."

6. T.R.B., "Washington Notes: Ordeal by Lung-Power," *New Republic* 100 (19 October 1939): 299. Possible members included aviators Charles A. Lindbergh and Eddie Rickenbacker, auto manufacturer Henry Ford, Herbert Hoover, and Charles A. Beard. *CT*, 23 September 1939, 1. See also KAOWC, *Newsweek*, 2 October 1939, 29; editor John C. O'Laughlin to Hoover, 9 September 1939, Hoover Papers; Drew Pearson and Robert S. Allen, "Washington Merry-Go-Round," [University of] *Michigan Daily*, 27 September 1939, 4; Chester Bowles to Philip La Follette, 28 September 1939, Philip La Follette Papers; Maney, *La Follette*, 231.

7. American Legion, *NYT*, 28 September 1939, 5; AFL, *NYT*, 3 October 1939, 1. White committee in Walter Johnson, *Battle*, 39–57; Jane Harriet Schwar, "Internationalist Propaganda and Pressure Groups in the United States, 1937–1941," Ph.D. diss., Ohio State University, 1973, chap. 6. Gallup poll, *NYT*, 24 October 1939, 14. For related polls, see Cantril, *Public Opinion*, 967–70, 1157–59.

8. See, for example, Raymond Moley to Jouett Shouse, 26 September 1939, Moley Papers; "Freedom of the Seas Again," *WTH*, 27 September 1939, 10; Amos Pinchot to Robert La Follette, 13 October 1939, Pinchot Papers; Hearst in Carlisle, *Hearst*, 202. Hugh Johnson claimed that he and his

patron, financier Bernard Baruch, had long worked to develop cash-and-carry. "Neutral Rights," *NYWT*, 23 September 1939, 1. For combining endorsement of cash-and-carry with mistrust of Roosevelt, see Harry Elmer Barnes, "Embargo Issue Realistic," *NYWT*, 29 September 1939, 22; Hoover to John C. O'Laughlin, 18 July 1939, Stanford Files.

9. Taft, *CR*, 13 October 1939, 358.

10. "National Unity Against War," *NYDN*, 22 September 1939, 29; "Our 'Neutrality' Act—A Help to Hitler," 5 September 1939, 27. See also "War Machines Need Fuel," 26 September 1939, 25; "Let's Tune Up Our Factories," 2 October 1939, 21.

11. See, for example, Taft, *CR*, 13 October 1939, 358; Waldrop, "European Reasons for Us to Say Out," *WTH*, 9 September 1939, A11.

12. "Our 'Neutrality' Act—A Help to Hitler," *NYDN*, 5 September 1939, 27; "What the Neutrality Debate Is About," 5 October 1939, 33.

13. Borah, *CR*, 2 October 1939, 71–73. On munitions plants, see also Senator Reed, *CR*, 16 October 1939, 476–77; Congressman William B. Barry (Dem.-N.Y.), *CR*, 31 October 1939, 1125; Congressman Dewey Short (Rep.-Mo.), *CR*, 1 November 1939, 1167. On immorality, see also "Keep the Arms Embargo!" *Christian Century* 56 (20 September 1939): 1126; Fish, radio broadcast, CBS, 26 September 1939, in *CR*, A67; Fish, radio speech, NBC, 28 October 1939, in *CR*, A701; Senator Charles Tobey, *CR*, 5 October 1939, 114; retired marine general Smedley Butler, "Arms Credits Sure Path to War," entered in *CR*, 14 October 1939, 409; "Keep the Embargo," *America* 62 (21 October 1939): 42; pacifist poet Sarah N. Cleghorn to Franklin D. Roosevelt (mimeographed), October 1939, WIL Papers; Sweeney, *CR*, 2 November 1939, 1314.

14. For foreign ships, see Vandenberg, *CR*, 4 October 1939, 102. For accidental sinkings, Walsh, 17 October 1939, 359; Congressman Leslie C. Arends (Rep.-Ill.), *CR*, 1 November 1939, 1253. For Declaration of Panama, see Schafer, *CR*, 11 October 1939, 305. For Allied factories, see Fish, speech, NBC, 28 October 1939, in *CR*, A701; Hiram Johnson, *CR*, 20 October 1939, 629; Vorys, *CR*, 1 November 1939, 1205. For U.S. shortages, see Reynolds, *CR*, 21 October 1939, 698; Congressman Thomas E. Martin (Rep.-Iowa), *CR*, 1 November 1939, 1265. For endangering Allies, see Shafer, *CR*, 31 October 1939, 1144.

15. See, for example, "Roosevelt vs. Roosevelt," *CT*, 29 September 1939, 18; B. C. Clark, *CR*, 11 October 1939, 276.

16. "We'll Need a Parachute," 2 October 1939, in *CR*, 327. For other warnings of a war boom, see T.R.B., "Washington Notes: The Peace-Party Republicans," *New Republic* 100 (27 September 1939): 213; meat packer Jay C. Hormel, "Proposal for Domestic Recovery," *CR*, inserted 28 September 1939, A68: constitutional scholar Edward S. Corwin, letter to *NYT*, 2 October 1939, 16; Wheeler, *CT*, 2 October 1939, 1; John T. Flynn, *Washington Daily News*, 3 October 1939; Downey, *CR*, 6 October 1939, 161; Maynard Krueger, [University of Chicago] *Daily Maroon*, 11 October 1939, 2; Congressman Andrew C. Schiffler (Rep.-W.Va.), *CR*, 19 October 1939, A376. For a focus on damage done to agriculture, see Fish, speech, CBS, 26 September 1939, in *CR*, A67; D. W. Clark, *CR*, 18 October 1939, 564; Reynolds, *CR*, 18 October 1939, 565.

17. Downey, *CR*, 6 October 1939, 169; Vandenberg, *CR*, 21 October 1939, 387; Congressman August H. Andresen (Rep.-Minn.), *CR*, 1 November 1939, 1229; Joseph P. Kennedy in Koskoff, *Kennedy*, 264.

18. Hiram W. Johnson to Hiram W. Johnson Jr., 24 September 1939, Johnson Papers; Hiram W. Johnson, *CR*, 10 October 1939, 249; Walsh, *CR*, 17 October 1939, 499; Robsion, *CR*, 2 November 1939, 1297; Castle Diary, 23 October 1939. Such pressure had some effect, for, on 24 October 1941, the Senate approved a state department amendment relaxing restrictions on American shipping. *NYT*, 25 October 1939, 1. Not all anti-interventionists concurred. Borchard said he hated to give up the right of U.S. vessels to trade with European belligerents, but he feared that the sinking of an American ship might "arouse a war spirit." Edwin M. Borchard to Hiram Johnson, 26 September 1939, Johnson Papers. Said Senator Bulow, "I would rather be a live coward on land than to be a dead hero in Davy Jones' locker." *CR*, 12 October 1939, 312.

19. See, for example, William R. Castle, *US News*, 11 September 1939, 4; Congressman James W. Mott (Rep.-Oreg.), *CR*, 1 November 1939, 1262; Dondero, *CR*, 31 October 1939, 1129; B. C. Clark, *CR*,

11 October 1939, 252; Shipstead, *CR*, 16 October 1939, 449; Hiram Johnson, *CR*, 20 October 1939, 630; professors Samuel Flagg Bemis, Philip Jessup, Charles Cheney Hyde, and Irwin N. Griswold as cited by Congressman Albert Engel (Rep.-Mich.), *CR*, 23 October 1939, 760; historian Max Savelle, *Stanford* [University] *Daily*, 20 October 1939, 10; Philip C. Jessup to Edwin M. Borchard, 12 October 1939, Borchard Papers.

20. Fish, radio address, NBC, 25 September 1939, in *CR*, A20; Borah, *CR*, 2 October 1939, 70.

21. Dondero, *CR*, 31 October 1939, 1129.

22. For examples, see references to Van Nuys by Senator John H. Overton (Dem.-La.), *CR*, 5 October 1939, 119; to Senator Warren R. Austin (Rep.-Vt.) by B. C. Clark, 11 October 1939, 267; to Edward R. Burke (Dem.-Nebr.) and Wallace W. White (Rep.-Maine) by Hoffman, 12 October 1939, 349.

23. For the variety of people offering this argument, see Norman Thomas to editor, *New York Herald Tribune*, 12 September 1939, Thomas Papers; Coughlin, "From the Tower: This Is Stalin's War," *Social Justice*, 9 October 1939, 5; Professor Herbert Briggs, *Cornell* [University] *Daily Sun*, 13 October 1939, 1; William Z. Foster, "The Arms Embargo," *Daily Worker*, 25 October 1940, 6; Dennis and Gravenhoff, *WFL* 60 (21 September 1939): 3; Holt, *CR*, 18 October 1939, 553; Congressman William J. Miller (Rep.-Conn.), *CR*, 25 September 1939, A47.

24. B. C. Clark, *CR*, 11 October 1939, 268. Particularly noted was a French military mission which, in May 1939, arrived to survey possible war orders. See Lundeen, *CR*, 14 October 1939, 415, quoting *Washington Post* of 4 May 1939. Also recalled was an air accident which exposed the presence of a French purchasing mission. See Rush Holt, *CR*, 18 October 1939, 552. *Uncensored* noted that despite the arms embargo, American airplane manufactures were filling Allied orders. See "More Cooperation," 3 (21 October 1939): 1.

25. See, for example, attorney William Potter Lage to James A. Shanley, 28 October 1939, copy in Borchard papers; Engel, *CR*, 2 November 1939, 1331–32; John Haynes Holmes to Edgar J. Fisher, 25 September 1939, Holmes Papers.

26. Nye cited Wilson's secretary of state Robert Lansing, who claimed that reduction of the new American trade would result in "industrial depression, idle capital, and idle labor," which in turn would cause "general unrest and suffering among the laboring classes." He also quoted Federal Reserve Board member Paul M. Warburg, who had found possible cuts in wartime trade jeopardizing America's potential "to become the masters of the world," and Walter Hines Page, American ambassador to Britain, who had claimed that credits to the Allies were needed to "prevent the collapse of world trade and of the whole European finance." Nye, *CR*, 13 October 1939, 373, 379. Nye had been chairman of a famous Senate committee investigating the role of the munitions industry in U.S. entry into World War I.

27. Barton, broadcast, NBC, 29 October 1939, in *CR*, A593. See also Philip La Follette, radio broadcast, 3 October 1939, in *CR*, A189.

28. C. Hartley Grattan, *The Deadly Parallel* (New York: Stackpole, 1939), 79; emphasis in original. For praise of Grattan, see Hiram Johnson, *CR*, 20 October 1939, 632; Ernest L. Meyer, "Fish Learn Quicker," *Progressive*, 20 September 1941, 4; Thomas, "Your World and Mine," *Call*, 4 November 1939, 3. For citation of Grattan, see Holt, *CR*, 18 October 1939, 562. For a positive review, see *Fellowship* 5 (December 1939): 19. For opposition to Grattan's interpretation of American entry into World War I, see reviews by Harvard historian Sidney B. Fay, "Recipes for Neutrality," *Saturday Review of Literature* 21 (4 November 1939): 3–4, 16, and S. T. Williamson, *NYT Book Review*, 19 October 1939, 16.

29. Roosevelt, speech, 21 September 1939, *CR*, 10–11.

30. For biographical material on Borchard, see Kendall, "Borchard," and Doenecke, "Edwin M. Borchard, John Bassett Moore."

31. For studies of Moore, see Megaree, "Moore," and Doenecke, "Edwin M. Borchard, John Bassett Moore," 1–34. For Moore on collective security, see "What of the Night?" *Virginia Quarterly Review* 17 (January 1941): 75–88.

32. For a study of Jessup's career, see Marshall R. Kuehl, "Jessup." Jessup's own works include Philip C. Jessup and Francis Deák, *Neutrality: Its History, Economic and Law*, vol. 1: *Its Origins* (New York: Columbia University Press, 1935); Jessup, vol. 4: *Today and Tomorrow* (New York: Columbia University Press, 1936).

33. Edwin M. Borchard to William E. Borah, 16 February 1939; Edwin M. Borchard to Elbert D. Thomas, 18 October 1939, Borchard Papers.

34. Borchard, speech to Council of Foreign Relations, Chicago, as cited by Borah, *CR*, 17 October 1939, 510; Edwin M. Borchard to Leslie H. Thompson, 12 October 1939, Borchard Papers; Divine, *Illusion*, 146–47. For fear of reprisal, see also William Potter Lage to John Bassett Moore, 11 September 1939, Moore Papers.

35. Edwin M. Borchard to William E. Borah, 20 and 29 September 1939, Borchard Papers; Borchard, address to the American Academy of Political and Social Science, 14 October 1939, in *CR*, A415–18. Many anti-interventionists adopted Borchard's reasoning. See Borah, *CR*, 2 October 1939, 72; Shanley, 31 October 1939, 1107; letters to Shanley by William Potter Lage, William C. Dennis, Frederick C. Dunn, and John Bassett Moore, 3 November 1939, A761–62; "American Peace and Neutrality," *CT*, 13 September 1939, 14; California attorney general Earl Warren to Hiram Johnson, 23 October 1939, Johnson Papers. Castle challenged the claim that it was illegal to revoke an embargo during a war, saying that Columbia scholar Charles Cheney Hyde confused the illegal with the inexpedient. "We still have a right to do anything we please with our own laws but it may be unwise at any time to do what we want to do." Castle Diary, 26 September 1939.

36. Philip C. Jessup and Charles Cheney Hyde, letter, *NYT*, 21 September 1939, 17; Pound cited by Vandenberg, *CR*, 4 October 1939, 100; Danaher, *CR*, 17 October 1939, 508.

37. Woodrow Wilson by Shanley, *CR*, 31 October 1939, 1112; Sir Edward Grey by Vandenberg, *CR*, 4 October 1939, 100; former secretary of state William Jennings Bryan by McCarran, *CR*, 19 October 1939, 598; Robert Lansing by Keefe, *CR*, 1 November 1939, 1185; Henry S. Frazer, technical expert to the League of Nations Committee for the Codification of International Law, by Vandenberg, *CR*, 4 October 1939, 100; Key Pittman by Congressman Joshua Johns (Rep.-Wis.), *CR*, 19 October 1939, 617; "Pittman vs. Pittman," *CT*, 26 September 1939, 1.

38. Edward S. Corwin, letter, *NYT*, 2 October 1939, 16; statements of Borchard, John Bassett Moore, and legal scholar Manley O. Hudson, in B. C. Clark, *CR*, 11 October 1939, 277; Congressman Frederick C. Smith (Rep.-Ohio), *CR*, 12 October 1939, 344–45; Walsh, *CR*, 17 October 1939, 494; Congressman Everett Dirksen (Rep.-Ill.), *CR*, 27 October 1939, 1045; John Bassett Moore's *Digest of International Law*, in *CR*, 27 October 1939, 1045.

39. See, for example, historian William B. Hesseltine, "How Much History Does Franklin Roosevelt Know?" *CT*, 22 October 1939, 16; historian Charles Callan Tansill to Harry Elmer Barnes, 30 October 1939, Barnes Papers; "Reciting History," *Saturday Evening Post* 212 (28 October 1939): 22; Holt, *CR*, 18 October 1939, 554; Vandenberg, *CR*, 4 October 1939, 103; Johns, *CR*, 19 October 1939, 617; Nye, *CR*, 20 October 1939, 654; Downey, *CR*, 6 October 1939, 165; Senator Clyde Reed, speech of 1 October 1939, in *CR*, A130; "Reciting History," *Saturday Evening Post* 212 (28 October 1939): 22.

40. Engel, *CR*, 23 October 1939, 760; Jessup, *Barnard* [College] *Bulletin*, 24 October 1939, 1.

41. Sargent, Bulletin #8, 28 September 1939, *Getting US into War*, 128; Beard, "'International Law' Complex and Shifting," *NYWT*, 26 September 1939, 18; "The Mirage of International Law," *Christian Century* 56 (27 September 1939): 1160. See also Charles Callan Tansill, "Neutrality Debate Speaks Peace, but Moves Toward War," *America* 62 (28 October 1939): 66; Coughlin, "From the Tower: 'A Greater Consistency'—Mr. President," *Social Justice*, 2 October 1939, 7.

42. C. Hartley Grattan to Edwin M. Borchard, 30 October 1939, Borchard Papers. See also Senator Bulow, *CR*, 12 October 1939, 315.

43. "Spot Cash," *America* 61 (7 October 1939): 614. See also Congressman Louis L. Ludlow (Dem.-Ind.), *CR*, 16 October 1939, 486.

44. Dorothy Detzer to Helen Essary, 11 September 1939, WIL Papers; John Haynes Holmes to Barnett Brickner, 24 October 1939; Holmes to Paul Crosbie, 2 October 1939, both in Holmes Papers. At one point Holmes found the embargo a symbolic issue, not really relevant to the underlying issues that determined American belligerency. Letter to Robert Whitaker, 31 October 1940, Holmes Papers.

45. Nye, *CR*, 5 October 1939, 114. In an article, he conceded that the nation had not yet found machinery to subsidize many industries that would certainly suffer at the result of trade curtailment. See "Keep Our Money Out of War," *Look* 3 (7 November 1939): 22–23. See also J. Max Weis, research director, World Peaceways, *United States News*, 11 September 1939, 4.

46. Thomas, *Vassar* [College] *Miscellany News*, 25 October 1939, 1; Lodge, speech to New York Herald Tribune Forum, 26 October 1939, in *CR*, A554. Borchard conversely favored exporting arms to all neutrals, even though he knew that such goods could ultimately reach the belligerents. "This would be not our problem, nor our fault." Letter to William E. Borah, 29 September 1939, Borchard Papers.

47. Hoover, in *CR*, 12 October 1939, 320; Hoover, radio address, 20 October 1939, in *CR*, A497–98. For discussion on the background of Hoover's proposal, see Castle Diary, 30 September 1939, 11 October 1939; Herbert Hoover to William R. Castle, 14 September 1939, the Papers of William R. Castle, HHPL (hereafter cited as Castle Papers). Hoover had made a similar proposal to the World Disarmament Conference in 1932 but lacked a consensus.

48. Lindbergh, entry of 2 October 1939, *Wartime Journals*, 267; Lindbergh, radio speech, 13 October 1939, in *CR*, A301–3. For White, see Best, *Hoover*, 1:136.

49. See, for example, Senator Alben W. Barkley (Dem.-Ky.), *CR*, 14 October 1939, 415; Senator Key Pittman, *CR*, 14 October 1939, 441–42.

50. Clark, *CR*, 14 October 1939, 416. See also Lundeen, *CR*, 14 October 1939, 415; "Ganging Up on Neutrality," *New Masses* 33 (24 October 1939): 21.

51. William P. Lage to Edwin M. Borchard, 16 October 1939, Borchard Papers; Herbert Hoover to Philip C. Jessup, 2 October 1939, Jessup Papers; Herbert Hoover to John C. O'Laughlin, 4 September 1939, Stanford Files.

52. Charles W. Tobey to Alben W. Barkley, Senate majority leader, and text of amendment, *CR*, 4 October 1939, 105. Cash-and-carry terminated only on 1 May 1939. For examples of support, see Nye, *CR*, 4 October 1939, 114; B. C. Clark, 11 October 1939, *CR*, 269–70; staff writer Gerald B. Donnelly, "Neutrality Planned to Keep Us Out of War," *America* 61 (23 September 1939): 556–57; Donnelly, "Neutral We Must Remain in the Truest Way," *America* 61 (30 September 1939): 580–81; report of Dorothy Detzer to WIL National Board, Detroit, 21–22 October 1939, WIL Papers, SCPC; Edwin M. Borchard to John A. Danaher, 7 October 1939, Borchard Papers; Edwin M. Borchard to Senator Francis T. Maloney (Dem.-Conn.), 7 October 1939, Borchard Papers; "Either-Or," *Uncensored* 1 (7 October 1939): 1; Norman Thomas, "Your World and Mine," *Call*, 14 October 1939, 2.

53. Taft, *CR*, 24 October 1939, 790–94. For a similar view, see William P. Lage to Edwin M. Borchard, 26 September 1939, Borchard Papers. Borah differed, saying Taft "would practically sink all our ships." *CR*, 24 October 1939, 792.

54. Taft, *CR*, 13 October 1939, 357. Lage had also suggested the ban on government agencies. William P. Lage to Edwin M. Borchard, 26 September 1939, Borchard Papers. For the House counterpart to Taft's amendment concerning the role of government agencies, see Jesse P. Wolcott, *CR*, 1 November 1939, 1209.

55. La Follette, *CR*, 25 October 1939, 846. For endorsements, see Capper, *CR*, 851; Frazier, 853; Nye, 854. Even before La Follette made his proposal, socialist leader Norman Thomas had offered a similar suggestion, saying that England and France could obtain their raw materials from their own "mighty empires." *United States News*, 11 September 1939, 4; Norman Thomas to Dorothy Detzer and Frederick J. Libby, 5 October 1939, WIL Papers. See also Lodge, address to New York Herald Tribune Forum, 26 October 1939, in *CR*, A553; Kirby Page, *Christian Century* 56 (1 October 1939): 1248; KAOWC position, A. L. Dodge to D. Detzer, 24 September 1939, WIL Papers; Dorothy Detzer, *United States News*, 18 September 1939, 10.

56. Johnson, *CR*, 25 October 1939, 830.

57. *CR*, 27 October 1939, 1023–24; 2 November 1939, 1344–45; Gallup poll, *NYT*, 29 October 1939, 29.

58. Hiram Johnson to Frank Doherty, 3 November 1939, Johnson Papers; Dorothy Detzer to Emily Greene Balch, 4 November 1939, WIL Papers; Edwin M. Borchard to William E. Borah, 3 November 1939, Borchard Papers.

59. Flynn, minutes, governing committee, KAOWC, 6 November 1939, KAOWC Papers; diary entry, 27 October 1939, in *The Private Papers of Senator Vandenberg*, ed. Arthur H. Vandenberg Jr. (Boston: Houghton Mifflin, 1952), 3; "Exit Embargo," *Uncensored* 6 (11 November 1939): 1.

60. *NYT*, 8 November 1939, 1, 12; Hull, *Memoirs*, 1:697–98; Roosevelt to William Allen White, 13 November 1939, *FDR: His Personal Letters*, 954. For general discussion, see Langer and Gleason,

*Challenge to Isolation*, 234; "Neutrality Striking Hardest at U.S. Ships and Seamen," *Newsweek*, 20 November 1939, 15–16.

61. Johnson, "One Man's Opinion," *SFN*, 9 November 1939, 15. See also 10 November 1939, 19; 13 November 1939, 13.

62. *Daily Worker*, 8 November 1939, 1; "Getting Around the Law," *New Republic* 101 (22 November 1939): 127; "Pecunia Non Olet," *NYDN*, 8 November 1939, 31; "Ships, Flags, and Men," *NYDN*, 13 November 1939, 21; Norman Thomas, "Your World and Mine," *Call*, 25 November 1939, 2. See also Congressman Shanley, *United States News*, 20 November 1939, 4.

63. Hiram Johnson to John Bassett Moore, 5 January 1940, Moore Papers; "The Arms Embargo Repeal," *Commonweal* 31 (17 November 1939): 86; "Under a False Flag," *New Masses* 33 (21 November 1939): 18; John Bassett Moore to Harlan Fiske Stone, 11 November 1939, Moore Papers; Edwin M. Borchard to John Bassett Moore, 8 November 1939, Borchard Papers.

64. Dallek, *Roosevelt*, 212; Reynolds, *Creation*, 69, 75–76, 90, 95; Divine, *Illusion*, 332.

65. Rock, *Chamberlain and Roosevelt*, 229, 246, 311; Kimball, *Forged in War*, 25.

66. Ponting, *1940*, 43–44, 60.

67. Gallup poll, 27 September 1939, in Cantril, *Public Opinion*, 1147.

68. "But Boake Carter Says," *SFE*, 9 September 1939, 9. See also "Americans Are Also Calm," *Christian Century* 56 (20 September 1939): 1123; "The 'Athenia,'" *New Republic* 101 (13 September 1939): 141; "It Seems to Have Been a Submarine," *NYDN*, 6 September 1939, 37. For original accounts of the sinking, see *NYT*, 4–9 September 1939.

69. Herbert Hoover to John C. O'Laughlin, 4 September 1939, Stanford Files; Reynolds, *CR*, 21 October 1939, 689. Bennett Clark concurred; see 690. Reynolds also suspected the Russians, who—he said—desired to pit Germany and Britain against each other; see 691. *Social Justice* featured Reynolds's comments. Issue of 13 November 1939, 4.

70. It cited an affidavit by Gus Anderson, Chicago travel agent, to the state department. Anderson claimed that the ship was not torpedoed, that it carried munitions and gun emplacements, and that on reaching Canada, it was to be outfitted as a British sea raider. Issue of 30 October 1939, 10. See also *NYT*, 18 October 1939, 6.

71. Hull, M*emoirs,* 1:677.

72. John Bassett Moore to Edwin M. Borchard, 24 February 1940, Borchard Papers. See also Edwin M. Borchard to John Bassett Moore, 22 February 1940, Borchard Papers. For a debate with a prominent maritime lawyer, see James Ryan, *NYT*, 25 February 1940, sect. 4, 8; Borchard, *NYT*, 10 March 1940, sect. 4, 8. See also Borchard, "Was Norway Delinquent in the Case of the *Altmark*?" *American Journal of International Law* 34 (April 1940): 289–94.

73. Jessup, letter to *New York Herald Tribune*, 22 February 1940; "America and Other Neutrals," *CT*, 21 February 1940, 120. See also "Report Russian Advances in Finland," *Christian Century* 57 (28 February 1940): 269; "Comment," *America* 62 (2 March 1940): 542; "Extending the War," *New Masses* 35 (5 March 1940): 20; "A Set-Back to the Imperialist War-Intrigues," *Daily Worker*, 27 February 1940, 6.

74. Edwin M. Borchard to John Bassett Moore, 14 September 1939, Borchard Papers; Borchard, memorandum to George Holden Tinkham, 23 December 1939, Borchard Papers; John Bassett Moore to Edwin M. Borchard, 19 September 1939, Borchard Papers. For U.S. policy, see "Hull Neutrality Statement," *NYT*, 15 September 1939, 14; Langer and Gleason, *Challenge to Isolation*, 283.

75. Johnson, "Rights at Sea," *NYWT*, 23 February 1940, 20; "But Boake Carter Says," *SFE*, 3 January 1940, 9; Langer and Gleason, *Challenge to Isolation*, 282–83. For the *Düsseldorf*, see *NYT*, 16 December 1939, 4.

76. "Neutral Navicerts," *Newsweek*, 11 December 1939, 16; "The Admirable Russian Friend," *CT*, 1 November 1939, 14; Engel, *CR*, 2 November 1939, 1333 (chart given).

77. Robert W. Matson, *Neutrality and Navicerts: Britain, the United States, and Economic Warfare, 1939–1940* (New York: Garland, 1994), 9, 12.

78. Langer and Gleason, *Challenge to Isolation*, 280; "British Orders on Blockade," *NYT*, 28 November 1939, 2.

79. See, for example, Roy W. Howard to Lord Beaverbrook, 27 January 1940, Howard Papers; Fish, *CR*, 12 March 1940, 2730–31.

80. Johnson, "U.S. Rights," *NYWT*, 27 November 1939, 17. For further protests of Johnson, see "British Racket," *Miami Daily Herald*, 29 December 1939; *SFN*, 8 January 1940, 13.

81. Edwin M. Borchard to John Bassett Moore, 29 September 1939, Borchard Papers. See also John Bassett Moore to Edwin M. Borchard, 6 December 1939, Borchard Papers; Coughlin, "The President's Message to Congress," *Social Justice*, 2 October 1940, 4.

82. Hull, "U.S. Note on Blockade," *NYT*, 9 December 1939, 4.

83. Langer and Gleason, *Challenge to Isolation*, 358; "Text of Hull Note to British," *NYT*, 6 January 1940, 2.

84. John Garry Clifford, "The Odyssey of *City of Flint*," *American Neptune* 32 (April 1972): 100–116. For a contemporary account, see "Neutral Problem Spotlighted by *City of Flint* Seizure," *Newsweek*, 6 November 1939, 13–15.

85. Laurence A. Steinhardt, U.S. ambassador to the Soviet Union, to State Department, "Text of Envoy's Report," *NYT*, 28 October 1940, 3; "U.S. Statement on Flint," *NYT*, 29 October 1939, 36. For Roosevelt's anger, see Roosevelt to Cordell Hull and Sumner Welles, 22 December 1939, *F.D.R.: His Personal Letters*, 974.

86. "*City of Flint*," *New Masses* 33 (7 November 1940): 19–20; "*City of Flint*," *New Masses* 34 (13 February 1940): 23; Clark, *CR*, 25 October 1939, 830; "The Flitting '*City of Flint*,'" *New Republic* 101 (8 November 1939): 5; Jessup, *Columbia* [University] *Spectator*, 26 October 1939, 1. See also Professor Edward S. Corwin, *NYT*, 24 October 1939, 6; Rich, *CR*, 25 October 1939, 4863.

87. See, for example, Shafer, *CR*, 1 November 1939, 1203; *Social Justice*, 6 November 1939, 8; Edwin M. Borchard to Bennett C. Clark, 27 September 1939, and Borchard to James A. Shanley, 6 October 1939, Borchard Papers.

88. Johnson, "Taking Sides," *NYWT*, 14 November 1939, 17; "The Pot and the Kettle," *SFE*, 27 November 1939, 8.

89. "U.S. Note on Mail Seizure," *NYT*, 30 January 1940, 10; Matson, *Neutrality and Navicerts*, 27; Truman, *NYT*, 16 February 1940, 9; Pittman, *NYT*, 19 February 1940, 8.

90. Borchard, memorandum to George Holden Tinkham, 23 December 1939, Borchard Papers; "Bermuda and American Mails," *CT*, 23 February 1940, 12; Clark quoted in *Time*, 4 April 1940, 13. For Associated Press report on use of bayonet, see *NYT*, 22 February 1940, 1, 2. For British denials, see *NYT*, 30 February 1940, 1; *NYT*, 27 February 1940, 3. For further protest, international law scholar Herbert Wright, testimony, SFRC, 5 February 1941, 461; Congressman Jacob Thorkelson (Rep.-Mont.), *CR*, 7 February 1940, A632; Thill, *CR*, 28 February 1940, A1041.

91. Maas, *NYT*, 16 February 1940, 9; Thorkelson, *CR*, 7 February 1940, A623; "Britain and the Mails," *New Republic* 102 (29 January 1940): 133.

92. "U.S. Note on Mail Seizure," *NYT*, 30 January 1940, 10; "The British Foreign Office to the United States Embassy at London, 17 January 1940," in *Documents on American Foreign Relations: July 1939–June 1940*, 2 vols., ed. S. Shepard Jones and Denys P. Myers (Boston: World Peace Foundation, 1940), 2:715–18; *NYT*, 20 January 1940, 1, 4; Pan American Airways, *NYT*, 26 February 1940, 1, 3.

93. "Business as Usual," *Uncensored* 16 (20 January 1940): 2; Edwin M. Borchard to Bennett C. Clark, 27 September 1939, and to James A. Shanley, 6 October 1939, Borchard Papers. For further protest, see *Social Justice*, 11 August 1941, 6; Congressman Dirksen, *SFE*, 19 November 1941, 19. For the blacklist, see Matson, *Neutrality and Navicerts*, 22–24.

94. *NYT*, 21 January 1940, 1; Langer and Gleason, *Challenge to Isolation*, 359; "Tobacco for Britain," *CT*, 20 January 1940, 10.

95. Reynolds, *Creation*, 78–79. Quotation of Chamberlain, 27 January 1940, 78. He was obviously incorrect about spending "all our dollars."

96. See, for example, Hugh Johnson, "U.S. Rights," *NYWT*, 27 November 1939, 17; Hugh Johnson, "Rights at Sea," *NYWT*, 23 February 1940, 20; "Ghost Writers," *Uncensored* 20 (17 February 1940): 1–2; *Social Justice*, 6 November 1939, 15; Borchard, memorandum to George Holden Tinkham, 23 December 1939, Borchard to John Bassett Moore, 3 January 1940, William P. Lage to Edwin M. Borchard, 24

January 1940, Borchard Papers; "Neutrality Violations," *New Masses* 34 (16 January 1940): 19. There was some support for Hull's approach. See "America Protests Against British Policy," *Christian Century* 56 (20 December 1939): 1565; "Trade or War," *America* 63 (18 May 1940): 156; "The British and the Mails," *New Republic* 102 (5 February 1940): 164.

97. Sargent, Bulletin #26, 12 January 1940, *Getting US into War*, 235; "Mr. Hull Protests to Britain," *CT*, 8 January 1940, 12; "British Ships and Sealing Wax," *CT*, 25 January 1940, 10; *Social Justice*, 6 November 1939, 15; "Page Mason and Slidell," *NYDN*, 24 January 1940, 29.

98. For administration, see Reynolds, *Creation*, 68; James MacGregor Burns, *Roosevelt: The Lion and the Fox* (New York: Harcourt Brace, 1956), 415. For Berle, see entry of 15 March 1940, *Navigating*, 296. For Hull, see Breckinridge Long, entry of 15 March 1940, *War Diary*, 65; Hull, *Memoirs*, 1:733–36. For Long, see entry of 4 March 1940, *War Diary*, 61. For Welles, see *NYT*, 22 November 1939, 3. For FDR, see Roosevelt to Winston Churchill, 1 February 1940, in *Churchill and Roosevelt: The Complete Correspondence*, vol. 1: *Alliance Emerging, October 1933–November 1942*, ed. Warren F. Kimball (Princeton, N.J.: Princeton University Press, 1984), 34.

99. For Moffatt, see Reynolds, *Creation*, 68. See also entries of 2, 6, and 22 November 1939, *Moffat Papers*, 276–79; 19, 20, and 25 January 1940, 286–87, 290; and 12 March, 300–301. For Berle, see memorandum, 20 January 1940, *Foreign Relations, 1940*, vol. 2: *General and Europe* (Washington, D.C.: U.S. Government Printing Office, 1957), 6–7. For Chamberlain, see Reynolds, *Creation*, 77.

100. Hull, *Memoirs*, 1:735–36; Matson, *Neutrality and Navicerts*, 51–52.

101. "Text of Minister Cromwell's Talk to Canadians," *NYT*, 20 March 1940, 6. For a similar Cromwell speech, see *NYT*, 4 March 1940, 2.

102. Hull, *NYT*, 22 March 1940, 1, 4; "Spanked Envoy," *Newsweek*, 1 April 1940, 14–15. See also "The Head of Cromwell," *Time*, 1 April 1940, 15; "Neutrality's Headaches," *United States News*, 29 March 1940, 12–13.

103. See, for example, "Jimmy Cromwell Tells 'Em," *NYDN*, 21 March 1940, 31; Hearst, "In the News," *SFE*, 23 March 1940, 1, 2; "Not Our War: Mr. Cromwell Twice Wrong," *SFE*, 25 March 1940, 16; Holt, *CR*, 4 April 1940, 4006; Ernest L. Meyer, "As the Crow Flies," *Progressive*, 4 May 1940, 8; Barnes, "Keep Out of War and Investigate the War-Mongers" [draft], 38, Box 252, Lundeen Papers.

104. See, for example, Congressman Sweeney, *CR*, 20 March 1940, 3161–62; "Minister Cromwell Spreads War," *Daily Worker*, 21 March 1940, 1, 6; "Through Cromwell, Britain Hopes to Get U.S. In," *Daily Worker*, 5 April 1940, 6; Bennett C. Clark, *Newsweek*, 1 April 1940, 14.

105. "Diplomatic Dope," *Uncensored* 26 (30 March 1940): 3–4; Fish, *CR*, 20 March 1940, 3165; letter, George Holden Tinkham to Cordell Hull, 20 March 1940, in *CR*, A1575.

106. "Playboy Diplomacy," *New Republic* 102 (1 April 1940): 424; "Cromwell Goes to War in Canada," *CT*, 21 March 1940, 13; Jennings, *CR*, 3 April 1940, 3966; Nye, *Newsweek*, 1 April 1940, 14; Edwin M. Borchard to John Bassett Moore, 20 March 1940, Borchard Papers; "Recall Cromwell," *New Masses* 35 (2 April 1940): 18.

107. "Minister Cromwell Makes a Speech," *Christian Century* 57 (3 April 1940): 436; Wiley, *CR*, 5 April 1940, 4073; Coughlin, "From the Tower," *Social Justice*, 25 March 1940, 5. Cromwell had written the books *The Voice of Young America* (New York: Scribner's, 1933) and *In Defense of Capitalism* (New York: Scribner's, 1937).

108. Joseph Alsop and Robert Kintner, *American White Paper* (New York: Simon & Schuster, 1940), 78, 81–82, 87. For the background of the book, see Robert W. Merry, *Taking on the World: Joseph and Stewart Alsop, Guardians of the Twentieth Century* (New York: Penguin Books, 1996), 79–81.

109. Lundeen, *CR*, 11 June 1940, 9511; "Ersatz White Paper," *Uncensored* 31 (4 May 1940): 1–3. Norman Thomas, press release, 11 May 1940, the Papers of the Socialist Party [microfilm], Hoover Institution (hereafter cited as Socialist Party Papers); Nye, *CR*, 8 March 1941, 2086. See also Bruce Minton, "American White Paper," *New Masses* 35 (14 May 1940): 23–24; Amos Pinchot, open letter to Franklin D. Roosevelt, 20 May 1940, in *CR*, A3378; Lawrence Dennis, *WFL* 93 (9 May 1940): 5; Frederick J. Libby to S. Foster Hunt, 1 June 1940, NCPW Papers; Libby to C. P. Jervey, 6 May 1940, NCPW Papers; Harry Elmer Barnes, "Keep Out of War and Investigate the War-Mongers" [draft], 10, Box 252, Lundeen Papers.

110. *The German White Paper: Full Text of the Polish Documents Issued by the Berlin Foreign Office* (New York: Howell, Soskin, 1940), 11.

111. For the contemporary debate concerning Bullitt and the white paper, see Orville H. Bullitt, ed., *For the President, Personal and Secret: Correspondence Between Franklin D. Roosevelt and William C. Bullitt* (Boston: Houghton Mifflin, 1972), 406–9; Will Brownell and Richard N. Billings, *So Close to Greatness: A Biography of William C. Bullitt* (New York: Macmillan, 1987), 250, 273.

112. Breckinridge Long, entry of 27 March 1940, *War Diary*, 74; Pearson and Allen, "Washington Merry-Go-Round," [University of] *Michigan Daily*, 4 April 1940, 4; Krock, "In the Nation: The Timing and Target of the White Paper," *NYT*, 3 April 1940, 22. "Statement by Secretary of State on Alleged Documents, 29 March 1940," in Jones and Myers, *Documents* 2: 364; Bullitt, Roosevelt, and Potocki, *NYT*, 30 March 1940, 1, 4; Kennedy in Lindbergh, entry of 29 November 1940, *Wartime Journals*, 420; Kennedy in Herzstein, *Luce*, 153, 449.

113. For affirmations of their veracity, see William P. Lage to Edwin M. Borchard, 4 April 1940, Borchard Papers, expressing mutual concurrence; Sidney Hertzberg to Harry Elmer Barnes, 3 April 1940, Barnes Papers; Oswald Garrison Villard, "Men and Events," *Nation* 150 (6 April 1940): 450.

114. Holt, *NYT*, 30 March 1941, 4; Lundeen, *CR*, 11 July 1940, 9510; "Did the United States Start the War?" *Christian Century* 57 (10 April 1940): 468; Fish, speech, NBC blue network, 30 March 1940, in *CR*, A1797.

115. "The Element of Truth," *Washington Post*, 31 March 1940; "Documents from Our Own Archives," *CT*, 31 March 1940, 18. See also "Our War Birds in the Polish Archives," *CT*, 1 April 1940, 12. Under the byline of Washington bureau chief Arthur Sears Henning, the *Tribune* carried a page one story declaring that both the foreign diplomatic community and American officialdom found the documents genuine. See "Capital Scents Ring of Truth in Nazi Charges: Notes Familiar Tone in Polish Papers," 1 April 1940, 1.

116. Reynolds, *CR*, 1 April 1940, 3745–46. See also Paul Mallon, "The News Behind the News," *SFE*, 3 April 1940, 13. Amos Pinchot, open letter to Franklin D. Roosevelt, 13 April 1940, Roosevelt Papers. Pinchot cited Bullitt's speech to Paris's American Club on 22 February 1939 and FDR's endorsement of a *Washington Post* editorial on 11 April 1939.

117. Reynolds, *CR*, 30 March 1940, 3747; *CR*, 2 April 1940, 3820; Fish, *CR*, 1 April 1940, 3803; Fish, speech, NBC blue network, 30 March 1940, in *CR*, A1796–98. In introducing his resolution, Reynolds asked the Senate Foreign Relations Committee to examine a number of matters: reasons for the Welles trip; complete information with respect to the *German White Paper*; copies of all speeches made by Bullitt, Kennedy, and Cromwell; and the circumstance of a recent Bullitt speech made in Bordeaux.

118. "A German White Book," *NYDN*, 30 March 1940, 15; "Paging Bullitt and Kennedy," *NYDN*, 15 January 1941, 29. See also Washington columnists John O'Donnell and Doris Fleeson, "Capitol Stuff," *NYDN*, 31 January 1941, 4; "Tragic Anniversary," 3 September 1940, 25; "Neville Chamberlain Dead," 12 November 1940, 25.

119. "Democracy's Parties," *Call*, 8 November 1941, 4. Both the *Daily Worker* and communist leader Earl Browder saw the documents as genuine and quoted such anticommunist journalists as Drew Pearson and Arthur Krock to this effect. See "What the Polish Documents Say About Mr. Bullitt," *Daily Worker*, 8 April 1940, 1; Browder, quoted in speech at Boston on 31 March in same editorial.

120. On Barnes and Grattan, see *PM*, 25 August 1940, 7. On Barnes endorsement, see Harry Elmer Barnes to *NYT*, 26 November 1940, Barnes Papers; Barnes, "Keep Out of War and Investigate the War-Mongers" [draft], 29, Box 252, Lundeen Papers. See also *NYT*, 22 November 1940, 13; 4 December 1940, 7.

121. Oswald Garrison Villard, "Men and Events," *Nation* 150 (6 April 1940): 450; Mallon, "The News Behind the News," *SFE*, 3 April 1940, 13. See also "Propaganda Trap," *Newsweek*, 8 April 1940, 17.

122. Seldes, *In Fact* 1 (3 June 1940): 1; "After the Nazi White Book," *New Masses* 35 (16 April 1940): 22. See also review by Joseph Starobin, *New Masses* 37 (1 October 1940): 18–19; Congressman John Main Coffee (Dem.-Wash.), [University of Wisconsin] *Daily Cardinal*, 12 April 1940, 1.

123. "Nazi White Book," *Time*, 8 April 1940, 15; "Propaganda Trap," *Newsweek*, 8 April 1940, 17.

124. Castle Diary, 31 March 1940. See also entry of 3 April 1940.

125. "The Nazi-Polish Documents," *Commonweal* 31 (12 April 1940): 521; "The White Book," *America* 63 (13 August 1940): 15. See also Danaher, *NYT*, 30 March 1941, 4.

126. See, for example, Thorkelson, *CR*, 3 April 1940, A1844; B. C. Clark, *CR*, 19 August 1940, 10,480; Senator Reed, 10,485.

127. See, for example, George Seldes, *In Fact* 1 (9 September 1940): 1–2; "Mr. Bullitt Likes French Fascism," *Daily Worker*, 22 July 1940, 6. Seldes quoted *Ambassador Dodd's Diary, 1933–1938* (New York: Harcourt Brace, 1941) to indicate that Bullitt opposed the French-Soviet understanding of 1935. *In Fact* 2 (24 February 1941): 1.

128. Castle Diary, 3 April 1940. See also entry of 7 January 1941, referring to Bullitt's personal life. For other claims that Bullitt was warlike, see *SFN*, 1 April 1940, 13; Holt, *CR*, 18 October 1939, 552; Holt, *CR*, 12 June 1940, 8056; Reynolds, *CR*, 3 April 1940, 3923; Amos Pinchot, open letter to Roosevelt, 20 May 1940, in *CR*, A3686; Nye, *CR*, 29 April 1941, 3382; Senator Wheeler quoted in Chamberlin Diary, 16 February 1941.

129. Fish, *CR*, 26 December 1940, A6977. Fish quoted from the *New York Herald Tribune*, 22 December 1940, which cited *Gringoire*. For another use of the *Gringoire* article, see "What About It, Mr. Bullitt?" *Scribner's Commentator* 9 (March 1941): 79. For quotations from another collaborationist paper, *Le Nouveau Temps*, concerning Bullitt, see *CT*, 9 November 1940, 5, and editorial "Busy Billy Bullitt," 10 November 1940, 10.

130. William Bullitt, speech, Philadelphia, in *CR*, 18 August 1940, A5074–76. For attacks on the August speech, see B. C. Clark, *CR*, 19 August 1940, 10,479; Schafer, *CR*, 19 August 1940, 10,519; Knutson, *CR*, 19 August 1940, 10,519; "Badly Timed: Bullitt's Speech Earned Rebuke," *SFE*, 22 August 1940, 10; "Comment," *America* 63 (31 August 1940): 562; "Orson Welles—Bullitt," *St. Louis Post-Dispatch*, 19 August 1940; "Internationalist Hall of Fame," *Scribner's Commentator* 9 (December 1940): 18; "Bullitt Orders the People to Shed Their Blood," *Daily Worker*, 20 August 1940, 1; "FDR's Trigger Man," *New Masses* 36 (27 August 1940): 15.

131. Hugh Johnson, "British Racket," *Miami Daily Herald*, 29 December 1940. See also Sargent, Bulletin #4, 23 June 1939, *Getting US into War*, 114.

132. "Our Envoy to Britain," *CT*, 25 November 1939, 8. For hostile linking of Bullitt and Kennedy, see Fish, speech, CBS, 2 March 1940, in *CR*, A1154; "Defense of Lord Lothian," *CT*, 29 October 1939, 16; "Our Hot Ambassadors," *CT*, 4 April 1940, 16.

133. "Kennedy Says, 'Stay Out,'" *Christian Century* 56 (27 December 1939): 1595–96. For other claims that Kennedy sought peace, see Dennis, *WFL* 85 (14 March 1940): 5; Castle Diary, 21 February 1940.

134. Hearst, "In the News," *SFE*, 12 March 1940, 2. See also "Kennedy's Refusal Reflects Character," *SFE*, 16 February, 1940, 7. In September, Hearst columnist Boake Carter suggested Kennedy for a new cabinet post, secretary for national defense. "But Boake Carter Says," *SFE*, 30 September 1940, 11.

135. Long, entry of 6 December 1939, *War Diary*, 39; Roosevelt policy, Travis Beal Jacobs, *America and the Winter War, 1939–1940* (New York: Garland, 1981), 129.

136. For examples of anti-interventionist opinion, see "Sibelius Is Forced to Decline . . . ," *Commonweal* 31 (25 December 1939): 173; Fish, *CR*, 27 February 1940, 2036.

137. Berle, *Navigating*, 275; Roy W. Howard to Madame De Polignac, 16 December 1939, Box 157, Howard Papers; Norman Thomas to Mary Fox, 4 December 1939, Thomas Papers. Thomas thought that in 1930 Finland might have gone fascist. He still found reactionary forces there but claimed that its turn to democracy had been "a magnificent performance." See Norman Thomas to David Dubinsky, 21 December 1939, Thomas Papers.

138. John Haynes Holmes to Roger William Riss, 6 December 1939; Holmes to Clarence R. Skinner, 11 December 1939, Holmes Papers.

139. See, for example, issues of the *Daily Worker* and *New Masses*.

140. Edwin M. Borchard to John Bassett Moore, 1 December 1939, Borchard Papers; Sargent, Bulletin #21, 8 December 1939, *Getting US into War*, 187–95; "Finland and Russia," *NYDN*, 17 November 1939, 35.

141. "Allies to Help Finland," *NYDN*, 20 December 1939, 35; "Finland's Fate Depends on Germany," *NYDN*, 22 January 1940, 19; "The War in Finland," *CT*, 20 December 1939, 18.

142. "The Problem of Aid to Finland," *CT*, 7 January 1940, 16; "Finland and Its Defenders," 12 January 1940, 14. See also "Reproaches from Mr. Stanley," *CT*, 24 March 1940, 14.

143. "Why Did Hore-Belisha Quit?" *NYDN*, 31 January 1940, 27; "The Finnish Theatre," *NYDN*, 8 March 1940, 33. For other defenses of British inaction, see "But Boake Carter Says," *SFE*, 22 March 1940, 9; Castle Diary, 14 March 1940; Cushman Reynolds, "General Mud," *Common Sense* 10 (August 1941): 232.

144. "Laudable: Right That U.S. Aid Finland," *SFE*, 14 December 1939, 16. However, the *Examiner* opposed anything smacking of a war loan. "War Loan: U.S. Must Avoid Involvement in War," *SFE*, 20 January 1940, 6; "War Loans," *SFE*, 8. See also C. David Tompkins, *Senator Arthur H. Vandenberg: The Evolution of a Modern Republican, 1884–1945* (East Lansing: Michigan State University Press, 1970), 176; Hiram Johnson and D. Worth Clark in Jacobs, *Winter War*, 107, 132.

145. Fish, *NYT*, 11 January 1940, 12; 28 February 1940, 5; 29 February 1940, 1.

146. See, for example, Congressman Robert M. Chiperfield (Rep.-Ill.), *CR*, 27 February 1940, 2058–59; Taft, *CR*, 13 February 1940, 1313. A dissident view was taken by the WIL, which claimed that Congress had a responsibility to declare that a state of war existed. Resolutions, National Board, 20–21 January 1940, Washington, D.C., WIL Papers. On 16 January 1940, Senator Danaher offered a concurrent resolution to invoke the 1939 neutrality act, so that neither belligerent would receive U.S. aid. See Porter, *Sixth-sixth Congress*, 110; *NYT*, 17 January 1940, 1.

147. See, for example, Congressman William A. Pittenger (Rep.-Minn.), *CR*, 23 January 1940, A319; Congressman Harold Knutson (Rep.-Minn.), *CR*, 27 February 1940, 2064; Frank Waldrop, "The Real Issue of Finnish Loans," *WTH*, 30 January 1940, 9; "Real Reason for Our Loan Dodging," *WTH*, 1 February 1940, 13.

148. Buckler, *CR*, 27 February 1940, 2080.

149. See, for example, Bennett C. Clark and Hiram Johnson in Porter, *Sixth-sixth Congress*, 102; Borah, Holt, and Congressman Clifford Hope (Rep.-Kans.) in Porter, *Sixth-sixth Congress*, 106; Hiram W. Johnson to Hiram W. Johnson Jr., 10 February 1940, Johnson Papers; Harry Elmer Barnes to Mr. Elliott, 14 February 1940, Barnes Papers; Nye, *CT*, 17 January 1940, 2.

150. On Constitution, see Wiley, *CR*, 18 January 1940, 1289.

151. On Export-Import Bank, see Congresswoman Jessie Sumner, *CR*, 28 February 1940, 2100; Danaher, *CR*, 9 February 1940, 1292; Hiram Johnson, *CR*, 13 February 1940, 1401; Fred Bradley (Rep.-Mich.), *CR*, 21 February 1940, A895.

152. Danaher, *CR*, 9 February 1940, 1293; Sargent, Bulletin #42, 6 March 1940, *Getting US into War*, 317–19; Vorys, *CR*, 27 February 1940, 2041; Barry, *CR*, 28 February 1940, 2112; "Look Out for Booby Traps!"—and That War Debt Gratitude," *New Republic* 101 (25 October 1939): 323–24. Congressman Keefe sought an amendment specifying that the Export-Import Bank could make no loan either directly to a government or indirectly to any agency established by that government, which was in default on its loans. Text, *CR*, 28 February 1940, 2100–2102. It was voted down the same day sixty-nine to ninety-eight. See 2102.

153. On British and French, see "Congress Ponders Loans to Finland," *Christian Century* 57 (31 January 1940): 131; "Thunder Heads," *New Republic* 102 (22 January 1940): 100. See also "Aid to Finland," *New Republic* 102 (29 January 1940): 132.

154. Thomas, [University of North Carolina] *Daily Tar Heel*, 31 January 1940, 1. See also Reynolds, *CR*, 13 February 1940, 139; Holt in Porter, *Sixth-sixth Congress*, 107; Oscar Ameringer, "This Thing of Worrying About Europe," *American Guardian*, 2 February 1940, 1.

155. On size of allocation, see Johns, *CR*, 27 February 1940, 2076; Congressman John Taber (Rep.-N.Y.) in Porter, *Sixth-sixth Congress*, 107.

156. On domestic communism, see Reynolds, *CR*, 13 February 1940, 1396. On Mexico, see Barry, *CR*, 17 February 1940, 2062; Sumner, 27 February 1940, 2060.

157. Borchard cited by Senator Alexander Wiley, *CR*, 9 February 1940, 1286. For other expressions of Borchard's opposition, Edwin M. Borchard to John Bassett Moore, 12 December 1939, and to John A. Danaher, 12 February 1940, Borchard Papers; Borchard, *United States News*, 26 February 1940, 23. For other anti-interventionists, see William P. Lage to Borchard, 4 January 1940, and John Bassett

Moore to Hiram Johnson [copy], 8 January 1940, Borchard Papers; Senator Clyde Reed, *Newsweek*, 29 January 1940, 13; Philip C. Jessup to James A. Shanley, 6 March 1940, Jessup Papers.

158.  Wiley, *CR*, 18 January 1940, 1289; Wiley, "American Forum of the Air," 28 January 1940, in *CR*, A617; Senator Alva Adams, *Newsweek*, 29 January 1940, 13; Hiram Johnson to John Bassett Moore, 10 and 16 February 1940, John Bassett Moore to Edwin M. Borchard, 19 January 1940, Moore Papers.

159.  See, for example, Rankin, *CR*, 28 February 1940, 2102; ed. Verne Marshall, *Cedar Rapids Gazette*, 15 January 1940; Norman Thomas, "Your World and Mine," *Call*, 13 January 1940, 2; Norman Thomas, "Your World and Mine," *Call*, 27 January 1940, 2; Frank Waldrop, [University of North Carolina] *Daily Tar Heel*, 19 January 1940, 1; "Will Scandinavia Become a Battleground?" *Christian Century* 57 (17 January 1940): 69; "How to Get into War," *America* 62 (17 January 1940): 435–36; memo of George Holden Tinkham, attached to letter to Borchard, 23 December 1939, Borchard Papers; Capper, *CR*, 13 February 1940, 1389; labor leader Leonard Woodcock as quoted by Ben Fischer to Travers Clement, 22 January 1940, Socialist Party Papers; Hugh Johnson, "One Man's Opinion," *SFN*, 19 January 1940, 19; "Congress Should Take a Long Think About This One," *NYDN*, 18 January 1940, 27; Bennett C. Clark, *Newsweek*, 29 January 1940, 13; "That of Our Own," *Saturday Evening Post* 212 (23 March 1940): 26; Nye, *NYT*, 11 January 1940, 12; Borah, *NYT*, 3 January 1940, 2.

160.  McCarran, *CR*, 13 February 1940, 1383. For pacifists, see Donovan E. Smucker, youth secretary of the FOR, "The Finnish Invasion," *Fellowship* 6 (February 1940): 21; Frederick J. Libby, "No War Loans to Finland," *Peace Action* 6 (February 1940): 2; Libby, *United States News*, 26 February 1940, 23; Dorothy Detzer to Emily Greene Balch, 13 February 1940, WIL Papers; John Haynes Holmes to John Macfarlane Howie, 5 February 1940, Holmes Papers.

161.  Gerry Allard, "Support the Finns!" *Call*, 9 December 1939, 4; National Executive Committee, Socialist Party, statement, Milwaukee, 10 December 1939, 4, Socialist Party Papers; Norman Thomas, "Your World and Mine," *Call*, 27 January 1940, 2; Thomas, *Yale* [University] *Daily News*, 20 January 1940, 2. See also pacifist and former Episcopal bishop Paul Jones, letter to *Call*, 6 January 1940, 3.

162.  See Borah and editorial, "America Honors Finland on Heroic Anniversary," *SFE*, 7 December 1939, 14; Norman Thomas, interview, *Yale* [University] *Daily News*, 20 January 1940, 1; James A. Shanley to Edwin M. Borchard, 16 January 1940, Borchard Papers. Not all anti-interventionists concurred. Borchard said that once further installments on Finland's debt were forgiven, it would be impossible to argue against the cancellation of all Allied debts to the United States. Edwin M. Borchard to James A. Shanley, 18 January 1940, Borchard Papers.

163.  Reynolds, citing *CT*, in *CR*, 13 February 1940, 1397–98. See also "Business as Usual," *Uncensored* 16 (20 January 1940): 2. Of the mainstream anti-interventionists who spoke on the matter, only Borchard opposed any moral embargo. Borchard declared that administration efforts to prevent rubber and tin dealers from making shipments to Russia violated the Sherman anti-trust act. Edwin M. Borchard to William P. Lage, 30 March 1940, Borchard Papers.

164.  Congressman Robert Secrest (Dem.-Ohio), *CR*, 27 February 1940, 2076; Daniel Reed, *CR*, 27 February 1940, 2082; "American Supplies for Red Josef," *CT*, 6 March 1940, 14; "American Aid to Stalin," *CT*, 14 March 1940, 14; Nye, "We're Already in the War," *Look*, 23 April 1940, 8. Not surprisingly, *New Masses* found no proof that any U.S. strategic materials sent to the USSR wound up in German hands. "And Churchill," 35 (9 April 1940): 22.

165.  Andresen, *CR*, 7 February 1940, 1179. For more stress on the gold trade, see *Social Justice*, 5 February 1940, 18; Danaher, *Wesleyan* [University] *Argus*, 15 January 1940, 1; Waldrop, "Why Stalin Doesn't Declare War," *WTH*, 13 January 1940, 11; "Russia Befriended," *CT*, 22 February 1940, 14.

166.  See, for example, Castle, *United States News*, 26 February 1940, 23; "Comment," *America* 62 (2 March 1940): 562; Edwin M. Borchard to Alexander Wiley, *CR*, 9 February 1940, 1286; Congressman Earl C. Michener (Rep.-Mich.), 27 February 1940, 2040; Norman Thomas interview, *Yale* [University] *Daily News*, 20 January 1940, 2; "Congress Ponders Loans to Finland," *Christian Century* 57 (31 January 1940): 131; John Bassett Moore to Hiram Johnson [copy], 18 January 1940, James A. Shanley to Edwin M. Borchard, 16 January 1940, Borchard Papers; Father Coughlin contribution of $1,000, *NYT*, 16 January 1940, 5; "But Boake Carter Says," *SFE*, 24 January 1940, 13; John Bassett Moore to Hiram

Johnson, 12 February 1940, Moore Papers; Robert James Maddox, *William E. Borah and American Foreign Policy* (Baton Rouge: Louisiana State University Press, 1969), 246. Wiley introduced a bill to permit contributions to Finland to be tax-deductible. *CR*, 18 January 1940, 456.

167. Best, *Hoover*, 1:141; "For Finland," *Time*, 11 March 1940, 16.

168. "Charity for Finland," *New Republic* 102 (5 February 1940): 163; Norman Thomas to David Dubinsky, 21 December 1939, Thomas Papers; "European Relief," *CT*, 19 December 1939, 16. See also "Brave Little Finland," *NYDN*, 14 December 1939, 39. Even the arch-rightist Ralph Townsend claimed that most of the publicity for Finnish relief "seemed worded, not so much to stir compassion for Finns, as to stir war hate against Russia." "Mercy—Strictly Political," *Scribner's Commentator* 9 (March 1941): 81.

169. Support for such a move came from such anti-interventionists as Hiram Johnson and Congressman Mason. Jacobs, *Winter War*, 69. See also *Social Justice*, 5 February 1939, 5.

170. Vandenberg, *CT*, 5 December 1939, 4; *CR*, 18 January 1940, 457. When Finland signed the armistice, Senator D. Worth Clark introduced a resolution calling on the United States to recall the American ambassador. *CR*, 15 March 1940, 2919.

171. *CR*, 12 February 1940, 1354. One hundred eight opposed the measure. See also Fish, *CR*, 25 January 1940, 689–90; Herbert Hoover in *Newsweek*, 11 December 1939, 24; *Social Justice*, 5 February 1940, 5, 18; Hamilton Fish and Congressman James A. Van Zandt (Rep.-Pa.), *United States News*, 2 February 1940, 25.

172. Entry of 30 November 1939, *Moffat Papers*, 280–81.

173. Wheeler, *United States News*, 2 February 1940, 24; Johnson, "One Man's Opinion," *SFN*, 6 December 1939, 15; Johnson, "Tom-Tom Beating," *NYWT*, 10 February 1940, 13; Thomas, "Finland's Fight: A World Cause," *Call*, 16 December 1939, 2; Reed in Porter, *Sixty-sixth Congress*, 106; William R. Castle to Herbert Hoover, 7 December 1939, Castle Papers. Hoover replied that while Castle theoretically was correct, "if we are going to pursue a course of conduct toward Germany, Mr. Roosevelt ought to take responsibility for his friendly leanings towards the Communists." Herbert Hoover to William R. Castle, 11 December 1939, Castle Papers.

174. "Break Off with the Soviets?" *NYDN*, 5 December 1939, 38; Steinhardt in Jacobs, *Winter War*, 93.

175. See, for example, "Finland Falls: But War Is Not Yet Over," *SFE*, 16 March 1940, 8; Coughlin, "From the Tower," *Social Justice*, 25 March 1940, 3. More than a year later, Hanson Baldwin wrote of the Finns, "Their cause was lost when the world cheered their victories but, cheering, delayed its help." See Baldwin, *United We Stand!* 10. The Allies, he said, could have reduced the amount of raw materials Russia was giving Germany, severed Germany's iron ore routes to northern Swedish towns, and established a northern front on Germany's exposed flank, thus forcing Germany into a major defensive effort. He did concede strategic difficulties but claimed "war cannot be won without taking risks." *United We Stand!* 10–11.

176. "Report Russian Advances in Finland," *Christian Century* 57 (28 February 1940): 269. See also Hugh Johnson, "Join or Die," *NYWT*, 23 January 1940, 17; Edwin M. Borchard to John A. Danaher, 9 February 1940, Borchard Papers; "But Boake Carter Says," *SFE*, 25 January 1940, 15; "Allies, Nordic Nations Can Wisely Aid Finland," *SFE*, 20 December 1939, 12; "England and France Must Fight in Finland's Cause," *SFE*, 6 February 1940, 8.

177. "War Proves Ships Helpless," 5 May 1940, in pamphlets of Al Williams columns, Box 276, Lundeen Papers (hereafter cited as Williams Pamphlets); "Duty Done," *Uncensored* 24 (16 March 1940): 1. See also "Johnny-Come-Lately," *Uncensored* 23 (9 March 1940): 9. *Uncensored* did concede that Britain could not have easily come to Finland's aid, for Norway and Sweden would not have allowed the passage of Allied troops, and an attack on Petsamo would have been folly.

178. Dennis, *WFL* 86 (14 March 1940): 1–2.

179. Flynn, *SFN*, 21 March 1940, 16; "Salute to Finland," *NYDN*, 14 March 1940, 29; Hearst, "In the News," *SFE*, 15 March 1940, 1. Such anti-interventionists were not alone. See, for example, Ickes, entry of 3 December 1939, *Secret Diary*, 3:75.

180. "Finland and Russia Make Peace," *Christian Century* 57 (20 March 1940): 371; "The Peace Crisis," *New Republic* 102 (18 March 1940): 363; Hoover, *Stanford* [University] *Daily*, 1 March 1940, 1; "Has War Tide Reached Its Peak?" *NYDN*, 14 March 1940, 29; John Bassett Moore to George H. Ryden, 2 May 1940, Moore Papers.

181. Jacobs, *Winter War*, 223–24, 235; Maddux, *Years of Estrangement*, 126–27.
182. Jacobs, *Winter War*, 231–38; Porter, *Sixty-sixth Congress*, 125–26; Matson, *Neutrality and Naviticerts*, 60–62; entry of 16 January 1940, *Moffat Papers*, 282–83.
183. Dallek, *Roosevelt*, 210; Maddux, *Years of Estrangement*, 112–13.
184. Entry of 30 January 1940, *Moffat Papers*, 290–91.
185. On the issue of farm and other nonmilitary supplies, those with opinions voted 58 percent in favor, 42 percent opposed. Nine percent had no opinion. On the matter of planes and other weapons, the tally was 61 percent opposed, 39 percent in favor. *NYT*, 7 February 1940, 4. There was a 73:27 ratio in favor of permitting Finland to sell bonds in the United States. *NYT*, 10 March 1940, 27.
186. The Fish bill was voted down eighty-two to thirty-five. *CR*, 28 February 1940, 2116.
187. Edwin M. Borchard to William P. Lage, 19 January 1940, 16 March 1940, Borchard Papers. Lage felt betrayed by the fact that Hiram Johnson, La Follette, and Vandenberg backed the Brown bill in the Senate Foreign Relations Committee. William P. Lage to Edwin M. Borchard, 8 February 1940, Borchard Papers. For Fish, see *NYT*, 11 January 1939, 12. Asked interventionist Congressman Albert A. Gore (Dem.-Tenn.) of Fish, "Where is the great isolationist now?" *CR*, 28 February 1940, 2113.

## CHAPTER 6: THE FALL OF WESTERN EUROPE

1. Weinberg, *World at Arms*, 115–18.
2. Anne Morrow Lindbergh, entry of 16 April 1940, *War Within*, 79. Among those who expected such a strike, see Charles A. Lindbergh, entry of 10 October 1940, *Wartime Journals*, 402; and author A. Fleming MacLiesh, memo [spring 1940], Hertzberg Papers.
3. Hoover cited in Castle Diary, 20 April 1940; Villard, "Issues and Men," *Nation* 150 (27 April 1940): 542. For Roosevelt's comments, see *NYT*, 14 April 1940, 1.
4. Swomley, *Wesleyan* [University] *Argus*, 22 April 1940, 3.
5. See, for example, Reynolds, Congressman Jacob Thorkelson, *CR*, 11 April 1940, 4353; Frederick J. Libby, "Calmly, Coolly, America Must Stay Out," *Peace Action* 6 (April 1940): 1; Edwin M. Borchard to James A. Shanley, 10 April 1940, Borchard Papers; "Britain's War Shadow," *Daily Worker*, 9 April 1940, 6; 10 April 1940, 1; Shipstead in *Daily Worker*, *CR*, 11 April 1940, 6; "The War Spreads," *New Masses* 35 (16 April 1940): 22; "A Policy for the American People," *New Masses* 36 (23 April 1940): 4; J. S. Barnes, "The Scandinavian Adventure," *Social Justice*, 3 June 1940, 13; Villard, "Issues and Men," *Nation* 150 (20 April 1940): 514; "This Is Not Our War," *Socialist Appeal*, 13 April 1940, 4; "The Sea Fights Off Norway," *CT*, 13 April 1940, 12; Professor Herbert Wright, testimony, SFRC, 5 February 1941, 454–55; Judge John A. Matthews, testimony, SFRC, 8 February 1941, 776; Ralph Townsend, testimony, SFRC, 8 February 1941, 809, 814. National Executive Committee, Socialist Party, *Progressive*, 11 May 1940, 7; William Randolph Hearst, "In the News," *SFE*, 10 April 1940, 2. Hearst did concede that Churchill in honor could not have refused to take action. "In the News," *SFE*, 6 May 1940, 1.
6. Dennis, *WFL* 89 (11 April 1940): 2; 95 (23 May 1940): 2; "Chronology," *Uncensored* 28 (13 April 1940): 3–6. See also Hugh Johnson, *SFN*, 10 April 1940, 15; "Scandinavia Between the Millstones," *Christian Century* 57 (17 April 1940): 502–3.
7. Welles and Long in Long, entry of 9 April 1940, *War Diary*, 76.
8. See, for example, "The War Spreads," *CT*, 10 April 1940, 18; National Executive Committee, Socialist Party, "The Nazi Invasion of Scandinavia," *Call*, 20 April 1940, 1; Albert W. Hamilton, "The Struggle for Control of Norway," *Call*, 4 May 1940, 5; "The War Begins," *New Republic* 102 (15 April 1940): 491. By the next issue, the *New Republic* was becoming interventionist. If British sea power could not keep Hitler out of Norway, so it reasoned, it could not exclude him from Sweden, Rumania, Holland, "or any other remote quarter." Moreover, it could not keep Spain out of Gibraltar, Japan out of Singapore and the Indian Ocean, or Italy out of Yugoslavia, Greece, "Asia Minor," or Africa. "Let Britain lose the Norway campaign, and the empire of the mistress of the seas will be eroded like a sandbag in a flooded torrent." "If Germany Wins," 102 (22 April 1940): 525.

9. "Comment," *America* 63 (20 April 1940): 30; "They've Found the Battleground," *NYDN*, 10 April 1940, 33; "The Rights of Small Nations," *NYDN*, 9 April 1940, 25.

10. "Scandinavia Between the Millstones," *Christian Century* 57 (17 April 1940): 502–3; "Strategy in Norway," *New Masses* 25 (7 May 1940): 21; "Sweden's Ore," *Uncensored* 28 (13 April 1940): 1–2; Dennis, *WFL* 90 (18 April 1940): 2; 89 (11 April 1940): 1; Burton Rascoe to Quincy Howe, 13 April 1940, Hertzberg Papers.

11. Hoover in Castle Diary, 20 April 1940; Hearst, "In the News," *SFE*, 10 April 1940, 3.

12. See, for example, Senator Guy Gillette, October 16, 1939, 465; Ludlow, 16 October 1939, 485; Capper, broadcast, CBS, 29 September 1939, in *CR*, A88.

13. "The Moral Right to Peace," *CT*, 26 January 1940, 12. See Churchill speech text, *NYT*, 21 January 1940, 30; Netherlands reply, *NYT*, 25 January 1940, 5.

14. John E. Kelly, "Ist Dies Nicht ein Cockeyed War!" *America* 62 (30 March 1940): 682; Hearst, "In the News," *SFE*, 13 March 1940, 2; Edwin M. Borchard to John Bassett Moore, 24 November 1939, Borchard Papers.

15. See, for example, "The Bulldog Breed," *Christian Century* 57 (22 May 1940): 663; Castle Diary, 31 May 1940. For lack of surprise, see John T. Flynn, *Call*, 1 June 1940, 1. Of all the anti-interventionists, only Hiram Johnson even hinted at Germany's defeat. Hiram W. Johnson to Hiram W. Johnson Jr., 11 May 1940, Johnson Papers.

16. "Comment," *America* 63 (18 May 1940): 142.

17. Anne Morrow Lindbergh, entry of 20 May 1940, *War Within*, 88; emphasis in original.

18. Charles A. Lindbergh in Anne Morrow Lindbergh, entry of 24 May 1940, *War Within*, 88. See also entry of 24 June 1940, *War Within*, 117.

19. A Gallup poll found 67 percent seeing the Germans as winning; 8 percent, the Allies. *NYT*, 19 May 1940, 16.

20. Reynaud, *NYT*, 29 May 1940, 4; Belgian premier Hubert Pierlot, text of statement, *NYT*, 29 May 1940, 4; "Leopold's Suppressed Letter," *CT*, 3 January 1941, 10. Hearst, finding the letter true, accused Roosevelt of suppressing its contents. "In the News," *SFE*, 28 April 1941, A.

21. Lawrence Dennis, *WFL* 96 (29 May 1940): 3; Castle Diary, 30 May 1940, 1 September 1940; "Justice for Leopold of Belgium," *CT*, 18 June 1941, 6; "Nations in Defeat," *CT*, 2 January 1941, 10; Schafer, *CR*, 10 June 1940, 7904; Congressman Thorkelson, *CR*, 10 June 1940, 7094; Coughlin, Memorial Day speech, *Social Justice*, 10 June 1940, 3; "Let's Hear from Leopold," *Social Justice*, 10 June 1940, 8; Devere Allen, *Yale* [University] *Daily News*, 4 November 1940, 3; Devere Allen, "Belgium and the War," *Unity* 126 (17 February 1941): 185–86; Herbert Hoover, *Life*, 25 November 1940, 75; Joseph P. Kennedy in Bilainkin, entry of 20 August 1940, *Diary*, 189–90.

22. "Leopold III Calls It Off," *NYDN*, 29 May 1940, 21; Cudahy, *Newsweek*, 19 August 1940, 13. See also Cudahy in Lindbergh, entry of 17 September 1940, *Wartime Journals*, 391; Cudahy, "Belgium's Leopold," *Life*, 25 November 1940, 75–83. The *Chicago Tribune* took Cudahy to task, saying that Cudahy regarded himself less as the representative of the American people in Belgium than as the representative of the Belgian crown to America. "Whose Ambassadors?" 3 December 1940, 14.

23. Carmer, "Leopold and Dunkerque," *Scribner's Commentator* 11 (December 1941): 65–68; Hearst, "In the News," *SFE*, 30 May 1940, 1–2. Hearst also claimed that King Christian surrendered Denmark without striking a blow in its defense. Similarly, Wilhelmena exhorted the Dutch to fight to the last ditch while herself fleeing to England. Hearst evidently soon mellowed, for he blamed Roosevelt for suppressing Leopold's letter to the American people. "In the News," *SFE*, 20 August 1940, 1.

24. Allen, *Brown* [University] *Daily Herald*, 23 April 1941, 1; Dennis, *WFL* 100 (27 June 1940): 4. See also Dennis, *WFL* 96 (29 May 1940): 1, 3; Dennis, *WFL* 94 (16 May 1940): 2.

25. Reynolds, *Creation*, 104; Reynolds, "Churchill and the British 'Decision,'" 150–53; Ponting, *1940*, 110. John Charmley finds such comments a momentary concession to Halifax and not indicative of his real views. *Churchill, the End of Glory: A Political Biography* (New York: Harcourt Brace, 1993), 405.

26. Hiram W. Johnson to Hiram W. Johnson Jr., 16 June 1940, Johnson Papers; William Henry Chamberlin, "France in June: The Collapse," *Atlantic Monthly* 166 (September 1940): 298.

27. David Reynolds, "1940," 326–27; R. H. S. Stolfi, "Equipment for Victory in France in 1940," *History* 155 (February 1970): 1–20; Ponting, *1940*, chap. 5.

28. "Busy Billy Bullitt," *CT*, 10 November 1940, 10; "State Trial in France," *CT*, 29 July 1940, 10; Hiram W. Johnson to Hiram W. Johnson Jr., 4 July 1940, Johnson Papers. See also Nye, *CR*, 21 June 1940, 8795.

29. See, for example, Al Williams, "Claims Proved," 5 June 1940, in Williams pamphlet, Box 276, Lundeen Papers; Hugh Johnson, "One Man's Opinion," *SFN*, 25 June 1940, 13; Devere Allen, "Why Did France Collapse?" *Unity* 125 (15 July 1940): 152; Lindbergh, entry of 10 October 1940, *Wartime Journals*, 402.

30. Colonel Robert R. McCormick, broadcast of 20 October 1940, in *Addresses by Colonel Robert R. McCormick* (Chicago: WGN, 1940), 68–69; William Henry Chamberlin, "France in June: The Collapse," *Atlantic Monthly* 166 (September 1940): 302; Dennis, *WFL* 96 (29 May 1940): 2; "Eighteen Days of War," *NYDN*, 28 May 1940, 23. Fuller's work is *Towards Armageddon: The Defence Problem and I* (London: Dickson, 1937). See also "Can Hitler Invade England?" *NYDN*, 11 May 1941, 17; "Confusion . . . Critical," *NYDN*, 22 May 1940, 31; "The Fall of France," *NYDN*, 14 July 1940, 35; "What France Lacks," *CT*, 16 June 1940, 14.

31. Harry Elmer Barnes to Mr. Elliott, 14 February 1940, Barnes Papers. See also John Bassett Moore to Edwin M. Borchard, 14 June 1940, Moore Papers; "What the Hitler–Stalin Pact Means to the World," *Social Justice*, 4 September 1939, 7.

32. Johnson, "Join or Die," *NYWT*, 23 January 1940, 17. See also "How France Was Betrayed," *New Masses* 36 (25 June 1940): 4; Henry Nelson Weiman and Arthur E. Holt, "Keep Our Country Out of War," *Christian Century* 56 (27 September 1939): 1162.

33. "Double Negative," *Uncensored* 16 (20 January 1940): 2; Carter, *Philadelphia Evening Ledger*, 29 September 1939.

34. Gillis, "France: God's Instrument?" *Catholic World* 151 (March 1940): 649. See also *Social Justice*, 22 July 1940, 3.

35. See, for example, Frank Hanighen, "Making the World Safe for Empire," *Common Sense* 8 (September 1939): 20; African American editor George Schuyler cited by Robert L. Birchman, "The Negro Question," *Socialist Appeal*, 15 June 1940, 3; "Shock-Troops," *Uncensored* 1 (7 October 1939): 2.

36. Lundeen, *CR*, 14 October 1939, 428; Norman Thomas to William Pickens, 25 September 1939, Thomas Papers; Holt, *CR*, 18 October 1939, 549.

37. Gish, speech to Executives' Club, Chicago, 9 May 1941, in *CR*, 9 May 1941, A2563. See also "What France Lacks," *CT*, 14 June 1940, 14; "When France Lost the War," *CT*, 31 July 1940, 10; "Comment," *America* 63 (9 June 1940): 310.

38. MacNider, speech to Young Republican League, Des Moines, Iowa, 12 June 1940, in *CR*, A3937; Dennis, *WFL* 105 (1 August 1940): 1–2.

39. Schafer, *CR*, 1 November 1939, 1277; "These Wrecked France" (photo essay), *Scribner's Commentator* 9 (February 1941): 13–20. See also Lois and Donaldson Thornburn, "Dear Elmer," *Scribner's Commentator* 8 (August 1940): 30–32, 41–42.

40. René de Chambrun, *I Saw France Fall: Will She Rise Again?* (New York: Morrow, 1940). For favorable treatment, see *Newsweek*, 21 November 1940, 50; "Concrete Guy," *Time*, 21 October 1940, 34, 36; George T. Eberle, *America* 64 (26 October 1940): 78; Stanton B. Leeds, "Chambrun—Soldier of France," *Scribner's Commentator* 9 (January 1941): 11–12, 21–23; Sargent, Bulletin #96, 30 December 1940, *Getting US into War*, 550; Gilbert Twiss, *CT*, 16 October 1940, 23. Joseph Barnes, foreign editor of the *New York Herald Tribune*, treated most of the book with respect but objected to Chambrun's praise of the Vichy government. "A Frenchman Speaks for Victory," *New York Herald Tribune Book Review*, 20 October 1940, sect. 9, 5.

41. Stanton B. Leeds, *These Rule France: The Story of Edouard Daladier and the Men Around Daladier* (Indianapolis: Bobbs-Merrill, 1940). Most reviews were critical, accusing him of an extreme rightist bias. See, for example, Leo Gershoy, "French Affairs," *Yale Review* 29 (Summer 1940): 823–24.

42. "French Plane Production," *Uncensored* 37 (15 June 1940): 3. For approval of *Uncensored*'s position, see "Blum's Government," *Call*, 29 June 1940, 4.

43. Hanighen, "Were the Social Reforms of the Popular Front Responsible for the French Defeat?" *Uncensored* 41 (13 July 1940): special supplement, 1–4. See also C. Hartley Grattan, letter to the editor, *New Republic* 103 (29 July 1940): 143.

44. "Campaign of Nonsense," *Progressive*, 9 November 1940, 8.

45. Wheeler, *CR*, 20 February 1941, A784; Clark, *CR*, 23 October 1939, 717; Norman Thomas, "Your World and Mine," *Call*, 30 December 1939, 7; Flynn, "Other People's Money: War on the Home Front," *New Republic* 100 (27 September 1939): 188. For similar accusations, see Villard, [University of Rochester] *Tower Times*, 23 February 1940, 1; Harry Elmer Barnes, "This Unholy War!" *NYWT*, 29 March 1940, 22; Pierre Crabites and John Earle Uhler, "France Is Not a Democracy," *Catholic World* 153 (March 1941): 665; Robson, *CR*, 2 November 1939, 1295; Reynolds, *CR*, 14 October 1939, 428; Reynolds, *CR*, 21 October 1939, 693. Ernest L. Meyer recommended journalist Pierre Van Paassen's *Days of Our Years* (New York: Hillman-Curl, 1939), a book that—as noted by the socialist journalist—denied that either France or Britain was a democracy. *American Guardian*, 15 September 1939, 4. Porter Sargent drew on André Simone's *J'Accuse! The Men Who Betrayed France* (New York: Dial, 1940). See Bulletin #96, 3 January 1941, *Getting US into War*, 548.

46. See, for example, Porter Sargent, Bulletin #22, 15 December 1939, *Getting US into War*, 200; Sargent, Bulletin #28, 15 January 1940, *Getting US into War*, 245; "Refugees," *Uncensored* 1 (7 October 1939): 1; "France Hunts Down Dissenters," *Christian Century* 56 (25 October 1939): 1291–92; Devere Allen, "Frenchmen Without Tears," *Fellowship* 6 (September 1940): 105; "Path of Resistance," *Uncensored* 9 (2 December 1939): 3; "French Liberties," *Uncensored* 31 (4 May 1940): 4.

47. "Fighting for What Democracy?" *New Republic* 101 (8 November 1939): 1; Barnes, "Debunking Holy War," *NYWT*, 5 February 1940, 5; "French Pacifists," *Uncensored* 4 (28 October 1939): 1; Detzer, WIL National Board meeting, 20–21 January 1939, WIL Papers.

48. Sargent, Bulletin #34, February 3, 1940, *Getting US into War*, 273; "Fighting for What Democracy?" *New Republic* 101 (8 November 1939): 1; "Toward Totalitarianism," *NYDN*, 11 February 1940, 47. Conversely, the *Chicago Tribune* had little sympathy for the French communists, accusing them of practically preparing for a French defeat by reducing production and presenting the country with an outmoded air force. "The End of the French Communists," 20 January 1940, 10. For other attacks on the French communists, see Hearst, "In the News," *SFE*, 25 June 1940, 1; William Henry Chamberlin, "France in June: The Collapse," *Atlantic Monthly* 166 (September 1940): 302–3.

49. See, for example, *American Guardian*, 3 November 1939, 1; *American Guardian*, 1 December 1939, 2; *Social Justice*, 23 September 1940, 3–4.

50. Barnes, "This Unholy War!" *NYWT*, 29 March 1940, 22; William Henry Chamberlin, "France in June: The Collapse," *Atlantic Monthly* 166 (September 1940): 301–2. See also Chamberlin, "Daladier: The Tragedy of France," *American Mercury* 50 (August 1940): 477–83.

51. Hanighen, "How France Is Taking the War," *New Republic* 101 (20 December 1939): 257; Hearst, "In the News," *SFE*, 26 March 1940, 1. See also *SFE*, 11 April 1940, 2.

52. "A Tisket a Tasket," *Uncensored* 25 (23 March 1940): 1; Hanighen memo, 18 May 1940, Hertzberg papers. See also Dennis, *WFL* 86 (21 March 1940): 4.

53. "Thieves Fall Out," *New Masses* 36 (6 August 1940): 16; Stanton B. Leeds, "Chambrun, Soldier of Fortune," *Scribner's Commentator* 9 (January 1941): 11; "The French Trials," *CT*, 19 November 1940, 12. For its initial disapproval of the trials, see "State Trial in France," *CT*, 29 July 1940, 10.

54. Holmes, "A Way to Stop It!" *Unity* 125 (2 September 1940): 4; emphasis in original.

55. Hanighen, "Selling to the Enemy," *Harper's Magazine* 180 (March 1940): 387; Allen, "Frenchmen Without Tears," *Fellowship* 6 (September 1940): 105. For indictments of the trade in raw materials, see "Business as Usual," *Uncensored* 12 (23 January 1939): 1–2; Leon Hamilton, "Profits of War Are Taken on Both Sides," *Social Justice*, 22 January 1940, 7; Dreiser, *America Is Worth Saving*, 255; Aaron Levenstein, "Business as Usual," *Call*, 6 January 1940, 4, all citing "Germany and France Exchange Ore and Coal Through Belgium," *Iron Age* 144 (7 December 1939): 87. See also Sargent, Bulletin #24, 29 December 1939, *Getting US into War*, 218; "What Price Patriotism?" *New Masses* 34 (9 January 1940): 21; Kelly, "Ist Dies Nicht ein Cockeyed War!" 682; Holmes, "Enemies Helping One Another," *Unity* 124 (19 February 1940): 184; Holmes, "The Munitions Scandal," *Unity* 125 (1 April 1940): 35–36.

56. Lindbergh, entry of 17 June 1940, *War Within*, 111; "Comment," *America* 63 (29 June 1940): 310.

57. For interventionist doubts concerning Pétain, see Ickes, entry of 3 August 1940, *Secret Diary*, 3:277.

58. "Congratulations to Britain," *NYDN*, 6 July 1940, 13; Holmes, "Men Who Live Too Long," *Unity* 125 (5 August 1940): 164; Dennis, *WFL* 100 (27 June 1940): 1.

59. *Social Justice*, 22 July 1940, 3; Herbert Hoover to John C. O'Laughlin, 8 July 1940, Stanford Files; "Fascist France," *Christian Century* 57 (17 July 1940): 894.

60. "The Future of France," *Christian Century* 57 (25 September 1940): 1166. It claimed that the papacy had hoped for a Latin bloc within the fascist order, one bound together by a religious tie and able to resist inundation by a culture based on state totalitarianism. Into such a bloc would enter Italy, Spain, France, and perhaps some of the succession states that Mussolini might create as spoils of war. Such a Latin bloc "would bring Europe back into sanity." Arguing to the contrary, *America*, in praising Vichy's opposition to divorce and birth control, questioned whether the government would become fascist. "Comment," *America* 63 (24 August 1940): 535.

61. Chamberlin, "Hitler's Alternatives: Is He a Prisoner of Conquest?" *Atlantic Monthly* 167 (January 1941): 8.

62. Sargent, Bulletin #96, 3 January 1941, *Getting US into War*, 562; "Comment," *America* 64 (22 February 1941): 53; Hearst, "In the News," *SFE*, 19 April 1941, A; *Social Justice*, 16 June 1941, 19; *Social Justice*, 21 July 1941, 7; *Social Justice*, 8 September 1941, 3; Norman Thomas to Ambassador Gaston Henry-Haye, 13 February 1941, Thomas Papers.

63. Mario Rossi, *Roosevelt and the French* (New York: Praeger, 1993), 155; Kimball, *Forged in War*, 87.

64. Roosevelt, *NYT*, 16 May 1941, 1, 4; Hull, *NYT*, 6 June 1941, 1.

65. Hearst, "In the News," *SFE*, 19 April 1941, H2; "France in a Tough Spot," *CT*, 9 June 1941, 12; "Herr Hitler's Union," *CT*, 26 April 1941, 10; Libby, "War Method Makes Enemies of Former Friends," *Peace Action* 7 (May 1941): 2. See also Congressman Karl Mundt (Rep.-S.Dak.), *CR*, 28 June 1941, A3157; Dennis, *WFL* 147 (22 May 1941): 3.

66. "France," *NYDN*, 17 May 1941, 15.

67. Pétain broadcast, text, *NYT*, 13 August 1941, 4; "Comment," *America* 65 (23 August 1941): 534; Castle Diary, 13 August 1941.

68. Roosevelt, address at Charlottesville, text, *NYT*, 10 June 1941, 6. Welles, who consistently had confidence in Mussolini, wanted the phrase omitted. See Berle, entry of 11 June 1940, *Navigating*, 322.

69. Barnes, "The War Profiteers," *Social Justice*, 11 December 1939, 11. See also Barnes, "Hope of Christian Europe Lies in Rome," *Social Justice*, 5 February 1940, 7.

70. Thomas, *Wesleyan* [University] *Argus*, 12 October 1939, 1; "Heirs of the British Empire," *NYDN*, 10 March 1940, 47; "The War on the Neutral Fronts," *NYDN*, 24 November 1939, 37. The *News* wavered over Italy's ultimate role in the conflict, at one time predicting that it would join the Allies, at other times Germany. See "What Will Mussolini Do?" *NYDN*, 2 March 1940, 15; "Is It a Deal?" *NYDN*, 6 March 1940, 33; "What Did Hitler and Mussolini Say," *NYDN*, 21 March 1940, 31.

71. Lundeen, *CR*, 5 June 1940, A3591.

72. Knutson, *CR*, 11 June 1941, 7997; Lindbergh, entry of 10 June 1940, *War Within*, 106; "Comment," *America* 63 (22 June 1940): 282. See also "The Hand and the Dagger," *America* 63 (22 June 1940): 294–95; "Mussolini Comes In," *NYDN*, 11 June 1940, 23.

73. Lindbergh, entry of 10 June 1940, *Wartime Journals*, 356; Castle Diary, 10 June 1940; Long, entry of 13 June 1940, *War Diary*, 104; Welles in Berle, entry of 11 June 1940, *Navigating*, 322.

74. "Daggers Made in U.S.A.," *Uncensored* 38 (22 June 1940): 1–2; "The Men Behind Mussolini," *New Republic* 102 (17 June 1940): 808; Lundeen, *CR*, 27 August 1940, 11,026.

75. Lindbergh, testimony, SFRC, 6 February 1941, 509; "Mussolini's Wars," *CT*, 19 November 1940, 12; Hearst, "In the News," *SFE*, 12 April 1940, 1–2.

76. *NYT*, 18 May 1940, 8; Hoover, speech in Lincoln, Nebraska, in *Addresses upon the American Road, 1940–1941* (New York: Scribner's, 1941), 50. He did stress that such aid must be given within the framework of existing loans that, at the time, prohibited loans to any nation, such as Britain, delinquent in war debts.

77. Wert, "Specter," 393; Wert, "Aid to the Poles," 511–24. For shadowboxing between FDR and Hoover concerning Hoover's possible leadership of an administration initiative, see Wert, "Specter," 81–92.

78. Wert, "Specter," 60. For the claim that relief efforts distracted Hoover from normal political activity, see Best, *Hoover*, 1:141–44.

79. Wert, "Specter," 4, 281; Belgium commission, *NYT*, 16 May 1940, 11. For British rationale, see Gordon Wright, *The Ordeal of Total War, 1939–1945* (New York: Harper & Row, 1968), 47.

80. Cudahy, *NYT*, 7 August 1940, 1, 3; *The Armies March: A Personal Report* (New York: Scribner's, 1941), chap. 14. In June 1940, Cudahy claimed that of some 8.4 million Belgians, some 8.3 million were subsisting on starvation rations. "Belgium Is Hungry," *Life* 10 (2 June 1941): 81. In October 1941, he told the SFRC that he had seen children in the first stages of pellagra, rickets, and other diseases of malnutrition. Testimony, 23 October 1941, 146.

81. For anti-interventionist endorsements of Cudahy's remarks, see, for example, "Jangling Ambassadors," *America* 63 (24 August 1940): 546; John Nevin Sayre, "Peace Is Not Built on Hunger," *Fellowship* 6 (September 1940): 125; McCarran, *CR*, 29 May 1941, 4553; Villard, "Chaos in the Cabinet," *Christian Century* 58 (25 June 1941): 828; Edward J. Skillin Jr., "Case Against," *Commonweal* 35 (5 December 1941): 181–82.

82. Hoover, press statement, "Starvation in the Occupied Democracies," 11 August 1940, *Addresses, 1940–1941*, 117–18; Wert, "Specter," 304–6.

83. Herbert Hoover to Raymond Graham Swing (copy), 19 August 1940, Castle Papers. See also Castle Diary, 21 August 1940 and 5 October 1940.

84. Hoover in Anne Morrow Lindbergh, entry of 12 August 1940, *War Within*, 136; Charles A. Lindbergh, entry of 12 August 1940, *Wartime Journals*, 378.

85. Churchill's speech, text, *NYT*, 21 August 1940, 4.

86. Hoover, "Reply to a Statement of British Refusal to Allow Relief of the Invaded Democracies," 6 October 1940, in *Addresses, 1940–1941*, 119–20; Hoover, speech at Poughkeepsie, New York, 15 November 1940, in *Addresses, 1940–1941*, 128; Hoover, "Feed Hungry Europe," *Collier's* 106 (23 November 1940): 72.

87. *Time*, 24 February 1941, 18. Among the interventionists backing Hoover's effort were David Lawrence, Raymond Gram Swing, Lowell Thomas, Clare Boothe Luce, Raymond Clapper, and the Luce publications. Publisher Henry Luce himself left the interventionist Century Group over the matter. Herzstein, *Luce*, 170. In an editorial dated December, the *NYT* declared that "it would be a bitter awakening for Great Britain, if . . . she were to win the war and discover that the democratic peoples . . . had been alienated." "Should We Feed Europe?" 10 December 1940, 24. In the Senate such individuals included Elbert D. Thomas, Francis T. Maloney, Charles O. Andrews (Dem.-Fla.), Joseph Ball (Rep.-Minn.), John H. Bankhead 2nd (Dem.-Ala.), William W. Barbour (Rep.-N.J.), Theodore G. Bilbo (Dem.-Miss.), Ralph Owen Brewster (Rep.-Maine), Harold Burton (Dem.-Ohio), and John Thomas (Dem.-Idaho). Signers to Thomas Resolution, *CR*, 2 June 1941, 4589. Interventionist columnist Dorothy Thompson toyed with a mild food relief plan. Herzstein, *Luce*, 184–85.

88. James H. George Jr., "Another Chance: Herbert Hoover and World War II Relief," *Diplomatic History* 16 (Summer 1992): 396–97.

89. Berle, entry of 8 July 1940, *Navigating*, 327. See also 28 September 1940, 339. For contrary views, see Roosevelt to Harry Hopkins, 1 March 1941, *F.D.R.: His Personal Letters*, 1129; Ickes, entry of 27 July 1940, *Secret Diary*, 3:274–75; 10 August 1940, 296; 1 December 1940, 385; Hull, *Memoirs*, 2:1052.

90. Hull, *NYT*, 12 December 1940, 12; Hoover in Chamberlin Diary, 10 January 1941.

91. Hoover, "The March of Hunger in Europe," Chicago, 16 February 1941, in *Addresses, 1940–1941*, 150. An NCFSD report maintained that the daily ration of bread and meat in Belgium was one-third that of the Germans. The British Ministry of Economic Warfare denied this, claiming that the daily ration was actually 79 percent what the Germans were allowed. While doubting all claims, Wert cites John Gillingham's *Belgian Business in the Nazi New Order* (Ghent: Jan Dhondt Foundation, 1977) to argue that while hunger was the rule for most Belgians, famine never occurred. As Hoover had predicted famine by 15 February, the British argument gained credibility. Wert, "Specter," 365–67. As Wert writes, "Without famine, there was no exigency, no need for intervention. The time factor, originally an ally of Hoover, now worked against him." 367.

92. Wert, "Specter," 352; Hoover, memorandum, conversation with Cordell Hull, 28 February 1941, 5, Hoover Papers.

93. Hoover, *An American Epic* vol. 4, *The Guns Cease Killing and the Saving of Life from Famine Begins, 1939–1963* (Chicago: Regnery, 1964), 40–41. For Hoover's confidence concerning the Germans, see Castle Diary, 28 February 1941. For popular mistrust, see Wert, "Specter," 372–73.

94. "Statement on the Blockade Policy of the British Government," 10 March 1941, in *CR,* 17 March 1941, 2293–94.

95. Hoover, "A Reply to British Refusal to Permit Relief," 10 March 1941, *Addresses, 1940–1941,* 159. See also Hoover, letter to [London] *Times,* 16 April 1941, in *American Epic,* 62–64; Herbert Hoover to Cordell Hull (copy), 24 April 1941; Cordell Hull to Herbert Hoover (copy), 10 May 1941, Castle Papers.

96. For concrete support of the NCFSD, see minutes, FOR Executive Committee, 11 March 1941, FOR Papers; A. J. Muste to Lord Halifax, 11 March 1941, FOR Papers; program, NCPW, 15 November 1941, *Peace Action* 7 (October 1941): 3. The WIL annual meeting, while not referring directly to the Hoover plan, appealed to the president to break "the hunger blockade" by using "his high influence upon the governments of Europe to allow ships to carry food and clothing to pass through the blockade." Minutes, 1–4 May, 1941, 3, WIL Papers. For examples of Roman Catholic opinion, see Edward S. Skillin, "Blockading the Conquered Peoples of Europe," *Commonweal* 32 (18 October 1940): 518; "The Food Blockade," *Catholic World* 153 (April 1941): 4–9; *Social Justice,* 2 September 1940, 8. Among the anti-interventionist Roman Catholic clergy, one finds Cardinal William Henry O'Connell of Boston and Archbishop John T. McNicholas of Cincinnati. In total, twenty-one bishops and archbishops supported the plan, as did eighty-four other prominent clergy.

97. For an example of the *Christian Century,* see "The Incomparable Atrocity," 57 (11 December 1940): 1543–45. The *Century* also published Devere Allen, "For Every Reason: Feed Europe!" 57 (20 November 1940): 1147–49; Ernest Fremont Tittle, "Stricken Souls and Empty Stomachs," 57 (27 November 1940): 1476–78; and Rose Wilder Lane, "A Question for Americans," 58 (23 April 1941): 558–59.

98. Diplomats included William R. Castle, J. Reuben Clark, and Henry P. Fletcher. Publishers and journalists included Boake Carter, William Randolph Hearst, Frank Gannett, George Sokolsky, Emil Hurja, Wheeler McMillan, Raymond Moley, Dorothy Dunbar Bromley, Roy Howard, and Freda Utley. See also "Why Starve Our Friends?" *CT,* 28 August 1941, 14; "Food for Europe," *NYDN,* 13 August 1940, 21. AFC national committee members included MacNider, Pinchot, Flynn, Villard, banker and former navy secretary Charles Francis Adams, aviator Eddie V. Rickenbacker, manufacturer Igor Sikorsky, manufacturer Edward L. Ryerson Jr., Methodist bishop Wilbur Emery Hammaker, novelist Kathleen Norris, and Alice Roosevelt Longworth, the outspoken daughter of Theodore Roosevelt. Charles and Anne Morrow Lindbergh supported the Quaker feeding of Europe. See Charles A. Lindbergh, entries of 5 September 1940 and 6 October 1940, *Wartime Journals,* 392, 397; Anne Morrow Lindbergh, entries of 27 October 1940 and 26 December 1940, *War Within,* 149, 156; *NYT,* 25 December 1940, 14. For AFC National Committee, see minutes, 27 October 1941, Box 337, AFC Papers.

99. See, for example, "Shall We Fight France?" *Progressive,* 31 May 1941, 8; "Just Let France Starve?" *NYDN,* 11 March 1941, 23; Villard, "Will France Fight England?" *Progressive,* 8 March 1941, 6; William Hague, "Should We Feed Europe?" *Scribner's Commentator* 9 (January 1941): 33.

100. Dennis, *WFL* 122 (28 November 1940): 4; "Hunger in France," *Christian Century* 58 (20 January 1941): 10; Johnson, *CR,* 17 March 1940, 2292. See also William Henry Chamberlin, *Yale Daily News,* 13 March 1941, 1; *Social Justice,* 24 March 1941, 8.

101. Edwin M. Borchard to John Bassett Moore, 6 June 1941, Borchard Papers. See also General Wood, *SFE,* 8 July 1941, 2.

102. Winston Churchill to Franklin D. Roosevelt, 3 June 1941, in Kimball, *Churchill and Roosevelt,* 1:125.

103. Gannett, speech at Rutland, Vermont, 7 June 1940, in *CR,* A3731; Ludlow, *CR,* 14 April 1941, A1675; "In Humanity's Name," *Christian Century* 57 (13 November 1940): 1407; "The Question of Food for Europe," *NYDN,* 4 December 1940, 39; "Passing of the Great Race?" *NYDN,* 24 March 1941, 19. See also "Belgian Belt Buckles," *NYDN,* 2 February 1941, 43.

104. See, for example, John Nevin Sayre, "Peace Is Not Built on Hunger," *Fellowship* 6 (September 1940): 125; Congressmen Barry, *CR,* 27 March 1941, 2677; Pittenger, *CR,* 3 March 1941, A953; Knute

Hill to NCFSD, 20 May 1941, the Papers of the National Committee on Food for the Small Democracies, Hoover Institution (hereafter cited as NCFSD Papers); Gerald P. Nye to NCFSD, 20 May 1941, NCFSD Papers.

105. Johnson, "One Man's Opinion," in *CR*, 20 March 1941, 1289. Earlier Johnson had been more fatalistic, doubting that Hoover could keep such food from reaching the Germans and claiming that the "dilemma" was an inescapable part of modern war. "One Man's Opinion," *SFN*, 29 November 1940, 21.

106. "Innocent Blood," *CT*, 27 October 1941, 12; Gillis, "The Food Blockade," *Catholic World* 153 (April 1941): 5; Aiken, *CR*, 25 February 1941, 1362; Burdick, *CR*, 22 May 1941, 4320. See also "Food for Europe," *NYDN*, 13 August 1940, 21; "Hunger in Europe," *CT*, 21 October 1941, 12.

107. Shipstead, *CR*, 17 May 1941, 2291; "Big Chance for Great Britain," *NYDN*, 21 November 1940, 31; "In Humanity's Name," *Christian Century* 57 (13 November 1940): 1407; Dennis, *WFL* 103 (18 July 1940): 3; 124 (12 December 1940): 4. See also William R. Castle to R. Douglas Stuart Jr., 11 March 1941, Box 63, AFC Papers; "Greece Starves," *NYDN*, 3 July 1941, 21.

108. Reynolds, *CR*, 8 August 1940, A4900; Barnes, cited by Nye, *CR*, 26 February 1941, 1431; "Pragmatism," *Uncensored* 62 (7 December 1940): 1–2; *Friday*, 3 January 1941, 5.

109. See, for example, Clay Judson to Page Hufty, 12 September 1941, Box 283, AFC Papers; Cudahy, testimony, SFRC, 23 October 1941, 146. See also John Finerty, testimony, HFAC, 14 October 1941, 57; "Washington Summary," *NYDN*, 15 November 1941, 15.

110. Wert, "Specter," 382–84; George, "Another Chance," 399; polls in Cantril, *Public Opinion*, 1103.

111. Arthur H. Vandenberg to R. S. Richmond, 17 July 1941, 15 September 1941, NCFSD Papers; Hoover, *NYT*, 20 October 1941, 1, 4. Hoover's own committee opposed hearings on the grounds that opponents of the plan would use them as a forum for their views, while pro-plan arguments would go unnoticed. Far better to have it brought out of committee and onto the House floor. This maneuver would have been quite unorthodox. Yet, if the plan's advocates were successful, a full debate, it was hoped, could bring about adoption of the pro-plan resolution by a handsome majority. Raymond S. Richmond to William B. Barry, 16 November 1941, NCFSD Papers.

## CHAPTER 7: PROTECTING THE REPUBLIC

1. Villard, *Our Military Chaos* (New York: Knopf, 1939), ii, 186; emphasis in original. The book was typeset just before the outbreak of war, but Villard was able to make minor alterations during proofreading and saw no need for substantive changes. See also "Issues and Men: The United States and the War," *Nation* 149 (23 September 1939): 324. Villard offered similar views in "Billions for What?" *Progressive*, 17 February 1940, 3; "True American Preparedness," *Progressive*, 28 September 1940, 6.

2. Fey, "We Recommend," *Fellowship* 6 (March 1940): 51. See also Paul Hutchinson, "Pouring Money down the Drain," *Christian Century* 56 (6 December 1939): 1507; Ruth Sarles, "Books in a World at War," *Peace Action* 6 (January 1940): 7.

3. Johnson, "Military Chaos," *NYWT*, 16. See also "Big-Navy Nightmare," *New Republic* 102 (22 January 1940): 103. Villard repeated his plea in "Issues and Men," *Nation* 153 (13 January 1940): 47.

4. Rogers, "Defense in a Vacuum," *Nation* 149 (4 November 1939): 501; Eliot, *New York Herald Tribune*, 19 November 1939, 6; Livingstone Hartley, "The Greatest Neutral," *New Republic* 102 (15 April 1940): 511; Dupey, "The Dilemma of Defense," *Saturday Review of Literature* 21 (4 November 1939): 18.

5. Villard, "Investigate the Army!" *American Mercury* 49 (April 1940): 427–34. The army replied that it was always under the scrutiny of efficiency experts, that the existence of General Marshall (not a West Pointer) disproved the caste charge, and that a plethora of officers was needed to build up a satisfactory number of well-schooled leaders for an emergency. *Newsweek*, 8 April 1940, 15–16. *Newsweek* conceded the existence of army posts in out-of-the-way areas rather than strategic ones.

6. Villard, "Issues and Men," *Nation* 150 (8 June 1940): 710. For Villard's continual pleas for modernization, see "Germany's Military Successes," *Atlantic Monthly* 166 (August 1940): 176; "The Wrong

Way to Prepare," *Christian Century* 58 (8 January1941): 57–58. On 28 May, Roosevelt announced the formation of a seven-person civilian board to fulfill the industrial side of the armament program. *NYT*, 29 May 1940, 1, 15. In some ways differing from Villard, Dennis said neither "the big shot business men" nor Roosevelt had any idea of "the social and industrial reorganization necessary for a modern war machine equal to that of Germany." *WFL* 100 (27 June 1940): 5.

7. Wiley, *CR*, 14 September 1940, 12,169. See also Wiley, *CR*, 31 May 1940, 7286.

8. See, for example, "To the Brink," *St. Louis Post-Dispatch*, 11 June 1940.

9. Pinchot, open letter to Franklin D. Roosevelt, in *CR*, 20 May 1940, A3685. See also Amos Pinchot to Roy Howard, 27 May 1940, Pinchot Papers; Lindbergh, speech, 19 May 1940, *The Radio Addresses of Col. Charles A. Lindbergh, 1939–1940* (pamphlet; New York: Scribner's Commentator, 1940), 11; Al Williams, speech to National Aviation Forum, 29 May 1940, in *CR*, A3401.

10. For resources, see Wiley, *CR*, 11 June 1940, 7918. For tanks, see Vorys, speech to War Veterans Republican Club of Ohio, Columbus, 25 May 1940, in *CR*, A3271. For rifles, see "It's Time to Think of America," *CT*, 18 June 1940, 12. For provisions, see Lundeen, speech, 10 June 1940, in *CR*, A3753.

11. Robsion, *CR*, 13 June 1940, A4168.

12. Danaher, *CR*, 3 June 1940, 7373; McCormick, broadcast of 15 June 1940, *Addresses*, 9.

13. Belgium comparison, "Arm Our Army at Once," *CT*, 13 May 1940, 1; Switzerland, Hearst, "In the News," *SFE*, 14 May 1940, 9; Lindbergh, "A Letter to Americans," *Collier's* 107 (29 March 1941): 15.

14. For general U.S. weakness, see David Reynolds, "1940," 334. For Marshall, see Bender, *CR*, 11 June 1940, 7998. For Johnson, see Vandenberg, radio address, 9 June 1940, in *CR*, A3691. For Drum, see "Second Rate Armies Aren't Armies," *CT*, 17 May 1940, 14.

15. See, for example, such FDR defense pleas as *NYT*, 31 May 1940, 1, 8; *NYT*, 29 June 1940, 1, 16. For Roosevelt's 1938 wishes, see Mark Skinner Watson, *Chief of Staff: Prewar Plans and Preparations* (Washington, D.C.: United States Army, 1950), 137.

16. Roosevelt address, text, *NYT*, 17 May 1941, 10.

17. Roosevelt address, text, *NYT*, 17 May 1941, 10; Roosevelt address, text, *NYT*, 26 May 1940, 12.

18. Dallek, *Roosevelt*, 223–24.

19. "National Defense," *Uncensored* 33 (18 May 1940): 1. See also Dennis, *WFL* 95 (23 May 1940): 3; Resolutions, WIL annual meeting, Pittsburgh, 27–30 April 1940, 3; "The WIL Today," n.d., attached to Mrs. S. Foster Hunt, 9 September 1940, WIL Papers; "Shotgun Defense," *Saturday Evening Post* 213 (31 August 1940): 28; Lindbergh, *CT*, 16 June 1940.

20. Waldrop, "Where Will Our Army Fight?" *WTH*, 7 June 1940, 11A; Dennis, *WFL* 148 (29 May 1941): 5.

21. See, for example, "Will We Do It?" *Saturday Evening Post* 213 (6 July 1940): 26; McCormick, broadcast of 14 July 1940, *Addresses*, 21; Hiram W. Johnson to Hiram W. Johnson Jr., 23 June 1940, Johnson Papers; Short, *CR*, 6 May 1941, 3666; Wheeler, speech, Floyd B. Olson memorial exercises, Minneapolis, 17 June 1940, in *CR*, A3961; Dennis, *WFL* 156 (24 July 1941): 2; *WFL* 157 (31 July 1941): 2.

22. Taft, address, "New Dealism or Real Defense?" 20 June 1940, in *CR*, A4111; Dennis, *WFL* 97 (6 June 1940): 4. See also *WFL* 156 (24 July 1941): 2.

23. Waldrop, "Where Will Our Army Fight?" 11A; "We'd Better Arm at Once," *NYDN*, 11 May 1940, 17; "West Point of the Masses," 19 May 1940, 41. See also *News* editorials "Close Up," 3 August 1940, 13; "Pass the Conscription Bill Now!" 26 August 1940, 19. For its concrete recommendations, see "An Army of 1,000,000 Sergeants," 12 May 1940, 43; "Whatever Happens, We Need an Army," 14 May 1940, 25; "Our Job," 29 May 1940, 21; "Hitler and Napoleon," 20 June 1940, 33; "Blitzkrieg Technic," 2 June 1940, 41.

24. McCormick, broadcast of 9 June 1940, *Addresses*, 7. He soon endorsed plans for the creation of nine regular army divisions, eighteen national guard divisions, five thousand new planes, thirteen thousand cannon, tanks, and antiaircraft artillery. Speech, 15 June 1940, *Addresses*, 9. For previous views of his newspaper, see "America's Defense," *CT*, 11 September 1939, 10; "Is It a New A.E.F.?", *CT*, 26 October 1939, 14; "No Army for Aggression," *CT*, 12 November 1939, 16.

25. Stimson, radio address at Yale University, NBC, *NYT*, 19 June 1940, 1.

26. His biographer Keith D. McFarland writes that "although the isolationists never counted Woodring among their number and while he never considered himself one of them, there is no doubt that they shared identical views when it came to the question of American involvement in a foreign war." *Harry H. Woodring: A Political Biography of FDR's Controversial Secretary of War* (Lawrence: University of Kansas Press, 1975), 201. Castle said Woodring was "just about as fond of Roosevelt as I am." Castle Diary, 3 February 1940.

27. Woodring, speech, Gridiron Club, St. Louis, 30 January 1940, in *CR*, A556; Woodring, *NYT*, 21 June 1940, 4; statement of 21 June in MacFarland, "Woodring," 231; speech, 9 July 1940, Woodring Testimonial Dinner, in *CR*, A4430.

28. David G. Haglund, *Latin America and the Transformation of U.S. Strategic Thought, 1936–1940* (Albuquerque: University of New Mexico Press, 1984), 204.

29. Knox, speech to bankers convention, Grand Rapids, cited by Wheeler, address to the American Anti-War Crusade of the Keep America Out of War Congress, Auditorium Theater, Chicago, 30 June 1940, CBS, in *CR*, A4313.

30. See, for example, Holt, *CR*, 8 July 1940, 9264; Dennis, *WFL* 100 (27 June 1940): 2.

31. Wheeler, *CR*, 20 June 1940, 8694.

32. See, for example, Holt, *CR*, 21 June 1940, 8820; Wheeler, Chicago speech, 30 June 1940, *CR*, A4313; Bone, *CR*, 9 July 1940, 9317.

33. Nye, *CR*, 9 July 1940, 9314; Holt, *CR*, 8 July 1940, 9267. See also "Stimson and Knox," *New Masses* 35 (2 June 1940): 25; Senator Dennis Chavez, *CR*, 9 July 1940, 9314; Lawrence Dennis, "Interventionist with a Record," 7 July 1940, in *CR*, A9315–16.

34. See, for example, B. C. Clark, *CR*, 20 June 1940, 8701; B. C. Clark, *CR*, 21 June 1940, 8809; Holt, *CR*, 20 June 1940, 8696; Fish, radio speech, 22 June 1940, NBC red network, in *CR*, 4186–87; Van Zandt, address to various state VFW conventions, entered in *CR*, 25 July 1940, A4573; Van Zandt, speech, Williamsport Consistory of the Scottish Rite Masonry, Williamsport, Pennsylvania, 28 June 1940, in *CR*, A5183. One dissent came from Villard, who considered Woodring "a lightweight." "Issues and Men," *Nation* 150 (8 June 1940): 710.

35. Castle Diary, 29 June 1940; Wheeler, Chicago address, 30 June 1940, in *CR* A4313. For Knox, see also Bone, *CR*, 9 July 1940, 9321.

36. "Secretary Knox, Secretary Stimson," *NYDN*, 22 June 1940, 13; Vandenberg, *CR*, 8 July 1940, 9261; roll call on Stimson, *NYT*, 10 July 1940, 13; on Knox, *NYT*, 11 July 1940, 3.

37. Reynolds, *Creation*, 110; Harper, *American Vision*, 69.

38. Schafer, *CR*, 12 March 1940, 2748. Schafer's amendment was rejected, after which the appropriation went through 305 to 37, with 88 not voting. See 2752–53. See also Al Williams, *Washington Daily News*, 24 April 1940.

39. Navy department announcement, *NYT*, 7 June 1940, 1, 14; Lundeen speech, Washington, D.C., 10 June 1940, in *CR*, A3753; Williams, "Courting Disaster," 13 June 1940, in Williams pamphlet, Box 276, Lundeen Papers. For other examples, see Shafer, *CR*, 10 June 1940, 7890–92; Lundeen, *CR*, 15 June 1940, 8334; Holt, *CR*, 12 June 1940, 8052; Holt, *CR*, 15 June 1940, 8337; Nye, "What Is Delaying the Defense Program?" address to New England Town Hall, Boston, 14 August 1940, in *CR*, A10821; Al Williams, "Keep Our Planes," 8 June 1940, in Williams pamphlets. The *Chicago Tribune* favored sending World War I Enfield rifles to the Allies but opposed the dispersal of first-line planes. See "American Arms and American Battles," 6 June 1940, 20.

40. *WTH*, 19 June 1940.

41. For France's fall, see Lundeen, *CR*, 19 June 1940, 8606. For Hague, see Case, *CR*, 20 June 1940, 8884. For legal action, see Fish, *CR*, 22 June 1940, 9055–56; "The *Alabama* Precedent," *CT*, 24 June 1940, 12; B. C. Clark, *CR*, 20 June 1940, 8698. For criminal codes, see Keefe, *CR*, 20 June 1940, A4045. For crews, see "Undeclared War," *CT*, 20 June 1940, 20. For act of war, see D. W. Clark, radio speech, "A Deadly Parallel," 20 June 1940, in *CR*, A4137.

42. Schafer, *CR*, 21 June 1940, 8885.

43. *NYT*, 25 June 1940, 1. Langer and Gleason, *Challenge to Isolation*, 522.

44. Walsh amendment, *CR*, 21 June 1940, 8828.

45. *Life*, 24 June 1940, 30; 15 July 1940, 17–23.

46. Kirk in James Leutze, *Bargaining for Supremacy: Anglo-American Naval Collaboration, 1937–1941* (Chapel Hill: University of North Carolina Press, 1977), 83; Long, entry of 13 June 1940, *War Diary*, 104.

47. Pittman, *NYT*, 26 June 1940, 6.

48. Long, entry of 12 June 1940, *War Diary*, 103; war department in Reynolds, *Creation*, 110; Marshall in David G. Haglund, "George C. Marshall and the Question of Military Aid to England, May–June 1940," *Journal of Contemporary History* 15 (October 1980): 745–60; Richard M. Leighton and Robert W. Coakley, *Global Logistics and Strategy, 1940–1943* (Washington, D.C.: Department of the Army, 1955), 33.

49. Arnold in John Morton Blum, *From the Morgenthau Diaries*, vol. 2: *Years of Urgency, 1938–1941* (Boston: Houghton Mifflin, 1965), 151, 163; Marshall, "Memorandum for the Secretary of War," 18 June 1940, in *The Papers of George Catlett Marshall*, vol. 2: *"We Cannot Delay": July 1, 1939–December 6, 1941*, ed. Larry Bland (Baltimore: Johns Hopkins University Press, 1986), 246–47; Watson, *Chief of Staff*, 305, 311.

50. Smith in Watson, *Chief of Staff*, 312; Morgenthau, *Diaries*, 142–43.

51. Clifford and Spencer, *First Peacetime Draft*, 246 n. 12; Berle, entry of 15 May 1940, *Navigating*, 314.

52. Poll of 23 May 1940, Cantril, *Public Opinion*, 973. For related polls, see 973, 1159–60.

53. The breakdown was as follows: to sell all U.S. planes, 9 percent; to sell some, 38 percent; to sell none, 49 percent; no opinion on the matter, 4 percent. The public was split over the matter of general aid, with 51 percent favoring U.S. credit for Allied air purchases and 49 percent opposed. Poll of 29 May 1940, Cantril, *Public Opinion*, 1159.

54. Gallup poll of 25 June 1940, Cantril, *Public Opinion*, 1186. In a *Fortune* poll, 40.1 percent predicted a German victory; 30.3 percent, a win for the Allies. See 1186.

55. Haglund, *Latin America*, 197. Reynolds dates Roosevelt's decision as early August. *Creation*, 68. Presidential aide Harry Hopkins told Churchill it was the British bombing of the French fleet at Oran, an event that took place on 3 July, that convinced Roosevelt that Britain would continue the fight. Gilbert, *Churchill*, 643–44.

56. Reynolds, *Creation*, 112; Leutze, *Bargaining*, 290 n. 53.

57. Clifford and Spencer, *First Peacetime Draft*, 257 n. 51; Leutze, *Bargaining*, 97–103. Donovan gave the British 60:40 odds in repelling an invasion. Entry of 2 August 1940 in *The London Journal of General Raymond E. Lee, 1940–1941*, ed. James Leutze (Boston: Little, Brown, 1971), 27–28.

58. For a wider context to the entire debate over defense, see John A. Thompson, "The Exaggeration of American Vulnerability," *Diplomatic History* 16 (Winter 1992): 23–43.

59. "Big-Navy Nightmare," *New Republic* 102 (22 January 1940): 103; "Another Scare from the Admirals," *Christian Century* 57 (4 January 1940): 99–100; Fish, *CR*, 29 April 1940, 4899; Fish, *United States News*, 10 May 1940, 25. See also Dennis, *WFL* 102 (11 July 1940): 5.

60. See, for example, *Social Justice*, 15 January 1940, 20.

61. "Big Ships: Superior Craft Seem Fantastic," *SFE*, 12 January 1940, 8. See also *SFE*, 30 December 1939, 11; Hearst, "In the News," *SFE*, 1 March 1940, 1.

62. See, for example, Burdick, *CR*, 19 June 1940, A3728; AFC, *Washington News Letter* 16 (4 June 1941): 4, Box 284, AFC Papers; Wiley, *CR*, 31 May 1940, 7280. For initial hesitancy of the aircraft–battleship issue, see "Sea Power vs. Air Power," *NYDN*, 20 September 1939, 35; "A Question Still Unanswered," *NYDN*, 11 December 1939, 31; Frank C. Waldrop, "European Reasons for Us to Stay Out," *WTH*, 9 September 1939, A11.

63. Lindbergh, speech at Hollywood Bowl, 20 June 1941, in *CR*, A3184; Reynolds, *CR*, 29 April 1940, A2442. See also Reynolds, *Washington Daily News*, 11 May 1940.

64. Edison, *NYT*, 2 May 1940, 14. See, for example, Danaher, speech to Republican State Convention, Hartford, 14 May 1940, in *CR*, A3053. For similar approval of Edison's remarks, see Hiram Johnson to Hiram Johnson Jr., 5 May 1940, Johnson Papers; "Design of Warships Needs Reconsid-

eration," *Christian Century* 57 (15 May 1940): 627–28; Alf Landon, speech, NBC, 17 May 1940, in *CR*, A3090.

65. Stirling, "Bureaucracy Rules the Navy," *Current History* 51 (March 1940): 50–52; Barnes, *NYWT*, 1 April 1940, 12.

66. For the *Royal Oak*, see Libby, "Proposed Naval Expansion Is Clearly without Excuse," *Peace Action* 6 (February 1940): 3. For the *Bismarck*, see "The *Hood* and the *Bismarck*," *NYDN*, 28 May 1940, 29; Al Williams, "Decline of Seapower," *Progressive*, 25 October 1941, 4. For Taranto, see "Design of Warships Needs Reconsideration," *Christian Century* 57 (15 May 1940): 627–28; "Taranto Revives an Old Debate," *Christian Century* 57 (27 November 1940): 1469; Villard, "Is Sea Power Tottering?" *Progressive*, 30 November 1940, 6. For stress on the limitation of air power at Taranto, see "Men and Machines in This War," *CT*, 21 November 1940, 16.

67. See, for example, Libby, "Vinson Naval Bill Made Foolish by Events," *Peace Action* 6 (April 1940): 3; Lundeen, *CR*, 21 May 1940, 6500.

68. Reynolds, *CR*, 29 April 1940, A2442; Danaher, speech, Republican State Convention, Hartford, 14 May 1940, in *CR*, A3053.

69. See, for example, Sargent, Bulletin #25, 5 January 1940, *Getting US into War*, 219; Johnson, "One Man's Opinion," *SFN*, 20 June 1940, 13. Libby was an exception among such people. He denied opposing a two-ocean navy, provided it was for defense and not aggression. Frederick J. Libby to Mrs. S. Foster Hunt, 1 June 1940, NCPW Papers.

70. McCormick, testimony, SFRC, 6 February 1941, 480; McCormick, broadcast of 29 September 1940, *Speeches*, 58; McCormick, radio speech, *CT*, 29 June 1941, 3. For varying views on naval expansion presented by McCormick's newspaper, see "America's Defense," *CT*, 11 September 1939, 10; "Behind the First Line of Defense," *CT*, 23 May 1940, 16; "Arm Our Army at Once," *CT*, 13 May 1940, 1.

71. See, for example, Fish, *CR*, 12 March 1940, 2749–50. In the Senate vote for a major naval bill, only Capper, Danaher, Reed, and Edwin Johnson were in opposition. *NYT*, 19 April 1940. 1. For further Senate action, see *NYT*, 22 June 1940, 6.

72. *NYT*, 29 May 1940, 14.

73. See, for example, Nicholas Broughton, "America in a Hostile World," *Scribner's Commentator* 9 (November 1940): 74.

74. Fish, *CR*, 12 March 1940, 2729. By June, Fish had claimed that the U.S. Navy possessed seven times the strength of the Germans. *CR*, 30 June 1940, 9696.

75. Wheeler, *CR*, 7 August 1941, 6873.

76. Fleming MacLiesh and Cushman Reynolds, *Strategy of the Americas* (New York: Duell, Sloan & Pearce, 1941), 105; Baldwin, "Wanted: A Plan for Defense," *Harper's Magazine* 181 (August 1940): 233–34. A unified enemy fleet might have twenty-five battleships to the United States's fifteen, but the sum would include two German "pocket battleships" and only three Russian battleships, the latter unable to cross the seas. *United We Stand!* 128. Baldwin did say the United States needed two to three more battleships, another aircraft carrier, more cruisers, submarines, and mine and net layers. The navy department also needed to change its design and procurement methods, slice the red tape, and shake up the navy yards. See 234. Baldwin called for increased shipbuilding facilities, greater speed in construction, and concentration on ships that could be built quickly. See 175. In April 1941, he claimed that the United States lacked sufficient ships to provide a battlefleet for both coasts. Furthermore, he said, some American battleships in the Pacific were in poor condition and possessed fleet auxiliaries that were too slow (e.g., cargo ships, tugs, seaplane tenders, etc.). See "The Naval Defense of America," *Harper's Magazine* 182 (April 1941): 453–54.

77. Baldwin, "What of the British Fleet?" *Reader's Digest* 39 (August 1941): 1–2. For positive references to Baldwin's article, see Robert La Follette Jr., *CR*, 29 October 1941, 8323; Waldrop, "They Weep," *WTH*, 2 November 1941, E1; O'Connor, *CR*, 6 October 1941, 7684; "Shipbuilding," *Uncensored* 102 (13 September 1941): 4; AFC Research Bureau, "One-Man War," *Did You Know?* 22 (September 1941, in Doenecke, *IDU*, 202–3; "Are American Bottoms Needed to Deliver Materials to Britain?" *Did You Know?* 28 (25 October 1941): 427–28.

78. See, for example, *Social Justice*, 15 January 1940, 20; 27 May 1940, 1.

79. Walsh, *CR*, 14 May 1940, 6081; Walsh, *Washington Daily News*, 11 May 1940.

80. Taft, speech, "Peace and Preparedness," 20 May 1940, in *CR*, A3178. See also speech of 29 May 1940, in *CR*, 3385.

81. Hearst, "In the News," *SFE*, 22 March 1940, 2. On 19 April 1940, he repeated his plea, then mentioned battleships as well. See 2.

82. Charles A. Lindbergh, testimony, HFAC, 23 January 1941, 377; Castle, "What about the Monroe Doctrine Now?" *Saturday Evening Post* 213 (27 July 1940): 40. See also "Design for Freedom," *Saturday Evening Post* 212 (11 November 1939): 24.

83. See, for example, "A 'Two-Ocean' Navy," *NYDN*, 23 October 1939, 23; "Let's Think about Ourselves," *NYDN*, 11 June 1940, 23.

84. "U.S. Siege Unworkable," *NYDN*, 6 November 1939, 33.

85. "A Two-Ocean Navy," *NYDN*, 22 July 1940, 19.

86. "Do We Have to Fight Japan?" *NYDN*, 17 February 1941, 19. See also "Article 8," *NYDN*, 25 June 1940, 32; "Keep It in One Ocean," *NYDN*, 15 July 1940, 21. "Two Ships for One," *NYDN*, 14 October 1940, 25; "Somebody Stumbled," *NYDN*, 11 June 1941, 33.

87. See, for example, Joseph P. Kennedy, in Breckinridge Long, entry of 7 November 1940, *War Diary*, 148; Rankin, *CR*, 19 March 1941, 2356; Wiley, *CR*, 6 June 1941, 4820; "The Long Range Bomber," *CT*, 1 June 1940, 10; MacLiesh and Reynolds, *Strategy*, 172; Stuart Chase to Dorothy Detzer, 3 October 1939, WIL Papers; Al Williams, *Airpower* (New York: Coward-McCann, 1940), 415. Even Villard, who claimed that the fall of France did not alter the nation's strategic situation, found that popular anxieties warranted a small, highly efficient air force. Letter to Norman Thomas, 16 July 1940, Thomas Papers.

88. Williams, *Airpower*, 405; "Wright's Foreign Policy as American as His Art," *Progressive*, 27 July 1940, 5.

89. See, for example, Hearst, "In the News," *SFE*, 24 May 1940, 1, 2; Michener, *CR*, 4 September 1940, 11,494; *Social Justice*, 1 July 1940, 8; Villard, "Germany's Military Success," *Atlantic Monthly* 166 (August 1940): 175; "The Rise and Fall of Billy Mitchell," *NYDN*, 19 June 1941, 31; Hearden, "Cudahy," 111.

90. Michael S. Sherry, *The Rise of American Air Power: The Creation of Armageddon* (New Haven, Conn.: Yale University Press, 1987), 53.

91. For biographical sketch, see "Alvord Joseph Williams, Jr.," *Current Biography, 1940*, 870–72. For resignation, see "Free Speech, Hell," *Time*, 22 July 1940, 17. For citations, see General Robert E. Wood, "Our Foreign Policy," speech to Chicago Council of Foreign Relations, 4 October 1940, in *CR*, A6301; "Major Williams Resigns," *CT*, 12 July 1940, 10; "The Waste of American Air Leadership," *CT*, 24 August 1941, 14; *Social Justice*, 29 July 1940, 5; Roy Howard to J. I. Miller, 24 March 1941, Howard Papers; Francis Neilson, entry of 14 February 1941, *Tragedy*, 2:146.

92. For Popular Front, see Williams, *Airpower*, 74, 76–78. For Ethiopia, see 18, 218, 334. For Spain, see 251. Quotation, 228.

93. On FDR, see Williams, *Airpower*, 395; on gold purchases, 403; on international politicians, 394.

94. Williams, *Airpower*, 405.

95. Williams, *Airpower*, 394, 405, 408, 410.

96. See, for example, George T. Eberle, *America* 63 (28 September 1940): 693; "A Few Determined Young Men," *NYDN*, 8 September 1940, 47; Eddie Rickenbacker, preface to Williams, *Airpower*, vii–viii. The *Chicago Tribune* offered lengthy quotations on its editorial page, 6 October 1940, 18.

97. Baldwin, "Down-to-Earth Air Talk," *Saturday Review of Literature* 170 (21 September 1940): 11. See also John Chamberlain, *Harper's Magazine* 181 (October 1940): front advertising pages.

98. *Newsweek*, 12 August 1940, 38–39; Eliot, "Apostle of Air Power," *New York Herald Tribune Book Section*, 1 September 1940, 6; Max Gissen, "The Eagles They Fly High," *New Republic* 103 (7 October 1940): 482.

99. "The Best Defense for U.S.," *SFE*, 14 November 1939, 10. In April 1940, Hearst cabled editorial supervisor Edmond D. Coblentz, calling for a campaign in his papers for air power. Cable, 19 April

1940, the Papers of Edmond D. Coblentz, University of California at Berkeley. See also "But Boake Carter Says," *SFE*, 24 September 1940, 13; Hearst, "In the News," *SFE*, 18 April 1940, 1.

100. Hearst, "In the News," 24 September 1941, 1A. For the original article, see *Army Ordnance* 22 (September–October 1941): 217–20, reprinted in "The Bombing Plane Has Made America Invasion-Proof," *Reader's Digest* 39 (November 1941): 64–66. For other references to Phillips, see Barry, *CR*, 16 October 1941, 9765; Wheeler, *CR*, 6 November 1941, 8553; John Haynes Holmes, letter to *Harvard* [University] *Crimson*, 3 October 1941, 2; "U.S. Impregnability," *Uncensored* 104 (27 September 1941): 3; Stuart Chase, "Forgotten Facts," *Progressive*, 18 October 1941, 5.

101. "Where the Blitzkrieg?" *NYDN*, 18 December 1939, 27. Its source was an article by Cy Caldwell in the December *Aero Digest*. See also "War in the Air," *NYDN*, 20 December 1939, 35. By May 1941, the *News* embraced the bomber. It warned, "We may be invaded from Canada or Mexico," as it called on the United States to rely on long-range bombers that would intercept enemy craft from coastal bases. "Why Not a Separate Air Force?" 5 May 1941, 19.

102. Reynolds, *CR*, 29 April 1940, A3175. For other references to Norway, see Al Williams, speech to National Aviation Forum, 29 May 1940, in *CR*, A3402; retired major general William C. Rivers, radio speech, "Europe's War and America's Security," 18 May 1940, in *CR*, A3039; MacLiesh and Reynolds, *Strategy*, 172–73. For other references to Poland, see Case, *CR*, 6 June 1941, 4819; Nye, *CR*, 26 February 1941, 1434; Williams, *Airpower*, 368–78.

103. Eben Emael, "Schmeling; Separate Air Force," *NYDN*, 30 May 1941, 17; Dunkirk, Villard, "No Defense Against Airplanes," *Progressive*, 7 September 1940, 6; Battle of Britain, Case, *CR*, 6 June 1941, 4819.

104. See, for example, AFC, *Washington News Letter* 16 (4 June 1941): 3–4, Box 284, AFC Papers; Congressman Melvin Maas, report of Fred Burdick, 3 June 1941, AFC Papers, Box 65; Sokolsky, "These Days: The Planes Have It," *New York Sun*, 5 June 1941, 22; Williams, "Brass Hats Die Hard," *Progressive*, 7 June 1941, 8.

105. See, for example, Taft, speech, 29 May 1940, in *CR*, A3385; Hearst, "In the News," *SFE*, 14 May 1940, 9; *Social Justice*, 19 August 1940, 20; Vorys, speech, War Veterans' Republican Club of Ohio, Columbus, 25 May 1940, in *CR*, A3271; Norman Thomas to Anton Gardon, 29 May 1940, Thomas Papers; Vandenberg, radio address, 9 June 1940, in *CR*, A3961; "It's Time to Think of America," *CT*, 18 June 1940, 12.

106. McCormick, broadcast of 15 May 1940, *Addresses*, 9; Williams, speech to National Aviation Forum, 29 May 1940, in *CR*, A3401; Williams, "British Orders," 29 July 1940, in Williams pamphlets.

107. Edison in Hearst, "In the News," *WTH*, 14 May 1940, 9; Arnold in Maas, address, Williamsport Consistory, Scottish Rite Masonry, Williamsport, Pennsylvania, 28 June 1940, in *CR*, A5182; Colonel George Chase Lewis, "The Truth about Our Air Defenses," *Scribner's Commentator* 8 (July 1940): 3–5.

108. Rickenbacker, "We Need 250,000 Planes and 500,000 Pilots," *Look*, 27 August 1940, 8–12. He had previously called for fifty thousand planes and twenty-five thousand pilots. *United States News*, 16 October 1939, 4.

109. "Rickenbacker Is the Man," *CT*, 15 May 1940, 12. See also "A Page of Comment," *Social Justice*, 3 June 1940, 5; 1 July 1940, 8; Don Rogers, "Rickenbacker—Air Lines Wizard," *Scribner's Commentator* 10 (June 1941): 45–52; "Why Not Ask the Air Men?" *NYDN*, 7 July 1941, 19.

110. Doenecke, *IDU*, 14. General Robert E. Wood, its national chairman, suspected that Rickenbacker feared losing valuable mail delivery contracts for Eastern Air Lines, the firm he headed. For Wood on Rickenbacker, see R. Douglas Stuart Jr. to Page Hufty, 2 February 1941, Box 64, AFC Papers.

111. Text, Roosevelt speech, *NYT*, 17 May 1941, 10.

112. See, for example, "West Point of the Masses," *NYDN*, 19 May 1940, 41; Robert E. Wood to Franklin D. Roosevelt, 17 May 1940, Wood Papers.

113. For stress on technical training, see "How to Get a Mechanized Army," *NYDN*, 9 July 1940, 23; "Why a Big Army?" 29 July 1940, 19; "Draft Bill Approved, 13–3," 7 August 1940, 2. For planes and pilots, see "Calling Out the Guard," *NYDN*, 31 July 1940, 25.

114. "The New Arms Program," *CT*, 17 May 1940, 14.

115. Lindbergh on cost and men, in Castle Diary, 19 May 1940; Flynn, "Other People's Money: Who's Going to Pay the Defense Bill?" *New Republic* 102 (10 June 1940): 792; Williams, "Real Air Power

for America," *Scribner's Commentator* 8 (August 1940): 107. For cost, see also Castle Diary, 27 May 1940. For manpower, see also Al Williams, "Real Air Power for America," *Scribner's Commentator* 8 (August 1940): 107. Both Marshall and General Hap Arnold, chief of the air corps, concurred on the need for trained pilots. Marshall to Bernard M. Baruch, 14 May 1940, in Marshall, *Papers*, 2:212.

116. Dennis, *WFL* 97 (6 June 1940): 4; Flynn, *SFN*, 24 May 1940, 22; Lindbergh radio broadcast cited in "The Roosevelt War Plan Exposed," *CT*, 16 October 1940, 16. For a previous example of such skepticism, see Fish, *CR*, 12 March 1940, 2729.

117. Baldwin, "Wanted: A Plan for Defense," *Harper's Magazine* 181 (August 1940): 235; Al Williams, "Real Air Power for America," *Scribner's Commentator* 8 (August 1940): 107.

118. Lindbergh, testimony, HFAC, 23 January 1941, 420; Lindbergh, "A Letter to Americans," *Collier's* 107 (29 March 1941): 15. In citing the Lindbergh article, Fish claimed that U.S. aircraft, when compared to first-line British and German planes, lacked self-sealing tanks, adequate gun power, and sufficient speed. *CR*, 21 March 1941, 2481. See also Wheeler, speech, Indianapolis, 28 May 1941, in *CR*, A2628.

119. AFC, *Washington News Letter* 16 (4 June 1941): 3, Box 284, AFC Papers; Williams, "Panicky Promises," *Progressive*, 13 September 1941, 4. For other Williams indictments, see testimony, SFRC, 7 February 1941, 583, 588; "I Rebuke Seversky," *Scribner's Commentator* 10 (July 1941): 10.

120. Lundeen, *CR*, 21 May 1940, 6499; Lundeen, *CR*, 19 June 1940, 8606; Lundeen, *CR*, 27 August 1940, 11,010; Van Zandt, "A Department of National Defense," speech, NBC, 23 May 1940, in *CR*, A3239; Williams, speech to National Aviation Forum, 29 May 1940, in *CR*, 3401; Williams, *Washington Daily News*, 14 June 1940, in *CR*, 5294; MacLiesh and Reynolds, *Strategy*, 164; Wheeler, *CR*, 24 August 1940, 10,730. For the support of Capper, General Rivers, General Johnson Haygood, Congressman Maas, and General Wood, who was uncertain about giving the office cabinet rank, see *United States News*, 13 September 1940, 27; *United States News*, 20 September 1940, 26. Hanson Baldwin was a lone dissenter, saying that a separate air force would simply create confusion in a time of crisis. *United We Stand!* 221. To Baldwin, its creation would only cause bitterness; if the U.S. Navy were deprived of its "flying fleets," the Allied ability to dominate the seas might be crippled. "Sea Power Is Dominant," *NYT*, 27 October 1941, 4.

121. See, for example, *News* editorials all titled "United States Air Force," 8 June 1941, 51; 17 June 1941, 19; 14 July 1941, 19; 20 July 1941, 37; 11 August 1941, 15; 8 September 1941, 19; 19 September 1941, 31; 30 September 1941, 21; 14 October 1941, 35.

122. "How about a Separate Air Force?" *NYDN*, 14 March 1941, 31. Al Williams denied that the British air force possessed real autonomy, a factor helping weaken that nation. "An Accounting Is Due," *Progressive*, 17 May 1941, 4.

123. "Why Not Ask the Air Men?" *NYDN*, 7 July 1941, 19.

124. McCormick, broadcast of 21 July 1940, *Addresses*, 26; McCormick, broadcast of 28 July 1940, *Addresses*, 29; "Bombs Wreck Commons Chamber," *NYDN*, 13 May 1941, 23; "The 'Bomb Hell Out of 'Em' Theory," *NYDN*, 18 May 1941, 43.

125. Dennis, *WFL* 145 (8 May 1941): 4; 125 (19 December 1940): 3; 77 (18 January 1940): 5; Johnson, "One Man's Opinion," *SFN*, 19 October 1939, 21.

126. For Spain, see Wood, Chicago Council on Foreign Relations speech, 4 October 1940, in *CR*, A6301. For Finland, see "Air Bombs on Finland," *CT*, 5 February 1940, 12; "The Purpose of the Air Bogy," *CT*, 26 February 1940, 10.

127. "Can We Lick Germany without Fighting?" *NYDN*, 16 February 1941, 41; Dennis, *WFL* 97 (6 June 1940): 4. For France, see also Charles A. Lindbergh, "A Letter to Americans," *Collier's* 107 (29 March 1941): 76; Baldwin, *United We Stand!* 118–19.

128. Japan, "Can We Lick Germany without Fighting?" 41; Hearst, "In the News," *SFE*, 14 September 1940, 13A.

129. See, for example, "Bombs Wreck Commons Chamber," *NYDN*, 13 May 1941, 23; Cudahy, testimony, SFRC, 23 October 1940, 140; Libby, HFAC, 14 October 1941, 60, 66; Gillis, "The 'Isolationist' Argument," *Catholic World* 155 (December 1941): 262.

130. Sherry, *Rise*, 85, 92. For Lindbergh, see testimony, HFAC, 23 January 1941, 425–26; SFRC, 6 February 1941, 520.

131. Ickes, entry of 18 September 1938, *Secret Diary*, 2:469; Morgenthau, *Diaries*, 2:48.

132. David Kahn, "United States Views Germany and Japan in 1941," in *Knowing One's Enemies: Intelligence Assessments Before the Two World Wars*, ed. Ernest R. May (Princeton, N.J.: Princeton University Press, 1984), 492; Ronald Lewin, *Hitler's Mistakes* (New York: Morrow, 1984), 89–93, 103–5; Milch quotation in Lewin, *Hitler's Mistakes*, 103; Sherry, *Rise*, 77.

133. R. J. Overy, "From 'Uralbomber' to 'Amerikabomber': The Luftwaffe and Strategic Bombing," *Journal of Strategic Studies* 1 (September 1978): 154–78; John Killen, *A History of the Luftwaffe* (New York: Doubleday, 1968), especially 101, 164, 183.

134. Clifford and Spencer, *First Peacetime Draft*, 110–11.

135. Roosevelt, acceptance speech, text, *NYT*, 12 July 1940, 2; Roosevelt, press conference, 1 August 1940, in *The Public Papers and Addresses of Franklin D. Roosevelt*, vol. 9: *War—and Aid to Democracies, 1940*, comp. Samuel I. Rosenman (New York: Random House, 1950), 320; Marshall in Charles E. Kirkpatrick, *An Unknown Future and a Doubtful Present: Writing the Victory Plan of 1941* (Washington, D.C.: Center of Military History, 1990), 44.

136. Lindbergh, speech, NBC, 15 June 1940, in "Radio Addresses," 14; Waldrop, "The U.S. Becomes a Nation in Arms," *WTH*, 29 July 1940, 7; Reynolds, *CR*, 21 August 1940, 10,669. See also General Robert E. Wood to Marvin McIntyre, 5 May 1940, Wood Papers; Maas, *CR*, 7 September 1940, A5672.

137. "Total War Is Here to Stay," *NYDN*, 12 September 1940, 31. For attacks on the *News* editorial, see "'Brutes Wanted'—Capitalism's Ideal for Civilization," *Daily Worker*, 13 September 1940, 1; letter of Frederick J. Libby to *Christian Century* 57 (16 October 1940): 1285; Wheeler, *CR*, 14 September 1940, 12,166; Sargent, Bulletin #80, 20 August 1940, *Getting US into War*, 431 n. 5. For the *News*'s defense of the word "brutality," see editorials "War *Is* Brutality," 17 September 1940, 21; "Not Enough Volunteering," 20 September 1940, 33.

138. "No Substitute for Men and Guns," *NYDN*, 5 July 1940, 21. See also "Make It Universal *Military* Training," *NYDN*, 23 June 1940, 37.

139. Johnson, "One Man's Opinion," *SFN*, 6 June 1940, 15. See also Johnson, *SFN*, 10 July 1940, 13; 30 July 1940, 13; "Selective Service Right Now," CBS speech, 23 August 1940, in *Vital Speeches* 6 (15 September 1940): 729–30. He was critical of aspects of the Burke–Wadsworth bill, for he wanted more stress on trained personnel. Johnson, "One Man's Opinion," *SFN*, 7 July 1940, 21; *SFN*, 3 August 1940, 11. For Johnson's hopes to direct selective service, see "One Man's Opinion," *SFN*, 10 August 1940, 11; 13 September 1941, 23. In 1941, the Roosevelt administration went even further, denying his application for a renewal of his military commission as brigadier general. Ohl, *Hugh S. Johnson*, 301–3.

140. See, for example, Wheeler, 13 August 1940, *CR*, 10,239; Congressman U. S. Guyer (Rep.-Kan.), *CR*, 4 July 1940, A5299; John Haynes Holmes to Walter Van Kirk, 11 July 1940, Holmes Papers; Fish, *CR*, 3 September 1940, 11,361; Flynn, *SFN*, 18 June 1940, 14; "No Conscription," *America* 63 (24 August 1940): 547.

141. Entry of 6–9 August, 1940, Chamberlin Diary; Barnes, statement to Sidney Hertzberg, 16 August 1940, Hertzberg Papers. See also Norman Thomas, "Your World and Mine: On the Road to American Fascism," *Call*, 14 September 1940, 5. For other anxieties concerning militarism, see Capper, *CR*, 19 August 1940, 10,477; "Conscription," *America* 63 (6 July 1940): 351; Fish, *CR*, 11 July 1940, 9534; William Hubben, "If Conscription Comes," *Christian Century* 57 (7 August 1940): 995; "Why Was Conscription Demanded?" *Christian Century* 57 (16 October 1940): 1269; Ludlow, *CR*, 4 September 1940, 11,466; Norman Thomas to Henry Sloane Coffin, 6 August 1940, Thomas Papers.

142. Wheeler claimed that though the Supreme Court, speaking through Justice Benjamin Cardozo, affirmed the government had a right to levy conscription in wartime, it was silent as to a peacetime draft. *CR*, 20 August 1940, 10,595. A lawyers' committee noted that even under Article I, Section 8, of the Constitution, there was neither an implied nor an expressed power to enact conscription ("Brief on the Peacetime Military Conscription [Burke–Wadsworth Bill] [S. 4164] and the Maloney Amendment"), prepared by the Lawyers' Committee to Keep the United States Out of War, inserted by Wheeler in *CR*, 23 August 1940, A5206–10.

143. See, for example, Max Frimmel, "Conscription and the Jones," *New Masses* 36 (9 July 1940): 21–22; Julian Webb, "Conscription: Straitjacket for 42,000,000," *New Masses* 36 (6 August 1940): 3–5;

Adam Lapin, "Prelude to M-Day," *New Masses* 36 (6 August 1940): 14; Wheeler, *CR*, 13 August 1940, 10236; Keefe, *CR*, 3 September 1940, 11,371; Norman Thomas to members, House Military Affairs Committee, 30 July 1940, Thomas Papers.

144. Taft, *CR*, 14 August 1940, 10,307. For similar anxieties concerning socialism, see entry of 26 July 1940, Chamberlin Diary.

145. For the salary issue, see newspaper column, former Congressman Samuel B. Pettengill (Dem.-Ind.), entered in *CR*, 19 August 1940, A5061. For the matter of arbitrariness, see Congressman Carl Hinshaw (Rep.-Calif.), *CR*, 14 September 1940, 12,217; Dennis, *WFL* 107 (15 August 1940): 2. For the rural issue, see Representative Henry C. Dworshak (Rep.-Ind.), *CR*, 4 July 1940, 11,476.

146. See, for example, Burdick, *CR*, 14 August 1940, 10,350; Nye, 23 August 1940, 10,810; Taft, speech, 5 September 1940, in *CR*, A5491.

147. For administrative problems, see Dennis, *WFL* 105 (25 July 1940): 4. For cost and provisioning, see Wheeler, *CR*, 5 August 1940, 10,223; author unknown, "Facts Underlying Peacetime Conscription," in *CR*, 9 October 1940, A6256. For weakening the economy, see "The Army and the Draft," *CT*, 25 July 1940, 10.

148. See, for example, Woodruff, *CR*, 1 August 1940, A4687; Burdick, *CR*, 1 August 1940, A4711; Edwin C. Johnson, *CR*, 7 August 1940, 10,973; Nye, broadcast, 9 August 1940, in *CR*, A4997; Bender, *CR*, 3 September 1940, 11,394; "Conscription Will Hamper Defense," *CT*, 24 July 1940, 10. For facilities, see "Men without Weapons," *CT*, 9 September 1940, 12; Reynolds, *CR*, 19 August 1940, 10,482; Wheeler, *CR*, 22 August 1940, 10,727; Knutson, *CR*, 3 September 1940, 11,402; Dennis, *WFL* 112 (19 September 1940): 5.

149. See, for example, "Expanding Our Armed Forces," *CT*, 31 July 1940, 10; Vandenberg, *CR*, 9 August 1940, 10,096; Vandenberg, *CR*, 12 August 1940, 10,128; "Knights without Armor," *Uncensored* 46 (17 August 1940): 2; Robsion, *CR*, 3 September 1940, 11,402; Congressman John M. Wolverton (Rep.-W.Va.), *CR*, 7 September 1940, A5533. Auto executive William S. Knutson, one of the seven members National Defense Advisory Commission and America's foremost production specialist, was frequently quoted on the two-year matter.

150. Wheeler, *CR*, 13 August 1940, 10,222; Wiley, *CR*, 28 August 1940, 11,086. See also "Bob La Follette Says: America Doesn't Want a Man-Power Muddle," *Progressive*, 27 July 1940, 1.

151. On Canada, see Fish, *CR*, 30 July 1940, 9688; Fish, *CR*, 6 August 1940, 9959. "Conscription—U.S. and Canadian Models," *CT*, 2 August 1940, 8. On Australia, see Wheeler, *CR*, 14 August 1940, 10,299. Congressman Thomas E. Martin noted that Britain enacted the draft only once it entered the war. *CR*, 4 September 1940, 11,458. Conversely, said Representative Frederick C. Smith, nearly all Latin American countries had conscription, yet that continent "teems with communism." *CR*, 11 July 1940, 9678.

152. See, for example, Taft, *CR*, 14 August 1940, 10,309; Walsh, *CR*, 21 August 1940, 10,654; Walsh, *CR*, 28 August 1940, 11,140; Dennis, *WFL* 106 (1 August 1940): 3.

153. See, for example, Wheeler, *CR*, 5 August 1940, 9838; "Expanding Our Unarmed Forces," *CT*, 31 July 1940, 10; "Conscription," *America* 63 (27 July 1940): 435; Dorothy Detzer to Hannah Clothier Hull and Emily Greene Balch, 21 August 1940, WIL Papers.

154. Fish, *CR*, 30 June 1940, 9696; Downey, *CR*, 15 August 1940, 10,391.

155. See, for example, Senator George Norris (Ind.-Nebr.), *CR*, 22 August 1940, 10,428; Taft, *CR*, 14 August 1940, 10,310; Lodge, *CR*, 22 August 1940, 10,729; Baldwin, "Wanted: A Plan for Defense," *Harper's Magazine* 181 (August 1940): 236.

156. Vandenberg, *CR*, 25 July 1940, 10,128. See also "Preparation for What?" *CT*, 10 July 1940, 10; "An Army for Europe," *CT*, 11 July 1940, 1; "An Army for a Caesar," *CT*, 18 September 1940, 14; "Conscripting Conscription," *Uncensored* 43 (17 July 1940): 4; "No Conscription," *America* 63 (24 August 1940): 547.

157. "'Good Neighbor' Gets Tough," *Call*, 7 September 1940, 1; Norman Thomas, "Your World and Mine: "War or Democracy," *Call*, 28 September 1940, 5.

158. Taft, *CR*, 21 August 1940, 10,654.

159. For a proposal of 150,000 to 200,000 men, see "Preparation for What?" *CT*, 10 July 1940, 10. For a proposal of 750,000, see Taft, *CR*, 14 August 1940, 10,308. For a proposal of 400,000, see Hanson Baldwin, "Wanted: A Plan for Defense," *Harper's Magazine* 181 (August 1940): 238; Baldwin, *United*

*We Stand!* 259. For excerpts from Baldwin's *Harper's* article, see "Rational Defense," *Uncensored* 42 (20 July 1940): 2–4; "Hanson Baldwin Rejects Conscription," *Peace Action* 6 (August 1940): 7. For left-wing use of Baldwin, see *In Fact* 1 (9 September 1940): 3.

160. See, for example, letter of Rush Holt, 8 August 1940, in *SFE*, 10 August 1940, 1; news story, *SFE*, 13 August 1940, 2; "But Boake Carter Says," *SFE*, 15 August 1940, 15; letter of Senator Millard Tydings (Dem.-Md.), *SFE*, 19 August 1940, 1–2; *SFE*, September 4, 1940; letter from Congressman Knutson, *SFE*, 7 September 1940, 1.

161. Fish, *CR*, 5 September 1940, 11,572; Fish, *CR*, 14 September 1940, 12,214; Clifford and Spencer, *First Peacetime Draft*, 216.

162. See, for example, "Peace-Time Conscription," *America* 63 (10 August 1940): 491–92; Chamberlin Diary, 22 July 1940; Philip Burnham, "Alternative to War," *Commonweal* 32 (12 July 1940): 246.

163. Norman Thomas to Wintrow Morse, 10 December 1940, Thomas Papers; Dorothy Detzer to Mrs. Louis M. Robinson, 21 August 1940, WIL Papers.

164. "Conscripting Conscription," *Uncensored* 43 (27 July 1940): 2–5. See also "Conscription Slowdown," *Uncensored* 44 (3 August 1940): 2–3; "Conscription Confusion," *Uncensored* 45 (10 August 1940): 2; "Knights without Armor," *Uncensored* 46 (17 August 1940): 2; Fish quoting Adjutant General E. S. Adams, *CR*, 11 July 1940, 9533; Frank Hanighen to Cushman Reynolds, n.d. [July 1940], Hertzberg Papers; Capper, *CR*, 5 August 1940, A4749; Wiley, *CR*, 28 August 1940, 11,086; "Conscription for the Third Term," *CT*, 31 August 1940, 10.

165. Dondero, *CR*, 7 August 1940, 10,000. See also author unknown, "Facts Underlying Peacetime Conscription," in *CR*, 9 October 1940, A6254; Vandenberg, *CR*, 25 July 1940, 9598.

166. Hugh Johnson, *SFN*, 9 September 1940, 14; Johnson, "Selective Service Right Now," 749. See also "Pass the Conscription Bill Now!" *NYDN*, 26 August 1940, 19; "Bunk about Bombing," *NYDN*, 10 September 1940, 23; "Politics and the Draft," *NYDN*, 11 September 1940, 31; "Not Enough Volunteering," *NYDN*, 20 September 1940, 33.

167. House vote, 5 September 1940, *CR*, 11,604; Roosevelt, "Proclamation Calling for Draft Registration on Oct. 16," *NYT*, 17 September 1940, 1; Gallup, *New York Times*, 11 August 1940, 6. For political maneuvering, see Clifford and Spencer, *First Peacetime Draft*, 220–21.

168. Lodge, "The Drift Toward War," radio broadcast, 25 September 1940, in *CR*, 5905; Dennis, *WFL* 132 (6 February 1941): 4.

169. "New Tactics, New Weapons," *CT*, 14 September 1940, 12; "While Yet There Is Time to Think," *Saturday Evening Post* 213 (7 September 1940): 26; Wiley, *CR*, 14 September 1940, 12,169. See also Wiley, *CR*, August 23, 1940, 10,794.

170. Baldwin, *United We Stand!* 250–52. MacLiesh and Reynolds differed, finding U.S. officers more imaginative, knowledgeable, and efficient than ever, though they did find coastal defenses dangerously inadequate. See 29, 131. For their own listing of army shortages, see *Strategy*, 235.

171. For CDAAA plan, *NYT*, 13 September 1940, 6. For internal dissidence, Johnson, *Battle*, 119–22. For CDAAA on draft, see Clifford and Spencer, *First Peacetime Draft*, 178–79.

172. See, for example, "Notes on a Day's News," *Uncensored* 49 (7 September 1940): 4; B. C. Clark, *CR*, 26 September 1940, 12,644; "Your Government," *Saturday Evening Post* 213 (12 October 1940): 30; Lodge, radio speech, "The Drift to War," 25 September 1940, in *CR*, A5906; Lodge, *CR*, 25 September 1940, 1589; *Social Justice*, 9 September 1940, 6.

173. "While Yet There Is Time to Think," *Saturday Evening Post* 213 (7 September 1940): 26; Johnson, *United States News*, 18 October 1940, 35; Libby, "France, Too, Went to War Unprepared," *Peace Action* 7 (October 1940): 3; Clark, *CR*, 25 September 1940, 12644. See also B. C. Clark and Holt, *CR*, 14 September 1940, 12,167. In November, Roosevelt denied that the Norden bombsight was attached to the forty-six bombers sent to Britain. Rather, Britain was receiving a more obsolete Sperry sight. *CT*, 22 November 1940, 4.

174. Johnson, "Defend America First," address delivered over NBC network, 5 September 1940, in *Vital Speeches* 6 (1 October 1940): 763; AFC advertisement, *NYT*, 3 October 1940, 21.

175. For Hague, see Short, *CR*, 3 September 1940, 11,364; Keefe, *CR*, 4 September 1940, 11,429. For act of war, see John Nevin Sayre, *United States News*, 18 October 1940, 35.

## CHAPTER 8: MILITARY DEFENSE OF THE HEMISPHERE

1. "Declaration of Panama," Jones and Myers, *Document,* 2:115–17. Canada and "the undisputed colonies and possessions of European countries" were excluded. For background, see Irwin F. Gellman, *Good Neighbor Diplomacy: United States Policies in Latin America, 1933–1945* (Baltimore: Johns Hopkins University Press, 1979), 83–85.

2. Bennett Champ Clark was an exception in praising Roosevelt and Hull for their "brilliant leadership" in the matter. *CR,* 18 February 1941, 1099. See also John Haynes Holmes, "Three Hundred Miles," *Unity* 124 (15 January 1940): 152, though Holmes claimed it could not be enforced "by guns."

3. Shafer, *CR,* 12 October 1939, A289; "Hostile Acts," *CT,* 4 October 1939, 16; "American Waters," *CT,* 9 October 1939, 10. See also "The War in American Waters," *CT,* 22 December 1939, 16; John Bassett Moore to Edwin M. Borchard, 11 March 1940, Borchard Papers; John Bassett Moore to Hiram Johnson, 8 January 1940, Moore Papers; Edwin M. Borchard to John Bassett Moore, 3 January 1940, Borchard Papers.

4. See, for example, Dorothy Detzer, minutes, WIL National Board, Detroit, 21–22 October 1939, WIL Papers; Alf Landon to Verne Marshall, 30 October 1939, the Papers of Verne Marshall, Herbert Hoover Presidential Library, West Branch, Iowa (hereafter cited as Verne Marshall Papers); John Bassett Moore to Edwin M. Borchard, 5 January 1940, Borchard Papers; "Design for Freedom," *Saturday Evening Post* 212 (11 November 1939): 24; John Bassett Moore to Rear Admiral William L. Rodgers, 21 December 1939, copy in Borchard Papers; "Is It a 'Safety' Belt?" *Christian Century* 56 (18 October 1939): 1261; "A Defense Belt for the Western Hemisphere?" *Christian Century* 56 (11 October 1939): 1228; Edwin M. Borchard to John Bassett Moore, 12 March 1940, Borchard Papers.

5. White, *CR,* 1 November 1939, 1237. See also Alf Landon, *NYT,* 2 November 1939, 11.

6. John Bassett Moore to Rear Admiral William L. Rodgers, 21 December 1939, copy in Borchard Papers; Edwin M. Borchard to John Bassett Moore, 3 January 1940, Borchard Papers. For similar accusations, see also Hugh Johnson, *SFN,* 22 December 1939, 13; Alf Landon, *NYT,* 2 November 1939, 11; Sargent, Bulletin #25, 5 January 1940, *Getting US into War,* 222. For U.S. announcement, see *NYT,* 21 December 1939, 1, 6.

7. "American Waters," *CT,* 9 October 1939, 10. Furthermore, the *Tribune* continued, Canada should acquire Newfoundland, Labrador, and Greenland; the United States should take over European-owned islands in North and Central America; Cuba or Haiti should possess Jamaica; and Argentina should receive the Falklands. "For an American Foreign Policy," *CT,* 22 October 1939, 16.

8. Haglund, *Latin America,* 149; Gellman, *Secret Affairs,* 169; Berle, entry of 6 October 1939, *Navigating,* 262.

9. Berle, entry of 30 September 1939, *Navigating,* 260.

10. For administration reaction, see "Statement on Safety Zone," *NYT,* 24 December 1939, 4; Haglund, *Latin America,* 157; Dallek, *Roosevelt,* 206; Hull, *Memoirs,* 1:691–92. Quotation from Gellman, *Good Neighbor Diplomacy,* 91.

11. Gallup poll, 3 July 1940, Cantril, *Public Opinion,* 1169.

12. Opposed were Republicans Bradley, Schafer, Hoffman, Thill, Hawks, John F. Harter (N.Y.), and John C. Kunkel (Pa.) and Democrat Andrew Edmiston (W.Va.). Answering present were Republicans Chiperfield, Thorkelson, Tinkham, Dworshak, Hinshaw, and Benjamin Jarrett (Pa.). See *CR,* 18 June 1940, 8560.

13. For a classic description of Hitler's policy, see Hans Louis Trefousse, *Germany and American Neutrality, 1939–1941* (New York: Bookman, 1951).

14. Vorys, *CR,* 18 June 1940, 8595. See also Vandenberg, radio speech, 9 June 1940, in *CR,* A3690; Villard, "Men and Events," *Nation* 150 (15 June 1940): 734.

15. Hull, text of statement, *NYT,* 6 July 1940, 6; German position, 1, 8.

16. Fish, *CR,* 18 June 1940, 8536. See also "Europe's Wars," *America* 63 (20 July 1940): 407.

17. *Washington Daily News,* 13 June 1940; Schiffler, *CR,* 18 June 1940, 2188; Chiperfield, *CR,* 16 June 1940, 8550. Unknown to Chiperfield, Hull told Ambassador Lothian in mid-April that Greenland lay within the Western Hemisphere and was hence protected by the Monroe Doctrine. Hull, *Memoirs,* 1:755.

18. Katherine Rodell, "How to Defend This Hemisphere," *Common Sense* 9 (July 1940): 12; Sargent, Bulletin #69, 20 July 1940, *Getting US into War*, 389. See also "Big Stick Policy," *New Masses* 35 (28 May 1940): 22.

19. "The Future of the Monroe Doctrine," *Christian Century* 57 (19 June 1940): 788; Gifford, *CR*, 18 June 1940, 8553. See also Warren Mullin, information letter, NCPW, 7 June 1940, NCPW papers; Congressman Daniel Reed, *CR*, 18 June 1940, 8554; "The Monroe Doctrine: A Cloak for Aggression," *Daily Worker*, 15 May 1940, 6.

20. *NYT*, 28 July 1940, 1, 13; Gellman, *Good Neighbor Diplomacy*, 100.

21. "Mr. Hull at Havana," *CT*, 26 July 1940, 8; Flynn, *SFN*, 3 August 1940, 12; Sidney Steinman, "American Imperialism Faces Southward," *Call*, 10 August 1940, 2; "Havana Conference Ends with United Action," *Christian Century* 57 (7 August 1940): 964. For further praise, see Isabel B. La Follette, "A Room of Our Own," *Progressive*, 27 July 1940, 7; "Bob La Follette Says: Havana Conference Is a Great Step Forward," *Progressive*, 3 August 1940, 1.

22. Lundeen, S.J. Res. 119, *CR*, 17 June 1940, 8392; Fish, *CR*, 18 April 1940, 4770. See also comments by William R. Castle, Senator Gillette, and author and public official Theodore Roosevelt Jr., *United States News*, 26 April 1940, 24.

23. Lundeen, *CR*, 6 June 1940, 7681; Fish, radio address, 18 April 1940, in *CR*, A2302–3.

24. See, for example, Lundeen, *CR*, 17 June 1940, 8392; "Greenland, Denmark, and the United States," *NYDN*, 13 April 1940, 15; Fish, radio address, 18 April 1940, in *CR*, A2302.

25. See, for example, "Curaçao and Iceland," *CT*, 13 May 1940, 12; Hearst, "In the News," *SFE*, 16 April 1940, 1–2; Philip C. Jessup to Lloyd K. Garrison, 20 May 1940, Jessup Papers.

26. Lundeen, *CR*, 17 June 1940, 8312; Fish, radio speech, 18 April 1940, in *CR*, A2302; "Our Problem of Upholding the Monroe Doctrine," *CT*, 11 August 1940, 7.

27. "Greenland, Denmark, and the United States," *NYDN*, 13 April 1940, 15; "Problem of Greenland," *NYDN*, 16 April 1940, 27.

28. Waldrop, "Hitler Still Far from Greenland," *WTH*, 10 April 1940, 13; Reynolds, *CR*, 11 April 1940, 4353; Lindbergh, testimony, HFAC, 373. See also Lindbergh in "Guarding the Americas," *CT*, 11 August 1940, 14.

29. See, for example, Bennett Clark, *NYT*, 5 October 1939, 14.

30. Niel M. Johnson, *George Sylvester Viereck: German-American Propagandist* (Urbana: University of Illinois Press, 1972), 198–99; Alton Frye, *Nazi Germany and the American Hemisphere, 1933–1941* (New Haven, Conn.: Yale University Press, 1967), 138; Kipphan, *Deutsche Propaganda*, 187.

31. See, for example, William E. Bullitt to Roosevelt, 22 February 1939, in *For the President*, 315–17; 23 March 1939, 326–27; 4 April 1939, 334–36. For British feelers, see Reynolds, *Creation*, 53–54.

32. Among the vice chairmen were Senator Reynolds, Congressman Sweeney, marine general Smedley Butler, Senator Jennings Randolph (Dem.-W.Va.), and former senator Smith W. Brookhart (Rep.-Iowa). Among the endorsers were congressmen Shafer, Ludlow, and John W. McCormack (Dem.-Mass.); former congressman Abe Murdock (Dem.-Utah); Governor John Moses (Dem.-N.Dak.); Governor E. P. Carville (Dem.-Nev.); Michael O'Reilly, editor of the *Gaelic American*; and John B. Patterson, director of the school of public affairs at American University. Historian Charles C. Tansill was director of historical research. Prescott Dennett, executive editor of the Columbia Press Service, was national secretary. Prescott Dennett to R. Douglas Stuart Jr., 7 October 1940, Box 284, AFC Papers; *CT*, 3 December 1939, 7. In April 1940, Lundeen resigned, pleading lack of time. Letter to Linn Gale and Prescott Dennett, 29 April 29, Box 234, Lundeen Papers.

33. Frank Knox to Prescott Dennett, 12 January 1940, Box 234, Lundeen Papers; McAdoo in undated press release, Make Europe Pay War Debts Committee (MEPWDC), Box 234, Lundeen Papers. See also Knox in Ickes, entry of 23 June 1940, *Secret Diary*, 3:213; Leutze, *Bargaining*, 104; *Crowded Years: The Reminiscences of William G. McAdoo* (Boston: Houghton Mifflin, 1931), 419–31.

34. Lundeen, *CR*, 14 October 1939, 411. See also 436.

35. Julian M. Pleasants, "The Senatorial Career of Robert Rice Reynolds," Ph.D. diss., University of North Carolina, 1971; "Robert Rice Reynolds," *Current Biography, 1940*, 680–82. One other legislator

from the Deep South, Representative Hugh Peterson (Dem.-Ga.), was somewhat anti-interventionist, voting against lend-lease and the arming of merchant ships.

36. Reynolds, *CR*, 14 October 1939, 412–13; 4 March 1940, 2285; 11 April 1940, 4343; American Forum of the Air, entered in *CR*, 2 May 1940, 5403–5; radio broadcast, Raleigh, entered *CR* 3 April 1940, A1839; text, S.J. Res. 221, *CR*, 17 June 1940, 8392; speech to American Defense Society, 13 April 1940, in *CR*, A2441. Hearst too sought Lower California, stressing a base at Magdalena Bay. "In the News," *SFE*, 12 March 1940, 1.

37. Such a move was favored by Wiley, *CR*, 11 April 1940, 4355; Waldrop, cited in MEPWDC release, entered in *CR*, 22 May 1940, A3309; Hearst, "In the News," *SFE*, 13 July 1940, 1; "Heirs of the British Empire," *NYDN*, 10 March 1940, 47; "World's Fare," *Social Justice*, 16 October 1939, 6; Edwin C. Johnson, Mutual network speech, 15 June 1940, in *CR*, A3918–20; Edwin C. Johnson, Louis Ludlow, Senator Homer Bone (Dem.-Wash.), and Arthur Capper in *United States News*, 17 July 1940, 26–27; William R. Castle, "What about the Monroe Doctrine Now?" *Saturday Evening Post* 213 (27 July 1940): 40; Philip C. Jessup to Lloyd K. Garrison, 20 May 1940, Jessup Papers.

38. "Islands for Defense," *CT*, 2 October 1939, 12. In August 1940, the *CT* called for a naval outpost and air base near Cape Farewell, Greenland; use of the Canadian naval base at Halifax; and air facilities at Labrador and Botworth Harbor, Newfoundland. It also sought control of the British naval base at Jamaica and the Dutch naval base at Curaçao, the latter dominating the Windward Strait; Bermuda, which stood directly in the way of an enemy frontal advance; and the Azores, which controlled the Atlantic sea lanes. The United States should also control the Dutch islands of Curaçao, Aruba, and Bonaire and the British islands of Trinidad and Tobago, which dominated Venezuelan oil output. It also sought U.S. bases on the Bahamas, Guadeloupe, and Martinique. To protect U.S. Caribbean bases and Latin America, the American powers should control British, French, and Dutch Guiana. A U.S. fleet should be based at Pernambuco, Brazil. "Guarding the Americas," 11 August 1940, 14; "Our Problem of Upholding the Monroe Doctrine," graphic section, 11 August 1940, 7.

39. Fish, *CR*, 28 May 1940, 7049. See also Fish, *United States News*, 26 July 1940, 26.

40. Plebiscite, Detzer, minutes, WIL executive board, 21 February 1940, WIL Papers; Latin American administration, Katherine Rodell, "How to Defend This Hemisphere," *Common Sense* 9 (July 1940): 11; repurchase, "Another Modest Proposal," *New Republic* 102 (3 June 1940): 744–45. The WIL annual meeting stressed that the interest of the inhabitants must be the primary consideration in any transfer. Minutes, 27–30 April 1940, 4, WIL Papers. For Norman Thomas endorsement of negotiations, see *United States News*, 26 July 1940, 26–27.

41. Poll, *NYT*, 12 November 1939, 30. The tally centered on a bill introduced by Representative Franck R. Havenner (Dem.-Calif.), which called for peaceful cession through negotiation.

42. *Washington Daily News*, 16 May 1940.

43. "West Indies Mystery," *CT*, 26 February 1940, 10.

44. See, for example, Wiley, *CR*, 23 August 1940, 10,796; Colonel McCormick, statement to resolutions committee, Republican national convention, *CT*, 20 June 1940, 12.

45. "Some West Indies Wards for U.S.A.," *NYDN*, 27 June 1940, 29. See also "Heirs to the British Empire," *NYDN*, 10 March 1940, 47. The *News* also urged U.S. bases in Natal, Chile, Peru, and Mexico. "Let's Get the Title First," 27 August 1940, 23; "Naval Bases from Britain," 21 August 1940, 29.

46. "Atlantic Outpost," *CT*, 23 July 1940, 10. Lundeen's committee cited FDR's statement, made to Congress on 16 May 1940, that Bermuda in hostile hands would greatly threaten the United States. Roosevelt, address to Congress, 16 May 1940, in *CR*, 6243; IFWDDC press release, entered in *CR*, 22 May 1940, A3309. See also "If Bermuda Fell into Hostile Hands," *CR*, 18 May 1940, 12.

47. "Atlantic Outpost," *CT*, 23 July 1940, 10.

48. Reynolds, American Forum of the Air, entered in *CR*, 2 May 1940, 5403. Reynolds also mentioned Curaçao. See *CR*, 6 June 1940, 7682–83.

49. For predictable attacks from the American left, see "U.S. Imperialism Out to Grab," *Daily Worker*, 2 May 1940, 6; *Daily Worker*, 18 May 1940, 6; James Burnham, "Their Government," *Socialist Appeal*, 20 October 1939, 4.

50. Edwin M. Borchard to James Shanley, 7 June 1940, Borchard Papers; Hugh Johnson, "Allied Debts," *NYWT*, 18 January 1940, 13.

51. Churchill to Roosevelt, 15 May 1940, in Kimball, *Churchill and Roosevelt*, 1:37.

52. Reynolds, *Creation*, 114, 127.

53. Leutze, *Bargaining*, 43–44; Kimball, *Forged in War*, 57.

54. "Roosevelt's Message and the Diplomatic Exchanges," *NYT*, 4 September 1940, 10; press conference, 3 September 1940, in Samuel I. Rosenman, comp., *Roosevelt Papers and Addresses*, 9:378. For a comprehensive study of the agreement, see Robert Shogun, *Hard Bargain: How FDR Twisted Churchill's Arm, Evaded the Law, and Changed the Role of the American Presidency* (New York: Scribner's, 1995).

55. Lawyers' letter, *NYT*, 11 August 1940, sect. 4, 8; "Text of Attorney General Jackson's Opinion Upholding the Transfer of Destroyers," *NYT*, 4 September 1940, 16.

56. For histories of the CDAAA and its more interventionist offshoot, the Fight for Freedom Committee, see Schwar, "Internationalist Propaganda"; Johnson, *Battle*; Mark Lincoln Chadwin, *The Hawks of World War II* (Chapel Hill: University of North Carolina Press, 1968). For a case study of the debate involving such groups and their foes, see James C. Schneider, *Should America Go to War? The Debate over Foreign Policy in Chicago, 1939–1941* (Chapel Hill: University of North Carolina Press, 1989).

57. CDAAA, "Progress Bulletin," 12 August 1940, 2, Box 34, CDAAA Papers; poll, 9 August 1940, Cantril, *Public Opinion*, 1160; polls of 22 October and 19 November 1940, Cantril, *Public Opinion*, 973.

58. For an example of an interventionist misgiving, see Breckinridge Long, entry of 19 December 1940, *War Diary*, 163.

59. See, for example, Wiley, *CR*, 23 August 1940, 10,798; Hugh Johnson, *SFN*, 5 September 1940, 19; "But Boake Carter Says," *SFE*, 4 September 1940, 7. Wheeler favored canceling part of Britain's war debt in exchange for the bases but opposed trading the destroyers. *NYT*, 18 August 1940, 1.

60. "The More We Think of It the Better We Like It," *NYDN*, 5 September 1940, 27.

61. "We Get the Bases," *CT*, 4 September 1940, 14. See also "The New North America," *CT*, 5 September 1940, 16; "America Second," *CT*, 1 October 1940, 14.

62. McCormick, radio address of 8 September 1940, *Addresses*, 46.

63. "Today the Strongest Nation in the World," *CT*, 13 October 1940, graphic section, 1.

64. See, for example, Knutson, *NYT*, 4 September 1940, 16; Lindbergh, testimony, HFAC, 23 January 1941, 391.

65. Flynn, in *Social Justice*, 23 September 1940, 7; Lodge, *CR*, 20 September 1940, 12,387; Rogers, *CR*, 12 September 1940, 12,047.

66. See, for example, Hugh Johnson, "One Man's Opinion," *SFN*, 6 August 1940, 13; Nye, *Newsweek*, 16 September 1940, 17; Walsh, "Our Navy for Our Own Defense," speech, CBS, 13 August 1940, in *CR*, A5226; Lundeen, *CR*, 24 August 1940, A5217; Sterling Morton to R. Douglas Stuart Jr., 23 August 1940, Morton Papers; "Scheming for War," *CT*, 6 August 1940, 10; *Social Justice*, 9 September 1940, 4; Marcantonio, *NYT*, 4 September 1940, 16; Johns, *CR*, 6 September 1940, 11,647; Hearst, "In the News," *SFE*, 6 September 1940, 11.

67. La Follette, AFC speech, in *CT*, 12 September 1940, 9.

68. "Dictator Roosevelt Commits an Act of War," *St. Louis Post-Dispatch*, 3 September 1940. For an endorsement of the editorial, see *CT*, 4 September 1940, 14. For other attacks on Roosevelt's supposed arbitrary power, Congressmen Wolcott, *CR*, 3 September 1940, 11,399; Sweeney, *CR*, 4 September 1940, 11,414; Fish, *CR*, 6 September 1940, 11,664; Earl R. Lewis (Rep.-Ohio), *CR*, 9 September 1940, 11,829; Taft, *CR*, 14 September 1940, 12,168; B. C. Clark, *CR*, 26 September 1940, 12,644; George E. Sokolsky, "These Days," *New York Sun*, 6 September 1940, 20; Castle Diary, 7 September 1940. Hiram Johnson said he did not object to aiding Britain but opposed the "manner" and "hypocrisy" of the deal. Hiram Johnson to John Bassett Moore, 4 September 1940, Moore Papers.

69. John Bassett Moore to Hiram Johnson, 17 September 1940, Moore Papers; Bone, *CR*, 15 August 1940, 10,406; undated memo, "The WIL Today," attached to Mrs. C. F. Hunt to G. C. Bussey, 9 September 1940, WIL Papers; Dorothy Detzer to Katherine Devereaux Blake, 31 October 1940, WIL Papers.

70. For Hague Convention, see "Dictator Roosevelt Commits an Act of War," *St. Louis Post-Dispatch*, 3 September 1940; Herbert W. Briggs, cited in "A Demolishing Indictment," *St. Louis Post-Dispatch*, 7 September 1940; Holt, *CR*, 26 September 1940, 12,644; Libby, "Shall the United States Discontinue Diplomatic Relations with the Axis Powers?" *American Forum of the Air* 2 (15 December 1940): 13;

Charles Cheney Hyde in *CT*, 8 September 1940, 6; Borchard, "The Attorney General's Opinion on the Exchange of Destroyers for Naval Bases," *American Journal of International Law* 34 (October 1940): 690–97; Norman Thomas, radio broadcast of 4 September 1940, *Call*, 14 September 1940, 1.

71. For Treaty of Washington, see Herbert W. Briggs, cited in "A Demolishing Indictment," *St. Louis Post-Dispatch*, 7 September 1940; "On Going to War," *Saturday Evening Post* 213 (19 October 1940): 26; Danaher, American Forum of the Air, 25 August 1940, in *CR*, A5393. Danaher noted the nontransfer agreement adopted by the Conference of Panama and signed on 3 October 1939.

72. For Walsh amendment, see Borchard, "Attorney General's Opinion"; Briggs cited in "A Demolishing Indictment"; Edward S. Corwin, letter to *NYT*, 13 October 1940, sect. 4, 6; Danaher, American Forum of the Air, 25 August 1940, in *CR*, A5393.

73. Borchard, "Attorney General's Opinion"; Congressman Earl Lewis, *CR*, 9 September 1940, 11,827; "Notes on a Day's News," *Uncensored* 49 (7 September 1940): 3; Briggs, "A Demolishing Indictment"; Danaher, American Forum of the Air, 25 August 1940, in *CR*, A5393.

74. See, for example, Congressman Dirksen, *CR*, 6 September 1940, 11,647; Congressman Earl Lewis, *CR*, 9 September 1940, 11,828; "Notes on a Day's News," *Uncensored* 49 (7 September 1940): 2; Castle Diary, 7 September 1940; Porter Sargent, Bulletin #87, 18 September 1940, *Getting US into War*, 459 n. 11; Edwin M. Borchard to John Bassett Moore, 4 and 28 September, 3 October 1940, Borchard Papers. Moore concurred, saying that "Nothing too unfavorable could be said of Jackson's opinion. . . . His so-called opinion was no opinion at all." Letter to Borchard, 5 October 1940, Borchard Papers.

75. Edward S. Corwin to *NYT*, 13 October 1940, sect. 4, 6. Charles Francis Adams in Castle Diary, 20 September 1940. For other criticism of Jackson, see William Dennis, president of Earlham College and former diplomat, to Frederick J. Libby, 6 September 1940, NCPW Papers.

76. Transient agreement, Hoffman, *CR*, 3 September 1940, 11,399; "But Boake Carter Says," *SFE*, 10 September 1940, 13. For similar comments, see B. C. Clark, *CR*, 14 September 1940, 12,168; Mencken, 6 October 1940, in Sargent, Bulletin #87, 18 September 1940, *Getting US into War*, 456 n. 4.

77. Clark, *CR*, 28 February 1941, 1536.

78. Reynolds, *CR*, 1 March 1941, 1598. For the Pearson-Allen column, undated, A937. See also Wheeler, *CR*, 1 March 1941, 1598. The *Chicago Tribune* suggested that the British government buy the needed real estate from its own subjects, then give it to the United States in exchange for more valuable ships. See "Payment for the Bases," 11 March 1941, 12.

79. See, for example, "Dictator Roosevelt Commits an Act of War," *St. Louis Post-Dispatch*, 3 September 1940; Lundeen, *CR*, 24 August 1940, A5217; Danaher, *CR*, 9 August 1940, 10,102; Hoffman, *CR*, 3 September 1940, 11,399; Dirksen, *CR*, 6 September 1940, 11,664; Edith Nourse Rogers, *CR*, 12 September 1940, 12,047; Hugh Johnson, *SFN*, 6 August 1940, 13; Edwin C. Johnson, American Forum of the Air, 1 September 1940, in *CR*, A5664; *SFE*, 10 September 1940, 13; "Fifty Destroyers to Britain?" *NYDN*, 6 August 1940, 21; Bone, *NYT*, 4 September 1940, 16.

80. Johnson, "One Man's Opinion," *SFN*, 17 August 1940, 13. William R. Castle presented the converse argument. If the destroyers, he said, could save England, he would have endorsed the gift. He claimed, however, that a "large part of our navy people" did not think the ships would affect the outcome. Castle Diary, 20 August 1941. The *New York Daily News* predicted that by the time the destroyers were reconditioned, the war would probably be over. "The Consequences of Stumble-Bum Diplomacy," 24 August 1940, 13. See also "Naval Ships for Britain," *NYDN*, 21 August 1940, 29.

81. Congressman Frederick C. Smith, *CR*, 4 September 1940, 11,413; Lodge, "The Drift Toward War," radio speech, 25 September 1940, in *CR*, A5905; "Those 'Obsolete' Destroyers," *Progressive*, 7 September 1940, 8.

82. Nye, *CR*, 23 August 1941, 10,811.

83. Edwin M. Borchard to Gerald P. Nye, 1 July 1941, Borchard Papers; Corwin, letter to *NYT*, 13 October 1940, sect. 4, 6. See also George E. Sokolsky, "These Days," *New York Sun*, 25 October 1940, 22; Bender, *CR*, 6 September 1940, 11,647; Hanson Baldwin, *United We Stand!* 49; Hugh Johnson, testimony, HFAC, 23 January 1941, 444.

84. Hugh Johnson, *SFN*, 25 September 1940, 13; Fish, *CT*, 24 November 1940, 10. If Britain turned the offer down, Fish would—with the consent of Congress—pay Britain a billion dollars and give her an additional fifty destroyers.

85. Lundeen, *CR*, 24 August 1940, A5217. For *New York Daily News* focus on Martinique alone, see "Better Take Martinique," 15 November 1940, 33; "Let's Take Martinique," 14 April 1941, 19; "To Make Crete Safe for Greece—or Martinique Safe for Democracy," 23 May 1941, 29. For addition of St. Pierre and Miquelon, see "British Bases for U.S. Destroyers," 4 September 1940, 35. For addition of other French islands, "Why Stall? Take Martinique Now," 5 January 1941, 41; "This Question of Aid to Britain," 27 November 1940, 35. For addition of Dutch Guiana, "Why the Guff about Guiana?" 26 November 1941, 37.

86. Baldwin, *United We Stand!* 52; Dorothy Detzer, report to WIL National Board, 30 October–1 November 1940, 7–8, WIL Papers.

87. "Bases, Destroyers, Empire," *New Masses* 36 (17 September 1940): 16. See also "Taking the Lion's Share," *New Masses* 36 (27 August 1940): 16; "Still Deeper into War," *Daily Worker*, 4 September 1940, 1.

88. Villard, "Should We Buy the West Indies?" *Christian Century* 58 (23 April 1941): 560–62. Villard was such a continentalist that he would not resist an enemy in Bermuda but would wait until it reached the U.S. Testimony, SFRC, 23 October 1941, 187.

89. Libby, "We Want No More Islands," *Peace Action* 7 (April 1941): 2; Roosevelt to Cordell Hull, 11 January 1941, *F.D.R.: His Personal Letters*, 1104–5.

90. James MacGregor Burns, *Roosevelt: The Soldier of Freedom* (New York: Harcourt Brace Jovanovich, 1970), 11. Reynolds, *Creation*, 113–30; Kimball, *Forged in War*, 57.

91. For the practical problems with the ships, see Philip Goodhart, *Fifty Ships That Saved the World* (New York: Doubleday, 1965), chap. 14. For delays, see Reynolds, *Creation*, 131.

92. Reynolds, *Creation*, 132, 287.

93. Hemispheric focus, Haglund, *Latin America*, 99; War College, Watson, *Chief of Staff*, 94; FDR noted in Berle, entry of 26 May 1939, *Navigating*, 223–24.

94. Haglund, *Latin America*, 185. For the argument that Roosevelt deliberately exaggerated the limited scope of the Nazi movement in the Americas so as to aid the Allies, see Gellman, *Good Neighbor Diplomacy*, 115–16.

95. See, for example, Livingstone Hartley and Donald C. Blaisdell, "Turning the Tables," CDAAA, *Washington Office Information Letter* 17 (9 May 1941): 4, Box 35, CDAAA Papers.

96. Drew Pearson and Robert S. Allen, "Can We Keep Hitler Out of the Americas?" *Look*, 16 June 1940, 20–22; "If Britain Should Lose," *Time*, 22 July 1940, 20; Bullitt in Long, entry of 13 August 1940, *War Diary*, 122.

97. Hartley and Blaisdell, "A Lesson from Crete," CDAAA, *Washington Office Information Letter* 20 (30 May 1941): 3, Box 35, CDAAA Papers. For concurrence, Breckinridge Long, entry of 21 April 1941, *War Dairy*, 199.

98. "Text of Colonel Lindbergh's Address," *NYT*, 16 June 1940, 37. See also Lindbergh, speech, 19 May 1940, "Radio Addresses," 10.

99. Lindbergh, testimony, HFAC, 23 January 1941, 384. He called for air bases in Hawaii, Bermuda, Alaska, Canada, and Newfoundland, then a separate dominion. See also Charles A. Lindbergh to R. Douglas Stuart Jr., 13 November 1940, Wood Papers.

100. Lindbergh, testimony, SFRC, 6 February 1941, 522. Walter Lippmann had written an article positing that only by controlling the seas could a nation supply such South American bases. "The Lindbergh Doctrine of United States Defense," *Washington Post*, 30 January 1941. Lindbergh replied that the very reason for installing such air bases was to assist the U.S. Navy in holding command of the sea. Testimony, SFRC, 6 February 1941, 539. For an endorsement of Lindbergh, see Fish, *CR*, 28 May 1940, 7049; Fish, speech, NBC, 22 June 1940, in *CR*, A4187.

101. For example, see Frank Gannett to Frank P. S. Glassey, 25 April 1940, Gannett Papers; Katherine Rodell, "How to Defend This Hemisphere," *Common Sense* 9 (July 1940): 12.

102. Van Zandt, address to Consistory of Scottish Rite Masonry, Williamsport, Pa., 28 June 1940, in *CR*, A5184. See also Capper, radio broadcast, 10 October 1940, in *CR*, A6296.

103. La Follette, address to annual law school dinner, [University of Chicago] *Daily Maroon*, 7 May 1940, 2. The anti-interventionist and architect Frank Lloyd Wright labeled La Follette's policy "out of the frying pan into the fire." Frank Lloyd Wright to Philip La Follette, 27 July 1940, Philip La Follette Papers.

104. Wiley, *CR*, 23 August 1940, 1079; Castle, "What about the Monroe Doctrine Now?" *Saturday Evening Post* 213 (27 July 1940): 38, 40.

105. "Mr. Hull at Havana," *CT*, 26 July 1940, 8; "Guarding the Americas," *CT*, 11 August 1940, 14. See also "Our Problem of Upholding the Monroe Doctrine," *CT*, graphic section, 11 August 1940, 7; "Hemispheric Defense," *CT*, 3 July 1941, 10. In October 1940, *Tribune* publisher McCormick claimed that the U.S. southern defense crescent protected oil deliveries from Mexico, Venezuela, and the Dutch West Indies. McCormick, "Today the Strongest Nation in the World," graphic section, 13 October 1940, 2. At one point, the *Tribune* downplayed any threat from Pernambuco. See "Let's Look at the Facts," 1 February 1941, 28. Publisher McCormick mentioned Natal as a good spot for a U.S. base. McCormick, *CT*, 1 June 1941, 3.

106. Ward, "Future for Americas," *Social Justice*, 10 June 1940, 15; "But Boake Carter Says," *SFE*, 19 February 1941, 13; Clark, *NYT*, 30 July 1941, 8. For an attack on Clark, see "In the News," *Call*, 9 August 1941, 1.

107. Fish, *United States News*, 6 June 1941, 26; Graeme Howard, *America and a New World Order* (New York: Scribner's, 1940), 86–90; Morton, *Let's Think This Matter Through* (pamphlet; Chicago: privately printed, 1941), entered in *CR*, 21 February 1941, A786; Wood, "Our Foreign Policy," address to the Chicago Council of Foreign Relations, 4 October 1940, in *CR*, A6302; interview with Kenneth Crawford, *PM*, 25 May 1941, 5. In words that were much attacked, Wood said, "Offhand, I would say only defend it to the bulge but that is not a settled opinion and it is only my personal opinion," meaning that he was not speaking for the America First Committee. The CDAAA accused him of permitting more than 70 percent of the Latin American people to fall under the Nazi regime, inviting German bombers within range of the Panama Canal, and abandoning the Monroe Doctrine. Livingstone Hartley and Donald C. Blaisdell, "A Sabotage Policy," CDAAA, *Washington Office Information Letter* 20 (30 May 1941): 4, Box 35, CDAAA Papers.

108. Baldwin, *United We Stand!* 96, 101–3, 107–9. Baldwin had mentioned the use of Valparaiso, Pernambuco, Belem, St. Paul Island, Aruba, Curaçao, Trinidad, and air bases in Venezuela. "Wanted: A Plan for Defense," *Harper's Magazine* 181 (August 1940): 230. For support for Baldwin, see Norman Thomas, "Your World and Mine: Into War through Hysteria," *Call*, 7 June 1941, 8.

109. MacLiesh and Reynolds, *Strategy*, 1–52. They also wrote of a supplementary base at Para, as it possessed an abundance of cranes, tugs, and marine railways. See 65.

110. Taft, *CR*, 26 August 1940, 10,901; Norman Thomas to John D. Luckey, 5 October 1940, Thomas Papers; Thomas, testimony, HFAC, 22 January 1941, 337. In November 1941, Thomas said that the U.S. arms program was laden with imperialist ambitions that would frighten, not gain, the support of Latin Americans. *Cornell [University] Daily Sun*, 20 November 1941, 1.

111. Rivers, radio speech, "Europe's War and America's Security," 18 May 1940, in *CR*, A3039; Downey, *CR*, 9 October 1939, 183; 6 October 1940, 171; Nye, *CR*, 26 February 1941, 1434; Taft, "Shall the United States Enter the European War?" radio address, 17 May 1941, in *CR*, A2344; Hearst, "In the News," *SFE*, 21 August 1940, 1. See also broadcaster Fulton Lewis Jr., [Dartmouth College] *The Dartmouth*, 9 January 1941, 1; Robert R. McCormick, broadcast, 23 June 1940, *Addresses*, 12.

112. Johnson, *SFN*, 8 June 1940, 11; Johnson, *SFE*, 24 August 1940, 11, 21; Chavez, "America Must Choose—Pan-Americanism or War," broadcast, NBC, 8 July 1940, in *CR*, A4351. See also Congressman Frederick C. Smith, broadcast, NBC, 11 July 1940, 9678.

113. Beals, *Pan America*, 450–51. Quotation, 429.

114. Marshall in Haglund, *Latin America*, 201–2; Marshall, "National Strategic Decisions," 22 May 1940, in Marshall, *Papers*, 2:218–19. For the "general agreement" of Roosevelt, Stark, and Welles, see Marshall, "Memorandum for the War Plans Division," 23 May 1940, in Marshall, *Papers*, 2:220.

115. "Joint Plan for the Occupation of Martinique and Guadeloupe," 8 July 1940, in *American War Plans, 1919–1941*, vol. 4: *Coalition War Plans and Hemispheric Defense Plans, 1940–1941*, ed. Steven T. Ross (New York: Garland, 1992), 169–76.

116. Marshall, *NYT*, 5 June 1940, 14; Norman Thomas to Bella Kussy, 11 June 1940, Thomas Papers. See also Norman Thomas to "Lyn," 17 July 1940, Thomas Papers.

117. Villard, "Issues and Men," *Nation* 150 (15 June 1940): 734.

118. Haglund, *Latin America*, 175–78; Hull, *Memoirs*, 1:820–21.

119. Frederick J. Libby to W. B. Wachter, 22 June 1940, NCPW Papers; Dorothy Detzer to Mary Far-quharson, 21 June 1940, WIL Papers; "Hemispheric Hysteria," *New Masses* 35 (11 June 1940): 21. The journal also pointed to American air missions already assigned to Brazil, Ecuador, Chile, Argentina, and Colombia. See also "Plus Battleships," *New Masses* 36 (2 July 1940): 24.

120. Taft, *CR*, 26 August 1940, 10,900.

121. For background, see Haglund, *Latin America*, 178–80; Watson, *Chief of Staff*, 95–96; Gellman, *Good Neighbor Diplomacy*, 136; Forrest C. Pogue, *George C. Marshall*, vol. 2: *Ordeal and Hope, 1939–1942* (New York: Viking, 1966).

122. See, for example, Villard, "Issues and Men," *Nation* 150 (15 June 1940): 734; "The Future of the Monroe Doctrine," *Christian Century* 57 (19 June 1940): 788.

123. Libby, report to executive board, NCPW, 18 September 1940, NCPW Papers. In November 1941, Libby's NCPW accused the United States of encouraging the Latin American countries to build up armaments, saying this move would only promote internecine strife. "Program Adopted by the National Council for the Prevention of War," 15 November 1941, *Peace Action* 7 (October 1941): 3.

124. *In Fact* 1 (17 June 1940): 2.

125. Detzer, report to WIL executive, December 1939, WIL Papers; Wheeler, American Forum of the Air, 12 January 1941, in *CR*, A179. See also Clarence Senior, "Will Pan Americanism Last?" *Call*, 16 August 1941, 2.

126. "Defending Democracy," *Christian Century* 57 (5 June 1940), 776–77; Bradley, address to Michigan Commercial Secretaries Association, Mackinac Island, 30 August 1940, in *CR*, A5440; Broughton, "America in a Hostile World," *Scribner's Commentator* 9 (November 1940): 73; Morton, *Let's Think This Matter Through* [pamphlet], entered in *CR*, 21 February 1941, A786. For focus on dictatorship, see also "Havana Conference Ends with United Action," *Christian Century* 57 (7 August 1940): 964; John T. Flynn, article datelined 24 August 1940, in *CR*, A5306; Robert E. Wood, interview, *PM*, 25 May 1941, 5; MacLiesh and Reynolds, *Strategy*, 243.

127. Johnson, *SFN*, 8 June 1940, 11; "Plus Battleships," *New Masses* 36 (2 July 1940): 16.

128. Arden, "Pan American Relations: Part I," *Scribner's Commentator* 11 (December 1941): 63; Dennis, *WFL* 100 (27 June 1940): 6; "The Mexican Mystery," *NYDN*, 25 May 1940, 15; Hearst, "In the News," *WTH*, October 4, 1940, 16; Hearst, *WTH*, 15 February 1941, 17. For Hearst in 1916, see Swanberg, *Citizen Hearst*, 296–98.

129. See, for example, Hearst, "In the News," *SFE*, 11 March 1940, 1; Reynolds, American Forum of the Air, 28 April 1940, in *CR*, 5045.

130. Reynolds, *CR*, 8 April 1940, 4131. For additional anxiety concerning Japan, see also "Alaska and the Far East," *Commonweal* 32 (16 August 1940): 339.

131. Johnson, "One Man's Opinion," *SFN*, 19 April 1940, 23.

132. The authors endorsed the current efforts to build bases at the panhandle, Sitka, Juneau, Ketchikan, Point Barrow, Nome, the Seward Peninsula, the Kodiak Islands, Dutch Harbor, and Kiska. Needed too was a military highway through British Columbia, so as to give the United States an overland supply line to Alaska. MacLiesh and Reynolds, *Strategy*, 69–71, 234.

133. Charles A. Lindbergh, testimony, HFAC, 23 January 1941, 37; Baldwin, *United We Stand!* 111, 114. Baldwin favored patrol plane bases at Sitka and Kodiak, submarine bases at Kodiak and Dutch Harbor, an advance base at Fairbanks, and a staging field at Annette Island near Ketchikan. He suggested an outpost for patrol bases and small bases farther down the Aleutian chain, perhaps at Agattu and Kiska. For anti-interventionist use of Baldwin on Alaska, see AFC Research Bureau, "Wings over Nome," *Did You Know?* 5 (1 July 1941), in Doenecke, *IDU*, 297–98; AFC Research Bureau, "Nobody Know the Trouble We're In," *Did You Know?* 12 (24 July 1941), in Doenecke, *IDU*, 363; "This Changing Hemisphere," *Uncensored* 93 (12 July 1941): 4.

134. Fish, *CR*, 28 June 1941, 6364; Adams, *CR*, 6 August 1941, 6820.

135. *New York Herald Tribune*, 30 June 1941.

136. Livingstone Hartley and Frank S. Goodwin, "Our North Pacific Front," CDAAA, *Washington Office Information Letter* 32 (22 August 1941): 1, Box 35, CDAAA Papers.

137. "Wings over Nome," 295–98; "Nobody Know the Trouble We're In," 363.

138. "Text of President's Address Depicting Emergency Confronting the Nation," *NYT*, 28 May 1941, 12. See also "President's Call for Full Response on Defense," *NYT*, 30 December 1940, 6. For further anxiety over Dakar, see Berle, entry of 10 September 1940, *Navigating*, 335; 14 February 1941, 357; 26 May 1941, 369.

139. Livingstone Hartley, "Threat to the South Pacific," CDAAA, *Washington Office Information Letter* 31 (15 August 1941): 2, Box 35, CDAAA Papers; Hartley, "Keys to the South Atlantic" (pamphlet; New York: CDAAA, 1941), 3–4; Hartley and Donald C. Blaisdell, "Danger from Drifting," CDAAA, *Washington Office Information Letter* 15 (25 April 1941): 2–3, Box 35, CDAAA Papers. For concurrence, see Breckinridge Long, entry of 25 April 1941, *War Diary*, 199. See also "The Danger," *Life*, 5 May 1941, 30; Ickes, entry of 4 May 1941, *Secret Diary*, 3:503; Lee, entry of 24 September 1940, *London Journal*, 69.

140. Office of Public Opinion Research, poll of 10 July 1941, Cantril, *Public Opinion*, 1061. For related polls, see 1061–62.

141. See, for example, Hugh Johnson, "One Man's Opinion," *SFN*, 8 July 1940, 13.

142. See, for example, *Social Justice*, 11 November 1940, 9; Ruth Sarles to Kendrick Lee, 20 April 1941, Box 34, AFC Papers; Sarles to Richard A. Moore, 4 June 1941, in Doenecke, *IDU*, 252; AFC Research Bureau, "Our Iceland Outpost," *Did You Know?* 7 (9 July 1941), in Doenecke, *IDU*, 312; Wheeler, *Time*, 21 July 1941, 16; "The Dakar Illusion," *NYDN*, 24 August 1941, 23. For doubts that the United States would occupy the Atlantic islands, see Warren Mullin, minutes, executive board, NCPW, 20 May 1941, 3, NCPW Papers.

143. "Freedom of FDR," 87 (31 May 1941): 3. See also AFC Research Bureau, "Our Iceland Outpost," *Did You Know?* 7 (9 July 1941), in Doenecke, *IDU*, 312.

144. "Islands," *Uncensored* 90 (21 June 1941): 4.

145. See, for example, Landon, *NYT*, 3 June 1941, 8; intelligence officer Truman Smith cited in Herbert Hoover, memorandum, 1 June 1941, Hoover Papers.

146. AFC Research Bureau, "Our Iceland Outpost," *Did You Know?* 7 (9 July 1941), in Doenecke, *IDU*, 312; Samuel B. Pettengill, "Heavy Weight Champ," Release 219, 23 January 1941, Box 11, the Papers of Samuel B. Pettengill, University of Oregon (hereafter cited as Pettengill Papers).

147. La Follette, [University of Wisconsin] *Daily Cardinal*, 10 May 1941, 1; "But Boake Carter Says," *SFE*, 28 May 1940, 19.

148. Lindbergh, "A Letter to Americans," *Collier's* 107 (29 March 1941): 77. See also Nye, *CR*, 26 February 1941, 1433.

149. Baldwin, "The Realities of Hemisphere Defense," *Reader's Digest* 39 (July 1941): 118. Baldwin did claim that St. Louis in Senegal afforded a quite defensible outpost but that if the United States did enter the conflict, it would be wiser to send troops to Alexandria, Egypt, for the fate of Africa would be decided there. "Potential U.S. Bases—III," *NYT*, 23 July 1941, 6.

150. Fish, *CR*, 20 May 1941, 4283; "The Dakar Illusion," *NYDN*, 24 August 1941, 23; Taft, *CR*, 22 February 1941, 1283. See also Senator Adams, *CR*, 6 August 1941, 6820.

151. AFC Research Bureau, "Our African Outpost," *Did You Know?* 8 (11 July 1941), in Doenecke, *IDU*, 306–7; "Items," *Uncensored* 96 (2 August 1941): 2.

152. Gilroy, "—And Willkie Threw It Away," *Scribner's Commentator* 9 (February 1941): 50–51; Flynn, *SFN*, 12 May 1941, 14.

153. "But Boake Carter Says," *SFE*, 24 May 1941, 7.

154. AFC Research Bureau, "Our African Outpost," *Did You Know?* 8 (11 July 1941), in Doenecke, *IDU*, 305; Baldwin, "The Realities of Hemisphere Defense," *Reader's Digest* 31 (July 1941): 118.

155. Marshall to Harold R. Stark, 27 June 1941, in Marshall, *Papers*, 2:551; *Fortune* poll, Cantril, *Public Opinion*, 783; 41.2 percent were in favor, 28.3 percent were opposed, and 30.5 percent had no opinion. For a earlier *Fortune* poll showing 56.9 percent in favor, see August 1941, Cantril, *Public Opinion*, 1170.

156. "1941 Campaign," *Uncensored* 80 (12 April 1941): 1–2.

157. AFC Research Bureau, "Our Iceland Outpost," *Did You Know?* 7 (9 July 1941), in Doenecke, *IDU*, 312.

158. McCormick, testimony, SFRC, 6 February 1941, 477–79, 483; "Let's Look at the Facts," *CT*, 1 February 1941, 28.

159. Reynolds, *Creation*, 201.

160. Marshall, *Papers*, 2:547; in Leighton and Coakley, *Global Logistics*, 68–71; Stetson Conn and Byron Fairchild, *The Framework of Hemisphere Defense* (Washington, D.C.: Department of the Army, 1960), 117–19, 121–22, 138–39; Hull, *Memoirs*, 2:941–42; "Joint Army and Navy Basic Plan for the Occupation of the Azores," May 1941, in Ross, *American War Plans*, 4:351–59.

161. Dallek, *Roosevelt*, 285.

162. Mark A. Stoler, *George C. Marshall: Soldier-Statesman of the American Century* (Boston: Twayne, 1989), 81; Conn and Fairchild, *Framework*, 139–41; "Joint Army and Navy Basic Plan for the Capture and Occupation of the Azores," 23 September 1941, in Ross, *American War Plans*, 4:342–50. For Roosevelt's lingering expectation of possible invasion, see his letter to Emory S. Land, 1 August 1941, *F.D.R.: His Personal Letters*, 1193.

163. For the Azores, one found 45.9 percent favoring defense, 24.7 percent opposed, and 29.4 percent having no opinion. For Dakar, the ratio was 41.2 percent, 28.3 percent, and 30.5 percent. Cantril, *Public Opinion*, 783.

164. Gallup poll, 22 September 1939, Cantril, *Public Opinion*, 782. For related polls, see 782–83.

165. Dallek, *Roosevelt*, 235–36.

166. Haglund, *Latin America*, 52, 116–19, 249–50 n. 24; Watson, *Chief of Staff*, 150, 371.

167. Thomas B. Buell, *Master of Sea Power: A Biography of Fleet Admiral Ernest J. King* (Boston: Little, Brown, 1980), 125; Marshall, *Papers*, 2:547–48; Conn and Fairchild, *Framework*, 119–21, 278–89; "Joint Army and Navy Plan to Provide Armed Support to Recognized Latin American Governments," 15 March 1941, in Ross, *American War Plans*, 4:207–13.

## CHAPTER 9: ECONOMIC SURVIVAL IN THE AMERICAS

1. See, for example, Breckinridge Long, entry of 23 March 1940, *War Diary*, 72; Hull, *Memoirs*, 1:814.

2. Ickes, entry of 29 January 1939, *Secret Diary*, 2:568; Haglund, *Latin America*, 137–38; Gellman, *Good Neighbor Diplomacy*, 9.

3. Welles, *NYT*, 31 January 1941, 6; *St. Louis Post-Dispatch*, 31 January 1941.

4. Douglas Miller, *You Can't Do Business with Hitler* (Boston: Little, Brown, 1941), 151–72; quotations, 153, 157.

5. "The President's Statement," *NYT*, 22 June 1940, 1, 9; Haglund, *Latin America*, 211.

6. "America Incorporated," *Uncensored* 40 (6 July 1940): 4; Flynn, *SFN*, 26 July 1940, 20; Chodorov, "South American Dynamite," *Scribner's Commentator* 8 (October 1940): 4. See also Hugh Johnson, "One Man's Opinion," *SFN*, 16 July 1940, 20; Flynn, *SFN*, 13 July 1940, 13; "Allies to the South," *CT*, 3 July 1940, 12.

7. Johnson, "One Man's Opinion," *SFN*, 20 June 1940, 13; "What Will Come Out of Havana?" *Christian Century* 57 (24 July 1940): 917. For Latin American reluctance, see also Flynn, *SFN*, 26 July 1940, 20; "America Incorporated," *Uncensored* 40 (6 July 1940): 3.

8. Press conference, *NYT*, 10 August 1940, 2; Gellman, *Good Neighbor Diplomacy*, 93–94; Haglund, *Latin America*, 212.

9. Roosevelt, message to Congress, text, *NYT*, 23 June 1940, 15; Hull, address to Foreign Minister's Conference, Havana, text, *NYT*, 23 July 1940, 14.

10. See, for example, Norman Thomas to John D. Luckey, 5 October 1940, Thomas Papers.

11. "Havana Conference Ends with United Action," *Christian Century* 57 (7 August 1940): 964. See also "Economic Solidarity with South America," *Christian Century* 57 (28 August 1940): 1043–44.

12. Frank C. Hanighen, "South of the Border," *Progressive*, 3 May 1941, 9. See also Frank Waldrop, "Hemisphere Security Must Be Bought," *WTH*, 1 August 1940, 14.

13. See, for example, Congressman Bradley, address to Michigan Commercial Secretaries Association, Mackinaw Island, 30 August 1940, in *CR*, A5440; "But Boake Carter Says," *SFE*, 30 July 1940, 11.

14. Flynn, *Washington Daily News*, 25 July 1940. See also Flynn cited by Reynolds, *CR*, 23 August 1940, 10,284. For earlier Flynn misgivings, "Other People's Money: South American Bubble," *New Republic* 101 (25 October 1939): 33.

15. "America Second," *CT*, 1 October 1940, 14. For more on cost, see also "A Half Billion for Good Neighbors," *CT*, 24 July 1940, 10; "The Half Billion for Latin America," 2 August 1940, 8.

16. Gellman, *Good Neighbor Diplomacy*, 162; Albert E. Eckes, *The United States and the Global Struggle for Minerals* (Austin: University of Texas Press, 1979), 98.

17. See, for example, Charles A. Lindbergh, testimony, SFRC, 6 February 1941, 538–39; John Cudahy to Claude Pepper, 15 October 1941, Flynn Papers; "Fair Deal for American Exports," *CT*, 30 December 1939, 6; "We Can Stay Out," *CT*, 11 January 1940, 12.

18. Peek, memorandum to America First Committee, in *CR*, 19 May 1941, A236; Johnson, *Hell Bent for War*, 100; AFC Research Bureau, "The Economics of Hemisphere Defense," *Did You Know?* 23B (19 September 1941), in Doenecke, *IDU*, 178. See also Philip La Follette, testimony, SFRC, 3 February 1941, 270.

19. See, for example, William Orton, *Williams* [College] *Record*, 23 April 1940, 1; Roger Wylie, "Latin America: Economic Pawn," *Scribner's Commentator* 10 (May 1941): 50; Williams, *Airpower*, 414; Robert La Follette Jr., *CR*, 12 October 1939, 334; Katherine Rodell, "How to Defend This Hemisphere," *Common Sense* 9 (July 1940): 12; Nye, *CR*, 23 October 1941, 743; "Gains in Exports Are Misleading," *CT*, 4 December 1940, 16. The *Tribune* did warn that much of this trade might revert back to Europe once the war ended.

20. "Citadel of Civilization," *NYDN*, 8 October 1939, 51; "We Can Get Used to It, Too," 18 October 1940, 37.

21. La Follette, *CR*, 12 October 1939, 15; Chase, "Four Assumptions about the War," *Uncensored*, 28 December 1940, special supplement, 3; "A Choice of Evils," *CT*, 9 February 1941, 16; Ward, "Future for Americas," *Social Justice*, 10 June 1940, 15; Klotsche, [Northwestern University] *Daily Northwestern*, 6 December 1940, 1; Wood, "Our Foreign Policy," address to Council of Foreign Relations, Chicago, 4 October 1940, in *CR*, A6302; Norman Thomas to John D. Luckey, 5 October 1940, Thomas Papers; Hutchins, "America Has a Choice," *Progressive*, 31 May 1941, 9.

22. For references to Latin American tin and rubber, see "Economic Solidarity with South America," *Christian Century* 57 (28 August 1940): 1044; Chavez, radio broadcast, NBC, 8 July 1940, in *CR*, A4352; Downey, *CR*, 6 October 1939, 117–18; MacLiesh and Reynolds, *Strategy*, 45. For rubber, see Downey, *CR*, 9 October 1939, 171; La Follette Jr., *CR*, 24 February 1940, 1306. For tin, see "America Incorporated," *Uncensored* 40 (6 July 1940): 4; Dorothy Detzer, report to WIL executive, Geneva, December 1939, WIL Papers; Hugh Johnson, "Pacific Trade," *NYWT*, 6 February 1940, 17; Baldwin, *United We Stand!* 54.

23. Christopher Thorne, *Allies of a Kind: The United States, Britain, and the War Against Japan, 1941–1945* (New York: Oxford University Press, 1978), 17.

24. AFC Research Bureau, "The All-American Front," *Did You Know?* 17 (8 August 1941), in Doenecke, *IDU*, 169; "Nobody Knows the Trouble We're In," *Did You Know?* 12 (24 July 1941), in Doenecke, *IDU*, 365; Johnson, "Anchors Away," *Saturday Evening Post* 213 (5 October 1940): 78; Fish, *CR*, 15 May 1940, 6195–96. Fish claimed Secretary of Agriculture Henry Wallace and Interior Secretary Harold Ickes backed his proposals. See also "Tin Tintype," *Uncensored* 46 (17 August 1940): 4–5. Hanighen privately reported that "the tin smelter people" wanted too much government money to establish their plants. Frank Hanighen to Sidney Hertzberg, ca. July 1940, Hertzberg Papers. "Our Tin Supply," *CT*, 13 August 1940, 10, also suggested building smelting plants in Bolivia.

25. Taft, *CR*, 19 September 1940, 11,846.

26. "America Incorporated," *Uncensored* 40 (6 July 1940): 4; La Follette, *CR*, 24 February 1940, 1306; MacLiesh and Reynolds, *Strategy*, 48. For manganese, see also Downey, *CR*, 6 October 1939, 172.

27. Chavez, 25 October 1939, *CR*, 825; Chavez, radio speech, NBC, 11 August 1940, in *CR*, A4923; Taft, *CR*, 10 September 1940, 11846.

28. Beals quoted in "Carleton Beals" in *Current Biography, 1941*, 60–62. For a scholarly biography, see John A. Britton, *Carleton Beals: A Radical Journalist in Latin America* (Albuquerque: University of New Mexico, 1987).

29. For endorsement of Beals's work, see AFC Research Bureau, "All-Out Aid for the Western Hemisphere," *Did You Know?* 23B (22 September 1941), in Doenecke, *IDU*, 181–82; Norman Thomas, testimony, HFAC, 22 January 1941, 338; Nicholas Broughton, "Books in a World at War," *Peace Action* 7 (December 1940): 7; Harry Elmer Barnes, *NYWT*, 17 April 1940, 22; memorandum introduced by Nye, *CR*, 9 November 1941, 8616. For critical reviews accusing him of being insufficiently aware of the Nazi menace, see Samuel Putnam, "Two Hearts That Beat as One," *New Masses* 39 (27 May 1941): 21–22; Samuel Guy Inman, *New York Herald Tribune Book Review*, 8 December 1940, 6. Economist Peter F. Drucker accused Beals of adopting the very economic imperialism be claimed to be condemning. "A Policy for the Americas," *Saturday Review of Literature* 33 (21 December 1940): 14.

30. See, for example, Sterling Morton, interview, Midsummer Industrial Conference, Illinois Industrial Council, Green Lake, Wisconsin, 22 August 1940, Morton Papers; Dennis, *WFL* 100 (27 June 1940): 5–6; Castle, "What about the Monroe Doctrine Now?" *Saturday Evening Post* 213 (27 July 1940): 38; Knutson, *CR*, 5 January 1941, 591; B. C. Clark, *CR*, 18 February 1941, 1099; Libby, "Which Way to the Brave New World?" *Peace Action* 6 (July 1940): 2; Taft, *CR*, 10 September 1940, 11,846; Hoover quoted by Libby, *Peace Action* 9 (October 1940): 1; AFC Research Bureau, "The Economics of Hemisphere Defense," *Did You Know?* 23A (19 September 1941), in Doenecke, *IDU*, 175–76; historian Arthur May, *This Bewildering Democracy: Reflections on American Foreign Policy* (pamphlet; Rochester, N.Y.: privately printed, 1941), 14; MacLiesh and Reynolds, *Strategy*, 44–45; "Beef and the Axis," *NYDN*, 22 March 1941, 15; Flynn, "Other's People's Money: South American Bubble," *New Republic* 101 (25 October 1939): 339.

31. "America Incorporated," *Uncensored* 40 (6 July 1940): 3; Lewis, [Dartmouth College] *The Dartmouth*, 9 January 1941, 1.

32. Wood, "Our Foreign Policy," A6302; "Wine, Lace and War," *NYDN*, 25 January 1941, 15; "South American Trade after the War," *NYDN*, 21 April 1941, 23.

33. Baldwin, "Wanted: A Plan for Defense," *Harper's Magazine* 181 (August 1940): 231; Kennedy, testimony, HFAC, 21 April 1941, 294; "South American Trade after the War," *NYDN*, 21 April 1941, 23.

34. See, for example, Mundt, *CR*, 21 April 1941, A1823; Nicholas Broughton, "America in a Hostile World," *Scribner's Commentator* 9 (November 1940): 7; D. W. Clark, *CR*, 24 February 1941, 1296; Charles A. Lindbergh, testimony, HFAC, 23 January 1941, 434; Beals, *Pan America*, 514; "The Latin American Trade Crisis," *CT*, 7 April 1941, 14; "Common Sense in Latin America," *CT*, 13 September 1940, 8; "Hitler's Speech," *NYDN*, 12 December 1940, 39; Hoover, "Our Future Economic Preparedness," 18 September 1940, in *Vital Speeches* 7 (15 November 1940): 94; Norman Thomas, testimony, SFRC, 27 January 1941, 297; Howard, *America and a New World Order*, 86–91; Flynn, *Washington Daily News*, 25 July 1940; Flynn, "Other People's Money: An American Bubble," *New Republic* 101 (25 October 1939): 339; Castle, address to Worcester Foreign Policy Association, 14 May 1940, in *CR*, A2999; Morton, speech, National Small Businessmen's Association, Chicago, 12 August 1940.

35. Dennis, *WFL* 111 (12 September 1940): 4; [Lawrence Dennis], "The Economic Consequences of American Intervention," unpublished manuscript [1941], in Doenecke, *IDU*, 201–2. In July 1940, Hitler did order the resumption of a huge "blue-water" naval construction program. By fall, he tabled the program to concentrate on the forthcoming war against the Soviets. Weinberg, *Germany, Hitler, and World War II*, 199.

36. Haglund, *Latin America*, 137; Gellman, *Good Neighbor Diplomacy*, 104.

37. Roosevelt to William Allen White, 14 December 1939, *F.D.R.: His Personal Letters*, 968; Roosevelt, text of address, *NYT*, 28 May 1941, 2.

38. Hull, address, text, *NYT*, 19 May 1941, 1, 2; Bullitt, "What Next?" *Life*, 21 April 1941, 95, 97; Lippmann, "The Economic Consequences of a German Victory," *Life* 9 (22 July 1940): 64–69; Thompson, "World Germanica," *Reader's Digest* 37 (July 1940): 115–18. See also historian Allan Nevins, "Facing the Nazi Revolution," *Reader's Digest* 37 (August 1940): 63–66; Wendell Willkie, "Americans, Stop Being Afraid!" *Collier's* 107 (10 May 1941): 65. Many such positions are summarized in Patrick J. Hearden,

*Roosevelt Confronts Hitler: America's Entry into World War II* (DeKalb: Northern Illinois University Press, 1987), and Paul A. Varg, "The Coming of the War with Germany," *Centennial Review* 20 (Fall 1976): 219–27.

39. *Fortune* poll, Cantril, *Public Opinion*, 1120. For related polls, see 1129–20.

40. Miller, *You Can't Do Business*, 87, 135–36, 205–11; quotation, 167.

41. Crowther, "We Don't Have To," in *CR*, 6 November 1941, 8565–66. For favorable reviews, see Gustav Stolper, Viennese economist and former member of the German Reichstag, *Yale Review* 21 (Autumn 1941): 182; William L. Shirer, *Saturday Review of Literature* 24 (5 July 1941): 7. For negative reaction, see Stuart Chase, "Must We Fight for Our Foreign Trade?" *Progressive*, 26 July 1941, 5; Norman Thomas, "Your World and Mine: Imperialism Rampant," *Call*, 16 August 1941, 5; Pettengill, "Post War Trade," Release 275, 7 August 1941, Box 11, Pettengill Papers; AFC Philadelphia chapter, *The Voice of the People*, 6 October 1941; *Social Justice*, 15 September 1941, 11; Wheeler, *CR*, 6 November 1941, 8565; Nock, review, *Scribner's Commentator* 11 (November 1941): 82–83; John Cudahy to Claude Pepper [copy], 15 October 1941, Flynn Papers; Norman Thomas, "Your World and Mine," *Call*, 16 August 1941, 5.

42. Jonathan Utley, *Going to War with Japan, 1937–1941* (Knoxville: University of Tennessee Press, 1985), 85, 86.

43. Moley, "Perspective: Why We Help England," *Newsweek*, 3 February 1941, 60. See also Senator La Follette, *CR*, 29 October 1941, 8322; Norman Thomas to Alfred P. Perkins, June 2, 1941, Thomas Papers.

44. Thorpe, "National Defense for War? For Peace?" *Nation's Business* 29 (February 1941): 13; Taft, "Shall the United States Enter the European War?" radio address, 17 May 1941, in *CR*, A2344–45. See also Robert M. Hutchins, "America Has a Choice," *Progressive*, 31 May 1941, 9.

45. Boeckel, "Lend-Lease Misses the Bus," *Peace Action* 7 (February 1941): 5; Kennedy, testimony, HFAC, 20 January 1941, 236. Senator George Aiken saw postwar agricultural markets as being destroyed beyond repair. *CR*, 25 February 1941, 1362.

46. See, for example, political scientist Landrum Bolling, *Brown* [University] *Daily Herald*, 23 November 1939, 1; Bulow, *CR*, 21 February 1941, 1254; Stuart Chase, "Must We Fight for Our Foreign Trade?" *Progressive*, 26 July 1941, 5.

47. For under 8 percent, see Ludlow, *CR*, 16 October 1939, 487. For under 7 percent, see Freda Utley, "How Could We Combat a Hitler-Dominated Europe?" *American Forum of the Air* 3 (16 November 1941): 5. For 7 percent, see General Wood, interview with Kenneth Crawford, *PM*, 25 May 1941, 5; Hoover, "A Call to Reason," speech, Chicago, 29 June 1941, in *Addresses, 1940–1941*, 96. For 5 percent, John Chamberlain, *The American Stakes* (Philadelphia: Lippincott, 1940), 152. See also Joseph P. Kennedy, speech at Oglethorpe University, 24 May 1941, in *CR*, A2492; farm editor Wheeler McMillen, "Hitler: Economic Threat?" *Scribner's Commentator* 9 (March 1941): 29. For 3 percent, see Nye, *Bryn Mawr College News*, 1 May 1941, 4. See also George Peek, address entered in *CR*, 21 July 1941, A3528.

48. Kennedy, *CR*, A2492; Wood, Crawford interview, 5; Emeny, testimony, HFAC, 22 January 1941, 466.

49. Peek said that rubber accounted for 12 percent of U.S. imports; tin, 5.1 percent; coffee, 5 percent; raw silk, 4.9 percent; cane sugar, 4.5 percent; newspaper print, 4.9 percent; and all other items, no more than 3 percent, except wool, which was 3.3 percent. Peek noted the possibility of producing substitutes, claiming that the United States could produce its own rubber, that rayon and nylon could replace silk, and that the United States was preparing itself to smelt tin from ore coming from Latin America. Address, in *CR*, 21 July 1941, A3528.

50. Flynn, *SFN*, 9 June 1941, 14; 9 August 1940, 22. In the 9 August column, he also warned against intervention and claimed that the United States had the option of economic isolation.

51. Chase, [Dartmouth College] *The Dartmouth*, 10 October 1940, 1; "We Can Get Along Alone," *Progressive*, 9 August 1941, 9. See also Chase, "Autarchy," *Progressive*, 23 August 1941, 5. For examples of anti-interventionist endorsement of Chase, see Barnes, "Keep Out of War and Investigate the War-Mongers" [draft], 56, Box 252, Lundeen Papers; Chamberlain, *American Stakes*, 150; Norman Thomas, "Your World and Mine," *Call*, 4 November 1939, 3.

52. Hoover, "A Call to Reason," Chicago, 29 June 1941, in *Addresses, 1940–1941*, 96; "Our Future Economic Defense," 18 September 1940, in *Addresses, 1940–1941*, 22. See also speech to Republican National Convention, 25 June 1940, in *Addresses, 1940–1941*, 221.

53. Lodge, *CR*, 10 February 1941, 825; Peek, address, entered in *CR*, 21 July 1941, A3528; [Dennis], "The Economics of American Intervention" [1941], in Doenecke, *IDU*, 204–5. See also Herbert Hoover, journal of Raymond Moley, 11 June 1940, Moley Papers.

54. Flynn, *SFN*, 24 September 1940, 14. See also Chodorov, "Germany: Economic Threat?" *Scribner's Commentator* 9 (March 1941): 34.

55. Flynn, "Nazi Economy: A Threat?" *Scribner's Commentator* 10 (August 1941): 21. For skeptical comments about the use of gold in commerce, see "Is Uncle Sam Gold-Poor?" *Christian Century* 57 (7 August 1940): 965; Danaher, *CR*, 25 August 1940, A5662; Norman Thomas, testimony, SFRC, 3 February 1941, 292. For a pro-gold position, see Ralph Townsend, *Seeking Foreign Trouble* (pamphlet; San Francisco: privately printed, 1940), 18.

56. The manuscript was read in draft by William R. Castle, Hoover's undersecretary of state; international lawyer John Foster Dulles; and James Mooney, head of General Motors Export Corporation and advocate of a negotiated peace in Europe. Major General James G. Harbord, board chairman of the Radio Corporation of America and chief of staff to General John J. Pershing during World War I, wrote the foreword.

57. For endorsements, see *Scribner's Commentator* 10 (July 1941): 59; Page Hufty, "America First Book List," *AFC Bulletin* 476 (7 August 1941), in Doenecke, *IDU*, 121; Neilson, entry of 6 June 1941, *Tragedy*, 2:362; Norman Thomas to Graeme Howard, 4 October 1940, Thomas Papers; Porter Sargent to Norman Thomas, 11 October 1940, Thomas Papers; Castle Diary, 30 July 1940; Robert E. Wood, "American Foreign Policy Today," in *We Testify*, ed. Doris Fielding Reid and Nancy Schoonmaker (New York: Smith & Durrell, 1941), 111; Moley, "Perspective: World Trade and the Future," *Newsweek*, 9 June 1941, 72. For more critical reactions, see political scientist Elizabeth M. Lynskey, "America's Part," *Commonweal* 33 (7 February 1941): 402–4; Nicholas Broughton, "Books in a World at War," *Peace Action* 7 (October 1940): 7. Interventionist political scientist Robert Strausz-Hupé found the work thoughtful but questioned whether tranquillity could exist among the large power blocs. "Brave New World Order," *Current History and Forum* 52 (24 December 1940): 24.

58. Howard, *America and a New World Order*, quotations respectively on 79, 115, 107, 109.

59. See, for example, Peek, address, in *CR*, 21 July 1941, A3258; Hanford MacNider, testimony, HFAC, 22 January 1941, 359; Taft, speech at Vienna, Illinois, 30 September 1939, in *CR*, A76; Taft, "Preparedness and Peace," speech at St. Louis, 20 May 1940, in *CR*, A3178; Taft, *CR*, 22 February 1941, 1282; Robert E. Wood, "Our Foreign Policy," A6302; "A World Divided," *NYDN*, 12 May 1941, 19; press release, Lundeen speech in honor of Duke Saxe-Coburg, Washington, D.C., 20 March 1940, Box 306, Lundeen Papers; Nye, speech, CBS, 21 June 1941, in *CR*, A307; Cudahy cited in Long, entry of 16 August 1940, *War Diary*, 123; Charles A. Lindbergh, "Speech Appealing for Peace Plea to Europe," *NYT*, 5 August 1940, 6.

60. Johnson, *Hell Bent for War*, 97–100. See also Verne Marshall, debate, "Aid to Britain: Give, Lend, or Withhold?" New England Town Meeting of the Air, 16 January 1941, Verne Marshall Papers; Nye, speech, CBS, 21 June 1941, in *CR*, A3075; Yale economist Richard Bissell, *Yale Daily News*, 16 October 1940, 1; Amos Pinchot to Burton K. Wheeler, 19 May 1941, Pinchot Papers; Wood, "Our Foreign Policy," A6302; Flynn, *SFN*, 9 August 1940, 22; Freda Utley, "How Could We Combat a Hitler-Dominated Europe?" 5.

61. Peek, address, in *CR*, 21 July 1941, A3527–28.

62. Flynn, *SFN*, 10 June 1941, 14; "Nazi Economy: A Threat?" *Scribner's Commentator* 9 (August 1941): 19–26.

63. See, for example, Nye, speech, CBS, 21 June 1941, in *CR*, A3075; Flynn, "Nazi Economy: A Threat?" 22; Broughton, "America in a Hostile World," *Scribner's Commentator* 9 (November 1940): 72; Chodorov, "Germany: Economic Threat?" *Scribner's Commentator* 9 (March 1941): 33–34. Emeny, testimony, HFAC, 22 January 1941, 466.

64. Cleona Lewis, *Nazi Germany and World Trade* (Washington, D.C.: Brookings Institution, 1941). For an endorsement of Lewis's study, see Anti-War News Service, "The Economic 'Menace' of Nazism,"

*Call*, 13 September 1941, 6. Commenting on the study, *Newsweek* claimed that isolationists were justified in pointing to it with pleasure. 23 June 1941, 40.

65. AFC Research Bureau, "Buy or Die," *Did You Know?* 6 (5 July 1941), in Doenecke, *IDU*, 159–63.

66. AFC Research Bureau, "Swastika over Sickle," *Did You Know?* 15 (1 August 1941), in Doenecke, *IDU*, 164–68.

67. Broughton, "America in a Hostile World," 72. See also Nye, *CT*, 17 June 1941.

68. For the interventionist argument, see Livingstone Hartley and Donald C. Blaisdell, "Wages in Conquered Countries," CDAAA, *Washington Office Information Letter* 22 (13 June 1941): 3–4, Box 35, CDAAA Papers. For example of opposition, see Norman Thomas, [University of Wisconsin] *Daily Cardinal*, 27 May 1941, 1.

69. See, for example, William Henry Chamberlin, "War: Short Cut to Fascism," *American Mercury* 51 (December 1940): 398; Barry, *CR*, 16 October 1941, 7965; Peek, address, in *CR*, 21 July 1941, A3528; Philip La Follette, testimony, 3 February 1941, SFRC, 269; Vorys, address, Charlottesville, Institute of Public Affairs, 24 June 1941, in *CR*, A3101; Norman Thomas, "Your World and Mine: Into War through Hysteria," *Call*, 7 June 1941, 8; Wheeler, address, Indianapolis, 28 May 1941, in *CR*, A2628; Freda Utley, "How Could We Combat a Hitler-Dominated Europe?" 5. Utley did assert that in products involving unskilled labor, such as timber produced by concentration camps, the Soviets could undersell the West.

70. Chodorov, "Germany: Economic Threat?" *Scribner's Commentator* 9 (March 1941): 33.

71. "All America," *Uncensored* 67 (11 January 1941): 2–3. As far as percentages went, the United States produced 30 percent of the world's iron ore, 32 percent of the copper ore, 22 percent of the lead, 30 percent of the zinc, 62 percent of the petroleum, 50 percent of the cotton, and 34 percent of the coal. It also produced three-fifths of the world's oil, at least a third of the world's electric power, and generated at least half of the world's total horsepower. See also Amos Pinchot to Renee von Eulenburg-Wiener, 10 October 1941, Pinchot Papers. For Roosevelt's address, see *CR*, 6 January 1941, 45.

72. See, for example, Hugh Johnson, "Anchors Away," *Saturday Evening Post* 213 (5 October 1940): 778; "Tin Tintype," *Uncensored* 46 (17 August 1940): 5; Flynn, *SFN*, 25 February 1941, 15; McCormick, "Today the Strongest Nation in the World," *CT*, 13 October 1940, graphic section, 5; MacLiesh and Reynolds, 12; AFC Research Bureau, "The All-American Front," *Did You Know?* 17 (8 August 1941), in Doenecke, *IDU*, 169–73; AFC Speakers Bureau, "What Strategic Materials Do We Lack in the United States?" [undated 1941], in Doenecke, *IDU*, 156–57; "The Strategic Materials"; "How Self-Sufficient Are We?" *Peace Action* 7 (March 1941): 6. *Peace Action* cited the statement of Secretary of Commerce Jesse Jones, as reported in *NYT*, 20 February 1941, 35, and the report of industrialist Edward Stettinius of the National Defense Advisory Commission, *NYT*, 14 July 1940, 1, 14, in which both spoke of domestic developments in tin, magnesium, and rubber.

73. Robert M. Hathaway, "1933–1945: Economic Diplomacy in a Time of Crisis," in *Economics and World Power: An Assessment of American Diplomacy since 1789*, ed. William H. Becker and Samuel F. Welles (New York: Columbia University Press, 1984), 303; Jeff Frieden, "Sectoral Conflict and Foreign Economic Policy, 1914–1940," *International Organization* 42 (Winter 1988): 64.

74. Stockpiling, Jonathan Marshall, *To Have and Have Not: Southeast Asian Raw Materials and the Origins of the Pacific War* (Berkeley: University of California Press, 1995), chap. 2; RFC, Mira Wilkins, *The Maturing of Multinational Enterprise: American Business Abroad from 1914 to 1970* (Cambridge, Mass.: Harvard University Press, 1974), 253–55; Roosevelt and Welles, Eckes, *Global Struggle*, 99.

75. Utley, *Going to War with Japan*, 85.


## CHAPTER 10: WAR, PEACE, AND ELECTIONS


1. Churchill to Roosevelt, 15 May 1940, in Kimball, *Churchill and Roosevelt*, 1:37; Lee, entry of 4 August 1940, *London Journal*, 29; Gilbert, *Churchill*, 6:408; Ponting, *1940*, 161.

2. Lee, entry of 5 September 1940, *London Journal*, 44; Gilbert, *Churchill*, 6:811. See also Lee, entry of 15 September 1940, *London Journal*, 58; 4 October 1940, 78.

3. Lee, entry of 24 June 1940, *London Journal*, 6; 15 July 1940, 16; 18 July 1940, 18.

4. Leutze, *Bargaining*, 96.

5. Berle, entry of 6 September 1940, *Navigating*, 334. See also 30 September 1940, 338.

6. Berle, entry of 21 September 1940, *Navigating*, 336; Bullitt in entry of Ickes, 22 September 1940, *Secret Diary*, 3:329.

7. *Fortune* in Cantril, *Public Opinion*, 1186. Thirty percent predicted a British victory. See also "What the U.S.A. Thinks," *Life*, 29 July 1940, 20, in which 56 percent predicted a German victory and just over 33 percent said the United States should surrender in the face of defeat. For related polls, which sporadically showed optimism concerning Britain, see Cantril, *Public Opinion*, 1186–87.

8. *Fortune* poll, Cantril, *Public Opinion*, 1108.

9. *Life*, 10 June 1940, 28; "The Defense of Britain," 15 July 1940, 17–23.

10. Sterling Morton to Ralph Church, 16 May 1940, Morton Papers; Joseph P. Kennedy to Cordell Hull, 27 May 1940, in *Foreign Relations, 1940*, 1:233; Kennedy in Koskoff, *Kennedy*, 257. For Kennedy's general pessimism, see Whalen, *Founding Father*, chaps. 17–20; Koskoff, *Kennedy*, 210–316; Beschloss, *Kennedy and Roosevelt*, 190–243.

11. See, for example, Williams, "Real Scrap Coming!" 28 May 1940; "Key to Invasion," 19 June 1940; "England by Fall," 25 June 1940; "Two Gladiators," 10 July 1940; "People's War," 22 July 1940, in Williams Pamphlets.

12. Williams, "Vital Lessons," 7 August 1940, in Williams Pamphlets.

13. Dennis, *WFL* 105 (1 August 1940): 2. See also 98 (13 June 1940): 5; 101, (3 July 1940): 1–2.

14. Hearst, "In the News," *SFE*, 24 June 1940, 1. The publisher even said Britain could cause a little trouble on its own. If it still wanted to fight, Hearst suggested that it could blockade Italy, stiffen Balkan resistance, and find a "true war leader" such as Lloyd George or former war secretary Leslie Hore-Belisha. See *SFE*, 6 May 1940, 1.

15. "An Overseas Army Needs Docks," *CT*, 16 June 1940, 14. For slightly more caution, see "Italy Enters the War," *CT*, 11 June 1940, 14.

16. McCormick, broadcast of 30 June 1940, in *Addresses*, 14–15.

17. "The Battle of Britain Begins," *NYDN*, 24 July 1940, 27. For a slightly more pessimistic estimate, see "Mahan Revised," 1 July 1940, 25; "War Jitters," 1 August 1940, 25; "Blitzkrieg on Britain," 13 August 1940, 21; "50–50," 13 September 1940, 33.

18. Taft, "Peace and Preparedness," 20 May 1940, in *CR*, A3148. For other Taft claims along this line, see *CR*, 22 February 1941, 1282; "Shall the United States Enter the European War?" radio address, 17 May 1941, in *CR*, A2344.

19. Johnson column, entered in *CR*, 13 June 1940, A4141; Flynn, *CR*, 8 May 1940, 14. See also Flynn, *CR*, 26 June 1940, 16.

20. Baldwin, "Wanted: A Plan of Defense," *Harper's Magazine* 181 (August 1940): 231.

21. See, for example, Herbert Hoover to John C. O'Laughlin, 15 August 1940, Stanford Files; Hugh Johnson, *SFN*, 27 August 1940, 19; Castle Diary, 14 September 1940; Charles A. Lindbergh in Castle Diary, 9 September 1940; General Wood, "Our Foreign Policy," speech to Chicago Council of Foreign Relations, 4 October 1940, in *CR*, 6301.

22. Hearst, "In the News," *SFE*, 12 September 1940, 1. In October, Hearst claimed that the Axis invasion of England was "off" for good. *SFE*, 12 October 1940, 15.

23. "The Coming Test of Air War," *CT*, 6 September 1940, 12; "Bombing Ranges," 22 September 1940, 16. See also "News from England," 29 September 1940, 14.

24. "Another War Winter," *NYDN*, 3 October 1940, 21. See also "What Would Napoleon Do Now?" *CT*, 7 October 1940, 10; "The Air Forces," *CT*, 6 December 1940, 16.

25. Howe, radio script, 4 October 1940, Jessup Papers.

26. Sterling Morton, "Let's Think This Matter Through" [pamphlet], in *CR*, 21 February 1941, 787; Landon, "Stand by the Neutrality Act," speech to Kansas City Cooperative Club, 26 November 1940, in *CR*, A6737. See also "Germans in Rumania," *CT*, 13 October 1940, 18; "Trying to Crack Hitler's Empire," *CT*, 26 November 1940, 11; "Rumanian Preview of Europe," *CT*, 25 January 1941, 8.

27. "Hitler in Control of Europe," *CT*, 23 November 1940, 8. For further optimism, see "The War Against Shipping," *CT*, 11 December 1940, 16; "The Italian Front," *CT*, 8 December 1940, 26.

28. Villard, "How Long Can Europe Endure?" *Christian Century* 57 (2 October 1940): 1207. See also Villard, "How Long Can England Stand It?" *Progressive*, 21 September 1940, 6. For a similar reference to the winter, see Morley Diary, 20 October 1940; "As the War Goes into Winter," *CT*, November 27, 1940, 12.

29. Villard, "Will Hitler Invade America?" *Christian Century* 57 (23 October 1940): 1313.

30. Leutze, *Bargaining*, 188.

31. Libby to executive board, NCPW, 18 September 1940, NCPW Papers; Castle Diary, 9 September 1940; Taft, *CR*, 14 August 1940, 10,307; Johnson, *SFN*, 28 September 1940, 14; Dennis, *WFL* 102 (11 July 1940): 1–3; 103 (18 July 1940): 3–4; 106 (8 August 1940): 1–2; 107 (15 August 1940): 2. For another prediction of social revolution, see *Social Justice*, 14 October 1940, 3. For general pessimism, see "The Outlook for Britain," *Christian Century* 57 (3 July 1940): 844.

32. "Gibraltar, Greece and the Blitzkrieg," *NYDN*, 22 August 1940, 29; C. Hartley Grattan, "If Britain Goes Under: A Speculation," *New Republic* 103 (1 July 1940): 20.

33. Hoover, "Our Future Economic Defense," 18 September 1940, *Addresses, 1940–1941*, 15. See also John Haynes Holmes, sermon, 29 September 1940, in *CR*, A6061; Dennis, *WFL* 112 (19 September 1940): 5; *Social Justice*, 16 September 1940, 3.

34. "Defeat at Dakar," *NYDN*, 27 September 1940, 37. See also *Social Justice*, 7 October 1940, 3; Kennedy to Hull, 27 September 1940, *Foreign Relations, 1940*, vol. 3: British Commonwealth (Washington, D.C.: Government Printing Office, 1958), 48–49.

35. See, for example, Morley Diary, 20 October 1940; Dennis, *WFL* 114 (3 October 1940): 3–4; 118 (31 October 1940): 3; 117 (24 October 1940): 2; 120 (14 November 1940): 4.

36. Anne Morrow Lindbergh to Robert E. Wood, 13 October 1940, Wood Papers; "Hold 'Em, Lion," *NYDN*, 4 October 1940, 37; "What Would Napoleon Do Now?" *CT*, 7 October 1940, 10. See also "Where Is Hitler Going Next?" *NYDN*, 28 December 1940, 13. Mention was made of Salonika, the Dardanelles, Istanbul, and Rumania.

37. Lindbergh, entry of 3 November 1940, *Wartime Journals*, 412. See also Lindbergh, testimony, HFAC, 23 January 1941, 398.

38. Charles A. Lindbergh to Robert E. Wood, 12 November 1940, Wood Papers. For stress on the heavy impact of German bombing, see "Kriegsozialismus," *New Masses* 37 (22 October 1940): 22; *Social Justice*, 7 October 1940, 3; *Social Justice*, 9 December 1940, 3.

39. Libby, [University of] *California* [Los Angeles] *Daily Bruin*, 4 December 1940, 1; memorandum of conversation, 22 December 1940, HHPL "Air Invasion of England," *CT*, 31 December 1940, 6.

40. See, for example, William Henry Chamberlin, "The Coming Peace," *American Mercury* 51 (November 1940): 267; Amos Pinchot to Edgar J. Cook, 28 November 1940, Pinchot Papers; "The Air Forces," *CT*, 6 December 1940, 16; "Loss from Air Bombing," *CT*, 10 December 1940, 16; "How Long a War?" *CT*, 21 December 1940, 10; Robert E. Wood to J. H. Meyer, 12 September 1940, Box 286, AFC Papers; "The Big Picture," *Uncensored* 63 (14 December 1940): 5.

41. "How Long a War?" *CT*, 21 December 1940, 10; Oswald Garrison Villard to Philip Bernstein, 4 December 1940, Villard Papers.

42. Rock, *Chamberlain and Roosevelt*, 278; Fulton Oursler Jr., "Secret Treason," *American Heritage* 42 (December 1991): 52–76.

43. FOR Council, 20 April 1940, *Fellowship* 6 (May 1940): 74; minutes, WIL annual meeting, 27–30 April 1940, Pittsburgh, 1, WIL Papers; Federal Council, "The Churches and the World Situation," *Peace Action* 6 (April 1940): 6; Libby, "Chaco Mediation Points Way Now," *Peace Action* 6 (April 1940): 3; "What Can America Do for Peace?" *Christian Century* 57 (15 May 1940): 631.

44. "The Wisdom of Pius XII," *NYDN*, 7 May 1940, 27. For Pius's statement, see *NYT*, 6 May 1940, 2.

45. "Hitler and Napoleon," *NYDN*, 14 April 1940, 45. On 1 June, the *News* declared the Allies "well advised" to make a negotiated peace before Hitler "starts slashing France to pieces as he did Belgium and Holland." As Hitler was fifty-one years old, it added, he could not last forever. See "Roll Up That Map," 1 June 1940, 13.

46. See, for example, John O'Brien, *Social Justice*, 3 April 1940, 10; Hearst, "In the News," *SFE*, 17 April 1940, 2; Hearst, "In the News," *SFE*, 24 June 1940, 1.

47. Robert Bendiner, "Men Who Would Be President: Burton K. Wheeler," *Nation* 150 (27 April 1940): 536; Dennis, *WFL* 100 (27 June 1940): 4; 97 (6 June 1940): 2; Mooney, "War or Peace in America?" address to Case Alumni Association, University Club, Cleveland, 1 June 1940, in *CR*, A4057; Waldrop, "The Peace Balance Sheet," *WTH*, 30 June 1940, C15. For similar optimism in June, see author Lincoln Colcord to Amos Pinchot, 28 June 1940, Pinchot Papers.

48. Albert W. Palmer, "The Road Away from War," *Christian Century* 57 (19 June 1940): 793.

49. "Democracy and Blitzkrieg," *Common Sense* 9 (June 1940): 17.

50. Libby, "Early Mediation Can Save Civilization," *Peace Action* 6 (April 1940): 2.

51. Hitler speech, text, *NYT*, 20 July 1940, 4–5.

52. Halifax speech conveying British refusal, text, *NYT*, 23 July 1940, 4. Halifax privately sought a German peace offer so as to gain time. If necessary both Halifax and Churchill would have agreed to a peace involving surrender of some British colonies, Mediterranean possessions, French overseas territory, and possible de jure recognition of Hitler's eastern conquests, although not conceding the British navy, air force, independence, or ability to wage a future war. Roberts, *Holy Fox*, 181, 214.

53. Reynolds, *Creation*, 105; Kimball, *Forged in War*, 54–55.

54. David Reynolds, "Churchill and the British Decision," 159–62.

55. Gallup poll, 20 July 1940, Cantril, *Public Opinion*, 1136. The breakdown: 70 percent for continued fighting, 22 percent for making peace.

56. Villard, "Should Britain Talk Peace?" *Christian Century* 57 (31 July 1940): 946; "Hopes of Peace," *NYDN*, 17 July 1940, 31. See also "Negotiated Peace Is the Alternative," *Peace Action* 6 (July 1940): 2.

57. Lindbergh, entry of 20 July 1940, *War Within*, 129.

58. "Hitler's Peace," *CT*, 22 July 1940, 10.

59. See, for example, Norman Thomas to H. L. Green, 3 July 1940, Thomas Papers; Norman Thomas to S. K. Ratcliffe, 8 October 1940, Thomas Papers; Thomas, testimony, HFAC, 22 January 1941, 320; Lindbergh, speech of 4 August 1940, "Radio Addresses," 18; *Social Justice*, 7 October 1940, 3; WIL Executive Board, minutes, 18 December 1940, WIL Papers.

60. "Christmas Truce—Why Not?" *NYDN*, 5 December 1940, 39; "The Pope Prays for Peace," *NYDN*, 3 October 1940, 21; "The Wisdom of the Pope," *NYDN*, 26 November 1940, 32; Hearst, "In the News," *SFE*, 25 July 1940, 9; Wood, *NYT*, 12 December 1940, 18; Wood, *CT*, 12 December 1940, 1; Wood, "America First," *Time*, 23 December 1940, 13; Frederick J. Libby to Harry Emerson Fosdick, 19 December 1940, NCPW Papers. The *Chicago Tribune* thought that Roosevelt himself might be disqualified. See "Peace by Spring or What?" 15 December 1940, 18.

61. Wood, speech to Chicago Council on Foreign Relations, 4 October 1940, in *CR*, A6302. The *Chicago Tribune* endorsed the speech. "A Negotiated Peace," 19 October 1940, 12. In November, Joseph P. Kennedy told Herbert Hoover that two months earlier Germany had offered Britain a peace based on "full maintenance of their empire, fleet, and everything else," although the Germans could, in Hoover's words, "make the entire Continental settlement without interference from the British." Memorandum, Hoover–Kennedy conversation, 22 November 1940, Hoover Papers.

62. Wood, *CT*, 12 December 1940, 1.

63. Robert E. Wood to Roy Howard, 14 December 1940, Wood Papers; Robert E. Wood to Horace Bowker, 19 December 1940, Box 22, the Papers of the Fight for Freedom Committee, Princeton University. See also Wood to Sterling Morton, 13 May 1941, Morton Papers; Wood to R. J. Finegan, 22 January 1941, Box 292, AFC Papers. In July 1941, Wood was more detailed. He endorsed the restoration of the Netherlands, France, Norway, Denmark, Greece, and Finland; denied that Czechoslovakia, Luxembourg, and Austria could be restored; and feigned ignorance about Poland, Yugoslavia, Estonia, and Latvia. Peace, he said, would be more sound if some smaller, economically unsound nations "were eliminated." Robert E. Wood to B. E. Maidenberg, 11 July 1941, AFC Papers.

64. Chamberlin Diary, 12 December 1940; "War to What End?" *CT*, 25 December 1940, 16; John Chamberlain to Mark Prentiss, 30 December 1940, in Doenecke, *IDU*, 220.

65. Morley Diary, 21 June 1940; 4 July 1940; 20 and 27 October 1940. Conversely, Dennis saw the British "lower classes" as the more restive element. *WFL* 102 (11 July 1940): 3.

66. In September, Castle, Lindbergh, and Cudahy all said privately they hoped Britain might somehow win, but they feared that a decisive victory would mean the wiping out of Germany and

general Bolshevism throughout Europe. Castle Diary, 20 September 1940. For Cudahy's claim that a German victory would bring no disadvantage to the United States, see Breckinridge Long, entry of 16 August 1940, *War Diary*, 123. For Moore, see John Bassett Moore to Nicholas F. Lenssen, 7 May 1940, Moore Papers.

67. Allen, "Peace Negotiations or War to the Death?" *Christian Century* 57 (30 October 1940): 1333. Hitler's terms supposedly included German control of all conquered territory in Europe, English domination of French colonies, a common military move against Russia, German economic control of Latin America, and North America as Britain's economic sphere.

68. Amos Pinchot to Edgar J. Cook, 28 November 1940, Pinchot Papers; Joseph P. Kennedy in memorandum of Hoover–Kennedy conversation, 11 November 1940, Hoover Papers; Herbert Hoover in Castle Diary, 21 September 1940. Castle concurred. For Kennedy Lloyd George, see Long, entry of 6 November 1940, *War Dairy*, 147.

69. Edwin M. Borchard to John Bassett Moore, 21 December 1940, Borchard Papers; "The Big Picture," *Uncensored* 63 (14 December 1940): 5.

70. Alexander, *CR*, 4 October 1940, 13,223; Alexander, radio broadcast, Mutual station WOL, 16 December 1940, in *CR*, A6912. For endorsements, see William B. Lloyd Jr., director of the Campaign for World Government, to Senator Rush Holt, 2 December 1940, in *CR*, A6807–8; Libby, "Why No Preparedness for Peace?" *Peace Action* 7 (November 1940): 1; WIL National Board meeting, resolutions, 30 October–1 November 1940, Washington, D.C., 3. Congressman Rich, in concurring, said only a new U.S. president, one "who can take a position whereby the people of the world will have confidence in him and faith in him," could take such action. *CR*, 4 October 1940, 13,224.

71. Wheeler, speech, NBC, 30 December 1940, in *CR*, A7031; Wheeler, *Newsweek*, 6 January 1941, 16. The same article reported that he was backed by senators Holt, Tydings, and Vandenberg. A few anti-interventionists were opposed. Philip Burnham, an editor of the *Commonweal*, stressed Hitler's untrustworthiness. "Peace and/or Appease—Senators," *Commonweal* 33 (10 January 1941): 293. The Trotskyist *Militant* claimed to concur with the Stalinist *Daily Worker* in declaring that Wheeler's peace would be made on Hitler's terms. Moreover, it said Wheeler wanted FDR to encourage a war between Germany and Russia. J. W., "What 'Negotiated' Peace Means," *Militant*, 5 May 1941, 5.

72. I. F. Stone, "Munichman from Montana," *Nation* 152 (11 January 1941): 36. Wheeler said he sought to make his proposal before the United States attempted lend-lease. *Washington Daily News*, 11 January 1941. Possibly Wheeler had little hope for his proposal, for he wrote Norman Thomas that he suggested the peace bid to "focus attention on the idea" that FDR was encouraging war. Burton K. Wheeler to Norman Thomas, 24 January 1941, Thomas Papers. In late February, Wheeler endorsed a British victory but hoped that a peace would introduce disarmament. Wheeler, *CR*, 27 February 1941, 1475.

73. Castle Diary, 14 April 1940; William Henry Chamberlin, "The Coming Peace," *American Mercury* 51 (November 1940): 271. See also Dennis, *WFL* 122 (28 November 1940): 4.

74. Roosevelt, speech, 28 December 1940, in *CR*, A6992.

75. Libby, "President's Speech Alters None of These Facts," *Peace Action* 7 (December 1940): 3; Thomas, "Your World and Mine," *Call*, 11 January 1941, 5; "We Go to War," *America* 64 (11 January 1941): 379. For criticism of FDR, see also "The President's War," *Christian Century* 58 (8 January 1941): 48; "If Not a Negotiated Peace," *Christian Century* 58 (15 January 1941): 79.

76. "Up from Plenty," *Time*, 29 January 1940, 22; Taft, "Peace and Preparedness," speech in St. Louis, 20 May 1940, in *CR*, A3177; Patterson, *Taft*, 217.

77. "Senator Taft Firm for Neutrality," *Christian Century* 57 (12 June 1940): 756; Chester Bowles to Robert A. Taft, 28 May 1940, the Papers of Robert A. Taft, Library of Congress (hereafter cited as Taft Papers); Dennis, *WFL* 108 (24 August 1940): 4. Among the anti-interventionists for Taft were Raymond Moley, George E. Sokolsky, Republican leaders John Hamilton and Mrs. Preston Davie, Congressman J. Edgar Chenoweth (Colo.), Congressman Knutson, banker and former U.S. vice president Charles G. Dawes, Chicago businessman Kent Clow, and public relations executive James T. Selvage. See Boxes 62–76, Taft Papers. Hoover told Castle he found Taft the best candidate as far as intellect and honesty were concerned but lacking, in Castle's paraphrase, a "fanatical corps who will direct and vitalize his campaign." Castle Diary, 20 April 1940. Castle himself favored Taft. Diary, 29 January 1940.

78. For details of the Dewey campaign, see Richard Norton Smith, *Thomas E. Dewey and His Times* (New York: Simon & Schuster, 1982), chap. 9; Barry K. Beyer, *Thomas E. Dewey, 1937–1947: A Study in Political Leadership* (New York: Garland, 1979), chaps. 7 and 8.

79. "Newsgram—Tomorrow," *United States News*, 19 April 1940, 4; see also *United States News*, 26 April 1940, 4.

80. Smith, *Dewey*, 298.

81. For Dewey speeches, see *NYT*, 21 January 1940, 32; 30 March 1940, 8; 31 March 1940, 7; 4 May 1940, 18; 22 June 1940, 11; 23 June 1940, 2.

82. Among the anti-interventionists supporting Dewey were Colonel Theodore Roosevelt Jr. (*SFE*, 13 April 1940, 8); Oklahoma Republican leader Herbert K. Hyde (*CT*, 18 June 1940, 13); and Hiram Johnson (John C. O'Laughlin to Herbert Hoover, 11 May 1940, Stanford Files; Hiram W. Johnson to Hiram W. Johnson Jr., 4 July 1940, Johnson Papers). For the prominent role of one stanch anti-interventionist in the Dewey campaign, see Kristie Miller, *Ruth Hanna McCormick: A Life in Politics 1880–1944* (Albuquerque: University of New Mexico Press, 1992), 257–79.

83. "Thomas E. Dewey," *NYDN*, 14 June 1940, 29. See also "An Isolationist," *NYDN*, 22 June 1940, 13.

84. *CT*, 18 June 1940, 12. See also "Dewey," *CT*, 22 June 1940, 10. In a news story of 22 June, the *Tribune*'s Washington correspondent Arthur Sears Henning called him the outstanding noninterventionist in the field of Republican aspirants. See 9.

85. For negative comments, see Dennis, *WFL* 84 (7 March 1940): 6; Flynn, "Other People's Money: The Republican Campaign Huddle," *New Republic* 102 (8 April 1940): 472; Amos Pinchot to "Sir," 19 March 1940, Pinchot Papers; Villard, "Issues and Men," *Nation* 149 (19 August 1939): 197; *Social Justice*, 25 December 1939, 5.

86. Castle Diary, 29 January 1940. Castle concurred with Longworth's opposition.

87. Tompkins, *Vandenberg*, 176. Tompkins offers the best discussion of Vandenberg's brief bid for the presidency. See 175–85.

88. Nye in Tompkins, *Vandenberg*, 178, 180; Flynn in Frey, "Flynn," 183; Milton S. Mayer, "Men Who Would Be President: VI. Try to Find Vandenberg," *Nation* 150 (11 May 1940): 587.

89. "Republican Politics," *NYDN*, 26 November 1940, 49; "Confidentially Washington Correspondents Think—," *Look*, 6 December 1939, 4. See also Kenneth G. Crawford, "War and the Election," *Nation* 150 (10 February 1940): 163–64.

90. Roosevelt in Ickes, entry of 26 August 1939, *Secret Diary*, 2:707.

91. Melvin Dubofsky and Warren Van Tine, *John L. Lewis: A Biography* (New York: Quadrangle, 1977), 351–52. For Hoover's attempt to receive the nomination, see Best, *Hoover*, 1:120–22 plus chap. 5; Richard Norton Smith, *An Uncommon Man: The Triumph of Herbert Hoover* (New York: Simon & Schuster, 1984), 281–86.

92. Amos Pinchot to Randolph Walker, 26 January 1940, Pinchot Papers. On Borah, see Frank Gannett to James O'Malley, 24 January 1940, Gannett Papers.

93. For MacNider, see *NYT*, 28 June 1940, 3. For Barton, see Burke, *NYT*, 7 February 1940, 14. For Fish, see Troncone, "Fish," 345–46; *NYT*, 25 February 1940, 1. For Capper, see *Social Justice*, 24 April 1940, 20. For Lindbergh, see *Social Justice*, 3 June 1940, 1.

94. The best account of the entire Willkie campaign is found in Donald Bruce Johnson, *Wendell Willkie and the Republican Party* (Urbana: University of Illinois Press, 1960), chaps. 2–4.

95. See, for example, *NYT*, 5 May 1940, 3; 12 May 1941, 3; 29 May 1940, 16; 19 June 1940, 17.

96. McNary had opposed repeal of the arms embargo in 1939 but voted for conscription in 1940.

97. Vandenberg, undated entry, *Private Papers*, 5–6; Johnson, *Willkie*, 9; Patterson, *Taft*, 228. See also Dennis, *WFL* 115 (25 September 1940): 2; Best, *Hoover*, 1:164. Richard Norton Smith notes that Dewey and Vandenberg made overtures to Taft on the fifth ballot but were stymied by Willkie backers. See *Dewey*, 313.

98. See, for example, "The Phenomenon of Wendell Willkie," *Christian Century* 57 (5 June 1940): 275; Norman Thomas to Wendell Willkie, 11 May 1940, Thomas Papers; Frank Hanighen, memo, 18 May 1940, Hertzberg Papers.

99. Johnson, *Willkie*, 77. The eight who signed the petition were Knutson, Mundt, Keefe, Woodruff, Cliff Clevenger (Ohio), George W. Gillie (Ind.), Stephen Bolles (Wis.), and Earl Lewis (Ohio).

100. "Republican Platform of 1940," in *National Party Platforms*, 2 vols., comp. Donald Bruce Johnson (Urbana: University of Illinois Press, 1978), 1:390; Landon, *Newsweek*, 8 July 1940, 15; Best, *Hoover*, 1:163.

101. Mencken, *Time*, 1 July 1940, 17. See also Norman Thomas to Alice Dodge, 8 July 1940, Thomas Papers; Dennis, *WFL* 100 (27 June 1940): 2; *Social Justice*, 8 July 1940, 3; Flynn, "Other People's Money: The Republicans Steal FDR's Issue," *New Republic* 103 (8 July 1940): 53–54; Wheeler, speech, American Anti-War Crusade, KAOWC, 30 June 1940, in *CR*, A4313; Edwin C. Johnson, "A Plea for a Peace Plank," address at Chicago, 14 July 1940, in *CR*, A4497; "The Republican Platform," *NYDN*, 28 June 1940, 27.

102. On London conference, China, air bases, and draft, see Willkie, acceptance speech, text, *NYT*, 18 August 1940, 3; on Britain, *NYT*, 22 September 1940, 1; on destroyer bases, *NYT*, 4 September 1940, 1, 14; on FDR, Johnson, *Willkie*, 155.

103. See, for example, Castle Diary, 29 June 1940; "The Third Term a Bugaboo," *Catholic World* 152 (November 1940): 129–38; Hugh Johnson, "One Man's Opinion," *SFN*, 19 June 1940, 13; Congressman Charles Halleck (Ind.), speech, Republican National Convention, 27 July 1940, in *CR*, A4252; Sterling Morton to *Chicago Herald-American*, 28 September 1940, copy in Morton papers; Oswald Garrison Villard to Harry Elmer Barnes, 19 August 1940, Barnes Papers; Felix Morley, *Haverford* [College] *News*, 5 November 1940, 6; novelist Kathleen Norris, *SFE*, 4 August 1940, 14; "Text of John L. Lewis's Appeal for the Support of Wendell Willkie," *NYT*, 26 October 1940, 12; Anne Morrow Lindbergh, entry of 28 June 1940, *War Within*, 119–20; Philip Jessup to Barton Leach Jr., 8 August 1940, Jessup Papers; John Bassett Moore to Hiram Johnson, 25 November 1940, Moore Papers. Among the prominent anti-interventionist Democrats endorsing Willkie were Senator Burke, a conservative defeated for renomination in 1940; former senator James A. Reed (Dem.-Mo.); former justice Daniel F. Cohalan of the New York Supreme Court; Alan Valentine, president of the University of Rochester; ex-governor William F. ("Alfalfa Bill") Murray of Oklahoma; and humorist Irvin S. Cobb. *Newsweek*, 29 July 1940, 17–18. Additional bolters included Dean George H. Whipple of the University of Rochester medical school, a Nobel Prize winner (*Newsweek*, 5 August 1940, 17), and General Robert E. Wood (*Newsweek*, 16 September 1940, 17). Among the American Writers for the Opposition or American Writers for Wendell Willkie, chaired by novelist Booth Tarkington, one found such anti-interventionists as O. K. Armstrong, Bruce Barton, George T. Eggleston, George Sokolsky, and anthropologist and author Daniel Gregory Mason. Letterhead, Flynn Papers.

104. *CT*, 16 September 1940, 12; *Social Justice*, 4 November 1940, 1. For Willkie renunciation of Coughlin, see *NYT*, 28 August 1940, 1, 12.

105. See, for example, "But Boake Carter Says," *SFE*, 9 October 1940, sect. SP, 5; Hearst, "In the News," *SFE*, 10 September 1940, 1–2; Raymond Moley to John Bassett Moore, 26 July 1940, Moley Papers; "Foreign Policy in the Campaign," *Christian Century* 57 (23 October 1940): 1302–4; Charles A. Lindbergh and Arthur Vandenberg in Lindbergh, entry of 17 September 1940, *Wartime Journals*, 390; Herbert Hoover to John C. O'Laughlin, 3 September 1940, Stanford Files; Philip Burnham, "Man for the White House: Willkie," *Commonweal* 33 (1 November 1940): 44–47; "Wendell Willkie," *America* 63 (6 July 1940): 350; J. H. Gipson, president of Caxton printers, to Frederick J. Libby, 26 October 1940, NCPW Papers; Jay Hormel to Wendell Willkie [copy], 26 October 1940, Wood Papers; Amos Pinchot to Wendell Willkie, 9 October 1940, Pinchot Papers. An unsigned memo in the AFC Papers said that Flynn was not personally voting for Willkie but would give a broadcast on 3 November stressing the dangers of FDR getting the nation into war. No date, Box 282. See also Frey, "Flynn," 184; Dorothy Dunbar Bromley, "The Lesser Danger" (special supplement), *Uncensored* 57 (2 November 1940): 1.

106. Hiram W. Johnson to Hiram W. Johnson Jr., 30 August 1940, Johnson Papers.

107. See, for example, insurance executive Asa V. Call to Hiram W. Johnson, 1 July 1940, Johnson Papers; "The Third World War," *NYDN*, 7 July 1940, 35; John Bassett Moore to Edwin B. Borchard, 5 October 1940, Borchard Papers; Edwin M. Borchard to John Bassett Moore, 3 October 1940, Borchard Papers; "Mr. Willkie's Speech," *Christian Century* 57 (28 August 1940): 1045–47; Harry Elmer Barnes, [George Washington University] *Hatchet*, 17 December 1940, 1.

108. Wheeler, speech to Anti-War Crusade, KAOWC, 30 June 1940, in *CR*, A4312.

109. Sterling Morton to Kenneth McEwen, 10 May 1939, Morton Papers; Harry S. Ashmore, *Unseasonable Truths: The Life of Robert Maynard Hutchins* (Boston: Little, Brown, 1989), 207–9; Milton Mayer, *Robert Maynard Hutchins: A Memoir* (Berkeley: University of California Press, 1993), 209–12, 222. For additional treatment of Hutchins's views, see Joseph E. Jaffe Jr., "Isolationism and Neutrality in Academe, 1938–1941," Ph.D. diss., Case Western Reserve University, 1979, chaps 1–3.

110. For Kennedy, see Beschloss, *Kennedy and Roosevelt*, 202–3; Koskoff, *Kennedy*, 234–37. For Garner, see *Social Justice*, 1 January 1940, 20. For Farley, see *Social Justice*, 29 July 1940, 6. Though he studiously avoided comments on public policy, Farley later claimed to be an anti-interventionist. James A. Farley, *Jim Farley's Story: The Roosevelt Years* (New York: Whittlesey House, 1948), 241.

111. Villard suggested Interior Secretary Harold Ickes, Agriculture Secretary Henry Wallace, Secretary of State Cordell Hull, Joseph Eastman of the Interstate Commerce Commission, Governor Herbert Lehman of New York, and Associate Justice William O. Douglas. Villard, "Issues and Men," *Nation* 150 (2 March 1940): 310.

112. For the best work on Wheeler, see John Thomas Anderson, "Senator Burton K. Wheeler and United States Foreign Relations," Ph.D. diss., University of Virginia, 1982. For the Wheeler campaign, see Cole, *Roosevelt*, 385–88.

113. "Evolution of a Senator," *Time*, 14 June 1940, 15–16.

114. Burton K. Wheeler with Paul F. Healy, *Yankee from the West* (Garden City, N.Y.: Doubleday, 1962), 363.

115. Wheeler's view in Frank Hanighen to Sidney Hertzberg, 8 July [1940], Hertzberg Papers.

116. Wheeler, *Yankee from the West*, 366–88, to Bernard F. Donahoe, *Private Plans and Public Dangers: The Story of FDR's Third Nomination* (South Bend, Ind.: University of Notre Dame Press, 1965), 14, 228–29 n. 56.

117. Robert Bendiner, "Men Who Would Be President: V. Burton K. Wheeler," *Nation* 150 (27 April 1940): 536.

118. Wheeler, *NYT*, 13 June 1940, 1, 8; *CR*, 12 June 1940, 8055; Wheeler, speech, American Anti-War Crusade, KAOWC, 30 June 1940, in *CR*, A4313. For other threats to bolt the Democratic Party over the war issue, see Bennett Champ Clark, *Newsweek*, 1 July 1940, 29; Edwin C. Johnson, "A Third Party May Be the Answer," radio address, Mutual Network, 15 May 1940, in *CR*, A3920.

119. Roy W. Howard in Wheeler, *Yankee from the West*, 363; Frank Hanighen to Sidney Hertzberg, 8 July [1940], Hertzberg Papers; *Social Justice*, 11 March 1940, 20; Robert E. Wood to Burton K. Wheeler, 14 June 1940, Wood Papers; Chester Bowles to Philip La Follette, 8 July 1940, Philip La Follette Papers; Edwin M. Borchard to R. Douglas Stuart Jr., 3 October 1940, Borchard Papers; Edwin Johnson, "A Plea for a Peace Plank," address at Chicago, 14 July 1940, in *CR*, A4498. The pro-Roosevelt *NYDN*, in endorsing Wheeler as vice-presidential candidate, saw his anti-interventionism as a positive factor. "Why Not Draft Wheeler?" 12 July 1940, 23.

120. Lewis, *NYT*, 27 January 1940, 1; *NYT*, 3 July 1940, 1.

121. "Democratic Platform of 1940," in Johnson, *Platforms*, 382–83.

122. Lindbergh, *NYT*, 15 October 1940, 1, 8.

123. See, for example, Hugh Johnson, *WTH*, 6 September 1940; merchandiser Ira Hirschmann to Dorothy Detzer, 7 September 1940, WIL Papers; Robert E. Wood, *CT*, 16 October 1940, 8; David I. Walsh, Castle Diary, 23 August 1940.

124. "An Ominous Nomination," *Christian Century* 57 (31 July 1940): 943; Rovere, "Campaign Caravan: Who's an Appeaser?" *Call*, 12 October 1940, 4.

125. Flynn, "Other People's Money: Happy Days Are Here Again," *New Republic* 103 (16 September 1940): 385; *Country Squire in the White House* (New York: Doubleday, Doran, 1940), 106, 113.

126. See, for example, Alf Landon to John T. Flynn, 3 September 1940, Flynn Papers; Hiram Johnson to William F. Knowland, 28 July 1940, Johnson Papers; John Haynes Holmes to Oswald Garrison Villard, 3 October 1940, Villard Papers; Castle Diary, 14 August 1940; John Haynes Holmes, "The Real Roosevelt," *Unity* 126 (16 September 1940): 30; Aaron Levenstein, "Roosevelt, the Militarist," *Call*, 10 August 1940, 4; Alf Landon to John T. Flynn, 19 September 1940, Box 18, Flynn Papers.

127. Sargent, Bulletin #82, 26 August 1940, *Getting US into War*, 439–41.

128. For endorsement, see *CT*, 1 September 1940, 6. For the beginning of serialization, see *CT*, 21 October 1940, 1.

129. See, for example, John C. Cort, *Commonweal* 33 (1 November 1940): 60–61; Hamilton Basso, "Books in Review: The Great Profile," *New Republic* 103 (29 July 1940): 146–47; anonymous writer, "The President," *NYT Book Review*, 14 July 1940, 15.

130. Chamberlain, "The New Books," *Harper's Magazine* 181 (October 1940), in advertising section.

131. See, for example, John Chamberlain and Stuart Chase in "Poll," *Uncensored* 57 (2 November 1940): special supplement, 2; Quincy Howe, "Roosevelt, Willkie, Thomas?" (special supplement), *Uncensored* 55 (19 October 1940); Will Durant to *NYT*, 31 October 1940, Roosevelt Papers; Alfred Bingham, "How They Are Voting: III," *New Republic* 103 (21 October 1940): 553; *St. Louis Post-Dispatch*, 13 October 1940; Charles A. Beard, [University of] *Rochester Tower Times*, 4 October 1940; Sidney Hyman, *The Lives of William Benton* (Chicago: University of Chicago Press, 1969), 238; "Bob La Follette Says," *Progressive*, 5 October 1940, 1; Harry Elmer Barnes to Lowell Mellett, 11 November 1940, Barnes Papers. Barnes had written Villard in August that Willkie was no more than "Coolidge with a goat-gland operation and a gardenia. We will have to vote for Norman [Thomas] and despair of the Republic." Letter, 16 August 1940, Villard Papers.

132. "Thinking Out Loud," *NYDN*, 30 July 1940, 19. See also "Should Draft Roosevelt," *NYDN*, 10 July 1940, 31. Cissy Patterson's *Washington Times-Herald*, whose editorials were usually direct reprints of those of the *NYDN*, was the only pro-FDR paper in the nation's capital.

133. See, for example, Usher Burdick, *CR*, 3 September 1940, 11,380.

134. "The Campaign," *Uncensored* 52 (28 September 1940): 1. See also "Voice of the People," *Uncensored* 39 (29 June 1940): 1.

135. Dennis, *WFL*, 31 October 1940, 3; Mencken, "Heil Roosevelt," *Baltimore Sun*, 25 September 1940.

136. A. J. Muste to Lucille B. Milner, 30 October 1940, WIL Papers. See also Norman Thomas, "Your World and Mine," *Call*, 9 November 1940, 6; Libby, "Willkie Is Surrounded by Interventionists," *Peace Action* 7 (September 1940): 2. Noting that the Senate was bound to remain Democratic, Libby hoped that the Republicans could capture the House, thereby restoring "checks and balances."

137. For example, see Cushman Reynolds, Burton Rascoe, Sidney Hertzberg, and Frank Hanighen, "Poll," *Uncensored* 57 (2 November 1940): special supplement, 2; John Haynes Holmes and critic Edmund Wilson, "How They Are Voting: III," *New Republic* 103 (21 October 1940): 554; *American Guardian*, 1 November 1940, 1; economist William Orton, *Smith College Weekly*, 11 October 1940, 2. Several anti-interventionists said they would vote for Thomas in protest if Roosevelt's election appeared certain. See Selden Rodman, "Poll," *Uncensored* 57 (2 November 1940): special supplement, 2; political scientist Fred Rodell, "How They Are Voting: III," *New Republic* 103 (21 October 1940): 553.

138. Rovere, "How They Are Voting: II," *New Republic* 103 (30 September 1940): 445; Burton K. Wheeler to Norman Thomas, 7 January 1941, Thomas Papers.

139. Roosevelt address at Boston, *NYT*, 31 October 1940, 14.

140. For stress on foreign policy, in particular the claim that the distressing European situation aided Roosevelt, see Johnson, *Willkie*, 162; Robert Divine, *Foreign Policy and U.S. Presidential Elections, 1940–1960*, 2 vols. (New York: New Viewpoints, 1974), 1: 85; Justus D. Doenecke, "The Election of 1940," in *Running for President: The Candidates and Their Images*, 2 vols., ed. Arthur M. Schlesinger Jr. (New York: Simon & Schuster, 1994), 2:209. For the claim that in some ways Willkie's anti-interventionist posture helped him, see Herbert S. Parmet and Marie B. Hecht, *Never Again: A President Runs for a Third Term* (New York: Macmillan, 1968), 276–77. In June, Gallup polls showed 66 percent ready to vote for the candidate standing for increased aid to the Allies. *Newsweek*, 10 June 1940, 32.

141. See, for example, Hanighen, "Capital Letter: Hard Words for the New Deal," *Common Sense* 9 (November 1940): 11; "President Roosevelt's Responsibility," *Christian Century* 57 (13 November 1940): 1408; Sargent, Bulletin #78, *Getting US into War*, 423; Hugh Johnson, "One Man's Opinion," *SFN*, 1 November 1940, 11; Chamberlin Diary, 5 November 1940. Amos Pinchot bore Willkie no bitterness, finding him "pretty nearly a great man." Amos Pinchot to Douglas Johnson, Columbia University, 7 November 1940, Pinchot Papers.

142. Dennis, *WFL* 119 (7 November 1940): 1; Hearst, "In the News," *SFE*, 7 November 1940, 1–2.

143. *Uncensored* noted the election of such senators as Johnson of California, Thomas of Idaho, Shipstead of Minnesota, Vandenberg of Michigan, Wheeler of Montana, Walsh of Massachusetts, Maloney of Connecticut, La Follette of Wisconsin, and Brooks (Rep.-Ill.). Both Jeanette Rankin (Rep.-Mont.) and Fish were sent to the House. See "The Mandate," *Uncensored* 58 (9 November 1940): 1–2. See also Sargent, Bulletin #94, 19 November 1940, *Getting US into War*, 516 n. 1; "President Roosevelt's Responsibility," *Christian Century* 57 (13 November 1940): 1408; "Election Postscript," *New Masses* 37 (26 November 1940): 11.

144. Libby, "Election Showed Nation Anti-War," *Peace Action* 7 (November 1940): 2, 8; "Discussion Outline," issues by National Education Committee of the Socialist Party and the Young People's Socialist League, [December 1940?], Socialist Party Papers. Mentioned were senators William H. King (Dem.-Utah) and Sherman Minton (Dem.-Ind.), and New Jersey Democrat James Cromwell, former minister to Canada who was nominated for the Senate.

145. Hiram W. Johnson to Hiram W. Johnson Jr., 9 November 1940, Johnson Papers. For other examples of such disillusion, see Yale economist Richard Bissell, *Yale Daily News*, 6 November 1940, 1–2; Dennis, *WFL* 119 (7 November 1940): 1; Castle Diary, 6 November 1940.

## CHAPTER 11: LEND-LEASE AND THE "FUTILE WAR"

1. For histories of the AFC, see Cole, *America First*, and Doenecke, *IDU*. For Flynn and the AFC, see Stenehjem, *American First*.

2. For portraits of Wood, see Justus D. Doenecke, "General Robert E. Wood: The Evolution of a Conservative," *Journal of the Illinois State Historical Society* 71 (August 1978): 162–75; Doenecke, "The Isolationism of General Robert E. Wood," *Three Faces of Midwestern Isolationism*, ed. John H. Schacht (Iowa City, Iowa: Center for the Study of the Recent History of the United States, 1981), 11–22.

3. Doenecke, *IDU*, 16, 57 n. 55. Lipsig was aided by Cushman Reynolds, who intermittently edited *Uncensored*.

4. Justus D. Doenecke, "Verne Marshall's Leadership of the No Foreign War Committee, 1940," *Annals of Iowa* 41 (Winter 1973): 1153–72.

5. Stimson in Edward R. Stettinius Jr., *Lend-Lease: Weapon for Victory* (New York: Macmillan, 1944), 65.

6. For Britain's condition, see Ponting, *1940*, 205–10; quotation, 209.

7. Winston Churchill to Franklin D. Roosevelt, 8 December 1940, in Kimball, *Churchill and Roosevelt*, 1:102–9.

8. *NYT*, 18 December 1940, 10; press conference, 17 December 1940, in Rosenman, *Roosevelt Papers and Addresses*, 9:604–15.

9. "President's Call for Full Response on Defense," *NYT*, 30 December 1940, 6; Reynolds, *Creation*, 159.

10. "Text of Lease-Lend Bill," *NYT*, 11 January 1941, 1, 3; *Newsweek*, 20 January 1940, 16; AFC, "A Factual Analysis of H.R. 1776," n.d. [1941], inserted by D. W. Clark, *CR*, 28 February 1941, A901–2; "No. 1776," *Time*, 20 January 1941, 15.

11. See, for example, Van Zandt, *CR*, 5 February 1941, 587; Amos Pinchot to John T. Flynn, 29 January 1941, Pinchot Papers; Fish, *CR*, 3 February 1941, 501; McCarran, *Time*, 3 March 1941, 16; Tinkham, *CR*, 5 February 1941, 627; Shipstead, *CR*, 26 February 1941, 1346; Danaher, *CR*, 8 March 1941, 2078.

12. Howard K. Beale to Charles A. Plumley [copy], 27 January 1941, NCPW Papers; "No Compromise!" *Christian Century* 58 (22 January 1941): 113.

13. Shafer, *CR*, 5 February 1941, 598; Lambertson, *CR*, 7 February 1941, A530; Marcantonio, *CR*, 4 February 1941, 560; "The Economic Consequences of the Lease-Lend Program," n.d. [1941], Box 279, AFC Papers. See also Maas, speech to sixteenth Women's Patriotic Conference on National Defense, 28 January 1941, in *CR*, A694; Robert Rice Reynolds, *Time*, 3 March 1941, 16.

14. For examples, see resolution, American Coalition of Patriotic Societies, 27 January 1941, SFRC, 656; Congressman Day, *CR*, 3 February 1941, 518; Congresswoman Rogers, *CR*, 6 February 1941, 654; Henry Cabot Lodge, *CR*, 10 February 1941, 627; B. C. Clark, *CR*, 18 February 1941, 1098; Wheeler, *CR*, 28 February 1941, 1520; "Spirit of '76," *Uncensored* 68 (18 January 1941): 3; "Power of the Purse," *NYDN*, 14 January 1941, 21; "Secretary Hull on the Dictatorship Bill," *NYDN*, 17 January 1941, 27; Roy W. Howard to Ralph Heinzen, 21 January 1941, Box 179, Howard Papers; Alan Valentine, testimony, SFRC, 5 February 1941, 401; Charles A. Beard, testimony, SFRC, 4 February 1941, 309; "Comment," *America* 64 (25 January 1941): 422; Waldrop, "What Are Munitions?" *WTH*, 7 March 1941, 12.

15. John Bassett Moore to Hiram Johnson, 25 January 1941, in *CR*, 653; Fish, 7 February 1941, *CR*, 769.

16. See, for example, Senator Tobey, *CR*, 5 March 1941, 1791; Norman Thomas, testimony, HFAC, 22 February 1941, 340; Thomas, testimony, SFRC, 3 February 1941, 301; John Danaher to Philip Jessup, 13 January 1941, Jessup Papers; Representative Thomas K. Winter (Rep.-Kans.), *CR*, 5 February 1941, 608.

17. Villard, "Crossing the Rubicon," *Progressive*, 15 February 1941, 6; "Secretary Hull on the Dictatorship Bill," *NYDN*, 17 January 1941, 27; Holmes, "Editorial Comment," *Unity* 127 (April 1941): 22; Peale, 14 February 1941, Box 62, AFC Papers. See also "Behold! The Brass Serpent," *Saturday Evening Post* 213 (15 February 1941): 26.

18. MacNider, radio broadcast over Washington, D.C., station WOL, 22 January 1941, in *CR*, A259; Joseph P. Kennedy to Congressman Louis Ludlow, 14 December 1940, in *CR*, 30 January 1941, 423; "The Economic Consequences of the Lease-Lend Program," n.d. [1941], Box 279, AFC Papers. See also "Butter or Guns," *Uncensored* 75 (8 March 1941): 3–4.

19. Lindbergh, testimony, SFRC, 6 February 1941, 526, 528; Fish, *CR*, 5 February 1941, 659; Wheeler, *CR*, 17 February 1941, 1045, 1052; Mundt, *CR*, 5 February 1941, 611; Keefe, *CR*, 30 January 1941, 420; Woodruff, *CR*, 7 February 1941, 774; Al Williams, testimony, SFRC, 7 February 1941, 578–79; Al Williams, "U.S. Air Power," *Progressive*, 15 February 1941, 5.

20. Walsh, *CR*, 7 March 1941, 2003. Walsh's amendment lost 33 to 56, with 6 not voting. *CR*, 8 March 1941, 2050. For support, see Taft, *CR*, 7 March 1941, 2039; AFC, *Washington News Letter* 4 (19 February 1941): 1, Box 281, AFC Papers.

21. See, for example, Van Zandt's use of Marshall and Stimson, *CR*, 5 February 1941, 558.

22. Lumber merchant George Cless, testimony, HFAC, 24 January 1941, 566; Congressman Frederick C. Smith, *CR*, 5 February 1941, 670; Sokolsky, "These Days: Merchants of Doom," *New York Sun*, 8 February 1941, 16; "These Days: Let There Be Light!" *New York Sun*, 15 February 1941, 16.

23. "The Economic Consequences of the Lease-Lend Program," n.d. [1941], 7–21, Box 279, AFC Papers; Frank Hanighen to *Uncensored*, received 20 December [1940], Hertzberg Papers; "Ubiquitous $$$," *Uncensored* 64 (21 December 1941): 2. See also "Our Passing Democracy," *America* 64 (25 January 1941): 435.

24. Danaher, *CR*, 7 March 1941, 1995. The amendment was defeated 33 to 48, with 14 not voting. See 1996–97. For similar concerns by Carl Ackerman, dean of the Columbia University School of Journalism, see Ackerman to Robert A. Taft, n.d., entered in *CR*, 3 March 1941, 1654.

25. See, for example, John A. Danaher to Edwin M. Borchard, 13 January 1941, Borchard Papers. Congressman Dworshak introduced an amendment prohibiting the authorization of any violation of international law. It was defeated 94 to 142. See *CR*, 8 February 1941, 814.

26. Dennis, "Memorandum on Certain Points Raised in Connection with the Lend-Lease Bill," entered in *CR*, 7 March 1941, 2005; Dennis, testimony, HFAC, 24 January 1941, 577.

27. For the Washington Treaty and the Hague Conference, see Danaher, *CR*, 24 February 1941, 1313. For the Kellogg–Briand pact, see Taft and Danaher, *CR*, 24 February 1941, 1319. For the Panama Declaration, see Chavez, speech, NBC, 1 March 1941, in *CR*, A934; Castle, testimony, HFAC, 23 January 1941, 518; Norman Thomas, testimony, SFRC, 3 February 1941, 291; AFC, "A Factual Analysis of H.R. 1776," inserted by D. W. Clark, 28 February 1941, A902.

28. See, for example, "Road Out of Crisis?" *Commonweal* 33 (24 January 1941): 339; "Is It a 'Go-to-War' Bill?" *Christian Century* 58 (12 March 1941): 347; Roy W. Howard to Nelson T. Johnson, 24 March 1941, Box 180, Howard Papers; Howard to Lord Beaverbrook, 14 May 1941, Box 180, Howard Papers;

William Dennis, testimony, HFAC, 24 January 1941, 580; Edwin M. Borchard, letter to SFRC, hearings, 25 January 1941, 653.

29. Thomas, HFAC, 22 January 1941, 349.

30. Signers included Wendell H. Furry, Frederick Merk, F. O. Matthiessen, Edmund S. Morgan, Mark Schorer, Carl E. Schorske, Delmore Schwartz, Paul M. Sweezy, Kirtley Mather, and Frederick B. Tolles. *Harvard* [University] *Crimson*, 7 February 1941, 1, 4.

31. Rankin, *CR*, 8 February 1941, 813. It was voted down 82 to 137. See 814.

32. See, for example, Jonathan T. Pratt, "War Partnership—It Can't Be Limited," *Scribner's Commentator* 9 (March 1941): 71–72; Hiram W. Johnson to Hiram W. Johnson Jr., 5 May 1941, Johnson Papers; Taft, *CR*, 22 February 1941, 1281; "Why Destroy Ourselves?" *CT*, 1 March 1941, 16; international law professor Herbert Wright in Frank Hanighen to Cushman Reynolds, n.d. [9 February 1941], Hertzberg Papers.

33. Wheeler, American Forum of the Air, 12 January 1941, in *CR*, A178; "Untruthful . . . Dastardly . . . Unpatriotic . . . Rottenest," *NYDN*, 16 January 1941, 25.

34. Vandenberg, *CR*, 18 February 1941, 1106. For another such reference to the Brooklyn Navy Yard, see "Our Passing Democracy," *America* 64 (25 January 1941): 435. During the appropriations debate, Mundt introduced an amendment banning the outfitting of foreign ships in U.S. ports. See support from Representatives Bolton and Francis H. Case (Rep.-S.Dak.). *CR*, 19 March 1941, 2367–70. The amendment was voted down 67 to 107. See 2372.

35. R. Douglas Stuart Jr. to Donald McDonald, 10 January 1941, Box 62, AFC Papers.

36. Taft, *CR*, 22 February 1941, 1281; 5 March 1941, 1823. Taft conceded that the president had some power to send naval vessels outside the Western Hemisphere. However, the bill, he claimed, would permit him to establish bases in Singapore, Gibraltar, Egypt, and even Britain itself. *CR*, 7 March 1941, 1971, 1973.

37. Taft, *CR*, 8 March 1941, 2079. Castle also recalled the *Alabama* claims issue. Testimony, HFAC, 23 January 1941, 501.

38. See, for example, Congressman Arends, *CR*, 29 January 1941, 383; Hugh Johnson, testimony, HFAC, 23 January 1941, 439; Castle, testimony, HFAC, 24 January 1941, 506, 513; General Wood, testimony, SFRC, 4 February 1941, 350; Professor Herbert Wright, testimony, SFRC, 5 February 1941, 457; Alf Landon, testimony, SFRC, 8 February 1941, 664; Robsion, *CR*, 5 February 1941, 641; Frank Hanighen to Cushman Reynolds, 9 January 1941, Hertzberg Papers; Edwin M. Borchard to James Shanley, 13 January 1941 and 8 February 1941, Borchard Papers; "Bad Logic by Morgenthau," *NYDN*, 30 January 1941, 23; Fish, *CR*, 13 January 1941, 136; Wheeler, *CR*, 1 March 1941, 1602.

39. Gillette, *CR*, 8 March 1941, 2064. It was voted down 33 to 55, with 7 not voting. See 2065.

40. *NYT*, 22 January 1941, 1; Warren F. Kimball, *The Most Unsordid Act: Lend-Lease, 1939–1941* (Baltimore: Johns Hopkins University Press, 1969), 180–81; Watson, *Chief of Staff*, 125.

41. *CR*, 6 February 1941, 749; Kimball, *Most Unsordid Act*, 201.

42. Kimball, *Forged in War*, 71; Morgenthau in *Newsweek*, "Battle of '1776,'" 27 January 1941, 14.

43. Beard, testimony, SFRC, 3 February 1941, 313. See also "Britain Has Resources in America," *Christian Century* 58 (19 February 1941): 245. For concrete estimates, see Robsion ($8 billion), *CR*, 8 February 1941, A577; Reynolds ($10 billion), *CR*, 20 February 1941, 1214; John T. Flynn ($4.5 billion), memo to HFAC, in *CR*, 18 February 1941, 1116; Fish ($3 billion), radio broadcast, 13 January 1941, in *CR*, A91; R. Douglas Stuart Jr. ($2 billion), letter to General Wood, 5 December 1940, Box 63, AFC Papers; Congressman Andresen (between $7 billion and $10 billion), *CR*, 7 February 1941, 767; *CT* (between $4 billion and $5 billion) in editorial "Britain's Financial Position," 12 December 1941, 16; *Uncensored* ($6 billion) in "Dollar Assets," 69 (25 January 1941): 4.

44. Wood, testimony, SFRC, 4 February 1941, 373; Kimball, *Most Unsordid Act*, 225.

45. See, for example, "Mr. Roosevelt's Lost Opportunity," *Christian Century* 58 (1 January 1941): 6; Congressman Fred L. Crawford (Rep.-Mich.), *CR*, 19 March 1941, 2360–1; Congresswoman Rogers, HFAC, 22 January 1941, 331; Maas, *CR*, 22 February 1941, 1276; Castle, testimony, HFAC, 24 January 1941, 532; Hanford MacNider to Milo J. Warner, 20 December 1940, MacNider Papers.

46. See, for example, B. C. Clark, *CR*, 18 February 1941, 1118; Senator Albert J. Ellender (Dem.-La.), *CR*, 5 March 1941, 1807–8; Bulow, *CR*, 21 February 1941, 1258.

47. Taft, *CR*, 22 February 1941, 1276. See also Shipstead, *CR*, 18 February 1941, 1119.

48. "Dollars vs. Empire," *Uncensored* 62 (7 December 1940): 2.

49. See, for example, Bone and B. C. Clark, *CR*, 20 February 1941, 1119, 1120; Reynolds, *CR*, 20 February 1941, 1213; Helen Essary, "Dear Washington," *WTH*, 28 January 1941, 8.

50. William Benton to R. M. La Follette Jr. 17 December 1940, in Doenecke, *IDU*, 100–101. See also Benton, *CT*, 8 January 1941, 1. The paper was friendly to the idea. "The Benton Test and Some Others," 11 January 1941, 10.

51. Nye, speech, Mutual network, 19 January 1941, in *CR*, A1334.

52. George N. Peek to R. Douglas Stuart Jr., 11 December 1940, AFC Papers. For additional mention of gold production, see Congressman John R. Jennings Jr., *CR*, 5 February 1941, 665.

53. Marcantonio, *CR*, 4 February 1941, 555. See also Maas, *CR*, 4 February 1941, 555; Flynn in Stenehjem, *American First*, 68. For similar concerns, see "Dollars vs. Empire (con't)," *Uncensored* 71 (8 February 1941): 2. R. Douglas Stuart Jr., however, stressed Britain's sorry plight. Shipping losses, he said, exceeded the rate of April 1917. Shipment of fruit had been curtailed entirely. Meat rationing had been severely increased. Several ports were closed. R. Douglas Stuart Jr. to Robert E. Wood, 5 February 1941, Box 63, AFC Papers.

54. "Status of British Shipping," *CT*, 16 December 1940, 16. See also "Mr. Roosevelt's Crisis," *CT*, 19 December 1940, 18.

55. "The British Ship Supply," *CT*, 23 December 1940, 10; Wheeler, *CR*, 18 February 1941, 1120. For reaction to the dominions, see "Canada Doesn't Lend-Lease," *NYWT*, 8 February 1941; Taft, *CR*, 18 February 1941, 1116; B. C. Clark, *CR*, 18 February 1941, 1118; Congressman Clifford Hope, *CR*, 7 February 1941, 775.

56. Hart, testimony, SFRC, 7 February 1941, 756.

57. See, for example, Hugh Johnson, testimony, HFAC, 23 January 1941, 441; William R. Castle, HFAC, 24 January 1941, 532; Congressman Walter C. Ploeser (Rep.-Mo.), *CR*, 4 February 1941, 568; Charles A. Beard, testimony, SFRC, 3 February 1941, 313; Professor Herbert Wright, SFRC, 5 February 1941, 453. Fish sought $2 million. Troncone, "Fish," 361. Rich suggested $5 billion. See *CR*, 4 February 1941, 560. Sokolsky suggested $10 billion. "Shall the Small Invaded Nations Be Fed?" *American Forum of the Air* 3 (23 February 1941): 9.

58. Taft added several qualifiers. First, the president must certify that the borrower nation is unable to provide for its U.S. purchases. Second, such sums can only be used for buying U.S.-made goods. Third, the president shall require either adequate security, territory and investments, or naval and military bases in South America or elsewhere. Fourth, the chief of staff and the chief of naval operations must certify to the president that the articles shipped are dispensable. If more money was needed, Taft said, he was willing to adjust the sum. His proposal was voted down 29 to 62, with 4 not voting. Taft, *CR*, 8 March 1941, 2080–82. Kimball claims that the figure of $2 billion appeared to hold some fascination for the Republicans. They introduced three amendments containing this amount. *Most Unsordid Act*, 201. See also Fish, *CR*, 3 February 1941, 488; Richard B. Wigglesworth (Rep.-Mass.), 5 February 1941, 610; House minority report in *CR*, 5 February 1941, 663–64.

59. See, for example, Joseph P. Kennedy, radio address, 28 January 1941, in *CR*, in testimony, HFAC, 261; Vermont manufacturer Ralph Flanders to Senator George Aiken, in *CR*, 13 February 1941, A635; Congressman Clifford Hope, *CR*, 5 February 1941, 607; Alf Landon, testimony, SFRC, 7 February 1941, 684; Landon to Verne Marshall, 30 December 1940, Verne Marshall Papers; Hugh Johnson, testimony, HFAC, 23 January 1941, 442.

60. Johnson, *CR*, 28 January 1941, 258; Herbert Hoover to William R. Castle, 1 March 1941, Castle Papers; Aiken, *CR*, 6 March 1941, 1869. Aiken said the United States could provide patrol bombers and supply shipbuilding funds, so Canada could recondition British warships and construct torpedo boats.

61. Wood, testimony, SFRC, 4 February 1941, 347–49. Robert E. Wood to R. J. Finnegan, 22 January 1941, Box 292, AFC Papers; debate with Senator Ernest W. Gibson Jr., Advertising Men's Post #38, American Legion, Chicago, 3 February 1941, in Box 35, AFC Papers. For another mention of gifts or loans, see "Aid to Britain Without H.R. 1776," *CT*, 3 February 1941, 12.

62. See, for example, Lindbergh, testimony, SFRC, 6 February 1941, 534; Merwin K. Hart, testimony, SFRC, 8 February 1941, 769; Barry, testimony, HFAC, 25 January 1941, 682; Jennings, *CR*, 5 February 1941, 665; Tobey, *CR*, 5 March 1941, 1790; John Chamberlain to Mark Prentiss, 30 December 1940, Box 35, AFC Papers; Frank Hanighen to *Uncensored*, received 20 February [1941], Hertzberg Papers.

63. "What Is Your Life Worth?" *NYDN*, 5 January 1941, 41; Wood, testimony, SFRC, 4 February 1941, 375–76.

64. Any further amount could be repaid in rubber, tin, or tea, or by a mortgage on British gold production. Fish, radio broadcast, CBS, 13 January 1941, in *CR*, A91. Once Britain could no longer supply securities and collateral, U.S. supplies should be given. Fish, HFAC, 21 January 1941, 315. A few anti-interventionists balked at taking Britain's hemispheric possessions. Norman Thomas called them "run-down slum property." Testimony, HFAC, 22 January 1941, 331. The *CT*, denying that any relationship could be forced, said that eventually the islands would gravitate naturally to the American flag. "British Citizens and American Bases," 28 January 1941, 10.

65. Maas, *CR*, 4 February 1941, 557. The *Washington Daily News*, a Scripps-Howard paper, found $16 billion to be overpayment but stressed the role of the British possessions in defending the Panama Canal. See "The Billion Dollars for Britain," 5 February 1941. See also Congressman Gerald W. Landis (Rep.-Ind.), *CR*, 4 February 1941, 563; Mundt, *CR*, 5 February 1941, 650. However, on 6 February the chair ruled that the amendment was not germaine to the bill. See 727. See also the amendment of Congressman John M. Costello (Dem.-Calif.), *CR*, 7 February 1941, 767. Andresen spoke for the amendment. *CR*, 767, 769.

66. Barry, *CR*, 4 February 1941, 528; Nye, speech, Mutual network, 19 January 1941, A1334; Wiley, *CR*, 4 March 1941, 1717.

67. Lincoln Colcord to Robert E. Wood, 6 January 1941, Box 59, AFC Papers. R. Douglas Stuart Jr. found Colcord correct in thinking an absolutely neutral stand more rational. However, he told Colcord to be aware of the intense public sentiment and the fact that "logical consideration *[sic]* do not prevent those who advocate strict neutrality from being widely and hopelessly discredited." R. Douglas Stuart Jr. to Lincoln Colcord, 8 February 1941, Box 59, AFC Papers.

68. Dennis, *WFL* 27, 2 January 1941, 2.

69. Wood, testimony, SFRC, 3 February 1941, 348.

70. McCormick, testimony, SFRC, 6 February 1941, 487.

71. Lindbergh, testimony, SFRC, 6 February 1941, 494. Senator Claude Pepper (Dem.-Fla.), a strong interventionist, doubted if Lindbergh's policies and judgments would have permitted the sending of one rifle or round of ammunition to Britain. Lindbergh concurred with Pepper. *CR*, 527.

72. For time limits, see, for example, William R. Castle, testimony, HFAC, 24 January 1941, 514; Benjamin Marsh, executive secretary, People's Lobby, testimony, HFAC, 550; "No Blank Check," *St. Louis Post-Dispatch*, 24 January 1941; "Bad Logic by Morgenthau," *NYDN*, 30 January 1941, 23; Fish, *CR*, 4 February 1941, 559. For spending limits, see Joseph P. Kennedy, testimony, HFAC, 24 January 1941, 231. The AFC mistrusted time limits on the grounds that they gave a false sense of security. *Washington News Letter* 1 (31 January 1941), in Doenecke, *IDU*, 226.

73. Vandenberg, *CR*, 7 March 1941, 1991–92. It was defeated 36 to 45, with 14 not voting. See 1994. For Vorys, see *CR*, 6 February 1941, 727. For support, see Raymond Moley, "H.R. 1776," *Newsweek*, 20 January 1941, 64. A similar amendment by Fish, centering on congressional consent for the transfer of any navy vessel, was defeated 123 to 183. See *CR*, 7 February 1941, 775.

74. Kimball, *Most Unsordid Act*, 210–11, 214–16.

75. *NYT*, 9 March 1941, 1; *NYT*, 12 March 1941, 1, 3.

76. Gallup poll, 7 March 1941, in Cantril, *Public Opinion*, 410. For related polls, see Cantril, *Public Opinion*, 409–10.

77. Diary entry, 8 March 1941, in *Private Papers*, 10. Emphasis Vandenberg's.

78. Land in J. Garry Clifford, "A Connecticut Colonel's Candid Conversation with the Wrong Commander-in-Chief," *Connecticut History* 28 (November 1988): 28.

79. Reynolds, *Creation*, 167, 273–82. For continued anxieties over the British closed economy, see Berle, entry of 17 July 1941, *Navigating*, 373.

80. Reynolds, *Creation*, 275–82.

81. Robert E. Sherwood, *Roosevelt and Hopkins: An Intimate History* (New York: Harper, 1948), 270.

82. Thomas A. Bailey and Paul B. Ryan, *Hitler vs. Roosevelt: The Undeclared Naval War* (New York: Free Press, 1979), 113.

83. Kimball, *Most Unsordid Act*, 241.

84. "Air Power and the Battle of Britain," *Uncensored* 76 (15 March 1941): 3–4; article by Sherman B. Altick in memo, Barbara McDonald, speaker's bureau, 27 February 1941, AFC Papers.

85. McCormick, *WTH*, 6 February 1941, 2. See also McCormick, testimony, SFRC, 6 February 1941, 485–86.

86. "Salonika: The Back Door," *CT*, 15 March 1941, 12. For other examples of *Tribune* optimism, see "An Excited Spokesman," 7 January 1941, 12; "Prospects in Africa and Elsewhere," 1 February 1941, 16; "British and Greek Victories," 10 February 1941, 10; "A Campaign of Fear and Hysteria," 6 March 1941, 14.

87. "The Big Spring Rush," *NYDN*, 30 January 1941, 23; "Will Hitler Invade?" *NYDN*, 15 March 1941, 15. See also "What Is Hitler Up To?" 28 January 1941, 19.

88. Lincoln Colcord to R. Douglas Stuart Jr., 12 February 1941, Box 69, AFC Papers; Libby, "Answers to Some Vital Questions," *Peace Action* 7 (January 1941): 2.

89. See, for example, Sauthoff, *CR*, 19 March 1941, 2377; Hugh Johnson, testimony, HFAC, 23 January 1941, 452. For American opinion, see Office of Public Opinion Research, 28 January 1941. Thirty-two percent saw Germany winning, 23 percent expected stalemate, and 16 percent were undecided. Cantril, *Public Opinion*, 1187.

90. McCormick, testimony, SFRC, 6 February 1941, 479. See also Sweeney, *CR*, 5 February 1941, 581; Flynn, *SFN*, 8 February 1941, 12.

91. Wheeler, *CR*, 17 February 1941, 1044. See also Morton, *Let's Think the Matter Through* [pamphlet], entered in *CR*, 21 February 1941, A787; Short, *CR*, 6 February 1941, 740.

92. Thomas, testimony, HFAC, 22 January 1941, 349. For more pessimistic views, see Thomas, *Wesleyan* [University] *Argus*, 9 January 1941, 1; Stuart Chase, "Balancing the Risks," *Progressive*, 17 May 1941, 5. For supposed opposition to the war inside Germany, see Nofrontier News Service, "Germany from the Inside," *Unity* 126 (3 February 1941): 173.

93. "The Search for a Lasting Peace, II: Germany and Europe's Chaos," *Christian Century* 58 (19 February 1941): 249.

94. Chamberlin, "Hitler's Alternatives: Is He a Prisoner of Conquest?" *Atlantic* 167 (January 1941): 7–8.

95. Bulow, *CR*, 21 February 1941, 1256; Castle Diary, 22 February 1941; Hearst, "In the News," *SFE*, 30 January 1941, extra, A.

96. "Can Blockade Win Victory?" *NYDN*, 22 January 1941, 29; Villard, "Disregarding War Facts," *Progressive*, 25 January 1941, 6; "The Long View," *Uncensored* 67 (11 January 1941): 1. See also "But Boake Carter Says," *SFE*, 21 February 1941, 7; "If Not a Negotiated Peace," *Christian Century* 58 (15 January 1941): 80.

97. Watson, *Chief of Staff*, 371. When Smith was military attaché to Germany, he showed himself to be a strong Germanophile, but he was most accurate in technical matters and hence highly respected by General Marshall. For Smith's technical competence, see Kahn, "United States Views," 489–90. For his prewar reports and a summary of his career, see Hessen, *Berlin Alert*. For praise by Marshall, Marshall to James G. Harbord, 17 February 1940, in Marshall, *Papers*, 2:161.

98. Dennis, *WFL* 131 (30 January 1941): 5. For Dennis on Italy, see also 124 (12 December 1940): 1; 125 (19 December 1940): 2; 133 (13 February 1941): 2; 140 (3 April 1941): 3.

99. See, for example, Dennis, *WFL* 127 (2 January 1941): 1–2; 130 (23 January 1941): 4; 133 (13 February 1941): 1.

100. See, for example, Edwin M. Borchard to John A. Danaher, 6 January 1941, Borchard Papers; Morley Diary, 30 January 1941; *Social Justice*, 27 January 1941, 9; Jonathan T. Pratt, "War Partnership—It Can't Be Limited," *Scribner's Commentator* 9 (March 1941): 73.

101. Cudahy quoted in William R. Castle to R. Douglas Stuart Jr., 14 February 1941, in Doenecke, *IDU*, 127; "Don't Kid Yourselves," *NYDN*, 19 March 1941, 31; Kennedy, radio address, 18 January 1941,

attached to testimony, HFAC, 21 January 1941, 263; Lindbergh, testimony, HFAC, 23 January 1941, 404, 415–16; Lindbergh in Castle Diary, 15 February 1941. For the argument that many overestimated the potential of the German air force, see Lewin, *Hitler's Mistakes*, 103–5.

102. General memo, AFC Washington Office, 29 January 1941 and 12 February 1941, in Doenecke, *IDU*, 225, 229–31. In other bulletins, the office noted the threat of a Turkish-Bulgarian nonaggression pact to Greece, temporary closing of the Suez Canal, Luftwaffe mastery over Libya, a German submarine drive, German troops in Bulgaria, the exposed position of Gibraltar, and the possibility that the British lacked the forces to back the Greeks effectively. General memos, AFC Washington Office, 18 February, 20 February, 23 February, and 4 March 1941, in *IDU*, 231–7.

103. Flynn, *SFE*, 20 January 1941, 14.

104. "England Is Faced with Revolution," *Social Justice*, 6 January 1941, 7–8; 20 January 1941, 4. See also 27 January 1941, 12.

105. Dennis, *WFL* 135 (27 February 1941): 3.

106. *Life*, 30 December 1940, 14; Roosevelt to Winston Churchill, 16 January 1941, in Kimball, *Churchill and Roosevelt*, 1:129.

107. Dwight William Tuttle, *Harry L. Hopkins and Anglo-American-Soviet Relations, 1941–1945* (New York: Garland, 1983), 69–70; George D. McJimsey, *Harry Hopkins: Ally of the Poor and Defender of Democracy* (Cambridge, Mass.: Harvard University Press, 1987), 146; Marshall, "Memorandum for General [Leonard T.] Gerow," 26 February 1941, in Marshall, *Papers*, 2:431.

108. Hull in Ickes, entry of 2 February 1941, *Secret Diary*, 3:422. See also Breckinridge Long, entry of 7 February 1941, *War Diary*, 175.

109. Lee, entry of 20 December 1940, *London Journal*, 183. He soon qualified this opinion. Entry of 22 December 1940, 185.

110. See, for example, Chamberlin Diary, 1 February 1941; "The 'Wave' of the Future," *Common Sense* 10 (March 1941): 81; NCPW official Paul Harris, [Northwestern University] *Daily Northwestern*, 19 February 1941, 1; Alfred Bingham, Brown [University] *Daily Herald*, 10 February 1941, 4; Lincoln Colcord to Edwin M. Borchard, 8 January 1941, Borchard Papers; Alanson B. Houghton, former U.S. ambassador to Germany, as noted in Castle Diary, 21 March 1941; "Welles Cold to Tokyo Plea; Warns Axis of Firm Stand," *NYDN*, 28 February 1941, 29; "Is It Table Stakes?" *NYDN*, 20 March 1941, 31; Robert E. Wood to R. J. Finnegan, 22 January 1941, Box 292, AFC Papers; Clay Judson to James B. Conant, 3 February 1941, in Doenecke, *IDU*, 125.

111. Vandenberg, *NYT*, 2 January 1941, 1, 6. *New Masses* claimed that Vandenberg was actually proposing a scheme, similar to the House–Grey understanding, for getting the United States into the conflict. "What 'About' the Peace Talk," 38 (14 January 1941): 19. For endorsement of Vandenberg's general call for negotiations, see "An Inquiry America Should Make," *CT*, 28 December 1940, 6; Senators Wheeler, Tydings, and Harry F. Byrd (Dem.-Va.), *CT*, 27 December 1941, 1.

112. Lindbergh, testimony, HFAC, 23 January 1941, 378. Such a negotiated peace, he continued, would not be a peace "that I would particularly approve of," but he found the alternative a disastrous war. See 413. Sterling Morton said Lindbergh expressed his own views poorly, for he probably meant that continued war meant ruin for all Europe. Morton to Amos Pinchot, 24 January 1941, Pinchot Papers.

113. Lindbergh, testimony, SFRC, 6 February 1941, 490. When asked by Senator Tom Connally (Dem.-Tex.) whether he would restore Denmark or Belgium, he said he would not attempt to suggest the concrete settlement. See 497. "The situation changes from week to week; and it depends a great deal on the status of the war." See 498. Such a peace would have to take in "realities" neglected at Versailles, such as the need to eliminate the Polish Corridor and alleviate the condition of minorities in Czechoslovakia. See 558.

114. See, for example, "Congress Should Summon Kennedy," *NYDN*, 10 January 1941, 27; "Britain's Stake in an Early Peace," *CT*, 22 February 1941, 10; "Prospects in Africa and Elsewhere," *CT*, 1 February 1941, 16.

115. William R. Castle to R. Douglas Stuart Jr., 14 February 1941, AFC Papers; Dennis, memo on lend-lease, in *CR*, 7 March 1941, 200; Libby, "Answers to Some Vital Questions," *Peace Action* 7 (January 1941): 8.

116. See, for example, "The Search for a Lasting Peace, IV: A Basis for Negotiations," *Christian Century* 58 (12 March 1941): 354; William R. Castle to R. Douglas Stuart Jr., 11 March 1941, AFC Papers; Taft, *CR*, 22 February 1941, 1276, 1281; Rankin, *CR*, 7 February 1941, 754; McCarran, *CR*, 22 February 1941, 1271; Bulow, *CR*, 21 February 1941, 1253.

117. "Is It Table Stakes?" *NYDN*, 20 March 1941, 31; Norman Thomas, *Wesleyan* [University] *Argus*, 9 January 1941, 2. See also Arthur J. May, *This Bewildered Democracy*, 15.

118. Lindbergh, testimony, HFAC, 23 January 1941, 378; SFRC, 6 February 1941, 490. See also "But Boake Carter Says," *SFE*, 16 January 1941, 9.

119. James M. Gillis, "Friendly Challenge to the Pope," *Catholic World* 152 (January 1941): 387; "The Search for a Lasting Peace, IV: A Basis for Negotiations," *Christian Century* 58 (12 March 1941): 354; "The Pope's Peace Effort," *NYDN*, 21 March 1941, 31; Lindbergh, testimony, HFAC, 23 January 1941, 378.

120. Bulow, *CR*, 21 February 1941, 1254; E. Stanley Jones, "What Is America's Role in This Crisis?" *Christian Century* 58 (19 March 1941): 389–90. Jones claimed to have reviewed the article with about twenty members of Congress, who—he claimed—were much in sympathy with his position. E. Stanley Jones to A. J. Muste, 18 April 1941, FOR Papers.

121. "The Search for Lasting Peace, I: Britain and the Future," *Christian Century* 58 (12 February 1941): 214; "The Search for Lasting Peace, V: A Basis for Negotiations," *Christian Century* 58 (12 March 1941): 351–53. Territorial readjustments might include restoration of Norway, Belgium, Denmark, and the Netherlands; an independent Poland, perhaps possessing new boundaries; internationalization of all colonies in North Africa under a mandate system; transfer of all other African colonies to mandate status; admission of India to the British Commonwealth; confirmation of the independence of Egypt, Iran, Iraq, and Syria; an independent Palestine; restoration of Czechoslovakia, with a plebiscite to determine the status of the Sudeten area; annexation of Austria to Germany; incorporation of the Hungarian parts of Transylvania into an independent Hungary; the establishment of a Balkan federation; restoration to Siam of territories taken by the European empires; immediate independence for the Philippines; withdrawal of Japanese troops from China and its restoration to full sovereignty; administration of Manchuria and Mongolia as mandates, with a plebiscite in fifteen years to determine their status; transfer of French Indochina, the Dutch East Indies, and Malaya to mandate status; a plebiscite in Burma to determine its fate; the dismantling of U.S. and Japanese island bases in the Pacific; and an American loan for world rehabilitation. See 354.

122. See, for example, Harry Elmer Barnes, "Where Are We Headed?" *Uncensored* 73, special supplement (21 February 1941): 2; *Social Justice*, 10 February 1941, 4.

123. "The Long View," *Uncensored* 67 (11 January 1941): 2; "If Not a Negotiated Peace," *Christian Century* 58 (15 January 1941): 80. See also Charles Clayton Morrison, testimony, SFRC, 7 February 1941, 626. The *Century* also noted such peace rumors as British efforts at Madrid through Samuel Hoare, British ambassador to Spain, and Lord Chancellor John Simon and German efforts through Franz von Papen, German ambassador to Turkey. "The Search for a Lasting Peace, V: A Basis for Negotiations," *Christian Century* 58 (12 March 1941): 351. For material on Tavistock, see *NYT*, 4 March 1940, 4. For Davis, see *NYT*, 31 December 1940, 1.

124. See, for example, Dorothy Detzer to Emily Greene Balch, summarizing their common position, 2 February 1941, WIL Papers; Henry Cabot Lodge, *CR*, 8 March 1941, 2061.

125. Kennedy, speech, 18 January 1941, in testimony, HFAC, 260. Several days later he claimed that Hitler sought to dominate the world. See testimony, 21 January 1941, 288.

126. Amos Pinchot to J. E. McEldowney, 11 March 1941, Pinchot Papers.

127. Gallup poll, 3 January 1940, Cantril, *Public Opinion*, 1108; Gallup poll, 9 January 1941, 1136; Gallup poll, *NYT*, 31 January 1941, 6. For related polls, see Cantril, *Public Opinion*, 1187.

## CHAPTER 12: A TROUBLED SPRING

1. B. Mitchell Simpson III, *Admiral Harold R. Stark: Architect of Victory, 1939–1945* (Columbia: University of South Carolina Press, 1989), 84.

2. Livingstone Hartley and Donald C. Blaisdell, "Threat to the Lifeline," CDAAA, *Washington Office Information Letter* 10 (21 March 1941): 1–2, Box 35, CDAAA Papers. See also Hartley and Blaisdell, "The Patrol System and the Atlantic Lifeline," *Washington Office Information Letter* 16 (2 May 1941): 1, Box 35, CDAAA Papers.

3. Hartley and Blaisdell, "Limitations on the Risk of War," *Washington Office Information Letter* 12 (4 April 1941): 2–3, Box 35, CDAAA Papers.

4. Hartley and Blaisdell, "Allied Ship Losses," *Washington Office Information Letter* 18 (16 May 1941): 1, Box 35, CDAAA Papers.

5. Hartley and Blaisdell, "Ship Losses," *Washington Office Information Letter* 24 (27 June 1941): 4, Box 35, CDAAA Papers; Hartley and Blaisdell, "Good News from the Atlantic," *Washington Office Information Letter* 27 (18 July 1941): 2–3, Box 35, CDAAA Papers.

6. See, for example, Nye, *CR*, 15 April 1941, 3113; O'Connor, *CR*, 17 April 1941, 3165; journalist Samuel Crowther to Charles W. Tobey, 1 May 1941, in *CR*, 3780; Bender, *CR*, 24 April 1941, 3281, 3283; Taber, *CR*, 29 April 1941, 3382.

7. Tobey, *CR*, 15 April 1941, 3110; 18 April 1941, 3176–78.

8. Tobey, *NYT*, 1 April 1941, 13. For other resolutions, see for example, Mundt, *CR*, 3 April 1941, A1628; Fish and Congressman Carl Curtis (Rep.-Nebr.), *CR*, 3 April 1941, 2949.

9. "Tobey's Nose," *Time*, 28 April 1941, 14. For endorsements of Tobey's position, see "Let the People Know the Truth," *Daily Worker*, 19 April 1941, 14; Waldrop, "For the Record," *WTH*, 25 April 1941, 12.

10. Tobey, *NYT*, 1 May 1941, 1.

11. Text of agreement, *NYT*, 11 April 1941, 4; press conference, 12 April 1941, *Roosevelt Papers and Addresses*, vol. 10: *The Call to Battle Stations, 1941*, comp. Samuel Rosenman (New York: Random House, 1950): 117–20.

12. Berle in Waldo Heinrichs, *Threshold of War: Franklin D. Roosevelt and American Entry into World War II* (New York: Oxford University Press, 1988), 87; entry of 6 February 1941, *Navigating*, 356. See also Livingstone Hartley and Donald C. Blaisdell, "Defeatism," and "Implications of Greenland," CDAAA, *Washington Office Information Letter* 15 (25 April 1941): 1, 3, Box 35, CDAAA Papers.

13. *Fortune* poll, August 1941, Cantril, *Public Opinion*, 782.

14. "Campaign 1941," *Uncensored* 80 (12 April 1941): 2. See also Bender, *CR*, 24 April 1941, 3284; Case, *CR*, 24 April 1941, 3284; "From Greenland to the Red Sea," *Christian Century* 58 (23 April 1941): 548; "War 1,000 Miles Closer as U.S. Takes Greenland," *U.S. Week*, 19 April 1941, 2; Castle Diary, 16 April 1941.

15. See, for example, "The United States Moves into Greenland," *CT*, 12 April 1941, 8.

16. *SFE*, 18 April 1941, 13; "U.S. Bases on Greenland," *NYDN*, 14 April 1941, 19; MacLiesh and Reynolds, *Strategy*, 53. The latter two authors suggested maintaining a seasonal base there. See 234.

17. "The President's Red Sea Order," text, *NYT*, 12 April 1941, 7; *Time*, 19 May 1941, 17; Wheeler, *CT*, 13 April 1941, 4. See also Woodruff, *CR*, 24 April 1941, 3284.

18. Heinrichs, *Threshold*, 47.

19. Bailey and Ryan, *Hitler vs. Roosevelt*, 134; William L. Langer and S. Everett Gleason, *Undeclared War, 1940–1941* (New York: Harper, 1953), 446.

20. Press conference, 25 April 1941, *NYT*, 26 April 1941, 1, 4. For criticism of Roosevelt's distinction between patrols and convoys, see "Washington Picture," *Uncensored* 85 (17 May 1941): 3; "Convoys Mean Shooting and Shooting Means War," *Christian Century* 58 (7 April 1941): 611.

21. Roosevelt, *NYT*, 30 April 1941, 1; "Pressure Parade," *Newsweek*, 2 June 1941, 17.

22. See, for example, R. Douglas Stuart Jr. to Robert E. Wood, 26 April 1941, Box 69, AFC Papers; William R. Castle to Sterling Morton, 8 August 1941, Morton Papers; Marcantonio, *CR*, 30 April 1941, 3465; Fish, *CR*, 5 May 1941, 3583.

23. Hoover, speech, New York, 11 May 1941, in *CR*, A2315. Endorsements included General Charles G. Dawes, *New York Herald Tribune*, 14 May 1941; Hearst, "In the News," *SFE*, 13 May 1941, 1; Rankin, *CR*, 14 May 1941, A2315. In private Hoover predicted that a warlike incident would occur, saying, "We will see our ships sunk and American boys killed." Letter to William J. Gross, 7 April 1941, Hoover Papers.

24. Villard, "The Truth about the Convoy Outcry," *Uncensored*, 10 May 1941, 4; AFC, *Washington News Letter* 16 (4 June 1941): 3; "Washington Picture," *Uncensored* 85 (17 May 1941): 3.

25. See, for example, Alf Landon and Frederick J. Libby cited in Libby, "Britain Can't Hold Out Many Months More," *Peace Action* 7 (May 1941): 2; "Washington Picture," *Uncensored* 85 (17 May 1941): 3.

26. Taft, radio address, "Shall the United States Enter the European War?" 17 May 1941, in *CR*, A2343. See also Villard, "Some Vital War Facts," *Progressive*, 24 May 1941, 5; Amos Pinchot to Lincoln Colcord, 13 May 1941, Pinchot Papers.

27. "Through Falsehood to War," *CT*, 5 April 1941, 12; Vandenberg, *CR*, 7 May 1941, 3693. Interventionists had often claimed 205 ships had been sunk.

28. *Christian Century* 58 (21 May 1941): 676. For other citations of the Land letter, see open letter, Amos Pinchot to Henry L. Stimson, 6 May 1941, in *CR*, 4097; Taft, radio address, "Shall the United States Enter the European War?" 17 May 1941, *CR*, A2343; "Convoys," *Uncensored* 84 (10 May 1941): 1–2; "The Convoy Fraud Exposed," *CT*, 9 May 1941, 14; Joseph Starobin, "The Convoy Conspiracy," *New Masses* 39 (20 May 1941): 4.

29. "Land and the British," *Time*, 19 May 1941, 17; *NYT*, 13 May 1941, 7; Roosevelt to Emory S. Land, 10 May 1941, *F.D.R.: His Personal Letters*, 1152–53. In a letter to anti-interventionist Bruce Barton, Roosevelt said that he was fully cognizant of the problems in getting goods to Britain, for the problem not only came from submarines, as in World War I, but from "the heavily armed fast surface raider, the bombing plane operating far off shore, and the night bombing of English, Scotch and North Irish ports after a ship actually gets there." He claimed that Land's figures were of "no value," being "foisted on him by a young statistician who made them up from newspaper stories." Letter dated 19 May 1941, Roosevelt Papers.

30. Admiralty statement, *NYT*, 9 May 1941, 7.

31. See, for example, "How Desperate Is Britain?" *Christian Century* 58 (7 June 1941): 614; "Sensational Charge by Maritime Union," *In Fact* 2 (21 April 1941): 2–3; "Through Falsehood to War," *CT*, 5 April 1941, 12; "Where the War Stands," *New Masses* 39 (6 May 1941): 4.

32. Bennett, *CR*, 23 April 1941, 3254. See also Sweeney, *CR*, 30 April 1941, 3437.

33. Shafer, *CR*, 22 May 1941, A2437.

34. *NYT*, 9 April 1941, 1, 4; Bland, *CR*, 5 May 1941, 3585; 6 May 1941, 3669.

35. See, for example, Bender, *CR*, 6 May 1941, 3589; Dondero, *CR*, 6 May 1941, 3590. Only one anti-interventionist backed the bill, claiming that any government could seize any property it deemed in the public need. "But Boake Carter Says," *SFE*, 5 April 1941, 7.

36. Fish, *CR*, 5 May 1941, 3582. See also Fish, *CR*, 6 May 1941, 3669.

37. Vorys, *CR*, 5 May 1941, 3592. See also Representative Francis Culkin (Rep.-N.Y.), 3589; Short, *CR*, 6 May 1941, 3665; Short in *Newsweek*, 19 May 1941, 17.

38. Edwin M. Borchard to William R. Castle, 5 May 1941, Borchard Papers. Borchard found legal the protests by Denmark and Italy. Edwin M. Borchard to George Holden Tinkham, 16 April 1941, Borchard Papers.

39. Allen, *CR*, 5 May 1941, 3584.

40. Bland, *CR*, 5 May 1941, 3587. House Republicans backed an amendment introduced by Congressman Culkin that would have prevented the president from transferring German and Italian ships to the British. It was defeated 222 to 160. *CR*, 6 May 1941, 3678. In the Senate Vandenberg offered an amendment similar to that of Culkin, which was voted down 38 to 43. *CR*, 15 May 1941, 4103–4. For general narrative, see "Overt Act," *Time*, 19 May 1941, 17.

41. Vandenberg, *CR*, 15 May 1941, 4068, 4099. For the accusation that the move was warlike, see also House Minority Report cited by Robsion, *CR*, 6 May 1941, 3657; Fish, 5 May 1941, 3580; Bradley, 5 May 1941, 3594; Raymond S. Springer (Rep.-Ind.), 8 May 1941, A2178; "Comment," *America* 65 (24 May 1941): 170.

42. Culkin, *CR*, 5 May 1941, 3590; Robsion, *CR*, 6 May 1941, 3659.

43. House roll call, *NYT*, 8 May 1941, 12; Senate roll call, 16 May 1941, 4.

44. Roosevelt address, text, *NYT*, 28 May 1941, 12; "Text of Proclamation," *NYT*, 1.

45. *NYT*, 29 May 1941, 1, 2.

46. Burns, *Soldier*, 91.

47. Frank Freidel, *Franklin D. Roosevelt: A Rendezvous with Destiny* (Boston: Little, Brown, 1990), 371.

48. AFC in *Newsweek*, 9 June 1941, 14; Doenecke, *IDU*, 49. For similar comments, see General Wood in AFC, *Washington News Letter* 15 (30 May 1941), in Doenecke, *IDU*, 262–63; "Mr. Roosevelt's Oration," *NYDN*, 29 May 1941, 19; "Freedom of FDR," *Uncensored* 87 (31 May 1941): 1, 3; Dennis, *WFL* 148 (29 May 1941): 3.

49. See, for example, Ruth Sarles to R. Douglas Stuart Jr., 31 May 1941, in Doenecke, *IDU*, 128.

50. Woodruff, *CR*, 29 May 1941, 4573.

51. AFC Research Bureau, "Freedom of the Seas," *Did You Know?* 3 (26 June 1941), in Doenecke, *IDU*, 276–78. See also Edwin M. Borchard to John A. Danaher, 30 May 1941, Borchard Papers; Herbert W. Briggs, *Cornell* [University] *Daily Sun*, 26 May 1941, 5; Waldrop, "The Free Seas," *WTH*, 11 June 1941, 12; Waldrop, "This Freedom," *WTH*, 17 September 1941, 12.

52. "Freedom of FDR," *Uncensored* 87 (31 May 1941): 2; Bennett, speech, NBC red network, 2 June 1941, in *CR*, A2654; Nye, "Fraudulent Freedoms," address of 12 June 1941, in *CR*, A2864. See also Robsion, *CR*, 12 August 1941, 7007.

53. Reynolds, *Creation*, 347 n. 38. For firsthand accounts, see, for example, Ickes, entry of 12 April 1941, *Secret Diary*, 3:466; 25 May 1941, 3:347.

54. Anthony Cave Brown, *The Last Hero: Wild Bill Donovan* (New York: Times Books, 1982), 156.

55. Roosevelt to Churchill, 10 May 1941, in Kimball, *Churchill and Roosevelt*, 1:184. On 2 May, Churchill had said to Eden, "There has been a considerable recession across the Atlantic," with the consequences that "quite consciously we are being left very much to our fate." Warren F. Kimball, "Churchill and Roosevelt: The Personal Equation," *Prologue* 6 (Fall 1974): 178.

56. Demaree Bess, "Our Frontier on the Danube: The Appalling Story of Our Meddling in the Balkans," *Saturday Evening Post* 213 (24 June 1941): 9, 118–20.

57. See, for example, Nye, *CR*, 23 May 1941, 4365–66; "But Boake Carter Says," *SFE*, 29 May 1941, 5; Case, *CR*, July 3, 1941, 5821.

58. See, for example, "Who Killed Yugoslavia and Greece?" *NYDN*, 26 May 1941, 21.

59. "Promises," *Uncensored* 80 (12 April 1941): 1. See also "The Big Picture," *Uncensored* 81 (19 April 1941): 1–2. Donovan called *Uncensored's* claims about him "wholly and completely untrue." William J. Donovan to Cushman Reynolds, 2 June 1941, Hertzberg Papers. Editor Cushman Reynolds replied that he was giving an objective appraisal of the situation. Cushman Reynolds to William J. Donovan, 13 June 1941, Hertzberg Papers. Donovan again denied the charges. William J. Donovan to Cushman Reynolds, 16 June 1941, Hertzberg Papers.

60. Fish, *CR*, 14 April 1941, 3084. For similar comments, see Charles Clayton Morrison, address, AFC, Chicago Rally, 27 April 1941, in NCPW Papers; Wheeler, *SFE*, 16 April 1941, 5. For a similar claim concerning both Greece and Yugoslavia, see "Comment," *America* 65 (26 April 1941): 59; Herbert Hoover to John O'Laughlin, 13 April 1941, Stanford Files.

61. See, for example, Demaree Bess, "The Battle of the Balkans," *Saturday Evening Post* 213 (26 April 1941): 14–15, 60–62; Nye, *CR*, 29 April 1941, 3382; Sokolsky, "These Days: Colonel Donovan's Mission," *New York Sun*, 29 April 1941, 20.

62. Hanighen, "Wild Bill at Large," memo, ca. April 1941, Hertzberg Papers.

63. For Teapot Dome, see Wheeler, *CR*, 31 July 1941, 6501. For the Nye Committee, see Hanighen, "Wild Bill at Large."

64. Gilbert, *Churchill*, 6: chaps. 55–58; Brown, *Last Hero*, chap. 10; Peter B. Lane, *The United States and the Balkan Crisis of 1940–1941* (New York: Garland, 1988), 248, 289–90.

65. "Facts about Yugoslavia," *Social Justice*, 21 April 1941, 11; *Social Justice*, 11 November 1940, 9.

66. Pettengill, "The 'Noble Democracies,'" Release 224, 11 February 1941, Box 11, Pettengill Papers; "Getting Ready for the Next War," *Christian Century* 57 (11 September 1940): 1103. See also Taft, "Russia and the Four Freedoms," speech, CBS, 25 June 1941, in *CR*, A3077; Nye, "Two Men in a Boat," speech to AFC rally, New York City, in *CR*, 13 November 1941, A1501; Devere Allen, "Some Dictators Are Nice," *Call*, 18 January 1941, 2; Wheeler, *CR*, 28 February 1941, 1522; Norman Thomas, testimony, SFRC, 3 February 1941, 305; Robert Rice Reynolds, SFRC, 8 February 1941, 683.

67. Herbert Hoover to William J. Gross, 7 April 1941, Hoover Papers; Dennis, *WFL* 138 (20 March 1941): 2. See also 139 (27 March 1941): 2.

68. "The Drive on Suez," *CT*, 16 April 1941, 12; "What Next?" *NYDN*, 2 May 1941, 29.

69. See, for example, *Social Justice*, 5 May 1941, 3; Sokolsky, "These Days: The Neo-Defeatists," *New York Sun*, 3 May 1941, 16; "A Possible Road to Peace," *Christian Century* 58 (11 June 1941): 775; Henry Haskell, "Stalin Bound to Axis; Looks to Middle East," *Call*, 31 May 1941, 2.

70. William R. Castle to Edwin M. Borchard, 9 April 1941, Borchard Papers. See also Castle Diary, 6 April 1941.

71. *CT*, 6 June 1941, 14. See also "The Lesson of Crete," *CT*, 3 June 1941, 12.

72. Mundt, *CR*, 22 May 1941, A2463; "A Black Day for the Axis," *NYDN*, 2 April 1941, 35.

73. Lindbergh, "Reaffirmation," *Atlantic Monthly* 167 (June 1941): 686; Wheeler, [University of] *Michigan Daily*, 6 May 1941, 1. See also Ernest L. Meyer, "The Man in the Alcove," *Progressive*, 24 May 1941, 4.

74. "After the Ball," *NYDN*, 9 June 1941, 19. For a similar prediction, see "Stalin Is 60, Hitler Is 50," *NYDN*, 22 December 1939, 23.

75. "Worse News," *Uncensored* 82 (26 April 1941): 4; "Bombing Results Compared," *CT*, 17 May 1941, 10; Ruth Sarles to R. Douglas Stuart Jr., 24 May 1941, in Doenecke, *IDU*, 249. See also "Peace Talk' Rumors Gain in Washington," *Call*, 14 June 1941, 8.

76. See, for example, Truman Smith cited in Herbert Hoover, memorandum, 1 June 1941, Hoover Papers; Morley Diary, 13 April 1941; John Haynes Holmes, "Editorials," *Unity* 127 (June 1941): 56; Charles A. Lindbergh cited in Chamberlin Diary, 3 June 1941; Lindbergh, entry of 28 June 1941, *Wartime Journals*, 511.

77. Nye, *Yale* [University] *Daily News*, 25 April 1941, 3; Baldwin, *Yale Daily News*, 24 April 1941, 1. In his book, Baldwin was slightly more optimistic. Underground resistance in Czechoslovakia and Poland, he said, could indicate the shape of things to come. *United We Stand!* 45–46.

78. Wood interview, *PM*, 25 May 1941, 4–5. See also Robert E. Wood to Sterling Morton, 25 May 1941, Morton Papers.

79. Frederick J. Libby to Gilbert Stinger, 22 May 1941, NCPW Papers.

80. *WFL* 149 (5 June 1941): 4–5; 150 (12 June 1941): 3; 141 (10 April 1941): 1; *Social Justice*, 7 April 1941, 6; *Social Justice*, 5 May 1941, 3; "Comment: The German Record," *Social Justice*, 16 June 1941, 4.

81. Herbert Hoover to William J. Gross, 7 April 1941, Hoover Papers; "The Immediate Relation of the United States to This War," address, New York City, 12 May 1941, in *CR*, A2315–16. For further stress on British weakness by Hoover and Lindbergh, see Charles A. Lindbergh, entry of 31 May 1941, *Wartime Journals*, 498.

82. For a denial that Britain would be invaded, see Berle, entry of 26 May 1941, *Navigating*, 369. For doubts of an invasion among British leaders, see entry of 22 April 1940, Lee, *London Journal*, 254.

83. See Kahn, "United States Views," 493.

84. Ickes, entries of 4 March and 30 May 1941, *Secret Diary*, 3:503, 527; *Life*, 21 April 1941, 96–99; polls of 25 April and 29 May 1941, Cantril, *Public Opinion*, 1187.

85. Waldo Heinrichs, "FDR and the Entry into World War II," *Prologue* 26 (Fall 1994): 124–26.

86. See, for example, Clay Judson to R. M. Hutchins, 19 May 1941, AFC Papers; Robert E. Wood to Sterling Morton, 25 May 1941, Morton Papers; Chiperfield, *CR*, 24 June 1941, A3026; Edwin Johnson and D. Worth Clark in *CT*, 2 June 1941, 5; "Why Short of War?" *Common Sense* 10 (May 1941): 145; Wheeler, *CT*, 22 June 1941, 3. For a more cautious estimate by *Common Sense*, see "Russia and the War," 10 (August 1941): 240, in which the liberal monthly said that such a peace could only serve as an armed truce among enemies and last only as long as it was mutually convenient.

87. Nye, *Yale Daily News*, 25 April 1941, 3; La Follette, [University of North Carolina] *Daily Tar Heel*, 15 May 1941, 1.

88. Hearst, "In the News," *SFE*, 25 April 1941, 1; Robert E. Wood to Sterling Morton, 25 May 1941, Morton Papers. For a similar view of the British Empire, see Rankin, *CR*, 4 June 1941, 4727; Edwin M. Borchard to Henry Houghton, 10 April 1941, Borchard Papers.

89. "Last Call," *NYDN*, 20 April 1941, 25.

90. See, for example, Chester Bowles to Roy Larsen, 30 April 1941, in Doenecke, *IDU*, 286; John T. Flynn to Robert E. Wood, 5 June 1941, in Doenecke, *IDU*, 112; Villard, "The Fate of England," *Christ-*

*ian Century* 58 (11 June 1941): 781; Dennis, *WFL* 149 (5 June 1941): 2; 147 (22 May 1941): 4; "Are We Afraid of Peace?" *Christian Century* 58 (18 June 1941): 795; Hoover in Lindbergh, entry of 31 May 1941, *Wartime Journals*, 498; Case, *CR*, 6 June 1941, 4820. For a rare example of pessimism, see Lincoln Colcord to Amos Pinchot, 14 May 1941, Pinchot Papers.

91. Wheeler, *Newsweek*, 2 June 1941, 14; "Peace Feelers," *NYDN*, 21 May 1941, 31. For Paris press, see *NYT*, 19 May 1941, 6.

92. Connally, *Newsweek*, 2 June 1941, 14. For rumors concerning Connally's statement, see Ruth Sarles to R. Douglas Stuart Jr., 24 May 1941, in Doenecke, *IDU*, 249; AFC, *Washington News Letter* 16 (4 June 1941), in Doenecke, *IDU*, 264; "War or Peace for America," *CT*, 24 May 1941, 8; "Peace," *Uncensored* 86 (24 May 1941): 2; "'Peace Talk' Rumors Gain in Washington," *Call*, 14 June 1941, 8.

93. See, for example, Villard noted in Chamberlin Diary, 31 May 1941. For Roosevelt's denial, see Ickes, entry of 8 June 1941, *Secret Diary*, 3:535; Lash, *Roosevelt and Churchill*, 347. For additional speculation concerning peace terms, see Ruth Sarles to R. Douglas Stuart Jr., 31 May 1941, in Doenecke, *IDU*, 129; AFC, *Washington News Letter* 16 (4 June 1941), in Doenecke, *IDU*, 264; Case, *CR*, 6 June 1941, 4820; Sokolsky, "These Days: The Peace Offensive," *New York Sun*, 10 June 1941, 10; Dennis, *WFL* 149 (5 June 1941): 2; "Peace in the Offing," *Social Justice*, 2 June 1941, 3.

94. For claims that Hess was offering a peace bid, see Rankin, *CR*, 20 May 1941, 4279; Hoffman, *CR*, 31 July 1941, 6561; Wheeler and Voorhis in *Newsweek*, 2 June 1941, 14; Herbert Hoover in Smith, *Uncommon Man*, 298.

95. Gabriel Gorodesky, "The Hess Affair and Anglo-Soviet Relations on the Eve of 'Barbarossa,'" *English Historical Review* 101 (April 1986): 405–20; Alan Bullock, *Hitler and Stalin: Parallel Lives* (New York: Knopf, 1992), 713–14.

96. "Washington Picture: Logic," *Uncensored* 85 (17 May 1941): 2; Hoover cited in Helen Essary, "Dear Washington," *WTH*, 3 July 1941, 10; *Daily Worker*, 21 June 1941, 1, 4. See also Frederick J. Libby to Cyrus H. Karraker, 22 May 1941, NCPW Papers; Libby to Gilbert Stinger, 22 May 1941, NCPW Papers; "Peace Discussions, Not Peace Negotiations, Have Begun," *Peace Action* 7 (May 1941): 1; Devere Allen, "Was Hess Visit His Third?" *Call*, 9 August 1941, 2; "Peace in the Offing," *Social Justice*, 2 June 1941, 3; Seldes, *In Fact* 3 (30 June 1941): 1.

97. Hess in *CT*, 29 October 1944, 19.

98. "Mystery Surrounds the Flight of Hess," *Christian Century* 58 (21 May 1941): 676. See also the Trotskyist *Militant*, 17 May 1941, 1.

99. "Nazi Madness," *Christian Century* 58 (28 May 1941): 712. See also Lincoln Colcord to Amos Pinchot, 14 May 1941, Pinchot Papers; Travers Clement, "Wishful Thinking Seen in Buildup Given Hess," *Call*, 24 May 1941, 1.

100. "Comment," *America* 65 (24 May 1941): 170; Dennis, *WFL* 146 (15 May 1941): 2. Similarly Cudahy saw no backing in Germany for the flight. Testimony, SFRC, 23 October 1941, 171.

101. "The Flight of Hess," *NYDN*, 14 May 1941, 29.

102. Oscar Mannheimer, "What Rudolph Hess Was After," *New Masses* 39 (27 May 1941): 68.

103. Report of Frederick J. Libby, 20 May 1941, NCPW Papers; report of John Nevin Sayre, 28 March–25 May 1941, FOR Papers; American Friends Service Committee, "A Call to Persons of Good Will," in *Christian Century* 58 (18 June 1941): 801.

104. Voorhis, *CR*, 19 May 1941, 4234.

105. For reference to H.J. Res. 131, see *CR*, 3 March 1941, 1699. For endorsement by the NCPW Council, see minutes, 29 May 1941, 6, NCPW Papers.

106. For endorsements of Vorys's effort, see Libby minutes, NCPW executive board, 20 May 1941, NCPW Papers; "Comment," *America* 65 (5 July 1941): 338–39. The AFC gave the proposal publicity while not endorsing a negotiated peace. See R. A. Moore, Bulletin #383, 2 July 1941, AFC Papers; AFC, *Washington News Letter* 16 (4 June 1941), in Doenecke, *IDU*, 264. Norman Thomas endorsed the general notion of a peace offensive but feared that if Roosevelt were involved, he would lead the nation into war. Norman Thomas to John M. Vorys, 8 May 1941, Thomas Papers. As late as November, Vorys pressed his peace offensive, declaring that a five-point program of Secretary Hull, the speeches of Undersecretary Sumner Welles, and the Atlantic Charter could become the basis of more concrete pro-

posals. Vorys, *CR*, 13 November 1941, 8883. The German people, he said, should be offered an alternative just so that their government would have to accept or face insurrection. If the United States refused to deal with Hitler, it should state the terms it would offer if he were overthrown. *CR*, 28 November 1941, 8883.

107. For Vorys's plan, see "An American Peace Offensive," speech at Williams College, 26 April 1941, in *CR*, A1984–86; Vorys, *CR*, 5 May 1941, 3592; 9 May 1941, 3880; "The United States, the War, and the Future," speech before the Institute of Public Affairs, University of Virginia, 24 May 1941, in *CR*, 3100–3101; John H. Vorys to Franklin D. Roosevelt, 3 May 1941, Roosevelt Papers. Roosevelt replied that he would take Vorys's views into account. FDR to John H. Vorys, 17 May 1941, Roosevelt Papers.

108. For Roosevelt, see Edwin M. Borchard to Henry Houghton, 4 April 1941, Borchard Papers; Robert A. Taft, speech, CBS, 25 June 1941, in *CR*, 3077; Ludlow, radio speech, WJSV, Washington, D.C., 27 May 1941, in Box 11, Pettengill Papers. For Pius, see *SFE*, 16 April 1941, 14; actress Lilllian Gish, speech, 9 May 1941, Executives' Club of Chicago, in *CR*, A2563.

109. Participants would include Pius XII, President Ernst Wetter of Switzerland, King Gustav of Sweden, President Ismet Inonu of Turkey, and a South American representative of the Pan-American conference. These five, or their personal representatives, could meet with a U.S. representative. Mundt, CBS broadcast "America's Rendezvous with Destiny," 20 May 1941, in *CR*, A2426. See also Mundt, *CR*, 22 May 1941, A2463; Mundt, *American Forum of the Air* 3 (8 June 1941): 8. Norman Thomas opposed Mundt's bid, fearing that Roosevelt would use it to issue an ultimatum to Germany and Japan, the rejection of which would be another reason for bringing the United States into war. Norman Thomas to Karl Mundt, 12 June 1941, Thomas Papers.

110. Sidney Bradshaw Fay, "Problems of Peace Sentiment," *Events: The Monthly Review of World Affairs* 9 (April 1941): 241–48; 9 (May 1941): 321–30; Gold, *Daily Worker*, 29 May 1941, 7. Gold stressed that communist-sponsored American Peace Mobilization included all of Fay's planks in its peace program.

111. Hull address, text, *NYT*, 19 May 1941, 1, 2; Ludlow, speech, CBS, "The Peace Side," 28 May 1941, in *CR*, A2599–2600, which also notes endorsements of Ludlow's resolution came from Harry Emerson Fosdick and William Cardinal O'Connell of Boston; Louis Ludlow to Samuel B. Pettengill, 30 May 1941, Box 11, Pettengill Papers; Mundt, CBS broadcast "America's Rendezvous with Destiny," 20 May 1941, in *CR*, A2426.

112. Sterling Morton to Robert R. McCormick, 23 May 1941, Morton Papers; "'Peace Talk' Rumors Gain in Washington," *Call*, 14 June 1941, 8.

113. "Text of President's Address Depicting Emergency Confronting the Nation," *NYT*, 28 May 1941, 12.

114. Gallup poll, 6 May 1941, Cantril, *Public Opinion*, 975. One Gallup poll, taken on 8 April 1941, showed 47 percent in favor of Britain negotiating with the Germans, 46 percent opposed, and 7 percent possessing no opinion. Other polls showed much stronger opposition. Cantril, *Public Opinion*, 1136.

## CHAPTER 13: GREAT BRITAIN

1. Manfred Jonas, "Pro-Axis Sentiment and American Isolationism," *Historian* 29 (February 1967): 221–37.

2. "No Hostility to England," *CT*, 1 November 1939, 14; Norman Thomas to Henry Sloane Coffin, 6 August 1940, Thomas Papers; "The Consequences of Stumblebum Diplomacy," *NYDN*, 24 August 1940, 13. For further endorsement of British victory, see "Dictator Churchill," *NYDN*, 24 May 1940, 29; "We're Not Anti-British," *NYDN*, 23 February 1941, 43.

3. Charles A. Lindbergh, "We Cannot Win This War for England," speech, New York AFC meeting, 23 April 1941, in *Vital Speeches* 7 (1 May 1941): 424; Hearst, "In the News," *WTH*, 2 April 1941, 9.

4. For a description of British efforts in this regard, see Nicholas John Cull, *Selling War: The British Propaganda Campaign Against American "Neutrality" in World War II* (New York: Oxford University Press, 1995). For the accusation that British intelligence successfully led in this enterprise, see Thomas

Earl Mahl, *Desperate Deception: British Covert Operations in the United States, 1939–1944* (Washington, D.C.: Brassley's, 1998).

5. Lindbergh, entry of 28 December 1940, *War Within*, 456.

6. For a full-scale treatment of the interwar period, see John E. Moser, *Twisting the Lion's Tail: American Anglophobia Between the World Wars* (New York: New York University Press, 1999).

7. Barnes, [University of] *Michigan Daily*, 17 May 1940, 2. See also John Haynes Holmes, address, "Getting America into War Has Started Again," 27 September 1939, in *CR*, A200.

8. Sidney Rogerson, *Propaganda and the Next War* (London: Bles, 1938). For citations, see Holt, *CR*, 18 October 1939, 542; Holmes, "Getting America into War Has Started Again"; Sargent, Bulletin #2, June 1939, *Getting US into War*, 102–3.

9. Dreiser, *America Is Worth Saving*, 71. For attacks on the book, see R. L. Duffus, "Dreiser to the Rescue," *NYT Book Review*, 9 February 1941, 22; "Counsel from Hollywood," *Time*, 3 February 1941, 76. For a mixed review, see Granville Hicks, "Dreiser to the Rescue," *Saturday Review of Literature* 23 (22 February 1941), 13. For praise, see Samuel Sillen, "Dreiser's J'Accuse," *New Masses* 38 (28 January 1941): 24–26.

10. For brief biographies of Sargent, see "Sargent's Bulletins," *Time*, 25 December 1939, 34; George H. Cless Jr., "Sargent: Oracle of Education," *Scribner's Commentator* 9 (February 1941): 58–63; "Porter (Edward) Sargent," in *Current Biography, 1941*, 751–52.

11. Among the bulletin's endorsers were such anti-interventionists as H. L. Mencken, Boake Carter, Alfred M. Bingham, Gerald P. Nye, Dorothy Dunbar Bromley, George Holden Tinkham, Hubert Herring, Burton Rascoe, Al Williams, Upton Close, Burton Wheeler, and Bennett Champ Clark. Educators included philosopher John Dewey, university president Robert Maynard Hutchins, Anglican educator Bernard Iddings Bell, historians Charles A. Beard and Will Durant, biologist Raymond Pearl, anthropologist Earnest Hooton, sociologist E. A. Ross, astronomer Harlow Shapley, and psychologist Goodwin Watson. See *Getting US into War*, passim. See also Norman Thomas to Porter Sargent, 28 February 1940, Thomas Papers; Oswald Garrison Villard to Porter Sargent, 30 July 1940, Villard Papers; Dorothy Detzer to Helen Lyle Creed, 4 April 1940, WIL Papers; John Haynes Holmes to Porter Sargent, 24 May 1940, Holmes Papers.

12. See, for example, Dennis, *WFL* 145 (8 May 1941): 5; *Social Justice*, 26 May 1941, 14; pacifist activist Edwin C. Johnson, *Fellowship* 7 (August 1941): 143; Morris H. Rubin, "The Last Column," *Progressive*, 7 June 1941, 12; Ernest L. Meyer, "Fish Learn Quicker," *Progressive*, 20 September 1941, 4; Albert Jay Nock, "Getting US into War," *Scribner's Commentator* 10 (September 1941): 81–84; Paul Hutchinson, "The Spirit of Sam Adams," *Christian Century* 58 (2 July 1941): 865.

13. See, for example, Holt, *CR*, 9 October 1939, 184; Theodore Dreiser to Frederick V. Field, 25 November 1940, Hertzberg Papers; "LET'S FIGHT FOR PEACE," *Social Justice*, 18 September 1939, 3.

14. Mencken, "Notes on a Moral War," *Baltimore Sun*, 8 October 1939. See also Mencken, [Princeton University] *Daily Princetonian*, 4 March 1941, 1.

15. "The War Parties," *CT*, 22 September 1939, 14. See also "Unequal Partners," *CT*, 29 November 1940, 12.

16. John Bassett Moore to Edwin M. Borchard, 6 December 1939, Borchard Papers. See also John Bassett Moore to Hiram Johnson, 28 March 1940, copy in Borchard Papers.

17. Bone, statement of 5 November 1940, cited in Sargent, Bulletin #12, 16 October 1939, *Getting US into War*, 151 n. 13; "The Status Quo—It Is Always to Be Maintained but Never Is," *NYDN*, 29 September 1940, 45; "Conversation Piece," *NYDN*, 18 September 1941, 31; John Haynes Holmes to Frederick J. Libby, 7 November 1941, NCPW Papers. See also "Cost of Saving British Empire," *NYDN*, 26 July 1941, 13; "Lafayette, We Are Here," *NYDN*, 21 September 1941, 41.

18. Ralph Townsend was an exception among the extreme anti-interventionists in finding relations "fairly good" between two nations. Testimony, SFRC, 8 February 1941, 812.

19. Downey, *CR*, 9 October 1939, 183; Beals, *Pan America*, 157.

20. Sargent, Bulletin #69, 20 July 1940, *Getting US into War*, 395 n. 12; Holt, *CR*, 9 October 1939, 18; *Social Justice*, 20 June 1940, 5. For other comments on the War of 1812, see Coughlin, "The President's Message to Congress," *Social Justice*, 2 October 1939, 4; Harrison George, "Change the World," *Daily Worker*, 17 January 1940, 7; Dreiser, *America Is Worth Saving*, 63.

21. For a general indictment, see Harvey Weston, "Anglo-American Relations," *Scribner's Commentator* 10 (September 1941): 67–80. Weston used as his source a book by Bull Moose political writer George Henry Payne, *England: Her Treatment of America* (New York: Sears, 1931). For American Revolution, see Short, *CR*, 5 February 1941, 600. For Monroe Doctrine, see Nye, *CR*, 7 November 1941, 8610; Vorys, *CR*, 18 June 1940, 8543; Chavez, *CR*, 27 February 1941, 1487. For Confederacy, see Vardis Fisher, *Idaho Daily Statesman*, 7 January 1941.

22. See, for example, "Nye vs. Morgenthau," *Scribner's Commentator* 9 (April 1941): 10.

23. Sweeney, *CR*, 14 August 1940, 10,359. See also *CR*, 4 September 1940, 11,511.

24. Churchill, *The Aftermath* (New York: Scribner's, 1929); Wheeler, *CR*, 5 November 1941, 8527.

25. Dreiser, *America Is Worth Saving*, 71; Chavez, *CR*, 27 February 1941, 1484; Barnes, "Course of U.S. in the War," *NYWT*, 16 January 1940, 14; La Follette, *CR*, 12 October 1939, 332. Conversely, Senator La Follette attacked both Britain and France for failing to work with the United States in 1937 in imposing an arms ban on Spain. *CR*, 12 October 1939, 332.

26. David A. Richards, "America Conquers Britain: Anglo-American Conflict in the Popular Media during the 1920s," *Journal of American Culture* 3 (Spring 1980): 95–103.

27. See, for example, Roger Wylie, "Latin America: Economic Pawn," *Scribner's Commentator* 10 (May 1941): 45.

28. For the complete text of Düsseldorf, see Leslie Gould, "Trade after the War—Is Düsseldorf Pact a Straw?" *New York Journal-American*, 10 February 1941.

29. Norman Thomas to Mr. Goldman, 19 January 1941, Thomas Papers; Norman Thomas, "Your World and Mine: The Problems We Face," *Call*, 17 May 1941, 8; Charles Tobey to Alfred E. Stearns, 10 May 1941, in *CR*, A2271; La Follette, testimony, SFRC, 3 February 1941, 268–69.

30. "Gold Mine," *Uncensored* 9 (2 December 1939): 1; William Philip Simms, "Britain's Demands," article dated 12 March 1940, in *CR*, 19 March 1940, A1514; Reynolds, *CR*, 29 March 1940, A1514.

31. Fish, *CR*, 12 March 1940, 2730–31. He also accused the British of holding goods that American merchants had bought in Germany and refusing permission to American exporters seeking to sell cotton to Finland. See also Judge John A. Matthews of New York Chancery Court, broadcast, 18 February 1940, in *CR*, A1770.

32. See, for example, anxieties voiced by Joseph P. Kennedy in Beschloss, *Kennedy and Roosevelt*, 197; "Cabbages and Kings: Beyond His Powers," *Scribner's Commentator* 11 (November 1941): 5–6; "The British Trade Offensive," *CT*, 25 March 1940, 8; "Various Trade Wars," *CT*, 11 December 1939, 14; "Fair Deal for American Exports," *CT*, 30 December 1939, 6.

33. Case, *CR*, 13 November 1941, 8859.

34. See, for example, Dennis, *WFL* 154 (10 July 1941): 2–3; "Cabbages and Kings: Patient Griselda," *Scribner's Commentator* 10 (October 1941): 5; Wheeler, *CR*, 5 November 1941, 8532; Wheeler in *Time*, 17 November 1941, 14.

35. "Competition from an Ally," *CT*, 21 September 1941, 16. See also "Is This a Serious War for Britain?" *CT*, 17 June 1941, 10.

36. Nye, *CR*, 7 November 1941, 8605; Jones, *CR*, 6 October 1941, 7801.

37. Reynolds, *Creation*, 273; Ponting, *1940*, 227.

38. Wheeler, *CR*, 28 February 1941, 152; "What America Needs from Britain," *CT*, 19 March 1941, 14; "Tin and the State Department," *CT*, 6 November 1940, 12; "Our Tin Supply," *CT*, 13 August 1940, 10. See also "Tin Tintype," *Uncensored* 46 (17 August 1940): 4–5. Shrewd bargaining, so Hugh Johnson claimed, could crack the British tin cartel. "Pacific Trade," *NYWT*, 6 February 1940, 17.

39. See, for example, Villard, "The Fate of England," *Christian Century* 58 (11 June 1941): 781; Congressman Harry Sauthoff (Prog.-Wis.), *CR*, 16 October 1941, 7994; "Ships for Britain," *CT*, 6 June 1941, 14; "It's Time to Think of Ourselves," *CT*, 23 September 1941, 12; Sweeney, broadcast, NBC, 6 May 1941, in *CR*, A3154.

40. "Dollars vs. Empire (Cont.)," *Uncensored* 71 (8 February 1941): 3. See also Frank Hanighen, "Capitol Letter: Minority Report on Lease-Lend Bill," *Common Sense* 10 (February 1941): 52.

41. See, for example, Dennis, *WFL* 163 (11 September 1941): 5; Congressman O'Connor, *CR*, 21 January 1941, 213; Robert La Follette, *CR*, 24 February 1941, 1303; "Q & A," *Uncensored* 66 (4 January 1941): 3.

42. Muste, [University of Wisconsin] *Daily Cardinal*, 7 May 1941, 1; La Follette, *CR*, 24 February 1941, 1303; Lindbergh, entry of 6 October 1941, *Wartime Journals*, 547 (emphasis his). See also Norman Thomas, testimony, HFAC, 22 January 1941, 343.

43. Callum A. MacDonald, "The United States, Appeasement and the Open Door," in Mommsen and Kettenacker, *Fascist Challenge*, 403, 407.

44. Kimball, *Juggler*, 49, 59; Theodore A. Wilson, *The First Summit: Roosevelt and Churchill at Placentia Bay, 1941*, rev. ed. (Lawrence: University Press of Kansas, 1991), 155–58; William Roger Louis, *Imperialism at Bay: The United States and the Decolonization of the British Empire, 1941–1945* (New York: Oxford University Press, 1978), 24.

45. Hull, *Memoirs*, 2:975–76; Graff, *Welles*, 391; Churchill in Thorne, *Allies*, 101; Kimball, *Forged in War*, 101.

46. J. G. Lockhart and C. M. Woodhouse, *Cecil Rhodes: The Colossus of South Africa* (New York: Macmillan, 1963), 57–58; Robert I. Rotberg, *The Founder: Cecil Rhodes and the Pursuit of Power* (New York: Oxford University Press, 1988), 101–2, 666.

47. Flynn, "Other People's Money: Fascists at Home," *New Republic* 103 (14 October 1940): 525; "The Death of Lord Lothian," *Christian Century* 57 (25 December 1940): 1603; Sargent, Bulletin #11, 16 October 1939, *Getting US into War*, 144. See also Holt, *CR*, 16 December 1940, 13,920; Edward Price Bell, letter to editor, *CT*, 29 April 1941, 10; Albert Hall, "Cecil Rhodes: Father of Union Now," *Scribner's Commentator* 10 (June 1941): 77–78.

48. Townsend, testimony, SFRC, 8 February 1941, 812; Lindbergh, *NYT*, 30 October 1941, 5. Lindbergh was undoubtedly referring to Britain's attack on the French fleet at Mers-el-Kebir, the British interception of three Finnish ships, and a blockade of the northern Finnish port of Petsamo.

49. Nock, review of Jawaharlal Nehru, *Toward Freedom* (New York: Day, 1941), in *Scribner's Commentator* 10 (August 1941): 91. See also Nock, review of Douglas Reed, *A Prophet at Home* (London: Cape, 1941), in *Scribner's Commentator* 10 (October 1941): 20.

50. Jerome Frank, *Save America First: How to Make Our Democracy Work* (New York: Harper, 1938); Chavez, *CR*, 25 October 1939, 821. For another positive reference to Frank, see Sargent, *Getting US into War*, 19. When conflict broke out in 1939, Frank himself switched to a more interventionist position. Jerome Frank to Louis Mumford, 30 September 1939, the Papers of Jerome Frank, Yale University Library.

51. Townsend, testimony, SFRC, 8 February 1941, 800. For Turks, see White, *CR*, 12 March 1940, 2749. For Weimar, see Henry Nelson Weiman and Arthur E. Holt, "Keep Our Country Out of This War," *Christian Century* 56 (27 September 1939): 1162; Devere Allen, "Why Did France Collapse?" *Unity* 125 (15 July 1940): 15; Sargent, *Getting US into War*, 20–23.

52. Dreiser, speech to American Peace Mobilization, CBS, 9 November 1940, clipping of *People's World*, n.d., Hertzberg Papers. See also economist William A. Orton, *Mt. Holyoke News*, 14 February 1941, 1.

53. For Rhineland, see Guyer, *CR*, 13 November 1941, 8838. For Ethiopia, see Reynolds, *CR*, 18 October 1939, 559. For Spain, see Weiman and Holt, 1162.

54. Borah, broadcast, NBC, 27 October 1939, in *CR*, A463.

55. Wheeler, *CR*, 6 August 1941, 9931. See also Tobey, address to the American Mothers of Massachusetts, Boston Commons, 11 May 1941, in *CR*, A2267; Sargent, *Getting US into War*, 21.

56. See, for example, Dwight Macdonald, "Sparks in the News," *Socialist Appeal*, 16 December 1939, 4; Boake Carter in Rock, *Chamberlain and Roosevelt*, 239 n. 52; "England Is Faced with Revolution," *Social Justice*, 6 January 1941, 8; Thomas, "Your World and Mine," *Call*, 4 November 1939, 3, citing [London] *Daily Telegram*; Aaron Levenstein, "Do Nazis Get British Arms?" *Call*, 25 November 1939, 2; Levenstein, "Bankers Do Business with Nazis," *Call*, 9 December 1939, 3.

57. Holt, *CR*, 18 October 1939, 549.

58. Sargent, *Getting US into War*, 20–23; William K. Hutchinson, "Hitler–British Tie Suspected by Borah," *WTH*, 2 February 1940.

59. "Business as Usual," *Uncensored* 8 (25 November 1939): 1. For similar indictments, see "Business as Usual," *Uncensored* 10 (9 December 1939): 2; *Socialist Appeal*, 16 December 1939, 4; Aaron Levenstein, "Trading with the Enemy," *Call*, 9 December 1939, 1.

60. Canada met with similar criticism. In January 1940, *Uncensored* noted that at the very time Britain was aiding Finland to resist Russian invasion, Canada was selling a million bushels of wheat to the aggressor. Such imports, it said, could release Russian-grown wheat for Germany's granaries, which in turn would operate to further Hitler's original strategy in making the Nazi-Soviet trade and mutual assistance agreements. "Business as Usual," *Uncensored* 16 (20 January 1940): 2. See also Sargent, Bulletin #30, 26 January 1940, *Getting US into War*, 248.

61. Nye, *CR*, 12 October 1939, 361. See also Senator La Follette, *CR*, 12 October 1939, 331; D. Worth Clark, *CR*, 16 October 1939, 447; "Is Britain Willing to Arm Her Enemies?" *Christian Century* 56 (25 October 1939): 1292; Aaron Levenstein, "Do Nazis Get British Arms?" *Call*, 25 November 1939, 1; "Merchants of Blood and Iron," *Call*, 30 December 1939, 4.

62. "Business as Usual," *Uncensored* 6 (11 November 1939): 1.

63. Dreiser, *America Is Worth Saving*, chap. 14; Nye, *CR*, 9 October 1939, 192; "Let's Put an End to This Hysteria," *Labor*, 11 June 1940; Clark, *CR*, 18 October 1939, 548; Barnes, "Keep Out of War and Investigate the War-Mongers" [draft], Box 252, Lundeen Papers.

64. "Blunder upon Blunder," *CT*, 2 October 1939, 12. See also Dennis, *WFL* 94 (16 May 1940): 1.

65. "Mr. Chamberlain in Peace and War," *CT*, 13 November 1941, 12.

66. See, for example, "Mr. Chamberlain's Record," *New Republic* 101 (13 September 1939): 142; "Guardians of Democracy: Chamberlain," *Uncensored* 15 (13 January 1940): 4; "Our Buzzards Come to Roost," *American Guardian*, 8 September 1939, 4; *In Fact* 1 (10 March 1940): 3.

67. "Exit Chamberlain and Enter Churchill," *CT*, 12 May 1940, 16; "Chamberlain Resigns," *NYDN*, 4 October 1940, 37. See also Lois and Donaldson Thorburn, "Beau Saboteur," *Scribner's Commentator* 10 (April 1940): 68–69.

68. Hearst, "In the News," *SFE*, 13 November 1940, 1; "What Hitler–Stalin Pact Means to the World," *Social Justice*, 4 September 1939, 7.

69. For rightist criticism, see Dennis, *WFL* 131 (30 January 1941): 1; *Social Justice*, 10 June 1940, 4.

70. See, for example, Catherine Curtis, chairman, Women's National Committee to Keep the United States Out of War, testimony, SFRC, 8 February 1941, 825; "Halifax, Propagandist," *SFE*, 18 July 1941, 10; "Cabbages and Kings: 'Quaint Yankee,'" *Scribner's Commentator* 10 (August 1941): 5.

71. "Guardians of Democracy: Halifax," *Uncensored* 15 (13 January 1940): 4. See also Jim Cork, "British Statesmen and India," *Call*, 12 April 1941, 2; Sargent, *Getting US into War*, 39. Idaho author Vardis Fisher said Halifax jailed one hundred thousand Indians at one time. See "Propaganda, Then and Now," *Idaho Sunday Statesman*, 20 April 1941.

72. See, for example, "The 'Reformed' Appeaser," *Daily Worker*, 24 December 1940, 7; Marcantonio, *CR*, 5 February 1941, 656; Sargent, *Getting US into War*, 39; "Halifax Is Real," *Militant*, 4 January 1941, 4; "Guardians of Democracy: Halifax," *Uncensored* 15 (13 January 1940), 4.

73. Wheeler, *CR*, 4 August 1941, 6673. See also speech, "Unity for Peace," 20 March 1941, in *CR*, A1341.

74. George Ambrose Lloyd, *The British Case* (New York: Macmillan, 1940). For attacks, see *In Fact* 2 (10 March 1941): 2; Sargent, *Getting US into War*, 39; "Mr. Brailsford's Appeal," *Christian Century* 57 (2 October 1940): 1200.

75. Sargent, *Getting US into War*, 38; Marcantonio, *CR*, 5 February 1941, 656.

76. John Haynes Holmes to Dr. Hedwig S. Kuhn, 10 October 1939, 6 December 1939, Holmes Papers. See also Helen Essary, "Dear Washington," *WTH*, 6 November 1941, 10; Merwin K. Hart, testimony, SFRC, 8 January 1941, 745; "Lord Halifax," *CT*, 10 May 1941, 10; "Britain's Spokesman," *CT*, 27 March 1941, 10.

77. Roberts, *Holy Fox*, chap. 30; Cull, *Selling War*, 126, 134. For the claim that Halifax got along well with government and press from the outset, see Kimball, *Forged in War*, 79.

78. FDR in Lash, *Roosevelt and Churchill*, 273; Ickes, entry of 8 February 1941, *Secret Diary*, 3:428; Hopkins in Sherwood, *Roosevelt and Hopkins*, 237.

79. Reynolds, *Creation*, 179.

80. For example, see Congressman Bartel Jonkman (Rep.-Mich.), *CR*, 4 February 1941, 530; "Man of Britain," *Saturday Evening Post* 213 (18 January 1941): 26; George Cless, testimony, SFRC, 8 Febru-

ary 1941, 706; Philip Jessup to Hiram Johnson, n.d., read to SFRC, 24 October 1941, 252; Hearst, "In the News," *SFE*, 2 February 1941, 1–2; Sargent, *Getting US into War*, 23, 28–31; "Lothian, Before and After," *NYDN*, 19 January 1941, 43; Nye, *CR*, 25 February 1941, 1365; Nye, *CR*, 4 August 1941, 6674; "Special Supplement: Lord Lothian," *Uncensored* 17 (27 January 1940): 3–4; Ferdinand Lundberg to Sidney Hertzberg, n.d. [ca. late January 1940], Hertzberg Papers.

81. Wheeler, *CR*, 4 August 1941, 6673. For a general attack by Wheeler, see "Unity for Peace," radio address, 20 May 1941, in *CR*, A1341.

82. James Burr Hamilton [George Sylvester Viereck], *Lord Lothian versus Lord Lothian* (Scotch Plains, N.J.: Flanders Hall, 1941), in *CR*, 19 June 1940, A4036.

83. See, for example, Borah, *NYT*, 23 October 1939, 1, 4; John Bassett Moore to Edwin M. Borchard, 26 October 1939, Borchard Papers.

84. Lothian, address, *NYT*, 5 January 1940, 4; George Holden Tinkham to Cordell Hull, 30 March 1940, entered in *CR*, 21 March 1940, A1575. For similar criticism, see also "Lothian, British Keynoter," *NYDN*, 8 January 1940, 17; Holt, *NYT*, 6 January 1940, 3; Frank Waldrop, "Ambassadors and Luncheon Clubs," *WTH*, 21 April 1940, C15.

85. Associated Press dispatch in *CR*, 20 November 1940, A6684. When the inevitable protests came, the British news agency denied that Lothian ever included the word "men." See *New York Sun*, 16 November 1940. For the controversy over the word "men," see B. C. Clark, *CR*, 26 November 1940, A6707. For an example of anti-interventionist outrage, see Holt, speech, Mutual network, 5 December 1940, in *CR*, A7054.

86. Hearst, "In the News," *SFE*, 20 December 1940, 1; Lindbergh, entry of 13 December 1940, *Wartime Journals*, 428. See also Roy Howard to Lord Beaverbrook, 11 May 1940, Howard Papers; Edwin M. Borchard to George Holden Tinkham, 12 September 1940, Borchard Papers; "Defense of Lord Lothian," *CT*, 29 October 1939, 16; "Lord Lothian," *CT*, 13 December 1940, 1; "Lord Lothian," *CT*, 4 January 1940, 12; Castle Diary, 12 December 1940; "Cabbages and Kings: He Knew What He Wanted," *Scribner's Commentator* 9 (February 1941): 5; "The Death of Lord Lothian," *Christian Century* 57 (25 December 1940): 1603.

87. For a positive view, see David Reynolds, "Lord Lothian and Anglo-American Relations, 1939–1940," *Transactions of the American Philosophical Society* 73 (pamphlet; Philadelphia: American Philosophical Society, 1983). For a negative one, see Rhodri Jeffreys-Jones, "The Inestimable Advantage of Not Being English: Lord Lothian's American Ambassadorship, 1939–1940," *Scottish Historical Review* 63 (April 1984): 105–10; Rhodri Jeffreys-Jones, "Lord Lothian and American Democracy: An Illusion in Pursuit of an Illusion," *Canadian Review of American Studies* 17 (Winter 1986): 411–22.

88. For negative reaction, see *Social Justice*, 30 October 1939, 20; Nye, *CR*, 25 February 1941, 1364; Nye, *CR*, 4 August 1941, 6673; G. S. Jackson, "Is Britain's Government Democratic?" *New Masses* 39 (8 April 1941): 9; *In Fact* 1 (1 July 1940): 3; Norman Thomas, "Your World and Mine: The Problems We Face," *Call*, 12 May 1941, 5; Holt, *CR*, 18 October 1939, 542.

89. "Peace and Power Politics," *Uncensored* 88 (7 June 1941): 4; "Text of Lord Beaverbrook's Speech," *NYT*, 24 March 1941, 4; "Union with Britain?" *NYDN*, 25 March 1941, 23; Hearst, "In the News," *SFE*, 7 August 1940, 1; "British Cabinet Changes," *CT*, 5 May 1941, 10.

90. Thomas, testimony, HFAC, 4 February 1941, 333. See also John Haynes Holmes to Alfred P. Perkins, 13 February 1941; Holmes to Max Tashna, 14 May 1941, Holmes Papers.

91. See, for example, Holt, "Is Churchill Good Enough for Roosevelt?" *Scribner's Commentator* 9 (July 1941): 35; Nye, *CR*, 26 February 1941, 1729; Nye, *CR*, 8 March 1941, 2083.

92. Holt, "Is Churchill Good Enough for Roosevelt?" 34–36. See also *Social Justice*, 17 March 1941, 13.

93. See, for example, Holt, *CR*, 18 October 1941, 558; Holt, *CR*, 12 December 1940, 13,897; AFC cited in *NYT*, 19 March 1941, 8; Wheeler, *NYT*, 21 March 1941, 8; Ralph Townsend, testimony, SFRC, 8 February 1941, 801; Sargent, Bulletin #32, 26 January 1940, *Getting US into War*, 257; Dennis, *WFL* 94 (16 May 1940): 1; "Winston Churchill," *NYDN*, 15 November 1939, 39.

94. See William Griffin, publisher of the *New York Enquirer*, "When Churchill Said Keep Out!" *Scribner's Commentator* 9 (2 February 1941): 25–28. For additional material on the interview from Griffin's standpoint, see Frazier and Reynolds, *CR*, 21 October 1939, 686–87; entries of Congressman

Michael J. Kennedy (Dem.-N.Y.), 10 April 1940, in *CR*, A1994. For a friendly sketch of Griffin's background, see Bill Cunningham, *Boston Post*, 20 January 1941. For anti-interventionist use of Griffin, see Nye, *CR*, 26 February 1941, 1412; Holt, *CR*, 12 December 1940, 13,896; Tobey, *CR*, 7 November 1941, 8647; "Then and Now," *Call*, 7 December 1940, 4; *Social Justice*, 14 April 1941, 15; Sargent citing himself and Villard, Bulletin #32, 26 January 1940, *Getting US into War*, 261 n. 1; John Haynes Holmes to Ralph Sussman, 17 February 1941, Holmes Papers. For British denials of the interview, see *NYT*, 11 October 1939, 2; 9 March 1940, 4; 29 March 1940, 5; 6 April 1940, 4.

95. For Churchill and Bolshevism, see G. S. Jackson, "Is Britain's Government Democratic?" *New Masses* 39 (8 April 1941): 8; Sherman Staley, "Who Is Winston Churchill?" *Socialist Appeal*, 9 September 1939, 3; Sargent, *Getting US into War*, 38. For Gandhi, see Vardis Fisher, "Propaganda, Then and Now," *Idaho Sunday Statesman*, 20 April 1941; Jim Cork, "British Statesmen and India," *Call*, 12 April 1941, 2. For Mussolini, see Nye, *CR*, 25 February 1941, 1364; Wheeler, radio speech, "Unity for Peace," 20 March 1941, in *CR*, A1341; Wheeler, *CR*, 15 July 1941, 6046; Richard Rovere, "Winston Churchill's 'Dusty Answer,'" *Call*, 4 January 1941, 4. For a claim that Churchill was insufficiently anti-Russian, see Symes, "Hold That Line," *Call*, 4 January 1939, 4.

96. "Winnie the Pooh," *Uncensored* 26 (30 March 1940): 4. For other references to Churchill on Hitler, see Nye, *CR*, 8 March 1941, 1364; "Comment," *Social Justice*, 8 September 1941, 9; Sargent, Bulletin #22, 15 December 1939, *Getting US into War*, 197. Yet Churchill's supposedly long-standing opposition to Germany was also stressed. General Wood recalled a conversation in 1936 in which Churchill allegedly had told him, "Germany is getting too strong. We must smash her." Testimony, SFRC, 4 February 1941, 389.

97. See, for example, Hearst, "In the News," *SFE*, 25 April 1941, 1; 28 May 1941, A; 11 June 1940, 1; 7 August 1940, 1; Hanighen, "Blood, Sweat and Illusions," *Progressive*, 14 June 1941, 9; Dennis, *WFL* 115 (10 October 1940): 3; 153 (3 July 1941): 2; Dwight Macdonald, editorial reply to Stephen Spender, *Partisan Review* 7 (September–October 1940): 407; Vardis Fisher, "Propaganda, Then and Now," *Idaho Sunday Statesman*, 20 April 1941; Ezra Pound, "The Inedible: Russia Has It," *America* 62 (9 March 1940): 594.

98. See, for example, "Why Did France Crack Up?" *NYDN*, 3 July 1940, 19; "The Fall of France," *NYDN*, 14 July 1940, 35; "Churchill as Orator," *NYDN*, 29 April 1941, 23; Hearst, "In the News," *WTH*, 3 May 1941, 3; *WTH*, 10 April 1941, 1.

99. See, for example, "Churchill's Old Age," *New Masses* 35 (18 June 1940): 21; Libby, letter to NCPW executive board and branch offices, 4 June 1941, NCPW Papers; Waldrop, "Child Eating Mother?" *WTH*, 28 September 1941, E1.

100. Kennedy in Costello, *Ten Days*, 50; "Churchill In," *NYDN*, 9 May 1940, 33. See also "The Consequences of Stumblebum Diplomacy," *NYDN*, 24 August 1940, 13. See also "Dictator Churchill," *NYDN*, 24 May 1940, 29.

101. See, for example, Dennis, *WFL* 118 (31 October 1941): 1.

102. "Exit Chamberlain and Enter Churchill," *CT*, 12 May 1940, 15. For previous tributes, see "Mr. Churchill Takes Over," *CT*, 5 April 1940, 16; "Chamberlain's Speech," *CT*, 8 May 1940, 18. *Tribune* publisher Robert McCormick said, "I have known Winston Churchill for 25 years. A more thoroughly honorable man never lived." McCormick, testimony, SFRC, 6 February 1941, 480.

103. "Mr. Churchill's Words and Deeds," *CT*, 6 June 1940, 20. See also Anne Morrow Lindbergh, *Wave*, 33.

104. Castle Diary, 16 April 1941; "Inside England," *Uncensored* 90 (21 June 1941): 1.

105. Reynolds, *Creation*, 114; W. Averell Harriman and Elie Abel, *Special Envoy to Churchill and Stalin, 1941–1946* (New York: Random House, 1975), 191; Kimball, *Forged in War*, 13. For other FDR criticism, see Lash, *Roosevelt and Churchill*, 273.

106. See, for example, Dennis, *WFL* 92 (2 May 1940): 1; *WFL* 94 (16 May 1940): 1; *Social Justice*, 10 June 1940, 4; Villard, "Issues and Men," *Nation* 150 (11 May 1940): 599; Jackson, "Is Britain's Government Democratic?" *New Masses* 39 (8 April 1941): 9; Lois and Donaldson Thornburn, "Beau Saboteur," *Scribner's Commentator* 8 (June 1940): 64–65. Yet it was not only such anti-interventionists who disliked Eden. Hopkins found him to be a man possessing "no deeply rooted moral stamina," whose lack of substance permitted Churchill to be his own foreign secretary. Ponting, *1940*, 75.

107. For Henderson, see Burton Rascoe to Quincy Howe, 13 April 1940, Hertzberg Papers; Sargent, *Getting US into War*, 38; critic Malcolm Cowley, "The Other England," *New Republic* 102 (29 April 1940): 581–82; Herbert Rosen, *Daily Worker*, 27 April 1940, 7; "War Aims," *Uncensored* 8 (25 November 1939): special supplement, 1. For both Stanley and Hoare, see "Guardians of Democracy," *Uncensored* 15 (13 January 1940): 4–5. On Stanley, see also "The Belisha Beacon," *New Masses* 34 (16 January 1940): 19.

108. Hearst, "In the News," *SFE*, 11 April 1940, 2. See also Hearst, *SFE*, 9 March 1940, 2. For further praise of Hore-Belisha, see "Chamberlain Drops a War Minister," *CT*, 9 January 1940, 14; "Mr. Chamberlain Doesn't Explain," *CT*, 18 January 1940, 12; "Hore-Belisha and the Generals," *CT*, 2 February 1940, 10; "Guardians of Democracy," *Uncensored* 15 (13 January 1940): 3; Sargent, Bulletin #26, 12 January 1940, *Getting US into War*, 233–34; "Why Did Hore-Belisha Quit?" *NYDN*, 31 January 1940, 27; Frank Waldrop, "The Man Behind the Blowup," *WTH*, 9 January 1940, 9.

109. "David Lloyd George," *NYDN*, 10 May 1940, 31. For a surprising endorsement, see Ickes, entry of 12 May 1940, *Secret Diary*, 3:176.

110. Dennis, *WFL* 105 (1 August 1940): 2; 115 (10 October 1940): 3. Conversely *Social Justice* found Bevin to be a carefully built-up front for Marxist powers that sought Britain's downfall. Issue of 14 October 1940, 4.

111. *Social Justice*, 24 June 1940, 20; Hearst, "In the News," *SFE*, 14 April 1940, 2; 23 December 1940, 1–2.

112. Francis X. Bushman to Verne Marshall, 23 December 1940, Verne Marshall Papers; Nock, Nehru review, *Scribner's Commentator* 10 (August 1941): 91; *Social Justice*, 1 July 1940, 4. For an example of AFC anti-British views, see Page Hufty, Bulletin #615, 9 October 1941, Box 279, AFC Papers. See also Congressman Lambertson, *CR*, 26 September 1940, 12,704; "Cabbages and Kings: Brussels Sprouts," *Scribner's Commentator* 10 (October 1941): 6.

113. Reynolds, *Creation*, 23. See, for example, Senator La Follette, *CR*, 12 October 1939, 332; Wheeler, *CR*, 28 February 1941, 1522; Norman Thomas to Robert Alexander, 19 June 1941, Thomas Papers; Thomas, testimony, HFAC, 22 January 1941, 325; Sweeney, *CR*, 5 February 1941, 581; Ernest L. Meyer, "'For Democracy'—'Oh Yeah'," *American Guardian*, 15 September 1939, 4; Villard, [University of Rochester] *Tower-Times*, 23 February 1940, 1; Theodore Dreiser to Frederick V. Field, 25 November 1940, Hertzberg Papers; Dreiser, *America Is Worth Saving*, chap. 7.

114. Williams, *Airpower*, 402; Barnes, "Political Rule in Britain," *NYWT*, 3 November 1939, 26. Barnes continued that according to "Britain's Unknown Ruler," an article in the London *Sunday Express* reprinted as "Persons and Personages" in *Living Age* 357 (October 1939): 145–48, the real ruler of Britain was Sir Horace Wilson, head of the three hundred thousand bureaucrats who ran the nation. Wilson appointed all the heads of government departments, was personally close to Chamberlain, and was the supreme economic adviser to the government.

115. For Priestley, see Sargent, Bulletin #15, 14 November 1939, *Getting US into War*, 165. For Wells, see Downey, *CR*, 9 October 1940, 190. For Eden, see Robert Maynard Hutchins, sermon at Rockefeller Memorial Chapel, 30 March 1941, in *CR*, A1580; Tobey, *CR*, 15 July 1941, 6046; Johns, speech, 11 June 1941, in *CR*, A2834.

116. Kennedy, interview, *Boston Globe*, 10 November 1940; Barnes, "The War and World Revolution," *Progressive*, 15 November 1941, 9.

117. See, for example, Reynolds, *CR*, 21 October 1940, 693; "NY Post Does Its Duty for War Propaganda," *Daily Worker*, 2 November 1939, 6.

118. "The War Parties," *CT*, 22 September 1939, 14. See also "War and Dictatorship," *CT*, 7 September 1939, 15; "Let's Have the Regular Order," *CT*, 25 September 1939, 12; Senator La Follette, *CR*, 12 October 1939, 329.

119. "A Democracy of Voteless Men," *CT*, 15 October 1939, 14. See also "People at War," *CT*, 10 March 1940, 18.

120. Johnson, "One Man's Opinion," *SFN*, 26 September 1939, 13; "Toward Totalitarianism," *NYDN*, 11 February 1940, 47. See also Vandenberg, *CR*, 4 October 1939, 97; Rankin, *CR*, 9 October 1939, A206.

121. *NYT*, 23 May 1940, 1, 4; A. J. P. Taylor, *British History: 1914–1945* (New York: Oxford University Press, 1965), 479; "Last Ditch," *Newsweek*, 3 June 1940, 18.

122. See, for example, "A Page of Comment," and "England Goes Totalitarian," *Social Justice*, 3 June 1940, 3, 6; Kennedy, testimony, HFAC, 21 January 1941, 237.

123. "Britain Establishes a War Dictatorship," *Christian Century* 57 (5 June 1940): 723.

124. "It Has Happened in England," *CT*, 24 May 1940, 14. For a similar claim that Britain was as totalitarian as Germany, see Neilson, entry of 9 August 1940, *Tragedy*, 1:579; "No Conscription," *America* 63 (24 August 1940): 457.

125. See, for example, "Toward Totalitarianism," *NYDN*, 11 February 1940, 47; Dennis, *WFL* 95 (23 May 1940): 1; Herbert Hoover to Edmond G. Lincoln, 5 August 1940, Hoover Papers. Joseph P. Kennedy was an exception, claiming that though such legislation could well be an inevitable by-product of any war, "that does not mean that some form of democracy could not come back at the end of the war." Testimony, HFAC, 21 January 1941, 237.

126. Dennis, *WFL* 95 (23 May 1940): 1. For the dictatorship theme, see also *WFL* 150 (12 June 1941), 3.

127. "M-Day in London," *New Masses* 35 (4 June 1940): 19. For other such left-wing comments on the condition of labor, see Marcantonio, *CR*, 5 February 1941, 657–58; Seldes, *In Fact* 2 (9 January 1941): 1; G. S. Jackson, "Is Britain's Government Democratic?" *New Masses* 39 (8 April 1941): 9.

128. Thomas, testimony, HFAC, 22 January 1941, 324–25, 343; Wheeler, speech of 25 June 1941, in Anderson, "Wheeler," 216. See also Vandenberg, *NYT*, 1 January 1941, 6; Koskoff, *Kennedy*, 287; "What's Coming in England?" *NYDN*, 15 September 1940, 47; Sokolsky, "These Days: The Four Freedoms," *New York Sun*, 5 December 1940, 24; Coughlin, "World Heads Towards Total War," broadcast of 12 May 1940, in *Social Justice*, 20 May 1940, 3; Merwin K. Hart, testimony, SFRC, 8 February 1941, 744.

129. See, for example, Sokolsky, "These Days," *New York Sun*, 12 April 1941, 18; Shafer, *CR*, 19 March 1941, A1419; *Scribner's Commentator* 9 (April 1941), inside front cover; Amos Pinchot, "The Roosevelt–Laski Scheme," *Scribner's Commentator* 8 (October 1940): 62–68.

130. Kennedy, testimony, HFAC, 21 January 1941, 237.

131. "Britain's Goal," *Progressive*, 5 April 1941, 12. It cited Geoffrey Crowther, "Is Britain Turning Socialist?" *NYT Magazine*, 23 March 1941, 3, 24.

132. See, for example, Catherine Curtis, "Washington Affairs and National Defense," speech to Mothers of the United States of America, Detroit, 13 June 1941, in *CR*, A5269; Wheeler, *CR*, 21 April 1941, 3; "Cabbages and Kings: Remember This Symbol: 18B," *Scribner's Commentator* 11 (December 1941): 5. Extremist anti-interventionists stressed the "persecution" of those whom they found kindred spirits overseas. See, for example, *Social Justice*, 15 July 1940, 6; "Duke of Buccleuch," *Social Justice*, 14 October 1940, 8; "The *Week* Suppressed," *New Masses* 35 (18 June 1940): 21.

133. Ponting, *1940*, 149.

134. Davis, *CR*, 23 October 1939, 913.

135. "Only by Peace Can Liberty Be Protected," *SFE*, 12 August 1940, 8.

136. "A Bill to Destroy the Republic," *CT*, 12 January 1941, 1.

137. See, for example, "Cabbages and Kings: Freedom," *Scribner's Commentator* 10 (June 1941): 3; Lillian Symes, "Hold That Line," *Call*, 26 July 1941, 5; Holmes, "Civil Liberties in Time of Crisis," *Unity* 126 (7 October 1940): 37; "Criticism Here and There," *CT*, 15 October 1941, 12.

138. "British C.O.'s," *Uncensored* 3 (21 October 1939): 2. See also "British Peace Sentiment," *Uncensored* 23 (9 March 1940): 3; Devere Allen, *Unity* 124 (20 November 1939): 96. For anxieties over British pacifists, see "Britain Bears Down on Opponents of War," *Christian Century* 57 (22 May 1940): 660.

139. Chamberlin, "War: Shortcut to Fascism," *American Mercury* 51 (December 1940): 394–95.

140. Hoover, memorandum of conversation with Joseph P. Kennedy, 22 November 1940, Hoover Papers.

141. Reynolds, *Creation*, 24–25; Kimball (with Fred E. Pollock), *Juggler*, chap. 7; Ickes, entry of 29 January 1939, *Secret Diary*, 2:571.

142. Harper, *American Vision*, 36–37; Roosevelt to editors, cited in Rock, *Chamberlain and Roosevelt*, 287; Roosevelt to Willkie in Thorne, *Allies*, 98.

143. Leutze, *Bargaining*, 176; Harper, *American Vision*, 54; Thorne, *Allies*, 99. For Berle's attacks on their entire diplomatic record, see entry of 3 May 1940, *Navigating*, 309.

144. Leutze, *Bargaining*, 179; Pogue, *Marshall*, 2:132–33; Stoler, "Embick"; Schaffer, "Embick," 89–95.

145. Gallup polls, 8 April and 20 May 1941, in Cantril, *Public Opinion*, 976. At the same time a July poll showed only 14 percent favoring immediate entrance into the war; of 86 percent who either opposed entry or had no opinion, 31 percent claimed the United States should fight only if invaded. Gallup poll of 9 July 1941, in Cantril, *Public Opinion*, 976. Even in a Gallup poll taken on 22 October, only 17 percent wanted immediate entry. Cantril, *Public Opinion*, 977. The highest record, 27 percent, was reached in a Gallup poll taken on 29 May 1941. Cantril, *Public Opinion*, 973.

## CHAPTER 14: THE BRITISH EMPIRE

1. Gillis, "All-Out Aid for Britain," *Catholic World* 153 (March 1941): 643; Burton Rascoe to Sidney Hertzberg, 6 July 1940, Hertzberg Papers. See also Knutson, *CR*, 10 October 1940, A6275; Congressman James P. McGranery (Dem.-Pa.), *CR*, 1 November 1939, 1213; Congressman Homer D. Angell (Rep.-Oreg.), *CR*, 1223–24; Alexander, *CR*, 1 November 1939, 1259; Voorhis, *CR*, 2 October 1939, A123; "All Is Not Lost," *Catholic World* 151 (July 1940): 133; Upton Close, "Common Sense for Americans," *Living Age* 358 (August 1940): 510.

2. "The Empires," *CT*, 18 October 1939, 16. On commonwealth, see Gillis, "Good Old Uncle Sam," *Catholic World* 153 (March 1941): 642. On dominion, see Dreiser, *America Is Worth Saving*, 104.

3. Wheeler, *CT*, 26 June 1941, 2. See also *CR*, 27 February 1941, 1488.

4. Nye, 4 March 1941, *CR*, 1722. See also Nye, [University of North Carolina] *Daily Tar Heel*, 19 November 1941, 1; *CR*, 26 February 1941, 1730.

5. Lundeen, *CR*, 18 October 1939, 547. See also speech, Washington, D.C., 9 June 1940, in *CR*, A3754; *CR*, 27 August 1940, 11,017.

6. Clark, *CR*, 4 November 1941, 8485. See also *CR*, 24 February 1941, 1297.

7. Sweeney, *CR*, 5 February 1941, 581; Robsion, *CR*, 2 November 1939, 1295. See also Ralph Townsend, testimony, SFRC, 8 February 1941, 798.

8. Mencken, "Notes on a Moral War," *Baltimore Sun*, 8 October 1939; "No Hostility to England," *CT*, 1 November 1939, 14. See also "How about It, Mr. Churchill?" *CT*, 2 October 1941, 12.

9. Chester Bowles to Phil La Follette, 28 September 1939, Philip La Follette Papers.

10. Thomas, letter to the editor, *New Republic* 104 (20 June 1941): 118–19.

11. Jim Cork, "'This England,'" *Call*, 6 December 1941, 2. See also Dreiser, *America Is Worth Saving*, 108–9.

12. Hanighen, "Making the World Safe for Empire," *Common Sense* 8 (September 1939): 22; Seldes, "Tuberculosis for Natives; $$$ for Britons," *In Fact* 2 (27 January 1941): 2–3.

13. "Double Talk," *NYDN*, 1 June 1941, 41; Townsend, testimony, SFRC, 8 February 1941, 798; Clark, SFRC, 8 February 1941, 709; Norman Thomas to Henry Pinski, 8 April 1941, Thomas Papers; Marcantonio, *CR*, 22 January 1941, 238. See also Dreiser as noted in "Books in a World at War," *Peace Action* 7 (February 1941): 7.

14. Fisher, *Idaho Daily Statesman*, 17 January 1941; Robsion, *CR*, 6 May 1941, 3660. For specific remarks concerning Egypt's apathy, see Wheeler, *CR*, 28 February 1941, 1522. For the demands of Burma, see "Freedoms in Burma and India," *CT*, 23 September 1941, 12; "U Saw's Own View of the Freedoms," *CT*, 6 November 1941, 14. For general comments, see "Poverty of India Monument to Empire," *Social Justice*, 27 October 1941, 11; Dreiser, *America Is Worth Saving*, 106.

15. Nye, *CR*, 26 February 1941, 1726–32; White, *CR*, 5 February 1941, 657. For further comments concerning opium, see Lutheran radio minister Walter Maier, *American Guardian*, 9 February 1940, 2; Marcantonio, *CR*, 5 February 1941, 581.

16. Nye, *CR*, 4 March 1941, 1731. See also Gillis, "What Are They Fighting For?" *Catholic World* 150 (December 1939): 259; Dreiser, *America Is Worth Saving*, 108.

17. Chester Bowles to Philip La Follette, 28 September 1939, Philip La Follette Papers. For further comment on the Boer War, see Lundeen, *CR*, 18 October 1939, 550; Holt, *CR*, 18 October 1940, 549–50; Marcantonio, *CR*, 5 February 1941, 657; Edwin M. Borchard to James A. Shanley, 30 August 1939, Borchard Papers; Walter Maier cited in *American Guardian*, 9 February 1940, 2; Dreiser, *America Is Worth Saving*, 69; Theodore Dreiser to Frederick V. Field, 25 November 1940, Hertzberg Papers; "A Page of Comment," *Social Justice*, 3 June 1940, 3; Sweeney, *CR*, 5 February 1941, 581; Nye, *CR*, 4 March 1941, 1729.

18. See, for example, Chester Bowles to Philip La Follette, 28 September 1939, Philip La Follette Papers; "Axis Cashing In on Blunders in Near East," *Social Justice*, 9 June 1941, 9; D. Worth Clark, *CR*, 16 October 1939, 448; John Arnold, "Mr. Chamberlain Looks at Zion," *New Masses* 34 (19 March 1940): 26–27.

19. Holt, *CR*, 18 October 1939, 551. See also Nye, *CR*, 4 March 1941, 1731; Sweeney, *CR*, 20 March 1940, 3162; Sweeney, speech, NBC red network, 6 May 1940, in *CR*, A2154; "But Boake Carter Says," *SFE*, 5 December 1941, 17.

20. Coughlin, "Shrine Dinner Chats," *Social Justice*, 5 June 1939, 3.

21. See, for example, Nye, *CR*, 4 March 1941, 1725; D. W. Clark, *CR*, 16 October 1939, 446; Marcantonio, *CR*, 5 February 1941, 657; Seldes, "Facts about 'Democracy' in India," *In Fact* 2 (27 January 1941): 3; "Washing the Empire Linen," *New Masses* 33 (31 October 1939): 16; Sweeney, *CR*, 5 February 1941, 581; James McCawley, "Under British Rule: A Study in 'Benevolent' Imperialism," *Catholic World* 150 (March 1940): 703–10.

22. Nock, review of Nehru, in *Scribner's Commentator* 10 (August 1941): 87–90; Tobey, *CR*, 4 March 1941, 1732; Townsend, testimony, SFRC, 8 February 1941, 798; Wheeler, *CR*, 28 February 1941, 1522; Wheeler, *CR*, 15 July 1941, 6047. For his firsthand observations, see Wheeler, *CR*, 24 February 1941, 1311–12.

23. For bombing, see *Social Justice*, 25 September 1939, 8; Nye, *CR*, 4 March 1941, 1732; Marcantonio, *CR*, 4 February 1941, 560; Marcantonio, *CR*, 5 February 1941, 657.

24. Chester Bowles to Philip La Follette, 28 September 1940, Philip La Follette Papers; Sterling Morton to Robert E. Wood, 3 April 1941, Morton Papers. See also *U.S. Week*, 22 May 1941, 7.

25. See, for example, Frazier, *CR*, 14 October 1939, 399; "India in This War," *CT*, 8 November 1939, 16; "India in the War," *CT*, 17 December 1939, 16; John Haynes Holmes, A. J. Muste, Roger Baldwin, J. Holmes Smith, and Gordon Halstead, letter to the editor, *New Republic* 102 (17 June 1940): 827; "War Aims," *Uncensored* 4 (28 October 1939): 2; "India Strikes for Freedom," *Christian Century* 56 (18 October 1939): 1260.

26. See, for example, Mrs. Kamaladevi, educator and a member of the Indian National Congress, to Youth Committee Against War, [City College of New York] *Main Events*, 13 November 1939, 1.

27. Patel, *Daily Worker*, 22 December 1939, 2. See also *Barnard* [College] *Bulletin*, 14 November 1939, 4; [University of Chicago] *Daily Maroon*, 8 December 1939, 1; [Dartmouth College] *The Dartmouth*, 15 November 1939, 1; [Bryn Mawr] *College News*, 29 November 1939, 1, 3; *Vassar* [College] *Miscellany News*, 6 December 1939, 1; [Northwestern University] *Daily Northwestern*, 7 December 1939, 2; [City College of New York] *Campus*, 8 March 1940, 1; [Clark University] *Scarlet*, 5 March 1940, 1; [University of North Carolina] *Daily Tar Heel*, 12 April 1940, 1. For Patel's background, see *Vassar Miscellany News*, 6 December 1939, 1.

28. Singh, [University of Chicago] *Daily Maroon*, 29 January 1941, 1. For Singh, see also [New York University] *Washington Square College Bulletin*, 6 November 1939, 1; [City College of New York] *Campus*, 8 November 1939, 1; 11 November 1939, 1; *Wesleyan* [University] *Argus*, 13 November 1939, 2; [Northwestern University] *Daily Northwestern*, 26 September 1940, 1; 3 October 1940, 2; 4 October 1940, 1; 8 October 1940, 3.

29. See, for example, Coughlin, "May India Succeed," *Social Justice*, 25 December 1939, 4; Gerald Griffin, "In Darkest India," *New Masses* 34 (27 February 1940): 12–14; Marion Greenspan, "India: 360,000,000 in Motion," *New Masses* 35 (28 May 1940): 13–14; Dennis, *WFL* 86 (21 March 1940): 5. Within a year, Dennis predicted that irrespective of the outcome of the war, Britain would not be ruling India much longer. *WFL* 134 (20 February 1941): 2.

30. Alexander, *CR*, 1 November 1939, 1259.

31. While most anti-interventionists said little about nationalist leader Mahatma Gandhi himself, some on the extreme left attacked him. See, for example, James Burnham, "Their Government," *Socialist Appeal*, 27 October 1939, 4; Greenspan, "India: 360,000,000 in Motion," 13–14; Andrew Roth, "Behind the Arrest of Nehru," *New Masses* 37 (26 November 1940): 12.

32. For protest from the extreme left, see Roth, "Behind the Arrest of Nehru," 12; Michael Sayers, "Nehru of India: Spokesman of Awakening Millions," *Friday*, 13 December 1940, 8–9; "How about India?" *Daily Worker*, 6 November 1940, 6. For others, see Robert Carroll, "Is This My War?" *Scribner's Commentator* 10 (July 1941): 61; Villard, "India: An Acid Test," *Progressive*, 20 September 1941, 4; Dorothy Detzer to Emily Greene Balch, 24 March 1941, WIL Papers; "Political Imprisonment Growing in India," *Christian Century* 58 (9 January 1941): 876.

33. Norman Thomas to Mirza Ahmad Schrab, 6 December 1940, Thomas Papers.

34. "British Empire Faces Growing Unrest in India," *Christian Century* 56 (1 November 1939): 1325. See also "Washing the Empire Linen," *New Masses* 33 (31 October 1939): 16; Lillian Symes to Oscar Lange, 7 November 1939, Thomas Papers.

35. "Bad News for India," *Christian Century* 57 (22 May 1940): 659; "No Democracy for India," *Christian Century* 57 (21 August 1940): 1022.

36. "Divided India: Natives Should Beware Russia," *SFE*, 18 March 1940, 16; "India's Opportunity," *NYDN*, 8 February 1940, 29; Waldrop, "The Man in the Loincloth," *WTH*, 16 August 1940, 16.

37. Thorne, *Allies*, 103; Louis, *Imperialism*, 8–10.

38. Kimball, *Juggler*, 132–40. See also Thorne, *Allies*, chaps. 8, 14, 21, pp. 710–11.

39. Clark, *CR*, 16 October 1939, 446; "No Hostility to England," *CT*, 1 November 1939, 14. See also Holt, *CR*, 18 October 1939, 549; Congressman McGranery, *CR*, 1 November 1939, 1215.

40. Chester Bowles to Philip La Follette, 28 September 1939, Philip La Follette Papers; Sweeney, *CR*, 5 February 1941, 581.

41. See McGranery, *CR*, 1 November 1939, 1214–15; Holt, *CR*, 2 December 1940, A6983–85. Nye quoted an address to the Congress of the United States issued in the early 1920s by Irish nationalists. *CR*, 4 March 1941, 1733.

42. Hanighen, "Making the World Safe for Empire," *Common Sense* 8 (September 1939): 21. For general comments, see William Griffin, "Churchill's Attack on Neutrality," *New York Enquirer*, 11 November 1940; Drieser, *America Is Worth Saving*, 110–11; "Irish Victory," *New Masses* 39 (10 June 1941): 21; Nye, *CR*, 25 February 1941, 1370.

43. See, for example, "The Irish Are Not Fooled," *Daily Worker*, 10 January 1940, 6; *Daily Worker*, 26 April 1940, 4; Holt, *CR*, 15 November 1940, A6590; Professor John O'Brien, speech to Catholic Women's Club, Madison, Wisconsin, in *CT*, 18 March 1941, 8. For the broader picture, see Raymond James Raymond, "American Public Opinion and Irish Neutrality, 1939–1945," *Eire-Ireland* 18 (Spring 1983): 20–45.

44. For Churchill's concern, see *NYT*, 6 November 1940, 25, 26. For Ireland's rejection, see *NYT*, 7 November 1940, 1, 6.

45. Sargent, Bulletin #26, 5 January 1940, *Getting US into War*, 231; *Daily Worker*, 17 February 1941, 6; Los Angeles lawyer Joseph Scott, address, San Francisco Civic Auditorium, in *CR*, 10 February 1941, A556; Congressman O'Connor, *CR*, 17 April 1941, 3166; William Griffin, *New York Enquirer*, 11 November 1940.

46. Editorial, *Saturday Evening Post* 213 (19 April 1941): 28; "Cabbages and Kings: Turning on the Heat," *Scribner's Commentator* 10 (June 1941): 5. For other intimations that Britain was starving Ireland, see "Irish Victory," *New Masses* 39 (10 June 1941): 21; "Ireland Menaced by Starvation," *U.S. Week*, 26 April 1941, 7.

47. "Irish Bases," *Uncensored* 64 (21 December 1940): 1. See also "Irish Bases," *Uncensored* 67 (11 January 1941): 2. Interventionist military writer George Fielding Eliot questioned *Uncensored*'s claim that the bases were not important to Britain. Blacksod Bay, he maintained, would be of great value. Eliot also disputed the claim that it would take six months to erect a temporary base. George Fielding Eliot to Sidney Hertzberg, 23 December 1940, Hertzberg Papers. Associate editor Cushman Reynolds replied to Eliot, saying that although bases in Eire would be assets, they would not necessarily break up Germany's intense submarine campaign. Letter of 31 January 1940, Hertzberg Papers.

48. Frank Hanighen to Cushman Reynolds, 9 January 1941, Hertzberg Papers.

49. "Ireland Next?" *CT*, 9 July 1940, 10; "When Eire Eyes Are Smiling," *NYDN*, 8 January 1941, 29; "Easter in Ireland," *NYDN*, 15 April 1941, 28. See also Castle Diary, 3 January 1941.

50. Taft and Wheeler, *Time*, 16 July 1941, 16; *Newsweek*, 21 July 1941, 11. See also rumors reported by Warren Mullin, minutes, NCPW executive board, 19 March 1941, NCPW Papers; Sargent, Bulletin #26, 5 January 1940, *Getting US into War*, 230–31 n. 4.

51. John A. Danaher to Edwin M. Borchard, 8 July 1941, Borchard Papers; R. A. Moore, Bulletin #415, 15 July 1941, Box 279, AFC Papers. See also AFC Research Bureau, "Another A.E.F.," *Did You Know?* 9 (15 July 1941), in Doenecke, *IDU*, 345.

52. "Addresses of President and Hull Before Pan American Union," *NYT*, 15 April 1939, 2; Gallup poll, 22 September 1939, Cantril, *Public Opinion*, 772. For other polls, see 772.

53. See, for example, Detzer, report to WIL National Board, 21–22 October 1939, WIL Papers.

54. Johnson, "War in America," *NYWT*, 12 September 1939, 17; Nye, *NYT*, 14 September 1941, 14; Edwin M. Borchard to John Bassett Moore, 27 September 1939, Borchard Papers. See also "The New War Propaganda," *America* 61 (20 September 1939): 613.

55. Barnes, "Russian Tie-Up with Nazis," *NYWT*, 3 October 1939, 18. Some anti-interventionists found Canada lacking in enthusiasm for the conflict. See "Canada Votes," *New Republic* 102 (5 February 1940): 165; "The War Is Unpopular in Canada," *Daily Worker*, 13 January 1940, 6.

56. Roosevelt, *NYT*, 13 September 1939, 1; Johnson, *SFN*, 26 September 1939, 13. See also Paul Blakely, "The Monroe Doctrine Is a Policy, Not a Law," *America* 61 (30 September 1939): 583; John Bassett Moore to William Potter Lage, 23 September 1939, Moore Papers.

57. Lindbergh, "Talk on Arms Embargo," text, *NYT*, 14 October 1939, 10.

58. "But Boake Carter Says," *SFE*, 26 October 1939, 15; Hugh Johnson, *SFN*, 21 October 1939, 13; 17 October 1939, 17. Castle read the speech as a clumsy attempt to state that Canada should not be under the protection of the Monroe Doctrine if it went to war whenever Britain did. Diary, 16 October 1939.

59. See, for example, "Shoot the Works," *New Republic* 101 (1 November 1939): 366; Walter Lippmann, "Today and Tomorrow," *New York Herald Tribune*, 17 October 1939, 21; Dorothy Thompson, "On the Record: Col. Lindbergh's Imperialism," *New York Herald Tribune*, 20 October 1939, 19.

60. "A Doctrine Should Work Both Ways," *American Guardian*, 6 October 1939, 4; "Heirs to the British Empire," *NYDN*, 10 March 1940, 47; typed memo on Dennett conversation with Tansill, enclosed in Prescott Dennett to Ernest Lundeen, 14 December 1939, Box 234, Lundeen Papers.

61. "Mr. Churchill Turns to the New World," *Christian Century* 57 (19 June 1940): 787. See also "Without Benefit of the Constitution," *Christian Century* 57 (18 September 1940): 1136.

62. See, for example, Philip C. Jessup to Lloyd K. Garrison, 20 May 1940, Jessup Papers; William R. Castle, "What about the Monroe Doctrine Now?" *Saturday Evening Post* 213 (27 July 1940): 40.

63. "A Defensive Alliance with Canada," *CT*, 19 June 1940, 14. See also "It's Time to Think of America," 18 June 1940, 12.

64. Hearst, "In the News," *SFE*, 7 June 1940, 2. For dissent, see Nye quoted by Herman C. Kudlich, "The Watch Tower," *Steuben News* (July 1940): 6.

65. Fred E. Pollock, "Roosevelt, the Ogdensburg Agreement, and the British Fleet: All Done with Mirrors," *Diplomatic History* 5 (Summer 1981): 203–19.

66. For example, see Capper, radio broadcast, 10 October 1940, in *CR*, A6296; MacNider, testimony, HFAC, 22 January 1941, 337; Charles A. Lindbergh, testimony, SFAC, 23 January 1941, 427; Vandenberg, *CR*, 18 February 1941, 1105; Stuart Chase, "Harsh Realism for America," *Progressive*, 22 March 1941, 1. One minority voice, Norman Thomas, denied that he favored the defense of Canada, particularly if the British fleet were lodged there. Testimony, HFAC, 22 January 1941, 337.

67. Hearst, "In the News," *SFE*, 21 August 1940, 1–2; 22 August 1940, 9; "Defense Plans with Canada," *CT*, 20 August 1940, 10; "Economic Results of the Alliance," 11 September 1940, 12; "North American Defense," 8 October 1940, 12. See also *CT*, "The United States and Canada," 2 December 1940, 16.

68. "Insurance Against Invasion," *NYDN*, 20 August 1940, 21. See also "The Consequences of Stumblebum Diplomacy," *NYDN*, 24 August 1940, 13; "Can the United States Be Invaded?" *NYDN*, 18 August 1940, 37.

69. McCormick, broadcast of 23 June 1940, in *Addresses*, 11–12 (emphasis in original); "Today the Strongest Nation in the World," *CT*, 13 October 1940, graphic section, 2; McCormick, speech, WGN, 8 September 1940, in *Addresses*, 46–47. In the Pacific, said McCormick, "sturdy Canadians of the northwest" would support American garrisons stationed in Alaska. For further comments on the strong defense potential of Newfoundland, Nova Scotia, and New Brunswick, see McCormick, SFRC, 6 February 1941, 478.

70. See, for example, Sokolsky, "These Days," *New York Sun*, 6 September 1940, 20; "Candor in the White House," *Christian Century* 57 (4 September 1940): 1067. For mild criticism, see Dorothy Detzer to Hannah Clothier Hull and Emily Greene Balch, 21 August 1940, WIL Papers. In October, Detzer found FDR to be acting unilaterally by not informing the public that the United States would conduct joint military and naval staff activities with Canada. Dorothy Detzer to Katherine D. Blake, 31 October 1940, WIL Papers.

71. Villard, "Our Canadian Alliance," *Christian Century* 57 (28 August 1940): 1054; Woodruff, *CR*, 22 August 1940, 10,777; "Zero Hour," *New Masses* 36 (3 September 1940): 3. See also "New Stage in Policy," *New Masses* 36 (27 August 1940): 16, which predicted joint U.S.-Canadian occupation of British territory in the hemisphere. In April 1941, *New Masses* claimed that Wall Street was obtaining a mortgage on Canada's raw materials and a firmer grip on its economy and politics while the Canadian working class was paying the heavy price. See "Pact with Canada" 39 (21 April 1941): 19.

72. "Candor in the White House," *Christian Century* 57 (4 September 1940): 1067.

73. Pollock, "Roosevelt," 219.

74. See, for example, Arthur Hale, "The World-Island," radio address, *Scribner's Commentator* 9 (December 1940): 86–88.

75. [Dennis], "The Economic Consequences of American Intervention," unpub. ms., n.d. [1941], in Doenecke, *IDU*, 203. See also *WFL* 108 (24 August 1940): 2.

76. Vandenberg and Ross, *United States News*, 30 May 1941, 24–25. See also Gerald P. Nye and Louis J. Taber, master of the National Grange and AFC national committeeman, *United States News*, 30 May 1941. Other calls for defending Canada came from Fish and General Wood. *United States News*, 6 June 1941, 26.

77. Clark, *NYT*, 30 July 1941, 8. For the embarrassment of one AFC staffer, see Ruth Sarles to R. Douglas Stuart Jr., 8 August 1941, Box 67, AFC Papers.

78. Libby, *United States News*, 6 June 1941, 26. For Wheeler and Morley as well as Senator Aiken and pacifist leaders Richard R. Wood and J. Barnard Walton, see *United States News*, 30 May 1941, 24–25.

79. Johnson, *SFN*, 26 September 1939, 13; Johnson, speech, American Legion, 27 September 1939, in CR, A96; Sargent, Bulletin #30, 26 January 1940, *Getting US into War*, 247–52; AFC, *Washington News Letter* 15 (30 May 1941), in Doenecke, *IDU*, 263; "War Dictatorship in Canada Claimed," *Call*, 17 May 1941, 8. The labor leader was Alexander Welch, secretary-treasurer of the Canadian Hosiery Workers.

80. Kimball, *Juggler*, 128; Rock, *Chamberlain and Roosevelt*, 237; Roosevelt quotation, Thorne, *Allies*, 103.

81. D. Cameron Watt, *Succeeding John Bull: America in Britain's War, 1900–1975* (New York: Cambridge University Press, 1984), 80–81, 100; Louis, *Imperialism*, 19.

82. Thorne, *Allies*, 100; Ponting, *1940*, 12–15.

## CHAPTER 15: THE SOVIETS

1. For a brief discussion of American opinion, see chapter 1 of George Sirgiovanni, *An Undercurrent of Suspicion: Anti-Communism in America during World War II* (New Brunswick, N.J.: Transaction, 1990).

2. "Text of Roosevelt's Address to the American Youth Congress," *NYT*, 11 February 1940, 44.

3. See in particular Ralph B. Levering, *American Opinion and the Russian Alliance, 1939–1945* (Chapel Hill: University of North Carolina Press, 1976), chaps. 2 and 3.

4. Al Williams, *Airpower*, 403; "What Are the Allies' War Aims?" *NYDN*, 17 September 1939, 33. See also Nielson, entry of 11 October 1939, *Tragedy*, 1:120; Fish, *CR*, 26 June 1941, 5553; Robsion, *CR*, 14 July 1941, 6016; "The Beast of Moscow Speaks," *CT*, 4 July 1941, 8; "How's the Nerves, Buddy?"

*NYDN*, 31 August 1939, 25; Rich, *CR*, 9 October 1941, 7798; John Cudahy, testimony, SFRC, 23 October 1941, 151; "Shall We Fight for Russia?" *Christian Century* 58 (10 September 1941): 1104; Frank Gannett, speech to Rochester American Legion and Chamber of Commerce, entered in *CR*, 3 January 1940, A16. Other anti-interventionists put both nations on the same plane. See, for example, Frederick C. Smith, 10 October 1941, 7825; A. J. Muste to Lucille B. Milner, 30 October 1940, WIL Papers; "But Boake Carter Says," *SFE*, 2 July 1941, 10; O'Connor, 9 October 1941, 7787; Tinkham, *CR*, 7 February 1941, 762; Melvin J. Maas, *United States News*, 4 July 1941, 23.

5. Freda Utley, "Russia and Germany," lecture, CBS, 1 July 1940, 9, the Papers of Freda Utley, Hoover Institution (hereafter cited as Utley Papers). For Utley's firsthand experiences, see Freda Utley, *The Dream We Lost: Soviet Russia Then and Now* (New York: John Day, 1940); *Lost Illusion* (Philadelphia: Fireside, 1948); *Odyssey of a Liberal*.

6. Utley, *Dream,* respectively 361, 359.

7. Utley, *Dream*, 365, 297 (emphasis in original), 298.

8. See, for example, Chamberlin Diary, 9–12 September 1940 and 28 September 1940; Travers Clement, "Dream into Nightmare," *Call*, 14 September 1940, 6; Villard, "Russia, Then and Now," *Common Sense* 9 (October 1940): 26–27. In her memoirs, Utley claimed that the book was praised by a variety of writers, not all anti-interventionists. They included Charles A. Beard, Dwight Macdonald, Selden Rodman, Alfred Bingham, Eugene Lyons, Ben Stolberg, Isaac Don Levine, and Norman Cousins. *Odyssey of a Liberal*, 259.

9. Thomas, "Your World and Mine: Questions for the War Makers," *Call*, 12 October 1940, 5; "Your World and Mine: Liberals and Some Delusions," *Call*, 26 October 1940, 5; Thomas, review in *Modern Quarterly* 15 (Summer 1940): 81–82.

10. For praise, see Stephen Naft, *Living Age* 359 (October 1940): 189–90; philosopher Bertrand Russell, "The Tragedy of Reality," *Saturday Review of Literature* 22 (28 September 1940): 6; Isabel Paterson, "Turns with a Bookworm," *New York Herald Tribune*, 22 September 1940, 19; Pearl Buck, *Asia* 40 (October 1940): 577–78; Margaret Marshall, "Books and the Arts: Notes by the Way," *Nation* 151 (7 September 1940): 197.

11. Florinsky, *NYT Book Review*, 6 October 1940, 5; Peffer, review in *New York Herald Tribune*, 22 September 1940, 8; Rovere, "Russia and the West," *New Republic* 103 (23 September 1940): 424.

12. "How's the Nerves, Buddy?" *NYDN*, 31 August 1939, 25; "The Beast of Moscow Speaks," *CT*, 4 July 1941, 8; Hiram Johnson, *CR*, 7 August 1941, 6848; Robsion, *CR*, 14 July 1941, 6016.

13. For example, see Freda Utley, "Russia and Germany," lecture, CBS, 1 July 1940, 11, Utley Papers; Utley, "The Great Russian Illusion," *Atlantic Monthly* 167 (April 1941): 477; Herbert Hoover to William J. Gross, 7 April 1941, Hoover Papers; Edwin M. Borchard to Henry Houghton, 10 April 1941, Borchard Papers; Dennis, *WFL* 113, 25 September 1940, 3; George Sokolsky, interview, *Brown* [University] *Daily Herald*, 21 March 1941, 4; Holmes, "Editorial Comment," *Unity* 127 (April 1941): 22; Norman Thomas, "Your World and Mine: Which 'American Century'?" *Call*, 22 March 1941, 8; Thomas, "Your World and Mine: Stalin's Role in World Tragedy," *Call*, 3 May 1941, 8.

14. William Henry Chamberlin, "Stalin in the War," *Yale Review* 30 (March 1941): 498. See also "The Coming Peace," *American Mercury* 51 (November 1940): 271; *Wesleyan* [University] *Argus*, 17 March 1941, 1–2.

15. Waldrop, "What Was Stalin's Price?" *WTH*, 1 October 1940, 12; "Russia: A Combat Estimate," 31 October 1940, 10.

16. See, for example, "Red Josef on Watch," *CT*, 26 January 1941, 14; Monsignor Fulton J. Sheen, "What Are We Fighting For?" sermon, "Catholic Hour," NBC, reprinted in *Scribner's Commentator* 10 (May 1941): 84; Wheeler, *CR*, 22 August 1940, 10729.

17. Barnes, "Where Are We Headed?" *Uncensored* 73 (21 February 1941): special supplement, 2; Wood, address to the Chicago Council of Foreign Relations, 4 October 1940, in *CR*, A6303; "If Not a Negotiated Peace," *Christian Century* 58 (15 January 1941): 79.

18. See, for example, D. W. Clark, *CR*, 16 October 1939, 446.

19. Lindbergh, "What Substitute for War?" *Atlantic Monthly* 165 (March 1940): 307. In a conversation among the three men, Castle and Cudahy concurred. See Castle Diary, 20 September 1940.

20. "Europe vs. Asia," *NYDN*, 19 October 1939, 35; "What Are Our War Aims as to Russia?" 12 January 1941, 43.

21. Morley, "The Formula of Federation," *Asia* 40 (June 1940): 293; MacNider, testimony, HFAC, 22 January 1941, 358; Villard, "The Fate of England," *Christian Century* 58 (11 June 1941): 780. See also Henry Haskell, "Russian Imperialism," *Call*, 11 November 1939, 4.

22. See, for example, "American Arms for Russia," *CT*, 16 March 1940, 10.

23. Holmes, "What Do You Mean—Neutral?" *Unity* 124 (19 February 1940): 183. See also Barnes, "Keep Out of War and Investigate the War-Mongers" [draft], 19, Box 252, Lundeen Papers.

24. Danaher, speech, Republican State Convention, Hartford, Conn., 14 May 1940, in *CR*, A3052; Hoover cited in editorial, "Our Foreign Policies," *America* 63 (4 May 1940): 100; Pettengill, "Airplanes for Russia," Release 225, 13 February 1941, Box 11, Pettengill Papers.

25. "On the Job," *Time*, 19 August 1940, 11.

26. Clark, letter to Joseph North and A. B. Magil, editorial board of *New Masses*, in *CR*, 17 October 1940, 13,585. For similar arguments, see "Guns for Comrade Joe," *CT*, 18 October 1940, 14; Libby, "Only Stalin Could Win," *Peace Action* 7 (October 1940): 1–2; Castle Diary, 11 August 1940; Hearst, "In the News," *WTH*, 29 October 1940, 9; Sokolsky, "These Days," *New York Sun*, 18 October 1940, 22; Sokolsky, "These Days," *New York Sun*, 25 February 1941, 20.

27. *NYT*, 22 January 1941, 1, 8.

28. See, for example, see Tinkham, *CR*, 29 January 1941, 384; Lindbergh, testimony, HFAC, 23 January 1941, 395; Congressman William W. Blackney (Rep.-Mich.), *CR*, 3 February 1941, 509; Robsion, *CR*, 5 February 1941, 642; D. W. Clark, *CR*, 24 February 1941, 1297; "Moral Embargo Against Russia Lifted," *Christian Century* 58 (5 February 1941): 174; B. C. Clark, SFRC, 4 February 1941, 385; "Chief Enemy: Why Should We Appease Russia?" *SFE*, 14 February 1941, 8; Herbert Wright, testimony, SFRC, 5 February 1941, 444; Ralph Townsend, "Mercy—Strictly Political," *Scribner's Commentator* 9 (March 1941): 83–84; Catherine Curtis, testimony, SFRC, 22 February 1941, 819; McCarran, *CR*, 22 February 1941, 1270.

29. Shanley, *CR*, 24 February 1941, 1309.

30. "Stalin Embraced by Our Way of Life," *CT*, 23 January 1941, 8. For a similar argument, see Castle, testimony, HFAC, 24 January 1941, 528.

31. See, for example, "Russia Makes a Record," 5 March 1941, 31; "The Allied Diplomacy," 18 March 1940, 21; "What Shall We Do about Russia?" 19 September 1940, 29; "The U.S., the Axis, and Russia," 30 September 1940, 23; "Let's Play Some Power Politics," 6 October 1940, 47; "Better Warm Up to Russia," 9 December 1940, 31; "Whither Stalin?" 3 January 1941, 27; "The President's Message," 7 January 1941, 19; "Good Day's Work, Mr. Welles," 23 January 1941, 37; "Our Russian Policy," 16 May 1941, 29.

32. "One at a Time," *NYDN*, 28 April 1941, 21.

33. See, for example, retired marine general Smedley Butler, quoted in *American Guardian*, 19 January 1940, 3; Nye, "Keep Our Money Out of War," *Look*, 7 November 1939, 22–25; Libby, "Is Hitler 'Coming Over Here'?" *Peace Action* 6 (May 1940): 2; Norman Thomas, "Your World and Mine," *Call*, 30 September 1939, 2.

34. "Of Things to Come," *Uncensored* 9 (2 December 1939), 3.

35. Flynn, *SFN*, 6 January 1941, 14.

36. Flynn, "Stalin Moves in Europe," *NYWT*, 13 December 1939, 30; Haskell, "Will War Spread to the Balkans?" *Call*, 20 January 1940, 2; "Red Josef in Rumania," *CT*, 2 July 1940, 12; "Another Austerlitz?" *NYDN*, 6 September 1940, 31; "They Spell It 'Romania,'" *NYDN*, 31 August 1940, 13. See also "Revelation," *Uncensored* 39, 29 June 1940, 3; "When Dictators Fall Out," *NYDN*, 2 July 1940, 23; "Drang nach Osten," *NYDN*, 11 October 1940, 31; "Getting Ready for the Next War," *Christian Century* 57 (11 September 1940): 1104. For subsequent indications of anxiety, see William R. Castle to R. Douglas Stuart Jr., 11 March 1941, Box 63, AFC Papers.

37. Utley, "The Great Russian Illusion," *Atlantic Monthly* 167 (April 1941): 471–74, 477. See also Utley, "Russia and Germany," lecture, CBS, 1 July 1940, 8–9, Utley Papers.

38. "When Dictators Fall Out," *NYDN*, 2 July 1940, 23.

39. Dennis, *WFL* 120 (14 November 1940): 1, 2; 121 (20 November 1940): 1. See also 104 (25 July 1940): 1; 116 (17 October 1940): 4; 126 (26 December 1940): 4; 134 (20 February 1941): 4; 141 (10 April 1941): 4.

40. "Mystery," *Uncensored* 90 (21 June 1941): 4; Norman Thomas, "Your World and Mine: War Front and Home Front," *Call*, 28 June 1941, 5. See also "Comment: Nazis Dictate Soviet Changes," *Social Justice*, 24 March 1941, 8; *Social Justice*, 19 May 1941, 9; Henry Haskell, "Stalin Bound to Axis; Looks to Middle East," *Call*, 31 May 1941, 2.

41. Dallek, *Roosevelt*, 215.

42. Barton Whaley, *Codeword Barbarossa* (Cambridge, Mass.: MIT Press, 1973), 37–40.

43. Berle, entry of 5 March 1941, *Navigating*, 362.

44. Flynn diary notes, 27 June 1941, Box 32, Flynn Papers.

45. "Statement of the New York Chapter," 23 June 1941, in Doenecke, *IDU*, 290; "'Greatest Struggle in the World,'" *NYDN*, 19 July 1941, 13; "Why Did Hitler Attack Russia?" *NYDN*, 22 September 1941, 17. See also "Fighting for Food," *NYDN*, 15 October 1941, 33.

46. Norman Thomas, "Your World and Mine: The Russian-German War," *Call*, 5 July 1941, 5.

47. Dennis, *WFL* 152, 26 June 1941, 1.

48. Hearst, "In the News," *SFE*, 23 June 1941, 2; Henry Haskell, "Behind Hitler's New Blitzkrieg," *Call*, 5 July 1941, 2.

49. Truman, *NYT*, 24 June 1941, 7.

50. See, for example, "Are the Germans Stopped?" *NYDN*, 25 July 1941, 21; Woodruff, *CR*, 24 June 1941, A3052; Fish, 5 August 1941, 6775; Jennings, 12 August 1941, 7054; Frederick C. Smith, 7 November 1941, 8673; Norman Thomas to B. J. O'Neill, 26 June 1941, Thomas Papers; "Our Alliance with Barbarism," *CT*, 2 September 1941, 14; Robsion and Rankin, *CR*, 14 July 1941, 6016. Robsion preferred to see the Russians win as he wanted to see a British victory. *CR*, 9 October 1941, 7789.

51. Woodruff, *CR*, 22 July 1941, A3052; Johnson, *CR*, 22 July 1941, 6244. See also Johnson, *CR*, 7 August 1941, 6848.

52. *NYT*, 26 June 1941, 1; "Aid-for-Russia Issue Flares to Complicate Foreign Policy," *Newsweek*, 7 July 1941, 12; Kimball, *Forged in War*, 90.

53. Tuttle, *Hopkins*, 82–85; Levering, *American Opinion*, 41–59; Bailey and Ryan, *Hitler vs. Roosevelt*, 215; Kimball, *Juggler*, 35.

54. "President's Lend-Lease Letter," *NYT*, 19 September 1941, 1, 12; Rich amendment, *CR*, 10 October 1941, 7823; final House vote, 14 October 1941, 7839; final Senate vote, 23 October 1941, 8209. Thirty-six House members did not vote.

55. For the prediction of a quick Soviet defeat, see Lieutenant Colonel Paul M. Robinett in Marshall, *Papers*, 2:161.

56. Livingstone Hartley and Donald C. Blaisdell, "The Widening of the War," CDAAA, *Washington Office Information Letter* 24 (27 June 1941): 1–2; Hartley and Blaisdell, "Hitler's Objectives in Russia," *Washington Office Information Letter* 25 (4 July 1941): 1–3, Box 35, CDAAA Papers.

57. Hartley and Blaisdell, "The Widening of the War," 2, Box 35, CDAAA Papers.

58. See, for example, Congressman John Taber, *CR*, 10 October 1941, 7823; Alf Landon, "The Contribution of the Republican Party to National Defense," speech, Second District Women's Republican Club, Kansas City, Kansas, 17 October 1941, in *CR*, A4726.

59. *Militant*, 28 June 1941, 1. Its victory program included release of all "pro-Soviet" political prisoners, democratically elected Soviets in factories and villages, legalization of all "pro-Soviet" political parties, an appeal to German workers to destroy Hitler, and the creation of the Socialist United States of Europe. Issue of 19 July 1941, 1.

60. "The Order of Belligerence," *Commonweal* 34 (4 July 1941): 224; "Russian Participation," *Commonweal* 34 (8 August 1941): 363; Villard, "Our Moral Confusion," *Christian Century* 58 (9 July 1941): 881.

61. Wheeler, *CR*, 5 November 1941, 8521. For an additional plea for the creation of a neutrality zone, see "American Aid For Russia?" *Christian Century* 58 (9 July 1941): 875. For other concerns about Vladivostok, see AFC Research Bureau, "Did You Know the Real Implications of the President's Refusal to Invoke the Neutrality Act Against the Soviet Union?" *Did You Know?* 4 (27 June

1941), in Doenecke, *IDU*, 294; Day, *CR*, 9 October 1941, 7796; Libby, "Vladivostok Is in the Japan Sea," *Peace Action* 7 (June 1941): 2.

62. "Hitler Attacks Stalin," *Christian Century* 58 (2 July 1941): 855; Taft, *Newsweek*, 29 September 1941, 14; Taft in AFC pamphlet, "Should America Fight to Make the World Safe for Communism?" (Chicago: AFC, 1941); Mundt, *United States News*, 17 October 1941, 28.

63. Lindbergh, speech of 2 July 1941, in *CR*, 7 July 1941, A3283.

64. "Text of Lindbergh's Address at America First Rally in Madison Square Garden," *NYT*, 31 October 1941, 4.

65. See, for example, Knutson, *CR*, 5 August 1941, 6775; Francis Case, 3 July 1941, 5821; Hiram Johnson to Hiram Johnson Jr., 24 June 1941, Johnson Papers; Nye, *United States News*, 4 July 1941, 23; Anton J. Johnson, speech, Mutual network, 14 October 1941, *CR*, A4642; James Gillis, "Covenant with Hell," *Catholic World* 153 (August 1941): 513–17; Hoover, *NYT*, 20 June 1941, 1; AFC memorandum, 23 June 1941, Box 337, AFC Papers. For views of the nondemocratic right, see Boris Brasol, "Aid to Russia? Incredible," *Scribner's Commentator* 10 (November 1941): 26; Coughlin, *United States News*, 4 July 1941, 23; Dennis, *WFL* 163, 11 September 1941, 2.

66. Fish, speech, NBC blue network, in *CR*, 30 June 1941, A3188; Sterling Morton to R. Douglas Stuart Jr., 26 June 1941, Box 61, AFC Papers; "Slav vs. Teuton," *NYDN*, 29 June 1941, 39; "Russia for the Russians," *NYDN*, 6 September 1941, 13; "But Boake Carter Says," *SFE*, 7 July 1941, 7; Chester Bowles to R. Douglas Stuart Jr., 2 July 1941, Box 59, AFC Papers.

67. Roosevelt, *NYT*, 1 October 1941, 9. See also Roosevelt to Pope Pius XII, 3 September 1941, *F.D.R.: His Personal Letters*, 1204–5.

68. For examples of anti-interventionist retorts, see AFC Bulletin #644, 21 October 1941, AFC Papers; John Haynes Holmes to Angelina Balabanoff, 7 October 1941, Holmes Papers; "Clergy Refute Claims on Soviet Religious Freedom," *AFC New York Chapter Bulletin*, 11 October 1941, 3; "Clerics Warn of Soviet Ties," *AFC New York Chapter Bulletin*, 18 October 1941, 3; "On the Peace Front," *AFC New York Chapter Bulletin*, 18 October 1941, 4. Wheeler, speech to AFC at San Diego, *In Fact* 4 (17 November 1941): 4; Hoffman, *CR*, 9 October 1941, 1169–70; Rich, 9 October 1941, 7798; Dworshak, 10 October 1941, A4602.

69. The Catholic Laymen's Committee for Peace, located in New York City and close to the anti-interventionists, polled some thirty-five thousand Catholic clergy. Of the 37.6 percent who responded, only 967 favored aiding "the communistic Russian government"; 11,860 were opposed and 328 had no opinion. *CR*, 16 October 1941, A4676–77.

70. "Are the Four Freedoms a Delusion?" *Christian Century* 58 (15 October 1941): 1262; Lillian Symes, "Hold That Line: A Don't for Dictators," *Call*, 18 October 1941, 5; "Heavenly Front," *Uncensored* 105 (4 October 1941): 1.

71. Fish, *Newsweek*, 13 October 1941, 62; Rogers, *CR*, 6 October 1941, 7684, 7825. See also Congressman Robert F. Jones, *CR*, 10 October 1941, 7821; O'Connor, *CR*, 6 October 1941, 7684; Vandenberg, *CR*, 27 October 1941, 8253.

72. "Atheists, Russian and German," *Catholic World* 153 (September 1941): 652; "What Is Religious Freedom?" *Commonweal* 34 (17 October 1941): 603. See also *Social Justice*, 13 October 1941, 3; D. W. Clark, *CR*, 4 November 1941, 8480.

73. "Uniate Unity," *Uncensored* 108, 25 October 1941, 2. On the Uniate Church, see also Dennis, *WFL* 167, 9 October 1941, 3.

74. "Aid to Russia," *CT*, 13 October 1941, 14.

75. AFC Research Bureau, "Russia Calls," *Did You Know?* 26 (4 October 1941), in Doenecke, *IDU*, 195; Wood, *Newsweek*, 7 July 1941, 12.

76. Herbert Hoover to John O'Laughlin, 28 June 1941, Hoover–O'Laughlin correspondence, Stanford Files. See also Congressman Chiperfield, *CR*, 24 June 1941, A3026; Frank Waldrop, "The Russian Retreat," *WTH*, 28 June 1941, 10; "Rush to Russia?" *NYDN*, 25 June 1941, 31.

77. Hiram Johnson to Hiram Johnson Jr., 6 July 1941, Johnson Papers. For similar comments in July, see Villard, *Progressive*, 5 July 1941, 8; Villard, "Germany in Russia," *Progressive*, 26 July 1941, 8; "Greatest Struggle in World History," *NYDN*, 19 July 1941, 17; Dennis, *WFL* 157 (31 July 1941): 1; Morley Diary, 16 August 1941.

78. Baldwin, "Soviet Debacle Is Seen," *NYT*, 2 July 1941, 6; George Sokolsky, "These Days: When Moscow Falls," *New York Sun*, 26 July 1941, 6.

79. "Political Commissars," *Uncensored* 97 (9 August 1941), 3; Flynn diary notes, 20 August 1941, Box 32, Flynn Papers; Herbert Hoover to John C. O'Laughlin, 23 August 1941, Stanford Files. See also *AFC New York Chapter Bulletin*, 16 August 1941, 3, AFC Papers; Morley Diary, 16 August 1941; Baldwin, "Blueprint for Victory," *Life*, 4 August 1941, 35; *Social Justice*, 18 August 1941, 3; Dennis, *WFL* 160 (21 August 1941): 3. Dennis soon conceded that the Russians were doing better than anyone predicted, but still claimed that Germany would win. *WFL* 161 (28 August 1941): 1–2.

80. See, for example, Charles A. Lindbergh to Robert E. Wood, 24 September 1941, Wood Papers; Dennis, *WFL* 163 (11 September 1941): 1; 164 (18 September 1941): 1; "The Battle of Russia," *NYDN*, 23 September 1941, 25; "Nazi-Soviet Situation," *Uncensored* 102 (13 September 1941): 3; "The Biggest Battle," *Uncensored* 103 (20 September 1941): 3; "Soviet Morale," *Uncensored* 104 (27 September 1941): 3.

81. "War Movement in U.S. Wanes as Soviet Defeat Looms," *AFC New York Chapter Bulletin*, 6 September 1941, 3, AFC Papers; McCormick, radio address, WGN, 20 September 1941, in *CT*, 21 September 1941, 3; Libby, "Where Would Russia's Collapse Leave U.S.?" *Peace Action* 7 (September 1941): 2.

82. Baldwin, "Russian Campaign—II," *NYT*, 6 September 1941, 4. See also "Hard Russian Campaign Brings Many Surprises," *NYT*, 21 September 1941, sect. 4, 4.

83. Freda Utley, "The Russo-German War," n.d., 1–2, Utley Papers; Utley, "Limits of Russian Resistance," *American Mercury* 53 (September 1941): 299–300.

84. See, for example, Dennis, *WFL* 167 (9 October 1941): 1–2; 169 (23 October 1941): 4; 170 (30 October 1941): 2; Felix Morley to Robert E. Wood, 14 October 1941, Box 66, AFC Papers; "But Boake Carter Says," *SFE*, 9 October 1941, 15; Castle Diary, 9 October 1941; Flynn, testimony, SFRC, 23 October 1941, 205; Flynn diary notes, 8 and 17 October, Box 32, Flynn Papers; "Terrestrial Front," *Uncensored* 105, 4 October 1941, 3–4; "Aid to Russia May Turn Against Us," *Social Justice*, 20 October 1941, 9.

85. Frank Waldrop, "Washington Notes," *WTH*, 1 October 1941, 14; R. Douglas Stuart Jr. to Robert E. Wood, 11 October 1941, Box 59, AFC Papers; "Supreme Errors," *Uncensored* 107 (18 October 1941): 3; Cudahy, testimony, SFRC, 23 October 1941, 165; Baldwin, "Hitler Has Won Much but Not All in Russia," *NYT*, 19 October 1941, sect. 4, 4.

86. "Where Russia Is Weak," *CT*, 19 November 1941, 12; "Soviet Prospects," *Uncensored* 109 (1 November 1941): 3.

87. Taft, address, CBS, "Russia and the Four Freedoms," 25 June 1941, in *CR*, A3077; "A Break for Britain," *NYDN*, 23 June 1941, 17; "The Heat Is Off," *CT*, 23 June 1941, 10. See also William Gellerman, associate professor of education at Northwestern, [Northwestern University] *Summer Northwestern Newsmagazine*, 1 July 1941, 4; Libby, letter to NCPW executive board and branch offices, 13 August 1941, NCPW Papers; Charles A. Lindbergh to Robert E. Wood, 24 September 1941, Wood Papers; Edwin M. Borchard to John Bassett Moore, 10 October 1941, Borchard Papers; investment banker Edward S. Webster to Robert E. Wood, 7 October 1941, AFC Papers; R. Douglas Stuart Jr. to Sterling Morton, 7 July 1941, AFC Papers.

88. "Swastika over Sickle," *Did You Know?* 15 (1 August 1941), in Doenecke, *IDU*, 164–68. See also McCormick, radio address, WGN, 20 September 1941, in *CT*, 21 September 1941, 3.

89. Chiperfield, *CR*, 8 August 1941, 6939; Herbert Hoover to John C. O'Laughlin, 28 June 1941, Stanford Files. See also Hoover to O'Laughlin, 3 August 1941, Stanford Files; Taft, *CR*, 1 August 1941, 6571.

90. "Nazi-Soviet Situation," *Uncensored* 102 (13 September 1941): 3.

91. O'Connor, *CR*, 9 October 1941, 7787. See also Castle Diary, 20 September 1941; Oswald Garrison Villard, "The Military Outlook," *Christian Century* 58 (8 October 1941): 1240.

92. "The Heat Is Off," *CT*, 23 June 1941, 10. See also "Stalin in Defeat," 5 July 1941, 6; "What Imminent Peril?" 23 July 1941, 10.

93. "Russian Adventures, 1912 and 1941," *NYDN*, 6 July 1941, 17. See also *News* editorials "Gen. Summer," 29 July 1941, 27; "Hold the Boys for the Duration?" 1 August 1941, 28; "Russia for the Russians," 6 September 1941, 13; "The Battle for Russia," 12 September 1941, 31; "Russian Riddles," 11 October 1941, 15; "The Battle of Russia," 23 October 1941, 33. For another example of the Napoleon analogy, see Congressman Case, *CR*, 3 July 1941, 5821.

94. Wiley, *CR*, 7 August 1941, 6851–52; Wheeler, *CR*, 7 August 1941, 6871; "Two Years of War," *Christian Century* 58 (3 September 1941): 1070. See also Norman Thomas, "Your World and Mine: The War Enters Its Third Year," *Call*, 13 September 1941, 5; "Your World and Mine: There's Still Time If . . . ," *Call*, 4 October 1941, 5.

95. Hiram Johnson to Hiram Johnson Jr., 8 November 1941, Johnson Papers; Baldwin, "Winter Balks Nazi Plans for an Early Knockout," *NYT*, 23 November 1941, sect. 4, 4; Baldwin, "Struggle for Moscow Crucial Point of War," *NYT*, 30 November 1941, sect. 4, 3; "Col. December," *NYDN*, 3 December 1941, 39.

96. See, for example, Alf Landon to Herbert Hoover, 1 November 1941, Hoover Papers.

97. Thomas, [University of California, Berkeley] *Daily Californian*, 20 October 1941, 2. Thomas did express sympathy for the Soviet peoples, particularly those living in the invaded Ukraine. See Thomas to B. J. O'Neill, 26 June 1941, Thomas Papers.

98. Igor Sikorsky to Herbert Hoover, 16 July 1941, Hoover Papers; Robsion, *CR*, 9 October 1941, 7790. See also Libby, "Churchill–Stalin Alliance Strengthens Anti-War Policy," *Peace Action* 7 (June 1941): 1.

99. John Haynes Holmes, "If Russia Wins," *Christian Century* 158 (30 July 1941): 954–55; "Russia Will Decide Germany's Fate," *Christian Century* 58 (3 December 1941): 1492; Bulow, quoted in bulletin of Fred Burdick, "Communists Plan World-Wide Revolution," 4 October 1941, materials of the America First Committee, on deposit at Firestone Library, Princeton University; Sokolsky, "These Days: Quo Vadis?" *New York Sun*, 26 June 1941, 18.

100. "If Russia Wins," *CT*, 10 July 1941, 10; "Playing the Red," *Saturday Evening Post* 214 (8 November 1941): 26. See also "No Paladins Here," *America* 65 (12 July 1941): 378.

101. For Chamberlin's odyssey, see Myers, "Chamberlin."

102. *Confessions of an Individualist*, respectively, 285, 275.

103. For sympathetic treatments of Chamberlin's anti-interventionism, see Paul Hutchinson, "A Journalism of Moral Values," *Christian Century* 57 (12 July 1940): 769–70; "More Than Streetlights Are Dimmed," *Progressive*, 29 June 1940, 6. For favorable mention of the book in general, see Nick Broughton, "Books in a World at War," *Peace Action* 7 (September 1940): 7; Thomas Fleming, "From Blind Alleys to Clearer Roads," *America* 63 (10 August 1940): 497–98.

104. Vera Micheles Dean, "If Hitler Had Fought Stalin," *New York Herald Tribune Book Review*, 2 June 1940, 9.

105. William Henry Chamberlin, *The World's Iron Age* (New York: Macmillan, 1942), 362.

106. William Henry Chamberlin, "The Struggle for Continents," *Atlantic Monthly* 168 (September 1941): 279–80; Chamberlin, speech, Progressive Club, 19 October 1941, as covered in *Amherst* [College] *Student*, 20 October 1941, 4; *Smith College Associated News*, 21 October 1941, 3; *Stanford* [University] *Daily*, 12 November 1941, 12.

107. See, for example, Congressman Harry Sautoff, *CR*, 16 October 1941, 7994; Bennett Clark, *CR*, 4 November 1941, 8491; *New York Enquirer*, 24 November 1941; "The New Western Front," *Christian Century* 58 (12 November 1941): 1399; Travers Clement, "How Gullible Are We?" *Call*, 25 October 1941, 4; Wheeler, *NYT*, 12 November 1941, 8; "Cabbages and Kings: Proof of the Pudding," *Scribner's Commentator* 11 (November 1941): 5; Norman Thomas, "Your World and Mine: U.S. Heads for Total War," *Call*, 6 December 1941, 5.

108. Samuel B. Pettengill to Robert E. Wood, 16 October 1941, Box 286, AFC Papers.

109. "The Churchill Chin Is Not His Shoulder," *CT*, 31 October 1941, 14. See also "The British Enigma," *CT*, 4 November 1941, 12.

110. Hearst, "In the News," *SFE*, 14 October 1941, 1. For a similar view, see Hanson Baldwin, *NYT*, 13 October 1941.

111. Jones, *CR*, 10 October 1941, 7821; Robsion, *CR*, 9 October 1941, 7790.

112. R. Douglas Stuart Jr. to Herbert Hoover, 30 June 1941, Box 3, subject file, Hoover Papers.

113. Gallup poll, *NYT*, 13 July 1941, 2. Seventeen percent asserted it made no difference who won the war, and 7 percent offered no opinion. For the August and September polls, see Raymond H. Dawson, *The Decision to Aid Russia, 1941: Foreign Policy and Domestic Politics* (Chapel Hill: University of North Carolina Press, 1959), 227–28.

114. Levering, *American Opinion*, 60.

115. In poll of 24 June 1941, 72 percent predicted a Soviet victory; in poll of 9 September, 70 percent. Cantril, *Public Opinion*, 1187.

116. Kimball, *Juggler*, 25; Maddux, *Years of Estrangement*, 149; Tuttle, *Hopkins*, 82. See also remarks of Colonel Paul M. Robinett, assistant chief of G-2, in Marshall, *Papers*, 2:565; Breckinridge Long, entry of 30 June 1941, *War Diary*, 207; Bullitt in Ickes, entry of 28 June 1941, *Secret Diary*, 3:550.

117. Laurence A. Steinhardt to Cordell Hull, 28 June 1941, *Foreign Relations, 1941*, vol. 1: *General and the Soviet Union* (Washington D.C.: U.S. Government Printing Office, 1958), 177.

118. Edward M. Bennett, "Joseph C. Grew: The Diplomacy of Pacification," in *Diplomats in Crisis: United States–Chinese–Japanese Relations, 1919–1941*, ed. Richard Dean Burns and Edward M. Bennett (Santa Barbara, Calif.: ABC Clio, 1974), 83–84.

119. Berle, letter to Harry Hopkins, 30 July 1941, *Navigating*, 374; Hull, *Memoirs*, 2:973; Hull in Dawson, *Decision*, 117.

120. Memorandum of conversation by Welles, 11 August 1941, *Foreign Relations, 1941*, 1:357–59.

121. Kimball, *Juggler*, 27; Gilbert, *Churchill*, 6:1143.

122. Marshall, Memorandum for General [Hap] Arnold, 16 July 1941, in Marshall, *Papers*, 2:567–68; Marshall to Robert A. Lovett, 18 July 1941, 569; Marshall to Henry L. Stimson, 29 August 1941, 595. In summer 1941 Colonel Philip Faymonville, special lend-lease representative in the Soviet Union, predicted Russia would survive. George C. Herring Jr., *Aid to Russia, 1941–1946: Strategy, Diplomacy, the Origins of the Cold War* (New York: Columbia University Press, 1973), 41. See also Lee, entry of 27 June 1941, *London Journal*, 319; Raymond E. Lee to William J. Donovan, entry of 14 July 1941, 337; entry of 12 August 1941, 367.

123. Marshall, "Memorandum for Mr. Welles," 10 July 1941, in Marshall, *Papers*, 2:564.

124. Stimson in Pogue, *Marshall*, 2:73; Herring, *Aid to Russia*, 13; Kimball, *Forged in War*, 110.

125. Kirkpatrick, *Unknown Future*, 65.

126. Heinrichs, *Threshold*, 146–48. See also Ickes, entry of 20 September 1941, *Secret Diary*, 3:617.

127. Bailey and Ryan, *Hitler vs. Roosevelt*, 216; Kimball, *Juggler*, 37.

128. John Lewis Gaddis, *Russia, the Soviet Union, and United States: An Interpretive History*, 2d ed. (New York: McGraw-Hill, 1990), 157; Peter G. Boyle, *American-Soviet Relations: From the Russian Revolution to the Fall of Communism* (New York: Routledge, 1993), 44; Herring, *Aid to Russia*, 286.

129. *NYT*, 27 June 1941, 1.

130. Langer and Gleason, *Undeclared War*, 827. See also Roosevelt to Cordell Hull, 6 September 1941, *F.D.R.: His Personal Letters*, 1207–8.

131. Hull, *NYT*, 4 November 1941, 1, 10; anti-Comintern pact, *NYT*, 26 November 1941, 12; British declaration, *NYT*, 7 December 1941, 1, 19.

132. "Harry and Joe in the Kremlin," *CT*, 6 August 1941, 12; "Scandinavia and the War," *Christian Century* 58 (9 July 1941): 875; "Outraged Finland Deserves U.S. Sympathy," *SFE*, 28 September 1941, sect. 1, 14; *SFE*, 24 July 1941, 8; Bradley, *CR*, 30 June 1941, A3207. See also Tobey, *CR*, 7 August 1941, 6849; Jonkman, *CR*, 8 August 1941, 6927; Hearst, "In the News," *SFE*, 8 August 1941, 1; Hiram W. Johnson to Hiram W. Johnson Jr., 10 August 1941, Johnson Papers; Otis T. Wingo, "Finland's Man of the Hour," *Scribner's Commentator* 9 (October 1941): 10–15.

133. Hoffman, *CR*, 7 November 1941, 8687; "Marked for Slaughter," *Call*, 15 November 1941, 4. See also Hoffman, *CR*, 4 November 1941, 8502; Rich, *CR*, 13 November 1941, 8877; B. C. Clark, *CR*, 19 November 1941, 9001; "Finland's Just Cause Before the World," *New York Journal-American*, 9 November 1941; Hearst, "In the News," *SFE*, 21 November 1941, 1.

134. Wheeler, *CR*, 6 November 1941, 8547; Hoover and Taft, *Time*, 17 November 1941, 15; Shipstead, *CR*, 19 November 1941, 9001. See also D. W. Clark, *CR*, 4 November 1941, 8485; "Mr. Hull Hits a New Low," *CT*, 15 November 1941, 14.

135. Johnson, "Peace or War," broadcast, NBC, 6 November 1941, in *CR*, A5042; Waldrop, "Independence Day," *WTH*, 6 December 1941, A12. See "British-Finnish Breach Most Tragic of War," *SFE*, 19 October 1941, 13.

136. Herring, *Aid to Russia*, 23, 47–48; Kimball, *Juggler*, 34; Maddux, *Years of Estrangement*, 151.

## CHAPTER 16: A PIVOTAL SUMMER

1. Heinrichs, *Threshold*, 110.

2. "Texts of Messages Relating to Occupation of Iceland," *NYT*, 8 July 1941, 3.

3. Livingstone Hartley and Donald C. Blaisdell, "Action in the Atlantic," CDAAA, *Washington Office Information Letter* 26 (11 July 1941): 1, Box 35, CDAAA Papers.

4. Gallup poll, 29 July 1941, Cantril, *Public Opinion*, 1128.

5. Hearst, "In the News," *SFE*, 16 April 1940, 1; Lundeen, *CR*, 6 June 1940, 7683. As his authority, Lundeen cited Arctic explorer Vilhjalmur Stefansson, author of *Iceland: The First American Republic* (New York: Doubleday, Doran, 1939). For direct quotations from Stefansson, see Shanley, *CR*, 17 April 1940, A2187.

6. "Guarding the Americas," *CT*, 11 August 1940, 14. Some other anti-interventionists found Iceland to be in the European sphere, not the American one. See Fish, radio speech, 18 April 1940, in *CR*, A2302; Taft, *CR*, 10 July 1941, 5926; Robsion, *CR*, 14 July 1941, 6015; Charles A. Lindbergh, entry of 8 July 1941, *Wartime Journals*, 515.

7. Waldrop, "Hitler Still Far from Greenland," *WTH*, 10 April 1940, 13. For similar dissent, see Philip C. Jessup to Lloyd K. Garrison, 20 May 1940, Jessup Papers.

8. "Iceland," *NYDN*, 9 July 1941, 29. See also "Toward a Shooting War," *NYDN*, 10 July 1941, 35; "The Road to War," 3 October 1941, 37.

9. Lindbergh, entry of 8 July 1941, *Wartime Journals*, 515; Norman Thomas, "Your World and Mine: There's Still Time If . . . ," *Call*, 4 October 1941, 5; *Christian Century* 58 (16 July 1941): 901–2; R. Douglas Stuart Jr. to Armand Gay, 19 July 1941, Box 61, AFC Papers.

10. Taft, *CR*, 7 July 1941, 5912; 10 July 1941, 5926. See also Charles A. Lindbergh, testimony, HFAC, 23 January 1941, 395.

11. McCormick, testimony, SFRC, 6 February 1941, 478; "This Changing Hemisphere," *Uncensored* 93 (12 July 1941): 3–4.

12. Castle diary, 8 July 1941; Taft, *CR*, 10 July 1941, 5926. See also Edward S. Corwin, *United States News*, 1 August 1941, 27; Amos Pinchot, open letter to President Roosevelt, 11 July 1941, Pinchot Papers; Edwin M. Borchard to Gerald P. Nye, 14 July 1941, Borchard Papers; R. Douglas Stuart Jr. to Armand Gay, 19 July 1941, Box 61, AFC Papers; "Shooting War," *Militant*, 12 July 1941, 6. For Taft's clash with Senator Connally over constitutional power, see *CR*, 10 July 1941, 5930–31.

13. Edwin M. Borchard to Gerald P. Nye, 21 July 1941, Borchard Papers; Finerty, testimony, SFRC, 23 October 1941, 198; Villard, SFRC, 23 October 1941, 184.

14. "But Boake Carter Says," *SFE*, 30 October 1941, 31; Detzer, report to WIL National Board, 18 October 1941, 41, WIL Papers.

15. Marshall, testimony, Senate Military Affairs Committee, 9 July 1941, 2; Marshall, *NYT*, 24 July 1941, 9; Pogue, *Marshall*, 2:151.

16. Roosevelt, message to Congress, *CR*, 21 July 1941, 6149–50.

17. Gallup poll, *NYT*, 30 July 1941, 9.

18. "But Boake Carter Says," *SFE*, 11 July 1941, 7. Similarly, Merwin K. Hart favored retaining all draftees or national guardsmen whom the army deemed essential for defense. Testimony, House Military Affairs Committee, 25 July 1941, 123.

19. "Marshall's Testimony," *NYDN*, 17 July 1941, 25. The *News* soon called for a compromise on Marshall's proposals: keep the fifty thousand reserve officers on active duty as trainers of incoming draftees, promote many sergeants to second lieutenants, and stagger the year's term for the draftees so that the United States would always have about 1.25 million men who had nine months of training. Draftees over age twenty-eight, those married before induction, and those whose families were in distress should all be mustered out. Of the six hundred thousand draftees currently in the army, fifty thousand men could be released each month and fifty thousand taken in. "How Grave Is Our Danger?" *NYDN*, 21 July 1941, 17.

20. Short, *CR*, 8 August 1941, 6918–19. See also Libby, "Keep Faith with Draftees," *Peace Action* 7 (July 1941): 2; Hart, testimony, House Military Affairs Committee, 25 July 1941, 122; statement of KAOWC, 163; Catherine Curtis, testimony, 134.

21. Vorys, *CR*, 8 August 1941, 6935. See also Hanighen, "The People Become Suspicious," *Progressive*, 16 August 1941, 1; Norman Thomas, "Your World and Mine: A Letter to the President," *Call*, 21 August 1941, 5.

22. "They Are Not on the Square," *CT*, 10 August 1941, 14; Williams, "All or Nothing," *Progressive*, 26 July 1941, 4.

23. Clark, *CR*, 1 August 1941, 6583; Wheeler, *CR*, 1 August 1941, 6584.

24. Danaher, *CR*, 1 August 1941, 6568. See also "War Bloc Pushes Draftee Bill," *AFC New York Chapter Bulletin*, 26 July 1941, 2.

25. For Wavell and Auchinleck, see *NYT*, 8 July 1941, 8. For negative reactions of anti-interventionists, see Wheeler, *NYT*, 9 July 1941, 12; *NYT*, 16 July 1941, 11; AFC Research Bureau, "Our Iceland Outpost," *Did You Know?* 7 (9 July 1941), in Doenecke, *IDU*, 312; Freda Utley, "An Englishwoman Pleads: Must the World Destroy Itself?" *Reader's Digest* 39 (October 1941): 18; "England, U.S. May Try Invasion of Nazi Europe," *Social Justice*, 21 July 1941, 8; Forrest Harness (Rep.-Ind.), *CR*, 8 August 1941, 6931; "Action Is Called For," *Peace Action* 7 (July 1941): 2; Wheeler, *CR*, 15 July 1941, 6044; Tinkham, *CR*, 10 July 1941, A3386.

26. "Text of Churchill's Statement in House of Commons," *NYT*, 30 July 1941, 6. Various anti-interventionists attacked Churchill's statement, including Nye, Bennett Clark, Woodruff, the Scripps-Howard press, and the *St. Louis Post-Dispatch*. See "Churchill Critics," *Newsweek*, 11 August 1941, 17–18.

27. Kenneth Foley, "AEF Looms behind 'War Verge' Talk," *Call*, 9 August 1941, 1; de Gaulle, *NYT*, 29 July 1941, 2.

28. See, for example, Representative Bender, *CR*, 24 July 1941, 6308; publisher J. H. Gipson to D. Worth Clark (copy), 22 July 1941, NCPW Papers; Libby, "Keep Faith with Draftees," 2; "Soldiers Until . . . ," *Did You Know?* 10 (17 July 1941): 2; "This Extraordinary Bad Faith," *CT*, 11 July 1941, 10.

29. For citations of Pepper, see Wheeler, *CR*, 7 August 1941, 6869; Fish, *CR*, 8 August 1941, 6908.

30. "You're in the Army Now," *NYDN*, 9 August 1941, 23.

31. Blackney, *CR*, 8 August 1941, 6941.

32. "This Is What Soldiers Complain About," *Life*, 18 August 1941, 17–21, as noted in "Report on Morale," *CT*, 19 August 1941, 10; Harold Lavine, "Why the Army Gripes," *Nation* 153 (30 August 1941): 179–80, as noted in "Mr. Roosevelt Talks About Unity," *CT*, 2 September 1941, 14. See also AFC endorsement of the *Life* article in Page Hufty, AFC Bulletin #506, 20 August 1940, Box 279, AFC Papers; editor Morris H. Rubin, "The Last Column," *Progressive*, 9 August 1941, 12.

33. For salaries, see Wheeler, *CR*, 31 July 1941, 6495; Harry Sauthoff, *CR*, 12 August 1941, 7047. For strike-breaking, Wheeler, *CR*, 1 August 1941, 6584.

34. Dennis, *WFL* 161 (28 August 1941): 2.

35. On Germany, see Sautoff, *CR*, 12 August 1941, 7047. On Canada, see Nye, *CR*, 4 August 1941, 6676; "This Cockeyed World," *NYDN*, 5 August 1941, 23.

36. Stephen D. Wesbrook, "The Railey Report and Army Morale, 1941: Anatomy of a Crisis," *Military Review* 60 (June 1980): 11–24.

37. Clark, *CR*, 6 August 1941, 6830. See also "A Concession to Bad Management," *Christian Century* 58 (13 August 1941): 995; testimony, Catherine Curtis, House Military Affairs Committee, 25 July 1941, 133.

38. "Do the Best with What We Have," *CT*, 7 July 1941, 10.

39. "Is the Nation in Peril?" *Christian Century* 58 (30 July 1941): 950; Adams, *CR*, 1 August 1941, 6819. See also Wiley, *CR*, 7 August 1941, 6851; Taft, *CR*, 1 August 1941, 6571; Walsh, *CR*, 5 August 1941, 6760; Bender, *CR*, 24 July 1941, 6308; Chiperfield, *CR*, 8 August 1941, 6939; Hart, testimony, House Military Affairs Committee, 25 July 1941, 122. The *NYDN* estimated that losses could have been as high as three million for Russia, two million for Germany. "The Battle of Russia," 7 August 1941, 23. See also "Marshall's Testimony," *NYDN*, 17 July 1941, 25; "How Grave Is Our Danger?" *NYDN*, 21 July 1941, 17.

40. Wiley, *CR*, 7 August 1941, 851. For a similar claim concerning British strength, see Amos Pinchot to Hamilton Fish, 1 July 1941, Pinchot Papers.

41. See, for example, Wheeler, *CR*, 6 August 1941, 6828; Sauthoff, *CR*, 12 August 1941, 7046; Springer, *CR*, 12 August 1941, 7003; "Congress Is Not Stampeded," *Christian Century* 58 (6 August 1941): 971; "The War Situation," *CT*, 20 June 1941, 10.

42. Page Hufty, "'DANGER' GREATER—OR A.E.F.," AFC Bulletin #433, 23 July 1941, in Doenecke, *IDU*, 357–59. See also "Appeal to Conscience," *CT*, 13 August 1941, 12.

43. Bender, *CR*, 24 July 1941, 6308; Wiley, *CR*, 7 August 1941, 8851.

44. Wiley, *CR*, 7 August 1941, 6851; Walsh, *CR*, 5 August 1941, 6761; Jonkman, *CR*, 8 August 1941, 6930. See also Norman Thomas, "Your World and Mine: Is Extension of the Draft Necessary?" *Call*, 9 August 1941, 5.

45. Reed, *CR*, 8 August 1941, 6933; Wood, *NYT*, 5 July 1941, 24. See also Hoffman, *CR*, 8 August 1941, 6951; Taft, *CR*, 1 August 1941, 6571.

46. AFC Research Bureau, "Nobody Knows the Trouble We're In," *Did You Know?* 12 (24 July 1941), in Doenecke, *IDU*, 361–65; AFC Research Bureau, "Another A.E.F.?" *Did You Know?* 9 (15 July 1941), in Doenecke, *IDU*, 345–46. For Baldwin, see "The Realities of Hemispheric Defense," *Reader's Digest* 39 (July 1941): 117.

47. AFC Research Bureau, "The Shape of Things to Come?" *Did You Know?* 13 (30 July 1941), in Doenecke, *IDU*, 366–72.

48. Wood in Cole, *Roosevelt*, 437, and Doenecke, *IDU*, 33–34; slogan, Page Hufty, AFC Bulletin #440, 25 July 1941, Materials of the American First Committee, Firestone Library, Princeton University, (hereafter cited as Princeton Files); AFC Research Bureau, "Long-Term Conscription," *Did You Know?* 17 (17 July 1941), in Doenecke, *IDU*, 351–57.

49. Robert E. Wood to Robert R. Reynolds, 17 July 1941, in Doenecke, *IDU*, 342–43.

50. Oswald Garrison Villard to R. Douglas Stuart Jr., 25 July 1941, Box 67, AFC Papers; Villard, "Let Congress Keep Control!" *Christian Century* 58 (13 August 1941): 1006; Hammond in Ruth Sarles, "A Story of America First," unpub. ms., AFC Papers, 231; Hearst, "In the News," *SFE*, 28 July 1941, A; Hearst, "In the News," *SFE*, 11 August 1941, A.

51. "Demobilize the Draft Army?" *Christian Century* 58 (1 October 1941), 1198–99; "Lippmann Proposal Is Inspired," *Christian Century* 58 (8 October1941): 1229.

52. Taft, *CR*, 1 August 1941, 6575; text, 5 August 1941, 6740. For an endorsement, see "The Taft Plan," *CT*, 25 July 1941, 8. It was voted down twenty-seven to fifty, with eighteen not voting. *CR*, 5 August 1941, 6741.

53. Johnson, *CR*, 7 August 1941, 6877. It was voted down thirty-six to thirty-seven, with twenty-three not voting. Other such defeated proposals included those by Downey, who sought a $30 per month bonus for each month in service beyond twelve months (by voice vote), and Senator William Langer (Rep.-N.Dak.), who wanted to raise the monthly bonus to a hundred dollars. *CR*, 7 August 1941, 6861. On 12 August. Voorhis proposed an amendment granting an extra pay allowance of $30. It too was defeated by voice vote. *NYT*, 13 August 1941, 1.

54. Fish, *CR*, 8 August 1941, 6909. See also Hanks, "Fish," 306.

55. House vote, *CR*, 12 August 1941, 7074–75; Sarles, 228; FDR, Clifford and Spencer, *First Peace-time Draft*, 233; poll, *NYT*, 11 August 1941, 6. See also overwhelming endorsement shown in government abstracts of editorial opinion. White, *FDR and the Press*, 84.

56. Clifford and Spencer, *First Peacetime Draft*, 232.

57. R. Douglas Stuart Jr., in Cole, *America First*, 102; Samuel Pettengill to Robert E. Wood, 14 and 15 August 1941, Box 292, AFC Papers; Page Hufty, Bulletin #503, 20 August 1941, Box 279, AFC Papers; Livingstone Hartley, "The Army Saved," CDAAA, *Washington Office Information Letter* 31 (15 August 1941): 1–2, Box 35, CDAAA Papers.

58. Theodore A. Wilson, *First Summit;* Theodore A. Wilson, "The First Summit: FDR and the Riddle of Personal Diplomacy," in *The Atlantic Charter*, ed. Douglas Brinkley and David R. Facey-Crowther (New York: St. Martin's, 1994), 1–31.

59. For the full text, see "The Official Statement," *NYT*, 15 August 1941, 1.

60. AFC Research Bureau, "Eight Points for War or Peace, 3: Can They Work?" *Did You Know?* 21A and 21B (2 September 1941), in Doenecke, *IDU*, 332.

61. "Platform," *Uncensored* 98 (16 August 1941): 1.

62. Flynn in "AFC Leaders Assay Pact," *AFC New York Chapter Bulletin*, 23 August 1941, 2. See also "Peace" in New York *AFC New York Chapter Bulletin*, 23 August 1941, 4; "Can They Work?" 333–34. To Dorothy Detzer, point 2 met a WIL principle but neglected the problem of population pressures, acute in the case of Japan. Report of national secretary, WIL, 18 October 1941, WIL Papers.

63. Hearst, "In the News," *WTH*, 26 August 1941, 9; "Can They Work?" 336. For other critiques of point 3, see "Platform," *Uncensored* 98 (16 August 1941): 1; Detzer, report of national secretary, WIL, 18 October 1941, WIL Papers; Sokolsky, "These Days: Said Winston to Franklin," *New York Sun*, 19 August 1941, 16.

64. "I Am the State," *NYDN*, 10 November 1941, 29. See also AFC Research Bureau, "Eight Points for War or Peace, 1: What Do They Mean?" *Did You Know?* 19 (23 August 1941), in Doenecke, *IDU*, 322; "Can They Work?" 336.

65. "Platform," *Uncensored* 98 (16 August 1941): 1; McCracken, testimony, SFRC, 22 October 1941, 103. See also James Gillis, "Equal Access" and "Weasel Word?" *Catholic World* 154 (November 1941): 7; Ruth Sarles to R. Douglas Stuart Jr., 3 October 1941, in Doenecke, *IDU*, 301; Libby, "Grave Questions Arise," *Peace Action* 9 (September 1941): 2; Libby, testimony, HFAC, 16 October 1941, 65. Congressman Ludlow dissented from the criticism. He saw Roosevelt and Churchill as seeking to cut the ground out from under Hitler, whose nation had long been demanding economic opportunity and access to raw materials. Ludlow, cited in report, Fred Burdick, 14 August 1941, Box 65, AFC Papers.

66. "What Do They Mean?" 323. For an endorsement of points 4 and 5, see Detzer, report of national secretary, WIL, 18 October 1941, WIL Papers.

67. "What Do They Mean?" 320, 323. For other critiques of point 6, see Hiram Johnson, *CR*, 19 August 1941, 7206; Detzer, report of national secretary, WIL, 18 October 1941, WIL Papers; Castle Diary, 16 August 1941; General Wood, AFC release, 14 August 1941, Box 278, AFC Papers; "What Has Roosevelt Promised Churchill?" *CT*, 15 August 1941, 8; "Mr. Churchill Tells Us," *CT*, 26 August 1941, 8.

68. "What Do They Mean?" 320; "Can They Work?" 338.

69. Ruth Sarles to R. Douglas Stuart Jr., 15 August 1941, in Doenecke, *IDU*, 314; Libby, "Churchill–Roosevelt Statement a Step Toward Peace," *Peace Action* 7 (August 1941): 1. See also "Platform," *Uncensored* 98 (16 August 1941): 2.

70. For critiques of point 7, see "Can They Work?" 341; Ruth Sarles to R. Douglas Stuart Jr., 3 October 1941, in Doenecke, *IDU*, 300; Henry Noble McCracken, testimony, SFRC, 22 October 1941, 103.

71. "Platform"; "What Do They Mean?" 323.

72. "War for Utopia," *NYDN*, 15 August 1941, 25. On 31 December 1940, Churchill had granted Roosevelt's request that minimal aid be given Vichy France. Wert, "Specter," 340.

73. "Comment," *America* 65 (23 August 1941): 534; Dennis, *WFL* 159 (14 August 1941): 4.

74. AFC Research Bureau, "Eight Points for War or Peace," in Doenecke, *IDU*, 323. See also Congressman Day, *CT*, 20 October 1941; Detzer, report of national secretary, WIL, 18 October 1941, 6, WIL Papers.

75. Norman Thomas, "Your World and Mine: Churchill Baits Hook; U.S. Labor Scene," *Call*, 6 September 1941, 5; Von Weigand, *SFE*, 17 August 1941, 1–2; "V for Communism," *Uncensored* 106 (11 October 1941): 4. See also "Platform," *Uncensored* 98 (16 August 1941): 2; "God, Inc.," *Uncensored* 109 (1 November 1941): 1.

76. Frederick J. Libby to Sarah J. Swift, 5 December 1941, NCPW Papers.

77. AFC Research Bureau, "Eight Points for Peace or War, 2: What Legal Effect Do They Have?" *Did You Know?* 20 (23 August 1941): 324–30.

78. See, for example, reporter Chesly Manly, who found Roosevelt "doing another Woodrow Wilson." *WTH*, 19 August 1941; Philip La Follette to Clay Judson, 18 August 1941, Box 283, AFC Papers; "War for Utopia," *NYDN*, 15 August 1941, 25; John Finerty, testimony, HFAC, 14 October 1941, 31; Finerty, testimony, SFRC, 23 October 1941, 199; Frank O. Lowden, former governor of Illinois, to John Foster Dulles, 25 October 1941, Dulles Papers.

79. "What Do They Mean?" 317–20; Fairbank in "AFC Leaders Assay Pact," *AFC New York Chapter Bulletin*, 23 August 1941, 2. For other comparison to the Fourteen Points, see Villard, "That View of Secrecy," *Christian Century* 58 (27 August 1941): 1052; Hearst, "In the News," *SFE*, 21 August 1941, 2;

Norman Thomas, "Your World and Mine: Roosevelt–Churchill Meeting and After," *Call*, 30 August 1941, 5.

80. Nye in "Peace," *AFC New York Chapter Bulletin*, 23 August 1941, 1; Dennis, *WFL* 159 (14 August 1941): 4; Castle Diary, 16 August 1941. See also "What Has Roosevelt Promised Churchill?" *CT*, 15 August 1941, 8; "Platform," 1.

81. Lindbergh, *War Within*, 216 (emphasis in original); Hearst, "In the News," *SFE*, 21 August 1941, 2; "After the Atlantic Conference, I: What Happened on the *Augusta*?" *Christian Century* 58 (27 August 1941): 1045–47. For similar arguments, see "The Roosevelt–Churchill Eight Points," *Commonweal* 34 (29 August 1941): 435–36; "How Are You Going to Kill the Bear?" *NYDN*, 16 August 1941, 18.

82. See, for example, Representative Mundt in report, Fred Burdick, 14 August 1941, Box 65, AFC Papers; Moley, "Perspective: War Aims," *Newsweek*, 25 August 1941, 56; Clay Judson to Phil La Follette, 15 August 1941, Box 283, AFC Papers.

83. General Wood, AFC press release, 14 August 1941, Box 278, AFC Papers.

84. See, for example, socialist leader Al Hamilton to Norman Thomas, 15 August 1941, Socialist Party Papers; Villard, "This Global War," *Christian Century* 58 (10 September 1941): 1108–9; Albert W. Palmer, testimony, SFRC, 22 October 1941, 92.

85. Dorothy Medders Robinson and Dorothy Detzer to FDR, 11 October 1941, WIL Papers; also in Roosevelt Papers. An actual WIL resolution endorsing the points regretted "the secrecy and undemocratic way" in which they were drafted. It opposed the unilateral disarmament of Germany, which, it felt, would merely repeat the mistake embodied the war-guilt clause of the Versailles treaty and hence stiffen German resistance. Resolutions, WIL National Board, WIL 18–19 October 1941, WIL Papers.

86. Libby, "Churchill–Roosevelt Statement a Step Toward Peace," 1. See also "Strictly within the Family," *Peace Action* 9 (October 1941): 2. Libby went so far as to claim, "In view of the sharp bargaining that is yet to come, I don't see how the British, backed by Roosevelt, could have gone any further in the direction of conciliation than they have done." Letter to Norman Thomas, 3 September 1941, NCPW Papers. Thomas thought Libby unwise to endorse the declaration, particularly as Churchill voiced imperialist sentiments in explicitly speaking of disarming "the wicked" alone. Norman Thomas to Frederick J. Libby, 8 September 1941, NCPW Papers.

87. Frederick J. Libby to Marshall B. Wyatt, 13 November 1941, NCPW Papers; A. J. Muste to Frederick J. Libby, 5 November 1941, NCPW Papers. Speaking at Cornell University, Muste called on the United States to offer an immediate peace proposal that would include the Eight Points. *Cornell* [University] *Daily Sun*, 31 October 1941, 1.

88. See, for example, Flynn, "AFC Leaders Assay Pact," *AFC New York Chapter Bulletin*, 23 August 1941, 2; Sokolsky, "These Days: No Nearer War," *New York Sun*, 21 August 1941, 14; *Social Justice*, 25 August 1941, 3; "Declaration of the Atlantic," *Saturday Evening Post* 213 (27 September 1941): 26; Villard, "Startling Peace Aims," *Progressive*, 30 August 1941, 8; Landon, *NYT*, 16 August 1941, 7; Maney, *La Follette*, 248; Morley Diary, 16 August 1941; Castle Diary, 16 August 1941. Castle later heard that the meeting was not a success, for Churchill supposedly had accused FDR of failing to keep promises concerning airplanes, tanks, and an army of two million men. Castle Diary, 4 September 1941.

89. "But Boake Carter Says," *SFE*, 13 August 1941, 7. For AFC promotion of Carter's remarks, see Page Hufty, Bulletin #489, 14 August 1941, AFC Papers. Villard also found the meeting "a poor copy of the Hitler–Mussolini meetings on the Brenner and elsewhere." See "That Veil of Secrecy," *Christian Century* 58 (7 August 1941): 1052.

90. Manly quoted by Senator Alben Barkley, 19 August 1941, *CR*, 7204.

91. Norman Thomas to Burton Wheeler, 25 August 1941, Thomas Papers. See also "Vague War Aims Cloak Far East Pact, Is Belief," *Call*, 23 August 1941, 1.

92. "After the Atlantic Conference," *Christian Century* 58 (27 August 1941): 1046.

93. See, for example, Arthur Capper in Fred Burdick, general report, 26 August 1941, in Doenecke, *IDU*, 450; B. C. Clark, *CR*, 19 August 1941, 7209; Taft in Wilson, *First Summit*, 231; Hiram W. Johnson, *CR*, 19 August 1941, 7206; Hiram W. Johnson to Hiram W. Johnson Jr., 17 August 1941, Johnson Papers.

94. Burdick report, 19 August 1941, Box 65, AFC Papers. Burdick had previously claimed that many congressional leaders did not believe that Roosevelt would launch the United States on a full belligerent

course unless the majority of its people expressed at least tacit approval. Burdick report, 14 August 1941, Box 65, AFC Papers.

95. Tinkham in Burdick report, 19 August 1941, Box 65, AFC Papers; Burdick report, 15 August 1941, Box 65, AFC Papers.

96. "What Do They Mean?" 316; Ruth Sarles to R. Douglas Stuart Jr., 15 August 1941 in Doenecke, *IDU,* 313; "Peace," *AFC New York Chapter Bulletin,* 23 August 1941, 1.

97. See, for example, Dennis, *WFL* 159 (14 August 1941): 1.

98. Knutson, in Burdick report, 14 August 1941, Box 65, AFC Papers; Wood, AFC press release, 14 August 1941, Box 278, AFC Papers; Wood, *CT,* 15 August 1941, 5. Yet, several days later, Wood feared that "America will soon follow up the proposed peace points by active participation in the war." AFC press release, 19 August 1941, AFC Papers.

99. Stuart, *CT,* 15 August 1941, 5; Clay Judson to Philip La Follette, 15 August 1941, Box 283, AFC Papers.

100. Reynolds, *Creation,* 213–16; Kimball, *Forged,* 103; Kimball, *Juggler,* 248 n. 83; Freidel, *Roosevelt,* 387; Reynolds, "The Atlantic 'Flop': British Foreign Policy and the Churchill–Roosevelt Meeting of August 1941," in Brinkley and Facey-Crowther, *Atlantic Charter,* 130.

101. White, *FDR and the Press,* 84; *Fortune* poll in Cantril, *Public Opinion,* 1083.


## CHAPTER 17: PROJECTIONS OF CONFLICT

1. See, for example, General Smedley Butler, address, Mutual, entered in *CR,* 18 October 1939, 568; Daniel Reed, *CR,* 16 October 1939, 477; *CR,* 2 November 1939, 1312; Reynolds, *CR,* 21 October 1939, 688; Holt, radio address, 1 June 1940, in *CR,* 3687; Verne Marshall, "Is a Hitler Defeat Essential to the United States?" Town Meeting of the Air, debate with Dean Acheson, 9 January 1941, in Verne Marshall Papers; Notre Dame theologian John C. O'Brien, "Can America Stay Out?" *Catholic Digest* 5 (November 1940): 18, originally in *Our Sunday Visitor,* 22 September 1940; Norman Thomas, *Barnard Bulletin,* 28 February 1941, 4.

2. Borah, *CR,* 2 October 1939, 74; Hugh Johnson to R. Douglas Stuart Jr., 8 January 1941, in Doenecke, *IDU,* 106; Thill, *CR,* 10 November 1941, 8748; Coffee, *CR,* 12 November 1941, 8792.

3. For favorable treatment of *Johnny Got His Gun* (Philadelphia: Stuart, 1939), see Stuart Chase to Sidney Hertzberg, 5 October 1939, Hertzberg Papers; "Tops in Horror Stories," *NYDN,* 9 October 1939, 31; Holt, *CR,* 31 October 1939, A853; Holt, *CR,* 2 January 1941, 14014; *Social Justice,* 5 May 1941, 3. Trumbo also wrote an antiwar novella, *The Remarkable Andrew, Being the Chronicle of a Literal Man* (Philadelphia: Lippincott, 1941), that was serialized in the *CT.* See issue of 1 February 1941, 1.

4. See, for example, B. C. Clark, *CR,* 18 February 1941, 1101; Frank Gannett to Dexter Perkins, 17 November 1941, Gannett Papers; Truman Smith cited in Herbert Hoover, memorandum, 1 June 1941, Hoover Papers; Dennis, *WFL* 156 (24 July 1941): 5; "British Offensive," *Uncensored* 72 (15 February 1941): 3.

5. Lindbergh, speech, Los Angeles, 20 June 1941, in *CR,* 3185. See also Lindbergh, testimony, HFAC, 23 January 1941, 385, 404, 424, 429; testimony, SFRC, 6 February 1941, 508; Lindbergh, entry of 10 October 1940, *Wartime Journals,* 403; 3 November 1940, 412. Hugh Johnson concurred. Testimony, HFAC, 23 January 1941, 437.

6. Williams, "Folly of Invasion Talk," *Progressive,* 2 November 1941, 5. See also Truman Smith cited in Herbert Hoover, memorandum, 1 June 1941, Hoover Papers.

7. Waldrop, "Who'll Do It?" *WTH,* 4 October 1941, 16.

8. "How Are You Going to Kill the Bear?" *NYDN,* 16 August 1941, 18. For another reference to Dunkirk, see AFC, *Washington News Letter* 16 (4 June 1941): 3.

9. Marshall, debate, Town Meeting of the Air, 9 January 1941, Verne Marshall Papers; *Social Justice,* 24 March 1941, 4; Dennis, *WFL* 106 (8 August 1940): 3. Congressman Jonkman thought in terms of four to ten times. *CR,* 6 May 1941, 3671. For a more modest but still formidable estimate, see "British War Aims . . . and Ours," *NYDN,* 27 February 1941, 27.

10. Villard, "The Military Outlook," *Christian Century* 58 (8 October 1941): 1240; Wheeler cited in Villard, "Our Incredible Overconfidence," *Christian Century* 58 (5 November 1941): 1371. See also Wheeler, speech, Indianapolis, 28 May 1941, in *CR*, A2628; Bennett, speech, NBC red network, 2 June 1941, A2654.

11. Fish, *CR*, 30 April 1941, 3465; Wheeler, debate, American Forum of the Air, 12 January 1941, in *CR*, A179.

12. For two million, see Al Williams, "Shore-Based Airpower," *Progressive*, 4 July 1941, 4. For four to five million, see Woodruff, *CR*, 29 May 1941, 4574; Morris Rubin, "The Last Column," *Progressive*, 25 October 1941, 12; Bennett, speech, NBC red network, 2 June 1941, in *CR*, A2654; Merwin K. Hart, testimony, SFRC, 8 February 1941, 744; John T. Flynn, testimony, SFRC, 23 October 1941, 206; Stanton B. Leeds, "The Real Pétain," *Scribner's Commentator* 10 (July 1941): 17; Rankin, *CR*, 24 April 1941, 3280; Hoover, speech, New York, 12 May 1941, in *CR*, A2315; Wheeler, *CR*, 6 November 1941, 8553; MacNider, testimony, HFAC, 22 January 1941, 353. For six to ten million, see Freda Utley, "Must the World Destroy Itself?" *Reader's Digest* 39 (October 1941): 18; Shipstead, *CR*, 3 November 1941, 8422; James Gillis, "The 'Isolationist' Argument," *Catholic World* 155 (December 1941): 262; Bulow, *CR*, 12 October 1939, 311–12; Congressman Johns, radio address, 11 June 1941, in *CR*, A2835; *Social Justice*, 27 October 1941, 3; B. C. Clark, *CR*, 4 November 1941, 8492; Cudahy cited by Villard, "Our Incredible Overconfidence," *Christian Century* 58 (5 November 1941): 1370; "Comment," *America* 66 (8 November 1941): 115. *Uncensored* estimated eight million, judging that one out of three men between ages eighteen and twenty-five would be called. It said its estimate came from the U.S. General Staff. "Strained Leash," *Uncensored* 107 (18 October 1941): 2; "Blueprint," *Uncensored* 108 (25 October 1941): 4. For twenty million, see Fish, *CR*, 11 March 1941, 2169.

13. For a minimum of 150 divisions, see "The Job of Beating Germany," *NYDN*, 3 March 1941, 19. For the estimate of 280 divisions, see Morris Rubin, "The Last Column," *Progressive*, 25 October 1941, 12.

14. Villard, "Blueprints for War," *Progressive*, 8 November 1941, 8. He was citing *Wall Street Journal* writer Eugene S. Duffield.

15. For estimates of one million casualties, see Lindbergh, speech, 15 September 1939, in *CR*, A16; Smedley Butler, address, entered *CR*, 18 October 1939, 567; Morton, *Let's Think This Matter Through* [pamphlet], in *CR*, 21 February 1941, A785. For an estimate of three million, see Fish, *CR*, 22 September 1941, 7509. For an estimate of five million, see Edwin Johnson, *CR*, 17 June 1940, A3919. For an estimate of ten million, see Verne Marshall, debate, Town Meeting of the Air, 9 January 1941, Verne Marshall Papers.

16. Baldwin, "Blueprint for Victory," *Life*, 4 August 1941, 47.

17. Johnson, speech, Minneapolis, Mutual, 18 September 1939, in *CR*, A62; Fish, *CR*, 9 October 1941, 7790. Fish quoted Senator Pepper, whom he called "an arch interventionist," as saying the war could cost $100 billion a year. Fish, speech, Mutual, 7 October 1941, in *CR*, A4629. For the sum of a hundred billion, see also Edwin C. Johnson, *CR*, 17 June 1940, A3919. For Baldwin, see "Blueprint for Victory," *Life*, 4 August 1941, 47.

18. See, for example, Castle, HFAC, 24 January 1941, 499; Baldwin, "Blueprint for Victory," *Life*, 4 August 1941, 47.

19. Chase, "Four Assumptions about the War," *Uncensored* 65 (28 December 1940): special supplement, 2; "American Inventory, November 1941," *Progressive*, 15 November 1941, 5. See also Taft, *CR*, 9 July 1940, 9311.

20. Fish, *CR*, 30 April 1941, 3465. Fish quoted Pepper as claiming the war could last up to twenty years. Speech, Mutual, 7 October 1941, in *CR*, A4629.

21. Hoover, speech, New York, 12 May 1941, in *CR*, A2315. For the estimation of ten years, see also Johns, radio address, 11 June 1941, in *CR*, A2835; "Not Ethics, but Mathematics," *NYDN*, 22 May 1941, 29.

22. McCormick, broadcast of 6 October 1940, in *Addresses*, 62–63. See also "A Choice of Evils," *CT*, 9 February 1941, 16. In July 1941, Colonel McCormick explicitly retracted his opinion that an army could be landed on the mainland, though at tremendous cost. The 640 miles between Iceland and Norway made that route impossible. The English Channel remained a serious obstacle. Were the United States to use Ponta Delgada and Cape Verde as bases to take Dakar, the invaders would still have to

cross a thousand miles of desert, an impenetrable barrier, and then fight the hostile nations of Spain, Portugal, and France. McCormick, address, WGN, *CT*, 27 July 1941, 5. For McCormick's newspaper, see "What We Know," *CT*, 19 May 1941, 1; "The Invasion of Europe," *CT*, 12 May 1941, 12.

23. Morton, *Let's Think This Matter Through* [pamphlet], in *CR*, 21 February 1941, A785.

24. "The Kings Depart," *NYDN*, 27 May 1941, 29. See also "After the Crusade, What?" *NYDN*, 17 July 1941, 27.

25. Mencken, "Sham Battle," *Baltimore Sun*, 1 October 1939.

26. Baldwin, *United We Stand!* 270–71, 301 n. 3.

27. Baldwin, *United We Stand!* 120, 128.

28. Livingstone Hartley and Donald C. Blaisdell, "The Spectre of an A.E.F.," CDAAA, *Washington Office Information Letter* 12 (4 April 1941): 1, Box 35, CDAAA Papers. For a proposal that "small invasions" take place in Norway and southern Italy, see Livingstone Hartley and Frank S. Goodwin, "Invasion of Europe," CDAAA, *Washington Office Information Letter* 32 (22 August 1941): 3, Box 35, CDAAA Papers.

29. [Plan Dog] Stark, "Memorandum for the Secretary," 12 November 1940, in *American War Plans*, vol. 3: *Plans to Meet the Axis Threat, 1939–1940*, ed. Steven T. Ross (New York: Garland, 1992): 229, 241, 248.

30. "Ultimate Requirements Study: Estimate of Army Ground Forces," in *American War Plans, 1919–1941*, vol. 5: *Plans for Global War: Rainbow Five and the Victory Program, 1941*, ed. Ross, 193–203.

31. Wilson, *First Summit*, 214–17; Langer and Gleason, *Undeclared War*, 738–40; Kirkpatrick, *Unknown Future*; "Joint Board Estimate of United States Over-All Production Requirements," 11 September 1941, in Ross, *American War Plans*, 5:162–201. For AFC sympathy, see Albert C. Wedemeyer, *Wedemeyer Reports!* (New York: Holt, 1958), 25.

32. Wilson, *First Summit*, 219; quotation from Leighton and Coakley, *Global Logistics*, 140.

33. *CT*, 4 December 1941, 1. For an interpretation of the leak, see Thomas Fleming, "The Big Leak," *American Heritage* 38 (December 1987): 65–71.

34. Reynolds, *Creation*, 42, 212; Sherry, *Rise*, 98; Dallek, *Roosevelt*, 285, 293; Kimball, *Juggler*, 34; Wilson, *First Summit*, 117; Kimball, *Forged in War*, 7, 113. Clifford and Spencer are slightly more cautious. See *First Peacetime Draft*, 45.

35. Heinrichs, *Threshold*, 159; Reynolds, *Creation*, 288–89, 350 n. 83.

36. Roosevelt in Leighton and Coakley, *Global Logistics*, 127.

37. Wilson, *First Summit*, 219.

38. Churchill in Reynolds, *Creation*, 213; Wilson, *First Summit*, 28, 94, 123. Marshall in Wilson, *First Summit*, 94, 118.

39. Ickes, entry of 2 September 1939, *Secret Diary*, 2:721. See also entry of 2 March 1940, 3:150.

40. Johnson attacked in B. C. Clark, *CR*, 11 October 1939, 282; *Call*, 21 October 1939, 3.

41. For Bullitt, see Ickes, entry of 10 March 1940, *Secret Diary*, 3:149.

42. Roosevelt to Harry H. Woodring, 11 March 1940, *F.D.R.: His Personal Letters*, 1007.

43. Roosevelt, press conference (excerpts), 22 September 1939, in *The Public Papers and Addresses of Franklin D. Roosevelt*, vol. 8: *War—and Neutrality, 1939*, comp. Samuel I. Rosenman (New York: Random House, 1950), 526. See also press conference, 13 October 1939, in Rosenman, *Roosevelt Papers and Addresses*, 8:543. For Holt, see *CR*, 18 October 1939, 546. For other direct references to submarines, see Porter Sargent, Bulletin #8, 28 September 1939, *Getting US into War*, 127–28; Wheeler, speech at Hudson, Massachusetts, 1 October 1939, in *CR*, A458; John T. Flynn, "Other People's Money: The South American Bubble," *New Republic* 101 (25 October 1939): 339–40; Amos Pinchot to Robert M. La Follette, 13 October 1939, Pinchot Papers.

44. Fish, *CR*, 12 March 1940, 2728; "Remember the Coulmore?" *Uncensored* 10 (7 December 1939): 1; "Wuxtry!" 22 (2 March 1940): 1–2; Sargent, Bulletin #18, 24 November 1939, *Getting US into War*, 172–73.

45. Entry of 26 June 1940, *Navigating*, 326. See also entries of 23 March 1940, 299, where Berle talks of a German naval strike against the Western Hemisphere; 17 April 1940, 305; 26 May 1940, 318.

46. Clifford and Spencer, *First Peacetime Draft*, 43.

47. *Life*, 24 June 1940, 16–18.

48. For the entire *Liberty* series, see Fred Allhoff, *Lighting in the Night* (Englewood Cliffs, N.J.: Prentice Hall, 1979). For Van Loon, see *Invasion* (New York: Harcourt Brace, 1940).

49. Chester Bowles to Robert La Follette Jr. [copy], 16 May 1940, Hertzberg Papers; Fish, CR, 6 June 1940, 4811–12; Wheeler, *CR*, 13 August 1940, 10237; "Fifth Column Hysteria," *Christian Century* 57 (12 June 1940): 758–59. See also "Increasing the War Jitters," *Christian Century* 57 (11 September 1940): 1101–2.

50. Holmes, "The Mania of War," *Unity* 125 (17 June 1940): 115. For Berle, see entry of 4 June 1940, *Navigating*, 321. See also Taft, "Peace and Preparedness," speech at St. Louis, 20 May 1940, in *CR*, A3177; "The War Draws Nearer," *America* 63 (25 May 1940): 182; Hiram W. Johnson to Hiram W. Johnson Jr., 9 June 1940, Johnson Papers; Robert R. McCormick, broadcast of 9 June 1940, in *CT*, 10 June 1940, 3; Wheeler, address, 7 June 1940, in *CR*, A3676; John Haynes Holmes, "As We Move Toward War," sermon, 29 September 1940, in *CR*, A6059; Hoffman, *CR*, 7 September 1940, A6259; "A Time for Cool Heads," *Christian Century* 57 (29 May 1940): 694; "The American Jitters," *Christian Century* 57 (7 May 1940): 712.

51. "British Navy Scare," *Uncensored* 35 (1 June 1940): 1–2; La Follette, SFRC, 3 February 1941, 664–65. See also Hiram Johnson, *CR*, 20 October 1939, 631; O'Connor, *CR*, 21 January 1941, 212.

52. Butler, broadcast, Mutual network, as inserted by B. C. Clark, *CR*, 18 October 1939, 567.

53. Hoover, memorandum, 28 February 1941, Hoover Papers.

54. Taft, "Shall the United States Enter the European War?" radio address, 17 May 1941, in *CR*, A2344.

55. See, for example, Marcantonio, *CR*, 22 January 1941, 238; Robert La Follette, *CR*, 24 February 1941, 1304; "Information, Please," *Peace Action* 6 (July 1940): 7; "Suppressed Document on Conscription," *In Fact* 1 (9 September 1940): 3–4; George H. Cless Jr., "The William Allen White Reign of Terror," *Scribner's Commentator* 9 (December 1940): 40; "The Truth behind 'If Hitler Wins' Bugaboo," *Daily Worker*, 8 June 1940, 7; B. C. Clark, *CR*, 3 June 1940, 7376; "Invasion: FDR's Gigantic Hoax," *New Masses* 35 (28 May 1940): 3; "The Senate Committee Contradicts FDR," *New Masses* 35 (28 May 1940): 5; Dorothy Detzer to Mrs. S. Foster Hunt, 18 September 1940, WIL Papers; "To the Brink," *St. Louis Post-Dispatch*, 11 June 1940; Wheeler, speech, Minneapolis, 18 June 1940, in *CR*, A3960; "Sensational Senate Report," *Progressive*, 10 August 1940, 3; Frank Hanighen to Sidney Hertzberg, 27 May 1940, Hertzberg Papers.

56. Conclusions, Senate Committee on Naval Affairs, in Walsh, *CR*, 4 June 1940, 7439.

57. "Baldwin, Hanson W(eightman)," in *Current Biography, 1942*, ed. Maxine Block (New York: Wilson, 1943), 52–55; Carol Hill, "Memorandum of Possible Profile on Hanson W. Baldwin," 2 June 1941, Moley Papers.

58. For sample endorsements of Baldwin, see "But Boake Carter Says," *SFE*, 1 August 1940, 19; "But Boake Carter Says," *SFE*, 2 August 1940, 9; Cushman Reynolds, "General Mud (II)," *Common Sense* 10 (September 1941): 266; Beale, "Some Fallacies," 20; La Follette, *CR*, 29 October 1941, 8323; Robert E. Wood to Hanson Baldwin, 8 May 1941, Wood Papers; Waldrop, "They Weep," *WTH*, 2 November 1941, E1; O'Connor, *CR*, 6 October 1941, 7684; "American Impregnability," *Uncensored* 5 (4 November 1939): supplement, 1; "Rational Defense," *Uncensored* 42 (20 July 1940): 2–4; various *Did You Know?* bulletins of the AFC in Doenecke, *IDU*, passim; Nye, speech of 1 August 1940, in *CR*, 10,819; "Do the Best with What We Have," *CT*, 7 July 1941, 10.

59. Baldwin noted in Edwin M. Borchard to John Bassett Moore, 23 April 1941, Borchard Papers.

60. *United We Stand!* 75.

61. *United We Stand!* 76, 128.

62. *United We Stand!* 128, 78 (quotation). For other comparisons to Gallipoli, see Reynolds, speech to American Defense Society, 13 April 1940, in *CR*, A2441; Nye, *CR*, 26 February 1941, 1425.

63. *United We Stand!* 92, 96, 107–8. He also mentioned Acapulco, Magdalena Bay, the gulf of southern California, and such islands as the Johnson chain, the French Frigate Shoals, Kigman Reef, Palmyra, Canton, and Rose. See 110.

64. Baldwin, "Blueprint for Victory," *Life*, 4 August 1941, 47.

65. For anti-interventionist endorsement, see Norman Thomas to Morris R. Cohen, 4 November 1941, Thomas Papers; "America First Book List," AFC Bulletin #476, 7 August 1941, in Doenecke, *IDU*, 120; Paul Hutchinson, "Should America Enter the War?" *Christian Century* 58 (7 May 1941): 623–24; John Haynes Holmes, "Editorials," *Unity* 127 (June 1941): 57; Pettengill, "United We Stand," 31 July 1941, Box 11, Pettengill Papers. For interventionist endorsement, see Walter Millis, *New York Herald Tribune Book Review*, 4 May 1941, 5; "The Job," *Time*, 28 April 1941, 89; Lindsay Rogers, "Divided We Are Falling," *New Republic* 104 (10 May 1941): 561; S. T. Williamson, *NYT Book Review*, 4 May 1941, 1, 18; "The Defence of America," *Times* [London] *Literary Supplement*, 2 August 1941, 374.

66. Cowley, "No Defense," *New Republic* 104 (26 May 1941): 734. For an exchange between Baldwin and Cowley, see *New Republic* 104 (30 June 1941): 889–90.

67. MacLeish and Reynolds, *Strategy*, 51–55, 64, 69–76, 234.

68. MacLeish and Reynolds, *Strategy*, 173, 217–19, 226–27.

69. For praise from anti-interventionists, see reference to John Chamberlain and Hanson Baldwin in Sidney Hertzberg to R. Douglas Stuart Jr., 6 February 1941, Box 61, AFC Papers; Paul Hutchinson, "Should America Enter the War?" *Christian Century* 58 (7 May 1941): 623–24; Norman Thomas to Cushman Reynolds, 7 April 1941, Thomas Papers; Norman Thomas to Ken Jefferson, 13 November 1941, Thomas Papers; Samuel Romer, "Books: Hemispheric Defense," *Call*, 12 April 1941, 8. For other favorable reviews, see journalist and former diplomat Nicholas Roosevelt, *New York Herald Tribune Book Review*, 6 April 1941, 5; S. T. Williamson, *NYT Book Review*, 18 May 1941, 12. One reviewer, Burton Ledoux, said the book could "serve well as a text book for isolationist and interventionist alike." *Common Sense* 10 (May 1941): 154.

70. Flynn, "Can Hitler Invade America?" *Reader's Digest* 38 (April 1941): 4, 2. For a somewhat similar scenario by Nye, see *CR*, 26 February 1941, 1434; Chamberlain, *American Stakes,* 174–77, drawing on Mauritz A. Hallgren, *The Tragic Fallacy: A Study of America's War Policies* (New York: Knopf, 1937), chap. 5.

71. See, for example, Smedley Butler, broadcast, Mutual network, as inserted by B. C. Clark, *CR*, 18 October 1939, 567; Downey, *CR*, 6 October 1939, 162; Villard, "Will Hitler Invade America?" *Christian Century* 57 (13 October 1940): 1312; Hanson Baldwin quoted in "Democracy: Conscription's Victim?" *Detroit Free Press*, 31 July 1940; Senator La Follette, *CR*, 24 February 1941, 1304; "If Worst Came to Worst," *CT*, 28 November 1939, 14; "A Still Bigger Army and What It Means," *CT*, 6 January 1941, 12.

72. Wheeler, [University of] *Michigan Daily*, 6 May 1941, 1. Wheeler estimated twenty-six tons of equipment and tanks for each invader. *CR*, 22 August 1940, 10,728.

73. Johnson, "Can Hitler Invade America?" *Peace Action* 6 (December 1939): 5. See also "Second Rate Armies Aren't Armies," *CT*, 17 May 1940, 14.

74. Walter Trohan, "Could the U.S. Be Invaded? Yes, but What a Job!" *CT*, 4 June 1940, 1.

75. "National Defense," *Uncensored* 33 (18 May 1940): 1. See also Fish, speech, CBS, 26 May 1940, in *CR*, A3270.

76. AFC, Bulletin #559, 18 September 1941, Box 279, AFC Papers. Quoted was Hagood, "Generals Never Learn," *Collier's* 108 (23 August 1941), 57. See also John Haynes Holmes, letter to *Harvard* [University] *Crimson*, 3 October 1941, 2.

77. For meaning of Lindbergh, see, for example, Jeanette Rankin, undated speech entered in *CR*, 16 January 1940, A209; Fish, *CR*, 28 May 1940, 7049; Fish, 6 June 1941, 4812; Walsh, 4 June 1940, 7445; Nye, 26 February 1941, 1432. For similar arguments, see "A Still Bigger Army and What It Means," *CT*, 6 January 1941, 12.

78. Lindbergh, "Text of the Speech," *NYT*, 20 May 1940, 8. For similar stress on Germany's lack of long-range bombers, see Nicholas Broughton, "America in a Hostile World," *Scribner's Commentator* 9 (November 1940): 71; Al Williams, "Oceans Wider Than Ever," *Progressive*, 9 August 1941, 4.

79. Lindbergh, speech, "Impregnable America," 30 October 1940, Yale University, in *Scribner's Commentator* 9 (January 1941): 5.

80. Nye, *CR*, 26 February 1941, 1433. Speaking over CBS in June 1941, Nye said that the Germans had a plane capable of flying to New York. It could, however, only carry a bomb of ten or twelve pounds and would be unable to return to its base. CBS speech, 26 June 1941, in *CR*, A3075.

81. "But Boake Carter Says," *SFE*, 28 May 1940, 19. See also "But Boake Carter Says," *SFE*, 24 January 1941, 11.

82. Nye, *CR*, 26 February 1941, 1433; Taft, *CR*, 10 July 1941, 5926.

83. Villard, "Will Hitler Invade America?" *Christian Century* 57 (13 October 1940): 1312.

84. See, for example, Waldrop, "Can They Really Gang Up on Us?" *WTH*, 4 October 1939, 11; "But Boake Carter Says," *SFE*, 24 January 1941, 11.

85. Colonel McCormick, broadcast of 9 June 1940, in *Addresses*, 6–7. For McCormick in World War I, see Smith, *Colonel*, chap. 7.

86. Johnson, "Can Hitler Invade America?" *Peace Action* 6 (December 1939): 5; Butler, broadcast, Mutual network, as inserted by B. C. Clark, *CR*, 18 October 1939, 567; Villard, "Will Hitler Invade America?" 1312. Hagood was frequently cited by anti-interventionists. See, for example, Holt, *CR*, 18 October 1939, 556; Nye, *CR*, 26 February 1941, 1425; Lundeen, *CR*, 27 August 1940, 11,009; Smedley Butler, *CR*, 3 November 1939, 815.

87. Clark, *CR*, 9 October 1939, 182.

88. See, for example, Norris, *CR*, 22 August 1940, 10,728; Lodge, *CR*, 22 August 1940, 10,729; Fish, *CR*, 4 December 1941, 9477.

89. Morton, *Let's Think the Matter Through* [pamphlet], in *CR*, 21 February 1941, A787.

90. Downey, *CR*, 9 October 1939, 182–83. In August, Downey predicted that within two years, the United States would have at least twenty-five thousand combat planes that would possess "ample power to pulverize any attack on the Western Hemisphere." *CR*, 27 August 1940, 11,039.

91. Rankin, undated speech, entered in *CR*, 16 January 1940, A209.

92. For Villard, see remarks, Conference on National Defense, School of Public and International Affairs, in [Princeton University] *Daily Princetonian*, 29 February 1940, 1. He did call for minefields and submarines. Letter to Norman Thomas, 16 July 1940, Thomas Papers. Congressman Woodruff recalled General Marshall's claim: 450,000 men, properly trained and equipped, could prevent any invasion. *CR*, 12 November 1941, 8786. For the number 400,000, see "Where Would We Send a Million Men?" *CT*, 15 April 1940, 10. It estimated that half a million men could prevent such ports as Halifax from falling into enemy hands. See "To Beat a Blitzkrieg," 4 June 1940, 14.

93. "Invincible Uncle Sam," *NYDN*, 7 April 1940, 43. See also "Strategy for Two Wars," *NYDN*, 3 February 1941, 19.

94. Waldrop, "Can They Really Gang Up on Us?" 11. For similar references to World War I, see Downey, *CR*, 6 October 1939, 162; Flynn, American Forum of the Air, 12 January 1941, in *CR*, A178; General Wood, testimony, SFRC, 4 February 1941, 356; Villard, "Will Hitler Invade America?" 1312.

95. Chavez, speech, Tucumcari, New Mexico, 11 May 1940, in *CR*, A2956. For similar references to Norway, see Norman Thomas, HFAC, 22 January 1941, 321; Flynn, "Other People's Money: Billions for Defense—Against What?" *New Republic* 102 (29 April 1940): 575.

96. "Conscript Confusion," *Uncensored* 45 (10 August 1940): 1. See also Congressman Philip A. Bennett, speech, Women's Republican Club, Warrensburg, Missouri, 16 May 1941, in *CR*, A2412; Burdick, *CR*, 12 August 1941, 7002.

97. Wheeler, *CR*, 7 August 1941, 6877. See also "British Navy Scare," *Uncensored* 35 (1 June 1940): 2.

98. General Wood said a year. See testimony, SFRC, 4 February 1941, 362. Charles A. Lindbergh said a year or two. Testimony, SFRC, 6 February 1941, 341.

99. Jennings, *CR*, 4 September 1940, 11,501; "Spirit of '76," *Uncensored* 68 (18 January 1941): 4.

100. Stimson, *NYT*, 17 January 1941, 6; CDAAA, "Progress Bulletin," 19 July 1940, 2, Box 34, CDAAA Papers; Chadwin, *Hawks*, 79, 81.

101. For historical references, see "Will We Do It?" *Saturday Evening Post* 213 (6 July 1940): 26; Shipstead, *CR*, 25 February 1941, 1346; Upton Close, "Common Sense for Americans," *Living Age* 358 (August 1940): 508; "Our First Line of Defense," *CT*, 6 February 1941, 12.

102. Nye, American Forum of the Air, 25 August 1940, in *CR*, A5660. See also Nye, *Yale* [University] *Daily News*, 24 April 1941, 1. For a massive memo inserted by Nye in the *CR*, see "The First-Line-of-Defense Argument," 7 November 1941, 8609–14, a lengthy record of British naval "aggression" in the Western Hemisphere.

103. Thomas, *Vassar* [College] *Miscellany News*, 21 May 1941, 1, 4; Baldwin, *United We Stand!* 41–42.

104. See, for example, Waldrop, "Would the British Navy Fight or Run?" *WTH*, 24 May 1940, 17; Al Williams, testimony, SFRC, 7 February 1941, 582.

105. Nye, *CR*, 26 February 1941, 1425; "Q and A," *Uncensored* 66 (4 January 1941): 3; "Spirit of '76," *Uncensored* 68 (18 January 1941): 4. Baldwin saw Britain either scuttling the fleet or moving it to such an empire stronghold as Canada. "Wanted: A Plan for Defense," *Harper's Magazine* 181 (August 1940): 231.

106. See, for example, "If Worst Came to Worst," *CT*, 28 November 1939, 14; "The Four False-hoods," *CT*, 1 April 1941, 12.

107. MacLiesh and Reynolds, *Strategy*, 191–94, 199. Two years was also noted in "Conscription Confusion," *Uncensored* 68 (18 January 1941): 4. Downey claimed eighteen months. *CR*, 27 August 1940, 11039. See also "Can the British Navy Be Captured?" *Call*, 15 June 1940, 3.

108. See, for example, Philip La Follette, testimony, SFRC, 2 February 1941, 282; Alf Landon, testimony, SFRC, 8 February 1941, 685; Baldwin, *United We Stand!* 39.

109. McCormick, testimony, SFRC, 6 February 1941, 48; Taft, *CR*, 22 February 1941, 1283. Taft noted FDR's address to Congress given on 6 January 1941. See also AFC Research Bureau, "Nobody Know the Trouble We're In," *Did You Know?* 12, in Doenecke, *IDU*, 361.

110. Broughton, "America in a Hostile World," *Scribner's Commentator* 9 (November 1940): 74.

111. Leutze, *Bargaining*, 209–10.

112. Roosevelt, *CR*, 6 January 1941, 45. For the admission of many interventionists, including President Roosevelt, that the United States could not be invaded by ground forces, see John A. Thompson, "The Downfall of Fortress America," *Journal of American Studies* 26 (December 1992): 393–408.

113. Gallup poll, *NYT*, 29 September 1939, 13, Cantril, *Public Opinion*, 775. In an exact breakdown of the April 1941 *Fortune* poll, one finds 56.1 percent in the negative, 33.0 percent affirmative, and 10.9 percent having no opinion. Cantril, *Public Opinion*, 1119.

## CHAPTER 18: TOWARD UNDECLARED WAR

1. Gilbert, *Churchill*, 6:1175.

2. Churchill in Reynolds, "Atlantic 'Flop,'" 133; Marshall in Lee, entry of 12 October 1941, *London Journal*, 423–24.

3. Norman Thomas, "Your World and Mine: Predictions and Conclusions," *Call*, 19 July 1941, 5; Hoover, *NYT*, 17 September 1941, 1; "Britain Doesn't Need Our Army," *CT*, 11 September 1941, 10. Al Williams was an exception among anti-interventionists in forecasting that the invasion of Britain lay ahead. "Folly of Avoiding Facts," *Progressive*, 12 July 1941, 4. The American army remained skeptical concerning Britain's anti-invasion defenses. Reynolds, *Creation*, 212.

4. A poll by the Office of Public Opinion Research released on 19 November 1941 showed 85 percent predicting German defeat; 5 percent, German victory; and 3 percent, stalemate; 7 percent had no opinion. For this and other polls, see Cantril, *Public Opinion*, 1187–88.

5. *Christian Century* 58 (8 October 1941): 1227–28. See also James Gillis, "Hitler's Troubles," *Catholic World* 153 (September 1941): 65; "Inside Germany," *Uncensored* 107 (18 October 1941) 4.

6. Shipstead, *CR*, 3 November 1941, 8423; Cudahy, testimony, SFRC, 22 October 1941, 148, 178; Fish, *Smith College Associated News*, 14 October 1941, 2.

7. Shanley, speech, Charles Carroll Forum, Palmer House, in *CT*, 29 September 1941, 6; Villard, "Will It Be a Stalemate?" *Progressive*, 6 December 1941, 10. For the Bess article, see *Saturday Evening Post* 214 (22 November 1941): 14–15, 84–88. See also Villard, "German Morale Hard Hit," *Progressive*, 9 August 1941, 8; Norman Thomas, letter to *NYT*, 6 December 1941, Thomas Papers.

8. See, for example, Robert E. Wood to S. Kent Costikyan, 18 November 1941, Box 56, AFC Papers; Castle Diary, 8 November 1941.

9. Hoover in Helen Essary, "Dear Washington," *WTH*, 3 July 1941, 10; "It May Be '43," *NYDN*, 14 November 1941, 37; Alf Landon to Herbert Hoover, 4 December 1941, Hoover Papers.

10. See, for example, Edwin M. Borchard to Tom Connally, 31 October 1941, Borchard Papers.

11. Freda Utley, "An Englishwoman Pleads: Must the World Destroy Itself?" *Reader's Digest* 39 (October 1941): 19; Morley Diary, 8 November 1941. In July, Morley had found the European continent to be steadily acquiring a vested interest in German victory. Hitler's "Holy War against communism," he said, would strengthen that interest, making it far more difficult for the United States to intervene directly on behalf of "the British Raj." Morley Diary, 7 July 1941. He endorsed a peace that would preserve the British Empire while letting Germany dominate a unified Europe. Entry of 28 July 1941.

12. Dennis, *WFL* 154 (10 July 1941): 2; 163 (11 September 1941): 4; 164 (18 September 1941): 4 (quotation). For more Dennis forecasts, see 160 (21 August 1941): 3; 163 (11 September 1941): 2; 168 (16 October 1941): 5; 169 (23 October 1941): 2.

13. "England, U.S. May Try Invasion of Nazi Europe," *Social Justice*, 21 July 1941, 8; 1 September 1941, 3; 15 September 1941, 3.

14. See, for example, Senator Edwin Johnson, in "Comment," *America* 66 (15 November 1941): 143.

15. Morrison, testimony, SFRC, 23 October 1941, 245; A. J. Muste to Mrs. H. W. Foote, 28 October 1941, FOR Papers.

16. Tittle, [Northwestern University] *Daily Northwestern*, 12 November 1941, 1.

17. See, for example, Norman Thomas, "Your World and Mine: Peace Rumors and War Facts," *Call*, 21 June 1941, 5; Cudahy, *CT*, 11 August 1941, 1; "Appeal to Conscience," *CT*, 13 August 1941, 12; Senators Nye and Adams, *CT*, 12 October 1941, 12; "Roosevelt Can Stop the War If He Wants To," *NYDN*, 12 August 1941, 27. Cudahy hoped the Vatican would join such an effort. Testimony, SFRC, 23 October 1941, 147. For further mention of Pius XII, see NCPW executive board, minutes, 17 September 1941, 1, NCPW Papers.

18. John Haynes Holmes to Edwin M. Borchard, 9 October 1941, Borchard Papers. Social worker Helen Alfred was secretary-treasurer. Sponsors included the FOR (Sayre, Muste), KAOWC (Mary Hillyer, Villard), NCPW (Libby), and WIL (Hannah Clothier Hull, Detzer). The AFC publicized the group. Doenecke, *IDU*, 61 n. 70.

19. R. Douglas Stuart Jr. to Robert M. Hutchins, 29 October 1941, in Doenecke, *IDU*, 137; Schneider, *Should America*, 205.

20. America First, said Flynn, could help finance the group and lend personnel. John T. Flynn to Robert E. Wood, 11 November 1941, in Doenecke, *IDU*, 138–39.

21. Wheeler, *Newsweek*, 14 July 1941, 15; Castle Diary, 16 August 1941; John Haynes Holmes to Bishop Edward L. Parsons, 8 October 1941, Holmes Papers. See also Vorys, *American Forum of the Air* 3 (16 November 1941): 10–11; "Russia and the War," *Common Sense* 10 (August 1941): 241.

22. Alfred M. Bingham to J. D. Frank, 6 August 1941, the Papers of Alfred M. Bingham, Yale University; "Is Peace Impossible?" *CT*, 9 August 1941, 6; "Roosevelt Can Stop the War If He Wants To," *NYDN*, 13 August 1941, 31; editorial, same title, *NYDN*, 14 August 1941, 23; Utley, "God Save England from Her Friends," *Common Sense* 10 (August 1941): 227–33; "Must the World Destroy Itself?" *Reader's Digest* 39 (October 1941): 17. For AFC publicity for the *Reader's Digest* version of Utley, see Page Hufty, AFC Bulletin #629, 14 October 1941, AFC Papers.

23. Taft, cited in Ruth Sarles to R. Douglas Stuart Jr., 3 July 1941, AFC Papers; Libby in Fred Burdick, report, 15 August 1941, Box 65, AFC Papers; Charles A. Lindbergh to Robert E. Wood, 23 September 1941, as reprinted in Ruth Sarles, "A Story of America First," 1942, AFC Papers. See also R. Douglas Stuart Jr. to J. C. Hormel, 19 September 1941, Box 60, AFC Papers; Catherine Curtis, testimony, House Military Affairs Committee, 28 July 1941, 134.

24. See, for example, Philadelphia attorney and AFC leader Isaac Pennypacker, testimony, SFRC, 22 October 1941, 109.

25. Cudahy, [University of Wisconsin] *Daily Cardinal*, 23 October 1941, 1; Cudahy, speech of 30 October 1941, in Anderson, "Wheeler," 255.

26. Edwin M. Borchard to John Haynes Holmes, 10 October 1941, Borchard Papers. See also Borchard to John Bassett Moore, 10 October 1941; Borchard to John A. Danaher, 13 October 1941, both in Borchard Papers.

27. Ruth Sarles to R. Douglas Stuart Jr., 16 October 1941 (Box 67) and 18 October 1941 (Box 41), AFC Papers. Libby, too, cited rumors that it was the German army, not the Nazi Party, that controlled the Reich and that Hitler would resign once the Battle of Russia was concluded. Frederick J. Libby to Mr. and Mrs. P. H. Gray Jr., 2 September 1941, NCPW Papers.

28. Dennis, *WFL* 167 (9 October 1941): 1; "Peace Is Not Far Distant," *Social Justice,* 10 November 1941, 3.

29. Chester Bowles to R. Douglas Stuart Jr., 16 October 1941, AFC Papers.

30. Libby, "Churchill–Roosevelt Statement a Step Toward Peace," *Peace Action* 7 (August 1941): 2; *NYT,* 7 August 1941, 4. Other terms involved a twenty-five-year German occupation of northern Russia and the Ukraine, the reestablishment of Poland, partial independence for Yugoslavia and Greece, and Italian control of Ethiopia, Libya, and Tunisia.

31. *CT,* 7 August 1941, 3; "Inside Germany," *Uncensored* 107 (18 October 1941): 4; Cudahy, [University of Wisconsin] *Daily Cardinal,* 23 October 1941, 1.

32. Libby, "Discussions of Post-War World Begin," *Peace Action* 7 (September 1941): 2, 4. See also Libby, "Strictly within the Family," *Peace Action* 7 (October 1941): 1–2; Libby, testimony, HFAC, 14 October 1941, 63; Libby to Norman Thomas, 3 September 1941, NCPW Papers.

33. "Suggestions of Dr. Edwin Borchard," enclosed with letter from Helen Alfred to Dorothy Detzer, 3 December 1941, WIL Papers.

34. Chester Bowles to Herbert Hoover, 28 November 1941, Hoover Papers, cited in J. Garry Clifford, "A Note on Chester Bowles's Plan to End World War II," *Peace and Change* 14 (January 1989): 106–22. Bowles asked Hoover to introduce these terms. He also wanted the former president to suggest that the Swiss, Swedish, and Turkish governments and perhaps the Vatican offer mediation services.

35. Herbert Hoover to Chester Bowles, 29 November 1941, Hoover Papers. See also Herbert Hoover to Alf Landon, 1 November 1941 and 3 December 1941, Hoover Papers. Just a month before, Hoover had predicted peace talks between Germany and Britain. Smith, *Hoover,* 303.

36. Hanford MacNider to Robert E. Wood, 11 July 1941, AFC Papers. Wood replied that a negotiated peace was not a prime objective of the AFC, though it had been mentioned by various AFC speakers. Robert E. Wood to Hanford MacNider, 14 July 1941, AFC Papers. According to Libby, Stuart opposed inclusion of a negotiated peace in the AFC platform on the grounds that it would be confused with appeasement. Frederick J. Libby to Charles A. Lindbergh, 29 July 1941, AFC Papers.

37. Lindbergh, entry of 14 November 1941, *Wartime Journals,* 557.

38. Livingstone Hartley and Donald C. Blaisdell, "Hitler's Objectives in Germany," CDAAA, *Washington Office Information Letter* 25 (4 July 1941): 2, Box 35, CDAAA Papers. See also Hartley, "The Coming Hitler 'Peace' Drive," *Washington Office Information Letter* 28 (24 July 1941): 3.

39. Ickes, entry of 12 July 1941, *Secret Diary,* 3:574; Roosevelt, *NYT,* 2 September 1941, 10; polls, Cantril, *Public Opinion,* 1136–37, 1166.

40. *NYT,* 10 June 1941, 1, 7; Bailey and Ryan, *Hitler vs. Roosevelt,* 138–39.

41. Livingstone Hartley and Donald C. Blaisdell, "Stop Press," CDAAA, *Washington Office Information Letter* 12 (13 June 1941): 5; Hartley and Blaisdell, "Policy," *Washington Office Information Letter* 23 (20 June 1941): 2, Box 35, CDAAA Papers.

42. AFC Research Bureau, "Freedom of the Seas," *Did You Know?* 3 (26 June 1941), in Doenecke, *IDU,* 276; David A. Reed, testimony, SFRC, 22 October 1941, 72. For other protests, see William Dennis to Frederick J. Libby, 20 June 1941, NCPW Papers; Taft, *CR,* 3 November 1941, 8430; minority report, HFAC, entered in *CR,* 16 October 1941, A4692; Danaher, *CR,* 6 November 1941, 8569; Nye, 29 October 1941, 8311; Vandenberg, *CR,* 27 October 1941, 8255. Nye had first suspected British treachery but, on learning the facts, withdrew his innuendo. *Newsweek,* 23 June 1941, 14.

43. "*Robin Moor* a New *Lusitania*?" *NYDN,* 13 June 1941, 29. See also Vandenberg's anxiety as noted in Robert A. Taft to Edwin M. Borchard, 3 July 1941, Borchard Papers.

44. *Daily Worker,* 11 June 1941, 6.

45. "Memorandum on Contraband Material in the Cargo of the Robin Moor," *Did You Know?* 1 (18 June 1941), in Doenecke, *IDU,* 268–71; Richard A. Moore, Bulletin #339, 20 June 1941, Box 279, AFC Papers. See also O'Connor, 9 October 1941, *CR,* 7685; Finerty, testimony, HFAC, 14 October 1941, 20;

Vandenberg, *CR*, 27 October 1941, 8255; HFAC, minority report, entered 16 October 1941, *CR*, A4692; Nye, *CR*, 29 October 1941, 8311; Frederick J. Libby to Frank J. Murray, 5 November 1941, NCPW Papers; Frank Waldrop, "What Is Contraband?" *WTH*, 14 June 1941, 13; Villard, testimony, SFRC, 23 October 1941, 183; Finerty, testimony, SFRC, 23 October 1941, 194; Edwin M. Borchard to John A. Danaher, 29 October 1941, Borchard Papers.

46. Roosevelt, *NYT*, 18 June 1941, 1; AFC Research Bureau, "Memorandum on Arming United States Merchant Vessels," *Did You Know?* 2 (21 June 1941), in Doenecke, *IDU*, 272–75.

47. Roosevelt, address to Congress, 20 June 1941, in *CR*, 5391–92. He referred to difficulties with the French in 1799, the war against the Barbary pirates, the War of 1812, and the U.S. role in ousting the French from Mexico.

48. James MacGregor Burns, *Soldier*, 101.

49. Sokolsky, "These Days: Freedom of the Seas," *New York Sun*, 10 July 1941, 26; AFC Research Bureau, "Freedom of the Seas," *Did You Know?* 3 (26 June 1941), in Doenecke, *IDU*, 275–78.

50. Bailey and Ryan, *Hitler vs. Roosevelt*, 147.

51. *NYT*, 9 September 1941, 1, 9; 10 September 1941, 1, 12; Bailey and Ryan, *Hitler vs. Roosevelt*, 180.

52. Finerty, testimony, HFAC, 14 October 1941, 20; Finerty, testimony, SFRC, 23 October 1941, 194; Villard, testimony, SFRC, 23 October 1941, 18; Wood statement in Sarles, "Story of America First," 280–81. See also AFC Research Bureau, "One-Man War," *Did You Know?* 22 (13 September 1941), in Doenecke, *IDU*, 403–4; O'Connor, *CR*, 9 October 1941, 7685; "Neither Cash nor Carry," *CT*, 10 September 1941, 20.

53. AFC Research Bureau, "Jekyll-and-Hyde Ships," *Did You Know?* 24 (23 September 1941), in Doenecke, *IDU*, 411–16 (quotation, 414; emphasis in original); Finerty, testimony, HFAC, 14 October 1941, 39, 46; Wood statement in Sarles, "Story of America First," 281.

54. News of sinking, *NYT*, 5 September 1941, 1, 4; McCarran and Danaher, *NYT*, 5 September 1941, 4.

55. Roosevelt, address, text, *NYT*, 12 September 1941, 4.

56. Livingstone Hartley and Frank S. Goodwin, "Hitler Forces the Issue," CDAAA, *Washington Office Information Letter* 35 (12 September 1941): 1, CDAAA Papers. In particular, the CDAAA cited the London Naval Treaty of 1930, which provided for the safety of the crews of all sunk merchant ships. Hartley and Goodwin, "Freedom of the Seas," *Washington Office Information Letter* 36 (19 September 1941): 2, Box 35, CDAAA Papers.

57. Gallup poll, *NYT*, 3 October 1941, 4. Twenty-eight percent disapproved; 10 percent had no opinion. See also White, *FDR and the Press*, 87.

58. Fish, *CR*, 22 September 1941, 7508. Attorney Pennypacker supported the arming of merchantmen, provided the ships were not permitted to carry contraband or enter combat zones or belligerent ports. Testimony, SFRC, 22 October 1941, 111.

59. Hoover, *NYT*, 17 September 1941, 1.

60. Lindbergh, entry of 11 September 1941, *War Within*, 221; Castle Diary, 14 September 1941; Philip C. Jessup to R. Douglas Stuart Jr., 26 September 1941, Jessup Papers. Nye, S.R. 164, 165, *CR*, 11 September 1941, 7393; Clark, *CR*, 7393–94; R. Douglas Stuart Jr. to Mary Hillyer, 10 September 1941 (Box 61) AFC Papers; R. Douglas Stuart Jr. to Mary Hillyer, 10 September 1941, Box 61, AFC Papers. Nye sought an investigation by the Senate Committee on Naval Affairs. Clark wanted the ship's log submitted to the Senate. At first the AFC said the German attack was unjustified. "One-Man War," in Doenecke, *IDU*, 404.

61. Norman Thomas to Burton K. Wheeler, 9 September 1941, Thomas Papers. See also Thomas to R. Douglas Stuart Jr., 10 September 1941, Thomas Papers. For similar attacks on the U.S. presence in Iceland, see "Declaration of Elimination," *Uncensored* 101 (6 September 1941): 2; "The Greer Incident," *CT*, 6 September 1941, 5.

62. "A Helpless Nation?" *Christian Century* 58 (24 September 1941): 1166.

63. For the full text of the Stark report and responses to questions by Senator Walsh, see *CR*, 29 October 1941, 8314–15.

64. Livingstone Hartley and Frank S. Goodwin, "The First Shot," CDAAA, *Washington Office Information Letter* 43 (7 November 1941): 2, Box 35, CDAAA Papers.

65. See, for example, Shipstead, broadcast, NBC, 31 October 1941, in *CR*, 8425; Congressman Bradley, *CR*, 16 October 1941, 8003–4; "President versus Admiral," *St. Louis Post-Dispatch*, 2 November 1941; "Mrs. Roosevelt," *NYDN*, 4 November 1941, 23; "An American Destroyer Is Torpedoed," *Christian Century* 58 (25 October 1941): 1324; "Comment," *America* 66 (25 October 1941): 59; "Memorandum concerning Ships Thus Far Attacked or Sunk," attached to Edwin M. Borchard to Herbert Hoover, 30 October 1941, Borchard Papers; John T. Flynn, testimony, SFRC, 23 October 1941, 214; "Navy Gets Green Light," *Call*, 20 September 1941, 1; Frank Gannett to Dexter Perkins, 17 November 1941, Gannett Papers (in which Gannett praises Perkins, a prominent historian, on the matter).

66. *CT*, 15 October 1941, 12.

67. Amos Pinchot, open letter to President Roosevelt, 24 October 1941, AFC Princeton file. See also "Bismarck and Roosevelt," *AFC New York Chapter Bulletin*, 25 October 1941, 4. For endorsement of the Pinchot letter, see "More about the U.S.S. *Greer,*" *NYDN*, 29 October 1941, 27; Frederick J. Libby to Frank J. Murray, 5 November 1941, NCPW Papers.

68. See, for example, "But Boake Carter Says," *SFE*, 22 October 1941, sect. 2, 5; Lincoln Colcord to Amos Pinchot, 28 October 1941, Pinchot Papers; General Wood, statement of 17 October 1941, in Sarles, "Story of America First," 253; Burdick, *CR*, 13 November 1941, 8863; "Planned U.S. Incidents," *AFC New York Chapter Bulletin*, 20 September 1941, 2.

69. John A. Danaher to Edwin M. Borchard, 29 October 1941, Borchard Papers; Nye, *CR*, 29 October 1941, 8307; Herbert Hoover to Edwin F. Borchard, 29 October 1941, Borchard Papers; Wheeler, *CR*, 5 November 1941, 8518.

70. See, for example, Hoffman, *CR*, 15 September 1941, 7413; Woodruff, *CR*, 17 September 1941, 7464; Rich, 7467.

71. Among the signers were Amos Pinchot, Philip C. Jessup, Charles A. Beard, George N. Peek, Johnson Hagood, Herbert W. Briggs, Kathleen Norris, Edwin S. Corwin, Edwin M. Borchard, journalist Samuel Hopkins Adams, former Oklahoma governor Murray, railroad financier Robert R. Young, and theology professor John C. O'Brien. Many were active in America First. See *AFC New York Chapter Bulletin*, 20 September 1941, 1–2; *NYT*, 15 September 1941, 2; Sarles, "Story of America First," 282.

72. Wood statement in Sarles, "Story of America First," 240. For a similar statement concerning undeclared war, see Capper, broadcast, WIBW and Kansas network, 12 September 1941, in *CR*, 7404.

73. "One-Man War," 401–8; "Peace," *AFC New York Chapter Bulletin*, 20 September 1941, 1, 4 (quotation).

74. Lincoln Colcord to Edwin M. Borchard, 16 October 1941, Borchard Papers; Clay Judson to Page Hufty, 12 September 1941, Box 283, AFC Papers; "The Hidden Purpose," *CT*, 13 September 1941, 1.

75. "One-Man War," 402–3, 406 (quotation); "Fact or Fancy," *Call*, 27 September 1941, 4. Cited by both was Hanson Baldwin, "What of the British Fleet?" *Reader's Digest* 39 (August 1941): 1–2.

76. News of sinking, *NYT*, 13 September 1941, 1, 2; Finerty, testimony, SFRC, 23 October 1941, 194.

77. Bailey and Ryan, *Hitler vs. Roosevelt*, 184; Reynolds, *Creation*, 216.

78. *NYT*, 23 September 1941, 1, 4; Bailey and Ryan, *Hitler vs. Roosevelt*, 188; Roosevelt to Tom Connally, 26 September 1941, *F.D.R.: His Personal Letters*, 1214.

79. See, for example, Finerty, testimony, HFAC, 14 October 1941, 20; Villard, radio broadcast, 12 October 1941, in *CR*, 76; Danaher, *CR*, 6 November 1941, 8569; Edwin M. Borchard to Herbert Hoover, 31 October 1941, Borchard Papers.

80. Fish, *CR*, 23 September 1941, 7516. See also attached memo, Edwin M. Borchard to Senator Brewster, 4 November 1941, Borchard Papers; AFC Research Bureau, "Jekyll-and-Hyde Ships," *Did You Know?* 24 (23 September 1941), in Doenecke, *IDU,* 411–16.

81. Bradley, *CR*, 24 September 1941, 7523; Amos Pinchot to Randolph Walker, 30 September 1941, Pinchot Papers.

82. For events, *NYT*, 4 October 1941, 1, 6. For anti-interventionists, see Finerty, testimony, HFAC, 14 October 1941, 20; Villard, radio broadcast, 12 October 1941, in Mary Hillyer, testimony, HFAC, 14 October 1941, 76. Congressman O'Connor claimed that the *I. C. White* was lent to Britain and was under British direction. *CR*, 9 October 1941, 7685.

83. Bailey and Ryan, *Hitler vs. Roosevelt*, 192.

84. Reynolds, *Creation*, 217.

85. Attorney James Lipsig, an AFC staffer, found it to be generally established under international law that when a merchant ship was armed, it took on the character of an auxiliary warship and hence was not subject to the geographic limitations of the neutrality act. The state department, said Ruth Sarles, believed that the president had the authority, on his own, to order ships into combat zones. See Ruth Sarles to R. Douglas Stuart Jr., 16 October 1941, in Doenecke, *IDU*, 21. Sarles also asserted that the Maritime Commission believed that legislation was not required to provide for arming merchant ships, for the old law on protection against pirates would suffice. Sarles to R. Douglas Stuart Jr., 19 September 1941, Box 67, AFC Papers. Samuel B. Pettengill claimed the president could eliminate all combat areas by proclamation. Pettengill to General Robert E. Wood, 16 October 1941, in Doenecke, *IDU*, 302. Historian Harry Rudin asserted the president possessed the authority to define war zones and send American ships into European waters. *Yale* [University] *Daily News*, 14 October 1941, 1.

86. Roosevelt, message to Congress, *CR*, 9 October 1941, 7757–58.

87. Livingstone Hartley and Frank S. Goodwin, "Points about Ship Arming," CDAAA, *Washington Office Information Letter* 40 (17 October 1941): 2, Box 35, CDAAA Papers; Hartley, "The Proof of the Pudding," *Washington Office Information Letter* 41 (24 October 1941): 3–4.

88. Fish, *CR*, 16 October 1941, 7954. See also Case, *CR*, 17 October 1941, 8040. Congressman Melvin J. Maas was one anti-interventionist who said the neutrality act should be repealed for; it "was never a workable law," "had no scientific basis," and "was contrary to all traditional policies." Maas, *United States News*, 3 October 1941, 28.

89. Wood in Sarles, "Story of America First," 254.

90. Shafer, *CR*, 16 October 1941, 7978; Short, *CR*, 17 October 1941, 8029; Beard, undated statement, inserted by La Follette, SFRC, 24 October 1941, 249. See also O'Connor, *CR*, 9 October 1941, 785; Vorys, *CR*, 13 November 1941, 8881.

91. Firing, Vandenberg, *CR*, 27 October 1941, 8257; targets, David A. Reed, testimony, SFRC, 22 October 1941, 51–52; mines, House report, 12 October 1941, in *CR*, A4692. Signers included Chiperfield, Vorys, Mundt, and Jonkman.

92. Congressman Frank Crowther (Rep.-N.Y.), *CR*, 10 November 1941, 8747. See also David A. Reed, testimony, SFRC, 22 October 1941, 51; AFC Research Bureau, "Did You Know These Things about Arming American Merchant Ships?" *Did You Know?* 27 (13 October 1941): 10, Box 280, AFC Papers.

93. B. C. Clark, *CR*, 1 November 1941, 8408. The *CT* predicted it would be seven months before some ships were armed. See "Experts for War," 15 October 1941, 12.

94. Shafer, *CR*, 16 October 1941, 7978. See also Chiperfield, *CR*, 16 October 1941, 7967; Colcord, testimony, SFRC, 24 October 1941, 219.

95. Finerty, testimony, HFAC, 14 October 1941, 22, 25.

96. AFC Research Bureau, *Did You Know?* 27 (13 October 1941): 15–16. See also La Follette, 29 October 1941, 8320, citing Arthur Krock, "In the Nation: The Value of Armament to Merchant Ships," *NYT*, 2 October 1941, 24; David A. Reed, testimony, SFRC, 22 October 1941, 51; Warren D. Mullin, "The Neutrality Law Should Stand," *Peace Action* 7 (September 1941): 3.

97. Knox cited by Robert La Follette, *CR*, 29 October 1941, 8320. For military columnists Frederick Palmer and George Fielding Eliot, see La Follette, *CR*, 8319. See also Lieutenant S. D. Willingham, "Modern Submarine versus Major Warship," *U.S. Naval Institute Proceedings* 67 (April 1941): 513–20, cited by B. C. Clark, *CR*, 1 November 1941, 8408.

98. Stark cited by La Follette, *CR*, 29 October 1941, 8321. For other citations of Stark, see O'Connor, *CR*, 15 October 1941, 7902; Mundt, HFAC, 22 October 1941, 41; Chiperfield, *CR*, 16 October 1941, 7967.

99. AFC Research Bureau, "Did You Know These Things About Arming American Merchant Ships?" *Did You Know?* 27 (13 October 1941): 17, Box 279, AFC Papers; Woodruff, *CR*, 15 October 1941; Congressman Charles S. Dewey, *CR*, 16 October 1941, 7965.

100. For Hyde, see Vandenberg, *CR*, 27 October 1941, 8256. For Jessup, see La Follette, *CR*, 29 October 1941, 8321; Jessup to Hiram Johnson, 18 October 1941, Jessup Papers. For Moore, see John Bassett Moore to Robert E. Wood, 14 October 1941, Box 66, AFC Papers. For Borchard, see Edwin M. Borchard

to James Shanley, 13 October 1941, in HFAC, appendix, 82. See also AFC Research Bureau, *Did You Know?*, "Did You Know These Things," 6–9. For affirmation of the continued viability of international law, see Vandenberg, *CR*, 27 October 1941, 8256; Finerty, testimony, HFAC, 14 October 1941, 35, 37–38; David A. Reed, testimony, SFRC, 22 October 1941, 52.

101. Edwin M. Borchard to Senator Tom Connally, 31 October 1941, Borchard Papers. Emphasis in original.

102. Wood statement, *NYT*, 10 October 1941, 4; Robert E. Wood to Burton K. Wheeler, 9 October 1941, Box 55, AFC Papers. For other apprehensions of war, see Congressman John Jennings Jr., *CR*, 16 October 1941, 7992; Rich, *CR*, 17 October 1941, 803; Robsion, *CR*, 13 November 1941, 8873.

103. Colcord, testimony, SFRC, 24 October 1941, 219; Finerty, testimony, SFRC, 23 October 1941, 191; AFC Research Bureau, "Did You Know That Elimination of the Neutrality Law Combat Zones Means War?" *Did You Know?* 28 (25 October 1941): 54, Box 280, AFC Papers.

104. For *Bold Venture*, see *NYT*, 22 October 1941, 1, 3. For *Teagle*, see *NYT*, 23 October 1941, 1, 6.

105. Finerty, testimony, SFRC, 23 October 1941, 194; Danaher, *CR*, 6 November 1941, 8569.

106. *NYT*, 18 October 1941, 1, 3; Bailey and Ryan, *Hitler vs. Roosevelt*, 197–98.

107. Villard, radio speech, WABC, 12 October 1941, reported in [New York University] *Heights Daily News,* 14 October 1941, 2.

108. Finerty, testimony, HFAC, 14 October 1941, 55; Finerty, testimony, SFRC, 23 October 1941, 189. See also Cudahy, testimony, SFRC, 23 October 1941, 155.

109. For minority report, see *CR*, 16 October 1941, 7967. For further endorsement of British registry, see R. Douglas Stuart Jr. to Alf Landon, 27 October 1941, Box 60, AFC Papers; Congressman Dewey, *CR*, 16 October 1941, 7975; Mundt, *CR*, 17 October 1941, 8013.

110. House vote, *NYT*, 18 October 1941, 1; Gallup poll, *NYT*, 19 October 1941, 5. On the war zone issue, 40 percent were negative and 6 percent were undecided. For related polls, see Cantril, *Public Opinion*, 1128.

111. Bailey and Ryan, *Hitler vs. Roosevelt*, 221.

112. See, for example, Edwin M. Borchard to James A. Shanley, 31 October 1941, in testimony, HFAC, 81; Senator Theodore Bilbo, *CR*, 4 November 1941, 8475; Cudahy, testimony, SFRC, 23 October 1941, 140; Flynn, testimony, SFRC, 23 October 1941, 203–4; Philip Jessup to Hiram Johnson, n.d., in testimony, SFRC, 252; Vandenberg, *CR*, 27 October 1941, 8251; Taft, *CR*, 3 November 1941, 8432; R. Douglas Stuart Jr. to Felix Morley, 16 October 1941, Box 66, AFC Papers; "Last Call for Congress," *NYWT*, 4 November 1941; Warren Mullin, "The Neutrality Act Should Stand," *Peace Action* 7 (September 1941): 3; FOR executive committee, 21 October 1941, 3, FOR Papers; "Comment," *America* 66 (18 October 1941): 30; "Neutrality Repeal," *SFN*, 26 September 1941, 14. Libby was less apocalyptic, denying that repeal of the neutrality act would lead to total war so long as the hemispheric restriction on draftees still stood. Frederick J. Libby to Frank J. Murray, 5 November 1941, NCPW Papers.

113. David A. Reed, testimony, SFRC, 22 October 1941, 66; *Christian Century* 58 (22 October 1941): 1294–96; "One Way Passage" [AFC leaflet], 1.

114. *NYT*, 22 October 1941, 1, 3; Bailey and Ryan, *Hitler vs. Roosevelt*, 198.

115. Villard, testimony, SFRC, 23 October 1941, 183; Vandenberg, *CR*, 27 October 1941, 8255; Taft, *CR*, 3 November 1941, 8430. See also Danaher, *CR*, 6 November 1941, 8569; Nye, *CR*, 29 October 1941, 8311; David A. Reed, testimony, SFRC, 22 October 1941, 74; Wheeler, *CR*, 5 November 1941, 8522. For more cautious statements, see Finerty, testimony, SFRC, 23 October 1941, 194; Edwin M. Borchard to John A. Danaher, 29 October 1941, Borchard Papers.

116. Roosevelt, Navy Day address, text, *NYT*, 28 October 1941, 4. For a critique of the speech, see Gellman, *Good Neighbor Diplomacy*, 114–15.

117. "Roosevelt's War," *NYDN*, 21 October 1941, 25; Herbert Hoover to Edwin M. Borchard, 29 October 1941, Borchard Papers; Wheeler, *CR*, 5 November 1941, 8528. See also Robert E. Wood, AFC press release, 27 October 1941, Box 278, AFC Papers; Vandenberg, *CR*, 27 October 1941, 8255; Nye, *CR*, 29 October 1941, 8311; Fish, *CR*, 17 October 1941, 8030; Frank Gannett to Dexter Perkins, 17 November 1941, Gannett Papers, acknowledging as well Perkins's concurrence; Burdick, *CR*, 13 November 1941, 8863; "But Boake Carter Says," *SFE*, 4 November 1941, 9; "We Read a Day's News," *Wall Street*

*Journal,* 21 October 1941; "An American Destroyer Is Torpedoed," *Christian Century* 58 (29 October 1941): 1324; Hoffman, *CR,* 30 October 1941, 8365; Edwin M. Borchard to John A. Danaher, 23 October 1941, Borchard Papers; Clay Judson to Amos Pinchot, 29 October 1941, Pinchot Papers; Amos Pinchot, open letter to Franklin D. Roosevelt, 24 October 1941, in *CR,* 8312.

118. "Get the British Out of Iceland," *CT,* 18 October 1941, 12; Vorys, *CR,* 17 October 1941, 8105. See also Mundt, *CR,* 17 October 1941, 8012; Short, *CR,* 8033.

119. See, for example, Hanford MacNider to Robert E. Wood, 28 October 1941, Box 286, AFC Papers; Raymond Moley, "Washington Tides," *Newsweek,* 10 November 1941, 21; Amos Pinchot to Elsie French Fitzsimon, 12 November 1941, Pinchot Papers; D. Worth Clark, Wheeler, and Taft, *CR,* 4 November 1941, 8479.

120. Wood, AFC press release, n.d., Box 278, AFC Papers; "A Policy of Suicide," *CT,* 29 October 1941, 16. See also Norman Thomas, "Your World and Mine: Presidential Demagogy," *Call,* 8 November 1941, 5.

121. John F. Bratzel and Leslie B. Rout Jr., "FDR and the Secret Map," *Wilson Quarterly* 9 (January 1995): 167–73; Cull, *Selling War,* 170–73.

122. Clark, *CR,* 4 November 1941, 8479; Allen, "FDR Finds 'Secret Plan' of Nazis 11 Years Late," *Call,* 22 November 1941, 2.

123. Wheeler, *CR,* 5 November 1941, 8529; La Follette, "What's Next for America?" 1 November 1941, in *CR,* A5043; Cudahy, testimony, SFRC, 23 October 1941, 153; AFC Research Bureau, "Did You Know That Elimination of the Neutrality Law Combat Zones Means War?" *Did You Know?* 28 (25 October 1941): 52–58, Box 280, AFC Papers. See also Wiley, *CR,* 30 October 1941, 8346; Capper, *CR,* 31 October 1941, 8385; Felix Morley quoted in "The Drift," *Saturday Evening Post* 214 (11 October 1941): 28.

124. Dennis, *WFL* 169 (30 October 1941): 3. Dennis, *WFL* 168 (23 October 1941): 3.

125. See, for example, see Wood, statement, 9 October 1941, in Sarles, "Story of America First," 285–86.

126. Taft, *CR,* 30 October 1941, 8338. Fish pegged U.S. shipping at seven million tons. *CR,* 12 November 1941, 8763.

127. "One Way Passage" [AFC leaflet], 4–5. It said that whereas in September 1939 Britain had 21,000,000 tons, or 31 percent of the world's shipping, it currently possessed 25,767,000 tons, or 45 percent of the world's shipping. Taft estimated the British shipping loss at 5 percent. *CR,* 30 October 1941, 8338. For additional use of British sources, see Mundt, *CR,* 12 November 1941, 8768; "The Inner Enemies of the Republic," *CT,* 9 October 1941, 1.

128. Wheeler, *CR,* 5 November 1941, 8517. The CDAAA conceded Churchill's claims but noted that winter months—with their long nights, rough seas, and bad visibility—were more favorable for submarine operations. Livingstone Hartley and Frank S. Goodwin, "Toward Victory in the Atlantic," CDAAA, *Washington Office Information Letter* 44 (14 November 1941): 3, Box 35, CDAAA Papers.

129. Congressman H. Carl Andersen (Rep.-Minn.), *CR,* 6 October 1941, 7684. Congressman O'Connor went so far as deny that the British Empire had ever attempted to draw on its pool of manpower. Of the four hundred million people in the empire, only four million were armed. See 7790.

130. *NYT,* 5 November 1941, 1, 3; Bailey and Ryan, *Hitler vs. Roosevelt,* 205–6.

131. *NYT,* 1 November 1941, 1, 3, 4; Bailey and Ryan, *Hitler vs. Roosevelt,* 205.

132. For samples of anti-interventionist comment, see "Mrs. Roosevelt," *NYDN,* 4 November 1941, 23; "The Americans Already Dead," *CT,* 7 November 1941, 14; Frank Waldrop, "Keep Cool," *WTH,* 1 November 1941, 14; Waldrop, "They Weep," *WTH,* 2 November 1941, E1; Taft, *CR,* 3 November 1941, 8430.

133. Aiken, *CR,* 31 October 1941, 8393; Wheeler, *CR,* 6 November 1941, 8550, citing "Text of Krock's Talk to Columbia College Alumni," *NYT,* 6 November 1941, 4; Rich, *CR,* 5 November 1941, 8538; Pinchot, memo to R. Douglas Stuart Jr., 3 December 1941, Box 284, AFC Papers; Nye, *CR,* 7 November 1941, 860; Norman Thomas to *Kansas City Times,* 7 November 1941, Thomas Papers.

134. Voting on bill, *CR,* 7 November 1941, 8680; voting on Clark motion, *CR,* 7 November 1941, 8675. On the latter, the vote was thirty-eight to forty-nine.

135. Hill, *CR,* 13 November 1941, 8867. See also Dondero, *CR,* 13 November 1941, 8853.

136. Pfeiffer, *CR*, 12 November 1941, 8767. See also Vorys, *Yale* [University] *Daily News*, 28 October 1941.

137. Roosevelt in *CR*, 13 November 1941, 8890–91; Dirksen, *CR*, 13 November 1941, 8880.

138. Voting, *CR*, 13 November 1941, 8891.

139. Wood statement, 14 November 1941, Box 23, AFC Papers; Cole, *America First*, 164; Cole, *Lindbergh*, 196.

140. Wilson, "FDR and the Riddle," 31. For Gallup poll of 5 November 1941 on AEF, see Cantril, *Public Opinion*, 978. The remaining 7 percent was undecided.

141. Bailey and Ryan, *Hitler vs. Roosevelt*, 213.

142. See, for example, Mundt and Woodruff in report of Fred Burdick, 16 November 1941, Box 284, AFC Papers; KAOWC press release, 14 November 1941, Socialist Party Papers; "Washington Summary," *NYDN*, 15 November 1941, 15; John Haynes Holmes, "Editorial Comment," *Unity* 127 (December 1941): 159; Burdick, report, 27 November 1941, Box 284, AFC Papers; Karl E. Mundt to Amos Pinchot, 4 November 1941, Pinchot Papers; Burton K. Wheeler to Norman Thomas, 25 November 1941, Thomas Papers.

143. "The Neutrality Act Is Discarded," *Christian Century* 58 (26 November 1941): 1459; John T. Flynn to Robert E. Wood, 11 November 1941, in Doenecke, *IDU*, 139. See also Flynn to Wood, 16 November 1941, in Doenecke, *IDU*, 434.

144. Amos Pinchot to Arthur F. Bronwell, 21 November 1941; Pinchot to Karl Mundt, 21 November 1941, both in Pinchot Papers.

145. *CT*, 14 November 1941, 14. See also Chamberlin Diary, 13 November 1941; Hiram W. Johnson to Hiram W. Johnson Jr., 16 November 1941, Johnson Papers; "Comment," *America*, 22 November 1941, 170; Castle Diary, 8 November 1941.

146. Reynolds, *Creation*, 218–20. For quotation, 220. For Churchill's confidence, see 214.

147. Kahn, "United States Views," 495.

## CHAPTER 19: THE DOMESTIC FRONT

1. "Mr. Flynn on War Hysteria," *New Republic* 103 (11 November 1940): 660. See also "The President's War," *Christian Century* 58 (8 January 1941): 47.

2. See, for example, Frank Hanighen, "Capitol Letter," *Common Sense* 9 (July 1940): 13–14; Walter C. Frame, *America* 63 (21 September 1940): 651; Villard, "Our Canadian Alliance," *Christian Century* 57 (28 April 1940): 1054; "Fifth Column," *Uncensored* 34 (25 May 1940): 3–4. See also "Short of Aid," *Uncensored* 37 (15 June 1940): 2; "Fifth Column Notes," *Uncensored* 38 (22 June 1940): 4; "Fifth Column News," *Uncensored* 40 (6 July 1940): 1.

3. "They Rifled My Office, Too," *New Masses* 36 (25 June 1940): 14–15; "News Notes of a Week," *New Republic* 103 (29 July 1940): 134. See also "The Witch Hunt Begins," *New Republic* 102 (3 June 1940): 745.

4. See, for example, John T. Flynn, "Other People's Money: Johnny, Get Your Gun," *New Republic* 102 (27 May 1940): 728; "Other People's Money: The Price of Hysteria Is Reaction," *New Republic* 102 (29 June 1940): 141; Dennis, *WFL* 95 (23 May 1940): 2.

5. C. Hartley Grattan to Sidney Hertzberg, 15 May 1940, Hertzberg Papers.

6. See, for example, Villard, "Rule by Fear," *Christian Century* 58 (26 February 1941): 288; Morton, *Let's Think This Matter Through* [pamphlet], in *CR*, 21 February 1941, A785.

7. Fisher, *Idaho Daily Statesman*, 17 January 1941. For other comparisons to Welles, see Congressman Noble H. Johnson (Rep.-Ind.), *CR*, 21 June 1940, A4083; MacNider, testimony, SFRC, 6 February 1941, 561; "Reaction," *Time*, 27 May 1940, 17; Holmes, "Nothing to Fear but Fear," *Unity* 125 (1 July 1940): 131.

8. Woodruff, *CR*, 3 February 1941, 503; Valentine, testimony, SFRC, 5 February 1941, 402.

9. Fish, *CR*, 28 April 1941, 3350. See also Nye, "Loyalty and Unity," speech to Steuben Society of America, 20 September 1941, in *CR*, 7626.

10. Edwin M. Borchard to John Bassett Moore, 19 February 1941, Borchard Papers; Wheeler, *CR*, 1 March 1941, 1607. See also "Are We to Have a New Spy Hunt?" *Christian Century* 56 (20 September 1939): 1124; Nye, *CR*, 29 October 1941, 8306.

11. Ickes, *NYT*, 14 April 1941, 19; Villard, [University of] *California* [Los Angeles] *Daily Bruin*, 24 April 1941, 1; William R. Castle to R. Douglas Stuart Jr., 17 September 1941, Box 63, AFC Papers.

12. Villard, "The Pattern for War Is Repeated," *Christian Century* 58 (22 January 1941): 119. For Roosevelt's reference to slackers, see message to Congress, *CR*, 6 January 1941, 6. For Hutchins, see "American Has a Choice," *Progressive*, 31 May 1941, 9.

13. See, for example, Wheeler, speech to antiwar mobilization, Washington, D.C., 7 June 1940, *CR* A3676; Hugh Johnson, 30 September 1940, in Sargent, Bulletin #34, 3 February 1940, *Getting US into War*, 276 n. 6; Mencken, *Baltimore Sun*, 29 September 1940; Fish, *Harvard Crimson*, 4 March 1940, 1.

14. See, for example, Frazier, *CR*, 14 October 1939, 397; Sterling Morton, *Let's Think This Matter Through* [pamphlet], in *CR*, 21 February 1941, A785; Sargent, Bulletin #34, 3 February 1940, *Getting US into War*, 278 n. 11.

15. Thomas, *Harvard* [University] *Crimson*, 5 November 1940, 3; Barnes cited by Nye, *CR*, 26 February 1941, 1431. See also Barnes, "Peace for Liberty: Menace Lies in War," *NYWT*, 19 February 1940, 16.

16. Herbert Hoover to William J. Gross, 7 April 1941, Hoover Papers.

17. Sargent, Bulletin #34, 3 February 1940, *Getting US into War*, 27; Barnes quoted by Nye, *CR*, 26 February 1941, 1431; Mayer, "I Think I'll Sit This One Out," *Saturday Evening Post* 212 (7 October 1939): 97. See also William Henry Chamberlin, "War: Shortcut to Fascism," *American Mercury* 51 (December 1940): 392; Norman Thomas to S. K. Ratcliffe, 8 October 1940, Thomas Papers.

18. Marcantonio, "There Shall Be No Gestapo in America," address, Mutual network, 12 June 1941, in *CR*, A2852; Krueger, [University of Chicago] *Daily Maroon*, 12 November 1941, 1.

19. Dennis, *WFL* 103 (18 July 1940): 1; 150 (12 June 1941): 1.

20. "Snoops Wanted," *Uncensored* 5 (4 November 1939): 1; "Who's Afraid?" *Commonweal* 31 (27 October 1939): 1; Sargent, Bulletin #35, 9 February 1940, *Getting US into War*, 280–82; Burnham, "Alternative to War," *Commonweal* 32 (12 July 1940): 245; Nye, *CR*, 23 August 1940, 10,807; Chamberlin diary, 28 August 1940.

21. Krock, "In the Nation: The Consolidation Plan for Official Press Agents," *NYT*, 2 April 1941, 22; "National Defense," *Uncensored* 79 (5 April 1941): 3; Julian Webb, "Conscripting the News," *New Masses* 39 (20 May 1941): 9.

22. Krock, *NYT*, 28 September 1941, 22, cited by Frank C. Hanighen, "The Coming Coup d'Etat," *Progressive*, 27 September 1941, 5; Norman Thomas to Morris R. Cohen, 4 November 1941, Thomas Papers. See also John Bassett Moore to Harlan Fiske Stone, 19 July 1940, Moore Papers.

23. Corwin, [Princeton University] *Daily Princetonian*, 31 October 1940, 2. For corroboration, see Cole, *Lindbergh*, 129; Richard W. Steele, "Franklin D. Roosevelt and His Foreign Policy Critics," *Political Science Quarterly* 94 (Spring 1979): 20–21. For protests, see Wheeler, *CR*, 3 March 1941, 1655; "Cabbages and Kings: Don't Be Afraid," *Scribner's Commentator* 9 (March 1941): 5–6; Norman Thomas, "Your World and Mine: Emotional Urges to War," *Call*, 1 November 1941, 5.

24. Sargent, Bulletin #35, 9 February 1940, *Getting US into War*, 282; Dorothy Detzer to Mrs. Mary Farquharson, 21 June 1940, WIL Papers.

25. For protests, see, for example, "Keeping Our Liberties," *New Republic* 101 (4 October 1939): 228; Sargent, Bulletin #35, 9 February 1940, *Getting US into War*, 282; resolutions, WIL annual meeting, Pittsburgh, 27–30 April 1940, 3, WIL Papers.

26. La Follette amendments, "American Casualties," *Uncensored* 35 (1 June 1940): 3; anti-sabotage and FCC, "Civil Liberty," *Uncensored* 122 (22 November 1941): 3; Sumners in Lawrence Dennis to Harry Elmer Barnes, 28 November 1941, Barnes Papers.

27. For examples of opposition to the Smith Act, see Warren Mullin, director of the NCPW's labor department, *Washington Information Newsletter* 8, 7 June 1940, 5, NCPW Papers; Maynard Krueger, [University of Chicago] *Daily Maroon*, 12 November 1941, 1.

28. Sargent, Bulletin #34, 3 February 1940, *Getting US into War,* 274; Thomas, [University of] *California* [Los Angeles] *Daily Bruin,* 23 September 1940, 1; Thomas, "Your World and Mine: America's Drift Toward Empire," *Call,* 19 October 1940, 5.

29. Norman Thomas to Tom Connally, 31 July 1940, Thomas Papers; passage of House version, *CR,* 1 July 1940, 9121–22; passage of Senate version, *CR,* 30 September 1940, 12,828; acceptance by House, *CR,* 7 October 1940, 13,344.

30. Burnham, "Alternative to War," *Commonweal* 32 (12 July 1940): 246; Dennis, *WFL* 121 (20 November 1940): 3–4.

31. MacLeish, "The Irresponsibles," address to American Philosophical Society, 19 April 1940, as reprinted in *Nation* 150 (18 May 1940): 618–23; "Post-War Writers and 'Pre-War Readers,' address to American Association for Adult Education, 23 May 1940, in *New Republic* 102 (10 June 1940): 790; emphasis in original. For background material, see Scott Donaldson, *Archibald MacLeish: An American Life* (Boston: Houghton Mifflin, 1992), 334–38.

32. See, for example, "From Philip Drunk to Philip Sober," *Christian Century* 57 (16 October 1940): 1269–70; Isidor Schneider, "Triumvirate of Disintegration," *New Masses* 36 (25 June 1940): 17; John Haynes Holmes, "MacLeish and the Martial Spirit," *New Republic* 102 (24 June 1940): 860; Norman Thomas, "Your World and Mine," *Call,* 6 July 1940, 2; Samuel Sillon, "Archibald MacLeish, the Irresponsible," *New Masses* 35 (11 June 1940): 24; Sillon, "Authors of Surrender," *New Masses* 37 (8 October 1940): 4–7; Sillon, "The Irrationals," *New Masses* 37 (29 October 1940): 20–22. For support of MacLeish, see Philip Jessup to Van Wyck Brooks, 5 September 1940, Jessup Papers.

33. "The Ghost of Randolph Bourne," *Uncensored* 39 (29 June 1940): 4; Morton Dauwen Zabel, "The Poet on Capitol Hill," *Partisan Review* 8 (January–February 1941): 2–19; Symes, "Hold That Line: Who Are the Irresponsibles?" *Call,* 5 October 1940, 5. For endorsement of Zabel, see Sargent, Bulletin #34, *Getting US into War,* 275 n. 4.

34. Butler, address, text, *NYT,* 4 October 1941, 14.

35. Clark, "Commotion at Columbia," *Newsweek,* 14 October 1941, 6; "Hail Columbia's Fuehrer," *CT,* 8 October 1940, 12; Holmes, letter to *Columbia Spectator,* 4 October 1940, Holmes Papers. See also Holmes, "Hitler Takes Over Morningside Heights," *Unity* 126 (21 October 1940): 52; Flynn, "Other People's Money: Fascists at Home," *New Republic* 103 (14 October 1940): 525; Edwin M. Borchard to John Bassett Moore, 14 October 1940, Borchard Papers; "Nicholas Murray Butler—Semper Idem," *Christian Century* 57 (16 October 1940): 1268; "Butler Heads War Drive in Universities," *Call,* 19 October 1940, 6; Quincy Howe, radio script, 4 October 1940, Jessup Papers; William Henry Chamberlin, "War: Shortcut to Fascism," *American Mercury* 51 (December 1940): 395.

36. *Columbia Spectator,* 11 October 1940, 1.

37. Sargent, Bulletin #37, 9 February 1940, *Getting US into War,* 284–85 n. 6. See also Lillian Symes, "Hold That Line," *Call,* 21 December 1940, 5.

38. "Advice for Radio Speakers—and Preachers," *Christian Century* 56 (20 September 1939): 1124.

39. Mellett, *NYT,* 23 February 1941, 23; Richard W. Steele, *Propaganda in an Open Society: The Roosevelt Administration and the Media, 1933–1941* (Westport, Conn.: Greenwood, 1985), 74.

40. "H.R. 3368," *Uncensored* 74 (1 March 1941): 4. See also Frank Hanighen to Cushman Reynolds, 27 February [1941], Hertzberg Papers.

41. YCAW, Frank Hanighen, "Capitol Letter: Minority Report on Lease-Lend Bill," *Common Sense* 10 (February 1941): 53; Thomas, [University of] *Michigan Daily,* 29 May 1941, 1; Thomas, [University of] *California* [Los Angeles] *Daily Bruin,* 17 and 20 October 1941, 1; Wheeler, *CR,* 5 November 1941, 8516.

42. Miami, *NYT,* 4 May 1941, 6; 6 May 1941, 8; 11 May 1941, 34; Oklahoma City, *NYT,* 27 August 1941, 7. For other instances, see Doenecke, *IDU,* 71 n. 146.

43. See, for example, Norman Thomas to Ben Fischer, 10 February 1940, Socialist Party Papers; "Mr. Jackson and the FBI," *New Republic* 102 (8 April 1940): 455.

44. "Policeman's Interpretation of History," *Uncensored* 16 (20 January 1940): 2. See also "Jottings," *Unity* 124 (5 February 1940): 170.

45. Nye, "We're Already in the War," *Look,* 23 April 1940, 11.

46. Nye noted in Reed Vernon, "Pro-War Forces Try to Smear Memory of Senator Lundeen," *Call,* 12 October 1940, 8; "Hoover Investigates Nye," *New Republic* 103 (22 July 1940): 101; Holmes, "Believe It or Not!" *Unity* 125 (5 August 1940): 165.

47. Flynn, "Other People's Money: Who's Behind Hoover?" *New Republic* 102 (11 March 1940): 345. See also John T. Flynn to Bennett C. Clark, 15 February 1940, Flynn Papers.

48. "Special Supplement: J. Edgar Hoover," *Uncensored* 20 (17 February 1940): 1–2. In a private letter to an NCPW official, editor Hertzberg said, "We are always anxious to do what we can to expose J. Edgar." Sidney Hertzberg to Clayton D. Coughran, 9 April 1940, Hertzberg Papers.

49. See, for example, "The Dies Committee's Third Term," *New Republic* 102 (29 January 1940): 132; Dorothy Detzer, minutes, WIL annual meeting, Pittsburgh, 27–30 April 1940, 4; "Rewrite Job," *Uncensored* 60 (23 November 1940): 4; Dennis, *WFL* 122 (28 November 1940): 3; *WFL* 117 (24 October 1940): 3; Sargent, Bulletin #35, 9 February 1940, *Getting US into War*, 280–82.

50. "Who's Afraid?" *Commonweal* 31 (27 October 1939): 1–2; Barnes, "Peace for Liberty: Menace Lies in War," *NYWT*, 19 February 1940, 16; "Nazified," *America* 63 (7 September 1940): 602–3.

51. Robert L. Bliss to Chicago FBI, 13 March 1941; W. S. Devereaux to Robert L. Bliss, 27 March 1941, both in Box 285; R. Douglas Stuart Jr. to Janet Ayer Fairbank, 9 June 1941, Box 60, all in AFC Papers.

52. Edwin S. Webster Jr. to J. Edgar Hoover, 28 March 1941; J. Edgar Hoover to Edwin S. Webster Jr., 9 April 1941; America First Committee case file, 100-4712-21, the Papers of the Federal Bureau of Investigation, J. Edgar Hoover Building, Washington, D.C. (hereafter cited as FBI Papers).

53. J. Edgar Hoover to Robert E. Wood, 17 October 1941, Box 60, AFC Papers; Lindbergh, entry of 7 June 1941, *Wartime Journals*, 515. For the findings of two historians, see Douglas M. Charles and John P. Rossi, "FBI Surveillance and the Charles Lindbergh Investigation, 1939–1941," *Historian* 59 (Summer 1997): 831–47.

54. See in particular the memorandum, J. Edgar Hoover to Stephen Early, 1 March 1941, Official File #4330, Roosevelt Papers. Thanks to the Freedom of Information Act, the author received several thousand individual items of FBI material contained in case files entitled "America First Committee" and "Charles Augustus Lindbergh." The files revealed that FBI field offices kept careful tabs on local AFC chapters and rallies. After the Japanese attack on Pearl Harbor, FBI reports on prewar AFC activities became even more extensive, sometimes taking the form of capsule histories, though at times these summaries were most inaccurate. See FBI Papers. For an account of the AFC's relationship to the FBI, see Cole, *Roosevelt*, 484–87.

55. Wood to Dies in Richard E. Moore, press release, 13 November 1941, Box 278, AFC Papers. For similar sentiments, see Amos Pinchot to Christopher Emmet, 26 March 1940, Pinchot Papers.

56. Sarles, "Story of America First," 329.

57. Steele, "Franklin D. Roosevelt," 15–32; Dallek, *Roosevelt*, 224–27; Charles F. Croog, "FBI Surveillance and the Isolationist–Interventionist Debate, 1939–1941," *Historian* 54 (Spring 1992): 441–58; Douglas M. Charles, "Informing FDR: FBI Political Surveillance and the Isolationist–Interventionist Foreign Policy Debate, 1939–1945," *Diplomatic History* 24 (Spring 2000): 211–32; Robert E. Herstein, *Roosevelt and Hitler: Prelude to War* (New York: Paragon, 1989), 338.

58. Ickes, entry of 2 June 1940, *Secret Diary*, 3:197. See also entries of 26 May 1940, 189; 15 June 1940, 211.

59. Leo P. Ribuffo, *The Old Christian Right: The Protestant Right from the Great Depression to the Cold War* (Philadelphia: Temple University Press, 1983), chap. 5. See also Geoffrey S. Smith, *To Save a Nation: American Countersubversives, the New Deal, and the Coming of World War II* (New York: Basic Books, 1973).

60. For the entire spectrum of accusations, see George Wolfskill and John A. Hudson, *All But the People: Franklin D. Roosevelt and His Critics, 1933–1939* (New York: Macmillan, 1969).

61. See, for example, Philip Jessup, speech, Peace Day Assembly, [Bryn Mawr] *College News*, 24 April 1940, 2; Hiram W. Johnson to Hiram W. Johnson Jr., 10 June 1940, Johnson Papers. For comments from more conservative figures, see Danaher, *CR*, 24 February 1941, 1312; Vandenberg, *CR*, 18 February 1941, 1107; Frank Lowden to Norman Thomas, 15 August 1941, Thomas Papers; Frank Gannett to Justin Nixon, 14 October 1941, Gannett Papers.

62. Flynn, "Other People's Money: War on the Home Front," *New Republic* 101 (20 September 1939): 188; "Other People's Money: Patriotism Backfires," *New Republic* 103 (9 September 1940): 352; Gustav Stolper, *German Economy, 1870–1940: Issues and Trends* (New York: Reynal & Hitchcock, 1940).

63. Holmes, "How Can Hitler Be Stopped?" *Fellowship* 5 (September 1939): 4; Frederick J. Libby to Mrs. S. Foster Hunt, 1 June 1940, NCPW Papers; Burnham, "Their Government," *Socialist Appeal*, 9 September 1939, 4; Hughes cited in Tobey, "A Reply to the War Cry," NBC red network, 7 July 1941, in *CR*, A3394; Kennedy, *Boston Globe*, 10 November 1940.

64. Hoover, "We Must Keep Out," *Saturday Evening Post* 212 (28 October 1939): 74.

65. La Follette, *CR*, 12 October 1939, 329; Libby, "The American Way: Say It with Votes," *Peace Action* 7 (November 1941): 2.

66. Barnes, [George Washington University] *Hatchet*, 17 December 1940, 1; Borchard, memo, 10 October 1940, Borchard Papers; Dennis, *WFL* 112 (19 September 1940): 4; Hutchins, speech, NBC red network, 23 January 1941, in *CR*, A304; Chase, "Four Assumptions About the War," *Uncensored*, special supplement (28 December 1940): 3. See also Chase, "Balancing the Risks," *Progressive*, 17 May 1941, 5.

67. Utley, "Can Democracy Survive Total War?" *Annals of the American Academy of Political and Social Science* 216 (July 1941): 14. Reprinted in part as "Whither Bound?" *Reader's Digest* 39 (December 1941): 9–15. Dennis assisted Utley in preparing the *Digest* reprint. Lawrence Dennis to John W. Blodgett Jr., 10 October 1941, Dennis Papers.

68. "Defending Democracy," *Christian Century* 57 (5 June 1940): 727; Macdonald, "National Defense: The Case for Socialism," *Partisan Review* 7 (July–August 1940): 260.

69. Johnson, "War in America," *NYWT*, 20 September 1939, 25; Landon, "The Contribution of the Republican Party to National Defense," speech to Second District Women's Republican Club, Kansas City, Kansas, 17 October 1941, in *CR*, A4726; Mundt, *CR*, 16 October 1941, 7952. For similar scenarios, see Morton, *Let's Think This Matter Through* [pamphlet], in *CR*, 21 February 1941, A786; Wood, "Our Foreign Policy," speech to Council of Foreign Relations Association of Chicago, 4 October 1940, in *CR*, A6302.

70. AFC Research Bureau, "Say, Is This the U.S.A.?" *Did You Know?* 14 (31 July 1941), in Doenecke, *IDU*, 372–79.

71. For an early detailed indictment, see Rose M. Stein, *M-Day: The First Day of War* (New York: Harcourt, Brace, 1936).

72. *NYT*, 10 August 1939, 1, 2.

73. Johnson, "One Man's Opinion," *San Francisco News*, 29 September 1939, 25. For other mentions of Morgan and the du Ponts, see "Overlooked," *Uncensored* 3 (21 October 1939): 2; B. C. Clark, *CR*, 11 October 1939, 282.

74. "Be Ready for M-Day!" *New Republic* 101 (4 October 1939): 230.

75. See, for example, Isabel Bacon La Follette, "A Room of Our Own: Mobilization Plan," *Progressive*, 4 November 1939, 7; Isabel Bacon La Follette, "A Room of Our Own: 'The War in Europe,'" *Progressive*, 11 November 1939, 7.

76. *Social Justice*, 30 October 1939, 19; "What War?" *Saturday Evening Post* 212 (25 November 1939): 22; Vandenberg, *CR*, 4 October 1939, 97; Clark, *CR*, 23 October 1939, 721; Downey, *CR*, 23 October 1939, 725; Villard, "Blueprints for War," *Progressive*, 8 November 1941, 8; Garrett, "How Are We Doing?" *Saturday Evening Post* 214 (4 October 1941): 14–15, 36–43; "War Plans," *Uncensored* 1 (7 October 1939): 2; "Too Much Secrecy," *WTH*, 17 October 1939, 10.

77. For Tobin, see Sargent, Bulletin #3, 15 June 1939, *Getting US into War*, 104–5. For Nixon, see his edited volume *What Will Happen and What to Do When War Comes* (New York: Greystone, 1939). For Tobin's article, see "Preparing Civilian America for War," *Foreign Affairs* 17 (July 1939): 686–98; Dorothy Dunbar Bromley, "After the Next War," *American Guardian*, 15 September 1939, 4.

78. "War Comes to America," *Look*, 7 November 1939, 33–37.

79. See, for example, "If M-Day Comes," *Progressive*, 31 August 1941, 6; B. C. Clark, *CR*, 11 October 1939, 282.

80. See Leo Cherne, *Adjusting Your Business to War* (New York: Tax Research Institute, 1939).

81. Sargent, Bulletin #8, 28 September 1939, *Getting US into War*, 128.

82. McFarland, *Woodring*, 173.

83. Langer and Gleason, *Challenge to Isolation*, 271; Roosevelt's letter to WRB, *NYT*, 25 November 1939, 2; Alan Brinkley, *The End of Reform: New Deal Liberalism in Recession and War* (New York: Knopf, 1995), 178–79. For Roosevelt's private reaction, see Jordan A. Schwarz, *The Speculator: Bernard M. Baruch in Washington, 1917–1965* (Chapel Hill: University of North Carolina Press, 1981), 361; Ickes, entry of 9 September 1939, *Secret Diary*, 2:719.

84. Kirkpatrick, *Unknown Future*, 48–49.

85. See, for example, Barnes, "Fascist Peril Seen in Bill," *NYWT*, 2 January 1940, 16; *Social Justice*, 22 January 1940, 1; Frank Waldrop, [University of North Carolina] *Daily Tar Heel*, 19 January 1940, 2; Shafer, *CR*, 26 August 1940, A5249; "War Department's M-Day Plans a Menace to Labor," *Call*, 24 February 1940, 2; Woodruff, *CR*, 28 February 1940, A2184.

86. Fey, "Defense or Despotism?" *Christian Century* 57 (24 January 1940): 110–14. For other summaries of the plan, see "Design for Living in War Time," *Peace Action* 6 (September 1939): 7; "They've Picked Your War Job," *Peace Action* 6 (November 1939): 6, based on Walter Davenport, "They've Picked Your War Job," *Collier's* 104 (4 November 1939): 9–11, 75–77; Warren D. Mullin, "Real Intent of M-Day Plan Concealed in Secret 'Annexes,'" *Peace Action* 6 (December 1939): 3, 7. For a similar claim that M-Day plans were copied from the Germans, see Warren Mullin, [University of California, Berkeley] *Daily Californian*, 2 July 1940, 1; George H. Cless Jr., "An Open Letter to the Glens Falls Chapter, National Committee to Defend America by Aiding the Allies," 10 July 1940, Box 222, Lundeen Papers; Barnes, "Keep Out of War and Investigate the War-Mongers" [draft], 2, Box 252, Lundeen Papers.

87. Villard, [University of Rochester] *Tower Times*, 23 February 1940, 1; Dennis, *WFL* 95 (23 May 1940): 2; *Call*, 12 April 1941, 1.

88. Flynn, "Can Hitler Beat American Business?" *Harper's Magazine* 180 (February 1940): 327; Page, *Johns Hopkins Newsletter*, 16 February 1940, 1.

89. See, for example, Taft, "Peace and Preparedness," speech, St. Louis, 20 May 1940, in *CR*, A3188; Taft, *CR*, 13 October 1939, 356; Arthur Capper, radio address sponsored by the American Coalition of Patriotic Societies, Washington, D.C., NBC, 17 May 1940, in *CR*, A3043–44; Flynn, "Other People's Money: Patriotism Backfires," *New Republic* 103 (9 September 1940): 352.

90. Edison, *NYT*, 4 January 1940, 1, 13; Borah, *NYT*, 12 January 1940, 2; "The Navy Wants a Dictator," *Christian Century* 57 (17 January 1940): 68. See also "'Joker' in Naval Bill Upsets Congress," *Christian Century* 57 (14 August 1940): 989; Jennings, *CR*, 3 April 1940, 3966; "Enter Decrees," *Uncensored* 14 (6 January 1940): 1–2; "In Washington," *Uncensored* 15 (13 January 1940): 1.

91. Russell–Overton bill, *NYT*, 29 August 1940, 1, 10; *Time*, 16 September 1940, 13; Flynn, "Other People's Money: Patriotism Backfires," *New Republic* 103 (9 September 1940): 352.

92. Lee and Pepper, *NYT*, 29 August 1940, 1; "Candor on the Prospects for Dictatorship," *Christian Century* 57 (11 September 1940): 1100; "Nazified," *America* 63 (7 September 1940): 603.

93. For varied projections of the debt, see Wood, "Our Foreign Policy," speech to Council of Foreign Relations Association of Chicago, 4 October 1940, in *CR*, A6302; Eddie Rickenbacker in Villard, "The Wrong Way to Prepare," *Christian Century* 58 (6 January 1941): 58; Amos Pinchot, open letter to President Roosevelt, 18 April 1939, Pinchot Papers; Holmes, "If We Go to War!" *Unity* 125 (1 July 1940): 132; William R. Castle to Edwin M. Borchard, 13 March 1941, Borchard Papers; "$132,000,000 a Day for the War," *NYDN*, 9 February 1940, 45; "After the Ball," *NYDN*, 9 June 1941, 19.

94. Borchard, memo, 10 October 1940, Borchard Papers; Lundeen, speech to Keep America Out of War Club and Debate Council, [George Washington University] *Hatchet*, 31 October 1939, 1; Dennis, *WFL* 115 (10 October 1940): 5.

95. Herbert Hoover to William J. Gross, 7 April 1941, Hoover Papers; Clark, *CR*, 11 October 1939, 268; La Follette, *CR*, 12 October 1939, 330; Meyer, "The Pendulum Swings," *Progressive*, 25 October 1941, 4. For additional anxiety concerning returning veterans, see Chester Bowles to R. Douglas Stuart Jr., 15 July 1941, in Doenecke, *IDU*, 279; Maynard Kruger, [University of Chicago] *Daily Maroon*, 11 October 1939, 2; Norman Thomas to Jerry Voorhis, 14 November 1941, Thomas Papers.

96. See, for example, Capper, "Time to Think American," *Scribner's Commentator* 9 (February 1941): 70; Capper, "Keep Out of Foreign Wars," radio address, 7 February 1941, in *CR*, A612; Sweeney,

speech, NBC red network, 6 May 1941, in *CR*, A2154; O'Connor, *CR*, 9 October 1941, 7787; Robsion, *CR*, 9 October 1941, 7789.

97. For 40 percent, see Holt, speech, Mutual network, 5 December 1940 in *CR*, A7055. For sixty-two million, see Burdick, *CR*, 4 February 1941, 540. For ten million, see La Follette, *CR*, 24 February 1941, 1308.

98. Hutchins, speech, NBC red network, 23 January 1941, in *CR*, A304. See also radio address, Sunday morning service, Rockefeller Memorial Chapel, University of Chicago, 30 March 1941, in *CR*, A1582.

99. Wheeler, speech, NBC, 30 December 1940, in *CR*, 7030–32; Chester Bowles to Philip La Follette, 28 September 1939, Philip La Follette Papers; Fish, *CR*, 12 March 1940, 2728; Lawrence Dennis to Dorothy Thompson, 9 December 1940, Dennis Papers.

100. See, for example, "A Peace or War Boom?" *Call*, 14 October 1939, 2; Hugh Johnson, "War in America," *NYWT*, 20 September 1939, 25; "The Long Arm of War," *New Republic* 101 (20 September 1939): 169; "Mobilize for Neutrality!" *New Republic* 101 (13 September 1939): 145; J. S. Barnes, "The War Profiteers," *Social Justice*, 11 December 1939, 2; "War Boosts Prices," *NYDN*, 8 September 1939, 37; Maynard Krueger, [University of Chicago] *Daily Maroon*, 31 October 1939, 1; Morton, interview, Midsummer Industrial Conference, Illinois Industrial Council, Green Lake, Wisconsin, 22 August 1940, Morton Papers.

101. "First Signs of a War Boom," *Christian Century* 56 (15 November 1939): 1336; Nye, *CR*, 29 April 1941, 3382; Hutchins, "The Proposition Is Peace," broadcast, Mutual network, in *Scribner's Commentator* 10 (July 1941): 95–96.

102. See, for example, Isabel Bacon La Follette, "A Room of Our Own," *Progressive*, 2 December 1939, 7; Norman Thomas, "Your World and Mine," *Call*, 25 November 1939, 2.

103. "'Ware the War Boom," *New Republic* 101 (4 October 1939): 227; "Storm Warning" (25 October 1939): 329. See also "Plan Neutrality!" (15 November 1939): 96.

104. Flynn, "Other People's Money: War—It's Wonderful!" *New Republic* 101 (27 September 1939): 214. See also Maynard Krueger, "The Myth of War Prosperity," *Call*, 16 September 1939, 4.

105. "War Business," *Uncensored* 19 (10 February 1940): 4–5.

106. "While We Wait for the War Boom," *Christian Century* 57 (21 February 1940): 236. See also Flynn, "Other People's Money: Hurray for War Profits!" *New Republic* 101 (1 November 1939): 367–68.

107. *Call*, 24 February 1940, 4. See also Norman Thomas, "Your World and Mine," *Call*, 2 March 1940, 1.

108. See, for example, Joseph Starobin, "FDR's Road to War," *New Masses* 35 (9 April 1940) 7–10.

109. War Business," *Uncensored* 19 (10 February 1940): 4–5.

110. Nye, *CR*, 29 April 1941, 3382; Dennis, *WFL* 137 (13 March 1941): 5.

111. See, for example, Sweeney, *CR*, 5 February 1941, 581; Villard, "An American Program for 1941," *Progressive*, 11 January 1941, 6; Wheeler, *CR*, 15 August 1940, 10,391.

112. Harrington in "Arms Employment," *Uncensored* 37 (15 June 1940): 4; Hanighen, "Capitol Letter: Unemployment and Defense," *Common Sense* 9 (July 1940): 15; Henderson and Nehemis in Wheeler, *CR*, 6 November 1941, 8558–59; OPM in AFC Research Bureau, "Priority Orphans," *Did You Know?* 25 (30 September 1941), in Doenecke, *IDU*, 187–88.

113. Dennis, *WFL* 98 (13 June 1940): 4.

114. "Butter or Guns," *Uncensored* 75 (8 March 1941): 3–4. See also "Butter and Guns (Con't)," *Uncensored* 78 (29 March 1941): 2–4; "Guns or Butter (Con't)," *Uncensored* 92 (5 July 1941): 2–4.

115. AFC Research Bureau, "Lease-Lend for War," *Did You Know?* 26 (4 October 1941), in Doenecke, *IDU*, 197–98.

116. See, for example, "More Than a Stock Market Boom," *Commonweal* 30 (15 September 1939): 465; Flynn, "Other People's Money: Hurray for War Profits!" *New Republic* 101 (1 November 1939): 367.

117. "War Boosts Prices," *NYDN*, 8 September 1939, 37; "Clear Conscience," *Uncensored* 14 (6 January 1940): 4.

118. See, for example, Libby, mimeographed letter to staff, 17 May 1940, NCPW Papers; Flynn, "Other People's Money: Business Warms Up to the War," *New Republic* 102 (24 June 1940): 857; "Dream Power," *Saturday Evening Post* 213 (8 February 1941): 26; Norman Thomas, "Your World and

Mine: Can We Have Guns *and* Butter?" *Call*, 20 March 1941, 4; Hanighen, "Capitol Letter: Are the New Dealers in Retreat?" *Common Sense* 10 (April 1941): 117.

119. "Keep the Arms Embargo!" *Christian Century* 56 (20 September 1939): 1126; "Munitions Makers Are Making Profits," *Christian Century* 57 (13 November 1940): 1405–6; Thomas, "Those False Illusions," *Progressive*, 4 January 1941, 2; Thomas, "Your World and Mine: Stumbling into Total War," *Call*, 10 May 1941, 5; Dennis, *WFL* 173 (19 November 1941): 5.

## CHAPTER 20: THE ASIAN CAULDRON

1. See various polls, Cantril, *Public Opinion*, 1081–82.

2. See, for example, Robsion, *CR*, 2 November 1939, 1296; Thorkelson, *CR*, 23 April 1940, A2320; Keefe, *CR*, 3 September 1940, 11,373; "Japan Still Means to Swallow China," *Christian Century* 57 (7 February 1940): 165; Philip Jessup to Toshi Go, 23 April 1940, Jessup Papers; Gillis, "Dollars First," *Catholic World* 150 (March 1940): 648; Edwin C. Johnson, American Forum of the Air, 6 October 1940, in *CR*, A61555; journalist Ira Bennett, unpub. ms., forwarded to AFC, 26 August 1941, Box 63, AFC Papers.

3. Hoover, address, Toronto, 22 November 1938, in *Further Addresses upon the American Road, 1938–1940* (New York: Scribner's, 1940), 185; "Roaring at Japan and Cooing at Mexico," *CT*, 15 February 1940, 14. See also "Our Relations with Japan," *CT*, 1 September 1939, 14.

4. Ralph Townsend, "Japan: Our Commercial Prize," *Scribner's Commentator* 9 (November 1940): 45. Convicted in 1942 of failing to register as a Japanese agent and sent to prison, Townsend always insisted that he was a genuine anti-interventionist. The Japanese, he said, had simply found his argument useful and had therefore published and distributed his writings. Cole, *Nye*, 209.

5. *AFC New York Chapter Bulletin*, 16 August 1941, 3.

6. Hearst, "In the News," *SFE*, 3 December 1941, 1.

7. Alfred L. Castle, "William R. Castle," 337–51; Castle, *Diplomatic Realism*, chap. 8.

8. Castle Diary, 11 September 1939 and 13 June 1940. He found the timing of the Japanese attack on China particularly poor, especially in light of the possibility of an accord with the United States, though he found no reason for Hull to again condemn the Japanese actions. For further condemnation of Japan, see Castle Diary, 29 February 1940.

9. Roy Howard to Y. Suma, consular of Japanese embassy, Washington, D.C., 28 August 1939; Howard to Yuriko-san [Miss Yuriko Go], Tokyo, 7 December 1939, Box 158, Howard Papers. See also Roy Howard to Matsuoka Yosuke, 11 September 1940; Roy Howard to S. Sheba, Tokyo, 30 September 1940, both in Box 170, Howard Papers.

10. "The Safest Time to Kick a Man Is When He Is Down," *NYDN*, 28 August 1939, 19; "The Japs Get Nice," 11 September 1939, 23; "Japan's 'Goom-By, Please,'" 25 September 1939, 21; "Put the Screws on Japan," 27 November 1939, 20; "Europe Grabs the Headlines," 4 December 1939, 27; "Modus Vivendi," 27 December 1939, 27; "Japan, China and World Conquest," 5 February 1940, 19.

11. "Lothian, British Keynoter," *NYDN*, 8 January 1940, 17.

12. "Are We Inconsistent?" *NYDN*, 2 February 1940, 21. See also "We're Called Inconsistent," *NYDN*, 4 March 1940, 21; "Our Real Problem," 11 March 1940, 21; "Our Real Problem," 18 March 1940, 21.

13. "Japan, China and World Conquest," *NYDN*, 5 February 1940, 19. See also "The Safest Time," *NYDN*, 28 August 1939, 19. For other anti-interventionist calls for aid to China, see Norman Thomas to Max Kaplan, 6 December 1940, Thomas Papers; Baldwin, *United We Stand!* 72–73; Hoover, speech of 29 June 1941, Chicago, in *Addresses, 1940–1941*, 101; Wheeler, *CR*, 1 August 1941, 6590.

14. "Our Relations with Japan," *CT*, 1 September 1939, 14; Dennis, *WFL* 173 (19 November 1941): 3. See also Dennis, *WFL* 85 (14 March 1940): 4; Castle, "Why War with Japan?" *New York Herald Tribune*, 7 December 1941.

15. See, for example, Fish, radio address, 18 April 1940, in *CR*, A2302; Lundeen, *CR*, 27 August 1940, 11,014; *Social Justice*, 26 August 1940, 5; "Japan Prepares to Seize Her Golden Opportunity," *Christian Century* 57 (31 July 1940): 941; "Uncle Sam, Receiver in Bankruptcy," *Christian Century* 57 (21 August 1940): 1020.

16. "We Have Nothing to Fight for in China," *CT*, 23 September 1939, 10; "Our Front in China," 15 November 1939, 12. See also "The Third Step?" *CT*, 27 November 1939, 10; "Take Our Army Out of China," 13 July 1940, 6; "Why Are Our Marines in Shanghai?" 24 July 1940, 10; "Wars 'On Order,'" 15 October 1940, 14.

17. "The War News," *NYDN*, 14 November 1939, 27.

18. Moley, speech, Harvard Club, 8 November 1939, Moley Papers; Wheeler, *CR*, 24 February 1941, 1312. See also Ralph Townsend, testimony, SFRC, 8 February 1941, 798.

19. John J. Whiteford, "The Paradoxical Chinese," *Scribner's Commentator* 9 (February 1941): 24. The author might have used a pseudonym, as the journal occasionally used this device.

20. "China as a Democracy," *NYDN*, 31 March 1941, 21; "$132,000,000 a Day for the War," 9 February 1941, 45; "Passing of a Great Race?" 24 March 1941, 19.

21. See, for example, Edwin M. Borchard to T. J. League, 3 April 1940, Borchard Papers; Castle Diary, 24 March 1940.

22. Johnson, "Tom-Tom Beating," *NYWT*, 10 February 1940, 13. Lawyer William P. Lage attacked Senators La Follette, Vandenberg, and Hiram Johnson for backing the China loan. Lage to Edwin M. Borchard, 8 February 1940, Borchard Papers.

23. Townsend, testimony, SFRC, 8 February 1941, 798; "China as a Democracy," *NYDN*, 31 March 1941, 21. See also Taft, "Russia and the Four Freedoms," broadcast, CBS, 25 June 1941, A3077; Wheeler, *CT*, 19 March 1941, 2; Wheeler, *CR*, 1 August 1941, 6590.

24. Burton Rascoe to Quincy Howe, 13 April 1940, Hertzberg Papers; Johnson, "Anchors Away," *Saturday Evening Post* 213 (5 October 1940): 78. See also Ralph Townsend, *America Has No Enemies in Asia!* (pamphlet; San Francisco: the author 1938); "China as a Democracy," *NYDN*, 31 March 1941, 21.

25. See, for example, Mark Shaw, "What Should Be Our Policy Toward Japan?" *American Forum of the Air* 3 (23 November 1941): 8; resolution, American Coalition of Patriotic Societies, 27 January 1941, SFRC, 656; Dennis and Gravenhoff, *WFL* 70 (30 November 1939): 4.

26. Hearst, "In the News," *SFE*, 26 April 1940, 2; 30 September 1940, 1. Hearst also included anarchy and provincial "outlaws" among China's woes. See "In the News," *SFE*, 3 December 1941, 1.

27. Dennis, *WFL* 115 (10 October 1940): 4; 133 (13 February 1941): 3; Ralph Townsend, "Must We Might Japan?" *Scribner's Commentator* 9 (June 1941): 98. See also Ralph Townsend, "Japan: Our Commercial Prize," 45.

28. See, for example, "The Search for a Lasting Peace, III: The Struggle for Power in the Far East," *Christian Century* 58 (26 February 1941): 279; "Do We Have to Fight Japan?" *NYDN*, 17 February 1941, 19.

29. Moley, "Perspective: Must We Fight Japan?" *Newsweek*, 22 July 1940, 60; Castle Diary, 19 December 1940; Bender, *CR*, 13 May 1940, A2895.

30. John Bassett Moore to Charles C. Tansill, 19 March 1940 [not sent], Moore Papers; Moore to Hiram Johnson, 17 September 1940, Moore Papers. For Moore on Asian exclusion, see Moore to Lincoln Colcord, 14 January 1941, Moore Papers. For Moore's pointing to his background, see John Bassett Moore to Raymond Moley, 24 July 1940, Moley Papers. For China as geographic entity, see also Moore to William T. Dewart, 15 April 1940, Moore Papers.

31. See, for example, Libby, "Time Approaches for Mediation in the Far East," *Peace Action* 6 (February 1940): 2.

32. Johnson, "Anchors Away," 78; Barnes, "Crisis in the Far East: Japan's New Attitudes," *New York Herald Tribune*, 8 March 1940, 22; Dennis, *Dynamics*, 9–10; Dennis, *WFL* 139 (27 March 1941): 4.

33. Tansill, "American Policy in the Far East," *Thought: A Review of Culture and Ideas* 15 (March 1940): 39–63; quotation, 40.

34. John Bassett Moore to Raymond Moley, 24 July 1940, Moley Papers; Hugh Johnson, "Anchors Away," 78. See also Townsend, "Must We Fight Japan?" 96–97. For more favorable references to the Nine Power Pact, see Roy Howard to S. Sheba, 30 September 1940, Box 170, Howard Papers; Edwin C. Johnson, American Forum of the Air, 6 October 1940, in *CR*, A6155; Capper, broadcast, radio station WINX, Washington, D.C., 8 March 1941, in *CR*, A1636; Reynolds, American Forum of the Air, entered in *CR*, 2 May 1940, 5405.

35. Wiley, *CR*, 23 January 1940, 542; Danaher, *CR*, 24 February 1941, 1311; Page, "How to Keep America Out of War" [study guide], *Fellowship* 6 (March 1940): 46. See also Mark Shaw, "What Should Be Our Policy Toward Japan?" 8; Roy Howard to Shigeyoshi Obata, San Francisco, 28 April 1941, Box 180, Howard Papers; Dennis, *WFL* 155 (17 July 1941): 1; "The Search for a Lasting Peace, III: The Struggle for Power in the Far East," *Christian Century* 58 (26 February 1941): 279.

36. Hearst, "In the News," *SFE*, 7 February 1941, 2. Hearst compared Japan's war in China to American acquisition of Arizona, New Mexico, and California. Hearst, "In the News," *SFE*, 30 September 1941, 1. See also John Bassett Moore to Hiram Johnson, 17 July 1939, Moore Papers.

37. Pinchot, confidential memo accompanying letter to R. Douglas Stuart Jr., 3 December 1941, Box 284, AFC Papers; Sargent, Bulletin #95, 30 December 1940, *Getting US into War*, 535.

38. Castle, "A Monroe Doctrine for Japan," *Atlantic Monthly* 166 (October 1940): 445–52; quotation, 447. Castle did admit that a Japanese Monroe Doctrine, if it involved cutting off Western trade, might be dangerous. The doctrine "must not threaten the political integrity of member nations" but rather "act as a guarantee to their security." See 449–50. For similar references to a Japanese Monroe Doctrine, see "Empire in Asia," *Christian Century* 57 (10 July 1940): 870; "International Finance Breaks Down," *Social Justice*, 4 August 1941, 3; Hearst, "In the News," *SFE*, 28 June 1940, 1; "Asia for the Asiatics," *NYDN*, 19 August 1940, 19.

39. Castle, *Yale* [University] *Daily News*, 17 December 1940, 1; "Why War with Japan?" letter to *New York Herald Tribune*, 7 December 1941.

40. Howard, *America and a New World*, 100, 107, 112. A visualized version of Howard's book was entitled "Permanent Peace Through Prosperity: Economic Cooperation of Regional Population Blocs." It contained a huge world map divided into continental spheres of influence. Japan, China, and the East Indies comprised one economic bloc. The accompanying text left little doubt as to the pacesetter. The Japanese, it said, "must either migrate, export, starve or conquer. The white race countries have blocked their migrating and their exporting. If the Japanese obtain a preferred position in the Orient, this region, rich in diversified resources, can achieve a much higher standard of living for the Oriental people." Copy in Box 34, AFC Papers.

41. Dennis, *WFL* 146 (15 May 1941): 4. See also *WFL* 139 (27 March 1941): 4.

42. "Do We Have to Fight Japan?" *NYDN*, 17 February 1941, 19; "War in the Pacific?" 26 July 1941, 13.

43. Morton, speech to Illinois Industrial Council, 22 August 1940, Morton Papers. See also Castle, "A Monroe Doctrine for Japan," 450; "China as a Democracy," *NYDN*, 31 March 1941, 21; Ralph Townsend, *Does Japan Slam the Door Against American Trade in Areas of Japanese Influence in China?* (pamphlet; San Francisco: Japanese Chamber of Commerce, 1938).

44. Hearst, "In the News," *SFE*, 17 June 1940, 1.

45. Townsend, testimony, SFRC, 8 February 1941, 798; "Fight Germany and Japan?" *NYDN*, 17 November 1941, 23; "Better Treat Japan Nicely," *NYDN*, 8 July 1940, 19; Shaw, "What Should Be Our Policy Toward Japan?" 7; Castle, "A Monroe Doctrine for Japan," 452.

46. Dennis, *WFL* 103 (18 July 1940): 4; 173 (19 November 1941): 2 (quotation). For earlier predictions of a national socialist revolution in Japan, see Dennis and Gravenhoff, *WFL* 57 (31 August 1939): 5; 70 (30 November 1939): 4–5.

47. Utley, *Going to War with Japan*, 79–80.

48. For Plan Dog, see Stark, "Memorandum for the Secretary," 12 November 1940, in Ross, *American War Plans*, 3:227, 231.

49. See, for example, "What's Up Now?" *CT*, 1 October 1939, 16; Norman Thomas, [University of Wisconsin] *Daily Cardinal*, 20 January 1940, 1; Holmes, "America in the Far East," *Unity* 126 (21 October 1940): 51; Flynn, "Other People's Money: Chestnuts, Money and Democracy," *New Republic* 103 (21 October 1940): 556; William C. Rivers, "The Embargo Resolutions and the Far East," *Peace Action* 6 (March 1940): 4; Wheeler, *CR*, 24 February 1941, 1311; Nye, *CR*, 26 February 1941, 1432.

50. Morton, *Let's Think the Matter Through* [pamphlet], in *CR*, 21 February 1941, A786–87. For similar sentiments, see "The New Order in Asia," *NYDN*, 5 August 1940, 19; "What Is Our Far East Policy?" *NYDN*, 28 October 1940, 23.

51. Chamberlin, "War: Shortcut to Fascism," *American Mercury* 51 (December 1940): 399.

52. "Crisis in Japan," *America* 66 (25 October 1941): 71.

53. Barnes, "Danger Point in the Far East," *NYWT*, 10 October 1939, 30; Johnson, *Chicago Herald-American*, 27 August 1941. See also "Review of the Month: Repercussions," *Common Sense* 9 (May 1940): 18; "A War on Two Fronts?" *NYDN*, 6 October 1941, 21; Congressman Tinkham, *Yale Daily News*, 1 March 1940, 1; "Various Trade Wars," *CT*, 11 December 1939, 14.

54. See, for example, Upton Close, "Must We Fight over Dutch Indies?" *Living Age* 358 (June 1940): 322.

55. "President to Renew Plan for A.E.F. to Dakar," *AFC New York Chapter Bulletin*, 16 August 1941, 3. See also "U.S. Interests Not at Stake in Japanese Crisis," *AFC New York Chapter Bulletin*, 6 December 1941, 3.

56. "Japan and Great Britain," *CT*, 22 January 1940, 12. Similarly the *Chicago Tribune* said that the Europeans had balked at pressing Japan when the Brussels conference of 1937 was called, though it did not regret the meeting's failure. For other references to Manchuria, see Hugh Johnson, "Anchors Away," 80; Barnes, "Danger Point in the Far East," *NYWT*, 10 October 1939, 30.

57. See, for example, resolutions, WIL annual meeting, 1–4 May 1941, 6, WIL Papers.

58. Tinkham, *CR*, 21 March 1940, 3238–42. See also *CR*, 16 January 1941, 178. Tinkham's position was noted in *Social Justice*, 4 March 1940, 4; Sargent, Bulletin #41, 6 March 1940, *Getting US into War*, 307–8; Bulletin #93, 31 October 1940, 493. Canton and Enderbury islands were members of the Phoenix group, some 1,300 miles southeast of Japan's mandated territory and 1,900 southwest of Hawaii. For the actual circumstances, see Francis X. Holbrook, "The Canton Island Controversy: Compromise or American Victory?" *Journal of the Royal Australian Historical Society* 59 (June 1973): 128–47; M. Ruth Megaw, "The Scramble for the Pacific: Anglo–United States Rivalry in the 1930s," *Historical Studies* 17 (October 1977): 458–73.

59. Williams, *SFN*, 29 May 1940, 14; Holt, *CR*, 21 July 1940, 8812. See also Holt, speech over NBC, 2 January 1941, in *CR, 1940*, A7053.

60. Robsion, *CR*, 19 March 1941, 2365. Offering a contrary view, Al Williams said of Singapore, "We may do a good bit of bluffing in the Far East, but I do not believe we will fight Japan in that corner of the globe." *Airpower*, 413.

61. See, for example, "The Alliance Against America," *CT*, 28 September 1940, 10.

62. Thomas interview, *Yale Daily News*, 20 January 1940, 1; Moley, *CT*, 19 April 1941, 4.

63. Gary R. Hess, "The Emergence of U.S. Influence in Southeast Asia," in *American, Chinese, and Japanese Perspectives on Wartime Asia, 1931–1949*, ed. Akira Iriye and Warren Cohen (Wilmington, Del.: Scholarly Resources, 1990), 185–86.

64. The exact ratio was 82:18. *NYT*, 30 August 1939, 8. See also Gallup's poll of 19 January 1940, Cantril, *Public Opinion*, 1159; *NYT*, 14 February 1940, 10; 30 September 1940, 1160.

65. National Convention, Socialist Party, "Socialist Resolution on War," *Call*, 20 April 1940, 2.

66. Barnes, "Keep Out of War and Investigate the War-Mongers" [draft], 18, Box 252, Lundeen Papers; Villard, "Our Wrecked Japanese Policy," *Christian Century* 57 (4 December 1940): 1509; Capper, radio broadcast, station WINX, Washington, D.C., 8 March 1941, in *CR*, A1636.

67. Secrest, *CR*, 27 February 1940, 2076. See also broadcast, 5 August 1940, in *CR*, A4815.

68. See, for example, Keefe, *CR*, 3 September 1940, 11,373.

69. Danaher, *CR*, 17 October 1939, 511; Arthur Stevens Phelps, "U.S.E. [United States of Europe]," *Fellowship* 6 (January 1940): 5; Marcantonio, 5 February 1941, *CR*, 658.

70. AFC, *Washington News Letter* 13 (15 May 1941): 2, Box 284, AFC Papers; Capper, radio address, WINX, Washington, D.C., 8 March 1941, in *CR*, A1637.

71. See, for example, Harry Emerson Fosdick noted in "Shall We Embargo Japan?" *Christian Century* 57 (28 February 1940): 271.

72. Utley, "Japan's Great Bluff," *Nation* 151 (12 October 1940): 321; Reynolds, American Forum of the Air, entered in *CR*, 2 May 1940, 5405. See also Robsion, *CR*, 2 November 1939, 1296.

73. "Quarantine Japan Now," *NYDN*, 1 February 1940, 27. See also "U.S. Oppressing Japan," 12 February 1940, 19; "On the Pacific," 19 February 1940, 21; "The Pittman Resolution," 26 February 1940, 19.

74. Andresen, *CR*, 7 February 1940, 1180.

75. William Henry Chamberlin, "What Should Be America's Policy in the Far East?" *American Forum of the Air* 3 (16 February 1941): 13; Sumner, *CR*, 13 May 1941, 400; Nye, broadcast, CBS, 21 June 1941, in *CR*, A3076; Wheeler, *CR*, 1 August 1941, 6590. On oil, see also Springer, *CR*, 13 June 1941, 2851; Robsion, 6 May 1941, 3660; Congressmen Edward H. Rees (Rep.-Iowa), Crawford, Coffee, Sumner, 13 May 1941, 3999–4000; Lamberston, *CR*, 10 October 1941, 7825; resolutions, WIL annual meeting, Washington, D.C., 1–4 May 1941, 6, WIL Papers.

76. See, for example, Danaher, *CR*, 17 October 1939, 511; Andresen, *CR*, 19 February 1941, 1185–86; Andersen, 9 May 1941, 3862.

77. He also noted that cotton, which was contraband, had not been embargoed, for no Democratic legislator wanted to prevent its shipment. Fish, *CR*, 23 April 1940, 4898. A month earlier, he had stressed that he opposed a total cessation of trade. Justin Harris Libby, "The Irresolute Years: American Congressional Opinion Toward Japan, 1937–1941," Ph.D. diss., Michigan State University, 1971, 182.

78. "Review of the Month: Repercussions," *Common Sense* 9 (May 1940): 18. See also "Bring On the Embargo," *NYDN*, 18 May 1940, 21.

79. "The Safest Time," *NYDN*, 28 August 1939, 19; "Why Not Blockade the Japs?" 19.

80. "Japan's 'Goom-By, Please,'" *NYDN*, 25 September 1939, 21. See also "Are We Inconsistent?" *NYDN*, 2 February 1940, 21.

81. "A Legislative Program for the Neutrality Bloc," 19 December 1939, KAOWC Papers.

82. See, for example, Wiley, *CR*, 23 January 1940, 541–42. Wiley did concede that arms traffic could be reduced without any congressional embargo, for the United States needed the matériel. For a similar fear about China, see Fish, *CR*, 12 March 1940, 2730.

83. See, for example, "While We Increase Pressure," *New Republic* 102 (22 January 1940): 101; Libby, "Shall the United States Discontinue Diplomatic Relations with the Axis Powers?" *American Forum of the Air* 2 (15 December 1940): 13. Within six months, Libby was talking of a general Japanese strike in the Far East. Letter to Constance A. Hulburt, 12 June 1941, NCPW Papers.

84. Castle, speech, American Town Meeting of the Air, text, *New York Herald Tribune*, 15 December 1939. See also Castle, speech to American Academy of Political and Social Science, *Philadelphia Inquirer*, 23 April 1940; Fish, *CR*, 12 March 1940, 2730. Challenging the statement that Japan might make overtures to the Soviet Union, Freda Utley noted that Japanese goods could not easily find a market there, for the Russians either made the items themselves or could not afford to buy them. Unlike Germany, Japan could not supply Russia with machinery, skilled workers, or engineers, as Japan's industry itself was suffering acutely from lack of qualified personnel. "Japan's Red Flirtation," *Nation* 150 (24 February 1940): 278.

85. Pettengill, "Meddlesome Mattie—Chapter 2," in *CR*, 19 August 1940, A5065.

86. May, "This Bewildered Democracy," 14; Baldwin, *United We Stand!* 69.

87. See, for example, "Sun-kissed Flagellants," *CT*, 19 November 1939, 12; "Mr. Knox Spies a War," *CT*, 27 October 1941, 12; John Bassett Moore to Hiram Johnson, 14 March 1941, Moore Papers; Johnson, "British Racket," *Miami Daily Herald*, 29 December 1939. For scholarly confirmation, see Hathaway, "Economic Diplomacy," 303.

88. "What the President Didn't Say," *NYDN*, 2 June 1941, 21. Another time it said that each Japanese bought $3 worth of goods from the United States, each Chinese $0.03. "Is Japan Quitting China?" *NYDN*, 4 November 1940, 35.

89. See, for example, "You Won't Forget Japan," *Peace Action* 6 (December 1939): 1; Barnes, "Crisis in the Far East: Japan's New Attitudes," *NYWT*, 8 March 1940, 22; "A Policy for the Pacific," *New Republic* 101 (22 November 1939): 126; Townsend, "Japan: Our Commercial Prize," 44–46.

90. Sargent, Bulletin #95, 30 December 1940, *Getting US into War*, 52; Cless, testimony, SFRC, 8 February 1941, 701; Johnson, "Anchors Away," 78; "But Boake Carter Says," *SFE*, 7 February 1941, 11. By 1941, Hugh Johnson was calling for an all-out embargo on Japan. Claiming that the United States permitted vast quantities of metals, fuels, and the constituents of explosives to reach Japan, he wrote, "We short-rationed our potential enemy, but we still supplied enough to tempt him to belligerence. It almost seems in retrospect as though we courted conflict." *Hell Bent for War*, 131–32.

91. "War in the Pacific?" *NYDN*, 26 July 1941, 13; "Friendship with Japan," *SFE*, 2 January 1940, 14.

92. Townsend, "Must We Fight Japan?" 98. See also "But Boake Carter Says," *SFE*, 24 January 1940, 13; Rivers, "The Embargo Resolutions," *Peace Action* 6 (March 1940): 4.

93. William J. Baxter, *Japan and America Must Work Together!* (New York: International Economic Research Bureau, 1940), especially 7, 9, 96.

94. See, for example, *Social Justice*, 10 March 1941, 4; Chamberlin, "What Should Be America's Policy in the Far East?" 13; Ralph Townsend, "Japan: Our Commercial Prize," 43–44. True, said Townsend, some American businesses—such as banking and insurance—had been at a disadvantage, but these losses had been more than compensated by other gains.

95. Hearst, "In the News," *SFE*, 3 December 1941, 1; "A Choice of Evils," *CT*, 9 February 1941, 16. See also *SFE*, 2 January 1940, 14.

96. "Do We Have to Fight Japan?" *NYDN*, 17 February 1941, 19. It did claim that Japan might engage in the common practice of taking a "jobber's commission"—that is, requiring the United States to ship all goods to Japan for reexport to Japanese-dominated countries.

97. Flynn, *SFN*, 9 June 1941, 14.

98. Townsend, testimony, SFRC, 8 February 1941, 799.

99. "Sun-kissed Flagellants," *CT*, 19 November 1939, 12; Johnson, "Anchors Away," 78. For another reference to cotton, see Castle, "A Monroe Doctrine for Japan," 451.

100. Townsend, "Japan: Our Commercial Prize," 42; "Professors Thirsting for Blood," *CT*, 24 November 1940, 14.

101. See, for example, "Paying a Debt by Rattling a Crowd," *Christian Century* 58 (14 May 1941): 645; Libby, "You Won't Forget Japan," *Peace Action* 6 (December 1939): 1.

102. See, for example, Chester Bowles to Robert La Follette Jr. [copy], 16 May 1940, Hertzberg Papers; Fish, *CR*, 6 June 1940, 4811–12; Wheeler, *CR*, 13 August 1940, 10,237; Wheeler, *CR*, 22 August 1940, 10,730.

103. Haskell, "We Can't Be Licked," *Call*, 18 October 1939, 4; Holt, *CR*, 18 October 1939, 556; MacLiesh and Reynolds, *Strategy*, 225; Castle, testimony, HFAC, 24 January 1941, 517.

104. See, for example, "At Sea," *Uncensored* 20 (17 February 1940): 3; Nye, *CR*, 6 October 1939, 162; Nye, *CR*, 26 February 1941, 1435; Holt, *CR*, 18 October 1939, 556; Villard, "A Primer of Invasion," *Christian Century* 58 (12 February 1941): 220. For Roosevelt's original article, see "Shall We Trust Japan?" *Asia* 23 (July 1923): 475–78.

105. "A Still Bigger Army and What It Means," *CT*, 6 January 1941, 12; Taft, *CR*, 14 August 1940, 10,308; Villard, "The Wrong Way to Prepare," *Christian Century* 58 (8 January 1941): 220. See also Nye, *CR*, 26 February 1941, 1435.

106. MacLiesh and Reynolds, *Strategy*, 221–24; Wheeler, *CR*, 24 February 1941, 1311.

107. For Taussig, Hull, and Stark, see *NYT*, 23 April 1940, 1, 8.

108. Clark, *NYT*, 25 April 1940, 7; Fish, *CR*, 23 April 1940, 4898. See also "War in the Pacific," *Socialist Appeal*, 27 April 1940, 8; Libby, *NYT*, 24 April 1940, 6; "Admiral Taussig Overplays the Navy's Hand," *Christian Century* 57 (1 May 1940): 563.

109. Flynn, "Other People's Money: Whom Are We Getting Ready to Fight?" *New Republic* 102 (22 January 1940): 115; MacNider, testimony, SFRC, 6 February 1941, 561. See also Holt, *CR*, 18 October 1939, 555; B. C. Clark, *CR*, 23 October 1939, 728; Fish, *CR*, 29 April 1940, 4899; Wheeler, *CR*, 24 February 1941, 1311.

110. Hagood, "When We Invade Japan," *Scribner's Commentator* 8 (June 1940): 5.

111. Hearst, "In the News," *SFE*, 26 April 1940, 1; 26 June 1940, 1–2 (quotation); 5 August 1940; 21 February 1941, 1A. Hearst also warned against a Soviet invasion of an undefended Alaska, saying the USSR could then proceed southward through British Columbia to the Pacific states. For another fear of Japanese invasion, see Short, *CR*, 29 May 1941, 4567.

112. "Our Secretary of War Outlines Our Naval Policy," *NYDN*, 8 May 1941, 21. See also "Do We Have to Fight Japan?" 17 February 1941, 1; "More and Better Shambles," 18 May 1941, 43.

113. See, for example, Hoover, speech, New York, 12 May 1941, in *CR*, A2315; "Appeasement for Japan?" *Christian Century* 57 (26 June 1940): 812.                                  •

114. Wheeler, speech, Minneapolis, 17 June 1941, in *CR*, A3961.

115. "How to Double the Fleet in a Week," *CT*, 30 May 1940, 14.

116. Dennis, *WFL* 126 (26 December 1940): 3; "Defense, 1933–1940," *NYDN*, 20 May 1940, 19. For Philippines, see also "South China Sea," *Uncensored* 69 (25 January 1941): 4.

117. Libby, "Only Stalin Could Win," *Peace Action* 6 (October 1940): 2; Downey, *CR*, 6 October 1939, 163. See also Downey, *CR*, 9 October 1939, 177; 27 August 1940, 11,038.

118. Barnes, "Realistic War View," *NYWT*, 19 April 1940, 26. See also Barnes, "No War with Japan," *Progressive*, 6 December 1941, 9. He had previously estimated $50 billion. "Crisis in the Far East: Japan's New Attitudes," *NYWT*, 8 March 1940, 22.

119. See, for example, William C. Rivers, "Situation in East," *NYT*, 1 September 1940, sect. 4, 7; "Invincible Uncle Sam," *NYDN*, 7 April 1940, 43; Amos Pinchot to Hiram Johnson, 2 October 1940, Pinchot Papers; "International Finance Breaks Down," *Social Justice*, 4 August 1941, 3; Sargent, Bulletin #95, 30 December 1940, *Getting US into War*, 533.

120. See, for example, Frank C. Hanighen, "Out on Two Limbs," *Progressive*, 2 November 1941, 2; "U.S. Interests Not at Stake in Japanese Crisis," *AFC New York Chapter Bulletin*, 6 December 1941, 3.

121. Walsh, *CR*, 3 March 1941, 1627, 1629. See also conclusions of the report of the Senate Naval Affairs Committee, 15 May 1940, in Walsh, *CR*, 4 June 1940, 7439.

122. Lundeen, *CR*, 27 August 1940, 11,015. See also Hearst, "In the News," *SFE*, 29 October 1941.

123. Villard, "The Wrong Way to Prepare," *Christian Century* 58 (8 January 1941): 58.

124. "South China Sea," *Uncensored* 69 (25 January 1941): 4. Ernest L. Meyer was an exception in predicting a quick American victory, ironically echoing the views of General Marshall. Meyer, "Working Pattern for 'The Next War,'" *Progressive*, 26 April 1941, 4. In a confidential meeting with seven Washington correspondents on 15 November 1941, Marshall foresaw a quick Japanese defeat due to air strikes from Alaska and Siberia. Herzstein, *Roosevelt*, 245.

125. Williams, *Airpower*, 412–13; *SFN*, 29 May 1940, 14. For additional anxiety over the Japanese leading the United States into their home waters, see Lincoln Colcord to Edwin M. Borchard, 16 October 1941, Borchard Papers.

126. "Strategy for Two Wars," *NYDN*, 3 February 1941, 19. See also "U.S. Oppressing Japan," *NYDN*, 12 February 1940, 19; "Uncle Sam," 7 April 1940, 43; "Two Ships for One," 14 October 1940, 25; "Is Japan a Pushover?" 29 July 1941, 19; "Back Door to War?" 29 August 1941, 27; "Via Boston to Archangel," 24 October 1941, 33; "An Alliance with Japan?" 19 November 1941, 28.

127. See, for example, Frank Cullen Brophy, "The Four Freedoms Ride Again," *Commonweal* 34 (13 June 1941): 180.

128. Baldwin, *United We Stand!* 70. After citing Baldwin on the Aleutian route, Thomas went further, warning against building American bases in Siberia on the grounds that these exposed salients could well lead to war with Japan. "Should the U.S. Act Now in Asia?" World Peaceways Forum, station WQXR, 27 July 1941, Socialist Party Papers. For another prediction of eventual U.S. victory, see Charles A. Lindbergh, "Impregnable America," speech at Yale University, 30 October 1940, in *Scribner's Commentator* 9 (January 1941): 4.

129. Baldwin, *United We Stand!* 69. Baldwin found Japan uneven in strength. It possessed considerable reserves of imports, a year's supply of oil, a goodly number of effective planes, and an army superior to that of the United States. However, its chief weakness lay in the huge casualties engendered by the China campaign; it probably could not muster more than three million people for army service. See 120, 122.

130. Downey, *CR*, 6 October 1939, 163. He did claim that by levying a naval blockade, the United States might be able to starve the Japanese within four years.

131. Hagood, "When We Invade Japan," *Scribner's Commentator* 8 (June 1940): 4–5; quotation, 4.

132. Hearst, "In the News," *SFE*, 29 October 1941, 1, A.

133. "The Crisis with Japan," *CT*, 2 December 1941, 14. For another comment on flimsy Japanese houses, see MacLiesh and Reynolds, *Strategy*, 225.

134. May, *This Bewildered Democracy*, 14; Libby, "Only Stalin Could Win," *Peace Action* 7 (October 1940): 2; "A War on Two Fronts?" *NYDN*, 6 October 1941, 21.

135. Johnson, "Anchors Away," 78; Hearst, "In the News," *SFE*, 21 February 1941, 1A; Rivers, radio address, "Europe's War and America's Security," entered in *CR*, 20 May 1940, A3039; Downey, *CR*, 9 October 1939, 177.

136. "A Legislative Program for the Neutrality Bloc," New York City, 12 December 1939, KAOWC Papers. See also FOR Council, 20 April 1940, in *Fellowship* 6 (May 1940): 74.

137. "Mr. Knox Spies a War," *CT*, 27 October 1941, 12; "What Next in the Pacific?" *NYDN*, 8 August 1941, 17.

138. Waldrop, "Who Really Owns the Philippines?" *WTH*, 4 August 1940, 10C. For critiques of the initial American involvement, see Hugh Johnson, "Anchors Away," 77; Fish, *CR*, 4 April 1940, 4028.

139. "Make Guam a Salient??" *NYDN*, 15 January 1940, 21. See also "What Is Our Far East Policy?" *NYDN*, 28 October 1940, 23; "Fight Germany *and* Japan?" *NYDN*, 17 November 1941, 23; Wheeler, *CR*, 28 October 1940, A6524.

140. Johnson, "Anchors Away," 75; "The Vassal Mind," *CT*, 3 October 1939, 10; "Filipino Hostages," *CT*, 25 January 1940, 10; "America in the Far East," *CT*, 20 August 1941, 12.

141. Barnes, "Japan's Power in Philippines," *NYWT*, 17 November 1939, 26.

142. "South China Sea," *Uncensored* 69 (25 January 1941): 3; Johnson, "Anchors Away," 77; Barnes, "Japan's Power in Philippines," *NYWT*, 17 November 1939, 26; Flynn, "Other People's Money: Whom Are We Getting Ready to Fight?" *New Republic* 102 (22 January 1940): 115; "But Boake Carter Says," *SFE*, 29 January 1940, 9. The Philippines are a rare instance when Carter differed with his employer William Randolph Hearst.

143. "Filipino Independence and the Democrats," *CT*, 30 April 1940, 10. See also "Big-Navy Nightmare," *New Republic* 102 (22 January 1940): 103; Downey, *CR*, 9 October 1939, 177; Bruce Barton, *CR*, 6 September 1940, 11,662; "War Madness," *Call*, 17 February 1940, 2; Barnes, "Keep Out of War and Investigate the War-Mongers" [draft], 38, Box 252, Lundeen Papers; Selden Rodman to Sidney Hertzberg, 22 May 1940, Hertzberg Papers; "Shall We Embargo Japan?" *Christian Century* 57 (28 February 1940): 271.

144. "Quarantine Japan Now," *NYDN*, 1 February 1940, 27; "Quezon Raises the Ante," 23 September 1940, 23; "The British Navy," 20 May 1940, 19.

145. Johnson, "Anchors Away," 75. General William C. Rivers gave a different distance, some 7,250 miles between the U.S. West Coast and the Philippines, but offered the same argument. See "Situation in East," *NYT*, 1 September 1940, sect. 4, 7.

146. Barton, *CR*, 6 September 1940, 11,662. The amendment was rejected. See 11,664.

147. See, for example, "Congress and the Militia," *CT*, 7 August 1940, 12; "Bombers in Manila," *CT*, 20 June 1940, 14; "Bringing in a New War Zone," *CT*, 29 August 1940, 10; "What Is Our Far Eastern Policy?" *NYDN*, 28 October 1940, 23; AFC *Washington News Letter* 12 (7 May 1941): 3, Box 284, AFC Papers.

148. Baldwin, *United We Stand!* 61–63, 73. For an endorsement of Baldwin's position, see AFC Research Bureau, "Nobody Knows the Trouble We're In," *Did You Know?* 12 (24 July 1941), in Doenecke, *IDU*, 366. For other endorsements of neutralization, see Arthur J. May, *This Bewildered Democracy*, 14; Norman Thomas, "Your World and Mine," *Call*, 2 November 1940, 5.

149. Rivers, letter to editor, *Christian Century* 57 (21 February 1940): 252; Rivers, "Are We Facing War in Asia?" radio speech, 8 October 1940, in *CR*, 6847–48; "Why Risk War with Japan?" 17 February 1941, in *CR*, A1099. Rivers was a vice chairman of Libby's NCPW, wrote for *Peace Action*, and served on the board of World Peaceways.

150. See, for example, Capper, *United States News*, 8 August 1941, 28; Chamberlin Diary, 16 February 1941.

151. Wheeler, *CR*, 6 March 1941, 1877. Fish, *CR*, 23 April 1940, 4899. Wheeler also said he would go to war if Japan interfered with U.S. citizens and property in Asia.

152. "Vital Outpost: Philippines Must Be Fortified," *SFE*, 24 April 1940, 1. See also "Planes: Thousands for Allies, Dangers for U.S.," *SFE*, 26 April 1940, 14; "For Our Good: Why Not Build Planes for U.S.!" *SFE*, 2 May 1940, 2.

153. Hearst, "In the News," *SFE*, 25 April 1940, 2; 10 October 1940, 1. For other Hearst warnings, see *SFE*, 26 April 1940, 1; 21 February 1941, 1A; 4 August 1941, 1–2; "In the News," *WTH*, 13 August 1941, 9.

154. For the most detailed account of the debates within the American military, see Brian McAllister Linn, *Guardians of Empire: The U.S. Army and the Pacific, 1902–1940* (Chapel Hill: University of North Carolina Press, 1997), chaps. 7–9. For Embick, see 178. For Stimson, see Ickes, entry of 10 May 1940, *Secret Diary*, 3:510.

155. Daniel F. Harrington, "A Careless Hope: American Air Power and Japan, 1941," *Pacific Historical Review* 48 (May 1979): 217–38; Ronald H. Spector, *Eagle Against the Sun: The American War with Japan* (New York: Free Press, 1985), 74–75; Sherry, *Rise*, 105–6; Utley, *Going to War with Japan*, 112.

156. Harrington, "Careless Hope," 224, 226, 229, 231; "Memorandum from Robert L. Shirred to David W. Hulburd Jr.," 15 November 1941, in Marshall, *Papers*, 2:676.

157. D. Clayton James, *The Years of MacArthur*, vol. 1: *1880–1941* (Boston: Houghton Mifflin, 1970), 583–84, 594–95, 609–10.

158. Langer and Gleason, *Challenge to Isolation*, 149–50.

159. "Japan Invites Us Out," *NYDN*, 7 October 1940, 21; Baldwin, *United We Stand!* 72–73. See also "Make Guam a Salient??" *NYDN*, 15 January 1940, 21; "Quarantine Japan Now," *NYDN*, 1 February 1940, 27; "Planes: Thousands for Allies, Dangers for U.S.," *SFE*, 26 April 1940, 14; Hearst, "In the News," *SFE*, 19 April 1940, 2; Hearst, "In the News," *SFE*, 26 April 1940, 1.

160. For the opposition of various neutrality organizations, see "A Legislative Program for the Neutrality Bloc," New York City, 19 December 1939, KAOWC Papers.

161. For example, see Al Williams, *SFN*, 29 May 1940, 14; "Big-Navy Nightmare," *New Republic* 102 (22 January 1940): 103; "We Fortify Guam and Samoa," *Christian Century* 57 (5 March 1941): 307.

162. Rivers, *Los Angeles Evening Herald and Express*, 3 March 1941. See also "Why Risk War with Japan?" A1099; "Europe's War and America's Security," A3039; William C. Rivers to Norman Thomas, 20 December 1940, Thomas Papers; letter to editor, *NYDN*, 20 January 1940, 15.

163. "But Boake Carter Says," *SFE*, 29 January 1940, 9; "West of Hawaii," *Uncensored* 73 (21 February 1941): 1.

164. Libby, "Are We Bluffing—or Aren't We?" *Peace Action* 7 (February 1941): 2. See also Edwin M. Borchard to William E. Borah, 16 February 1939, Borchard Papers; "Make Guam a Salient??" *NYDN*, 15 January 1940, 21; "The War Birds Hover over Guam," *CT*, 20 April 1940, 10.

165. "Guam in Pacific Power Politics," *CT*, 27 April 1940, 8. It saw such projects as cooperation over Singapore and Canton and Enderbury islands and the use of the American and British fleets as an international police force to be further evidence that the United States sought control of the Pacific and the "bottling up" of Japan.

166. See, for example, B. C. Clark, *CR*, 23 October 1939, 728; Reynolds, American Forum of the Air, entered in *CR*, 2 May 1940, 5404; Colonel Robert R. McCormick, broadcast of 9 June 1940, in *Addresses*, 6–7; McCormick, "Today the Strongest Nation in the World," *CT*, 13 October 1940, graphic section, 2; Karl von Wiegand, *SFE*, 24 November 1940, 1. While Hearst expressed alarm that half of Hawaii's population was Japanese, he claimed that the islands were well defended against capture. "In the News," *SFE*, 22 February 1941, 1.

167. Downey, *CR*, 6 October 1941, 163; "Mr. Knox Spies a War," *CT*, 27 October 1941, 12.

168. MacLiesh and Reynolds, *Strategy*, 71–74; "A New Base for the Fleet," *NYDN*, 8 July 1940, 19. See also "Snappers-Up of Unconsidered Trifles," *NYDN*, 27 June 1940, 29; "Japan Invites Us Out," 21.

169. "Q & A," *Uncensored* 66 (4 January 1941): 2; Rivers, "Are We Facing War in Asia?" radio speech, 8 October 1940, in *CR*, 6847.

170. Norman Thomas to Toshu Go, 25 September 1939, Thomas Papers. See also comment of E. Stanley Jones, *Peace Action* 7 (October 1941): 4.

171. Wiley, *CR*, 23 January 1940, 542. Wiley also endorsed the proposals of missionary executive A. L. Warnshius, who spoke in terms of reciprocal naval reduction and more advantageous commercial access for Japan. See A. L. Warnshius, "The Way to Peace in East Asia," *Christian Century* 57 (3 January 1940): 11–13.

172. Howard, editorial statement of 30 January 1940, in *CR*, A6033.

173. "The Search for a Lasting Peace, III: The Struggle for Power in the Far East," *Christian Century* 58 (26 February 1941): 280. See also Shaw, "What Should Be Our Policy Toward Japan?" 8.

174. Resolutions, WIL annual meeting, Washington, D.C., 1–4 May 1941, 6, WIL Papers.

175. "A Policy for the Pacific," *New Republic* 101 (22 November 1939): 127. See also "While We Increase Pressure," *New Republic* 102 (22 January 1940): 101; "The War of Nerves in the East," *New Republic* 102 (5 February 1940): 164.

176. See, for example, FOR Council, 20 April 1940, in *Fellowship* 6 (May 1940): 74; Detzer, confidential memorandum to WIL Board, 27 September 1941, WIL Papers; WIL National Board, Swarthmore, Pennsylvania, 18–19 October 1941, 3, WIL Papers; NCPW program, 15 November 1941, *Peace Action* 7 (October 1941): 3.

177. "Japan Treaty Ends—What Now?" *NYDN*, 29 January 1940, 19. It continued that France, because of its ownership of Indochina, could participate. If Japan desired, the trade agreements might be extended to Burma, India, and the Malay states. If Japan refused, the United States could clamp down on Japan's imports.

178. "Couldn't Uncle Sam Mediate?" *NYDN*, 16 September 1940, 21. See also "Prelude to War," *NYDN*, 28 April 1941, 21.

179. "What Next in the Pacific?" *NYDN*, 4 August 1941, 17.

180. Statement of purpose, 9 September 1941; mimeograph letter, O. K. Armstrong to supporters, 4 October 1941; O. K. Armstrong to Frederick J. Libby, 9 October 1941, all in NCPW Papers. On 6 November, Shaw wrote Armstrong, announcing his resignation as acting chairman, claiming lack of time. Mark R. Shaw to O. K. Armstrong, 26 November 1941, NCPW Papers. Members included acting chairman Mark R. Shaw (associate NCPW secretary for the Boston area, former Methodist missionary in Japan); acting secretary O. K. Armstrong (erstwhile organizer for the No Foreign War Committee and the American First Committee); program chairman Elizabeth B. (Mrs. Joseph A.) Schumpeter of Taconic, Connecticut (author, expert on Far Eastern research, and wife of prominent economist); Frederick J. Libby; William J. Baxter; William Henry Chamberlin; Ralph Townsend; Rev. John Cole McKim of Peekskill, New York (for thirty years involved in educational work in Japan); Paul Hutchinson (associate editor of the *Christian Century*); Mrs. Mary Walters Brooks of Gainesville, Florida (former Baptist missionary in Japan); T. T. Brumbaugh of Columbus, Ohio (former missionary to Japan); and Payson Treat (historian, Stanford University). O. K. Armstrong to supporters, 4 October 1941, NCPW Papers. Historian Paul Clyde was also listed as a member.

181. See, for example, "A Legislative Program for the Neutrality Bloc," 19 December 1939, New York City, KAOWC Papers; FOR Council, 20 April 1940, in *Fellowship* 6 (May 1940): 74; Minutes, FOR Council, 29 November 1941, 4, FOR Papers; resolutions, WIL National Board, Swarthmore, Pennsylvania, 18–19 October 1941, WIL Papers; NCPW program, 15 November 1941, *Peace Action* 7 (October 1941): 3. Not all proponents were pacifists. See, for example, Sterling Morton, address, National Small Businessmen's Association of Chicago, 12 December 1940, Morton Papers; Arthur J. May, *This Bewildered Democracy*, 14; "Clipper Trip," *Commonweal* 35 (21 November 1941): 108.

182. Thomas, "Should the U.S. Act Now in Asia?" radio broadcast, WQXR, 27 July 1941, Thomas Papers; Detzer, confidential memorandum to WIL Board, 27 September 1941, WIL Papers; FOR Council, 20 May 1940, in *Fellowship* 6 (May 1940): 74.

## CHAPTER 21: TOWARD THE PACIFIC WAR

1. See, for example, Felix Morley, "The Formula of Federation," *Asia* 40 (June 1940): 291–94; Castle Diary, 29 February 1940.

2. Villard, "Issues and Men: The United States and the War," *Nation* 149 (23 September 1939) 234.

3. "America in the Far East," *CT*, 18 January 1940, 12. See also "Far Eastern Doublecross," *New Masses* 35 (28 June 1940): 22.

4. "Japan on the Ragged Edge," *NYDN*, 4 March 1940, 21. See also "Good News for China," 16 January 1940, 27; "Quarantine Japan Now," 1 February 1940, 27; "Japanese in Swatow," 1 April 1940,

21; "Strange Doings in China," 8 April 1940, 21; "The Japanese Didn't Win," 15 April 1940, 21; "A Broadcast from Chungking," 22 April 1940, 21. "War Weariness in Japan," 27 May 1940, 25.

5. Langer and Gleason, *Challenge to Isolation,* 158. For the text of the agreement between Sir Robert Craigie, British ambassador to Japan, and Arita Hisharo that prompted American concern, see *NYT,* 23 July 1939, 1.

6. "Text of 1911 American-Japanese Treaty," *NYT,* 27 July 1939, 8.

7. *NYT,* 27 July 1939, 1, 8; "Dead Hare, Weeping Fox," *Time,* 7 August 1939, 12.

8. Utley, *Going to War with Japan,* 79; poll, *NYT,* 30 August 1939, 8. The exact ratio was 81:19.

9. Roy Howard to Nelton T. Johnson, 19 January 1940, Box 169, Howard Papers; "Why Not Blockade the Japs?" *NYDN,* 28 August 1939, 19.

10. Dorothy Detzer to Emily Greene Balch, 7 August 1939, WIL Papers.

11. Vandenberg, *NYT,* 27 July 1939, 8; text of Vandenberg resolution, *NYT,* 19 July 1939, 6; Lippmann, "Today and Tomorrow: The Seriousness of the Far Eastern Question," *New York Herald Tribune,* 30 January 1940, 19; Vandenberg, *CR,* 1 February 1940, 886. For Vandenberg's hostility to embargo threats, see *CT,* 7 November 1939, 5.

12. Tompkins, *Vandenberg,* 166. For reiteration of his position, see Vandenberg, *CR,* 9 June 1940, A3691. Conversely, the *Christian Century* opposed concluding a new commercial treaty, claiming that further trade restrictions were needed to check Japanese aggression. See "Appeasement for Japan," *Christian Century* 57 (26 June 1940): 811–12.

13. See, for example, "The War of Nerves in the East," *New Republic* 102 (5 February 1940): 164; Sokolsky, "Japan Moves a Castle," *New York Herald Tribune,* 27 November 1939, 14. Libby, "You Won't Forget Japan," *Peace Action* 6 (December 1939): 1.

14. Maddox, *Borah,* 246; Marian C. McKenna, *Borah* (Ann Arbor: University of Michigan Press, 1961), 367.

15. "Japanese Trade Treaty to Lapse," *CT,* 16 January 1940, 10.

16. Castle Diary, 16 January 1940. For further Castle reaction, see Castle Diary, 24 December 1939 and 12 January 1940; America's Town Meeting of the Air, *New York Herald Tribune,* 15 December 1939; Castle, *NYT,* 15 December 1939, 2.

17. Borchard, speech to Yale alumni, Orange, New Jersey, 27 January 1940, in *CR,* A603. See also memorandum to George Holden Tinkham, 23 December 1939; Edwin M. Borchard to John Bassett Moore, 3 January 1940, Borchard Papers. As late as October 1940, both in Borchard hoped for a general accommodation with Japan that would include a new commercial treaty. Borchard, *United States News,* 25 October 1940, 26.

18. "Friendship with Japan," *SFE,* 2 January 1940, 14.

19. Tansill, "American Policy in the Far East," *Thought: A Review of Culture and Ideas* 15 (March 1940): 39–63 (quotation, 40); Dennis and Gravenhoff, *WFL* 72 (14 December 1939): 2.

20. "Japan and Great Britain," *CT,* 22 January 1940, 12; Burton Roscoe to Quincy Howe, 13 April 1940, Hertzberg Papers; "Charlie McCarthy at Nanking," *New Masses* 25 (9 April 1940): 21. On 28 March, Sir Robert Leslie Craigie had said that Britain and Japan were "ultimately striving for the same objective— namely lasting peace and the preservation of our institutions from extraneous and subversive influences." *NYT,* 29 March 1940, 8. William P. Lage feared that Britain was again making peace with Japan at American expense. Letter to Edwin M. Borchard, 4 April 1940, Borchard Papers.

21. Hull, *NYT,* 31 March 1940, 1, 38.

22. Edwin M. Borchard to T. J. League, 3 April 1940, Borchard Papers. The British did not recognize Wang's government.

23. "Victorious China," *CT,* 1 April 1940, 12.

24. Arita, *NYT,* 16 April 1940, 9; "Hull Statement on the Indies," *NYT,* 18 April 1940, 6; Japan spokesman, *NYT,* 19 April 1940, 6.

25. See, for example, Lundeen, *CR,* 19 April 1940, 4; Hoover cited in entry of 11 June 1940, Journal of Raymond Moley, Moley Papers; "Mr. Roosevelt as the Buckler and Spear," *CT,* 19 April 1940, 16; Amos Pinchot to Karl Bickel, 25 April 1940, Pinchot Papers; Norman Thomas, "Your World and Mine," *Call,* 5 May 1940, 2.

26. Edwin M. Borchard to George Holden Tinkham, 30 April 1940, Borchard Papers. Borchard preferred that the Indies remained under Dutch sovereignty but said that such a condition could not possibly be guaranteed in perpetuity.

27. Fish, *CR*, 18 April 1940, 4747; radio address, 18 April 1940, in *CR*, A2302.

28. "A Cloud Much Larger Than a Man's Hand," *Christian Century* 57 (1 May 1940): 564; Castle Diary, 20 April 1940. See also Castle, "A Monroe Doctrine for Japan," *Atlantic Monthly* 166 (October 1940): 446; Castle, address, Worcester Foreign Policy Association, 14 May 1940, in *CR*, A2300.

29. "Right or Wrong," *NYDN*, 19 April 1940, 29; "The Dutch East Indies Question," *NYDN*, 17 April 1940, 35. See also "Japan and the Dutch East Indies," *NYDN*, 18 May 1940, 21. For more anxiety about war, see Senator Bone, *CR*, 19 April 1940, 4; Libby, "Survey of the International Situation," 22 April 1940, 1, NCPW Papers; Nye, [University of] *Michigan Daily*, 20 April 1940, 1.

30. "Right or Wrong," 29. See also "How to Double the Fleet in a Week," *NYDN*, 4 June 1940, 23. In the bulletin of the New York AFC chapter, some two hundred thousand Dutch were accused of "lording it over" fifty-three million "orientals." See "Peace," issue of 2 August 1941, 2.

31. Close, "Must We Fight Over Dutch Indies?" *Living Age* 358 (June 1940): 322; Flynn, "Other People's Money: Chestnuts, Money and Democracy," *New Republic* 103 (21 October 1940): 556.

32. Livingstone Hartley and Donald C. Blaisdell, "Danger from Drifting," CDAAA, *Washington Office Information Letter* 15 (25 April 1941): 2, Box 35, CDAAA Papers; Close, "Must We Fight Over Dutch Indies?" *Living Age* 358 (June 1940): 323; "War with Japan," *Social Justice*, 29 April 1940, 6.

33. Johnson, "Pacific Trade," *NYWT*, 6 February 1940, 17; Chamberlain, *American Stakes*, 156. See also Flynn, "Other People's Money: Chestnuts, Rubber and Democracy," *New Republic* 103 (20 October 1940): 556; Robert E. Wood, address before Council of Foreign Relations of Chicago, 10 October 1940, in *CR*, A6302; "From Washington," *Uncensored* 34 (25 May 1940): 1; Waldrop, "We Needn't Fight for Tin or Rubber," *WTH*, 17 September 1940, 11; "Would Our Industry Collapse?" *CT*, 11 May 1941, 16; "War in the Pacific?" *NYDN*, 26 July 1941, 13; Taft, *CT*, 26 August 1941, 4; "But Boake Carter Says," *SFE*, 7 February 1941, 11; *Social Justice*, 10 February 1941, 4; memo, W. R. Castle to F. J. Hall (response to Hall's letter to Castle, 24 February 1941) n.d., Castle Papers; Brooks Emeny, testimony, HFAC, 23 January 1941, 469; Burton K. Wheeler to Norman Thomas, 7 August 1941, Thomas Papers.

34. "The New Order in Asia," *NYDN*, 5 August 1940, 19; "A War on Two Fronts?" 12 June 1940, 31; "'How to Double the Fleet in a Week,'" 4 June 1940, 23. See also "Japan," 17 June 1940, 21; "Asia for the Asiatics," 19 August 1940, 19.

35. Wood, address before Council of Foreign Relations of Chicago, 10 October 1940, in *CR*, A6302; Downey, CR, 9 October 1939, 171; MacLiesh and Reynolds, *Strategy*, 21; "An Appeal from Japan," *Christian Century* 58 (17 September 1941): 1135; Johnson, *SFN*, 2 July 1940, 13; Chamberlain, *American Stakes*, 180. For use of MacLiesh and Reynolds, see "Nobody Knows the Trouble We're In," *Did You Know?* 12 (24 July 1941), in Doenecke, *IDU,* 361. The AFC also cited "Synthetic Rubber," *Fortune* 22 (August 1940): 70–71, 112–20.

36. "International Finance Breaks Down," *Social Justice*, 4 August 1941, 3. For similar stress on U.S. dependence on outside rubber, see Flynn, *SFN*, 25 February 1941, 15.

37. For claims that the United States could manufacture its own tin, see Downey, *CR*, 9 October 1939, 170–71; "But Boake Carter Says," *SFE*, 26 February 1941, 13; Clevenger, *CR*, 3 September 1940, 11,383. For claims that the United States could provide substitutes for both tin and rubber, see Norman Thomas, "Should the U.S. Act Now in Asia?" broadcast, station WQXR, 27 July 1941, Thomas Papers; "Tin and Rubber," *CT*, 24 November 1940, 14.

38. Hugh Johnson, "Anchors Away," *Saturday Evening Post* 213 (5 October 1940): 78. See also Waldrop, "We Needn't Fight for Tin or Rubber," *WTH*, 17 September 1940, 11.

39. MacLiesh and Reynolds, *Strategy*, 27; *Social Justice*, 13 August 1940, 4. For similar stress on U.S. dependence on outside tin, see Flynn, *SFN*, 25 February 1941, 15.

40. *NYT*, 26 July 1940, 1, 7. For the private dissent of Sumner Welles, see Ickes, entry of 27 July 1940, *Secret Diary*, 3:273.

41. "Text of the Decision," *NYT*, 21 December 1939, 1, 10.

42. See, for example, "Shall the 'Moral Embargo' Be Made Legal?" *Christian Century* 57 (10 January 1940): 36; Fish, *CR*, 23 April 1940, 4898.

43. See, for example, Chamberlin Diary, 26 July 1940; Wheeler, *CR*, 8 August 1940, 10,129; Herbert Hoover to John C. O'Laughlin, 5 August 1940, Stanford Files.

44. "A Two Ocean War for a One Ocean Fleet," *CT*, 29 July 1940, 10. In June 1940, it called for settlement with Japan, followed by moving the navy into the Atlantic. "It's Time to Think of America," 18 June 1940, 12. See also Colonel McCormick, broadcast of 9 June 1940, in *Addresses*, 7.

45. Edwin M. Borchard to John Bassett Moore, 26 July 1940, Borchard Papers; "Japan Marches on," *NYDN*, 12 August 1940, 19; Castle Diary, 2 August 1940. For Castle's endorsement of a firmer stand against Japan, see Castle Diary, 8 November 1940.

46. "No More Aviation Gas for Japan," *Christian Century* 57 (14 August 1940): 988; "No Embargo," *New Masses* 36 (6 August 1940): 16. The communist weekly endorsed a "real" embargo on scrap iron, which—it said—should be coupled with major economic and financial assistance to China. "No Embargo Yet," *New Masses* 36 (17 September 1940): 17. See also "Wang Humbug," 35 (2 April 1940): 20; "No Embargo," 36 (6 August 1940): 16.

47. Dallek, *Roosevelt*, 240–41; Langer and Gleason, *Undeclared War*, 21.

48. For Roosevelt's continued linkage of American oil and the Dutch East Indies, see Franklin D. Roosevelt to Eleanor Roosevelt, 13 November 1940, *F.D.R.: His Personal Letters*, 1007; Roosevelt to Harold L. Ickes, 23 June 1941, 1173; Ickes, entry of 24 December 1939, *Secret Diary*, 3:96; 11 February 1940, 132; 8 September 1940, 314; 1 December 1940, 388.

49. Reynolds, *Creation*, 137; Chihiro Hosoya, "Miscalculations in Deterrent Policy: Japanese-U.S. Relations," *Journal of Peace Research* 5 (1968): 97–115.

50. Reynolds, *Creation*, 135.

51. Dorothy Detzer to Hannah Clothier Hull and Emily Greene Balch, 21 August 1940, WIL Papers. Detzer also claimed that Britain had withdrawn its marines from Shanghai without giving "ten minutes notice" to the United States. Though Britain consulted the United States over the Burma Road matter, the United States did not approve. *Challenge to Isolation*, 719–20.

52. Edwin M. Borchard to Eugene Davidson, 17 July 1940, Borchard Papers; Castle, "A Monroe Doctrine for Japan," *Atlantic Monthly* 166 (October 1940): 447; "A Two Ocean War for a One Ocean Fleet," 10.

53. "Mr. Roosevelt's Wars on Order," *CT*, 25 October 1940, 12. For similar sentiments, see Tinkham, *CR*, 14 October 1940, 6324A.

54. Lincoln Colcord to Amos Pinchot, 19 October 1940, Pinchot Papers. See also Lincoln Colcord to Wendell Willkie, 9 October 1940, copy in Pinchot Papers.

55. Wheeler, *CR*, 25 February 1941, 1367.

56. For Berle's apprehension, see entry of 11 October 1940, *Navigating*, 343.

57. For Churchill's bid, see Churchill to Roosevelt, 4 October 1940, in Kimball, *Churchill and Roosevelt*, 74. For the opposition of the U.S. military, see Maurice Matloff and Edwin M. Snell, *Strategic Planning for Coalition Warfare* (Washington, D.C.: Department of the Army, 1953), 34–38. See also Leutze, *Bargaining*, 166; Marshall, *Papers*, 2:327, 410; Stark, "Memorandum for the Secretary," 12 November 1940, in Ross, *American War Plans*, 3:240.

58. Hull, *Memoirs*, 1:897.

59. Stimson quoted in Langer and Gleason, *Undeclared War*, 21.

60. See, for example, *Social Justice*, 30 September 1940, 3.

61. "Toward War in Asia," *CT*, 27 September 1940, 14. See also "Mr. Roosevelt Arranges a Crisis," 9 October 1940, 10.

62. "The Alliance Against America," *CT*, 28 September 1940, 10; "Still Jabbing Japan," *NYDN*, 9 September 1941, 21. See also "Stumblebum Diplomacy Here," *NYDN*, 24 July 1940, 21; "Our Far Eastern Policy," 9 December 1940, 31; "What'll We Do with Siberia?" 29 September 1941, 21.

63. William R. Castle to R. Douglas Stuart Jr., 9 December 1940, Box 282, AFC Papers. See also Castle Diary, 26 September 1940; William R. Castle to R. Douglas Stuart Jr., 7 December 1940, Box 282, AFC Papers.

64. See, for example, "A War on Two Fronts," *NYDN*, 25 September 1940, 33; "For Whom Are Saving Indo-China?" *NYDN*, 27 September 1940, 37; Flynn, "Other People's Money: Chestnuts, Money and Empire," *New Republic* 103 (21 October 1940): 556; "War with Japan—For What?" *CT*, 26 July 1941, 6; "Mr. Knox Spies a War?" *CT*, 27 October 1941, 12.

65. Sargent, Bulletin #95, 30 December 1940, *Getting US into War*, 553–54; "But Boake Carter Says," *Chicago Herald-American*, 7 February 1941.

66. Kimball, *Juggler*, 152–53.

67. Roosevelt quoted in "Text of Tri-Power Accord," *NYT*, 28 September 1940, 3.

68. Franklin D. Roosevelt to Joseph C. Grew, 21 January 1941, in Joseph C. Grew, *Ten Years in Japan: A Contemporary Record Drawn from the Diaries and Private and Official Papers of Joseph C. Grew* (New York: Simon & Schuster, 1944), 361. See also Roosevelt to Francis B. Sayre, 31 December 1940, *F.D.R.: His Personal Letters*, 1093–95.

69. Moley, "Perspective: The New Axis," *Newsweek*, 7 October 1940, 64. For earlier anxieties concerning war with Japan, see Moley, "Perspective: "Must We Fight Japan?" 22 July 1940, 60.

70. See, for example, Frederick J. Libby to Philip H. Gray, 27 September 1941, NCPW Papers; Merwin K. Hart, testimony, SFRC, 8 February 1941, 749; Charles A. Lindbergh, "Impregnable America," address at Yale University, in *Scribner's Commentator* 9 (January 1941): 4; "Peace and U.S.," *CT*, 19 October 1940, 2; Nye, *CT*, 28 September 1940, 1; Fish, *CR*, 1 October 1940, 12,944. See also the more interventionist Breckinridge Long, entry of 28 September 1940, *War Diary*, 133.

71. "A Pact Against America," *Christian Century* 57 (9 October 1940): 1238–39; Villard, "Our Wrecked Japanese Policy," *Christian Century* 57 (4 December 1940): 1509; Dennis, *WFL* 113 (25 September 1940): 3.

72. Borchard, memos to T.R. Armstrong, 3 and 10 October 1940, Borchard Papers. Yet he still hoped for an agreement with Japan that would include a new commercial treaty. *United States News*, 25 October 1940, 26.

73. Wesley Winans Stout to R. Douglas Stuart Jr., 30 September 1940, Box 289, AFC Papers; Baldwin, *United We Stand!* 71–72.

74. See, for example, Norman Thomas to Hartley Cross, 4 October 1940, Thomas Papers; Hiram Johnson and Nye in *Newsweek*, 21 October 1940, 14; "Mr. Roosevelt Arranges a Crisis," *CT*, 9 October 1940, 10; "Wars 'On Order,'" *CT*, 15 October 1940, 14; "Registering for What?" *CT*, 16 October 1940, 16; Upton Close, speech to Institute of Arts and Sciences, *Columbia* [University] *Spectator*, 27 November 1940, 1; "But Boake Carter Says," *SFE*, 11 November 1940, 7; "Is Japan Quitting China?" *NYDN*, 4 November 1940, 35; "Whither Japan?" *NYDN*, 18 November 1940, 23.

75. Dennis, *WFL* 114 (3 October 1940): 4. For predictions of a Japanese strike on British and Dutch possessions, see *WFL* 120 (14 November 1940): 1.

76. "Is It an Election Crisis in the Far East?" *Christian Century* 57 (16 October 1940): 1267.

77. Hoover in Castle Diary, 2 October 1940. See also Nye and Bennett Clark, *CT*, 28 September 1940, 1. For interventionist concurrence, see Breckinridge Long, entry of 11 February 1941, *Wartime Diary*, 177.

78. William R. Castle to F. J. Hall, 2 October 1940, Castle Papers. See also debate with Adolf A. Berle, *PM*, 25 October 1940, 7.

79. Castle Diary, 2 October and 8 November 1940; William R. Castle to F. J. Hall, 1 October 1940, Castle Papers. See also Castle Diary, 18 October 1940.

80. See, for example, Hugh Johnson, "One Man's Opinion," *SFN*, 30 September 1940, 13; Edwin C. Johnson, "Hate War, My Countrymen," radio address, 5 October 1940, in *CR*, A6244.

81. Wheeler, *CT*, 28 September 1940, 1; Rivers, "Are We Facing War in Asia?" 8 October 1940, radio speech, station WQSR, in *CR*, A6848.

82. "Japan Invites Us Out," *NYDN*, 7 October 1940, 21. For accusations of U.S. provocation, see also "Have We a Far East Policy?" 25 December 1940, 23; "Nomura Talks Sense," 2 December 1940, 25; "What the President Didn't Say," 2 June 1940, 25. For earlier anxieties, see "How to Double the Fleet in a Week," 4 June 1940, 23.

83. Hearst, "In the News," *SFE*, 30 September 1940, 1. See also Hearst, *SFE*, 7 February 1941, 2.

84. Harold E. Fey, "Scapegoat for Stalemate," *Christian Century* 57 (11 December 1940): 1554; Dennis, *WFL* 120 (14 November 1940): 1.

85. Akira Iriye, "U.S. Policy Toward Japan Before World War II," in *Pearl Harbor Reexamined: Prologue to the Pacific War,* ed. Hilary Conroy and Harry Wray (Honolulu: University of Hawaii Press, 1990), 23–24.

86. Gallup poll, 30 September 1940, in Cantril, *Public Opinion,* 775.

87. The exact figures were 49.4 percent in favor, 24.2 percent opposed, and 26.4 precent having no opinion. Cantril, *Public Opinion,* 1076. For related polls, see 1076–77.

88. *Fortune* poll, October 1941, Cantril, *Public Opinion,* 1162.

89. For examples of apprehension over growing tension, see Felix Morley to Robert E. Wood, 4 January 1941, Morley Papers; Robert E. Wood, speech, Mutual, *SFE,* 8 July 1941, 2; William Henry Chamberlin, review of Claude Buss, *War and Diplomacy in Eastern Asia* (New York: Macmillan, 1941) in *NYT Book Review,* 13 July 1941, 6.

90. Castle Diary, 26 January 1941. In February, he said the same thing to Nomura himself. Though he was hopeful of peace, he always found the Japanese army doing "something stupid." Castle Diary, 18 February 1941. See also entry of 9 March 1941.

91. *Social Justice,* 27 January 1941, 9; "But Boake Carter Says," *Chicago Herald-American,* 25 February 1941; Dennis, *WFL* 134 (20 February 1941): 1, 2. Dennis soon claimed that Roosevelt sought to stop Japan if it moved southward from Indochina, although he doubted whether the American general staff had any plans for hindering a Japanese invasion. *WFL* 135 (27 February 1941): 5. See also *WFL* 146 (15 May 1941): 4.

92. Poll of 27 February 1941, Cantril, *Public Opinion,* 975; general report, Washington Office, AFC, 21 February 1941, in Doenecke, *IDU,* 449. See also AFC *Washington Newsletter* 8 (21 March 1941), Box 281, AFC Papers; AFC *Washington Newsletter* 11 (29 April 1941): 3, Box 284, AFC Papers; AFC manual cited in Stenehjem, *American First,* 113.

93. Sayre, report, 15 December 1940–25 March 1941, FOR Papers.

94. See, for example, Sokolsky, *Brown* [University] *Daily Herald,* 21 March 1941, 4; Herbert Hoover to William J. Gross, 7 April 1941, Hoover Papers; "Pacific Picture," *Uncensored* 89 (14 June 1941): 2–3; Ruth Sarles to R. Douglas Stuart Jr., 31 May 1941, Box 67, AFC Papers; Ruth Sarles to Kendrick Lee, 7 June 1941, Box 67, AFC Papers; Sarles to R. Douglas Stuart Jr., 3 July 1941, in Doenecke, *IDU,* 133; "Part of the Axis Is Sprung," *CT,* 25 July 1941, 8.

95. "But Boake Carter Says," *SFE,* 19 April 1941, 7.

96. Hearst, "In the News," *SFE,* 17 April 1941, A. See also Fish, *CR,* 14 April 1941, 3084. For anxieties concerning any Japanese-Soviet rapprochement, see Castle Diary, 18 November 1939; Sargent, Bulletin #85, 30 December 1940, *Getting US into War,* 541.

97. For early fears, see "Crisis in the Orient," *New Masses* 38 (25 February 1941): 18.

98. "Eastern Munich?" *U.S. Week,* 7 June 1941, 7; "Mr. Hull's Gesture," *New Masses* 39 (10 June 1941): 20.

99. *Social Justice,* 23 June 1941, 5; Dennis, *WFL* 155 (17 July 1941): 1.

100. Baldwin, *United We Stand!* 72–73; Baldwin, "Blueprint for Victory," *Life,* 4 August 1941, 30.

101. "Text of Welles's Statement on Japan," *NYT,* 25 July 1941, 5; Roosevelt, "Freezing Statement's Text," *NYT,* 26 July 1941, 5; Langer and Gleason, *Undeclared War,* 708. For the argument that Roosevelt's mid-level bureaucrats levied sanctions of far greater scope that the president intended, see Utley, *Going to War with Japan,* 151–56. For a challenge to Utley's position, see Heinrichs, *Threshold,* 246–47 n. 68; Waldo Heinrichs, "Franklin D. Roosevelt and the Risks of War," in *American, Chinese, and Japanese Perspectives on Wartime Asia, 1931–1939,* 164.

102. Livingstone Hartley, "Far East," CDAAA, *Washington Office Information Letter* 28 (24 July 1941): 4. See also Hartley, "Action to Halt Japan" and "The Freezing Order," *Washington Office Information Letter* 29 (1 August 1941): 1–3, Box 35, CDAAA Papers.

103. Harrington, "Careless Hope," 221; Gallup poll, 29 July 1941, in Cantril, *Public Opinion,* 1077. For similar polls, see 1168. For government survey, see White, *FDR and the Press,* 85.

104. "More Stick," *Commonweal* 34 (15 August 1941): 388; Thomas, "Should the U.S. Act Now in Asia?" address over World Peaceways Forum, WQXR, 27 July 1941, Thomas Papers. See also Norman

Thomas to Burton K. Wheeler, 25 August 1941, Thomas Papers; Ira Bennett, special correspondent for McClure's syndicate, unpub. ms., forwarded by William R. Castle to AFC offices, 26 August 1941, Box 63, AFC Papers.

105. "Two-Faced Role in East Mocks '4 Freedom' Talk," *Call*, 2 August 1941, 1; George Stern, "Japan's Next Southward Move Would Bring War," *Militant*, 2 August 1941, 6.

106. See, for example, "War with Japan—For What?" *CT*, 26 July 1941, 6; "Mr. Knox Spies a War?" *CT*, 27 October 1941, 12.

107. "AFC Hits Welles on Indo China," *AFC New York Chapter Bulletin*, 2 August 1941, 1. The executive committee was composed of John T. Flynn, Edwin S. Webster Jr., Adelaide (Mrs. John P.) Marquand, Amos Pinchot, and investment banker H. Dudley Swim. Castle claimed to understand why the Japanese compared their occupation of Indochina bases to the U.S. expedition to Iceland. Castle Diary, 3 October 1941.

108. "Peace," *AFC New York Chapter Bulletin*, 2 August 1941, 1–2. See also Fish, *NYT*, 11 August 1941, 3.

109. Edwin M. Borchard to Eugene Davidson, 28 July 1941, Borchard Papers.

110. Castle Diary, 24 July 1941; "Fighting for Food," *NYDN*, 15 October 1941, 33.

111. "War with Japan—For What?" *CT*, 26 July 1941, 6.

112. See, for example, Castle Diary, 26 and 28 July 1941. Anti-interventionists long had had anxieties concerning U.S. involvement over Singapore, particularly the possibility of sending the American fleet there. See, for example, Dennis, *WFL* 112 (19 September 1940): 1; "Asia's War Moves Southward," *Christian Century* 57 (2 October 1940): 1196; William C. Rivers, "Are We Facing War in Asia?" radio address, station WQSR, 8 October 1940, in *CR*, A6847; George Holden Tinkham to Edwin M. Borchard, 11 December 1940, Borchard Papers; *Social Justice*, 9 December 1940, 9; "Yunnan-Hainan-Singapore," *NYDN*, 11 November 1940, 23; "But Boake Carter Says," *SFE*, 7 February 1941, 11; Frederick J. Libby, "Are We Bluffing—or Aren't We?" *Peace Action* 7 (February 1941): 2; physiologist Anton J. Carlson, *CT*, 22 February 1941, 4; Capper, Tinkham, Castle, and Sayre in *United States News*, 7 March 1941, 26–27; Villard, "Watch Singapore," *Progressive*, 22 March 1941, 5; WIL annual meeting, Washington, D.C., 1–4 May 1941, WIL Papers.

113. Hartley, "Singapore" (leaflet; New York: CDAAA, 1941), Box 36, CDAAA Papers; Livingstone Hartley and Donald C. Blaisdell, "Danger from Drifting," CDAAA, *Washington Office Information Letter* 15 (25 April 1941): 2, Box 35, CDAAA Papers.

114. Hearst, "In the News," *SFE*, 4 August 1941, 1; "Trade as Usual," *Call*, 9 August 1941, 4; Dennis, *WFL* 157 (31 July 1941): 2–3. See also 158 (7 August 1941): 3. Dennis was soon accusing Britain and the United States of attempting "to goad Japan into a war of desperation or to force her into a suicidal peace." His evidence included their encouragement of militancy within China and the Netherlands East Indies and the closing of the Panama Canal, the latter move in violation of treaty obligations. Dennis, *WFL* 160 (21 August 1941): 2.

115. "What Next in the Pacific?" *NYDN*, 4 August 1941, 17.

116. Hull, *NYT*, 7 August 1941, 1, 6; "Resident to Renew Plan for A.E.F. to Dakar," *AFC New York Chapter Bulletin*, 16 August 1941, 3; Chester Bowles to R. Douglas Stuart Jr., 8 August 1941, Box 59, AFC Papers. See also Villard, "Those False 'Menaces,'" *Progressive*, 23 August 1941, 8; Ruth Sarles to R. Douglas Stuart Jr., 9 August 1941, in Doenecke, *IDU*, 135. For an expression of earlier alarm, see "Peace," *AFC New York Chapter Bulletin*, 2 August 1941, 2.

117. *Call*, 23 August 1941, 1; Wheeler, *CT*, 26 August 1941, 1; *SFE*, 28 August 1941, 8; *NYT*, 28 August 1941, 3. Wheeler had first approved of Roosevelt's freezing order, saying, "I think it will slow up Japan from an economic standpoint and call their bluff so they will not start anything." Wheeler, *CT*, 27 July 1941, 3.

118. Ruth Sarles to R. Douglas Stuart Jr., 15 August 1941, in Doenecke, *IDU*, 313; Hearst, "In the News," *Social Justice*, 28 August 1941, 1; AFC executive committee in Cole, *America First*, 192.

119. Reynolds, *Creation*, 23; poll of 5 August 1941, in Cantril, *Public Opinion*, 975.

120. Livingstone Hartley and Frank S. Goodwin, "United Front in the Pacific," CDAAA, *Washington Office Information Letter* 34 (5 September 1941): 2, Box 35, CDAAA Papers.

121. See, for example, R. Douglas Stuart Jr. to William R. Castle, 5 August 1941, Box 63, AFC Papers; John T. Flynn in Stenehjem, *American First*, 113–14; Fred Burdick, general letters, 26 and 29 Au-

gust 1941, Box 65, AFC Papers; "War Movement in U.S. Wanes as Soviet Defeat Looms," *AFC New York Chapter Bulletin*, 6 September 1941, 3; Ruth Sarles to R. Douglas Stuart Jr., 3 October 1941, Box 285, AFC Papers. For pessimistic views, see "International Finance Breaks Down," *Social Justice*, 4 August 1941, 3; Harold E. Fey, "Do We Want Peace with Japan?" *Christian Century* 58 (1 October 1941): 1196.

122. Frederick J. Libby to Mr. and Mrs. Philip H. Gray Jr., 2 September 1941, NCPW Papers; "Peace in the Orient," *Uncensored* 102 (13 September 1941): 1–2; "How Many Wars?" *CT*, 21 September 1941, 16; "Negotiations with Japan Offer a New Hope," *Christian Century* 58 (3 September 1941): 1069. See also "President Roosevelt and Prince Konoye Negotiate," *Christian Century* 58 (10 September 1941): 1099. The Protestant journal did express concern when Japan threatened Thailand, for the United States would find its seizure a menace to Singapore, which in turn threatened Malaya and the Netherlands East Indies. That move endangered "white Australia." "An Appeal from Japan," *Christian Century* 57 (17 September 1941): 1135.

123. Fish and Vorys, "What Should Be U.S. Policy Toward Japan?" *American Forum of the Air* 3 (10 August 1941): 5–6, 8, 13–14.

124. Herbert Hoover to John C. O'Laughlin, 30 August and 6 September 1941, Hoover Institution; Hoover to William R. Castle, 4 September 1941, Castle Papers. For Desvernine effort, see Smith, *Hoover*, 304–5.

125. "Do We Want Peace with Japan?" *Christian Century* 58 (1 October 1941): 1196; Dennis, *WFL* 164 (18 September 1941): 4.

126. Concerning the Dutch East Indies, one found 39.9 percent in favor of defense, 29.1 percent opposed, and 31 percent in the "don't know" column. For Singapore, the respective figures were 34.6 percent, 33.0 percent, and 32.4 percent; Burma Road, 29.8 percent, 37.1 percent, and 33.1 percent; Thailand, 28.4 percent, 36.8 percent, and 34.8 percent. See Cantril, *Public Opinion*, 783.

127. See, for example, Congressman Knute Hill, *CR*, 13 November 1941, 8857.

128. Diary entry, 17 October 1941, Flynn Papers; Lincoln Colcord to Edwin M. Borchard, 16 October 1941, Borchard Papers; "Mr. Knox Spies a War," *CT*, 27 October 1941, 12. The *Chicago Tribune* cited its Washington correspondent, Arthur Sears Henning, who reported that Japan had offered considerable concessions to FDR, including close to total withdrawal from China, ending further moves toward British and Dutch possessions in the East Indies, abandoning the Axis alliance, and pledging not to interfere with U.S. shipments to Russia via Vladivostok. In return, Japan sought mutual rescinding of the freezing orders, restoration of normal trade, and probably recognition of the Manchurian conquest. Supposedly, according to Henning, the matter of the Chinese air bases wrecked the negotiations.

129. See, for example, Albert W. Palmer, president of Chicago Theological Seminary, testimony, SFRC, 22 October 1941, 89; "Drumming Up a War in the Pacific," *Christian Century* 58 (25 October 1941): 1325.

130. Dennis, *WFL* 169 (23 October 1941): 5; Herbert Hoover to John C. O'Laughlin, 19 October 1941, Stanford Files.

131. Resolutions, WIL National Board, Swarthmore, Pennsylvania, 18–19 October 1941, 3, WIL Papers; NCPW program, 15 November 1941, in *Peace Action* 7 (October 1941): 3; Fey, "Reconciliation with Japan," *Fellowship* 7 (September 1941): 148–49. In somewhat the same spirit, Libby expressed birthday greetings to Hirohito. Frederick J. Libby to Admiral Nomura Kichisaburo, 3 November 1941, NCPW Papers.

132. U.S. Department of State, *Papers Relating to the Foreign Relations of the United States: Japan: 1931–1941*, 2 vols. (Washington, D.C.: Government Printing Office, 1943), 2:709–10, 715–17.

133. State, *Foreign Relations: Japan*, 2:755–56; Langer and Gleason, *Undeclared War*, 284–85.

134. See, for example, Wheeler, *NYT*, 17 October 1941, 8; 19 October 1941, 10; 20 November 1941, 10; John T. Flynn to Robert E. Wood, 11 November 1941, Box 55, AFC Papers.

135. "Fight Germany *and* Japan?" *NYDN*, 17 November 1941, 23. For further calls for peace, see "An Alliance with Japan?" *NYDN*, 19 November 1941, 23; "Come On—Let's Appease Japan," 24 November 1941, 21.

136. See, for example, "Whose War with Japan?" *CT*, 18 November 1941, 14; "The Crisis with Japan," *CT*, 2 December 1941, 14; "One Chance in Ten," *Christian Century* 58 (19 November 1941): 1432–34; "But Boake Carter Says," *SFE*, 18 November 1941, sect. 2, 5.

137. Nye, *NYT*, 21 November 1941, 5; Robert A. Taft to Norman Thomas [copy], 24 November 1941, KAOWC Papers. On 11 November, Taft claimed to have learned that the administration had rejected Japan's proposals for a settlement. Their terms included the maintenance of Japanese garrisons in five major Chinese cities as possible places from which to attack Vladivostok. *NYT*, 12 November 1941, 8. At that point he backed the administration.

138. Dennis, *WFL* 172 (13 November 1941): 3. See also 174 (27 November 1941): 3.

139. U.S. Department of State, *Papers Relating to the Foreign Relations of the United States, 1941*, vol. 4: *The Far East* (Washington, D.C.: Government Printing Office, 1956), 661–64.

140. State, *Foreign Relations: Japan*, 2:768–70; *NYT*, 27 November 1941, 1.

141. See, for example, Lincoln Colcord to Edwin M. Borchard, 26 November 1941, Borchard Papers; "East Meets West," *Uncensored* 113 (29 November 1941): 1–3. According to *Uncensored*, Hull proposed that Japan would maintain neutrality in the Nazi-Soviet war, leave the Axis, guarantee free passage of munitions from Vladivostok, and withdraw from Indochina, Thailand, and China. Once Japan accepted these terms, the United States would lift the commercial blockade, unfreeze credits, help finance Japan's shift to a peacetime economy, and guarantee Japanese markets in the United States, Latin America, and the Far East.

142. Minutes, FOR National Council, 29 November 1941, 3–4, FOR Papers; Dennis, *WFL* 175 (4 December 1941): 1–2; Burdick, general letter to AFC, 4 December 1941, in Doenecke, *IDU*, 438–39. On 4 December, the *Chicago Tribune* and the *Washington Times-Herald* published war department contingency plans that involved the drafting of ten million men, a joint U.S.-British invasion by 1 July 1943, and a five-million man AEF assigned to 215 divisions. See 1, 10.

143. Mallon, "The News Behind the News," *SFE*, 22 November 1941, 7; Rizley in Fred Burdick, general report to AFC, 2 December 1941, in Doenecke, *IDU*, 452. See also "War Medicine Everywhere," *NYDN*, 5 December 1941, 39; "War with Japan? Who Says So?" *CT*, 29 November 1941, 12.

144. See, for example, "Let's Let Congress In on the War," *NYDN*, 2 December 1941, 29; Taft in Fred Burdick, general letter to AFC, 3 December 1941, in Doenecke, *IDU*, 452–53; Hearst, "In the News," *SFE*, 3 December 1941, A. The Gallup poll of 25 November 1941 showed 52 percent predicting war with Japan in the near future, 27 percent opposing the proposition, and 21 percent having no opinion. Cantril, *Public Opinion*, 975.

145. Herbert Hoover to Alf Landon, 29 November 1941, Hoover Papers; Burdick, general letter, 2 December 1941, in Doenecke, *IDU*, 451. Among those endorsing a mail campaign were Woodruff, Johns, and Pheiffer. See also Taft and Keefe in Burdick, general letter, 3 December 1941, in Doenecke, *IDU*, 453.

146. For Mundt, see Doenecke, *IDU*, 153. For Ludlow, see Burdick, general letter, 3 December 1941, in Doenecke, *IDU*, 452–53. Ruth Sarles promoted a resolution calling on the president to inform the SFRC on U.S. policy. See letter to R. Douglas Stuart Jr., 6 December 1941, in Doenecke, *IDU*, 440.

147. J. Garry Clifford and Robert Griffiths, "Reflections upon an Ante–World War II Letter: John A. Danaher and United States Intervention in World War II," *Connecticut History* 23 (April 1982): 52; Castle Diary, 1 December 1941; Lambertson, *CR*, 1 December 1941, 9255. See also Lambertson in Burdick, general letter, 2 December 1941, in Doenecke, *IDU*, 451; Lambertson, *CR*, 4 December 1941, 9449; 5 December 1941, 9480.

148. "The Far Eastern Crisis," *Christian Century* 58 (10 December 1941): 1531. See also "When Negotiators Rattle the Sword," *Christian Century* 58 (3 December 1941): 1493.

149. *AFC New York Chapter Bulletin*, 6 December 1941, 1.

150. Raymond A. Esthus, "President Roosevelt's Commitment to Britain to Intervene in a Pacific War," *Mississippi Valley Historical Review* 50 (June 1963): 28–38; Reynolds, *Creation*, 246; Gilbert, *Churchill*, 1263; Kimball, *Forged in War*, 119.

151. See, for example, "Crisis in Japan," *America* 66 (25 October 1941): 71; Bender, *CR*, 13 November 1941, A5183; Wiley, *CR*, 30 October 1941, 8346; Mundt in Ruth Sarles to R. Douglas Stuart Jr., 6 December 1941, Box 284, AFC Papers; Castle, letter to editor, *New York Herald Tribune*, 7 December 1941; "But Boake Carter Says," *SFE*, 18 November 1941, sect. 2, 5; "U.S.-Japan War," *NYDN*, 3 December 1941, 39; Edwin M. Borchard to John Bassett Moore, 2 December 1941, Borchard Papers.

152. Herbert Hoover to John C. O'Laughlin, 19 October 1941, Stanford Files; Wiley, *CR*, 30 Octo-

ber 1941, 8343. See also "Must We Fight Germany *and* Japan?" *NYDN*, 1 December 1941, 27; Amos Pinchot to William R. Castle, 5 August 1941, Castle Papers.

153. Colcord, testimony, SFRC, 24 October 1941, 225. See also Hearst, "In the News," *SFE*, 30 November 1941, A.

154. Long, entry of 14 September 1940, *War Diary*, 129; Berle, entry of 29 September 1940, *Navigating*, 340. See also Berle, entries of 7 July 1940, *Navigating*, 328; 27 September 1940, 338.

155. Utley, *Going to War with Japan*, 89–93.

156. Marshall and Stark to Roosevelt, 27 November 1941, in U.S. Senate and House of Representatives, *Pearl Harbor Attack: Hearings and Report*, 14 vols. (Washington, D.C.: Government Printing Office, 1946), 14:1083. For Stark's earlier apprehension, see Stark, "Memorandum for the Secretary," 12 November 1940, in Ross, *American War Plans*, 3:238, 240.

157. See, for example, Dennis, *WFL* 176 (11 December 1941): 1; AFC statement in Cole, *America First*, 193; "Comment," *America* 66 (13 December 1941): 254; "Cabbages and Kings," *Scribner's Commentator* 11 (January 1942): 3; Hoover, *Time*, 15 December 1941, 17; "We All Have Only One Task," *CT*, 8 December 1941, 1.

158. Wheeler, *NYT*, 8 December 1941, 6; Burton K. Wheeler to John T. Flynn, 22 December 1941, Box 20, Flynn Papers.

159. "An Unnecessary Necessity," *Christian Century* 58 (17 December 1941): 1565; John A. Danaher to Edwin M. Borchard, 9 December 1941, Borchard Papers; "Well, We're in It," *NYDN*, 8 December 1941, 31. See also Lindbergh, entry of 8 December 1941, *Wartime Journals*, 561.

160. See, for example, Hiram W. Johnson to Hiram W. Johnson Jr., 13 November 1941, Johnson Papers; Charles Callan Tansill, "The United States and Japan, 1854–1941," *Thought: A Review of Culture and Ideas* 17 (March 1942): 104; "Our Country! In Her Intercourse with Foreign Nations May She Always Be in the Right; but Our Country, Right or Wrong," *NYDN*, 9 December 1941, 37.

161. Sterling Morton to Robert E. Wood, 8 December 1941, Morton Papers; Robert E. Wood to Otto Case, 31 March 1941, Wood Papers; Norman Thomas to Maynard Krueger, 11 December 1941, Thomas Papers.

162. "Japan's Perfidy United the American People," *CT*, 9 December 1941, 1; W. R. Castle to R. Douglas Stuart Jr., 8 December 1941, in Doenecke, *IDU*, 454; Hearst, "In the News," *SFE*, 8 December 1941, 1.

163. Libby, "Our Task and Yours," *Peace Action* 8 (December 1941): 1; Villard, "The Japanese Infamy," *Progressive*, 20 December 1941, 8; John Haynes Holmes to Henry Hitt Crane, 18 December 1941, Holmes Papers. See also John Nevin Sayre, "Japan Attacks Us," *Fellowship* 8 (January 1942): 4.

164. National Action Committee, "Socialist Statement on War," *Call*, 20 December 1941, 1.

165. See, for example, Herbert Hoover to Boake Carter, 11 December 1941, Hoover Papers; "We're at War!" *Social Justice*, 15 December 1941, 3.

166. Minutes, AFC National Committee, 11 December 1941, in Doenecke, *IDU*, 469. For claims that America First's cause was just, see Burton K. Wheeler to Robert E. Wood, 22 December 1941, Box 55, AFC Papers; Samuel Pettengill to Robert E. Wood, 12 December 1941, Box 55, AFC Papers.

167. Minutes, executive committee, KAOWC, 8 December 1941, KAOWC Papers; Chester Bowles to John T. Flynn, 22 December 1941, Flynn Papers. See also Karl Mundt to Hanford MacNider, 23 December 1941, MacNider Papers.

168. Amos Pinchot to Art Young, 30 December 1941, Pinchot Papers; "Cabbages and Kings," *Scribner's Commentator* 11 (January 1942): 3.

169. Moley, "Unity in War," *Newsweek*, 15 December 1941, 84; Sokolsky, "These Days: It Is Better So," *New York Sun*, 11 December 1941, 30; Detzer to WIL branches, 8 December 1941, WIL Papers; Vandenberg, diary entry of 8 December 1941, *Private Papers*, 17; Robert E. Wood to Otto Case, 31 March 1941, Wood Papers. See also Lincoln Colcord to Edwin M. Borchard, 9 December 1941, Borchard Papers; Edwin M. Borchard to Lincoln Colcord, 12 December 1941, Borchard Papers; Dennis, *WFL* 179 (2 January 1942): 1.

170. See, for example, Francis Neilson, entry of 12 December 1941, *Tragedy*, 3:12.

171. John A. Danaher to Edwin M. Borchard, 18 December 1941, Borchard Papers; Lindbergh, entry of 8 December 1941, *Wartime Journals*, 560; Herbert Hoover to William R. Castle, 8 December

1941, Castle Papers; Herbert Hoover to Frank R. McCoy, 17 December 1941, Hoover Papers. Technically the 26 November message was not an ultimatum, for no deadline was set, it presented options to Japan, and it was not phrased in such a way as to present a final offer. Norman Hill, "Was There an Ultimatum Before Pearl Harbor?" *American Journal of International Law* 42 (April 1948): 355–67; Hans L. Trefousse, *Pearl Harbor: The Continuing Controversy* (Malibar, Fla.: Krieger, 1982), 35.

172.  Libby, "Our Task and Yours," *Peace Action* 8 (December 1941): 1; "An Unnecessary Necessity," 1565–66; "The Course Before Us," statement of FOR executive committee, 10 December 1941, *Fellowship* 8 (January 1942): 2. See also Sayre, "Japan Attacks Us," 4.

173.  Herbert Hoover to James B. Howell, 26 December 1941, Hoover Papers; William R. Castle to R. Douglas Stuart Jr., 8 December 1941, in Doenecke, *IDU,* 454; Hearst, "In the News," *SFE,* 8 December 1941, 1.

174.  Minutes, AFC National Committee, 11 December 1941, in Doenecke, *IDU,* 469; Frederick J. Libby to Philip Bernstein, 18 December 1941, NCPW Papers; Dorothy Detzer to WIL branches, 8 December 1941, WIL Papers; "The War," *Commonweal* 35 (19 December 1941): 212.

175.  Robert E. Wood to Charles A. Lindbergh, 3 January 1942, Wood Papers; Robert E. McCormick to Robert E. Wood, 2 January 1942, Wood Papers; "Hawaii Investigation," *NYDN,* 11 December 1941, 39. See also "How Did It Happen?" *NYDN,* 10 December 1941, 39.

176.  Dennis, *WFL* 176 (11 December 1941): 2.

177.  Edwin M. Borchard to John A. Danaher, 12 December 1941, Borchard Papers; Herbert Hoover to Frank R. McCoy, 17 December 1941, Hoover Papers. See also Hoover to John C. O'Laughlin, 31 December 1941, Stanford Files.

## CONCLUSION

1.  Wayne S. Cole, "What Might Have Been," *Chronicles* 15 (December 1991): 22.

2.  Elmer Davis, "The War and America," *Harper's Magazine* 180 (April 1940): 458.

3.  Beals, *Pan America,* 157.

4.  Short, *CR,* 5 February 1941, 600.

5.  Macdonald, editorial reply to Stephen Spender, *Partisan Review* 7 (September–October 1940): 407.

6.  Vandenberg, *CR,* 4 October 1939, 97.

7.  John Bassett Moore to Edwin M. Borchard, 6 December 1939, Borchard Papers.

8.  Waldrop, "Child Eating Mother?" *WTH,* 28 September 1941, E1.

9.  Charles Callan Tansill, *Back Door to War: The Roosevelt Foreign Policy, 1933–1941* (Chicago: Regnery, 1952).

10.  *CT,* 1 February 1941, 1, 12; "Why They Are Sore at Their Lindbergh," *Daily Worker,* 21 May 1940, 6. For typical communist reaction to mainline anti-intervention, see Carl Harris, "'America First,' White Committee Alike Under Skin," *Daily Worker,* 26 December 1940, 5; "Col. Lindbergh—An Imperialist in Robes of Peace," *Daily Worker,* 25 April 1941, 6; "The APM Mobilization," *New Masses* 38 (31 December 1940): 19.

11.  Justus D. Doenecke, "Rehearsal for Cold War: United States Anti-Interventionists and the Soviet Union, 1939–1941," *International Journal of Politics, Culture, and Society* 7 (Spring 1994): 375–92; Doenecke, *Not to the Swift: The Old Isolationists in the Cold War Era* (Lewisburg, Pa.: Bucknell University Press, 1979).

12.  Doenecke, *IDU,* 49.

13.  Islands-for-war-debts, *NYT,* 12 November 1939, 2285; negotiated peace, *NYT,* 10 March 1940, 27; lend-lease, Cantril, *Public Opinion,* 409–10.

14.  Norman Thomas to Maynard Krueger, 11 December 1941, Thomas Papers; John Haynes Holmes to John T. Flynn, 16 January 1942, Flynn Papers; Anne Morrow Lindbergh, entry of 9 December 1941, *War Within,* 242 (emphasis in original).

# Bibliography

## MANUSCRIPTS

Materials of the America First Committee, Firestone Library, Princeton University, Princeton, New Jersey

The Papers of the America First Committee, Hoover Institution on War, Revolution and Peace, Stanford, California

The Papers of Harry Elmer Barnes, University of Wyoming, Laramie, Wyoming

The Papers of Alfred M. Bingham, Yale University, New Haven, Connecticut

The Papers of Edwin M. Borchard, Yale University, New Haven, Connecticut

The Diary of William R. Castle, Houghton Library, Harvard University, Cambridge, Massachusetts

The Papers of William R. Castle, Herbert Hoover Presidential Library, West Branch, Iowa

The Diary of William Henry Chamberlin, Providence College, Providence, Rhode Island

The Papers of Edmond D. Coblentz, University of California, Berkeley, California

The Papers of the Committee to Defend America by Aiding the Allies, Princeton University, Princeton, New Jersey

The Papers of Lawrence Dennis, Hoover Institution on War, Revolution and Peace, Stanford, California

The Papers of John Foster Dulles, Princeton University, Princeton, New Jersey

The Papers of the Federal Bureau of Investigation, J. Edgar Hoover Building, Washington, D.C.

The Papers of the Fellowship of Reconciliation, Swarthmore College Peace Collection, Swarthmore, Pennsylvania

The Papers of the Fight for Freedom Committee, Princeton University, Princeton, New Jersey

The Papers of John T. Flynn, University of Oregon Library, Eugene, Oregon
The Papers of Jerome Frank, Yale University Library, New Haven, Connecticut
The Papers of Frank Gannett, Cornell University, Ithaca, New York
The Papers of Sidney Hertzberg, New York Public Library, New York, New York
The Papers of John Haynes Holmes, Library of Congress, Washington, D.C.
The Correspondence of Herbert Hoover and John C. O'Laughlin, Hoover Institution on War, Revolution and Peace, Stanford, California
The Papers of Herbert Hoover, Herbert Hoover Presidential Library, West Branch, Iowa
The Papers of Roy W. Howard, Library of Congress, Washington, D.C.
The Papers of Philip C. Jessup, Library of Congress, Washington, D.C.
The Papers of Hiram W. Johnson, University of California, Berkeley, California
The Papers of the Keep America Out of War Congress, Swarthmore College Peace Collection, Swarthmore, Pennsylvania
The Papers of Philip La Follette, Wisconsin Historical Society, Madison, Wisconsin
The Papers of Ernest Lundeen, Hoover Institution on War, Revolution and Peace, Stanford, California
The Papers of Hanford MacNider, Herbert Hoover Presidential Library, West Branch, Iowa
The Papers of Verne Marshall, Herbert Hoover Presidential Library, West Branch, Iowa
The Papers of Raymond Moley, Hoover Institution on War, Revolution, and Peace, Stanford, California
The Papers of John Bassett Moore, Library of Congress, Washington, D.C.
The Diary of Felix Morley, Herbert Hoover Presidential Library, West Branch, Iowa
The Papers of Felix Morley, Herbert Hoover Presidential Library, West Branch, Iowa
The Papers of Sterling Morton, Chicago Historical Society, Chicago, Illinois
The Papers of the National Committee for the Prevention of War, Swarthmore College Peace Collection, Swarthmore, Pennsylvania
The Papers of the National Committee on Food for the Small Democracies, Hoover Institution on War, Revolution and Peace, Stanford, California
The Papers of Samuel B. Pettengill, University of Oregon, Eugene, Oregon
The Papers of Amos Pinchot, Library of Congress, Washington, D.C.
The Papers of Franklin D. Roosevelt, Roosevelt Presidential Library, Hyde Park, New York
The Papers of the Socialist Party (microfilm version), Hoover Institution on War, Revolution and Peace, Stanford, California
The Papers of Robert A. Taft, Library of Congress, Washington, D.C.
The Papers of Norman Thomas, New York Public Library, New York, New York
The Papers of Freda Utley, Hoover Institution on War, Revolution and Peace, Stanford, California
The Papers of Oswald Garrison Villard, Harvard University, Cambridge, Massachusetts
The Papers of the Women's International League for Peace and Freedom, American Section, Swarthmore College Peace Collection, Swarthmore, Pennsylvania
The Papers of Robert E. Wood Papers, Herbert Hoover Presidential Library, West Branch, Iowa

## U.S. GOVERNMENT DOCUMENTS

*Congressional Record.*

Department of State. *Papers Relating to the Foreign Relations of the United States, 1939,* vol. 1: *General.* Washington, D.C.: Government Printing Office, 1956.

——. *Papers Relating to the Foreign Relations of the United States, 1940,* vol. 1: *General.* Washington, D.C.: Government Printing Office, 1959.

——. *Papers Relating to the Foreign Relations of the United States: 1941,* vol. 4: *The Far East.* Washington, D.C.: Government Printing Office, 1956.

——. *Papers Relating to the Foreign Relations of the United States: Japan: 1931–1941,* vol. 2. Washington, D.C.: Government Printing Office, 1943.

House of Representatives. Committee on Foreign Affairs. *Arming American Merchant Vessels.* Washington, D.C.: Government Printing Office, 1941.

——. *Lend-Lease Bill.* Washington, D.C.: Government Printing Office, 1941.

House of Representatives. Committee on Military Affairs Washington. *Remove Restrictions on National Defense.* Washington, D.C.: Government Printing Office, 1941.

Senate Committee on Foreign Relations. *Modification of Neutrality Act of 1939.* Washington, D.C.: Government Printing Office, 1941.

——. *To Promote the Defense of the United States.* Washington, D.C.: Government Printing Office, 1941.

Senate and House of Representatives. Joint Committee on the Investigation of the Pearl Harbor Attack. *Pearl Harbor Attack: Hearings and Report,* vol. 14. Washington, D.C.: Government Printing Office, 1946.


## PUBLISHED DIARIES, JOURNALS, MEMOIRS, AND DOCUMENTS

Ameringer, Oscar. *If You Don't Weaken: The Autobiography of Oscar Ameringer.* New York: Holt, 1940.

Berle, Beatrice Bishop, and Travis Beal Jacobs, eds. *Navigating the Rapids, 1918–1971: From the Papers of Adolf A. Berle.* New York: Harcourt Brace Jovanovich, 1973.

Bilainkin, George. *Diary of a Diplomatic Correspondent.* London: Allen & Unwin, 1942.

Bland, Larry, ed. *The Papers of George Catlett Marshall.* Vol. 2, *"We Cannot Delay": July 1, 1939–December 6, 1941.* Baltimore: Johns Hopkins University Press, 1986.

Bliven, Bruce. *Five Million Words Later: An Autobiography.* New York: Day, 1970.

Blum, John Morton. *From the Morgenthau Diaries.* Vol. 2, *Years of Urgency, 1938–1941.* Boston: Houghton Mifflin, 1965.

Bullitt, Orville H., ed. *For the President, Personal and Secret: Correspondence Between Franklin D. Roosevelt and William C. Bullitt.* Boston: Houghton Mifflin, 1972.

Chamberlin, William Henry. *Confessions of an Individualist.* New York: Macmillan, 1940.

Chatfield, Charles, and Charles DeBenedetti, eds. *Kirby Page and the Social Gospel: An Anthology.* New York: Garland, 1976.

Detzer, Dorothy. *Appointment on the Hill.* New York: Holt, 1948.

Dodd, William E. *Ambassador Dodd's Diary, 1933–1938.* New York: Harcourt Brace, 1941.

Doenecke, Justus D., ed. *In Danger Undaunted: The Anti-Interventionist Movement of 1940–1941 as Revealed in the Papers of the America First Committee.* Stanford, Calif.: Hoover Institution Press, 1990.

Eggleston, George T. *Roosevelt, Churchill, and the World War II Opposition: A Revisionist Autobiography.* Old Greenwich, Conn.: Devin-Adair, 1979.

Farley, James A. *Jim Farley's Story: The Roosevelt Years.* New York: Whittlesey House, 1948.

Fey, Harold E., ed. *Kirby Page, Social Evangelist: The Autobiography of a Twentieth-Century Prophet for Peace.* Nyack, N.Y.: Fellowship, 1975.

Fish, Hamilton. *FDR: The Other Side of the Coin.* New York: Vantage, 1976.

———. *Memoir of an American Patriot.* Washington, D.C.: Regnery Gateway, 1991.

*The German White Paper: Full Text of the Polish Documents Issued by the Berlin Foreign Office.* New York: Howell, Soskin, 1940.

Grew, Joseph C. *Ten Years in Japan: A Contemporary Record Drawn from the Diaries and Private and Official Papers of Joseph C. Grew.* New York: Simon & Schuster, 1944.

Gronowicz, Anthony, ed. *Oswald Garrison Villard: The Dilemma of the Absolute Pacifist in Two World Wars.* New York: Garland, 1983.

Harriman, W. Averell, and Elie Abel. *Special Envoy to Churchill and Stalin, 1941–1946.* New York: Random House, 1975.

Hessen, Robert, ed. *Berlin Alert: The Memoirs and Reports of Truman Smith.* Stanford, Calif.: Hoover Institution Press, 1984.

Holmes, John Haynes. *I Speak for Myself.* New York: Harper, 1959.

Hooker, Nancy Harvison, ed. *The Moffat Papers: Selections from the Diplomatic Journals of Jay Pierrepont Moffat, 1919–1943.* Cambridge, Mass.: Harvard University Press, 1956.

Hoover, Herbert. *Addresses on the American Road, 1940–1941.* New York: Scribner's, 1941.

———. *An American Epoch.* Vol. 4, *The Guns Cease Killing and the Saving of Life from Famine Begins, 1939–1963.* Chicago: Regnery, 1964.

———. *Further Addresses upon the American Road, 1938–1940.* New York: Scribner's, 1940.

Hull, Cordell. *The Memoirs of Cordell Hull.* 2 vols. New York: Macmillan, 1948.

Ickes, Harold L. *The Secret Diary of Harold L. Ickes.* Vol. 2, *The Inside Struggle, 1936–1939;* Vol. 3: *The Lowering Clouds, 1939–1941.* New York: Simon & Schuster, 1954.

Israel, Fred L., ed. *The War Diary of Breckinridge Long: Selections from the Years 1939–1944.* Lincoln: University of Nebraska Press, 1966.

Jacobsen, Hans-Adolf, and Arthur L. Smith Jr., eds. *World War II Policy and Strategy: Selected Documents with Commentary.* Santa Barbara, Calif.: ABC-Clio, 1979.

Johnson, Donald Bruce, comp. *National Party Platforms.* Vol. 2. Urbana: University of Illinois Press, 1978.

Johnson, Walter, ed. *Selected Letters of William Allen White.* New York: Holt, 1947.

Jones, S. Shepard, and Denys P. Myers, eds. *Documents on American Foreign Relations: July 1939–June 1940.* Vol. 2. Boston: World Peace Foundation, 1940.

Kimball, Warren F., ed. *Churchill and Roosevelt: The Complete Correspondence.* Vol. 1, *Alliance Emerging, October 1933–November 1942.* Princeton, N.J.: Princeton University Press, 1984.

Lerski, George J., comp. *Herbert Hoover and Poland: A Documentary History of a Friendship.* Stanford, Calif.: Hoover Institution Press, 1977.

Leutze, James, ed. *The London Journal of General Raymond E. Lee, 1940–1941.* Boston: Little, Brown, 1971.

Libby, Frederick J. *To End War: The Story of the National Council for the Prevention of War.* New York: Fellowship Publications, 1969.

Lindbergh, Anne Morrow. *The Flower and the Nettle: Diaries and Letters, 1936–1939.* New York: Harcourt Brace Jovanovich, 1976.

———. *War Within and Without: Diaries and Letters, 1939–1944.* New York: Harcourt Brace Jovanovich, 1980.

Lindbergh, Charles A. *Wartime Journals of Charles A. Lindbergh.* New York: Harcourt Brace Jovanovich, 1970.

McAdoo, William G. *Crowded Years: The Reminiscences of William G. McAdoo.* Boston: Houghton Mifflin, 1931.

Morley, Felix. *For the Record.* South Bend, Ind.: Regnery Gateway, 1979.

Neilson, Francis. *The Tragedy of Europe: A Day-to-Day Commentary of the Second World War.* 5 vols. Appleton, Wis.: C. C. Nelson, 1940–1946.

Noakes, Jeremy, and Geoffrey Pridham, eds. *Documents on Nazism, 1919–1945.* New York: Viking, 1974.

Pepper, Claude Denson, with Hays Gorey. *Eyewitness to a Century.* New York: Harcourt Brace Jovanovich, 1987.

Roosevelt, Elliott, ed. *F.D.R.: His Personal Letters, 1928–1945.* New York: Duell, Sloan & Pearce, 1950.

Rosenman, Samuel I., comp. *The Public Papers and Addresses of Franklin D. Roosevelt.* Vol. 8, *War—and Neutrality, 1939.* Vol. 9, *War—and Aid to Democracies, 1940.* Vol. 10, *The Call to Battle Stations, 1941.* New York: Random House, 1950.

Ross, Steven T., ed. *American War Plans, 1919–1941.* Vol. 3, *Plans to Meet the Axis Threat, 1939–1940.* Vol. 4, *Coalition War Plans and Hemispheric Defense Plans, 1940–1941.* Vol. 5, *Plans for Global War: Rainbow Five and the Victory Program.* New York: Garland, 1992.

Seldes, George. *Never Tired of Protesting.* New York: Stuart, 1968.

Stettinius, Edward R., Jr. *Lend-Lease: Weapon for Victory.* New York: Macmillan, 1944.

Straight, Michael. *After Long Silence.* New York: Norton, 1983.

Utley, Freda. *Odyssey of a Liberal: Memoirs.* Washington, D.C.: Washington National Press, 1970.

Vandenberg, Arthur H., Jr., ed. *The Private Papers of Senator Vandenberg.* Boston: Houghton Mifflin, 1952.

Wedemeyer, Albert. *Wedemeyer Reports!* New York: Holt, 1958.

Wheeler, Burton K., with Paul F. Healy. *Yankee from the West.* Garden City, N.Y.: Doubleday, 1962.

## NEWSPAPERS

*Baltimore Sun*
*Boston Globe*
*Boston Post*
*Cedar Rapids Gazette*
*Chicago Herald-American*
*Chicago Tribune*
*Christian Science Monitor*

*Daily Telegram* [London]
*Daily Worker* [New York]
*Detroit Free Press*
*Idaho Daily Statesman*
*Los Angeles Evening Herald and Express*
*Miami Daily Herald*
*New York Daily News*
*New York Enquirer*
*New York Herald Tribune*
*New York Journal-American*
*New York Sun*
*New York Times*
*New York World-Telegram*
*Philadelphia Evening Ledger*
*Philadelphia Inquirer*
*PM*
*St. Louis Globe-Democrat*
*St. Louis Post-Dispatch*
*San Francisco Examiner*
*San Francisco News*
*Times* [London]
*Washington Daily News*
*Washington Evening Star*
*Washington Post*
*Washington Times-Herald*

## COLLEGE NEWSPAPERS

*Amherst* [College] *Student*
*Barnard* [College] *Bulletin*
*Brooklyn College Vanguard*
*Brown* [University] *Daily Herald*
[Bryn Mawr] *College News*
[City College of New York] *Campus*
[City College of New York] *Main Events*
[Clark University] *Scarlet*
*Columbia* [University] *Spectator*
*Cornell* [University] *Daily Sun*
[Dartmouth College] *The Dartmouth*
[Georgetown University] *Hoya*
[George Washington University] *Hatchet*
*Harvard* [University] *Crimson*
*Haverford* [College] *News*
*Johns Hopkins* [University] *Newsletter*
*Mt. Holyoke* [College] *News*
[New York University] *Heights Daily News*

[New York University] *Washington Square College Bulletin*
[Northwestern University] *Daily Northwestern*
[Northwestern University] *Summer Northwestern News Magazine*
[Princeton University] *Daily Princetonian*
*Smith College Associated News*
*Smith College Weekly*
*Stanford* [University] *Daily*
[University of California, Berkeley] *Daily Californian*
[University of] *California* [Los Angeles] *Daily Bruin*
[University of Chicago] *Daily Maroon*
[University of] *Michigan Daily*
[University of North Carolina] *Daily Tar Heel*
[University of Rochester] *Tower Times*
[University of Wisconsin] *Daily Cardinal*
*Vassar* [College] *Miscellany News*
*Wesleyan* [University] *Argus*
*Williams* [College] *Record*
*Yale* [University] *Daily News*

## CONTEMPORARY PERIODICALS

*America*
*American Forum of the Air*
*American Guardian*
*American Journal of International Law*
*American Mercury*
*Annals of the American Academy of Political and Social Science*
*Army Ordnance*
*Asia*
*Atlantic Monthly*
*Call*
*Catholic Digest*
*Catholic World*
*Christian Century*
*Collier's*
*Common Sense*
*Commonweal*
*Communist*
*Congressional Digest*
*Current History*
*Current History and Forum*
*Events: The Monthly Review of World Affairs*
*Fellowship*
*Fortune*
*Forum*
*Friday*

*Harper's Magazine*
*In Fact*
*Iron Age*
*Labor*
*Life*
*Living Age*
*Look*
*Militant*
*Modern Quarterly*
*Nation*
*Nation's Business*
*New International*
*New Masses*
*New Republic*
*Newsweek*
*Our Sunday Visitor*
*Partisan Review*
*Peace Action*
*Progressive*
*Propaganda Analysis*
*Public Opinion Quarterly*
*Reader's Digest*
*Rotarian*
*Saturday Evening Post*
*Saturday Review of Literature*
*Scribner's Commentator*
*Scribner's Magazine*
*Socialist Appeal*
*Social Justice*
*Southern Economic Journal*
*Steuben News*
*Survey Graphic*
*Thought: A Review of Culture and Ideas*
*Time*
*Times* [London] *Literary Supplement*
*Uncensored*
*United States News*
U.S. Naval Institute *Proceedings*
*US Week*
*Unity*
*Virginia Quarterly Review*
*Vital Speeches*
*Weekly Foreign Letter*
*Yale Review*

## CONTEMPORARY BOOKS AND PAMPHLETS

Allhoff, Fred. *Lighting in the Night.* Englewood Cliffs, N.J.: Prentice Hall, 1979.

Alsop, Joseph, and Robert Kintner. *American White Paper.* New York: Simon & Schuster, 1940.

Baldwin, Hanson. *United We Stand!: Defense of the Western Hemisphere.* New York: McGraw-Hill, 1941.

Barnes, J. S. *Fascism.* New York: Holt, 1931.

Baxter, William J. *Japan and America Must Work Together!* New York: International Economic Research Bureau, 1940.

Beale, Howard K. *Some Fallacies of the Interventionist View.* Pamphlet. Washington, D.C.: author, 1941.

Beals, Carleton. *Pan America: A Program for the Western Hemisphere.* Boston: Houghton Mifflin, 1940.

Beard, Charles A. *A Foreign Policy for America.* New York: Knopf, 1940.

———. *Giddy Minds and Foreign Quarrels: An Estimate of American Foreign Policy.* New York: Macmillan, 1939.

Bingham, Alfred M. *Insurgent America: Revolt of the Middle-Classes.* New York: Harper, 1935.

———. *The United States of Europe.* New York: Duell, Sloan & Pearce, 1940.

Block, Maxine, ed. *Current Biography.* Annual. New York: Wilson, 1941–44.

Bryant, Arthur. *Unfinished Victory.* London: Macmillan, 1940.

Buell, Raymond Leslie. *Isolated America.* New York: Knopf, 1940.

Burnham, James. *The Managerial Revolution.* New York: Day, 1941.

Buss, Claude. *War and Diplomacy in Eastern Asia.* New York: Macmillan, 1941.

Candee, Marjorie Dent, ed. *Current Biography.* Annual. New York: Wilson, 1957.

Carter, Boake. *Why Meddle in Europe? Facts, Figures, Fictions and Follies.* New York: McBride, 1939.

Carter, Boake, and Thomas H. Healy. *Why Meddle in the Orient? Facts, Figures, Fictions and Follies.* New York: Dodge, 1938.

Chamberlain, John. *The American Stakes.* Philadelphia: Lippincott, 1940.

Chamberlin, William Henry. *The World's Iron Age.* New York: Macmillan, 1942.

de Chambrun, René. *I Saw France Fall: Will She Rise Again?* New York: Morrow, 1940.

Chase, Stuart, and Marian Tyler. *The New Western Front.* New York: Harcourt Brace, 1939.

Cherne, Leo. *Adjusting Your Business to War.* New York: Tax Research Institute, 1939.

Churchill, Winston. *The Aftermath.* New York: Scribner's, 1929.

Cromwell, James H. R. *In Defense of Capitalism.* New York: Scribner's, 1937.

———. *The Voice of Young America.* New York: Scribner's, 1933.

Cudahy, John. *The Armies March: A Personal Report.* New York: Scribner's, 1941.

Day, Stephen. *We Must Save the Republic: A Brief for the Declaration of Independence and the Constitution of the United States.* Washington, D.C.: Shaw, 1941.

Dennis, Lawrence. *The Coming American Fascism.* New York: Harper, 1936.

———. *The Dynamics of War and Revolution.* New York: Weekly Foreign Letter, 1940.

Dreiser, Theodore. *America Is Worth Saving.* New York: Modern Age Books, 1941.

Engelbrecht, H. C., and Frank Hanighen. *Merchants of Death: A Study of the International Armament Industry.* New York: Dodd, Mead, 1934.

Fish, Hamilton. *The Red Plotters.* New York: Domestic and Foreign Affairs Publishers, 1947.

Flynn, John T. *Country Squire in the White House.* New York: Doubleday, Doran, 1940.

Frank, Jerome. *Save America First: How to Make Our Democracy Work.* New York: Harper, 1938.

Fuller, J. F. C. *Towards Armageddon: The Defence Problem and I.* London: Dickson, 1937.

Grattan, C. Hartley. *The Deadly Parallel.* New York: Stackpole, 1939.

Hallgren, Mauritz A. *The Tragic Fallacy: A Study of America's War Policies.* New York: Knopf, 1937.

Hamilton, James Burr [George Sylvester Viereck]. "Lord Lothian versus Lord Lothian." Pamphlet. Scotch Plains, N.J.: Flanders Hall, 1941.

Howard, Graeme. *America and a New World Order.* New York: Scribner's, 1940.

Jessup, Philip C. *Neutrality: Its History, Economic and Law.* Vol. 4, *Today and Tomorrow.* New York: Columbia University Press, 1936.

Jessup, Philip C., and Francis Deák. *Neutrality: Its History, Economic and Law.* Vol. 1, *Its Origins.* New York: Columbia University Press, 1935.

Johnson, Hugh S. *Hell-Bent for War.* Indianapolis: Bobbs-Merrill, 1941.

Johnson, J. Percy, ed. *Directory of Newspapers and Publications.* Annual. Philadelphia: Ayer, 1940–44.

Leeds, Stanton B. *These Rule France: The Story of Edouard Daladier and the Men Around Daladier.* Indianapolis: Bobbs-Merrill, 1940.

Lenin, V. I. *Imperialism: The Highest Stage of Capitalism.* New rev. ed. New York: International Publishers, 1939.

Lewis, Cleona. *Nazi Germany and World Trade.* Washington, D.C.: Brookings Institution, 1941.

Lindbergh, Anne Morrow. *The Wave of the Future: A Confession of Faith.* New York: Harcourt Brace, 1940.

Lindbergh, Charles A. *The Radio Addresses of Col. Charles A. Lindbergh, 1939–1940.* Pamphlet. New York: Scribner's Commentator, 1940.

Lloyd, George Ambrose. *The British Case.* New York: Macmillan, 1940.

MacLiesh, Fleming, and Cushman Reynolds. *Strategy of the Americas.* New York: Duell, Sloan & Pearce, 1941.

Markham, Reuben H. *The Wave of the Past.* Chapel Hill: University of North Carolina Press, 1941.

May, Arthur J. *This Bewildered Democracy: Reflections on American Foreign Policy.* Pamphlet. Rochester, N.Y.: privately printed, 1941.

McCormick, Robert R. *Addresses by Colonel Robert R. McCormick.* Chicago: WGN, 1940.

Miller, Douglas. *You Can't Do Business with Hitler.* Boston: Little, Brown, 1941.

Millis, Walter. *Road to War: America, 1914–1917.* Boston: Houghton Mifflin, 1935.

Morrison, Charles Clayton. *The Outlawry of War.* Chicago: Willett, Clark & Colby, 1927.

Morton, Sterling. *Let's Think This Matter Through.* Pamphlet. Chicago: privately published, ca. 1941.

Muste, A. J. *Nonviolence in an Aggressive World.* New York: Harper, 1940.

Nehru, Jawaharlal. *Toward Freedom.* New York: John Day, 1941.

Nixon, Larry, ed. *What Will Happen and What to Do When War Comes.* New York: Greystone, 1939.

Page, Kirby. *How to Keep America Out of War.* Pamphlet. Philadelphia: American Friends Service Committee, et al., 1939.

Patterson, Jean Rushmore. *Letter to Anne Lindbergh.* Pamphlet. New York: Lenox Hill, 1940.

Payne, George Henry. *England: Her Treatment of America.* New York: Sears, 1931.

Rauschning, Hermann. *The Revolution of Nihilism.* Garden City, N.Y.: Garden City, 1939.

——. *The Voice of Destruction.* New York: Putnam, 1940.

Reed, Douglas. *A Prophet at Home.* London: Cape, 1941.

Reid, Doris Fielding, and Nancy Schoonmaker, eds. *We Testify.* New York: Smith & Durrell, 1941.

Rogerson, Sidney. *Propaganda and the Next War.* London: Bles, 1938.

Rothe, Anna, ed. *Current Biography.* Annual. New York: Wilson, 1950.

Salter, Arthur. *Security: Can We Retrieve It?* London: Macmillan, 1939.

Sargent, Porter. *Getting US into War.* Boston: Porter Sargent, 1941.

Schoonmaker, Edwin D. *Democracy and World Dominion.* New York: Smith, 1939.

Seldes, George. *Iron, Blood, and Profits: An Exposure of the World-Wide Munitions Racket.* New York: Harper, 1934.

Simone, André. *J'Accuse! The Men Who Betrayed France.* New York: Dial, 1940.

Stefansson, Vilhjalmur. *Iceland: The First American Republic.* New York: Doubleday, Doran, 1939.

Stein, Rose M. *M-Day: The First Day of War.* New York: Harcourt, Brace, 1936.

Stolper, Gustav. *German Economy, 1870–1940: Issues and Trends.* New York: Reynal & Hitchcock, 1940.

Streit, Clarence K. *Union Now with Britain.* New York: Harper, 1941.

Thomas, Norman. *We Have a Future.* Princeton, N.J.: Princeton University Press, 1941.

Thomas, Norman, and Bertram D. Wolfe. *Keep America Out of War: A Program.* New York: Stokes, 1939.

Townsend, Ralph. *America Has No Enemies in Asia!* Pamphlet. San Francisco: the author, 1938.

——. *Does Japan Slam the Door Against American Trade in Areas of Japanese Influence in China?* Pamphlet. San Francisco: privately printed, 1938.

——. *Seeking Foreign Trouble.* Pamphlet. San Francisco: privately printed, 1940.

Trumbo, Dalton. *Johnny Got His Gun.* Philadelphia: Stuart, 1939.

——. *The Remarkable Andrew, Being the Chronicle of a Literal Man.* Philadelphia: Lippincott, 1941.

Utley, Freda. *The Dream We Lost: Soviet Russia Then and Now.* New York: Day, 1940.

——. *Lost Illusion.* Philadelphia: Fireside Press, 1948.

Van Loon, Hendrick. *Invasion.* New York: Harcourt Brace, 1940.

Van Paassen, Pierre. *Days of Our Years.* New York: Hillman-Curl, 1939.

Villard, Oswald Garrison. *Our Military Chaos.* New York: Knopf, 1939.

——. *Within Germany.* New York: Appleton-Century-Crofts, 1940.

Williams, Al. *Airpower.* New York: Coward-McCann, 1940.

Welles, Sumner. *The Time for Decision.* New York: Harper, 1944.

## BOOKS (SECONDARY SOURCES)

Ashmore, Harry S. *Unseasonable Truths: The Life of Robert Maynard Hutchins.* Boston: Little, Brown, 1989.

Bailey, Thomas A., and Paul B. Ryan. *Hitler vs. Roosevelt: The Undeclared Naval War.* New York: Free Press, 1979.

Bell, Daniel, ed. *The Radical Right.* Garden City, N.Y.: Doubleday, 1963.

Bell, P. M. H. *The Origins of the Second World War in Europe.* London: Longman, 1986.

Berg, A. Scott. *Lindbergh.* New York: Putnam's, 1998.

Beschloss, Michael J. *Kennedy and Roosevelt: The Uneasy Alliance.* New York: Norton, 1980.

Best, Gary Dean. *Herbert Hoover: The Postpresidential Years, 1933–1964.* 2 vols. Stanford, Calif.: Hoover Institution Press, 1983.

Beyer, Barry K. *Thomas E. Dewey, 1937–1947: A Study in Political Leadership.* New York: Garland, 1979.

Black, C. E., and E. C. Helmreich. *Twentieth-Century Europe.* 3d ed. New York: Knopf, 1966.

Blumenthal, Henry. *Illusion and Reality in Franco-American Diplomacy, 1914–1945.* Baton Rouge: Louisiana State University Press, 1986.

Boyle, Peter G. *American-Soviet Relations: From the Russian Revolution to the Fall of Communism.* New York: Routledge, 1993.

Brinkley, Alan. *The End of Reform: New Deal Liberalism in Recession and War.* New York: Knopf, 1995.

Britton, John A. *Carleton Beals: A Radical Journalist in Latin America.* Albuquerque: University of New Mexico, 1987.

Brown, Anthony Cave. *The Last Hero: Wild Bill Donovan.* New York: Times Books, 1982.

Brownell, Will, and Richard N. Billings. *So Close to Greatness: A Biography of William C. Bullitt.* New York: Macmillan, 1987.

Buell, Thomas B. *Master of Sea Power: A Biography of Fleet Admiral Ernest J. King.* Boston: Little, Brown, 1980.

Bullock, Alan. *Hitler and Stalin: Parallel Lives.* New York: Knopf, 1992.

Burns, James MacGregor. *Roosevelt: The Lion and the Fox.* New York: Harcourt Brace, 1956.

———. *Roosevelt: The Soldier of Freedom.* New York: Harcourt Brace Jovanovich, 1970.

Cantril, Hadley and Mildred Strunk. *Public Opinion, 1935–1946.* Princeton, N.J.: Princeton University Press, 1951.

Carlisle, Rodney P. *Hearst and the New Deal: The Progressive as Reactionary.* New York: Garland, 1979.

Castle, Alfred L. *Diplomatic Realism: William R. Castle, Jr., and American Foreign Policy, 1919–1953.* Honolulu: Samuel N. and Mary Castle Foundation, 1998.

Chadwin, Mark Lincoln. *The Hawks of World War II.* Chapel Hill: University of North Carolina Press, 1968.

Charmley, John. *Churchill, The End of Glory: A Political Biography.* New York: Harcourt Brace, 1993.

Chatfield, Charles. *For Peace and Justice: Pacifism in America, 1914–1941.* Knoxville: University of Tennessee Press, 1971.

Clifford, J. Garry, and Samuel R. Spencer Jr. *The First Peacetime Draft.* Lawrence: University Press of Kansas, 1986.

Cohen, Robert. *When the Old Left Was Young: Student Radicals and the First Mass Student Movement, 1929–1941*. New York: Oxford University Press, 1994.

Cohen, Warren I. *The Chinese Connection: Roger S. Greene, Thomas W. Lamont, and George E. Sokolsky and American–East Asian Relations*. New York: Columbia University Press, 1978.

Cole, Wayne S. *America First: The Battle Against Intervention, 1940–1941*. Madison: University of Wisconsin Press, 1953.

———. *Charles A. Lindbergh and the Battle Against American Intervention in World War I*. New York: Harcourt Brace Jovanovich, 1974.

———. *Gerald P. Nye and American Foreign Relations*. Minneapolis: University of Minnesota Press, 1962.

———. *Roosevelt and the Isolationists, 1932–1945*. Lincoln: University of Nebraska Press, 1983.

Conn, Stetson, and Byron Fairchild. *The Framework of Hemisphere Defense*. Washington, D.C.: Department of the Army, 1960.

Costello, John. *Ten Days to Destiny: The Secret Story of the Hess Peace Initiative and British Efforts to Strike a Deal with Hitler*. New York: Morrow, 1991.

Crunden, Robert M. *The Mind and Art of Albert Jay Nock*. Chicago: Regnery, 1964.

Culbert, David H. *News for Everyone: Radio and Foreign Affairs in Thirties America*. Westport, Conn.: Greenwood, 1976.

Cull, Nicholas John. *Selling War: The British Propaganda Campaign Against American "Neutrality" in World War II*. New York: Oxford University Press, 1995.

Dallek, Robert. *Franklin D. Roosevelt and American Foreign Policy, 1932–1945*. New York: Oxford University Press, 1979.

Davis, Kenneth S. *The Hero: Charles A. Lindbergh and the American Dream*. Garden City, N.Y.: Doubleday, 1959.

Dawson, Raymond H. *The Decision to Aid Russia, 1941: Foreign Policy and Domestic Politics*. Chapel Hill: University of North Carolina Press, 1959.

Divine, Robert. *Foreign Policy and U.S. Presidential Elections, 1940–1960*. 2 vols. New York: New Viewpoints, 1974.

———. *The Illusion of Neutrality*. Chicago: University of Chicago Press, 1962.

———. *Second Chance: The Triumph of Internationalism During World War II*. New York: Atheneum, 1967.

Doenecke, Justus D. *Anti-Intervention: A Bibliographical Introduction to Isolationism and Pacifism from World War I to the Early Cold War*. New York: Garland, 1987.

———. *The Battle Against Intervention, 1939–1941*. Malabar, Fla.: Krieger, 1997.

———. *Not to the Swift: The Old Isolationists in the Cold War Era*. Lewisburg, Pa.: Bucknell University Press, 1979.

Donahoe, Bernard F. *Private Plans and Public Dangers: The Story of FDR's Third Nomination*. Notre Dame, Ind.: University of Notre Dame Press, 1965.

Donaldson, Scott. *Archibald MacLeish: An American Life*. Boston: Houghton Mifflin, 1992.

Dubofsky, Melvin, and Warren Van Tine. *John L. Lewis: A Biography*. New York: Quadrangle, 1977.

Eckes, Albert E., Jr. *The United States and the Global Struggle for Minerals*. Austin: University of Texas Press, 1979.

Edwards, Jerome E. *The Foreign Policy of Col. McCormick's Tribune, 1929–1941*. Reno: University of Nevada Press, 1971.

Egan, Eileen M. *Class, Culture, and the Classroom: The Student Peace Movement of the 1930s*. Philadelphia: Temple University Press, 1980.

Elson, Robert T. *Time, Inc.: The Intimate History of a Publishing Enterprise, 1923–1941*. Vol. 1. New York: Atheneum, 1968.

Fecher, Charles A. *Mencken: A Study of His Thought*. New York: Knopf, 1978.

Feinman, Ronald L. *Twilight of Progressivism: The Western Republican Senators and the New Deal*. Baltimore: Johns Hopkins University Press, 1981.

Flynn, George Q. *Roosevelt and Romanism: Catholics and American Diplomacy, 1937–1945*. Westport, Conn.: Greenwood, 1976.

Foster, Carrie A. *The Women and the Warriors: The U.S. Section of the Women's International League for Peace and Freedom, 1915–1946*. Syracuse, N.Y.: Syracuse University Press, 1995.

Freidel, Frank. *Franklin D. Roosevelt: A Rendezvous with Destiny*. Boston: Little, Brown, 1990.

Frye, Alton. *Nazi Germany and the American Hemisphere, 1933–1941*. New Haven, Conn.: Yale University Press, 1967.

Gaddis, John Lewis. *Russia, the Soviet Union, and United States: An Interpretive History*. 2d ed. New York: McGraw-Hill, 1990.

Gellman, Irwin F. *Good Neighbor Diplomacy: United States Policies in Latin America, 1933–1945*. Baltimore: Johns Hopkins University Press, 1979.

———. *Secret Affairs: Franklin Roosevelt, Cordell Hull, and Sumner Welles*. Baltimore: Johns Hopkins University Press, 1994.

Gies, Joseph. *The Colonel of Chicago*. New York: Dutton, 1979.

Gilbert, James Burkhart. *Writers and Partisans: A History of Literary Radicalism in America*. New York: Wiley, 1968.

Gilbert, Martin. *Winston S. Churchill*. Vol. 6, *Finest Hour, 1939–1941*. Boston: Houghton Mifflin, 1983.

Gillingham, John. *Belgian Business in the Nazi New Order*. Ghent: Jan Dhondt Foundation, 1977.

Goodhart, Philip. *Fifty Ships That Saved the World*. New York: Doubleday, 1965.

Graff, Frank Warren. *Strategy of Involvement: A Diplomatic Biography of Sumner Welles*. New York: Garland, 1988.

Green, James R. *Grass-Roots Socialism: Radical Movements in the Southwest, 1845–1943*. Baton Rouge: Louisiana State University Press, 1978.

Griffiths, Richard. *Fellow Travellers of the Right: British Enthusiasts for Nazi Germany*. London: Constable, 1980.

Guinsburg, Thomas N. *The Pursuit of Isolationism in the United States from Versailles to Pearl Harbor*. New York: Garland, 1982.

Haglund, David G. *Latin America and the Transformation of U.S. Strategic Thought, 1936–1940*. Albuquerque: University of New Mexico Press, 1984.

Hänel, Wolfgang. *Hermann Rauschnings "Gesprache mit Hitler": Eine Geschichtsfälschung*. Ingolstadt, Germany: Zeitgeschichte Forschungstelle, 1984.

Harper, John Lamberton. *American Vision of Europe: Franklin D. Roosevelt, George F. Kennan, and Dean G. Acheson*. New York: Cambridge University Press, 1994.

Healy, Paul F. *Cissy: The Biography of Eleanor M. "Cissy" Patterson*. Garden City, N.Y.: Doubleday, 1966.

Hearden, Patrick J. *Roosevelt Confronts Hitler: America's Entry into World War II*. DeKalb: Northern Illinois University Press, 1987.

Heinrichs, Waldo. *Threshold of War: Franklin D. Roosevelt and American Entry into World War II.* New York: Oxford University Press, 1988.

Herring, George C., Jr. *Aid to Russia, 1941–1946: Strategy, Diplomacy, and the Origins of the Cold War.* New York: Columbia University Press, 1973.

Herrmann, Dorothy. *A Gift for Life: Anne Morrow Lindbergh.* New York: Ticknor & Fields, 1993.

Herzstein, Robert E. *Henry R. Luce: A Political Portrait of the Man Who Created the American Century.* New York: Scribner's, 1994.

———. *Roosevelt and Hitler: Prelude to War.* New York: Paragon, 1989.

Hofstadter, Richard. *The Progressive Historians: Turner, Beard, Parrington.* New York: Knopf, 1968.

Hunt, Michael H. *Ideology and U.S. Foreign Policy.* New Haven, Conn.: Yale University Press, 1987.

Hyman, Sidney. *The Lives of William Benton.* Chicago: University of Chicago Press, 1969.

Isserman, Maurice. *Which Side Were You On? The American Communist Party During the Second World War.* Middletown, Conn.: Wesleyan University Press, 1982.

Jäckel, Eberhard. *Hitler's* Weltanschauung: *A Blueprint for Power.* Middletown, Conn.: Wesleyan University Press, 1972.

Jacobs, Travis Beal. *America and the Winter War, 1939–1940.* New York: Garland, 1981.

James, D. Clayton. *The Years of MacArthur.* Vol. 1, *1880–1941.* Boston: Houghton Mifflin, 1970.

Johnpoll, Bernard K. *Pacifist's Progress: Norman Thomas and the Decline of American Socialism.* Chicago: Quadrangle, 1970.

Johnson, Donald Bruce. *Wendell Willkie and the Republican Party.* Urbana: University of Illinois Press, 1960.

Johnson, Niel M. *George Sylvester Viereck: German-American Propagandist.* Urbana: University of Illinois Press, 1972.

Johnson, Walter. *The Battle Against Isolation.* Chicago: University of Chicago Press, 1944.

Jonas, Manfred. *Isolationism in America, 1939–1941.* Ithaca, N.Y. Cornell University Press, 1966.

Kershaw, Ian. *The Nazi Dictatorship: Problems and Perspectives of Interpretation.* 2d ed. London: Arnold, 1989.

Killen, John. *A History of the Luftwaffe.* New York: Doubleday, 1968.

Kimball, Warren F. *Forged in War: Roosevelt, Churchill, and the Second World War.* New York: Morrow, 1997.

———. *The Juggler: Franklin Roosevelt as Wartime Statesman.* Princeton, N.J.: Princeton University Press, 1991.

———. *The Most Unsordid Act: Lend-Lease, 1939–1941.* Baltimore: Johns Hopkins University Press, 1969.

Kipphan, Klaus. *Deutsche Propaganda in den Vereinigten Statten.* Heidelberg: Winter, 1971.

Kirkpatrick, Charles E. *An Unknown Future and a Doubtful Present: Writing the Victory Plan of 1941.* Washington, D.C.: Center of Military History, 1990.

Klehr, Harvey. *The Heyday of American Communism: The Depression Decade.* New York: Basic Books, 1984.

Koskoff, David E. *Joseph P. Kennedy: A Life and Times.* Englewood Cliffs, N.J.: Prentice Hall, 1974.

Lane, Peter B. *The United States and the Balkan Crisis of 1940–1941.* New York: Garland, 1988.

Langer, William L., and S. Everett Gleason. *The Challenge to Isolation: The World Crisis of 1937–1940 and American Foreign Policy.* New York: Harper, 1952.

———. *The Undeclared War, 1940–1941.* New York: Harper, 1953.

Lash, Joseph P. *Roosevelt and Churchill, 1939–1941: The Partnership That Saved the West.* New York: Norton, 1976.

Leighton, Richard M., and Robert W. Coakley. *Global Logistics and Strategy, 1940–1943.* Washington, D.C.: Department of the Army, 1955.

Leutze, James. *Bargaining for Supremacy: Anglo-American Naval Collaboration, 1937–1941.* Chapel Hill: University of North Carolina Press, 1977.

Levering, Ralph B. *American Opinion and the Russian Alliance, 1939–1945.* Chapel Hill: University of North Carolina Press, 1976.

Lewin, Ronald. *Hitler's Mistakes.* New York: Morrow, 1984.

Link, Arthur S. *Wilson.* Vol. 4, *Confusion and Crises, 1915–1916.* Princeton, N.J.: Princeton University Press, 1964.

Linn, Brian McAllister. *Guardians of Empire: The U.S. Army and the Pacific, 1902–1940.* Chapel Hill: University of North Carolina Press, 1999.

Lockhart, J. G., and C. M. Woodhouse. *Cecil Rhodes: The Colossus of South Africa.* New York: Macmillan, 1963.

Louis, William Roger. *Imperialism at Bay: The United States and the Decolonization of the British Empire, 1941–1945.* New York: Oxford University Press, 1978.

Lower, Richard Coke. *A Bloc of One: The Politics and Career of Hiram W. Johnson.* Stanford, Calif.: Stanford University Press, 1993.

Lubell, Samuel. *The Future of American Politics.* 3d ed., rev. New York: Harper, 1965.

Lukacs, John. *The Hitler of History.* New York: Knopf, 1997.

MacDonald, C. A. *The United States, Britain and Appeasement, 1936–1939.* New York: St. Martin's, 1981.

Maddox, Robert James. *William E. Borah and American Foreign Policy.* Baton Rouge: Louisiana State University Press, 1969.

Maddux, Thomas R. *Years of Estrangement: American Relations with the Soviet Union, 1933–1941.* Tallahassee: University Presses of Florida, 1980.

Mahl, Thomas Earl. *Desperate Deception: British Covert Operations in the United States, 1939–1944.* Washington, D.C.: Brassley's, 1998.

Maney, Patrick J. *"Young Bob" La Follette: A Biography of Robert M. La Follette, Jr., 1895–1953.* Columbia: University of Missouri Press, 1978.

Marcus, Sheldon. *Father Coughlin: The Tumultuous Life of the Priest of the Little Flower.* Boston: Little, Brown, 1973.

Marrus, Michael R. *The Holocaust in History.* Hanover, N.H.: University Press of New England, 1987.

Marshall, Jonathan. *To Have and Have Not: Southeast Asian Raw Materials and the Origins of the Pacific War.* Berkeley and Los Angeles: University of California Press, 1995.

Martin, Ralph G. *Cissy.* New York: Simon & Schuster, 1979.

Matloff, Maurice, and Edwin M. Snell. *Strategic Planning for Coalition Warfare.* Washington, D.C.: Department of the Army, 1953.

Matson, Robert W. *Neutrality and Navicerts: Britain, the United States, and Economic Warfare, 1939–1940.* New York: Garland, 1994.

Mayer, Milton. *Robert Maynard Hutchins: A Memoir.* Berkeley and Los Angeles: University of California Press, 1993.

McCoy, Donald. *Landon of Kansas.* Lincoln: University of Kansas, 1966.

McFarland, Keith D. *Harry H. Woodring: A Political Biography of FDR's Controversial Secretary of War.* Lawrence: University of Kansas Press, 1975.

McJimsey, George D. *Harry Hopkins: Ally of the Poor and Defender of Democracy.* Cambridge, Mass.: Harvard University Press, 1987.

McKenna, Marian C. *Borah.* Ann Arbor: University of Michigan Press, 1961.

Merry, Robert W. *Taking On the World: Joseph and Stewart Alsop, Guardians of the Twentieth Century.* New York: Penguin, 1996.

Meyer, Donald B. *The Protestant Search for Political Realism.* Berkeley and Los Angeles: University of California Press, 1960.

Miller, Donald L. *The New American Radicalism: Alfred M. Bingham and Non-Marxian Insurgency in the New Deal Era.* Port Washington, N.Y.: Kennikat, 1979.

Miller, Kristie. *Ruth Hanna McCormick: A Life in Politics 1880–1944.* Albuquerque: University of New Mexico Press, 1992.

Moser, John E. *Twisting the Lion's Tail: American Anglophobia Between the Two World Wars.* New York: New York University Press, 1999.

Muresianu, John M. *War of Ideas: American Intellectuals and the World Crisis, 1938–1945.* New York: Garland, 1988.

Myers, Constance Ashton. *The Prophet's Army: Trotskyists in America, 1928–1941.* Westport, Conn.: Greenwood, 1977.

Nore, Ellen. *Charles A. Beard: An Intellectual Biography.* Carbondale: Southern Illinois University Press, 1983.

Offner, Arnold A. *The Origins of the Second World War.* New York: Praeger, 1975.

Ohl, John Kennedy. *Hugh S. Johnson and the New Deal.* DeKalb: Northern Illinois University Press, 1985.

Parmet, Herbert S., and Marie B. Hecht. *Never Again: A President Runs for a Third Term.* New York: Macmillan, 1968.

Patterson, James T. *Mr. Republican: A Biography of Robert A. Taft.* New York: Knopf, 1972.

Pogue, Forrest C. *George C. Marshall.* Vol. 2, *Ordeal and Hope, 1939–1942.* New York: Viking, 1966.

Ponting, Clive. *1940: Myth and Reality.* Chicago: Dee, 1990.

Porter, David L. *The Seventy-sixth Congress and World War II, 1939–1940.* Columbia: University of Missouri Press, 1979.

Randall, Mercedes M. *Improper Bostonian: Emily Greene Balch.* New York: Twayne, 1964.

Reynolds, David. *The Creation of the Anglo-American Alliance, 1937–1941: A Study in Competitive Co-operation.* Chapel Hill: University of North Carolina Press, 1982.

Ribuffo, Leo P. *The Old Christian Right: The Protestant Right from the Great Depression to the Cold War.* Philadelphia: Temple University Press, 1983.

Roberts, Andrew. *"The Holy Fox": A Life of Lord Halifax.* London: Macmillan, 1991.

Roberts, John W. *Putting Foreign Policy to Work: The Role of Organized Labor in American Foreign Relations, 1932–1941.* New York: Garland, 1995.

Robinson, Joann Ooiman. *Abraham Went Out: A Biography of A. J. Muste.* Philadelphia: Temple University Press, 1981.

Rock, William R. *Chamberlain and Roosevelt: British Foreign Policy and the United States, 1937–1940.* Columbus: Ohio State University Press, 1988.

Rogge, O. John. *The Official German Report: Nazi Penetration, 1924–1942; Pan-Arabism, 1939–Today.* New York: Yoseloff, 1961.

Rossi, Mario. *Roosevelt and the French.* New York: Praeger, 1993.

Rotberg, Robert I. *The Founder: Cecil Rhodes and the Pursuit of Power.* New York: Oxford University Press, 1988.

Ryant, Carl. *Profit's Prophet: Garet Garrett.* Selinsgrove, Pa.: Susquehanna University Press, 1989.

Schaffer, Louis. *Vito Marcantonio: Radical in Congress.* Syracuse, N.Y.: Syracuse University Press, 1966.

Schieder, Thedor. *Hermann Rauschnings "Gesprache mit Hitler" als Geschichtsquelle.* Opladen, Germany: Westdeutscher, 1972.

Schmitz, David F. *The United States and Fascist Italy, 1922–1940.* Chapel Hill: University of North Carolina Press, 1988.

Schneider, James C. *Should America Go to War? The Debate over Foreign Policy in Chicago, 1939–1941.* Chapel Hill: University of North Carolina Press, 1989.

Schott, Linda K. *Reconstructing Women's Thoughts: The Women's International League for Peace and Freedom.* Stanford, Calif.: Stanford University Press, 1997.

Schwarz, Jordan A. *Liberal: Adolf A. Berle and the Vision of an American Era.* New York: Free Press, 1987.

———. *The Speculator: Bernard M. Baruch in Washington, 1917–1965.* Chapel Hill: University of North Carolina Press, 1981.

Sherry, Michael S. *The Rise of American Air Power: The Creation of Armageddon.* New Haven, Conn.: Yale University Press, 1987.

Sherwood, Robert E. *Roosevelt and Hopkins: An Intimate History.* New York: Harper, 1948.

Shils, Edward A. *The Torment of Secrecy.* Glencoe, Ill.: Free Press, 1956.

Shogun, Robert. *Hard Bargain: How FDR Twisted Churchill's Arm, Evaded the Law, and Changed the Role of the American Presidency.* New York: Scribner's, 1995.

Simpson, B. Mitchell, III. *Admiral Harold R. Stark: Architect of Victory, 1939–1945.* Columbia: University of South Carolina Press, 1989.

Sirgiovanni, George. *An Undercurrent of Suspicion: Anti-Communism in America During World War II.* New Brunswick, N.J.: Transaction, 1990.

Smith, Geoffrey S. *To Save a Nation: American Countersubversives, the New Deal, and the Coming of World War II.* New York: Basic Books, 1973.

Smith, Richard Norton. *The Colonel: The Life and Legend of Robert R. McCormick, 1880–1955.* Boston: Houghton Mifflin, 1997.

———. *Thomas E. Dewey and His Times.* New York: Simon & Schuster, 1982.

———. *An Uncommon Man: The Triumph of Herbert Hoover.* New York: Simon & Schuster, 1984.

Spector, Ronald H. *Eagle Against the Sun: The American War with Japan.* New York: Free Press, 1985.

Steele, Richard W. *Propaganda in an Open Society: The Roosevelt Administration and the Media, 1933–1941.* Westport, Conn.: Greenwood, 1985.

Stenejem, Michele Flynn. *An American First: John T. Flynn and the America First Committee.* New Rochelle, N.Y.: Arlington House, 1976.

Stoakes, Geoffrey. *Hitler and the Quest for World Domination: Nazi Ideology and Foreign Policy in the 1920s.* New York: Berg, 1986.

Stoler, Mark A. *George C. Marshall: Soldier-Statesman of the American Century.* Boston: Twayne, 1989.

Swanberg, W. A. *Citizen Hearst.* New York: Scribner's, 1961.

———. *Norman Thomas: The Last Idealist.* New York: Scribner's, 1976.

Taylor, A. J. P. *British History: 1914–1945.* New York: Oxford University Press, 1965.

Thorne, Christopher. *Allies of a Kind: The United States, Britain, and the War Against Japan, 1941–1945.* New York: Oxford University Press, 1978.

Tompkins, C. David. *Senator Arthur H. Vandenberg: The Evolution of a Modern Republican, 1884–1945.* East Lansing: Michigan State University Press, 1970.

Trefousse, Hans Louis. *Germany and American Neutrality, 1939–1941.* New York: Bookman, 1951.

———. *Pearl Harbor: The Continuing Controversy.* Malibar, Fla.: Krieger, 1982.

Tull, Charles J. *Father Coughlin and the New Deal.* Syracuse: Syracuse University Press, 1965.

Tuttle, Dwight William. *Harry L. Hopkins and Anglo-American-Soviet Relations, 1941–1945.* New York: Garland, 1983.

Utley, Jonathan G. *Going to War with Japan, 1937–1941.* Knoxville: University of Tennessee Press, 1985.

Van Allen, Rodger. *The* Commonweal *and American Catholicism: The Magazine, the Movement, the Meaning.* Philadelphia: Fortress, 1974.

Waldrop, Frank J. *McCormick of Chicago: An Unconventional Portrait of a Controversial Figure.* Upper Saddle River, N.J.: Prentice Hall, 1966.

Warren, Donald. *Radio Priest: Charles Coughlin, the Father of Hate Radio.* New York: Free Press, 1996.

Watson, Mark Skinner. *Chief of Staff: Prewar Plans and Preparations.* Washington, D.C.: United States Army, 1950.

Watt, D. Cameron. *Succeeding John Bull: America in Britain's Wars, 1900–1975.* New York: Cambridge University Press, 1984.

Weinberg, Gerhard L. *Germany, Hitler, and World War II: Essays in Modern German and World History.* New York: Cambridge University Press, 1995.

———. *A World at Arms: A Global History of World War II.* New York: Cambridge University Press, 1994.

———. *World in the Balance: Behind the Scenes of World War II.* Hanover, N.H.: Brandeis University Press of New England, 1981.

Wendt, Lloyd. *Chicago Tribune: The Rise of a Great American Newspaper.* Chicago: Rand McNally, 1979.

Whalen, Richard J. *The Founding Father: The Story of Joseph P. Kennedy.* New York: New American Library, 1964.

Whaley, Barton. *Codeword Barbarossa.* Cambridge, Mass.: MIT Press, 1973.

White, Graham J. *FDR and the Press.* Chicago: University of Chicago Press, 1979.

Wilkins, Mira. *The Maturing of Multinational Enterprise: American Business Abroad from 1914 to 1970.* Cambridge, Mass.: Harvard University Press, 1974.

Wilson, Theodore A. *The First Summit: Roosevelt and Churchill at Placentia Bay, 1941.* Rev. ed. Lawrence: University Press of Kansas, 1991.

Wiltz, John E. *In Search of Peace: The Senate Munitions Inquiry, 1934–1936.* Baton Rouge: Louisiana State University Press, 1963.

Wolfskill, George, and John A. Hudson. *All But the People: Franklin D. Roosevelt and His Critics, 1933–1939.* New York: Macmillan, 1969.

Wreszin, Michael. *Oswald Garrison Villard: Pacifist at War.* Bloomington: Indiana University Press, 1965.

———. *A Rebel in Defense of Tradition: The Life and Politics of Dwight Macdonald.* New York: Basic Books, 1994.

———. *The Superflous Anarchist: Albert Jay Nock.* Providence, R.I.: Brown University Press, 1972.

Wright, Gordon. *The Ordeal of Total War, 1939–1945.* New York: Harper & Row, 1968.

## SCHOLARLY ARTICLES

Addison, Paul. "Lloyd George and the Compromise Peace in the Second World War." In *Lloyd George: Twelve Essays,* ed. A. J. P. Taylor (London: Hamish Hamilton, 1971): 361–84.

Bennett, Edward M. "Joseph C. Grew: The Diplomacy of Pacification." In *Diplomats in Crisis: United States–Chinese–Japanese Relations, 1919–1941,* ed. Richard Dean Burns and Edward M. Bennett (Santa Barbara: ABC-Clio, 1974): 65–89.

Billington, Ray Allen. "The Origins of Middle Western Isolationism." *Political Science Quarterly* 60 (March 1945): 44–64.

Blackorby, Edward C. "Usher Lloyd Burdick." In *Dictionary of American Biography: Supplement 6, 1956–1960,* ed. John A. Garraty (New York: Scribner's, 1980): 85–87.

Bratzel, John F., and Leslie B. Rout Jr. "FDR and the Secret Map." *Wilson Quarterly* 9 (January 1995): 167–73.

Carleton, William G. "Isolationism and the Middle West." *Mississippi Valley Historical Review* 33 (December 1946): 377–90.

Castle, Alfred L. "William R. Castle and Opposition to United States Involvement in an Asian War, 1939–1941." *Pacific Historical Review* 54 (August 1985): 337–51.

Charles, Douglas M. "Informing FDR: FBI Political Surveillance and the Isolationist–Interventionist Foreign Policy Debate, 1939–1945." *Diplomatic History* 24 (Spring 2000): 211–32.

Charles, Douglas M., and John P. Rossi. "FBI Political Surveillance and the Charles Lindbergh Investigation, 1939–1941." *Historian* 59 (Summer 1997): 831–47.

Clifford, John Garry. "A Connecticut Colonel's Candid Conversation with the Wrong Commander-in-Chief." *Connecticut History* 28 (November 1988): 24–38.

———. "A Note on Chester Bowles's Plan to End World War II." *Peace and Change* 14 (January 1989): 106–22.

———. "The Odyssey of *City of Flint.*" *American Neptune* 32 (April 1972): 100–116.

Clifford, John Garry, and Robert Griffiths. "Reflections upon an Ante–World War II Letter: John A. Danaher and United States Intervention in World War II." *Connecticut History* 23 (April 1982): 46–54.

Cogley, John. "James Martin Gillis." In *Dictionary of American Biography: Supplement 6, 1956–1960,* ed. John A. Garraty (New York: Scribner's, 1980): 237–38.

Cole, Wayne S. "America First and the South, 1940–1941." *Journal of Southern History* 22 (February 1956): 36–47.

———. "What Might Have Been," *Chronicles* 15 (December 1991): 20–22.

Croog, Charles F. "FBI Political Surveillance and the Isolationist-Interventionist Debate, 1939–1941." *Historian* 54 (Spring 1992): 441–58.

De Benedetti, Charles. "John Haynes Holmes." In *Biographical Dictionary of Modern Peace Leaders,* ed. Harold Josephson (Westport, Conn.: Greenwood, 1985): 422–44.

Dilliard, Irving. "Roy Wilson Howard." In *Dictionary of American Biography: Supplement 7, 1961–1965,* ed. John A. Garraty (New York: Scribner's, 1981): 369–70.

Doenecke, Justus D. "The Anti-Interventionism of Herbert Hoover." *Journal of Libertarian Studies* 8 (Summer 1987): 311–40.

———. "Charles Clayton Morrison." In *Biographical Dictionary of Modern Peace Leaders,* ed. Harold Josephson (Westport, Conn.: Greenwood, 1985): 664–66.

———. "Edwin M. Borchard, John Bassett Moore, and Opposition to American Entry in World War II." *Journal of Libertarian Studies* 6 (Winter 1982): 1–34.

———. "The Election of 1940." In *Running for President: The Candidates and Their Images,* ed. Arthur M. Schlesinger Jr., vol. 2 (New York: Simon & Schuster, 1994): 201–15.

———. "Frederick Joseph Libby." In *Biographical Dictionary of Modern Peace Leaders,* ed. Harold Josephson (Westport, Conn.: Greenwood, 1985): 562–64.

———. "General Robert E. Wood: The Evolution of a Conservative." *Journal of the Illinois State Historical Society* 71 (August 1978): 162–75.

———. "The Isolationism of General Robert E. Wood." In *Three Faces of Midwestern Isolationism,* ed. John H. Schacht (Iowa City, Iowa: Center for the Study of the Recent History of the United States, 1981): 11–22.

———. "The Isolationist as Collectivist: Lawrence Dennis and the Coming of World War II." *Journal of Libertarian Studies* 3 (Summer 1979): 191–207.

———. "Non-interventionism of the Left: The Keep America Out of the War Congress, 1938–1941." *Journal of Contemporary History* 12 (April 1977): 221–36.

———. "Rehearsal for Cold War: United States Anti-Interventionists and the Soviet Union, 1939–1941." *International Journal of Politics, Culture and Society* 7 (Spring 1994): 375–92.

———. "*Scribner's Commentator,* 1939–1942." In *The Conservative Press in Twentieth-Century America,* ed. Ronald Lora and William Henry Longton (Westport, Conn.: Greenwood, 1999): 273–282.

———. "Verne Marshall's Leadership of the No Foreign War Committee, 1940." *Annals of Iowa* 41 (Winter 1973): 1153–72.

———. "*Weekly Foreign Letter,* 1938–1942." In *The Conservative Press in Twentieth-Century America,* ed. Ronald Lora and William Henry Longton (Westport, Conn.: Greenwood, 1999): 283–94.

Dubofsky, Melvyn. "John L. Lewis and American Isolationism." In *Three Faces of Midwestern Isolationism,* ed. John H. Schacht (Iowa City, Iowa: Center for the Study of the Recent History of the United States, 1981): 23–33.

Esthus, Raymond A. "President Roosevelt's Commitment to Britain to Intervene in a Pacific War." *Mississippi Valley Historical Review* 50 (June 1963): 28–38.

Fensterwald, Bernard, Jr. "The Anatomy of American 'Isolationism' and Expansion." *Journal of Conflict Resolution* 2 (June 1958): 111–39; (December 1958): 280–307.

Fleming, Thomas. "The Big Leak." *American Heritage* 38 (December 1987): 65–71.

Frieden, Jeff. "Sectoral Conflict and Foreign Economic Policy, 1914–1940." *International Organization* 42 (Winter 1988): 59–90.

George, James H., Jr. "Another Chance: Herbert Hoover and World War II Relief." *Diplomatic History* 16 (Summer 1992): 389–407.

Gorodesky, Gabriel. "The Hess Affair and Anglo-Soviet Relations on the Eve of 'Barbarossa.'" *English Historical Review* 101 (April 1986): 405–20.

Haglund, David G. "George C. Marshall and the Question of Military Aid to England, May–June 1940." *Journal of Contemporary History* 15 (October 1980): 745–60.

Harrington, Daniel F. "A Careless Hope: American Air Power and Japan, 1941." *Pacific Historical Review* 48 (May 1979): 217–38.

Hathaway, Robert M. "1933–1945: Economic Diplomacy in a Time of Crisis." In *Economics and World Power: An Assessment of American Diplomacy,* ed. William H. Becker and Samuel F. Welles (New York: 1984): 277–331.

Hauner, Milan. "Did Hitler Want World Domination?" *Journal of Contemporary History* 13 (January 1978): 15–32.

Hearden, Patrick J. "John Cudahy and the Pursuit of Peace." *Mid-America* 68 (April–June 1986): 99–114.

Heinrichs, Waldo. "Franklin D. Roosevelt and the Risks of War." In *American, Chinese, and Japanese Perspectives on Wartime Asia, 1931–1939,* ed. Akira Iriye and Warren Cohen (Wilmington, Del.: Scholarly Resources, 1990): 147–78.

Heinrichs, Waldo. "FDR and the Entry into World War II." *Prologue* 26 (Fall 1994): 119–30.

Hess, Gary R. "The Emergence of U.S. Influence in Southeast Asia." In *American, Chinese, and Japanese Perspectives on Wartime Asia, 1931–1939,* ed. Akira Iriye and Warren Cohen (Wilmington, Del.: Scholarly Resources, 1990): 179–221.

Hill, Norman, "Was There an Ultimatum Before Pearl Harbor?" *American Journal of International Law* 42 (April 1948): 355–67.

Hilton, Stanley E. "The Welles Mission to Europe, February–March 1940: Illusion or Realism?" *Journal of American History* 58 (June 1971): 93–120.

Holbrook, Francis X. "The Canton Island Controversy: Compromise or American Victory?" *Journal of the Royal Australian Historical Society* 59 (June 1973): 128–47.

Hosoya, Chihiro. "Miscalculations in Deterrent Policy: Japanese-U.S. Relations." *Journal of Peace Research* 5 (1968): 97–115.

Howlett, Charles F. "John Nevin Sayre and the International Fellowship of Reconciliation." *Peace and Change* 15 (April 1990): 123–49.

Iriye, Akira. "U.S. Policy Toward Japan Before World War II." In *Pearl Harbor Reexamined: Prologue to the Pacific War,* ed. Hilary Conroy and Harry Wray (Honolulu: University of Hawaii Press, 1990): 17–25.

Jeffreys-Jones, Rhodri. "The Inestimable Advantage of Not Being English: Lord Lothian's American Ambassadorship, 1939–1940." *Scottish Historical Review* 63 (April 1984): 105–10.

———. "Lord Lothian and American Democracy: An Illusion in Pursuit of an Illusion." *Canadian Review of American Studies* 17 (Winter 1986): 411–22.

Jonas, Manfred. "Pro-Axis Sentiment and American Isolationism." *Historian* 29 (February 1967): 221–37.

Kahn, David. "The United States Views Germany and Japan in 1941." In *Knowing One's Enemies: Intelligence Assessments Before the Two World Wars,* ed. Ernest R. May (Princeton, N.J.: Princeton University Press, 1984): 476–501.

Hanks, Richard Kay. "Hamilton Fish and American Isolationism, 1920–1944." Ph.D. diss., University of California, Riverside, 1971.

Jaffe, Joseph E., Jr. "Isolationism and Neutrality in Academe, 1938–1941." Ph.D. diss., Case Western Reserve University, 1979.

Kaner, Norman Jay. "Vito Marcantonio and American Foreign Policy." Ph.D. diss., Rutgers University, 1968.

Kendall, Richard H. "Edwin M. Borchard and the Defense of Traditional American Policy." Ph.D. diss., Yale University, 1964.

Kent, Alan Edmond, Jr. "Portrait in Isolationism: The La Follettes and Foreign Policy." Ph.D. diss., University of Wisconsin, 1956.

Kuehl, Marshall R. "Philip C. Jessup: From America First to Cold War Interventionist." Ph.D. diss., Kent State University, 1985.

Lanier, James Carpenter. "Stuart Chase: An Intellectual Biography (1888–1940)." Ph.D. diss., Emory University, 1972.

Libby, Justin Harris. "The Irresolute Years: American Congressional Opinion Towards Japan, 1937–1941." Ph.D. diss., Michigan State University, 1971.

Marabell, George Peter. "Frederick J. Libby and the American Peace Movement, 1921–1941." Ph.D. diss., Michigan State University, 1975.

McGreen, John Dennis. "Norman Thomas and the Search for an All-Inclusive Socialist Party." Ph.D. diss., Rutgers University, 1976.

Megaree, Richard. "Realism in American Foreign Policy: The Diplomacy of John Bassett Moore." Ph.D. diss., Northwestern University, 1963.

Myers, Robert Hobbs. "William Henry Chamberlin: His Views of the Soviet Union." Ph.D. diss., Indiana University, 1973.

Pleasants, Julian M. "The Senatorial Career of Robert Rice Reynolds." Ph.D. diss., University of North Carolina, 1971.

Pois, Anne Marie. "The Politics and Process of Organizing for Peace: The United States Section of the Women's International League for Peace and Freedom, 1919–1939." Ph.D. diss., University of Colorado, 1988.

Sarles, Ruth. "A Story of America First." Papers of the America First Committee, Hoover Institution, Stanford University.

Schwar, Jane Harriet. "Internationalist Propaganda and Pressure Groups in the United States, 1937–1941." Ph.D. diss., Ohio State University, 1973.

Troncone, Anthony C. "Hamilton Fish, Sr., and the Politics of American Nationalism." Ph.D. diss., Rutgers University, 1993.

Turnbaugh, Roy Carroll, Jr. "Harry Elmer Barnes: The Quest for Truth and Justice." Ph.D. diss., University of Illinois, 1977.

Weinrich, William Arthur. "Business and Foreign Affairs: The Roosevelt Defense Program, 1937–1941." Ph.D. diss., University of Oklahoma, 1971.

Wert, Hal Elliott. "The Specter of Starvation: Hoover, Roosevelt and American Aid to Europe, 1939–1941." Ph.D. diss., University of Kansas, 1991.

Ziegler, John Alan. "*The Progressive*'s Views on Foreign Affairs, 1909–1941: A Case Study of Liberal Economic Isolationism." Ph.D. diss., Syracuse University, 1970.

## ORAL HISTORY

Interview with Lawrence Dennis, 1967, Columbia Oral History Project, Columbia University.

# Index